AN ANECDOTAL HISTORY
OF OLD TIMES
IN SINGAPORE

AN ANECDOTAL HISTORY OF OLD TIMES IN SINGAPORE

FROM THE FOUNDATION OF THE SETTLEMENT
UNDER THE HONOURABLE THE EAST INDIA COMPANY
ON FEBRUARY 6TH, 1819
TO THE TRANSFER TO THE COLONIAL OFFICE
AS PART OF THE COLONIAL POSSESSIONS OF THE CROWN
ON APRIL 1ST, 1867
BY
CHARLES BURTON BUCKLEY

KUALA LUMPUR
UNIVERSITY OF MALAYA PRESS
1965

SOLE DISTRIBUTORS

Oxford University Press, Amen House, London E.C.4

GLASGOW   NEW YORK   TORONTO   MELBOURNE   WELLINGTON
BOMBAY   CALCUTTA   MADRAS   KARACHI   LAHORE   DACCA
CAPE TOWN   SALISBURY   NAIROBI   IBADAN   ACCRA
KUALA LUMPUR   HONG KONG

● *University of Malaya Press 1965*
This edition reproduced by
kind permission of Fraser & Neave, Ltd.
Singapore

REPRINTED PHOTOGRAPHICALLY IN HONG KONG BY
SOUTH CHINA PHOTO-PROCESS PRINTING CO. LTD.

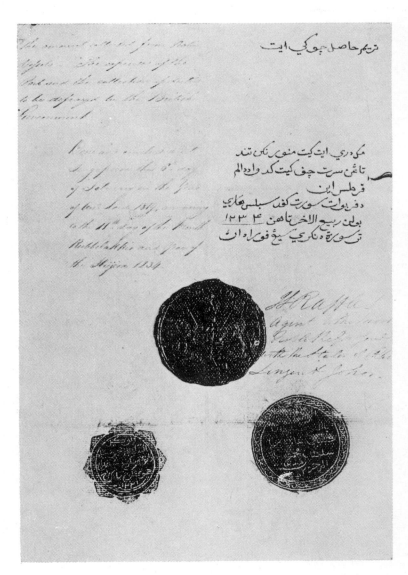

THE LAST PAGE OF THE TREATY OF 6TH FEBRUARY, 1819.

An Anecdotal History
Of Old Times . .
In Singapore . . .

(With Portraits and Illustrations)

FROM

The Foundation of the Settlement under the Honourable the
East India Company, on February 6th, 1819,

TO THE

Transfer to the Colonial Office as part of the Colonial
Possessions of the Crown on April 1st, 1867,

BY

CHARLES BURTON BUCKLEY.

IN TWO VOLUMES—VOLUME I.

SINGAPORE :
PRINTED BY FRASER & NEAVE, LIMITED.

[Original Title Page]

"I was curious to see how he manufactured his wares. He dipped into various books, fluttering over the leaves of manuscripts, taking a morsel out of one, a morsel out of another, here a little, and there a little. The contents of his book seemed to be as heterogeneous as those of the witches' caldron in Macbeth. After all, thought I, may not this pilfering disposition be implanted in authors for wise purposes; may it not be the way in which Providence has taken care that the seeds of knowledge and wisdom shall be preserved from age to age, in spite of the inevitable decay of the works in which they were first produced? Generation after generation, both in animal and vegetable life, passes away, but the vital principle is transmitted to posterity, and the species continue to flourish. Thus do authors beget authors, and in a good old age they sleep with their fathers, that is to say, with the authors who preceded them, and from whom they had stolen.—WASHINGTON IRVING.

PREFACE.

◆

THIS book is in great part a revision with many additions of a series of articles which appeared under the same title in the weekly *Singapore Free Press* newspaper, from the time I re-established that paper in 1884, until it became a daily paper in 1887, when I gave it over into other hands. There had been for several years only one newspaper in Singapore, and it was desirable to have a second. The papers about the old history of the place were written with a view to have matter always ready for the paper, to be used in case of need; but in that respect it turned out unnecessary, because it was intended that each issue should consist of 8 pages, while the first number filled 24, and it never was reduced to the size originally intended. The history papers thus printed only reached to the year 1856.

I had the columns of the history cut out of the newspaper, sewn into a book, and interleaved. This was sent to Mr. W. H. Read, who passed it on to Mr. James Guthrie, who died lately at an old age. Their remarks, additions, and corrections were added to others which came in from various quarters, owing to the publicity in the newspaper. The result was that by the kindness and good-nature of many of the old residents of the place, I had the loan of a great number of papers, books, documents and pamphlets, of all kinds, age, and descriptions; some coming to pieces with usage, some eaten through by white ants, and all more or less suffering from the mis-directed energy of insect life. All these papers, with much other material that came to light after the papers were first written, have been worked into this book. It has been carried down to the Transfer in 1867, as the principal mark of an epoch in the story of the place. Occasionally later events have been added, where they seemed likely to be useful, as showing the result at the present time of what was then done.

This work then had been in gradual growth for over twenty years when the first chapter was put in the hands of the present printers; and has been over a year in the press, from various causes, which may explain some of the allusions to the present day, which vary from July, 1901 to September, 1902.

It is unnecessary to say that it is only a compilation, but trouble has not been spared to make it as correct as the existing means of knowledge would allow. It was intended at one time to note the various sources from which the statements were derived, but it was soon found that this would cause such a number of side-notes, and such a mass of inverted commas, as to be impracticable, and was therefore abandoned. The language and even the spelling of Malay names and places have not been altered, with any attempt at correction, and if some may think that the sentences could occasionally be better expressed, or names spelt differently, the only answer is that they are intentionally left as they were found. Square brackets have been used to explain any allusion in quoted passages by reference to the present time, as for example on page 57, in paragraph 6 of Raffles's letter of instructions, words have been put in brackets to explain what part of the present town his words referred to.

It has long been a matter of regret to me that the writings of Crawfurd, Logan, Braddell and others, who gave so much time to writing about Singapore and the neighbouring countries, should be so soon forgotten, and the books scarcely to be obtained. When a copy is found on the bookshelves of some old library here, it is generally tumbling to pieces. I thought time would be well spent in the attempt to collect the information of the old days that was contained in them, and, as they were not likely to be seen much longer, it would be no literary piracy to reprint their contents just as they were written, when their length allowed it in a book like this, which soon showed signs of becoming much larger than was intended.

For the history of the earlier years of the Settlement, the book is largely indebted to a number of notes made by Mr. Braddell, probably about fifty years ago, when he contemplated writing a book about the Settlements. Other work of a more useful kind to the community afterwards occupied his time so fully, that his intention was not carried out; and it is pleasant to think that this book is carrying on the project of one who gave up so much of his time for many years to enrich the local literature, and brought to bear upon it a knowledge of the Malay language and writings which was at that time very rare.

The book is certainly made up largely of scraps, and it was at one time suggested to collect the various subjects under distinct heads; but it was thought that the chronological way in which it was begun was better, except in a very few instances; and the Index goes far to overcome any difficulty. Still I feel that it reminds one of the story of the boy who, asking for a book to read, was given a dictionary by mistake, and being asked how he liked it, replied that it might be very interesting to grown-up people, but he thought it changed the subject too frequently.

It is a book that will interest those only who have some association with Singapore; and, even to them, many of the details may well seem of little interest, as matters of no importance, or as stories of people of whom they have never heard. But I would suggest to them that such details could never again be found, and, if not kept now, can never be recorded hereafter; and that they may be of interest or possible use to some others for various reasons. Also that it is such details which help to keep alive the memory of those who, in the early days of Singapore, helped to make it what it has become, although at the time they could not have realised what it was to be. Now that eighty-three years have passed away since the Settlement was established, such details of the present time should have much less interest.

It may be that there is no other place, probably no other place that has attained in so short a time the wonderful prosperity of Singapore, that has a record of the details, even to unimportant matters, of its growth from its very birth, and, through babyhood and boyhood, up to manhood ; and for this reason also it seemed to me better to err on the side of including too much, rather than to omit any information that was still to be found. It may be that it is only Singapore that has the materials still available for such a record, and, as the place continues to grow, so may the contents of such a book continue to be of interest.

If this book succeeds in keeping alive the contents of many of the old papers, though necessarily in a briefer form, it is only due to the time, thought, trouble, and expense, freely given by the old writers about Singapore, whom I have named. I came to Singapore in 1864, a time when some of the first residents were alive ; a few here and many more in Europe. I have sat at dinner, in Governor Cavenagh's time, at Government House in Grange Road, with Mr. Ibbetson, a very old man, who had been Governor of the Straits in 1829, but long resided in Penang; and I had known of the place, as a boy, from a lady in England (mentioned at pages 155 and 297) from whom and her husband, Mr. Seymour Clarke (both long since dead), my brothers and sisters and I received much kindness as children ; through whom and Mr. W. H. Read, Mrs. Clarke's brother, it was that I came to Singapore, rather than to India, when I had to leave the climate of England ; and it was their children who gave the beautiful peal of bells which hang in St. Andrew's Cathedral. That lady, as a child, used to play about in the garden of her father's house on the slope of old Government Hill, now called Fort Canning, close to where the Freemasons Hall now stands. So I did not undertake the task without some personal knowledge of older days, and some appreciation of the meaning and allusions contained in such old papers as were still to be traced ; while it has been to me a work of gratitude to many I have known here, to record what they have done, and a labour of love.

My very warm acknowledgments and those of the readers of the book, are due to Mr. A. W. Bean, an amateur photographer of unusual experience, who has taken the photographs of many old pictures, to be reproduced as illustrations to this book. The result has been better than was anticipated, as some of the originals were old and much defaced, but he took infinite pains to produce the best result possible, which the pictures certainly show.

I wish (solely for my own satisfaction, and on the principle that he who pays the piper has the right to call the tune) to close this preface with a passage from the translation of the *Hikayat Abdullah* (see page 28), which always makes me laugh. It is the end of old Munshi Abdullah's preface or introduction to *his* work about Singapore and matters connected therewith? It is as follows :—

"No doubt there will be found many mistakes, lapses, and things forgotten, both in style and narrative, as well as in junction of the letters or in the entanglement of words. Now may I bow my head before the Europeans and native gentlemen who take the trouble to read my story, so as properly to have acquaintance therewith ; and as thus at the very beginning of my book I have acknowledged my deficiencies and ignorance, I all the more heartily and willingly ask pardon and forgiveness ; and I further state that it has no claim to the name of being a clever one, but, on the contrary is full of stupidities and errors in every time and period."*

SINGAPORE, *December, 1902.*

---

* *N.B.*—This has the same weight as " Your most obedient, humble servant " at the end of an English letter !

ILLUSTRATIONS.

VOLUME II.

CONTENTS.

CONTENTS—*contd.*

SOME OF THE STORIES IN THIS BOOK.

ADDITIONS AND CORRECTIONS.

Page.	Para.	Line.	
21	2	last	*After* " Chapter IV," *add* " on page 35. "
52	last	8	*For* " ask reinforcements " *read* " ask for reinforcements. "
75	last	6	*For* " former years " *read* " after years. "
76	3	10	*For* " McSwiney " *read* " Coleman. "
95	2	last	*After* " related hereafter " *add* " on page 651. "
111	2	2	*For* " Superintendence " *read* " superintendence.
140	3	14	*For* " Journey " *read* " Journal. "
145	2	5	*For* " Zero " *read* " Zeta. "
146	6	2	" Come to Rhio from Tringanu. " Mr. Read writes : " This must be a mistake, as it was Sultan Hussein who went to Pahang not to Tringanu. Abdul Rahman remained at Peningat and Rhio as usual. " *See* " Play and Politics, at page 10.
151	3	15	*For* " former years " *read* " after years. "
157	3	6	*For* " contained is, " *read* " contained in. "
164	3	last	*After* " another chapter " *add* " at page 242. "
175	4	14	*For* " power us over, " *read* " power to hand us over. "
177	2	17	*For* " exporation, " *read* " exportation. "
177	2	last	*After* " first chapter " *add* " on page 7. "
187	2	1	*For* " when son " *read* " when his son. "
193	4	5	*For* " John Spottiswoode, " *read* " William Spottiswoode."
199	4	3	*For* " masts, " *read* " mast."
200		footnote	*For* " Crawford, " *read* " Crawfurd. "
201	4	6	*For* " John Price, " *read* " John Prince. "
202	—	7	*For* " W. Holloway, " *read* " Charles Holloway. "
205	last	2	*After* " Straits, " *add* ;—He had landed at Penang on his way, and dismissed nearly the whole staff the first day. He landed quite quietly early in the morning, and met several officials in gorgeous uniform, who did not recognise him. He determined to put down their plumes and uniforms and otherwise reform the staff.
207	2	—	Mr. Read writes : "It was brilliant moonlight the morning of George's walk. The same thing happened to Archie Spottiswoode and John Connolly who went their usual morning ride, and as they reached the Square, where they lived, the 5 o'clock gun fired. Ships anchoring used occasionally to fire a gun, as a sign they had arrived. "
208	2	5	Mr. Schwabe died in London, not Liverpool.
208	2	16	*For* " Mr. Bain " *read* " Mr. Gilbert Bain," and strike out the words " some years. "
208	2	19	*For* " James Young " *read* " Jasper Young. "

Page.	Para.	Line.	
208	3	2	Mr. Read writes: "Surely the statement that pirate prahus were from six to eight tons and sixty to seventy feet long is a mistake? I should have thought them to be 25 to 30 tons, and some 20 feet shorter." The statement was found in an old paper, but Mr. Read is much more likely to be correct.
219	1	13	*After* "5th September" *add* "1832." (The "Magicienne" came at the time of the second Naning expedition).
219	3	3	1849 (the figures have a broken letter.)
221	2	8	Strike out the words "now Woodsville Cottage." Mr. Balestier's house was on his plantation, near where the Rifle Butts are now; Woodsville Cottage was Dr. Montgomerie's house, still standing.
230	5	5	*For* "present days" *read* "present day."
233	last	4	*Add* that Mr. William Paterson came to Singapore in 1843.
234	last	10	*After* "the two partners" *add* "in Shaw Whitehead & Co"
257	5	3	Mr. Read writes: "Sister St. Joseph was from America, a sister of Mr. Spooner of Russell & Co. of Canton."
269	3	7	*For* "buildings has" *read* "buildings have."
281	6	1	*For* "Marryatt" *read* "Marryat."
297	3	13	*For* "Lucy Julia Beamont," *read* "Lucy Julia Beaumont."
297	5	7	*For* "five last" *read* "four last." Mrs. A. S. Saunders is the daughter of Mr. W. H. Read.
297	5	16	*For* "Lancashire" *read* "Lancaster."
310	3	7	*For* "the Settlement" *read* "that Settlement." Captain C. M. Elliot used to call William Scott the "Ancient of Days."
328	2	last	Mr. Read writes: "Keppel's band struck in the middle of a quadrille. He addressed the band-master, 'Eager, what is this?'—'Cannot get anything to drink, Sir.' Mr. Church said 'Nonsense, I gave them three bottles of beer.' The later party was not given by Napier, but at W. W. Ker's house on Beach Road. It is quite true that the band played the Rogues March opposite Church's house."
382		end	The following paragraph, intended to conclude this Chapter, was accidentally omitted from the copy sent to the printers:—Mr. George Henry Brown came to the Straits from Calcutta in or about the year 1840, settling first in Penang. About 1842 he removed to Singapore, where he acquired by grant the property on Thomson Road to which he gave the name of Mount Pleasant. This was then clothed with virgin forest, haunted by tigers. He cleared a large part of it, made roads, built houses, and planted nutmegs. The nutmeg plantation ultimately failed, like all the others in Singapore, though more gradually than some. Mr. Brown was a man of great versatility. He possessed great mechanical ability. During some periods of his career he engaged in carriage-making, and constructed carriages of much finish and durability. He became an expert in

Page. Para. Line.

gutta percha, and was very successful in mixing various qualities to render them more workable. He was one of the earliest shipowners in Singapore, and had at one time three sailing vessels trading to China and Japan. Mr. Brown was an enthusiast in music, and was a fair performer on the pianoforte and the violin. For some years he had meetings at his house for the practice of instrumental music, which were frequented by the d'Almeida's and other musical amateurs, and at which public performances were sometimes prepared. He was for some years honorary organist of the old St. Andrew's Church. When the Presbyterian congregation was formed, in 1858, Mr. Brown joined it. About the same time, or shortly afterwards, the old Church had to be removed, and during the erection, on the same site. of the present St. Andrew's Cathedral the congregations of both the English and the Presbyterian Church met (at different hours) in the old Mission Chapel belonging to the London Missionary Society, at the angle formed by North Bridge Road and Bras Bassa Road. To that Chapel the old organ was removed, and when the new St. Andrew's was opened, Mr. Brown purchased it for the use of the Presbyterian Church, and from that time, and for many years, was honorary organist, using the same organ until a new one was obtained, which he himself erected in the existing building. (This latter instrument was afterwards taken into the Cathedral of the Good Shepherd, where it is still in use.)

In his latter years Mr. Brown started the growing of tapioca on his estate, and had works for the manufacture of the root. In September, 1881, he had a terrible accident with the machinery, in which he lost his left arm. He never regained his strength, and died in October, 1882, in the 65th year of his age, at Penang, where he had gone in the hope that the air of the hill would revive him.

419	Names	7	*Read* "Cumming, J. B.," *and take out the* "B" after Crane T. O.
437	7	2	*For* "Curteis" *read* "Curties."
477	1	2	*For* "Indian Cavalry" *read* "Bengal Cavalry," and for daughter *read* "step-daughter," Mrs. Seymour was a daughter of Mrs. Burton, who was one of the daughters of Colonel Farquhar, and married W. R. George after Burton's death, who had been in A. L. Johnston & Co.'s office. Andrew Farquhar was a son of the Andrew Farquhar mentioned on pages 98 and 166 and a grandson of Colonel Farquhar.
512	1	10	*For* "all good work done Mr. Thomson" *read* "all the good work done by Mr. Thomson."

Page.	Para.	Line.	
514	last	5	*For* "Plumb and Rule" *read* "Plumb-rule."
557	4	5	*For* "Inchi Abdullah" *read* "Moonshi Abdullah."
573	—	—	Monk's Hill House was built by C. A. Dyce who lived in it for some years.
602	1	8	*For* "and the manœvres" *read* "and to the manœvres."
605	2	2	*For* "of the name" *read* "if the name."
611	3	last	Mr. Read writes: "Poor Mauduit fell into a tiger pit, the stake ran through him, and he died shortly afterwards.'
628	1	15	*For* "bowstay" *read* "bobstay."
629	2	2	*For* "Ariel" *read* "Frolic."
631	4	3	Mr. Read writes: "Punch said £2,000. It was a misprint in the Singapore paper."
650	2	—	Mr. Read writes: "Naval charts were funny things in the forties. In his book called 'Rajah Brooke's Journal' published in 1845, Keppel said that he sailed sixty miles inland, according to the Admiralty charts, on his first visit to Borneo in the *Dido*. I had for a long time in my office in Singapore a chart of the China sea on which every shoal or island reported by captains for about 25 years was marked down. I showed it to Raynell of the *Waterwitch*, and he would not look at it, saying that if he did, he would not dare to beat up the China sea against the monsoon. One half of the dangers did not exist. Captains thought they were dangers, but did not verify them."
723	3	3	*For* "Sir William Jeffcott" *read* "Sir William Norris."
789	1	2	*For* "over a quarter" *read* "nearly a quarter." The last census gave the population of Singapore as 228,555.
Index	—	—	Under Keppel, for "403" *read* "405."

INTRODUCTORY.

CHAPTER I.

Sir Stamford Raffles.

CHAPTER I.

SIR STAMFORD RAFFLES.

THE very remarkable prosperity and continually increasing progress of Singapore are so entirely to be traced to the great ability and noble character of Sir Thomas Stamford Raffles, that it seems impossible to commence the story of the place without speaking of him.

He was born on board-ship off the island of Jamaica on July 5th, 1781. His father was one of the oldest captains in the West India trade, sailing out of London. The boy was sent to a boarding school at Hammersmith, near London, but he had been there hardly two years when he was placed, at the age of fourteen, as a clerk in the large offices of the Honorable East India Company in Leadenhall Street, in the City of London, where the vast political and commercial interests of the East India Company were supervised from England. He never ceased to regret the necessity which took him so early from school, and throughout his life seemed to feel as if he considered himself in some ways deficient in education, though his published correspondence shews that there was no need for such a feeling, as it is a model of correct and forcible language.

After leaving school, he gave up his time, before and after office hours, to the study of languages and science, and taught himself French so thoroughly that it was of great service to him in after years in Java. All he earned was carried home to his parents, who were at that time in difficulties, which no doubt accounts for his being started so early in life. A little story that is told of his mother complaining of his extravagance in burning a candle in his room at night in order to study, after having been in office all day, tells a pathetic tale of the way the daily wants of the family were supplied. While in his young days he deprived himself of every indulgence for their sake, he delighted, in the after days of comparative affluence, in surrounding his mother with every comfort he could give her.

In 1805 the Directors determined to increase their establishment at Penang, and Raffles, although he was unusually young for such a post, was sent out as Assistant Secretary. On the voyage he taught himself the Malay language, and soon after his arrival, Mr. Dundas, the Governor of Penang, received a letter from Mr. Marsden asking some questions about Malay literature.

William Marsden was the son of English parents of good family who had settled in Ireland in the reign of Queen Anne. He was at school in Dublin, and when he was sixteen, in 1771, went out to Bencoolen, where he was for eight years. Three years afterwards he wrote his " History of Sumatra " which made his reputation. He became Chief Secretary to the Admiralty, where he was for twelve years. He then returned to his favourite studies, and wrote the Malay Grammar and Dictionary. He was the first literary and scientific Englishman, with the advantage of local knowledge, who wrote about the Malay countries, with laborious care and scrupulous fidelity. He died in 1836, eighty-two years old, and left his library to King's College, London, and his Oriental manuscripts, medals, &c., to the British Museum.

Mr. Marsden's letter was at once handed to Raffles, as the person best qualified to answer it, and Mr. Marsden, after receiving the Governor's reply enclosing Raffles' answers to the enquiries in the letter, wrote to Raffles and a brisk correspondence was kept up between them, until he returned to England in 1816, when they met and became warm personal friends. The reply to the letter in question, written so soon after his arrival in Penang, shows how complete his knowledge of the language had become. Three years afterwards, Raffles sent Mr. Marsden a sketch of a Malay grammar he had drawn out and wrote to say that he was compiling a dictionary which Mr. Marsden was welcome to, if it was of any service to him; and two years afterwards he wrote " How goes on the dictionary?" alluding to Marsden's Malay Dictionary which is still indispensable to students of Malay here. While Raffles was in Penang, two Governors died, and he himself was so seriously ill, in the new climate, that little hopes were entertained of saving his life. In 1808 he went for a short trip to Malacca and returned to Penang, and it was entirely in consequence of a long and very able letter he then wrote to the Bengal Government that the intention was abandoned to destroy all the public buildings in Malacca, to take all the inhabitants to Penang, and to abandon the place, in the hope of improving Penang. This had been absolutely decided on but Raffles' despatch prevented what, it can now be seen, would have been a very foolish, unnecessary, and discreditable policy. He afterwards was sent back to Malacca to collect information and to prepare the way for Lord Minto, and left there on the 18th June, 1811, with him on the expedition to Java.

During the first decade of the nineteenth century much damage was done to the English trade in the Archipelago by French privateers which found refuge in the Dutch possessions. The Dutch had been forced by the French into the European wars and the Dutch Colonies had passed into the power of the French when Holland became dependent upon France during the wars of Napoleon; and Lord Minto, the Governor-General of India, had determined to attack Java. The English fleet which numbered ninety vessels, carrying 6,000 European and 6,000 native troops, left Malacca on the 11th June, 1811, and the army landed in Java near Batavia on the 4th August. On the 9th the troops occupied Batavia unopposed, and on the 26th at the great battle of Cornelis, seven miles from Batavia, (in which the English loss was

500, and the enemy's loss was 4,000 and 5,000 were taken prisoners) the English rescued Java from the French, and it became British territory.

Lord Minto remained six weeks in Java, and left Raffles there as the Lieutenant-Governor. The accounts of his extraordinary energy and judgment in the government of six millions of people, divided into thirty residencies, all chafing under former mismanagement, cannot be mentioned here; but when he left Batavia in March, 1816, the roads were filled with boats, crowded with people of all nationalities, who came to see his departure. The deck of the vessel was quite covered with fruit and flowers and offerings of every description; and it was said that it was impossible to describe the scene which took place when the vessel weighed anchor; the people declaring that Java had lost the greatest friend she had ever possessed.

He sailed for England, calling on the way at St. Helena, and having an interview with Napoleon Buonaparte whom he was anxious to see. The ex-Emperor refused to see any visitors, but on being told it was Raffles, late Governor of Java, he immediately consented to receive him. Raffles was told to address him as General, not Emperor, and if Buonaparte received him with his hat on, Raffles was not to continue the conversation uncovered. Buonaparte asked a number of questions about Java and its trade, with which he seemed to be well acquainted. Raffles reached England in October, 1816, and was knighted in the following summer.

In October, 1817, he was appointed Lieutenant-Governor of Bencoolen, and embarked on board the "Lady Raffles" at Portsmouth, and reached Bencoolen on the 22nd of March, 1818. It was then a most wretched place, and the shocks of earthquakes had so damaged the house he had to live in, that no one else would trust himself in it. It was while he was there in April, 1818, that we find him writing about the necessity for such a port as Singapore. He wrote that it was indispensable that the British government should have regular authority in the Archipelago to declare and maintain British rights; that these at that time extended no further south than Malacca; and that the Dutch wanted to confine Bencoolen to the almost inaccessible and rocky shores of the west coast of Sumatra; that it would be desirable to fix a convenient station, which would probably be somewhere in the neighbourhood of Bintang, or Bentan, (an island opposite Singapore) known to navigators by its hill. He said that the object was not territory; it could be confined to a simple commercial station, with a military guard; and when once formed would soon maintain a successful rivalry with the Dutch, who would be obliged either to adopt a liberal system of free trade, or see the trade of those seas collected under the British flag. How true this has proved, the history of Singapore has amply shown.

This seemed to him a matter of such supreme importance, that he determined to go to Bengal, and urge it in person; and having no choice, and not considering his own comfort, he went with Lady Raffles in a very small vessel with only one little cabin, where centipedes and scorpions roved about at their pleasure. The vessel lost a mast in the Bay of Bengal, and to crown her misfortunes a drunken pilot put her on shore on a bank at the mouth of the Hooghly, where she literally upset, and Sir Stamford and Lady Raffles were taken up to Calcutta in a boat.

The result of his interviews with Lord Hastings, then Governor-General, was that Sir Stamford was appointed Agent to the Governor-General to occupy some central station within the Archipelago, to the southward of Malacca, so as to secure free trade with the Archipelago and China through the Straits of Malacca, and to concede to the Dutch their pretensions in Sumatra. The effect of this appointment was to render Raffles quite independent of the government of Penang, and to place the management of British interests to the South of Malacca under his government at Bencoolen. Colonel Bannerman was Governor of Penang, and as will be shewn presently, he tried, from jealousy, to mar the efforts of Raffles, and behaved (to use the words of Mr. Boulger) with extraordinary baseness. Colonel Bannerman died on the 8th August, 1819, at Penang. He had been made Governor of Penang on 24th November, 1817. In January, 1819, Raffles had arrived at Penang from Calcutta, and wrote to Mr. Marsden that he was yet uncertain how far he might be successful in his mission, and said that Rhio had been lost by the English neglecting to occupy it, and that there would be difficulty in founding an establishment elsewhere, but that he should certainly attempt it. He also had a mission to Acheen (which we do not enter on here), which gave him much anxiety.

In the *Singapore Chronicle* of 1831, we have found a letter, re-printed from the Asiatic Journal, written by Colonel William Farquhar of the East India Company's service, in which he claims to have had at least a large share in the merit attributed to Sir Stamford Raffles for founding Singapore. Major Farquhar had been for several years Resident and Commandant at Malacca, which he had handed over again to the Dutch in September, 1818. He was on his way home when he met Raffles on his way from Penang to the south. Raffles had brought a complimentary letter from Lord Hastings, the Governor-General, say-ing that he hoped that circumstances would admit of Major Farquhar accompanying Sir Stamford Raffles, in order to assume the control of the new establishment, at least during its infancy. So he turned back again, and he and Sir Stamford discussed the position of the most advan-tageous site for the projected settlement.

Major Farquhar says that the Carimon Islands appeared to him to be the best, as they were in the direct track of all ships passing up and down the Straits, but that Sir Stamford thought the old Malay Settlement of Johore, upon the peninsula, was better. On visiting the Carimons on their way, they were found not to afford the local advantages he had expected, so he, Major Farquhar, suggested that it might be advis-able to stop at Singapore on the way to Johore. This appears to be very improbable, because we find no trace of this in any of Raffles' writings, and we do find traces of his attention having been attracted, no doubt in his eager studies of Malay literature, to the old sea-port of Singapore. Lady Raffles says " before he left England, Sir Stam-ford contemplated Singapore, a classical spot, as a place favorably situated to have a British station." And in a letter Raffles wrote on board-ship off Calcutta on December 12th, 1818, to Mr. Marsden, he said that his attention was principally turned to Johore, and that Marsden must not be surprised if his next letter was "dated from the site of the ancient city of Singapura."

The Major goes on to say that on the following day he went to Rhio for the purpose of endeavouring to obtain permission from the native viceroy to form a new Settlement in Singapore in place of the Carimons, and after some difficulty the viceroy so far acceded as to say that, as far as he was concerned, as governor of the dominions of Johore, he had no kind of objection, but that he had already been *obliged* to sign a treaty with the Dutch by which he was restricted from granting permission to any European power to have a footing within any part of the territory of Johore; but as he had, before the treaty was signed, granted Major Farquhar permission to form a settlement upon the Carimon Islands, he left him and Sir Stamford Raffles to the use of their own discretion in establishing a settlement at Singapore.

So the Major returned there, and in conjunction with Sir Stamford concluded a treaty, which was signed by Sir Stamford alone with both the Native Chiefs who were then present at Singapore. The treaty was signed on the 6th February, and the British flag was formally hoisted, and the island taken possession of, and Sir Stamford sailed the very next day on his return to Penang.

Since the above passages were written in 1884, about Colonel Farquhar's claim to take the credit of the selection of Singapore, a Memorial sent by him to the Court of Directors in London, and of Sir Stamford's reply have came to light in Mr. Boulger's book, but they only bear out what was said. The letter in the *Singapore Chronicle* (which can no longer be found) was probably a reprint of part of the Memorial. Mr. Boulger's conclusion is that Farquhar had no pretension even to a minor contributory part in the acquisition of Singapore.

From Penang in the same month of February, Sir Stamford wrote to the Duchess of Somerset in England, with whom he kept up a continual correspondence, and he explained to her how to find Singapore on the map (which directions have had to be given to many others since, but are yearly becoming less necessary; the English idea that the place is somewhere in the centre of India being less frequent than formerly). He says, in the letter, that on the spot—the site of the ancient maritime capital of the Malays, and within the walls of those fortifications, raised not less than six centuries ago—he had planted the British flag, where he trusted it would long triumphantly wave.

On the 10th June he was again writing from Singapore. He wrote: "I shall say nothing of the importance which I attach to the permanence of the position I have taken up at Singapore; it is a child of my own. But for my Malay studies, I should hardly have known that such a place existed; not only the European, but the Indian world was also ignorant of it. I am sure you will wish me success; and if my plans are confirmed at home, it is my intention to make this my principal residence, and to devote the remaining years of my stay in the East to the advancement of a Colony which, in every way in which it can be viewed, bids fair to be one of the most important, and at the same time one of the least expensive and troublesome, which we possess. Our object is not territory but trade; a great commercial emporium and a fulcrum, whence we may extend our influence politically as circumstances may hereafter require. By taking immediate possession, we put a negative to the Dutch claim of exclusion; and, at the same time, revive the drooping confidence of our allies and friends. One free port in these seas must eventually destroy the spell of Dutch monopoly."

In these passages about the old Malay capital, Sir Stamford alluded to the Malay history or tradition to be found now at length in the books of Mr. Marsden and Mr. Crawfurd and in Mr. Braddell's translations in Mr. Logan's Journal.

Four months afterwards, Sir Stamford had returned to Singapore, having only stayed at Acheen and Penang a sufficient time to settle the troublesome point he had been deputed in Calcutta to take in hand; and on the 10th June he wrote from Singapore to another friend: "Our station completely outflanks the Straits of Malacca, and secures a passage for our China ships at all times, and under all circumstances. It has further been my good fortune to discover one of the most safe and extensive harbours in these seas, with every facility for protecting shipping in time of war. In short, Singapore is everything we could desire, and I may consider myself most fortunate in the selection: it will soon rise into importance; and with this single station alone I would undertake to counteract all the plans of Mynheer; it breaks the spell; and they are no longer the exclusive sovereigns of the Eastern Seas.

Five days later he wrote: "Everything is going on well here, it bids fair to be the next port to Calcutta; all we want now is the *certainty of permanent possession,* and this, of course, depends upon authorities beyond our control. You may take my word for it, this is by far the most important station in the East; and as far as naval superiority and commercial interests are concerned, of much higher value than whole continents of territory."

Certainty of permanent possession! It is difficult to state shortly what difficulties were thrown in his way, and how (as Mr. Earl wrote in 1838) "Singapore was established, without the concurrence, indeed with the decided disapprobation of the Home Government." A letter had been sent after him by the Supreme Government from Calcutta, after he had started for Penang, which fortunately he did not receive till too late, and Singapore had been founded. The letter ordered him to desist from the attempt to found a station. The Government in Calcutta were afraid of the action of the Dutch. Colonel Bannerman heard in Penang that the Dutch were preparing to seize Singapore by a coup-de-main, and (in his efforts to prevent Raffles carrying out the project) wrote an abject letter to the Dutch Governor of Malacca entreating him to do nothing till he could refer Raffles' action to Calcutta; and a nice letter he wrote to Calcutta! To Major Farquhar in Singapore he wrote advising him to abandon the place at once as it was impossible to resist the overpowering armament at the disposal of Batavia, and saying that *defeat would tarnish British honour more than the retreat of the small party at Singapore.* He refused to send any assistance. The Dutch did not come, the few Englishmen did not go, and here we are still. All that was required was time for Singapore to show what it was worth. The expense of a whole year, Mr. Egerton says, was less than that of one month in Bencoolen, and no one talked any more about "running away."

It was not until Singapore had been established for three years, and the trade had reached a value of several millions of dollars in the last year, that it was recognised by Great Britain; and it was not until April, 1826, and only three months before his death, that the Court of Directors acknowledged that Sir Stamford had been a match for the Dutch and that the Company were greatly indebted to him for establishing the Settlement of Singapore. His view of responsibility was expressed in his own words, in reference to another matter altogether, when he said that it was true that, by incurring responsibility, a man might lose both his fortune and his fame, but that no man was fit for high station anywhere who was not prepared to risk even more than fame and fortune at the call of judgment and his conscience.

Sir Stamford returned to Bencoolen in a vessel with Lady Raffles and one of their children of four months old, after staying two or three months in Singapore. The ship struck on a bank in the Straits of Rhio, it was feared she could not be got off, and a small boat was got ready to endeavour to take them back to Singapore. Just as they were leaving the vessel, hopes were entertained that by throwing all the water overboard to lighten the vessel still more, she might be got off, and before morning the attempt succeeded. They thought it fortunate it had happened so near Rhio, and stopping there, sent a boat on shore stating what had happened and requesting a supply of water. The Dutch Resident refused all intercourse, asserted that Sir Stamford came as a spy, and would not give the assistance that was urgently needed by Lady Raffles and the baby. The voyage was continued with considerable anxiety, when, in the Straits of Banca, the Captain of an American vessel stopped, at some risk, and, with great difficulty, by means of ropes, conveyed to them some casks of water. Lady Raffles adds that his name was forgotten, but his kindness was always remembered.

For years afterwards, the Dutch refused to allow any person of his name or his family to enter Java unmolested, and when Sir Stamford was going to Bencoolen in June, 1823, the vessel had to put into Batavia to land some cargo from Bengal. Lady Raffles was very unwell, and Sir Stamford asked permission for her to land for two or three days, and received a reply allowing it in very grudging terms and expressing the greatest possible surprise at their coming into the port. Sir Stamford never left the ship but the people were not to be restrained, and the vessel was the scene of a crowd of visitors of all ranks flocking to see him. That Sir Stamford was far above any such ill-natured feelings, on his side, is shown by one anecdote. Some time after this, the Java Government were in distress for money (as Lady Raffles and her child had been in distress for want of water to drink), and it was sought to raise a loan of thirty lacs of rupees in Bengal. But there was a feverish anxiety in Calcutta as to the security of the Dutch, and the loan was closed, when the only subscription to it, actually realized, was that of Thomas Stamford Raffles.

Another anecdote will show the influence Sir Stamford Raffles was possessed of in other parts of the world than in this Archipelago, where he was principally known. In 1880, two boys, born in Singapore, and sent to school in England, were taken to see the Zoological Gardens in London. The party were in the large new lion house that had been lately built, and were passing along the front of the cages, where the boys were interested in noticing that some of the tigers had been sent from Singapore by the Maharaja of Johore. When they reached the middle of the hall one of the boys suddenly stopped and pointed to a bust placed in the most conspicuous part of the room on the wall over the front of the cages, and said to his brother that it was like that in Singapore. And so it was, for it is a duplicate of the bust made by Chantrey which is in the Raffles Institution, where the boys had been at school. Under the bust is an inscription to the effect that Sir Thomas Stamford Raffles was the Founder and first President of the Society, which has now a world-wide name and reputation.

In an article in the London *Daily Telegraph* of 12th July, 1886, it speaks of this bust, and says that Sir Francis Chantrey took extreme interest in the Zoological Gardens and contributed not a little towards it. It also says that the Gardens were instituted by Sir Stamford Raffles, Sir Humphrey Davy, Lord Darnley, Sir Everard Home, and other distinguished naturalists; placing Raffles first. It seems more than likely that the meeting of Raffles and Chantrey about the affairs of the Society led to the making of the bust. The article concludes by saying, "when the managers of the Zoological Gardens set up the bust of Sir Stamford Raffles in their new "Lion House," they paid a just and graceful compliment to one of the first and most distinguished founders of their Society."

Sir Stamford returned to Bencoolen in August or September, and in November, 1820, he considered it indispensable to proceed again to Calcutta, where he arrived in the same month. He was received with great enthusiasm by the mercantile community, which, like the mercantile community of Singapore, recognised, many years before the Government, the great benefit he. had bestowed upon trade. They gave him a public dinner, and made every possible demonstration to please him; and, after he left, sent a representation to Government supporting what he had done. The old saying, that it is astonishing with how little wisdom the world is governed, would never have been better exemplified than if the Government had given orders to break up the establishment at Singapore; which would have been given if it had not been for the steady persistence of Sir Stamford; and the courage, he so strongly possessed, of his own opinions.

In a letter written in 1820 to his cousin, he said: "Singapore continues to thrive most wonderfully, it is all and everything I could wish, and if no untimely fate awaits it, promises to become the emporium and pride of the east. I learn with much regret the prejudice and malignity by which I am attacked at home, for the desperate struggle I have maintained against the Dutch. Instead of being supported by my own Government, I find them deserting me, and giving way in every instance to the unscrupulous Dutch. All, however, is safe so far, and if matters are only allowed to remain as they are, all will go well. The great blow has been struck, and though I may personally suffer in the scuffle, the nation must be benefited; and I should not be surprised were the Ministers to recall me, though I should, on many accounts, regret it at the present moment. Were the value of Singapore properly appreciated, I am confident that all England would be in its favour; it positively takes nothing from the Dutch, and is to us everything."

Then a series of domestic calamities fell upon them in Bencoolen, of the most distressing kind. In 1850, Dr. Robert Little, of Singapore, wrote in Logan's Journal some lengthy papers on the subject of fever, and in Volume 4, at pages 711 and 715, are remarks upon the reasons for the unhealthiness of Bencoolen at that time. In October, Lady Raffles' brother died there from the effects of an illness occasioned by the fatigue and exposure of a campaign. In 1821 their eldest boy Leopold, named after the Prince, died after a very short illness; in the January following two more of their children were buried in Bencoolen. No one reading Sir Stamford's letters written at that time, interspersed with long letters on affairs of State and frequent reference to Singapore, can fail to see how much his life was affected by these trials; and no wonder that, in their consternation, the parents lost all confidence in the climate, and after a struggle sent away to England, in the very first vessel, with their old nurse, their only remaining child at that time, an infant named Ella. One of the boys that died was named Marsden, after Mr. Marsden his godfather. Lady Raffles' health was in a very precarious state.

In January, 1822, Sir Stamford wrote: "We have, thank God, recovered very much of late, and Sophia (Lady Raffles) is quite herself again. I am but a crazy mortal at best, but, on the whole, am quite as well in health as I have any right to expect in a climate which is anything but congenial to my constitution. We still hold our determination of quitting India for Europe about the end of next year; neither of us can hold out longer. We now pass our time in great retirement." On the 15th September, the day they left Bencoolen for Singapore, they buried another dear and invaluable friend, Dr. Jack, who died on board a vessel in the harbour, to which he had been taken to sail for the Cape after a serious illness.

On the 10th October, 1822, Sir Stamford again landed, for the third time, in Singapore. He wrote: "It is imposible for any one to see it, after Bencoolen, without surprise and emotion. And after the loss of almost everything that was dear to me on that ill-fated coast, and after all the risks and trials to which Singapore has been exposed, what must be my feelings to find it grown and advanced beyond measure, and even beyond my warmest anticipations and expectations— in importance, wealth and interest, in everything that can give it value and permanence. I felt, when I left Bencoolen, that the time had passed when I could take much active interest in Indian affairs, and I wished myself safe home; but I already feel differently. I feel a new life and vigour about me; and if it please God to grant me health, the next six months will, I hope, make some amends for the gloom of last sixteen."

Sir Stamford remained in Singapore until the 9th June, 1823, having been there for eight months, and never returned. He went to Bencoolen, and waited for the arrival of a vessel called the *Fame*, which was to take him to England. She did not arrive when expected, and at last, wearied out by disappointment, and beginning to think (as he wrote) that they seemed doomed to end their days in Bencoolen, for Lady Raffles had had another severe illness, and another infant, the last one remaining with them in Bencoolen, had been lost, they decided to leave in the *Borneo*, the same small vessel in which they had sent away their little child Ella, and the nurse, two years before. The vessel was ready for sea when the *Fame* arrived, fortunately as they supposed. The *Borneo* made a safe passage, the fate of the *Fame* we shall give in some of Sir Stamford's own words. It may be added that the *Fame* was insured, so the owner suffered no loss; that the East India Company had only a few tons of saltpetre on board for ballast, so they suffered no loss: and all the loss fell, as a last reminiscence of unhappy Bencoolen, on the man who met with an almost overwhelming calamity.

Throughout Sir Stamford's life in the East, he had taken a great interest in science, and had made collections of many different kinds, which could never be made again; he carried on a large correspondence with Mr. Marsden and others on scientific subjects, and on this his last voyage to England, after so many years, he took all his treasures with him.

The vessel sailed at daylight, and in the evening she was on fire, which was caused by the steward going with a naked light to draw some brandy from a cask, which took fire. They had just time to get clear of her in the boats, without time even to put any clothes over their sleeping dresses, when the vessel blew up. The first alarm was given at twenty minutes past eight; at half past eight there was not a soul on board, and soon after the magazine exploded, leaving them in open boats at sea, fifty miles from land, at night. There were two children with them, whose names are not mentioned. Their last child in Bencoolen had died shortly before. One of the two children was snatched out of bed when it was already on fire. This, it is thought, was William Charles Raffles Flint, afterwards Vicar of Sunningdale in England, and the subsequent heir to Sir Stamford's property, part of which is known as Flint Street here now. Ella Raffles, the child who was sent home in the *Borneo* died in 1841 at St. Leonards-on-Sea of consumption under twenty years of age, and Mr. Flint came into the property. The other was probably a child of Dr. Jack, who had died shortly before. The two children were wrapped up in the sailors' neckcloths, and everything else was swallowed up in one big ruin, as Sir Stamford expressed it.

After this chapter appeared in the *Free Press* newspaper in 1884, a letter was received from old Mr. Thomas Dunman in England, who is often referred to further on. He wrote "Will you allow me to tell you a story, told me by my dear late friend Captain William Scott of

Singapore. It may interest those who read your papers about old Singapore. In the *Free Press* of October 4th, I read this—"The other was probably a child of Dr. Jack," &c. Not so I think, for William Scott told me that on board the *Fame*, which was burnt to the water's edge, his son David was rescued from death by Sir Stamford Raffles. It was thought all hands were safe and in the boats, when it was discovered the child David was still on board. Raffles rushed back, found him and took him to the boat; David Scott was afterwards an officer in the Indian Army, and came to Singapore to see his father, and I was at his father's house on the last day, and we had a very pleasant evening together. The next morning he left in a sailing vessel for Calcutta to join his regiment and she was never heard of." And old Mr. James Guthrie, since dead, added under Mr. Dunman's note (which had been sent to him to look at) "Guthrie & Co. had a small shipment on board, insured with the Commercial Insurance Company, you might find the name of the ship, which Tom Dunman forgets, in their books. Besides Lieut. Scott, Mr. Lewis of the Bengal Civil Service was on board. She must have gone down in a hurricane in the Bay of Bengal."

They reached Bencoolen in safety after much anxiety and discomfort. The description written by Sir Stamford, two days afterwards, of the fire and of his loss, is too long to be printed here, but it should be read by every one who can admire a steady mind and quiet courage in the face of a great calamity. When he reached shore, he says that he went to bed at three o'clock in the afternoon and never woke until six the next morning. The only portion of the account which we reprint is Sir Stamford's remarks upon his loss; he wrote on the day after he reached the shore: "The loss I have to regret, beyond all, is my papers and drawings; all my notes and observations, with memoirs and collections, sufficient for a full and ample history, not only of Sumatra, but of Borneo, and almost every other island of note in these seas; *my intended account of the establishment of Singapore*; the history of my own administration; eastern grammars, dictionaries, and vocabularies; and last, but not least, a grand map of Sumatra, on which I had been employed since my arrival here, and on which, for the last six months, I had bestowed almost my whole undivided attention. This, however, was not all; all my collections in natural history; all my splendid collection of drawings, upwards of two thousand in number; with all the valuable papers and notes of my friends, Dr. Arnold and Dr. Jack; and, to conclude, I will merely notice that there was scarcely an unknown animal, bird, beast, or fish, or an interesting plant, which we had not on board—a living tapir, a new species of tiger, splendid pheasants, &c., domesticated for the voyage; we were in this respect a perfect Noah's ark. All—all has perished; but, thank God, our lives have been spared, and we do not repine; our plan is to get another ship as soon as possible. Make your minds easy about us, even if we should be later than you expected. No news will be good news."

In the Hakayit Abdulla, of which we shall often have occasion to speak further on, is a passage in which Abdulla, who was the Malay writer for Raffles and was much attached to him, wrote of the loss of the *Fame*. His words were spoken of, many years ago, as giving " a literary photograph of the collection of treasures that were lost." The following translation was made by Mr. J. T. Thomson:—Abdulla says, " I learnt from Colonel Farquhar that the ship in which Mr. Raffles was a passenger, having sailed from Bencoolen, had on the same evening been burnt with all his baggage and collections. When I heard the news I was breathless, remembering all the Malay books of ancient date collected from various sources; all these lost with the wonderful collection. As to his other property I did not care, for, if his life were spared, he could reinstate this. But the books could not be recovered, for none of them were printed, but in manuscript; they were so rare that one country might have only two of them. That is what distressed me. I further remembered his intention of composing a work on these countries, and his promise to put my name in it. All this was gone! When I thought of him I was the more grieved, because it not only was a great personal loss to him, but to Europe, as he had materials for several histories; one on Celebes, one on Borneo, one on Singapore, besides many other subjects. But the material of all these was now gone! My thoughts then turned to the origin of his taking them, but I consoled myself that he himself was saved. In this there was praise due to God, who orders to be and not to be, and acknowledgments are due to his power over his slaves."

It was very characteristic of the wonderful character and indomitable energy of Raffles that the next day after the loss of all that he had been collecting for so many years, he recommenced sketching the map of Sumatra, set all his draftsmen to work on new drawings of some of the most interesting specimens of natural history, sent numbers of people into the jungle to collect more animals, and, instead of any complaints or lamentations, he returned thanks, on the ensuing Sunday, for having preserved the lives of all on board, who had at one time scarcely contemplated escaping death in the open boats so far from shore.

This was not the end of their troubles, for another vessel was engaged, and when they were prepared to embark, her commander went quite suddenly and unexpectedly raving mad. At last, two months after the *Fame* had started on her short voyage, they left by the fourth vessel they had engaged, and reached England safely in August.

He reached England on Sunday the 22nd August, 1824, and only lived for two years, dying suddenly on the stairs from an apoplectic attack, with no one near him, having risen before five o'clock in the morning. His two years in England were clouded over with troubles with the Court of Directors regarding his pecuniary claims on the East India Company and his administration of Java and the establishment of Singapore, all of which will be found fully explained in Mr. Boulger's book. He died at his house, Highwood, Middlesex, on the 5th July, 1826, on his forty-fifth birthday, a young age for one who had done so much for the good of all around him, and for his fellow countrymen after him.

Soon after these papers appeared in the *Free Press*, Mr. Bicknell, who is now the Government Auditor at Penang, was going on leave, and he offered to try to find the grave of Sir Stamford and to copy the inscription. He afterwards wrote the following, which was put in the *Free Press* on the 28th November, 1885:—"I found the walls of the small Parish Church of Hendon covered with tablets, and memorials, but neither in the Church nor in the Churchyard could I find any record of Sir Stamford Raffles. The curate, who was a new arrival, and the old sexton, could give no definite information, but the latter said he was probably buried at Mill Hill, a village not far from Hendon. I accordingly made my way to Mill Hill, which is near Highwood, where the Raffles' family seat was situated. Here also I was unsuccessful in finding the grave of Raffles, but on a stone which was much worn, I found the following hardly legible inscription: "Here resteth the body of Sophia, widow of Sir T. Stamford Raffles, of Highwood, Kt., who departed this life December 12th, 1858, aged 72 years." The sexton of Mill Hill Church, who had been on the place for over 40 years, maintained that Raffles was not buried there, but, as Sir Stamford died even before his time, he may be wrong, especially as the condition of Lady Raffles' grave would justify one in thinking that all traces of her husband's resting place, who died many years before her, might have passed away. Hearing that there was no Church at all at the hamlet of Highwood, I was reluctantly compelled to give up my quest."

In Mr. Boulger's book, written twelve years later, he says, on page 387, that the exact position of the grave at Hendon Church is unknown; and that in 1887 the Rev. R. B. Raffles and his brother erected out of their slender means a brass tablet on the wall of the Church with the following inscription:—

In Memory of

SIR THOMAS STAMFORD RAFFLES, F.R.S., LL.D.,

STATESMAN, ADMINISTRATOR, AND NATURALIST, FOUNDER OF THE COLONY AND CITY OF SINGAPORE, 29TH JANUARY, 1819;

BORN 5TH JULY, 1781, DIED AT HIGHWOOD, MIDDLESEX, 5TH JULY, 1826, AND BURIED NEAR THIS TABLET.

ERECTED IN 1887 BY MEMBERS OF THE FAMILY.

Sir Stamford was twice married. First on 13th March, 1805, at St. George's, Bloomsbury. His wife died quite suddenly in Java in November, 1814, and was buried in the cemetery at Batavia, and a handsome monument was erected in the Government Gardens at Buitenzorg. Lord Minto described her as an accomplished and clever lady. Abdulla in the Hakayit Abdulla spoke very highly of her, saying she was always busy and a great help to her husband. He married his second wife, Sophia, before leaving England the second time in 1817, and had five children, four of whom died in his lifetime. Lady Raffles died in 1858. Four years after his death the widow published the Memoir of his Life and Public Service. The book has been useful as preserving materials that would otherwise have been lost, but it was written with an unfortunate determination to entirely omit any reference to any papers or letters which contained any allusion whatever to the first wife, who is only mentioned in a very short foot-note at page 234, which as Mr. Boulger shows is itself incorrect and misleading. The omissions detract from the value of the book.

Two editions of this Memoir were published. The first by John Murray in 1830, dedicated to Gilbert, Earl of Minto, the son of the Governor-General of India at the time Raffles went to Java. It is in one large volume, and has a picture of Chantrey's Bust, a sketch map of Singapore island, a view taken from Government Hill (now Fort Canning) a picture of the Rafflesia Arnoldi flower, some pictures of Java and Sumatra, and a map of the Eastern Archipelago. The second edition was published by James Duncan, 37 Paternoster Row, in June, 1835. It was dedicated to Chevalier Bunsen, and is in two smaller volumes with the same portrait, and a facsimile of a letter of Raffles written in Java in 1814.

Since 1884, when these papers were first written, two more lives of Raffles have been published. One by Mr. Boulger in one large volume by Horace Marshall & Son in 1897, which has eighteen illustrations and maps. The views of Singapore town are taken from modern photographs, a picture of The Raffles Library and Museum being wrongly called The Raffles Institution, a very different building. It has also a facsimile of Raffles' hand-writing, and a portrait, sitting in a room, which is in the National Portrait Gallery at Trafalgar Square. There are some inaccuracies in the book which should be corrected if it is reprinted. On page 34 it is said that Penang is seven miles distant from the mainland. On page 339 it speaks of Singapore being not quite one degree north of the equator.

This book is very complete and interesting and must have been the result of much labour and research. The author tells us that Sir Stamford had always been one of his heroes, and the work was certainly taken up with enthusiasm. When it was intended to republish those papers it became a question whether it was worth while to reprint this first chapter, now that Mr. Boulger's book tells the whole story of Raffles' life so much more fully ; but it was decided to leave it in, as it is part of the object of this book to show who and what the founder of Singapore really was, and those who read it may well be led to read Mr. Boulger's book which contains the account of all Sir Stamford's life, and not merely that part of it connected with Singapore as this book does.

Another life of Raffles was published in May, 1900, by T. Fisher Unwin, in one small volume, in the edition called The Builders of Greater Britain. It is written by Hugh E. Egerton, and has a picture of Chantrey's bust and two maps. It has an appendix which reprints part of the instructions given by Raffles on November 4th, 1822, which it says were obtained from the Acting Governor in Singapore as they had not been published before. This was not so. They had been printed in Volume 8 of Logan's Journal at page 102 in 1854; they were printed in these papers in the *Free Press* in 1884; and were afterwards printed in a pamphlet about the Verandah Question in 1896, and in the Municipal Report for that year; and have been frequently referred to for the last fifty years. The paper is again given in this book at full length in its proper place.

On the south side of the North Aisle of Westminster Abbey near the Transept is the large statue of Raffles. Over his head is the tablet to the Musician Purcell, with the well-known quaint inscription about his having "gone to that blessed place where only his harmony can be exceeded." Under the statue of Raffles is this inscription:—

To the Memory of

SIR THOMAS STAMFORD RAFFLES, LL.D., F.R.S.,

Lieut.-Governor of Java

and First President of the Zoological Society of London,

Born 1781. Died 1826.

Selected at an early age to conduct the Government
of the British conquests in the Indian Ocean
By Wisdom, Vigour and Philanthropy
He raised Java to Happiness and Prosperity
unknown under former rulers.

After the surrender of that Island to the Dutch
And during his Government in Sumatra,
He founded an Emporium at Singapore
Where in establishing Freedom of Person as the right
of the Soil
And Freedom of Trade as the right of the Port
He secured to the British Flag
The Maritime Superiority of the Eastern Seas.

Ardently attached to Science
He laboured successfully to add to the knowledge
And enrich the Museums of his native land.

Promoting the welfare of the people committed
to his charge
He sought the good of his Country
And the Glory of God.

In 1889 the compiler of this book had a photograph taken by the Photographer to the Queen, with the consent of the Dean, of the monument, and gave it to the Raffles Library where it is placed. It was said to be an absolutely permanent photograph, and was of the largest size, 4 feet by 2 feet, that could then be made, but it is already beginning to discolour. Might not a replica of the Monument be placed in the centre of the large domed hall of the Museum, how few people here know that the name of Singapore is to be found in Westminster Abbey?

On Jubilee Day, Monday the 27th June, 1887, the day on which was celebrated the 50th anniversary of Queen Victoria's reign, the statue of Sir Stamford Raffles on the Esplanade was unveiled. It is of bronze, eight feet high, with head a little bent and folded arms as if in thought, with a map of the Settlement at his feet. On comparing it with Chantrey's bust the features seem harder, but it was said that they represent his expression more truly than the bust, which seems very unlikely, as Sir Francis Chantrey, R.A., saw Raffles, and Mr. T. Woolner, R.A., the sculptor of the statue never did. No inscription has been placed on the pedestal. The sculptor executed the statue of Lord Lawrence at Calcutta and several statues at Sydney and Christchurch. The statue was then close to the chains on the Esplanade enclosure; the reclamation from the sea made three years afterwards had not then been made; it now stands in the centre of the plain. The total cost of the statue was $20,446.10.

The following particulars of the various portraits of Sir Stamford Raffles were obtained by Mr. W. H. Read from Mr. S. Raffles Flint in June, 1901. He says that the large portrait was painted by Mr. George Francis Joseph, A.R.A., in 1817 (when Sir Stamford was in England before his first visit to Singapore), and was hung in the dining room at Highwood. At Lady Raffles' death, in 1858, the Rev. W. C. Raffles Flint, finding that it was a larger picture than he could manage to house, presented it to the National Portrait Gallery. The reason, Mr. Flint supposes, why Lady Raffles had the bust engraved for the frontispiece for her book was that Chantrey's work was a better portrait and gave more of the character of the man. Mr. Hugh Egerton consulted Mr. Flint as to the portrait he should reproduce for his book in 1900, and Mr. Flint suggested the engraving of the bust for the above reasons. There is another three-quarter portrait, also by Joseph, which belonged to Captain Travers, who was A.D.C. to Sir Stamford in Java, which was left to Mr. Flint some years ago by Mrs. Travers, his daughter-in-law. Mr. Flint has also a miniature by Chalon taken, he believes, in 1817. All these portraits Mr. Woolner had when he was at work on his statue.

Singapore, as is well known, was fondly looked to by Raffles as a fit spot in which to plant a torch that would send its rays into the depths of native ignorance, idolatry and superstition; and his expectations, although slowly realized, have not been altogether frustrated or disappointed; for the career of improvement has set in with assured and steady steps from Singapore, as far as Borneo on the one side, to the Native States in the Malay Peninsula on the other. It is often the act of one generation merely to strike out principles which it is the fortune of the next to put in play, and Singapore of the present day is carrying out her part in what Sir Stamford projected. Sir William Norris, the Recorder, in his charge to the Grand Jury in 1837, said that he could not better conclude his address than with some of the words of Sir Stamford Raffles when he founded the Singapore Institution in 1823, when he said: "If commerce brings wealth to our shores, it is the spirit of literature and philanthrophy (and his Lordship added, of religion and justice) which teaches us how to employ it for the noblest purposes. It is this that has made Britain go forth among the natives, strong in her native might to dispense blessings to all around her. Let it still be the boast of Britain to write her name in characters of light; let her not be remembered as the tempest whose course was desolation, but as the gale of spring reviving the slumbering seeds of mind, and calling them to life from the winter of ignorance and oppression. If the time shall come when her empire shall have passed away, these monuments will endure when her triumphs shall have become an empty name."

Before the story of Singapore is begun, it is wished to refer briefly to the names of three persons who afterwards were so very well

To face page 16.

SIR THOS. STAMFORD RAFFLES, KT., PRESIDENT OF THE ZOOLOGICAL
SOCIETY, LL.D., F.R.S., S.A.L.S., &C.

known in Singapore, where they met and became very close friends, and whose names will be so prominently mentioned in our stories of later years. When the British flag was hoisted here, a boy named James Brooke had been born sixteen years before, at a place now called Secrose, a suburb of Benares in India. A boy named Henry Keppel the third son of the Earl of Albemarle, was ten years old, and soon afterwards joined the navy. On 7th February, 1819, the day after the flag was hoisted here, a boy was born in London, whose name is known to all our readers as William Henry Macleod Read.

Sir James Brooke, Rajah of Sarawak, first landed at Singapore on 28th May, 1839; he died in England in 1868; The Hon. Sir Henry Keppel first came here on 5th September, 1832, and is now an Admiral of the Fleet, the highest rank in the British Navy and at the very top of the Active List. He came back to Singapore on the 31st December, 1899, when over ninety years of age, to revisit for a short time the place he liked so well; and Mr. W. H. Read, who was the first unofficial member of the Legislative Council when it was established in the Colony, is now living in England.

CHAPTER II.

1511—1818

F OR the purposes of this book it is not desirable to refer except in the briefest way to the old history, if it can even properly be so called, of Singapore. It is, as Mr. John Crawfurd wrote in his Dictionary of the Indian Islands, published in 1856, " full of obscurity."

Captain Newbold in his book on the Straits of Malacca, published in 1839, at page 272 of the first volume, speaks of the subject. Munshi Abdulla in his book gives a most interesting account of Newbold and of the great pains he took in Malacca to enter deeply into the history and usages of the Malay countries, so that he probably learned all that could then be ascertained from the old books and from the Malays themselves on the subject. He tells us that the Island of Singapore is celebrated in the Malayan history as being the first place of settlement of the early Malay colonists, who afterwards founded the Empire of Malacca. It is said in the Malay history, called the *Sejara Malayu*, that Sang Nila Utama, supposed by Mohammedan historians to have been a descendant of Alexander the Great, settled on the island with a colony of Malays from Palembang in Sumatra and founded the city of *Singhapura* in A. D. 1160, when they changed the original name of *Tamasak* to *Singhapura*, the city of the Lion; from the tradition of Sang Nila Utama having seen a *Singha*, or Lion, near the mouth of the river. This lion is described in the *Sejara Malayu* as an animal very swift and beautiful, its body red, head black, and its breast white; very active, and in size larger than a he-goat.

The derivation of the name of Singapore has caused a discussion for many years. One month after these papers commenced to appear in 1884, Mr. William E. Maxwell, Mr. W. H. Read and others were waking it all up again in the correspondence columns of the *Free Press* in November. It was suggested that it was derived from *singgah*, to touch at, and *pulau*, an island, which became changed to *pura ;* which derivation one correspondent preferred to Mr. Crawfurd's opinion, which was the Sanscrit word *singha*, a lion, and *pura*, a city. To which Mr. Maxwell (afterwards Sir William Maxwell) retorted that " Crim Tartary " was not derived from " Cream of Tartar " nor was Singapura (the Malay spelling) derived from *singgah* to stop. He said that it did not follow because the word was Sanscrit that the island was called after the animal, as it was possible that it was named after a legendary king, who was called Raja Singa. Mr. Maxwell was satisfied that Mr. John Crawfurd was right. An intelligent Malay nobleman said that the tradition among the natives was that a Rajah on landing here saw a wild animal on shore and asked what it was, and was told *Singha*, a lion; and he said *pura-pura* which means

" gammon "; as it was impossible, in his opinion, there could be such
an animal in the island; so it was called at first *Singapura-pura*. There
is a somewhat similar tradition in regard to Malacca, where it is said
that a Rajah on landing, saw a pelandok (mouse deer) attack a dog
and drive it into the water, so he said " This is a fine place where
the very pelandoks are full of courage, let us found a city here," and
asking the name of a tree under which he was standing, was told
it was the *Malacca* tree, *Phyllanthus emblica* so he called the name of
the place Malacca. In the old books the name is spelt in various
ways, such as Sinkepure, Sincapoor, Sincapura, and Singapoura. The
French official letters to the Post Office are even now addressed to
Sincapour, and Admiral Keppel still addresses his to Sincapore, as Sir
Stamford Raffles himself spelt it at first (*see* Boulger page 304).

It is certain that Singapore, though not reclaimed to civilization
for 220 years afterwards, bore in 1598 the same name that it does
now and gave its name to the Straits at the foot of the Peninsula.
This is shown by the inscription on a tombstone in the old ruined
Church of the Visitation of Our Lady, afterwards called St. Paul's
Church, on the hill at Malacca. Begbie wrote that it lies in the
centre of the Church opposite the door or principal entrance, and that
the inscription, though much worn, was still (in 1833) legible, as
follows :—

> HIC JACET DO
> MINVS PETRVS
> SOCIETATIS
> JESV SECVN
> DVS EPISCOPVS
> JAPONENSIS
> OBIIT AD FRE
> TVM SINGAPV
> RA MENSE FE
> BRVARIO AN
> NO 1598.

The principal thing observable, Begbie remarks, being the studied
division of the words. He gave a translation (for the information of
the fairer sex) as follows.—Here lies (the body of) Lord (Bishop) Peter,
of the Society of Jesuits, (and) the second Bishop of Japan. He died
at the Straits of Singapore in the month of February in the year
1598." In the Journal of the Straits Asiatic Society, No. 34 for 1900,
is a complete account and plan of the graves and the inscriptions in
the old Church, the above being the oldest of all. It was compiled
by Mr. E. M. Merewether, and contains some very interesting matter,
which would otherwise have been lost.

In a very old book published by a Captain Hamilton called a
" New Account of the East Indies " he says " In the year 1703 I
called at Johore on my way to China, and he (the King of Johore)
treated me very kindly and made me a present of the island of
Singapore but I told him it could be of no use to a private person,
though a proper place for a company to settle a colony in, lying

in the centre of trade, and accommodated with good rivers and a safe harbour, so conveniently situated that all winds served shipping both to go out and come into these rivers." Mr. Crawfurd, in re-printing this in his Dictionary at page 403, says it is remarkable that Singapore was so unmistakably pointed out over a century before, and that this striking recommendation did not occur to Sir Stamford Raffles when he went to look for a suitable locality; but in this Crawfurd may have been mistaken, as Sir Stamford was so well acquainted with the old histories, and it may have been one of the passages he alluded to in his letters to Marsden.

The lines of the old city and its defences were still to be traced in 1819, according to a passage in a letter of Sir Stamford Raffles to Mr. Marsden at page 376 of his Memoirs by his widow; but Mr. Crawfurd (Dictionary page 402) wrote that the remains discovered in Singapore were certainly not such as to convey a high opinion of what De Barros calls " the celebrated city of Singapura, to which resorted all the navigators of the western seas of India, and of the eastern of Siam, China, Campa and Camboja, as well as of thousands of islands to the eastward," because there was not a vestige of granite used which abounds in the neighbourhood and was in Mr. Crawfurd's time so largely employed.

Captain Newbold tells us that in 1252, the Javanese invaded Singapura, destroyed the city and dispersed its inhabitants over various parts of the Malay Peninsula, the majority going to Muar and Malacca where they settled and founded that city. The Javanese did not remain on the island, and Crawfurd says it remained submerged (as he terms it) for about five and a half centuries without being occupied, being only the occasional resort of pirates. In 1811 the Tumongong of Johore came to Singapore with about 150 followers, a few months before the British expedition passed Singapore on the way to conquer Java. Mr. Crawfurd says that the Tumongong himself told him this in 1823.

In order to understand the necessity which Raffles foresaw for establishing a settlement at Singapore it is necessary to refer to the history of Malacca which was again in the hands of the Dutch in 1818, whose object was to create a monopoly of all the trade to the south of that place.

The Malays having been driven to Malacca in 1252, were attacked by the Portuguese in 1511. Albuquerque, who was Governor or Viceroy of the Portuguese possessions in the East, disembarked his troops from Cochin, consisting of 800 Portuguese and 600 Malabars, or native soldiers, from nineteen vessels on the 24th July, the eve of Saint James the Apostle (Begbie.) He did not succeed and had to re-embark with a loss of ten men from poisoned arrows. A few days afterwards he made another attack and occupied the town. It is said in one account that Albuquerque built the fortress and the old Church now in ruins on St. Paul's Hill, and the Convent of the Visitation of Our Lady close by, and that St. Francis de Xavier arrived at Malacca in the year 1547. In 1641 the Dutch, with the help of Johore, after a siege of six months' duration, took Malacca from the Portuguese, which was a fatal blow to them, and they never recovered their footing in this quarter of the globe.

The Dutch retained possession till August 1795, when they surrendered the town to the expedition of the British under Captain Newcome, R.N.
of H. M. S. *Orpheus* and Major Brown of the East India Company's
service.   Malacca was to have been restored to the Dutch at the peace of
Amiens in 1802, but war recommenced before it was done, and the Dutch
Settlements falling into the power of France it remained under the British
until September, 1818, when it was restored to the Dutch in accordance
with the Treaty of Vienna.   The Dutch did not lose a month in obtaining
a footing in Rhio, which is 45 miles to the south from Singapore, with a
view to establish a monopoly from Malacca to the southward, which led to
the disputes which afterwards arose about our occupation of Singapore.
In order to understand the difficulty which Raffles met with, and the
clever way in which he took advantage of the peculiar circumstances of
the case to overcome them, it is necessary to state as briefly as possible
how the Dutch claim over Rhio gave them an excuse to object to what
Raffles did, and even for threats to drive out the British from Singapore
by force of arms.   It may be called "The Story of the Two Sultans;"
and although events have settled down for many years in such a way as to
prevent any possible good arising from further discussion on the subject,
which created more argument and dispute than probably any occurrence in
Singapore, it should not be passed over here.

The Malay countries are usually ruled by a Rajah, (in the case of
Singapore he was in 1819 called the Tumongong) in whom the real power
of government rests, and to whom the soil of the country belongs, on the
principle that he holds the country in trust for the people, which is clearly
and emphatically laid down by the Mohamedan law.   But in these
countries in the Malay Peninsula there was also a Suzerain or Lord
Paramount, called the Sultan, whose position and dignity were recognised,
but whose rule was purely nominal.   Colonel Low in an article
on the Straits says "The Sultan of Johore was formerly and still
considers himself, perhaps, the nominal superior of the Peninsula states."
Captain Begbie says that in 1758 the Rajah of Johore (that is the Sultan)
assigned the nominal authority which he possessed over the states of
Rumbow, Sungei Ujong, Johole, and Nanning, to the Dutch.   He further
says, speaking of the Penghulu of Nanning, which lies between Rumbow
and Malacca, adjoining the same countries, "Notwithstanding this extent
of authority (on the part of the Chief of Nanning) the whole acknowledge
a superior influence which is vested in an individual named the Iang de
Pertuan Besar.   This personage may be denominated a titular chief, who
receives his honours from Menangkabow (in Sumatra, whence the Malays
originally came) but derives neither power nor fixed revenue from the
office."   Mr. Cameron says in his book, "It would appear from the first
that the Tumongong had more voice in the government than the Sultan,
especially in all that regarded Singapore, the soil of which appears to
have been his property;" and again on page 137, "With respect to the
island of Singapore, it is beyond doubt that the Tumongong's family had
great claims, both because they so cordially assisted our settlement, and
because, although subject to the seignory of the Sultan, the soil appears
to have been their property."   See also the remarks in Chapter IV.

There is therefore reason to doubt whether it was necessary to have
the concurrence of the nominal Sultan in obtaining the settlement of

Singapore. But it was desirable for political reasons and the question arose as to who was the proper individual to assent. The Dutch insisted that one Abdul Rahman, their *protege*, was the proper man; Raffles said it was one Hoosain, generally known as Tunku Long; and the question was which of these two half-brothers was the Simon Pure.

Sultan Mohamed Shah of Johore and Lingga, under whose authority, whatever it may have been, the island of Singapore was included, had in the year 1809, four wives. The first and fourth of these were of royal blood, and had no children. The second and third were of low extraction. The second was the mother of Hoosain or Tunku Long; the third was the mother of Abdul Rahman. Objections were afterwards made that neither of the two being of royal blood, but being of low birth, could in accordance with the Malay custom succeed their father. But this was not much insisted on. The Sultan intended his first born son Hoosain to succeed him and told him to go to Pahang to marry the sister of the Bandahara or Chief of that country there. Before he left the Sultan went with him from Lingga, an island south of Rhio and 125 miles from Singapore, to one of the islands at Battang opposite Singapore town, and as a proof of his intention that Hoosain should succeed him, the Sultan caused him to hoist the royal flag, while he himself hoisted the white flag which was emblematical of his retirement from the cares of government. This was surely good ground for Raffles insisting that *his* Sultan was the real man.

Hoosain sailed for Pahang and the Sultan returned to Lingga, where he almost immediately died, not without suspicion of having been poisoned by Rajah Muda Japhar, who was then in Lingga. He had been appointed Raja Muda by the deceased Sultan; in effect he was the viceroy or governor at Rhio appointed by the Sultan to act for him. He had a quarrel with Hoosain, and was afraid of losing his power if he became Sultan, while he had great influence over the younger brother Abdul Rahman.

Hoosain was out of the way, and he only heard of his father's death a few days after he landed at Pahang, and then it was only a rumour. Subsequently he got a crafty letter from Rajah Japhar who antedated his letter and told him nothing about the attempt to instal his brother Abdul Rahman in his stead. Besides this, Hoosain could not then leave Pahang on account of the monsoon.

What took place at Lingga on the morning after the Sultan's death is so well told by Captain Begbie, and is so interesting as to the ways of the Malays in appointing a sovereign that it is now taken at length out of his book :—

"On the morning subsequent to the demise of Sulthaun Mahomed Shah, the Rajah Moodah assembled such of the chiefs as were either able or willing to attend, and thus addressed them—

"'Our Sulthaun is no more. He died yesterday evening, but he has left us two sons—say which of the two will you choose as your sovereign ?'

" Two of the oldest and most influential of the chiefs, named Dattoo Pengawa Bukka and Dattoo Hadgi Peng-Hadgi, thus replied, ' Agreeably to the constitution of the Empire, the eldest son must ever be selected to fill the vacant throne. We therefore wish that

Tuankoo Houssain may be proclaimed Sulthaun of Johore.' Upon hearing this speech Rajah Japhar exclaimed in a peevish and discontented tone, ' Your wishes run exactly counter to my own.' The two chiefs replied, ' If your highness be desirous of acting contrary to the custom established by law, and of subverting the fundamental principles of the empire, why did you assemble us for the purpose of learning our sentiments. The desire that we have expressed is in strict accordance with the law of the state, and if your Highness, Iyang de Pertuan Moodah, persist in your endeavour to set it aside, we must solemnly protest against it as a violent infraction of the constitution.'

" The firm tone in which this speech was delivered, and the force of the argument it contained, overpowered the Rajah Moodah, who quitted the council without reply, the other chiefs following him, so that the agitating question of the succession was left undecided ; and, had Rajah Moodah been the only person concerned in the intrigue, it had probably fallen to the ground. But, although Tuankoo Abdul Rachman himself was thoroughly destitute of any hankering after empire, his immediate relatives eagerly thirsted after that reflected power which they would derive from his exaltation. Accordingly, two of his uncles, named Ibrahim and Mahomed, alarmed at the indecision and agitation which Rajah Japhar had displayed, proceeded, directly the assembly had thus abruptly broken up, to the house of their sister Inchi Mariam, Tuankoo Abdul Rachman's mother, and carried her along with them to the step-sister of the Rajah Moodah, Tuankoo Boontet, both of which ladies possessed great influence with him. The whole party, accompanied by a chief, named Inchi Kaloo, called upon Rajah Moodah Japhar that evening, and eventually succeeded in binding him firmly to the cause of Tuankoo Abdul Rachman, whom the junto proclaimed as sovereign that evening.

" The following morning the members of the cabal proceeded to the residence of the newly elected monarch, who, having heard somewhat of the intrigues that were carrying on in his favor, had closely secluded himself since the death of his father, in the hope that when not encouraged by him they would die away.

" When the door of his room was opened (Rajah Moodah is accused of having forced it) this chief thus addressed him :—' The body of your late father, and our sovereign, lies still unburied. You are aware that according to our custom, it cannot be committed to the earth, until the successor to the throne be appointed. Your brother is still absent, and who can tell when he will arrive ? There is consequently no one but yourself eligible to the crown and the election has fallen unanimously on you.'

" Tuankoo Abdul Rachman thus replied,—' My father, the late sovereign, expressed his earnest desire that my brother Tuankoo Houssain should succeed him according to custom, as well as that I should devote myself to the priesthood, and with that view I should proceed to Mecca on pilgrimage. I dare not consequently, and positively declare that I will not, disobey his wishes, lest I draw down a curse from heaven, and not a blessing. I therefore request you, Rajah Japhar, to act as Regent until the return of my brother.'

"Rajah Japhar Moodah, whose real reasons for wishing to substitute Tuankoo Abdul Rachman for his brother were that there was an existing feud between his family and that of Tuankoo Houssain, in consequence of which he feared a serious diminution of his authority in the event of that prince's succession; while the weakness and vacillation of Tuankoo Abdul Rachman's character held out to him a prospect of great power, especially as he was his own nephew, exclaimed, in a tone of apparently great surprise, 'How can I venture to assume the authority of the Sulthaun, when one of his sons is actually on the spot?' He was joined strongly in his remonstrances by the party, who accompanied him, and the weak and wavering Abdul Rachman, whose actions invariably took on the colour imparted to them by his advisers of the hour, felt his good resolves yield to the impulse of the moment, and after a few faint struggles consented to his nomination as Sulthaun.

"This advantage gained, the faction was by no means dilatory in improving it. That very evening, as many of the people of Lingga as could be assembled together, were apprized of his election by the zealous Rajah Moodah, who rebelled in the anticipation of unlimited sway under his imbecile master. This ceremony having been undergone, the remains of the deceased Sulthaun Mahomed Shah were committed to the dust with all the pomp becoming his rank. On the third day subsequent to the funeral, the new Sulthaun ascended the throne of his forefathers with all the solemnities usually observed on such occasions, and received the homage of his subjects, the fealty of the Malayan nations going with the stream.

"As soon as the monsoon changed Hoossain sailed back to Lingga, but found he was comparatively friendless. He went to his brother Abdul Rahman who at first received him very kindly, but Rajah Japhar had too much influence over Abdul Rahman, and threatening him with being left without means like his brother was, induced him to treat Hoossain with coldness and neglect."

The fourth widow of the dead Sultan was a spirited old lady, who lived where she had been born on the island of Pinigad, opposite Rhio, and she strongly supported Hoossain, saying, "Who elected Abdul Rahman as sovereign of Johore? Was it my brother Rajah Japhar, or by what law of succession has it happened? It is owing to this act of injustice that the ancient empire of Johore is fast falling to decay." The old Sultan, on his last visit to Pinigad, had left the regalia with this wife, who was called Tuanku Putri, and the old lady absolutely refused to give them up to Abdul Rahman, the Malay tradition being that the possession of the regalia was necessary to constitute a Sultan.

In the year 1818, Sir Stamford Raffles commenced those negotiations which ended in Singapore being established. Under ordinary circumstances a reference to England would have been indispensable, but Colonel Low remarks that Raffles foresaw that before any reference home could be replied to, the Dutch would have perfected their long cherished scheme of repressing the British name and influence in the eyes of the Malayan States, and of monopolizing a very disproportionate share of the Eastern trade. Raffles also justly argued that the Dutch could not fairly claim Singapore on the plea of prior engagements which they might have entered into with native princes before the transfer of Malacca to the British in 1795; because the Dutch authorities who transferred Malacca in that year had declared that Rhio, Johore, Pahang and Lingga were *not* dependencies of Malacca, while it was on the ground that Rhio *was* a dependency that the claim had now been set up; and also that engagements had been entered into by the English with the Rajah of Rhio, to retract from which would have been an acknowledgment of inferiority to the Dutch.

Major Farquhar had been sent to Rhio in August, 1818, from Penang, to see what could be done. He found the Rajah Muda Japhar, who has been spoken of, to be the only person with whom he could negotiate, and made a Treaty with him at Rhio on the 19th August, 1818, which it is not necessary to print here as it can always be found in the printed copies of the books relating to Treaties with the Native States. It was made between the East India Company and Jaffir, Rajah Muda of Rhio on behalf of Sultan Abdul Rahman, King of Johore, Pahang and Dependencies. It was not signed by Abdul Rahman. It provided for mutual liberty of navigation and commerce in the ports and dominions of Johore, Pahang, Lingga, Rhio and other places subject to the Sultan. In Mr. Cameron's book he says that the treaty also secured a right to build a factory on the island of Singapore, but the name of Singapore is not in the treaty at all. It was part of Johore, and therefore was impliedly affected, but it was not mentioned by name.

Sir Stamford Raffles afterwards used this as a second string to his bow in answer to the Dutch objections, by saying that the English had obtained the consent of the Dutch protege, Sultan Abdul Rahman, as well as of his elder brother Hoossain.

It is worth recording as it does not seem to have been mentioned in other books, in connection with the scheme of Sir Stamford Raffles to form a station to cope with the Dutch, that, some time before, he had said that Bencoolen was far out of the way of the great trade routes through the Sunda and Malacca Straits and its position was therefore unfavorable to trade. On this account he had obtained an anchorage (so it is written) at Simangka Bay in the Sunda Straits, his idea being to establish a commercial *entrepot* to rival Batavia. The Simangka Bay settlement proved a failure and then Raffles began afresh to secure some position in the narrow passage at the foot of the Malay Peninsula between India and China; which led to his visit to Calcutta and the eventual settlement at Singapore.

Colonel Low says (9 Logan's Journal, 313) that the Penang Government had attempted to form an establishment on the island of Bentan, opposite Singapore, but before their measures were taken the Dutch had occupied Rhio, and Colonel Bannerman retired from any further attempt, thinking it useless. Raffles was to succeed where he had failed.

CHAPTER III.

1819

---◆---

S IR STAMFORD RAFFLES left Calcutta for Penang about the 10th
December, 1818.   His instructions from Lord Hastings, the Governor-
General, as to the establishment of a port at the south end of the
Malacca Straits, at Rhio or elsewhere, are printed at length at page
298 of Mr. Boulger's book.   He was told to attend to this after the
conclusion of the negotiations he was to conduct at Acheen.   It is said
in the letter that the proceedings of the Dutch left no room for doubt
as to their policy of possessing themselves of all the commanding stations
in the Archipelago, and so completely excluding British shipping
and commanding the only channels for direct trade between China and
Europe.

Raffles arrived at Penang on the 31st December, 1818, and hearing of the proceedings of the Dutch regarding Rhio, he let the
mission to Acheen stand over and went to the south.   He was blamed
afterwards for having overruled his instructions by not going to Acheen
first, but in the end the Court of Directors exonerated him from all
blame, and admitted that he had acted wisely.   If he had not gone to
Singapore until after he had been to Acheen, there is good reason to
think that Singapore would have fallen under the control of the Dutch
as Rhio had done already.

Sir Stamford Raffles left Penang on the 19th January, 1819.   It
was thought to be impossible after this lapse of time to find out the
number of the vessels, or their names, which formed the expedition.
Abdulla mentions four ships and two ketches or schooners, and in some
correspondence the name of a brig *Ganges* and a ship *Nearchus*, and
two hired vessels called the *Mercury* and *Enterprise*, were mentioned.
The matter has now been ascertained from a very dilapidated Directory of Penang for 1820.   This contains a great deal of interesting and
amusing information which concerns Penang and not Singapore, but it
has a full list of all Arrivals and Departures of vessels at and from
Penang, which is headed "The Naval Register for 1819."   From this
can be seen the arrivals and departures of all vessels between Penang
and Singapore in that year, which throws a lot of light upon how
communication was first carried on, and the length of voyages.   There
was a distinction in the way of naming the East India Company's
ships.   Some were styled H.C.S. meaning the Honorable Company's
Ships, and in the column of the commanders, the Captains are always
described as Esquire.   For instance H.C.S. *Warren Hastings*, G. Wels-
tead, Esq., sailed from Penang on 7th September, 1819, for China.
Other ships were described as H.C.C. which meant Honourable Company's Cruisers, and in their case the commander was always styled

Captain or Lieutenant. We know that Raffles left Penang on the 19th January, and the following is the list of departures from Penang on that day as it is printed in that Directory—

Name of Vessel.		Commander.	Destination.
January 19 H.C.C. Nearchus		Captain Maxfield	Sea
Do.	Do. Minto	Lieut. Criddle	do.
Do.	Mercury	J. R. Beaumont	do.
Do.	Indiana	James Pearl	do.
Do.	Ganges	F. J. Barnard	do.
Do.	Enterprise	R. Harris	do.

This shows that Abdulla was right as to the number. From the same Directory it is possible to gather more information about the ships. The *Nearchus* and *Minto* had arrived at Penang before January, as they are not in the list for 1819; and we know that Raffles arrived in Penang on 31st December, 1818. In the letter of instructions given to Raffles in Calcutta on 28th November, it was said that a frigate would be appointed to convey him to Rhio and eventually to Bencoolen. Whether the *Nearchus* or the *Minto* was a frigate, or what class they were, is not now known. It is probable that Raffles came from Calcutta to Penang with these two ships which were to take him to Acheen from Penang. He did afterwards go from Penang to Acheen in the *Minto* accompanied by the *Indiana*. And the list shows that the *Minto* took him from Singapore on 7th February, the day after the Treaty was signed, accompanied by the *Indiana*, reaching Penang on the 14th, a passage of seven days. The *Nearchus* afterwards made two voyages between Singapore and Penang, and left Penang for Calcutta on 10th October, and does not appear again in the list. The *Minto* left Penang for Acheen, with Sir Stamford on 8th March; and on 22nd May left Penang for Singapore. On 23rd September she left Singapore for Penang and arrived there on 2nd October, a passage of nine days. She left Penang again on the 10th October for Singapore, so that she was evidently employed in connection with the place.

The *Mercury* left Calcutta on 10th December, and reached Penang on 12th January, a passage of thirty-three days. She left Singapore on 15th February and reached Penang on the 23rd, in eight days. She left Penang for Calcutta on 7th March; left Calcutta on 28th May reaching Penang on 19th June in 22 days, and left there for Singapore on the 25th June.

The *Indiana* left Calcutta on 20th December, 1818, and reached Penang on 1st January, 1819, in eleven days. She left Singapore with the *Minto* for Penang and accompanied her to Acheen. The two vessels left Acheen on the 26th April and reached Penang together on the 29th. On the 22nd May she left for Singapore, and left there on 15th October reaching Penang on the 27th. On 16th November she sailed for Calcutta.

It is probable from this knowledge of the voyages of these two vessels, that they were hired to carry the troops and stores. They were most likely country ships trading out of Calcutta, and when matters had somewhat settled down in Singapore they returned to Calcutta.

The other two ships are to be found in the same Directory in a list headed "Ships and Vessels belonging to the port of Prince of Wales Island," that is, Penang. There are twenty-seven vessels. The *Ganges* was a brig of 130 tons, owned by Bapoo Doory; and the *Enterprise* was a schooner of 85 tons owned by Alexander John Kerr, who we see in another place in the Directory was then the Registrar of the Court of Judicature. The book among many other odd things contains a list of the Executors, &c., of Estates in 1819, and it appears that Bapoo died and Mr. Kerr, the owner of the other vessel, was the Administrator of his estate.

The *Ganges* left Singapore for Penang on the 11th August, making the passage in six days, and in December sailed from Penang to Bombay. The *Enterprise* made several trips during the year to Singapore, and went once from Penang to Calcutta, and once to Bencoolen.

So the expedition consisted of two of the East India Company's men-of-war; two ships engaged in Calcutta; and two local vessels chartered in Penang.

On the way south they met Major Farquhar returning to Penang, and at his request Raffles went to view the Carimons, where Captain Ross of the surveying ship *Discovery* had been sent previously. This must be the Captain Ross mentioned in Newbold's book as being at Singapore when Sir Stamford reached there. The Carimons were not found suitable. It was the place which Farquhar had warmly recommended, as he did again a year or two afterwards, as a more central position than Singapore. The result has shown that Raffles was unquestionably right in his judgment. The ships anchored off St. John's Island on the evening of the 28th January. That island lies about five miles from the town on the west side of the harbour. It is said in Moore's book that "it was called by the Malays Si Kijang or 'the roe' an animal to which it had no resemblance, and the name having fallen upon the obtuse ears of some person who did not understand Malay, has ever since been called St. John's by Europeans."

The best account of the first landing at Singapore is in Munshi Abdulla's Hakayit Abdulla (or Autobiography of Abdulla) but as he did not come to Singapore until four months afterwards, he only tells what he had been told and is certainly incorrect in some particulars, but on the whole he probably gives a very good idea of what took place.

It will be well to explain here who Munshi Abdullah was, as his book gives so much interesting information about Malacca and Singapore which could not be found elsewhere. It is a book of his personal reminiscences, and is for a native Mohamedan a remarkable work. Parts of the book have been translated many times, that by Mr. Braddell in Logan's Journal, in 1852, and that by Mr. J. T. Thomson in his book called "Translations from the Hakayit Abdulla," published in 1874, are the only ones likely to be now obtainable. The whole of the book has not yet been translated. It is a standard reading book for students of Malay. Abdulla was an Arab of Yemen of mixed race, three removes from a pure Arab. His father and mother were both born in Malacca; his grandfather on the father's side (to which alone the Malays give importance) was the son of an Arab of Yemen and had been born at Nagore, South India, and married a Malay in Malacca. He was a tall, slightly bent, spare man, very energetic as his book shows, with a bronze complexion, and an oval face, as Mr. Thomson, who learned Malay from him, tells us. When he was a boy of 11 or 12 years old he was a Malay writer for Raffles in Malacca, and was much attached to him. He did a great deal of work in translating for the Missionaries at the Anglo-Chinese College in Malacca, and was the Malay teacher to the Europeans in Singapore in its early days, and to Mr. Keasberry. Abdulla's father had been Malay teacher to Marsden. Raffles wanted him to go to Java with the expedition, but his mother would not part with him as he was the only son and then only fourteen years old. In later years he was a master in the Raffles Institution. He sailed from Singapore in an Arab ship for Jeddah in February, 1854, intending to go to Mecca and then to pay a visit to Europe; but he died in Mecca on the 27th October in that year. His son Ibrahim bin Abdullah is now the Dato Bintara Dalam of Johore, an official of high rank, who accompanied the late Sultan Abubakar to Europe in 1878. Several passages from his book are quoted further on; they are examples of the manner of his writing, and of the thoughts of a Mohamedan. The stories are told in a very amusing way.

There is one other account by a Malay of what took place when Raffles landed for the first time. It is to be found in the Journal of the Straits Asiatic Society, No. 10 for 1882, and was taken down by Mr. H. T. Haughton of the Straits Settlements Civil Service, who died to the great regret of all in the Straits, in 1897, while still a young man. He took it down from an old Malay, said to be then about eighty years old, which would make him about fifteen in 1819, but as usual with these people, his age was quite uncertain. In the following number was a note by Mr. W. H. Read giving his reasons for thinking that the old man could not be very correct in his recollections. However that may be, his account in many ways coincides with Abdulla's, and taking the two together we can arrive at a pretty good idea of what took place.

Before doing this let us try to form a picture of what the entrance to the river looked like when Sir Stamford Raffles and Major Farquhar rowed into its mouth. There are little statements in several of the old books, besides these two accounts, which help in this. The right bank, which is the proper name for the side of the river where the Square is now, was a rising hill covered with jungle, and beyond the hill in the direction where the Police Courts are now and beyond, was what Abdulla calls a marsh. There was no one living on that side of the river then. On the left bank of the river (the Esplanade side as it is now called) the bank was covered with low jungle. On that bank, most probably somewhere between the present site of the Court House and Elgin Bridge, though some have thought as far up as the Ice House at Hill Street, were a few houses. Abdulla says four or five small huts, with six or seven cocoanut trees, and one larger house for the Tumongong; while the old Malay called Wa Hakim told Mr. Haughton that there were under a hundred small huts with a large one for the Rajah. It was probably between the two, as the Tumongong four years after-wards told Mr. Crawfurd that 150 Malays had accompanied him from

Johore in 1811. Abdulla tells us that the plain (the Esplanade) was covered with Kamunting and Kadadu plants. The river in fact was just what may be seen at other places round the island where a great town such as Singapore is now has never been commenced. Both Abdulla and Wa Hakim speak of the *orang laut* (men of the sea) and Abdulla as a Malay, (and in his own estimation a most superior being for which he had some reason), speaks of them in a contemptuous manner, as being like wild beasts. These were the descendants of the aborigines of Johore before the Malays crossed from Sumatra, and were born, lived and died in boats, a sort of sea-gipsies. One prow often contained, besides the head of the family, a grandmother, mother and several young children, who were left in some place of safety when the men went out on piratical expeditions. They were radically Malays, speaking the language and nominally Mohomedans, but really believing in a sort of fetishism like all untutored peoples. The place where their boats lay was called, Wa Hakim says, Kampong Tumongong. Such boats full of these people may still be seen occasionally in the river; they were very numerous forty years ago round the island at Telok Blangah and Selitar. Abdulla says. "There were also only two or three small huts at the extreme end of Campong Glam, belonging to the Glam tribe or clan who made their living by making kadjangs and mat sails, hence the name of the place." Captain Begbie says, "The Malay town is generally called Campong Glam on account of the Glam trees in its neighbourhood. The Glam is a species of the Kayu Putih whose leaves yield the well-known medicinal oil commonly contracted into Cajeput. It is called white wood from its bark being white. The rind peels off in ragged paper like shreds." The huts Abdulla speaks of were probably put up after the English came; he himself did not come until four months afterwards.

Such was the condition of the place and the people when Raffles and Farquhar landed in the morning, with one sepoy carrying a musket, as Wa Hakim says. The orang laut, frightened, all ran away, and Raffles walked up to the Tumongong's house. Abdulla says Farquhar sat down under a *Kalat* tree on the plain, and waited till the Tumongong came. Wa Hakim says he followed Raffles to the house to the edge of the verandah, as a Malay boy would do. The Tumongong gave them rambutans and other kinds of fruit, and then Raffles went inside. He explained why they had come and that it would be a good thing for the Malays in carrying on their traffic. The Tumongong made a speech of his own unworthiness (as usual) and said the question of the succession to the late Sultan was still unsettled, and that Tunku Putri had all the regalia; but he was the inheritor of the island by the Malayan law. Colonel Farquhar said " Sir Stamford Raffles has well considered, and he will put all straight." Being asked what was the name of the hill behind the plain (Fort Canning now) he said it was called Bukit Larangan, "Because the Rajah resided there in old times and erected his palace there, and would allow no one to go up, so it was called the Forbidden Hill."

They returned on board at 4 o'clock, and afterwards (Wa Hakim says twelve days which is out of the question, but such a Malay has very little idea of time) it was no doubt the next morning, the 29th

January, the tents and baggage were brought ashore, and half of the
Malay sailors commenced to cut down the scrub on the plain while the
other half put up the tents. This took two hours. Then a well was
dug below the *Kalat* tree, from which they all drank. Thirty Malacca
Malays were landed, and relieved each other in keeping guard near
the tents that night. The people of Singapore were too frightened to
approach at first, and one boy was drowned off Teluk Ayer; for, meeting one of the ship's boats, he became so alarmed that he jumped overboard, and the tide was running so strong that he was overpowered
and drifted out to sea.

We cannot doubt that Raffles spent the afternoon in talking to the
Tumongong and the Malays, and interesting them in his proposals. It
is a pity that little Abdullah did not come with him from Malacca or
we should have had a most amusing account of the conversation.
Raffles speedily convinced the Tumongong of his friendship and good
intentions and Farquhar went away to Rhio to see about the regalia.
Sir Stamford made the Preliminary Arrangement mentioned in the next
chapter on the following day, and waited for the return of Major
Farquhar. Begbie says that Raffles sent Farquhar to endeavour to persuade
Tunku Putri to give up the regalia but the old lady was inflexible.
She is described as a fine intelligent lady, whose countenance lit up
with great animation, when talking of old days. She was residing in
Malacca in 1833. Farquhar returned with Sultan Hoossain on the
evening of 5th February, and the treaty which concluded—what Raffles
had tried to accomplish, in the face of so many difficulties, was made
the next day.

The remainder of this chapter relates to the controversy that has
gone on for many years and still keeps occasionally cropping up, in
the most hopeless way, about the true date of the foundation of the
Settlement. It is not of the least practical importance, and those who
attach no interest to it can turn over to the end of the chapter.

After spending much time in hunting into it, the conclusion seems
to be irresistible that the 6th February, which has always been kept
as the anniversary is beyond any reasonable doubt, the proper date.

Sir Stamford Raffles and Major Farquhar were the only persons
actually present in Singapore at the time, who have left anything in
writing about the date when the British flag was hoisted. If the
diary and all the papers of Raffles had not been burnt in the *Fame* the
question would never have arisen. Unfortunately in a memorial Raffles
addressed to the Court of Directors, when in England not long before
his death, he had given the date as the 29th February. Lady Raffles
was in Penang at the time and could not speak from her own
recollection, and in her book she copied the same date, which was
repeated in the second edition. The 29th February was impossible,
there could be no such day, as 1819 could not be a leap year, and if
Lady Raffles had turned over two pages of her own book she would
have seen that her husband was back again in Penang writing letters
on the 19th February. We know that he left Singapore on 7th
February and did not return until June. There is one other passage
relating to the matter in the writings of Raffles; a letter he wrote to
Marsden, which is printed in Lady Raffles' book, dated 31st January, in

which he said " The lines of the old city and its defences are still to be traced and within its ramparts the British Union waves unmolested." This language in a private letter to his friend is certainly somewhat imaginative when it speaks of ramparts, because in April 1821 it was written in a despatch that " the place was covered with jungle with the exception of a small spot on the eastern side of the river, barely large enough to pitch the tents on." It may have been Raffles' way of expressing to his friend that there the English were and they were going to stop. Mr. Egerton tells us in his very recent work that a letter by a member of the expedition dated 29th January, showed ignorance still of its exact object, which would have been known to him at once if he had seen the British flag flying on shore; and that Captain Butler of the *Hope* who passed Singapore on the 31st, saw tents pitched on shore but made no mention of any flag there.

Now we come to what Major Farquhar wrote on the subject. In a long memorial which he addressed to the Board of Directors in 1824 he said, " On the 5th February I returned to Singapore and on the morning of the 6th the British flag was formally displayed. On the following day Sir Stamford Raffles left the Settlement, after having placed me in charge as Resident and Commandant with a letter of general instructions."

The Major had a good reason to remember the date as he had been to Rhio to fetch Sultan Hoosain. We know, as will be explained in the next chapter, that Raffles made a provisional agreement (as he styled it) with the Tumongong alone on the 30th January, and that the treaty which Sultan Hoosain himself signed together with the Tumongong, was made on the 6th February, the day the proclamation by Raffles was issued which is printed in the next chapter. There would have been no right (as Mr. Egerton suggests) to hoist the flag until the treaty was concluded, or to put it at the best, before the preliminary arrangement was made on the 30th. We know also that Raffles only arrived at Singapore on the evening of the 28th January, and then most probably Raffles sent some Malay on shore to tell the Tumongong who he was, and to prepare him for his visit the next day; which would be the usual course on such an occasion. We are told that he and Major Farquhar landed in the morning, which would then be the 29th, and if the date so often insisted on, and again repeated in 1887 in the inscription in Hendon Church is correct, the flag must have been hoisted at once, before the preliminary agreement was made. It seems incredible that the flag should have been hoisted with any pretensions to any right to do so, on the very day Raffles landed, and while he was discussing the terms of the arrangement that was only signed the next day, and while Sultan Hoosain was expected from Rhio to support it. It is possible that Sir Stamford hoisted a flag over a tent as a precaution in case the Dutch should hear of his arrival and try to hoist a flag themselves under a pretext of authority from the Raja Muda of Rhio and his *protege* Sultan Abdul Rahman, and the Malays on shore may not have cared whether a flag was put up or not, but it could not have been hoisted under any claim of right, or with any proper authority. As well might a foreigner go and hang up his country's flag in the middle of the Esplanade at this day.

On the 6th February the right to do so was given, and Major Farquhar's statement that the flag was formally hoisted on that day seems conclusive. Only five years after, on 6th February, 1824, the Governor, John Crawfurd, gave the first anniversary dinner at Government House, and he especially was not likely to make any mistake about the matter, nor the small European community who dined there, and the first words were "To-day being the anniversary of hoisting the British flag on this island," which appears in a diary written at the time. In Mr Read's book at page 12, he says "Sultan Houssein came at once to Singapore and a definite treaty was drawn up, signed and sealed by Raffles and the two chiefs, on February 6th, 1819, when the British flag was formally hoisted and saluted;" and Mr. Read was one, for reasons that will appear afterwards in this book, with particular means of being well acquainted with the history of the place.

There seems to have been an actual fatality in the misprints about the date, which began in Lady Raffles' book, and continues to this day. In Moor's book published in 1837, it says the flag was hoisted on 20th January, which in 1844 was remarked to be a misprint. In the Glossary by the late Sir Henry Yule, who travelled in Java in 1860, and is spoken of in Mr. Boulger's book, page 306, as "so careful a writer" it is printed as the 23rd February.

In a little book printed at the Malacca Mission Press in 1823, about the formation of the Singapore Institution in that year, it says at page 91, in Rules drawn up for the management, that the Annual General Meeting shall take place on the 29th day of February being the Anniversary of the establishment of Singapore. It does not seem improbable that, after the *Fame* was burned, a copy of that pamphlet may have been sent to Sir Stamford and that he copied the date from it in England.

In John Crawfurd's Journal of an Embassy to Siam, &c., published in 1830, he says:—"On 6th February, two days after the arrival of the expedition, the British flag was hoisted and the Settlement duly formed." In 1834, in Captain Begbie's book, he says, "In February Sir Stamford Raffles founded the Settlement of Singapore." In Newbold's book, in 1839, he gives no date of the month, but says that Singapore was ceded in February. Mr. Boulger's book in 1897, sticks to the 29th January. Mr. Egerton does not commit himself to any date, but says it is not clear by what right the flag could have been hoisted as early as the 29th January. The contention that the proper date should be the 29th January probably arose from the assumption that in Lady Raffles' book the word February must have been a misprint for January, and that the day of the month was correct because Raffles was here on that day in the month of January.

After the above was written attention was called to a "Note" printed at page 114 of the number of the Notes and Queries of the Journal of the Straits Branch of the Asiatic Society No. 4 for 1887, which had escaped notice when this chapter was written. It throws light upon the "various errors" and the way in which they arose. It is a letter written in 1886 or 1887 (the Governor gave no date) by the Rev. R. B. Raffles to the Governor at Singapore, which said that Mr. Raffles hoped the error as to the date of the foundation of

Singapore which had crept into many books (the 29th February) would not be reproduced on the pedestal of the statue which was to be erected in Singapore; in connection with which date he had seen *various errors*; and that Colonel Yule in his glossary "Hobson Jobson" had given the date as 23rd February, but had now accepted "without controversy" the correction which Mr. Raffles submitted. This was only a case of the blind leading the blind, unless Mr. Raffles could establish his case. His argument was that there could be no 29th February in 1819, which no one has ever doubted, and then he says that a letter (which has been quoted above) was dated Singapore, 31st January, 1819, announcing the occupation of the island. This is not so, the word occupation, or any similar expression is not used in the letter. And then he draws this conclusion: "It is thus plain that in the sentence in Lady Raffles' Book, giving the 29th February, the date '29th *January* 1819' should be read instead of '29th *February*, 1819.'" The italics are his own. The only thing that is plain is, that there is a mistake somewhere in the sentence. It is not plain that it is in the name of the month. Both Raffles and Farquhar are at one about that. It is common experience that misprints in figures are infinitely more likely than misprints in words, because there is no context to point to the error, and it is solely a question of careful reading, not correcting. An example of it is in Mr Boulger's book on page 306, where the date of the Treaty is printed 5th February, and the correct date, 6th February, is printed on page 313. Sir Stamford Raffles when he wrote his memorial had lost all his papers, and there is no reason to suppose Colonel Farquhar was wrong when he wrote the 6th February. The whole thing is explained if Mr R. B. Raffles' conjecture that the misprint could only have occurred in the name of the month has been the cause of all the previous "various errors." It is to be hoped that the day which has from the first been kept as a holiday for the anniversary may not be again questioned. *Requiescat in pace!*

CHAPTER IV.

THE Treaty made on the 6th February states in Article 1 that a Preliminary Agreement had been made on the 30th January. There had been no trace of that agreement for many years. Mr. Braddell made a note over fifty years ago that it could not be found; and in all the printed copies of the treaty that have been published, there is a foot-note to that Article in the treaty that "No copy of these Preliminary Articles is to be found." As will be explained presently the counterparts of these old documents which had been kept by the Tumongong, have, since the preceding chapter of this book was in print, very unexpectedly come to light in Johore, while the information obtained has thrown some further light upon matters that have been already spoken of. This agreement made with the Tumongong alone is on one side of a large piece of foolscap; it is in fair preservation though not as good as that of the treaty signed eight days afterwards. The thick, heavy sealing-wax of the large seal of the East India Company having broken and torn away part of the writing. It is in Malay only; there is no English counterpart as there is in the treaty : the Arabic writing is in the same hand as that in the treaty. It is the writing of a native, and was no doubt written by one who accompanied Raffles, as neither the Sultan nor Tumongong could write; and the old Malays say now that there would not, probably, have been anyone with the Tumongong who was able to do so. Munshi Abdulla was not with Raffles, as he lived in Malacca, then in the hands of the Dutch, for which reason he came to Singapore in June, four months later, as Raffles had then returned to the place, and the English had formed the settlement.

It will be seen that Sir Stamford Raffles treated on the 30th January with the Tumongong alone (the Sultan did not arrive till the 5th February) giving him a yearly sum of $3,000 for the privilege of establishing a Factory, and the opinion of the Sultan was to be taken when he arrived. In addition to what has been said on page 21 as to the practical independence of the Tumongong, Raffles wrote in a letter (see Lady Raffles' Memoir page 398) "As the land was the property of the Tumongong we did not hesitate to treat for the occupation of the port." And it will be noticed that in the Treaty the Tumongong is described as Chief of Singapore and its dependencies, and he, and not the Sultan, is dealt with as exercising sovereign rights with respect to a portion of his own "Dominions." (Article 3) ; and in the last article it provided that one half of the duties were to be paid to him alone, the Sultan receiving no share. In 1824 when it was desirable to make a further treaty for the whole of the island, Mr. Crawfurd in a despatch to Bengal, quoted further on, in order to furnish information regarding the position of the Native authorities, said, "The principal Officers of the Government of Johore from early times were the Bandahara or Treasurer, and the Tumongong or First Minister of Justice. These offices appear to have been for a long time hereditary in the families of the present occupants, who were indeed virtually independent chiefs; the former of them residing and exercising authority at Pahang, and the other at Singapore." In another despatch to Bengal he spoke of the Tumongong as "Not only exercising his powers of Government, but being, like other Asiatic sovereigns, *de facto* the real proprietor of the soil." Mr. Crawfurd was a man of great knowledge regarding the Malay countries, and he expressed in 1824 the same opinion as Sir Stamford Raffles had done in 1819.

The following is a translation of the agreement, the first few words have been torn away by the sealing wax :—

[Agreement made by?] the Dato Tummungung Sree Maharajah, Ruler of Singapore, who governs the country of Singapore and all the islands which are under the government of Singapore in his own name and in the name of Sree Sultan Hussein Mahummud Shah, Rajah of Johore, with Sir Thomas Stamford Raffles, Lieutenant Governor of Bencoolen and its dependencies on behalf of the Most Noble the Governor General of Bengal.

On account of the long existing friendship and commercial relations between the English Company and the countries under the authority of Singapore and Johore it is well to arrange these matters on a better footing never to be broken.

Article 1. The English Company can establish a factory (logi) situated at Singapore or other place in the Government of Singapore-Johore.

Article 2. On account of that the English Company agree to protect the Dato Tummungung Sree Maharajah.

Article 3. On account of the English Company having the ground on which to make a factory they will give each year to the Dato Tummungung Sree Maharajah three thousand dollars.

Article 4. The Dato Tummungung agrees that as long as the English Company remain and afford protection according to this Agreement he will not enter into any relations with or let any other nation into his country other than the English.

Article 5. Whenever the Sree Sultan, who is on his way, arrives here, all matters of this Agreement will be settled, but the English Company can select a place to land their forces and all materials and hoist the English Company's flag. On this account we each of us put our hands and chops on this paper at the time it is written on the 4th day of Rabil Ahkir in the year 1234.

Seal of the East India Company. (Signed) T. S. RAFFLES.
Chop of the Tummungung.

The Treaty of Saturday, the 6th February, is written on rough, thick, white, foolscap paper. The writing on the left side of half the page being in English and in Malay on the right. The following is a correct copy, with the spelling, capital letters, and all marks of punctuation exactly followed. The printed copies in use in Singapore are all incorrect, as was suspected but could not be shown until the

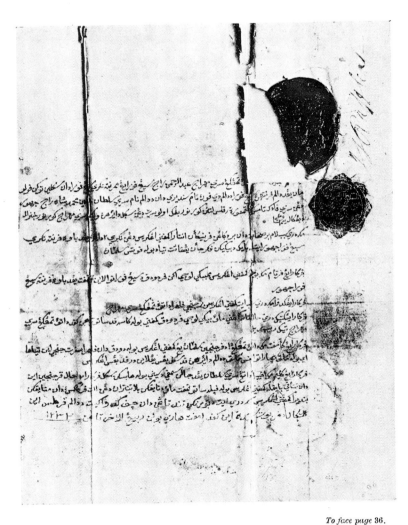

PHOTOGRAPH FROM THE ORIGINAL AGREEMENT OF JANUARY 30TH, 1819.

original counterpart kept by the Tumongong was found. Words had been spelt differently, some omitted, some displaced; and the Malay date was wrong, which led to the original being traced.

There are some curious things to be noticed. The East India Company is throughout styled the *English* East India Company, in one place the English Government is mentioned, and the last words speak of the *British Government.* These particular words were no doubt used purposely. The word Johore is spelt throughout with a final e, as it is spelt in Johore to this day, but Sir Stamford Raffles. after his signature spelt it Johor, which may please some small minds, but does not prove it is correct. The seal of the East India Company is two and a half inches in diameter, of thick red sealing wax. The English ink has somewhat faded, but the Malay in Indian ink is as black as the day it was written. The signatures are on the sixth page.

The way in which the original came to light after so many years was rather curious. It will be seen that the Mohamedan date is the 11th of the month. In the copy made in Mr. Braddell's notes, the date was given as the 11th. But in the printed copies of Government and also in the Book of Treaties, Part III, published by the *Straits Times* Press in 1877, the date was given as the 19th, or eight days later. There was of course no question as to the English date, the 6th February, and the Malay date would not have signified but for a reason that will more fully appear in the next chapter. The Malay chiefs who signed the treaty wrote letters to Rhio dated the 20th day of the same Malay month, saying that soldiers had been landed at Singapore. without their consent and that they had not acted voluntarily. If the date given in the Government copy was right those letters were written on the 7th February, the day after the treaty was signed and the very day Raffles left for Penang, just as his back was turned. This seemed unlikely. On the other hand, if Mr. Braddell's date was correct, the letters were not written until the 15th February, eight days later, and there was plenty of time for the Dutch to have heard of what Raffles had done, and to seek means to found an objection. Enquiry was first made in Singapore, but not one of these old documents is in existence. White ants, insects, and a damp climate account for a good deal, and mistakes or carelessness may account for more. It was also said that there was no means of ascertaining with any certainty the equivalent Malay date for any English date so long back as 1819. It was useless to search further in Singapore, so enquiry was made at the Government offices at Johore, on the Bank holiday in August, 1901. There again it was said that the Mohamedan Calendar was very erratic but it might perhaps be worked out; still it would not have been decisive of the question, without which it was no use. The Dato Bintara Dalam (the only surviving son of the old Munshi Abdulla) asked why so much trouble need be taken about it, why not look at the original? This sounded absurd, but he said it was in the safe. It has been said that truth lies at the bottom of a well, and it might be at the bottom of an iron safe. So a large safe was opened and the papers laid out on a big office table, and the Malay endorsements looked through. Near the bottom were some large folded pieces of parchment; the ink had entirely disappeared to the naked eye, the parchment was discoloured, and broken up into pieces like thin glass. One of these seemed to be about the year 1824, from the remains of a seal hanging to it, and it was said that it was no use looking any further, because the treaty of 1819 would be in the same state. But then Raffles may not have had any parchment with him. Soon after in a bundle of old papers the treaty was found, together with all the other original documents of that time. It seemed almost like a voice from the dead (or, as a Malay said, like unwrapping an Egyptian mummy) to open it out on the table and see the signature of Raffles and the chops of the chiefs which had been made in the attap house in the jungle on the bank of the river on that eventful day, on a site which is now the very centre of the large town of Singapore. The Dato Dalam was quite right, and also Mr. Braddell, and the question was at rest. Two counterparts of the treaty were of course made, one Sir Stamford Raffles or Major Farquhar kept, and the other was given to the Tumongong. The one copy, in the hands of English clerks, with secure safes, had not been forthcoming for many years and the copies of it were incorrect, while the copy that had been handed to the Malay chief who had not a table, chair, envelope, or safe, had been kept carefully wrapped up and preserved, and handed down through four generations and nearly a century to the hands of his great grandson, now styled the Sultan of Johore. The document it will be observed was not kept by the Sultan but by the Tumongong. If the Sultan had ever had it, it would have been lost without delay. It was the old story again of misprints of figures, but the result of this instance was to bring to notice this very historical document, and the trouble the misprint caused was turned to an excellent and most unexpected purpose.

THE TREATY.

Treaty of Friendship and Alliance concluded between the Honorable Sir Thomas Stamford Raffles Lieutenant Governor of Fort Marlborough and its Dependencies, Agent to the Most Noble Francis Marquess of Hastings Governor General of India &c., &c., &c., for the Honorable English East India Company on the one part and their Highnesses Sultan Hussein Mahummud Shah Sultan of Johore and Datoo Tummungung Sree Maharaja Abdul Rahman Chief of Singapoora and its Dependencies; on the other part.

ARTICLE 1ST.

The Preliminary Articles of Agreement entered into on the 30th of January 1819 by the Honorable Sir Stamford Raffles on the part of the English East India Company; and by Datoo Tummungung Sree Maharajah Abdul Rahman Chief of Singapoora and its Dependencies, for himself and for Sultan Hussein Mahummud Shah Sultan of Johore, is hereby entirely approved, ratified and confirmed by His Highness the aforesaid Sultan Mahummud Shah.

ARTICLE 2ND.

In furtherance of the objects contemplated in the said preliminary agreement; and in compensation of any and all the advantages which may be foregone now or hereafter by His Highness Sultan Hussein Mahummud Shah Sultan of Johore, in consequence of the stipulations of this Treaty; the Honorable English East India Company agree and engage to pay to His aforesaid Highness the sum of Spanish Dollars Five Thousand Annually; for and during the time that the said Company may, by virtue of this treaty, maintain a Factory or Factories on any part of His Highness's hereditary Dominions,; and the said company further agree to afford their protection to His Highness aforesaid as long as he may continue to reside in the immediate vicinity of the places subject to their authority. It is however clearly explained to and understood by His Highness that the English Government in entering into this alliance and in thus engaging to afford protection to His Highness is to be considered in no way bound to interfere with the internal politics of his States, or engaged to assert or maintain the authority of His Highness by force of Arms.

ARTICLE 3RD.

His Highness Datoo Tummungung Sree Maharajah Abdul Rahman Chief of Singapoora and its Dependencies having by Preliminary Articles of Agreement entered into on the 30th of January 1819 granted his full permission to the Honorable English East India Company to establish a Factory or Factories at Singapoora or on any other part of His Highness's Dominions; And, the said Company having in recompence and in return for the said Grant settled on His Highness the yearly sum of Spanish Dollars Three Thousand and having received His Highness into their Alliance and protection, all and every part of the said Preliminary Articles is hereby confirmed.

ARTICLE 4TH.

His Highness the Sultan Hussein Mahummud Shah Sultan of Johore and His Highness Datoo Tummungung Sree Maharajah Abdul Rahman Chief of Singapoora engage and agree to aid and assist the Honorable English East India Company against all enemies that may assail the Factory or Factories of the said Company established or to be established in the Dominions of their said Highnesses respectively.

ARTICLE 5TH.

His Highness the Sultan Hussein, Mahummud Shah Sultan of Johore and His Highness Datoo Tummungung Sree Maharajah Abdul Rahman Chief of Singapoora agree, promise and bind themselves their heirs and successors, that for as long time as the Hon'ble the English East India Company shall continue to hold a Factory or Factories on any part of the Dominions subject to the authority of their Highnesses aforesaid, and shall continue to afford to their Highnesses support and protection, they their said Highnesses will not enter into any treaty with any other Nation and will not admit or consent to the Settlement in any part of their Dominions of any other power European or American.

ARTICLE 6TH.

All persons belonging to the English Factory or Factories or who shall hereafter desire to place themselves under the protection of its flag, shall be duly registered, and considered as subject to British authority.

ARTICLE 7TH.

The mode of administering Justice to the native population shall be subject to future discussion and arrangement between the contracting parties, as this will necessarily in a great measure depend on the Laws and usages of the various tribes who may be expected to settle in the vicinity of the English Factory.

ARTICLE 8TH.

The port of Singapoora is to be considered under the immediate protection and subject to the regulation of the British Authorities.

ARTICLE 9TH.

With regard to the duties which it may hereafter be deemed necessary to levy on Goods, Merchandize, Boats or Vessels, His Highness Datoo Tummungung Sree Maharajah Abdul Rahman is to be entitled to a moiety or full half of all the amount collected from Native Vessels. The expenses of the Port and the collection of duties to be defrayed by the British Government.

Done and concluded at Singapoora this 6th day of February in the year of Our Lord 1819, answering to the 11th day of the Month Rubbelakhir and Year of the Hujira 1234.

Seal of the East   T. S. RAFFLES
India Company.   *Agent to the Most Noble the*
                  Gov. Genl. with the States of
                  Rhio Lingin and Johor.

Seal of the   Seal of the
Tummungung.   Sultan.

The impression of the native chops on the paper is made by holding the brass seal in the smoke of a flame until it is covered with lamp-black, and then pressing it on the paper.

Mr. John Crawfurd, writing in about 1828, spoke of this treaty as follows:—"In the first agreement with the native chief, the arrangement amounted to little more than a permission for the formation of a British factory and establishment, along two miles of the northern shore, and inland to the extent of the point-blank range of a cannon shot. There was in reality no territorial cession giving a legal right of legislation. The only law which could have existed was the Malay code. The native chief was considered to be the proprietor of the land, even within the bounds of the British factory, and he was to be entitled, in perpetuity, to one-half of such duties of customs as might hereafter be levied at the port. In the progress of the settlement, these arrangements were of course found highly inconvenient and embarrassing, and were annulled by the subsequent treaty." Mr. Crawfurd in speaking of the subsequent treaty means that of the 2nd August, 1824, which is printed on page 168, by which the whole island of Singapore with the adjacent seas, straits, and islets within ten miles from the Coast of the island, was ceded to the East India Company for ever.

On the same day the following Proclamation was issued by Raffles :—

PROCLAMATION.

A treaty having been this day concluded between the British Government and the native authorities, and a British establishment having been in consequence founded at Singapore, the Honourable Sir T. S. Raffles, Lieutenant-Governor of Bencoolen and its Dependencies. Agent to the Governor-General, is pleased to certify the appointment by the Supreme Government of Major Wm Farquhar, of the Madras Engineers, to be Resident, and to command the troops at Singapore and its Dependencies; and all persons are hereby directed to obey Major Farquhar accordingly.

It is further notified, that the Residency of Singapore has been placed under the Government of Fort Marlborough [Bencoolen], and is to be considered a dependency thereof; of which, all persons concerned are desired to take notice.

Dated at Singapore, this 6th day of February, 1819.

By order of the Agent of the Most Noble
the Governor-General.

(Signed) F. CROPLY,
Secretary.

On the day this was published, Sir Stamford addressed a letter to Major Farquhar giving him general instructions as Resident and Commandant of the station. It is impossible to read the letter without remarking the great foresight and high-minded policy of the writer. It contained instructions of a political nature, which after-events proved to have been almost prophetic*; it made all necessary provisions for finance, and for the appointment of a Master Attendant, and this in a port which, with the exception of his own vessels and a few native boats, was then empty; but which, in a short time, was to become a very busy harbour. He arranged for a watering place for the shipping that was to come, and established a European boarding officer with a boat and a crew for it. He said that Captain Ross having surveyed the coast, and he himself having inspected the nature of the ground, he had determined upon the site, and gave authority for the immediate erection of a small fort on the hill overlooking the Settlement [now Fort Canning] with a barrack for 30 European Artillery, and several batteries on positions he pointed out. He arranged for a garrison and stores and provisions.

The letter is printed at length, as it is of much interest :—

SINGAPORE, *6th February,* 1819.

To MAJOR WILLIAM FARQUHAR,
    Resident and Commandant,
        Singapore.

SIR,

Herewith I have the honor to transmit to you one of the copies of the treaty this day concluded between the Honorable the East India Company, and their Highnesses the Sultan of Johore, and the Tummungong of Singapore and its dependencies.

2. As the object contemplated by the Most Noble the Governor General in Council, namely the establishment of a station beyond Malacca, and commanding the southern entrance of the Straits, has thereby been substantially accomplished, I proceed to give you the following general instructions for the regulation of your conduct in the execution of the duties you will have to perform as Resident and Commandant of the station which has been established.

3. As you have been present at and assisted in the previous negociations, and are fully apprized of the political relations existing between the states in the immediate vicinity of this island, it is only necessary for me to direct your particular attention to the high importance of avoiding all measures which can be construed into an interference with any of the states where the authority of His Netherlands Majesty may be established. Whatever opinion may be formed with regard to the justice or nature of the proceedings of the Dutch authorities in these seas, it is not consistent with the views of His Lordship in Council to agitate the discussion of them in this country; and a station having been obtained which is properly situated for the securing the free passage of the Straits, and for protecting and extending the commercial enterprizes both of the British and native merchant, all questions of this nature will necessarily await the decision of the higher authorities in Europe.

4. It is impossible, however, that the object of our establishment at Singapore can be misunderstood or disregarded, either by the Dutch or the native authorities; and while the former may be expected to watch with jealousy the progress of a settlement which must check the further extention of their influence throughout these seas: the latter will hail with satisfaction the foundation and the site of a British establishment, in the central and commanding situation once occupied

---

* This passage, written in 1884, is quoted in Mr. Boulger's book (1897) at page 313.

by the capital of the most powerful Malayan empire then existing in the East, and the prospect which it affords them of the continuance, improvement and security of the commercial relations by which their interests have been so long identified with those of the British merchant. It is from the prevalence of this feeling among the natives and the consequences which might possibly arise from it, that I am desirous of impressing on your mind the necessity of extreme caution and delicacy, not only in all communications which you may be obliged to have with the subjects of any power under the immediate influence of the Dutch, but also in your intercourse with the free and independent tribes who may resort to the port of Singapore either for the purposes of commerce or for protection and alliance. The offer which is understood to have been made to the Sultan by the Bugguese, is a sufficient proof that in all communications regarding the proceedings of the Netherlands Government we should carefully guard against the expression of any sentiment of dislike or discontent, however justly those feelings might be excited, lest our motives be misconstrued, not only by the Dutch but by the natives themselves.

5. With regard, however, to those states which have not yet fallen under their authority, it is justifiable and necessary that you exert your influence to preserve their existing state of independence. If this independence can be maintained without the presence of an English authority it would be preferable, as we are not desirous of extending our stations; but as from the usual march of the Dutch policy, the occupation of Tringano, and the extension of their views to Siam, may be reasonably apprehended, a very limited establishment in that quarter may become ultimately necessary. It is at all events of importance to cultivate the friendship of these powers, and to establish a friendly intercourse with them ; and as the recent application from the Sultan of Tringano for a small supply of arms affords us a favorable opportunity of advancing towards this object, you will avail yourself of the first opportunity to comply with his request.

6. A similar line of policy in relation to the states of Pahang and of Lingin will be conducive to the maintenance of the influence and just weight which the English nation ought properly to possess in these seas. As it is my intention to return to this island after the completion of the arrangements at Acheen, I shall then be able to avail myself of the information you may have collected in the intervening period, relative to the political state of Borneo Proper, Indragiri and Jambi. In the meantime, it is probable that a knowledge of our establishment at this station will have considerable weight in preventing these powers from falling under the influence of the Dutch.

7. With reference to the native authorities residing under our immediate protection, it is only necessary for me to direct your attention to the conditions of the treaty concluded with these chiefs; which it will be incumbent on you to fulfil, under any circumstances that may arise, in a manner consistent with the character and dignity of the British Government. In the event of any question of importance being agitated by the Dutch Government at Batavia, or the authorities subordinate to it, you will refrain from entering into any discussion that can be properly avoided, and refer them to the authority under which you act.

8. To enable you to conduct the civil duties of the station with efficiency, I have appointed Lieutenant Croply your assistant; and that officer will conduct the details of the Pay Department, Stores and Commissariat with such other duties as you may think proper to direct. The allowances for your assistant have been fixed at Spanish dollars 400 per month, subject to the confirmation of the Supreme Government.

9. As the services of Lieutenant Croply as my acting Secretary, will be for some time required under my immediate authority, Mr. Garling of the Bencoolen Establishment will officiate until his return. In the event of its being necessary for you to leave the station or of any accident depriving the Company of your services, your assistant is appointed to succeed to the temporary charge until further orders.

10. Mr. Bernard has also been appointed to take charge provisionally of the duties of the port as Acting Master Attendant and Marine Storekeeper, and in consideration of the active duties that may be required in this department, and the general services which this officer may be required to perform, he is allowed provisionally to draw a monthly salary of 300 dollars per month.

11. As the convenience and accommodation of the port is an object of considerable importance, you will direct your early attention to it, and to the formation of a good watering place for the shipping. You will also be pleased to establish a careful and steady European at St. John's with a boat and small crew, for the purpose of boarding all square sailed vessels passing through the Straits and of communicating with you either by signals or by a small canoe as you may find most advisable.

12. It is not necessary at present to subject the trade of the port to any duties; it is yet inconsiderable, and it would be impolitic to incur the risk of obstructing its advancement by any measure of this nature.

13. In determining the extent and nature of the works immediately necessary for the defence of the port and station, my judgment has been directed in a great measure by your professional skill and experience. With this advantage and from a careful survey of the coast by Captain Ross, aided by my own personal inspection of the nature of the ground in the vicinity of the Settlement, I have no hesitation in conveying to you my authority for constructing the following works with the least delay practicable:—

On the hill overlooking the Settlement, and commanding it and a considerable portion of the anchorage, a small Fort, or a commodious block-house on the principle which I have already described to you, capable of mounting 8 or 10 pounders and of containing a magazine of brick or stone, together with a barrack for the permanent residence of 30 European artillery, and for the temporary accommodation of the rest of the garrison in case of emergency.

Along the coast in the vicinity of the Settlement one or two strong batteries for the protection of the shipping, and at Sandy Point a redoubt and to the east of it a strong battery for the same purpose.

The entrenchment of the Cantonment by lines and a palisade, as soon as the labor can be spared from works of more immediate importance.

14. These defences, together with a Martello tower on Deep Water Point, which it is my intention to recommend to the Supreme Government, will in my judgment render the Settlement capable of maintaining a good defence. The principle on which works were charged for at Malacca, is to be considered as applicable to this station, and it is unnecessary for me to urge on you the necessity of confining the cost of these works within the narrowest limits possible. As the construction of them, however, will necessarily demand a greater portion of care and superintendence than the performance of your duties will permit you to devote to them, I have appointed Lieutenant Ralfe of the Bengal Artillery to be the assistant Engineer. This officer will likewise have charge of the ordnance and military stores, and for the duties attendant on both these appointments conjoined I have fixed his salary at Spanish dollars 200 per mensem, to commence from the 1st instant, and subject to the confirmation of the Supreme Government.

15. As you will require the aid of a Staff officer to conduct the duties of the garrison, I have thought proper to authorize the appointment of a cantonment adjutant on the same allowances lately authorized at Malacca. As this officer may be considered your personal staff, I shall not make any permanent arrangement regarding it, but have appointed Lieutenant Dow to the temporary performance of its duties.

16. The indent for ordnance and stores which you have handed to me shall be transmitted to Bengal without delay, and I request you will lose no time in the erection of store-houses for their reception. An application for the number and description of troops which you have recommended to form the garrison of the residency will accompany the indent, together with an application for provisions equal to their supply for 12 or 15 months.

17. I should not think myself justified at the present moment in authorizing the erection of a house for the accommodation of the chief authority, but I shall take an early opportunity of recommending the adoption of that measure, or in the event of the Supreme Government declining to authorize it, the grant of a monthly allowance sufficient to compensate for the inconveniences to which, in the infancy of the Settlement, the Resident is necessarily liable. A store-house for the Commissariat department is at present of indispensible necessity, and you will accordingly be pleased to erect a house of this description, of such materials as can be procured, and as soon as you may find practicable. A maga-

zine built of such materials, for the military stores, would be subject to some risk; and I therefore confide to your professional judgment the adoption of such measures for their security as you may judge most expedient under the circumstances.

18. For a very short period it may be necessary to retain the brig *Ganges* as a store vessel, but I rely on your discharging her the moment her services can be dispensed with.

19. In the event of your adopting this arrangement, you will be pleased immediately to tranship to that vessel the public property now on board the H. C. hired ship *Mercury*, whose charter expires on the 24th instant, previously to which you will accordingly be pleased to discharge her from the public service. You will inform the commander, that I am entirely satisfied with his conduct while he was under my authority, and that as tonnage will probably be required to convey troops and stores from P. of W. Island, I shall be happy, in the event of his early arrival at that port, to consider his request for the further employment of his ship to be entitled to some consideration.

20. You are already apprized that the H. C. ship *Nearchus* has been put under your orders, and the services of the schooner *Enterprize* will be also available by you, during the remainder of the period of two months for which she was engaged.

21. The accounts of the residency are those which detail the receipt and disbursement of the public money. These are principally :—

(i.) An account particulars of military disbursements in which every military abstract and disbursement is clearly and correctly entered.

(ii.) A general account particulars, which will comprize the particulars of every disbursement of whatever nature, and containing also, under the head of "Military Establishment," a correct copy of No. 1, and,

(iii.) A general treasury account, shewing on the one side the general amount of the disbursement made on each particular account or head, with the balance remaining on hand; and on the other, the balance which remained on the 1st of the month, together with all the sums which may be received during the course of it.

22. The accounts of the commissariat cannot at present be arranged according to the established forms, they can however be kept with correctness by Mr. Garling, and I shall take care to procure and to forward from Pinang the necessary forms under which the first assistant will probably be able to arrange them on his taking charge of his appointment. You will of course exercise a strict superintendence over this department, no disbursements from which are to be made without your authority; and you will be pleased to examine the accounts rendered to you previously to transmitting them to Fort Marlborough.

23. A quarterly account of expenditure and remains of military stores will be transmitted to me. You will also be pleased to forward the usual returns to the Presidency of Fort William [Bengal] agreeably to the regulations of the service.

24. It does not occur to me that there is any other point of importance on which it is necessary at present to give you any instructions. I shall probably return to this residency after a short absence, and if in the meantime any important matter should occur, which I have not anticipated in this letter, I have the satisfaction afforded me by a perfect reliance on your acknowledged zeal, in the advancement and protection of the honor and interests of our country, moderated by the prudence and judgement which the infancy of our present establishment so particularly demands.

I have, &c.,

(Signed) T. S. RAFFLES.

Sultan Hussein died at Malacca in September, 1835, and was buried at the Tranquera Mosque. On his death no steps were taken as to the succession. The old empire, Mr. Braddell writes, was too far gone to admit of any hope of regeneration, and without the aid of the English Government, the Sultan's son could not attain a position of authority. The slight degree of influence attained by the late

Sultan, through the countenance of Sir Stamford Raffles and the East India Company, died with him. He had benefited by the pension which gave him means he could not otherwise have hoped to obtain. The whole influence over the mainland of Johore remained in the hands of the Tumongong, to the exclusion of the Sultan, who fell into indolent habits. Sultan Hussein was living, Mr. Earl says in his book, in a large, rambling attap habitation at Campong Glam, and could not attend to his own affairs, which were administered by several hadjees and petty chiefs attracted about him by the government pension. He was succeeded by his son Sultan Allie who was then fifteen years of age, and died in Malacca in 1877.

Mr. Earl speaks of Sultan Hussein as being so enormously stout that he appeared constantly on the point of suffocation, and Munshi Abdulla in his book described him thus:—"I now must ask pardon of such gentlemen as read my story, for it is necessary that they should know the disposition and appearance of Sultan Hussein; for new comers have not seen him. For this reason I must describe him. When he first arrived in Singapore from Rhio, he was not stout, but thin, but when he had become Sultan at Singapore, his body enlarged with his days and his size became beyond all comparison. He was as broad as he was long, a shapeless mass. His head was small, and sunk into his shoulders from fat, just as if he had no neck; his face was square, his nose was moderate, his mouth wide, his breast proportionate; he was pot-bellied in folds, his legs were thin, without contour; his feet were wide, his voice husky, with an awful sound; and it was his custom to fall asleep wherever he sat down. And when he was speaking, strangers were startled at the clashing sounds. His complexion was light yellow; but I need not dilate on this, as many know it, and have seen his appearance; but as far as my experience has gone, I have never seen so unwieldy a man, he could not even carry his own body. And, to my apprehension, in such enormity there can be no pleasure or ease to the body, but nothing but trouble."

Tumongong Abdul Rahman died in Singapore on the 8th December, 1825, and was buried in the *makum,* or Rajah's burial ground, at the mosque at Telok Blanga. He was succeeded by his second son named Ibrahim, because his elder son, Abdulla, did not wish to rule. Ibrahim was then fifteen years of age. He died in 1862 and was buried at the same place. He was succeeded by his eldest son Abubakar, who died at the age of 63 in London, while on a short visit to England, on 4th July, 1895, and his body was brought to Johore, being carried in an English man-of-war from Penang, and buried in Johore on 7th September with much ceremony. His son, Ibrahim, succeeded him, being named after his grandfather. He was born on 17th September, 1873, and is the present Sultan. The ruler of Johore was styled Tumongong until 1868, when with the approval of the British Government he was styled Maharajah; and subsequently, at the expressed wish of the people, it was agreed by the treaty with the British Government of 11th December, 1885, that the ruler should in future be recognised as the Sultan of the State and Territory of Johore. It was shown in some correspondence with the Secretary of State for the Colonies in July, 1878, when the question of the assumption of the title of Sultan of Johore by the Maharajah first arose, that the Tumongongs were lineally descended from the Sultan Abdul Jaleel (the third of the name) who was killed at the mouth of the Pahang river in resisting an invasion from Siak about 1726. Suleiman, one of his sons succeeded him as Sultan, while another, named Abbas, was the common progenitor of the lines both of the Bandaharas of Pahang and the Tumongongs of Johore. The first of the Tumongongs was named Abdul Jamal, while the second in succession, named Ibrahim, was the father of Tumongong Abdul Rahman who made the treaty with Raffles. There was Bugis blood in the family, as the death of Sultan Abdul Jaleel, in 1726, was avenged by a Bugis chief called Jaya Putra, who with his followers drove out the Siak chief, and restored the government to Suleiman the eldest son of the late Abdul Jaleel; in reward for this he was made the first Rajah Muda of Rhio, an office not before known, and married into the Sultan's family. A long account of the genealogy of the Johore Royal Families, written by Mr. Braddell, is in 9 Logan's Journal, page 66.

Abdulla's description of Sir Stamford Raffles has been printed more than once, part of it is in Mr. Boulger's book. As Mr. Thomson remarks, Raffles probably little thought that the young native boy writing in his office was so apt a sketcher. This is a part of Mr. Thomson's translation of Abdulla's chapter upon Sir Stamford:—

"When I first saw Mr. Raffles, he struck me as being of middle stature, neither too short nor too tall. His brow was broad, the sign of large heartedness; his head betokened his good understanding; his hair being fair, betokened courage; his ears being large, betokened quick hearing; his eyebrows were thick; his nose was high; his cheeks a little hollow; his lips narrow, the sign of oratory and persuasiveness; his mouth was wide; his neck was long; and the colour of his body was not purely white; his breast was well formed; his waist slender; his legs to proportion, and he walked with a slight stoop.

"Now I observed his habit was to be always in deep thought. He was most courteous in his intercourse with all men. He always had a sweet expression towards European as well as native gentlemen. He was extremely affable and liberal, always commanding one's best attention. He spoke in smiles. He also was an earnest enquirer into past history, and he gave up nothing till he had probed it to the bottom. He loved most to sit in quietitude, when he did nothing else but write or read: and it was his usage, when he was either studying or speaking, that he would see no one till he had finished. He had a time set apart for each duty, nor would he mingle one with another. Further, in the evenings, after tea, he would take ink, pen, and paper, after the candles had been lighted, reclining with closed eyes in a manner that I often took to be sleep; but in an instant he would be up, and write for a while till he went to recline again. Thus he would pass the night, till twelve or one, before he retired to sleep. This was his daily practice. On the next morning he would go to what he had written, and read it while walking backwards and forwards, when out of ten sheets, probably he would only give three or four to his copying clerk to enter into the books, and the others he would tear up.

" Now, Mr. Raffles took great interest in looking into the origin of nations, and their manners and customs of olden times, examining what would elucidate the same. He was especially quick in the uptake of Malay with its variations. He delighted to use the proper idioms as the natives do; he was active in studying words and their place in phrases; and not until we had told him would he state that the English had another mode. It was his daily labour to order post letters to the various Malay countries to support their good understanding with his nation, and increase the bond of friendship; this with presents and agreeable words. This gained the good will of the various Rajas, who returned the compliment with respect and thanks and moreover with presents. There also came a great many presents of books from various countries.

" Mr. Raffles's disposition was anything but covetous, for, in whatever undertaking or project he had in view, he grudged no expense so that they were accomplished. Thus his intentions had rapid consummation. There were numbers of people always watching about his house, ready to seek for whatever he wanted, to sell to him or take orders; so that they might obtain profit. Thus loads of money came out of his chest daily, in buying various things, or in paying wages. I also perceived that he hated the habit of the Dutch who lived in Malacca of running down the Malays. But Mr. Raffles loved always to be on good terms with the Malays, the poorest could speak to him; and while all the great folks in Malacca came to wait on him daily, whether Malays or Europeans, yet they could not find out his object of coming there—his ulterior intentions. But it was plain to me that in all his sayings and doings there was the intelligence of a rising man, together with acuteness. If my experience be not at fault there was not his superior in this world in skill or largeness of heart."

There is a short, appreciative note of Mr. Braddell's, at page 602 of 6 Logan's Journal, in which he says that Abdulla's description of Sir Stamford Raffles contained a portrait of the man, which was said, by those who knew him, to be as faithful as it was striking.

48

CHAPTER V.

1819—*Continued.*

THE exact position of Singapore has been frequently mistated in the books that refer to the place. The little observatory house at the point of the river near the Master Attendant's Office is accurately in Latitude N. 1°: 17'. 13.7" and Longitude E. 103°: 51': 15.7', or about 77 geographical miles north of the Equator, and in time 6 hours 55 min. 25.05 seconds east of Greenwich.

This book contains no description of its scenery, but **Mr.** Cameron's book has much on the subject which is charmingly expressed. He says that he had seen both Ceylon and Java and admired their many charms in no grudging measure, but for calm placid loveliness he placed Singapore high above them both. The view from the top of Bukit Timah cf the panorama of the magnificent tropical forest and jungle, with the numerous little green islands scattered like gems over the sea surrounding Singapore, and the large hills of Johore to the North is ample confirmation of Mr. John Cameron's opinion.

In a letter of 31st January, Sir Stamford mentioned the excellent harbour, and said that he had six draftsmen employed from eight o'clock to four, and that he expected to be able to leave, in the course of a few days, to return to Penang, where he was very anxious to rejoin Lady Raffles. He said that if he could keep Singapore, he would be quite satisfied, and in a few years British influence over the Archipelago, as far as regards commerce, would be fully established.

Major Farquhar, as has been said, wrote that Sir Stamford Raffles left Singapore on the day after the flag was formally hoisted and this is now confirmed by the old Penang Directory. In the list of shipping before referred to, are the arrivals at Penang on 14th February of H.C.C. *Minto* and the *Indiana* which left Singapore on February 7th. The same torn pages show that the two vessels left again for sea on March 8th, which is the day other accounts say that Raffles left for Acheen.

At this time the Indian Government and its Presidencies are set out in the same Directory, as follows:—

Supreme Government of Fort William at Calcutta.
Government of Fort St George at Madras.
Government of Bombay.
Government of St Helena.
Government of Ceylon.
Government of Mauritius.
Government of the Cape of Good Hope.
Island of Sumatra. The Hon. T. S. Raffles, Lieutenant Governor at Bencoolen.
Government of Fort Cornwallis, Prince of Wales' Island.

Singapore was under Bencoolen; and the only mention of it is under the heading of " Fort Marlbro', Bencoolen " as " Singapore, Major W. Farquhar, Resident and Commandant."

Major Farquhar, being installed as the first Resident and left in charge of Singapore, must have been very much occupied in a manner that has seldom, if ever, fallen to the lot of another. The fishing village grew into a town in the most unexampled manner. He sent the news of the Settlement to Malacca by a sampan, asking the Malays to come, and urging them to bring fowls, ducks, fruits, and provisions of all kinds, for which they would obtain a large profit. And others who had gone to Singapore with the expedition sent letters to the same effect.

Abdulla tells us that the news soon spread over the bazaar there, and numbers of persons started from Malacca, but pirates cut many boats off (forty Malacca Malays were all murdered in one boat) and although many were stopped, he says, by the Dutch, who did all in their power in Malacca, and by stationing a gunboat in the Straits, to prevent any person reaching Singapore, yet many hundreds reached there safely; and provisions being very dear, a fowl being sold for two rupees and a duck for a dollar, they made large profits. In the course of a year, the population had risen from 150 to 5,000, and a large trade was springing up, and that of Malacca and Rhio sinking fast.

This is Mr. Braddell's translation of a capital descriptive passage from the Hakayit Abdulla; it reads like a passage from the Arabian Nights. " At this time no mortal dared to pass through the Straits of Singapore. Jins and Satans even were afraid, for that was the place the pirates made use of, to sleep at and divide their booty, after a successful attack on any ship's boats or prahus. There also they put to death their captives, and themselves fought and killed each other in their quarrels on the division of the spoil."

Abdulla tells us of a remarkable conversation about this time between Sir Stamford and the native chiefs. Raffles had proposed that Mr. Palmer of Calcutta should send down goods for the Sultan and Tumongong to sell on commission for him, and that premises should be erected to store the goods and carry on the business and they might rise to riches. " They laughed and said that such was not their custom, for the Malay princes to trade would be a disgrace to them. Mr Raffles' countenance altered and became quite red, but he replied smilingly ' I am astonished to hear of such a foolish and improper custom : so that to trade is a disgrace but to pirate is not a disgrace.' The Sultan replied that pirating had descended from their forefathers, and therefore it was not a disgrace; and furthermore pirating had not its origin with the Malays."

It has been remarked that while Sir Stamford was founding a station to be second to none in Asia, and while he seemed fully to anticipate the extraordinary success that afterwards attended it, the first Resident, Major Farquhar, seems, from the records of his rule, to have scarcely seen beyond the prospect of a mere village fitted for the accommodation of a limited supply of goods and the temporary residence of traders. There is no doubt that the presence of Mr. Farquhar, and his influence after having been fifteen years among the Malacca Malays, induced many of them to come to Singapore and settle there to supply provisions, but it is added that it may well be doubted whether the irregularities that were admitted in his administration, which was not a strong one, peculiarly subject to native influence, and largely controlled by native ideas, did not counterbalance such benefits.

The following interesting account of Major Farquhar's services is found in a note made by Mr. Braddell. Farquhar, appointed cadet in 1791; arrived Madras 19th June, 1791; ensign, 22nd June; joined Lord Cornwallis' Grand Mysore Army, August, present at storming of Nundy Droog, Savern Droog, seige of Seringapatam 1792; taking of Pondicherry 1793; Lieutenant, 16th August 1793; appointed Chief Engineer, July 1795 to expedition to proceed to Malacca; surrender of Malacca 18th August, 1795; appointed to Manila expedition, but that given up recalled to Madras, 25th April, 1798. Returned to Malacca 29th May, 1798; full Captain 1st January, 1803; succeeded Colonel Taylor 12th July in Civil and Military authority at Malacca, Brevet Major 25th June, 1810; Major in Corps 26th September, 1811. Appointed to join the expedition to Java under Sir S. Auchmuty. Appointed by him in charge of intelligence and guides. Landed at Chillinching near Batavia, present at Weltevreden; Cornelis carried by storm 26th August, 1811. Surrender of Soerabaya 22nd September. Appointed by Admiral Stopford to chief civil authority at Soerabaya, but did not assume charge. Returned to Batavia, offered British Residency at Joejocarta, but refused and returned to Malacca 31st October, 1811.

Abdulla described him as "A man of good parts, slow at fault finding, treating rich and poor alike, and very patient in listening to the complaints of any person who went to him, so that all returned rejoicing."

After Raffles had left, Sultan Hoossein and the Tumongong began to be a little nervous about their proceedings in allowing him to open the settlement, and the three following letters were written to Rhio, trying to throw the responsibility off their own shoulders and pleading compulsion. Mr. Boulger says there was nothing strange in this, considering the influence and reputation of the Dutch. These letters are to be found in Malay with an English translation at page 104 of the Notes and Queries of the Straits Asiatic Society's Volume for 1887, being considered apparently as something that had not been published before. They were in the original of these papers on 11th October, 1884, and were then taken from a translation by Mr. Braddell, which was published in 1855 in the 9th Volume of Logan's Journal at page 444. The only date is in the second letter as the 20th day of Rubil Akir, which we now know was the 15th February, eight days after Raffles had left for Penang and Acheen :—

From the Tumongong Abdulrahman, residing at Singapore. To the Iang De Per Tuan Mudah of Rhio. (Tuanku Jaffar, the Rajah Mudah.)

After compliments.

"Your son informs his father that a party of English, having at their head Mr. Raffles and the Resident of Malacca, arrived at Singapore; the latter went on to Rhio, the former remaining. Their coming was quite without your son's knowledge, and it is by compulsion only that he has been necessitated to admit them to reside at Singapore, for he could not prevent their landing their men and stores, and proceeding to establish themselves, by constructing quarters, as they consulted their own inclinations only. At this time your son Tuanku Long (otherwise called Hoossein) arrived from Rhio, having been surprised by the reports of the arrival of so many vessels and ships at Singapore. As soon as he landed he met Mr. Raffles, the latter forcibly laid hold of him, and declared him Rajah, giving him the title of Sultan Hussain, and confirming the same by a written instrument (chop). Your son was thus compelled to a compliance with all their wishes."

From the Iang De Per Tuan of Singapore (Hussain). To the Iang De Per Tuan Besar, Sultan of Lingin (Abdulrahman).

" Your elder brother informs his younger brother that, by the dispensation of Almighty God towards his slave, things have turned out entirely beyond his previous conception. Abang Johor, being deputed by the Tumongong, came in the middle of the night, and acquainted him that a great number of vessels had lately arrived at Singapore, and, without the Tumongong's consent, had landed a large party of soldiers. Your brother was thrown into great agitation and per-plexity of mind by the suddenness and unexpected nature of the intelligence, and apprehensive only for the safety of his son (who was at Singapore) without reflecting, he forthwith quitted Rhio without giving notice to his father and mother. As soon as your brother arrived at Singapore he was met by Mr. Raffles, who immediately laid hold of him and declared him Rajah. Your brother had no choice left; indeed, being in the power of Mr. Raffles, what could he do? He was therefore necessitated to fall in with the views of this gentleman; had he not com-plied his ruin must have followed, as my brother will know. Although my brother may (seem) to comply with their views, never fear, nor entertain the least sus-picion that he intends to do anything that will cause future ill or animosity. God avert this! Such is your brother's situation, for being in the hands of the English, they would not let him go: they even refused his request to return for a short time to fetch his wife and children, desiring him to send for them."

Written at Singapore, 20th day of the month Rabil Akir, in the year of Mahomed 1234.

From the Iang De Per Tuan of Singapore (Hussain). To the Iang De Per Tuan Mudah of Rhio (Tuanku Jaffar).

After compliments and formalities.

" Your son informs his father that Abang Johor arrived in the middle of the night, and acquainted him that several ships had lately arrived at Singapore, and disembarked soldiers and stores. Being greatly surprised, perplexed, and agitated by the suddenness of the news, your son quitted Rhio that very night, scarcely possessing the use of his senses, without giving his father and mother notice of his departure. On his arrival at Singapore he met Mr. Raffles, who forcibly de-tained him and made him Rajah, by the title of Sultan Hussain Mahomed Shah, giving him a patent or chop to that effect. Your son now begs pardon, assured that it will be granted, both as it respects this and the world to come. Your son will never lay aside his respect for his father. With regard to your son's family, Mr. Raffles requests they may be sent to Singapore, and Rajah Tuah and Inche Saban are sent for the purpose of escorting them hither, and further, Inche Saban will receive charge of all the property inherited from his late father, whether it consists in duties received from China vessels, or from the China bazaar, or from the Custom House. These are required to pay your son's debts and defray the expenses of removing his family. Your son puts his trust in Almighty God and his Prophet, and then in his father, under all circumstances (meaning the Rajah Mudah)."

The Dutch had by this time seen the advantage that Sir Stamford had gained over them, and began to make a stir. On the 1st March Major Farquhar wrote as follows to Colonel Bannerman, Governor at Penang, as Raffles had left Singapore in order to proceed to Acheen : " Having obtained what I conceive to be authentic information that the Governor of Malacca has addressed a letter to you intimating that the British Establishment recently formed at Singapore has been effected

in a forcible manner without the previous consent of the Local
Authorities of the country, and having at the same time ascertained
that this information has been grounded on a letter from hence
by his Highness the Tumongong to Mr. Adrian Koek [then senior
Member of the Dutch Council at Malacca] of Malacca, I beg leave
herewith to transmit an explanatory document, signed by
Tunkoo Long, Sultan of Johore, and the Tumongong of Singapore,
which will no doubt remove every doubt which may have arisen in
your mind relative to the proceedings which have taken place. I
must also take the liberty to request that in the event of the erroneous
statement the Hon'ble Mr. Timmerman Thyssen [the Dutch Governor
of Malacca] is said to have transmitted having been received and
subsequently forwarded on to the Supreme Government, you will have
the goodness to transmit a copy of the present despatch for the
information of the Most Noble the Governor-General by the first
opportunity."

Enclosure.

"This is to make known to all whom it may concern, that our
friend Major William Farquhar, British Resident of the Settlement of
Singapore, has called upon me to declare whether or not any letter
or letters have been written by me to the Governor of Malacca, or to
any person under his authority, or to the Rajah Mudah of Rhio, intimating that the factory which the English have recently established
here was forcibly formed entirely against my will; I hereby freely acknowledge that I did write a letter to Mr. Adrian Koek of Malacca, and
one to the Rajah Mudah of Rhio, to the above effect, but my motive
for so writing arose solely from the apprehension of bringing on me
the vengeance of the Dutch at some future period. But I here call
God and His Prophet to witness that the English established themselves at Singapore with my free will and consent: and that from the
arrival of the Honorable Sir Thomas Stamford Raffles no troops or
effects were landed, or anything executed but with the free accord of
myself and of the Sultan of Johore. In token of the truth whereof
we have hereunto affixed our respective Seals."

At Singapore this first day of March, 1819. A true translation,
W. Farquhar, Resident, &c."

The Dutch Government at Malacca had written protesting against
the action of Raffles, and Colonel Bannerman sent the letter on to
Calcutta, with a minute of his own, supporting the Dutch complaint, and
afterwards hearing that the Dutch were fitting out an expedition to
attack Singapore, he wrote to the Dutch Government at Malacca asking
him, *from motives of humanity,* to wait until an answer could be received
to a letter he had sent to the Governor General at Calcutta. Major
Farquhar had written to Penang on the 6th March to ask reinforcements to meet any hostile attack. Colonel Bannerman, as has been said in
the first chapter, refused to send any help and advised Farquhar to
send back all the party from Singapore in the *Nearchus* and the *Ganges.*
All this will be found told with telling effect in Mr. Boulger's book at
pages 314 to 318.

Sir Stamford, as soon as he arrived in Penang in February, sent down tools for building, and provisions to the value of about $5,500.

A plague of rats set in at this time, and they are described as very large ones, which used to attack cats and get the better of them. Major Farquhar, as they became quite unbearable in his tent, offered a reward of one anna for each dead rat, and every morning the people came, some with 50 or 60, and some with 6 or 7. It soon, therefore, became an expensive matter, and the reward was much reduced; but they were still brought in, until they ceased to be troublesome; and so, Abdulla says, "the rat disturbance or war ceased." After this, great numbers of centipedes appeared, and stung people, so Major Farquhar paid for them also, and they gradually diminished, until Abdulla says "the lipan (centipede) disturbance and war also ended, and people ceased to mourn from the pain of their stings." The rat nuisance (bandicoots) appeared again in the merchants' houses on Kampong Glam Beach in 1845.

Shortly afterwards, Major Farquhar wanted to ascend Bukit Larangan. The tombs of the old Rajahs were there, and it was considered sacred, as it is to the present day. Malays were frequently seen until late years crowding up the hill and decorating old graves there. This is the hill now called Fort Canning. As the Tumongong's people would not go up on account of their fear of ghosts, Mr. Farquhar went up with his Malacca Malays, and drew up a gun, but not a single Singapore man went up. There was not much jungle, nor many large trees on the hill. When the gun was got up, a salute of twelve guns was fired, and a post set up to hoist the flag. After this, orders were given to clear the hill and a road was made up it. Government House was afterwards built on the hill, as will be mentioned further on. Major Farquhar's temporary house was near the place where the cricket pavilion is now, near the Town Hall. A house was made for the Master Attendant, Captain Flint, Sir Stamford's brother-in-law, at the end of the point near the present Master Attendant's Office. The houses were built with attap roofs and kajang (mat) walls. The large, old angsana trees at the river end of the Esplanade, were brought at this time from Tanjong Kling at Malacca in the boat of one Rajah Hadjee. The road from Malacca to Tanjong Kling, seven miles from the town, used to be lined with these beautiful trees, but they all died together about the same time, some twenty-five years ago. The handsome trees at the corner of the Esplanade in Singapore were fast decaying in 1882 when the first one was cut away altogether, and those still remaining will soon become things of the past. When they were all in full bloom, and covering the road with the golden leaves of their flowers they were very handsome. When the Esplanade was widened about 1890, some persons were much opposed to trees being planted along the side of the Esplanade facing the sea, as it was thought they would shut out the view of the sea. The trees are now well grown up, and the lower branches are well up from the ground and the view of the sea is open beneath them. When the trees grow to their full size it will be as handsome a sight as the famous avenue was in Malacca thirty-five years ago.

On the 5th April the *Mary Ann*, Webster, master, left Singapore for Penang and arrived there on the 14th. This was the first vessel,

other than those in the Expedition, to leave Singapore for Penang.
Besides the six vessels of the Expedition, some of which, as has been
said, went to and fro, only six other vessels sailed between Penang and
Singapore during the year.   The only other East India Company's
man-of-war that came to Singapore during the year, had left England
on 23rd April, reached Penang on 30th September, (five months) and
left Penang on 29th October for Singapore.   It was H.C.S. *Bridge-
water*, C. S. Timins, Esq., commander.   On 18th November there sailed
from Singapore the *Singapore*, which reached Penang on 17th December.
Her commander was Inchee Alley, and she must have been the first
ship with that name.

Mr. Francis James Bernard, the son-in-law of Major Farquhar,
was made Assistant to the Resident and put in charge of the Police,
as a Magistrate. He became the first Master Attendant until Captain
Flint arrived. Mr. Bernard had been the master of the *Ganges*,
but had appeared in the Penang shipping list as F. J. Barnard. The
vessel sailed in August from Singapore to Penang and the commander
was then changed.   Several of the first members of the mercantile
community and officials had been sailors, as was most likely to be
the case, as it was the cause of their being so far away from
England.

Abdulla tells us that one of Major Farquhar's dogs was taken
by an alligator one morning when he was at the Rochore river. The
alligator was surrounded and killed. It was eighteen feet long and the
body was hung on the banyan tree at Bras Basah. This referred to
a large and semi-sacred tree at Institution Bridge, which was accidentally
burnt and was taken away about twenty years ago.

On the 29th May, 1819, the Rev. Dr. Milne, of the Anglo-Chinese
College at Malacca applied for ground to build a school. He had
established a Christian Mission at Malacca in the year 1815, when
there were no schools there for the gratuitous instruction of children. He returned to Malacca in 1823, as Abdulla tells us, with his
wife and children.   Abdulla says " I observed the bearing and de-
portment of Mr. Milne to be those of a gentleman; his conversation
was polite and refined," and tells a great deal about him.   Dr.
Morrison the famous Chinese scholar came to stay with Dr. Milne at
Malacca. Abdulla says that if Dr. Morrison had worn a Chinese dress
no one would have taken him for a European; as he spoke Chinese so
well, and his manner, voice and the pen he wrote with were all like
the Chinese. Dr. Morrison, of the University of Glasgow, was sent out
to Macao in 1807, by a Society of Members of various British Churches
for the purpose of acquiring the Chinese language; as is stated
in the Deed drawn up at Canton on 21st March, 1820, regarding the
Anglo-Chinese College at Malacca, to which he gave £1,000 which he
had saved. It says that he entrusted the building of the College, the
foundation stone of which was laid in Malacca on 11th November,
1818, to Dr. William Milne, his first associate, he says, in the Chinese
Mission. Dr. Morrison was the first Vice-President of the Raffles
Institution in 1823, and drew up a long paper of suggestions for Sir
Stamford Raffles respecting it, which is found among some old papers
printed at the Malacca Mission Press in 1823 from which the above

particulars about these two prominent Missionaries, the pioneers in the Straits and China, have been found. Another old Malacca book printed at the Anglo-Chinese Press in 1819, called the Indo-Chinese Gleaner, contains a long memoir of Mrs. Milne, who died in Malacca on 20th March, 1819, 36 years of age.

The Reverend Robert Morrison, D.D., wrote at Macao his grammar of the Chinese language and his Dictionary, the expense of printing, £12,000, being paid by the East India Company. It was on his suggestion that Sir Stamford Raffles called the meeting on 1st April, 1823, to found the Singapore Institution. He was the first European who prepared documents in Chinese which they would consent to receive, and the first paper he wrote was supposed to have been the production of a learned Chinese, so means were taken to try to discover its author, as it was an act then regarded in China as treason. Dr. Morrison died at Macao on 1st August, 1834, and a long memoir appeared in the London Asiatic Journal for March, 1835.

When Raffles was Governor of Java, in a letter written at Buitenzorg in February, 1815, he wrote to his cousin Thomas: "The Rev. Mr. Milne is attached to the Mission in China. He is a liberal well-informed, excellent man. He is now in China, having touched at Malacca on the way. Such men do good wherever they go, and are an honour to their country and to the cause they espouse. As you are a Director of the Missionary Society you may possibly be able to promote his views, and I am anxious you should do so. Modest, unassuming, strictly kind and conciliating in everything he does, conviction is carried before the head enquires why." And in January 1823, Raffles wrote at Singapore: "The death of my friend, Dr. Milne of Malacca, has for a time thrown a damp upon missionary exertions in this quarter, but I expect Dr. Morrison here from China in March and I hope to make some satisfactory arrangement with him for future labours. The two missionaries who are here are not idle; Messrs. Milton and Thomson, the former in Chinese and Siamese, the latter in Malay and English printing." The Rev. J. Milton, who was the first missionary sent out by the London Missionary Society, established a school for Chinese and Malay children in this year. He was four years afterwards one of the Trustees of the Singapore Institution. Sir Stamford gave him $150 on condition that he would perform the usual Church Services.

Raffles was back again in Singapore in June as we find from his letters in the Memoirs. There is a letter to the Duchess of Somerset written in Penang on the 22nd February, and the next is dated Singapore, June 10th. From the shipping list, which has turned out so useful, it is seen that the *Minto* left Penang on 22nd May and as Lady Raffles says (on page 379) that her husband "was most agreeably occupied for some time in marking out the future town and giving instructions for the arrangement and management of the new colony," it may be that he remained until the 23rd September, when the *Minto* sailed to Penang, but he wrote the letter quoted presently on 25th June, speaking of his intending to leave. It is uncertain how long he remained. When he left he took back with him to Bencoolen a printing press and native type.

On the 11th June Raffles wrote to the Duchess of Somerset " My new colony thrives most rapidly. We have not been established four months and it has received an accession of population exceeding five thousand, principally Chinese, and their number is daily increasing. It is not necessary for me to say how much interested I am in the success of the place: it is a child of my own, and I have made it what it is."

In laying out the town, six building lots were reserved by Raffles :—One for Carnegy & Co., one for F. Ferrao, one for T. Macquoid, one for Captain Flint, and two to be disposed of by Raffles himself. Twelve lots along the North Beach were only to be sold to Europeans. Six were disposed of as above, and the other six were to be sold on application. It is almost certain no leases were ever drawn up, and no records exist now of any counterparts before 1826.

On the 4th June, the Rajah of Tapamana wrote to the Sultan of Johore, that the Rajah Mudah of Rhio has gone over to the Dutch, and was against his countrymen. The Rajah asked the Sultan to join forces and drive the Rajah Mudah and the Dutch out of the place and to instal a new Rajah Mudah, and to be careful above all things not to let him levy heavy duties. On 16th June, the Resident (Farquhar) wrote to Calcutta to request that some arrangements might be made at Singapore as otherwise in the event of anything occurring to him, the settlement would be left in charge of Mr. Montgomerie, a very young Assistant Surgeon.

Mr. Garling, of the Bencoolen Establishment, had been sent on a mission to Pahang. He was directed to return, and Mr. D. Napier, who was then expecting an appointment as writer in the Bencoolen service, was directed to be sent to Pahang as Resident. On the 6th of July, Captain Maxfield of the *Nearchus*, in a letter to the Resident, pointed out the existence of a good harbour between Point Romania and the Island.

On the 25th June, Raffles wrote to Major Farquhar as follows :—

1. Previous to my departure, I think it necessary to call your particular attention to the 11th para, of my letter of the 6th February, and to the importance of immediately improving the conveniences of the port for shipping, an object to which in the present advanced state of the Settlement all others ought to give way.

2. Points of primary importance to be attended to, should be the construction of convenient watering places, and affording to ships the means for watering, ballasting, as well as loading, with the least possible delay. The want of these conveniences has already been felt in several instances which have occurred during my stay here, and I feel satisfied that you will concur in the necessity of giving your early attention to this subject, as well as to the removal of the present temporary buildings between the stores and the river, and the erection of a convenient shed or bankshall at which merchants may load their goods. The removal of the bazaar from its present site is indispensible.

3. With regard to Police and the Administration of Justice, it does not appear to me necessary in the present state of the Settlement that any precise regulations should yet be laid down. As Resident, you are necessarily vested with the authority of chief magistrate and will of course exercise that authority, as is usual in places subject to British control, but where British laws may not have yet been introduced. As also the larger portion of the population may in a certain degree be considered as camp followers and consequently subject to your military authority as commandant, it will be left to your discretion to act in either of these capacities according to circumstances, by which, with the

assistance of the native authorities, you will be fully competent to provide for an efficient police and the settlement of such matters as do not require a more regular judicial proceeding. The Chinese, Bugguese and other foreign settlers are to be placed under the immediate superintendence of chiefs of their own tribes to be appointed by you, and those chiefs will be responsible to you for the police within their respective jurisdictions.

4. In higher cases of a criminal nature for which the military regulations or usage may not provide, the law of the country as it exists must necessarily be considered in force. The mode in which this law is to be carried into effect, will hereafter be defined as experience may direct, and in the meantime the present mode may be observed as far as in your judgment may appear advisable for the attainment of substantial justice. In the conduct of these proceedings you will of course exercise a personal superintendence and your sanction and confirmation is to be considered necessary to all decisions. It is to be hoped that cases of this nature will be of rare occurrence, and it is considered of importance that disputes between natives should as far as possible be left to be settled among themselves, according to their respective usages and customs.

5. These duties as above directed must in all cases be exercised by yourself or your assistant, as your representative, and cannot be delegated to any separate authority.

6. The whole space included within the Old Lines and the Singapore river [that was about between where the Cathedral compound and Elgin Bridge are now] is to be considered as Cantonments and of course no ground within this space can be permanently appropriated to individuals. Whenever you may have planned the lines, parades, &c., for the troops and set apart sufficient accommodation for magazine, &c., it will be necessary to allot sufficient space in a convenient and proper situation for officers' bungalows. The extent of each to be regulated by you according to circumstances, and the ground to be occupied by the officers as is usual in other Cantonments. The residency of the Tumonggong [this was on the river bank somewhere between where the Court House and Hill Street are now] is of course to be considered the only exception. The whole of the hill extending to the fort within the two rivers and the fresh water cut is to be reserved for the exclusive accommodation of the Chief Authority and is not to be otherwise appropriated except for defences.

7. Beyond these limits, the opposite point of the river, including the whole of the lately cleared high ground, and a space of 200 yards from the old lines, should also be reserved entirely for public purposes and no private building whatever for the present allowed within the same. In the native towns, as they have been and will be marked out, proper measures should be taken for securing to each individual the indisputive possession of the spot he may be permitted to occupy, which should be regularly registered in your office, certificates of which may be granted.

8. The European town should be marked without loss of time; this should extend along the beach from the distance of 200 yards from the lines as far eastward as practicable, including as much of the ground already cleared by the Bugguese as can possibly be required in that direction, re-imbursing the parties the expense they have been at in clearing and appropriating to them other ground in lieu. For the present the space lying between the new road and the beach is to be reserved by government, but on the opposite side of the road, the ground may be immediately marked out into twelve separate allotments of equal front, to be appropriated to the first respectable European applicants. To these persons a certificate of registry and permission to clear and occupy may be granted, according to the following form:—" No.—This is to certify that A. B. has permission to clear a spot of ground situated   and of the following dimensions and to occupy the same according to such general regulations as are now or may hereafter be established for the Factory of Singapore."

9. Whenever these allotments may be appropriated, others of convenient dimensions may in like manner be marked out in line and streets or roads formed according to regular plan.

10. It would be advisable that a circular carriage road should be cut in each direction from the cantonments during the present dry season.

11. A bridge across the river so as to connect the cantonments with the intended Chinese and Malay towns on the opposite side of the river, should be constructed without delay and as soon as other more immediate works are complete a good bungalow for the residence of the chief authority may be constructed on the hill.

T. S. RAFFLES.

Singapore, 25th June, 1819.

On the 26th June the following Arrangement was made with the Sultan and Tumongong. It is in Malay only, the following is a translation :—

JOHORE   1819.

ARRANGEMENTS MADE FOR THE GOVERNMENT OF SINGAPORE, IN JUNE 1819.

No. 1.

Be it known to all men, that we, the Sultan Hussain Mahomed Shah, Ungko Tumungong Abdool Rahman, Governor Raffles, and Major William Farquhar, have hereby entered into the following arrangements and regulations for the better guidance of the people of this Settlement, pointing out where all the different castes are severally to reside, with their families, and captains, or heads of their campongs.

ARTICLE 1.

The boundaries of the lands under the control of the English are as follows : from Tanjong Malang on the west, to Tanjong Katang on the east, and on the land side, as far as the range of cannon shot, all round from the factory.   As many persons as reside within the aforesaid boundary, and not within the campongs of the Sultan and Tumungong, are all to be under the control of the Resident, and with respect to the gardens and plantations that now are, or may hereafter be made, they are to be at the disposal of the Tumungong, as heretofore ; but it is understood, that he will always acquaint the Resident of the same.

ARTICLE 2.

It is directed that all the Chinese move over to the other side of the river, forming a campong from the site of the large bridge down the river, towards the mouth, and all Malays, people belonging to the Tumungong and others, are also to remove to the other side of the river, forming their campong from the site of the large bridge up to the river towards the source.

ARTICLE 3.

All cases which may occur, requiring Council in this Settlement, they shall, in the first instance, be conferred and deliberated upon by the three aforesaid, and when they shall have been decided upon, they shall be made known to the inhabitants, either by beat of gong or by proclamation.

ARTICLE 4.

Every Monday morning, at 10 o'clock, the Sultan, the Tumungong, and the Resident shall meet at the Rooma Bechara ; but should either of the two former be incapable of attending, they may send a Deputy there.

ARTICLE 5.

Every Captain, or head of a caste, and all Panghulus of campongs and villages, shall attend at the Rooma Bechara, and make a report or statement of such occurrences as may have taken place in the Settlement ; and represent any grievance or complaint that they may have to bring before the Council for its consideration on each Monday.

ARTICLE 6.

If the Captains, or heads of castes, or the Panghulus of campongs, do not act justly towards their constituents, they are permitted to come and state their grievances themselves to the Resident at the Rooma Bechara, who is hereby authorized to examine and decide thereon.

ARTICLE 7.

No Duties or Customs can be exacted, or farms established in this Settlement without the consent of the Sultan, the Tumungong, and Major William Farquhar, and without the consent of these three nothing can be arranged.

In confirmation of the aforesaid Articles, we, the undersigned, have put our seals and signatures, at Singapore, the 2nd day of the month of Ramzan 1234, answering to 26th June, 1819.

Seal of the SULTAN.   [L. S.] (Signed) T. S. RAFFLES.
Seal of the TUMUNGONG.   [L. S.] (Signed) W. FARQUHAR.

The Arrangement speaks of a large bridge, which must mean the place where Elgin Bridge is now, and the Chinese campong evidently became the present Boat Quay as it occupies the position pointed out. These plans could only be carried out in course of time, as the site of Boat Quay was a swamp which had to be filled up with the earth taken from the hill where the Square is now.

In August an invoice of civil stores, amounting to $42,963, was sent from Bencoolen. Many of the articles were stated to stand in the books at rates far beyond their value, and the Resident was instructed if possible to sell them for prime cost and charges, if not they were to be reduced to the level of prices at Penang and Batavia.

Mr. Dunn, a gardener, arrived with letters of recommendation from Raffles, and with a supply of spice plants, which were planted out on the Government Hill; near where the S. P. G. Mission House now stands, a few remained till late years. In this year 125 trees were planted. In 1848 the number of nutmeg trees planted in the island was over 7,000, and about that time nutmeg plantations became a sort of mania in Singapore, even private gardens close to European dwelling houses being given up to make room for more trees. The cause of the death of the trees was never accurately known, but the bad result and the heavy pecuniary loss is well described in Mr. Cameron's book at page 168.

A letter from the Supreme Government, dated 15th October, contains the following directions regarding the Government Establishments:—The Resident's salary to remain as fixed, but his successor to be Commandant, with Staff pay for civil duties. The Assistant to the Resident to be discontinued. Store-keeper and Master Attendant to be united on $150 salary. The Resident to take charge of Pay Office. Mr. Read, of the Bencoolen Service, may stay till required at Bencoolen. Resident's Establishments pay to be $130; Master Attendant's $110.

A subsequent letter, dated 11th January, 1820, directed the Resident to take the Police and Magistrate's duties; and remarked that Singapore was to be considered rather as a military post than as a fixed settlement, that artificial encouragement was not to be given to the immigration of natives, that if many people settled a magistracy might be formed if necessary, and moderate import dues fixed, taking care to prevent shackles to trade. Commerce, which formed the chief object of eastern settlements, not to be lost sight of in local revenue; but if a revenue could be had then it ought to be levied. The Resident proposed on 2nd November to appoint an Officer to act as Registrar of the Court of Justice; and also proposed to put restrictions on the sale of opium and spirits and on the practice of gaming, to sell the exclusive rights and to apply the proceeds one-third to the Sultan, one-third to the Tumongong, one-third to Government, the latter one-third to pay Police, allowances to the Captains of Tribes, &c.

A Bugis prince was summarily put to death by the Dutch at Rhio for alleged treason. His brother Balana rebelled and when finally driven out of Rhio took refuge in Singapore with 500 of his followers. The Malacca authorities demanded the person of the prince, but the demand was rejected by the Resident, and his refusal was afterwards approved by the Supreme Government.

The troops stationed in the Straits and Bencoolen in 1819 were the 2nd Battalion of the 20th Regiment of Bengal Native Infantry. Colonel T. Shuldham was Commandant at Penang, Major R. Hampton at Bencoolen, and Captain J. Seppings commanding the detachment at Singapore with Second Lieutenants W. Bonham and H. D. Coxe, and Dr. Montgomerie, so well known in Singapore for many years afterwards, as Assistant Surgeon.

The Governor-General of Java complained to the Governor-General of India that the Tumongong, with the sanction of the Singapore authorities, had sent a letter to the Sultan of Sambas exciting him against the Dutch. The Resident (Colonel Farquhar) denied the charge. The Governor-General in Calcutta wrote that he was anxious to prevent any fresh misunderstanding, as commissioners were engaged at home looking into the differences between the Dutch and English in the Eastern Seas.

At the beginning of October, Raffles was writing letters at Bencoolen. He heard there of the death of Colonel Bannerman, the Governor of Penang, on 8th August, and he went again to Calcutta to urge his views about Singapore and the general administration of the eastern islands. There was only one ship likely to touch at Bencoolen for some months, which was the vessel that brought the news of Colonel Bannerman's death, and as she had only one cabin, of which he could only have part, he was obliged to leave Lady Raffles behind. On the way, at sea, in the Bay of Bengal on the 9th November he wrote: "You will be happy to hear that the occupation of Singapore has been a death-blow to all the Dutch plans, and I trust that our political and commercial interests will be adequately secured." In Calcutta in January, 1820, he wrote: "Singapore continues to rise most rapidly in importance. It is already one of the first ports in the East. I could write volumes in its favor, but it may suffice to say that it has in every respect answered beyond my most sanguine expectations."

The following paper was written in 1819 by the eminent Hydrographer James Horsburgh, F.R.S., after whom the lighthouse on Pedra Branca is named. It is worth preserving as the opinion, even at that early period, of the estimation in which Singapore was held in England by those who were able to judge of its value from personal knowledge. Horsburgh was at this time (as appears from the old Penang Directory) in England as Hydrographer to the Court of Directors:—

"The settlement of Singapore, lately established by Sir Stamford Raffles being, in my opinion, of the utmost importance both in a political and commercial point of view to the British empire, particularly in the event of a war with France, Holland, or America, the Dutch Government will no doubt strongly remonstrate against that measure, and endeavour to make us relinquish it; but I think every possible argument, founded on truth and experience, should be brought forward in order to secure to us that valuable settlement.

"The Bugguese prows from Celebes and other parts of the Eastern Islands, will resort to the settlement of Singapore with their goods, and barter them for our manufactures, in preference to going to Malacca or Batavia, and it will soon become a depôt for the Eastern traders.

"The Straits of Sunda and Malacca are the two gates or barriers leading into the China Sea for all the commerce of British India, Europe, and the Eastern coasts of North and South America, which gates the Dutch fully command, if we do not retain the settlement of Singapore; for our settlement of Prince of Wales' Island being situated far to the northward and on the coast of an open sea, it affords no protection to our China trade, nor to ships passing through Malacca Straits, whereas the possession of Malacca and Rhio by the Dutch, also of Java and Banca, gives them the complete command of the Straits of Sunda, Banca and Malacca.

"If we retain the settlement of Singapore, great security will be afforded to our China trade in the event of war; for by possessing a naval station at the entrance of the China Sea, no enemy's cruisers will ever dare to wait off Pulo Oar to intercept our ships from China, which Admiral Linois did with the Marengo line-of-battle ship and two frigates, when he attacked the valuable fleet under the command of Captain Dance: and it was fortunate for the Company and the commerce of British India, that Linois had not a larger force.

"I trust you will excuse the liberty I have taken in addressing you on this subject; but considering it of great importance, I thought it right to do so in case you deem it proper to communicate it to Mr. Canning, or any others of those concerned."

J. HORSBURGH.

CHAPTER VI.

1820—1821.

1820.

SIR STAMFORD was strongly opposed to Singapore being placed under the orders of the Penang Government, and the Government at Calcutta in making arrangements at this time for the establishment of Singapore as a British settlement, and for the proceedings of the Resident, determined that the administration of affairs should be distinct from that of Penang, on account of the great difference between the previous governments and the commercial policy of the two islands.

Abdulla tells us:—" Every morning Mr. Farquhar was accustomed to walk about to examine the country, but it was covered with large jungle, except the centre of the plain where there were only kurmunting and sikadudu bushes, with some kalat trees, and the sea beach was covered with ambong and malpari and bulangan trees, and branches of them were strewed about. On the other side of the river nothing was seen but mangrove trees and jeraja. There was not a spot of good land, except a place ten fathoms wide, the rest was a mud flat except the hills. There was a large hill at the end of the mouth of the Singapore river."

This year found people of all nations coming to Singapore, Chinese, Arabs, and a few Europeans. Among the earliest of the Arabs was Syed Omar Bin Ally Al Junied who came from Palembang; he had been trading at Penang, and settled at Singapore with his uncle as a partner, named Syed Mahomed Bin Haroun Al Junied. Syed Omar was the innocent means of the attack upon Major Farquhar by a man who ran amok in 1823, of which the story is told among the events of that year. It was during 1820, or more probably in 1819, that Mr. Alexander Laurie Johnston came to Singapore. When he left Singapore in 1841, he said, in reply to an address that was presented to him, that he had been longer in Singapore than any one he left behind him, and that he had witnessed its rise from little better than an uninhabited jungle. He was a native of Dumfrieshire in Scotland, and belonged to a highly respectable family of that country. He first went out to India in the Merchant Navy of the East India Company, and when he had risen to the rank of Chief Mate, he left the service and took the command of a vessel of which he was owner. He enjoyed the especial friendship, and was much in the confidence, of Sir Stamford Raffles, who placed his name, as we shall see, at the head of the first list of Magistrates who were appointed to administer the laws of the infant Settlement. The letters and notes addressed by Sir Stamford to Mr. Johnston bear ample testimony to the frequency and benefit with which his advice and assistance were sought in all matters affecting the interests of the Settlement. In almost every public transaction, Mr. Johnston was at the head. He was one of the first Trustees of the Raffles Institution, he was the first Chairman of the

ALEXANDER LAURIE JOHNSTON.

To face page 62.

Chamber of Commerce, and the precedence which was always accorded to him on all public occasions showed the respect and esteem with which he was regarded and the kindliness of his manners and disposition. The natives and Chinese readily sought his advice, and in cases of dispute his decision was as much respected as a judgment of the Court, so highly was he appreciated by them. It was said that no Court was required in his day, as no one thought of going to law while there was Mr. Johnston to determine the matter, and all disputes of importance were laid before him as a matter of course. He was liberal and hospitable in the extreme, and in the earliest cash book that seems to have been opened when he commenced business here, the first entry to his personal debit is as follows:—"A. L. Johnston,— Paid subscription for release of a female European slave, $10." He established the house of A. L. Johnston & Co., the pioneer European mercantile firm in the place. He died in Scotland in 1850, and was spoken of by the *Free Press* at that time as one of the most sterling of the "worthies" of Singapore. Johnston's Pier was named after him.

One of the objections raised by the dissatisfied authorities in Calcutta against the settlement at Singapore was that the harbour was not defensible, and it is fortunate for the place that even up to the present time, the dispute has never been, in any way, elucidated by forcible example. Major Farquhar, now promoted to Lieutenant-Colonel, answered by a denial of the assertion, and said that New Harbour was capable of containing the largest ships, while smaller vessels could take refuge in the Singapore river and behind Sandy Point, which were all easily defensible. It is evident from this that the Resident in no way contemplated the crowd of vessels which (until the much later days of steamers at the wharves) filled the open anchorage. The Penang merchants objected to the position of Singapore, and recommended the Carimons, and Colonel Farquhar was sent again to visit them. Their argument was that, while Singapore only commanded one entrance to the Straits of Malacca, the Carimons commanded four, namely, Sabon, Dryon, the Old Straits round by Johore, and the New Straits round by St. John's Island.

In March the Resident proposed establishing Opium and Spirit farms, but Raffles wrote from Bencoolen to say that he considered it highly objectionable (although there were such farms at Penang and Malacca) and inapplicable to the principles on which the establishment at Singapore was founded. The farms were however sold, and $395 was received monthly for four opium shops, $160 for arrack shops, and $95 for gaming tables. The money was spent in paying the Superintendent of Police and Assistant Resident $200; twelve constables, a sergeant and a tailor $100; and $325 was paid to the Sultan and Tumongong for assisting in Police duties. Colonel Farquhar sent in his resignation during this year, and Captain Travers, who was Superintendent of Convicts at Bencoolen, was appointed Resident in his place, but Colonel Farquhar withdrew his resignation in time and continued in charge.

Complaints had been made about undue restrictions on trade. The Resident called a committee to enquire into it, and they reported on 13th April that there were no grounds for complaint, as the former

practice of the Nakodahs of native vessels making presents to the
Sultan and Tumongong had been discontinued. But a proclamation
in November 1822 showed that the practice was not altogether stopped.
This was the first of the contests by the mercantile community to
maintain entire free trade.

On the 24th April, Captain Flint, Sir Stamford's brother-in-law,
arrived and took charge of the Master Attendant's Office. He had
married in Malacca in 1811, one of the three sisters of Sir Stamford.
She was the widow of Mr. Thompson, an official in Penang, whom she
had married there. His salary was $250, and $181 allowed for the
establishment. Port charges on vessels were collected from the 1st
May from $5 on brigs to $10 on vessels over 400 tons. The gaming
tables were placed under the special supervision of the "Captain
China" and a tax levied on them. The proceeds of the gaming tax
were to be applied to keeping the streets clean. Two of the opium
shops were in Kampong Glam where a sufficiently large native town
had already sprung up by the 1st of May to call for their introduction. The farm revenues were kept as a separate fund and applied
to local purposes until May 1823, when they were ordered to be paid
into the Treasury.

The Bengal Government was always dissatisfied about the expenditure, and on the 20th October the Secretary wrote quarrelling
about the expense of a shroff and two coolies in the store department, and in the next month wrote deprecating expenses on any
public works "under the present circumstances of the Settlement."
In September a petition from the Sultan, Tumongong and representatives of all the tribes in Singapore was presented, stating that there
were reports that the place was to be given up, and earnestly begging
the Government not to abandon it to the Dutch "from whom God defend us." They attributed much evil to the Rajah Muda of Rhio.
They asked Captain Holt M'Kenzie, the Secretary to Government at
Bencoolen, then on his way to Bengal, to take charge of their petition
and present it to the Governor-General.

On the 12th August in this year Raffles issued a proclamation at Fort
Marlborough, as Bencoolen was officially . called, giving notice that the
custom duties there, with the exception of that on opium, were abolished from that date. And regulations about pilotage and boat-hire were
officially made; the latter on pepper was fixed at 16 cwt. to the ton, as
it remains here to this day. Demurrage was allowed at the rate of
double boat-hire if the boat was not discharged the first day. Mr.
Thomas Church, afterwards Resident Councillor of Singapore, was
Assistant Judge and Magistrate at this time in Bencoolen, where there
was a large staff of officials, about thirty-six Europeans in all, including a Chaplain, a School-master and a Printer, and three European
Residents in the interior. In the Memoirs will be found a long and
very interesting account of a remarkable expedition Mr. Church made
with Sir Stamford Raffles into the interior of Sumatra from Bencoolen.
Mr. Presgrave was an official in Bencoolen then and also went on
such expeditions.

While Singapore was a free port and attracting the trade of all
the surrounding places, a revised scale of duties on goods imported in

Penang by private merchants was published there, calculated on the price which they realised when sold at the Company's sales, and on the estimated value when sold by private bargain. The rates varied on different goods, that on piece-goods being two per cent. The business at the Penang Post Office must have been very small in those days, as an alphabetical register was kept of all letters that passed through the office, and a stamped receipt was given for each letter posted. This practice was carried on in Singapore for many years.

In a private letter Colonel Farquhar wrote to Sir Stamford on 21st March, he said: "Merchants of all descriptions are collecting here so fast that nothing is heard in the shape of complaint but the want of more ground to build upon. The swampy ground on the opposite side of the river is now almost covered with Chinese houses, and the Bugis village is becoming an extensive town."

The story of the mysterious disappearance of treasure from the Bencoolen chest, told first in Mr. J. T. Thomson's book at page 152 and afterwards in Mr. Cameron's book at page 13, and the bad character given to white ants in consequence, is so well known, that it may be interesting to some persons to learn that in the London *Globe* of October 22nd, 1828, also in 3 Carrington and Payne's Reports, page 358, is the report of a trial before Lord Tenterden, in the Court of King's Bench, Guildhall, between the East India Company and Mr. E. J. Lewis, the Sub-Treasurer at Bencoolen from 1814 to 1818, to recover the amount of a deficiency in the treasure under his charge. Mr. Brougham and several very eminent lawyers were engaged in the case. The plaintiffs were non-suited on the ground that the defendant was a covenanted servant of the Company, which in the form in which the action was brought, lost them their case, a result which in these days would not prevail. This shows that the old story of the Company having sent some files to be used against the teeth of the white ants, and being satisfied with that explanation, is not likely to be true. The discovery was made, when there should have been about $150,000 in the chest, on a surprise survey being held by Captain T. O. Travers, the Superintendent of Convicts at Bencoolen, soon after Raffles' arrival there in 1818. Mr. Lewis died in Paris about 1874.

It was in the year 1820 that Mr. Alexander Guthrie came to Singapore. He had been at the Cape of Good Hope. He started in business in his own name, and on the 1st February, 1823, issued a circular stating that he had joined Captain T. T. Harrington under the name of Harrington & Guthrie. Captain Harrington used to sail to neighbouring places, and from the old letter book of Mr. Guthrie, in which the letters were copied in his own writing (as were the letters of A. L. Johnston & Co., by Mr. C. R. Read) it appears that Harrington had some property in Malacca, and that his family were residing there. Letters used to be sent in triplicate in those days, all copied by hand; and an answer from Europe received in eighteen months was the usual course of business. Captain Harrington went to Malacca in November, 1823, and on the 8th of that month Harrington & Guthrie sent round a circular stating that the firm was dissolved, and that the business would be carried on by Mr. Guthrie in his own name.   On the 7th March, 1824, Mr. Harrington who is said to have always afforded plenty of amusement with his jokes and hearty laugh, went on board the *Fassel Kerrim* at 9 p.m. after a farewell dinner at Mr. Johnston's, and the vessel sailed in the morning. He was on his way to England.   In February, 1824, a fresh notice was issued that Mr. Clark had joined Mr. Guthrie, and it became Guthrie & Clark. It was Mr. Clark who built the present house at the Esplanade at the corner next to High Street, now part of the Hotel de l'Europe, where he lived for some time.   In January 1833, Mr. Clark left the firm, and Mr. Guthrie alone continued business as Guthrie & Co., which it is to this day.   Mr. James Scott Clark continuing business in his own name by himself.

Mr. Guthrie left Singapore on the 8th February, 1847, after having resided here for twenty-seven years.   He was spoken of by the *Free Press* when he left, as one of the earliest of the European merchants who settled in Singapore, and as distinguished for sound judgment and sterling integrity, and as having always occupied a high standing in the estimation of the community, whether as a member of society, a merchant, or a magistrate.   He died. in London in the year 1865.

Mr. James Guthrie, a nephew of Alexander Guthrie, arrived in Singapore in 1829, became a partner in Guthrie & Co., in January, 1837, and afterwards was head of the firm, from which he retired in 1876.   He died at Tunbridge Wells on 4th September, 1900, in his eighty-seventh year.   He came to Singapore when he was fifteen years old, having been born on 14th February, 1814.   He was twice married, and was survived by Mrs. Guthrie and two daughters.   His only son, who was for a short time in the business in Singapore, died while a young man, over twenty years ago.   Mr. James Guthrie was buried at Kensal Green Cemetery, London, where a number of old Singaporeans attended the funeral.

As a contrast to the quiet state of affairs in Singapore, and the contentment of the natives who were increasing so quickly in number, may be mentioned a report made by Captain Campbell of H.M.S. *Dauntless*, which had come from Ceylon to Penang in December, 1819, and had afterwards passed through Singapore on her way to Manila. The Captain reported on 3rd December, 1820, that a massacre had occurred in Manila, in which the natives had slaughtered all the English, French, Danes, and Americans whom they could find, and he lamented to say that twenty-six Europeans, a large proportion of whom were British, had fallen victims.

The following are interesting passages taken from the private letters of Sir Stamford written to friends in England in 1820:—"It will be satisfactory to Your Grace to know that the Dutch authorities in this country have at length been brought to their senses; and if what has been done here is supported and followed up with common prudence and decision we may at least save our commercial interests from the ruin which so lately impended.   Singapore continues to rise as rapidly as the out-stations of the Dutch decline.

"After all, it is not impossible the ministry may be weak enough to abandon Singapore, and to sacrifice me, honour, and the Eastern Archipelago to the outrageous pretentions of the Dutch.   My settlement continues to thrive most wonderfully; it is all and everything I could wish. If no untimely fate awaits it, it promises to become the emporium and pride of the East.

"Were the value of Singapore properly appreciated, I am confident that all England would be in its favour. It positively takes nothing from the Dutch, and is to us everything. It gives us the command of China and Japan, with Siam and Cambodia, to say nothing of the Islands themselves.

"We are very anxiously awaiting the decision of the higher powers on the numerous questions referred to them. It appears to me impossible that Singapore should be given up, and yet the indecisive manner in which the ministers express themselves, and the unjust and harsh terms they use towards me, render it doubtful what course they will adopt.

"Notwithstanding the uncertainty which must prevail pending the decision of the higher powers in Europe, and the circumstances of its being still held solely on my personal responsibility, against all the efforts of our own government as well as that of the Dutch, the settlement has advanced in the most rapid manner. From an insignificant fishing village, the port is now surrounded by an extensive town, and the population does not fall short of ten or twelve thousand souls, principally Chinese. The number is daily increasing, and the trade of the place has already induced the establishment of several mercantile houses of respectability. Should the decision from home prove favourable, I hope to go there next year to establish such municipal and port regulations as may provide for the increasing population and trade.

"My health I am sorry to say is not so good as it was. I feel the effects of climate very seriously and if I had no other inducement I should hasten home. In a public point of view, all I wish is to remain long enough to see my settlement at Singapore firmly established, and lay something like a substantial foundation for the future civilization of Sumatra. Two or three years will be sufficient for this, and then I shall have an object at home in endeavouring to uphold and further what will have been so far proceeded on. My great object, the independence of the Eastern Isles, has been attained."

1821.

The public works which had been erected at a cost of about $36,000, were valued at $30,000. This amount must have included one or two houses, and the erection of the batteries and huts for the troops. The lines for the troops were at the foot of the hill, between it and the Esplanade, where the Cathedral, Coleman Street, and other buildings are now.

In February the first junk arrived from Amoy, and the Merchants and the Resident fell out. The Sultan's Malays had put the nakodah of the junk in the stocks because he had refused to wait upon the Sultan with presents, which was practically a breach of the free trade of the port, and the merchants remonstrated. The Resident wrote to Sir Stamford Raffles at Bencoolen that it was an improper, premature, and very unnecessary interference on the part of the merchants, to which remark they objected. The Sultan's explanation was that the nakodah had been impudent.

On the 20th March, a general meeting was held with Mr. Johnston in the chair, about the police force, and it was decided that subscriptions should be made to provide funds for increasing the strength of the Police establishment, and that a committee of three Europeans and three native merchants should be formed to take into consideration all points connected with the Police, and that a general meeting of the subscribers should take place quarterly. At the request of the Resident on the 13th September, Mr. Johnston, Mr. Alexander Guthrie, Mr. Charles Scott and Mr. Claude Queiros, met on the same subject, and the proceedings of the previous meeting were confirmed, and it was decided to request the Resident to suggest to the inhabitants of Kampong Glam and China Town the propriety of entering into the subscription to extend the police system to those Kampongs. At that time Mr. F. J. Bernard was in charge of the Police, with a Malay writer, a jailor, a jemadar or sergeant, and eight peadas or constables. These were all paid by Government ; and one jemadar and nine peadas were paid by a mercantile subscription, called the Night Watch Fund, which amounted in the average to $54 a month. Up to this time robberies had not been numerous, only two having occurred of any consequence.

On the 17th April the Resident made a report upon the town and public works. He said that at first the place was covered with jungle, with the exception of a small spot on the eastern bank of the river [Esplanade side] barely large enough to pitch the tents on. Sepoys were employed to clear a space for cantonments, and a battery was raised by them. Ground had been cleared for the Chinese and Bugis Kampongs, and materials had been prepared for a bridge, but its erection as well as the powder magazine and other permanent buildings had been postponed. Reservoirs had been made for the supply of water to the ships and town, and Colonel Farquhar said that greater facilities existed in this respect than in any town in India. He proposed to levy a tax for the supply of water. He said that the river bank on the north side [Esplanade] was the only place eligible for English merchants, the other side being marshy and unfit for building. He proposed to set aside a place for the merchants between the Tumongong's kampong and the sea [where the Public Offices are now] and, as the space was limited, to remove the Tumongong higher up the river [to Kampong Malacca now]. Except these lots and one on the sea side of the road, used for the Police Office [near the end of the river on Esplanade side] no grants were made on the Singapore [Esplanade] side, and the squatters were informed they remained at their own risk. The Bugis had requested that the Rochor River should be cleared out ; which was done to the great advantage of the kampong on its banks. In May, 1821, about fifteen miles of road had been made, of which about half were carriage roads, forty to fifty feet in width. They extended from the river to Rochor ; round the hill, afterwards levelled, where Circular Road is now ; and out to Selegie, which is no doubt what is now called Selegie Road. The cost of the

roads was $6,447; of aqueducts $2,500; and $4,980 had been spent on
military buildings, $270 on a jail, $3,000 on fortifications, $600 on
bridges and $80 on the spice garden bungalow. The following is a
list of the roads that were made from the first establishment to May,
1821. The details as to the length are not without interest as they
show how far they went from the Esplanade. A good deal had been
done in the two years.

Yards.	Yards in width.	Remarks.
2,500 in Cantonment	16	Carriage road.
1,800 to Rochor and Campong Glam	16	Do.
2,650 Do. do.	15	Do.
600 Do. do.	10	Lined out.
1,800 round Singapore Hill ...	8	Nearly cut round.
1,200 over top of Singapore Hill	7	Small drains cut.
1,176 round Old Lines	2¼	Horse road.
800 to Selligie	12	Carriage road.
1,380 round Selligie	3½	Horse road.
1,675 from Selligie to farthest gambier (sic.)	3	Horse road.
3,100 Circular Road round west hills	4	Do.
1,440 along Rochor River ...	3	Do.
3,374 Roads and Streets in China Town	15	Carriage road.
2,396 over Teluk Ayer hills ...	2¼	Foot path.
156 Katong point at Paggar do.	2	Do.
100 Teluk Ayer to Sungei Kayah	2	Do.
140 Singapore and Selegie Hill	4	Horse path.

26,475 yards of road at a cost of $6,447.

In May, between the 7th and 9th, the Government Treasury was
robbed of $1,650, which was attributed to the guard being implicated
in it. The Madras Government wrote to enquire whether some convicts could not be advantageously introduced at Singapore, as they
escaped so frequently from Penang; and Colonel Farquhar replied that
a few could be received. A Singapore price current of 1st October,
1821, contains the following quotations: Banca tin $19. Beer $8 a
dozen. Canvas $10 a bolt. Cocoanut oil $8 a picul. Benares Opium
$1,625 a chest. Pepper $9.50. Rattans $1.50 Hats $8 each. Sago
$28 a koyan. Tobacco, Bengal Cigars $2.50 a thousand. Exchange
on Calcutta Rs. 206; on Madras and Bombay 220, on China and
Batavia at par, all at 30 days. No quotations on Europe, for no bills
of exchange existed. Goods from Europe and India were sold and the
nett proceeds remitted by shipments of produce, or specie.

The effect of the trade of Singapore upon that of Malacca and
Rhio was already very marked. The export and import duties and
harbour fees in Malacca, in 1819, were $50,000; in 1821 they were
only $23,000, and two years later only $7,000, while Singapore was

growing rapidly. Although it was established in 1819, and its trade during the first four years was considerable, it was found impossible in 1834 to make up any returns of imports and exports from an earlier period than May, 1823, owing to the records not having been kept.

A Court of Enquiry was held in May at the instance of the merchants on Captain C. Methven, 20th Bengal Native Infantry, for improper dealings with Tringanu traders, and after repeated attempts to get justice at the Civil Court had failed. He had been in the Bencoolen Detachment in 1819. In July the List of occupiers of lands was as follows:—

Claude Queiros, J. Morgan, A. Guthrie, G. Mackenzie, Williamson, Lackersteen, Hay Mackenzie, F. Ferrao, J. Almeida, Baron Jamearil, F. J. Bernard, Dunn, Captain Flint, Lieutenant Crossley, Captain Methven, Lieutenant Davis, Colonel Farquhar.

There were frequent reports of robberies, and the Chinese at Kampong Glam agitated the question as to the propriety of getting up a night watch similar to that supported by the Europeans. In the government report of 10th July, credit is taken for the fact that from July 1820 to July, 1821 only 47 cases of robbery and larceny were brought to the police, with two cases for attempting to steal slaves.

Circular orders were received to assist the Crown Commission in England to enquire into the subject of weights and measures, by sending home models of all in use, with explanations and information. Besides Singapore, the Resident was to take the Indian Archipelago and the East Coast of Sumatra. The result of these enquiries was published in "Kelly's Universal Cambist."

Measures were taken to prevent competition of foreign or other opium with that of Bengal. The Bencoolen opium regulations of 9th September, 1817, were extended to Singapore. Sir Stamford Raffles was anxious to prevent the regulation from interfering with the trade in opium.

CHAPTER VII.

1822.

THIS is the first year for which it seems possible to obtain the number of vessels coming into Singapore harbour, which was 139 square rigged vessels and 1,434 native crafts. This unparalleled rise of commerce was due to the principle of free trade, which was first tried at Singapore. The port was open to the vessels of all nations alike, as it has been ever since; in spite, as we shall see in later years, of not infrequent attempts to levy duties, which the mercantile community have from time to time opposed tooth and nail, by the most earnest and consistent means. The proposed evil was first mentioned soon after the Settlement commenced to attract attention, and we shall see from time to time how petitions were sent by the merchants in any direction likely to use influence to prevent it; urging in the strongest terms the ruin that it would bring upon a port, which was then, and always will be, practically, a mere warehouse for supplying the surrounding countries, which would not seek to purchase here if the goods could reach them direct or from other sources without the enhanced price caused by the duty which would benefit Singapore alone. The following report of a speech in the House of Lords on the 14th March, 1826, shows how soon attention was prominently attracted to the new Settlement, even in England :—

"The Marquis of Lansdowne said, that he had yesterday given notice of his intention to move for an account of the imports and exports of Singapore in the East Indies. He had been induced to make this motion in consequence of understanding that the East India Company had entertained a design of imposing duties upon that port, the effect of which would be to stifle the trade of that country, which, if these papers were produced, would appear from them to be flourishing with a degree of increasing prosperity since its cession to this country, that was likely in a short time to render it an acquisition of the greatest importance. All the advantages anticipated from our possession of that country had been fully realized by every circumstance which had since taken place; and he was certain that they would continue to increase rapidly if Singapore were retained as a free port. Should their lordships agree to the production of these papers, they would see from them, that in that part of the world, composed as it was of various and numerous tribes and nations, some of them barbarous, some civilized, such was the quick apprehension which prevailed of the advantages of a free trade there, and the permission granted them of frequenting that place, that its trade, which in 1822 had amounted to 8,468,000 dollars, in 1824 had increased to the enormous sum of 15,773,000 dollars; thus in three years doubling its amount, which had considerably increased before, since the occasion to which he had referred. It was impossible to consider this extensive trade, drawn from so many different quarters, without feeling that it must have operated a most material effect upon our great empire in the east, as well as upon that of China by producing a commercial spirit in that quarter of the world of which this country ought to avail itself, and turn to its advantage. But if the East India Company were to seek to derive a pitiful revenue from that island, it would have the effect, by cramping and reducing its trade, of at once closing those prospects upon us, which, connected as we were with that part of the world, its present state held forth to our view. In the course of two years and a half 2,889 vessels had entered that port, only 333 of which were manned by Englishmen, the remaining 2,506 being manned by natives of other nations. Such was the flourishing state of its commerce, carried on by various nations of different habits and manners, who, attracted by the establishment of a mild code of laws, contrived to live there most happily together, and avail themselves under the protection of this country, of the advantages of a free course of trade. He trusted they would be suffered to continue to do so, in despite of the short-sighted policy which would sacrifice such important advantages to the paltry lucre to be derived from the imposition of duties, which would only have the effect of annihilating its trade in a short time; under these circumstances he begged leave to move for the production of an account of the imports and exports of Singapore in the years 1822, 1823 and 1824, together with the amount of the tonnage and its value in each of these years, distinguishing the different countries to which it belonged —Ordered."

The last time the often vexed question arose between the Government and the mercantile community was in the days of Governor Ord, the first Governor after the Transfer to the Colonial Office in 1867, who was probably ignorant of the firebrand he took in his hand when he spoke of imposing customs duties here. He very soon abandoned the mere mention of it.

In November, 1822, in consequence of complaints having been made to Sir Stamford Raffles at Bencoolen that a Malay in Singapore named Wan Allee had assumed to establish a monopoly of selling attaps for roofing houses, Sir Stamford issued a proclamation giving notice that, with the exception of the regulations for restricting the consumption of opium and spirits, and the vice of gambling; and respecting the markets, and the sale of pork among the Chinese; which were all adopted as matters of policy for the general benefit of the whole community; the trade in all articles whatever was in every respect *open and free to all persons without imposition of any kind.* And in order that no one should plead ignorance of the entire free trade of the port, he had the proclamation translated into the native languages and explained and published by beat of gong, and placards affixed throughout the town.

In this year Colonel Farquhar proposed to establish a Court of Requests, which he thought the advancing state of the trade rendered necessary. He also referred the question whether the European merchants could be allowed, with propriety, to correspond with the Native States. Sir Stamford, in reply, said he was surprised at what he termed an extraordinary enquiry, and that he saw no reason why the Singapore merchants should not do what every European vessel navigating the seas had the privilege to do. The next time such a question was raised was in the time of Sir Harry Ord, the first Governor appointed by the Colonial Office in 1867, when he said that if the merchants of Singapore chose to do business in the Native States they did it at their own risk and could expect no support from the government. Fortunately more able and thoughtful men succeeded him, and the result was the commencement of the opening up of the Native States in 1875, one result alone of which has been that the value of exported tin from Singapore in 1898 was over two millions sterling.

Sir Stamford arrived at Singapore from Bencoolen on 10th October. On the 17th October a committee was formed, of three disinterested persons; Dr. Wallich, of the Gardens, Dr. Lumsdaine and Captain Salmond, the harbour-master of Bencoolen; to fix on the new site for the town, rendered necessary by the original plan [to keep the Esplanade side for government purposes] having been broken through.

In October fifty slaves were imported and sold by the Bugis in the river close to the Resident's house and some were sent as presents to Raffles and the Resident. Raffles called the notice of the Resident to the Act of Parliament which made it felony for any British subject to be concerned in slave dealing. The Resident replied that he allowed the practice, under the oft repeated plea of "the circumstances of the Port, &c." This was one of the reasons which Raffles afterwards gave of his want of confidence in Colonel Farquhar.

On 29th October an Advertisement was published, ordering all builders to discontinue work pending the orders of the town committee. In November a petition was presented by the Chulias praying that a headman or Captain should be appointed for the mercantile and labouring classes. The lower classes of Chulias were prohibited from living in verandahs of houses or anywhere on the northern side of the town and a Chulia campong was marked out for them. [This was probably where Cross Street is now.]

The Chuliahs were afterwards called Klings in Singapore. In Crawfurd's Dictionary, page 198, he says it was the name given by the Malays and Javanese to the Telinga nation of Southern India, and appeared to be a corruption or abbreviation of the genuine name of the country of that people, Kalinga. Being the only Indian nation known to the Malays, the word was used by them both for the people of India in general and for the country itself. The trade of the Telingas with the Archipelago was, he says, of great antiquity.

The day after Raffles returned, he wrote a letter in which the following passage occurs about the action of the Dutch: "You must be aware that the grounds on which I maintain our right to Singapore rested on the following facts, which it has never been in the Dutch power to disprove.

1. That subsequent to the death of Sultan Mahomed, about twelve years ago, there has been no regular installation of a successor, nor has any chief been acknowledged as such, with the essential forms required by the Malay custom.

2. That the regalia (the possession of which is considered essential to sovereignty) still remained in the custody of Tunku Putri, widow of the deceased Sultan.

3. That the Rajah of Lingin had never exercised the authority of Sultan of Johore, and explicitly disclaimed the title, and

4. That the prince whom we supported was the eldest son of the late Sultan and was intended for the succession. That he was acknowledged by one at least, if not both, the constituting authorities of the empire, and that he himself stood in no way committed to the Dutch, when I formed the treaty with him.

"The Dutch have allowed nearly four years to pass since our occupation of Singapore, in trying to prove that the Sultan of Lingin was actually invested with the authority of Johore: but finding our Ministry more firm than they expected, and their assertions not admitted as proofs, have at last given up the point and actually proceeded to the seizure of the regalia from the hands of Tunku Putri."

In November a Committee was formed of Captain Flint, the Harbour Master, Captain Salmond, and Mr. Maxwell, a merchant, with the Assistant Engineer, to enquire into the state of the bar at the mouth of the river, and to report on the means to be used to prevent an increase of the bar. To obviate which, steps were not taken until 1884; and the river wall extended seawards. On a site being fixed for the market by Colonel Farquhar, who after going round with some of the inhabitants had found a better place than that first proposed by the Committee, Che Sang, the principal Chinese merchant in the place at that time, agreed to build it at his own expense, if he was allowed to hold it free of tax for a certain number of years. This is the same Chinaman whose will occupied much of the time of the Court here for very many years, and only reached a final result after 1880, the Singapore "Jarndyce v. Jarndyce." Botanical gardens were now established, and a Dr. Wallich of the Botanical Gardens at Calcutta was appointed Superintendent. Raffles gave him forty-eight acres more land for the gardens, and a bungalow was built on the hill for his accommodation, as he said the matchless climate had restored him to health, and he would occupy it on his occasional visits to superintend the work. Raffles gave up the Government House Garden, and told Dr. Wallich to take as much more as he required to the northeast, which was the forty-eight acres for which a grant was given on 20th November, 1822, to the superintendent and his successors in office. The Gardens were, however, discontinued in 1829.

Sir Stamford found, on his return to Singapore, that several European merchants had built houses near the river on the Esplanade side in the space he had reserved for public purposes, so he gave notice that the Government did not insist upon the immediate removal of the buildings unless the ground became indispensable for public purposes, but the owners were warned not to spend any more money upon them. In order to prevent confusion and disputes in laying out the town and appropriating places for the different classes of natives, Sir Stamford in October appointed a Committee consisting of Captain Charles Edward Davis of the Bengal Native Infantry, Samuel George Bonham (afterwards Governor) who was a Civil Servant, and

Mr. A. L. Johnston, to act with a representative from each of the
principal classes of Arabs, Malays, Bugis, Javanese, and Chinese; and
he gave notice that while this Committee was sitting all persons were
required to stop building and to attend the Summons of the Committee and to give all the information and assistance they could.
He wrote a long minute on the subject of the laying out of the
town, which is published at the end of this Chapter.

Raffles' original plan in laying out the town had been to keep
the ground near the river where the public offices are now, as a
reserve for Government purposes, and to give the European merchants
the land next to it as far as the Rochor river, which would have
included the present Esplanade. After he left Singapore in 1819, and
before his return in October, 1822, the merchants told the Resident,
Colonel Farquhar, that it would be very inconvenient for the shipping
to build along the north beach [where the Esplanade is] as it was
flat and there was generally a surf. So Colonel Farquhar let them
build on the left bank of the river, where the public offices are,
but said they must be prepared to move if required. When Raffles
returned he found houses built, as we have said, on the reserved
ground, and after much consideration he resolved to alter his original
plan, and employed all the coolies he could get to level the small
hill on the south side, which made the site of Commercial Square.
The earth was used to fill up where Boat Quay is, which thus became
suitable for building. In October, the place where Circular Road
and Boat Quay are now was occupied solely by a few native traders
whose *roomah rackits*, as somebody called them, or rickety tenements,
or raft houses, were built over the swamp where the tide rose ten
feet and extended to some distance.

Those who had built houses by the Resident's permission on the
north bank were bought out, and had lots given them on the other
side of the river. Some of the houses on the north side were allowed
to remain and one was used for many years for the Land Office,
Import and Export Office, &c., and another as Post Office. The
Brass Bassa Canal, which is spoken of by Raffles as the fresh water
cut (by which he thought boat communication might be made with
the interior) was already made, and Colonel Farquhar finding that Sir
Stamford was giving away land very fast, protested, and desired Raffles
to make a reference to Bengal on his proposition to retain eight
hundred yards on the north beach. Sir Stamford did not forward the
reference, but reserved the ground from Singapore River to the
Brass Bassa Canal, and it should be added, (Mr. Braddell remarks)
that we are indebted, therefore, to Colonel Farquhar for the present
Esplanade.

In later years the Government wanted to place the Church on the
Esplanade, and appropriate the site where the first Church was built
and the Cathedral is now. On that occasion some of the residents explained
to the Bishop how very undesirable and one-sided a project it was,
and as he refused to consecrate the proposed ground, we have the
Esplanade to this day. In former years, on the Queen's birthday, a
review of all the Troops and Volunteers was always held on it. And
in the China war it was covered with tents for the troops. It is the

best place possible for our local Athletic Clubs, and for the New Year Sports, but we should not have it now, if it had not been for Colonel Farquhar and Bishop Wilson, and the mercantile community protesting against the proposed sale for building purposes, and a deputation telling the Governor, Mr. Fullerton, that if put up for sale it would be purchased by them and held for the public.

Mr. William Gordon Mackenzie, one of the merchants, received $2,175 as compensation for his house on the reserved land, and Mr. Queiros, the agent of Palmer & Co., of Calcutta, the largest mercantile house there in those days, received $3,000. The houses were pulled down and the materials sold. There was a long correspondence regarding one house belonging to Captain Methven who was absent, for whom Mr. Queiros was agent, and it led to a proclamation being issued directing that the house should be taken possession of by force if necessary, on which Mr. Queiros protested, and made a public address to the inhabitants.

Abdulla says : " Every day the quantity of goods for sale increased. It is impossible to describe the wonderful variety of the goods brought for sale by the Europeans, such as our fathers had never seen before. Auctions were held constantly where the goods were sold wonderfully cheap. At that time the auctioneer's gongs were not beaten, nor was notice sent round, the custom was simply to paste up notices at the several street corners that to-morrow morning at 10 o'clock an auction would be held at Mr. So and So's house, with a list of the articles for sale. The houses were all attap, except one built of brick by Mr. McSweeny who soon afterwards returned to England and it was then used for the police office. There was not a single house on the other side of the river. It was a mangrove swamp and all lived on the Plain side of the river. The Sultan wished to commence building his palace in Campong Glam, but the place was covered with jungle and there was no road through it, only round by the beach, as people were afraid to go through the jungle. The Sultan's family and all his followers now came over from Rhio. A Malacca man put up the first fishing stake off Teluk Ayer. There were continual disturbances between the Malacca Malays and the Chinese and Klings, and if they had not been afraid of Mr. Farquhar there would have been murders among them every day."

The population in this year had increased to 10,000 in November. It was in this year that Mr. Christopher Rideout Read, the partner of Mr. A. L. Johnston, came to Singapore. He had been to Bencoolen, and came here on the advice of Sir Stamford Raffles. Mr. John Purvis also came and established his firm here in this year. He had gone to China with Mr. Matheson, afterwards Sir James Matheson; and Mr. Purvis thought Singapore was a better opening than China and returned here, leaving Mr. Matheson who commenced business in Canton and joined Mr. Jardine.

Doctor Montgomerie, who is said to have first introduced Gutta Percha to the notice of Europeans, stated that he obtained the name of it, at Singapore, in 1822, while making enquiries relative to caoutchouc, but he lost sight of the subject, having returned to the Bengal Residency for a time. Some gutta was taken to England by Dr.

d'Almeida in 1842, but did not attract much attention, and it was brought into notice practically, at last, by Dr. Oxley and Dr. Little's discoveries about the year 1845.

The story of what was being done in Singapore town in 1822 was, no doubt, to be best found in the papers of Sir Stamford, which were burnt in the *Fame*, the only ones remaining being the letters written at this time from Singapore to his friends in England. He wrote in December that there were then 10,000 people, and that the enterprise and activity which prevailed were wonderful, and the effects of free trade and liberal principles had operated like magic. He speaks in the same letter of sending home the skeleton of an enormous ape, five feet six inches high, lately obtained from Borneo, the first specimen, probably, of an Orang Outan or Mias. In the last letter we have found that he wrote in this year, December, 1822, he said that a few spots of land before considered of no value, and passed over by Colonel Farquhar, had sold in the course of an hour for $50,000; and said that he had been cautious in wording the grants of land so as not to alarm the anti-colonists in England. The few spots of land he mentioned would of course be considered now very considerable quantities. He said that at Bencoolen the public expenses were more in one month than at Singapore in twelve; and while the capital turned at Bencoolen did not exceed $400,000 in a year, and nearly the whole of that was in the Company's bills on Bengal (the only returns that could be made), at Singapore the capital turned in a year exceeded eight millions, without any Government bills or Civil establishment whatever.

There were two missionaries in Singapore at this time, one was the Rev. Mr. Milton who knew Chinese and Siamese, and had brought a printer with him; so Mr. Milton took charge of the printing presses for Chinese type; the other missionary was the Rev. G. H. Thompson, who knew Malay and English printing. He was in connection with the London Missionary Society, and had a house near the corner of Brass Bassa Road and North Bridge Road, where the Society's chapel afterwards stood. He had a class of six boys, one of whom was named Monteiro, who came from Malacca and afterwards was clerk to the present Mr. Whampoa's grand-uncle at Teluk Ayer; Monteiro who remembered the commencement of the building of the Institution in 1823 died in Singapore in 1891. Mrs. Thompson had a class of about half a dozen girls in a room on the upper floor of the same house. This was the beginning of schools in Singapore.

At the end of this year Sir Stamford built a small bungalow where Fort Canning at present is, which afterwards became Government House, and he looked after a botanic and experimental garden on the hill. Mr. Earl wrote of this "The Government House is erected on the top of a hill at the back of the town, from which there is a fine prospect of the Straits. As it was completed within a fortnight after the first arrival of the British, it is not to be expected that it can be very substantial. The sides are rough planks and venetian windows, the roof is attaps. It is withal so unsubstantial that after a Sumatra squall inquiring glances are cast up to discover whether the house is still there or in the valley behind it. At the foot is a botanical garden, with several nutmeg trees planted by the founder of the Settlement."

On 28th November Raffles issued an advertisement establishing a Pork farm, and called on the Resident to frame rules. The following are extracts from Sir Stamford's letters written at the end of this year, and in January, 1823 :—" I am at present engaged in establishing a constitution for Singapore, the principles of which will I hope ensure its prosperity. The utmost possible freedom of trade and equal rights to all, with protection of property and person, are the objects to be attained. In Java I had to remodel, here the tax is new.

" Here all is life and activity, and it would be difficult to name a place on the face of the globe with brighter prospects or more present satisfaction. In little more than three years it has risen from an insignificant fishing village to a large and prosperous town, containing at least 10,000 inhabitants, of all nations, actively engaged in commercial pursuits, which afford to each and all a handsome livelihood and abundant profit. There are no complaints here of want of employment, no deficiency of rents, or dissatisfaction at taxes. This may be considered as the simple, but almost magical result of that perfect freedom of trade, which it has been my very good fortune to establish.

" I have nearly got over the job of undoing and am steadily going on with the establishment of something like a constitution for the place, on the principle of a free port in every sense of the word. The active spirit of enterprise among all classes is truly astonishing and, for its extent, I believe I may safely say that no part of the world exhibits a busier scene than the town and environs of Singapore. The Dutch have been obliged to take off their duties at Java and elsewhere on native prows

" I am now busy in allotting the land and laying out the different towns, defining rights, and establishing powers and rules for their protection and preservation. The task, though an arduous and serious one, is not one that I find unpleasant. What I feel most is the want of good counsel and advice, and of sufficient confidence in my own experience and judgment to lay down so broad and permanent a foundation as I could wish. I have already upwards of 10,000 to legislate for, and this number will, I doubt not, be increased during the next year. The enterprise and activity which prevail are wonderful, and the effects of a free trade and liberal principles have operated like magic. But that the past prosperity of the place may not prove ephemeral, it requires that I be more careful in what I do for the future: for if the past, under all our uncertainty of possession, has so far exceeded my expectations; what may not be calculated on hereafter when our principles are better understood, when our possession is considered secure, and when British capital and enterprise come into full and fair play.

" My time is at present engaged in remodelling and laying out my new city, and establishing institutions and laws for its future constitution. A pleasant duty enough in England where you have books, hard heads, and lawyers to refer to, but here by no means easy, where all must depend upon my own judgment and foresight. Nevertheless I hope that though Singapore may be the first capital established in the nineteenth century, it will not disgrace the brightest period of it."

The total tonnage, importing and exporting in 1822, was 130,689 tons. The total value of imports and exports was $8,568,172. Nearly the whole of the trade was carried on by borrowed capital, on which interest was paid from nine to twelve per cent. Not one ship arrived direct from England, notwithstanding European goods were in constant demand. All the goods had come by circuitous routes. Four free ships, that is not the East India Company's traders, loaded home during the year, and Raffles wrote that six more could have been laden if they had been there.

A detailed account of shipping had been kept during the year, which Raffles says was accurate. He added that during the two and a half years since the establishment of Singapore, by which he probably meant up to the end of 1821, 2889 vessels had entered and cleared, of which 383 were owned and commanded by Europeans, and 2,506 by natives, and that their united tonnage was 161,000 tons. This averages 56 tons each, so many were small native crafts. During the same period the value of merchandise, arrived and cleared, in native vessels was $5,000,000 and in ships not less than $3,000,000, giving a total amount of about eight millions as the capital turned, as Sir Stamford expresses it.

The following papers written by Sir Stamford Raffles himself regarding the laying out of the Town were collected by Mr. Braddell and were given in full in his notes, an ample reason for reprinting them here at length. They contain matter which has been usefully referred to, many times since, especially regarding the Verandah question, and they fill up the remainder of this chapter. The last letter is dated in February, 1823, but they all refer to this matter:—

LAND ALLOTMENT COMMITTEE.
To James Lumsdaine, Esq.
Nathaniel Wallich, Esq. and
Captain Francis Salmond.

Gentlemen,—It having been determined on the first establishment of this Settlement that the whole space included within the old lines and the Singapore river should be reserved exclusively for public purposes, and His Excellency the Governor General in Council having directed that the land subsequently occupied by individual settlers on the north bank of the Singapore river should be resumed, it has become necessary to fix upon another site on which the European merchants may construct adequate warehouses for the accommodation of the different descriptions of goods collected by them, and no spot has appeared better calculated for this purpose than the opposite bank of the Singapore river now in part occupied by Chinese.

Having consulted with Mr Coleman, by profession an architect, and with others and having myself partially examined the ground, I am not aware of any objection to the plan of building the warehouses on this line, except such as may arise from the additional expense which will be necessary in raising the ground and from some moderate compensation which it may be just to make to the Chinese on account of this removal. Hitherto the European merchants would seem to have laboured under an erroneous impression that they would eventually be allowed to have their warehouses on the side reserved by Government, which on many accounts was naturally preferred by them, but this delusion being now at an end, it is to be expected that they will gladly enter into the plan now under consideration and that the activity and energy which is now so conspicuous will easily overcome all minor and comparative disadvantages.

No title whatever can be granted to those individuals who have built store houses on the ground reserved for the Company and they will not have the power to transfer them as property, neither will any new buildings whatever be allowed to be erected thereon by individuals, and with the view of placing the mercantile community with regard to advantage for building, on the most equal footing possible, it is proposed to levy by way of ground rent or otherwise such a tax on the ground temporarily occupied by the existing buildings as shall be equivalent to the greater expense which may be incurred in laying the foundations on the opposite side of the river.

It is proposed that an embankment, which may at the same time serve to confine the river and drain the adjacent ground and afford the convenience of a long line of wharf in front of the warehouses, should in the first instance be constructed along the south side of the river, from the road opposite Ferry point to that which has been marked out for the intended bridge, so as to form an extensive crescent of about six or seven hundred yards, in the rear of which the range of the warehouses may be built on one uniform and approved plan.

In prosecution of the plan above stated, it is further proposed that with the view of preserving uniformity and ensuring the goodness of the materials and workmanship, this embankment or line of wharf should be constructed under the immediate superintendence of Government, the expense to be repaid by the individual, as the lots may be appropriated. Allowing sixty feet for the front of a warehouse and a space of 12 feet between each, it is estimated that the projected site is calculated to afford room for between 20 and 30 separate and commodious buildings. The depth proposed to be allotted to the range of buildings is 100 feet from the wharf for the warehouses and 50 feet in the rear for a yard, at the back of which will run a High Street, so as to admit of a back front to the buildings on the land side.

Previously, however, to the adoption of a plan involving such important interests, I am desirous of obtaining the best and most competent advice which circumstances admit, and with this view, I have appointed you to be a committee for the purpose of taking into your most deliberate consideration the plan now proposed, in all its bearings, and reporting in how far you deem the same advisable and advantageous and as preferable to any others which offer.

In selecting you for this important duty, I have been influenced no less by a full confidence in your peculiar qualifications and ability to form a correct judgment on the subject, than by the circumstance of your being wholly unconnected with any of the local parties, or conflicting interests which have heretofore so unfortunately prevailed at this Settlement.

I am, &c.,

(Signed) T. S. RAFFLES.

Singapore, 17th October, 1822.

TOWN COMMITTEE.

Proclamation by the Hon'ble Sir Thomas Stamford Raffles, Lieutenant Governor of Fort Marlborough and its Dependencies.

Whereas several European Merchants and others having occupied and constructed buildings of Masonry on portions of ground on the North Bank of the Singapore River and elsewhere, within the space intended to have been reserved exclusively for public purposes, viz., between the old lines and Singapore River from the sea inland to the back of the hill:

Under the present circumstances of the Settlement it is not the desire of Government to insist on the immediate removal of such buildings as may have been constructed of Masonry by Europeans and completed before the 10th April last, unless the same may become indispensible for the public service, but the parties interested are warned of what is intended, and the construction by individuals of all further buildings whatever, as well as the outlay of all further sums of money on those already constructed within the limits aforesaid, after this date, is most strictly prohibited.

The terms on which the above indulgence will be granted to present occupants will be hereafter made known.

These orders have application principally to the ground near the River occupied or intended to be occupied for commercial purposes and have no immediate reference to officers' Bungalows, for which, being a public purpose, an express provision was made, but it is clearly to be understood that all dwelling houses or buildings whatever situated within the limits aforesaid, whether the same may be in the actual occupation of Military Officers or of private individuals, are considered to be on the same footing and alike subject to the cantonment regulations.

That no person may plead ignorance hereof, the Resident will cause this Proclamation to be duly promulgated and copies affixed at the usual places for general information.

Given under my hand, at Singapore, this 29th day of October, 1822.

(Signed) T. S. RAFFLES.

Notice is hereby given, that in order to afford comfort and security to the different descriptions of inhabitants who have resorted to this Settlement, and to prevent confusion and disputes hereafter, it is the intention of Government forthwith to appoint a competent Committee, with such advice and assistance as may be necessary, for appropriating and marking out the quarters or departments of the several classes of the native population.

This committee will consist of three European Gentlemen and of a Representative from each of the principal classes of Arabs, Malays, Bugis, Javanese, and Chinese, and it will hold its first sitting on Monday next.

Pending the sitting of this Committee and until further orders all persons are required to suspend the construction of whatever buildings they may have in hand, whether of stone, brick or wood.

It is required of all persons to attend the summons of the said committee and to afford all possible information and assistance in their power that may be demanded of them.

That no one may plead ignorance of this advertisement, the same is to be translated into the native languages, published by beat of gong, and affixed at the usual places in Campong China, Campong Glam, and elsewhere.

By order, &c.,

(Signed)   L. N. HULL,

Acting Secretary.

To Captain C. E. Davis, President.

George Bonham, } Esquires, Members.
Alex. L. Johnston, }

Gentlemen,—The extent of the native population which has already accumulated at Singapore and the rapidity with which it daily increases, render it expedient that in providing for its accommodation a timely attention should be paid to its future regulation, with reference to the circumstances of the place and the peculiar character and institutions of the several classes of inhabitants of which the society will be composed.

1. It has been observed by the Supreme Government "that in the event of Singapore being permanently retained, there seems every reason to believe that it will become a place of considerable magnitude and importance, and it is essential that this circumstance should be constantly kept in mind, in regulating the appropriation of land. Every day's experience shews the inconvenience and expense that may arise out of the want of such a forecast" and in this respect an economical and proper allotment of the ground intended to form the site of the principal town is an object of the first importance, and one which under the present circumstances of the Settlement will not admit of delay.

2. In order to provide for this object in the best and most satisfactory manner which our present means admit, I have appointed you to be a committee for the purpose of suggesting and carrying into effect such arrangements on this head, as may on the whole appear to be most conducive to the comfort and security of the different classes of inhabitants and the general interests and welfare of the place, and in the performance of the duty you will be assisted by the Assistant Engineer and Assistant in the Police Department, and guided by the following instructions.

EXTENT OF THE TOWN GENERALLY.

3.　In considering the extent of ground necessary to be appropriated for the town generally, reference must be had not only to the numbers of the present inhabitants and the probability of their future increase, but to the nature and occupation of the several classes of which it is composed and the demands they may respectively have to preference in regard to advantageous sites for trade, &c., and it will be a primary object to secure to the mercantile community all the facilities which the natural advantages of the port afford.　At present a considerable portion of the sea and river face, which may hereafter become important for mercantile purposes, is occupied by the lower classes of Chinese, and as might be expected many of the early settlers have occupied positions and extent of ground which are now urgently demanded by a higher and more respectable class.　A line must be drawn between the classes engaged in mercantile speculation and those gaining their livelihood by handicrafts and personal labour; the former, and particularly the principal merchants, will require the first attention, and there does not appear any reason why the latter should in any instance be allowed to occupy those situations which are likely at any time to be required by the commercial community.　The cultivators form a third and interesting class, particularly of the Chinese population, but as no part of the ground intended to be occupied as the town can be spared for agricultural purposes they will not fall under your consideration, except in as far as it may become necessary to exclude them.

4.　The town may already be considered to occupy an extent of the sea face, from Tulloh Ayer to the large inlet formed by Sandy Point, of nearly three miles, and it may be presumed that if a space is reserved from thence inland in every direction of from half a mile to a mile, as the ground may admit, it will be sufficient for all the purposes required in a principal town.　A second town is gradually rising near the Salat or Malay Straits, and as soon as the road of communication is opened it may be expected that a very considerable population will collect in that quarter, but this does not fall under your immediate consideration.

5.　Along this line of sea face it will be expedient to preserve for the public all the space between the road which runs parallel to the beach and the sea, and generally deemed advisable in the neighbourhood of the Settlement to reserve an open space along the beach, excepting where it may be required by individuals for special purposes.　With this view the Chinese artificers and others who have settled on the beach near Tulloh Ayer and Campong Glam will be required to remove from thence without delay.

GROUND RESERVED BY GOVERNMENT.

6.　In the distribution of the ground intended to form the site of the town, you will most particularly observe that the whole of the space included between the Singapore river and the old Lines, inland from the sea face to the back of the hill, including a space of 200 yards East of the old lines, is reserved for the immediate purposes of Government.

7.　You will further keep in mind that Government also necessarily reserves all such commanding points in the town and its vicinity which may be useful for the defence of the place, such as the point at the entrance of the river, and the high grounds to the westward as well as the space between Sandy and Deep Water Points to the eastward, which it is intended to appropriate as a Marine Yard.　With these exceptions the whole of the space above pointed out may be allotted to individuals.

EUROPEAN TOWN AND PRINCIPAL MERCANTILE ESTABLISHMENTS.

8.　In fixing the site of the European town to the eastward of the cantonments, it was in the first place considered that the north east bank of the Singapore river as far as the hill would, with the whole of the space included within the old lines of Singapore, be indispensible for the public service, whenever the permanence of the settlement might be established; and in the second it was obvious that if relinquished by Government its extent was too limited to admit of its affording accommodation to all the European and other merchants who might be expected eventually to settle, and experience has already abundantly verified these presumptions.　It is admitted that the N. E. bank of the river and space occupied as cantonment possess peculiar advantages for the public in general and for the particular use of Government, and it is deeply to be regretted that any deviation should have been allowed from the original plan; under existing circumstances, however, some modification is thought advisable, and with the view of affording every possible accommodation to the trade of the port, it is proposed that in addition to the sea face to the eastward of the cantonments, the whole of the S. W. bank of the Singapore river with a circular road round the hill between the point and Tulloh Ayer, shall be appropriated for the use of European and other merchants.

9. Under this arrangement and the immediate accommodation which has been afforded to the principal part of the European merchants already settled, it is concluded that individuals will no longer feel an inclination to intrude on what may be considered the peculiar property of Government, but that those who may have planted themselves within its precincts will be sensible of the impropriety, and zealous in repairing the inconvenience they have occasioned, by an early removal of the materials of which their buildings are composed.

10. The necessity of draining the ground on the south west side of the river, is no less indispensible for the health of the Settlement than for securing the foundations of whatever permanent buildings may be erected thereon, and it is intended to proceed on the operation with the least delay practicable. In the meantime however, and during its progress, it is necessary that the present temporary buildings along the banks of the river should be removed, a measure which it will be your duty to carry into effect under the advertisement of this date, in such manner as shall be least inconvenient to the parties concerned.

11. To the Eastward of the Cantonments as far generally as the Sultan's, and inland to the bank of the Rochor river and the foot of the hills, including the whole of the great Rochor plain, is to be considered as set apart exclusively for the accommodation of European and other principal settlers.

NATIVE DIVISIONS OR CAMPONGS.

12. Your attention however is to be more exclusively directed to the proper allotment of the Native divisions of the town, and the first in importance of these is beyond doubt the Chinese.

CHINESE CAMPONG.

From the number of Chinese already settled, and the peculiar attractions of the place for that industrious race, it may be presumed that they will always form by far the largest portion of the community. The whole therefore of that part of the town to the south west of the Singapore river (not excepted as above) is intended to be appropriated for their accommodation. They will be permitted to occupy the south west bank of the river above the intended bridge on certain conditions, and the highroad leading from the bridge to the present Chinese campong, as well as the banks of the small inlet to the southward of it, will offer many advantageous situations as yet unoccupied. These will be particularly pointed out to you by the executive officer and you will proceed to mark out this division of the town generally inland as far as practicable up the slopes of hills, as may appear to be likely to be required, reserving an appropriate place above the bridge for the accommodation of the lower classes of Chuliahs and others employed in boats, cooly work, &c.

13. In establishing the Chinese campong on a proper footing, it will be necessary to advert to the provincial and other distinctions among this peculiar people. It is well known that the people of one province are more quarrelsome than another, and that continued disputes and disturbances take place between people of different provinces; it will also be necessary to distinguish between the fixed residents and itinerants,—between the resident merchants and the traders who only resort to the port for a time. Of the latter those from Amoi claim particular attention, and it may perhaps deserve consideration whether on account of their importance it may not be advisable to allot a separate division for their accommodation even to the westward of the Cantonments, beyond the European town and the Sultan. The object of Government being to afford the utmost accommodation to every description of traders, but more particularly to the respectable classes, you will always keep this in view, and while you generally direct

your attention to the importance of concentrating the different classes of the population in their separate quarters, you are not to lose sight of the advantage which may arise from deviating from this rule in special cases where the commercial interests of the Settlement are concerned. Few places offer greater natural facilities for commerce than Singapore and it is only desired that the advantage of these facilities be afforded to all who are competent to avail themselves of them in the proportion to their relative importance and claims to consideration.

14. It being intended to place the Chinese population in a great measure under the immediate control of their own chiefs, you will fix up such centrical and commanding sites for the residence of these authorities and appropriate to them such larger extent of ground, as may tend to render them efficient instruments of police, and at the same time raise them in the consideration of the lower classes.

15. You will also line out the different streets and highways, which should as far as practicable run at right angles and in no instance be less than — feet in breadth. To preserve uniformity and regularity hereafter, you will be pleased to class the streets according to their relative advantages of situation under the heads of 1st, 2nd and 3rd class, determining the least space along the street which shall be occupied by each house and consequently fixing the exact number of houses which each street will contain. It is proposed to fix a small ground rent on the spot occupied by each house, of one, two and three dollars for every fathom of front, according to the above classes, to be collected annually on the 1st of January and you will inform the parties that prior to the 1st of January next arrangements will be made for numbering the houses and granting them certificates of possession. Each street should receive some appropriate name and it will become the duty of the police to see them regularly numbered. Each street or division should also have a portion set apart for a police station.

16. The danger and apprehension of fire is at present so great that the most respectable of the inhabitants, including all the native merchants, seem desirous of constructing buildings of masonry with tiled roofs, and it will be at any rate necessary to stipulate for this in the immediate vicinity of the allotments set apart for the larger commercial store houses

17. The concentration of the different descriptions of artificers, such as blacksmiths, carpenters, &c., in particular quarters should also be attended to.

DESCRIPTION OF HOUSES TO BE CONSTRUCTED, EACH HOUSE TO HAVE A VERANDAH OPEN AT ALL TIMES AS A CONTINUED AND COVERED PASSAGE ON EACH SIDE OF THE STREET.

18. It will further be advisable that for the sake of uniformity and gaining as much room as possible a particular description of front for all brick or tiled houses should be attended to, and it is conceived that while the breadth of the streets is strictly preserved as above directed, a still further accommodation will be afforded to the public by requiring that each house should have a verandah of a certain depth, open at all times as a continued and covered passage on each side of the street.

19. In fixing a proper site for the principal church, theatre, &c , care should also be taken that it be in a central and open situation and that a considerable space be kept clear in the vicinity.

20. Although the object of your appointment does not include the details of police it will nevertheless be incumbent on you to suggest any general regulations which may appear to you as advisable in this respect, as far as the same may be connected with the plan of the town and the nature of the buildings of which it will be composed; under this head may be included draining, lighting, watching, cleansing and the like.

BUGIS CAMPONG.

21. Next to the Chinese your attention will be directed to the Bugis settlers. They at present occupy the whole extent from Campong Glam to the mouth of the Rochor River, but it is conceived that they may be more advantageously concentrated on the spot beyond the residence of the Sultan. In this case a part of Campong Glam, immediately adjoining the Sultan's residence, may be occupied by the Arabs according to a plan that will be submitted by Lieutenant Jackson, who has instructions to mark out the European town in that direction.

22. In the allotment of the Bugis town it will be equally necessary to attend to economy in the distribution of ground by laying out regular streets inland towards the river and obliging the inhabitants to conform thereto. At present the houses are scattered without any attention to order or convenience. This will become the more necessary in the event of its being determined to allow a Campong in this direction to the Amoi Chinese, as alluded to in a former paragraph.

ARAB CAMPONG.

23. The Arab population will require every consideration, and their expected numbers should not be estimated at less than from 1 to 2000. No situation will be more appropriate for them than the vicinity of the Sultan's residence, and it will only be necessary in providing the accommodation they require to keep in view the convenience of separating them as far as practicable from the European dwellings, with which they will in such case come nearly in contact.

MARINE YARD.

24. It being intended to appropriate the space between Sandy and Deep Water Points as a Marine Yard, permission will be given to Chinese artificers to settle in the vicinity of the public works on certain conditions, and by this arrangement it is calculated that accommodation will be afforded for a large portion of that description of people who will now be required to remove from the opposite beach. A moderate compensation to such Chinese settlers as may be required to remove their dwellings, under the arrangement now generally directed for the native town, will not be objected to, but the same must be defined and in no case exceed the actual expense to which they may be put to in removing.

25. The beach from the extremity of the European town will still continue open for the repair and building of native vessels as at present, and it is proposed that hereafter a public pier should be thrown out in this quarter in the most convenient spot for trade.

CHULIAH CAMPONG.

26. Reference has already been had to the advantage of allotting a separate division for the town class of Chuliahs up the Singapore river, and this will of course be done with a due consideration of their expected numbers, and the necessity of their residence being in the vicinity of the place where their services are most likely to be called for.

MALAYS.

27. The Malay population being principally attached to the Tumongong, or engaged in fishing, may not require any very extensive allotment. It is probable the larger portion of the former will settle near Panglima Prang's and the upper banks of the river; and the latter will find accommodation for themselves in the smaller bays and inlets beyond the immediate line of beach reserved for the town, but you will of course advert to the same as far as may be necessary.

MARKETS.

28. As a measure of police it is proposed to remove the fish market to Tulloh Ayer without delay and it will be the duty of the committee to consider in how far the general concentration of the fish, pork, poultry and vegetable markets, in the vicinity of each other, may not be advantageous for the general convenience and cleanliness of the place.

29. The importance of early provision for Mohametan and Chinese burial grounds, particularly the latter, at a suitable distance from town, will necessarily fall under your consideration.

30. You will assemble as early as practicable and as soon as you shall have decided on some general mode of proceeding for the despatch of business, you will be pleased to call upon the heads of the principal classes of natives to be present at your deliberations, explaining to them the object of your appointment and the desire of government, in associating them with you, that the interest of all should be duly considered in the arrangements adopted.

31. With reference to the extent and nature of the duties required it will be advisable that you should report your proceedings from time to time for con-

sideration and confirmation, and that whenever you have generally defined the arrangement to be adopted in any particular division, you leave the detail to be carried into effect by the Executive Officer or Police Department, or some subordinate committee, who will as occasion requires receive especial instructions for the purpose from Government, according to your recommendation.

32. In conclusion, it may be only necessary to observe that in imposing such extensive and varied duties on your committee, I feel fully confident that they will be performed in the manner most advantageous to the general interests of the Settlement and most creditable to yourselves and that you will duly appreciate their importance and necessity.

I am, &c.,

(Signed) T. S. RAFFLES.

Singapore. 4th November. 1822.

To

G. Bonham, Esq., Lieutenant Jackson, and F. Bernard, Esq.

Gentlemen,

1. It being essential that the several arrangements for the improvement of the town of Singapore should be carried into effect with the least delay practicable, I am directed to inform you that the Lieutenant-Governor has been pleased to appoint you to be a committee for the purpose of superintending these arrangements and carrying them into effect forthwith, conformably to the plan laid down, with such modifications as may from time to time be communicated to you by the Lieutenant-Governor.

2. The general plan of the town, shewing the allotment of the different Campongs, principal roads and streets, and ground reserved for public purposes, is in possession of the assistant Engineer who will from time to time communicate with the Lieutenant-Governor personally on any modifications that may become necessary.

3. The first and most important point to be attended to is the removal of the native population and buildings from the space on the north bank of the river between the Tumongong's and the sea, to the opposite side of the river, and a date should be fixed at which the present buildings, if not removed by the present occupants, will be pulled down by Government.

4. I enclose for your information the report of the Resident on the value of these buildings and the progress made by the parties in removing, and it will be your duty to see that a proper allotment of ground on the opposite side be made for all persons obliged to remove and who may not already have provided themselves with lots.

5. In the event of any question arising relative to the amount of valuation of any particular property, you will give due consideration to the same and submit your opinion thereon for the further orders of the Lieutenant-Governor.

6. The principle on which it has been resolved to proceed in granting remuneration to the parties, is to advance them one half of the estimated value of their present buildings immediately, and to pay the remainder at the expiration of six months if a brick building, or of three months if of plank, to be calculated from the 1st of February, provided the buildings are then removed or transferred to Government.

7. It is probable that to some of the parties advances have been made on this account, as the Resident was long since authorized to grant to them whatever remuneration he deemed the parties entitled to, the particulars of these you will of course ascertain and attend to.

8. The Resident will now be authorized to make such further advances on this account as may be required, on bills from the parties countersigned by the members of the committee.

9. The removal of the Chinese houses on the sea face at Campong Glam, the formation of the Chuliah campong there, and the laying out and appropriating of Bugis town will also deserve your early attention.

10. The removal of the Chuliah and Dhoby encampment near the Sepoy Lines should be immediately effected, in order that the ground may be appropriated for the purposes for which it is intended.

11. During the progress making by your committee the assistant Engineer will use every exertion in his department, and on reference to the Sitting Magistrate, you will at all times obtain the most ready and efficient assistance from the police, and as all parties have long had notice of the intentions and views of Government, there seems no occasion longer to delay the adoption of any measure of general improvement on account of the particular accommodation of individuals.

12. The formation of the new streets with the construction of the markets are objects deserving your early attention, and as the object of your appointment is to enable you not only to prosecute but complete all the arrangements for laying out the town, you are authorized to make such appropriation of ground to natives as may be entitled to consideration, and finally to do all such things in view, (*sic*) reporting your proceedings from time to time for the information of the Lieutenant-Governor.

13. The Lieutenant-Governor feels satisfied that the members of this committee will both individually and collectively feel the high importance of the trust reposed in them, and execute the same with zeal and ability.

I am, &c.,

(Signed)   L. N. HULL,

Acting Secretar

Singapore, 28th February, 1823.

CHAPTER VIII.

COMMERCIAL SQUARE AND THE OLD ROCK.

IN the Hikayat Abdulla it says:—"Mr. Raffles and Mr. Farquhar consulted together about the town, and Mr. Farquhar thought the mercantile buildings and markets ought to be on the Campong Glam side, while Mr. Raffles thought they ought to be on the other side of the river. Mr Farquhar said that on that side the traders would meet many difficulties, as the place was a low swamp, with bad water, and the expense of raising the levels of the ground would be very great, besides the difficulty of getting earth for filling up. Mr. Raffles said that if the Campong Glam side was chosen, the other side of the river would be deserted, and would not be settled for a hundred years. They were both full of projects and ideas on the subject, until three days after, when it struck Mr. Raffles that he could break up the hill at the end of Singapore point and fill up that side of the river [Boat Quay and up to the Police Court] with the material. The next day they met and made arrangements, and sent for coolies, greatly to the surprise of everyone. Two or three hundred coolies, Chinese, Malays and Klings, were employed at the rate of one rupee a day each man, chunkolling and carrying earth. Some were breaking up the rocks, of which there were very many in the hill. There were many tindals overlooking them, labour became dearer, although every evening bags of money were brought and each man got his payment for the day. Mr. Raffles came twice a day to give directions about the work. After about three or four months the hill was completely cut down, and all the hollows and streams and drains and valleys filled up. There only remained one rock about the height of an elephant but a great deal larger. The Chinese removed this for nothing, on getting the stone for their trouble."

The rise in Battery Road and the other streets leading up to the Square show where the hill was, and until late years there was a large round boulder, probably part of the large rock Abdulla speaks of, which kept cropping up through the road metal in Battery Road, very awkward for horses, which only disappeared when the road was widened and raised. A part of the rock was built into the front wall of Maclaine Fraser & Co.'s godown in Battery Road.

Abdulla then tells us:— "After the low marshy land [Boat Quay, Circular Road, &c.] was filled up, raised and embanked, it was measured out into lots and sold by auction. If any one wishes to know the locality of the hill, which was thus removed by Mr. Raffles, to fill up the ground on this side of the river, it was at the end of Singapore point, at the place now called Boat Street. [Boat Quay?] It was at first made into a garden, and all manner of flowers and trees planted.

I recollect hearing formerly that this spot was chosen as a site to erect a building in which to place a portrait of Mr. Raffles, as a memento that it was he who had formed the Settlement, but for some reason unknown to me it was not carried out, and the place now remains a garden opposite the house of Messrs. Spottiswoode and Connolly."

This is the present Commercial Square, an open space of about 200 yards long by 50 wide, with gardens in the centre. At the south corner of Change Alley (which might more appropriately have been called Spottiswoode Alley) where the building generally known as the old Oriental Bank now stands, was Mr. Spottiswoode's garden, with the house and godown standing further back inside the compound.

Abdulla then gives an amusing account of his own want of enterprise. He tells us that he had bought a piece of ground, on Colonel Farquhar's advice, at Campong Glam and built a plank house with attap roof, but lived there in terror as the place was surrounded with jungle. Afterwards he says: " When they were selling the filled up ground [near the Square] Mr. Raffles advised me to buy four or five lots, as afterwards this part of the town would become valuable. I answered where could I get money enough to pay for the land. I saw the lots selling at auction for $1,200 and $1,150, and there was besides the expense of building. Mr. Raffles smiled and said, never mind about the money, take the land first and we can talk about payment hereafter. In my stupidity and want of judgment, I thought of the difficulty I might experience if I got into debt, in case I wished to return to Malacca ; and besides money at that time was not easily earned in Singapore; in fact so much so, I made it a rule to go home to Malacca every six months. If I should buy land and build houses I would not be able to go home. In fact I really did not think at that time that Singapore would succeed. Before that I was not aware that the land sales were mere formalities, and that the price of lands was not paid, and I saw at once the deep cleverness of the idea. If Mr. Raffles was to give the land for nothing all manner of paupers would come, and when could he expect to see *pucka* houses rising. So he put the lands at such high rates that only wealthy people bought who could afford to build proper houses. It was solely on account of my own stupidity and want of judgment that I lost this opportunity of purchasing land, by following Tuan Raffles' advice, and I now repent, but what's the use of that. As the Malays say 'Repent before you do a thing, for it is no use afterwards.'"

Then Abdulla tells us of the rock at the mouth of the river, about which much has been said by all the writers about Singapore. The following is Abdulla's account of the discovery of it.

" At the end of the point there was another rock found among the brushwood; it was smooth, of square form, covered with a chiselled inscription which no one could read, as it had been worn away by water for how many thousands of years who can tell. As soon as it was discovered people of all races crowded round it. The Hindoos said it was Hindoo writing, the Chinese that it was Chinese. I went among others with Mr. Raffles and the Rev. Mr. Thompson. I thought from the appearance of the raised parts of the letters that it was

Arabic, but I could not read it, as the stone had been subject to the rising and falling tides for such a long time. Many clever people came, bringing flour and lard, which they put in the hollows and then lifted out in the hope of getting the shape of the letters. Some again brought a black fluid which they poured over the stone but without success. Ingenuity was exhausted in trying to decipher the inscription. The stone remained there till lately. Mr. Raffles said the inscription was Hindoo, because the Hindoo race was the earliest that came to the Archipelago, first to Java and then to Bali and Siam, the inhabitants of which places are all descended from the Hindoos. But not a soul in Singapore could say what the inscription was. During the time Mr. Bonham was Governor of the three settlements this stone was broken up by the Engineer. This is very much to be regretted, and was in my opinion highly improper; perhaps the gentleman did it from ignorance or stupidity, and now, from his conduct, we can never know the nature of this ancient writing. Did he not think that persons sufficiently clever might come and disclose the secret so long concealed? I have heard that in England there are persons very clever in deciphering such inscriptions with the aid of all manner of curious devices. Well may the Malays says 'What you can't make, don't break.' "

From what has been written since on the subject it is clear that Abdulla was pretty correct in his facts and his deductions; and it is an example of the general correctness of his recollections of what he himself saw. The next extract is from Lieut. Begbie's book :—" The principal curiosity of Singapore is a large stone at the point of the river, the one face of which has been sloped and smoothed, and upon which several lines of engraven characters are still visible. The rock being, however, of a schistose and porous nature, the inscription is illegible. It is said that Sir Stamford Raffles endeavoured, by the application of powerful acids, to bring out the characters with the view of deciphering them, but the result was unsuccessful. Where such an eminent person has failed, it may be thought presumptuous in me to hazard a conjecture on the subject of the language in which the inscription was penned, but I may perhaps be permitted to make an attempt to throw some light upon a subject so confessedly obscure. Resorting to the Malayan Annals, which, clouded as they undoubtedly are by fable and allegory, yet contain many a valuable piece of information, we find therein mention made of three remarkable stones at Singhapura. The first that I shall mention is that recorded at page 82 of Leyden's Malay Annals, in which the translator, following his author, tells us " that there was a man of Pasei, named Tun Jana Khateb, who went to Singhapura with two companions, named Tuan de Bongoran, and Tuan de Salangor. One day Tun Jana Khateb was walking in the market place of Singhapura, and drew near to the palace of the Rajah, where one of the Rajah's women observed him. He was looking at a betel tree, when it suddenly broke. This was observed by the Rajah, who was enraged at it, conceiving it to have been done solely for the purpose of attracting the lady's attention, and displaying his skill. He accordingly ordered him to be put to death. The executioners seized him, and carried him to the place of execution and stabbed him near the house of a seller of sweetmeats. His blood flowed on the ground, but his body vanished from their ken, and his blood was covered up by the sweetmeat seller, and was changed into stone and still remains at Singhapura.

"The second instance that I shall adduce is also recorded by the same author, who informs us that, during the reign of Rajah Secander Shah, the Javanese conquered Singhapura, principally by means of the treachery of Sang Ranjuna Tapa, who invited the enemy to the conquest in revenge for the Rajah having directed Tapa's daughter, who was one of the royal wives, to be impaled on suspicion of infidelity. As a judgment on his perfidy the historian says that 'By the power of God Almighty, the house of Sang Ranjuna Tapa faded, and its pillars were overturned, and rice ceased to be planted in the land, and Sang Ranjuna Tapa, both husband and wife, were changed into stone, and those are the two stones which appear beside the moat of Singhapura.

"The third, though first in order of record, I have reserved for the last because I am inclined to think that the evidence is fully presumptive in favour of its being the stone now visible at Singapore; it is to be met with at pages 62 and 63 of the Annals. The preceding pages inform us that in the reign of Sir Rajah Vicrama, there was a redoubtable champion of the name of Badang. Several remarkable feats of strength are recorded of him, but I will merely select the one in point. The fame of Badang having reached the land of Kling (Coromandel) the Rajah of that country despatched a champion, named Nadi Vijaya Vicrama, to try his strength with him, staking seven ships on the issue of the contest. After a few trials of their relative powers, Badang pointed to a huge stone lying before the Rajah's hall, and asked his opponent to lift it, and to allow their claims to be decided by the greatest strength displayed in this feat. The Kling champion assented, and, after several failures, succeeded in raising it as high as his knee, after which he immediately let it fall. The story then says that Badang, having taken up the stone, poised it easily several times, and then threw it out into the mouth of the river, and this is the rock which is at this day visible at the point of Singhapura, or Tanjong Singhapura After some other recitals, the Annals state that 'after a long time, Badang also died, and was buried at the point of the straits of Singhapura; and, when the tidings of his death reached the land of Kling, the Rajah sent two stone pillars, to be raised over his grave as a monument, and these are the pillars which are still at the point of the Bay.'

"Now, the first two instances are totally destitute of presumptive evidence; this last is, on the contrary, full of it. At the mouth of the river there is a large rock, which is concealed at high water, and on which a post was erected four or five years ago by, I believe, Captain Jackson of the Bengal Artillery, to warn boats of the danger; this is the rock fabled to have been hurled by Badang: He is said to have been buried at the point of the straits of Singhapura, the scene of this wonderful exploit; and there, the very spot where this record is to be still seen, the Rajah of Kling, who had been so serious a loser by it, ordered his monument to be erected. Fabulous and childish as the legend is, it brings us directly to the point. Sri Rajah Vicrama, called by Crawfurd (Indian Archipelago, Vol. 2, p. 482) Sri Rama

Wikaram, reigned in the year of the Hegira 620, or A.D. 1223, and was succeeded in Heg. 634, or A.D. 1236 by Sri Maharaja. The Annals state, after recording the death of Badang, that this king reigned a long time; consequently the occurrence must be placed early in his reign. The Annals were written in the year of the Hegira 1021, or A.D. 1612, nearly four centuries afterwards, and the original circumstance thus became obscured by legendary traditions; but I think that we are fairly warranted in concluding that there was a remarkable wrestler of the name of Bandang existing at that period, and that this inscription contained a recital of his feats, &c.

"This supposition naturally leads me to enquire what is the language in which these actions, recorded about A.D. 1228, could have been written. At the period of the transaction, the Malays were destitute of a written language, as it was not until between forty and fifty years afterwards, when the Mahommedan religion became the popular one, that the Arabic character was introduced. It appears to be probable that the Kling Rajah, aware of this destitution of a written character, employed a sculptor of his own nation to cut the inscription on the rock, and that, from the epitaph being in an unknown language, the original story as therein related, being necessarily handed down by oral tradition, became corrupted in every thing but its leading features. This supposition is borne out by the form of the characters, which more resembles that of the Malabar language than any other oriental tongue that I am acquainted with. I do not mean to say that the words are essentially Tamil, but merely to express an opinion that the inscription is couched in an obsolete dialect of that language. Language, as a nation progresses to civilization, sustains serious alterations, which, barely noticed at the time, or viewed as merely slight and necessary changes in order to meet the influx of new ideas and new wants, nevertheless, in the lapse of years, almost substitute a different dialect to that originally used by the community. The Tamil of A.D. 1228 may be easily conceded to be an obsolete tongue in A.D. 1830, although we are unable to trace the successive changes which it may have sustained in the revolution of six centuries. As a proof of this assertion I have merely to mention that the earliest Dutch Records at Malacca, which could not have been written before A.D. 1596, when the Dutch arrived in Java under Hautman, are now unintelligible, even to the best informed of the residents of that nation. Thus, in the course of less than two centuries and a half, a European language has been lost, much more guarded by adventitious circumstances against corruption than any native tongue could possibly be, in countries where the constant intercourse and the similarity of dialect would naturally lead to a fusion of Asiatic languages."

When the above passages appeared in the original of these papers, Mr. W. E. Maxwell wrote as follows regarding them in the *Free Press* of 15th November, 1884 :—

"If you have access to a complete set of the Journal of the Asiatic Society of Bengal, which I have not, you will find some information about the inscription which was formerly to be read on the rock at the mouth of the Singapore river, and about a similar inscription in Province Wellesley. Some of the fragments of the Singapore rock were, I think, sent to the Asiatic Society's Museum at Calcutta. See Journal, Asiatic Society Bengal, VI., 680; XVII., Part I., 154 and 232; Id., Part II., 62, 66. Lastly, as to the legends which connect the strong man Badang with Singapore and Johore. These are, I fancy, only a localised version of a popular legend which may be found in many Malay countries. I have heard the story of how Badang obtained his strength, told, *mutatis mutandis*, of a Perak hero, Toh Kwala Bidor. There are points of resemblance between the Malay Hercules and the Scandinavian Odin."

Sir William Maxwell afterwards collected all the papers he refers to from the Journal of the Society, and published them in 1886 in the first volume of Miscellaneous papers in Tribner's Oriental Series, which were issued in two volumes by the Straits Branch of the Royal Asiatic Society. From these papers which are of considerable length and contain two curious pictures of the inscription on the rock, the following remarks are taken :—

Dr. Montgomerie said that the rock was brought to light by some Bengal sailors employed by Captain Flint, R.N., the first Master Attendant. The men were much frightened on seeing the inscription and could not be induced to go on with the clearing, which had to be completed by Chinese. Dr. Montgomerie added that it was a pity that those who afterwards authorised the destruction of the ancient relic were not themselves prevented by some such wholesome superstition.

There is also a paper written by Mr. James Prinsep, a famous antiquarian of Calcutta; who said that several enquiries had been made about the inscription, and that he had made numerous attempts to procure a copy from some of the visitors to Singapore either for amusement or for their health. This paper was published in 1837, and says that Dr. William Bland of H.M.S. *Wolf* had at last made a facsimile of all that remained in any way perceptible on the rocky fragment. It was a rock, Dr. Bland wrote, of coarse red sandstone about ten feet high, two to five feet thick and nine or ten feet in length. The surface was an irregular square, with a space of about thirty-two square feet with a raised edge all round. There had been about fifty lines of inscription, the greater part illegible. He says he made frequent pilgrimages to the rock, and describes how he made as accurate a copy as possible of the marks on the stone. Eleven years afterwards there is another paper, which says that Dr. Montgomerie having mentioned that the rock had been blasted, application was made from Bengal to the Governor to send any legible fragments that might still exist, and he replied: "The only remaining portion of the stone you mention, except what Colonel Low may have, I have found lying in the verandah of the Treasury at Singapore, where it was used as a seat by the Sepoy guard and persons waiting to transact business. I lost no time in sending it to my house, but alas, not before the inscription was nearly erased. Such as the fragment was then however it is now, for I have preserved the stone with much care, and shall have pleasure in sending it for your museum, having failed to establish one, as I hoped to have done, in Singapore."

Governor Butterworth having sent the seat of the Sepoy guard to Calcutta, a Mr. J. W. Laidlaw writes a paper about it, and also about three other pieces sent by Colonel Low, and he explains what he did to try to make the characters legible enough to be copied. It shows from the various accounts that Abdulla's quaint description of the various "curious devices" was correct. Some tried with "well made and soft dough"; and by observing the shadows thrown into the letters when "the sun was descending into the west"; others by painting the stone exactly over with white lead; others by strewing over the stone finely powdered charcoal (animal being better than vegetable as being specifically heavier!) and then sweeping it gently to and fro with a feather. Raffles had tried acid, but this, one remarked, was quite useless, as it could have no effect on such stone. As one reads all this, one cannot help remembering the famous antiquity which Mr. Pickwick discovered at Cobham.

Colonel Low wrote that he was an unwilling and pained witness of the demolition of that memorial of long past ages, his petition to have it spared being met by the reply that it was in the way of some projected Bungalow. On the explosion taking place he had crossed the river from his office, and selected such fragments as had letters on them. The Governor, Mr. Bonham, sent to ask him to preserve a piece for him, and this was the portion sent by Colonel Butterworth to Calcutta. As the fragments were very bulky, Low had them, at considerable cost, gradually chiselled by Chinese into the shape of slabs, which were still ponderous. He presented them to the Society in Bengal. It seemed to him that the inscription might probably date from an early century of the Christian era. He had consulted Buddhist priests without success, as he found he knew as much as they did, being, as he says, a sadly ignorant set. There are drawings of the inscriptions on the three pieces of stone sent to Calcutta by him, and the conclusion in Bengal was a conjecture that the inscription was a record of some Javanese triumph at a period anterior to the conversion of the Malays to Mohammedanism.

Mr. W. H. Read writes: "I remember a large block of the rock at the corner of Government House, where Fort Canning is now; but during the absence of the Governor at Penang on one occasion the convicts requiring stone to replace the road, chipped up the valuable relic of antiquity, and thus all trace of our past history was lost. It was destroyed when the sea-wall was built round Fort Fullerton, where the Club, Post Office, and Master Attendant's Office now are. It used to be decorated with flags and offerings when at the entrance of the Singapore river. The immediate consequence of the removal of the stone, an act of vandalism, was the silting up of the river. I have been told that an inscription in similar characters, which I always understood were "cuneiform," still exists (1884) in the Carimon Islands."

If the story of Mr. Badang is true, we see there were sports on the Esplanade about six hundred and fifty years ago, which is the time when Badang is said to have lived.

CHAPTER IX.

1823.

ON 23rd January, Sir Stamford wrote to the Duchess of Somerset and Mr. Marsden about his house. He said he had had another very severe attack in his head in December, which nearly proved fatal, and the doctors were for hurrying him on board ship for Europe without much ceremony. However, as he could not reconcile himself to become food for fishes, he preferred ascending the hill of Singapore where his bones, if they remained in the East, would have the honour of mixing with the ashes of the Malayan Kings; and the result was that he had almost entirely recovered. He went on to say that he had built a very comfortable house, a small bungalow, on the hill, sufficient to accommodate his sister's family as well as his own, where, though the height was inconsiderable, he found a great difference of climate. Nothing could be more interesting and beautiful than the view, and the tombs of the Malay Kings were close at hand. He said the house which was one hundred feet in front and fifty feet deep was finished in a fortnight from its commencement.

This was the first Government House, and it occupied the site until 1859, when Fort Canning was made, and Government House was moved to the large house called Leonie Hill in Grange Road, rented from Mr. Campbell of Martin Dyce & Co., which was used until the present Government House was ready for occupation in 1869. In 1826 the cost of the house stood in the books as $916, but there is a note that Mr. Crawfurd had improved and enlarged it at his own expense; he having received $150 a month for house allowance in 1823, pending reference to Calcutta as to building a suitable house for the chief authority. In Captain Begbie's book there is a description of the first house in 1833. He says that it was a neat wooden bungalow with venetians and attap roof; and consisted of two parallel halls with front and back verandahs, terminated by two square wings which comprised the sleeping apartments. It seems probable that the centre part he speaks of was the original house of Raffles, more substantially constructed, which became the drawing and dining rooms, with the long verandahs at back and front, and that the wings were built on to it to provide sleeping apartments. It has always been a matter of tradition that Lord Elgin walked up and down all night on the long front verandah of the centre building, and decided in the morning to divert the troops going to China, and to send them to Calcutta on the rumour of the Mutiny having broken out in India, as will be related hereafter.

Begbie says that the drive up the hill in those days was exceedingly romantic, a spiral carriage road winding up the hill, and fresh beauties attracting the eye at each progressive step. Eminences, undulating above each other, displaying broad patches, either cleared for cultivation or shining in the bright green livery of clove plantations, or yielding a prospect of inviting coolness by the forest clumps with which they were chequered. Standing on the hill at the present time, in front of the fort and looking towards the sea, the town extends for some miles on either side at its base and round the back of the hill, while the hills that Captain Begbie spoke of are cleared and dotted with houses for several miles in each direction.

In January Raffles wrote to Calcutta requesting to be relieved, as he intended to go to England, and he suggested that a Resident should be appointed and Singapore placed under Bengal.

The European burial ground had been placed just in front of the Government bungalow, so a better place was looked for, and the present site of the old burial ground (which was used until 1865 when that in Bukit Timah Road was opened) was selected. Very few persons ever visit the old Cemetery now, and yet there is a history to be read in the tomb-stones, which however are fast decaying and tumbling down. The inscriptions in granite are almost effaced by time, and those on plaster have all tumbled away. The names on marble plates have lasted by far the best. One of the tomb-stones of 1821 must have been moved into this Cemetery from the former one where the flagstaff is now.

The license fund had been established to pay the police and other similar local charges. The Sultan and Tumongong were to be paid partly by allowances and partly by the half of the port dues. When those duties were foregone they had a claim on other revenues and were paid one-third of the license fund, but in December, 1822, these were commuted with them for $500 a month. The sums intended for public buildings were paid as compensation for the houses improperly allowed by Colonel Farquhar to be built on the north bank of the river, which had been reserved by Raffles for the Residency house, Church, Police Office and other public buildings; and after the erection of these buildings the local revenue would have been sufficient to meet the expenses if the compensation had not been paid, but now this could not be done during this year. In Mr. Braddell's Notes is this memorandum of the expenses:—

6th Feb., 1819 to 30 April, 1820	Rs. 188,244
May, 1820 to 30 April, 1821	105,954
1821 to 1822	103,343

The following letter was written to the Resident on 4th February by the Governor's Secretary:—

"I have the directions of the Lieutenant-Governor to request you will take immediate measures for preventing the Chinese from continuing the practice of letting off fire works at the Kramat you have allowed to be erected on the Government hill. He regrets exceedingly that any such establishment should have been permitted by you, on a spot so close to the site which has been set apart for the residence of the chief authority, and he trusts you will see the propriety of causing the discontinuance of the nuisance. The Lieutenant-Governor desires me to state that he was disturbed during the whole of last night by the nuisance complained of. I am at the same time directed to request you will cause the removal of the Chinese moveable temple and lights from the great tree near the lines and which is included within the space proposed to be reserved for the Church."

On the 18th February, the Goa Island signal post was directed to be removed to St. John's Island, which was cleared for the flagstaff station, and might afterwards be required for a lighthouse. Goa Island is to the eastward of St. John's.

The first sale of lands on the Salat road, south of Scott's Hill, in lots of 50 to 200 acres for cultivation, was made on the 23rd February.

In February, the committee (Messrs. Davis, Bonham and Johnston) on the subject of the town, spoken of in the last chapter, was dissolved with the warm thanks of Raffles, and their duties were made over to the first Magistrates, who were then appointed. Sir Stamford nominated them under Regulation No. 3 of 1823, by which they had the same powers as Justices of the Peace in England. The commission ran thus, after setting out the title of Sir Stamford and the authority under which it was issued: "And I do hereby order, require, and command all persons now resident or who may hereafter come within the jurisdiction of Singapore to show due respect and obedience to A. L. Johnston, John Argyle Maxwell [merchants], David S. Napier [Napier and Scott], A. F. Morgan, John Purvis, Alexander Guthrie, Graham Mackenzie [merchants], William Montgomerie [the Residency Assistant Surgeon], Charles Scott [Napier and Scott], John Morgan [merchant], Christopher Rideout Read [A. L. Johnston & Co.], Andrew Hay [A. L. Johnston & Co.], in the execution of the duties of their office accordingly." The explanations in the brackets are, of course, inserted now. These gentlemen were appointed for the year 1823, and the Resident had authority to appoint others annually on the 1st of January in each year; the commission was to remain in force until the establishment of a regular Court of Judicature.

Two of these Magistrates were to sit with the Resident in Court, to decide in civil and criminal cases, and two were to act in rotation each week for the minor duties of this office. Juries were to consist either of five Europeans, or four Europeans and three respectable natives. The Resident's court was to assemble once a week; the Magistrate's twice, but their office was to be open daily. Gambling and cock-fighting were strictly prohibited.

On the 11th March, Colonel Farquhar was severely stabbed by an Arab named Syed Yassin, who ran amok. On that morning, Syed Omar, who has been spoken of before, had sued Syed Yassin for the value of some goods he had sold to him; for Syed Yassin was a native of Pahang and traded between there and Singapore. Colonel Farquhar gave judgment for Syed Omar for $1,400, and Syed Yassin said he had not the money to pay. Syed Omar replied that he had the money, but would not pay, and Colonel Farquhar said that he must either pay, or give proper security, or go to jail, for imprisonment for debt was, of course, then in force.

The imprisonment of a Syed (or Holy man) was an insult to a descendant of the Prophet which could not be wiped out, as Syed Yassin thought, and he planned his revenge, as we shall see, in an artful way. He was taken to the jail, which was near the present

Public Offices by the river side, near the mouth of the river, about two o'clock, and no one thought of searching him; but he had hidden his kris inside his coat. About five o'clock he asked Mr. Fred. James Bernard, the Magistrate, to allow him to see Syed Omar, and try to prevail on him to give him time to pay. Syed Omar lived in High Street, on the same side as the present Court House, and Mr. Alexander Guthrie lived opposite in a house in a compound on the other side of the road, behind where the Hotel de l'Europe is now. Mr. Bernard allowed it, and sent a Hindoo peon in charge of him, for which he was afterwards blamed by Sir Stamford.

It was getting dark when Syed Yassin entered the compound of Syed Omar's house to kill him. The peon stopped at the outer gate, and when Syed Omar saw Syed Yassin coming in, he guessed his intention from his countenance, and ran out of the back door and along the river to Colonel Farquhar's house, which was near where the present Cricket Pavilion is, and told him that Syed Yassin had rushed at him at his house with a drawn kris. Colonel Farquhar, who was certainly a brave man, took up his stick, and went out to Syed Omar's house. In the meantime, the peon finding that Syed Yassin did not come out, called to him to come away, as it was getting dark; and Syed Yassin went to the gate and stabbed the peon, who fell down dead at his feet. He then went back again into the house to look for Syed Omar, but did not find him as he had run to the Colonel's.

Just at this time Abdulla, the Moonshi, was on his way to Mr. John Morgan's house to give him a lesson in Malay, and he met the Colonel and his son Andrew and Captain Davis who commanded the Sepoys, who was followed by four of his men with their muskets, and another Sepoy carrying a pole. The Colonel asked Abdulla where he was going; and then said he had better not go to Mr. Morgan's, as there was a man running amok at Syed Omar's house; so Abdulla went with the party. They all went into the compound, in the centre of which, in the front of the house, was the usual square place, where natives used to sit and talk, called the *balei*. The Colonel walked round the compound and into the house several times, but saw no one; for the murderer when he saw them approaching, had hidden under the *balei*, which was in the dark, being surrounded by mangosteen trees.

Colonel Farquhar walked away from the house for some little distance (as far as the bridge, where Elgin bridge is now) and then he went back to the house. When he reached the centre of the lawn he went up to the *balei* and pushed about with his stick underneath it, when Syed Yassin suddenly made a crouching spring at him and stabbed him in the chest, the blood from the wound quickly covering his coat and shirt. Abdulla and Andrew Farquhar ran up and supported him, and the latter having a sword in his hand cut Syed Yassin's mouth right through to his ear, and the Sepoys seeing this thrust him through with their bayonets. Captain Davis rushed off to the Sepoy Lines, near where the Cathedral is now, and soon afterwards returned with the Sepoys, without uniforms, some with only a cloth on, but all carrying their arms in their hands, and dragging several cannon which were loaded and primed and drawn up opposite the Tumongong's fence which was higher up the river.

The Colonel could not walk from loss of blood, so his son and Abdulla, and the Sepoy who had carried the pole, supported him into Mr. Guthrie's house opposite, and laid him on a sofa. Dr. Montgomerie soon came running in; he examined the wound, and told the Colonel's daughters that it was not very serious, as it was luckily not more than a bad flesh wound, so he bound it up, and told the people, who were in a great consternation, that it was not so serious as had been thought. A crowd of Europeans and Natives had assembled round Syed Omar's house. There was no moon that evening, and the occurrence happening after dark, the natives brought torches and candles, and very few persons knowing what the cause of the disturbance was, hastened to the place, numbers from the other side of the river coming across it. Not a single Malay was to be seen, as they had all been chased away by the Sepoys.

The general impression among the Europeans was that the Tumongong's followers had stabbed the Resident, and in order to understand what followed, we must remember that the Settlement was only just four years old, and there was a very small number of Europeans in the midst of a native community of some ten thousand persons, and that it occurred, suddenly, after dark. Sir Stamford Raffles came in his carriage, and in great haste ran into the Colonel's house, and finding that he was not killed, as he had been told he was, took up a candle and went to see the body of Syed Yassin.

Just at this time, a person going with a torch into Syed Omar's compound, stumbled over the dead body of the Hindoo peon, and then a fresh hubbub arose. Sir Stamford, who seems to have been (as Mr. Thomson remarks in his book) the only person who kept his wits about him, asked who Syed Yassin was, but his body by this time was so cut about by the infuriated people that it could not be recognised. Captain Davis had laid the guns on the Tumongong's quarters, but the Malays had all run away across the river, and he asked Raffles to let him fire into the kampong, but Sir Stamford told him to wait until he found out what it was all about. Mr. Bernard came up then, and when he saw the dead peon's body he remembered that he had sent him with Syed Yassin; and the other body was recognised as that of the Syed. It soon became clear that it was Syed Yassin that had stabbed Colonel Farquhar and not the Tumongong's people, and so things quieted down. When the people had cleared away, they carried the Colonel in a carriage to his own house, and Raffles ordered Captain Davis to take back the cannons and the Sepoys to the cantonment. Four of the convicts came and tied a rope to Syed Yassin's feet, and dragged the corpse to the centre of the plain. Raffles then ordered a blacksmith to be called, and when he came with three others, he scored on the sand a thing in the shape of a box, to be made of iron bars like a cage, about the height of a man, and said it must be made that night and brought by seven in the morning.

The next morning Sir Stamford went to the Colonel's house, and the Sultan and Tumongong and their chiefs came, and all the Europeans. The natives were called, and it was decided that the corpse should be sent round the town, in a buffalo cart, and the gong beaten to tell the people what he had done; and after that hung up in the iron cage at Tanjong Malang now known as Teluk Ayer point, on a mast; which was done, and it remained there for a fortnight. On the 14th March, Raffles published a proclamation stating that the Sultan in the name of the Malays had requested pardon of the King of England and the body was allowed to be removed, but all must take notice that amokers would be hung in chains and their bodies given to the winds. The body was then buried at Tanjong Paggar, where the result of the proceedings was (which Sir Stamford did not anticipate) that it became a place of pilgrimage, and Syed Yassin was considered a great saint, because the holy Syed had only killed a Fakir (the Hindoo) and wounded a Nazarene (Colonel Farquhar).

By one of those coincidences that all experience occasionally, the following passage was found in a little book that reached Singapore after the first sheets of this book were in the press. It is a little book published by Dent & Co., London, in 1901, called *The Story of Perugia,* written by Margaret Symons and Lina Duff Gordon, as one of the guide books to the old towns of Umbria :—"The street which runs from the *Piazza* down into the *Via dei Priori* is still called the *Via Della Gabbia* because of the large iron cage which used to hang above it from the upper windows of the palace. In this cage the Perugians were want to imprison thieves and other malefactors. * * * In 1442 we read of a sacrilegious robber, 'who was put into a round cage, and with a cord he was dragged up into a corner wall of the Palace of the Podesta, and there he remained for two days, and in the night he was put into prison; and in the loggia of that palace twelve sacks of the stolen goods were stored and round that cage there was a garland of false keys * * * and on the 28th January the said Angelo was again put back into the cage at midday, and it was very cold and there was much snow, and he remained there till the first day of February, both night and day, and that same day he was brought out dead and laid upon his bier on the Piazza, and he was buried in the passage of San Lorenzo which leads into the cloister.' " An interesting story of medieval times in the old-world town of Italy, and if it was not a custom that was known in other towns, is it possible that Sir Stamford may have heard of the cage at Perugia ?

This was the first *amok* we have any record of here. They are now rare, although in former times, and not very long ago, they were frequent enough. Mr. Thomson mentions the cases of two of the Dutch Governors of Bencoolen, and a Dutch Admiral, and of Lord Mayo at the Andamans, and Chief Justice Norman at Calcutta, as remarkable instances of what we know as amok, but the last two were rather murders of an individual than amok.

Mr. John Crawfurd says that the word in which the k at the end is mute and is pronounced by the Malays *amo,* means a desperate and furious charge or onset, either of an individual or body of men. The charge of the English at Waterloo, or the French over the bridge at Lodi would be considered, he says, by a Malay as illustrious *pengamoks.* Dr. Johnson in his Dictionary says he "knows not from what derivation the word is made to mean to run madly and attack all he meets." Crawfurd says it is the result of a sudden and violent emotion wholly unpremeditated, and is most frequent among the Bugis (4 Logan's Journal, 184). There is a paper on the subject (3 Logan's Journal, 532) by Dr. Oxley, who had great experience. He says that there are instances which require discrimination to prevent irresponsible persons suffering the penalty of the injured law. And that he had found cases where the monomaniac was suffering from some gastric disease or troublesome ulcer, and these fearful ebullitions broke out on some exacerbation of the disorder. Their friends said they generally appeared melancholy a few days before the outbreak; and that monomania among the Malays almost invariably took this terrible form. He said three-fourths of the cases he had seen were by Bugis. There is another paper in the same volume without the writer's name (p. 463) in which the amok is said to be the act of a monomaniac, and the mental condition is quite inconsistent with a regard for consequences; the pleasures of life have no attractions, and its pains no dread; the man being reduced to the gloomy despair and inward rage of the *pengamok.**

The first step therefore for the suppression of amoks was the abolition of the habit of carrying weapons by causing the Malays to trust for protection to the Government, for there was no security that if subjected to misfortune, insult, or oppression, an amok would not result. In those days when a Malay of Singapore could not go in his boat to the back of the island, to Johore or over to Siak, without a risk of being robbed and killed by pirates, he could not go unarmed; and of a hundred murders in Singapore in those days very few of the perpetrators were apprehended. The same article questions whether justice which seems to closely resemble revenge is advisable, and Mr. Thomson speaking of the hanging of Syed Yassin's body in the cage, expresses the same opinion. The case that is often mentioned on this subject occurred in Penang, and the judgment has been mentioned lately in a book on matters connected with the Native States. As the judgment of Sir William Norris is given in full in the same volume of Logan's Journal, it may be interesting to reprint it here. It reads somewhat curiously half-a-century later.

The case occurred on the 8th July, 1846, when a respectable house-builder in Penang ran amok in Chuliah Street and Penang Road, and killed an old Hindu woman, a Kling man, a Chinese boy and a Kling girl of three years old in the arms of her father, and wounded two Hindus, three Klings, and two Chinese, only two of whom survived. The witnesses said that after the recent loss of his wife and child he would not drink or smoke, and they thought he was mad. He said to the jury that he did not know what he was about, but as the jury said he had committed so many murders he supposed it must have been so. The amok took place on the 8th, the trial on the 13th, and the execution on the 15th July; all within eight days. It is said that amoks, which had been frequent in Penang, became almost unknown there afterwards, so that if one of the principal objects of punishment is the prevention of crime by others, it succeeded in its object. Still it seems somewhat pitiful in the light of Dr. Oxley and Mr. Thomson's remarks and the prisoner's statement.

---

* *Amok*; *mengamo'* to run amuck; *pengamo'* the person who runs amuck.

It is quite certain, however, that the interpreter could never have interpreted such a homily, and that the prisoner and the natives in Court never understood what it was all about*; and if the days for such a sermon from the Bench have not yet passed away, they are certain do so in the light of advancing intelligence.

The judgment was as follows :—

"Sunan, you stand convicted on the clearest evidence of the wilful murder of Pakir Sah on Wednesday last and it appears that on the same occasion you stabbed no less than ten other unfortunate persons, only two of whom are at present surviving. It now becomes my duty to pass upon you the last sentence of the law. I can scarcely call it a painful duty, for the blood of your innocent victims cries aloud for vengeance and both justice and humanity would be shocked were you permitted to escape the infamy of a public execution. God Almighty alone, the great 'searcher of hearts,' can tell precisely what passed in that wretched heart of yours before and at the time when you committed these atrocious deeds ; nor is it necessary for the ends of justice that we should perfectly comprehend the morbid views and turbulent passions by which you must have been actuated. It is enough for us to know that you, like all other murderers, 'had not the fear of God before your eyes,' and that you acted 'of malice afore-thought and by the instigation of the devil' himself, who was 'a murderer from the beginning.' But all the atrocities you have committed are of a peculiar character and such as are never perpetrated by Christians, Hindoos, Chinese, or any other class than Mahomedans, especially Malays, among whom they are frightfully common, and may therefore be justly branded by way of infamous distinction, as *Mahomedan Murders*. I think it right, therefore, seeing so great a concourse of Mahomedans in and about the Court, to take this opportunity of endeavouring to disabuse their minds and your own of any false notions of courage, heroism, or self devotion which Mahomedans possibly, but Mahomedans alone of all mankind, can ever attach to such base, cowardly and brutal murders ; notions which none but the devil himself, 'the father of lies,' could ever have inspired. But if such false. execrable and dangerous delusions really are entertained by any man or body of men whatever, it may be as well to show from the gloomy workings of your mind, so far as circumstances have revealed them, that not a particle of manly courage or heroism could have animated you, or can ever animate any man who lifts his cowardly hand against helpless women and children. You had lately, it seems, been greatly afflicted by the sudden deaths of your wife and only child, and God forbid that I should needlessly harrow up your feelings by reverting to the subject. I do so merely because it serves in some degree to explain the dreadful tragedy for which you are now about to answer with your life. Unable or unwilling to submit with patience to the affliction with which it had pleased God to visit you, you abandoned yourself to discontent and despair, until shortly before the bloody transaction, when you went to the mosque to pray !!—to pray to whom or to what? Not to senseless Idols of wood or stone which Christians and Mahomedans equally abominate—but to the one omniscient, almighty, and all merciful God in whom alone Christians and Mahomedans profess to believe ! But in what spirit did you pray, if you prayed at all? Did you pray for resignation or ability to 'humble yourself under the mighty hand of God'? Impossible. You may have gone to curse in your heart and gnash with your teeth, but certainly not to pray, whatever unmeaning sentences of the Koran may have issued from your lips. Doubtless you entered the Mosque with a heart full of haughty pride, anger and rebellion against your Maker, and no wonder that you sallied forth again overflowing with hatred and malice against your innocent fellow-creatures ; no wonder that, when thus abandoned to the devil, you stabbed with equal cruelty, cowardice and ferocity, unarmed and helpless men, women and children, who had never injured, never known, probably never seen you before.

---

* There is an old story that in Malacca after a long moral discourse by the Judge, it was interpreted as "*Suda Sala, gantong besok*" (you are guilty, and will be hung to-morrow). The Judge asked the interpreter whether he had explained it all. and being told that it was all right, seemed very much surprised at the brevity of the Malay language.

Such are the murders which Mahomedans alone have been found capable of committing. Not that I mean to brand Mahomedans in general as worse than all other men, far from it; I believe there are many good men among them,— as good as men can be who are ignorant of the only true religion. I merely state the fact that such atrocities disgrace no other creed, let the Mahomedans account for the fact as they may. But whatever may be the true explanation; whether these fiendish excesses are the result of fanaticism, superstition, overweening pride or ungovernable rage, or, which is probable, of all combined, public justice demands that the perpetrators should be visited with the severest and most disgraceful punishment which the law can inflict.

The sentence of the Court therefore is, that you, Sunan, be remanded to the place from whence you came, and that on the morning of Wednesday next you be drawn from thence on a hurdle to the place of execution, and there hanged by the neck until you are dead. Your body will then be handed over to the surgeons for dissection. and your mangled limbs. instead of being restored to your friends for decent interment, will be cast into the sea, thrown into a ditch, or scattered on the earth at the discretion of the Sheriff. And may God Almighty have mercy on your miserable soul!"

Among some very old papers collected by Mr. Braddell is a translation of the proceedings held in Dutch on the trial for amok at Malacca in 1803 of a man called Tjin Tjay, described as a slave. It is mentioned here to show how the Dutch dealt with the case. The prisoner said he was despairing, so he took a parang and cut at the Chinese woman and her children, and appeared very indifferent to the proceedings. The record shows that the trial was held before "De Groot, President, and other members of the College of Justice." The English had been in possession of Malacca since 1795, but the law of Holland continued to be administered, and was carried on as usual by the Dutch authorities in the name of their High Mightinesses (see Newbold p. 126 and 151). In a despatch by Mr. Crawfurd at Singapore, written on 13th November, 1824, he spoke of this, and said "Under our administration at Malacca which lasted upwards of twenty years matters were kept as much Dutch as possible, Dutch laws having been strictly administered by the same Court of Justice of three judges with salaries of 60 to 100 guilders a piece!" The note of exclamation is Mr. Crawfurd's.

The record ends, "Wherefore it is resolved that the prisoner be carried to the place of execution, and there being delivered over to the executioner he be bound to a cross and suffer until death, and that afterwards his body be taken down and exposed as a prey to the birds of the air." This was confirmed six days afterwards at an Extraordinary Meeting of the Court "on the part of their High Mightinesses the States" which recommended that the sentence be addressed to Colonel Taylor, who was the English Resident who was succeeded by Major Farquhar.

CHAPTER X.

1823—*Continued.*

ON the 14th March, a location was given to the Sultan as follows:—
To the east of the European town and lying between Rochore
river and the sea; measuring in front along Beach Road 731 feet; at
back of Chuliah Campong and along Rochore river about 1,200 feet; in
depth from Beach Road to Rochore river 2,100 feet. Estimated to
contain 56 acres. To the Tumongong was allotted a space of 6,000
feet along the Beach from Tanjong Pagar to Teluk Blangah and 1,200
feet deep. Estimated to contain 200 acres.

On the 1st April, a meeting was held about the founding of the
building to be called "The Institution," which afterwards was called
the Raffles Institution. The whole subject is dealt with in a subsequent
chapter.

In April, in consequence of the scarcity of labour, the local convicts
were ordered to work on the roads.

On the 1st day of May, Sir Stamford and Colonel Farquhar fell
out, and the former deposed the Resident from his authority. It seems
that the Colonel understood that the accounts were to be sent by him
direct to Bengal, instead of to Bencoolen as had been the case. To
this Raffles objected, and the Resident finding the control of Raffles
unpleasant, became contumacious, and called upon Raffles, who was
Lieutenant-Governor, to shew his authority for sitting in the Court of
Justice, and refused to obey his orders. Raffles could not stand this,
and took over charge of the civil duties of the station himself. Mr.
Braddell in a pencil note says that Colonel Farquhar was summarily
removed by an official notification intimating that his resignation, sent
in as far back as 23rd October, 1820, had been accepted. In a copy
of a letter in Mr. Guthrie's letter book, addressed to his partner,
Captain Harrington, at Malacca, dated 2nd May, Mr. Guthrie said that
on the previous day Colonel Farquhar had been deposed by Sir Stamford; he gave no reason, as Harrington was probably aware of what
had been going on. The Resident had a party led by Mr. Queiros,
who was agent for Palmer & Co. of Calcutta, the agents of the Dutch,
against whose authority Raffles' most strenuous opposition had been
carried on for years. On 23rd June, in a despatch to Calcutta, Raffles
said: "It is impossible not to respect Mr. Palmer as an individual, but
it is to be recollected that he is now the avowed agent of the Netherlands Government in these seas, and that it is very possible his mercantile interests may frequently be at variance with the principles which
an enlightened government may wish to adopt in its dependencies."

On the 11th January Raffles had written to Calcutta that he
requested to be relieved on account of bad health, but that if the two
offices of Resident at Singapore and Governor General's Agent in

Eastern Seas were to be united, he would not leave Singapore till he could transfer charge to a more competent successor than Lieutenant-Colonel Farquhar, in whom he had little confidence. On the 27th January he wrote again, saying that he was anxious to make arrangements for his successor. " I feel myself called upon to state in general terms that I consider Colonel Farquhar to be totally unequal to the charge of so important and peculiar a charge as that of Singapore has now become. However competent that officer may have been for the charge in the earlier stage of the Settlement, it is obvious that it has for some time past grown beyond his management, and that he neither entertains such general views nor can enter upon those principles of general government which now mark the character of the British Indian Administration. Having passed nearly the whole of his public life in the Dutch Settlement of Malacca his views are confined to his experience at that place, where the duties were insignificant, and where, from long neglect of the higher authorities, little like regular government existed except in the forms of a Dutch Court and the partial continuance of regulations established in the plenitude of the Dutch monopoly. The circumstances of Singapore are perfectly incompatible with these, and the consequence is confusion and general dissatisfaction. The Malay connection in which Lieut -Col. Farquhar is involved, and the general weakness of his administration afford an opening for such an undue combination of peculiar interests, as not only to impede the progress of order and regularity, but may lay the foundation of future inconvenience which it may hereafter be difficult to overcome." The letter then goes on to complain that under the weak and inconsistent rule of Colonel Farquhar, favouritism and irregularities were daily arising and, now that the Settlement was growing larger, would be inconvenient if not checked, and therefore asked that on his (Raffles) approaching departure a more competent officer should be appointed to succeed as Resident. He added that he had formerly said that he might remain in the East till 1822, but that time had passed and there was still no prospect of any final arrangement being arrived at in England about Singapore. The result was that Mr. John Crawfurd was appointed Resident, and Singapore was placed directly under Bengal.

In a letter written at Bencoolen in November (Memoirs, page 555) Raffles wrote, " I had only one object in view, the interests of Singapore, and if a brother had been opposed to them I must have acted as I did towards Colonel Farquhar, for whom I ever had, and still retain a warm personal affection and regard. I upheld him as long as I could, and many were the sacrifices I made to prevent a rupture. In Mr. Boulger's book at page 357 will be found a long letter by Raffles to the Court of Directors on the subject.

Captain Davis married one of the daughters of Colonel Farquhar; Mr. Bernard married another; and Mr. W. R. George, who was so very well known in Singapore, and died here in 1873, at the age of 77 years, married another. Major-General Farquhar died in Perth, in Scotland, on the 13th May, 1839, in his sixty-ninth year.

The system of slavery and slave-debtors prevailed in Singapore and Malacca to some extent at this time. The former was abolished by Raffles in 1823; who carried into effect the provisions of the Act of Parliament for the abolition of slavery, and considerably modified the system of slave-debtors. The claim of the creditor was in no case to be considered to exceed the services of the debtor for a period of five years, the debt being considered as worked out at the rate of one-fifth each year. The Magistrates made a presentment against the whole system of slave-master and slave-debtors on the 7th March, and Raffles acted upon it at once, the regulation being dated 1st May, 1823. It may be found at length in the appendix to Sir Stamford's Memoirs. The gaming licenses were stopped in May, the Magistrates having in a memorial of the 9th April strongly objected to their continuance. On the 17th May, $250 were given to the Rev. Mr. Thompson from the License Fund towards building a Malay Chapel.

In May the Java Government renewed its complaints and carried on a correspondence with the British Indian Government in such a tone that that authority declined entering further into the matter. The Dutch complained that Raffles had allowed the British flag to be hoisted on the mainland at Johore. Sir Stamford had done so on the requisition of the natives because Tunku Jaffar in the name of Sultan Abdul Rahman, at the instigation of the Dutch, had sent a party to take possession of the mainland of Johore. Without the English influence Sultan Hoossain would have been quite unable to hold the mainland, and Raffles thought it politic to allow its nominal use. The Calcutta Government in a letter dated 21st May, 1824, did not approve of this, but said that the subsequent measures of the Dutch Government deprived them of all right to apology. With the light of future events it is evident that Raffles did a very wise thing. The Dutch got possession of the regalia of Johore when the Governor of Malacca and a Dutch gentleman of influence went to Pulo Peningat, and after trying persuasion in vain, are said to have marched a body of soldiers with loaded arms into the chamber of Tunku Putri, and to have taken the regalia by actual force.

In June, Raffles was making preparations for leaving Singapore for the last time, and he made a fresh agreement with the Sultan and Tumongong. The Sultan was to receive $1,500, and the Tumongong $800, monthly. The whole island of Singapore (with the exception of the land appropriated to the chiefs) and the islands immediately adjacent to be at the entire disposal of the British. The following is a translation of the arrangement, the Straits Government printed copy of which says it has no date but was concluded about the beginning of June. In a despatch from Calcutta of 16th August, 1823, it speaks of the convention of 7th June, 1823, which unquestionably refers to this document and a letter of Raffles also mentions that date. The original counterpart has been found in Johore. It is in Malay only, has no date, and is on one side of a large piece of foolscap paper:—

Their Highnesses the Sultan and Tumongong having solicited that the Lieutenant Governor would, previous to his departure, lay down such general rules for their guidance as may be most conducive to the general interests of Singapore, and at the same time serve to define the rights of all parties, that there may be no dispute hereafter: The following rules are laid down by the Lieutenant-Governor, and concurred in by their Highnesses, to form the basis of the good understanding to be maintained in future:—

1st. In order to contribute to the personal comfort and respectability of their Highnesses, and at the same time to afford them an ample and liberal compensation for any advantage either expected or foregone by them, on account of port duties, tribute, or profits on monopolies, which are found to be inconsistent, and at variance with the principles maintained by the British Government, their Highnesses are, from the 1st instant, to receive a monthly payment, His Highness the Sultan of 1,500 *dollars, and His Highness the Tumongong 800 dollars per month, on the following conditions:—

2nd. Their Highnesses to forego all right and claim to the monopoly of Kranjee and Baloo wood within Singapore, and the islets immediately adjacent, as well as all claims to presents and customs upon Chinese junks and Chinese generally coming and going.

3rd. With the exception of the land appropriated to their Highnesses for their respective establishments, all land within the island of Singapore, and islands immediately adjacent, to be at the entire disposal of the British Government.

4th. As a further accommodation to their Highnesses, the Resident will be authorized to advance such further sums of money as may be sufficient for the completion of a respectable mosque near the dwelling of His Highness the Sultan, and also to assist His Highness the Tumongong in removing and establishing himself on the ground recently selected by him.

5th. Under these arrangements their Highnesses will be relieved from further personal attendance at the court on every Monday, but they will always be entitled to a seat on the bench, and to all due respect when they think proper to attend.

6th. In all cases regarding the ceremonies of religion, and marriages, and the rules of inheritance, the laws and customs of the Malays will be respected, where they shall not be contrary to reason, justice, or humanity. In all other cases the laws of the British authority will be enforced with due consideration to the usages and habits of the people.

7th. The British Government do not interfere at present in the local arrangement of the countries and islands subject to their Highnesses' authority, beyond Singapore and its adjacent islets, further than to afford them general protection as heretofore.

Chop of the Sultan.   T. S. RAFFLES.
Chop of the Tumungong.

The expense of the Civil Establishment when Sir Stamford left, amounted to $3,500 a month; the Resident, Mr. Crawfurd, drawing $1,400 (being salary $750, table allowance $500, and allowance for house rent $150); Mr. Bonham, the Assistant Resident, $300; Captain Flint, R.N., Master Attendant, $300; the Police Department, $450; the acting Chaplain, $100; Lieutenant Jackson for the Surveying Department, $200, which, however, was to include the establishment; and the Botanical Gardens $60; the rest was for clerks, boatmen and interpreters. In June, Raffles applied for a vessel to cruise against pirates, whose attacks on vessels he described as extremely frequent, and affording serious obstacles to native trade with Singapore.

During his last visit to Singapore, Sir Stamford had appointed committees of merchants and officials for various purposes, and had set the example of entrusting the un-official residents with a degree of power commensurate with their position in the community. In March, 1823, he wrote to Bengal: "I am satisfied that nothing has tended more to the discomfort and constant jarrings which have hitherto occurred in our remote settlements, than the policy which has dictated the exclusion of the British merchants from all share, much less credit, in the domestic regulations of the settlement, of which they are frequently its most important members." Words on which much might be said, in commenting on the history of later years, and attention to which by men, not similarly gifted, in later times, might have saved a good deal of irritation on both sides, and materially advanced the interests of the place.

On Sir Stamford's departure, the following address was presented to him by the entire mercantile community, through Mr. Crawfurd:—

"To Sir T. S. Raffles, Lieutenant-Governor of Fort Marlborough.

"Honourable Sir, The period of your approaching and final departure is one of peculiar interest to the commercial community of this place, and we, the undersigned, members of it, gladly seize the opportunity which it affords us of indulging in the expression of those feelings towards your person, which the occasion is so well calculated to excite.

"At such a moment, we cannot be suspected of panegyric, when we advert to the distinguished advantages which the commercial interests of our nation at large, and ourselves more specially, have derived from your personal exertions. To your unwearied zeal, your vigilance, and your comprehensive views, we owe at once the foundation and maintenance of a Settlement unparalleled for the liberality of the principles on which it has been established; principles, the operation of which has converted, in a period short beyond all example, a haunt of pirates into the abode of enterprize, security and opulence.

"While we acknowledge our own peculiar obligations to you, we reflect at the same time with pride and satisfaction upon the active and beneficent means by which you have promoted and patronized the diffusion of intellectual and moral improvement, and we anticipate, with confidence, their happy influence in advancing the course of humanity and civilization.

"We cannot take leave of the author of so many benefits without emotion, or without expressing our sorrow for the loss of his protection and his society. Accept, Sir, we beseech you, without distinction of tribe or nation, the expression of our sincere respect and esteem, and be assured of the deep interest we shall ever take in your own prosperity, as well as in the happiness of those who are most tenderly related to you.

> "We remain, with the deepest respect,
> "Your most obedient Servants,
> (Signed by the European and Native
> Merchants of Singapore).

Singapore, June 5th, 1823.

To which Sir Stamford sent the following reply:—

"Gentlemen,—Mr. Crawfurd has delivered to me the address, which you have so kindly and delicately drawn up on the occasion of my departure.

"Under the peculiar circumstances of my personal connection with the establishment of Singapore, it is impossible to suppose that I can be indifferent to any of its interests, far less to its commercial interests, of which I consider you to be the representatives.

"It has happily been consistent with the policy of Great Britain, and accordant with the principles of the East India Company, that Singapore should be established as a Free Port; that no sinister, no sordid view, no considerations either of political importance or pecuniary advantage, should interfere with the broad and liberal principles on which the British interests have been established. Monopoly and exclusive privileges, against which public opinion has long raised its voice, are here unknown, and while the Free Port of Singapore is allowed to continue and prosper, as it hitherto has done, the policy and liberality of the East India Company, by whom the Settlement was founded, and under whose protection and control it is still administered, can never be disputed.

"That Singapore will long and always remain a Free Port, and that no taxes on trade or industry will be established to check its future rise and prosperity, I can have no doubt. I am justified in saying thus much, on the authority of the Supreme Government of India, and on the authority of those who are most likely to have weight in the councils of our nation at home.

"For the public and peculiar mark of respect, which you, Gentlemen, have been desirous of shewing me on the occasion of my departure from the Settlement, I beg that you will accept my most sincere thanks. I know the feeling which dictated it, I acknowledge the delicacy with which it has been conveyed, and I prize most highly the gratifying terms to me personally in which it has been expressed.

"During my residence among you, it has afforded me the highest satisfaction to witness the prudence, the regularity, the honourable character of your proceedings, and when I quit you for other lands, I shall be proud to bear testimony in your favour, not only as your due, but as the best proof of the sure and certain result which the adoption of liberal and enlightened principles on the part of Government must always ensure.

"There are some among you, Gentlemen, who had to encounter difficulties on the first establishment of the freedom of the Port, and against whom party spirit and its concomitant, partial judgment, was allowed for a time to operate. In the commanding station in which my public duty has placed me, I have had an opportunity of, in a great measure, investigating and determining the merits of the case, and the result renders it a duty on my part, and which I perform which much satisfaction, to express my most unqualified approbation of the honourable principles which actuated the merchants of Singapore on that occasion.

"I am not aware, Gentlemen, that I have done any of you a favour, that is to say, that I have done to any man amongst you, that which I would not have done to his neighbour, or more than what my duty required of me, acting, as I have done, on the liberal and enlightened principles authorized by my superiors. My best endeavours have not been wanting to establish such principles, and to sketch such outlines, as have appeared to me necessary for the future prosperity of the Settlement, and in doing this it has been most satisfactory to me to have found in you that ready concurrence, and at all times that steady support, which was essential to my government and authority.

"May you, Gentlemen, English and Native, and as the language of your address expresses it, without class or distinction, long continue in the honourable and distinguished course which you have so happily commenced, and may the principles which you respect and act upon, long distinguish you among the merchants of the East.

"I can never forget that the Singapore Institution could not have been founded without your aid. The liberal manner in which you came forward, to spare from your hard earnings so large a portion for the improvement and civilization of the surrounding tribes, and in the furtherance of general knowledge and science would at once stamp the character of the Singapore merchant, even if it did not daily come forward on more ostensible occasions.

"I am grateful for the kind expression of your personal regards to me, and those who may be dear to me; and, in return, beg you will accept my most sincere and heartfelt wishes for your health, comfort, and prosperity.

"I have the honour to be,
"Gentlemen,
"Yours most faithfully,
T. S. RAFFLES."

Singapore, June 9th, 1823.

The following resolutions of the Bengal Government show the reason for placing Singapore under that government, to which it was transferred from Bencoolen :—

Fort William, 29th March, 1823.

"The first question for consideration is the nature of the control to be exercised henceforward over the affairs of Singapore, and the proceedings of the local Resident. The arrangement under which that trust was vested in the Lieutenant-Governor of Fort Marlborough originated in the circumstances under which the settlement was founded, and the temporary convenience resulting from it will cease with the relinquishment of the charge by Sir Stamford Raffles, under whose immediate direction the settlement was established, and whose personal superintendence of it, in its early stage, therefore possessed a peculiar value.

"It would seem more naturally to fall within the range of the Government of Penang, but there are objections of a different kind to that arrangement. There is a general impression that the prosperity of Singapore must in a great degree be attended with a proportionate deterioration of Penang. As far as the information furnished by the records of the custom house at the latter place affords the means of judging, it would not appear that this has yet been the case; but there is no doubt that the feeling prevails among the inhabitants of both settlements generally, and without supposing that it reaches the Government, or that if it did, it would bias their conduct, there seems no such advantage to be contemplated in rendering Singapore dependent on Penang, as to justify the risk of injury to the interests of the rising establishment, from the direct or incidental consequences of such an arrangement. The system of government and the principles of commercial policy prevailing at the two settlements are moreover radically different, and it is not reasonable to expect that each could be administered under the direction of a subordinate and limited authority with equal effect.

"On the occasion of relieving Sir Stamford Raffles from the Superintendence of Singapore, the Governor-General in Council deems it an act of justice to that gentleman, to record his sense of the activity, zeal, judgment, and attention to the principles prescribed for the management of the settlement, which has marked his conduct in the execution of that duty.

"On placing Mr. Crawfurd in charge of the settlement of Singapore, you will be pleased to communicate with him fully on all points, and furnish him with such instructions as you may deem necessary for carrying into effect the orders which are now communicated to you, in reply to your several despatches relative to the affairs of that settlement."

The rest of this chapter consists of the papers referring to the arrangements Sir Stamford made for establishing the constitution he spoke of in his letters in November, 1822. The greater part of them have been preserved in Mr. Braddell's Notes, but the Proclamation was sent to the Straits Branch Asiatic Society's Journal for 1891, by the late Mr. H. A. O'Brien. He was Treasurer of the Colony and found it among some old documents in the Singapore Treasury. He was apparently, unaware that it was printed at page 66 of the Appendix to Lady Raffles' book in 1830.

PROCLAMATION.

Provision having been made by Regulations Nos. III. and VI. of 1823 for the establishment of an efficient Magistracy at Singapore and for the mode in which local Regulations having the force of Law should be enacted, and by whom such Laws should be administered, it now becomes necessary to state the principles and objects which should be kept in view in framing such Regulations, and, as far as circumstances may admit, to apprize all parties of their respective rights and duties, in order that ignorance thereof may not hereafter be pleaded on the part of any individual or class of people.

The Lieutenant-Governor is, in consequence, induced to give publicity to the following Minute containing the leading principles and objects to be attended to :—

MINUTE BY THE LIEUTENANT-GOVERNOR.

1. As the population of Singapore will necessarily consist of a mixture, in various proportions, of strangers from all parts of the world having commercial concerns at this Port, though chiefly of Chinese and Malays, it would be impracticable for any Judicial Authority to become perfectly acquainted with the Laws and Customs having the force of Law which are acknowledged in their own countries respectively by the varied classes of so mixed a population, and to administer them in such a manner as to preserve them inviolate even in the mutual intercourse of those classes severally amongst themselves, far more so when justice is to be done between the Englishman and Chinese, the Bugguese and Hindoo, and the like. On the other hand, to apply the law of Europe direct, with all its accumulated processes and penalties, to a people of whom more than nine-tenths will probably be natives of China and the Malay Archipelago, would be as repugnant to universal and natural justice as it would be inconsistent with the benevolence and liberality which has ever marked the British rule in India.

2.   Under these circumstances, nothing seems to be left but to have recourse to first principles, to use every precaution against the existence of
temptation to crime that is found consistent with the perfect liberty of those
who have no evil intentions, and when these precautions fail, to secure redress
to the injured party, when possible, and such punishment as will be most
likely to prevent a repetition of the crime, either by the party himself offending,
or by those who may be inclined to follow his example. Nothing should be endured in the Settlement, however sanctioned by the local usage of particular
tribes who resort to it, that has either a direct effect, or notoriously strong
tendency to endanger the safety or liberty of person or the security of property,
and in the same manner. no want of what are considered legal formalities in
any country should debar a person from having substantial justice rendered
to him, *so that legal and moral obligation may never be at variance.*
3.   Taking this as the fundamental principle for the Laws of the Settlement,
it may be presumed that no local Regulation would be enacted that the society
if left to themselves would not desire to see carried into effect; no public
institution or source of expense would exist of which the benefit was not obvious
to the enlightened part at least, if not to the whole body of the community, who
would therefore soon feel that the Government was not made to tyrannize over
the people, but for their protection and happiness.
4.   Under such a system of administration, it is not unreasonable to expect that
every facility would be afforded by the mass of the population to the Executive
in carrying the Laws into effect, for even the midnight robber and swindler have
no desire that their own persons or property should be liable to those evils
which they inflict on the rest of the community, and will readily join in their
suppression when other delinquents are the objects of the terrors of the
Law.
5.   In carrying such a system into effect, it ought to be fully understood
and maintained on all occasions, that while individuals are allowed to *protect*
themselves as far as possible against wrongs, the *redress* of wrongs cannot be
left to the resentment or the revenge of the parties conceiving themselves injured.
That must be done solely by Government through the instrumentality of the
Judicial and Executive Officers whom it appoints for that purpose.
6.   No one therefore being allowed to be a judge in his own case, or to
revenge his own quarrel, arms or weapons capable of inflicting instant death
as habitually worn by the Malays become unnecessary, and, by dispensing with
them, the greatest temptation to and power of doing to others the greatest and
irremediable wrong in depriving them of life is in a great measure removed.
If a man takes another's horse or cow by robbery or theft or under a mistaken
idea that he has a right to the property in question, redress can be afforded to him
as soon as he is convicted of his crime or discovers his error, but if from revenge
or under false impressions a man is suddenly excited to take the life of a fellow
creature, it is in vain that he afterwards discovers that he was misled by passion
or had been deceived by appearances. It often happens too in these countries
that a man who considers himself aggrieved by a particular individual and finding
himself in possession of a sharp weapon, attempts the life of every one he meets
indiscriminately, and without having any wrong at their hands to complain of.
It is impossible to see who may or may not be guilty of such acts of inhuman
cruelty, and therefore all should agree to lay aside the use of the weapon that is
commonly employed by persons who then transform themselves to wild beasts by
giving way to brutal passion.
7.   On the same principle, it has been found by experience that those who indulge
frequently in gaming and cock-fighting, are not only liable to engage in quarrels
with those who have won their money, but also that they are incited to acts of fraud
and robbery in order to obtain the means of amusement or of attempting to retrieve
their losses; it is therefore the duty of Government to suppress both gaming and
cock-fighting as far as possible without trespassing on the free will of private
conduct. No man should be allowed to receive any money either directly or indirectly for conducting a gaming table or cock-pit, and winners of money at such
places should be compelled to restore the amount to the losers, and should on no
account be permitted to enforce payment from those with whom they have
gambled on credit.

8.   Intoxication being a source of personal danger to the community, and the indulgence in that vice being a frequent cause of betraying those who are addicted to it to the commission of acts of dishonesty, it is the duty of a good Magistracy to throw every obstacle in the way.   In the first place the Officers of Police should be required to place in constraint any person seen in public in a state of intoxication until he becomes sober, and in the next place the vendor of intoxicating articles who supplied him with the means of inebriety, should be visited with reproof and fined, and be liable to make good the amount of any loss which the person so intoxicated can prove he suffered during his inebriety from being unable to take care of himself; the extent of this fine must necessarily be discretionary on the part of the Magistrate, depending principally on the degree of inebriety produced; it should always be of such an amount that the fear of being subject to it may be sufficient to outweigh in the mind of the vendor the temptation of profit in the sale of his goods; of course if it should appear in evidence that the individual was supplied with the means of intoxication for the purpose of taking advantage of him in that state, the object converts the simple misdemeanour into a crime according to the particular purpose contemplated, and further punishment to the guilty as well as redress to the individual injured must be awarded accordingly.   The use of spirituous liquors, though innocent in moderation, becomes vicious when indulged in to excess: the consumption may be diminished by the enhancement of price: and in this way the indulgence may be made so expensive as to be only attainable beyond the bounds of moderation by those whose means give them a station in society that induces them to be guarded in their conduct for the sake of preserving the respect of those whose eyes are turned upon them; thus, while gaming as practised by the Chinese and cock-fighting by the Malays are absolutely pernicious in every degree in which they come under public cognizance, the use of opium and spirituous liquors may be repressed by exacting a heavy tax in the way of License from the vendors.

9.   There are many important considerations that stand in the way of enacting laws against prostitution, indeed it would, in a country where concubinage is not forbidden, be difficult to draw a line between the concubine and the common prostitute; it is practicable however in some degree, and highly desirable, that the temptation to profit should not exist to induce the seduction of women into this course of life by others of their own sex; the unfortunate prostitute should be treated with compassion, but every obstacle should be thrown in the way of her service being a source of profit to any one but herself.   It should therefore be declared unlawful for any person whatever to share the hire or wages of prostitution or to derive any profit or emolument either directly or indirectly by maintaining or procuring prostitutes, as for any parent or guardian of a female or any other person to ask or receive directly or indirectly any reward for bestowing a female in prostitution, any custom, law or usage of the country in which such female or her parents or her guardians were born notwithstanding, reserving only for a jury to advise what constitutes a legal obligation on the man to support the woman thus bestowed, or in other words a contract of marriage by local usage, and what a connection of prostitution; the penalty must be here also be modified by circumstances.   It is much more criminal to induct a girl into prostitution than to facilitate her pursuit of vice after she has entered upon it as a profession.

10.   It may be necessary to make specific Regulations for the protection of the community generally against fire, both with regard to the construction of buildings, the storing of gun-powder and combustibles, the manufacture of arrack, &c., &c., the power of infringing on a neighbour's property after a fire has broken out either for the purpose of access to the means of extinguishing it or to prevent its spreading to a greater distance.

11.   Boatmen and parties offering themselves publicly for hire may also be subjected to regulation with the view of facilitating the attainment of redress when they are guilty of fraud and negligence.

12.   Weights and measures of the acknowledged standard should be accessible to all, and those used in purchases and sales ought to be in strict conformity with such standards.   Certain Magisterial Officers, therefore, should be employed to examine those used by persons who openly keep goods exposed for

sale. When found defective the person in whose behoof they are used should be liable to fine proportioned to his supposed means and the apparent degree of fraud resorted to.

13. Fraud with respect to the quality of articles is a crime more readily detected, and may be left to private prosecution. In giving redress to the individual, punishment ought to be annexed in proportion as the fraud is of an injurious nature.

14. As a great check to fraud and falsehood, a general Registry Office for all written agreements or engagements which are liable to be made the ground of dispute before a Court of Justice, should be opened for the public. Regulation should be made for the authenticity of the document in the first instance, and either party or any party interested should be entitled to a copy, paying for the same a moderate fee as a compensation for the trouble given to the Registrar and his Establishment. Precaution must of course be taken against the falsification or abstraction of such documents from the Registrar's Office. All deeds which may be so registered should have an avowed preference over one that is not so registered, unless the holder of the latter can shew a clear, distinct and satisfactory cause why he has not been able to have his deed registered and the *onus* of establishing this ought decidedly to rest on him.

15. Nuisances generally speaking may be safely left to complaint of individuals in each particular instance where the cause of nuisance is not obvious to all, or directly injurious to particular individuals, as crowding the river with vessels, &c., when it may be made subject of special regulation.

16. All house-holders should be registered and all houses numbered; auctioneers and pawnbrokers should be placed under specific regulations, and none allowed to act as such without giving security for complying with the same and taking out a license for the purpose.

17. With respect to the employment of informers, it may be observed that Magistrates must have information, but no bad passion should be elicited in the procuring of it. No temptation to lead others to vice for the sake of reward for informing, no inducement to betray confidence, and the act of giving information should be treated as a public and honourable duty.

18. Precautionary measures being taken on the above principles for preserving the peace and good order of society and removing as far as practicable the immediate temptations to crime and violence, it next becomes necessary to define what shall be considered Crimes, what lawful punishments, and how injuries shall be redressed.

19. By the constitution of England, the absolute rights of the subject are defined as follows:—

    1st. "The right of personal security; which consists in a person's legal uninterrupted enjoyment of his life, his limbs, his body, his health and his reputation."

    2nd. "The right of personal liberty; which consists in the power of locomotion, of changing situation or removing one's person to whatever place one's own inclination may direct, without imprisonment or restraint, unless by due course of Law."

    3rdly. "The right of property; which consists in the use, enjoyment and disposal of all acquisitions without any control or diminution save only by the Laws of the Land."

20. There seems no reason for denying corresponding rights to all classes of people residing under the protection of the British Flag at Singapore, the Laws of the Land being such as are or may be enacted under the provisions of Regulation No. III. of 1823, dated the 20th January last, with such others of a more general nature as may be directed by a higher Authority or which may necessarily accrue under the provisions of the Legislature and the political circumstances of the Settlement as a Dependence of Great Britain. Admitting these rights to exist, it follows that all acts by which they are invaded are wrongs, that is to say, crimes or injuries.

21. In the enactment of Laws for securing these rights, legal obligation must never supersede or take place of or be inconsistent with or more or less onerous than moral obligation. The English practice of teaching prisoners to plead not guilty, that they may thus have a chance of escaping from punishment, is incon-

sistent with this and consequently objectionable. It is indeed right and proper that the Court should inform itself of all the circumstances of a crime from witnesses as well as from the declaration of the prisoner himself. Denial is in fact an aggravation of a crime according to every idea of common sense. It disarms punishment of one of its most beneficial objects by casting a shade of doubt over its justice.

22. The sanctity of oaths should also be more upheld than in the English Courts. This may be done by never administering them except as a *dernier resort*. If they are not frequently administered, not only will their sanction be more regarded and in this way their breach be less proportionately frequent, but of necessity much more *absolutely* uncommon and consequently much more certainly visited with due punishment in all cases of evidence given before a Court of Justice.

23. The imprisonment of an unfortunate debtor at the pleasure of the creditor, by which the services of the individual are lost to all parties, seems objectionable in this Settlement, and it is considered that the rights of property may be sufficiently protected by giving to the creditor a right to the value of the debtor's services for a limited period in no case exceeding five years, and that the debtor should only be liable to imprisonment in case of fraud, and as far as may be necessary for the security of his person in the event of his not being able to find bail during the process of the Court and for the performance of the decree after judgment may be passed.

24. It is well known that the Malay race are sensibly alive to shame, and that in many instances they would prefer death to ignominy. That is a high and honourable feeling and ought to be cherished; let great care be taken to avoid all punishments which are unnecessarily degrading. Both the Malays and Chinese are a reasoning people, and though each may reason in a way peculiar to themselves and different in some respects from our own way of reasoning, this germ of civilization should not be checked. Let no man be punished without a reason assigned. Let the principles of British Law be applied not only with mildness but with a patriachal kindness and indulgent consideration for the prejudices of each tribe as far as natural justice will allow, but also with reference to their reasoning powers however weak, and that moral principle which, however often disregarded, still exists in the consciences of all men. Let the native institutions as far as regards religious ceremonies, marriage and inheritance be respected when they may not be inconsistent with justice and humanity or injurious to the peace and morals of society.

Let all men be considered equal in the eye of the law.

Let no man be banished the country without a trial by his peers or by due course of law.

Let no man be deprived of his liberty without a cause, and no man detained in confinement beyond 48 hours without a right to demand a hearing and trial according to due course of law.

Let the people have a voice through the magistracy by which their sentiments may at all times be freely expressed.

25. In fixing a scale of punishments, the first principle to be attended to is that they should be so graduated as to attach to each particular crime its due and relative punishment according to its enormity, and with regard to the nature of the punishments they should be as mild and humane as the general security of person and property will admit. Severity of punishment defeats its own end, and the laws should in all cases be so mild that no one may be deterred from prosecuting a criminal by considerations of humanity. No feeling interferes with justice in behalf of a murderer, let this crime be punished by death, and no other. Banishment is the next in order. Solitary confinement proportioned to the degree of the offence or pertinacity of the offender in his criminal course seems the least objectionable of all sorts of punishment. Disgrace may also be a form of punishment, but much caution is required in this respect lest a too frequent enforcement of the punishment destroy the feeling which can alone make it a punishment. Personal chastisement is only for the lower orders who are incapable of feeling the shame of disgrace, and may probably be had recourse to in cases of wilful perjury where the falsehood of the witness is palpable and his object particularly mischievous. In all cases let it be considered as no less an object of the Law

to afford redress to the party injured, than to punish the offender. Compensation should in all cases, where it is possible, be made to the injured party to the extent of the means of the offender, as in the case of the Malay *Bangoon* where when the father is murdered, the family are entitled to pecuniary compensation for his loss.

T. S. RAFFLES.

With these views and principles the Lieutenant-Governor has this day transmitted to the Acting Magistrates such a graduated Scale of Crimes and Punishments as appears to him sufficient to meet the existing circumstances of the Settlement and to answer the end of substantial justice, with instructions that they will duly deliberate on the subject and after such revision as their local knowledge and experience may suggest, submit the same to the Chief Local Authority with their opinion, and in the form of a Code of Laws to be established for the Settlement and to be in force after publication by the Resident until rescinded by a higher Authority, or altered under the provisions laid down for the enactment of local Laws and Regulations.

The Magistrates have further been required to frame in the form of a Police Regulation, to be approved and published by Government, such further Regulations as may be advisable in that department.

It is to be hoped that the provisions that will be thus made will be found sufficient for the public peace and the protection of person and property until circumstances may admit of the establishment of a more regular Court of Judicature, every arrangement that can be now made being necessarily of a provisional nature.

Dated at Singapore 6th of June, 1823.

By the Lieutenant Governor of Fort Marlborough and its dependencies.

T. S. RAFFLES.

Letter of Instructions to Mr. Crawfurd on Raffles' departure.

To JOHN CRAWFURD, Esq.,
        Resident of Singapore.

Sir,

Having communicated so fully with you personally, on the affairs of Singapore and our interests to the eastward, and so entirely concurring as we do in all general questions of policy relating to them, it is only necessary that in transfering to you the future administration of this Settlement, I should advert to such points of detail as may require to be particularly defined.

Pars. 2-6 Relate only to form of accounts.

7. The Governor-General in Council having authorized the appointment of a responsible assistant to the Resident, Mr. Bonham, of the Bencoolen Civil Service, has been appointed to that situation, and I trust his conduct will merit your confidence; as, however, he is a young man and cannot be expected at present to have that weight in society that so experienced and responsible an officer as Captain Murray must have, it is left to your discretion to make such temporary provisions to supply your place in case of accident, or of your leaving the settlement, as may be necessary for the public service, pending the orders of the Governor-General on the subject, it being understood that your Civil Assistant is the proper officer to supply your place when absent, if he is competent to the duty.

8. The peace of small settlements being frequently disturbed by disputes concerning rank, particularly of the ladies, I think it would be advisable for you to avoid fixing any real rank whatever. Good breeding will always pay due deference to those who have any particular claims to precedence, at the same time that it will prevent the latter from claims it may not be agreeable to others to acknowledge, and as far as the public service is concerned your particular instructions according to the occasion will define what may be necessary.

9. The proclamation of 1st January, defines the form in which all regulations of a general nature are to be drawn out, and the several provisional regulations of 1823, contain all such general laws and regulations as are now in force.

10. With regard to the allotment of ground already granted, every detailed information will be found in the office of the Registrar and Executive Officer. The last grant issued by me is No. 574.

11. The enclosed extract of the resolutions of the Governor-General in Council, will place you in possession of (the opinion of) that authority regarding the principle on which ground should in future be disposed of, and you will of course pay particular attention to the same. The advertisement of the 31st ultimo provides for the cases particularly referred to by the Supreme Government, in which I have substituted an annual quit-rent for the payment of a capital sum as purchase money. On a reference to the register of grants it appears that the quit-rents for grounds in the vicinity of the town, already amount to an annual sum exceeding 3,000 Spanish dollars, which affords a permanent interest of 5 per cent. on a capital of 60,000 Spanish dollars, and exceeds by 20,000 dollars, the amount for which these particular lots were disposed of, after deducting for these lots which were granted in lieu of others and for which no purchase money was to be exacted.

12. By the accounts of the Town Committee, just delivered, you will perceive that the amount advanced by Government as compensation for removing these houses to make room for the Commercial establishments, on the opposite side of the river, will be dollars 10,259 for the China campong and dollars 1,704 for the Chuliah campong, and enclosure No. 4 contains the plan proposed by the Town Committee for recovering those amounts for the parties who are now enjoying the benefit of it. You will adopt this or such other arrangement as you may deem most just and proper and at the same time calculated to meet the convenience of the parties.

13. With regard to the ground between the Tumongong's and the sea, you will also perceive on reference to the same accounts, that the total amount stipulated for by the Committee is 25,706½ Ct. dollars, and that of this sum 14,756½ has already been paid, and 10,950 remain due to the parties, exclusive of the compensation granted to Mr. Quieros, Captain Methuen and Mr. Bernard. regarding which I have addressed you in a separate letter of this date.

14. It will further be seen by the said accounts that a sum of Ct. dollars 6,305 has been stipulated by the Committee to Chinese and others removing from the beach at Campong Glam, &c., and that of this sum there remains still due dollars 4,133.50.

15. The total amount compensations sanctioned by the Committee therefore amount in the whole to Ct. dollars 43,974.50, of which sum dollars 24,886 has been already paid and dollars 19,088.50 still remain due, and for this amount of balance due, you will be pleased to make such advances from the Treasury to the License fund, as may be required from time to time in fulfilment of the engagements entered into, it being desirable that until the accounts of compensation are finally closed, the whole should stand as disbursements from the License fund as heretofore.

16. Whenever the License fund shall have satisfied all these demands, and repaid into the Treasury the amounts from time to time advanced into it, you will be pleased to receive the amount so falling due as the revenue of Government, and carry it to account in the Treasury accordingly.

17. The remaining duties to be performed by the Committee may I conceive be conducted by your assistant and the executive officer, who are well acquainted with the details.

18. The ground plan of the town and its vicinity with which you have been furnished, with the explanations which I have personally given, will have placed you fully in possession of the arrangements I have had in view in this respect, and for all further details and information, I refer you to Lieutenant Jackson, the executive officer, who fully comprehends them and will be able to give you every satisfaction.

19. In laying out the town, I particularly recommend to your attention the advantage of an early attention (not only) to the provision of ample accommodation for the public service hereafter whenever it may be required, but to the beauty, regularity and cleanliness of the settlement; the width of the different roads and streets should be fixed by authority, and as much attention paid to the general style of building as circumstances admit.

20. The only public works of importance at present in hand, are the bridges and Sepoy lines, the former is executed by contract and the latter on estimate by the executive officer.

21. For your information respecting the form to be observed in the execution of public works, I enclose copy of a letter from the Secretary to the Governor-

General in Council, in the Territorial Department, under date the 20th January last. There are other points in this letter which will deserve your attention and particularly its conclusion, where a principle is laid down of which you should never lose sight, namely, that advantages in a financial point of view "must chiefly be looked for in a careful system of economy, avoiding unnecessary expense, rather than seeking revenue to cover it."

22. Enclosure No. contains the agreement this day entered into with their Highnesses the Sultan and Tumongong, and which it is trusted will prove satisfactory to all parties. I have had reason to be much satisfied with the honest intentions of these chiefs and particularly of their attachment to our Government, and I recommend them particularly to your personal kindness and attention. There are not wanting mischievous people, however, to mislead them and you should be on your guard against these.

23. Their Highnesses the Sultan and Tumongong seem to be under some apprehension regarding the safety of Johore, Rajah Moodah of Rhio, under the direction of the Dutch authorities, having made several attempts to enforce his authority there. You are recommended to take an early opportunity of conferring with their Highnesses on the subject, and adopting such provisional arrangements for the security of the place as may be prudent, without involving us in any new question with the Dutch.

24. You are personally so well acquainted with the politics of Singapore, the nature of our term and the importance of avoiding all further clashing with the Dutch authorities, that it is unnecessary for me to give you particular instructions on this head.

25. I shall make a point of forwarding to you for record in the Resident's Office at Singapore, copies of all correspondence which has taken place with the Supreme Government respecting the settlement, and in the event of my immediate departure preventing my communicating with the Governor-General in Council the particulars of the transfer until your monthly accounts are forwarded, you will be pleased to transmit with the same to that authority a copy of the instructions now given to you, with an intimation, that it is my will to address the Governor-General in Council more fully on the subject by an early opportunity.

26. Should I have omitted any particular points, I shall hereafter communicate with you further, and in the meantime I trust the above will be sufficient for your guidance as far as concerns the immediate management of Singapore.

27. Having given you these instructions as far as regards your situation as Resident of Singapore, I am desirous also of calling your attention, on some points, to the line of policy which it appears to me advisable for you to pursue more generally in your political capacity in the Archipelago. On this subject one of the most material points is our political relations with Siam and the Malayan States alleged to be tributary to it. On this point it is incumbent upon me to state with candour that the policy hitherto pursued by us has in my opinion been founded on erroneous principles. The dependence of the tributary states in this case is founded on no national relation which connects them with the Siamese nation. These people are of opposite manners, language, religion and general interests, and the superiority maintained by the one over the other, is so remote from protection on the one side or attachment on the other, that it is but a simple exercise of capricious tyranny by the stronger party, submitted to by the weaker from the law of necessity. We have ourselves for nearly forty years been eye witnesses of the pernicious influence exercised by the Siamese over the Malayan States. During the revolution of the Siamese government these profit by its weakness, and from cultivating an intimacy with strangers, especially with ours over other European nations, they are always in a fair train of prosperity. With the settlement of the Siamese government, on the contrary, it invariably regains the exercise of its tyranny and the Malayan States are threatened, intimidated and plundered. The recent invasion of Quedah is a striking example in point, and from the information conveyed to me it would appear that that commercial seat, governed by a prince of most respectable character, long personally attached to our nation, has only been saved from a similar fate by a most unlooked for event. By the independent Malayan States, who may be supposed the best judges of this matter, it is important to observe that the connection of the tributary Malays with Siam is looked upon as a matter of simple compulsion. Fully aware

of our power and in general deeply impressed with respect for our national character, still it cannot be denied that we suffer, at the present moment, in their good
opinion by withholding from them that protection from the oppression of the
Siamese which it would be so easy for us to give; and the case is stronger with
regard to Quedah than the rest, for here a general impression is abroad amongst
them, that we refuse an assistance that we are by treaty virtually bound to give,
since we entered into a treaty with that state, as an independent power, without
regarding the supremacy of Siam or ever alluding to its connection for five and
twenty years, after our first (establishment at Penang). The prosperity of the
Settlement under your direction is so much connected with that of the Malayan
nations in its neighbourhood, and this again (so much depends) upon their liberty
and security from foreign oppression, that I must seriously recommend to your
attention the contemplation of the probable event of their deliverance from the
yoke of Siam, and your making the Supreme government immediately informed
of every event which may promise to lead to that desirable result.

28. The suppression of piracy in the sea of the Archipelago is the second
point to which I would call your attention. It would be extremely desirable that
a general plan having this in view were put in force in conjunction with the government of Prince of Wales Island, the Dutch authorities, and the principal native
independent states. Your centrical position at Singapore will afford you superior
means for submitting such a plan to the supreme authorities. It is true that since
the establishment, of late years, of vigorous and powerful governments in these
seas, on our part and that of the Dutch, piratical attacks on European vessels
have become comparatively rare. They continue however extremely frequent on
native vessels, and afford serious obstacles to that intercourse by which the productions of the neighbouring nations are collected at this emporium, and our wares
and manufactures disseminated in return. Piracy for example is so frequent in
the Straits of Malacca, between Malacca and Pinang, that the square-rigged vessels
of the Chuliahs or natives of the Coromandal Coast, a timid people, are on this
account precluded from coming further than Pinang and Achin, and thus the
trade of fifty or sixty brigs and ships are in a great measure lost to Singapore,
for an inconsiderable portion of these people, only, tranship themselves and their goods
on British vessels for security and thus find their way to us. This peculiar obstacle
may be remedied by directing the vessel, for which application is made to the
Supreme government, to afford them convoy once a year from Penang, an employment which will not materially interfere with the other duties to which it may
be appointed.

29. The most formidable piratical depredations here, are committed by the
hardy and ferocious races which inhabit the Sooloo and other islands lying between
Borneo and the Philippines. These portions of the east insular seas are little
known to us, and the first object will be to obtain some accurate knowledge respecting their social and political condition. I especially recommend this subject
to your attention; valuable information regarding them may be collected from
the numerous native traders already frequenting Singapore, and a personal visit to
the countries in question may hereafter be deemed advisable. In the meantime
the maintenance of a friendly and conciliating correspondence with the chiefs of
the tribe and nations in question, and generally with all independent tribes of the
Eastern islands within the limits of the authority given to you by the Supreme
Government, will strengthen the confidence of the native inhabitants in general
and promote the important purpose of your appointment.

I am, &c.,

(Signed) T. S. RAFFLES.

Singapore, 7th June, 1823.

Sir T. S. Raffles's Letter to the Supreme Government, 7th June, 1823.

Allotment of Ground.

The principle laid down in the Resolution of the Supreme Government in the
Political Department of the 21st March last, and transmitted with Mr. Secretary
Swinton's letters of the same date, regarding the manner in which ground should

be disposed of at Singapore, has been duly make known, and the public have been apprized that all ground will be considered as let on a perpetual lease or for a term of years, that the plan of disposing of the ground to the highest bidders is approved, and that the biddings for the same in future are to be made in quit-rent, the lease being granted without any present payment to the parties who may offer the largest amount of annual rent.

This arrangement had previously occurred as the most convenient, and with the exception of the particular lots alluded to, all other allotments made by me were disposed of for the annual quit-rent offered, so that no inconvenience has resulted from this modification of the original plan.

With regard to the particular cases referred to, in which the Supreme Government has directed that the amount of purchase money should be commuted for an annual quit-rent, I have the satisfaction to report that the same has been carried into effect on the following principle.—The total amount of purchase money, agreeably to the account already transmitted to the Supreme Government, was 56,000 Spanish Dollars, but of this amount nearly one-half was purchased by persons who were compelled to remove from the opposite side of the river, in favor of whom it was a condition that purchase money would be foregone.

On reference to the registry of grants already transmitted to the Supreme Government, it will appear that the quit-rents for ground in the town and its vicinity already amount to upwards of 3,000 Spanish Dollars, which affords a permanent interest of 5 per cent. on a capital of 60,000 Spanish dollars, exceeding by one-half the amount due on account of purchase money for the particular lots in question, and which may be considered as by far the most valuable portion.

Under these circumstances, and as I had in the grants provided for either alternative by including a fixed quit-rent corresponding with the particular value of each lot, I have not found it necessary to do more with regard to allotments for commercial purposes than to declare that government has foregone the purchase money in consideration of the quit-rents, the ground being considered as let on a perpetual lease as directed by the Supreme Government.

One of the conditions on which this ground was disposed of, was, that the purchasers should compensate the occupants of temporary buildings who were obliged to make room for them, and the removal of these persons having been conducted by a committee appointed by government, the disbursements on this account have amounted to current dollars 10,159; this amount has been advanced by government but it will be re-imbursed by the parties and the resident has been recommended to adopt such arrangement for this purpose as may be most convenient for them.

With regard to the compensation to be paid by government to individuals removing from the space between the Tumongong's and the sea, I shall have the honour to address the Supreme Government more fully in a separate letter, and it may suffice to observe in this place,. that notwithstanding the various difficulties thrown in my way by the local authority, I have eventually had the satisfaction of completing this important arrangement to the satisfaction of all parties, and so as to render all further reference or dispute on the subject unnecessary.

Arrangements with the Sultan and Tumongong.

The advantage which had been taken of the general terms in which, from political considerations, it was deemed most advisable that the treaty with their Highnesses the Sultan and Tumongong should in the first instance be expressed, and the extraordinary principle assumed by Lieutenant-Colonel Farquhar, and maintained by him in opposition to my authority, that the disposal of the land was vested in the native chiefs, that the government of the country was native and the port a native port, rendered it indispensable that these points should be fully explained and more clearly defined, and as that officer had also permitted various exactions and privileges to be enjoyed by their Highnesses incompatible with the freedom of the port, I have availed myself of the opportunity offered in negociating with their Highnesses for the payment of an equivalent for the port duties, to stipulate such arrangements as seem essential to form the basis of the good understanding to be maintained for the future. With reference to the political discussions which have taken place regarding the Settlement, and the questions which have arisen regarding its tenure, I did not deem it prudent in any way to alter or revise the original treaty, but the conventional agreement now made may be considered equally binding on the parties, and may of course be hereafter adopted as the basis of any more definite treaty to be entered into, after the permanency of the Settlement has been established.

The amount stipulated to be paid to their Highnesses is,—to the Sultan 1,500 current dollars and to the Tumongong 800 current dollars per month, or in the whole current dollars 2,300, equal to Spanish dollars, at 15 per cent. premium (the present rate) 1,955. This is somewhat in excess of the 500 dollars originally intended for each, but I found it impracticable to effect the arrangement in a satisfactory manner for less, the demands of the parties or rather of their advisers having been materially influenced by the countenance which the chief local authority had so injudiciously and improperly given to their claims in opposition to the essential interests of government. The rapid increase in the value of property of every description rendered it however indispensable that no time should be lost in fixing the amount of compensation, and having waited the arrival of Mr. Crawfurd and conferred with him on the subject, I lost no time in completing the arrangement which upon the whole seemed most advantageous, and which I trust will meet the approbation of the Governor-General in Council.

Extract of Letter from Sir T. S. Raffles to the Secretary to the Supreme Government.

The information which must be before the Supreme Government from Prince of Wales Island, as well as in the reports of the late Mission to Siam, renders it unnecessary that I should enter at any length on the actual condition of the Malay States on the Peninsula, but I have thought it advisable to direct Mr. Crawfurd's attention to the subject, with the view of his keeping the Governor-General in Council regularly advised of the progress or otherwise of the Siamese influence among them.

The conduct and character of the Court of Siam offer no opening for friendly negociations on the footing on which European States would treat with each other, and require that in our future communications we should rather dictate what we consider to be just and right, than sue for their granting it as an indulgence. I am satisfied that if instead of deferring to them so much as we have done in the case of Quedah, we had maintained a higher tone and declared the country to be under our protection, they would have hesitated to invade that unfortunate territory. Having however been allowed to indulge their rapacity in this instance with impunity, they are encouraged to similar acts towards the other States of the Peninsula, and if not timely checked may be expected in a similar manner to destroy the truly respectable state of Tringanu, on the eastern side of the Peninsula.

The blockade of the Menam river, which could at any time be effected with the cruisers from Singapore, would always bring the Siamese Court to terms as far as concerns the Malay States, and from the arrogant and offensive tone recently assumed by the Siamese, some measure of the kind will I fear ere long become indispensable, unless the possible apprehension of our adopting such a measure may bring them to terms of more accommodation than they have yet shewn.

The only remaining point to which I have directed Mr. Crawfurd's attention, has been the consideration of such measures as it may be hereafter advantageous to adopt for the more general suppression of piracy in the eastern seas.

I have honor to be, &c.,

Singapore, 7th June, 1823.   T. S. RAFFLES.

Mr. Crawfurd arrived at Singapore on the 27th May, was received by a guard of honour and a salute of fifteen guns, and took charge of the Resident's Office. Colonel Farquhar left Singapore for England, the natives accompanying him to the ship in the harbour with numbers of boats decorated with flags and accompanied by music. Abdulla gives an account of his departure, and in a letter of the Colonel's we find an allusion by him to the number of addresses he received from the inhabitants on leaving the Settlement.

CHAPTER XI.

THE RAFFLES INSTITUTION.

ON 12th January, 1823, Sir Stamford Raffles wrote that he had selected a spot for the College he intended to establish. He had proposed to the Sultan and Tumongong that their sons should be sent to Calcutta for education, but they would not consent, so he decided to establish a school in Singapore. From a pamphlet printed at the Mission Press at Malacca in 1823 it is seen that a meeting was held at Raffles' House on Government Hill on 1st April when a very long and able minute, written by Sir Stamford Raffles, from which sentences have been often quoted, was read, in which he stated that there were three objects in view. (1) To educate the sons of the higher order of natives and others. (2) To afford means of instruction in the native languages to such of the Company's servants and others as may desire it. (3) To collect the scattered literature and traditions of the country with whatever may illustrate their (*sic*) laws and customs, and to publish and circulate in a correct form the most important of these, with such other works as may be calculated to raise the character of the institution and to be useful and instructive to the people.

A long paper written by Dr. Morrison was then read, suggesting the scheme for removing the Anglo-Chinese College from Malacca and uniting it with the Institution in Singapore. The Rev. R. S. Hutchings, who was the Chaplain at Penang, then spoke, and after him Dr. Morrison. These speeches were all reprinted in a pamphlet in Singapore in 1838, with the annual report of the Institution Free School. The officers were nominated, including the principal inhabitants, and among the Patrons was William Wilberforce, M.P. of England.

On 15th April the first meeting of the Trustees was held, Mr. J. A. Maxwell being the Honorary Secretary and A. L. Johnston & Co. the Honorary Treasurers. The subscriptions had amounted to $17,495; being $9,670 for the Institution generally, $1,075 for the Scientific Department, and $6,750 for the Malayan College. The Anglo-Chinese College house at Malacca was intended to be sold, and $4,000 was included in the above amount as its probable proceeds, the East India Company contributing $4,000, Raffles $2,000, Dr. Morrison $1,200, Colonel Farquhar $1,000, the Sultan and Tumongong $1,000 each, and Lady Raffles $400. The other subscribers were Mr. Bonham, F. G. Bernard, Captain Davis, Captain Flint, D. A. Fraser, G. Gordon, Thomas Howard, Lieut. L. N. Hull, Rev. R. S. Hutchings, Lieut. Jackson, A. L. Johnston, the Malay College, J. A. Maxwell, G. Mackenzie, Dr. Montgomerie, D. S. Napier, Charles Scott, and Rev. G. H. Thomson. A monthly subscription of $300 had been promised by Government for the schools, and $25 yearly for the library. Lieutenant

Jackson made a plan and estimate of the proposed building, which he said could be constructed in twelve months, this was approved, and $15,000 was voted for the purpose.

The building was then erected. It was not a well-constructed building, the roof especially being unskilfully erected, which caused frequent expense. It was originally built in the form of a cross and a wing was subsequently added at each arm. The addition and the three-storied wing at the Brass Bassa Road end were not erected until 1875, at the entire cost of the Government. Abdullah gives a short account of the laying of the foundation stone, which was attended by all the Europeans and the Native Chiefs and Malays; some money (he says a golden rupee, probably a sovereign) was put by Raffles, and $80 by the Europeans, under the door; a salute was fired, and Raffles named the building. Abdullah says that during the progress of its erection three Chinese fell from the scaffolding and were killed.

On 20th May, 1823, Raffles wrote a long despatch to the Governor-General at Bengal, calling attention to the advantage and propriety of educating the natives who came to Singapore. He said that all were in favour of it, but some wanted it delayed until the question of the permanency of the Settlement was decided with the Dutch. But as Dr. Morrison had arrived from China, and there was a question of moving the Anglo-Chinese College from Malacca now that place was under the Dutch, quick measures had been necessary to take advantage of this. After much deliberation with Dr. Morrison and Mr. Hutchings, the Penang Chaplain, who was in Singapore, he had decided to remove the College to Singapore and unite it under the general designation of the Singapore Institution, to be connected with branch schools in the Chinese and Malay languages, with a library and museum, as means admitted. He also said that he had appropriated for the use of the Institution and schools an advantageous allotment of ground near the town, and had endowed each of the Departments with 500 acres of uncleared ground on the usual terms. On 6th November the Governor-General wrote in reply that he did not approve of haste, and it would have been better if sanction had been asked before promising the grants of money; because Singapore was not settled yet. The scheme for removing the Anglo-Chinese College to Singapore fell through and in the *Free Press* of 12th December, 1839, it was spoken of as having proved a total failure, which had dwindled down into, if indeed it ever rose beyond, a small school, used merely as a dwelling house for the Principal.

On the 8th April, 1823, a lease of land, which cannot now be found, was promised by Raffles to the Trustees for the Institution, described as measuring 600 feet on the sea-side, and 1,140 feet inland to Rochore Street and bounded on the side (sides?) by College Street and the Fresh Water Stream; estimated to contain acres 15.2.32½. If these measurements are compared with the present map of the town, it will be seen that it was the large block of land now occupied by the Raffles Institution and the Convent, and now bounded by Beach Road, Brass Bassa Road, Victoria Street and Stamford Road. What was called Rochore Road in 1823 is now known as Victoria Street. North Bridge Road was not then made, nor was the line of that road reserved for a road in the lease to the trustees. What was described in the lease as College Street is now called Brass Bassa Road (it was always spelt so until quite lately, now it is written as Bras Basah) ; in an old lease of 1826 this road was called Cross Road. The name College Street was probably a suggestion by Raffles which was afterwards forgotten. What was described in the lease as Fresh Water Stream was a curious name, considering the great complaints that were made subsequently about the foul state of the water that still runs alongside Stamford Road.

In 1840 being in want of funds the Trustees retained only the large block between what is now North Bridge Road and the Sea, but only extends now to Beach Road, as the Reclamation from the sea was made many years afterwards. They disposed of the whole of the other (the Convent) block, at auction on 7th January, 1840, for $3,150 and a yearly quit-rent of $135, for the residue of the term of 999 years, in nine lots, each containing about 3,600 square yards, as follows :—

> Lot 1   to Syed Omar bin Alley al Junied.
> Lots 2, 3, 4 to Jozé d'Almeida & Sons.
>   „   5   to T. O. Crane.
>   „   6   to Antonio Jozé de Vasconcellos.
>   „   7   to Antonio d'Almeida.
>   „   8, 9   to Joseph Melany.

In 1860 the Rev. J. M. Beurel had acquired nearly the whole of these for the Convent. There remains in other hands to this day only a small portion at the corner of Stamford Road and Victoria Street; the rest is all occupied by the grounds and buildings of the Convent.

In addition to that large block of land, "a hill with the land adjacent to it to the northward at the back of Government Hill, to include an area of 100 acres," was also promised to the Trustees, on 8th April, 1823. These two grants it is said were issued as No. 1 dated 20th March, 1823, and No. 419 dated 10th April, 1823, but if this is correct they were issued before the promise made by Raffles on April the 8th; there is probably some mistake, and no copies of the grant are now to be found to correct it, nor any other record than the paper from which these particulars are taken.

The grant of the hill (afterwards called Institution Hill at River Valley Road) was for acres 28.1.31, and not for 100 acres; and the Trustees, saying that the land had been lying waste and producing no revenue, decided in December, 1844, to dispose of it. It was suggested to sell it to Chinese for a burial ground; on which the *Free Press* remarked as follows :—" We think the sale of the Institution Hill for any such purpose is much to be deprecated, and we trust the Trustees of the Institution will not dispose of it to any parties who would allow it to be applied in such a manner. It is too near the town to have a burial ground upon it, and it would give visitors a very unfavourable impression as to the unhealthiness of the place were they, on entering the Roads, to see this conspicuous hill, in addition to those in the vicinity of the town already appropriated to such purposes, covered with tombs. We do not think that the Trustees will lend themselves to this object ; but, perhaps, the best plan to avert any chance of the thing happening would be for our correspondent to buy up the hill. The Trustees would, we think, be inclined to take a fair and reasonable price from him, rather than accept the extravagant sum, which the eligibility of the situation for their purposes would, perhaps, induce the Chinese to offer." Luckily, the sale was never carried out, and the hill is now covered with European houses. One of the finest hills in Tanglin is occupied solely by Chinese graves, and it was fortunate that Prinsep's Hill and Institution Hill never shared the same fate. In the following January 1845, the Trustees advertised the hill to be let as follows :—

"The Trustees of the Singapore Institution invite offers to rent the hill belonging to the Institution, which adjoins the River Valley Road, for a term of 10 years at an annual quit-rent of $100 ; upon expiry of the leases the hill with all buildings and fixtures thereon to revert to the Institution. Or for the whole term of the Government lease (viz., 999 years) at an advanced rent. Tenders will be received until the first Friday in February, when the one approved of by the Committee will be accepted. The hill is well adapted for building lots. A stipulation will be entered in the lease prohibiting the hill being converted into a burying ground by the Tenant. Tenders to be sent to T. Oxley, Secretary."

As no offers were made to rent it, it was advertised in the following April by Mr. F. Martin for sale for the whole term of the lease at the highest annual rent. The result of the sale was told in the *Free Press* as follows :—

"On Monday, the 7th April, the remainder of the term for which the Institution Hill is held—about 990 years—was exposed at public auction, and knocked down for the annual sum of $225. This is a very high price indeed, and were it to be taken as a criterion of the general value of land in the island, might be held as bearing out, in a great degree, the extreme notions of certain parties on this point. We believe, however, that the high rate obtained was entirely owing to the peculiar situation of the hill which so completely overlooks the neighbouring properties, on which there are several houses, so that if the owners of the latter had allowed the hill to get into other hands, they would have been constantly exposed to the close oversight of the inhabitants of the hill, a situation which would have been anything but pleasant. It was this fact, and to prevent it being used as a situation for manufactures which might have made it a very unpleasant neighbourhood, that induced the owner of the adjacent property to secure the hill, which we suppose he will keep in grass." It was bought by Adam Sykes and Mungo Johnston Martin, on the 30th December, 1845. Dr. Robert Little afterwards purchased it and lived on the land for about thirty-five years in one house, a record probably for Singapore. Thus the Trustees parted with a considerable quantity of the land contained in these two grants (the block where the Convent stands and Institution Hill), which is now of very great value, for the small yearly sum of $360.

Sir Stamford Raffles, however, had given the Institution even more than this. He had also given orders, and Bengal had approved, to appropriate 1,500 acres of uncleared ground, on the usual terms, for the use of the School, which would appear to have been done, though the position of the land granted as Nos. 499, 500 and 501 referred to presently, cannot now be traced. It seems that on 9th January, 1827, a Government Notice was issued that all persons who failed to fulfil the terms of their contract to clear and build on land would forfeit their right if they did not comply before the 1st May. On the 27th February the following letter was sent to the Resident Councillor by Mr. J. A. Maxwell, the Honorary Secretary to the Singapore Institution :—

" Sir, on behalf of the Trustees of the Singapore Institution, I have the honour to enclose a document under their signature by which they renounce all claim to the lot of ground referred to in your favour of the 19th January, and I trust the same may be considered satisfactory with a view to the object for which it has been framed. The Grants referred to, viz., 499, 500 and 501 are in my possession and are ready to be delivered up if necessary."

A great deal has been said since about the Government having " illegally " resumed the land. At that time the Institution was serving no purpose ; no classes, as far as can be seen, were held ; the roof was tumbling in, and it may well be that the Trustees considered it could only be preventing the use of the land for a useful purpose if they held on to it when they could not fulfil the conditions under which it had been granted. It would be interesting to know where that land was. There is good reason to think that it was at the top of Orchard Road where Abbotsford, Nassim Hill, and part of the Tanglin Barracks are now. It was no doubt looked upon then as only jungle of problematical value, and not worth spending money to clear. There is no doubt that the lands given to the School, if they had remained in the hands of the Trustees would now be of very great value, beyond any possible conception at that time, and that the Report of the Trustees in 1845, in congratulating themselves on having secured a permanent monthly addition to the income of $18.75, by disposing of the lease of Institution Hill, reads curiously by present lights. But it is useless to judge of those things solely from the glare of the present day. In 1873 the Trustees wrote to the Government about the resumption of these lands in 1827, and eventually a fixed yearly grant of $5,940, and an undertaking to keep the Institution building in repair, were given by Government as compensation for lands resumed by Government in 1827. This appears in the foot note to the yearly account published in the annual report of the School, and in a letter of the Colonial Secretary to the Honorary Secretary of the Institution dated 3rd November, 1885, printed in the yearly report of the School.

Having now explained about the lands given to the School, the story of its progress is resumed. In May, 1825, the Court of Directors of the East India Company wrote to Singapore that they considered the establishment of the Institution (however useful in itself) was premature, as it was uncertain whether Singapore would continue to form a part of the British Dominions; but they did not disapprove of what had been done, so far as to stop supplies, and did not refuse to sanction the grants of land and the subscription promised by Sir Stamford Raffles, if the Governor considered the amounts unobjectionable.

The Court of Directors called upon Mr. Crawfurd, the Governor, for a report, and he sent a long despatch dated 7th February, 1826. After three years experience of Singapore, he thought the scheme of the Institution had been on too extensive a scale for the times, and the means were not sufficient to carry out the object. He recommended Government to confine the aim to elementary education, in the first place, since the present inhabitants of Singapore were utter strangers to European education and methods of instruction. He proposed that it be confined to reading and writing in Malay and Chinese (the most numerous and influential classes) and perhaps Arabic; but above all to reading, writing and arithmetic in English. The chief benefit of instruction in Asiatic languages was to reconcile the natives to European education and accustom them to regular habits of subordination and study. One great obstacle was the fear by the parents of conversion. The Rev. Mr. Thomson had long tried to get up a school without interference with religious matters. It would be better to wait until this feeling was allayed, and to have only laymen as masters. Chinese, Arabs and Malay teachers could be got; the difficulty was to find competent and respectable men, as the success would depend upon this. The originating of the schools would depend upon the patronage of the Government. The Court had authorised $300 a month; and arrears from April, 1823 to February, 1826, would amount then to $10,200, which with private subscriptions would suffice to endow and carry it on. He also asked for land for the school, and power to invest the money in buildings upon it; and for permission to occupy a Government building at present vacant. And generally he proposed to exclude the original scheme altogether for the present, as quite beyond any probable means of carrying it out, and if hereafter there were better prospects, the schools could then be joined to the Institution. The present building was too far from the town for the convenience of the children, so their parents did not send them, and they also objected to any religious teaching in the school, as in the Anglo-Chinese College.

There is a short note by Mr. Braddell, no doubt an extract from some Government correspondence, that on 18th August, 1827, the Trustees tendered the Institution to Government to purchase it or rent it, which was declined on the 6th September.

At the end of 1832, the *Free Press* said:—"The unfinished building, or rather ruin, so well known as the Singapore Institution, stands in a conspicuous situation at the head of Kampong Glam, on the town side fronting the sea-beach. To strangers it is often a matter of astonishment that a building in such an eligible site, and in the neighbourhood of so many respectable and new habitations, should be suffered to remain in its present dilapidated condition, especially when a comparatively small sum would suffice to put it in repair, and make it habitable. For several years, it has been an eye-sore to the inhabitants of the Settlement, from the desolate and neglected appearance of the building and premises; and latterly it has become a nuisance, in some degree, as it affords a convenient shelter for thieves, a class of beings whom the benevolent founders of the Institution never contemplated should be supported on its foundation. The ground attached is nearly all covered with stagnant marsh, and jungle, which must in some wise affect the air in that neighbourhood."

Mr. Fullerton had proposed buying the ground and converting the house into a Church. At another time it had been proposed to make a Public Library and Town Hall of it, and to sell part of the ground to finish the building. Some of these proposals were referred to Dr. Morrison in China, and he replied: "I would rather, even if it were a hundred years hence, have the land and building reserved for the original purpose of native education, than for the sake of any other object consent to alienate it."

It was said in an old report of the School that had Sir Stamford Raffles remained longer in Singapore, or the Institution proceeded on the plan he laid down, most of the objects he proposed might have been accomplished, but after his death no influential person was found able and willing to follow up his views and plans, and nothing but an unfinished building of eleven years standing remained in 1834 to show that such a project had been contemplated. The intention had been to instruct the better class of natives, and there were not sufficient of them to form classes, and nothing was done beyond framing an elaborate scheme, with European teachers for Malay, Siamese and Chinese, who would have had no scholars to teach. As far as can be traced now, no classes were actually formed, the masters in the College at Malacca not coming to Singapore.

In February, 1834, Mr. Darrah, the Chaplain, began writing about the subject of the neglected education of the children in the Settlement, and on 3rd May made the proposal to establish elementary schools in different places with native masters, with a central school at which the descendants of Europeans could attend, with some of the more advanced boys from the minor schools. Mr. Darrah circulated a paper, and $335 were subscribed towards erecting a building, and $45 was promised in monthly subscriptions. Until the building of planks and attap, which was estimated to cost $600, should be erected, the Government gave the use of an unoccupied house near the foot of Fort Canning, nearly opposite (Mr. James Guthrie wrote) to the top of High Street. Another account says that the Government only gave the use of the ground, and a building 70 feet long by 22 feet wide was built for $600. However this may have been, the school was opened on the 1st August, 1834, and managed by Mr. J. H. Moor. There were 46 boys, and before long the number increased to 80. On the 25th September a meeting was held of the subscribers and it was decided to form an association called the "Singapore School Society." The schools to be under the direction of the Chaplain in their religious and literary details, and the Bible to be used generally as a class book, but not to be indispensable for children of any sect of religion different from the Established Church. The Committee consisted of Messrs. Johnston, Wingrove, Scott, Darrah, Oxley and Napier. Mr. Moor was the first European Master at $75 a month and there were two native masters at $12 each. The Governor and the Recorder were Patrons. The school had 32 boys in the English classes, of whom 12 paid; but the whole fees only amounted to $3 a month. There were 18 boys in the Tamil class, 12 in the Malay, and 12 in the Chinese, but the report says

"The American Missionaries, the Rev. Tracy and Parker, having opened a Chinese Free School in a central part of the town, the boys went there as it was near their homes, and they avoided the real or imaginary danger incidental to crossing the wooden bridge which led to the Singapore school from the town!"

On the 27th August, 1835, a meeting was held at the Court House, Mr. Alexander Guthrie in the chair, at which it was resolved that the original scheme of the Institution should be rescinded and another adopted more consonant to the general sense of the supporters and better adapted to the object in view. That children of any country should be taught without regard to any exclusive course of religious instruction. The salary of the head master not to exceed $100, and for native teachers $15. The Patrons to be the Governor, Recorder and the Resident Councillor, and a Committee of five was appointed, of Messrs. Wingrove, W. Napier, G. D. Coleman, Thomas McMicking and Thomas Oxley. Dr. Oxley became Honorary Secretary. A Government allowance of $100 a month was granted, and the subscription list amounted to $81, but the Government allowance for the first year was appropriated towards the completion of the Institution building, which was in such a bad state. The house that had been lent by the Government in High Street for the school was in such bad repair, that it was only fit for another year, and the Committee proposed that the Institution building should be repaired and used by the "Singapore School Society" as it was now termed, though the name "Singapore Free School" seems to have been generally used. On the 1st January, 1836, there was a public meeting held at the Reading Room, of the subscribers to the monument that it had been intended to erect to the memory of Sir Stamford Raffles. It was decided "that it is the opinion of this meeting that they will best perpetuate the remembrance of the eminent services rendered to this Settlement, and the commercial world generally, by this distinguished individual, by endeavouring to complete the Institution founded by him for the purposes of education. That as the meeting finds the funds already collected for the monument amount to $1,827, and that there is nearly $1,000 more subscribed, which it is expected will be paid immediately, it is resolved that as soon as it is found a sufficient sum can be raised by additional subscriptions for the purpose of completing the buildings and making them fit for schools on an extended scale, they will place at the disposal of the Trustees of the Institution the whole sum subscribed for the erection of the monument."

The amount necessary for the purpose was estimated at $5,000, and Dr. Montgomerie undertook to superintend the repairs and completion. It was then mentioned that the bust of Raffles by Chantrey, which Lady Raffles had presented to the Institution, would be placed in a conspicuous spot in the completed building, with an inscription in English, Latin, Chinese and Malay. The inscription was never made.

On the 5th of the same month, a meeting of the Trustees of the Singapore Institution was held in the Resident Councillor's Office, and the following resolutions were passed. " 1st.—That the plan proposed by the subscribers to the monument of Sir T. S. Raffles of giving their funds for completing the Institution for Schools be approved of and thankfully accepted, and that a Subscription List be opened at the Reading Room immediately for further donations from the European and Chinese inhabitants to finish the building on a plan and estimate already furnished by Mr. Coleman.

"2nd.—That the Institution having been founded jointly by Sir T. S. Raffles and Dr. Morrison, a communication be immediately made of these proceedings to the son of the latter, Mr. J. R. Morrison, now Interpreter to H. M. Superintendent in China, requesting that he will be pleased to name such persons, as he may be desirous should act as Trustees.

"3rd.—That the Hon'ble Kenneth Murchison, Governor, and the Hon'ble J. E. Gambier, Recorder, be requested to become Patrons of this Institution, and that the following gentlemen be nominated Trustees according to the Regulations provided at the founding of the Institution: Messrs. R. F. Wingrove, W. Montgomerie, Jas. Fraser, W. D. Shaw, A. Guthrie, G. D. Coleman, T. McMicking, Wm. Napier, and the Rev. S. Wolfe, and that Thomas Oxley, Esq., be requested to act as Secretary."

At a meeting called by the Trustees of the Raffles Institution in May, a letter from Dr. Morrison was read, stating that he had already collected upwards of $1,000 by subscriptions in China, and that he had received a promise of $400 additional, whenever the building was completed, and the education of the natives actually commenced; also, a statement of the funds then available and accumulating having been submitted by the Treasurers, and plans and estimates for finishing the building with suitable out-offices on a scale adequate to present resources, and adapted for immediate objects, as well with a view to its future extension and enlargement in accordance with the original objects of the Founders, having been laid before the meeting by Mr. Coleman, who declared himself willing to contract to finish the whole in two years from this time for the sum of $5,700, and it further appearing to the meeting that the funds will be sufficient for the purpose, and the building when completed in every way suitable for the objects contemplated,—it was unanimously resolved that a committee, consisting of Alex. L. Johnston, Esq., Wm. Montgomerie, Esq., and W. D. Shaw, Esq., be empowered to make a contract with Mr. Coleman for finishing the building and out-offices for the sum specified, and on the plans submitted. It was further resolved, that every effort should be made to increase the subscriptions collectively and individually by the Trustees, and that those already subscribed be immediately collected.

The paper spoke as follows of the meeting:—" It is proposed to appropriate one of the upper rooms as a Library and Museum, where all meetings of the Committee or of the Trustees can be held. Donations of books should be forthwith solicited, to form the Library and Museum, as also specimens of the Natural History of the Archipelago, and the countries in our vicinity. If only a little zeal be displayed in accomplishing these two desirable objects, collections would soon be made, which would form perhaps some of the principal attractions of the Institution after its completion. The building which is of considerable extent, although not nearly approaching in magnitude to the original plan, will be a handsome and striking object, constructed according to scientific principles, in which that part of the building which had been completed under the original design showed a lamentable defect. It is also built so as to be capable of receiving such additions as will bring it to the dimensions of the original plan without any disfigurement of its parts, or detraction from its symmetry. With a proper degree of support, there is every reasonable hope that this establishment, on the scale on which it is at present proposed to be conducted, will not only effect its more immediate objects, but be the means, slow perhaps, but sure, of realising and embracing the more extensive and advanced system of education which its gifted and lamented founder had so much at heart, and which it is still so important an object to secure. It is stated that one gentleman at Canton promised $400 on the completion of the building, and we have reason to believe that there are several others in this Settlement who withhold their contributions until they can see that their money is likely to be well applied. As the workmen have already commenced on the repairs, we trust not many months will elapse before they will be able to satisfy themselves on that point."

In May, 1837, the *Free Press* said that the Institution building was nearly finished, and in December the classes were removed to it from High Street and the building was first used as a School. The arrangement being that the building was lent to the School Committee but that if funds should afterwards be provided to carry out the original proposal of Sir Stamford Raffles, the Trustees of the Institution should give one year's notice before resuming the building, and should repay the money advanced for repairs from the School funds, which had then amounted to $1,800. The upper school then contained 50 boys, taught by Mr. Moor and Mr. Fitzpatrick, who came from Calcutta. There was a Library, the first in Singapore, open free to all, in one part of the building; but only subscribers to the school fund could borrow the books. It was proposed to commence a museum, but this was never done. A large attap shed was put up for play, with a gymnasium, a small fives court and quoit ground, which the boys and their friends subscribed to pay for. There were 102 Chinese, 46 Klings and 51 Malays. A Bugis class was started but was unsuccessful. The Rev. Edward White, Residency Chaplain, gave great assistance and partly furnished the lower English class at his own expense.

In April, 1838, the Committee sent a Memorial to Lord Auckland, the Governor-General, asking for Rs. 5,000 to purchase scientific apparatus, of which they sent a list, including a telescope, microscope, electrical machine, surveying instruments and many other things. The only result was that the Government allowance was increased from $93.53 to $187.27; the Government accounts being kept in rupees. At this time a circular letter was drawn up in Malay urging the Malay Chiefs to send their children for instruction. The Rajahs of Kelantan, Tringanu and Quedah answered that they approved highly of the object and system of the school; but nothing came of it. To leave nothing untried, another address to Malays in general was drawn up, and the son of the Sultan and some other influential Malays attended a meeting at the school on 15th September, 1838, and signed the paper.

Five hundred copies were printed and placarded over Singapore and Kampong Glam, and sent to no less than thirty different places round the coast and Borneo and Celebes by the nakodas of trading vessels, but it led to no result. The following are passages from the address :— Our friend has undoubtedly heard of the eminent and enlightened Sir Stamford Raffles and how anxious he was to promote the intellectual improvement of the Malays, and add to their happiness. To help the desirable and benevolent object the late Sultan of Johore and the Tumongong, with Sir Stamford Raffles and other gentlemen, subscribed a large sum of money to erect a handsome edifice in Singapore to serve as an Institution for the instruction of Malays and other neighbouring natives. We have to acquaint our friend that the Singapore Institution is now completed. It is of brick, 120 feet long and 60 feet broad, two-stories high. Competent masters have been engaged, and we invite our friend to send his sons, relations, and the sons of some of his nobles to Singapore to be taught to read and write both the Malay and English languages, and to acquire much useful knowledge." It then spoke of the advantages of education, and said that students could reside in the building, or be boarded with respectable Malays and attend as day scholars.

In November, 1838, a letter was sent asking the Secretary of the British and Foreign School Society in London to engage a teacher at a salary of $100 a month, with a house, and accommodation to take in boarders ; and £100 was sent for the passage money. In anticipation of his arrival it was proposed to erect a bungalow behind the school, but it was thought better to build one of the wings contained in the original plan of the building. The foundations had been laid at first for both the proposed wings. Mr. Coleman estimated the cost at $2,800, and a memorial was sent to Calcutta asking for $1,000 towards it. The Trustees of the Institution consented that the sum spent by the Committee should be treated in the same way as the previous $1,800 for repairs. Bengal did not allow the $1,000, and subscriptions were asked from Canton, Batavia and Manila. Mr. Thomas McMicking, who had gone to reside at Manila, collected $170, and Mr. Oliphant of Canton gave $500. The new wing was finished in May, 1839.

In August, 1839, it was decided at a meeting held at the Institution that as considerable inconvenience had arisen from there being two authorities (the Trustees of the Institution itself and the School Committee) connected with the Singapore Institution, whose views and interests were entirely similar in every respect, it was desirable to vest the whole in the Trustees alone ; and that the School Committee should deliver all funds and property to the Trustees, which should appoint a school committee of a certain number from their body annually. After a long delay it was found that a master had not been engaged in England, and the Rev. J. T. Dickenson, of the American Foreign Missions in Singapore, was engaged at $100 a month in April, 1840, and he occupied the upper part of the new wing; one large room downstairs being used for a Chinese school-room, and the other for the printing room, where printing was done for the benefit of the Institution, but did not bring in much. There were then 14 boarders living with Mr. Moor, paying $3 each a month. Mr. Keasberry was Superintendent of the Malay classes. The Tamil class was closed as it did not succeed for want of a competent master. There were 208 boys on the list, average attendance 160 to 170, including 38 Roman Catholic and 25 Protestant Christians.

In December, 1839, some Siamese noblemen sent $194 from Bangkok towards the expense of erecting a wing to the building, and Prince Momfanoo said he would send two Siamese youths of respectable family to be educated at the Institution, but this does not seem to have been done.

There was a hillock then just behind the school, and in 1840 the Trustees advertised that persons buying land near the school and desiring to erect substantial buildings could take stones from the hillock immediately behind the Singapore Institution. It was about fifty feet high, and an account of the geological formation of it will be found in the first volume of Logan's Journal at page 88.

The second wing was now built and was finished towards the close of 1841. The Supreme Court gave $50 a month from the interest on some funds at its disposal which assisted in paying the expense, which was about $3,030. School hours were then from nine to two o'clock, with only five minutes interval at noon, as some parents objected to their children playing in the sun at mid-day. The wing (it is called in the Report the right wing, whatever that may mean) was occupied by one of the masters and his family, and the large rooms in the main building were exclusively appropriated to the general purposes of the Institution, one being used as a Committee Room, the other as a Library.

In May, 1843, Mr. J. H. Moor, the first master died suddenly at the early age of forty and a subscription was made for his widow and children, which amounted to $6,700. It was invested in three mortgages on houses in the town at 12 per cent., and a monthly allowance was received by the widow until she died in Singapore in November, 1884.

Mr. Moor was born in Macao, whence he proceeded at an early age to Ireland, where he received his education. He was sometime at Trinity College, Dublin, with the view of qualifying himself for taking orders, but an unfortunate impediment in his speech ultimately led to Mr. Moor abandoning his intention. While in Dublin Mr. Moor served an apprenticeship to a respectable book-seller there and might afterwards have advantageously followed that business in Britain, but he preferred returning to the East. He came out to Madras on chance, and after remaining there a short time proceeded to Malacca, where, soon after his arrival in 1826, he originated the Free School under the auspices of Mr. Garling, then Resident Councillor at Malacca. Mr. Moor continued to conduct that school for four years, and during that time it was in a flourishing condition, being numerously attended. In September, 1826, Mr. Moor established the *Malacca Observer* which he carried on until October, 1829, when, in consequence of the paper having incurred the disapprobation of Government from the zeal with which the editor had exposed the system of slavery which then prevailed in Malacca, it was discontinued. In 1830, Mr. Moor came to Singapore where he taught a private school until 1834, when he was appointed Head Master to the Singapore Free School. Shortly after his arrival, Mr. Moor became editor of the *Singapore Chronicle*, which he conducted for four years, and only resigned on the establishment of the *Free Press* in October, 1835, the sub-editorship of which he held for about two years. After that he devoted himself chiefly to the duties of his situation in the Institution. In the latter end of 1837, Mr. Moor published the quarto volume entitled " Notes of the Malayan Archipelago," which consisted chiefly of articles which had appeared in the different Straits papers, of which Mr. Moor had been editor. This work, which was accompanied by a number of maps, contained much valuable information regarding the Native States and places adjacent. In a pecuniary point of view, however, it was very unprofitable work to Mr. Moor, from the expense incurred in engraving the charts, and the difficulties attendant on bringing out a work of any size with the limited materials at command in such a place as Singapore, and also from the slow and small sale. In the end a considerable loss was sustained, which pre-vented the appearance of the continuation of the work, which was at one time contemplated. From his long residence in the Straits Mr. Moor possessed much knowledge of the history both of the British possessions and the neighbouring states, which it is a pity he did not embody in a permanent form. Mr. Moor contributed largely to promote a taste for reading in the Settlement and adjacent stations by procuring consignments of books from the London publishers, which were disposed of at the English prices. A large number of books were, through Mr. Moor's instrumentality, sold in Singapore, and also in Java and China, but in this instance also the public were the only party benefited, as on account of the difficulty of procuring returns from the different places to which he sent the books, Mr. Moor was considerably out of pocket by the speculation. The above account of Mr. Moor's life is taken from the *Free Press* at the time of his death.

The Rev. J. T. Dickenson took charge of the school for four months, when he returned to America on account of his health and Mr. John Colson Smith, master of the Free School in Penang, was made Head Master of the Institution, and Mr. R. W. Wiber from the Penang Chinese Mission School was second master from January, 1844. Mr. Smith was very popular, and was a prominent Freemason. In 1852 he left the school and was Deputy Sheriff and in 1860 was appointed Magistrate and Commissioner of the Court of Requests, and left Singapore in 1862 for England, and afterwards died in Mauritius.

Mr. Fitzpatrick left in July the same year, and a system of monitors for teaching the lower classes was established as more useful, and by reducing expenses it was possible to establish a Girls' School, which was opened on 4th March, 1844.

The Rev. Alexander Stronach of the London Missionary Society had given much assistance, and done a great deal of good to the school. The Resident Chaplain had fallen out with the Committee on the subject of religious teaching, and nearly filled up the *Free Press* newspaper in August, 1844, with a very long correspondence on his side of the question. The Committee in their report said it was a matter of great regret that the Chaplain of the station neglected so interesting a field of usefulness and benevolence, having that time to attend to such an important duty which no other member of the Committee possessed. The Bishop of Calcutta was appealed to, and at his desire the Chaplain again resumed his connection with the school : but he contented himself with taking some little interest in the lower native classes only, and what was done was due to Mr. Stronach, who had worked continuously for nearly six years until he was removed to China in 1844. At this time there were 195 boys in the school.

In 1852, the Rev. W. B. Wright became Head Master. He had been a missionary in Sarawak ; his wife was a connection of Governor Butterworth. Mr. George Rappa had been at the Bishop's College, Calcutta, and returning to Singapore with very good testimonials, was appointed second master, and continued in the school until 1856. Mr. Wright remained until 1857 when he went to Malacca, to the great regret of the Committee.

The report for 1856 says that the Government of India had intimated the intention to contribute to every educational charity an amount equal to that subscribed or collected from the scholars in shape of fees, and that the Tumongong had agreed to give $1,500 annually for the support of vernacular schools. At the meeting of the subscribers, Mr. J. J. Greenshields and Dr. R. Little proposed, and it was adopted, that the land in rear of the Institution (the present play-ground) which belonged to the school, might be made available towards the support of the schools, (meaning disposing of the land) and Mr. R. C. Woods and Mr. W. Napier proposed that the Committee should consider the propriety of disposing of the existing building and ground to the Government and applying the proceeds to the establishment of schools in central positions of the town. Fortunately neither of these schemes came to anything, and the only sale that was made was never completed and the Girls' School now stands on the site. It was a curious fact that in 1855, at the request of the Ladies' Committee, Mr. Whampoa arranged to provision the Girls' School at an average charge of $4 a month for each child. On the 20th March, 1857, the new Head Master, Mr. John Barrett Bayley, arrived from England, and was Head Master until 1870.

The report of 1857 gives a list of the continuing Trustees of the Singapore Institution as distinct from the Committee of the School. They were William Napier, appointed 5th January, 1836; T. O. Crane, 6th February, 1842; M. F. Davidson, 6th February, 1844; W. H. Read, 27th March, 1846; John Harvey, 31st March, 1842; and Mr. Humphrey, the Residency Chaplain, 12th February, 1857.

In this year the question of the legal position of the Trustees was brought before the Supreme Court in a friendly suit between the Governor and two of the Trustees, W. Napier and T. O. Crane. It hung on for over four years, and ended by the Recorder on 27th April, 1861, confirming a long report by Mr. Christian Baumgarten, the Registrar of the Court, by which the matter was put on a settled footing. It provided for twelve Trustees, with a quorum of four for ordinary business and seven for the election of a Trustee or for voting extraordinary disbursements. An attempt was made to set aside the sale of the land that had been made, as already described, but lapse of time, if no other reason, prevented this. The first Trustees appointed under this order, besides the Resident Councillor, Residency Chaplain and Surgeon, who were appointed *ex-officio*, were W. Paterson, W. H. Read, C. H. Harrison, J. J. Greenshields, T. H. Campbell, C. H. H. Wilsone, N. B. Watson, the Rev. M. Fraser and Captain C. A. Purvis, Madras Artillery. They took charge of the building and its affairs on 15th June, 1861.

In August, 1863, a second European Master, Mr. George Williams, was engaged in England through the Queen's Inspector of Schools. In order to meet financial difficulties the trustees in that year accepted an offer of $4,000 from Mr. Joseph Joshua for "one third part of the land in the rear of and adjoining the Institution." This is the land on which the present Girls' School is built, and part of the play ground. Very fortunately the sale was never completed, and in 1875 the land was resumed as it had not been built on. In 1866 Mr. Bailey went to Europe on leave for two years, and Mr. George Brown was appointed second master. He had been a school master in the Navy, and being on board a surveying vessel stationed here, he left the service in Singapore to join the School. He afterwards took orders in Singapore, being ordained in St. Andrew's Cathedral, and went afterwards to Australia, where he was Rural Dean at Penrith and has now a parish church in the town of Sydney.

Mr. Bayley remained head master of the Institution until October, 1870. He earned the gratitude of the school boys of Singapore who owed much to him. He was a practical teacher, and the boys learned to write and cipher well, which was necessary for earning their living as clerks in Government and mercantile offices, their principal means of employment. From a comparatively small school, Mr. Bayley during thirteen years raised it to a large and flourishing one, (to quote the words of a report of the trustees) and it was ill-health which compelled him to leave Singapore. He went to Europe, and some years afterwards he came out for a short time as master of the School in Sarawak. He died in England on 16th July 1893, the Trustees recording on their minutes that he had for twelve years discharged the onerous duties of Head Master with great ability and success, and expressing their regret at his death.

At various times before 1854 the sum of $4,000 had been subscribed for a Scholarship Fund, Mr. R. C. Woods giving a yearly sum of $50 for some time. The interest on this sum is now applied in payment of the School-fees of some of the scholars, which is probably not what the subscribers intended to be done with the money.

In 1859 Mr. W. W. Shaw of Boustead & Co., gave $500 as the foundation of a fund for prizes for European, Eurasian or Portuguese boys studying Chinese, in order to provide better interpreters in the Courts. Some Chinese residents added $500, and subsequently Messrs. Alexander and James Guthrie gave $1,000. The interest on this was applied for a long time to the Chinese Class, which did not prove successful. Nor did the Malay Class, towards the support of which Messrs. Guthrie had also given $1,000. In 1890 the interest on the whole $3,000 was appropriated with the consent of the donors towards the expenses of the Girls' School.

In 1872 Mr. Jasper Young, of Boustead & Co., and Mr. Oscar Mooyer, of Behn, Meyer & Co., gave a sum of $2,000, the interest on which forms a yearly Prize-Fund.

In 1871 the Trustees congratulated themselves that seventeen boys had been sent to the School by the King of Siam, and expense was incurred to make arrangements to receive them; and to make more room a house was rented for the Girls' School which had occupied part of the building since its commencement, but never afterwards occupied any part of the Institution building. After six months all the Siamese boys went back to Siam and never returned to the School, and nothing came of it.

In 1875 the Government erected the two story extension and the large three-story wing at the end of the Building at Brass Bassa Road. The intention was that it should be occupied by the sons of Malay Chiefs, in accordance with the original scheme of Sir Stamford Raffles. This was the third time the proposal was brought forward, and for the third time it failed to succeed, and the building after being used for some years for the Library and Museum was given over in 1887 to the Institution for class rooms. Whether the scheme to educate the better class of Malays and Siamese did not succeed in any of these instances because it had inherent impossibilities, or whether there was not sufficient care in arranging the details, or a want of proper supervision in the school, the result remained that it failed each time.

As has been seen, the Institution began unsuccessfully, and now, nearly eighty years afterwards, it is possible to judge of what has been done, and what advantage has been taken of the opportunities it has had to promote education in the place, which, after all, was the real object of Sir Stamford Raffles.

When Mr. Bayley left in 1870 the number of boys was 410. The Brothers School, St. Joseph's, of which an account is given in another chapter, was then much smaller. The Anglo-Chinese School was commenced in 1886. The following were the numbers of the average enrolment of these three schools in the following years:—

		RAFFLES.	ST. JOSEPH'S.	ANGLO-CHINESE.
1870	...	410	190	—
1880	...	513	250	—
1887	...	—	—	85
1890	...	400	312	372
1900	...	431	426	590

This is the last year for which the Annual Report of the Government Inspector of Schools is available when this is printed. Notwithstanding the very large increase in the population during the last thirty years, and consequently in the number of boys able to attend school, the Institution has not increased its numbers, while the other schools have grown largely. With the exception of the addition made at the sole cost of Government, the buildings have not been enlarged since 1841. The Anglo-Chinese School has had large additions made to it, and the Brothers School is again to be enlarged at once with large and airy class rooms and dormitories. In each case these schools were cramped for land, while the Institution has very large grounds available for the purpose. The Institution has the considerable endowment of $500 a month and the interest on some invested funds; the buildings are kept in repair at Government expense: it has a splendid situation and a fine play-ground, while the other two schools have none : it has the scholarship funds already described, which the other Schools are without ; and it has the prestige and position naturally attaching to it. In 1880 there were over 500 boys, and at that time the large school rooms in the addition and the three-storied wing were occupied by the Library and Museum, now they are used as class-rooms. It is therefore no question of room for classes. But it may be said that by teaching smaller numbers the education may be better, which is undoubtedly very desirable. This can be tested by the results of the examinations for the Government Scholarships. The Higher Scholarships were instituted by the Government, in 1885, in order to encourage education in the Colony, and in 1889 the name was changed to the Queen's Scholarship. There are two each year of the value of £250 each, a year, for not more than five years, a princely scholarship. There are also Government Local Scholarships which are given with the object of inducing boys to remain longer in school. Since 1897 the examinations for all these Scholarships have been conducted by the Cambridge Local Examination Syndicate by papers sent out from Cambridge and returned there for examination. The impartial character of the result is unquestionable. Until 1890 the Institution gained the Higher Scholarships. In 1891 the Brothers School took one, and in 1893 and 1894 the Institution took one, the Anglo-Chinese School one, and the Penang Free School two. In 1895 and 1896 only one scholarship was given each year on the score of Government retrenchment, but the two were resumed in 1897. There were thus twelve Scholarships in the seven years from 1895 to 1901 inclusive, of which the Institution took four, the Penang Free School having taken five, the Penang Brothers School two, and the Anglo-Chinese School, Singapore, one. As to the Local Scholarships, the Institution took them until 1892 (they were established in 1882) and in the last four years from 1898 to 1901 the Institution has taken five out of twenty. The annual Government Report of the Inspector of Schools shows that in 1899, the average cost of each pupil in average attendance at the Institution was $64.05 : at the Brothers School $31.97 : and at the Anglo-Chinese School $27.42. As the accounts of that year might have included some unusual expenses, the average of expenses for the last five years has been taken out, and it shews the three Schools respectively, $56.12, $25.42, and $24.26. With its advantages and its larger expenditure it is a question whether it should not by this time have grown to three or four times its present size, as well in numbers as in buildings. Where others have done so much, the Institution has left it to others to shew the way, and while they have advanced, finds itself just where it was thirty years ago.

The Raffles Girls' School was opened on the 4th March, 1844, in the Institution building with six boarders and five day scholars.

In 1847, the School was removed from the centre of the building to the wing next to Brass Bassa Road, suitable out-offices were erected, and the wall, which is still standing, was built across the back part of the compound to make a separation between the schools and play grounds of the Boys and Girls. The centre rooms of the building, which had been used for the Girls, were then used for the Singapore Library.

In 1871, to make room for expected boy pupils from Siam, the Girls' School was moved into a house, rented at $55 a month on the opposite side of Brass Bassa Road, where the Raffles Hotel is now built. In 1877, as an increased rent was asked for that house, the school was moved to the last house in Beach Road, the one built by Dr. d'Almeida in 1825. In 1881 the new Girls' School building on the Institution land behind the Boys' School was commenced : it cost $12,008, of which the Government paid $6,000. The School was moved into the new building on 23rd July, 1883. In 1888 a wing was added to the end towards the sea : it cost $2,628, of which the Government paid $1,250.

Sir Stamford Raffles intended the name "The Institution" to be used. It was afterwards spoken of, and printed in the Annual Report as "The Singapore Institution" until after 1867, when for some reason that does not appear, in the Annual Report for that year printed in 1868, it was called "The Raffles Institution." No Annual Reports are to be found between 1848 and 1854 and probably none were issued. The previous Reports for the four years 1845 to 1848 were all printed together in 1849.

CHAPTER XII.

1823—Resumed.

MR. CRAWFURD took charge of the Resident's Office, and on the 9th June Raffles gave over to him full charge of the Settlement. Sir Stamford sailed the same day and reached Bencoolen on 18th July. He never returned to Singapore. The usual circular letter which had been sent to inform neighbouring States that he had given over charge to Mr. Crawfurd was returned unanswered by Van der Capellan, the Governor-General of Java.

It may be useful here to note the periods when Sir Stamford Raffles was actually in Singapore. He arrived in the harbour to establish a settlement on 28th January, 1819, and left on the 7th February. He returned in the beginning of June, after having been to Acheen, and left again either in July or September. He arrived for the third and last time on the 10th October, 1822, and left on the 9th June, 1823.

Mr. John Crawfurd had belonged to the Bengal Medical Service. He passed three years in Penang as a civil surgeon, and the next six in Java as British Resident at the Court of the Sultan when it was occupied by the British under Raffles. In 1820 he published his History of the Indian Archipelago, and in the following year he went as Envoy from the Indian Government to the Court of Siam and Cochin-China where his missions were not very successful; but his visits proved advantageous afterwards in opening up communication and obtaining information about those countries which were then very little known. In Cochin-China the King would not grant him an audience or receive the letter from the Governor-General, and the only result was that the British should be allowed to trade on the same terms as the French. His work on the subject of this Embassy was published in 1830. In 1834 he published the Journey of his Embassy to Ava where he went as Ambassador in 1827. He was said to be no mean diplomatist. He also wrote some valuable articles in the *Singapore Chronicle* on scientific subjects and there are several papers of his in Logan's Journal. All his books were said to be very useful and extremely laborious works. A review of his Descriptive Dictionary of the Indian Isles, published in 1856, is in Logan's Journal for the same year.

Crawfurd was famous both as an administrator and an author, but he was not a popular man, and succeeded two men of singular popularity. Raffles especially was a great favourite with all classes of the community, both European and native; his easy manners and courteous demeanour captivating all hearts; and Farquhar was very much liked. Mr Crawfurd's manner was against him and obscured the great qualities he evidently possessed. He was a typical Scotchman, and it was said of him that frugality, which is virtue in a poor but high spirited people, is apt to degenerate into parsimoniousness. He was very cautious, but managed the affairs of the settlement with energy and ability.

Abdulla speaks of him thus: "On looking at Mr. Crawfurd's disposition, he was impatient and of quick temper, but in what he was engaged he acted slowly and not immediately. Further, it could be perceived that he was a man of good parts, clever and profound. Yet it was equally true that he was much bent down by a love for the goods of this world. His hand was not an open one, though he had no small opinion of himself. Further, his impatience prevented him from listening to long complaints, and he did not care about investigating the circumstances of the case. As sure as there was a plaint he would cut it short in the middle. On this account I have heard that most people murmured and were dissatisfied, feeling that they could not accept his decision with good will, but by force only."

Mr. Crawfurd and Raffles (to use Sir Stamford's own words) ran too much on the same parallel not to be now and then jostling each other; and they were not always pulling easily together. There was much rivalry in authorship, probably, and they criticised each other pretty freely in the English reviews.

When Raffles came from Bencoolen to Singapore, in 1822, he was accompanied by an assistant, a civilian of the Bencoolen establishment; this was Mr. Edward Presgrave who had been the Judge and Magistrate in Bencoolen. Mr. Presgrave and Mr. Bonham became assistants to Mr. Crawfurd. Mr. Bonham was a very young man in those days; he had come out to Bencoolen when a boy of fifteen, and was afterwards Police Magistrate here for a long time, and eventually Governor in 1837. Mr. Crawfurd's portrait is hung in the Town Hall. He is represented in a sitting posture.

Mr. Crawfurd was in charge of the Settlement from 9th June, 1823 to 14th August, 1826, when he was succeeded by Mr. Prince. He then was appointed Civil Commissioner on the part of the British Government at Rangoon and in the following year went to Burmah as Ambassador. The *Glasgow Evening Post* of 11th September, 1830, contained a long account of a dinner given to Mr. John Crawfurd, by the Lord Provost and upwards of one hundred Glasgow merchants and others. It published a list of the forty-two toasts, among which one was "The free port of Singapore, and may its rising prosperity add another proof of the advantages to commerce which result from freedom." In 1833 he was a candidate for the new Parliament after the Reform Bill, as the representative of Glasgow, his principal reasons for obtaining support being his warm advocacy for the commercial interests of England upon matters connected with India; but he was not successful. Mr. Crawfurd continued to take a warm interest in the affairs of the Settlement to the very end of his life, and in his last year, on 31st January, 1868, when the Straits Settlements Association was formed in London, he was the first President. Mr. William Napier was Chairman, and Mr. James Guthrie, Deputy-Chairman. A clear proof that the best of the old Singaporeans did not neglect the interests of the place after they had left it. He died in 1868 at the age of eighty-five years.

In May, Raffles had asked the opinions of the Magistrates about the desirability of gambling licenses, and they unanimously represented their great and growing evils. So the system was abolished, and public gaming prohibited. It was alleged, in support of the gambling farm, that, by putting it under regulations, the quantity of vice was diminished, but Raffles said that independently of the want of authority in any Government to countenance evil for the sake of good, he could not admit that the effects of any regulation whatever, established on such a principle, could be put in competition with the solid advantages which must accrue from the administration of a Government acting on strict moral principles, discountenancing vice, and exercising its best efforts to repress it. He utterly repudiated the principle that it was necessary to relax the rules of government and morality in order to induce the immigration of Chinese and other traders. And Mr. Braddell remarks that Sir Stamford, convinced of the natural advantages of Singapore, and foreseeing its future prosperity, anxiously endeavoured to protect it from the inconvenience which must arise from sacrificing principle to expediency.

On the other hand Mr. Crawfurd took an entirely different view of the subject, and addressed the Magistrates asking for their advice and co-operation for his plan of legalizing gambling. The non-officials unanimously protested against the principle of legalizing vice in any shape, as likely to be detrimental to the best interests of the Settlement. Mr. Crawfurd, however, persisted, and on the 23rd August he wrote to the Magistrates as follows:—

"Gentlemen, I have the honour to inform you, that in consequence of an extensive conspiracy being discovered amongst the native police to defeat the regulations for the extirpation of gaming, the repeated and earnest representations of the principal Chinese inhabitants in regard to the existing system, and the object itself being found at present of difficult attainment, it has been deemed necessary, pending a reference to the Supreme Government, to license gaming, under the system of restraint and regulation which is detailed in the advertisement, a copy of which is herewith transmitted. You will have the goodness, therefore, to suspend all proceedings in regard to the regulation against gaming, until the pleasure of the Honourable the Governor-General in Council shall be received."

And on the 18th September he wrote to the Secretary to Government at Bengal explaining his reasons, as follows;—"Sir,—In a despatch of the 15th of July, I had the honour to bring to the notice of Government the circumstances relating to gaming at this Settlement. Since that period, a conspiracy amongst the native police has been discovered to defeat the regulations for its suppression, and three convictions have in consequence taken place. The penalties attached to a breach of the regulation are at the same time so extremely heavy and severe and, as it appears to me, so much at variance with the habits and manners of the inhabitants, that I have felt myself by no means warranted in carrying them into effect before they receive the confirmation of the Supreme Government.

"2. In the meantime, the principal natives and Chinese made repeated applications for the suspension of the regulation, stating a fact, the accuracy of which could not be questioned, that many of the lower classes had quitted the Settlement on account of being deprived of a customary amusement.

"3. Urged by these reasons, and feeling the impossibility, under the existing circumstances of the Settlement, of suppressing gaming, I have adopted as a temporary alternative, the plan of licensing it to a certain extent and placing it under a system of control and restriction, on the following conditions:—The number of gaming houses and of the houses of play are limited; no gaming is permitted but for ready money; no person gaming is permitted to wear arms; no gaming is permitted in private houses or in the street, the latter practice hitherto being very frequent; and finally the gaming licenses are to cease in forty-eight hours after the receipt of orders to that effect from the Supreme Government."

In a paper he wrote two years afterwards, Mr. Crawfurd explained his views as follows:—" The arguments for restoring the gaming farm are given at length in the papers submitted to Mr. Fullerton. The attempts made to put down the practice of gaming appear to me little better than charlatanerie in such societies as those of our eastern settlements, where the mass of the inhabitants is habitually addicted to play, and where it is viewed only as a harmless amusement. It is said to be disgraceful to gain a revenue by gaming. Not surely more so than making a revenue by drunkenness, for both as far as regards gaming and the consumption of wine and spirits, it is impracticable to distinguish between vicious and harmless indulgence. At all events it is consistent with every principle of wise legislation, that that which cannot be prevented ought to be regulated. The gaming farm of Singapore is divided into twelve licenses. The houses are all in one street and contiguous to each other, so as to be under the immediate eye of the police. This is the farm in which the greatest augmentation of revenue has taken place, and owing, as I conceive, entirely to the minute subdivision of it. The increase amounts to very little less than 300 per cent. I ought to mention that during two years and a half not a single quarrel or accident has taken place in the gaming houses."

On the 1st December, 1823, Raffles wrote from Bencoolen to Calcutta protesting against Mr. Crawfurd's action regarding gambling, and asking the Governor-General in Council to uphold the principle which he had felt it his duty to lay down and had been concurred in and approved by high authority. He said it involved no less the character of the place than the interests of those who resided in it. In a previous despatch written in Singapore on 22nd April, 1823, the following passage occurs, it is now copied from a manuscript note made by Mr. Braddell, in which he had himself copied out the whole passage, no doubt because it expressed Sir Stamford's views on the subject and so was sufficiently important to be quoted at length:—

" On the establishment of the Settlement I thought it my duty to declare that the vice of gaming was strictly prohibited, but licences having been subsequently granted by the Resident, I regret to say that they soon degenerated into the farming system as practised in the Dutch Settlements with all its attendant evils. Under these circumstances I could not do more on my arrival than attempt the modification of the existing system, leaving the future consideration of the subject until the end of the present official year, when my own experience would be enlarged, and something like an efficient Police established. That period having now arrived, a decision has become necessary, and on the representation made by the Magistrates I have not hesitated to abolish the farm altogether from the 1st May, notwithstanding the opposition to the measure which I have met with on the part of the Resident. That to give a license for gaming does give a countenance to the vice cannot I think be denied ; that it does so abstractedly is evident from no one ever arguing that a license may be given to robbers and pirates ; and that it is considered a justification in the apprehension of those who practise the vice is equally evident from the shameless audacity with which they bring their gambling disputes into open court. It is alleged in support of the Gaming Farm that by placing it under regulation, the quantity of vice is diminished, but independent of the want of authority of any human government to countenance evil for the sake of good, I cannot admit that the effects of any regulation whatever established on such a principle are to be put in competition with the solid advantages which must accrue from the administration of a government acting on strict moral principles, discountenancing vice, and exercising its best effects to suppress it."

Then follows a note of a despatch from the Governor-General to the Resident dated 11th September, 1823, in which it said : " With respect to gaming, it has been already intimated to the Lieutenant-Governor (Raffles) in reply to his letter of 22nd April last, that the sentiments of the Government coincided with his in regard to the propriety of abolishing the farm. The decision had been founded on the persuasion that the sanction of licensing public gaming houses tended to encourage and increase the vice, and that government seriously injured its respect in the eyes of the people, and brought the reproach of countenancing vice for sake of profit. Also that Raffles had stated that measures adopted by him at Bencoolen and Java had been entirely successful and produced a marked impression on the habits of the people. The Governor-General was averse to penal enactments for private gaming where there was no fraud ; and if not mischievous it was probably nugatory. But he considered it to be proper that public gaming and the establishment of professed gaming houses should be prevented, and, consequently, that the farm should not be reinstated. If, however, on further experience Mr. Crawfurd was satisfied that relinquishing the gaming farm would not be advantageous and its restoration not injurious to the morals of the people, or the respect to the British Government, the Governor-General would be prepared to re-consider the question."

The following were the annual revenues received from the Opium and Gambling Farms in the following years :—

		Opium.		Gambling.
1820	...	$ 7,345	...	$ 5,275
1821	...	9,420	...	7,335
1822	...	14,200	...	9,500
1823	...	22,830	...	15,076
1824	...	24,000	...	25,630
1825	...	24,030	...	33,657
1826	...	24,600	...	30,390

When in 1827 the Grand Jury presented the Gambling Farm as an immoral nuisance the remark was made by the Recorder (as Mr. W. H. Read thinks) or by Dr. Montgomerie (as Mr. James Guthrie thought) that "I did not think there were thirteen such idiots in the Island." Sir Stamford Raffles who was *tant soit peu cafard* (by no means a hypocrite) and had to propitiate Sir Robert Inglis, Mr. Wilberforce and others, (Exeter Hall), set his face against the Farm. Mr. Crawfurd who had a thorough knowledge of the Chinese and Native characters, and had no prejudices to contend with, was strongly in favour of it. It was finally abolished by the Court of Directors in 1829 when it brought in $2,922 a month, being $100 above the sum then paid for the opium farm. The consequence was corruption of the police, and surreptitious gambling worse than ever, even up to the present day.

The question of the gambling farm was for years a subject of continual discussion in the newspapers, and a bitter war waged between those who advocated a farm as a moral duty and those who discountenanced it on sentimental scruples. Mr. W. H. Read as *Delta* took up the former and Dr. Little as *Zero* opposed it. The question was thrashed out at great length in the *Free Press* from June to September, 1860; and in March, 1885, when the originals of these papers appeared in the Anecdotal History in the same paper, *Delta* wrote to say that he was still of the same mind, because a farm was the only way to *control* what all admitted to be a vice, and Dr. Little as *Zeta* replied that he was still alive and kicking, and his opinion (*suppression*) remained unchanged.

It will have been seen from Sir Stamford's letter quoted above that he spoke of an efficient police being established. Gambling may be controlled through a farm because it is then necessarily conducted in public and the farmers (like the Opium and Spirit farmers) protect their own interests in preventing private gaming; while it cannot be suppressed by an inefficient police, who are exposed to unlimited corruption. In the Protected Native States now there are gambling farms, and always have been. The great preponderance of opinion among those who had the means of acquainting themselves with the practical side of the subject has, probably, always been in favour of Mr. Crawfurd's view and not of that of Raffles.

In October Mr. Crawfurd wrote to Bengal saying that he was going to spend $900 on a new gaol, as the old one was only a temporary building, too small and insecure; it was a wooden building near the end of the east bank of the river, close to where the stone landing steps are now. He also proposed to spend $1,200 on a dredging machine to clear away the accummulation of sand at the mouth of the river, which he said had arisen owing to the injudicious manner in which some of the wharves and warehouses had been built, the effect of which had been to obstruct the natural course of the stream, and that if some scheme was not carried out, the navigation would be entirely obstructed. He also intended to spend $1,000 on a water-course and reservoir, as the wells and a small reservoir which had been constructed had fallen so much into decay that twelve of the East India Company's vessels which had touched at Singapore in the month of

September had experienced serious inconvenience for want of proper arrangements to supply water, and the advantages of the port depended, he said, very much upon its ability and convenience as a place of refreshment.

In February the native chiefs had asked permission to hoist the British flag in Johore to protect them against the risk of an attempt by their rivals at Rhio to occupy Johore. In August, a confidential order came from Bengal to strike the flag there, and Mr. Crawfurd told the native chiefs to do so, and thought it had been done. In November the Rhio chiefs, assisted by the Dutch authorities at that place, actually attempted to occupy Johore, and messengers were sent from there to Mr. Crawfurd, who now learnt that the flag had not been struck, and the native chiefs refused to do so, in spite of his remonstrances and explanations that no clause of any treaty bound the British to maintain the authority of the Sultan and Tumungong beyond the limits of the island of Singapore, but his directions were at last complied with. The native chiefs appealed to the Governor-General, which, of course, came to nothing. The Dutch had offered the most obstinate resistance to the Settlement at Singapore, and had it not been for the influence secured at home by Sir Stamford Raffles, who lost no opportunity of making friends for Singapore in official and mercantile circles, the place would probably have been soon given up. The opposition of the Dutch remained unabated until 1824, when the treaty of London of 17th March, the exchange of Bencoolen for Malacca, and other arrangements, ended the dispute.

Mr. Braddell made a note that on the 18th November the Resident was alarmed at the proceedings of the Dutch, and the following letter written by Mr. Crawfurd to the Secretary of the Government at Calcutta on that day explains the matter:—

Political Department.

Sir,—The Commissioners of the Dutch Government, whose arrival at Malacca I had the honor to report in a former despatch, passed this place about ten days ago on their way to Rhio.

At Malacca the Commissioners have nearly taken off all port charges and reduced the duties on native vessels to one per cent., an impost, however, still sufficient to prove irksome to the native traders and therefore equal to a direct encouragement to this port. The duty of 25 per cent. imposed on British woollens and cottons at Batavia is by the present arrangement extended to Malacca.

The Dutch Commissioners, while at Malacca, invited the rival brother of the Sultan who is connected with us, to come round to Rhio from Tringanu, where he had been residing for several years, and sent a ship of war for his accommodation. This invitation was accepted of, and about three weeks ago the native prince in question arrived at Rhio, where he was put in possession of what are called the regalia, and raised to the Throne of Johore.

The two native chiefs connected with us sent me a messenger yesterday, who had arrived from Johore itself, now a fishing village upon a large river on the Peninsula, 20 miles distant from this place. This person informed me that the newly created Sultan of Johore, in concert with the Dutch, had sent over a party of his own people, accompanied by two Europeans, to hoist his own and the Netherland flag and take possession of Johore as the legitimate prince.

The natives chiefs in connection with us have upon this occasion come forward to claim our active assistance, on the faith of promises alleged to have been made to them. I have declined on the part of Government to interfere in this transaction in any respect whatever, and recommended to the parties to rest satisfied in the meantime with the ample allowance which they derive from the bounty of the British Government.

The Netherland Government has resolved upon forming an establishment on the large island of Lingin which is a portion of the Johore territory. This will be detrimental to the interests of this place, only in as far as it may obstruct a growing trade in tin from a small island on the Coast of Lingin and dependent upon it, called Singkep. When Singapore was taken possession of on our part, the produce of Singkep in this metal was very inconsiderable, but in consequence of the high prices given at this port, it has since increased so much as at present to be estimated at little less than 5,000 piculs annually.

The activity of the Netherland Government has also been directed to other quarters in our vicinity. They have within the last 12 months formed a Settlement upon the Island of Billiton, which has claims to be considered as a British possession in consequence of a cession from the Sultan of Palembang in the year 1812, sanctioned by the silence of the convention of the Netherland Government of 1814, by which Banca, a cession of the same treaty, was given in exchange for Cochin. I submit this fact with the more confidence, as it chanced to come within the range of my own personal knowledge that the Island of Billiton was actually viewed as a British possession by the British Commissioners who conducted the discussion of the Dutch claims in London, in the year 1820.

The Batavian Government have from all accounts also obtained a cession of the Carimata Islands, which lie between Billiton and Borneo, and where it is said they contemplate forming a Settlement. Should this be effected they will be in an attitude in some respects to control every navigable channel leading from the Straits of Malacca and the China Sea, to the Java and Amboyna Seas and the Straits of Sunda.

It seems probable that one object at least of the policy in question, is so far to control the native trade as to give it a direction towards their own ports, and force it out of its present channels. In furtherance of this principle they have indeed already imposed heavy and almost prohibitory duties on all native vessels belonging to their own Settlements which shall trade or even touch at any foreign European ports.

Well authenticated accounts have been received at this place, that the Dutch Government in the month of September last, undertook an expedition for the conquest of Sangau. This is a Malay State situated on the Island of Borneo, about 300 miles up the great river of Pontianak, and in the heart of the country which has of the late years produced so much gold. The expedition consists of 3 gun-boats and 400 troops, principally Europeans, and it will require a voyage of two months to take it to its destination, as the ascent of the river is against a rapid stream and very difficult.

It may be worth remarking that Sangau is but one out of eight Malay States of considerable size, scarcely known by name to Europeans, all situated on the same river, which appears to be navigable for native vessels for little less than 1,000 miles.

I have received accounts from Sangora, the first Siamese province bordering on the Malay countries. The person who furnishes me with this information was in the presence of the Rajah of Sangora, on or about the 20th of October, and declares that although rumours were abroad of an intended invasion of Siam by the British, he had not heard a word of any meditated attack on Prince of Wales Island, or even of any preparation making by the Siamese which appeared to have that object in view.

                                        I have, &c.,
                                (Signed)   J. CRAWFURD,
                                                    Resident.

Singapore, 18th November, 1823.

The following correspondence found in Mr. Braddell's notes contains a good deal of information on many matters, with Mr. Crawfurd's reasons for the steps he took. The regulations for the sale of the various farms are all to be found in 8 Logan's Journal pages 339 to 347, but would take up too much room here. They show the conditions under which the licences were issued for the manufacture of gunpowder, the pawnbrokers' shops, gaming houses and cockpits, and the sale of spirits and opium.

Territorial Department.

To
HOLT MACKENZIE, ESQ.,
                    Secretary to the Government, Fort William.

Sir,—I have the honor to lay before the Honorable the Governor-General in Council a sketch of the available revenue of this Settlement, with a short estimated comparison of our probable future resources and disbursement.

2. It may be necessary to premise that the principal sources of revenue in the eastern islands are an excise or tax on the consumption of opium, spirituous liquors, pork and fish. To these may be added taxes on gaming, pawnbrokers' shops, &c., &c.

3. These taxes are commonly rendered a monopoly, and under the name of *Farms* disposed of to one person, who again sublets his privilege, according as he judges best for his own convenience and advantage. In this manner each particular branch of the revenue is sold at Prince of Wales Island to one individual, and even in the large Island of Java, where there are several millions of inhabitants, there are not in all above five or six farms for each distinct subject of revenue.

4. Having been for some years accustomed to the consideration of questions of the nature and viewing the vicious principle of establishing monopolies as equally prejudicial to the Government and the public, I have ventured in the arrangement of the revenues of this Settlement upon some considerable changes, which I trust will meet the approbation of the Supreme Government.

5. Instead of a monopoly in favor of an individual, I have decided upon establishing a certain number of licenses for each branch of revenue, on an estimate of the wants and consumption of the place, and these have been disposed of by public outcry to the highest bidder, substantial security being taken for prompt monthly payment. There is nothing new in this arrangement, being the same with the licenses in England for the retail of wine and spirits, substituting the public sale for the discretion vested in the Magistrates. It will not be necessary in this place to describe the specific conditions of the licenses so disposed of. As an illustration of the general principle and as an example of the whole I have the honor to append to this letter the conditions of the arrack license.

6. The licenses disposed of on these principles are those for opium, Asiatic spirits, pawnbrokers, and the manufacture and retail vend of native gunpowder.

7. The advantage of substituting licenses for the former farms or monopolies, will I hope appear evident from a comparison of the sale of the two principal licenses, those of opium and spirituous liquors, at the present and preceding sales, where there is shewn an advantage in favor of the license system for the first of 83 per cent. and for the second of 125 per cent.

8. The detailed results of the present and preceding sales are as follows:—

		The preceding sale	Present sale.
Opium, Spanish dollars		1,615	$ 2,960
Arrack	,,	682	,, 1,540
Pork	,,	302	,, 302
Gunpowder	,,	...	,, 217
Pawnbrokers	,,	...	,, 175
Gaming	,,	778	,, ...
Spanish dollars...		3,377	$ 5,194

9. From this statement it will be observed that two small additional licenses have been created, that one has been abolished, and that another remains without alteration. The monthly increase upon the whole is $1,817 per mensem, or exclusive of the abolished farm $778. I may further remark on this point,

that on the supposition of the abolished license being restored and its selling upon terms equally advantageous with other licenses, which was to be reckoned upon, the actual monthly revenues arising from these farms would have amounted to $6,718.

10. On the subject of the abolished license, viz., that for gaming and the two new ones established, viz., those for pawnbrokers and for the manufacture and vend of native gunpowder, as well as that for the vend of pork, I respectfully submit the following explanations.

11. The license for gaming houses was abolished at the end of April last, under impressions and opinions which have already been submitted to the Supreme Government by the Lieutenant-Governor of Fort Marlbro'. Differing wholly on this question with Sir S. Raffles, it will be the more necessary that I offer a full explanation, a matter which I am enabled to accomplish with the more satisfaction, as I have already frankly explained my sentiments and dissent to himself in person.

12. The gaming licenses have been abolished by Sir S. Raffles under a belief that to license gaming was to encourage the vice, and that the revenue which government received from this source must necessarily be obtained at the expense of the morals of the people, and therefore unworthy of the character of the Government. If the actual circumstances of the case really warranted this inference, I should be heartily prepared to join the Lieutenant-Government of Fort Marlbro' in recommending the permanent abolition of the gaming license, but after a long and attentive consideration of this question I am inclined to come to a very different conclusion.

13. The passion for gaming prevades all ranks of the two principal classes of our population, the Chinese and the Malays, to a most unusual and extraordinary extent, and I am clearly of opinion that in the relation which we stand to them, and the slender opportunities which we possess of reforming their manners and habits, the propensity, as far as our influence is concerned, is incurable.

14. If our population, even with the habits I have ascribed to it, were of a stationary nature there might be fair hopes, with time and pains, to improve it, but the fact is, that by far the greater proportion of the people who are found here are not permanent inhabitants of the place, but individuals who make a temporary convenience of it for a few weeks, for a few months, or at most for a few years. To attempt the reformation of a people so circumstanced appears to me to be utterly hopeless.

15. It is necessary, besides, to observe that the practice of gaming, especially in reference to the Chinese, is not a vice of the same character which Europeans are accustomed to contemplate it. It is in fact an amusement and recreation which the most industrious of them are accustomed to resort to.

16. Having few holidays and scarcely any amusements besides, they consider being debarred from gaming as a privation and a violence in some measure offered to their habits and manners.

17. It is true, indeed, that gaming is proscribed by their code of laws. The prohibition in this case however seems a dead letter, and perhaps scarcely more valid than that interdiction of foreign trade and emigration, to the disregard of which we owe at this very Settlement one of the principal branches of our trade and the most numerous and industrious class of our population.

18. The real effect which I am inclined to believe the prohibition of gaming must produce, while the propensity to indulge in play is so habitually strong, will be, that gaming instead of being publicly carried on will be pursued clandestinely, that instead of being subjected to a wholesome control, all restraint will be removed from it, that the price of conniving at the practice will always be a source of temptation and corruption to the inferior officers of the police, and that, finally, although perhaps less worthy of consideration, a large revenue will be very unnecessarily sacrificed for an imaginary benefit.

19. In support of the opinions now offered I may safely quote the results of the abolition of the gaming licenses, at Prince of Wales Island, which took place about 13 years ago on a representation from the Grand Jury, shortly after the establishment of the King's Court at that place. The gaming, notwithstanding the abolition, is admitted to have gone on undiminished, large fines have been weekly levied on account of illegal gaming, and about three years ago the whole police, including the European Constables, were discovered in a conspiracy to

defeat the laws against gaming and convicted of having been concerned for years in taking large bribes for conniving at illicit play, while in point of revenue a loss of not less than half-a-million dollars, has been experienced. A reference in consequence of the discovery of this abuse was made to the Hon'ble Court of Directors, and, as I understood from the best source, authority has recently been given to reconsider and re-establish the licenses.

20. If the statements and reasonings which I have now respectfully submitted be considered of any weight, I trust I shall have the authority of the Hon'ble the Governor-General in Council for restoring the licenses in question, if only with a view to objects of police, and so that the gaming may at least be made to defray a part of the charge of those establishments which the exercise of it, either openly or clandestinely, must always in a great measure create a necessity for supporting.

21. On the subject of the two new licenses, those for pawnbrokers and the manufacture and retail of native gunpowder, not much explanation I hope will be necessary. They were chiefly instituted as a measure of police. It is evident that both are of a nature that would render them serious nuisances if under no control. The manufacture of gunpowder requires a few more words. It was found that no less than five manufactories of this article existed and that they were carried on in the immediate precincts of the town, to the imminent danger of the place, as they were necessarily without restraint or inspection on the part of the public authorities.

22. With reference to the farm for the vend of pork, this is a recent branch of revenue, created as I understand for a temporary and specific purpose and which expires at the end of the year. I trust Government will favor me with an authority not to restore it, viewing it as I do, as an extremely injudicious tax, affecting one of the principal necessaries of life of the most numerous and industrious class of our population, and this too under aggravated circumstances, since the whole of the article is imported and from its nature at a very heavy expense. The inconsiderable revenue derived from it, it will be observed, is more than compensated by the two new licenses which are on the present occasion submitted for approval.

23. The quit-rents of lands disposed of on the principle laid down by the Supreme Government will constitute another item of revenue, On the first of January I am in hopes that four thousand Spanish dollars, or thereabout, will be realized from this scource, giving a monthly revenue of 333 dollars.

24. The rents of houses purchased by the government and of which an account has been rendered in the correspondence of the Lieutenant-Governor of Fort Marlbro', form at least a temporary source of revenue. Both with a view to re-imburse the Government, and as the best means of preserving the buildings themselves, I have considered it the most eligible plan to let them on short leases of six months to the highest bidder, as they are from time to time vacated by the present occupants. When the whole are let in this manner, it is estimated they will bring a monthly revenue of somewhat more than 1,000 Spanish dollars. At present two only have been vacated by the occupants and let, and these, besides affording offices for the Magistrates and Master Attendant. a boat office, and room for the military stores, bring a monthly rent of dollars 300.

25. Should government be pleased to give their sanction to the revenue measures which I now have had the honor to propose, the actual receipts will amount to 7,749 Spanish dollars a month. This revenue appears in no respect to press upon the industry of the place and from the nature of the principal branches of it may be expected to increase from year to year, to keep pace with the prosperity of the Settlement, and ultimately to meet our disbursements, of which at present it falls very considerably short.

26. To place this subject in one view before the government, I shall here beg leave to exhibit a short sketch of the ordinary expenses of the Settlement. They are as follows:—

Civil establishment	$3,923
Stipends to native princes	2,000
Military establishment	3,349
Total	9,272

27. By this statement it will appear that the actual deficiency is 3,445 dollars and that with the prospective improvement in the revenue, which I contemplate will be the result of the measures I have recommended, not more than 1,500 dollars.

I have, &c.,

(Signed) J. CRAWFURD,

Resident.

Singapore, 15th July, 1823.

The imports in Singapore in this year were £1,200,000, and the exports £950,000. The actual revenue of the Farms for the year ending 30th April, 1823, was $25,796, and the population then was 10,683.

The firm of Syme & Co., which continues under the same name to this day, was established in this year, by Mr. Hugh Syme. It was in this year also that Seah Eu Chin came to Singapore from Swatow. He worked his passage down by keeping the accounts of the junk he sailed in, and on reaching Singapore he took two shares in a boat that rowed and sailed to Klang and other places. After two years he stayed in Singapore as the agent for this and other boats, in Kling Street and afterwards in Circular Road. He was, it is said, the first to start gambier and pepper planting in Singapore. We are told that he tried planting tea, nutmegs and other things, and not succeeding as he expected, he gave them up and tried gambier. The price was then so low, that he was going to discontinue that also, but Mr. Church persuaded him to persevere, and he made a large fortune by it. At that time gambier was 75 cents, and pepper $1.50 a picul. In former years, during the time of Sir Richard McCausland, it was not unusual for the Court to advise Chinese suitors to refer their cases to Eu Chin. And years ago, when the Chinese Secret Societies were troublesome, he was the person who had most control over the headmen of them. In 1850 he headed the deputation of the Chinese which waited upon the Governor-General, Lord Dalhousie, on his visit to Singapore, and Governor Butterworth wrote to him expressing his grateful acknowledgments for the assistance he had given in welcoming His Lordship. In December, 1853, the Governor gave him a certificate of naturalization, adding that it gave him much satisfaction to enrol the name of so talented and highly respectable a resident, since 1824 in Singapore, among the naturalized British in the Straits of Malacca. In 1837 he married the eldest sister of Mr. Tan Seng Poh, whose father was the *Captain China* of Perak. His wife died and a year after he married her younger sister, and the old lady is still alive. Their eldest son, Seah Cho Seah, died in 1885, at thirty-nine years of age, and his second son, Seah Leang Seah, has been one of the unofficial members of the Legislative Council. Eu Chin died in Singapore at the age of 79, in September, 1883. Mr. James Guthrie made this note to the original of these papers :—" Seah Eu Chin was book-keeper to Kim Swee, who did a large business on Boat Quay between Market Street and Bonham Street; and between 1832 and 1834 built the houses that he occupied, at the end of the Bridge. Eu Chin, if I am not mistaken, then purchased the property. He was one of the best educated Chinese in Singapore, and was always ready to make himself useful." In 1 Logan's Journal, page

35 and in Volume 2 page 283, are two papers by Eu Chin upon the remittances made by the Chinese to their parents, and on their numbers, tribes, and habits in Singapore.

On 20th November a committee of military officers assembled to consider the best site for cantonments, the place used near Stamford Road, on the north bank of the river under Government Hill, being wanted for other purposes. They were then removed to Rochore, but the ground was found to be too low. After that they were removed to the Sepoy Lines, where they continued until the European regiments took the place of the native troops, and occupied the barracks at Tanglin in 1868.

In December the Rev. Mr. Robinson of Bencoolen having published a work on Malayan orthography, Raffles sent six copies to the Supreme Government at Bengal and thirty copies to the Court of Directors in London.

CHAPTER XIII.

1824.

I N January Mr. Frederick James Bernard established a newspaper, *The Singapore Chronicle*. He had applied in the preceding July, to the Governor-General, through the Resident, for leave to do so, and on the 10th January the first number was sent to Bengal. It was, probably, published once a fortnight, because in January, 1831, it was increased in size to a paper of four pages, the whole sheet being 20 inches long by 25 inches wide, and the Editor wrote that the increasing importance of the Settlement (in 1831) as to its commerce, and the consequent progressive addition to its population, demanded from the Singapore Press a paper more worthy of the place than the former one, and published at shorter intervals. The principal contributor to the paper, for the first two years, was Mr. Crawfurd himself, the Resident. In 1884 it was not possible to find any copy of the paper before 1831, and there is not one, probably, in existence. In 1833 there is a note in the *Singapore Chronicle* that the Editor had been unable to make up a complete file of the paper for 1824, 1825 and 1826, so it is not likely that copies are in existence now, nearly eighty years later.

A short notice of the newspapers of years ago in the Straits may be of interest here. *The Prince of Wales Island Gazette* began in 1805, and ceased in August 1827, after twenty-two years. On the 22nd August, 1827, another paper, called *The Penang Register and Miscellany,* was started, and after a short life, expired in September, 1828; this had been a weekly publication. On 25th October, 1828, *The Government Gazette of Prince of Wales Island, Singapore, and Malacca* was started in Penang, published weekly, and it ceased in its turn in July, 1830. On 20th July, 1833, *The Prince of Wales Island Gazette* was started; and on the 7th April, 1838, *The Penang Gazette and Straits Chronicle* was established; these were both weekly papers.

Malacca had also had its newspapers, *The Malacca Observer,* published fortnightly, having commenced in September, 1826, and stopped in October, 1829; it was a small paper about the size of *Punch*, of four pages. After a long interval, *The Weekly Register* started as a weekly publication, and two volumes were published in 1839 and 1840.

The *Singapore Chronicle* continued the only paper in the place until October, 1835, when the *Singapore Free Press* started, and proved too much for the vitality of the *Chronicle*, which ceased, after attempting to get support by lowering its subscription, on Saturday, the 30th September, 1837, and the press and type were shipped to Penang to start the *Penang Gazette and Straits Chronicle* there. The *Free Press* was then the only paper until 1845, when the *The Straits Times and Singapore Journal of Commerce* published its first number on Tuesday, the 15th July, as a weekly paper of eight pages.   In 1824 the news-papers had to be submitted to Government before publication, under what was called the "Gagging Act." As long as Mr. Crawfurd edited the *Chronicle*, this gave no inconvenience, of course; but afterwards the paper used to have large blank spaces in it, where paragraphs or articles had been taken out, and their places supplied by a few stars, to show that it was not a mistake in the printing. That Act was abolished in 1835, and the new paper was consequently called *The Free Press*.

In January, 1824, the first census was taken, and the population then was 10,683, of which there were 74 Europeans, 16 Armenians, 15 Arabs, 4,580 Malays, 3,317 Chinese, 756 Natives of India, and 1,925 Bugis, &c.

In a report Mr. Crawfurd made in January he said that those natives who lived in boats occupied themselves with fishing and piracy, and lived on sago brought from Sumatra. The cost of clearing land for gambier and pepper, for which the soil was good, was $35 an acre. The Chinese were of two classes, Macao and Hokien, the latter the most respectable and the best settlers; all the merchants and most of the good agriculturists were Hokien. The Klings were numerous and respectable as traders. The Bengalees few, and only as menials. The Bugis were numerous and distinguished from other islanders by in-dustry and good conduct, but all traders, not agriculturists. The Malays of Malacca were useful settlers; those of Johore and other native states more a nuisance than a benefit. Except the fishing Malays, all the natives appreciated the advantage of a good land tenure under a European Government, and the Chinese particularly.

In Mr. Crawfurd's opinion the principle to be followed in order to attract agriculturists, was to give a good and permanent tenure, simple and with few formalities on transfer; a good plan either to make grants, an estate for years, or leases for fifty or sixty years renewable on fine, or say at once, a thousand years. Title not to convey real property rights as in England, such as immunity from personal debts, &c., but to be merely chattels.

As there was no power to lay a tax upon Europeans, Mr. Crawfurd proposed that power should be given for the East India Company to assess rates for general municipal purposes, police, roads, lighting, cleansing, nuisances, &c.

The Resident asked permission to forward a gold cup, with a letter dated 23rd December, 1823, presented to Colonel Farquhar, the late Resident, by the Chinese inhabitants of Singapore.

On the 18th January there was a very high tide, rising two feet above the usual highest spring tides. It overflowed into the shops of the Chinese, and into A. L. Johnston & Co.'s godown, which was the nearest to the sea in Battery Road. Sampans were going along the streets at Boat Quay, as they were the only means for people to leave the houses. All Mr. Johnston's out-houses were thrown down by the water washing away the foundations. His house was in a compound, where the building of the Chartered Bank is now. There was a fence along the front in what is now called Battery Road, and steps on the river side, where he used to get into his boats.

In January the Resident reported the discovery of antimony in Borneo, to the north of Sambas, and also that it was found at Bulang, twenty miles from Singapore. In the next year 30 to 40 tons were imported for trial.

The Resident in a judicial report, of 9th January, stated that he was engaged in administering Chinese and Malay law. "The case with respect to Europeans is very different; there exists no means whatever in civil cases of affording the natives any redress against them, nor in criminal cases any remedy short of sending them for trial before the Supreme Court of Calcutta. It is unnecessary to dwell upon the great inconvenience of such a state of things, &c."

In a report of land tenures the Resident gave a list of grants already issued by Raffles from No. 1 to 576, and location tickets from 1 to 158.

On the 6th February Mr. John Crawfurd gave a dinner to all the Europeans, it being the anniversary of hoisting the flag in the island. "The dinner was at 7-30 p.m. and there were about fifty persons present including the ladies. There was plenty to eat but it was so much later than usual that few felt inclined to partake and some took nothing at all. There was a double row of tables. It was a stupid sort of affair altogether. They drank "The Prosperity of Singapore" and of Sir Thomas Raffles, besides all the usual loyal toasts. They rose from the table a little after ten, the Resident's frugal store of wine being apparently exhausted." This account of the first "official dinner" of Singapore is quoted from a diary of Mr. Walter Scott Duncan, which was in the possession of the late Mr. Gilbert Angus twenty years ago. Duncan was the son of the Sheriff substitute of Shetland, and came out to Singapore in 1823, in a vessel which brought out the wife and young daughter of Mr. C. R. Read of A. L. Johnston & Co., and Duncan became a clerk in that firm. He remained here a few months and then went to Rhio, where the firm had an agency, and remained there for some time. He afterwards returned to Singapore where he was a ship-chandler, and finally bought a plantation at Siglap, next to Dr. Little's, which he called Mount Thule, near the 7th mile on Changie Road, where he died in 1857.

At this time dinner was at 4 or 4.30 p.m. and people used to go out for a walk or a drive afterwards, or sometimes danced to the music of two or three fiddlers. At 9.30 there was a supper, and parties always broke up about ten o'clock. The streets were lighted for the first time on the evening of the 1st April, but there were very few lamps and they had only a single glass in front, so the light was little use. As if to show this, Mr. Purvis's godown was broken into that same night and robbed of goods worth $500.

On the 23rd February Mr. Spottiswoode and Mr. and Mrs. Connolly arrived from Padang in the brig *Guide*. They had left Madras in July, 1823, and had been selling the cargo at different places along the West Coast of Sumatra when there was any prospect of doing business. They had not been very successful and had still 300 packages of goods they had been unable to get rid of. They had been expected in Singapore for several months, as it was their intention to settle here, which they did. Mr. Duncan remarked in his diary that "they will add another firm to the already too great number established."

In February the Resident intended to stop the natives carrying their krisses and a peon was sent to proclaim it in Campong Glam. The man was afraid to do it, and went and told the Sultan, who was very indignant and told the peon that if he attempted to do it he would order him to be krissed on the spot. Mr. Crawfurd allowed the matter to stand over, in which the Europeans thought he showed weakness and want of decision. The Sultan very strongly insisted that it would be contrary to the stipulations at the time of our taking possession of the Island. A few days afterwards Mr. Crawfurd told the Sultan that the Tumongong had no objection, but the Sultan said he was a silly fellow, afraid to speak his own mind and did whatever the Resident wished. An armed guard of Sepoys had accompanied the Resident in case of any disturbance, and the police peons privately carried pistols. The regulation was afterwards carried out without difficulty. One necessary result of the Malays carrying krisses was frequent amoks.

On the 21st February, at three o'clock in the morning, occurred the first fire there is any notice of. It took place in the Dhobies' houses, and the Sepoys went with two engines and buckets. It was a moonlight night, and the fire was put out without any serious damage. About twenty houses were burnt.

On the 22nd February Syed Mahommed died. "He was a much respected Arab merchant, whose death is greatly lamented both by natives and Europeans. He was a man of great honesty, and fair and open in his transactions with all classes. He is supposed to have left considerable property."

On the 17th April the American brig *Leander* arrived from Batavia and brought the news of the loss of the *Fame* off Bencoolen, with all Raffles's collection; but the story was that she had sunk in Bencoolen roads only a few hours before the time Sir Stamford had fixed for embarkation, and so suddenly that the people on board had barely time to save their lives. The *Fame* had been of course burned at sea.

On the King's birthday, 23rd April, a salute was fired by the artillery on the Plain, and another at noon. "There was a dinner on the Goverment Hill at seven o'clock, which was so ill attended and stupid it scarce merits notice."

In those days the flagstaff was eagerly watched, and the signal for a ship to the eastward infused new life into all, as letters from Europe usually arrived *via* Batavia. A voyage from England took four or five months, and an answer within nine months was considered very punctual. It is worth noting that Duncan paid eighty guineas for his passage money from London to Singapore by the Cape and Batavia.

In May the farms were let for one year, and fetched $60,672, against $25,796 in 1823. This year the Opium farm fetched $23,100, Spirits $10,980, Gaming $26,112, and Pawnbrokers $480. By order of the Supreme Government the fines levied in the Court were to be applied to the improvement of the town.

The Dutch Resident at Rhio wrote to the Tumongong asking for a copy of the genealogy of the Royal Family of Johore. The Resident wrote to Bengal, on 10th May:—"The circumstance of carrying on a secret correspondence with a stipendiary of the British Government, living under its immediate protection, appearing to be a breach of that rule of forbearance with respect to the mutual claims of both governments in the Eastern Archipelago, I recommended the Tumongong not to reply to the Dutch Resident's letter."

The Sultan and Tumongong sent in a long memorial, complaining of the British flag and protection having been removed from Johore. The following is the Resident's report to the Supreme Goverment on the document. It is at full length in Mr. Braddell's Notes, so it is evident he thought it of enough value to be preserved. It is of considerable length, but is of much interest, as it shows how the English had been treating the Malay chiefs, and how they had risen by degrees to appreciate the importance of the place in which they had allowed the " Factory " to be established. As the place grew, their sense of their own consequence, and of the advantage they might take of it, increased. The letter is undoubtedly a very able one, and the future of Singapore depended upon the question it discussed. It will be seen from the treaty, set out in the next chapter, and made by Mr. Crawfurd as soon as he received an answer to this letter from the Supreme Government in Calcutta, that all his suggestions were carried out. His remark that Sir Stamford Raffles could probably have bought the whole island outright for a small sum, was no doubt correct, but on the whole, as events have turned out, through the gradual concurrence of the chiefs, and their consequent appreciation of the behaviour of the English towards them, it was to the advantage of the place that Raffles acted as he did. This is the letter:

"Sir,—I have had the honor to transmit by this opportunity to the Persian Secretary, a joint letter from the native chiefs with whom we are connected at this place, and a separate one from the Tumongong, with translations of both. On the subject of these communications it becomes necessary that I should offer some explanation. The first matter contained is the joint letter—that which refers to the fact of the British flag having been hoisted at Johore,—is probably not known to the Government, unless by rumour. The circumstances attending this transaction are shortly as follows:—

"In the month of February. 1823, the native chiefs connected with us, expressed to the local authority their apprehension that their rivals at Rhio intended to occupy Johore, and they solicited permission to hoist the British flag there to secure them against this risk. Their request was acceded to, and a flag supplied to them, which their own followers erected. In the month of August I received a confidential order to strike the British flag at Johore, in the possible event of its having been erected. On the receipt of these instructions, the necessary directions were communicated to the native chiefs for striking the flag, and I entertained at the time no doubt but that they had been strictly complied with, having been assured that they were.

"In the month of November, however, the apprehended occupation of Johore on the part of the rival chiefs at Rhio, assisted by the Dutch authorities at the settlement, was actually made. Messengers were dispatched from Johore to communicate this information to me, and I now not only learnt that the flag had not been struck, but that even a demand was set up for a right to our assistance in driving away the people of Rhio. It was in vain that I gave the most peremptory orders to strike the British flag, and that I explained that no clause of any treaty bound the British Government to maintain the authority of the Sultan and Tumongong in any place beyond the limits of the island of Singapore. My directions were disregarded, until I found myself compelled to make a threat of sending a force to remove the flag, when they were at length complied with.

"The object of the present address of the native chiefs to the Right Hon'ble the Governor-General, appears to be to complain of our withdrawing our protection by striking the flag at Johore, and to claim the fulfilment of some supposed treaty or promise which binds us to assert and maintain their authority by force of arms. It is scarcely necessary for me to state that no such engagement exists, but that, on the contrary, the second article of the treaty made in February, 1819, expressly provides that we are not bound to interfere in the internal political concerns of their government, nor to aid them by force of arms in asserting their authority, while every other engagement with them is altogether silent on this subject.

"I have been at much pains in explaining this matter to the native chiefs, but my efforts have not been attended with all the success I could have desired, for the subject is most repugnant to their wishes, and to certain ambitious views which they have been led to entertain. It will, therefore, be extremely desirable and satisfactory that the principles of the political connexion which subsists between them and our Government should be made known to them for their guidance from the highest authority.

"The second matter of the joint letter of the native chiefs refers to the question of slavery. The claim made here is that the Malayan law, which admits the existence of slavery, should not be altered or infringed. I presume to consider this as a demand utterly inadmissable. Singapore, however anomalous its situation in some respects, exists only through British protection, and is therefore virtually a British possession for the time. Slavery, therefore, in any form in which it is expressly contrary to law cannot be tolerated.

"The only individuals who can be considered as slaves in this island, according to our laws, are such persons as were in a state of slavery before the place was made over to the British Government and the British flag hoisted. This would include several of the slaves of the Tumongong, as this chief with many of his followers were actually on the island when we received possession of it. It would, however, perhaps exclude all the followers of the Sultan, as he was not present at the period in question, and did not come over with his retainers until some time thereafter.

"The difficulty is greatly enhanced by the impossibility of determining who is and who is not a slave. The chiefs insist that every person belonging to them is a slave, and in no respect master of his own property or actions, and they by no means confine this monstrous pretension to their own retainers at Singapore, but make the same over every native of the numerous islands and straits in our immediate vicinity, nominally or otherwise dependent upon them, who comes to sojourn or reside at this settlement. The Tumongong at least declares, at the same time, that he has no slaves in the sense in which we understand the term—that is, persons who can be bought or sold for money. It is true, indeed, that these chiefs are not in the practice of selling their people for money, but it is equally certain that their retainers cannot rid themselves of their allegiance, or rather of the condition of villinage in which they exist, without the payment of a fine, and this too only as a matter of especial favor.

" From the circumstances of this settlement, the nature of our relations with the native chiefs, and the serious although unavoidable inconvenience of their living amongst us or in our immediate vicinity, the question of slavery is frequently agitated, and unless settled and defined from the highest authority is likely to become the subject of considerable vexations and embarrassment. The temptations to the followers of the native chiefs to quit them are very great. The reward of labour and the comfort of the free labouring classes which they see before them, are all sufficient inducements to the men. The female portion have the additional one arising from the disproportion of the sexes which exists among the different classes of the inhabitants. Amongst the followers of the Sultan and Tumongong the proportion of women to men is two to one. Amongst the free settlers of every other description, this proportion is even more than inversed, the men being more than double the number of women, and in the case of the Chinese the disproportion is so great that there are at least eight men to every woman.

" The least degree of ill-treatment, and a considerable share of it has come to our knowledge, is sufficient under the circumstances I have stated, to induce the followers of the native chiefs to quit them. Whenever such an event takes place, their persons are demanded, remonstrances follow, and some dissatisfaction has been expressed in many cases where no claim of servitude could be made, and where it would have been a flagrant injustice to have remanded the parties.

" The easy remedy for the inconvenience now complained of appears to me to be that the Resident should open a register for the admission of the names of all persons who are *bona fide* slaves of the native chiefs, or who, being of mature age, acknowledge themselves to be so in the presence of impartial witnesses. In the same register might be inscribed the names of all the followers of the native chiefs who are their debtors, a class that from the poverty and improvidence of this race of people is very numerous. The amount of the debt should be inserted, and the parties not at liberty to quit the service of the chiefs until they have either discharged the full amount of the debt, or served such a reasonable length of time as might justly be considered equivalent to its liquidation.

" I have often proposed this plan to the native chiefs, and although they apparently acquiesced at first, they have not failed in the event to evade it, no doubt receiving it with jealousy as an irksome restraint upon their authority.

" Should the Right Hon'ble the Governor-General be pleased to approve of the suggestion now offered of forming a Registry, it might be carried into effect without any difficulty, by an expression of his approbation in the reply to the letter of the native chiefs.

"The breach of engagement apparently referred to in the concluding part of the letter of the native chiefs, has reference only to the subject of slavery. I am not aware of the existence of any treaty or engagement by which the right of perpetuating slavery while they live under the protection of the British flag is guaranteed to them, and I rest most fully satisfied that the concession of such a right, or of any other which implied a violation of the law of the realm, could not have been in the contemplation of any British authority. By the convention concluded in June, 1823, the only concessions made to the institutions of the Malays are in regard to the ceremonies of religion, marriage, &c., the rules of inheritance, and even these are to be respected where they shall not be contrary to reason, humanity, &c.

"The subject of the separate letter of the Tumongong, refers to a general and indefinite engagement to assist him in removing and establishing himself at his present residence. A similar engagement for the construction of a mosque was entered into with the Sultan, and a specific verbal promise of $3,000 made to him by Sir T. S. Raffles in my presence, during an interview which took place for this and other purposes. At this interview, however, the Tumongong although invited did not personally attend, owing to a temporary indisposition. His confidential advisers, however, attended for him, but made no claim whatever in my presence, and it was not until a month after the departure of Sir T. S. Raffles, that this chief urged a claim of similar amount to that of the Sultan. He has already received on account of himself or his followers, either for the removal or the construction of a new dwelling, $3,000. Yet I have most respectfully to recommend that his present demand, although not extremely reasonable, be also complied with, that even a possible suspicion of ill-faith may not attach to the Government from anything which may be supposed to have taken place, even through misapprehension.

"The demand made by the same chief for a residence in the town of Singapore has placed me in the same awkward situation as his pecuniary one. The matter was never hinted to me, either verbally or in writing, from the source of my instructions on other points, and it was with a good deal of surprise that I first heard the demand. The residence of the Tumongong and his numerous and disorderly followers was a nuisance of the first magnitude. Three thousand dollars had actually been paid for his removal. Three thousand more are demanded for the same object, and yet he wished to preserve a temporary residence in the very same spot, and to occupy all the ground which he had ever occupied. This would have been to have perpetuated every nuisance, for abating which so large an expense had been incurred. The matter would probably have been aggravated, when the followers of the Tumongong were living in his enclosure removed from the control of their chief.

"The inconveniences which arise from the present unsettled nature of our arrangements with the native chiefs, lead me to suggest for the consideration of the Right Hon'ble the Governor-General the expediency of entering into new engagements with them, in which the relations in which they are henceforth to stand with the European Government may be laid down with precision, and a termination put to the hopes which they have been led to entertain of aggrandising themselves abroad at our expense, or embarrassing our local administration.

"I beg for a moment to bring to the recollection of the Right Hon'ble the Governor-General the situation of this island and of the other countries in its neighbourhood constituting the nominal principality of Johore, when we formed our settlement in the year 1819. This principality extends on the continent from Malacca to the extremity of the peninsula on both coasts. It had several settlements on the island of Sumatra, and embraced all the islands in the mouth of the Straits of Malacca with all those in China seas, as far as the Natunas in the latitude of 4° N. and longitude 109° E. These countries are all sterile, thinly inhabited here and there on the coast only, and commonly by a race of pirates or fishermen, whose condition in society, ignorant of agriculture and without attachment to the soil, rises very little beyond the savage state; neither is there any good evidence of there ever having existed a better or more improved order of society.

"The condition of the island of Singapore itself may be adduced as an example of the whole. There was not an acre of its surface cultivated and not a dozen cleared of forest. The inhabitants, amounting to a few hundreds, commonly lived only in their boats, and finally the place had, not groundlessly, the reputation of being one of the principal piratical stations in these seas. The father of the present Sultan, being a person of some strength of mind, addicted himself to commercial pursuits and enjoyed more consideration than his predecessors, and consequently had a more extensive influence. He had no acknowledged successor, however, in his government. The individuals recognized both by ourselves and the Dutch were illegitimate children, and being both of them destitute of energy, made no attempt to assume his authority. The principal officers of the Government of Johore from early times were the Bandahara or treasurer, and Tumongong or first minister of justice. These offices appear to have been a long time hereditary in the families of the present occupants, who were indeed virtually independent chiefs, the first of them residing at and exercising sovereignty at Pahang, and the other, the individual with whom the British Government is now connected, doing the same thing at Singapore.

"The present Sultan when he connected himself with us was not only destitute of all authority but living in a state of complete indigence. It is unnecessary, therefore, to dwell on the comfort and respectability which this chief has derived since he placed himself under our protection. The condition of the Tumongong has not been ameliorated to the same extent, but I am not aware of any honest emolument which he has forfeited by his change of circumstances, and it may be added, although he is perhaps not entirely convinced of the beneficial nature of the change, that he has been rescued from a course of life of not the most respectable description. He is, at all events, unquestionably at present living in a greater state of affluence, security, and comfort than it was possible for him to have enjoyed without our protection.

"I have no hesitation in submitting it to the Right Hon'ble the Governor-General as my firm opinion, that men born and educated with such habits and prejudices as belong to men in the state of society which I have just described, ought in no respect to be associated with us in the Government of a settlement, nine-tenths of the inhabitants of which it may be fairly asserted have an utter repugnance and perhaps even contempt for their Government and Institutions. It appears to me that any participation whatever in the administration of the place on their part would be the certain source of trouble and embarrassment, nor am I able to conceive even any contingent advantage which can be expected to result from such a connexion.

" The principal stipulation of any future engagement with the native chiefs ought, as it appears to me, to be the unequivocal cession of the island of Singapore in full sovereignty and property for which the equivalent will be the payment of a sum of ready money and a pension for life. The payment in ready money need not be large, and in it may be included the pecuniary demands at present made by the native chiefs. The pensions should not exceed the present amount, which is $2,000 to both chiefs.

" It should be another stipulation that the British Government should not afford personal protection to the chiefs, except when they reside at Singapore ; leaving them, however, the unrestrained right, without forfeiture of their pensions, of residing at whatever other part of their territory they may think proper, with the single condition of their not entering into any political arrangements tending to involve the British Government or engaging in any enterprise tending to disturb the public tranquility.

" The minor arrangements for defining the situation and duties of the native chiefs when residing in the island, were the point of sovereignty once established, would evidently be a matter of no difficulty. They would then be viewed as independent princes occasionally residing amongst us as visitors, and as such entitled to be treated with such marks of respect and such forms of courtesy, as would gratify their feelings without proving injurious to the good government of the Settlement.

" However desirable such an arrangement might be, I am bound to state to the Government that I anticipate considerable difficulty in carrying it into effect. There will not be wanting the persons who will throw obstacles in the way of the negotiation amongst the retainers and parasites with whom they are surrounded. It is further necessary to mention that the chiefs themselves have been unaccountably led to entertain unfounded hopes of aggrandisement and support through our means. They are at the same time not without some desire to participate in our authority, although the singular indolence and incapacity both of themselves and of their followers render them utterly unfit for any useful employment.

" In the formation of the settlement an opinion seems to have been prevalent that the support of the native chiefs was indispensable to its success, although considering their character, their indigence, and their general destitution of useful influence, it is not easy to trace it to any substantial foundation. The first treaty with them conceded to them one-half of the duties on native vessels. The commanders of these vessels were then ordered to wait upon them, when presents were expected, and this continued until it was greatly abused. An exclusive right to all the lime on the island held valuable for exportation, seems afterwards to have been yielded to them, and a proposition is on record for levying a fine on all the Chinese returning to their native country for their exclusive benefit. These facts are evidences of the opinion to which I have alluded.

" It does not appear to me that the influence of the native chiefs has in any respect been necessary or even beneficial in the formation, maintenance, or progress of this settlement, the prosperity of which has rested solely and exclusively on the character and resources of the British Government. If I may presume to offer an opinion, the easy and obvious course to have pursued in first forming our establishment, would have been to have given at once a valuable pecuniary consideration for the complete sovereignty of the island, a stipulation which would have left us in every respect free and unencumbered, and conveyed a title of such validity as would not afterwards have been cancelled by any art of the native chiefs, wherever residing, or under whatever influence acting In this early stage, the sum which would have sufficed for such an object would certainly not have equalled one-half of what has already been disbursed to the native chiefs, and which has not fallen short of $60,000. It will perhaps be considered that the sooner we revert to this principle, the less exceptionable will be our title and the more easy and unfettered our future relations with the native chiefs.

" Should the Right Hon'ble the Governor-General be pleased to authorize me to negotiate for an engagement with the Sultan and Tumongong of Johore on the principles which I have had the honour to suggest, or on any other less exceptionable which the wisdom of Government may be pleased to point out, it will be my endeavour to smooth every obstacle which may be opposed to its successful termination.

JOHN CRAWFURD.

Singapore, 10th January, 1824.

On the 10th August a difficulty in dealing with recalcitrant Europeans arose, and Mr. Bonham, the assistant to the Resident, wrote to one individual as follows:—" Sir,—The Resident directs me to inform you that he has given the most serious consideration to the whole line of conduct lately pursued by you, and that considering the incompetency of the local rules in existence at this Settlement to afford security against so marked a spirit of insubordination as you have displayed, he has determined upon sending you to Calcutta, by an early opportunity, with a view of placing you at the disposal of the Governor-General in Council, and in a situation where you will be amenable to the authority of regular law. The Resident directs me further to state to you that this measure has been most reluctantly forced upon him by a consideration of the various outrages committed by you on the persons or property of private individuals—British as well as native—the insults and contempts offered by you to the local rules for the administration of justice and towards the persons whose duty it is to administer them, your sedulous perseverance in those proceedings after ample time and opportunity have been afforded you for making atonement or offering reparation, and finally by the fact of your being, contrary to law, in the East Indies, that is, without a license from the Court of Directors, and without the necessary certificate from the Chief Secretary to Government. The Resident directs me in conclusion to say that he considers it fair to inform you that he will strongly recommend to the Government not to permit your return to Singapore, until a regular administration of justice shall have been established within the Settlement."

This was Mr. J. Morgan, one of the merchants, who put himself in opposition to all law and control, and fired a morning and evening gun from his schooner in the river, and put the master of a vessel, consigned to his house, in confinement. The merchant was at last ordered to be put in the main guard and sent to Bengal, but through the intercession of his friends, he was released on making an apology. Mr. Crawfurd wrote to Calcutta on the subject in this way :—" In one respect especially the inadequacy of the jurisdiction of this Court has been most lamentably felt. This refers to the case of British subjects, who are at present amenable to no authority at this place, and the ill-disposed among whom have it always in their power to set the authority of Government at defiance, and to render themselves a bane to the peaceable inhabitants. I shall not at present enlarge upon this unpleasant topic, as I humbly trust it will shortly be in the power of Government to put an end to this very serious evil, equally prejudicial to the national character and to the prosperity and respectability of the Settlement."

In July a Portuguese Priest arrived and held Chapel in Dr. Jozé d'Almeida's house. About this time there was a small Roman Catholic community, and they applied to the Bishop of Siam and a priest came to Singapore. In 1823 or 1824 a small Chapel was built, where the St. Joseph's Boys School buildings are now, and the congregation soon increased by new arrivals of Christians. Chinese were converted, and in 1832 the Chapel was too small, as there were some six or seven hundred Chinese. In 1844 the present Church was commenced; in 1845 the Church at Bukit Timah; and in 1852 that at Serangoon. These matters are also referred to at length in another chapter.

Mr. Crawfurd at this time wrote about the necessity of a proper judicial system, which was the commencement of the introduction of the Supreme Court. Part of his letter to Bengal on 23rd August is as follows :—

" A third difference will arise from the want of a professional lawyer of high character and respectable qualifications, which can only be secured under the circumstances of this Settlement in the person of a judge nominated by the Crown. Independently of the impracticability of administering English law anywhere without a judge so qualified, the magnitude and intricacy of the business, which, from the growing commerce of this Settlement, is likely to be brought under the cognizance of a Court of Justice, render such a provision absolutely necessary. The Charter of Justice for Prince of Wales Island has been in operation for 16 years and I am led to believe has given satisfaction and answered every purpose of substantial justice. It will therefore afford a safe precedent for any enactment in respect to this island. The union of the executive and judicial authority, however, under that Charter, appears decidedly objectionable, and would be much more so at this place, where the executive administration is entrusted to a subordinate officer of government. For this reason, I would respectfully suggest that the judicial authority should be separate and distinct from the executive, as the surest means of rendering it independent and respectable."

The Resident then went on to propose that in mercantile cases the judge should have the assistance of a jury, and, as it would require two or three years to get a King's Court, a draft regulation for establishing a Civil Court and a Court for Small Debts was sent up for sanction. The first to have a respectable Solicitor as Registrar. The Court to consist of the Resident, the two Assistants and two inhabitants. The Small Debts Court to be under the two Assistants and to proceed summarily. A code of police regulations was also sent up for revision, nearly as complete as the draft Acts for the same purpose afterwards prepared. A short time after, the Resident received the following law opinion on this subject which was written either by the Recorder of Penang or the Advocate-General of Bengal: "With respect to the natives he (the Resident) should make them pay their debts by selling their property and by occasional incarceration; with respect to Europeans, and particularly Englishmen, I should recommend the Resident to assume only the authority of sending them from the island, when by getting into debt or general misconduct they impeded the objects of government."

On the 4th November some riots occurred among the Chinese, the first heard of, and several were killed and wounded. Ten tons of copper cents, intended for Bencoolen, were landed at Singapore, in all $11,840 worth. About this time, the mercantile community subscribed $1,255 for a proportion of the expense of draining the town, to be paid by each person in proportion to the degree of advantage he derived from it.

It was in this year that the name of Singapore was first heard in the House of Commons; Mr. Canning stated there that Singapore, after six years, would produce spices sufficient for the consumption of Great Britain and her Colonies. The result did not equal his anticipation, at least in the way he expected.

From a report of the Resident in this year, it appears there were twelve European firms in Singapore in the beginning of the year, either agents of, or connected with, good London or Calcutta houses, some with branches in Batavia, and not one that could be called an adventurer. He said that the only land that was of any value was that suited for godowns and dwelling houses, the best nearest the river, where the value of the best lots, 50 feet frontage and 150 feet deep from river was $3,000 and $38 yearly quit rent. Lots of 1,200 square yards, for dwelling houses, worth $400 and $28 quit rent. And he gives the names of a few of the owners of land at this time, dividing them into:—(1) Merchants Resident; (2) Merchants Non-Resident; (3) Government Officers; and (4) Missionaries. The names are as follows. They are here arranged alphabetically.

1.—MERCHANTS RESIDENT.

Captain Jozé d'Almeida.　　W. G. Mackenzie.
J. Clark.　　　　　　　　　F. Maclaine.

Andrew Farquhar.
— Fletcher
Alexander Guthrie.
Captain Harrington.
Alexander Hay.
Andrew Hay.
Alexander Laurie Johnston.
T. King.
Captain Howard.

J. A. Maxwell.
Alexander Morgan.
David S. Napier.
— Pearl.
John Purvis.
Claude Queiros.
Christopher Rideout Read.
Charles Scott.

2.—Merchants Non-Resident.

Barretto & Co. of Calcutta.
Carnegy of Penang.

G. D. H. Larpent of Calcutta.
John Palmer of Calcutta.

3.—Government Officers.

F. G. Bernard, Magistrate.
Samuel George Bonham, Assistant Resident.
Captain C. E. Davis, Bengal Native Infantry.
Hon. J. J. Erskine, Member of Council, Penang.
Colonel Farquhar, late Resident.
Captain W. Flint, r.n., Master Attendant.

Lieut P. Jackson, Executive Engineer and Surveyor.
Captain Methven.
Dr Montgomerie, Assistant Surgeon.
Captain Murray, Commanding Officer.
Mr Ryan, Store-keeper.
Captain Salmond, Harbour Master of Bencoolen.

4.—Missionaries.

Rev. Robert Morrison, d.d.
Rev. S. Milton.

Rev. G. H. Thomson.

CHAPTER XIV.

1824—Continued.

THE TWO TREATIES OF 1824.

A DESPATCH from Bengal of the 16th August contained the Advocate-General's opinion upon the convention with the Sultan and Tumongong of 7th June, 1823, saying that it was not an express declaration but a near approach to it, and that it was desirable to have a more direct and unequivocal abrogation of the native authority; probably as much had been done as the circumstances admitted, and now Singapore might be considered a British Settlement; but nothing could be satisfactory until the attention of the English authorities had been called to the matter, and an Act of Parliament passed.

On the 5th March the Governor-General wrote in answer to the despatch from Mr. Crawfurd of 10th January printed in the preceding chapter, that he agreed with him that it was desirable to obtain an immediate cession of Singapore, which ought to have been done at first, and now that it must be done there would be greater difficulties every day. The second agreement of Sir Stamford Raffles on 7th June had improved matters, but still left sovereignty, tenure, and political rights in a bad state. Authority was therefore given to Crawfurd to negotiate as proposed by him on the basis of the form of treaty sent privately, with authority to offer most liberal terms pecuniarily as an equivalent for the desired advantage.

Mr. Braddell says of this, "Ultimately on the 2nd August, 1824, Mr. Crawfurd concluded a Treaty by which the chiefs alienated for ever all right and title to Singapore, and assumed the position of private individuals while residing within the island. This favorable result was not arrived at without much trouble and the exhibition of great talent and patience. Both chiefs finding they had a strong hold on the English Government, were determined to make the best use of it. The bad arrangement on this head had been brought forward against Raffles as showing a want of foresight on his part, but the real explanation of that, as well as of many other consequences of an inconvenient nature, will be found in the fact that, pending the reference to Europe, his hands were tied, and a rapidly advancing Settlement was confined within the cramping limits of first arrangements, without having the advantage of improving and extending these arrangements to meet advancing requirements." The following is the form of the Treaty under which Singapore has been held to the present day. In November, 1861, it was ruled in the Supreme Court that the right of the British Government over the waters within ten miles of Singapore must be limited by a distance of three miles from any coast either of mainland or island within a circle of ten miles of which Singapore is the centre.

A TREATY of FRIENDSHIP and ALLIANCE between the HONOURABLE THE ENGLISH EAST INDIA COMPANY on the one side. and their HIGHNESSES the SULTAN and TUMONGONG of JOHORE on the other, concluded on the Second day of August, One Thousand Eight Hundred and Twenty-four (1824), corresponding with the Sixth day of the month of Zulhaji, in the year of the Hejira One Thousand Two Hundred and Thirty-nine (1239) by the above Sultan of Johore. HIS HIGHNESS SULTAN HUSSAIN MAHOMED SHAH, and the above TUMONGONG of JOHORE, HIS HIGHNESS DATU TUMONGONG ABDUL RAHMAN SRI MAHARAJAH on their own behalf, and by JOHN CRAWFURD. ESQ.. British Resident of Singapore, vested with full powers thereto, by the Right Honourable WILLIAM PITT, LORD AMHERST, Governor-General of and for Fort William in Bengal, on behalf of the said HONOURABLE ENGLISH EAST INDIA COMPANY.

ARTICLE 1.

Peace, friendship, and good understanding shall subsist for ever between the Honourable the English East India Company and their Highnesses the Sultan and Tumongong of Johore and their respective heirs and successors.

ARTICLE 2.

Their Highnesses the Sultan Hussain Mahomed Shah and Datu Tumongong Abdul Rahman Sri Maharajah hereby cede in full sovereignty and property to the Honourable the English East India Company, their heirs and successors for ever, the Island of Singapore, situated in the Straits of Malacca. together with the adjacent seas. straits, and islets, to the extent of ten geographical miles, from the coast of the said main Island of Singapore.

ARTICLE 3.

The Honourable the English East India Company hereby engages, in consideration of the cession specified in the last Article. to pay to His Highness the Sultan Hussain Mahomed Shah, the sum of Spanish Dollars thirty-three thousand two hundred (33,200). together with a stipend, during his natural life, of one thousand three hundred (1.300) Spanish Dollars per mensem, and to His Highness the Datu Tumongong Abdul Rahman Sri Maharajah, the sum of twenty-six thousand eight hundred (26,800) Spanish Dollars, with a monthly stipend of seven hundred (700) Spanish Dollars during his natural life.

ARTICLE 4.

His Highness the Sultan Hussain Mahomed Shah hereby acknowledges to have received from the Honourable the English East India Company in fulfilment of the stipulations of the two last Articles, the sum of thirty-three thousand two hundred (33,200) Spanish Dollars. together with the first monthly instalment of the above-mentioned stipend. of Spanish Dollars one thousand three hundred (1.300), and His Highness the Datu Tumongong Abdul Rahman Sri Maharajah also hereby acknowledges to have received from the Honourable the English East India Company, in fulfilment of the stipulations of the two last Articles, the sum of twenty-six thousand eight hundred Spanish Dollars (26,800), with one month's instalment of the above stipend of seven hundred Spanish Dollars.

ARTICLE 5.

The Honourable the English East India Company engages to receive and treat their Highnesses the Sultan Hussain Mahomed Shah, and Datu Tumongong Abdul Rahman Sri Maharajah, with all the honours, respect. and courtesy belonging to their rank and station. whenever they may reside at, or visit the Island of Singapore.

ARTICLE 6.

The Honourable the English East India Company hereby engages in the event of their Highnesses the Sultan and Tumongong, their heirs or successors. preferring to reside permanently in any portion of their own States, and to remove for that purpose from Singapore. to pay unto them, that is to say, to His Highness the Sultan Hussain Mahomed Shah, his heir or successor, the sum of twenty thousand (20,000) Spanish Dollars, and to His Highness the Datu Tumongong Abdul Rahman Sir Maharajah, his heir or successor, the sum of fifteen thousand (15,000) Spanish Dollars.

ARTICLE 7.

Their Highnesses the Sultan Hussian Mahomed Shah and the Datu Tumongong Abdul Rahman Sri Maharajah, in consideration of the payment specified in the last Article, hereby relinquish for themselves, their heirs, and successors, to the Honourable the English East India Company their heirs and successors for ever, all right and title to every description of immoveable property, whether in lands, houses, gardens, orchards, or timber trees, of which their said Highnesses may be possessed within the Island of Singapore or its dependencies at the time they may think proper to withdraw from the said island for the purpose of permanently residing within their own States, but it is reciprocally and clearly understood that the provisions of this Article shall not extend to any description of property which may be held by any follower or retainer of their Highnesses beyond the precincts of the ground at present allotted for the actual residence of their said Highnesses.

ARTICLE 8.

Their Highnesses the Sultan Hussain Mahomed Shah, and the Datu Tumongong Abdul Rahman Sri Maharajah hereby engage that, as long as they shall continue to reside within the Island of Singapore, or to draw their respective monthly stipends from the Honourable the English East India Company, as provided for in the present Treaty, they shall enter into no alliance and maintain no correspondence with any foreign power or potentate whatsoever, without the knowledge and consent of the said Honourable the English East India Company, their heirs and successors.

ARTICLE 9.

The Honourable the English East India Company hereby engages, that, in the event of their Highnesses the Sultan Hussain Mahomed Shah, and the Datu Tumongong Abdul Rahman Sri Maharajah removing from the Island of Singapore, as contemplated in the 6th Article, and being distressed within their own territories on such removal, to afford them, either at Singapore or Prince of Wales' Island, a personal asylum and protection.

ARTICLE 10.

The contracting parties hereby stipulate and agree, that neither party shall be bound to interfere in the internal concerns of the other's government, or in any political dissensions or wars which may arise within their respective territories, nor to support each other by force of arms against any third party whatever.

ARTICLE 11.

The contracting parties hereby engage to use every means within their power respectively, for the suppression of robbery and piracy within the Straits of Malacca, as well as the other narrow seas, straits, and rivers bordering upon, or within their respective territories, in as far as the same shall be connected with the dominions and immediate interests of their said Highnesses.

ARTICLE 12.

Their Highnesses the Sultan Hussain Mahomed Shah, and the Datu Tumongong Abdul Rahman Sri Maharajah hereby engage to maintain a free and unshackled trade everywhere within their dominions, and to admit the trade and traffic of the British nation into all the ports and harbours of the kingdom of Johore and its dependencies on the terms of the most favoured nation.

ARTICLE 13.

The Honourable the English East India Company hereby engages, as long as their Highnesses the Sultan Hussain Mahomed Shah and the Datu Tumongong Abdul Rahman Sri Maharajah shall continue to reside on the Island of Singapore, not to permit any retainer or follower of their said Highnesses who shall desert from their actual service, to dwell or remain in the Island of Singapore or its dependencies. But it is hereby clearly understood, that all such retainers and followers shall be natural born subjects of such parts of their Highnesses' dominions only in which their authority is at present substantially established, and that their names, at the period of entering the service of their

Highnesses, shall have been duly and voluntarily inscribed in a register, to be kept for that purpose by the chief local authority for the time being.

ARTICLE 14.

It is hereby mutually stipulated for and agreed, that the conditions of all former Conventions, Treaties, or Agreements entered into between the Honourable the English East India Company and their Highnesses the Sultan and Tumongong of Johore, shall be considered as abrogated and annulled by the present Treaty, and they are hereby abrogated and annulled accordingly, always, however, with the exception of such prior conditions as have conferred on the Honourable the English East India Company any right or title to the occupation or possession of the Island of Singapore and its dependencies, as abovementioned.

Done and concluded at Singapore, the day and year as above written.

SULTAN HUSSAIN MAHOMED SHAH.

J. CRAWFURD.

DATU TUMONGONG ABDUL RAHMAN SRI MAHARAJAH.

By another treaty made with the Tumongong on 19th December, 1862, Articles 6 and 7 of the above treaty were annulled as far as related to the Tumongong. He gave up the right to the $15,000, and received a title in fee simple for lands at Telloh Blangah, while he gave the Government the piece of land on which Mount Faber flagstaff had been erected, with a right of way to it, and a carriage road along the shore, and some other pieces of ground.

The two following despatches to the Government at Calcutta were written by Mr. Crawfurd:—

SINGAPORE, *3rd August*, 1824.

Sir,—In obedience to the instructions contained in your despatch of the 5th of March, and which arrived at this place on the 11th of May, I beg leave to report for the information of the Right Honorable the Governor-General that I lost no time in opening a negociation with the Sultan and Tumongong for the cession of this island. The result has been the treaty which is herewith transmitted, and which I respectfully submit for the approval and ratification of the Right Honorable the Governor-General.

Upon the different provisions of this convention, I beg to lay before the government the following short comment. The heading and first articles scarcely demand any particular remark. The names of the native princes are given at full length and their legitimate titles of Sultan and Tumongong of Johore, under which alone they can be supposed to have power to yield to us the sovereignty of the island, are given to them to the exclusion of more limited designation.

The 2nd, 3rd and 4th articles of the treaty convey to the Honorable East India Company as complete a cession of the sovereignty and property of the Island of Singapore and places adjacent to it, as I could find words to express it in. In framing these conditions I have received the Sultan as possessing the right of paramount dominion, and the Tumongong as not only virtually exercising the powers of government, but being, like other Asiatic Sovereigns, *de facto* the real proprietor of the soil, a principle the more satisfactorily established in the present instance, since the whole ceded territory when it came into our occupation was unreclaimed, in a state of nature and strictly destitute of permanent inhabitants. Government will have the goodness to notice that the cession made is not confined to the main island of Singapore alone, but extends to the Seas, Straits and Islets (the latter probably not less than 50 in number), within ten geographical miles of its coasts, not however including any portion of the continent. Our limits will in this manner embrace the Old Straits of Singapore and the important passage of the Rabbit and Coney, the main channel through the Straits of Malacca, and the only convenient one from thence into the China Seas. These extended bounds appear to me to be absolutely necessary towards the military protection of the Settlement, towards our internal security, and towards our safety from the piratical hordes that surround us, against whose incursions and depredations there would be no indemnity if we were not in the occupation of the numerous islets which lie upon the immediate coast of the principal Settlement. Accompanying this despatch, I beg to lay before government an outline Chart of the British Settlement as it will exist after the ratification of the present treaty.

The amount value stipulated to be paid by the East India Company for the cession of Singapore and its Dependencies, it will be seen by the third article of the treaty, is nominally sixty thousand Spanish dollars, in ready money, with a pension for life to the native princes of two thousand Spanish dollars per mensem. The real amount of ready money to be paid, however, is considerably short of this sum and is in fact only forty thousand, the difference of twenty thousand being the balance between the sum of eight thousand paid under the original treaty and the higher salary paid under the convention of June, 1823, from the period of its signature. This engagement was never ratified, for which reason I have naturally considered the sums heretofore paid on account of it as part and portion of the purchase money now given for the island. Besides this sum of 40,000 Spanish dollars, some contingent expences not exceeding in all 3,500 Spanish dollars and which will be particularized in a separate despatch, will be incurred.

The monthly stipends to be paid to the two native princes are the same as under the convention of 1823, viz., two thousand dollars between them. They had been accustomed indeed to the receipt of this large sum during the last twelve months, their expences and establishments had been measured accordingly and there was therefore no possibility of reducing it. Indeed great efforts were made to render this pension hereditary and perpetual, and the steady resistance made to this demand, which had no foundation in any former treaty or promise, formed for a long time the principal obstacle to the success of the negociation.

The 6th and 7th articles leave to their Highnesses the option of quitting the island of Singapore for the purpose of residing permanently within their own dominions. The sum to be paid to them in this case will amount to 35,000 Spanish dollars, and could we disencumber ourselves of them at such a price. I am of opinion that the advantage would be cheaply purchased. The object indeed which I had in view in naming so large a sum was to hold out some inducement to their removal, although, at the same time, considering the repose and security which they at present enjoy, and which the dispositions evinced by them in the progress of this negociation show clearly that they little wish to relinquish, I cannot look to the event as a very probable one. The benefits of this article are purposely made to extend to the heirs and successors of the princes, and with them of course there can be no difficulty in carrying its intentions into effect. One evident advantage to our administration will in the meanwhile attend this stipulation, that it will have a tendency to abate any temporary dissatisfaction which the princes and their followers might otherwise feel disposed to entertain while living under our immediate protection, as the option of retiring to their own states without loss or inconvenience will always be within their power.

While on this particular subject I have great satisfaction in being enabled to state for the information of government, that since the receipt of the letters addressed to the Sultan and Tumongong by order of the Right Honorable the Governor-General, a marked and very favorable change has taken place in their conduct. That of the Tumongong in particular, the most influential and intelligent individual of the two, has been highly respectable and steady throughout the whole of the present negociation, and I owe in a great measure to his support such success as I may venture to anticipate as the result of my own efforts.

The 8th, 9th and 10th articles make provision for the political relations which are henceforth to subsist between the native princes and ourselves, while they reside within our territories and are our pensionaries. The stipulation that they shall hold no correspondence with any foreign nation without our especial consent seems equally fair and indispensable. To this article indeed they were far from offering any objection, for their evident desire throughout was to engage themselves in a close alliance with us, and to render us, if possible, a party offensive as well as defensive to their quarrels. This was a point to be cautiously guarded against, and I have endeavoured to make the necessary provision for such a purpose in the 9th and 10th articles, which secure to the native princes, without putting us to political inconvenience, a personal asylum in case of need and effectually protect us, at the same time, from the necessity of interfering in their unprofitable quarrels among themselves or their neighbours, as well as from the more serious evil of being committed with European powers through their imprudence.

The 11th article provides for suppression of robbery and piracy. In this matter it is not much that the native princes in connexion with us have in their power, but it is always something at least that they should be bound down to the good conduct of their own immediate dependents, amongst whom there are to be found some depredators of considerable notoriety and the majority always more disposed to plunder than to labour when an opportunity offers.

The 12th article provides against the pernicious practice on the part of the native princes of establishing petty monopolies, towards which a strong propensity always exists. A free intercourse with our immediate vicinity, the whole of which is under their sway, is indispensable to a cheap supply of crude and raw produce, and the necessity of this to the prosperity of the Settlement seemed especially to call for the present stipulation, independent of its justice and propriety on general principles.

In explanation of the 13th article I may observe that possessing the sovereignty and property of the island, the followers and retainers of the princes will of necessity be as completely amenable to such laws as may be established by the sovereign power as any other class of the inhabitants. This right however will require to be exercised with delicacy and discretion. Something similar to the jurisdiction which is conceded to Ambassadors over their families in the international policy of European states, may in general be allowed to the native princes by courtesy, without at the same time permitting their residences to become a sanctuary for criminals of any order or description.

The only concession made upon a subject upon which the native princes were extremely urgent and importunate, the desertion of their retainers, is contained in the same article of the treaty. The class of persons comprehended in this provision are strictly subjects of the native princes, and aliens with respect to us, so that I am in hopes that the stipulation in regard to it, is of a strictly legal character.

I have had the honor, in a former despatch, of bringing to the notice of the Supreme Government the question of slavery as connected with the native princes. I have not permitted the present treaty to be polluted even by the mention of the subject, I must do the chiefs the justice indeed to say that they did not urge it. Under these favorable circumstances, when the present convention is ratified, slavery may be said to be banished from the island, where its illegality, whether our sovereignty, the condition of our Asiatic Colonists, or of the British settlers be considered, will be as complete as on the soil of Great Britain itself. I have the more satisfaction in making this report, since the practice of introducing slaves had at one time become too common and called for frequent punishment. I have now respectfully to solicit the permission of government to publish a formal denunciation against the practise in question, with an explanation of the state of the law as regards the question of slavery in general.

The 14th and last article annuls all former treaties and conventions, and I have only thought it prudent, chiefly in reference to our connexion with European powers, to make an exception for such rights of occupation as were conferred upon us by the engagements in question.

I have throughout the whole negociation, which is now being brought to a conclusion, carefully warned the native princes and the individuals who are in their confidence that no stipulation of the present treaty could be binding until the whole was duly ratified by the Right Honorable the Governor-General. The whole, therefore, is completely open to alteration and amendment, either in substance or expression, without any compromise of the character of the agent employed in carrying it into effect. I humbly trust, however, from the pains which have been taken both with the English copy and its Malayan version, that no serious revision will be necessary, and that the important objects contempled by the Right Honorable the Governor-General in Council, in opening the negociation, will be found expressed in the convention with adequate precision and comprehensiveness.

J. CRAWFURD,
Resident.

Sir,—I have the honor herewith to transmit a copy in English and Malay of the treaty just concluded with the Sultan and Tumongong of Johore, to which the seals of these chiefs are affixed. Much pains have been taken with the Malayan version of the treaty, and I am in hopes it will be found to express with accuracy and sufficient propriety the stipulations of the convention.

I have respectfully to propose, that should the treaty be ratified by the Right Honorable the Governor-General in Council, three copies of it should be engrossed upon parchment in half margin, leaving a column for the Malayan version, in the manner followed with the copy now submitted. Should these be transmitted with the Governor-General's ratification, the Malay will be added at this place, and one copy will be returned by the first opportunity to Bengal to be deposited among the Records of Government, while the other two will be presented as a mark of attention to their Highnesses the Sultan and Tumongong.

Singapore, 1st October, 1824.   J. CRAWFURD,

Resident.

THE TREATY WITH HOLLAND.

This year was also made memorable in the history of the Straits by the famous treaty between Great Britain and Holland of the 17th March, 1824. It was signed in London by Canning for the former, and Baron Fagel for the Netherlands. When Java and its dependencies were delivered over to the Dutch by the British, after the peace of 1814, and the congress of Vienna, (the English having defeated the French who had taken possession of Java, in the name of Napoleon) the first act of the Dutch, who had been thus restored to their former possessions, was, with proverbial ingratitude, to impose restrictions on British commerce in the Archipelago. The aggressions of the Dutch on our commerce in the East were very injurious, and this treaty was the consequence of the equivocal situation of affairs. The spirit of the treaty of 1824 was that the manufactures of each nation should not be liable to more than double the rate of duty charged on those of the country to which the port belonged, but this condition was not fulfilled by the Dutch and led to constant disputes.

The Dutch ceded to England all their petty establishments in India, and England gave up Fort Marlborough (Bencoolen) and all possessions in Sumatra, with an agreement that no British Settlement should be formed there or treaty concluded with any chief in the island. The Dutch ceded Malacca, which the English took charge of again, having left the Dutch there since 1818; and the Dutch agreed to abstain in a similar manner from all political intercourse with the Malay Peninsula. The Dutch also (very generously!) withdrew the objections which had been made to the occupation of Singapore by the British. But the British (and this was the part of the agreement which has led to frequent question and been the cause of loss not only to ourselves but to native countries) engaged that no British establishment should be made on the Carimon Islands, Battam, Bintang, (opposite Singapore harbour) Lingga, or any of the other islands south of the Straits of Singapore, nor any treaty concluded by British authority with the chief of those islands. To read this literally, Australia is an island south of Singapore, but the Dutch endeavoured in the most futile way to apply the terms of the treaty to Borneo. Sarawak is a native state under a British subject as native Rajah, appointed by the people, the North Borneo Company is a corporation of private individuals, but in each of these instances the Dutch have raised objections founded on this clause of the Treaty. The Dutch received other advantages under the treaty, and England, no doubt, sacrificed large interests by her concessions in yielding Sumatra. Bencoolen was, as Sir Stamford described it, an almost inaccessible and rocky shore, but other parts of Sumatra afford opportunities for much commerce, and the success of the pepper and tobacco plantations in the north show how much might be done if it was under British rule, and the country in a tranquil state.

The Treaty contained other provisions regarding the suppression of piracy, and for license for all the inhabitants of the territories affected to dispose of their property, as they pleased, for the term of six years, and for the payment of £100,000 to the Dutch to settle all accounts and reclamations arising out of the restoration of Java. The fortifications were all to remain intact, and the actual cession to take place on the 1st of March, 1825.

To the Treaty was attached a note by the British Plenipotentiary respecting (among other matters) the treaty that had been concluded in 1819 by Sir Stamford Raffles, in the interval between his first and second visits to Singapore, with the King of Acheen, and expressing a hope that no measures hostile to him would be adopted by the Dutch, or against any other Native Chiefs with whom the Bencoolen Government had made treaties. The Dutch Plenipotentiaries in their note said that the individuals interested in the existing order of things might cherish the hope that the Dutch would respect their acquired rights and their welfare. About fifty years after these words were written followed the present interminable Acheen War.

A few words more as to the result of the Treaty. The little sentence " islands south of the Straits of Singapore " politically closed up to England, as we have said, part of Borneo. But it also excluded the tin countries of Banca, the islands of Billiton, Bali, and nearly all the Celebes, in addition to Acheen and all Sumatra. In giving Bencoolen for Malacca, England perhaps has been in the end the gainer, and the unexampled progress of government, population and trade in the Malay Peninsula, is in marked comparison with the state of Sumatra, but the only advantage to her, from an impolitic treaty, as it was then thought in the Straits, was the greater consolidation of India, and the more complete command of the Straits of Malacca, of which the strategic importance is now being fully recognised.

The encroachments by the Dutch on British trade, which this treaty was intended to prevent, drew to a head in 1837, and on the 12th of August in that year the matter came before the House of Commons, on a petition from merchants connected with Singapore. Lord Palmerston, who on several occasions took up our cause very warmly, concurred in the statements of grievances alleged in the petition, and in effect stated pretty plainly that it was a matter of national importance, and that unless Holland intended to carry out the fulfilment of a treaty solemnly confirmed and ratified, it would have to be ultimately referred to Parliament and the question of peace or war with Holland would depend upon it.

Colonel Low in 1850 wrote of the treaty as turning the people of Sumatra and the island unceremoniously over to the Dutch influence, and saying that the statesmen who originated such an act of political and mercantile suicide must have been ignorant of the value of the regions which were to be affected by the treaty, or quite unmindful of the results of British generosity. It was not thought enough to perform an act of generosity by restoring Java to the Dutch in 1816, but also to exhibit an uncalled for liberality in 1824 at the expense of British trade. And he asked what right any nation in the 19th century could possibly have to barter away thus extensive countries, with their independent populations, without their consent. In which opinion, it may be, some, in this century, may probably concur.

A curious commentary on Colonel Low's remark is a passage in the book of G. F. Davidson, spoken of elsewhere.

He was present at Bencoolen when that place was handed over to the Dutch in 1825, and he says :—"The transfer to the Dutch was a severe blow and great disappointment to all the natives, both high and low. At a meeting of chiefs held at the Government House, at which the English and Dutch authorities were both present for the purpose of completing the transfer, the Senior Raja rose to address the assembly. He was an old man with whose power and will for mischief in former days the British had good cause to be acquainted. Spoken in Malay his words sounded stronger than when they are translated. He spoke to the following effect:—'Against this transfer of my country I protest, who is there possessed of authority to hand me and my countrymen like so many cattle over to the Dutch. If the English are tired of us let them go away, but I deny their power us over. When the English first came here they asked for and got a piece of land to build godowns and dwelling houses on; that piece of land is still shown by its stone wall, and is all they ever got from us. We were never conquered, and I now tell the English and Dutch gentlemen here assembled that had I the power, as I have the will, I would resist this transfer to the knife. I am however a poor man, and have no soldiers to cope with yours, and must submit.'"

No doubt it was considered an advantage that the two powers, whose system of government are so essentially different, should not have conterminous boundaries, or exist on the same island. The result would, it might well be thought, be a comparison in favour of the English which would bring the natives into their territory, to the obvious disadvantage of the other nation. And it is probable that (as in the cession of Java to the Dutch after the short occupation of the British) it was a point of English policy to uphold Holland, who without her colonies would have, practically, ceased to exist as a European power. The story is often told that Java was restored to the Dutch because a letter from Sir Stamford Raffles was mislaid, and never opened in the Foreign Office until some time afterwards, when the matter was all settled. But it appears more probable that Lord Castlereagh looked at the question from the view of an English politician, regarding it solely as one of European importance, and the letter in question was taken as not read, for, as Mr. Boulger says, Lord Castlereagh's administration was a *war* administration, and he neither knew nor cared about the commerce of the country.

One result of the treaty was that it gave occasion for public attention being pointedly drawn to the restoration of Java to the Dutch in 1816, in an article which appeared in the *Monthly Scottish Magazine* of October, 1836, published in Glasgow. It attracted much attention and was reprinted in full in the *Free Press* of 30th March, 1837. The writer, after discussing the whole question at length, wound up by saying that Great Britain could not be considered as acting beyond the necessities of the case, were she even to resort to the extreme measure of repossessing herself of Java. This, it was known afterwards, was written by Mr. John Crawfurd, who was then in Scotland. It refers to the story of Raffles' unopened letter concerning Java. The following is a short passage from the paper;—" The Island of Java was captured by the English in 1811, and held by them till 1816, when it was again ceded to Holland in consequence of arrangements entered into at the Congress of Vienna in the preceding year. It may seem strange that this country should have consented to give up a possession of so much value, and so capable of promoting our commercial objects. Some explanation seems indeed necessary, why settlements of less importance should have been retained, while that fertile and populous island, the resources of which were or ought to have been, known to British statesmen was thus heedlessly gifted away. It has been stated in apology, that in those stirring times (Anno 1815) and among the military " *diplomates* " who were assembled at Vienna, no foreign station was looked upon as valuable, excepting such as possessed importance as a military position. Twenty years of war had fairly convinced the assembled leaders of the Holy Alliance that European nations were willing, in all time to come, to play at their bidding the same deadly game which had just been finished. And under such a delusion what wonder is it if Java, possessing no military value, should have been overlooked? It has also been said that the then British Secretary for Foreign Affairs amid the many avocations with which he was occupied, had mislaid or left unread important documents which had been transmitted by Sir Stamford Raffles from Batavia, and which placed the value of the island of Java in a proper point of view, and that the error which he had committed was found out when it was too late to remedy it. "

The good work of Sir Stamford Raffles in Java was as remarkable as his sagacious foresight with regard to Singapore. Many Dutch writers have spoken of him with admiration and respect. This is not the place to enlarge upon it and it is to be found well told in Mr. Boulger's book.

But it is not altogether foreign to the object of this book to recapitulate very briefly from that work some of the good he did.

When he took charge of the government under such very exceptional circumstances, the natives had been so oppressed that in one province the population, which had exceeded eighty thousand in 1750, had been reduced to eight thousand in 1811. Other rich provinces had been brought to poverty and insurrection by oppression and misrule, and large cultivated tracts had become wildernesses. The inhabitants of whole districts had migrated into the native provinces. The forced cultivation of coffee had produced the most dreadful sufferings. There had been an insurrection in 1800 caused by oppression. It was said that in a few years the lives of at least ten thousand natives had been destroyed by forced labour on public roads made for purely military purposes and useless for agriculture. The Government had no silver in the Treasury, and the currency was depreciated paper forced into circulation under severe penalties. The whole situation, as Mr. Boulger remarks, bristled with difficulties.

Raffles introduced justice and trial by jury; and a very radical reform in the revenue by which means it was raised to nearly four millions sterling. The land returns in the Eastern districts, as appears from a paper by Mr. John Crawfurd (then a civil commissioner in Java under Raffles) rose from 818,218 guilders in 1808 under Daendels, the highest ever reached up to that time, to 5,368,085 in 1814 under Raffles. The transit dues, which made trade almost impossible, were reduced from the average of 47 per cent. to a level of 10 per cent. A law was made forbidding slavery; an end was put to the practice of compulsory labour, proper wages being paid for labour on the roads and in the postal service; the toll-gates which frequently raised the price of articles sent inland by seventy per cent. were totally abolished; the people obtained legal protection and the right to follow and enjoy the fruits of their own industry without paying the excessive exactions of an embarrassed Government; and before Raffles left and Java was restored to the Dutch, unconditionally and without price to Holland, the exporation of coffee amounted to an annual output of ˙fifty million pounds, with a free population, while under the Dutch system it had been limited to ten million pounds. All this in four years and a half. No wonder the natives three years afterwards crowded the ships in Batavia Roads where the Dutch refused to give Raffles leave to land, as has been said in the first chapter.

Mr. Boulger says that in the native courts of Java there still survive memories of that Governor Raffles who made himself equally loved and feared, and that the tradition is not altogether sentimental or devoid of practical value : and then Mr. Boulger adds the following, which we take leave to reprint in full, because it is very interesting to those in Singapore, many of whom no doubt think that if Java were in the rapid march of events in these days to fall into the power of another European nation (as it did into that of England in 1811) the Dutch might look in vain for such generosity a second time, and would not have the opportunity to treat their benefactors with ingratitude :—" Should events in Europe place the Netherlands in the possession of a stronger continental power, as was the case in the beginning of the century, the recollection of Raffles's wise and benevolent rule will serve to direct Dutch colonial opinion, so that it may seek that sure haven of British protection, freedom of trade and of institutions, which it found in the days of Minto and Raffles, rather than again become subject to a military despotism. This is no random or hasty thought. Not so many years ago there was a spasm of fear in Holland and throughout her colonies that they might be absorbed in the German Empire; and I have high authority for saying that when that apprehension reached the colonies, the Governor of the Dutch East Indies declared that as soon as the Black Eagle was hoisted at the Hague he would run up the Union Jack at Batavia. It is to Raffles that we should owe what I will venture to call the moral reversion to Java by the free action of its inhabitants, whenever violence or ambition shall snap the link with Holland."

On 1st October, 1824, Mr. Crawfurd wrote the following despatch to the Secretary to Government at Calcutta on the subject of the treaty:—

Sir,—An authentic copy of the Treaty concluded in London in the month of March last with the Government of the Netherlands, having been received at this place, through the medium of the Dutch Official newspaper, I beg respectfully to lay before the Right Hon'ble the Governor-General in Council such observations as are suggested by it, principally in its bearings on the local arrangements recently made with the native chiefs at this place.

By the 10th article of the treaty with the Netherland Government which touches the Town and Fort of Malacca, "His Netherland Majesty engages for himself and his subjects never to form any establishment in any part of the Peninsula of Malacca or to conclude any treaty with any native Prince, chief, or state therein." On the authority of this article, the designations of Sultan and Tumongong of Johore given in the local arrangement to the native chiefs appears to be unquestionable and appropriate.

By the 12th article of that treaty, His Britannic Majesty engages that no British establishment shall be made on the Carimon Isles, or the islands of Battam, Bintang, Lingin, or on any of the other islands south of the Straits of Singapore, nor any treaty concluded, by British authority, with the chiefs of those islands. The cession made to us by the native Princes of the main island of Singapore and the islets adjacent to it, to the extent of ten geographical miles from its coast, is in no respect impugned by the condition in question, as by the most liberal interpretation, the whole cession is strictly north of the southern limits of the Straits of Singapore.

I beg respectfully to state for the information of the Right Hon'ble the Governor-General in Council, a few doubts which it is probable may arise in the interpretation of the 10th and 12th articles of the treaty with the Netherland Government. By the former the Town and Fort of Malacca and its dependencies are ceded to the British Government. At the period of the conclusion of the treaty, the Settlement of Rhio, situated upon the island of Bintang, was strictly and in all respect a dependancy of Malacca as in every period of its connexion with the Dutch Government. By this article, therefore, it would become a British possession, but this is again precluded by the 12th article, which provides expressly against any British Settlement being formed on the island of Bintang or any treaty concluded by the British authority with its chief. Under these circumstances the only question is whether the Settlement of Rhio is to be retained or relinquished by the Dutch authorities.

It does not upon the whole appear to me that the occupation of Rhio could be beneficial to the British Government, yet its retention on the part of the Netherland Government, and our exclusion from entering into political relations with the chiefs of all the islands lying south to the Straits of Singapore and between the Peninsula and Sumatra, may prove a matter of some inconvenience to us, as it in fact virtually amounts to a dismemberment of the principality of Johore, and must thus be productive of some embarrassment and confusion. This may be easily illustrated by an example. The Carimon islands and the Malayan Settlement of Bulang are two of the principal possessions of the Tumongong of Johore or Singapore, and his claim to them is not only allowed by the rival chiefs, but more satisfactorily ascertained by the voluntary and cheerful alliance yielded to him by the inhabitants. By the present treaty, however, he must either forego all claims to these possessions, or removing to them, renounce his connexion with the British Government.

J. CRAWFURD,
Resident.

CHAPTER XV.

1825.

IN February, 1825, it was proposed to build a new market to cost $4,316. 60, as the market was too small. In April, 80 Madras convicts and 120 Bengal convicts arrived from Bencoolen. Lines were built for 600 to 700 at the cost of $13,199, but leaving room for extending the buildings for 1,200 to 2,000. Lieutenant Chester of the 23rd Bengal Native Infantry was appointed Superintendent, with $150 staff salary, and provision was made for an overseer at $50, a native doctor at $12, a writer at $7, and one peon for every 25 convicts at $6 a month. There is a note in some statistics regarding Penang that the occupation of Singapore caused a loss to the revenue at Penang between 1821 and 26th July, 1825, of $152,734.

In the months of March and April in this year Malacca was re-occupied by the English.

In the *Singapore Chronicle* there was a paper by Mr. Crawfurd on Agriculture in Singapore, which is reprinted in 3 Logan's Journal, page 508; experience has since shewn that his condemnation of the soil was well founded, coffee, cotton, sugar, and nutmegs having all failed to prove successful. Mr. Crawfurd said that the soil and climate were perfectly adapted for the cocoanut, orange, mangoe, durian and pineapple, as it was rather climate than soil that is required for such productions; and it appeared singular, and yet unexplained in vegetable physiology, that while the poorest wilds are sufficient for the growth, not only of the luxuriant plants which afford the rich fruits in question, but also for that of the most stupendous trees in the forest; the richest are indispensable to the successful culture of the lowly plants which afford the principal necessaries of life.

A despatch from the Court of Directors in London of 6th April, said that they had been much gratified by the information afforded of the flourishing condition of the commerce of Singapore, the value of which in imports and exports had amounted in 1822 to $8,568,172; and were happy to perceive that the establishments of the Settlement had been revised with a view to greater efficiency without any additional expense being entailed on Government.

It has been said before that in 1820 the expenses of Singapore for one year were less than those of Bencoolen for a month, and one most remarkable thing about Raffles's management was the extremely small number of civilians as compared with both Bencoolen and Penang. The expenditure at Bencoolen was £100,000 a year, and the return in pepper was altogether inadequate. As to Penang, the Governor and Council sent out from England to constitute the Presidency there in 1805 consisted of twenty-six Englishmen, whose salaries amounted to an aggregate of £43,500 a year, from the Governor with £9,000 to the school-master at £225. In Singapore there were only some three or four officials, whose monthly salaries including the clerks and peons amounted to a little under $4,000 a month.

In June Mr. Crawfurd sent to Calcutta a general report on the Eastern Seas from which the following notes are taken:—The Dutch charge 35 per cent. on all English cotton and woollen goods imported into Batavia, the only port at which Europeans can trade; and all the native ports over which the Dutch influence extends have the same regulations. The only effect of the treaty of 1824 had been to raise the duty on the export of coffee in Dutch ships to 2½ guilders, which made it half of the foreign duty, instead of reducing it. The trade which was increasing had been injured by these restrictions. Under English rule the Javanese had been becoming accustomed to a cheap and regular supply of English goods. The trade continued good until 1823, when the imports amounted to 7,000 cases of piece goods, valued at $2,100,000. The import duties had been then gradually raised from 6 to 12 per cent. and in 1823 to 25 per cent. from European, and 35 per cent. from foreign ports. The high duties checked the trade and now in 1825 the imports were only 3,000 cases. The Batavia customs duties rose from 432,109 guilders in 1817, and 996,556 in 1818, to 2,622,241 in 1823. They fell in 1824 to 2,399,943 though duties were raised retrospectively in that year.

The report also said that the Dutch regulations destroyed the trade from India to the native ports under their influence. Pontianak in 1812 took British goods to the value of $311,275. The place was then under native rule and the duties levied were 3 per cent. The trade increased until 1817 when the Dutch interfered with their regulations, and in 1824 the trade was extinct. The treaty of 1824 which stipulated that the Dutch native ports should not charge more on English than on Dutch imports was disregarded. The Dutch got over the difficulty by boldly calling the ports Dutch, though notoriously governed by native rulers and having no further power than the presence of a few soldiers.

The report said that the French had great influence in Cochin-China under the late king, but the present king who ascended in 1819 was not favourable to them. In 1822 there were eight Frenchmen in the public service, but now all were gone, the two last, Messrs. Vannier and Chaigneau, having passed through Singapore in April, 1825, on their way home.

Mr. Chaigneau having returned to France from Cochin China in 1821, was sent out again by King Louis XVIII. as Consul for France, with a number of presents, such as a large gilt clock, pistols, pictures of battles, and a very large mirror. The King for whom they had been intended, and who had treated him and the missionaries very well, died before Mr. Chaigneau's arrival. His successor took the presents, but refused to recognise him, and he was forced to leave the country. The French missionaries, however, insisted on remaining, and the persecutions then commenced and missionaries and converts were put to death. This continued until February, 1859, when a priest was beheaded near where the present Cathedral now stands in the town of Saigon, the evening before the French Expedition took the citadel.

In the same report the Resident said that the Sultan of Brunei had offered him Labuan, which place was formerly occupied by the English, and that the Dutch within the last two years had made two unsuccessful attempts to establish themselves at Brunei. They offered protection, but the Sultan answered that he was able to protect himself, and if not he would give due notice.

On the 2nd August, exactly one year after the date of the treaty, Mr. Crawfurd started in the ship *Malabar* for a trip round the island, to take formal possession. The Bengal Government had instructed him to do this. An account of the "voyage," as it was then called, was published in the *Singapore Chronicle*, and re-printed in Mr. Moor's Notices of the Indian Archipelago, where it is still to be found, although the *Chronicle* is not. The vessel was 380 tons, and they left at 6 a.m. going round to the eastward, arriving off Johore Hill the next morning at 10 o'clock. Mr. Crawfurd landed and went up the hill. While they were on shore, a heavy squall split the vessel's topsails, and they were unable to get off to the ship, and did not get on board till after dark, and well drenched. The next morning they got as far as Pulo Obin, and hoisted the British flag there, and fired a salute of 21 guns. The next day they got a little further, and went ashore on the mainland. The account says:—"Bukit Timah, although not above seven or eight miles from the town has never been visited by a European, seldom by a native; and such is the character of the intervening country, that it would be almost as easy a task to make a voyage to Calcutta as to travel to it." Two days afterwards they got out of the Straits to the west, and it says, "We thus took four days passing through the Straits, and our voyage upon the whole may be considered as rather expeditious. This was the only route of the first European navigators, and it seems singular that the present more obvious, safer and shorter passage should not have been earlier followed. Pursuing the old passage, four or five days at least are lost, and although there be always, except at the western extremity, from five to thirteen fathoms water, the navigation, from the occasional narrowness of the Strait, and the occurrence, now and then, of sunken rocks, is by no means free from danger. It is certainly never likely to be frequented again by the general navigator, but might occasionally be made available in time of war to avoid a superior enemy in the main channel, a view of its utility which an Englishman is little disposed to look to."

The account says that no huts were to be seen in the Straits, except some lately occupied by Singapore wood-cutters on Pulo Obin. The vessels then went to the Carimons and they visited the tin mines. Then they landed on the Rabbit and Coney Islands and took possession under a salute of 21 guns. They beat into the harbour at midnight, and landed at day-break after a trip of ten days, which is done now in a steamer in the course of eight or ten hours.

In September Mr. Crawfurd (who, as has been said, formerly held high office under Sir Stamford Raffles in Java, as Resident at Soerabaya and Samarang) reported to Bengal the unsatisfactory state of affairs in Netherlands India. Insurrections in Java, Borneo, Sumatra and Celebes. All the troops had been called in to defend Batavia. The open country as far as Soerabaya was in the hands of the insurgents. "I do not hesitate to report that the very existence of the Netherlands authority in India appears to me to be in imminent danger."

On 23rd September the Resident proposed to employ the Rev. Mr. Thomson, a missionary, to translate a good code of Malay laws. Raffles had formed a Committee at Bencoolen on 31st October, 1823, to report on native laws.

A company was started in Singapore this year to put on a steam vessel between Batavia and Penang, calling at Singapore. The Resident promised to assist and offered to subscribe $2,000 on the part of Government. It did not come to anything.

In February Sir Stamford Raffles, while in England, wrote a long letter to the Committee of the British and Foreign Bible Society on the continuance of its operations which had been under his care at Bencoolen, and were now changed owing to the return of Sumatra to the Dutch. He said that much good had been done in Bencoolen, and advised an agent being appointed to proceed to Singapore. As soon as Singapore became a settlement, Raffles had connected the Society with the place, and wrote to his cousin the Rev. Dr. Raffles, asking him if he knew of any layman who would come to Singapore as Agent to the Society, on a salary of £100 a year and all travelling expenses. Soon afterwards an Auxiliary Society was formed, which continued for many years, the Protestant clergymen generally forming the most active members of the Committee. The depot was in a small building of two stories at the corner of Brass Bassa Road and North Bridge Road where the Raffles Girls' School stands now. The care taker and books occupied the ground floor, and the upper floor was used for holding mission services and meetings of the committee. About 1882, on the suggestion of the local Society, the London Society established an Agent of their own.

Mr. Crawfurd in his book on the Embassy to Siam (1830) at page 357, made some remarks on the trade of Singapore and gave some statistics, as follows:—" It appears that in the years 1825 and 1826, which were so calamitous to the general commerce of the world, the value of the trade of Singapore, before so rapidly progressive, suffered some slight diminution ; but on inspecting the returns, however, it appears that the real quantity of goods had considerably increased, and that the diminution in amount arose from depreciation.

	Imports.		Exports.		Total.
1824	... $ 6,914,436	...	$ 6,604,601	...	$ 13,519,037
1825	... 6,289,396	...	5,837,370	...	12,126,766
1826	... 6,863,581	...	6,422,845	...	13,286,426

1822	Pepper exported	...	2,327,000	lb.
1823	,,	...	4,672,500	,,
1824	,,	...	3,104,400	,,
1825	,,	...	5,272,850	,,

1823	Tin exported	...	1,100	tons
1824	,,	...	1,000	,,
1825	,,	...	740	,,
1826	,,	...	1,230	,,

He said that the first direct arrival from Singapore to England was in 1821. In 1822 four ships cleared out with cargoes for Europe; in 1823, nine; 1824, twelve; 1825, fifteen; and in 1826, fourteen ships. The greater part of these were for London and Liverpool; some for Stockholm, Hamburg and Bordeaux.

Among the names of the land-holders in 1824, which is printed on page 70, was that of J. d'Almeida. Dr. Jozé d'Almeida had been a surgeon on board a Portuguese man-of-war, and, while he was passing through Singapore, was struck by the advantages of its position and prospects. It is said that before he decided to settle here he made some voyages between Macao and Calcutta in a Portuguese barque called the *Andromeda* of which he was the super-cargo and generally called the captain. Whether this was so or not, there is no doubt that he left money with Mr. F. J. Bernard to secure a piece of land and build a house for him. Mr. Bernard acquired the land at Kampong Glam, now numbered Lot 207, and the house then built on it was the last compound house on the Beach towards Kampong Glam, on the next plot but two from Middle Road. It was at one time from 1878 rented for the use of the Raffles Girls' School, and was purchased by the King of Siam. When the house was finished, Mr. Bernard and his family lived in it until December, 1825, when Dr. d'Almeida and his family came from Macao. There were some political disturbances there at the time and it was said that the Doctor had to leave very hurriedly in cnsequence. The same old house is now used by Chinese stone masons, with a number of sheds in front of it in the compound.

Dr. d'Almeida's dispensary was then in the Square where the back of Guthrie & Co.'s godowns is now, the rest of the building was occupied by four or five Chinese shops. The origin of the commencement of his mercantile business shows how unexpectedly some of the well established firms began. In consequence of the north-east monsoon, which vessels in those days did not try to face, two large vessels were detained in the harbour; one was a Portuguese, the other a Spanish vessel, bound for Macao and Manila, respectively. As they could not proceed on their voyage for four or five months, they determined to sell the greater part of their cargoes here to meet their expenses, and they consulted Dr. d'Almeida about it, and he consented to act as the agent of the vessels. He helped to sell the cargoes, mostly at auction, and finding it successful, determined to start in business, which was the commencement of the firm of Jozé d'Almeida & Sons, as it was afterwards known, which was established in 1825, and at the time of his death in Singapore in 1850, was one of the largest and most important firms in the place. The market was suitable for many articles of Portuguese industry and production, and during the first China War the firm did a very large business in raw silk and other Chinese merchandise.

In its day the Doctor's residence in Beach Road was a famous house in Singapore, the centre of Singapore social life. Very large parties were given in the old times by Dr. d'Almeida, and, after him, by Mr. José and his wife, whose house was always the rendezvous of all social amusement. All those who were thrown into personal contact with the d'Almeida family were not likely to forget

To face page 184.

Dr. Jose d'Almeida.

[*Photograph from an old oil painting.*]

their great kindness and hospitality and what they did to make Singapore, when it was a very much smaller place than it is now, a pleasant home for those who were resident here.

Mr. Earl, in his book on " The Eastern Seas and Singapore," published in London in 1837, speaks of him in the warmest terms, and dedicated the book to him. He says in one place, " Although the mercantile transactions carried on by Dr. d'Almeida were too extensive to permit him to devote much time to medical practice, yet they did not prevent him from employing the experience, which he had acquired during his service as a Surgeon in the Portuguese navy, in alleviating the sufferings of his fellow-creatures. Scarcely a native chief or nakodah, visits the Settlement without at least once paying his respects to Dr. d'Almeida, who had proved himself to be their sincere friend and benefactor."

One of Dr. d'Almeida's great friends was Mr. John Henry Velge. He was born in Malacca on 19th December, 1796, and lived to a great age. He remembered the blowing-up of the Malacca fort in 1807. He had been a sailor, and had married in Samarang. He sailed in his own ship, and, leaving the sea, settled down in Singapore, and towards the end of his life in Malacca, where he died on the 14th April, 1891, at the age of 95 years. His friends hoped, and half-expected, that he would see out a century, as he was a wonderfully active old gentleman. In the old days, he had a large house on the Beach, one of the biggest houses (years afterwards it was Emmerson's Hotel) and at Malacca he built, and lived in, the large house at Banda Elier which has since been bought by Government, and is now used as the Library and Rest House. In these two houses, at Singapore and Malacca, Mr. & Mrs. Velge, like the Doctor and his wife, used to show great hospitality. Both houses were admirably adapted for dances, which were quite a feature in the social life of both places.

Dr. d'Almeida and his family were admirable musicians, and his musical evening concerts were frequented by all who delighted in listening to the rendering of some of the best composers. His name coupled with that of Doctor Montgomerie, will always be connected with the discovery of gutta-percha, and he was constantly endeavouring to find out some new products for our markets. As an agriculturist he was indefatigable, but more enterprising than successful. Sugar, coffee, cocoa-nuts, cotton, all had his attention, and a great deal of his money. Before roads were opened out into the interior he began to plant at Tanjong Katong by laying out a plantation of cotton, and he introduced cotton seeds from the South Sea Islands, and tried North American, Brazilian, Egyptian, and Bourbon cotton. But the cotton failed, and the cleared ground was planted with cocoanuts and is now known as the Confederate Estate. He had a large plantation called Bandula about $4\frac{3}{4}$ miles from town on the right hand side of Serangoon Road, afterwards owned by Mr. Robert Jamie. He tried cochineal, vanila, cloves and gamboge trees from Siam. His experience as a traveller had made him acquainted with various trees and different kinds of fruit, which he planted here, and he also introduced teal and quail from India and China. Open-handed, generous and hospitable, he was a general favourite, whilst his unostentatious, but extensive, charity and benevolence endeared him to the lower classes.

On his visit to Europe in 1842 he was knighted by the Queen of Portugal and was appointed Consul-General in the Straits, and received several honorary titles and distinctions; and shortly before his death he was made a member of the Queen's Council in Portugal, a dignity with corresponds with that of our Privy Councillors. Spain also conferred on him the Order of Knighthood of Charles III.

Dr. d'Almeida was married more than once, and had a very large family of nineteen or twenty children. His eldest son Joaquim d'Almeida was married on 5th February, 1838, in the Roman Catholic Church in Calcutta to Rose Maria, the youngest daughter of Captain W. Barrington. He died in London about 1870. His younger brother José was born in Macao on 19th July, 1812, and came to Singapore with his brother Joaquim in November, 1825, to stay with Mr Bernard until his father arrived here on Christmas Day in that year. Their sister Carlotta came down with her father. She had been born in Macao in 1819, and never afterwards left Singapore. She died at 373, Victoria Street, on the 11th September, 1901, at 82 years of age. She was married to Mr. Maximiliano Miranda, a resident of Singapore, whom she survived nearly sixteen years.

There are still two sons of Dr. d'Almeida alive in Singapore, Mr. Edward and Mr. William d'Almeida, and one daughter, Mrs. Pereira, who married Mr. Francisco Evaristo Pereira, a well-known legal practitioner in former years in Singapore. These are the only surviving children of the Doctor. The eldest daughter, Marianne, was married to Mr. Thomas Owen Crane, three of whose daughters, afterwards Mrs. Thomas Dunman, Mrs. H. W. Wood, and Mrs. W. W. Shaw, were all very well-known and among the most highly respected residents in Singapore for many years. Mr. T. O. Crane had fourteen children, and thirteen are still alive. They were all born in Singapore, and speak well for the healthiness of the place. The history of many of the families best known in Singapore in former days was therefore largely mixed up with the family of Dr. d'Almeida.

Dr. d'Almeida died at Singapore and it was written at the time that nearly every European in the community attended his funeral, the Governor being one of the pall-bearers, and the attendance of the Chinese and native merchants was very large. His tomb which is now falling into decay, with the inscription almost illegible, is at the top of the hill in the old cemetery nearly in the centre of the block appropriated to the Roman Catholic Community, there are tombs of some of his children surrounding it, and not far away to the right is the tomb of Mr. Coleman, who was a Roman Catholic. The inscription on Dr. Almeida's tombstone is as follows; it is worth printing as it was deciphered with some difficulty, and is a record of one of the most prominent of the old Singapore pioneers:—

"Sacred to the memory of
Sir Jozé d'Almeida Carvalho E. Silva,
Knight, Commander of the Portuguese Orders
Of Christ and Conception, and

Knight of the Order of Charles the III. of Spain,
Member of the Privy Council of the Most Gracious Majesty
Queen Dona Maria II.,
Portuguese Consul-General in the Straits;
Born at St. Pedro Do Sul in Portugal
On the XXVII November, 1784, and
After a residence of XXV years in Singapore,
Departed this life on the XVII day of October, 1850,
In the LXVI year of this age.
The Lord is nigh unto all those that call upon him:
To all that call upon him in truth." Ps. 145, v. 18.

The firm was afterwards called Jozé d'Almeida & Son, when son
Joaquim joined; and in January, 1837, it was Jozé d'Almeida &
Sons, as the younger brother joined it, and it continued so until 1865.
It was not unknown for bills in Calcutta to be drawn upon Sir Jozé
d'Almeida & Sons after his Spanish decoration, but it was not usually
done. Mr. Joaquim was a very good man of business, but inclined to
be too speculative, while Mr. José was said to be too careful, and
the two together, years after the old man's death, brought the old
business to an end. There were many funny stories told of the
way the two brothers used to play at cross purposes. One instance
may be mentioned. Mr. José came into town early one morning
and found a letter, just arrived, that told of an earthquake in
Manila. His firm had a large stock of corrugated iron on hand,
and he decided to go out and buy up the stock in other people's
hands so as to made a "corner" in the article. So he went out
without saying anything about it in the office, putting the letter
carefully in his pocket, and bought up all he could on the quiet.
He was away from office for some time, and while he was out another
smart merchant who had also heard of the earthquake and of Mr.
José's proceedings, went round to the office, and finding that Mr.
Joaquim had just come in, asked him if he had a small quantity
of corrugated iron to sell. Joaquim said that they had had a large
stock of it for some time and could not dispose of it, but if he
would make an offer to clear out the whole lot he would be glad
to sell it cheap, which he did. Mr. José returned soon afterwards
to find that he had been buying at higher prices than his brother
had sold at, and his "corner" broken up. Mr. G. H. Brown was
too many for Mr. José on this occasion.

Young Mr. José d'Almeida a few years after his arrival here in
1825, went to Bali in a sailing ship (there were no steamers then)
to load rice; and from Bali he proceeded to Whampoa, the port of
Canton, where Jardine Matheson & Co. sold the cargo of rice, Mr.
d'Almeida acting as super-cargo of the vessel. From Canton he
sailed for Bali, then back again to Canton, after which he set out
for Macao, where he remained for four and a half months. Leaving
Macao in a vessel named the *Mermaid*, he was caught in the tail
of a typhoon, experiencing very violent weather. The vessel was blown
all the way down to Manila, and when she arrived in harbour, she
had lost all her boats and sails and masts. In fact Mr. d'Almeida
in the course of that eventful voyage on more than one occasion

abandoned all hopes of ever reaching land, and the vessel was so badly damaged that she took no less than 45 days to repair. Travelling about in this way on behalf of his firm he finally reached Singapore, preparatory to a journey to Calcutta, where he resided for five months. On his return he settled down here for some time, but in 1843 he went on a voyage to Sydney, Adelaide, Melbourne and Hobart Town, and it was at Sydney that he met the late Mrs. d'Almeida. He returned to Singapore to obtain his father's sanction to the marriage, and was married on the 28th September, 1845, at Trinity Church, Sydney, by the Lord Bishop of Australia, to Augusta, the second daughter of the Rev. J. C. Grylls, M.A., the minister of Trinity Church, and his wife's sister was married at the same time to the minister of Penrith, as appears from the advertisement in the *Free Press.* He took up his abode in Singapore until 1857, when just before the mutiny he made a voyage to Europe, remaining there some twelve months, which was said to be the only leave he was known to have taken.

Mr. and Mrs. José, as they were usually known, were most hospitable people. He built the first house on Mount Victoria. It had a ball-room attached to it on one side. The road at the foot of the hill was called Almeida Road after him. They had many daughters, most of whom were married in Singapore, and two sons, but all his family have left the Settlement. After the firm was dissolved, business was carried on under other names by the two brothers and some others for a few years, but during the latter years of his life Mr. José was a broker, and in spite of his great age, was most hardworking and persevering to the last, until he lost his wife, when he quite broke down. No one could doubt that they had always been very much attached to one another. There was a pathetic coincidence in their deaths. Mrs. d'Almeida died at the age of 70 years on Saturday the 7th January, 1894, and was buried on Sunday afternoon. Exactly one week afterwards, Mr. José died at the age of 81 years, and was laid by her side at the same hour on the following Sunday. To the older residents it seemed like the snapping of one of the last links of the chain between the commencement of Singapore and its far different modern life, and by them the names of the d'Almeida family will always be held in affectionate remembrance.

Mr. Thomas Owen Crane came to Singapore in 1824 or 1825. He had left England on his way to India, but the vessel was wrecked off the coast of Spain. He managed, with a few others, to swim to a barren rock, where they remained for over a month, eating shell-fish, rats, and chewing shoe leather. They were reduced to such straits that some of the sailors wanted to cast lots, as has been done in similar extremities, but a vessel sighted them and they were rescued. The ship was bound to Singapore, and so Mr. Crane remained here, and started in business as Thomas O. Crane in 1825. About 1842 his brother William came up from Australia, and they carried on business together as Crane Brothers, as auctioneers and land agents. William returned to England about 1857, and Mr. Crane continued in business as Thomas O. Crane & Co. His name is frequently mentioned in the old papers; he was a Justice of the Peace, a member for many years of the Raffles

School Committee; was one of the Wardens of the first Freemason's Lodge and assisted in many useful undertakings.

He commenced planting in May, 1836, and at the end of that year had seventeen acres planted with cotton at Tanjong Katong. The undertaking was abandoned, because the crops failed, owing, as he considered, to the want of a regular season, together with the variableness of the weather, so that the crop instead of coming forward at one time of the year, continued scantily all the year 'round, and was thus damaged by rain, beside causing expense in gathering in small quantities. He had the soil analysed in Calcutta, and it was reported to be of the best kind for the plant in its native localities. He then planted cocoanuts, and had a large plantation at Tanjong Katong in 1850, of which he gave a number of particulars, as to the method of planting, care of the trees, crops, &c., which are to be found by those interested in cocoanut plantations, in an article by Mr. J. T. Thomson in 4 Logan's Journal at page 103. About 1850, Mr. Crane sent some coprah to a firm at Marseilles, which had asked him to prepare a small quantity as a trial, which he did. The cost was said to be too high, and nothing was done in the article for over twenty years, when it began to be a principal article of export.

Mr. Crane married, as has been said, one of the many daughters of Dr. d'Almeida, in 1826, and had a family of fourteen children, only one of whom, the eldest daughter, is dead. The eldest son, William, went to Japan in 1861 and has resided there continuously up to the present time. Mr. Crane retired from business about 1864. He had lived for very many years at his large house at Gaylang, the only house near there at that time, a little beyond the Police Station on the right hand side, where the family had been brought up. He remained in Singapore for thirty-five years, when he made a short visit to England; and left here for the last time in 1866, dying in London in the following year. The business was carried on under the name of Crane Brothers, by sometimes one, sometimes two, of his sons, until July, 1899, when his son Mr. Charles Crane retired to England and the business was closed after seventy-four years. Mr. Henry Crane is the only one of his sons now in Singapore; his daughters Mrs. Dunman, Mrs. H. W. Wood, and Mrs. W. W. Shaw have already been referred to.

The following letter of Sir Stamford Raffles to Mr. A. L. Johnston was printed in the *Free Press* in 1885.

LONDON, *January 2nd*, 1825.

"My dear Sir,—I have received your kind letters of the 25th of April last, as well as one from the House of the 16th June. The latter I have answered in a separate letter. I have also to thank you for the *tripang,* specimen of Carimon tin, &c., which are in course of delivery.

"The wretched state of my health rendered it necessary that I should abstain as much as possible from public business for some months after my arrival, and had it been otherwise, the season of the year was unfavourable to any progress, London being quite deserted. I have, therefore, nothing very important to communicate to you as to what is actually done respecting Singapore. There is, as you may suppose, a lively interest taken in its future welfare, and you may be assured that I am not lukewarm on the subject.

"The necessity of a Court of Judicature is universally admitted, and the only question is the nature of the establishment required for the purpose. The idea of uniting the jurisdiction of Singapore with that of Pinang was early adopted, and the authorities at home have come to the conclusion that the civil as well as the judicial jurisdiction of Pinang might be advantageously extended to Singapore. With this view, I have reason to believe the Government of Pinang has been called upon to report on the practicability and advantages of the plan, and by this time it may probably have become matter of local discussion.

"Nothing, however, has yet been done of a decisive nature, and if I have done no other good, I believe I may have been the means of postponing a decision until the question can be viewed in all its bearings.

"By the Charter for the Recorder's Court at Pinang, a provision is made for the extension of its jurisdiction to any places in the vicinity of Pinang, which may hereafter become a Dependency on that Settlement, and nothing has appeared to the Court of Directors so easy as to make Singapore a Dependency on Pinang, and thus to provide a judicial jurisdiction at once. The idea also of making a respectable government at Pinang by uniting all the Eastern Settlements under one authority, affords a plea for continuing and extending an establishment of civil servants in that quarter whereby patronage ensues; and really, to a person resident in this country, and possessing only general information as to local interests in the East, there seems to be something much more simple in the plan of one government and jurisdiction for the Settlements to the eastward, than in the maintenance of several separate jurisdictions.

"My notion, as you must be aware, was to place all our stations to the eastward on the footing of commercial ports, and immediately dependent on the Supreme Government of India, and in furtherance of this plan I proposed that instead of Singapore giving way to Pinang, the latter should rather be placed on the same footing as Singapore and immediately subordinate to Bengal. Our recent treaty with the Dutch, whereby we have entirely shut ourselves out of Sumatra, and from the countries south of the Straits of Singapore, added to the political changes which may result from the present contest with the Burmans, as it may affect our Siamese neighbours, in some measure alters the state of the question, and I confess, when I reflect on the arbitrary proceedings which a local Resident may adopt, and the little interest which the Bengal Government is inclined to take in the local concerns of the place, that I am less tenacious of my former position than I once was, and that if a *due* and *permanent* provision could be made for the independence of Singapore as a *free* port, and for its Municipal regulation as a *free* town, there might be some advantages in connecting it with Pinang.

"Parliament will meet early in next month, and the subject will, no doubt, be discussed there, as well as in the Court of Proprietors. Nothing will be done in a hurry, and, therefore, it is possible letters from Singapore may arrive in time to assist our judgment. Under this possibility, I urgently request your opinion by the first conveyance that offers, and in the meantime, although I have thus given you confidentially the grounds on which I now feel inclined to come round to the opinion in favour of uniting Pinang and Singapore, I would wish you to understand that, as far as I have yet gone in my communications with the public authorities, I have expressed myself decidedly against such a measure, declaring that it would be at once to put an extinguisher on the rising prosperity of the place.

"If anything is decided upon, before I hear from you on the subject, I think it will be on the principle of establishing Pinang, Malacca, and Singapore—all as free ports—and under such regulations for their internal police as shall secure the rights and liberties of Englishmen to the population—European as well as Native. These points laid down by Parliament, it matters little whether the Civil Government is under one authority or several; an appeal will always lie to Bengal, and it may be an advantage that the public in Europe are from time to time informed how you are going on. At present, everything centres and rests in Bengal, whence but little impartial information is derived.

"On the subject of the clause in the treaty which restricts Americans from visiting Singapore, nothing can be more ridiculous. I have conferred with the American Minister and our own authorities on the subject, and I hope I shall succeed in removing this bar to your commerce. The treaty will, I understand, expire in two or three years, when, of course, the objectionable clause, as far as it affects Singapore, will not be renewed, and the only question is whether it is now worth while stirring a point which will soon be renewed. There are so many national jealousies, that the *British* merchant may possibly conceive that his interests would be injured by such a concession to Americans, and this is an argument likely to be used by the East India Company. Nevertheless, I should think that with the present *Liberal* administration, such arguments would not be much attended to, and that no serious difficulty will exist in obtaining an Order in favour of the American Trade.

"I am sorry to observe your Resident has had recourse to so vicious and objectionable a mode of raising a revenue as the establishment of the Gaming Farms. I think it likely the subject will attract public attention here and become matter for discussion in the Court of Proprietors, if not in a higher Court. My sentiments on the subject are on record, and I see no reason to alter them, and whenever the fit time comes I shall be prepared to support them.

"Accept my best thanks for the information you have furnished respecting the trade, &c., of Singapore; every particular is interesting to me, and possibly may be valuable in the discussions which will take place as to the future management of the Settlement.

"It is only of late that I have had an opportunity of seeing Dr. Morrison. His time has been partly taken up in a matrimonial arrangement which he has concluded much to his satisfaction, and he proposes returning to China by one of the direct ships in April. Before that time, I hope we shall be able to do something effectual regarding the Institution. As yet I have not moved in it.

"With regard to my own affairs and views, I have only to state that my severe losses by the *Fame* are likely so far to interfere with my plans of retirement, which I once fondly indulged, that it is possible I may, against my inclination, be forced into public life in this country. My friends assure me that the Direction is open to me, and I have no reason to expect difficulty in getting into Parliament; but the anxiety, fatigue and responsibility in which such a course would involve me, make me hesitate at present, and particularly while my health is so precarious. Were I to consult my personal happiness and comfort alone, I think it would be a wiser course to take a tour to the Continent for a year or two, and quietly retire into the country, where I might enjoy peace and tranquillity with the advantage of good society in men and books, and a visit to London for a few months in the year only. The only arrangement of a permanent nature which I have yet made, has been the purchase of the lease of a house in Grosvenor Street for thirty years, which looks a little like the tiding of my mind being to that quarter as a permanent residence for the rest of my life.

" With regard to the state of our account, I have written to the House all that appears necessary, and will only add in this place my earnest desire that you will complete the remittances as soon as you can, as I am anxious to invest my little property as early as possible. Until this is done, I hardly know how to make up my mind whether I must again accept employment or not.

" As to general news, it is hardly worth while sending you any in this form, as you will have abundant and perhaps later intelligence from the public prints.

" The overflow of capital in this country has occasioned a degree of gambling that some steady people think will end in something like the South Sea Bubble. Independent of the foreign loans, which are to an enormous extent, there is an association for almost every possible speculation that can be conceived, and vast sums of money have been made by the rise in the value of shares. Among those which have been proved most advantageous are the Mexican mines. At the present moment, public attention is principally attracted to the *Locomotive* Steam Engines, which are to propel carriages without horses from one part of the country to the other at the rate of ten to twelve miles an hour! A considerable opposition is expected on the part of the holders of canal shares.

" I have lately seen an article in what is called the *Helter Skelter Magazine* published at Calcutta, and which is attributed to Crawfurd. It is written in such bad taste, and with so much ill-humour, that I can hardly believe it to be his; for the rest it is amusing enough.

" Remember me kindly to all friends, and believe me

Yours very sincerely,
T. S. RAFFLES.

A note by Mr. Crawfurd said that the annual charge of the Civil Establishment in 1825 was about $50,000. The Military consisted of about 150 Sepoys and Native Artillery, with no Europeans except the Officers; and the expense was less than $35,000 a year.

CHAPTER XVI.

1826—1827.

1826.

IN January Mr. Crawfurd, in imitation of a similar scheme at Penang, asked leave from Calcutta to establish a lottery, the profits to be applied to town improvement. He and Lieutenant Jackson had prepared a chart of the Archipelago in Chinese and Bugis characters. He asked to have it lithographed at Calcutta and sold to natives, whom he described as very desirous to have it. He recommended that three Beacons should be lit up at night; one at Tree Island, one at St. John's, and one at Singapore town. Mr. Crawfurd also asked to be allowed to draw the allowance of Governor-General's Agent, as he was doing the duty formerly done by Raffles, who was now in England. The Resident's salary was $750, table allowance $500, and house rent allowance $150, total $1,400. The salary of Raffles as Lieutenant-Governor of Bencoolen had been Rs. 2,735, allowances Rs. 3,841, Governor-General's Agent Rs. 1,000, total Rs. 7,576 (say $2,900) a month.

Upon the expectation that the Recorder's Court at Penang would be extended to Singapore, the Resident recommended the following gentlemen, then on the Magistrates' list, to be included in a Commission of the Peace :—

Civil Servants.

Samuel George Bonham	John Patullo
Samuel Garling	Edward Presgrave

Merchants.

Charles Chester	John Argyll Maxwell
Thomas Davis	William Paton
James Innes	William Scott
Alexander Laurie Johnston	John Spottiswoode
Alexander Kyd Lindsay	Hugh Syme
William Gordon Mackenzie	William Vincent

Medical Officers.   Officials.

John Crawfurd (Resident)	Captain Edward Davies, B.M.I
William Montgomerie, M.D.	Captain William Flint, R.N.

From 1st February Lieutenant Jackson was appointed Surveyor, to survey lands, register grants, transfers, &c., on a salary of Rs. 300. The fees were $1 each for register and transfer, and 25 cents an acre for making survey, with a minimum charge of $1 for four acres.

In August the importation of military arms was advertised as illegal. The imports of arms and ammunition in the four years, 1823 to 1826, amounted to $276,411.

On the 14th August Mr. Prince was in orders at Singapore as a Senior Member of Council and Resident Councillor at Singapore, and Mr. Crawfurd went to England. Raffles in a letter to Bengal, speaking of Mr. Prince wrote:—

"After a service of thirty-five years during the largest portion of which time he maintained himself without any charge to Government." This is explained by the fact that Civil Servants at Bencoolen were allowed to trade. It appears that Mr. Prince had a river there to himself and no one else was allowed to trade or interfere. In fact for some, but it does not appear exactly for what services to the Company, further than keeping up the influence of the name, Mr. Prince had the monopoly of buying and selling in a district. The remark is not personal to Mr. Prince, it seems to have been the custom of the service. Mr. Prince only remained a little over a year, as Mr. Murchison took his place as Resident Councillor on 29th November, 1827, and his name does not appear prominently in any way. Mr. Presgrave was acting Resident until Mr. Prince took up the appointment, which he does not seem to have done for some months after August, 1826.

There was inconvenience at this time from want of suitable public offices, those in use being in merchants' godowns not built for offices, and the Resident, Treasurer and Accountant held office in their own private houses. When Raffles was in Singapore, he had used the upper floor of Captain Flint's house as an office.

In this year the three places, Penang, Malacca and Singapore, were incorporated as one Settlement consisting of the three Stations under the Government of Penang; with this difference: that whereas before the incorporation the three members of Council resided at Penang, two of the Councillors were now sent to the other stations, one to Singapore and one to Malacca under the title of Resident Councillors. At the same time Penang, which up to this period had been a customs port, was declared to be a free port, as was also Malacca, so that all three places were placed on an equal footing as regards all absence of customs duties. This form of government remained in operation until 1829, when the Court of Directors sent out positive orders to reduce the establishment, as the expenses at Penang were not considered to be justified. Mr. Robert Fullerton was appointed in this year, 1826, the first Governor of the Incorporated Settlements of Prince of Wales Island, Singapore, and Malacca, as he was officially styled. He had been a Madras civilian, and a member of the Council of that Presidency in 1819. His abilities, it has been said, should have placed him in a much wider field of action than that which the Straits afforded. He returned to Europe in 1829 and died in London on 6th June, 1831.

Mr. Presgrave, the Acting Resident, in a report on land said that the tenure was a lease for years subject to a small annual quit-rent. The Governor-General had proposed 99 years, but this was objected to by the inhabitants and 999 years had been allowed. On the 26th August, 1826, the register contained only lists of lands granted by Raffles. Mr. Crawfurd had disapproved of Raffles's grants as informal and sent up his own draft to Calcutta. The Advocate-General objected to Mr. Crawfurd's form, and made out a draft of his own, which was sent down. The Governor-General confirmed Raffles's grants, and directed fresh papers to be issued. The total number was 500, of which the quit-rent amounted to about $3,000. Mr. Crawfurd had given numerous location tickets, no list of which was kept, to clear unreserved lands. All the land was granted under conditions to clear or cultivate.

There was a minute by Governor Fullerton on 29th August that the Civil Servants were expected to pass examinations in the Chinese and Siamese languages.

On the 21st November a Penang Government Notification was issued abolishing port duties. In December the Penang Government called on the Resident Councillor at Singapore for his opinion as to assessing property. The Resident on the 14th January following stated that houses in Singapore were already assessed $322.90 monthly, and he amended it to $400.37. He objected to any tax on lands, as the produce was of trifling value.

In May the Dutch schooner *Anna* left Singapore for Batavia. Seven Malays or Javanese (one of whom was found afterwards to have been a fisherman in Singapore who left without paying his debts) went on board as passengers, saying they were pilgrims returning from Mecca. They rose on the crew after leaving Singapore, nearly killing the Captain and driving the crew on deck into the rigging, but some passengers on board and the rest of the crew killed them or drove them into the sea, where it is supposed they were drowned. This seems to be the first recorded instance of a piratical attempt on a European vessel sailing out of Singapore. In the 5th number of the *Singapore Chronicle* was an article on Malay piracy which was known to be written by Mr. John Crawfurd.

By the Letters Patent of 27th November, 1826, the Court of Judicature of Prince of Wales' Island, Singapore and Malacca was established. At the end of the year a subscription was raised for the purpose of erecting a monument to Raffles "as a testimony of gratitude from the inhabitants for the great and important benefits he conferred upon Singapore." Over three thousand dollars were subscribed, and Messrs. A. L. Johnston & Co. were appointed the Treasurers, but the scheme was not carried out, and eventually as has been already explained, the money was spent in repairing Raffles Institution. The resolutions passed at a meeting on the 30th January, 1827, were to the effect that a monument should be erected on some conspicous and suitable spot within the precincts of Singapore, with an inscription in English, Latin, Chinese and Malay. The plan and estimate to be prepared by Mr. Coleman, the Architect.

In the *Navy League Journal* for May, 1901, is a note of what was thought to be the record voyage of one of the East India Company's ships, the *Thomas Coutts*. In this year, she entered Bombay Harbour on June 2nd, 1826, after a passage of eighty-two days from England. Sailed from Bombay for China, August 2nd. Arrived at Singapore on the 26th. Sailed from Singapore for Macao, August 28th. Arrived there, September 11th. On her return voyage she sailed from China, November 23rd. Passed Java Head on December 10th. Arrived at St. Helena, January 22nd, 1827. Sailed on January 24th, and arrived in the Downs on March 2nd, 1827, having made thé quickest voyage out and home on record—ten days within the year. She carried fourteen long guns on each side on the main deck and four on the quarter deck. It is added that the old *Vindictive*, a 50-gun frigate, taking Rear-Admiral Sir Thomas Cochrane out to China in 1842, made the passage from Plymouth to Hongkong in eighty days; all studding-sail booms being carried away and the main-trysail mast on the foreyard as a boom. This was considered a fast passage.

1827.

It is in this year that we find the first trace of the subsequent Municipalities in the Settlements. A regulation was made, under Mr. Fullerton, on the 1st January, 1827, which was sanctioned by the Court of Directors and Board of Control, for the appointment of a body designated "The Committee of Assessors," framed for the purpose of providing the means of clearing, watching, and keeping in repair the streets of the town of Penang. The committee were to be chosen annually from the land-holders and house-holders of the island.

On the 27th February Mr. Prince, the Resident Councillor, sent round a circular inviting the inhabitants to make drains opposite their own premises. Great damage had been done by heavy rains, and to obviate future inconvenience it was proposed that drains should be made to carry off the water, and, in order to have the levels uniform, to allow the work to be done by Government officers at a fixed rate of $27.75 per 100 feet. A committee composed of Messrs. Bonham, Johnstone, Maxwell, Syme, and Scott was appointed when the work was completed, to assess the cost among the various proprietors. They reported in August that 5,088 feet of open, and 113 feet of covered drains had been completed.

Dr. Montgomerie was now superintending the Botanical Experimental Garden on the Government Hill, and wrote a report upon its state on the 1st February, which is at page 62 of Volume 9 of Logan's Journal. He had turned his attention solely to spices, nutmegs, and cloves, which promised well, and he proposed that Government should employ convicts in clearing ground and cultivating the spices until the trees began to bear, when the land might be divided up among the industrious Chinese. Dr. Montgomerie was in hopes, as Bencoolen had been given up, and Penang could only supply a small part of an article so much in demand, that it might be made a permanent source of profit in Singapore, but it never led to any result as the trees did not prosper in the island.

In March, the Resident Councillor sent round a circular to all the Europeans, saying that he was directed by the Governor in Council to call upon them to state the date of their arrival and their occupation and the license under which they resided. The circular was signed by the Europeans, a list of whose names may be found in Mr. Braddell's Notes in Mr. Logan's Journal, Vol. 9. The same question had been raised in Penang, and in 1796 the Government there had called upon all the Europeans to produce their authority for residence, and got some very amusing answers in reply, some of the merchants keeping

up a warm correspondence about it, after having purchased land and
property to a considerable extent, and having been encouraged to settle
there. One of them wrote that he had stayed there in the hazardous
attempt to cultivate a vile jungle and in the full assurance that he
had been *induced* to come and settle, and by that means he and
others had formed the most flourishing settlement in the world.
Under the Act of Parliament, of 1813, (53 Geo. 3, c. 155) continuing the East India Company's exclusive privileges, by Sections
XXXIII. to XL., any person desiring to go to or remain in India
had to obtain a certificate or license from the Board of Commissioners in London, the supreme authority for the management of the
affairs of India, under whom was the Board of Directors. There
was power for a Governor to give a special license in particular
instances, the reasons for which had to be entered upon the minutes
of the Council, which held good until the matter had been laid before the Court of Directors and notice was given to the applicant
that it was revoked. These rules had not been enforced, either in
Penang or Singapore, and nothing at all came of it, as was to be
expected; and, as far as is known now, no one in Singapore even
answered the circular, but among some old papers is a copy of the
following letter to Mr. W. R. George by John Anderson, the Secretary
to Government, dated Singapore, 10th May, 1827: "Sir, I am directed
to acquaint you that the Honourable the Governor has been pleased
to permit you to reside at this settlement, pending a reference to
the Honourable Court of Directors, and subject to all the Regulations of Government. If the Honourable Court's sanction should
eventually be withheld, you will of course be prepared to return
to Europe on the shortest notice." Two years afterwards on the 30th
September, 1829, the Court of Directors, in a long letter, approved
of the Government having made known to Europeans that they were
here liable to removal at the pleasure of the East India Company;
but said at the same time that under the peculiar circumstances of
the place, the resort of Europeans to follow creditable occupations
had not been discouraged, and they might be allowed to remain
as long as they conducted themselves, in the opinion of Government,
with propriety.

The Court of Judicature of Prince of Wales Island, Singapore, and
Malacca was opened on the 6th March by a Notification of Govern-
ment, the Resident's Court was closed, and suits for sums above $32
were removed and entered in H. M. Court. The Resident Councillor
had reported to Government the great inconvenience arising from
the want of a resident Judge at Singapore. Sir John Thomas
Claridge, Kt., took up his office as Recorder in August; and he and
Lady Claridge arrived at Singapore on the 4th September from
Penang. This was the first visit of H. M. Court. They left again for
Malacca four days afterwards, where they landed under a salute of 13 guns,
as the *Malacca Observer* records. Until the Transfer, and for a short
time afterwards, the Judges were always received with salutes from the
shore at the various Settlements. Sir John Claridge in this year gave
the opinion that the Resident Councillor could sit as Judge at each
place in the absence of the Recorder, and gave a long letter of

instructions to the Resident Councillor as to the way of conducting business, but he afterwards withdrew his opinion, and said that it could not be so as there was only one Court.

Mr. Prince sent round a circular to the natives, pointing out the great advantages of education, and calling on them to cooperate in getting up schools. The population in this year was 13,732.

On the 12th March the Supreme Government took exception to an article which had appeared in the *Singapore Chronicle* of the 15th February, which they said was written in a very objectionable style,—"The Governor in Council cannot avoid expressing his regret that the present editor should have deviated so widely from the discreet and prudent line of conduct invariably pursued by his predecessor; that he should have entered into the petty disputes of Calcutta editors and making common cause with them, who appear to have justly incurred the censure of the Supreme Government; instead of confining himself to the republication of interesting intelligence on passing events and to objects of direct local interest, calculated to promote the commerce and prosperity of the Settlement at which he resides, the unceasing attention to which has hitherto distinguished the *Singapore Chronicle* and peculiarly entitled it to the support of the Government."

On the 30th March a gunboat armed with lelahs and muskets was fitted with native sails and went out to cruise near Singapore against pirates. On the 10th April, with a view to assessment, a return was sent round to be filled up as to carts, carriages and ponies. The Bengal troops were relieved by troops from Madras in April.

Governor Fullerton landed for the first time at Singapore on the 3rd May, and returned to Penang on the 21st June. The houses of Captain Flint and Mr. Napier were rented for his accommodation; the former at about $190 and the latter at $260 a month (Rupees 500 and 687).

In May a Court of Requests was established, and three Commissioners appointed, Messrs. Presgrave, Bonham, and Wingrove.

On the 4th May a number of spice plants arrived from Penang on Government account and were offered gratuitously to any persons who would engage to take care of them and bring them to perfection.

In May the police was re-organised; 3 constables, 5 jemedars and 24 peons. On the 28th June Mr. Prince visited Bukit Timah preparatory to having roads made. He went on foot accompanied by the contractor of the roads. They had a five hours' walk, first W.S.W. and latterly N. E. [? W. N. W.]. The distance cut through undulating hills, marshes and rills was fourteen miles; three fourths in gambier and pepper cultivation. A *balei* was built on the top of the hill. A contract could not be got for less than $440 a mile, while the amount sanctioned by government was only 500 rupees a mile ($190).

On the 6th June Captain (afterwards Major-General) Blundell sailed from Penang, to which garrison he was then attached, with half a company of European Artillery to reinforce the garrison at Singapore, when war with France was threatening on account of Portugal.

On the 11th June the lease was issued by the Land Office for 999 years of the ground where the Court House now stands. Mr. Maxwell, the merchant, built the house which now forms part of the present building, and he leased the house to the Government for three years at 500 rupees a month. On 1st September, 1841, it was put up by public auction by Guthrie & Co. The house was described in the advertisement as having been erected during the years 1826 and 1827 under the superintendence of Mr. Coleman, the architect, and built of the best materials. It was contained in Grant No. 243, extending from High Street to the river, with a frontage on the river side of 240 feet, which at the expiry of the existing lease would afford a very superior situation for the erection of godowns or shops, as there was sufficient vacant ground without encroaching on the Court House or its out-offices. It contained 82,080 square feet, with an annual quit-rent of $85, and was let to the East India Company on a lease which would expire on 30th April, 1844, and afforded a *most favorable opportunity* for investing capital, &c , &c., (like Powell & Co.'s tempting notices at the present day). The Government bought it for $15,600. The original building was standing until the structure was altogether altered in 1901, but the large Court had been built on to the back of it, towards the river, in 1875. In the old days the Court was held in the centre room upstairs and the side rooms were used for the Resident Councillor's office and some of the officials : the land office being downstairs. For many years the Court was not held in the building, but in the one floor building at the side, which is now used as a store-room for the Government Printing Office, at which time the whole of the Court House was used for public offices. The large clock placed in the facade towards the Esplanade, and taken down in 1901 when the whole building was altered, was a gift to the first St Andrew's Church by Mr. Thomas Church, and when that building was pulled down, being unsafe, it was put in the Court House and not taken back when the present Cathedral was built.

A despatch of the Governor-General of the 12th July spoke of the necessity to endeavour to retrench the expenditure. A list of state papers was sent to the Court of Directors on 21st October. A lengthy report was sent by Mr. Presgrave on slavery in the place.

In September the Governor ordered three lots of land on the Esplanade to be sold for building land, to which the Resident Councillor objected, and Mr. Prince (who was spoken of as the general economical schemer) proposed that the military establishment in Singapore should be reduced to what it had been when under Bengal.

On a Sunday evening there was a severe thunderstorm in the harbour, and the East India Company's vessel *Buckinghamshire* was struck by lightning and her masts shivered and a seaman killed, while several others scarcely escaped. The storm reached as far as Malacca, and a large Dutch vessel on her way from Singapore was dismasted.

On the 18th November Mr. Prince left Singapore and Mr. Presgrave was deputy Resident Councillor in charge until the 29th when Mr. Murchison, the new Resident Councillor, arrived from Penang.

An Englishman named Mr. Charles Grey left Malacca on 2nd January and went across the Peninsula to Pahang. He fell, however, a sacrifice to his exertions, dying of jungle fever, contracted during the journey, twenty-five days after his return to Malacca. His account

of the journey is in Volume 6 of Logan's Journal, page 369. It is
méntioned here because he was probably the first European to penetrate
into the interior of the Peninsula.

In consequence of the great increase in the number of Chinese
vagrants, the Resident Councillor recommended Government to give them
an allowance of rice for one year and to send them into the interior
to clear jungle.

It was hoped that the labours of the Commissioners in Europe
which resulted in the London Treaty of March, 1824, would end all
disputes with the Dutch, but unfortunately a fresh cause of offence
broke out in connection with Singapore on the subject of the Carimon
Islands, and it woke up again the old question of the two rival Sultans.
The result of what had been done in 1819 was that Johore became
split up into two governments; one under Sultan Hoosein in Singapore,
and the other under his younger brother Sultan Abdulrahman in Rhio.
This was not very fair to Johore, but so far as the English action
went, it undoubtedly resulted in placing the Sultan and Tumongong
of Johore in a much more comfortable and secure position than they had
occupied before. The Tumongong considered the Carimon Islands as part
of his territory, as they had undoubtedly belonged to Johore, and had
been (or were still) made use of by the Malays on the mainland of
Johore as convenient stations for piratical purposes, while the islands were
not in any way connected with Rhio. It so happened at this time that
some Chinese had found tin at the Carimons; it never amounted to
much, for in four years the average output only came to 205 piculs a
year. An Englishman having heard of the mines, obtained permission
from Sultan Hoosein to work them. The Dutch Resident of Rhio looked upon the Carimons as part of the territory of Sultan Abdulrahman,
and still affected to deny the rights of Hoosein, whom he still asserted
was an illegitimate impostor (which was nonsense, as he was of exactly
similar birth to Abdulrahman) and as a dependent on his younger
brother Abdulrahman at Lingga for his daily bread (which was also
nonsense, as he was receiving a handsome pension from Singapore).

On the 23rd July news from Rhio reached Sultan Hoosein at
Singapore that Abdulrahman had made over the Carimons to the
Dutch, and that the Dutch Resident wanted Hoosein to withdraw
the Johore people. Sultan Hoosein appealed to the Resident of Singapore, who said he could not interfere, but wrote to Rhio protesting
against the Dutch taking the Carimons without authority from Europe,
as an infraction of Clause 6 of the Treaty of 1824. On the
17th September Hoosein told the Resident that he was informed the
Raja Muda of Rhio had gone with twenty sail to take forcible possession
of the Carimons, but that on their arrival Hoosein's followers had
refused to allow them to land, so they went to the south-east of the
island and hoisted a flag and returned to Rhio. Hoosein then wrote
to his brother Abdulrahman remonstrating with him for trying to
exclude him from his rights.*

There was then correspondence between the Residents of Singapore
and Rhio, in which the Resident of Rhio referred to the letters written

---

*Crawford had foreseen this, see foot of p. 178

by the Singapore Chiefs in February, 1819, which are printed at page 50 of this book, as a proof of their refusal to allow the English Settlement at Singapore. He said he was bound to interfere, and he would send two Dutch ships-of-war to reinforce the large fleet sent by the Raja Muda from Rhio. The Singapore Resident in reply confined himself to saying that the Singapore Sultan was entirely independent, and the Government did not interfere with his movements beyond the limits of the island; a fact which though often repeated to the Dutch they would not credit, not being able to discriminate in the difference of circumstances between the English in Hindustan, where the policy of interference was a necessity, and those in the Straits where such a policy was earnestly deprecated. To which the Rhio Resident replied that the Dutch had no idea of establishing a factory at the Carimons, but as Abdulrahman, the Sultan of Lingga, was a vassal of the Netherlands Government, he was bound to protest and preserve to him all that remained after the arrangement (Treaty of London) by which he lost so much, and the Resident added he was much more inclined to view the Singapore Sultan as a pirate than Sultan Abdulrahman of Lingga!

It is amusing to find the assertion that the Sultan of Lingga (who had, by means of the Dutch, taken away half of the territory of Johore from the authority of his elder brother) had been prejudiced by the treaty of 1824 which secured Rhio to him; but it is still more amusing to find in a letter of the Resident of Rhio to Singapore in connection with this matter, dated 12th October, 1827, the following expression used by a Dutch official: "After the King of England had magnanimously restored Java to the Dutch!"

In October an expedition from Rhio, headed by a Dutch schooner, anchored off the stockade at the Carimons and opened fire. The Dutch Resident with two officers and fifty Dutch European troops landed and took the place It was said by them that two pirate boats had joined the defenders, but soon afterwards a peaceable trading boat returned to Singapore, which had been on its way from Singapore to Kampar, and the crew said they had been wantonly fired into by the Dutch and two of their number shot. The Carimons were thus taken and have remained in the hands of the Dutch ever since, but have not been turned to any useful purpose.

In Mr Braddell's notes there is a list of Public Servants and European inhabitants residing at Singapore in March, 1827. There is also another notification signed by forty-two of the Europeans, which helps to complete it, and the following is probably an accurate Directory at the time, as it even includes police constables and "punch-house" keepers:

Hon'ble John Price, Resident Councillor.

Edward Presgrave, Esq, Deputy Resident, Malay Translator.

S. G. Bonham, Esq., Assistant Resident, in Charge of the Police and Convicts.

Rev. R. Burn, Chaplain.

Captain W. Flint, R.N., Assistant Master Attendant and Postmaster.

Captain C. E. Davis, Garrison Staff.

Lieut. P. Jackson, Executive Officer.

W. Montgomerie, M.D., Residency Assistant Surgeon.

R. G. Perreau, Extra Covenanted Servant from Bencoolen.

Assistants in Resident's and Secretary's Office.
J. F. Burrows, W. Hewetson, J. D. Remedios.

Assistants in Accountant's and Pay Office.
R. Winter | T. H. Bell

Assistants in Police Office and Convicts Department.
W. Campbell | J. Salmon
W. Holloway.

Constables.
Henry Gilbert | Francis Cox
Robert Macquire.

Overseer of Convicts.
Hilton.

Assistants in Master Attendant's Office.
Edward Coles | John Leyden Siamee

Post Office.
Edward Coles.

Commissioners : Court of Requests.
Edward Presgrave | S. G. Bonham
Clerk—W. Holloway ; *Bailiff*—Francis Cox.

Merchants and Agency Houses.

Almeida & Co.	Maxwell & Co.
Armstrong, Crane & Co.	Morgans, Hunter & Co.
Dalton, J.	Napier, Scott & Co.
Farquhar, A.	Purvis, J.
Guthrie & Clark	Spottiswoode & Connolly
A. L. Johnston & Co.	Syme & Co.
Mackenzie & Co.	Thomas & Co.

European Inhabitants.

D' Almeida, Jozé	Almeida & Co.
Armstrong, George	Armstrong, Crane & Co.
Bernard, F. J.	Agent to Lloyds, Notary Public.
Brown, J.	Employ of Mackenzie & Co.
Bruce, James R.	Employ of Armstrong & Co.
Clark.	Guthrie & Clark
Coleman, George D.	Civil Architect.
Connoly, John	Spottiswoode & Connolly
Crane, Thomas Owen	Armstrong, Crane & Co.
Dalton, John	Merchant.
De Silva, Martinus	Employ of Lieut. Jackson.
Douwe, P. E.	
Dunman, W.	
Ellis, John	Employ of A. L. Johnston & Co.

Farquhar, Andrew	Merchant.
Francis, J.	Tavern Keeper.
Frazer, J.	Employ of Maxwell & Co.
Freeze, Fred.	
George, W. R.	Employ of Thomas & Co.
Gorden, James	
Gummer, John (probably John Gemmill)	
Guthrie, Alexander	Guthrie & Clark.
Hallpike, Stephen	Shipwright.
Hansen, H. F.	
Hawthorn, Daniel	Ship-carpenter.
Hay, Andrew	A. L. Johnston & Co.
Holloway, C.	
Hunter, Robert	Morgans, Hunter & Co.
Johnston Alex. Laurie	A. L Johnston & Co.
Laby, Thomas	Punch-house Keeper.
Lardner, Thomas	Employ of Mr. Temperton.
Loch, John	Editor of *Singapore Chronicle*
Macdonald, William	Employ of Morgans, Hunter & Co.
Macintosh, J.	Employ of Spottiswoode & Connolly
Mackenzie, Graham	Mackenzie & Co.
Maia, F. de Silva Pinto	Roman Catholic Priest.
Martin, A.	Surgeon.
Matti, Miguel	Watchmaker.
Maxwell, J. D.	Maxwell & Co.
Merryweather, W.	Employ of Syme & Co.
Milton, Rev. S.	Missionary.
Moore, R.	Employ of Maxwell & Co.
Napier, W.	
Napier R.	
Page, W.	Employ of Morgans, Hunter & Co.
Patton, William, P.	Employ of Morgans, Hunter & Co.
Pelling, R. E.	Employ of Guthrie & Clark.
Purvis, John	Merchant.
Read, Christopher Rideout	A. L. Johnston & Co.
Ryan, C.	Employ of Napier, Scott & Co.
Shaw, W. D.	Mackenzie & Co.
Solomon, J.	
Spottiswoode, William	Spottiswoode Connolly
Sweeting, S.	Employ of Syme & Co.
Swinton.	Shipwright.
Syme, Hugh	Syme & Co.
Temperton, William	Shipwright.
Thomas, Charles	Thomas & Co.
Thomas, C. S.	Thomas & Co.
Thomas, Josiah	Thomas & Co.
Thomsen, Rev. C. H.	Missionary.
Westerburg.	Punch-house Keeper.
Wright, John	

Total—ninety-four Europeans.

CHAPTER XVII.

1828—1829.

1828.

IN June, 1828, the first Criminal Sessions were held in Singapore. There were twenty-seven indictments, of which six were for murder, one for manslaughter, ten for burglary and six for assaults. In the six murder cases two prisoners only were convicted, one Kling and one Chinese, and they were hanged on Monday, the 26th June, the first executions in Singapore. A Sessions was held in the next month at Malacca, but there were only three cases, comprising the whole accumulation of crime during the three years since the re-transfer by the Dutch in 1825. One Chinese convicted of murder hanged himself in his cell the night after the trial. The Judge had commuted his sentence to transportation to Bombay, as he had been two years in prison waiting for a trial, but the prisoner said in the Court that he preferred to be hanged and carried it out himself.

It was in this year that steamers began to be talked about. In 1826 a proposal was made in Bengal to establish a steam-vessel to run between India and the Straits, and a subscription list was sent round Singapore, Penang, and Malacca, but it all came to nothing. In 1828, Mr. Waghorn, who was the originator of the Overland Route, went to Calcutta from England and endeavoured to establish steam communication between England and India in seventy-two days *via* Cairo. The vessels were to carry letters and packages only, but no passengers, because he said they would incommode the seamen and retard the vessel's speed. The *Singapore Chronicle* was of opinion that it might prove not only agreeable but useful to have a steam-vessel in the Straits, but was of opinion that it would never pay, as the population of the Straits was too limited to support such a vessel.

The *Malacca Observer* and the *Singapore Chronicle* had an editorial combat over the question. The *Observer* asserted that a steamer might have the marvellous effect of increasing or doubling the commerce, which the *Chronicle* considered ridiculous. The *Observer* retaliated by saying that in 1770 it took more than a fortnight to go from London to Edinburgh by land, and that the proprietors of the waggon had to advertise some days before starting in order to obtain passengers ; and that now (in 1828) not less than 2,000 coaches ran daily to London from all parts of the kingdom ; and that tug-boats had been established on the Clyde, and that the increase of commerce in Glasgow was owing to their assistance ; and communication might be made, in time, between England and the Straits in eighty days ; besides which Singapore and Malacca could do a large business in the superabundance and cheapness of firewood. But the *Chronicle* said that steamers would lead to the resort of penned-up, bilious individuals to Singapore.

The *Chronicle* mentions that the Censor had struck out some paragraphs from the *Penang Register* of the 17th September, and the editor had printed them on a separate slip and sent it out with the

paper : which the *Chronicle* called a very bold step, as it certainly was ;
what the consequences were does not appear.

The population in this year was 15,834, exclusive of floating population, military and convicts.

On 17th June Mr. Murchison reported the great want of an interpreter in French, Spanish, and Portuguese, as so many foreign ships
were constantly coming to Singapore. He said that Doctord Almeida
was willing to accept the office for $100 a month.

In the same month the Governor wrote to China about interpret-
ers, and the matter was referred to the Rev. Dr. Morrison there, who
reported that he was not able to get trustworthy men, and if they
could be got, three or four dialects would be required, and the
Chinese could not speak English. He referred to the Anglo-Chinese
College at Malacca which had been founded ten years before ; the
small result of which (Mr. Braddell remarks) must have been mortifying
to the Doctor.

On the 3rd September Mr. Murchison pressed the adoption of
the plan of gunboats with native rig being adopted against pirates, as
previously contemplated ; he did not recommend steamers as they
were always out of order, and if engineers were shot they could not
be replaced.

Governor Fullerton at this time proposed making Malacca the
capital of the Straits Settlements. He said that it had been the
ancient seat of European Government for more than 200 years, was
a more healthy climate, more centrally situated, within two days sail
of Singapore and Penang, had more resources for supplies to troops,
and although the forts had been destroyed it was a more central
station and depot for whatever force might be collected together for
the defence of the whole. Being on the continent it commanded an interior,
and owing to the shoal water no ship could approach near enough
to bring its guns to bear on the shore, it had an indigenous and
attached population which the other two stations did not possess,
and in a political point of view it was conveniently situated for
maintaining such influence over all the Malay States as would prevent
their falling under Siamese dominion, and was near enough to the
south end of the Straits to watch the proceedings of the Dutch
[the two Straits bugbears of those days]. It was said in 1848 by
Mr. Blundell, afterwards Governor, that it could not be denied that
there was force in the arguments, but that it had become so much
the habit to decry Malacca and to pity the state into which it
was supposed to have fallen, that the argument would at that time
only excite a smile of ridicule, but that the policy of withdrawal
from all interference with the neighbouring Malay States was extremely
doubtful. A remark which the experience of the present time shows
to have been very true.

1829.

In March, 1829, Lord William Bentinck, the Governor-General,
came to the Straits. He landed at Malacca in the H. E. I. C. Steam-
vessel *Enterprize*, on the 10th March, and left for Singapore the
same evening. He came here to remodel the Government and reduce the

alleged overgrown civil and military establishments. He went into such sweeping measures that he proposed to abolish the Governor, but it was found that it was necessary for the chief authority to have that title, as the King's Charter of 1807 was so worded that the Court of Judicature in the Straits could not be held without it.

Mr. Fullerton returned to Europe, and was succeeded by Mr. Ibbetson, who resided at Penang, and was an energetic Governor. The salary for the Governor was Rs. 36,000 a year, (about \$16,400), and of the Recorder (Judge) 37,893 sicca rupees, or about 40,419 rupees. These two salaries were contributed in equal shares by the three Settlements.

Mr. Murchison, the Resident Councillor, went to Batavia in anticipation of leave on the 21st April for four or five months, to reside in the interior of Java. He returned in September, Mr. Presgrave acting during his absence. On the 30th April the flagstaff on Goa Island was withdrawn. On the 30th June the establishment for the Botanical Gardens was discontinued and ten convicts were put on to keep the grounds in order. The reason for this is not to be found; it was probably part of the economical retrenchment mania that is mentioned elsewhere.

In June we find an account of a piracy, which is only one of a number that were continually occurring. A man was brought up at the Police Court charged with having been the commander of one of five prahus which had attacked a boat bound from Lingga to Singapore, the throats of twelve people on board being cut to prevent anything being known of it. But there was a young boy on board, whom they sold as a slave, for the sake of the money, and he recognised the prisoner five months afterwards. His story was corroborated by one of the pirate's crew, also a boy, who turned evidence against his master.

On the 1st September the government allowance of \$50 a month to the *Singapore Chronicle* newspaper was withdrawn. On the 4th September the Rev. Mr. Thomsen reported that there was a Cantonese school at Kampong Glam of twelve boys. Another at Pekin Street of eight boys. A Hokien school at Pekin Street of twenty-two boys, and an English school of 48 boys, The cost of three native masters was \$26, of one English master \$60, and rent \$100. The English scholars paid \$15, natives \$4, and for extra subjects \$10. There was a wooden bridge across the river at this time, near where Elgin Bridge is now. It was always being patched up, and was described as having a brokenbacked appearance, with a curious variety of undulations.

On the 1st of October, 1829, a meeting was held at the house of Mr. E. Boustead, at seven o'clock in the evening, to consider the desirability of establishing a Billiard Club. This was the beginning of Singapore Clubs. Six persons attended, Mr. John Ellis, of A. L. Johnston & Co., was made Secretary, and a number of rules were passed. The admission fee was \$50, and the subscription \$4. No smoking was allowed in the Billiard Room, which was to be opened every day except Sunday, from six in the morning till ten at night. Any member not attending at a meeting was liable to be fined \$2, and any one who was absent three consecutive times without giving

an explanation was to cease to be a member of the Club. Soon
after it started, Mr. W. Merryweather, of Syme & Co., having been
absent three times, was turned out; but he was re-admitted at the
next meeting, so it had not much effect, as is generally the case
with such rules. At the close of the year Mr. W. R. George was
elected Secretary, and the subscription was raised to $6, and Mr.
George Armstrong was appointed Treasurer. Soon after this Mr. George
was fined for being absent, and in the minute book he has entered
the remark: "I protest against the resolution condemning me to pay a
fine for non-attendance, upon the plea that the members of the Club
present did not consider sickness a sufficient excuse. Perhaps at the
next meeting some member will produce his diploma, otherwise I must
be permitted to doubt the medical knowledge of the Club in toto."
The minute book, which is in Mr. George's writing, ceases in October,
1830, and what became of the Club afterwards is not known. The last
minute approves of the purchase of one dozen tumblers and two
water-goblets for the use of the members. The book has written on
the cover "Journal of the Singapore Billiard Club."

Mr George lived in Singapore until his death in 1873. He retired
from business during the later years of his life, but before that had
been book-keeper in Wm. Spottiswoode & Co., for many years. He is
the gentleman spoken of in Mr. Cameron's book at page 292 as "going
out for a walk every morning at five o'clock and coming back to his
tea at half-past six, which he had done during forty years of residence
(in 1863) and had reaped his reward in still robust health, strong nerve,
clear head, and a yet lively enjoyment of the good things of life."
These morning walks were thought in the young days of Singapore to
be a necessity for a healthy life, but there were then some who laughed
at the habit, and experience has seemed to agree with them. Active
exercise in the afternoon, at cricket, lawn-tennis, football and golf, has,
probably, been found equally useful. There was a very oft-told story
of Mr. George, which perhaps shows that it is more convenient. He
was living during the latter years of his life at a boarding-house, the
only one then in Singapore, kept by Mrs. Nugent in River Valley Road,
and always started out for his walk directly he heard the five o'clock
gun. He did so one morning and walked along Bukit Timah Road as
usual. The sun did not get up as it usually did when he had walked
about two miles, and he walked on until he thought something must
have happened to the sun, and gave it up as a bad job and turned
back. When he reached home he found it was half-past three. A gun
had been fired off near the house in the middle of the night, and
he had mistaken it for the five o'clock gun. His son Mr. John
Chadwick Farquhar George, since dead, was for many years in the
old Oriental Bank as Manager in Singapore and Ceylon.

Mr. Boustead's firm at this time was Boustead, Schwabe & Co.,
which was established first, as far as is known now, as Boustead & Co.,
about 1827, and became Boustead, Schwabe & Co., on 1st January
1834. Mr. Boustead had been to China, and returned and established
himself here. Mr. Boustead came to Singapore as the Manager of
a new firm of Robert Wise & Co., and occupied the godown and
house on the river next that which was then occupied by Mr. Johnston

and A. L. Johnston & Co., through to Battery Road, and lived there until he started on his own account as Boustead & Co., and moved to near Elgin Bridge in what was called the seven-and-twenty pillar house. Mr. Sykes then managed Robert Wise & Co. for a few years, when the firm was closed in Singapore about 1837 or 1838, both Mr. Sykes and Mr. Wise joining Mr. Boustead. Mr. Boustead was editor of the *Singapore Chronicle* for some years, and when Mr. Carnegy (who came from Penang,) and Mr. W. S. Lorrain bought that paper, then Mr. Boustead, Mr. Coleman and Mr. William Napier started the *Singapore Free Press* in 1835, as is mentioned further on under that year.

In 1846 there were four partners in Boustead, Schwabe & Co., Mr. Edward Boustead in China, Benjamin Butler in Manila, Gustav Christian Schwabe in Liverpool, and Adam Sykes in Singapore. Mr. Joseph Wise, Robert Duff and Abraham A. De Wind were then clerks. In 1848 Mr. Schwabe left the firm, he died in Liverpool at a great age about 1896. The firm was then styled Boustead & Co., in 1849, and for three years Mr. Boustead was the sole partner. In 1850 he went home at the time of the Great Exhibition in London and never returned to Singapore. He died in London on 29th February, 1888, and the Boustead Institute was built from a charitable legacy under his will, and also £1,000 was given towards building St Andrew's House in Armenian Street. In 1852 Joseph Wise and William Wardrop Shaw, who had been clerks in the house for several years became partners with Mr. Boustead, but Mr. Wise left in 1853 and Mr. Robert Bain became a partner. He had been a partner in A. L. Johnston & Co. for several years. Mr. Bain left in 1855 and some years afterwards was a partner in Maclaine, Fraser & Co. In 1856 the firm consisted of Mr. Boustead, W. W. Shaw, and Archibald Buchanan Brown; Mr. George Lipscombe, Henry Frolich and James Young were then clerks. The firm continued so till 1867 when Mr. Brown left, and Messrs. Lipscombe and Jasper Young became partners, and the firm then consisted of Messrs. Boustead, Shaw, Lipscombe and Young, and continued so for many years.

There was a remarkable story of piracy in this year. It may be interesting to say that the Malay piratical prahus were from six to eight tons burden and from sixty to seventy feet long. They carried one or two small guns with four swivels or *rantakas* on each side, and a crew of twenty to thirty men. When they attacked ships they put up a strong bulwark of thick planks. They had, of course, spears and krisses and as many fire-arms as they could procure. A vessel, the name of which is not given, but is described as Captain Gravesome's vessel, left Penang or Malacca on a trading voyage in 1819 and was not heard of until 1829. In 1827, Mr. John Dalton, the merchant, left Singapore in a Bugis prahu, and was detained as a prisoner for a considerable time by the Sultan of Koti. The remains of Captain Gravesome's vessel were lying in the river Koti, and among the Sultan's slaves were six persons of her crew. She had carried a valuable cargo of opium and piece-goods, and two European passengers, a young lady of twenty and a boy of fifteen years of age. A pirate of Borneo advised the Captain to go to Koti, where he could get a good market for his cargo: and offered to pilot the vessel up to Koti.

The Captain unfortunately believed him, and the Sultan's consent being soon obtained on the promise of half the spoil, the pirate returned to the ship and commenced the massacre by stabbing Captain Gravesome in his cabin. The crew were then attacked and all murdered but six, who leapt overboard and hid themselves in the jungle. The young woman and the boy, who were severely wounded, were taken to the Sultan, whose mother interposed on their behalf and took care of them. The Sultan told Mr. Dalton they had died of small-pox, but others said they had been poisoned, as the Sultan did not feel himself safe as long as they lived. The six guns belonging to the ship were lying in front of the Sultan's house. It would be easy to make a very long chapter of the stories of pirates in the early days of Singapore. It seems almost incredible now that such practices should have been so common as to excite only a passing remark, while in these days any similar occurence would excite universal horror, and speedy retribution. If Mr. Dalton had not found himself in a tight corner at Koti, and got back safely to Singapore in 1829, this story would, like many others, never have been known.

1830.

At the Chinese New Year, on a Sunday in the beginning of February, a great fire broke out in a blacksmith's shop in Circular Road, burned down Philip Street and one side of Market Street, and nearly got to Commercial Square. The loss was said to be $350,000. It cleared away a lot of badly constructed houses, and led to a great improvement in the streets. The Magistrates on the 10th February published an advertisement tendering their warmest thanks to the Madras Native Infantry and all those who had "come forward so promptly and rendered efficient aid for three successive nights and days." And a notice appears that "In consequence of the late calamitous fire there has been a complete suspension of business during the week, nearly the whole of the commercial community having been engaged in searching almost every house in town as well as the China junks and native boats for stolen property." A quantity of property was carried out of the burning godowns and it had, of course, to be identified by the proper owners after the fire was over. A Chinese claimed a quantity of various boxes and bundles, which others said belonged to them; but the first pointed triumphantly to his chop which he was able to point out on the packages. At last, in the height of the discussion, a European said that he remembered seeing the same Chinaman going about with a chop, very busy among the packages, during the fire; and this being corroborated by others, the man was taken to the police station.

The fire was much extended by an explosion which was caused in rather a curious way. A Chinaman had some barrels of gunpowder in his shop, and not being able to carry them away he threw them down the well, thinking very sensibly that they would be safe there. But the fire dried up the water there was in the well, and the powder blew up. No one was hurt at all, but pieces of the burning houses were blown by the explosion across the road on to the houses opposite, which were very hot and caught into a blaze immediately. There were no fire engines, of course, and the only water supply was by buckets carried by the convicts. The houses in the Square at the back of Market Street were not burnt, and the middle of the Square was covered with goods carried from the burning houses. One chest of opium was carried away by Chinese coolies and was never recovered, the owner, a Jew, being afraid to follow the coolies who ran off into the Chinese houses in the dark. The fire began about 8 o'clock in the evening, owing to some accident in cooking in the blacksmith's house. There was a Chinese New Year procession going through the street at the time the alarm was first given. The houses on the side of Market Street next the Square were partly built of brick, but those on the other side were all of wood.

In March the Government published a proclamation setting forth that the attention of the Governor in Council had lately been called to the practice which prevailed of importing persons under the denomination of slave-debtors, but which in reality was only a cover for slave-dealing, and it was therefore notified that the practice was illegal. It was said by the *Chronicle* at the time that the Bugis, by the aid of the Chinese, had been in the habit of importing slaves, under the name of slave-debtors, into the Eastern Settlements, and disposing of them to the Chinese, who actually purchased them or redeemed the alleged debts, and retained the persons as their slaves; a considerable number being taken to Malacca.

In September the boats of H. M. S. *Southampton* and the H. C. Schooner *Diamond*, while cruising in the Straits of Malacca for pirates, had an engagement with a fleet of piratical prahus, about thirty in number, which lasted for several hours.

At the point of the Singapore River were the Artillery barracks, and house of the officers, with a few pieces of ordnance, called Fort Fullerton after Governor Fullerton. Captain Begbie, speaking of about this time, writes in his book that there were some good shops at this time kept by Europeans, and he described Boat Quay as having a curve similar to the Regent Street Quadrant! But Mr. James Guthrie writes that there was only one European shop then, which was kept by George Armstrong & Co., at the end of Market Street, near the river, next to Guthrie & Clark's godowns and was removed to the new buildings in 1831 or 1832. In Mr. Duncan's diary in 1824 he wrote that he went to Armstrong's to buy some curry-dishes and was disappointed to find they were all disposed of Begbie speaks also of a road then being constructed, which was the commencement of the road to New Harbour. He says that Singapore had a Chaplain, but no Church, the only place of worship being the Mission Chapel, towards which the East India Company had liberally contributed.

The business of George Armstrong & Co. was commenced in 1822, and became (as several other stores have done) a mercantile house. At one time Mr. John Myrtle was a partner, but from about 1847 the business was carried by Mr. George Armstrong's widow and one or both of her sons. In 1857 John and Farleigh were the partners. but latterly it was carried on by Mr. John William Armstrong alone for about six years, and ceased in 1867. Mr. Farleigh Armstrong was afterwards a partner in Boustead & Co. Mr. George Armstrong was an assistant in

Syme & Co., from 1856 to 1862, and was a member of the first Singapore Volunteer Corps. He was very tall and a remarkable athlete. He died at Manila on 13th November, 1901, where he had lived for many years and had been secretary of the Manila Club.

CHAPTER XVIII.

1831.

IN January, 1831, substantial and uniform houses and shops had been erected where the fire had occurred ; and George Armstrong & Co. opened an Exchange Room, Reading and News Room, and Circulating Library on the 1st of January; a prospectus was issued, but no copy of it is now to be had. It was intended principally, apparently, for the use of Captains and Supercargoes of vessels.

The public complained that, although the town had been much improved by the new buildings, the Government did nothing to assist, and that Circular Road, which was then the most public thoroughfare, was in a shameful and dangerous state, and that South Bridge Road was overflowed knee-deep at high tides. When the road and wharf between Circular Road and the Canal were made, the lots were sold at prices that left a handsome surplus after paying expenses, although the purchasers were aware of the extraordinary outlay that would be required to build houses on a marsh which was overflowed in many places to a depth of seven feet. At Kampong Glam two hundred convicts in eight months, with an outlay of $500 for covered gutters, drained twenty-eight acres marsh land and intersected it with roads. It was sold at good prices, and in January one-fifth of it was covered with good upper-roomed houses, which were let readily. The writer of the letter from which these particulars are taken said that Government should have spent the money raised by the sale of the land in essentially benefiting the town, and especially in building a good substantial bridge, which he said would be the greatest boon that could be conferred upon it.

On a Sunday night in January, some thieves took off part of the roof of Guthrie & Clark's godown, and stole a quantity of piece-goods.

On the 7th January Doctor Alexander Martin died. He had come to the Settlement with Raffles. The notice of his death, which occurred in Singapore, describes him as Surgeon and Senior Sworn Clerk of the Court of Judicature; which sounds a curious combination in these days. He was succeeded by his brother Dr. M. J. Martin, who returned home in 1836, and was succeeded by his nephew Dr. Robert Little who retired in 1892 and died at Blackheath on 11th June, 1888.

There were between 400 and 500 acres of land under rice cultivation at this time, and it was proposed to have roads made by the convicts from Kampong Glam across the Kallang and Gaylang rivers (the two bridges being estimated to cost $500 each) so as to increase the cultivation. The roads are now main roads, with very substantial stone and iron bridges, but rice planting is a thing of the past. Mr. Fullerton had put on a tax or quit rent of one dollar per acre per month, which the *Chronicle* said completely prohibited the coolies who

came from China taking up any agricultural employment, as they found
it impossible to make the jungle produce sufficient to meet such a
heavy impost, and the gardens which had been prospering were
neglected.

The place was in a very lawless state at this time, several murders
being reported in one week, and no proper measures being available to
trace the criminals or to secure life and property in the out-lying parts
of the town. Very little was known of Singapore beyond the hills
behind the town; the rest of the island was covered with jungle with
a few isolated reclaimed spots. While a gang of Chinese convicts were
working on a road, a number of Chinese ran out of the jungle and
rescued ten of the convicts by carrying them off and knocking off their
irons. The whole police force, eighteen strong, was mustered and recovered five of the convicts. It was said at the time that a Secret
Society exceeding one thousand men, was established in the jungle, and
that they had actually an armed fort there. There is a note of Mr.
Braddell's that in July, 1830, there was activity in the Resident Councillor's office on the subject of Chinese Hoeys, or Secret Societies, and
that a letter was written with a list of questions to the Superintendent
of Police. This seems to have been the first mention of the Secret
Societies in Singapore.

In April, on a Sunday morning at two o'clock, a remarkable
robbery, or rather burglary, was perpetrated at the Singapore Institution. The Raffles Institution was then in an unfinished and decaying
state, and was repaired a few years afterwards, with money that
had been subscribed towards a statue for Sir Stamford Raffles. The
Rev. Mr. Milton with his wife and family were occupying the only
habitable room in the building. The following account was in the
newspaper :— ' The thieves, to the number of between 20 and 30,
came, as usual, armed with spears and axes, and had their faces
blackened; we believe some of them carried torches. Finding Mr.
Milton resolutely bent on not opening the door of the room, at their
summons, they broke it open with an axe, but were unable to
effect an entrance, as he had posted himself near the door behind
a chest of drawers, and prevented them from coming in with a
long pole (such as is generally used in carrying water) with which
he dealt not a few severe and well-directed blows amongst them.
His only servant, a Chinese cook, who usually slept at the door
inside the room, had posted himself at the other side, and assisted
materially in repelling the gang with an iron spit, but on his receiving a cut on the forehead from a spear, he retreated. The
thieves at length, betook themselves to throwing fragments of broken
pavement found outside the door, and compelled Mr. Milton also to
retreat. They then came in, and commenced smashing the chest of
drawers and other pieces of furniture in search of money; but their
principal object of search was an iron chest which lay at
the farthest end of the room, and which it is thought had
been seen by one of them previous to the attack, and he conjec-
turing, though very erroneously, that there was money in it, had
concerted with others to rid Mr. Milton of it and its supposed
contents.'

"The gang had just packed up some articles of clothing, and were carrying away the iron chest, when Mr. R. Wingrove, the Assistant Resident, who was living in a bungalow close to the Institution, having heard the noise, crossed Brass Bassa Road, and came promptly with his servants and one or two peons. The thieves on perceiving him dropped their burdens and betook themselves to flight, but they did not escape before Mr. Wingrove had fired a shot amongst them, which from their proximity must have done some execution; one of them, however, in retreating, made a thrust at Mr. Wingrove with a spear, which might have injured him seriously had not the blow been warded off by one of his servants. Another servant, with a bludgeon, knocked one of the thieves off his legs, but before a seizure could be made, a number of his companions ran up and carried him away. From the quantity of blood found sprinkled about the hall and in the room, it is pretty evident that Mr. Milton had done considerable damage to the thieves; he himself received but a slight injury on the hand from a stone. Mrs. Milton, who was of course much alarmed and had hidden herself with her two children, received also some slight injury from a similar missile. To behold the disordered state in which the dastardly ruffians left the room was truly pitiable for the unfortunate family. Most of the panes in two bookcases were broken; the table, chest of drawers, and other articles of furniture were broken to pieces, while books, glasses, and stones lay scattered about the room."

Shortly after the burglary at the Institution the night watch was started again. There had been some misunderstanding about it between the Government and the Merchants, and it had been abolished. The Magistrates in Quarter Sessions had levied an assessment of five per cent. to keep it up, for the sweeping reforms that had been made in the Government had abolished the Court, and some of the merchants agreed to carry on the subscription voluntarily. A meeting was called, but owing to some misunderstanding it fell through.

The Reverend Samuel Milton was one of the first Missionaries sent out by the London Missionary Society to the Straits and China. The following is a list of the first sixteen who were sent out, in the order of their appointment. It has been found in a long list of Missionaries including 65 names, which appeared in the *Free Press* on 13th March, 1845

NAME.	ENTERED.	RETIRED.	DIED.	STATION.
Robert Morrison, D.D.	1807	—	1834	Canton
William Milne, D.D.	1813	—	1831	Malacca
W. H. Medhurst, D.D.	1817	—	—	Shanghai
John Slater	1817	1823	—	Batavia
John Nice	1818	—	1825	Penang
Samuel Milton	1818	1825	—	Singapore
Robert Fleming	1820	1823	—	Malacca
James Humphreys	1822	1830	—	do.
David Collie	1822	—	1828	do.
Samuel Kidd	1824	1832	—	do.
John Smith	1826	1829	—	do.
Jacob Tomlin	1826	1836	—	Singapore
Samuel Dyer	1827	—	1843	Penang

NAME.	ENTERED.	RETIRED.	DIED.	STATION.
John Evans	1833	—	1841	Malacca
Samuel Wolfe	1835	—	1837	Singapore
Alex. Stronach	1837	—	—	do.

The list of American Missionaries sent to the Straits, appears in the same list as follows:—

	ENTERED.	RETIRED.	DIED.	STATION.
Ira Tracy	1833	—	—	Singapore
J. T Dickenson	1837	1840	—	do.
M. B. Hope, M D.	1837	1838	—	do.
George W. Wood	1838	18 0	—	do.
Robert W. Orr	1838	1841	—	do.
John A Mitchell	1838	—	—	do.

The Reverend Samuel Milton died in Singapore on 5th September, 1848. His widow lived in the place till an old age, and also died here.

At this time there were two signal flag-staffs. one on Government Hill as at present, and the other on St. John's Island. There was no town clock, and a proposal to have one ended in nothing. In 1830 ten junks had arrived in Singapore from China. In 1831 eighteen came, of which two had sailed from Seang Hai, which was described as being near Ningpo. It is better known now as Shanghai. They were of 500 and 175 tons respectively. The whole 18 junks were 3,713 tons, and the value of their cargoes was $200,200.

In May Mr. Hallpike started a boarding house in High Street. Mr. Stephen Hallpike had bought about half of the land belonging to Morgan & Co.'s estate, extending from the corner of High Street near the Court House to the bridge on the river side. The other half was bought by Kim Swee, and has been owned until now by the Eu Chin family. Mr. Hallpike continued his business, while his wife conducted the boarding house. He had a blacksmith's shop and shipyard at the back, and repaired carriages by which he made a good deal of money. He died at Singapore on the 27th June, 1844. at 61 years of age, and his widow married Mr. J. B. Gordon (who had been Hallpike's partner) in London in 1846.

In February an American vessel was loading pepper in Sumatra, and the master and four of his crew were on shore when she was attacked by Malays, all the officers and crew murdered, the vessel plundered, and seven or eight thousand dollars carried off. The Captain got assistance from some other American vessels and remained in the vessel. An American frigate went a year afterwards and burnt the houses, killing two hundred of the inhabitants. Pirate prahus in fleets of as many as twenty-two boats, were known to be not many miles from the outer harbour of Singapore.

On the 8th June Chong Long, one of the principal Chinese merchants of Singapore, gave a great dinner on his 44th birthday, which all the influential residents attended. There were a number of toasts, as usual in those days, including the health of Mr. Ibbetson the Resident, and the memory of Sir Stamford Raffles. It reads rather funnily now, that Chong Long made a speech at a late period of the evening proposing the health of the Duke of Wellington. Chong Long was the son of the Captain China of Malacca when it was under the Dutch. He lived in the

Square and sometimes gave entertainments in European style to the British inhabitants, and was a very intelligent and wealthy man. He went to China in 1838, and was murdered in a house in Macao by some ruffians who broke into it at night, in the middle of December. Mr. William Spottiswoode was his Executor. The Malacca-born Chinese, such as Chong Long, held more direct intercourse with Europeans than the other Chinese. Many were born of Malay mothers, but as they wore the dress of their fathers they were scarcely to be distinguished from the actual natives of China, and although less active and energetic than the latter, they were more enlightened and made better merchants. They acquired in some degree the general habits of Europeans and their mode of transacting business, which made them more agreeable to the latter. Many were independent merchants, and others were cashiers and under-clerks in European godowns. Chong Long was the most intelligent and perhaps the most wealthy of this class.

There was another Chinaman, said to be a wealthier man, whose name was Che Sang. He kept his money, as every one else did in those days, in iron chests, for there were no banks, and he always slept among them. He was said to be a great miser, but addicted to gambling; in fact it is said in Mr. Earl's book that he had acquired a considerable part of his fortune by it. One day he lost a considerable sum, which put him out terribly, so he cut off the first joint of one of his little fingers with an oath not to play anymore, but the remedy was not effectual, for he returned to it again.

There was a long account of the funeral of Che Sang, written by a missionary, in the *Friend of India*, of Calcutta, on 17th May, 1836. He was described as a miser, 73 years of age. He was born at Canton, and had gone to Rhio as a boy of fifteen, then to Penang where he was for ten years, then to Malacca for some years, and then to Singapore. He died there on 2nd April, and was buried on the 13th, the funeral going about through the commercial part of the town on the way to the Hokien burial ground, attended by ten to fifteen thousand persons. Che Sang used to boast that he had so much influence over the Chinese that any day he said the word, he could empty the place of all the Europeans—but he never tried.

Both Chong Long and Che San built houses at Campong Glam, but neither of them were ever occupied. The first was purchased and rebuilt by Mr. Carnie, and the latter by Mr. Ker. Mr. Carnie's was purchased and occupied by Mr James Fraser of Maclaine, Fraser & Co., in 1840, and Mr Ker's by Mr Christian Baumgarten.

The first public entertainment in Singapore was given in this year by Signor Masoni, a violinist; and in June, the Officers of the 29th Madras Native Infantry, who had just come, allowed their band to play once a week on the plain, which is now called the Esplanade. As long as the Native Regiments were stationed here, the band used to play, latterly twice a week; the chains were taken down opposite Coleman Street and the carriages were driven in, and stood in a circle round the bandstand. Theatricals were proposed as an additional amusement, which led to much correspondence in the *Chronicle*. One writer, who objected to theatrical performances as tom-fooleries which no rational man would waste his time in, proposed that a fives court should be built instead.

In August the newspapers first mentioned the dispute with the Pungulu of Naning at Malacca, which led to the so-called Naning War, and as it attracted a very great deal of attention in Singapore, it is mentioned here. The English took possession of Malacca from the Dutch, and with it of Naning upon the terms on which the Dutch had held possession of it, one of the stipulations being for the payment of a certain duty. By a treaty made by Colonel Taylor, the British Resident at Malacca, with Pungulu Dholl Syed and the chiefs of Naning, dated 16th July, 1801, it was agreed that the Pungulu should come yearly in person, or send one of his chiefs, to Malacca to pay homage to the Company, and, as a token of submission, to present one-half coyan of the first fruits of the crop of paddy (400 gantangs). These were then worth about $12. There was a dispute at this time also about the Pungulu having forcibly seized a piece of land within the Malacca boundary which belonged to one Inche Surin. The two things together led to the quarrel, but in a paper by Colonel Low, and in another by Mr. Blundell, written in 1848 and 1850, they each ascribe the cause to the non-payment of the ridiculously petty claim for the padly; Colonel Low remarking that the cost of the war was somewhat about twenty lacs of rupees and that it ended in pensioning the rebel chief on a hundred rupees a month, a larger sum of money than the man had ever before possessed at one time. Mr. Blundell had a note that the original estimate of proposed cost of the expedition was $1,929 41; and the actual expense from August, 1831, to April, 1833, was Rupees 89,301.6.7 for local charges alone.

On the 6th August, 1831, the first expedition started from the town of Malacca under the command of Captain Wyllie, Madras Native Infantry. His subalterns were Lieutenant Milnes, Lieutenant Begbie who commanded the artillery, Ensign Short, and Assistant-Surgeon Smith. Mr. W. T. Lewis, Assistant Resident of Malacca went as Commissioner. A detailed account of the expedition was written by Begbie and published in a pamphlet at the Malacca Mission Press in the same year, which was much laughed at by the Madras newspapers. The chief of Rambau joined the Pungulu of Naning and the expedition met with so much unexpected opposition that it returned to Malacca, leaving the heavy luggage and two guns behind them, and throwing Malacca into a tremendous state of alarm as they thought they were left at the mercy of the Malays, whom, apparently, they thought a much more courageous people than they were.

Early in January, 1832, a force of Madras troops was sent to Malacca, under Lieutenant Colonel Herbert, consisting of a regiment of native infantry, a company of rifles, two companies of sappers and miners, and some Europeans and native artillery. They got on very slowly, as they proceeded to cut what they called a military road, eighty yards wide, up the country by felling the trees, and at last accomplished what (it was afterwards said) a hundred of Rajah Brooke's Dyaks from Borneo would have settled in a week. Lieutenant Harding and Ensign Walker of the Madras Native Infantry were killed and two of the Ensigns were wounded. Mr. Begbie in his book, page 234, says, "A handsome monument designed by Lieutenant

Symthe of the Engineers, was erected to the memory and over the remains of Mr. Walker by his brother officers of the 5th. Visitors to Malacca often pass the tombs on their way up country. The troops were ten weeks going only twelve miles, not including a stoppage of about a month on the way at Alor Gaja.

The Pungulu ran away; but soon afterwards Mr. J. B. Westerhout of Malacca was sent up. He was, Mr. Newbold says, eminently qualified by his perfect knowledge of the Malay character, and his influence with the principal persons of the neighbouring independent states, to end the dispute satisfactorily. The result was which might have been arrived at in the first instance, and the $12 realized for the Malacca Treasury) that the ex-Pungulu came down to Malacca on the 5th February, 1834, and lived in great comfort in Malacca on the Government allowance. where his house was the daily resort of health-seeking followers of Mohamed, as he set up as an unqualified medical practioner and was believed to have a miraculous power in the cure of diseases. This man, Pungulu Dholl Syed, died at Malacca in August, 1849, and was buried at Tabu in Naning.

It was the Naning expedition that led to Admiral Keppel coming to the Straits for the first time. He had joined the *Magicienne* 24 guns, as a young lieutenant, at Woolwich, and on reaching Madras sailed for Malacca in May, as the news had reached Madras of the need for reinforcements at Naning. They anchored off Malacca on 6th June, and Keppel was sent in charge of a small force to blockade the Lingy river. It is mentioned in Begbie's book, and he says that while the boats were blockading the mouth of the Lingy, arms, ammunition and provisions were passed round another way and conveyed into the interior with as little difficulty as if no blockade had existed. In Admiral Keppel's book, published in 1899, is an account of his doings, and a picture of his boats firing a salute opposite the house of the Raja in the Muar river up country. He was away on this duty from 10th June to 23rd August. In that book, also, "A Sailor's Life under Four Sovereigns," at page 145, is the following:—"The Naning War was now over. I was very loth to part with my good friend the Rajah. So persuaded was he of my merits, that he solemnly offered me the hand of his daughter in marriage, on condition that I would become his heir and succeed him on the throne of Moowar (Muar). It was no idle jest. He wrote officially to the Powers at Penang, and for some years the document was to be seen in the Government offices. I have endeavoured to obtain a copy of this flattering proposal; but the lapse of time, the changes of administration in the affairs of the Straits Settlements, to say nothing of the ravages of white ants, preclude my presenting it to my readers."

The compiler of this book tried, in common with others, in 1888, to find any trace of the paper or the facts, but, as the Admiral says, it was hopeless after so many years to expect it. One cannot help wondering what the result would have been if he had accepted his offer, which was of course quite impracticable, but it was, except for the daughter, exactly what afterwards took place with Rajah Brooke, who took up the Government of Sarawak

To face page 218.

ALMIRAL OF THE FLEET, SIR HENRY KEPPEL, G.C.B., D.C.L.
From a photograph taken in 1900.

at the request of the Rajah and his people there, and led to the great good that resulted from it. It is known in Singapore how annoyed Sir Henry Keppel was when Governor Sir Harry Ord, about the year 1868, on some British merchants applying to him about the disturbances in Selangor, which seriously affected the trade of Singapore, told them that if the British merchant chose to trade in the Peninsula, it was his own business, and he must expect no assistance from Government; and how Sir Henry Keppel, who was then Admiral on the station, offered to give all the help the Navy could properly give. And if there had been such a Rajah Brooke of Sarawak, as Lieut. Keppel would have proved himself in Muar in 1837, the Native States might have been opened up forty years before they were. The *Magacienne* arrived at Singapore on the 5th September, which was the first time Admiral Keppel landed there, and went on to Batavia at the end of the month, Mr. Bonham being a guest of the Captain, as far as that place, and the ship then returned to the Indian Station. Admiral Keppel tells us in his book that Mr. Bonham could not do without his smoke, and the Captain of the *Magicienne* objected to the smell, and smoking was not allowed. So Lieutenant Keppel, when officer of the watch, gave orders to close the Captain's skylight as he *thought* a squall was coming on, and after Mr. Bonham had his smoke the squall had passed over, and the skylight was opened again. The ship returned to Singapore for three weeks in April, 1832, and on reaching Madras at the end of May, Lieutenant the Hon. Henry Keppel heard he had been promoted to Commander on 30th January.

The first mention of tigers is in the *Chronicle* of the 8th September, when a Chinaman was killed by one near the road leading to New Harbour, not far from the Sepoy Lines. And shortly afterwards a native was killed in another direction, probably by the same animal. A few months later (in November) Mr. & Mrs. Armstrong, while taking a drive on the road leading towards New Harbour, observed a tiger crossing the way, at a short distance in front of them. It is stated in Mr. Cameron's book that no tiger was known in the island until 1835, when one was seen by Mr. Coleman when he was surveying about four miles from town in the jungle. The tiger had jumped into the middle of the party and landed on the theodolite, and as soon as Mr. Coleman came into town, the people went out at once to see the place, and the marks of the tiger and the broken theodolite. But Mr. Cameron was mistaken, as the newspaper of 1831 contains the account of the cases that have just been mentioned.

These seem to have been exceptional cases, because it was usual to say in Singapore that no tigers were known on the island before 1835. Dr. Oxley in a paper on the zoology of Singapore, written in 1849, said that not many years before, the existence of a tiger on the island was firmly disbelieved. It must be remembered that in 1831 the island was thick jungle except near the town, and there were, and are to this day, so many deer and pig that the tigers were not likely to venture near human habitations. There is no reason whatever to think that they were attracted by human beings; and as little reason to think that they had not always been on the island, swimming across the narrow

Straits from Johore in search of the pig and deer, as there is no doubt they do to this day. In the Straits there are islands dotted about, and it is no long swim to cross over, with an island as a resting place on the way. In some notes on Penang and Province Wellesley, written by Mr. J. D. Vaughan in 1857, he said that tigers were known to swim across to Penang from Province Wellesley, and the distance there is very much greater than the narrow Strait between Singapore and the mainland of Asia. The Penang newspaper of 18th June. 1859, said that one or two more tigers had obtained a footing in Penang, and from the distance they had to swim in crossing from the mainland they were generally pretty well tired when they landed, and had frequently been killed whenmet with in that condition. Two at least, however, appeared to have escaped into the jungle and unless they were at once destroyed they would do much mischief. The passage was copied into the *Free Press* of 30th June. If true, it is remarkable, and puts beyond question the great ease with which tigers could cross into Singapore island from the mainland.

It was when the gambier and pepper plantations began to extend beyond the town that tigers commenced to be so dangerous. The *Free Press* in May, 1839, said that it had only been within the last year or two that human life had been taken by tigers in the settlement, and that during the week two Chinese had been carried off near town in the neighbourhood of the new road called the Kangong Road [Serangong Road] and that the government reward of $20 was not sufficient, as the number of casualties within the preceding year had been over twelve. After this the paper contained continual notes of death from tigers, in all cases close to town, or within two miles, and the reward was increased to $50, the paper remarking, that "It was singular that the settlement should have existed for about eighteen years before any occasion of death by tigers was heard of, and that fatal accidents of the kind should happen now (1839) just as the island began to be cleared of jungle, and roads carried into the interior in various directions."

This would rather seem to explain the matter than to occasion surprise. The Chinese coolie working in the jungle on a gambier plantation is just the chance a tiger will take to pounce upon him from behind, the way in which they always attack a human being. The truth of the statement that the loss of life through tigers on the island reached at one period the extent of one man every day has often been doubted; but five men in eight days, as early as 1840, seems to show that it was not improbable. Dr. Oxley says that it was found on careful enquiry that 300 human beings were killed by tigers in 1857, of whom only seven were reported to the police; and in later years, about 1860, over two hundred deaths were reported to the police in one year; and as the gambier-planters only reported those which were likely to become known to the police, it is certain that very many more, and probably double that number, were lost. The difficulty of obtaining coolies to work on the plantations in the jungle, as it was then, was a strong inducement to the towkays to keep the deaths as little known as possible, and in 1860 there were plantations in all directions over the island, whereas in 1840 the country was only opened for a very few miles, except along Serangoon Road, where coffee and sugar were planted.

The government reward was afterwards increased to $100, and many of the more distant gambier plantations were deserted in consequence of tigers. Pits were dug and traps set, but on two occasions the tigers took the men when they went to see whether their traps were successful. Mr. Balestier, who had the sugar plantation three miles from town on Serangoon Road, called Balestier Plain, said that it was no uncommon thing to see the tracks of tigers about his house (now Woodsville Cottage) in the morning, and he used to point out the spot where two of his men had been killed in 1842.

The pits were dug 14 or 15 feet deep, a lot of tree trunks were thrown over the mouth as soon as a tiger was found inside, and he was shot at from between them. In later years the tigers were drawn alive into thick rattan baskets, made like the baskets in which pigs are carried. The basket was closed at one end only, and a strong rattan which the tiger cannot bite through was passed through it. The basket was then placed on the ground near the top of the pit, and a running noose made on the end of the rattan after it had passed through the basket. The noose was then placed over a long pole, and one end was pushed down into the pit. Directly the tiger saw the pole it naturally sprang up, catching it between his fore-paws and biting at the end. The noose was then allowed to slip down the pole, and therefore went over the tiger's head and fore-paws, and was drawn tight under its arms. The tiger was then hauled up by main force, and as the rope passed through the closed end of the basket, the tiger was dragged into the basket head first, and once inside there was so little room to move that he was a close prisoner.

From time to time in this book some of the best known tiger stories will be told in their turn, but it may be mentioned here that there were two men who were very remarkable for their pluck in this respect. One was a French Canadian, named Carrol, who left his country during the disturbances in 1838. He used to live in the jungle almost altogether, and he made tiger hunting a business for the sake of the rewards, which were considerable at one time, about 1860, as the Chamber of Commerce gave a reward as well as the Government, and the body was also worth money. Carrol died in the General Hospital. He was an elderly man; a very fine rifle shot, and was known because he always wore a gold ring half way up a long greyish beard, like a necktie ring. The other man was a Eurasian named Neil Martin Carnie, who was born in Singapore. He was of a roving frame of mind, and never settled down to a steady life; for a time he would be the chief clerk in the Municipality, then he would become an Inspector, and then something else, but the moment he heard of a tiger his office saw him no more. He used to roam about the jungle at night with a retired Sergeant-Major of police, a Malay, who lived down at Serangoon, near the 5th mile. That man had one day shot a tiger, and he found the reward so much easier earned than his pay, that he left the police and started a cattle farm, joined with it tiger hunting, and was very successful. Carnie was a man of great pluck, as the story of the tiger he shot in 1864 shows, which will be told hereafter The tigers are few now in Singapore island, but there are always some to be heard of, though difficult to find, as Mr. G. P. Owen and Mr. D. Maw have found, who have shot so many. It is well to remark that tiger-shooting in Singapore is a very different thing to the sport in India, where the sportsman is up on the back of an elephant or high up in a tree. Here it is a much more dangerous and adventurous matter; on foot, in a jungle, face-to-face at a moment's notice with a tiger. Only bold-spirited men have been successful in Singapore, and there have not been many of them.

In September, a meeting of the mercantile community was held to draw up a Petition to Parliament on the subject of the Court of Justice, as no Court had been in operation in any of the three Settlements for fifteen months, and the evils arising from this circumstance had been felt to be of a very serious nature. A copy of the Petition to the House of Commons was to be found in the *Chronicle* of the 13th October, and of that to the House of Lords in the paper of 24th November, which gave the list of the signatures, comprising almost every gentleman in the Settlement acquainted with English.

In October a burglary was committed in Dr. Oxley's house, and a convict, a servant of the Doctor, caught the man, a Malay of Bencoolen, after the Doctor had shot at him with some small shot just as he was getting out through the window. The burglar wounded the convict with a kris, and he then jumped out of a window in the Doctor's room, fifteen feet from the ground. Dr. Oxley was Government Surgeon, and the story was often told that on going to the hospital the next morning, a man had to have a lot of shot picked out of his back; and it is said the doctor, who knew how the shot got there, was a long time getting out the pellets.

In September, 1831, the Privy Council (in England) held a meeting to hear an appeal from Sir John Claridge (the Recorder) against his removal from the office of Recorder of the Straits at the instance of the East India Company, who had made six charges of wrongful conduct against him, the principal one being on the ground of his refusal to go circuit in consequence of a dispute between him and Mr. Fullerton as to certain expenses of the Court. The result was that Sir John Claridge was removed from the office of Recorder, but the Privy Council said that no imputation rested on his capacity or integrity in the exercise of his judicial functions, or to preclude him from further employment. The effect was the re-establishment of the Court under the old Charter, and until the arrival of the Recorder, Sir Benjamin Malkin, in February, 1833, Mr. Fullerton, Mr. Ibbetson, Mr. Bonham, Mr. Murchison and Mr. Garling, held the Courts in the three Settlements from the 10th April.

Against this paragraph written in 1884, Mr James Guthrie wrote the following note:—"The Recorder misunderstanding, I believe, is correct, but the Court continued until Mr. Fullerton went home, when to reduce expenditure, the Governor-General in Calcutta proposed doing away with the Governorship of the Straits, and the community were indebted to Mr. K. Murchison, then Resident Councillor in Singapore, who agreed to take the responsibility of opening the Cou·t, if the Europeans bound themselves to give their support. Mr. Ibbetson was then Resident Councillor of Penang, and after a time he was appointed the Governor.

———

CHAPTER XIX.

1832 and 1833.

1832.

IN January, John Francis, who had kept a sort of public house, opened what he called a Hotel at the north end of the Square, with a Billiard Room and a Refreshment Hall, as he styled it in the advertisement. This seems to have been the first of the kind. In 1840 he opened a butcher's shop in Teluk Ayer Street.

Mr. Thomas Owen Crane and his wife were living in the upper part of the house where the Mercantile Bank now stands, at the centre end of the south end of the Square. The lower part was occupied by the offices of Mr. T. O. Crane and Dr. d'Almeida.

On the 7th May the Criminal Assizes were held by Mr. Ibbetson and Mr. Bonham. There were in all nearly forty prisoners, including four murder cases, and the Assizes lasted seven days. The Grand Jury presented the state of the large bridge, a long standing grievance, and complained of the Government neglecting to maintain it when they had sold the land near it on the express undertaking to do so. They also mentioned the number of Chinese beggars in the streets, and the state of the Teluk Ayer Market, which was covered with attap, and not kept clean, also the silting up of the mouth of the river, and lastly the numerous burglaries that had been committed by gangs of Chinese in bodies of fifty to one hundred men. They said that the atrocities of the villains had increased to such an alarming extent that if some active measures were not taken to put a stop to their career, there was every probability of their becoming so powerful that it would not be safe for any one to reside at a distance from town or to settle as cultivators in the interior.

In May, the paper contained long accounts of the second Naning Expedition, already spoken of. In June the Chinese in Singapore, with the sanction, but not the aid of Government, subscribed to fit out four large trading boats with thirty Chinese each, well armed and carrying several guns, to go out and attack the pirates, which were lurking outside the harbour. This was a grave reflection on the vigilance and exertion of Government, which, from the support it derived from the Chinese trade, ought to have been foremost in endeavouring to protect the native ships from pirates who, emboldened by impunity, continued to attack traders, even close to the harbour and inside it. The Chinese boats went out, and fell in with two pirate prahus, one large and one small, and sank one, but the other escaped. One or two of the Chinese were killed. The agreement the towkays made was that two hundred dollars were to be paid for each pirate boat attacked, and two hundred dollars given to the relations of any man who was killed.

In July, at a General Quarter Sessions, the Magistrates levied a rate of five per cent. on the rent of all houses in the town, for six months, to repair and cleanse the roads, and for other purposes mentioned in the Charter. Canton advertisements were published in the Singapore paper at this time, and in June one is published stating that on the 15th February, William Jardine and James Matheson had established the firm of Jardine, Matheson & Co., the former firm of Magniac & Co. having then ceased.

The Government having been shamed, apparently, by the Chinese, had two boats built at Malacca carrying 12 pounder guns, manned by nineteen Malays (trustworthy characters, not pirates) to act in Singapore against the pirates.

In September it was suggested to make a further collection towards the monument to Sir Stamford Raffles, and to erect a substantial stone bridge to be called "Raffles Bridge." The amount of the previous subscription was still in the hands of the Treasurers. To this it was objected that Government were bound to build the bridge; and towards the end of the year orders came from Bengal to do this, but the engineer had left Singapore before the orders were received.

On the 15th September a Dutch schooner, the *Reliance*, blew up in the harbour, the gunpowder kept in the vessel having exploded in some way that was never explained. The Captain, two European mates, and five of the native crew were killed, and the rest seriously injured.

In November, a sampan-pukat belonging to Singapore sailed for Pahang, having a cargo valued at $10,000 to $12,000, consisting of opium (of which there were seven chests), raw-silk, piece-goods, rice, tobacco and sundry other articles. This vessel had thirty-three Chinese sailors on board, and carried seven lelahs or small guns. About 10 o'clock, when off Pulo Tingy, she fell in with a fleet of pirate boats 15 or 16 in number. An attack was soon made on the pukat, when after a fight of two hours, four of the Chinese were killed. Shortly after, by some accident, the small quantity of gunpowder which remained in the pukat blew up and set fire to the sails, so that the crew could not fight nor the vessel escape. The pirates then came near, and attacked the Chinese with spears and darts, and the latter, being overpowered by numbers, threw themselves into the water, where most of them met their death, either by drowning, or from the spears of the pirates.

By this time it was sun-set, and twelve of the crew, including the nacodah or commander, having contrived to evade the pirates, continued floating on pieces of wood, during the whole night and until early the next morning, when they were picked up by some Malay fishermen who lived on the coast nearly opposite to where the piracy occurred. The name of this place was stated to be Qualla Soodili. The Chinese were well treated by the Malays, who would have brought them round to Singapore by sea, but the pirates, having had intimation that some of the survivors were there, watched for them. The Malays, however, conducted them overland to Johore, from whence they were passed to Singapore. The Chinese on arrival rewarded their preservers with sixty rupees.

In December a reply was received to the Petitions that had been addressed to the two Houses of Parliament in the preceding year, and the appointment of the new Recorder was made known.

It was about this time that an alteration in the seat of Government took place which was transferred from Penang to Singapore, as the most important of the three Settlements.

The following statistics are taken from Mr. Earl's book:—"The amount of goods imported from Great Britain into the chief British Settlements in India in the year 1832, was as follows:—

Bengal, Madras and Bombay ...	£2,592,530
Singapore ...	„ 340,799
Ceylon ..	„ 47,792

"I cannot readily obtain estimates of the trade of Penang and Malacca for the same year, but in 1829 the former imported from Great Britain to the amount of £16,767, and the latter to £10,166."

1833.

In January the Rev. Robert Burn, the Chaplain of Singapore, died in Dr. Oxley's house. He was said to be a man of unusual attainments. Mr. G. F. Davidson says in his book:—"There seems to be some fatality attaching to clergymen at Singapore, as three following incumbents the Revs. Burn, Darrah and White, all died young, and of the same complaint. My own opinion is they were all too strict adherents to teetotalism." An opinion formed sixty years ago with which he would find many now to disagree, after a more lengthy experience of the climate. There was still no Church in the Settlement.

In the same month a census was taken, but as it was collected by the two constables who were attached to the Settlement and had many other duties to do, it was not considered as very correct, as they could not possibly make minute enquiries at every house and in every district, especially those situated beyond the limits of the town. The population was put down at 20,978, of whom 119 were Europeans and Armenians. This did not include the Military or the Convicts, and showed an increase of 1,263 over the year 1832. The population had increased during the preceeding five years about fifty per cent.

It was about this time that two midshipmen of an English Man-of-War, the *Curacoa*, had a duel on shore here, from which one of them died a few days afterwards. The surviving principal, and both the seconds, were committed for trial afterwards in Bombay, and acquitted.

In February a proposal was made to establish a Singapore Bank, by subscription, to consist of two thousand shares of two hundred dollars each (a capital of $400,000) with a first call of $50 a share, in order to make advances on property, to discount at 12 per cent., with a commission of $\frac{1}{4}$ to $\frac{1}{2}$ per cent. on sums drawn out in current accounts, to pay the expenses of the establishment. It was considered quite a new proposition, and nothing was done in the matter. No local bank has been started in Singapore yet, except a small business called a Bank that we shall come to a few years later. In April the proposal had reached Calcutta, and there was a very long article in the papers there headed

" Singapore Bank," which said that it might be useful, but not in the way it was proposed, because a bank of deposit and loan was not required in Singapore, as there were no capitalists for whom it could keep accounts, no rich proprietors to offer substantial security, and no manufacturers requiring long-winded advances. And it suggested another expedient by which the business of local circulation could be effected, without any bank at all, by the issue of local paper on the part, and for the profit, of Government.

In April it was proposed to establish a Singapore Marine Insurance Society, which came more nearly to a successful issue than the Bank did. It was estimated that the merchants paid about sixty thousand dollars annually for premiums of insurance to Societies of Calcutta, and it was argued that so much money should be retained in the place. It was suggested to commence with a first subscription of $10,000. This came also to nothing. In 1883, fifty years later, a local Insurance Company was started, but it no longer exists.

In May an agreement was made with Mr. Coleman to build a pauper hospital for $11,402. It does not appear where the site was.

In October after many attempts of Mr. Bonham, Mr. George Drumgold Coleman was finally appointed Superintendent of Public Works, Overseer of Convict Labour and Land Surveyor. He first began the employment of the convicts on large outside works, by reclaiming land from the sea and marshes. Roads were first made along the sea fronts, and North and South Bridge Roads, now the main thoroughfare through the town from north to south, where the names meet at Elgin Bridge. He designed the first St. Andrew's Church. Coleman Street at the south end of the Cathedral compound, and Coleman Bridge, were named after him.

Mr. Coleman died in Singapore on the 27th March, 1844, and is buried in the Old Cemetery on Fort Canning where the inscription on his tomb is still legible. He was born at Drogheda in Ireland, and was one of the oldest residents in Singapore at the time of his death. The *Free Press* spoke of him in the following terms :— "Mr. Coleman, for many years, was employed under the Government as Superintendent of Convicts and Public Works, and to his good judgment and untiring energy we mainly owe the great extent of good roads on this island, and to his taste and skill as an architect we are also indebted for many of the elegant buildings, both public and private, which adorn Singapore. In June, 1841, he embarked for his native country, and after visiting all that is interesting in Europe, he had but recently returned here, with a view to a permanent residence, when he fell a prey to fever, brought on by exposure to the sun." His widow married Mr. William Napier.

A number of piracies were continually reported. A large trading schooner was attacked on her way from Malacca, and ten of her crew killed by five pirate prahus. The pirates were said to belong to Singapore, Padang and Lukut. The Company's gun-boat *Hawk* was attacked near Penang by upwards of twenty prahus, well armed, with guns, and she had to retreat, after expending nearly all her ammunition. An English brig was attacked by three large prahus and the vessel waited until they came close, and then fired a twelve-pounder at them.

The pirates replied with grape shot, and a breeze springing up, the brig was enabled to proceed, but they followed her up, and would have attacked her again at night, but for a schooner coming up; the pirates then made off. The newspaper remarked that it was certain that many piracies, attended with horrible atrocities, occurred in the vicinity of Singapore, of which no tidings were ever heard.

The Jail at this time was on the site of the present Central Police Station, where the Magistrate's Court was afterwards held until the building was pulled down in 1884 to erect the present station. It was built, as has been said before, on a swamp, and was inundated at every high tide, which was very prejudicial to the health of the persons confined or supposed to be confined in it, for it was a very insecure place; the safe custody depending principally upon the inability of any absconders to avoid being hunted down in the small Settlement; in fact the Grand Jury "presented" during this year that the prisoners who had escaped had done so because they were permitted to go a considerable distance outside the Jail, without any guard, to fetch water for their own use. The wall round it was only a few feet high, and on Sundays those in Jail for debt used to go out for a walk after stepping over the wall. The floor had sunk at this time upwards of a foot, and was raised in 1834 when the building was completed, but it is said that it sank much more afterwards, and when the surrounding compound was filled up, the prisoners were put in what had been the upper story of the building.

In March Mr. Bonham, the Resident Councillor, wrote to the Editor of the *Chronicle* that the Supreme Government had, on his recommendation, sanctioned the discontinuance of the censorship of the Press in Singapore, so that the proof-sheet need not be sent to him any more. The Editor wrote an article on the subject, in which he quoted an old remark of Blackstone that to subject the press to the restrictive power of a licenser was to make all freedom of sentiment liable to the prejudice of one man and make him the arbitrary judge of controverted points.

In April appeared the first notice found of stray dogs being liable to be destroyed, in the streets, for ten days. On the 5th of this month, Singapore was startled by a Government Notification, sent out as a sort of *Gazette Extraordinary*, that all Dutch vessels were to be seized in the harbour, and that His Majesty's ships of war were instructed to detain and bring all Dutch vessels into port. This was in expectation of war with Holland. But a postscript stated that the Governor-General had given orders that it should not be carried into effect until further directions from England, or unless the Dutch commenced measures, in these seas, of hostilities or annoyance. In Batavia, notice was given that Dutch vessels on the coast exposing themselves to the danger of being captured if war should be declared with England, should proceed immediately to Soerabaya, as a place of safety. The Dutch fleet in Java then consisted of two frigates, one of 32, the other of 23 guns, and two brigs, and some small gun-boats, or cutters. The frigates were at once sent to Soerabaya to protect the shipping. It all came to nothing, and the embargo was taken off in the month of

May, and did not reach Singapore until September, but one immediate
effect was the detention in Java of the Dutch rice-carrying vessels,
which caused the price of rice in Singapore to rise considerably within
a few weeks.

There were four of H. M. Ships in the harbour soon after the
notification was received from Calcutta, but only one, the *Harrier*, when
it arrived. The *Alligator* came down from Penang, the *Wolf* from
Madras, and the *Magicienne* from Calcutta. In March or April, when
the rupture with Holland was expected, a flagstaff was erected on Blakan
Mati island, in order to signal the approach of vessels. Begbie
says that the island was so called because tradition said that a Malay
had been murdered behind the hill, the words meaning literally "behind
dead," but Mr. Haughton in an interesting paper in the Journal of
the Straits Asiatic Society for 1889, No. 20, on the names of places
here, gives the meaning as "dead-back island," so called from the
sterility of the soil on the hills. There is a place with a similar name
in Batavia (2 Logan, 572). The flagstaff was removed in 1845 on account
of the unhealthiness of the site.

On the 25th April, Sir Benjamin Malkin, the new Recorder, and
Lady Malkin, with Mr. A. J. Kerr, the Registrar of the Court of
Judicature, arrived in Singapore. The Judge was received with a
salute of 15 guns from the ship and from the fort. The Assizes were
opened in May, and lasted a week, there being twenty-four cases. The
Grand Jury made a long presentment as usual, the tumble down bridge
being made a great deal of again, and the increasing bar at the
mouth of the river. It sounds curious to find that the Judge promised
the interference of the Court to have the latter removed as a nuisance.
They also referred to the very great evils of piracy, and its serious
effect upon the trade of Singapore, to which the Recorder replied
(as Sir John Claridge had done before in Malacca) that by an
unfortunate oversight in framing the Charter, the Straits Court had not
the power even to try offences of this nature, but that he was aware
of the urgency and importance of the subject, and would willingly
impress the same upon the attention of Government.

It was the custom at this time in Singapore for the Government to
grant a free license to the Chinese to gamble for fifteen days at the
commencement of every Chinese New Year. It was given under the
impression that it formed part of their religion, or at least was considered
a religious ceremony by them. It was attended by all the pernicious
evils which accompany unrestricted gaming, and on reference to Canton
it was found that it was never sanctioned there at the New Year, any
more than at any other time.

The Chinese made a long petition to the Government on the subject of
piracy, giving numerous instances which were continually occurring, proposing certain measures for its suppression. The Government, as usual,
talked, but did not act; and the Chinese again took measures themselves,
with the sanction of Government, and chartered a vessel to go and cruise
against them, at their own expense. The natives could get no credit for
opium, owing to the great risk of its being taken by pirates on the way to the
neighbouring places. This woke the authorities up, and the H. C. schooner
Zephyr was despatched up the East Coast, but did not meet with success.

There were pirates of another sort, also, in those days, for the paper contains an account of a vessel from Calcutta being chased for four hours by a brigantine, evidently filled with armed men. The English vessel was fully prepared to resist the pirate, if she had attempted to board, but she did not come up to her.

The new Chaplain, Mr. Darrah, applied to Government for an allowance to establish a Free School, as there was no school of any consequence in the place, and he also asked Government for a grant of a small sum for the purpose of opening a lending library. The Government replied that there could be but one opinion as to the utility of the objects he proposed, but, on the score of the economy, so rigidly enforced by the Government in Calcutta, they could not assist him, but would request leave from Calcutta.

However, Mr. Darrah started at once by opening a school in the Mission Chapel, on Sunday afternoons in July from four to six o'clock, taught by himself and two others, which was the first Sunday School in Singapore. There was no Church at this time, the only place of worship being the Mission Chapel.

The house at New Harbour lately known as the Malay College was built about this time. Begbie says that the Sultan of Singapore (he meant the Tumongong) had erected a very neat house at New Harbour, built and furnished after the English style. The artillery barracks and house of the officer had already been erected at the point of the river, called Fort Fullerton, where the Marine Office, Post Office and Club now stand.

The overland route question began again in this year, and a meeting was held in Bombay at which it was proposed to have three voyages a year, each way; and one advantage proposed in the report of the Committee appointed by the meeting is so very original, looking at it from the light of the present days, that we quote it:—" Of these sources of profit the principal may be found in the conveyance of respectable native pilgrims to and from Jedda, and in the numbers of Civil and Military Officers of this country, who will gladly avail themselves of a regular and certain communication with the Red Sea Ports, to visit on furlough the attractive and healthy regions of Egypt and Syria from November to March. Nowhere else, within the limits prescribed by the Absentee Regulations, can so extensive and beneficial a change of climate be attained in so agreeable a manner, or on such economical terms, after having spent little more money than would have been required for a passage to the Cape, not to say anything of the return passage, and the enormous expenses of living there, contrasted with the difficulty of spending money in Egypt. By remaining during one intermediate trip of the steamer in Egypt, the whole country from the borders of Abyssinia to Aleppo, with the splendid monuments of antiquity of Syria and Egypt, Damascus, Palmyra, Baalbec, Jerusalem, Cairo and the Pyramids, Dendera, Thebes, Phile and Mount Sinai might be visited for one-tenth part of the expense, with far less danger, and in nearly the same period that would be necessary to cross the continent of India from Bombay to Calcutta, and back again, or for a visit to the Neilgheiries. During the whole of which, the absentee's Indian term of service will not only be untouched, but he will continue to receive his Indian allowances. When all the advantages afforded by this communication are taken into consideration, the Committee feel confident that there is scarcely an individual of the British community on the Indian Continent, who will not give his mite towards its establishment, and that their present appeal to the public will meet with the liberality which a measure of such importance deserves."

The Singapore paper published this report at the request of the Bombay Committee, and said that considerable sums had been subscribed in India, and that Singapore ought not to be behind-hand in supporting an object so likely to prove of ultimate benefit to this place, as well as to India in general, especially as the plan seemed to bid fair for completion. It remarked that there was no reason why a good steamer could not make four trips from Bombay to Suez in twelve months. At a meeting held in Calcutta about the same time for the same object, Bishop Wilson, at the general request, took the chair and subscribed one thousand rupees to the fund. The amount of the former subscriptions to Mr. Waghorn's fund was added to this one. Similar meetings were held in Ceylon.

In October a London tailor opened a shop, and also a European hair-dresser, both in Malacca Street, but in different houses. In November, on a Sunday night, about ten o'clock a shock of an earthquake lasting for more than a minute was felt in Singapore, and two slighter shocks were perceptible in the early morning. The punkahs were set moving by the motion. It was the first phenomenon of the kind that had occurred since the formation of the Settlement, and it was conjectured the volcano Gunong Berapi, in Sumatra, was in violent eruption. Similar shocks were felt at Malacca and Penang, at the same time, allowing for the difference of a few minutes.

On Saturday, 7th December, Mr. Murchison was sworn in as Governor of the Settlements, as Mr. Ibbetson was going on leave to England, and Mr. Murchison immediately left for a trip to the Cape; the late and newly sworn-in Governors both leaving the harbour in the same vessel on that day, to go to Muntoh to sail in other vessels from there. The Government devolved on Mr. Garling, the Senior Resident Councillor, who was then at Malacca. The European hair-dresser left Singapore in the same vessel as the two Governors, but at whose expense, or why, does not appear. A European hair-dresser set up a shop in Battery Road forty years later, and he made no better business of it than his predecessor seems to have done.

Mr. Ibbetson was one of the first who had set up the example, in Penang, in 1821, of cultivating on a large scale, which to the great advantage of that island, was afterwards followed. At that time the Indian Government encouraged the Straits Officials to invest their savings in cultivation, but afterwards, following the rules it had laid down in India itself, the encouragement was succeeded by a positive prohibition, and a very great loss was sustained by those who held land, for which the Government gave no compensation, as it should in fairness have done.

A Government Savings Bank was established in Calcutta in this year, and it was proposed to open one in Singapore, as it had been done in Penang. But nothing came of it, and the first Savings Bank was established here in the Post Office in 1874. The Bank in Penang had just been started by the Recorder, Sir Benjamin Malkin, who had been one of the active Managers of the Marylebone Savings Bank in London, and he drew up rules, called a public meeting, and set the bank going. He was described as one who took a very active interest in the good of the population.

The *Chronicle* mentions that in this year, in September, the grove of trees leading up to the top of the hill at Malacca had been cut down by a goth. It was, however, the Governor, who suggested they obstructed the view of the lighthouse to ships entering the harbour, the fact being that some of them interfered with an official's view of the flag-staff. The article said " The trees referred to were rendered venerable, as they formed a regular and magnificent avenue up the Government Hill, to the porch of the ancient ruined Church which stands on the summit. The ruin is famous, as the celebrated St. Francis Xavier, a zealous Jesuit Missionary, ministered in it for several years."

The European Overseer of Convicts was murdered by one of the convicts in December, and the murderer refusing to surrender, and attempting to stab a European Officer, and actually wounding one of the sepoys, the guard shot him.

On the 29th November, the ship *Ann* from Macao, eight days out, arrived in the harbour with the Chief Officer, Carpenter's mate, a Parsee passenger and three sailors murdered; and the second mate and seven others severely wounded. The Manila seamen on board rose on the ship for the sake of a large quantity of specie on board. They were detained on board and taken to Bombay for trial, there being no jurisdiction here to try them. It was remarkable that the father of the principal offender (who died himself from wounds inflicted upon him by the Captain with a teak awning stanchion seized in the hurry of the moment), was the son of a man who was in a Bombay ship which was nearly cut off some years before by Manila sailors, under very similar circumstances of time and place. The insurance offices had refused after that to take risks on vessels on which Manila men were employed, but the rule fell into disuse.

In November orders arrived from Bombay to make tidal observations, but it was not done on account of the expense. The orders were renewed in August, 1834, but the result was defective as the local authorities refused the necessary expense for an efficient establishment.

About this time there were twenty European Mercantile houses in Singapore, seventeen British, one Portuguese, one German, and one American; and three extensive Armenian firms to whom it was said Singapore was indebted for the re-opening of the trade with Borneo.

As to the European firms, in addition to Messrs. A. L. Johnston & Co., Guthrie & Co., and Jozé d'Almeida and Sons, which have been already spoken of, the following had been established.

The firm of John Purvis & Co., was started in 1822. Until 1855 Mr. John Purvis was the sole partner. In 1856 John Murray Purvis joined as a partner; Mr. T. S. Thomson, a first cousin of Mr. J. T. Thomson, the Government Surveyor, joined as a clerk, in 1860. Mr. John Purvis left the firm 31st March, 1862.

The firm of Syme & Co. commenced in Singapore in 1823 and the firm was appointed Lloyds' Agents in 1828, and are so still. In 1846 there were four partners, Robert Ker in Glasgow, Edward Doering in Liverpool, Thomas McMicking in Singapore, and Joseph Cheney Bolton in Manila. In 1851 William Ker, Jun., who had been a clerk since 1848, and William McMicking became partners, and in 1852 Gilbert McMicking, who had been a clerk previous to 1846. In 1852 Mr. W. Mactaggart was a clerk, and he and Mr. Robert Jardine were partners on 1st January, 1857. In the previous year the clerks had been W. Mactaggart, H. W. Wood, James Murray and G. M. Dare. In 1858 the partners were William Mactaggart, Robert Ker, J. C. Bolton (afterwards Chairman of the Caledonian Railway and M.P. for Stirlingshire). William Ker, G. Scholfield, Gilbert McMicking, Robert Jardine (who is still a partner) and William Ker, Junior, (Mr. Paton Ker's father).

The firm of Spottiswoode & Connolly was started in 1824. In 1846 the partners were William Spottiswoode in England, and John Connolly and Charles Spottiswoode in Singapore. In 1848 Mr. William Mactaggart was a clerk, with John Connolly, Jun., Andrew Connolly and A. J. S. Spottiswoode. On 13th August, 1849, the name was changed to William Spottiswoode & Co. The office was where Change Alley is now. In 1854 the partners were William, Charles and Archibald Spottiswoode, Mr. James Weir becoming a clerk. On 31st December, 1856, William Spottiswoode left the firm and Charles Archibald carried on the business. In 1859 A. J. Spottiswoode was the only partner, and in 1860 he was joined by Mr. Weir, and in 1863 by Charles Grey McClellend.

In 1827 the firm of Maclaine, Fraser & Co. began. The partners were James Fraser in London, Lewis Fraser and Gilbert Angus Bain in Singapore, and John Purss Cumming in England; James B. Cumming being a clerk. In 1854 Mr. Bain left the firm and Simon F. Cumming became a clerk; Mr. R. O. Norris was a clerk for many years from 1848. From 1855 the two Frasers and J. P. and J. B. Cumming were the partners, Mr. N. B. Watson who was very popular (and always known as *Nota Bene*) being a clerk. On 24th September, 1858, Mr. J. P. Cumming died, and Mr. Robert Bain became a partner on 1st January, 1859; he had been in A. L. Johnston & Co., and afterwards in business on his own account. In 1860 Mr. N. B. Watson became a partner, and in 1861 James Bannerman Cumming left. Mr. Charles Dunlop, who had come out to the firm in 1857, became a partner in 1st January, 1864, and in the next year Mr. Lewis James Fraser.

In 1828 the firm of Ker, Rawson & Co. was established by Mr. William Wemys Ker in Singapore, Mr. Thomas Sam Rawson in London, and Christopher Empsan in China. Mr. William Paterson was a clerk, and Mr. Henry Minchin Simons was a clerk in 1849. In 1853 the firm was composed of Messrs. Ker, Rawson, Paterson, and Simons, and continued so until the 30th April, 1859. At that time the old name was dropped and Messrs. W. W. Ker, Paterson, and Simons continued under the name of Paterson, Simons & Co., which is the same at this day. Mr. Thomas Shelford and Mr. W. G. Gulland appear for the first time as clerks in the firm in 1863. Mr. William Paterson died at Eastbourne in January, 1898, at the age of 75 years. He had been for over twenty years Chairman in London of the Chartered

Bank of India, Australia and China. Two of his sons are partners now in the firm. Mr. Thomas Shelford, c.m.g., died near Guildford in January, 1900, sixty one years of age. He was a member of the Legislative Council of the Straits Settlements for many years. One of his sons is a partner in the firm. Mr. Henry Minchin Simons died in London in December, 1901, at the age of seventy seven years, and his only son is also a partner in the firm.

In 1832 the firm of Hamilton Gray & Co. commenced business. In 1846 the partners were Walter and William Hamilton and William Macdonald in England, and Ellis James Gilman and George Garden Nicol in Singapore. Ed. Loze was a clerk. The firm continued so until 1852, when the partners were Walter Buchanan, William Hamilton, and G. G. Nicoll; the next year John Jarvie, who had been a clerk since 1849, became a partner. In 1854 Reginald Padday and C. H. H. Wilsone joined as clerks. Mr. Padday became a partner in 1857, and Mr. Wilsone in 1863.

The firm of Shaw Whitehead & Co., was originally called Graham Mackenzie & Co., and on 31st December, 1834, Mr. Colin Mackenzie left the firm and it was changed to Shaw Whitehead & Co. with Mr. J. H. Whitehead as a partner. The tombstone in the old Cemetery shows that Mr. John Horrocks Whitehead died in Singapore on 21st September, 1846, at the age of 36 years. In 1846, the first date which can be traced, the partners were J. H. Whitehead and Michie Forbes Davidson in England, and James Stephen in Singapore. In 1847 J. H. Whitehead had left the firm. The next year Mr. Davidson left and joined A. L. Johnston & Co. and the two partners were Stephen and Robert Duff. Garlies Allinson was then a clerk. In 1852 Mr. Duff was the only partner, and the name was changed to William Macdonald & Co. on the 1st July of that year, the partners being Robert Duff and William Macdonald; the clerks were Garlies Allinson, Farleigh Armstrong and Alexander Rodger. In 1855 Mr. Allinson became a partner. In 1859 William Ramsay Scott was a clerk. In 1860 the three partners were Messrs. Duff, William Macdonald, and J. E. Macdonald.

CHAPTER XX.

1834.

O N New Year's day the first Regatta was held. There were, in the third race, five boats, the property of European gentlemen, which composed the "Singapore Yacht Club." The race was six and a half miles round the harbour. Their names were *Waterwitch, Maggie Lauder, Shamrock, Hawk's Hill,* and *Jenny dang the Weaver.* A salute was fired at day-break by the man-of-war, the *Magicienne,* and also from the battery, which was the custom in those days.

On the 3rd January, Mr. Bonham, the Deputy Resident, was sworn in as Acting Governor of the Settlements, having been appointed Resident, and acting for the absent Governor, and Mr. Wingrove was appointed acting Resident Councillor of Singapore.

A gang robbery, which excited a great deal of attention, took place in this month, of which the *Chronicle* had the following account :— " A most daring burglary and robbery was committed between two and three o'clock on Tuesday morning, by a formidable gang of Chinese bandits who issued from the jungle, in the house of a dhobie, named Manook, residing in the Dhobie village at Campong Glam. The gang consisted of about 50 men, armed with spears and other weapons, some carrying torches. Having broken open the door with great violence, they proceeded to plunder, and succeeded in carrying away a chest, a large bundle of clothes, and a quantity of silver ornaments which they compelled the women and children residing in the house, to deliver up, on pain of death. The immediate neighbourhood had been alarmed early, but although the inhabitants were numerous, they afforded so little assistance, through fear, that the robbers retreated, with their booty, towards the jungle, almost scathless, and at a slow pace.

Fortunately a gentleman residing in the vicinity of the road they took, had been apprised of their first approach, and was ready, with about a dozen natives, hastily collected in the neighbourhood, to meet them on their return. He was armed with a double-barrelled gun and a pistol loaded with balls, and two of the party had a blunderbuss and a musket. The robbers were summoned to stand, but they only answered with the cry to strike, when the gentleman fired one barrel at the whole body, and one man was observed to fall. He discharged the other barrel, and the pistol, the blunderbuss and the musket were likewise fired; and some of the natives, inhabitants of the Buffalo village, who were of the party, attacked the robbers with great vigour. The latter, however, escaped, but left the chest and a bundle of clothes on the road.

Mr. R. F. Wingrove and Mr. A. J. Kerr, who had left their residence on the alarm reaching them, shortly after came up with the Constable and some peons, and dividing themselves into two or three separate parties, they set out in pursuit by different tracks leading into the jungle. On one track a table cloth, a pair of trousers and a bundle of spears were found, and there was every indication of the gang being a little in advance; but the party (no doubt like the one in Oliver Twist after Bill Sykes, and for possibly similar reasons) considering themselves too small and too weak to penetrate further during the dark, without incurring danger, returned at day-break towards the town. The line of retreat of the robbers was pointed out by the clothes scattered along the road. A number of European ladies had afterwards to sort out their wardrobe and take it away.

In February, Mr. Darrah, the Chaplain, began writing on the subject of the neglected education of the children in the Settlement, and the necessity of establishing schools, as has been stated on page 128.

In April the Governor-General turned the tables round again, and Mr. Church was appointed to officiate as Governor, and Mr. Bonham as Resident. Mr. Church had been Deputy Resident Councillor at Penang and it had been said in Singapore that he had a better right, from longer service, than Mr. Bonham, who had been appointed in January. Mr. Murchison, the Governor, was still on leave at the Cape.

In May the first mention of Gambier is found, as being likely to become a staple article of export from Singapore to England, and the paper gave an account of it and its properties, describing it as a valuable astringent in cases of dysentery in doses of twelve grains to one drachm. And it also spoke of sago as being prepared exclusively in Singapore, for consumption in Europe and India.

An aggrieved individual wrote to the paper that the centre of the Square was made a rubbish heap, and that a Chinaman had turned it into a depot for old timber and rubbish from a building he was re-erecting, and had broken down the railing, and complaining that no one seemed to stir in the matter.

In this year, Mr. Bonham, in writing to the Supreme Government, complained of the expense of a professional Judge, and asserted that the presence of a Recorder was not necessary. He proposed that the business of the Court should be carried on by the Governor and Resident Councillors, with an occasional visit from one of the Calcutta Judges. And that if the system in force was to be continued, it was hardly fair that the European inhabitants should not contribute for the protection they received, and he suggested that a duty on trade should be immediately imposed.

Lord William Bentinck, the Governor-General, was of opinion that some tribunal like a Court of Requests was all that was necessary; while Lord Auckland, in a very long minute, was of opinion that the system then in force ought to be abolished, and considered a proper substitute would be by employing the Malay language in all the Courts, and administering the law of England with some modifications on particular points; with a paid Magistrate, and an Assistant Magistrate with power to try petty cases, and a jury of five for small felonies. The Magistrates and their assistants to be Commissioners of a Court of Requests, and one Resident to be placed over the three Settlements, to visit them alternately, holding civil and criminal Courts, hearing appeals from

Magistrates, and trying civil cases, with a jury when either of the parties wished it, and to try all criminal cases, except British subjects charged with capital crimes; and lastly, that a Judge of the Supreme Court of Calcutta should visit the Straits once a year, or oftener, to hear appeals, to review the proceedings of the Resident and Magistrates, and to try all civil and criminal cases that were referred to him.

Sir Benjamin Malkin, the Recorder, also stated his views at considerable length. He was favourable to the existing system with some improvements and reduction in the expense. The Court continued as it was until after the Transfer in 1867, Admiralty jurisdiction being added in September, 1837; but it may be useful to explain how judicial matters had progressed in the Settlement up to this time; and what had been proposed in the early days of the Settlement.

Various suggestions for the amendment or alteration of the Straits Judicial System had been made during the course of the fifteen years. In 1829, Mr. Fullerton, in a long minute on the subject of the economical administration of the Straits Settlements, had proposed three schemes:—the first of which was that the whole duties of the executive and judicial at each Settlement should be discharged by the Residents and their assistants. The Residents to be judges and magistrates, hearing themselves all causes above 500 rupees; referring those under that sum to their assistants, with an appeal to the residents; and that all misdemeanours, affrays, petty assaults, &c., the punishment of which would not exceed 36 stripes, imprisonment with hard labour for two years, or fine as far as 200 rupees, should be cognizable by the Residents; offenders of a graver nature committed for trial before the Court of Circuit. The Governor to proceed on circuit twice a year, whose duty it should be to try all criminals committed; hear all appeals from the Resident in causes exceeding 2,000 rupees, with an appeal to the King in Council in causes above 3,000 rupees. In all cases of importance, where either party wished it, a jury of four or seven to be impannelled; British-born subjects to be amenable to these Courts, but in cases exceeding 2,000 rupees to have an appeal to the Supreme Court at Calcutta instead of the Governor.

The second plan was, that the Residents should be assisted by five merchants, settlers, as assessors; the Governor and Council holding only Courts of Oyer and Terminer, which should try all the inhabitants, except British-born European subjects, who were to be sent to Calcutta for trial.

The third plan proposed by Mr. Fullerton was that the Government should be constituted like the other Governments of India; to fix on one of the Settlements (Malacca for example) as the Presidency. To have there a Governor and two Councillors; those at the other two stations to have the rank of Residents only, with powers of Zillah Judges; to establish the King's Court on its former scale (the Governor and Councillors being the Judges) with jurisdiction at the Presidency, and for four miles round, over natives; and with the same power over European British subjects, the Company and their servants, as was held by the Supreme Courts; or, if unadvisable to make the Governor, &c., the Judges, to make a Mayor's Court of it, as formerly at Madras and Bombay, leaving justice to be administered at the other two places, and beyond five miles from the Presidency town, by provincial Courts; three Zillah Courts, one Judge of Appeal and Circuit, and the Governor in Council the Sudder Adawlut.

The necessity of making provision for the administration of justice in the two Settlements, whose distance from Bengal put them beyond the sphere of the Courts there, led, in the year 1825, to the passing of an Act by which His Majesty was empowered to make provision for the administration of justice in the Settlements of Singapore and Malacca, and it was also declared lawful for the Court of Directors to annex Singapore and Malacca to the Settlement of Prince of Wales' Island, or any of the Presidencies, or to erect them into dependent Settlements.

In virtue of this power, the Court of Directors on the 12th October, 1825, declared that Singapore and Malacca should cease to be Factories subordinate to Bengal, and annexed them to Prince of Wales' Island, uniting the whole into one Government, consisting of a Governor or President and three Councillors, one of whom was to reside at each of the three Settlements, with the official designation of Resident Councillor, and the Governor was appointed to visit the different stations to assist in the administration of justice, or as other circumstances might suggest.

On the 27th November, His Majesty, by his Letters Patent, established the Court of Judicature of Prince of Wales Island, Singapore and Malacca. This Charter was nearly a transcript of the one constituting the Court of Judicature of Prince of Wales Island, which Sir Edmond Stanley had taken with him to Penang, when he, as Recorder, constituted the Court there in 1807, and only differed from it by attempting to make some provision for the administration of justice in Singapore and Malacca, as well as Penang.

To this end, it seems to have been contemplated that the Court should be held at the three Settlements alternately. Thus, in the clause specifying who were to be Judges of the Court, it was said that the Court should consist of and be holden before the Governor or President and the Resident Councillor for the time being of the station where the said Court should be held, and before one other Judge to be called the " Recorder of Prince of Wales Island, Singapore and Malacca," who was to be a Barrister of not less than five years standing, to be appointed by His Majesty and his successors from time to time.

The presence of the Recorder was essential to the holding of a Court if he should be resident within the Settlement, unless the Governor authorised the Courts to sit and act in the absence of the Recorder. This was evidently meant only to be done where the Recorder's absence proceeded from indisposition or other cause rendering his presence impossible, but it was soon found that such time as the Recorder could give to each of the stations was utterly inadequate to the proper dispensation of justice, and that very great inconvenience would arise were the Court only to be open during the actual residence of the Recorder there. The proper remedy would, of course, have been a modification of the Charter by the appointment of an additional Judge, but this does not seem ever to have been thought of; or, if thought of for a moment, rejected on account of the expense.

It was, therefore, necessary to devise some other means of providing for the difficulty. A forced interpretation was put upon the last mentioned provision of the Charter, which had only been intended to be available in cases of urgent emergency, and advantage was taken of it to keep Courts open at Singapore and Malacca, at the same time that the Recorder was actually holding his Courts at Penang. From this it followed that, though provision had only been made by the Charter for one Court, three Courts had grown up in the Straits; different Courts to all intents and purposes, except in so far as they all enjoyed one common name, had a concurrent jurisdiction in the different stations; and that the Courts at Singapore and Malacca were occasionally, once or twice in the year, favoured with a visit from the Recorder, who ordinarily officiated as Judge in the Court at Penang. They had each their Judge and their establishment of Registrar (although only the Penang officer was honoured with that title), Clerks, Interpreter, Sheriff, Coroner, &c.

The new Court of Judicature was opened at Penang in August, 1827, in presence of the Governor, Mr. Fullerton, the Recorder, Sir John Thomas Claridge, and the Resident Councillor.

Shortly after the opening of the new Court, disputes to which we have already referred, arose between the Governor, Mr. Fullerton, and the Recorder, in regard to the charges of the Court Establishment, the Recorder's travelling expenses, and other subjects, which led to much unpleasant altercation between them, and were detrimental to the public interest, causing an interruption of the business of the Court, the Recorder at one time refusing to sit unless his views were adopted. He also refused to proceed on circuit to Singapore and Malacca, and, in consequence, after much delay, and its being at one time prosposed to send the prisoners from these two places to Penang for trial, Mr. Fullerton was obliged to proceed on circuit alone, and to hold Courts at Singapore and Malacca.

Sir John Claridge afterwards went on circuit; and in August, 1829, as he was on his way to Singapore, he received despatches recalling him to England to answer charges which had been preferred against him by the Court of Directors. Sir John immediately proceeded home, and the business of the Court was carried on by the Governor and Resident Councillors, the former making circuits for the purpose of holding Sessions of Oyer and Terminer at the different stations.

On the 29th June, 1830, the Straits Government was dissolved, and with it also terminated, for the time, the Court of Judicature, as then constituted, it being closed in consequence of the opinion entertained that the members of the Government having lost the official designations by which they are mentioned in the Charter, they could no longer act under that instrument.

Great inconvenience was felt from this suspension of the judicial power, and business transactions were much impeded, it being found that where goods were sold to the natives on credit, many were disposed to resist or delay payment knowing that the creditor had no means of enforcing his demands. At the request of a large proportion of the European merchants at Singapore, Mr. Murchison, the Resident, opened a Court, called the "Resident's Court," which remained in operation for some time, and tended much to facilitate business, but, in consequence of some misunderstanding between the Resident and the inhabitants on the subject of raising a fund for the payment of a night watch (which we mentioned as occurring in the year 1830), the Resident closed his Court, and the inhabitants were left without any mode of obtaining redress.

The inhabitants both in Penang and Singapore met and petitioned Parliament on the subject, setting forth the serious effects produced on commerce by the want of the Court, as well as the injustice inflicted in there being no means of bringing to trial persons who had been committed for offences, many of whom had lain in jail for a long time. These petitions were sent home, but in the meantime the Court of Directors having resolved to continue the old Charter, they, in order to remove all doubts, ordered that the Resident at Singapore should be designated Governor, and that the Deputy Residents at the different stations should be called Resident Councillors. The Court was again re-established, and a Recorder, Sir Benjamin Malkin, arrived in the beginning of 1833.

The following were the subsequent Recorders of the Court of the incorporated Settlements. Sir Benjamin Heath Malkin, February, 1833, afterwards Chief Justice at Calcutta. Sir Edward John Gambier, June, 1835, afterwards Chief Justice at Madras. Sir William Norris, September, 1836. Sir Christopher Rawlinson, August, 1847, who succeeded Sir E. Gambier as Chief Justice at Madras. Sir William Jeffcott, February, 1850, who died at Penang on 22nd October, 1855. The Court was then divided into two Recorderships, at Penang and Singapore. Sir Richard Bolton McCausland was Recorder of Singapore and Malacca in 1856, and Sir Peter Benson Maxwell, Recorder of Penang in the same year. Sir R. McCausland retired in 1866 and Sir Benson Maxwell was Recorder of Singapore and Malacca, Sir William Hackett succeeding him at Penang.

On the 15th May, 1834, Mr. Bonham, the Resident Councillor suggested the re-introduction of the Gambling Farm, he said:—"I need scarcely remark that I should not venture on this suggestion were I not thoroughly convinced of the total impracticability of suppressing the vice. This from many years experience in the police office at this Settlement, and from a close intercourse with the natives engendered by a residence among them from nearly the very first formation of the place, I conscientiously believe impossible." Of course it was not done.

On the 1st September, Mr. Montgomery applied for a piece of ground at Blakan Mati to form docks, and soon after Mr. W. S. Lorrain for Messrs. Douglas, Mackenzie & Co., applied for land at Sandy Point for a similar purpose. That firm had houses at Canton, Singapore and Batavia, but in 1837 was confined to Batavia alone. Mr. Lorrain had been the manager in Singapore. He was afterwards a partner in Brown & Co., Penang.

In the whole week ending 8th May, only one vessel arrived at Singapore, a Dutch brig from Samarang and Rhio. This was noticed in the newspaper at the time, and is a curious comparison with the present days. The total number of square-rigged vessels entering Singapore during the year was 517, of 156,513 tons. The total revenue for the year was equivalent to $131,687, and the expenditure to $112,836. The total quantity of gambier was entered as piculs 10,549, of the value of $16,609. In the following year, 1835, it was piculs 13,624 for $16,786, about $1.20 a picul. The population in 1834 was 26,329, the population having trebled in the preceding ten years.

In June, Mr. Church, who was acting Governor, proposed to assist the revenue by levying dues on the shipping. It was not carried out.

In October the Governor-General turned the ruling authority back again, and Mr. Bonham resumed charge as Acting Governor, superseding Mr. Church. A series of "perplexing changes," as they were called at the time. Mr. Church had been in Malacca, though Acting Governor of the Straits.

It was in this year that Captain Begbie published his book at Madras, printed at the Mission Press there. He was an artillery officer, and accompanied, as has been said, the first expedition to Naning, of which he wrote an account published in a pamphlet in Malacca. His book contains an account of the second expedition. While he was in Malacca he searched into the old Dutch records there, which filled six large chests, and like Captain Newbold collected a quantity of information about the Malay Peninsula, the relations of Siam with the Malay States, the rulers and government of the various countries from Kedah to Lingga, the natural history of the country, and much other matter. The book had several pictures of views in the Straits and some charts which are of use as showing the names and position of places which are now called by other names. The book is now very rare, but is of value as a record of matter that cannot probably be found elsewhere. The Singapore newspapers for 1835 contained long extracts from the book, but did not consider it of much value, nor very correct.

CHAPTER XXI.

The Roman Catholic Church.

THE first Roman Catholic Missionary who seems to have visited Singapore was the Rev. Mr. Imbert, who being on his way to China in 1821 had been asked by the Bishop of Siam to obtain information about the state of religion in the new settlement. He remained a week, and wrote to Bishop Florens that there were only twelve or thirteen Catholics in Singapore, who led a wretched life.

M. Laurent Marie Joseph Imbert, of Aix in Provence, of the Société des Missions Etrangères had left France on 20th March, 1820, the 278th Priest sent out to the Far East since the commencement of the Society. In 1837 he was made Bishop of Corea, where he was tortured and beheaded by the Natives on 21st September, 1839, at 42 years of age.

A Native Priest of Malacca, called Padre Jacob, visited Singapore about 1822 and obtained a site from Sir Stamford Raffles to build a Roman Catholic place of worship (see the Gazette of 6th September, 1832), but there is nothing to shew that even a small shed was erected.

The Bishop of Siam was the Superior of the Mission at Penang but there were few missionaries there, and one could not be spared for Singapore. In 1824 the Catholics in Singapore wrote to the Bishop to send a Priest, but he, fearing he might be said to have no jurisdiction in the place, applied on 22nd September, 1827, to the Sacred Congregation of the Propagation of the Faith in Rome, which had been established by Pope Gregory XV. on 22nd July, 1622, and a decree was sent in the name of Pope Leo XII. giving him jurisdiction. The correspondence is, of course, in Latin.

In the meantime a Portuguese Priest named Francisco da Silva Pinto e Maia had come from Goa, where he had been sent from Macao for some explanations about his duties. It appears from an advertisement in the *Free Press* on 23rd May, 1838, in which he offered to give lessons gratis in Latin, &c., that he had been educated in Portugal; and in September, 1845, the *Singapore Free Press* stated that he had resided in Singapore since 1826, and had been made a Knight of the Order of Christ by the Queen of Portugal. He stopped and established himself in Singapore as the Catholic Pastor of the place.

In 1831 Bishop Bruguière, the Coadjutor Bishop of Siam, passed on his way from Siam to Penang. M. Barthelemy Bruguière, of Carcassonne in Languedoc, left France on 5th February, 1826, for the Mission at Siam. In 1830 he was Bishop of Corea, and died at Sivang in Tartary, after a very exhausting voyage of three years, on 20th October, 1835, at the age of 38 years, before he could take up the mission.

He called on Padre Maia and showed him the Decree of the Sacred Congregation of 1827, by which spiritual jurisdiction was given to him in Singapore as the Vicar Apostolic of Siam. Padre Maia acknowledged the Decree to be authentic, but afterwards declined to admit that the Bishop had any jurisdiction; which led to what Singapore looked on as a continually recurring, and, to the Protestants most amusing, contention . between the French and the Portuguese Clergy in Singapore, which was only ended in 1886. Mr. Earl said in his book (in 1837) " The head of the Portuguese Church is an Apostolic Vicar under the diocese of Goa. He is extremely jealous of the French Jesuits [Mr. Earl was wrong in this, there were not, and have not been, any Jesuit Clergy in Singapore] who have drawn from him the greater part of his flock, and he is in the habit of making protests against their performance of religious rights by advertisements in the newspapers, which however are perfectly unheeded by the missionaries. Two only of the latter are established in the town, but it is occasionally visited by others from Cochin–China, Siam, and other parts of Eastern Asia."

The ecclesiatical dispute was by no means confined to Singapore, it was much more warmly carried on in Ceylon, Bombay, and other places in India. Similar trouble had occurred in Africa, in regard to the Spanish priesthood. The Pope by the Bull *Inter Cætera*, dated 4th May 1493 (issued between the first and second voyages of Christopher Columbus) had in the old days given the Portuguese Church jurisdiction on the eastern side of an imaginary line drawn from the North to the South pole, and on the western side of that line to the Spanish Church, but it was found that the Portuguese ecclesiastical authorities had not the means to carry out the work of the Church in India and China, for which purpose the exclusive authority had been given. Macao, for example, and Goa, had never risen to the opportunity, and in Singapore there was neither a Church nor a School.

In the time of Pope Leo XII (1829-31), jurisdiction was given in Singapore to the Bishop of Siam, the head in that part of the world of the French Société des Missions Etrangères. The Portuguese Priests demurred to this, as they considered that the Pope could not derogate from the authority given long before to the Sovereign of Portugal, and the Portuguese and French Priests each denied the authority of the other. To make matters still more involved, a Spanish priest called Padre Yegros came from Goa, asserting that he had the ecclesiastical jurisdition in Singapore, and the two Churches already on the spot denied his authority and he in turn denied theirs.

Padre Maia then celebrated Mass in Dr. d'Almeida's house in Beach Road; the French Bishop in Mr. McSwiney's house opposite the present Church in Brass Bassa Road, at the corner of Queen Street; and Padre Yegros in some other house.

On the 24th April, 1838, Pope Gregory XVI declared by his celebrated Bull, *Multa Prœclaré*, (the authenticity of which was acknowledged at the time by the British authorities and the East India Company in London and Madras to be beyond question) that for good reasons the right claimed by the Portuguese did not exist in the Crown, in countries not subject to Portugal. In 1862 Pope Pius IX made a Concordat with the King of Portugal by which the right of patronage over the Roman Catholic Church in British India was acknowledged to be in the Crown of Portugal, but the French Church argued that as it was given on certain conditions which had not been fulfilled, it had no effect.

The result of this, as Mr. Earl wrote, was the publication of long advertisements in the *Singapore Free Press* which died away for a time, and woke up again at intervals for many years, until 1886 in fact, when the whole matter was finally set at rest by a long Concordat by Pope Leo XIII., dated Rome, 23rd June, 1886, which gave ordinary jurisdiction to the French Mission, but exempted from it the jurisdiction over the Portuguese Congregation only and the premises actually occupied by the Portuguese Clergy, which was given to the Bishop of Macao. That Portugal should have strenuously striven for her own side was not to be wondered at; and the result has been that all has since worked with great harmony in Singapore for the good of both the communities. Besides that Concordat there was issued a Bull *Humanœ Salutis Auctor* dated 1st September, 1886, a purely ecclesisatical document dealing with the jurisdiction.

Bishop Bruguière left Singapore for China, leaving the Rev. Mr. Clemenceau, who had lately arrived from France, in charge of the Church. The Rev. Pierre Julien Marc Clemenceau, of Poitiers in Poitou, left France on 4th July, 1831, worked 32 years in the Mission of Siam, and died at Bangkok, at the age of 58 years, on 18th January, 1864, having suffered from leprosy in the latter years of his life.

The Rev. Mr. Boucho (afterwards the Bishop) then came to Singapore. M. Jean Baptiste Boucho, of Bayonne in Gascony, left France on 11th January, 1824; he was made Bishop of Atalie in 1845, and died at Penang on 6th March, 1871, at the age of 75 years, after working in the Mission in the Straits for 47 years.

He was able to arrive at an understanding with Padre Yegros to labour amicably in the Church until matters should be authoritatively settled.

On 18th October, 1832, Mr. Bonham, the Resident Councillor, set aside the piece of ground in Brass Bassa Road (now occupied by the Brothers School) for the site of a Catholic place of worship, saying that no quit-rent would be charged as long as it was used for the purpose of religious instruction. The letter was addressed to the Rev. J. B. Boucho and Anselmo Yegros. In November, 1832, Father Boucho and Padre Yegros signed a Circular, stating the need of a decent place of worship, the want of means of their own congregations, and asking for help from the community.

At this time the Rev. Mr. Courvezy was Vicar. M. Jean Paul Hilaire Michel Courvezy, of Carcassonne in Languedoc, left France on 12th March, 1832, for the Siam Mission, became Bishop in 1834, and left the Society in 1845. He died in 1857.

In the newspaper of 11th December appeared the following notice :—After a lapse of many years, the Catholics of Singapore have become desirous of possessing a Church for the celebration of Divine Service, and have been grieved for the want of such. Divine Providence has, at length, come to their aid. Through the medium of an open subscription towards this object, the greatest part of the obstacle has been surmounted. On Sunday last, the 9th inst, we enjoyed the consolation of solemnizing and laying the first stone of an edifice which is being erected for the glory of the true God, upon a spot of ground granted by the bounty of the Government, and which, according to the contract with the builder, is to be finished on the 5th of May, 1833. That it will not be large, is our only regret; but it will suffice. Moreover, the Church of our Lord Jesus Christ usually consists of small communities. The first desire of our hearts, under these circumstances, is to express, publicly, our gratitude to those persons who have, with good will taken a part in the above-mentioned subscription. May they enjoy in their conscience those delicious sentiments which accompany the performance of a good action, and may God grant them a recompense, by shedding over them the blessings of His goodness and mercy. This letter will not prevent us from testifying our acknowledgements to each subscriber individually when we can have the honour of a visit. We would voluntarily publish their names, but we fear to offend their modesty and delicacy.

Receive, Mr. Editor, the renewed duty of our respect and regard.

A. Yegros, Superior of the Portuguese Mission, Judicial Vicar, and Delegate of the Chapter of Goa.

H. Courvezy, Apostolic Missionary, Canon of Chartres, and Parish Minister of Singapore.

The result was a subscription of about $450, largely collected among the merchants. There are the names of Mr. Bonham, A. L. Johnston, John Purvis, Connolly, Cunningham, Melany, and Napier. Padre Maia, to his praise be it said, appears as a subscriber for $20, and $145 was subscribed by the Chinese.

A little Chapel, sixty feet long and thirty feet wide only, was put up in the centre of the land. When the new Church was afterwards built, the Chapel was used for the first Boys School in 1852. It cost about $700. There is a copy of the contract with a Chinese, for the labour only, for $250; it was signed by the Vicar, the Rev. H. Courvezy, Padre Yegros, D. McSwiney, A. F. Francis, J. J. Woodford, and George Godfrey, on 5th December, 1832. On the 9th June, 1833, the Rev. Mr. Albrand being Vicar at the time, the Church was blessed and opened, and those who had signed the contract dined with the Vicar, the accounts were gone through, and it was found that Mr. McSwiney had paid out of his own pocket about $50 more than had been collected, which he added to his subscription; but some subscriptons not having been paid, it was thought that he might receive it eventually.

A small Parochial House, which stood at the corner of the compound at Brass Bassa Road and Queen Street, had also been built, of wood on brick pillars, at a cost of about $500, but this had been paid for at the joint expense of Father Albrand and the Missions Etrangères in equal shares.

The Rev. Etienne Raymond Albrand, of Gap in Dauphine, left France on 12th March, 1832. He died a Bishop at the age of 48 years, on 23rd April, 1853, at the capital of Kouy-tcheou, after having worked 21 years, first at Singapore and then at Siam.

In the beginning of 1833 the Rev. H. Courvezy went as Coadjutor to the Bishop at Siam, and Padre Yegros having no means at his disposal to live upon, left Singapore altogether and went to Manila. Father Albrand succeeded Father Courvezy as Vicar, and he really began the mission in Singapore, the little Chapel being completed a few months after his arrival. The Chinese members of the congregation rapidly increased, as they had much respect for him. No sooner was the Chapel approaching completion than Padre Maia fired off long Latin dissertations and lengthy letters of complaint to the newspaper.

In March, 1835, Father Albrand was moved to Siam. The Rev. Mr. Barbe was then appointed Vicar. M. Jean Pierre Barbe, of Tulle in Limousin, left France on 5th February, 1826, for the Mission of Siam; he afterwards was sent to Burmah, and died at Rangoon on 27th May, 1861, at the age of 59 years. He collected money to plaster the ceiling of the Chapel and to build a portico at the front entrance, which cost $198.50: this time the subscribers seem to have been all members of the congregation. Father Barbe only remained until the end of the year, and was succeeded by the Rev. Mr. Renier.

The Rev. Joseph Florentin Etienne Renier, of Chartres in Orleans, left France on 15th March, 1835, for the mission of Siam. He died at Moulmein, at the age of 60 years, on the 4th January, 1871, having been in the Straits and Burmah for 36 years. The name is spelt Regnier in the Register of the Missionaries, but his signature in the Church baptismal registers is spelt Renier. He raised a subscription to pave the floor with Malacca tiles, as the white ants had eaten the plank floor which had been put down for economy. There was never any spire or tower to this building.

In August, 1837, the Rev. Mr. Galabert was appointed Vicar, and remained until December, 1839, when he left for Bourbon, because Bishop Courvezy then came to Singapore intending to remain permanently.

The Rev. Noel Alexandre Galabert, of Carcassonne in Languedoc, left France on 22nd April, 1833, and quitted the Society (according to the register of members) in 1835. But this must be a mistake, and Father Beurel's book must be correct, as the old baptismal register in the Church has Father Galabert's signatures in the year 1839.

Bishop Courvezy was alone in Singapore till February, 1839, when the Rev. Mr. Galy came from Macao.

The Rev. Jean Paul Galy, of Toulouse in Languedoc, left France on 15th May, 1838. He was for many years in Tongking and Cochin-China. In 1841 he was beaten, put in a cage and condemned to death, but after a detention of 22 months, he recovered his liberty by the intervention of the commander of a French man-of-war which visited the place. He died on 15th October, 1869, at Saigon, 59 years of age.

In June 1839, a Chinese Catholic Priest named John Tschu came from Siam. He was born in the Province of Canton of a respectable Chinese family, his father being a literate Mandarin. He had been sent when young, by a French Missionary, to the college in Penang, and after doing mission work there, he was sent to open another mission in Siam which became very flourishing, and he was ordained in Siam in 1838 by Dr. Courvezy, who appointed him head of the Chinese mission in Singapore. He died on the 13th July, 1848, to the great loss of the mission, after working nine years in Singapore, and having formed a flourishing and numerous congregation of Chinese, who were much attached to him. The *Singapore Free Press* contained an account of his life, from which the above particulars are taken, and said that his loss was much felt by the Roman Catholic Community. He was buried in the Church at the altar of St. Joseph, where a granite stone was placed over his tomb. When the new Church was built, the coffin was opened and the bones were placed in the St. Joseph Chapel in the new Church, and a marble slab with an inscription was put on the side wall.

On the 29th October, 1837, two missionaries intended for the Mission at Siam arrived from France, and Mr. Galy went to Macao, expecting to penetrate into Cochin-China to which he had been first destined by the Directors of the Mission in Paris. One of those two missionaries was the Rev. J. M. Beurel, to whom the Roman Catholic Community of Singapore owe an incalculable debt of gratitude. Dr. Courvezy arranged for Father Beurel to remain in Singapore, and his companion, the Rev. A. Dupond, went on to Siam. In this year, 1839, the compound of the Chapel was surrounded with a wall, built partly at Bishop Courvezy's expense and partly by subscriptions he raised among the Catholic Community.

The Rev. Jean Marie Beurel, of St. Brieuc in Brittany, left France on 28th April, 1839, and was in the Mission at Singapore for 30 years. He left Singapore on 4th December, 1868, and went to Paris, ill with paralysis, and died there, at the age of 60 years, on 3rd October 1872, after four years illness.

A pastoral letter was addressed on 6th October, 1840, by Dr. Courvezy to the congregation regarding the feasts and fasts to be observed in the Mission, having regard to the different conditions of life in this climate, on which account the Pope had granted certain modifications. It also provided for the day of observance of some of the greater feasts to take place on the Sunday following the day of the feast.

On 3rd January, 1840, the Mission of Siam was sub-divided, owing to the difficulty of communication with Siam, and the different language used in the Malay Peninsula. Dr. John Paul Hilary Michael Courvezy was appointed Vicar Apostolic of the new division of the Malay Peninsula, and his Coadjutor Dr. Pallegoix became Bishop of Siam alone.

From the first establishment in 1832 to the end of 1839 there had been in the congregation 130 baptisms, 64 deaths, and 20 marriages. The whole of the expenses has been met by the collections made every Sunday at the Parochial Mass, and by subscriptions occasionally circulated in the congregation, chiefly at Christmas, Easter and Corpus Christi.

Bishop Courvezy proposed to enlarge the Chapel by adding transepts to form a cross, but adopted Father Beurel's proposal to endeavour to raise funds to build a new Church and to use the Chapel for a school.

An appeal was issued on 23rd April, 1840, drawn up by the Bishop in French, and translated into English by Lieut. Jerningham of H. M. S. *Wellesley* which was here at the time, stating that the Chapel was much too small, and in bad repair, and asking for subscriptions towards a new building. In the succeeding four years $5,105.72 was collected, chiefly among the European community, though belonging (as Father Beurel wrote) to Protestantism. In 1841 Queen Amelia of France gave 4000 francs, and the Bishop of Manila about $3000 in 1842, which latter sum was left by the Bishop in the hands of the Armenian Merchants, Seth Brothers, who failed, and only $215 was eventually recovered.

The congregation thought the loss was owing to the want of care by the Bishop, and it unfortunately became the cause of very considerable trouble in the congregation and of delay in commencing the building, and also to Father Beurel going away to Burmah, to work with his friend Bishop Bigandet there, in November 1842, owing to a misunderstanding with the Bishop on this subject, and not returning until April, 1843, when he came back at the earnest request of the congregation who had addressed letters to the Superior in Paris, and to Dr. Boucho in Penang, pointing out the great loss to the Church if Father Beurel did not return.

Before he left he had asked Governor Bonham for land for the new Church, and Mr. Bonham offered four acres of ground on the slope of Government Hill between the Cemetery and the Convict Lines, which would be near where the American Methodist School and St Andrews House and the Masonic Lodge are now. This would have been very suitable (as Father Beurel wrote) for all the buildings, such as schools and dwelling house, but Bishop Courvezy rejected it.

An application was them made in writing for the ground opposite the row of three houses in Brass Bassa Road between Victoria Street and Queen Street, then occupied by Messrs. Caldwell at the corner of Victoria Street, Cunningham in the centre, and McSwiney at the corner of Queen Street. The application was accompanied by a commendatory letter signed by many of the leading Protestants, including Messrs. George Armstrong, J. Balestier, E. Boustead, W. S. Duncan, J. Guthrie, J. Purvis, W. Napier, W. and T. Scott, and Maclaine Fraser & Co. After some trouble, as the Government at first wanted to give only a small piece of ground, the present site was given on 20th July, 1842, being 211 feet by 313, (which was afterwards added to) on the condition that it was not to be used as a Burial Ground on any occasion whatever, and that no buildings should be erected upon it except for ecclesiastical purposes connected with the Chapel. The term was 999 years.

Mr. J. T. Thomson made a plan which was approved by the Governor, but it was afterwards superseded by one made by Mr. McSwiney, as being less expensive and easier to keep in repair.

On Sunday, the 18th June, 1843, the foundation stone of the Church was laid. The following is an account of the ceremony in the *Free Press*:—" On Sunday last the Catholic community of Singapore had the gratification of witnessing the solemn ceremony of blessing and laying the " Corner Stone " of their new Church of the " Good Shepherd." It began at half past six a.m. The congregation being assembled in the present chapel, the Right Revd. D. D. Hillary Courvezy, robed in his Pontificals, proceeded in procession to the spot, where the Church is to be raised. The procession was formed by a Cross-bearer, two acolytes and nine children, all robed in white; by the Wardens and Trustees of the Church, with their insignia; by the Architect Mr. D. L. McSwiney, carrying a Silver Trowel; John Connolly, Esq., the gentleman appointed to lay the Corner Stone; and the Right Revd. Dr. Hillary Courvezy supported by the Revd. J. M. Beurel and the Chinese Clergyman the Revd. John Tschu, followed by the rest of the faithful. His Lordship the Bishop, being on the spot, addressed the assembly in a brief but very impressive and edifying discourse, explaining why the place where a Temple is to be erected to Almighty God ought to be blessed and sanctified by prayer, and thanking God for the various donations received from charitable persons, which had enabled the Catholic community to begin such an undertaking, &c.

"After the discourse, the Right Revd. Doctor performed the prescribed religious ceremony. When the corner stone was blessed, it was carried by two Chinese Christians from the Altar erected for the occasion to the left corner of the frontispiece of the proposed edifice. Then the Revd. J. M. Beurel read in an audible voice the following inscription :—

To the Greater Glory and Honour
Of the Holy and Undivided Trinity.
In the year of our Redemption

MDCCCXLIII.

On the Feast of Corpus Christi.
The Eighteenth day of June;
In the thirteenth year of the Pontificate
Of our Holy Father

GREGORY THE SIXTEENTH ;

In the sixth year of the happy reign
Of Her Most Gracious Majesty

VICTORIA,

Queen of Great Britain and Ireland;
In the thirteenth year of the reign
Of His Christian Majesty

LOUIS PHILLIPE,

King of the French;
And during the Governorship of
The Honourable SAMUEL GEORGE BONHAM.
In the presence and with the approbation
Of the Right Revd. D. D. Hilary Courvezy,
Bishop of Bidopolis, and
Vicar Apostolic, &c., &c., of the Malay Peninsula,
Of the Revd. John M. Beurel, M. Ap.,
Of the Wardens and Trustees of the Church,
And of the Architect Denis McSwiney,
John Connolly, Esq.
Laid the Corner Stone of this Church,
Which is to be dedicated to
Our Divine Saviour
Under the title of
"The Good Shepherd,"
Complete, O Lord, this undertaking
And when completed, protect it."

"This inscription was translated into five other languages, viz., into Latin, French, Portuguese, Chinese and Malay and signed by Dr. Courvezy, Revd. J. M. Beurel, John Connolly, D. L. McSwiney, by the Wardens and Trustees of the Church and some other gentlemen. These documents together with British, French, Spanish, and various other coins, and a copy of the *Singapore Free Press*, the *Straits Messenger*, the *Bengal Catholic Herald*, the *Madras Catholic Expositor*, &c., were put into vases which were deposited in a place beneath the corner stone, prepared for their reception. Immediately after, the corner stone was laid by John Connolly, with the approbation of His Lordship the Bishop, that gentleman reciting at the same time the following prescribed prayer:— 'In the faith of Jesus Christ we lay this first stone in this foundation in the name of the Father and of the Son and of the Holy Ghost; that the true faith and the fear of God and fraternal charity may flourish here and that this place be dedicated to prayer and to invoke and praise the name of our Lord Jesus Christ, who liveth and reigneth with the Father and the Son and the Holy Ghost, world without end. Amen.'

"The remainder of the ceremony being performed the procession returned to the old Chapel in the same order in which it had first proceeded to the site of the intended Church, when the Bishop ascended the altar and celebrated a Pontifical High Mass."

On the 21st December, 1843, Bishop Courvezy left for France and did not return to Singapore, and the Rev. J. B. Boucho, the Pro-vicar Apostolic, became Superior of the Mission, after he had been twenty years in the Straits. Father Beurel at this time paid a visit to Malacca, and made arrangements to have a Chapel established there, on the site of which the present Church now stands.

In 1844, a further amount of $2,557.80 was raised by subscriptions in Singapore for the new building, and unexpectedly $1,467 was received from the Directors of the Seminary of Foreign Missions in Paris who had heard of the loss of the $3,000, which had caused so much trouble.

Governor Butterworth, on Mr. Beurel's application explaining that the land given for the Church was smaller than was necessary to provide against buildings being erected close to the Church, and so occasioning disturbance to the services, increased the land by making it a square of 313 feet.

In 1845 the Rev. P. Galy went to Bourbon to collect subscriptions for the church building, and brought back nearly $1,000 after paying the expenses of the voyage. In August about $800 was collected in the congregation to build the steeple, and in the same month Mr. Boucho was appointed Bishop, which greatly pleased the congregation. The ceiling of the old Chapel fell in immediately after service on the feast of the Epiphany and several persons were hurt, but not seriously. There were only a few persons remaining in the Church, or the accident would have been very serious.

The Rev. John Baptist Boucho went to Calcutta by the steamer *Fire Queen* in September, 1845, and was consecrated there as Bishop of Athalia and Vicar Apostolic of the Malayan Peninsula, and arrived at Singapore on 25th May, 1846.

In June Father Beurel wrote to the Government asking for the lease to be issued for the Church compound in the name of Bishop

Boucho and himself, saying that it was called the Church of the Good Shepherd, at Father Beurel's wish. In 1846, Father Beurel went to Manila and China to collect money for the Church building, as all the funds were exhausted and the Church was not finished. He collected about $1,800.

In this year the Chapel was built at Bukit Timah for the Chinese congregation, and was called St Joseph at Father Beurel's wish. The Rev. Mr. Manduit was the priest, and he went to live permanently among the Chinese when the building was completed about the end of the year. The Rev. Anatole Manduit, of Coutances in Normandy, left France on 26th December, 1843, and died, 41 years of age, in Singapore, after fifteen years work among the Chinese, on 1st April, 1858. He was buried in the Church at Bukit Timah where there is a lengthy inscription on the granite stone over his grave.

The *Free Press* of 23rd April, 1846, contained the following :— " The Rev. Gentlemen of the Catholic Mission, to whose care we are indebted for the conversion of so many Chinese, are trying to raise beyond Bukit Timah a small Chapel, on a spot liberally granted to them by the local Authorities, from whom they have always experienced kindness, particularly from his Honor the Governor. This chapel is to be solely used for the Chinese Converts. They would like to request the kind assistance of all the friends of civilisation here to enable them to carry out their intention properly; but they feel rather backward in introducing the subject as they have already called once or twice on the charity of the public for their New Church. Yet they would feel very thankful, if some charitable persons would enable them to raise a substantial and respectable building, instead of one of planks and attaps, which they are compelled to do now from want of means."

In April, 1847, the Rev. Mr. Issaly came to Singapore and took the place of Father Manduit at Bukit Timah.

The Rev. Marie Francois Adolphe Issaly, of St Brieuc in Brittany, left France on 21st October, 1846, and died in the Procure House in Hongkong, where he had gone because he was ill, on 27th May, 1874, at the age of 52 years, after 28 years work in the Straits. He was first buried in Hongkong. In March, 1879, his remains were exhumed and were buried in the Church of SS. Peter and Paul in Singapore.

In June, 1846, the new Church was nearly completed and Bishop Boucho being unable to come to Singapore from Penang, the ceremony of opening the Church fell on Father Beurel, who was accompanied by the Revs. Manduit, Issaly and John Tschu. It took place at 7 a.m. on Sunday the 6th June. The corner stone had been blessed by Bishop Courvezy; the Cross on the top of the steeple by Bishop Pallegoix; and the whole building was now blessed by him who had, through his unceasing efforts, caused it to be erected. There was a procession outside and inside the new Church, where Psalms were sung, followed by a procession to the old Chapel for removing the Holy Sacrament from there to the new Church; and a sermon by Father Beurel.

The accounts kept, in the most methodical method possible, by Father Beurel, show that the total expense of the building, from the making of the plan and laying the foundations to the completion of the building and the furniture, was $17,128.76, and $1,206.46 was remitted to Paris for all the candlesticks, some vestments, the statue of the Virgin, and numerous ornaments for the service of the Church. The total payments amounting to $18,335.22, which left a debt on the building of $4,434.50.

The total receipts were $13,900.72, which was all collected in Singapore including the interest received upon it, except the following sums; from Bourbon, $1,200; Calcutta, $412.83; Manila, $2,310 60 (which included the $1,467 that had been received from the Mission in Paris on account of the loss by Seth Brothers) and from Siam $100.

Mr. Connolly advanced $1,800 to complete the urgent payments for the construction, and it was decided to repay this and the balance (for which Father Beurel became the only person responsible) out of the pew rents and collections; and he wrote to Queen Amelia and the ministry in France, asking for money to help to pay the debt, but owing to the political revolution, the only answer received was from the Minister of the Interior to say that he would, if possible, obtain a picture of the Good Shepherd for the Church, which Father Beurel had asked for, but this never came. Mr. McSwiney, the Architect, left Singapore in October, 1847. Soon after this Messrs. Cunningham and Connolly built the two gates of the compound in Victoria Street at their own expense and a subscription was made to complete the large front steps and drains round the Church. The Steeple had been erected from a design by Mr. Charles Dyce, and a subscription amounting to $700 had been made towards it.

In 1845 the Chinese Congregation made a subscription to erect a house in the School compound where religious instruction might be given to the Chinese. The cost was $700.

In the beginning of 1858 Father Beurel established canonically the Way of the Cross in the Church. The pictures were oil paintings, and cost about $250; Mr. Benjamin De Souza promised to pay for them. The statues of the Good Shepherd, St. Joseph, St. Peter, and St. Paul were also received from Paris at the same time as the pictures. The first cost $40, and was given by Mr. Cunningham; and that of St. Peter, $35, by Mr. Blanco. In August Mr. L. Cateaux, of Messrs. Hinnekindt's firm, gave the picture of the Martyrdom of St. Sebastian, which had been painted by Mr. Jules Pecher of Antwerp, who had gained a gold medal for it at the Brussels Exhibition. Mr. Cateaux gave it on the condition that if the Church should at any time pass to any other body than that of the Mission, the priests should remove it and place it in one of their own Churches.

In 1859 the Parochial House was completed, which was considered a great event in the Roman Catholic Community. Father Beurel had made a contract with a Chinaman to build it for $2,500, which the Congregation undertook to subscribe. The result was that it nearly ruined Father Beurel, as he writes, for he had the not unusual experience in Singapore of finding that it cost very much more before he could get it finished, for it cost $8,100.55 when it was done; and it is amusing to read in Father Beurel's Annals, that he "had a great deal to suffer from this Chinaman, who acted the part of a first rate hypocrite and rogue."

In 1860 the Church was paved with marble, got from Antwerp through Mr. L. Cateaux. Some of it turned out to be very inferior, and some of the congregation said it was mere trash and not fit to be seen in the Church, which caused more trouble to Father Beurel, as some of the congregation declined to subscribe. The cost of the marble, and the Font and other things came to $1,986.17 which was raised by subscription; three Chinese members of the Congregation, Pedro No Kea and two others, giving $200 each, Mr. J. Woodford $300, and others subscribing handsomely.

In 1888 the building, now made the Cathedral, was considerably enlarged, being extended at the west end.

When Bishop Boucho died he was succeeded by Bishop Michel Esther Le Terdu, of St. Brieuc in Brittany. He had left France for the Straits on 10th April, 1850. He resided at Penang. He died in the Seminary at Paris, a few weeks after he arrived in France, having gone home ill, after 27 years work in the Straits, on 10th May, 1877, at 51 years of age. He wrote a Catechism and several books of devotion. He had been Parish Priest at Pulo Tikus at Penang, and was consecrated in the church there by Bishop Bigandet. He came to Singapore on 3rd July, 1871, and resided there.

He was succeeded by Mgr. Edward Gasnier, of Angers in Anjou. He had left France on 19th July, 1857, to the mission at Mayssour (Bangalore) in Southern India and came to the Straits as Bishop in 1878. He died in Singapore, after several years illness and a voyage to France in search of health, on 8th April, 1896, and was buried in front of the High Altar in the Cathedral of the Good Shepherd. By an Ordinance of 15 November, 1885, the Bishop was then designated "The Titular Roman Catholic Bishop of Malacca resident in the Straits Settlements."

Bishop Gasnier, to whom the Congregation were very much attached, had a thorough knowledge of English which was a great advantage to the community. He was succeeded by Mgr. Michel Marie Fée, of Laval in Maine, who left France on 16th April, 1879.

Mention should be made here of Bishop Bigandet, as he was well known in the Straits, though he was never Bishop in the diocese. Paul Ambroise Bigandet of Besancon in Franche Comte, left France on 12th June, 1837, and was in Siam until 1842 when he came to the Straits, being principally at Penang, and remained until 1856, when he went to Burmah as Apostolic Administrator and in 1870 was made Bishop of Burmah.

In Volumes, 4, 6, 7, 8, 9, and 11 of Logan's Journal are many lengthy papers by Mr. Bigandet on the subject of the Budhist Monks or Talapoins, the Legend of Budha, and the dialects of Siam and Burmah.

When Father Beurel died he was succeeded as Vicar by the Rev. Louis Armand Daguin, of Séez in Normandy, who left France on 15th July, 1860, and was 26 years in the Straits. He died at Paris on 5th June, 1886, at the age of 50 years, having gone home on account of illness.

He was succeeded by the Rev. Jean Pierre Rêmes, of Bayonne in Gascony, who left France on the same day with Father Daguin in 1860. He returned to France on account of illness in 1888, and is now the Superior of the Sanatorium of the Mission at Mombeton in Tarn and Garonne in France, which had been installed there in 1886.

The next Vicar was Father Elysee Ferdinand Delouette, of Rheims in Champagne, who left France on 3rd July, 1872. He died in Singapore on the 29th March, 1897, and was buried in the Church of St. Joseph at Bukit Timah.

He was followed by the Rev. Christophe Mazery, of Nantes in Brittany, who left France on 15th March, 1868. He died in Singapore on 12th February, 1900, and was buried in the same Church at Bukit Timah. His successor, the present Vicar is the Rev. Henri Pierre Rivet, of Nantes in Brittany, who left France on 2nd August, 1882, and was appointed Vicar in February, 1900.

A remarkable character in Singapore was the Rev. Pierre Pâris, who was born on 19th January, 1822, at Fontenis, Haute-Saone, and was a peasant boy working in the fields, which was no doubt a good preparation for the work he afterwards did in Singapore, where he spent long hours trudging about in the jungle between the different huts of his congregation. He went into the priesthood, commencing to learn Latin at eighteen years of age, and after being a vicar in a country parish for four years joined the Society of Foreign Missions in 1854. On 27th June, 1855, he left Antwerp for the Straits. After a short time in Penang he went to Malacca, where he learnt the patois spoken by the Portuguese there, and Tamil and Chinese. He was a good linguist, speaking several dialects of Chinese. As an example of the way he used to move about, he might be seen on Sunday morning walking into town along Serangoon Road, for there were no jinrikishas then, with his Chinese umbrella in one hand and a stick in the other. He had said mass and preached in Chinese at Serangoon, and was walking seven miles into town to hold the service in Tamil at eleven o'clock. After that he would hold a service in the jail; at 2 o'clock he had Catechism for the Chinese children, and at 3 o'clock evening service in the Chinese Church of S.S. Peter and Paul. It had been through his exertions that this fine Church had been built in the town in 1871, to which Pedro No Kia had subscribed very liberally.

On Monday he rested in the Parochial House and read the papers, &c., and saw Chinese who came to consult him about their affairs. Tuesday he spent in trudging about the jungle, resting from time to time in the huts of the Chinese whom he went to visit. Wednesday he spent among the Chinese in the town. Thursday he remained at home at Serangoon teaching the Catechumens, who used to come long distances to him, having three rooms in which were large pictures sent by Chinese from Shanghai. In each room there was a catechist speaking one of the three Chinese dialects which Father Pâris knew. The last two days of the week were given to confessions, &c., and he was sometimes so engaged from the morning until late at night, for there was a very large Chinese congregation. Everyone knew Father Pâris with his stick and his Chinese umbrella. From 1874 he was Pro-vicar of the Mission. He died at the age of· 61 years, on 23rd May, 1883, in the Parochial House, Singapore, after six months illness, having been very feeble for some time. He was buried in the Church of S.S. Peter and Paul, having worked in the Straits for 28 years.

On the 23rd April, 1866, being St. George's Day, the Rev. J. M. Beurel held a Meeting with the object of establishing a Society to be called the St. George Singapore Catholic Young Men's Society. He was the President, the Rev. A. L. Daguin and Mr. F. E. Pereira the lawyer, who had a large practice at that time, were Vice-Presidents, and the Committee consisted of Messrs. Paul Brasier; J. J. Woodford, W. Lecerf, L. C. Masfen, J. F. Hansen, W. J. Valberg, L. J. Scheerder H. D. Chopard, A. Pilliet, J. Cazalas, J. Eade, and G. Reutens. Twenty eight members joined on the first occasion. Monthly Meetings were held in the Parochial House. There was a Library for which papers and books were ordered from England. Papers used to be read on various subjects. Mr. J. J. Woodford gave three lectures with experiments on the Atmosphere. Mr. A. McIntyre read two papers, one on Perseverance. Mr. H. B. Woodford held forth on Intemperance, Mr. C. De Menzies on Education, and Father Beurel and Mr. F. E. Pereira each gave four addresses on various subjects. The minute book ends abruptly in June of the following year. It remained for Father Rivet, in 1900, to found a similar Club, in very good premises, and with many more members, now the Congregation has increased so much, with billiard tables and other amusements for the young men in the evenings, which are much more likely to continue to call them together than reading very long and scientific papers.

On 1st January, 1897, Monseigneur Zaleski, the Archbishop of Thebes, arrived in Singapore. It was the first time a visit of a Papal Delegate to Singapore took place, and he was received with great ceremony by the members of all the Romen Catholic Churches in Singapore. A joint address was presented to him by all the Churches including the Portuguese Church of St. Joseph. On 14th February, 1897, the Cathedral was consecrated by Bishop Fee. There is a rule that Churches cannot be consecrated as long as any debt remains on the building, and on 31st December, 1897, there was still a balance of $2,000 due after paying for the extension, which was paid by special subscriptions. In order to consecrate the Church some repairs and painting were necessary, costing $1,345.18 for which a further subscription was made, and the debt which had existed since the commencement of the building was finally paid off.

THE PROCURE.

On the 17th March, 1857, the Procure House was established in Singapore. Father Beurel had, until that time, done the work of Procureur as well as that of Missionary, but the administration of the Mission had become too large to admit of this being done satisfactorily.

The word Procureur in French means one who has power to act for another, as an agent or manager; and in the Religious Societies the word means one who has charge of their temporal concerns. In the large English Missionary Societies the clergy who do such work are usually called the Secretaries. The Procure Houses are also used as stopping places for the clergy passing from one diocese to another, or as resting places for invalids; and the money matters and general business affairs of the mission are transacted through the Procureur.

The Society had established a Procure House in Macao in 1732, which had been transferred in 1847 to Hongkong. Father Libois, of Séez in Normandy, who had left France in 1837, being the first Procureur in Hongkong. He was Director in Paris in 1866, and died at Rome, as Procureur there, on 6th April, 1872, at the age of 67 years, having been 35 years in the Mission.

In 1857 he came to Singapore to establish the Procure House, and brought with him from Hongkong Father Osouf, of Coûtances in Normandy, who had come out from France the year before. They built the present House at the corner of River Valley Road and Oxley Road, and in October Father Libois returned to Hongkong, leaving Father Osouf as Procureur, who in 1863 went as Sous-Procureur at Hongkong and was afterwards Procureur there from 1866 to 1875, when he became Director at Paris, and in 1877 was a Bishop in Japan and is now Archbishop of Tokyo.

He was succeeded by Father Cazenave, of Bayonne in Gascony, who left France in 1858 to go to Tongking, and was Procureur in Singapore from 1863 to 1864 and was then Procureur at Shanghai. Father Patriat, of Dijon in Burgundy, succeeded him. He left France in 1862, and was Sous-Procureur in Singapore, and Procureur from 1864 to 1874, when he went as Superior to the Sanatorium at Hongkong, and died at the Sanatorium at Monbeton in France on 21st November, 1887, after 25 years service.

In 1874 he was succeeded by Father Martinet, of Verdun in Lorraine, who left France in 1870, and had been Sous-Procureur in Hongkong until 1872, when he came to Singapore as Sous-Procureur, and was Procureur from 1874 to 1876 when he went as Procureur to Shanghai, and in 1891 to Hongkong.

In 1876 Father Holhann, of Verdun, who left France in 1874, came from Hongkong, where he had been Sous-Procureur, to Singapore, and was Procureur from 1876 to 1881, when he went to Penang as Director of the College there.

Father Nicolas Justin Couvreur, of Langres in Champagne, who had left France on 16th October, 1878, and had been Sous-Procureur in Hongkong for three years, was appointed Procureur in Singapore in 1881, and is so to this time.

It may be of interest here to give some particulars about this Society of Foreign Missions. The "Société des Missions Etrangeres" was begun in 1659 at Paris, in the Rue du Bac, where it still has its large establishment. It was in the Chapel there, which is still standing, that Fenelon preached his famous sermon, which is said to have been a model for all missionary sermons afterwards. It seems to have been difficult to find out the exact date of the beginning of the Society, but it is certain that the two first priests left France on 18th June, 1660. The first of these, Pierre de la Mothe Lambert, was then 35 years of age, and he died at Iuthia, the then capital of Siam, as Bishop, on 15th June, 1679, at the age of 54 years. He came from Lisieux in Normandy.

King Louis XIV. issued his Letter of Patents, equivalent to a Charter of Incorporation, in July, 1663. The Seminary, or College for the training of missionaries, was formally opened on 27th October in that year.

During the first ten years 23 Missionaries went from France; by the end of that Century there had been 96; by the end of 1800, 264; and in 1892 the total had amounted to 1968. Between 1840 and 1888, 64 had been sent to the Straits; 13 had died in Singapore, 3 in Malacca, and 20 at Penang. Before 1840 the names of the Clergy in the Straits were included in the Mission of Siam, and the names are not tabulated separately.

For 240 years the Society has carried on the mission in the Far East, and has establishments now in Japan, Tongking, Cochin-China, China, Siam, Corea, Thibet, Pondicherry, the Malay Peninsula and Burmah. The report of the Society for 1900 shows that there are at present in these missions 35 Bishops and 1,117 European missionaries, of which one Bishop and 32 clergy are in the Straits

In consequence of the French revolution, the Church in France had been despoiled of its funds, and a Society called the Propagation of the Faith was established in Lyons. Collections were made throughout France, and in less than fifty years, largely from the constant collection of a few sous among the poor throughout the Churches, a fund was established even larger than that which had been at disposal for the foreign Missionaries in the previous century.

The Association was started in Lyons in 1821 by Mademoiselle Jaricot, and gradually developed into what it is at the present day. The annual funds now amount roughly to 6,000,000 francs, distributed among the Roman Catholic Missions throughout the world. Accounts are published yearly in French, English, and some other languages.

From this fund each Missionary of the Society of Foreign Missions receives 660 francs (£26.8.0, or say at the present exchange about $22 a month) the Bishops receiving 1,320 francs, or twice that amount. On this the Clergy have to depend for their support. The only addition is what they may receive for stipends for masses, and for marriage, baptism, and other fees.

The following memorandum relating to the Roman Catholic clergy in the Straits, written over half a century ago, and headed "Bigandet, Malacca," is found among the rough manuscript notes of Mr. Braddell, and fits in curiously in the present place :—"Priests, nearly all French secular clergy, belonging to the Society or Congregation des Missions Etrangères. Sole object religious, no earthly motives. No political intercourse with their country, no interference in political service. They are priests, and profess to belong to no party, no political creed, no ambition but propagation of Christian religion, and with it education and civilization. For maintenance they receive $120 a year. There are twenty in the Straits with a Bishop. Admission to the Society a great favour. Small pay, no pension. When coming out, expected that they entertain no idea of ever quitting it, and that they are prepared to die in the scene of their labours." One hundred and twenty dollars was then the value of the six hundred and sixty francs already mentioned.

The object of referring to the matter is, that the extent of the work that is to be seen in Singapore is often thought to have been due to other sources, such as funds from the Society of Foreign Missions in Paris, and not to the energy and devotion of the clergy and the generosity of the community of the place. The following sentence, in a foot note at page 35 of the second volume of a book "La Cochinchine Religieuse" published in Paris in 1885, and sent to the Singapore newspaper for review, goes some way to explain the matter. "Grâce à l'œuvre de la Propagation de la foi, les simples missionnaires recoivent six cent soixante francs, et les vicaires apostoliques treize cents francs par an. C'est peu, mais c'est suffisant pour des hommes qui n'envient ni les riches traitements, ni le confortable des clergymans protestants."*

It can be seen from the history of the Society published in Paris in 1894, in three volumes (Vol II. page 417), that the members are secular priests making no vows of poverty or of obedience, but making a promise before leaving France that they will, as far as they are able, follow the rules of the Society touching their manner of living, dress and other similar matters. They are therefore free to give up their work, as has been shewn to have been the case with some of those who have been mentioned in this chapter, much in the same way as some of the Missionaries of the London Missionary and American Societies are shewn on page 214 of this book to have retired.

The principles upon which the Society is conducted seem to be that each Priest must be satisfied with his yearly allowance for his support, and with the assurance that in case of extreme old age or illness he will not be neglected. It is an inherent obligation that no Missionary can possess landed property of his own, in the Mission to which he is appointed, unless with the consent of the Bishop, and that after his death it must pass to the Mission, or to a Church or School, or some work of the Mission. It is a principle of the Society that a Mission should be self-supporting as far as it can become so; therefore whenever a Mission is able to support itself without the aid of the Society, the Missionaries will willingly leave all behind them, and begin new work where such aid is more required. It has been said that it is to these principles that the Society has owed its success, and Singapore has shown how well, in one instance, it has been deserved.

The Diocese of Malacca receives yearly at the present time, 1901, the following amounts from France:—

From the Propagation of the Faith—

For the Bishop and Clergy	Frcs.	24,475.00
For the Catechists, School-masters and grants to open new Schools, &c.	,,	11,643.95
Total	Fcs.	36,118.95
From the Sainte Enfance for children not in the Convents	,,	12,000.00
From the Sainte Enfance for all the Convents	,,	21,000.00
Total ...	Fcs.	69,118.95

---

* "Thanks to the work of the Propagation of the Faith the plain Missionaries receive 660 francs and the Bishops 1,300 (? 1,320) francs a year. It is little, but it is enough for men who do not seek the costly living, nor the comfort of Protestant clergymen."

The allotment of the sum for Catechists, &c., is entirely under the control of the Bishop in Council with his Clergy. The grants from the Sainte Enfance (the Holy Childhood) are given for the support of orphans.

These amounts vary very little from year to year. There is now a slight tendency to decrease, owing to the fact that the annual increase in the funds of the Societies for the Propagation of the Faith and of the Sainte Enfance is less than the increase in the number of calls upon the Societies.

Both these Associations receive help from other nations. France contributes about two-thirds of the funds of the Propagation, and about one-third of those of the Sainte Enfance. Germany and Belgium take the lead in the subscription to the Sainte Enfance.

In addition to these funds the Clergy have, as has been said, the *Stipendia Missarum*, and any money they may possess as family inheritance, besides contributions, if any, from their friends or benefactors in Europe. The local contributions provide the rest.

Some of this matter does not fall strictly within the intention of this book; but the facts came to the surface in hunting into the history of the older buildings, and the interest that must attach to it among the congregation of the Church, is a ready excuse for it, and must give them cause for grateful appreciation of the work that is carried on in their midst, in a way that seems, to the Protestant compiler of this book, to hold out a great example to others.

THE BROTHERS SCHOOL.

The establishment of this school was entirely due to the Rev. J. M. Beurel. He had originally wished to be admitted into the Society of the Brothers of the Christian Schools, but was refused because he was in sacred orders. In 1841 he wrote to the Rev. J. B. Boucho, Penang, to consult him on the subject, but he was told that there were very great difficulties which seemed insurmountable; that it would require a large outlay of money which Father Beurel would not have at his disposal; and it was not likely the Superior General in Paris would send his subjects to this extremity of the world; besides how would the masters bear the climate under the severity of their rules; and it was suggested that laymen as school masters would be better than a body of men under a Religious Order.

The proposal had to drop for the time, but when the ground was given by the Government for the new Church, Mr. Beurel arranged that the old chapel and compound should remain for the future school, and informed Governor Bonham that it was his earnest desire to establish schools for the boys and girls of Catholic parents and the public in general, and that the chapel and buildings would perfectly answer for the purpose.

At this time, 1843 to 1845, attention could only be given to procuring means for building the new Church; but in February, 1846, seeing this on the way to completion, Mr. Beurel wrote to the Superior of the Brothers of the Christian Schools in Paris saying that he dreamed day and night of establishing schools at this furthest extremity of the East Indies, under their direction, and that he hoped to see it realised, and that as soon as the new Church was finished he would apply again for help. The Superior General replied that they would willingly assist, but they could not hold out much hope of doing so, because the number of masters was small, especially of those who were thoroughly acquainted with English.

On Sunday, the 6th June, 1847, when the Church was finished and blessed, Father Beurel, after the Gospel, announced to the Congregation that he had the positive intention to establish schools under the direction of the Christian Brothers, and of some nuns or sisters. That he took the great Patriarch Saint Joseph for the Patron of the undertaking, and would set his hand to the work. In July he wrote to the Queen of France asking for help, and to the Minister of the Interior and the Minister of Foreign Affairs, but the revolution of 1848, which had just taken place and had driven King Louis Philippe out of France, prevented any replies. The Bishop also objected to any Brothers being brought from Europe unless Father Beurel could show that he had sufficient means to maintain the establishment.

The *Singapore Free Press* of the 22nd June, 1848, contained the following—"Below we publish a paper which has been handed to us by the Reverend Mr. Beurel, and contains the prospectus of a school which, if properly carried out, will be productive of much usefulness not only in Singapore, but in the neighbouring native states. It is intended not only to educate such children as may be sent to the school by their parents and guardians in Singapore, but to procure children to be sent from the various native states, who will receive at the hands of the instructors such tuition as will introduce them to a higher state of civilization, and fit them for being the instruments of spreading it amongst their countrymen. This school, as the plan has been explained to us, will in a great measure afford the means of accomplishing the purposes which Sir T. S. Raffles had in view in founding the Singapore Institution, but which none since his departure have possessed sufficient zeal and influence to carry out. The indefatigable energy and perseverance of the Missionaries of the Society for the Propagation of the Faith will probably enable them to undertake this successfully. Regarding it as of the greatest importance to a proper civilization and conversion of natives, that a sound education should be the fore-runner or accompanier of such, we cordially recommend Mr. Beurel's prospectus to the most favorable consideration of our readers :—

"The Revd. J. M. Beurel having, through God's blessing, completed his Church, purposes now establishing in this Settlement a Boys' School to be placed under the direction of the 'Christian Brothers.' These Teachers are well known in many parts of Europe to be thoroughly qualified to instruct youth, as they are specially brought up for the purpose, and bind themselve by vow to devote their lives to the furtherance of this most eminently Christian and civilizing call, asking no remuneration for their labours beyond what may be necessary for their food and dress.

"They have many flourishing Schools not only in Europe but also in the United States of America. In the East Indies they are but little known, though their services are much required. The Revd. J. M. Beurel has then full hope and confidence that the public at large and especially his liberal friends who have so kindly lent him assistance in the building of his Church, will promote and patronise by some pecuniary assistance his views of introducing these enlightened and disinterested teachers of youth into this part of the world, where Christianity and civilization are yet so little diffused among the natives. What he requires at present is sufficient funds for the necessary expenses of their passage to this place.

"The Central School, which is to be established at Singapore, will be at first opened by three of these European Masters in the old Roman Catholic Chapel, which is in every respect well adapted for a School-Room. English, French, Chinese and the Malay languages, together with the various branches of mathematics, book-keeping, drawing, &c., &c., &c., will be taught in the school. The principles upon which it is to be conducted will be as liberal as possibly can be: thus it will be open to every one, whatever his creed may be; and should, for instance, a boy of a persuasion different from that of Roman Catholics attend it, no interference whatever will take place with his religion, unless his parents or guardians express their wishes to have him instructed in the Catholic religion. Public religious instruction will be given to Roman Catholic boys either before or after the hours for School: but at all times the Masters will most carefully watch over the morals of the whole, whatever their religious persuasion may be."

The result was a sum of $1,352.50, and looking through the list of subscribers it is seen that there is scarcely a member of the commercial community left out. E. Boustead, J. Guthrie, W. H. Read, M. F. Davidson, G. G. Nicol, D. Fraser, J. Steel, J. Connolly, C. Carnie, Raja Brooke, W. Mactaggart, W. Napier, A. Logan, J. Armstrong, and many other well-known names, heading the list.

In 1849 there seemed no chance of getting Brothers from France owing to the revolutionary upheaval, but on the 2nd July the Bishop. being in Singapore from Penang, on his third visit, gave Father Beurel written permission to establish the School under the Christian Brothers "on condition that the said Reverend Gentleman will defray all expenses of establishing and keeping up such a School out of his own resources without entailing any burden either upon the Bishop or his successors." There is a note of Father Beurel, "I accepted it with joy, in the hope that, through God's blessing, it would become light, but however the event has proved it to have been rather heavy."

In 1850 nothing could be arranged in Singapore, and it was decided in September that Father Beurel should go to France to try to carry out this important undertaking. He sailed on the 25th October in a French vessel, *L'Artilleur*, and reached Havre on 14th March. He returned with six Brothers, four sisters, a lay sister, and two young missionaries. They all went to Antwerp to join a vessel there on 3rd December, and reached Singapore on 28th March, 1852. Three of the Brothers were for Penang; the three for Singapore were Brothers Liefroy the Director, Gregory the Sub-Director, and Lothaire. Brother Antoine Liefroy was born at Auch in France on 9th August, 1809. He left Singapore in 1862 for Mangalore. He was the Brother Director and Visitor of Singapore, Penang, and Colombo. He died at Cairo in 1867.

Brother Gregory was born in Ireland in 1820, was in Singapore until 1863, when he went to India, and died there of Cholera in 1865.

Louis Antoine Combes, Brother Lothaire, was born in Loire in France in 1827. He returned from Singapore to France in 1872, and was in Singapore for a short time in 1875 and in 1877, having been in Hongkong. From 1880 to 1884 he was Director of the School in Liverpool, and then for a short time Director in London. Between 1881 and 1884 the Brothers School in Singapore was conducted by lay teachers under the direction of the Missions Étrangères. The Brothers came back again in 1885 under Brother Lothaire as Superior and the secular teachers left. Brother Lothaire died at the Sanatorium of the Mission at Fleury Meudon, near Paris, in 1899. He is remembered with much affection by his pupils.

The Christian Brothers School had been founded about 1680 at Rheims in France by John Baptist de La Salle. He was born there on 30th April, 1651, the son of the Chancellor of State to the King and President of the High Court of Rheims. The schools spread rapidly in France, extending to Paris, Chartres, Calais and Avignon, and to Rome before the close of the century.

On 2nd July, 1725, King Loius XV. issued the Letters Patent constituting the Institute, and on 26th September in the same year Pope Benedict XIII. approved by a Bull the " Institute and Rule of the Brothers of the Christian Schools." It was one of the strict rules of the Founder that no priest was received into the community; he thought that the mixing of Priests and Brothers might be a cause of division, and that the Brothers would be aspiring to be priests and prefer preaching to the humble but useful work of the Schools and the community might die out for want of teachers.

In 1886 in France alone there were 308,000 boys and 8,859 teachers. In Paris there were then 96 Schools, some of the buildings being very extensive, with gymnasiums and large military bands formed by the boys.

The founder now known as Saint De La Salle, as he was canonized on 24th May, 1900, died at Rouen on 7th April, 1719, 68 years old, on the night between Good Friday and Saturday, the large history of the Institute remarking that he went to celebrate the Paschal Feast in Paradise. He was buried on the Saturday, and in 1734 the body was exhumed and re-interred in the chapel of the Brothers, and in 1881 the remains were again removed to the chapel in the Boarding School. On Sunday, 19th February, 1888, the first ceremony of canonization took place at St. Peter's at Rome, and the following is a translation of one of the four Inscriptions, in Latin, which decorated the building on that day :—

To John Baptist De La Salle
Founder and Father
Of the Brothers of the Christian Schools
Raised to the honours of the Blessed
The whole Catholic World
Sends up prayer and supplication
Mingled with tears
That the Education of Youth
Placed in great peril by impiety
May not Deviate
From the Holy Laws of Religion.

The Schools spread over the continent and reached Ireland in 1804, Reunion in 1816, and Montreal in Canada in 1838. As far as can be gathered from the history, it was Father Beurel who first led to their coming further abroad, because in a map of the Schools in India and China printed on page 602 of the large and very handsome life of the founder, published in Paris in 1888, it says that the communities there were founded from 1852, and that is the year that Father Beurel brought out the first Brothers for Singapore. Algiers was not begun until 1853, and Saigon in 1866. So that Singapore seems to have been the commencement of the Schools which have now so largely spread in the East. Bishop Boucho's remark, already mentioned, that it was not likely the Superior General in Paris would send the teachers so far, seems to bear this out.

Father Beurel used to remark that it was on 6th June, 1847, the feast of Corpus Christi, at High Mass, that he first spoke about the Schools, and began to say a public prayer for their success at the High Mass on every Sunday; and that it was on the same day of the year in 1851 that the Superior General in Paris gave his consent, against almost all expectation.

On the 22nd July, 1852, a Prospectus was issued of the school. It said that it was to be a free school, to be held in the large and airy premises, lately used as the Catholic Church, No. 3, Brass Bassa Road, and as the teachers received no more than their support for their pious labours it was hoped the generous and enlightened public would support it according to their means. Every care would be taken to form the Catholic children in the solid maxims of Christian piety, but there would be no interference with the religious tenets of other creeds. This had been headed "St. John's School," the reason for which does not appear. The Director objected to the name as he wanted it called the Christian Brothers School. Messrs. G. W. Lecerf, James Isaiah Woodford, and Patrick J. Cunningham, were the first Committee, but the Director objected to a Committee, and the school was practically left under the management of the Brothers.

The School was opened on 1st May, there were three European masters. One French Brother Liefroy, and two Irish Brothers, Gregory and Swedbert. The latter died in Singapore on 1st April, 1855. Brother Lothaire had stayed at Penang. In 1860 two more masters had been added. The number of pupils at the end of the first year was 110.

The grant of land where the Boys' School now stands was dated 28th May, 1863, of the area of acre 1.3.5, and is given in trust for the Roman Catholic Community of Singapore so long as the Christian Brothers shall maintain a school.

In 1853 the French Government gave a grant of 1,000 francs a year, and the Tumongong having won a bet of $100 from the Sultan of Lingga, it was given to Father Beurel for the school. The French Government allowance gave $151.80, the Masonic Lodge gave $25, other subscriptions $792, and the Church Mission in Singapore $60. The school was in debt at the end of the year to Father Beurel for $1,528.52. In 1855 he bought the large piece of ground at the north-east corner of the compound belonging to the Society of Foreign Missions. It had been intended to build the Procure House there, but after the arrival of the Brothers it was found necessary to buy it for their use or there would have been no compound behind the school.

At the end of 1861 the school owed Father Beurel $2,977.57. He had given $900 in donations to the School during these first ten years; $1,260 had been collected in France; $7,862 subscribed in Singapore including subscriptions for the new house; and $160 received in donations from the Masonic Lodge.

From 1854 Father Beurel received a few boarders in his house who went to the school as day scholars. In the beginning of 1855 he received 26 or 27 Boarders from Manila and Macao. Father Beurel had lived in a house in the School enclosure, and he removed in 1857 to the house at the east corner of Brass Bassa Road and Queen Street where the Catholic Club is now. At Easter the Brothers wished to take the boarders into their house. It was done, but the boys did not like the change and it led to a good deal of trouble, which Father Beurel had anticipated as there was not sufficient room to accommodate them, and the boys twice walked off in a body, and eventually the greater number returned as boarders to Father Beurel.

On Monday the 19th March, 1855, on a beautiful evening at 6 o'clock after Vespers, the corner stone of the intended new school was laid. The Sisters with all the girls from the Convent and a number of other persons were present. In a bottle laid in a granite stone in the foundation was the following paper:—" In the year of of Our Lord 1855 on the 19th of March, the feast of St. Joseph, the Glorious Patron of this Mission and especially of all the undertakings of the Rev. J. M. Beurel, for the Propagation of the Catholic Faith, the first stone of this building to be erected for the use of the venerated and pious Brethren of the Christian Schools established in the town of Singapore in the year 1852, has been laid by the Rev. Father Hypolito Huerta, of the Order of the Hermits of St. Augustin, under the patronage of and with the blessing of the Right Rev. Dr. J. B. Boucho, Bishop of Italia, the Venerable Vicar Apostolic of this Mission. Complete, O Lord, this work which is undertaken for Thy Glory and the salvation of souls in this place, under the protection of the Blessed Virgin Mary and her glorious spouse St. Joseph. Amen. "

The subscription had amounted to $842 and the expense of laying the foundations for the large house was about $700. The Bishop, however, afterwards thought that it was better to delay the actual building, as Father Beurel had already undertaken much pecuniary responsibility for the Convent building, and the expense of building the Brothers' School might be more than he was able to meet for the present. The Bishop wrote that he thought there should be a little breathing time, and that it should stand over for two or three years. The result was that the building was not proceeded with until the end of 1866.

In the beginning of 1865 the Brother Director, Brother Lothaire, determined to set to work to provide a new schoolhouse, to be used as a school and a dwelling house for the Brothers. In February, 1865, he wrote to the Government that he had been promised $4,500 for the purpose, and sent a plan of the proposed building. He asked Government for assistance, but the only result was the grant of Government bricks at the cost price to Government, and even this was not fully carried out, as the building of the new Government House required so many bricks that the promise to the School was set aside before the building was finished.

On 8th November, 1866, Brother Lothaire made a contract with a Chinese for the construction of the building, by which the contractor was to pull down the then existing class rooms, the old residence occupied by Father Paris, and the house formerly occupied by Father Beurel, and to erect a building 149 feet long, 61 feet wide, and 32 feet high, to be finished on 15th August, 1867. The contract price was $8,600, but the tiles of the old buildings and the materials for the chapel, which was to be fitted like the one in the Convent, were to be supplied by the Brothers. While the building was being erected the classes were held in Father Beurel's house, and in attap buildings as circumstances allowed.

THE CONVENT.

On the 7th July, 1849, Mr. Beurel wrote to Governor Butterworth that it was intended, now the Boys' School was in a fair way to be established, to found another charitable institution " on behalf of the females of all classes and conditions in the Island, including a school for respectable ladies, an orphanage, and an asylum for destitute widows, the whole to be placed under the care and direction of the Sisters of Charity." He asked for the ground next the Church in Victoria Street. The Governor in reply wrote that a large piece of land has already been given for the Church, in addition to the land on the other side of Brass Bassa Road, which was now to be used for the Boys' School ; and that the ground Mr. Beurel now applied for appeared to be the only eligible spot for a new Court House, should one be erected.

On 15th July, 1852, Father Beurel again applied for the same land, to Governor Blundell, urging that the intention to build a new Court House had been abandoned, and that the land was being only used by the convicts to store firewood and cut up timber, which disturbed people in the Church. The Governor replied that the land could not be parted with.

On 18th August, 1852, Father Beurel bought with his own money, for $4,000, the house at the corner of Victoria Street and Brass Bassa Road. It is the large house that is still standing next the main entrance, and was built by Mr. Coleman for Mr. Caldwell. This was the beginning of the Convent buildings, which now cover so large a space, being much larger than those of any other ecclesiastical body in Singapore, and having a large open space with grass and trees in the centre.

Father Beurel afterwards bought, with his own monies, four of the lots of land which were sold by the Trustees of the Raffles Institution as already stated on page 124. These comprised 14,200 square yards or 127,800 square feet ; and on 27th December, 1863, he conveyed it, as a gift of his own, to "the Reverend Mother St. Mathilde and her successors in office as Superior of the Convent, in order to establish a Convent and charitable Institution for the Sisters of the Charitable Institution of the Holy Infant Jesus."

On 20th December, 1853, Father Beurel bought an adjoining house for $3,000, which was to become the Orphanage. This has long been pulled down.

The Society to which Father Beurel applied in France for help in finding Sisters for the Convent, is called the Institute of the Charitable Schools of the Holy Infant Jesus of St. Maur. [L'Institut des Ecoles Charitables du Saint Enfant Jésus de Saint Maur.] It was founded by the Rev. Father Nicolas Barré, at Rouen in 1666, and in 1673 he founded the Seminary at Paris in the Rue St. Maur, where it still stands; but the street is now called Rue de l'Abbé Grégoire. Abbé Tiberge in 1670 purchased the land, and nine years afterwards bought adjoining properties which he left by his will to the Sisters for the instruction of poor children. He had been the Director in Paris of the Missions Etrangères, and was one of its great benefactors, and a well-known author. He died on 9th October, 1730, at the age of 79 years, and was buried with much ceremony in their Chapel.

It seems to have been due to Father Beurel that the Society of St. Maur sent the first Sisters away from France. It is certain that the first Mission founded at a distance was that of the Straits. On 17th November, 1851, the first four sisters left Paris, the Mother of the Society going with them from the Rue de l'Abbé Grégoire to Antwerp to see them off under care of Father Beurel. This is stated at length in the History of the Society, which says in a footnote, that the foundation proposed for Singapore was first begun at Penang, and that the work in Singapore started a little later in 1854. It also says that between 1851 and 1877, twelve departures of sisters for the East succeeded each other at intervals; the Superior, Mother de Faudoas, in religion, Sister St. François de Sales, always accompanying them to the ship. She died on 27th August, 1877, at the age of 70 years, having been 56 years in the Society, and its head for forty years. The history attributes chiefly to her the founding of the convents at Penang, Singapore, Malacca, Yokohama, Tokio, and the first arrangements for that at Bangkok.

It has been said on page 261 that when Father Beurel returned from France in 1852 he was accompanied from Antwerp by four sisters. Among these was Mother St. Paulin, the Superior, who died and was buried at sea about fifteen days before the vessel arrived at Singapore. On their arrival in Singapore the Bishop, to the great disappointment of Father Beurel, sent the Sisters to Penang after they had only been about eight days in Singapore, and suggested to Father Beurel to write to Calcutta to try and get some Irish Sisters, who were at Dacca and wished to leave there. Father Beurel did not like the proposal, which was not carried out, and he wrote to France to try to induce others to come.

Very soon a second party left France, starting from Southampton and crossing the desert in caravans. On their way they met Father

Bigandet in the desert who was very much astonished to see them, and was not pleased because they could not all speak English. In this party there were Mother St. Mathilde, who came as Superior to take the place of Mother St. Paulin who had died at sea; Sister St. Apollinaire, Sister St. Damien, and Sister St. Gregoire. It has been thought in Singapore that Mother St. Mathilde (to whom, as will be shewn presently, the Convent and Singapore owe so much) came out with Father Beurel, but it was not the case. She was the first Superior who arrived in Singapore for the Convent, as her predecessor had died on the voyage, which has probably led to the mistake.

Mother St. Mathilde stayed first at Penang, as Superior, with all the Sisters, and after a year she came to Singapore, on 6th February, 1854, with Sisters St. Gaetan, Apollinaire, and Gregoire. Mother St. Damien remained at Penang as the Superior there.

The third party left France in 1853, and arrived in Singapore in February 1854. There were three Sisters, of whom two, Sisters St. Patrick and St. Leonard remained in Penang, and the other was Sister St. Gaetan, who came to Singapore, and was, for twenty years, Mother Superior of the Convent.

Mother St. Mathilde remained in Singapore, until 20th June, 1874, when she went to Yokohama and there founded the two Convents at Yokohama and Tokio which have since increased so largely. She has since made two short visits to Singapore, and is at the present time living in the Convent at Yokohama, at the very advanced age of eighty-eight years, after being half a century in the East. So it seems likely that, like Father Beurel, she will die far away from the place where she laid the solid foundations for the good work of the Convent in Singapore, which owes as much to her as the other institutions of the Church do to Father Beurel.

When Mother St. Mathilde went to Japan, with Sister St. Gregoire, in 1874, Mother St. Gaetan became Superior. In 1858 an English Lady, called in religion Sister St. Joseph, had come out to the Convent. She had been a Protestant, and two of her sisters, who came to Singapore on two occasions to see her, used to go to St. Andrew's Church. She died of consumption, on 31st May, 1883, after many years illness, during which she persistently strove to carry on her work in the class-rooms with the pupils who were very much attached to her. These two ladies, working together, (the French lady with her musical ability and very refined manners, and the English lady with her experience of life outside a convent's walls, having been brought up in a Protestant family), made the Convent a perfect home for the large number of pupils and orphans who lived in it. After Sister St. Joseph's death, Mother St. Gaetan used to say that she seemed to have lost half of herself, and she certainly felt her loss very much. Mother St. Gaetan herself went to Europe in ill-health, and died in London in 1892, where she had gone to found the first Convent of the Society there.

During these years the buildings had grown. In 1855 a small house was built for boarders. Afterwards it was pulled down and the long building behind Mr. Caldwell's house was put up. Then the Chapel and the schoolrooms were built, as money could be collected to pay for them. At last, in 1891 and 1892, the long, large building at the southern boundary of the land was put up. It cost $30,000, of which the Government gave $10,000, as it was then the rule for the Government to aid towards school buildings. The rest of the money was raised by subscriptions. Cheang Hong Lim, a rich Chinese, since dead, gave $3,000; considerable sums were added by the liberality of Protestants in Singapore; the Congregation of the Church, which is far from as well off as the Protestant community, gave little by little, but constantly, of their means, and the required sum was eventually raised.

There is a Religious Society in France called La Sainte Enfance, the published accounts of which, issued each year, can be seen by all. The funds, collected in many cases in very small weekly or monthly subscriptions of a few sous, are devoted to paying for the keep of children of heathen parents; a certain sum being allowed per head to the Convent which provides for them. The amount allowed in 1900, and it varies very little, was 21,000 francs for all the Convents in the Straits, at Singapore, Malacca, Kuala Lumpor, Taipeng and Penang. It is in this way only that the Convent in Singapore receives any money help from France, and a very small sum it is, compared with the necessary expense of keeping up such an establishment as the Convent, which at the time when this is given to the printer at the end of 1901 has within its walls from 300 to 320 inmates.

Where then, it may be asked, does the rest of the money come from day by day to provide for so many? Consider the money spent on salaries in the other charitable institutions and schools in the Straits, and then seek to know, which there is no difficulty in ascertaining, what is the corresponding expense in the Convent of those who devote their lives to their work for the work's sake; and there is half the answer. There is the Government Grant, as in the Schools of other denominations; and, for the rest, it is sometimes said that the Roman Catholic communities are good beggars, and given a certain proportion of paying pupils (but a great number of orphans and children for whom nothing can be expected to be paid, but are willingly gathered in,) and day by day the needful food is found. The work may be carried on under difficulties, but it never fails, and continues to grow. It requires little discrimination on the part of children or their parents to appreciate the advantage of being under the instruction of refined and well-educated ladies whose only aim, it is apparent, is the good that they are doing, and who are without any motive of self-interest or self-advantage, for where can this find place in their dependent lives; and when for such good reasons, some Protestant parents are glad to send their children as day scholars to learn their lessons or their music there, they know that the school fees go to help to feed and clothe another class of children who badly need it.

———

This Chapter would seem very imperfect if it did not emphasize the long and arduous work of Father Beurel in the interest of the Roman Catholic Church and of the Congregation during thirty-five years. He carried out the work of the Parish as regards its pecuniary affairs in the most business-like way, and left behind him most accurate accounts and details in writing of all that took place, which have all been placed at the disposal of the compiler of this book while writing this chapter. At the beginning of the first book, a large volume, he has written in French "The Annals of the Catholic Mission at Singapore, written by the undersigned in his moments of leisure. J. M. Beurel, M. Ap."

In reading the books one is struck with the difficulties he met with, and the way he surmounted them. We find the Bishop objecting to his going on with buildings because he was, not at all unreasonably, afraid of the responsibility of Father Beurel incurring liabilities which he would not have the means to meet, and quoting the text in Luke xiv., about a man building a tower without counting the cost and not having wherewith to complete it, at which those that behold him, mock.

It has sometimes been thought in Singapore that all these buildings and the schools, and the work of the Church, had been very largely due to pecuniary help from France, without which they would not have existed, nor the work of the clergy carried on. The documents and accounts show exactly the opposite, and it is for this reason that so many details of the expense and the source of the money for the buildings has been given in this chapter The local Government gave the land free, as it has done to all charitable bodies for churches and schools, but the church received no money aid from Government, like the Raffles Institution and the Church of England. We have seen how on one occasion Father Beurel found so many difficulties in his way that he went to Burmah to join Father Bigandet, not intending to return, but doing so, at the earnest request of the Congregation, to continue the work he had taken in hand, which he lived to see completed.

The third volume of the History of the Society, at page 247, contains a special account of Father Beurel, as he was considered to have done remarkable work for the Mission. The following is a translation of one passage; " of an unalterable calm, a combination of human philosophy and saintly resignation, of perseverance that nothing could deter, neither blind opposition nor active hostility; neither the anger of the great nor the menaces of the small; he was one of those who know that in the affairs of this life a direct line is not necessarily the shortest road from one point to another; when an obstacle stood in his path and he could not clear it in a single bound, he would go round it gently and quietly, with a smile which bore witness to his confidence in the future."

He spent the whole of his private means, which were not inconsiderable, in Church buildings, and he was not the only instance of the kind among the Roman Catholic clergy in the Straits.

Bishop Bigandet, then Bishop of Burmah, was in Singapore for one week in October, 1884, on his way to Rangoon; and on Sunday the 12th, at High Mass in the Church of the Good Shepherd, when there was a large congregation, for he was very much respected, he said on going up into the pulpit and turning to the congregation, that before commencing his sermon, he wished to recall to the minds of them all, the memory of Father Beurel, and of all he had done for the congregation. And then, after a pause, he commenced his sermon.

Father Beurel was ill in Paris for about three years before he died. He was buried there, and not, as all the congregation would have wished, in the Church he had built. There is a portrait of him in the Parochial House, but the best remembrance of him is the large Church, the Convent and the Brothers' School close by.

Some of the older members of the congregation at this time were boys taken by him into his house and brought up by him for useful work in the place. Among them an old Chinese resident, while this chapter was in the printer's hands, has given the names of Mr. John Scheerder, Mr. Martia, Buan Seng the shipping clerk of a large European firm, and Tan Hay Seng, the son of Pedro No Kia, a wealthy Chinese member of the congregation in the older days.

There is an old and true story of how Governor Butterworth thought Father Beurel had outwitted him by building the Parochial House on the ground that had been given only for the Church; but Father Beurel always said that it was an ecclesiastical building connected with the Church and therefore was within the meaning, if not the letter, of the lease. It used therefore to be thought by some in Singapore that Father Beurel was rather too clever a man of business; but this was only one side of the matter. When one looks at the large buildings just spoken of, and then at the Churches at Bukit Timah, Serangoon and Johore, the large Church of S.S. Peter and Paul for the Chinese behind the Brothers' School, and the Church of St. Mary of Lourdes for the Tamils at a short distance from it, the work that has been done is as striking as the small remuneration for which their Clergy do such willing work, giving their own private means, as well as their whole lives, to the calling they follow. When remembering the number of those who have ended their lives in Singapore, and looking at the long rows of tombs of Sisters of the Convent at the Cemetery in Bukit Timah Road, there are many (not of their communion alone) who will echo the words which are put at the end of "The Obituary" at the close of the yearly report of the Société des Missions Etrangères for 1900, *"Sit Memoria illorum in benedictione."*

THE PORTUGUESE MISSION.

The Rev. Francisco de Silva Pinto e Maia of Porto, who has already been spoken of in this chapter, is shown by the records of the Portuguese Church to have arrived at Singapore on 7th April, 1825, and commenced the Mission which still exists under the patronage of the Portuguese Crown. He built a parochial house with a small chapel attached to it, and worked indefatigably for twenty-five years. Father Maia died in Singapore on 17th February, 1850. He was buried at the old cemetery, and his remains were transferred to the Church of St. José after that Church was built. He left all he had, including some land he had bought, for the erection of the Church.

The Rev. Vincente de Santo Catharina succeeded Father Maia, and he erected the main building of the present Church of St. José in Victoria Street, which cost about $15,000. The greater part of the money was derived from the gifts of Father Maia, supplemented by a sum of $2,000 from the King of Portugal and by local subscriptions. The foundation stone was laid on the 14th December, 1851, the following inscription being made upon it :—

"The first stone of this Portuguese Roman Catholic Church at Singapore, consecrated to the service of the ALMIGHTY GOD, in honour of the HOLY VIRGIN and St. JOSEPH, was laid by the Vicar VICENTE DE SANTA CATHARINA on the 14th day of December, A. D. 1851, and the Church erected by contribution from the fund of the Mission of St. Joseph of Macao and those of the inhabitants of Macao and of this island, raised through the instrumentality and noble zeal of JOAQUIM D'ALMEIDA, Esq., and the aforesaid Vicar, in the 5th year of the Pontificate of Pius IX., the 25th year of the reign of DONA MARIA II. Queen of Portugal, the 14th year of the reign of Her Britannic Majesty Queen VICTORIA, and the 9th year of the administration of Colonel WILLIAM JOHN BUTTERWORTH, C.B., Governor of Prince of Wales' Island, Singapore and Malacca."

In 1868 the Church was enlarged by the addition of two wings, and the Parochial House was repaired and extended. The Portuguese Government gave $9,000, and a subscription was raised among the community.

A School for children was established by Father José Pedro Sta Anna de Cunha in June, 1879, in a shop-house in Middle Road opposite the Parochial House. In 1880 it was moved into a compound house in Victoria Street, near the Church, and in 1886 to the new building specially erected for the purpose in the Church compound, towards the expense of which the local government contributed $4,000, as it had done to other schools. In 1893 the Girls' School was separated from the boys, the ground floor of the Parochial House being fitted as a school for boys, and in 1894 the Society of the Conosianas Sisters in Italy took charge of the Girls' School.

The Portuguese Mission was under the Archbishop of Goa until 1887, when the jurisdiction was transferred to the Bishop of Macao.

CHAPTER XXII.

1835.

IN February the flag-staff at Blakan Mati was given up. In August, 1834, orders had been received from Bengal for Mr. Coleman to prepare plans and estimates for an iron suspension bridge, and on the 28th February, 1835, the bridge arrived from Calcutta on board the *Will Watch*. The estimate was $10,680.

In May, petitions were signed by all the European Mercantile Community addressed to the King and to the Governor-General of India on the subject of piracy, which was very bad at this time, even at a short distance outside the limits of the harbour, some Europeans being attacked in sampans when going out to board vessels; also as to the want of Admiralty Jurisdiction; and also regarding the restriction against American vessels being allowed to trade with Singapore.

The latter had been a vexed question for several years. Soon after the termination of the American War, a convention was made at London in July, 1815, by which the trade by American vessels were restricted to the principal settlements of the East Indies, viz., Calcutta, Madras, Bombay, and Prince of Wales' Island, which latter was, at the time, the only British Settlement in the Straits of Malacca. Singapore was not established and Malacca was about to be restored to the Dutch. The Americans, under this convention, resumed their trade with the British possessions in India, which had been interrupted by the war of 1812, and, after the expiration of the time to which the convention was limited, they still followed their trade with these countries as usual.

In 1819 Singapore was added to the British Possessions in India, with the avowed purpose of making it a Free Port, and a general depot of British trade in the Far East. Moreover, it became a principal Settlement under a Governor of its own, subject only to the authorities at home and to the Supreme Government of Bengal. The Americans came to trade at Singapore, and their merchant ships added to the number of foreigners who habitually frequented the port, and as they most commonly brought specie to invest in eastern commodities brought to the Settlement, they were among its most valuable customers.

They believed and so did the inhabitants of the place, that a fair construction of former treaties and past practice (although after the expiration of the term for which such treaties were made), allowed for their trading still to the possessions of the East India Company, and they accordingly came here under the same security as they went to other principal places in the East Indies.

Things remained in this harmonious state till the Commander of H. M. S. *Larne*, in 1825, taking a different view of the subject, thought proper to detain the American ship *Governor Endicott*, found in the neighbourhood and avowedly bound to this place. She was sent to Calcutta, and there put under trial; but as she had *not traded* in this port, that important question did not come up, and the Court had no opportunity of giving an opinion. The ship having committed no alleged breach of law, was acquitted, and damages were adjudged against the Commander of the *Larne*.

The detention of the *Governor Endicott* had the effect of deterring the Americans from trading with this place as formerly, under an apprehension of being seized and sent to a distant port to undergo a long and expensive trial, and perhaps not realize one shilling of any damages which might be adjudged to them by the Court, as in the case of the *Governor Endicott*, the owners of which were said never to have received any part of the amount of damages recovered against the Captain of the *Larne*. To avoid, therefore, any such difficulty, they had resorted to the indirect practice of effecting their purpose through the neighbouring Dutch Port of Rhio, or other adjacent places.

The American vessels used to anchor in a bay called *Boolang* on the island of Battam, opposite Singapore, about fourteen miles E. S. E. from the roads, and beyond British jurisdiction. The cargo was sent out in boats from Singapore, and the only result of a foolish system was the delay and expense of conveying the produce by boats to Boolang. In 1830, Mr. C. R. Read had been to England to try to get the trade allowed, and there was only one opinion as to the inconsistency of the regulation.

Mr. Balestier, who was the American Consul, lived in Singapore, but ostensibly had his office at Rhio, styling himself Consul for the port of Rhio, in the Island of Bintang and such other ports as were nearer thereto than to the residence of any other Consul for the United States. In November, 1836, he was recognised by the Court of Directors in London, and became Consul at Singapore in June, 1837, and American ships were allowed to trade on the same footing as those of other nations. The result was a large increase in the trade with America, nearly 8,000 tons of shipping visiting the port in the year ending 30th June, 1837.

In this year Captain Newbold says it was proposed by an American Missionary that Colonies of young men and women should come to the Straits to spread science and civilisation! Each Colony of these philanthropists was to comprise five to fifteen families, or thirty to ninety individuals, to include agriculturists, carpenters, goldsmiths, shoemakers and a religious pastor. They were to rely on their own resources, and have a sort of common stock. It was thought that such colonies would be highly serviceable to the Straits. This remarkable scheme to found families who were to remain in this country, and their descendants after them, did not come to a practical trial. The result in such a climate could easily have been foreseen.

In June Governor Murchison returned from leave and resumed charge of his office. Mr. Bonham and Mr. Wingrove being the Resident Councillor and Assistant Resident at Singapore.

In July the garden in Commercial Square was enclosed with a dwarf wall with wooden railing, and the ground levelled, planted with ornamental trees, and laid out with paths.

In August a prospectus was published of a Bank, proposed to be established in Singapore, to be called the Singapore and Ceylon Bank, with a Board of Directors in London, with a Capital of £200,000 divided into five thousand shares of £40 each. The responsibility of the shareholders to be limited by the Charter. It came to nothing.

On the 26th September, a very daring burglary, long remembered in Singapore, took place at Mr. McMicking's house at Duxton, near Spottiswoode Park. A numerous gang of Chinese broke into the bed-room of Mr. McMicking, and inflicted such severe wounds on him that he was unable to offer any resistance, and the gang plundered the room of everything they could lay their hands on, and decamped. There were two other gentlemen in the house, but they were not in the room in time to be of service either in the apprehension or identification of the robbers. Several Chinese were arrested, among others the water-carrier, who was recognised by the syce, and was arrested the next morning; he was hiding in the jungle, instead of being at his usual occupation.

A fire took place in the same week near Cross Street and seventy-seven native houses were burnt, and property destroyed, estimated in value at five thousand dollars.

In October a gang of fifty or sixty armed Chinese attacked the house of a Bengalee named Sarawan, at the new kampong, called Buffalo Village, now called Kandang Kerbau. The inmates were awakened by the barking of their dogs, and were prepared with loaded fire-arms, as after the attack on Mr. McMicking's house, people were on the alert. The robbers attempted to break in, when one of the Bengalis fired a musket from an upper window and killed one of the gang, who was carried off by his companions. The inmates then sallied out, accompanied by several neighbours, who had caught the alarm, and gave chase. They succeeded in capturing one of the gang, and found the one that had been shot lying dead on the road. The one they caught tried to fight, and was so severely beaten with clubs by the Bengalis that he died in the hospital two hours after, and two others of the gang were shot by some Javanese, who had gathered close by.

A Coroner's Inquest brought in a verdict of justifiable homicide; and the authorities rewarded the most active of the men who had been concerned in it. The police thought that a further attack would be made the following night, and a body of peons were concealed in the jungle. They apprehended three Chinese who were lurking about with arms. Those engaged in the burglary were supposed to be the same as those who were concerned in the attack on Duxton, and the leader of the gang was a man formerly employed as a gardener there. It was generally thought that the very low and unremunerative wages for agricultural labour at the time were the cause of the existence of such organised bands of Chinese, but others said that they were men who came to Singapore purposely to plunder. The effects of these attacks was to prevent the extension of the town, as life and property were not considered safe beyond its immediate precincts.

In October the *Singapore Free Press and Mercantile Advertiser*
issued its first number. It was started by Mr. William Napier, the
lawyer, Mr. Lorrain, Mr. Boustead and Mr. Coleman. Mr. Boustead,
in addition to his mercantile work, had been helping to edit the
Singapore Chronicle for some time, and when Mr. Carnegy came from
Penang and purchased the paper, it was agreed to start the new paper
to advance the interests of the place. It was a weekly paper of four
pages, published on Thursdays, the last page containing a price current,
shipping reports, and mercantile information. The first number contained a curious advertisement by a priest of the Portuguese Mission
in Malacca, protesting against certain acts of the Vicar of St. Peter's
Church in Malacca for having rashly arrogated to himself an unlimited power in selling a garden (which cost $200) and a gold crown
(which cost $80) the property of the Church; contrary to the laws,
statutes, and determinations of the Holy Canons and the Sacred Council,
and to the injury of the rights of the Bishop of Goa. It also contained the prospectus of a work to be called "Notices of the Indian
Archipelago," afterwards published by Mr. Moor. The first numbers
contained a series of letters on the subject of the cultivation of land
in Singapore, which the writer considered would be fertile if a few
of the largest trees were left to prevent the soil being parched up
by the sun and to attract moisture from the clouds. He recommended
sugar-cane as likely to yield an abundant crop, but it was tried on
a large scale afterwards at Balestier Plain, and resulted in great loss.

On St. Andrew's day, a large dinner was given by the Scotchmen
of Singapore; Dr. Montgomerie and Mr. William Napier presided, and
Messrs. Spottiswoode, Lorrain, Carnie and Stephen were stewards. It
was given in the upper rooms of the Court House, and the hour was
half-past six. The Malacca Band had been learning some appropriate
airs for the respective toasts, which the *Straits Chronicle* said were
an ineffable treat to all admirers of music! There were about seventy
subscribers. On the following evening a ball was given by them, and
the ladies wore tartan scarves, and several gentlemen appeared in the
garb of old Gaul, and the party did not break up till daylight. This
(said the paper) was the first celebration of the Feast of St. Andrew
at Singapore.

In November the Canton authorities affected to be alarmed at the
appearance of the first steamer, the *Jardine*, in China, and the Hoppo
issued orders to her to *spread her sails* and return to her own country,
which however, was not complied with, but in the following January
the owners were obliged to send her away, and she came down to
Singapore. The following is the concluding passage in the edict issued
at Canton on the 7th January, 1836:—"Further, the Acting Governor
and myself have corresponded (on the subject); and if the said foreigner's *smoke-ship* arrives (at the Bogue) immediately open and attack
her hull with a thundering fire, and those who succeed in knocking
her to pieces shall certainly be promoted (over others). If the orders
are disobeyed and she enters, the least guilty shall be reported to the
Emperor, degraded from office and wear the wooden collar; the most
guilty shall be punished according to military law (*i.e.*, exiled to the
frontiers as slaves to the army). No indulgence will be shown to

any through the whole affair. Now, at this time, the Imperial orders are sternly severe; she (the steamer) cannot be allowed to linger about until some disturbance happens. Besides replying to and ordering the said Macao Custom House Weiyuen strictly to enjoin the pilots, morning and night, to be on the look out, and on no account to be negligent in their guard; it is proper to proceed to drive her out. When these orders reach the said hong merchants, let them respectfully obey, and send them immediately to the foreigners, who manage the affairs of the said nation, to issue urgent orders to the said ship to fix a day for spreading her sails and returning to her own country; she is not allowed to make pretexts, linger about, and cause a disturbance.—A Special Edict."

The *smoke-ship* afterwards came to Singapore, and her singular adventures are related in a future chapter.

Towards the end of this year, it was known that the Local Government had received orders from Calcutta to frame a schedule of duties to be levied on trade, to provide means to put down piracy. It was said that such a scale of duties might be made as would answer that object, and yet, at the same time, preserve native trade from the vexatious interference of a Custom House, and this double object was to be attained by imposing a duty on a certain class of shipping only. It was said, on the other side, that the imposition of duties threatened more serious injury to trade than piracy itself, and that the increasing trade of Singapore, which was the resort of numbers of natives who had been formerly traders with Dutch ports, was due to the facility with which they were allowed to trade here.

In November it was advertised that Mr. Thomas McMicking had been admitted a partner in Syme & Co.'s firm at Singapore, Batavia and Manila, and that Andrew Hay and Walter Scott Duncan commenced the firm of Hay and Duncan. In December the Church services were held in the Court House instead of in the Mission Chapel, as before, as the Rev. Samuel Wolfe, of the London Missionary Society, held services in that Chapel on Sunday evenings at seven o'clock.

On Tuesday, 22nd December, an attempt was made to set fire to the town. In Market Street there were a number of wooden houses belonging to Chong Long, all tenanted except one, in which some persons had piled up a quantity of dammar and other combustible materials. The peons in going their rounds at night noticed smoke coming from the vacant house, and knowing it to be unoccupied they broke in and extinguished the fire, which in a few minutes, as there was a strong wind blowing, would have consumed, the paper said, a great part of the town. The Magistrates issued a notice offering a reward for information regarding the incendiaries.

PIRACY.

It was about this time that serious efforts were made to stop piracy. The numerous islands and little rivers afforded a hundred shelters, and the natives on the coasts were barbarous, rapacious, and poor, which tended strongly to beget a piractical character, and it was not surprising (Mr. Crawfurd remarked in an article he wrote on the subject) that the Malays should have been notorious for their depredations. They formed large fleets, as in September, 1830, the boats of H. M. S. *Southampton* and the East India Co.'s Schooner *Diamond* had an engagement in the Straits of Malacca with a fleet of about thirty piratical prahus which lasted for several hours, as has been said on page 210. Mr. Earl says in his book that in 1835 the Malay pirates absolutely swarmed in the neighbourhood of Singapore, and carried it on in a perfectly systematic manner.

On the 23rd April, 1835, a public meeting was held in Singapore and a memorial was sent to the Governor-General and to the King in Council on the subject.

The result of the complaints was that H. M. Sloop *Wolf*, which had been commissioned in England in May, 1834, arrived in Singapore from Madras and Penang on the 22nd March, 1836. She was commanded by Captain Edward Stanley, and the first Lieutenant was Mr. Henry James, who died, a retired Commander, in his ninety-ninth year, in 1898. His son Mr. H. G. James, is now in Singapore. In 1899 Captain James's life entitled "A Midshipman in Search of Promotion" was published in London, and it gives an account, taken from his logs and letters, of the services of the *Wolf* at Singapore at this time.

She went twice to Calcutta to take pirates from Singapore to be tried there, as the Court in Singapore had no jurisdiction to try them until, by Letters Patent of 25th February, 1837, Admiralty Jurisdiction was given to the local Court for the purpose. On one of these occasions, the 29th May, 1837, just as the vessel was leaving Singapore for Calcutta, eleven Malay prisoners, who had been captured at Pulo Tinggi, taking advantage of the carelessness of the sentry, jumped overboard in the harbour and swam away. Five of them were caught by the ship's boats, but the rest escaped. On the morning of Wednesday, 4th October, 1836, two pirates, who had been convicted at Calcutta, were hung on the sea beach in Singapore.

The newspaper in 1836 contained numerous accounts of pirates, and remarked that, if fully detailed, their frequency would furnish matter for a paper to be exclusively devoted to their notice. The Opium brig *Lady Grant*, carrying four hundred chests, was attacked off the Sambilang Islands in the Straits of Malacca by five large prahus, and followed for some distance until it fell calm at midnight. The brig fired broadsides of grape and canister, and disabled the boats, one of which was of very large size carrying a black flag, and full of men. Native traders and even fishing boats coming into Singapore were continually attacked.

The pirates had a regular station at the Dindings where they went to refit, and kept their stores, plunder and captives. At one time, there were eighty men, women and children kept captive there, when H. M. S. *Rosa* went and attacked them.

The day the *Wolf* arrived at Singapore a bad case of piracy had occurred off Point Romania, the entrance to the China Sea, and the ship, accompanied by the East India Co.'s Schooner *Zephyr*, Captain Congalton, went off at once on a cruise to the eastward, and chased three large pirate prahus which were attacking a native vessel under Dutch colours at Point Romania, but the pirates escaped. The next day thirteen large prahus were attacked, and musketry fire was briskly exchanged between the ship's boats and the pirates.   As there was no wind the vessels could not follow the boats up, and five more prahus came out of a river near Point Romania, and joined the thirteen. They all escaped, as the ammunition in the boats was exhausted, and the men-of-war were too far away to give assistance.   Some of the prahus were of considerable size, with cloth sails, and were rigged as three-masted schooners.

The following is an account that appeared in the *Free Press* of one of the pirate boats captured by the *Wolf*, on one of these occasions :—" The prahu captured was 54 feet in length and fifteen feet beam, but their general length was 56 feet.   They were strongly built, with a round stern, and the stern post, having a considerable curve, on which the rudder, made to fit, was hung on a pintle and gudgeon.   The decks, after the same fashion as the Malay prahus, were made of split neebong, being cut into convenient lengths, so that any part of the deck could be rolled up.   The depth of hold was about six feet.   From the upper edge of the prahus a projection of bamboo, nearly two feet broad, was made all round the vessel, from the stockade near the bow to the stern, on the outer edge of which was raised, of the same material, a breastwork about three feet high, and outside this their rattan plaited cables were placed around, one coil above another, an excellent protection against shot.

" These vessels were double-banked, pulling 36 oars, 18 on each side, nine of which rested on the edge of the prahu, passing through the projecting raised work already alluded to ; the upper tier of nine oars, being worked over all the lower tier, were pulled by men sitting on the deck inside the boat itself, the upper by others sitting on the projecting bamboo work, whose heads could barely be seen above it.   The oars were worked diagonally in the style, as has been supposed by some authors, of the ancient war galleys, by which contrivance considerable room was saved.   Indeed this work projecting from the side of the vessel favoured in some measure the ingenious theory of the late General Melville in his essay on the galleys of the Greeks and Romans.

" The rowers among these pirates were of the lower castes, or slaves captured in their cruizes; hence a strong Chinese became a valuable acquisition to them ; and the oars could admit of two men pulling at each if necessary.   Their rigging was of the most simple kind, a large sail forward and a smaller sail abaft, made of light mats sewed together, stretched on bamboos above and below, having cross pieces at intervals from top to bottom in the foresail only, which was hoisted on a triangle of stout bamboos forming the fore-mast.   This was done exactly like the Bugis boats, a bamboo lashed close to the outer edge of the vessel on each side ; and a third, fastened to the deck amidships immediately behind the stockade, is brought up to meet the two upright pieces, and all are lashed together at the top, forming a very efficient support to the sail, and excellently adapted for resisting shot; in fact it was found very difficult to shoot them away, for when struck by shot they were only split and still stood as well as before.   The small mast behind was a spar.

" The working of their sails was likewise very simple, for when the prahu went about, the tacks and braces were let go, the bow pulled somewhat round, and the sail turned round to the other side of the mast, fore the tacks, boused down; and the braces, which led aft, made fast, and so the vessel was on the other tack.

"Each prahu had a stockade, not far from the bow, through which was pointed an iron four-pounder; another stockade abaft, on which was stuck two swivels, and around the sides were from three to six guns of the same description, all brass, stuck upon upright pieces of wood; they had likewise muskets, spears, &c., and many of the pirates wore very large bamboo shields covering all the upper part of the body. The fighting men wore long hair which they let loose in the battle, to give them a savage appearance. It may be mentioned that the orang kaya's prahu was armed with brass guns, according to the report of his son, who was one of the captives."

In May, 1836, H. M. S. *Andromache* came from Trincomalee. She was commanded by Captain Chads, a very distinguished man; he died Sir Henry Ducie Chads, G.C.B., near the top of the Admiral's list. On the 29th December, 1812, he had been first lieutenant of the frigate *Java* of 36 guns, 18 pounders, Captain Henry Lambert, which was burnt and sunk in action with the American ship *Constitution* in the war with America. The Captain was killed, and there is a monument to him in St. Paul's Cathedral. The command then devolved on Lieutenant Chads, who was promoted in consequence. A great number of officers, sailors and marines were killed and wounded in the action.

Captain Chads afterwards commanded the *Cambrian* in Singapore and China, and Mr. W. H. Read says that he was on board her in the harbour in Singapore when the *Constitution*, years afterwards, came round St. John's Island. The old Captain got quite excited and exclaimed "What would I give to have twenty minutes with her *now!*" His son Henry Chads, still alive, is now Sir Henry Chads, K.C.B., an Admiral on the retired list. He was afterwards first lieutenant of the *Harlequin*, and was desperately wounded, losing his left arm, in an attack on Acheen pirates. Sir James Brooke was wounded at the same time. This was in 1844. Mr. R. O Norris writes "I remember Lieutenant Chads, because Padre White used to give lectures in Coleman Street, which the boys from the Institution and the girls from Miss Whittle's School attended. Probably Miss Coleman, Miss Ryan, and myself are the only ones now in Singapore who remember Lieutenant Chads, who came to the lectures. We boys noticed that he had lost his left arm, and thought him a hero." Mr. Earl says in his book, page 383, that the *Andromache* made some very formidable attacks on the pirates, and adopted a very successful ruse by disguising the vessel so that it was mistaken for a native merchant ship. She had passed through the harbour to the west, and came back the next day through the harbour disguised as a Dutch trader, came across pirates outside, and gave them a lesson as they ranged alongside his ship. The Malays then fancied that every square-rigged vessel which they met was a man-of-war.

The *Andromache* went to attack a noted stronghold on the island of Gallang, in the Rhio Archipelago. A great quantity of things, the result of piracy, were found, and a junk of 300 tons which had been captured on her way from Cochin-China. About thirty large boats and fifty smaller ones were destroyed, and a very large quantity of ammunition was found. The boats were fitted with large guns and all sorts of piratical contrivances, and there was not the least trace on the island of any cultivation or industry, although there were large villages sufficient to contain several thousand inhabitants.

An old Singapore paper speaks of a midshipman then on board the *Andromache*, named Henry Chads. This was the present Sir Henry Chads, just spoken of.

The *Free Press*, in connection with piracy, spoke of the slave traffic that was then carried on; one writing from personal knowledge saying that the island of Nias, Sumatra, in particular, the largest and most populous opposite that coast, was the place where the curse seemed to exist most; that on board any of the numerous small prahus going in the direct route from that island to the North West Coast, young boys and girls would be found, either kidnapped by the dealers, or purchased by them for the numerous petty Rajahs. And at any of the settlements in Sumatra, these unhappy victims were exposed for sale in the ships like any other goods. The writer said that he had happened in 1835 to see four young women, just imported for sale in this way, their owner answering enquiries from intending purchasers with the same indifference as he answered those of another customer who was buying a piece of cloth.

The third man-of-war which was in Singapore for the same purpose, was the *Raleigh*, Captain Michael Quin, a famous character, who also was on the Admiral's list when he died, as was also Captain Stanley of the *Wolf*.

On the 7th September, 1837, a public dinner was given to Captain Stanley and the Officers of the *Wolf* by the Chamber of Commerce at Calcutta, for their services against pirates in the Straits.

At the Assizes which were held in June, 1838, the jury were mostly occupied with piracy cases, and on the last day, which was a Saturday, eighteen Malays were tried and convicted, three others were so ill of their wounds that their trial was postponed. Some of the men were executed on the following Monday.

On Thursday, 14th June, a public dinner was given by the mercantile community to Captain Stanley and the officers of the *Wolf*, in testimony of the sense entertained of their services in the suppression of piracy. Mr. Spottiswoode gave his house, and it was said to be the largest party that had been assembled in Singapore. The Governor and Resident Councillor were present, and Mr. Shaw was Chairman. Captain Congalton of the *Diana*, was away, but his health was drunk also with much enthusiasm.

The Chamber of Commerce presented an address to Captain Stanley, and a sword with the following inscription:— " Presented to Captain Edward Stanley, by the European and Chinese Mercantile Community of Singapore, in testimony of the grateful sense entertained by them of his unwearied and successful exertions for the suppression of piracy in the Straits of Malacca and adjacent seas, during the years 1836, 1837 and 1838, while commanding Her Majesty's Sloop *Wolf*." The value of the sword was one hundred guineas.

It was the first occasion that any similar mark of public approbation had been bestowed by the community on any of the vessels employed in the suppression of piracy, but the *Wolf* with the assistance of Captain Congalton, had adopted systematic and energetic measures.

The encounter of the first steamer, the East India Company's *Diana*, with the pirates in 1837, is worth telling. H. M. S *Wolf* was a sailing vessel, of course, so Captain Congalton in the little steamer *Diana* went ahead, and the pirates in six large prahus, seeing the smoke, thought it was a sailing ship on fire, so they left the Chinese Junk which they were attacking, and bore down on the steamer, firing on her as she approached. To their horror, the vessel came close up *against the wind*, and then suddenly stopped opposite each prahu, and poured in a destructive fire, turning and backing quite against the wind, stretching the pirates in numbers on their decks. A vessel that was independent of the wind was, of course, a miracle to them.

In 1811, in a letter to Lord Minto, Sir Stamford Raffles had made numerous allusions to piracy and slavery. He described piracy as "An evil of ancient date, which had struck deep in the Malay habits," and said the old Malay romances and fragments of traditional history constantly referred to piratical cruises. He said that piracy was a source of slavery, and that the practice was an evil too extensive and formidable to be cured by reasoning and must be put down by a strong hand. There were a number of very able and long articles in the third, fourth, and fifth volumes of Logan's Journal. The author is not named, but they are full of details of old piracy stories from the earliest days.

The account of the commencement of the suppression of piracy in Singapore would be very incomplete without special reference to Captain Samuel Congalton, whose portrait is in the Singapore Library.

Captain Congalton was born in Leith on 23rd March, 1796. He ran away to sea in a collier when a young boy, but his eldest brother found him and brought him back. He again ran away to sea, and eventually got a place as gunner on a ship bound to Calcutta. The vessel was sold there, and joining a country ship he arrived at Penang in 1821. Captain Poynton of the East India Co.'s armed Schooner *Jessy* wanted a mate, and he joined her and remained in the Straits until his death in 1850.

While he was in the *Jessy*, Captain Marryatt, the famous novelist, of H. M. S. *Larne*, gave him great praise for his services in the Rangoon War.

In March, 1826, Captain Poynton was made Harbour Master at Malacca, and Congalton took command of the sailing schooner *Zephyr*, on a salary of $100 a month, and was blockading the Lingy river, with H. M. S. *Magicienne*, and Lieutenant the Hon. Henry Keppel, in the Naning War.

At the end of 1836 the Government determined to sell the *Zephyr*, and in the beginning of 1837 the East India Co.'s steamer *Diana* was sent to the Straits and Congalton was appointed Captain at a salary of Rs. 350. The *Diana* was the first steamer constructed in India, she was 160 tons and 40 horse-power and attained the great speed (*at that time*) of five knots an hour. She carried the Captain, two European officers, and thirty Malays.

The *Nemesis* came out round the Cape of Good Hope soon afterwards, and the Captain of her was very proud of having brought her out.

On 2nd January, 1846, the East India Company's steamer *Hooghly* arrived at Singapore to relieve the *Diana*. Captain Congalton declined the command of one of the larger steamers, and preferred to remain in the Straits, and his salary was advanced to Rs. 500 a month. His services in the employ comprised a period of twenty-eight and a half years, and he said in a report that he had never been absent from his duties, either on sick leave or on account of private affairs, for a single day, until a few months before his death, when attacked by a dangerous illness.

He was frequently employed in political missions to the Native States, and in conjunction with Mr. J. T. Thomson he made a chart of the Singapore Straits. A handsome silver jug was given him by Captain Stanley and the Officers of the *Wolf*, another by Sir William Norris, the Recorder, and a third by Governor Butterworth. Mr. J. T. Thomson in his book speaks very highly of him. His memory was cherished by many friends in the Straits, as a very brave and generous-minded sailor. Mr. Read writes of him as " a fine old fellow and a great favorite with everybody " and old Admiral Keppel who returned to Singapore in November, 1901, when this chapter was ready for the printer, spoke of him as " a rough and ready old fellow, a thorough sailor, and a great character in the Straits."

His thorough knowledge of the Malays and their haunts made him invaluable in attacking the pirates, but he often did the hard work, and others in the Men-of-war got the credit and the rewards.

The *Diana* was the first steamer that ever appeared in Borneo, and was an object of great curiosity to the Natives. Crowds visited her, and when a number of chiefs were down below, the machinery was set in motion, to their great horror. They flew on deck crying out *dya bergrak! dia bergrak!* (it stirs, it stirs) thinking it was a living monster, fed in the hold to move the vessel as it was ordered.

Captain Congalton was a short man, but compact and active. He was a man of high principles, blunt and honest. The copy of his portrait which is now in the Raffles Library was purchased after his death by his friends in Singapore and was intended to be hung in the public hall. It was painted by a Mr. Berghaus about 1847, and was engraved. In the first volume of Logan's Journal is an article by Captain Congalton on a search for Coal deposits on the coasts of the Peninsula.

The Newspaper remarked afterwards that Captain Congalton's many actions against pirates did not rival the deeds of Sir James Brooke and Sir Henry Keppel, in after years; yet there was no doubt that the first check was due to him and that he initiated a new state of things. It was he who first met them with an energy that paralyzed them, and it was difficult perhaps to realize what they meant in those days to the trade of Singapore and to the safety of human life in the locality. On Captain Congalton's death at Penang in April, 1850, everyone attended his funeral and all flags were hoisted at half-mast.

THE ARMENIAN CHURCH.

The beginning of the Armenian Church services in Singapore was in the year 1821. There was then three Armenian firms here, Aristarchus Sarkies, Arratoon Sarkies of Malacca, and another; they were trading with Malacca at the time. The priest, the Revd. Eleazar Ingergolie, died in Singapore in the year 1826, after having been several years here.

The old minute book of the Armenian Church shows that on 8th January, 1825, a meeting was held and a letter was written to one of the Archbishops in Persia asking that a priest might be sent to Singapore. The letter was signed by Johannes Simeon, Carapiet Phanos, Gregory and Isaiah Zechariah, Mackertich M. Moses, and Paul Stephens. On June 23rd, 1826, there was further correspondence with the Archbishop. On 23rd September, 1827, there was a meeting to decide about a place to hold the services when the priest should arrive; and subscriptions were collected. In July, 1827, the Rev. Gregory ter Johannes, the priest, had arrived, and a meeting was held to provide for the ecclesiastical vessels and ornaments that were required. The services were first held in a room behind where John Little & Co. are now. Soon afterwards the Archbishop Gregory came on a visit to Singapore. In September a small room was rented for the services in what was spoken of as "the Merchant's Square," where Powell & Co. are at present. A minute says that the expenses for rent, servants, and the salary of the Priest amounted to $63 a month. The minutes until 1833 contain many records of subscriptions received in Singapore and from Calcutta and Java for the fund for building a Church. In March, 1833, an appeal was made to their friends in the European community, and on 29th March a letter was written to Mr. Bonham, the Resident Councillor, asking for the grant of a piece of land for the Church, facing the Esplanade or at the foot of the Government Hill. This was not successful, and on 23rd April another letter was sent asking for another piece of ground "lying at the Botanical Gardens facing the public road called "the Hill Street." This was granted, and the Church now standing was built there. In January, 1835, the Church was finished and ready to be consecrated. The total cost was $5,058.30, which was made up by the contract price to a Kling contractor, $3,500; Mr. Coleman, the Architect and Engineer, $400; sundry expenses for materials, &c., $708.36; and vestments, ornaments, &c., $449.94. The amount subscribed was $3,224.52 of which $466 was by European residents in Singapore; $573.22 from Calcutta; $402.88 from Java, and $173 from Armenians passing through Singapore. The rest was from the Armenian community in the place.

The Church was originally built with a high dome, but it became unsafe and was altered into the present roof. Mr. Catchick Moses at his own expense built the wall round the compound, except the railing in Hill Street; and he also enlarged the Priest's house, and built the back porch. The minutes shew that considerable sums were collected at various times and sent to Persia for schools there.

The building of the Church had been commenced on the 1st January, 1835, and was consecrated on the 26th March, 1836, being the anniversary of St. Gregory, the Illuminator and first monk of the Armenian Church, to whom it was dedicated. The *Free Press* spoke as follows of the building :—"This small, but elegant, building does great credit to the public spirit and religious feeling of the Armenians of this Settlement; for we believe that few instances could be shewn where so small a community have contributed funds sufficient for the erection of a similar edifice. The interior of this Church is a complete circle of thirty-six feet diameter, with a semi-circular chancel of eighteen feet wide on the east front; four small chambers, two of which are intended for staircases, and two for vestries, are designed, so that the body of the Church forms an equilateral square ; from these project three porticos of six columns each, which shade the windows and entrances, and afford convenient shelter for carriages in rainy weather. The principal order is Doric, surmounted by a balustrade, the top of which is twenty-three feet high; the roofs of the porticos, vestries, and chancel are flat, and that of the body of the Church a truncated cone rising ten feet with a flat space of twelve feet diameter on which is erected a Bell-turret, with eight arches, and as many Ionic pilasters ; the height of these pilasters, with their entablature, is eleven, and that of the dome which they support six feet, the whole being surmounted by a ball and cross, the top of which is fifty feet above the floor of the Church. The above are the general measurements of the building, and we regret the absence of mechanical means to enable us to present our distant readers with a drawing which might convey a correct idea of its appearance. The design was by Mr. G. D. Coleman, and whether owing to the abilities of the workmen, or the vigilance with which that gentleman superintended them, we know not; but it appears to us that the Armenian Church is one of the most ornate and best finished pieces of architecture that this gentleman can boast of. One only regret attends a survey of this building, which is that a rigid compliance with the old custom that directs the chancel to face the East, has caused the principal front to be placed in a totally opposite direction to that which the architect intended, and which would have presented it in a more conspicous and desirable point of views."

The ceremony of consecration was attended by a large number of the English community, and the paper gives a long account of it, from which we take the following:—"The Rev. Johannes Catchick, accompanied by the officiating deacons and clerks, one of them carrying the dresses and the foundation stone (emblematical) of the altar, on a silver tray, and all dressed according to the ranks of the Armenian Church, walked from a vestry to a table, placed for the purpose, in the north portico (the main entrance) where the 119th to the 122nd Psalms were read, verse by verse, by a deacon and clerk, followed by a prayer by the clergyman. The doors of the portico were then closed, while the 117th Psalm was read, and a hymn sung; and after another prayer by the clergyman, the doors were re-opened for the admission of the congregation.

"The curtain or veil of the chancel having been drawn up, the altar was exposed to view, having over it a picture of the Lord's Supper (merely as an altar-piece and an ornament). The 147th Psalm was then read, and a hymn sung, followed by the reading of several chapters from the Book of Kings, relative to the building of the Temple at Jerusalem, also from the Prophesies of Isaiah, Micah and Jeremiah, with parts of the 1st Chapter of St. Paul's Epistle to the Philippians, and 16th Chapter of St. Matthew's Gospel. Then followed the 25th Psalm, and, while reading this, some of the clerks proceeded to wash, first by water, then by wine, the sides of the altar, the wall of the two small alcoves in the chancel, in one of which the sacrament of the Lord's Supper is prepared, then the four sides of the body of the Church and head of the vestry door; after which the clergyman, accompanied by the senior deacon and clerk, went round to the spots so washed, and anointed them with Holy Oil from a silver cup making the Sign of the Cross : the clerks chaunting at the time. The four sides of the Church were then blessed by the clergyman with a golden cross, held in his hand, who dedicated the Church to Saint Gregory the Illuminator, and first monk of the Church of Armenia.

"The 92nd Psalm was then read, and a hymn sung, while the assistants were clothing the altar with the usual dresses. The curtain was afterwards let down for a few minutes to enable the clergyman to prepare himself for addressing the congregation, which he did from the steps of the altar. The service of the consecration having thus ended, the usual performance of the Mass took place (which is certainly quite distinct from that of the Roman Catholic Church) being interspersed with singing of hymns, reading of portions of the Prophets, Epistles, and Gospels, and the recital of the Apostles' Creed. The service was in the Armenian language and occupied about three hours and a half."

CHAPTER XXIII.

St. ANDREW'S CHURCH.

THE following is a translation of a passage from the Hikayat Abdulla:—"The place where the Church stands was the centre of a plain. When I first saw the ground the jungle had been cleared off and only small bushes remained. When cleared by Mr. Farquhar the plain was occupied for Sepoy Lines and for the residence of the principal Europeans, and continued to be so used until Mr. Crawfurd's time, when the Sepoys were removed along the road to Teluk Blanga, where lines and fine *pucka* houses were built for the men and officers. The plain then continued vacant, and was used as a place for exercising horses, and an evening lounge for Europeans to take the air After a short time, houses were built, one by one, till six or seven were finished for the Europeans. In the year of the Hejira 1234 (1838) when Mr. Bonham was Resident, and Mr. Wingrove was at the head of the police office, it became known that the Europeans intended to erect a large Church. Previous to this time they had been in the habit of attending at the small Chapel built by the Rev. Mr. Thompson. When everything was arranged subscriptions were collected from the residents, the Government, and strangers; and the work was finished as it now stands, by Mr. Coleman, the Architect."

In July, 1834, a meeting, which was well attended, was called in the vestry of the Mission Chapel by Mr. Darrah, the Chaplain, to consider a proposal to erect a suitable Church on the land given ten years before by Government for the purpose. A committee was appointed, and in October the Bishop of Calcutta arrived in Singapore, having called at Penang on his way. Bishop Wilson was the fifth Bishop of Calcutta, and first Metropolitan of India. He left England to take up the Bishopric in 1832, and was succeeded by Bishop Cotton in 1858. The Church services were at that time held in the Mission Chapel, and two days after his arrival, Bishop Wilson presided at a meeting, of which the following report was published at the time:—

"On Monday, the 6th October, a meeting of the European inhabitants of Singapore, the most numerous ever yet witnessed here, was held at the Court House, at 10 o'clock, for the purpose of taking into consideration the best means of erecting a suitable and commodious place of worship, for the use of the Protestant community of the Settlement. On the proposal of the Hon'ble S. G. Bonham, who was the Acting Governor, the Bishop of Calcutta took the chair. His Lordship stated that he understood the inhabitants had been desirous, from the commencement of the Settlement, to devise measures for the erection of a Church for their beautiful country, and he could not but feel anxiety that their wishes should be accomplished. He had had an opportunity of seeing the building which was used temporarily for divine worship, which was not at all suitable for the purpose. It would require very considerable alterations and a large outlay even if it could assume an ecclesiastical appearance; and supposing these were managed, the structure itself was of so slight a nature, that it could not be expected to last for any length of time, and thus their money and trouble would be wasted.

"The plan he would suggest, would be something like the following:—The structure must be neat, convenient, commodious and elegant; such as would adorn the neighbourhood, and be suitable for that very admirable site which had already been allotted, and was long ago intended for the purpose. The difficulty was as to means. Now, he would suggest, first of all, that from the letting of the seats when the Church was built and opened for divine worship, a certain income would arise. This might be appropriated to the payment of the interest of whatever money it might be necessary to borrow, and to the gradual liquidation of the principal itself. This was one source. Then, what might the Government be expected to do? In former times, when measures of strict economy were less essential, he should have said they would have built a Church; but now, he hoped he might still say that they would willingly assist in building it. Already $20 a month were paid by them for the rent of the missionary place of worship to which he had referred; and, he thought that Government would gladly make such a grant for the new Church as would redeem this monthly payment. Then he himself was the depository of a sum of money from the Society for Promoting Christian Knowledge. It was but small, but he felt authorised in offering £100 or $500, on their behalf. His Chaplain also was Secretary to the Church Building Fund for India, and he thought a small grant of Rs. 500 might be made from that fund. He (the Bishop) was encouraged, last of all, to hope that, from the appearance and high respectability of the Meeting, something might be done to give the plan a start, and to show that the inhabitants were in earnest. If this should be the case; and he would leave it to the Governor and themselves to propose and carry it into effect; a beautiful structure would soon be erected to ornament their town, daily increasing in importance, and their noble harbour; as also, above all, to promote the glory of God on the very confines of the civilized world.

The Governor next addressed the meeting by saying that, as far as laid in his power, he would strongly urge the Supreme Government to give a capital sum in lieu of the $20 a month which was now allowed. But the meeting should not be too sanguine in expecting that the recommendation would be complied with. It rested with the Supreme Government. At the same time, the question was entirely of a local nature, and he thought the inhabitants themselves should come forward, and, in a more tangible manner than by mere words, prove the desire they had for the construction of a proper place of worship, befitting the Settlement, now rapidly rising in importance.

The result of the appeal for the building fund for the Church was an instant and most liberal subscription amounting to $3,460.

The following are the names of the first subscribers:—The S. P. C. K. £100, Church Building Fund for India $250, Bishop Wilson £25, Mr. Bonham $250, Mr Wingrove and the Rev. F. J. Darrah, the Chaplain, $100 each, Messrs. Douglas Mackenzie & Co., Hamilton Gray & Co., Holdsworth Smithson & Co., Graham Mackenzie & Co., A. L. Johnston & Co., Maclaine Fraser & Co., Spottiswoode &

Connolly, and Syme & Co., subscribed $100 each firm, and Messrs. J. & G. Zechariah (Armenians) subscribed $50. The other subscribers were Messrs. J. Armstrong, R. Bruce, H. Caldwell, J. S. Clark, G. D. Coleman, T. O. Crane, G. F. Davidson, W. S. Duncan, W. R. George, S. Hallpike, Andrew Hay, W. Hewetson, W. S. Lorrain, M. J. Martin, J. H. Moor, M. Moses, William Napier, Thomas Oxley, John Poynton, John Purvis, J. Rappa, Thos. Scott, G. C. Swaabe, C. Spottiswoode, C. Thomas and J. Whitehead. There being so many Scotchmen among the subscribers, the Church was to be called after St. Andrew.

On the following morning, the 6th October, the Bishop consecrated the Burial Ground on the hill [near Fort Canning], and in the evening fourteen persons were confirmed, the first service of the kind, it is supposed, in Singapore. The Bishop left for Malacca two days afterwards, and did not return to Singapore until 1838 when he consecrated the first St. Andrew's Church.

On Friday the 16th October, 1835, a meeting was held at the Court House, to consider the erection of the Church, and several plans obtained from Calcutta were examined, and set aside, because they were not designed with verandahs or any other contrivances for shading the body of the Church from the glare and heat. A design by Mr. G. D. Coleman was approved, and it was determined to commence building at once. The body of the Church was forty-seven feet between the pedestals of the interior columns, and was semi-circular at the end next the middle entrance, which was fifty feet from the front of the chancel. The staircases, which led to the galleries, were placed in the angles cut off by the semi-circle. The chancel was twenty feet wide by sixteen feet from back to front, with a room on each side, like in the present Cathedral, of thirteen feet by ten. The whole was shaded by porticos, twenty feet wide, extending the full length of the building on each side, and making the extreme measurement one hundred and two feet by ninety-five. The porticos enclosed carriage roads, and over them on three sides were galleries. The one opposite the chancel was to be occupied by the organ and school children. The whole was to cost ten thousand dollars. The following engraving was drawn by Mr. James Miller, of Messrs. Gilfillan Wood & Co., from an old picture by Mr. Carpenter, an artist who visited Singapore about 1854, and included it in one of his views of the place.

On Monday the 9th November, 1835, a large number of persons assembled on the plain, on the site where the present Cathedral stands, to witness the laying of the foundation stone. There was no masonic or other ceremonial observed (the newspaper remarked) with the exception of a short service by the Residency Chaplain, preceded by a short address.

On Thursday, 8th June, 1837, a distribution of the sittings in the new Church was made by the Church Committee, and it was understood that Mr. White was to hold the first service on Sunday, the 11th; but at the last moment the Chaplain said that he could not officiate until he had been called upon by the community, by letter, to procure its consecration as soon as a fit opportunity offered. As soon as the condition became known, the Committee addressed the following letter on the 10th June, to the Resident Councillor, Mr. Church:—
" Sir, the new Church being completed and ready for performing Divine Service, we the undersigned, members of the Committee, request the Government to take charge of the same for the space of one year, it being understood, that the Church is not to be consecrated during that period, without the sanction of a majority of the subscribers to the building.

A. L. Johnston, R. F. Wingrove, J. H. Whitehead."

Mr. White, thereupon, commenced to officiate under an order from the Resident Councillor, the community not having consented to the conditions Mr. White had tried to impose about consecration, as it was said that in cases of there being no Chaplain, (as had been the case for seventeen months at that time) no other form of worship could be used in the building. Under these circumstances the first service took place on Sunday, the 18th June.

In August, 1838, Bishop Daniel Wilson came again to the Straits, visiting Penang and Malacca on his way to Singapore. He arrived in Singapore on Saturday, the 1st September, and conducted the service the next day. On Wednesday, a meeting was held to resume the proceedings commenced at the meeting in 1834, and after a very lengthy address and explanation by the Bishop, a petition for the consecration of the Church was signed by a good many of those present, and on Monday, the 10th September, the Church was consecrated. The paper contained no account of the ceremony.

Bishop Wilson of Calcutta, returned for the third time to the Straits in October, 1842. At his first visit subscriptions had been raised to build the Church; at his second visit, he consecrated it; and on this his third visit he sent out the following circular, on 31st October, 1842.

" The Bishop of Calcutta takes the liberty of circulating this paper with the view of ascertaining how far it may be agreeable to the gentry of this station to complete the beautiful and commodious body of their Church by the addition of a small but appropriate tower and spire, such as shall distinguish the sacred edifice from secular buildings in a manner usual in all parts of India, as well as at home. At present the Church may be mistaken for a Town Hall, a College or an Assembly Room. The strangers resorting to this great emporium of commerce have no means of knowing for what it is destined. By the

erection of a tower and spire, rising about 50 feet above the balustrade of the roof, its sacred design will be manifested, and the
surrounding heathen will see the honour we put upon our religion, and the
care we take to mark the reverence for the solemn worship of Almighty
God by the appropriate distinctions of its outward appearance. The
only four Churches in India built originally without the ecclesiastical
decoration of a spire or tower, were those of Kuruaul, Agra, Ghazee-
pore and Dinapore. Three of these have now the needful additions,
raised by the subscriptions of the several stations, and the fourth,
Dinapore, has its fund ready for the same purpose. The new Cathedral at Calcutta will have a tower and spire 200 feet high. The Scotch
Churches at Calcutta, Madras and Bombay have noble spires. Nor is
there any station in the territories of the East India Company so likely
to rise into distinguished importance as Singapore; the vicinity of which
to China and the accessions of commerce which may be expected from
the blessing of peace, just established in that Empire, render such an
Act of piety as the due completion of their Church peculiarly appropriate. National mercy calls for expressions and acts of gratitude to
the Giver of all good, and none is more suitable than this. The Bishop
is indeed persuaded that he is only anticipating the almost universal
wishes of the Community of Singapore in circulating this paper.
And, though the sum to be raised is large, in consequence of the
high price of labour and materials in this place, yet he feels confident
that the united and hearty and generous subscriptions of all classes of
persons will overcome the difficulties of completing the Sacred Edifice
now, as the difficulties in the commencement and progress of the work
were overcome before. One unanimous final effort will now crown the
preceding labours and give to Singapore a Church scarcely inferior
to any in the Eastern world."

Mrs. Balestier, the wife of the American Consul, gave a Bell to the
Church, which was afterwards used in the present Cathedral until the
peal of bells was given. It was cast by Revere at Boston, and was
given on condition that the curfew should be rung for five minutes
every evening at eight o'clock, which was done until 1874. It is a
large and heavy bell, 32 inches in diameter and 26 inches high. The
following words are cast on it. "Revere Boston 1843. Presented to
St. Andrew's Church, Singapore, by Mrs. Maria Revere Balestier of
Boston, United States of America." Mrs. Balestier, who had been Miss
Revere, died in Singapore on 22nd August, 1847, having been thirteen
years in the place. Mr. Thomas Church, the Resident Councillor,
gave a Clock, which was put up on the facade of the Court House, as
a temporary resting place, when the Church was pulled down.

When the Court House was being enlarged in 1901, the clock was
taken down, and the opportunity was taken to find out what kind of
clock it was that Mr. Church had given. It has on it the name of
the makers, Barraud & Lund, Cornhill, London, very eminent clock
makers, so that it is evident Mr. Church bought the best clock he
could obtain. The dial is 4 feet 6 inches in diameter, the figures are
6¾ inches long, and the long hand is 25 inches. The bell is 20 inches
diameter, and weighs probably about one and a half hundred weight.
It has the date 1839 cast on it. It is a very well made clock, and it

is still in very good condition after over sixty years work, and seems never to have been taken to pieces since it was put up. It ought to be replaced in the Cathedral tower, for which Mr. Church gave it.

The bell and the clock were both costly gifts to the Church, and intended to remain in the building or its successors. If they had been given to the Roman Catholic Church they would have been taken care of, and would have been put up, long since, in one of the steeples of their four other Churches, if they could not have been kept, as the donors intended, in the Cathedral. The clock could easily be set up now in the Cathedral tower, facing the Esplanade, where it would be very useful; the dial could be made larger and the hands longer without difficulty. The bell is in a shed in the Public Works Store at Kandang Kerbau, and may be forgotten there till it is broken up for old metal.

Mr. Richard O. Norris, who was then a boy attending Raffles School, sent the following amusing account of his recollections of the old Church to the *Free Press* in 1885:—

"Talking about the Church which I see mentioned in your History, I can give you some old recollectons of mine, which must soon lapse into the past. In the old days we had a barrel organ, and old Anchant, as he was called, was organ turner and singer. The organ was described in the paper as having a handsome Gothic oak base, twelve feet high, six wide and four deep; forty-two keys; with two ranks of pipes in the base, and three in the treble; and four barrels of twelve tunes each. We, Institution boys, used to sing. Then Anchant died, and one of the boys was the organ man, and the rest of us used to sing without any leader as best we could. I remember at the time of the China War, Sir Hugh Gough and all his staff attending Church in full uniform, and sitting in the Governor's and Resident Councillor's seats. The transports came pouring in, all in one day, and the harbour was full. But to return to the organ; the old machine got very wheezy and went to Malacca, and a subscription was collected for a new organ, which Bishop Wilson announced in his sermon on the last Sunday in October, 1842, and the money was sent home in 1843, and an organ made by Holditch of London came out, which cost £260. This passed in course of time to the Scotch Church, and eventually in extreme old age, it was bought by Mr. G. H. Brown for old acquaintance sake, and it expired at his house on Mount Pleasant. It had one row of keys and pedals. On the opening morning, and for some time, Mr. Keasberry played it, and some ladies made a choir. Then Mr. Charles A. Dyce came from Calcutta, and was amateur organist, and eventually married one of the young ladies who sang. Then Mr. G. H. Brown came from Penang, and he initiated a choir of boys from Raffles School, and girls from the School in North Bridge Road kept by Mrs. Whittle, whose husband was a surveyor. This did not last very long. Mr. Tom Church used to sing loud, and we boys in the gallery did hear him well. Church-going in the old days was better regulated than now, as all lived within a short distance from the Church. Both services were well attended, and Christenings always took place in the middle of the evening service. The Church was lit by candles in iron stands, which were used in the new Church until gas came out in 1864. The Communion Service was quarterly at first, and afterwards once a month, until about 1860. The notices of it, when once a quarter, used to be gummed on the walls. The pulpit was on one side, the reading desk, a little shorter, on the other, and the clerk's desk was close to the reading desk. After evening service the people walked home, and if it was a dark night, a lantern used to head the procession. I should like to mention that there were many prayer books and Bibles marked " Fort Marlborough, Bencoolen " a reminiscence of Sir Stamford Raffles, relics of the good old days, not one left now, no doubt. There were two tablets with the ten Commandments on them in gold letters, with two doves over them, at the sides of the Communion Table. They were made by man-of-war sailors during Padre White's time; they worked at them in the gallery behind the old hand-organ, but the tablets were not very artistic, especially the doves, though they were good enough for the old days. From the organ gallery we looked out upon the two pairs of gates at Mr. Coleman's two buildings, afterwards the Hotels in Coleman Street; part of the out-buildings were first covered with slates, a novelty here at the time."

In August, 1845, the steeple was struck by lightning, which splintered one of the tablets next to the Communion Table; and again on the 4th April, 1849, at about 2 o'clock in the afternoon, the spire was struck. The electric fluid descended the tower, and then took a playful direction, part proceeding to the earth down the inside front of the Church, but the greater portion took a two-fold lateral direction, then passed down the punkah rods, distant from each other about 20 feet, and destroyed the punkahs. Both currents again took a lateral direction, tearing off the mortar on the walls; that to right passed along the floor of one of the pews, and that to the left of the Communion Table escaped through and greatly injured the vestry door. The steeple, roofs and walls, down which the electric fluid passed perpendicularly, appeared as if riddled by swan shot. Fortunately the accident did not happen during Divine Service, or it is highly probable several lives would have been lost. There was no conductor fixed until after this occurence. In 1852 the Church ceased to be used, as it was in a dangerous state, and the Mission Chapel at the corner of Brass Bassa Road was used for the services. In 1854 the Grand Jury "presented" the ruinous state of the Church as a disgrace to the Settlement, and this led to the erection of the present Cathedral.

A discussion was raised in 1856 regarding the duties of the Trustees of St. Andrew's Church, and it was remarked in the newspaper that they had been spoken of as Churchwardens, which it said was as novel in Singapore as it would have been in India; that it was not sanctioned by the East India Company's charter; and was contrary to the letter and spirit of the rules laid down by the Government for the guidance of Chaplains in India. The rules made by the Governor in Council for Madras were printed at length. They provided for two lay trustees, who formed a committee of management with the Chaplain. One of them was to be the Senior Civil Servant, or the Officer Commanding the Garrison if a purely military station, provided the person appointed was a communicant of the Church of England and had no objection to hold the office. The other lay trustee was to be a gentleman in the service of the Queen or the E. I. Company, nominated by the Chaplain with the approval of the Bishop. The following were their duties, printed in full from the newspaper :—

"DUTIES OF THE LAY TRUSTEES.

1. It shall be the duty of the Lay Trustees to present to the Bishop, or his Archdeacon, at their Visitation, or immediately by letter, and at any time on the requisition of the Lord Bishop or his commissary, any irregularity or scandal on the part of the Chaplain, or in connection with the Chaplaincy, which may have occurred within the District.

2. To aid and assist the chaplain in the performance of his duties.

DUTIES OF THE STANDING COMMITTEE OF MANAGEMENT.

The Committee of Management shall take charge of the School and Charity Funds connected with the Chaplaincy ; see that the Church Yard and Burial Ground are kept in becoming order : take charge of the Plate, and the care of the goods, repairs and ornaments of the Church, or other building appropriated to the performance of Divine Service, and represent to Government, through the Ecclesiastical Head, any deficiency in these particulars, which they may think necessary or desirable to supply.

The Chaplain, as President, will report to Government any vacancy in the office of Lay Trustee."

In May, 1855, the Bengal Government approved of the proposal to build a new Church, and sanctioned an expenditure of Rs. 47,000 in cash for the purpose.

The newspaper of March, 1856, contained the following :—

" On Tuesday evening the 4th March, the Lord Bishop of Calcutta laid the foundation stone of a Church intended to replace St. Andrew's Church, which was sometime ago taken down on account of its insecure condition. The ceremony took place in presence of the Civil and Military authorities and a considerable number of the community. The following is a copy of the inscription placed below the stone :—

The first English Church of Singapore, commenced A. D. 1834 and consecrated A. D. 1838, having become dilapidated, this first stone of a new and more commodious edifice, dedicated to the worship of Almighty God according to the rites and discipline of the Church of England, under the name of St. Andrew, was laid by the Right Rev. Daniel Wilson, D.D., Lord Bishop of Calcutta and Metropolitan, on the 4th day of March, 1856, in the 24th year of his Episcopate.

The Hon'ble Edmund Augustus Blundell, being the Governor of the Straits Settlements,

The Hon'ble Thomas Church, being Resident Councillor of Singapore,

Lieut.-Col. Charles Pooley, of the Madras Army, Commanding the Troops,

The Reverend William Topley Humphrey being Chaplain,

And Captain Ronald Macpherson, of the Madras Artillery, being Architect.

The building to be erected at the charge of the Hon'ble East India Company.

Full estimate of cost, Co.'s Rupees 120,932 or with use of convict labour 47,916 Rupees. "

An account of the building of the present Cathedral is to be found in Major McNair's latest book published in 1897, "Prisoners their Own Warders," written in conjunction with Mr. W. D. Bayliss, who was Superintendent of Works and Surveys and Superintendent of Convicts. He says that it was designed by Colonel Macpherson, who was Executive Engineer at the time, and reproduced to some extent the character of old Netley Abbey in Hampshire. Mr. John Bennett, a civil and mechanical engineer, who had come out to Singapore to seek employment as a young man on Mr. A. L. Johnston's recommendation, of whom he was some connection, was largely concerned in the erection, and did most of the detail work of the building. He had been for a time a partner with Thomas Tivendale and James Baxter as shipwrights on the River near the Court House, as appears from an advertisement in 1852. He afterwards went to Burmah and the Andamans and occupied an important position there.

The building is 225 feet long, by 115 feet wide, with a nave and side aisles, and a north and south porch, having somewhat the appearance of transepts, which carriages can enter. The roof is of teak and slates. There is a gallery at the west end, approached by a circular iron staircase which was entirely made by the convicts, by whom the whole Church was erected, and it was said by Dr. Mouatt, the Inspector-General of Jails, Bengal, in a paper read by him before the Statistical Society, that the Cathedral built by Major McNair, entirely by convict labour, struck him as one of the finest specimens of ecclesiastical architecture which he had seen in the East, and a most remarkable example of the successful industrial training of convicts. The interior walls and columns were coated with a composition which has kept its colour, and has set so very hard that it is almost impossible to drive a nail into it. Major McNair's book gives the particulars of it, which we reprint, as an engineer in Singapore was very pleased when it was pointed out to him in the Major's book, and said he had often wished to know how it had been made:—

"It is Madras chunam made from shell lime without sand; but with this lime we had whites of eggs and coarse sugar, or "jaggery" beaten together to form a sort of paste, and mixed with water in which the husks of coconuts had been steeped. The walls were plastered with this composition, and after a certain period for drying, were rubbed with rock crystal or rounded stone until they took a beautiful polish, being occasionally dusted with fine soapstone powder, and so leaving a remarkably smooth and glossy surface." The Major does not give the height of the spire, nor does he relate what was said at the time, that he was on the top when the large iron cross was put in place, and slipped, or one of the lashings gave way, and he might have fallen, but he shut his eyes and held on for a few seconds where he was, and then quietly got into a safe place and came down.

It was originally intended to carry up the tower, but the foundations (which gave a good deal of trouble and are very deep, on account of the swampy nature of the ground) were found insufficient, and it was decided to put a light spire from a certain height. Search has been made among the old plans in the Government Office to try to

To face page 294.

St. Andrew's Cathedral and Raffles Monument on the Esplanade.

find the original plan and the proposed height of the tower, but without success. Before erecting the spire the same weight was piled up on the top of the tower to test the strain, and as it was found to stand, the spire was constructed of hollow bricks. A few years afterwards the foundations of the tower settled down further, and a crack gradually formed in the side walls of the aisles a few feet from the tower. The walls were then, about 1865, cut through and separated from the tower. The crack so made was filled in, and iron bands or ties inserted, and no further settlement has taken place. The height to the top of the cross has been given as 125 feet in one book and as 225 in another book about Singapore, and other measurements of the building have been stated equally incorrectly. The following details have now been carefully taken by the Public Works Department, and are correct.

The building is 181 feet 4 inches long, internal measurement from the west door, when closed, to the wall behind the Communion Table. Including the tower it is 226 feet 3 inches from the exterior points of the building. The nave and side aisles are 55 feet 4 inches wide. Including the two porches the building is 114 feet wide, internal measurement. The spire to the centre of the iron cross is 207 feet 6 inches from the ground. The tower is 38 feet 9 inches square at the base. The handsome chancel arch is 55 feet 6 inches from the floor-level to the apex, and 20 feet 4 inches wide at the foot. The interior height of the nave from floor to the under side of ridge is 74 feet. The enclosure or compound is about 660 feet by 540. A monument to Colonel Macpherson stands on the side towards the sea. He was buried at the cemetery at Bukit Timah Road.

Mr. John Cameron in his book speaks of it as a noble pile and one of the largest Cathedrals in India; and Major MacNair remarks that owing to the simplicity of its tracery and mouldings it really appears much larger than it actually is, and being built upon an open space, its proportions at once strike the eye of every visitor to the Colony. In another book it is spoken of as the most striking and beautiful Church east of the Cape of Good Hope.

In December, 1860, the building was ready to be used, and there was some correspondence in the paper about the delay in opening it. It appears from this, that the Mission Chapel which had been used for the Church services after the old Church was unsafe, was too small to hold the congregation, and two services were held, one after the other to make room for all, and it was also suggested to hold two evening services on Sunday. The reason for the delay was said to be owing to the windows and lamps not having arrived from England, which some of the congregation thought was a bad excuse, and offered to pay for temporary screens until the stained glass windows arrived. There was such a great demand for seats that a ballot was held at the Masonic Lodge for their disposal, and there was an advertisement in the *Free Press* in September, 1861, signed by Mr. John Colson Smith, as Treasurer, in which it was said that applications could be made for seats at $1 or 50 cents a month, according to their position. The seating at present with broad, wide seats, accommodates about 300; but on the occasion of the Memorial Service on the day of Queen Victoria's funeral, on 2nd February, 1901, when chairs were as far as possible substituted for the large seats, and advantage was taken of every inch of floor space, and over 300 persons occupied the gallery, there were about 1,400 persons in the congregation.

The Church was opened for service on 1st October, 1861, and was consecrated by Bishop Cotton of Calcutta, on Saturday, 25th January, 1862. The seats were first placed facing the east, as at present, but at one time, about 1871, they were placed towards the centre facing each other, and the pulpit was put at the pillar nearest the central gangway on the north side. In a few months it was found unsatisfactory, and the seats were replaced as at first. The Governor's seat properly speaking is on the south side of the centre passage, and was always so used until Sir Cecil Smith became Governor and preferred to remain in the seat he had occupied while Colonial Secretary, which is the corresponding seat on the opposite side. It really arose in consequence of the Chief Justice having been accustomed to sit at that time in the Governor's seats, as the Governor was a Roman Catholic, and Sir Cecil did not like to ask him to move, as he had become accustomed to the place. Consequently the alteration has been perpetuated, which is a mistake, as strangers properly expect to see the Governor in the right position, on the south side, as in other places.

The organ, which is an unusually good instrument, was built by John Walker of London, a first class maker, and was paid for by subscription at a cost of £600. It had the following specification :—

Swell Organ.	Great Organ.
Clarion	Trumpet
Oboe	Mixture, 4 and 5 ranks
Cornopean	Fifteenth
Mixture, 3 ranks	Twelfth
Fifteenth	Principal
Principal	Flute
Stopped Diapason	Stopped Diapason
Open do.	Dulciana
Double do.	Open Diapason
Couplers	Bourdon
Swell to Great	Pedal Organ
Pedals to Swell	Violoncello
Pedals to Great	Open Diapason 16 feet,

Mr. Terry, a very accomplished organist, who is now a manager in a very large Music establishment in Bond Street, London, came out with the organ, and first put it up between two of the pillars next the northern porch. Soon afterwards it was moved up into the gallery. In a few years it was decided that the small choir was too far away from the Congregation, so a subscription was made and a smaller organ was ordered from Bryceson Brothers, London, which cost £252.9.0. It had one manual, with seven sets of pipes and open 16-feet pedals. It was placed in what is now the northern vestry, with a reversed keyboard, so that the player sat facing the choir in the chancel. It was sold to the Penang Church when the large organ was again moved, and is the foundation of the organ now in use there, having been considerably enlarged. The money received for it was spent in repairing the large organ. In 1888 Walker's organ was again moved down-stairs, and placed where it is now at the east end of the north aisle. At the same time the floor level of the chancel was extended to the end of the organ case.

In 1889 a peal of eight bells, cast by the famous makers, Taylors of Loughborough, who founded "Big Ben" of St. Paul's Cathedral, London, was given to the Cathedral. The bells are of large size, the tenor, the largest, being as big as the No. 8 in the peal at St. Paul's. A clergyman of Oxford, an authority on the subject, said that they were in remarkably good tune and an excellent peal. The names of the donors are recorded on a brass near the west door as follows:—

† To the glory of God
The Peal of Bells
In this Cathedral Church
Of S. Andrew was dedicated
In Memory of
John Small Henry Fraser,
Captain H.E.I.C.S.
By His Heirs
William Henry McLeod Read,
K.C.N.L., C.M.G.
Amelia Sophia Saunders
Arthur Frederic Clarke
Lucy Julia Beamont
Denison Leslie Clarke
Anna McLeod Luttman Johnson
On the Seventieth Anniversary
Of the Foundation of the Settlement
6th February, 1889.

A special form of prayer was used on the afternoon of Wednes-, day, 6th February, at the dedication of the Peal of Bells and the Pulpit, which is mentioned further on.

In the earliest days of the Settlement Captain Fraser commanded one of the large sailing vessels of the East India Company, the *Marquess of Huntly*, and about 1826 and 1827 owned land in various parts of the town, in Kling Street, Boat Quay, High Street, and the whole of the piece of land on which the Hongkong and Shanghai Bank now stands. In course of years it passed to those whose names are men-tioned on the tablet, the five last being the children of Mr. and Mrs. Seymour Clarke. Mrs. Clarke was the daughter of Mr. C. R. Read, and came out with her mother in 1824, as has been mentioned on page 155. Mr. Clarke was the first Manager of the Great Western Railway, the pioneer of railways, and afterwards of the Great Northern Railway, and had a great deal of influence, which he used in pro-moting the Transfer of the Settlements in 1867. Queen Victoria never liked to make a railway journey unless Mr. Clarke went with the train, and the watch he always wore had been given to him by her. The Rev. Arthur Clarke is now Archdeacon of Lancashire. When the property was sold, the value had then advanced very largely, and those who had benefited by it presented the Bells.

There are three fine stained glass windows in the Apse, which were erected at the same time as the Church, and cost a large sum of

money. That in the centre has at the foot the following inscription :—
" To the Memory of Sir Stamford Raffles, Kt., the illustrious founder
of Singapore, A. D. 1861. "

The window on the north or left hand side of that one has the
following :—" To the Honour and Glory of God, and as a testimonial
to John Crawfurd, Esq., Governor of Singapore from 1823 to 1826,
whose sound principles of administration during the infancy of the
Settlement formed a basis for that uninterrupted prosperity which the
Colony thus gratefully records." Mr. Crawfurd was then alive.

The third window, that on the other (the right hand) side has
the following words:—" To Major-General William Butterworth, c.b.,
who successfully governed these settlements from 1843 to 1845, this window
is dedicated by the citizens of Singapore." There is an unfortunate
mistake in the second date, which should have been 1855, not 1845,
as pointed out by Major McNair in his book. The tablet close by
on the wall of the Sacrarium on its South side prevents any misunderstanding. It has the inscription :—" Sacred to the Memory of Major-
General William John Butterworth, c.b., of the Madras Army, for
nearly twelve years Governor of Prince of Wales Island, Singapore
and Malacca, who departed this life on the 4th November, 1856, at
Millhead House, Guildford, in the County of Surrey, England, in the
56th year of his age, distinguished alike in his civil and military
career for courage, zeal and integrity."

Opposite this tablet on the north side is one with the following
words :—" Sacred to the Memory of the Reverend Edward White, m.a.,
of the Bengal Establishment. His unwearied devotion to His Master's
service, during the eight years he was chaplain at this station, mingled
with his singular personal humility, won the deepest respect and
affection of his flock. Forgetful of self in zeal for their good, and
unmindful of the frailty of a constitution exhausted by previous
attacks and long residence in India, he sank under a brief illness and
in simple trust in Him who is the Resurrection and the Life. He
breathed his last in perfect peace on the 7th April, 1845, at Singapore,
in the 52nd year of his age. In sympathy with the bereaved widow
and fatherless children, and as a token of respect for their own loss, this
tablet is placed here by those who were allowed the benefit of his
ministry and the advantage of his example." He was buried with
military honours, and Mr. Church read the service. Over the door at
the west end of the building is a window, the subject of which is
the Four Evangelists, put up in 1872 in memory of Colonel Macpherson
who designed the Church.

At the west end of the north aisle there is a window with the
inscription : " In Memoriam David Rodger, obiit October 11th, 1867, œtat
37. " He was a partner in the firm of Martin, Dyce & Co. Two tablets
to Naval Officers were removed from the old Church and placed in the walls
near the east end of the aisles ; one was erected by the Commander and
Officers of H. M. Sloop *Harlequin* in Memory of George Samuel Berens, an
Officer who died at sea, on 11th September, 1843, aged 25 years, and was
buried off Tanjong Dattoo, Borneo ; and another tablet to the Memory of
Commander William Maitland of H. M. steamer *Spiteful*, who died in
the Roads of Singapore on 10th August, 1846, aged 40 years. There are

a few other tablets of modern date, but the construction of the building, with so many openings for windows, does not lend itself conveniently for the purpose, and they detract from the appearance of the building.

The handsome brass lectern was the gift of Mr. Thomas Shelford in 1873, in memory of his first wife, and the brass rails in front of the Communion Table were given by his family after his death in 1900. The pulpit was given by Sir C. C. Smith, when he was Governor, on 8th February, 1889. It was made in Ceylon. The set of choir stalls was given by Mr. J. J. Macbean in 1900. A handsome Communion Service was given by Mr. Arnold Otto Meyer and his son Edward Lorenz Meyer to the congregation. And an illuminated paper, hung in the vestry, says that it was "a thank offering and in remembrance of the goodwill and prosperity experienced by the House of Behn, Meyer & Company, during fifty years, on November 1st, 1890." Mr. Norris says that when he was a choir boy and Mr. G. H. Brown was organist, Mr. A. O. Meyer used to sing in the choir.

Until 1869 the Straits Settlements had been in the diocese of Calcutta, and on the consecration of the Ven. W. Chambers, Archdeacon of Sarawak, as Bishop of Labuan and Sarawak in that year, the Settlements were transferred to that diocese.

The Rev. F. T. McDougall, M.A., of Magdalen Hall, Oxford, and a Fellow of the College of Surgeons was, in 1847, appointed by the Archbishop of Canterbury and the Bishop of London to be the head of a new Mission to Sarawak. He was afterwards consecrated Bishop at Calcutta in 1855, which was the first consecration of a Bishop of the Church of England, out of England. He was styled Bishop of Labuan and Sarawak. He resigned in 1868, the year of the death of Rajah Sir James Brooke, and was succeeded by Archdeacon Chambers, advantage being taken, as has been said, of the vacancy of the See, to withdraw the Straits Settlements from the Diocese of Calcutta and include them in that of Labuan and Sarawak. St. Andrew's Church was then formally declared the Cathedral of the See, on 20th December, 1870. Bishop Chambers retired in 1879, and was succeeded in 1881 by the Ven. G. F. Hose, of St. John's College, Cambridge, who had been Colonial Chaplain and Archdeacon in Singapore. The style of the Diocese was then changed to Singapore, Labuan and Sarawak, being intended to give prominence to the position of Singapore, as the head-quarters of the work.

The St. Andrew's Church Mission was begun with one catechist at Whitsuntide, 1856. Bishop McDougall of Sarawak had joined with Mr. Humphrey, the Chaplain, in its establishment, and it was carried on by a committee. The Bishop, when in England, recommended the Society for the Propagation of the Gospel to assist the local mission by sending out an ordained missionary, and about the beginning of 1862 the Rev. E. S. Venn was sent by the Society to Singapore. On 11th May, 1863, at a meeting of the subscribers to the mission held at the Raffles Institution, at which the Governor, Colonel Cavenagh, presided, and Bishop McDougall was present, it was decided that it would be desirable to join the local mission with that of the S. P. G. to bear the name of the St. Andrew's Church Mission to the Heathen in connection with the S. P. G. ; the united mission to be under the management of the S. P. G. in communication with the Residency Chaplain. Mr. Venn, of Wadham College, Oxford, was the first missionary of the Society to the Straits. He died in Singapore on 19th September, 1866. After his death there was no resident missionary until 1872, when the Rev. William Henry Gomes was appointed. He was born in Ceylon in 1827, was educated at the Bishop's College, Calcutta, and went to the S. P. G. mission at Sarawak in 1852. He left Sarawak in 1867, and was appointed Acting Colonial Chaplain of Malacca. In 1868 he returned to Ceylon, and after working among the coffee planters there, he came back to the Straits in 1871 as acting Chaplain of Penang. In June, 1872, he became S. P. G. missionary at Singapore. In 1878 the Archbishop of Canterbury bestowed upon Mr. Gomes the decree of a Bachelor of Divinity of Lambeth, in recognition of his missionary and literary services. He translated the Prayer Book and a number of Hymns into native languages, Chinese, Dyak, and Malay, which were printed in Singapore at his own expense, aided by contributions from the congregations. The last edition of the Chinese Prayer Book was published with the sanction of the Archbishop of Canterbury under the auspices of the Society for Promoting Christian Knowledge. Mr. Gomes died on the morning of Sunday, 2nd March, 1902, 75 years of age, from failure of the heart, after being ill for a year. He was very much respected in Singapore, and his loss was much felt.

The Chapel in Stamford Road was built in 1875, the house for the missionary in 1877, and the school house in 1900. They all stand on the ground on the side of Fort Canning Hill, given by the Government to the Society for the purpose. In 1882 Mr. Gomes opened a branch mission for the Chinese living at Jurong, and a Church was built there. It is about fourteen miles by road from Singapore on the west side of the island.

CHAPTER XXIV.
1836.

O N New Year's Day, there was a regatta in the harbour, in which six yachts took part, and there were a number of boat races. An Artillery man, in firing a gun at sunrise, shot away his right arm.

On Monday, the 25th January, a private meeting was held, at the Reading Room, of the Mercantile community to consider the question of the imposition of duties, about which the following correspondence had taken place :—

" To

The Hon'ble KENNETH MURCHISON, Esquire,

Governor of Prince of Wales' Island,

Singapore and Malacca,

&c., &c., &c.

" Sir,—We the undersigned, Merchants of Singapore, having heard that the Supreme Government has it in contemplation to levy duties at this port, and being of opinion that such a measure will materially affect the trade of the Settlement, respectfully request that you will inform us if such be the case ; and if so, that you will be pleased to favour us with the particulars of such instructions as you may have received on the subject, in so far as you feel yourself at liberty to communicate the same.

We are, &c.

Joaquim d'Almeida.	A. Guthrie.	S. A. Seth.
Jose d'Almeida.	J. Hamilton.	W. D. Shaw.
E. Boustead.	A. Hay.	W. Spottiswoode.
C. Carnie.	R. C. Healey.	J. Stephen.
T. O. Crane.	A. L. Johnston.	S. Stephens.
J. S. Clark.	W. S. Lorrain.	J. H. Whitehead.
W. S. Duncan.	T. McMicking.	J. Wise.
J. Fraser.	G. Martin.	G. Zechariah.
W. R. George.	T. Scott.	I. Zechariah.

Singapore, 11th January, 1836."

" To Messrs. A. L. Johnston & Co., and the other Merchants of Singapore.

" Gentlemen,—In reply to your letter to my address, dated the 11th instant, I have the honour to apprize you that the Supreme Government has directed me to submit the draft of an Act and Schedule for levying a duty on the Sea Exports and Imports of the three Settlements, to meet the expense of effectually protecting the trade from Piracy.

The above comprises the directions of the Supreme Government ; the rate of the duties will be regulated by the estimated expenses of a Flotilla and a Custom House, on neither of which points can I, at present, give you any precise information. I may, however, state, that on the best procurable information, I am of opinion that a duty of 2½ per cent. on the articles enumerated in the annexed List (square-rigged vessels under foreign colours being liable to double duties) will raise a sufficient fund to meet the object in view. In framing the Schedule now laid before you, it has been my endeavour to render the system of duties as little obnoxious as possible to the local peculiarities of the Trade, and I shall be happy to pay every respect to any observations your experience may suggest upon points in which alteration or modification may be advantageously applied.

I have the honour to be, &c.,

K. MURCHISON,

Singapore, 13th January, 1836."   *Governor.*

A public meeting was then called on the 4th February, by the Sheriff, Mr. Wingrove, as was the custom in those days, and the following is an account of what took place:—

"A. L. Johnston, Esq., having been unanimously called to the Chair, briefly stated the object of the meeting, when the following Resolutions were unanimously agreed to:—

1st.—Proposed by Mr. J. Hamilton, and seconded by Mr. J. Fraser—That it is the opinion of this Meeting that this Settlement owes the commercial eminence it now enjoys to its having been established and continued a Free Port.

2nd.—Proposed by Mr. W. D. Shaw, and seconded by Mr. E. Boustead—That it is the opinion of this Meeting that the Imposition of Duties will be productive of serious injury to the Trade of this Settlement.

3rd.—Proposed by Mr. A. Guthrie, and seconded by Mr. R. C. Healey—That having been informed that the Supreme Government have it in contemplation to levy Duties here, it is the opinion of this Meeting that means should be taken for the purpose of obviating the purposed measure.

4th.—Proposed by Mr. T. McMicking, and seconded by Mr. R. C. Healey—That it is the opinion of this Meeting that the best means that can be adopted for the end, would be to petition both Houses of Parliament and the Supreme Government on the subject.

5th.—Proposed by Mr. J. Stephen, and seconded by Mr. E. J. Gilman—That Messrs. Johnston, Boustead, Hamilton, Guthrie and Shaw be appointed a Committee to draw up Petitions in conformity with the resolution now passed.

(The Petition having been previously prepared was read by the Chairman.)

6th.—Proposed by Mr. W. S. Lorrain, and seconded by Mr. José d'Almeida—That these Petitions having been adopted shall lie for signature ten days in the Singapore Reading Room, and that the one to the House of Lords be forwarded to Lord Glenelg, that to the House of Commons to the Members for Manchester and Glasgow, and that to the Supreme Government, direct.

7th.—Proposed by Mr. J. Fraser, and seconded by Mr. A. Guthrie—That a copy of the Petition to the Supreme Government be transmitted to the Local Government, with a request that, if they concur in the views of the Petitioners, they will second the·prayer of the Petition.

The following was the text of the Petition :—

" That your Petitioners having learnt with great regret that it is
the intention of the Supreme Government to establish a Custom House
and levy duties at this place to provide means for the suppression of
Piracy in these seas ; a measure, in the opinion of your Petitioners, that
will have a most injurious effect on the commercial prosperity of the place.

" That your Petitioners are confidently of opinion that the present
commercial importance of Singapore is entirely owing to its having
been continued a Free Port, without any obnoxious restrictions on its
Trade ; that most of the Native Traders have been induced to this Port,
in preference to others on the Island of Java and elsewhere, solely on
that account.

" That your Petitioners humbly beg to bring to your notice the
advantages of Singapore as a commercial depot, both to Great Britain
and British India ; the imports being composed to a large extent of the
Produce and Manufactures of these two Countries ; and considerably
promote the national industry of both in various branches. The return
exports are composed of articles which pay a large amount of duties
and thus add considerably to the revenue of both countries.

" That your Petitioners further beg to represent that a considerable
branch of the Trade here is the transhipment of goods sent solely for
the purpose of being forwarded to their ultimate destination ; which
branch would be completely destroyed by the imposition of any duties
whatsoever.

" That the Dutch Port of Rhio is but one day's sail from Singapore,
and is a Free Port. Your Petitioners, therefore, humbly submit that
the levying any duties on the trade of this place would have the
effect of transferring a considerable portion of the native trade to
that port. For, though by the schedule furnished by the Honourable
the Governor to your Petitioners, the native boats are freed from
paying duties, it would be necessary, to prevent smuggling, to subject
them to the forms of a Custom House establishment, which would be
nearly as obnoxious to them as the payment of duties.

" Your Petitioners also represent the large expense that would be
incurred by having a Custom House with an efficient establishment to
prevent smuggling, and submit that from local causes the facility of
smuggling would be so great, that a very large proportion of the
amount of Duties collected would have to be expended in the Custom
House establishment.

" Your Petitioners submit that this settlement has, since its establishment, been rapidly increasing in Population and Revenue ; that the
former has doubled itself within the last seven years, and the latter
for the official year ending 1834-35, shews an excess of Rs. 40,000
over the preceding year.

" That many of your Petitioners have been induced on the faith of
this Settlement being continued a Free Port, to invest large sums of
money on buildings for commercial and other purposes, the value of
which will, in their opinion, be much deteriorated by the falling off of
the trade consequent on the imposition of duties.

" Your Petitioners are of opinion that a Steam Boat would be most
efficacious in suppressing Piracy, and might also be employed occasionally

in the conveyance of the Court on Circuit and other Government purposes, thereby saving the Government a considerable amount annually expended for these purposes.

"Your Petitioners, therefore, humbly pray that the valuable Trade of Singapore may not be endangered by any duties being imposed thereon; but that it may be allowed to remain in the same free state it has hitherto done."

In this year the Fives Court was established, owing to the exertions of Dr. Montgomerie, who was a very popular man in Singapore. The Fives' Players gave him a dinner in February, in testimony, as they said, of the obligation they owed him for the introduction of such a wholesome and exciting sport. At that time they used to play fives in the early morning, instead of going for the usual constitutional walk. The Court was where part of the building of the Government Offices now stands, and in later years, and down to the year 1866, or thereabouts, there used to be always a dozen players in the Court between five and half-past six o'clock in the afternoon, and there were some very good players. In the course of time, the Court was pulled down to make room for the new buildings, and a Court was built in Armenian Street by the Government to replace it, but it was the death-blow to the history of Fives, and was pulled down in 1886 to make room for St. Andrew's House.

In March two strangers arrived from Borneo, being a pair of *Orang Outans*, brought from the interior, which excited a good deal of curiosity. The paper this year contained accounts of what Lieutenant Waghorn was doing to establish the Overland Route, which was called a very visionary scheme. He had persuaded an English woman to open an inn in Cairo, and steam-packets were started between Malta and Alexandria. He proposed to charge $60 for each passenger, without wine, for going from Alexandria to Suez, and he appointed Agents at Jedda, Cairo and Alexandria, and proposed to reside at Suez himself. The charge then for the postage of a letter from Plymouth to Alexandria was three shillings and sixpence, and a letter through Egypt to Bombay cost, in some instances, as much as £4. The paper does not mention what the weight of the letters was, but does not say anything to show that they were unusually heavy.

In May there was a fire at Kampong Glam, which burnt down a number of attap-roofed houses, occupied by Chinese shop keepers. The Convicts were quickly on the spot, and prevented the fire from spreading; without their help it was thought several streets would have been destroyed.

The *Singapore Free Press* on 12th May, said:—"The Supreme Government have authorised pensions to the family of the late Sultan of Johore. The family consists of two sons and two daughters, and the pension is $70 each, a sufficiently liberal allowance, but merely a gratuity to which no claim could be made with any shew of right. The Company, however, having lately granted pensions, $4,200 yearly, to the family of the late Tumongong, that of the Sultan is of course entitled to the benefit of the precedent. To the families of these two princes the Company is now paying $8,160 per annum."

On the 24th May, a public meeting was held at the Reading Room to form the Singapore Agricultural and Horticultural Society, with a subscription of $2 quarterly, to meet at seven o'clock in the evening of the first Saturday of every month. A Committee was appointed with the Governor as President, and Messrs. Balestier, Montgomerie, Almeida, Brennand and T. O. Crane, as members. The meetings were held regularly at the houses of the Members of Committee in turn, for some time, papers being read upon various subjects, one, the first, being by Dr. Oxley on the objects of the Society, and one by Dr. Montgomerie on the expense of clearing and draining the jungle to increase the cultivation in the island.

The paper of 2nd June, contained a very long article by Mr. J. Clunies Ross of the Cocos Islands on the formation of the Oceanic Islands, which were spoken of as " his very remote and isolated abode."

In June, Mr. Bonham, the Resident Councillor, was joined in a Commission with Captain Henry Ducie Chads, of H. M. S. *Andromache,* to arrange measures with a view to the suppression of piracy in the neighbouring seas.

In July, Boustead, Schwabe & Co., were advertising in the newspapers, bills on London or Manchester at 3 or 6 months' sight; and the Government advertised Bills on Bengal for sale at exchange 219.

A notice was inserted in the newspaper on 16th July, by the creditors of Mr. Mackertich Moses, signed by most of the principal European firms in the place, saying that reports had been circulated that Mr. Moses was kept in the jail for the purpose of oppressing him, which was not the case. He had made no offer to compromise or settle with the creditors, but had shut himself up in his house and held them at defiance. He was entitled to no indulgence, but if he would do as many Chinese merchants had done, and give a proper statement of his affairs with a fair offer of a composition, and security that he would not go away until his affairs were arranged, the creditors would let him out of jail. He was no relation of Mr. Catchick Moses.

Soda water was first advertised for sale, made at the Singapore Dispensary, on 31st August, the price was $1.50 a dozen, without the bottles.

In August, Lord Glenelg wrote to say that he was much gratified in presenting the petition already referred to, and that he was happy to say the measure which it deprecated would find no countenance from the home authorities; and in November, the East India and China Association in London, which had taken the matter up on behalf of Singapore, wrote to Messrs. C. R. Read, T. Fox, and E. Boustead that they had learned from the India Board that despatches were being forwarded to India directing the Government to suspend, if not already enacted, and to repeal, if enacted, the proposed impost.

On the 15th September, Dr. M. J. Martin was married to Miss Bell, of Westmoreland, by Mr. Bonham, the Resident Councillor. There was, presumably, no Chaplain in Singapore.

In October, Mr. Gilman published an account of the adulteration he had found in a parcel of tin he had purchased direct from a boat from Pahang. It had been usual to cut the slabs in half, but he happened to have two split open at the sides, and found the centres of all the slabs filled with dross, dirt, and a great number of Tringanu pice, which were made of spelter or lead. Tin was then worth $20, and lead $6. Another lot in another boat was found by the purchasers of it to be just the same, and it was taken to the Police Office and melted down to get the tin separated.

There were very many complaints about the defective state of the regulations regarding the disposal of Government land, and the Agricultural Society drew up a petition to the Governor-General, which was brought forward by Mr. Balestier and Mr. Boustead, and was sent to Calcutta through the local authorities. It was as follows:—"That your Petitioners lately formed themselves into a Society for the purpose of promoting and encouraging undertakings of an Agricultural and Horticultural nature generally in this Island.

"That your Petitioners humbly represent that their efforts in the above object are checked by reason that waste and vacant lands on this Island cannot be obtained either by purchase or on long leases.

"That your Petitioners are satisfied, from recent experiments, that the soil of this Island is generally adequate to the successful cultivation of cotton, sugar, pepper, nutmegs, the finer spices, and other articles of tropical produce, of which the increased production would eminently contribute to the general interest of the Settlement.

"That your Petitioners beg to represent that a great portion of the Island is likely to remain, as at present, an impervious jungle, unless a more liberal system as respects the sale or leasing of lands be adopted, which, in the opinion of your Petitioners, is essentially necessary, if the operations of agriculture are ever to be considered as of any importance in promoting its general welfare.

"Your Petitioners, therefore, humbly pray that your Lordship in Council will be pleased to take the premises into consideration, and to authorize the sale or leasing of lands at this Settlement or the leasing thereof for a term not less than ninety-nine years."

On St. Andrew's Day a public dinner was given, and the company finally broke up at sunrise after having partaken of a third supper.

It was towards the end of this year that the new Recorder, Sir William Norris, came into the Straits, and in his first charge to the Grand Jury, he took the opportunity of expressing his preference for the system of a public prosecutor instead of a Grand Jury, as was the case in the Colonies which had formerly been in the possession of the Dutch or French. There was no regular Bar in those days, none of the law agents having been professionally educated, and the Magistrates did all manner of work besides their own. The Recorder said that no permanent good could be expected until the interests of the stipendiary Magistrates were limited to, and their energies concentrated on, the discharge of their duties. The usual sitting Magistrate was a civil servant, who by the occasional absence of his superiors, acted sometimes as Judge, and always as Commissioner of the Court of Requests; and the remaining Justices of the Peace were mercantile men, who attended occasionally when the presence of two Justices was required by law. The Prisoner's Counsel was not allowed to speak on behalf of his client, nor was the prisoner allowed even to have copies of the depositions made by the witnesses against him; he had to rely upon his own memory.

It was at this time that gambier and pepper plantations began to be of importance in Singapore, the yearly production of gambier being about 22,000 piculs, and of pepper about 10,000. The largest gardens producing about 200 piculs of gambier, and 100 of pepper. On a plantation producing from 100 to 110 piculs, the average size of the gardens, six coolies were employed, at wages of $4 to $4.50 each. The price of gambier was then about $3 a picul. Complaint was already being made about the jungle being all cut down for firewood, and about plantations being deserted and allowed to run to lalang grass, while a fresh plantation was made in the nearest favourable site, and further devastation commenced.

Mr. John Palmer who was called "The Father of the Indian Mercantile Community," and whose name has been mentioned in the earliest days of the Settlement, died at Calcutta in 1836, seventy years old.

On the 17th November, Mr. Murchison, Governor of the Incorporated Settlements, left Penang for Calcutta on his final departure for England. Mr. Bonham acted in his stead, and Mr. Wingrove was sworn in as Resident Councillor of Singapore.

On 22nd November Captain John Poynton, the Harbour Master, died, aged 35 years. He had been in the Navy, and then joined the East India Company's service, and served with distinction. In 1822 he was Deputy Harbour Master in Penang, and was in the war at Rangoon in 1824, when Captain Marryat (the novel writer) of H. M. S. *Larne* gave him great credit. In 1832 he was appointed Harbour Master of Malacca, when William Scott was the same in Singapore, and being friends, as everyone was with William Scott, they exchanged places with each other. He left a widow and several children, and W. S. Lorrain and James Stephen settled up his affairs.

On New Year's Day in this year, at Canton, a party of gentlemen had made an attempt to proceed to Whampoa in the steamer *Jardine,* ostensibly for the purpose of having her measured and examined by the Chinese. The whole of the Europeans had tried to obtain permission from the Chinese authorities for the steamer to ply with passengers between Canton, Whampoa, Macao and Lintin. They went up the entrance of the Canton River, and one of the forts at the Bogue commenced firing upon her, but it was supposed the guns were not shotted. Three of the gentlemen got into a boat with four lascars and pulled to the fort, where there was a formidable turn out of the war-boats and junks. They were taken to the Admiral, and asked him to send up for orders that the steamer might be examined there, instead of at Whampoa, but he said his orders were express and he could not do it. He was invited on board, and came with about one hundred attendants, and the curiosity of all was unbounded. He was towed to and fro in his own vessel in the presence of thousands of spectators, and said he was quite satisfied it was only a passenger vessel, and unarmed, but he could not disregard his orders. As soon as the Chinese had left the vessel, she returned to Lintin, and the passengers proceeded to Canton in sailing boats. At night the forts at the Bogue were still firing, and the war junks exchanging signals and rockets and making much ado about nothing.

So the steamer was sent to Singapore for sale and arrived here on the 28th February, 1836, and was described in the shipping report for the day as a British schooner. They had not had a steamer to notify before this, as far as is known, as the *Diana* did not come until 1837. She was advertised for sale by A. L. Johnston & Co. The *Jardine* was 115 tons, builder's, or 56 tons steam, measurement, and 48 horse power, and was "considered to be the finest steam vessel hitherto built." Her speed was something over seven knots. The paper spoke of her as being a nine days' wonder, and every voice was raised against her, nothing but denunciations being expressed against her qualities. The reason of this was her misadventures on a trial trip she made, which was the first steam picnic in Singapore. The following passages from a letter written at the time contain an account of what had happened :—

"You must know we got under half steam (for the kettle did not boil) at about 6 A.M., on Friday (ominous day) and steered (lop-sided) direct for Goa Island [this is near St. John's Island]. Found the wood fuel too heavy, so threw a great part of it overboard; this eased her much, and we afterwards steamed away (for the kettle now boiled) very merrily; when, I suppose, the Captain wanted to make a short cut, and consequently stuck us in the mud. All hands were immediately employed in getting out an anchor and heaving off, which, after some trouble, was accomplished, and away we steamed again; but whether the tide was against us, or what else was the matter I know not, but certain it is, we did not get on so fast as some of us expected, and there were consequently a few black looks and a little growling; when, behold, as if to punish us for our impatience, snap went the newly repaired lever, and there we were, helpless. Misfortune never comes alone, for, besides the fracture to the lever, one of the iron boat davits broke and let the only boat we had into the sea (that is, only part of her, as she held on by the other davit). There was now nothing for it, but to get sails bent, when we discovered that lots of ropes were wanting, we had no clue-lines, and no many other things. Nevertheless amidst all our misfortunes, we did not forget good living, and beer, champagne, claret, &c., were in great request; our larder, too, was well supplied, so that we did pretty well in that particular. We got back to our homes in the *Snipe* and *Miss Maggie* [two yachts] which came out from the harbour to our rescue."

In March a circular was issued proposing to purchase the *Jardine* by a company in shares of $100 each and to run her between Singapore and Penang, and in May the paper contained an account of a trip to Malacca. The Company was not formed apparently. The paper contained the following account:—"The steamer *Jardine* has frequently been under steam for a few hours during the week, and we learn with much satisfaction that her engine is found to work admirably, which reflects great credit on Mr. Hallpike, who, with very inadequate means, has succeeded in putting the engine in the best of order. The *Jardine* starts this evening for Malacca with a party of gentlemen, and is expected to be back here on Monday morning. The *Isabella Robertson* has arrived since our last, but without bringing the new levers. They may, however, be expected very shortly."

And the account of the second voyage of this wonderful steamer, on a trip to Malacca, on Thursday, 26th May, is contained in a letter from which we make the following extracts:—

"We did not get off till nearly six. At half past seven, the moon rising, we struck hard, and ran, I should say a dozen yards, on a coral reef, I think off Pulo Sala; Mohamet said he went down to change his baju, and while off deck the course was altered. Captain Greig went out in the boat to sound, and found deep water on each side and behind us, backed her off with the paddles; this detained us twenty minutes. We had supper about nine, and shortly afterwards all of our party lay down to sleep, some below and others on deck; but Greig, Hallpike, and I remained up. About half past three on Friday morning, the 27th, Hallpike and I talking, the boat stopped, I said, 'Whatever is the matter now.' We ran to the engine and found the men below just rousing from sleep. They had let the fires get so low that the steam was off. We soon got on as well as ever. About half past six we were abreast Formosa. At a little after eight, most of us were dressed, and talking about breakfast in high spirits, and some said we should be in by 10, others 11, others 12. By this time Moar was before us, probably distant eight miles. We observed smoke coming out of the fore-hatch, from the engine room and the deck on each side of the main hatch, a little forward; it looked like steam at first, but it was soon found that the vessel had caught fire.

"All the passengers and servants ran aft and assisted to lower the boat into the water, the only boat we had. It was a common ship's boat, and I think would not have floated with more than about half our number. We pumped an immense deal of water into the engine room. I tried, and saw others try, to go forward at first, but the smoke was so suffocating that I was driven back, the deck forward was very hot. We got the awning down with very great difficulty, and covered the main hatch with it and soaked the water on it; we also kept the fore hatch to the engine room, a skylight, and the companion to cabin, covered with sails and tarpaulins. We had about seven buckets. McMicking and some of us went into the cabin (he first) and we stood by to haul him up, thinking it would be full of smoke if the flames had not yet reached it, but to our surprise and delight there was no smoke, and the bulkhead was quite cool. Before this, the deck was burst in on each side of the main hatch with the long heavy iron lever which sets the engine going, and we threw water down. I think the fire was out by half past nine to ten o'clock. Hallpike went down at the beginning, and got several bottles of gunpowder which were thrown overboard; he also secured some dollars that he had, saying that they spoke a language understood all the world over. The Captain tried to stop the engine and could not; she stopped of herself, from what cause I know not.

"When the fire was out, I saw what was the means of saving us aft of the boiler; a strong bulkhead, thick planking lined with tin on both sides, and with a space in the middle, and the fire had no strength to get through this, as there was no draught for it. What time we sat down to eat, I cannot tell, but we did, and then set to work and lighted the fires to get steam up as soon as the water was pumped out. I think about half past three or four the steam was got up; she went for seven minutes, then stopped. Water was pumped in, the fires made fierce, and the steam got up again, and then she went for five to seven minutes; we went on this way, probably 10 to 15 times, until we got to windward of the outer Water Island, and the fires were raked out to my great delight at about half past seven to eight o'clock. We supped and sang, and all went to sleep. We anchored a long way out, I think in 6½ fathoms, at four o'clock. The report boat came and I went in her, to my great joy, and got on shore by a quarter to seven." The paddles and paddle boxes were afterwards unshipped in Malacca and the steamer came back to Singapore under sail.

In this year the descendants of a male and female Jackall, that an individual had brought from Bengal, became very noisy and trouble-some animals, and killed fowls in people's compounds, and were said to be the progenitors of mongrel dogs here in the jungle.

Captain William Scott, the harbour master who has been spoken of in this chapter, was one of the most respected residents here, whose worth, gentleness, charity, and disinterested benevolence were widely known over the Far East. He was a first cousin of Sir Walter Scott the Novelist, and was the son of Mr. James Scott, the pioneer settler of Penang, who was the close friend and adviser of the first Governor and founder of the Settlement. He was born on 3rd May, 1786, and died 18th December, 1861, in Singapore and is buried in the old cemetery on Fort Canning. He was a very benevolent, hospitable, kind-hearted man, and all Singapore were his friends. As a boy he was in the Edinburgh High School, and, as a young man, was in the Volunteer Cavalry and Royal Archers of that city. Misfortunes came upon his father's house, whose estates passed into other hands, and he came out to the East. He was the Harbour Master and Post Master and was very regular at his office work. The best time to see him was in the early morning, cutting, planting and gardening in his plantation, at the corner of what is still known as Scott's Road, at the corner of Orchard Road opposite the Police Station and extend-ing up to the Tanglin Club. He lived in a small attap house called Hurricane Cottage, close to where Hurricane House is now. He grew there all kinds of fruits, native and exotic, the purple cocoa, the grace-ful betel-nut, a maze of rambutans, dukus, mangoosteens and durians, besides sea-cotton, arrowroot, and many more. His garden afforded one of the most picturesque, shady, pleasing retreats that could be imagined, illuminated as it was by the old man's lustrous blue eyes, silver hair, and warm hearty welcome. In the times of Sir George Bonham he was a constant guest at Government House, who had the training and experience to appreciate the value of such a man, and felt that his hospitality was graced by the presence of the cousin of Sir Walter. But times altered, and a new Governor "who knew not Joseph" a son of a shop-keeper, spoken of as "a compound of ignorance and pomposity," could not appreciate these things. It sounds paltry to speak of it, but the fact remains that Captain Scott one day, in 1847, walked into the Governor's Office, which was next to his own, in his usual every day suit of plain white clothes. This was considered a mortal affront; and the old faithful servant was ousted, and a young man, with peculiar interest, put in his place, and the older man's means of livelihood swept from under his feet. These sentences are abridged, but without alteration of words, from an old account by one of his friends, who were legion, and he added that Captain Scott felt the injustice most acutely "for he had a great deal of Sir Walter in him." The plantation is now sold for building purposes, but some of the old cocoa plants which Captain Scott introduced are still there. Scott's Road was named after him, and he was the uncle of Mr. William Ramsay Scott, who left Singapore to reside in England many years ago. The *Free Press* remarked at the time of Captain Scott's death, after speaking of his great kindness of disposition, that his long residence in the Straits made him an authority on all matters connected with its history, while he possessed a fund of anecdote regarding its earlier annals which rendered his conversation at once instructive and entertaining. And it said that his features bore a great likeness to his celebrated cousin, Sir Walter Scott. His portrait is in the Freemason's Lodge.

It was about this time that an Oriental Merchant, Abraham Solomon, came to the place. He was born in Bagdad, and after being about five years in Calcutta he came to reside permanently in Singapore. He lived on the river side, about the middle of Boat Quay, and died on 19th May, 1884, at 86 years of age, and was buried in the Jewish Cemetery in Orchard Road. It was said of him by Mr. Thomson, that he might have sat to a sculptor for a model of the father of the faithful. He dressed in the long flowing robes of the East, with a large turban; and his beard, as large and long as is seldom seen, flowed down over his breast. He was a man of large stature, and a notable person in the place. He was a leading man among his tribe and had much to do with the synagogue, and took an enthusiastic interest in the manners, customs, and literature of the East. He used sometimes to entertain Europeans, but was careful to remark that he could not dine with a Christian, so it was not a frequent occurrence. He did not speak English and conversation was carried on in Malay, which would not be the case at the present time. His children were educated at English teaching schools here, an advantage Bagdad did not offer to Abraham Solomon.

The European vessels in these days always engaged Malay sampans to wait on the ship, to avoid making the European crews row backward and forwards in the sun. The Malays learned to build very perfect boats, about twenty feet long and four feet in width, very unlike the tubs they had used before the Europeans came, and they were able to hold their own against European boats, which it was said never beat them. They had a crew of three to five men, and the charge was sixty cents a day. For $30 they would convey letters to Penang, nearly four hundred miles.

In Mr. Earl's book is a description of a Sumatra Squall, which is well worth reproducing. He said "The Sumatra squalls which were formerly, and are still in some degree, the terror of those who navigate the Straits of Malacca, are caused by the South-west Monsoon being obstructed in its course by the mountains of Sumatra. The appearance of the squall is betokened by a dense black cloud which rises from behind the opposite island of Battam and soon overspreads the sky, casting a dark shadow over the Strait, within which the sea is lashed to foam. Its effect is first felt by the ships in the roads, which heel over and swing to their anchors. There is always as much bustle on the river as on shore, for the cargo boats manned with noisy Klings come flying into the river before the squall, and putting up kadjang mats before the descent of the rain. The squalls seldom last more than half an hour, when, after a smart shower, the sun again breaks out and the wind subsides to a pleasant sea-breeze, leaving an agreeable freshness in the atmosphere."

These squalls prevail during the south-west monsoon between the beginning of April and the end of October. The north-east monsoon, Dr. Little remarks (2 Logan's Journal, 451) blow more steadily and with more force than the south-west, which he attributes to less high land intervening being the China Sea and Singapore, while the south-west Monsoon has to pass over Sumatra. He says the temperature of Singapore is lower by one or two degrees during the north-east monsoon (October to March) than during the south-west (April to September) and that more rain falls between October and March for the same reason.

CHAPTER XXV.

1837.

THE first paper for this year contained a long account of the New Year Sports. A meeting was held in the vestry of the Mission Chapel to open a branch of the British and Foreign Bible Society to be called "The Singapore Bible Auxiliary." The Resident Councillor, Mr. Wingrove, was President, and Dr. Oxley and many others joined the Society. In the number for October, 1884, of the Monthly Reporter of the Society, it says that the Rev. F. B. Ashley of Wooburn, in England, joined the Association in Singapore, when he was commanding the Artillery here, and the first contribution of £100 was sent to London in 1838.

The following paragraph about Chinese crackers at the New Year appeared in the *Free Press* in February: it shows how much worse matters were then than they are now, in this respect. " It has been brought to our notice that the firing of noisy crackers by the Chinese, with or without the permission of the Police, in the streets of the town during this season of their New Year's festivals, occasions so much alarm to the owners of carriages, that they are compelled to forego their use, unless they prefer to risk their necks. The burning of large heaps of gilded Joss-paper in the middle of the street may be a very harmless amusement and no wise dangerous to pedestrians, but firing crackers which resemble and equal in report a *feu de pelorin* is rather a more serious matter, and may very easily lead to damage of limb, if not to loss of life, especially as the little Chinese urchins, like little boys everywhere else who are allowed to have their own way, think it a very fine piece of fun to plant one right in the track of your passing or advancing vehicle. This ought not to be permitted, or if it does seem meet to shew respect for the ' customs of the natives,' they should be restricted at least to particular hours and places."

On the 8th February, at a meeting of the merchants, agents, and others interested in the trade of Singapore, convened by circular and held at the Reading Room for the purpose of taking into consideration the propriety of establishing a Chamber of Commerce at this Settlement, A. L. Johnston in the Chair, it was proposed by Ellis James Gilman, seconded by R. C. Healey and unanimously resolved :—

> (1) That an Association be formed under the designation of "The Singapore Chamber of Commerce " for the purpose of watching over the commercial interests of the Settlement.

Proposed by E. Boustead, seconded by W. S. Lorrain, and unanimously resolved :—

> (2) That all Merchants, Agents, Ship-owners, and other interested in the trade of the place, be eligible to become Members of this Association.

Proposed by Thos. Scott, seconded by J. S. Clark and unanimously resolved :—

> (3) That a Provisional Committee be now appointed to draw up Rules and Regulations for the government of the Chamber, and to report thereon to a General Meeting to be convened as soon as the same are prepared.

Proposed by W. S. Duncan, seconded by Lewis Fraser and unanimously resolved :—

> (4) That the said Provisional Committee consist of the following five gentlemen :—Messrs. Edward Boustead, Thomas McMicking, Alexander Guthrie, Ellis James Gilman, and William Renshaw George.

On the 20th February a set of regulations was drawn up. Mr. Johnston was the first President, and the Committee were T. McMicking, R. C. Healey, E. J. Gilman, Syed Abubakar, Kim Guan, I. Zechariah, E. Boustead, J. Balestier, Gwan Chuan and A. Guthrie. The regulations may be found printed at length in Mr. Newbold's book. One of the first acts of the Committee was to take up the question of the infringement by the Dutch of the treaty of 1824 by a prohibition of the introduction of British manufactured goods into Java, and a petition was forwarded to England on the subject. The papers were full of the question for some months. At a meeting of the Library Committee in the News-room it was decided, in consequence of the reduction in the price of newspapers in England, to reduce the rate of subscription to $24 a year.

In March, Mr. Bonham (afterwards Sir Samuel George Bonham) was appointed Governor to date from 25th December, 1836, when Mr. Murchison left for Europe; and Mr. Church was appointed Resident Councillor of Singapore from 4th March.

In the same month some Europeans played cricket on a Sunday afternoon on the Esplanade, which was objected to.

The rainfall in 1836 had been only 59.7 inches for the year. The following remarks upon the rainfall were written in April.—"The oldest European resident in the Settlement does not recollect any year, the first quarter of which can be compared with the last three months, so very unusual has the season been. Instead of heavy and continued rains, which might have been expected, particularly during January and February, the drought has been unprecedented even for our least rainy months : and we understand that a similar deficiency of rain has been experienced both at Penang and Malacca, these Settlements being even worse off than ourselves. The total fall of rain here from the 1st January to the 31st March amounted only to 6 inches and nine-tenths, whereas the table for the first quarter of 1835 exhibited a fall of 31 inches : and that of 1836 something less than 18 inches. During the past month dense fogs covered the face of the country almost every morning until two or three hours after sunrise, a rather unusual appearance with us."

In May, the Reverend Edward White, newly appointed Chaplain to the Settlement, arrived from Bengal. The Rev. F. J. Darrah died in Madras on the 29th September following.

In the same week, the first Annual Meeting of the Agricultural and Horticultural Society was held, Dr. Oxley in the chair, and it was decided to keep only the horticultural garden, under his management. The Society had held regular monthly meetings during the year, and had obtained cotton seeds for distribution to planters, and issued a letter to the Chinese containing suggestions and advice regarding planting other produce besides gambier and pepper. Dr. Oxley, Dr. Montgomerie, and Mr. T. O. Crane, the Secretary, were the prominent members of the Society.

In July, two Chinese, members of the Chamber of Commerce, were expelled from it, for having sold to a Jew four cases of opium, after putting in spurious contents of an inferior quality and weight.

A Memorial was sent by the Merchants and Mariners to the Governor-General asking that lighthouses might be erected near Romania Point and the Coney Island. On 30th July the Rajah of Selangor came to Singapore in his own brig, and was received with a salute of 15 guns. The Sultan of Lingga paid a visit to Singapore at the same time, so the *Free Press* remarked there were "two crowned heads" in the place : but both more than suspected of giving countenance to piracy.

The following is an account of a visit, probably the first of its kind, to Rhio, in the steamer *Diana*, Captain Congalton. "I was one of the party that went a steaming to Rhio on Monday last. It was a very rainy morning when those who had slept on board the steamer during the night were awoke by the arrival of those who had slept on shore. It was a very wet morning but we got under steam, notwithstanding, at a little before five o'clock, there being no less than nineteen of us altogether. We now proceeded gaily along, each step of our progress bringing us in sight of some piece of scenery worthy of notice, and most beautiful certainly was our sail through the Straits, where the eye wantoned over the glories of a smooth blue sea washing the sides of islets which sparkled in all the green and luxuriant verdure with which the imagination of a poet may be supposed to array the dwellings of the Fairies. We anchored at one o'clock. The place looks pretty, and H. N. M. Frigate *Ajax* lying at anchor in the roads did not, of course, detract from the beauty of the scene. The party were not long in landing, some of us proceeding to pay our respects to the Resident, some to take a look at the fort, and we were everywhere met with civility and polite attention from all the gentlemen of the station whom we met, and I believe we saw them all, for there is no great number of them. We then, all in a body, made our way to the house of the China Captain, accompanied by several of the Dutch military Officers, where a splendid tiffin awaited us, to which every one shewed his readiness to do honour. But the recall gun from the steamer broke in upon the harmony of the entertainment and compelled us to retrace our steps on board, leaving our worthy host, Ban Hok, filled with regret at our departure. I ought not to forget that on our visit to the fort the troops were turned out in honour of the visitors, and put through sundry well-executed manoeuvres, and also that a salute of nine guns was fired. We were also shewn the Government School, where, among other things, the children are taught music, and gave a proof of their proficiency by singing with great sweetness, an accomplishment of which, by the way, I would recommend the acquisition in the schools here, if the thing is possible, as besides having an excellent moral effect upon the children, we might have a little decent singing in Church of a Sunday. We returned to the steamer, and got under way for Singapore at four o'clock."

On Monday, 26th August, the first meeting was held of the Singapore Temperance Society, which began very successfully, with Lieut. Ashley of the Artillery as Secretary, and the Hon. T. Church as President, and the clergy and Dr. Oxley on the Committee. Three months afterwards Mr. John Gemmill, who was then a store-keeper and the first auctioneer in Singapore, published the following amusing advertisement:—

CIRCULAR.

The Temperance Society is making such rapid strides in this Settlement that it is useless to advertise Brandy for sale, although I have got some very good of an old stock, which I wish to get rid of, and leave off selling the article, there being little, or no consumption of it since the above society has commenced operations, and so effectually so that the spirit trade is very unprofitable, at least so I find it, and if all here tell the truth they will confess the same. Nevertheless, may the Temperance Society go on, and prosper, say I, although it hurts my trade. I have, however, just received a superior lot of very old Malmsey Madeira, that I can confidently recommend, also a fresh batch of genuine old Port Wine for sale by

JOHN GEMMILL

A Malacca Temperance Society was formed about the same time, with the Resident Councillor as President. There was an advertisement in the *Free Press* in August by Syme & Co., that they were prepared to advance in cash to the extent of nine-tenths of the value of Produce consigned to their Agents in London or Liverpool.

A new Cattle disease, which was very fatal, was first noticed at this time, and it was thought to be caused by the animals swallowing a small poisonous insect when eating grass, which produced violent irritation of the stomach. It caused great distress among the cattle-owners.

On Saturday, the 16th September, news was received by H. M. Sloop *Zebra* from Penang, of the death of King William the Fourth; and on Sunday, at 1 p.m. seventy-two minute guns, the year of his age, were fired from the battery on shore and from the *Zebra* in the roads. On Monday, at noon, a Royal salute was fired in honour of the accession of the Princess Victoria to the throne. The following was the proclamation, which is interesting to those who have not seen it before, from its quaint legal language. The form was followed on the death of Queen Victoria in 1901, being found printed in the original of these papers.

"Whereas it has pleased Almighty God to call to His Mercy our late Sovereign Lord King William the Fourth, of Blessed and Glorious Memory, by whose decease the Imperial Crown of the United Kingdom of Great Britain and Ireland is solely and rightfully come to the High and Mighty Princess Alexandrina Victoria, saving the Rights of any issue of his late Majesty King William the Fourth which may be born of his late Majesty's Consort: therefore, the Governor and Members of Council of Fort St. George in Council assembled, do now hereby, with one Voice and Consent of Tongue and Heart, publish and proclaim that the High and Mighty Princess Alexandrina Victoria, is now, by the death of our late Sovereign of Happy Memory, become our only lawful and rightful Liege Lady Victoria by the Grace of God, Queen of the United Kingdom of Great Britain and Ireland and of the British Territorries in the East Indies, Defender of the Faith, saving as aforesaid: to whom, saving as aforesaid, we do acknowledge all Faith and constant Obedience, with all hearty and humble affection: beseeching God, by whom Kings and Queens do reign, to bless the Royal Princess Victoria, with long and happy Years to reign over us.

Given at Fort St. George this twenty-fifth day of August, in the year of Our Lord One thousand eight hundred and thirty-seven.

GOD SAVE THE QUEEN.

All the pages of the *Free Press* were put into mourning borders for three weeks, and a notification was issued that the Governor in Council requested that mourning should be worn by all British subjects residing in the Presidency.

On Saturday, 30th September, the *Singapore Chronicle* issued its last number.

A Government notification appeared on 18th October, giving the reasons for passing the Indian Act No. 20 of 1837, regarding the transmission of land. It said that land could only be lawfully bequeathed and inherited according to English law, but in practice that had been little regarded. Freeholds had been equally divided between the members of a family instead of descending to the heir-at-law; and also bequeathed by will not executed with the formalities of a devise; and immigrants from different countries had introduced their own natural usages. If the English law were enforced under these circumstances great confusion, distress, and insecurity would result. It was desirable therefore to secure the present holders of land in their possession; all land in the Eastern Settlements (the Straits) would be treated as being, and as having always been, of the nature of personal property. At this time all the lands in Singapore were of a leasehold tenure (*Free Press*, 19th October, 1837) and the irregularities mentioned in the notification or preamble to the Act, had no existence here, it was only then applicable to Penang and Malacca.

Gambling was rampant at this time, and two cases of suicide by women in consequence occurred. It was remarked by the newspaper that the police peons were looked upon and generally found to be the most substantial people of any of their walk of life in Singapore, and were as inefficient as they could be; which was all that was got in exchange for the abolition of the gambling farm.

Prince William Hendrick Frederick, son of the Prince of Orange, a lieutenant on board H. N. M. frigate *Bellona*, came to Singapore in October, the first Royal Visitor, and after a complimentary reception, he visited Penang and Malacca on his way to Calcutta.

The Chamber of Commerce held a meeting on the 24th October, to protest against a proposal of the Supreme Government at Bengal to introduce a Rupee circulation. The following resolutions were passed:—

1st. That it is the opinion of this meeting, that the plan proposed by the Right Hon'ble the Governor-General in Council in a letter to the Hon'ble the Governor of the Straits Settlements, dated 16th August last, of substituting Company's Rupees as the only legal currency of these Settlements, in place of Spanish dollars and Dutch guilders—the present currency—would be highly injurious to the commerce of the said Settlements, besides entailing considerable expense on the Government.

2nd. That it is the opinion of this meeting, that the present currency is better adapted for the trade carried on at this place than any which can be substituted; Dollars and Guilders being almost the only coins which pass current in the neighbouring native states.

3rd. That should the Government carry into effect the proposed measure of making Company's Rupees the only legal tender, it is the opinion of this meeting that they would still not become current, nor remain in the Settlement, but be shipped to Calcutta, Madras, and Bombay as remittances, when the Government Treasury is shut, or when open at an unfavourable rate of exchange.

4th. That should the measure be adopted, this Meeting is of opinion that it would cause numerous difficulties to the Merchants in their intercourse with the native traders bringing produce to the place, who will receive payment in dollars and guilders only, and it would thus be productive of endless disputes and litigation.

5th. That it is the opinion of this meeting, that Government might issue a copper currency for the Straits, consisting of cent, half-cent and quarter-cent pieces (the Bengal copper coins not being adapted) with advantage to these Settlements; the present copper currency, either from short supplies or from the monopoly of the native shroffs, being subject to great fluctuation, which is severely felt by the labouring and poorer classes of the community who are usually paid in copper.

6th. That should Government issue a new copper currency for the Straits, it is the opinion of this meeting, that it would be necessary, in order to prevent, as far as possible, any fluctuation in the value of the coin, to have a considerable stock at each Settlement to enable the local Government to keep the market steadily supplied.

7th. That this meeting is of opinion that no means should be taken to prohibit the importation of copper tokens as an article of commerce, for the supply of the neighbouring native states, but that the Company's coin only should be permitted to pass current in these Settlements.

At this time the local Government officially recognised for copper coin, only the old coin struck for Bencoolen, and cents made for Penang, and all sorts of spurious and worthless coins were used for small change.

At the end of October, the number of cattle carried off by the disease we have mentioned, rose to considerably over five hundred, and a subscription was made for the natives who owned them, as they were reduced to destitution.

The Government having given way as to the imposition of duties, turned from the miscarriage of that plan to injure the trade of Singapore, to the formation of another. The second scheme of taxation was a tonnage duty on all square-rigged vessels coming to the port, whether with cargo or as a port of call. It was supposed that it would produce an annual revenue of Rs. 50,000. It came to nothing, but it was allowed by the mercantile community at the time that if it were suggested for the purpose of maintaining a light-house in the Straits for the security of navigation, they would not hesitate to recognise the propriety of it, but there was no light-house then, and no pilots, and no dock establishment in any of the three Settlements, nor any establishment maintained to carry on surveys in the neighbourhood, which the occurrence of frequent accidents proved to be necessary, and nothing had been done for the benefit of the class of shipping it was proposed to tax.

Sir Benjamin Malkin who had been promoted to the Calcutta Bench as Chief Justice died there in October. He had left the Straits on 29th June, 1835. The *Englishman* spoke of him as a man of extensive learning, and ever ready to open his purse-strings for useful and charitable objects.

From time to time various suggestions were made about steam communication, and in November a proposal was originated in Singapore to establish a line between Calcutta and the Straits, and the following outline of the scheme was published :—

"It is proposed to establish a monthly communication by Steam between this Port and Calcutta, and thus to extend to the Straits, and in some degree also to China, the benefits of the communication opened between England and India by the Red Sea. To effect this desirable object, a plan is now in circulation to form a Joint-Stock Association. It is intended to purchase a steam vessel fitted up chiefly for the accommodation of passengers, but to carry also a small quantity of freight. The time occupied in the voyage between Calcutta and Singapore, allowing her to touch for a few hours at Penang and Malacca, would not much exceed eight days, and would certainly not be more than ten. She would then have five days to remain here and fifteen days for her return voyage (touching, of course at Malacca and Penang) and for her stay at Calcutta before the month was finished. The time of her departure from Calcutta would be regulated by the arrival of the Mails by the Red Sea. If time permitted it, and freights or a sufficient number of passengers offered, she might touch occasionally at any of the ports on the eastern side of the Bay of Bengal, or her voyage might be extended to Java, but such deviations would only be permitted, if they could be made without fear of their interrupting the regular monthly communication between Calcutta and the Straits.

"The benefit which the scheme, if it succeeds, will confer on the settlers in the Straits, are too obvious to require to be pointed out; to the residents in Bengal they would be also great, but of a different nature. It is believed that if the advantages which the climate of the Straits and the voyage hold out to the Indian invalids were more generally known, and a regular monthly communication once established, the numbers who now resort here would soon be greatly increased. The certainty of being able to get back within the month would induce numbers to visit the Straits in search of health, who now remain in India, until a voyage to the Cape or Europe, and an absence of many months, or even of some years, is rendered necessary. Besides, there are many who, for recreation, would gladly absent themselves from Calcutta for a month, but who now cannot do so, on account of the uncertainty of getting back again within a reasonable time.

"No hopes are hold out to subscribers that much profit will at first result from the undertaking, though it may reasonable be expected that after the first year, the increased number of passengers would enable it to pay pretty well. It is hoped that the Government of India will pass an Act limiting the liability of the subscribers to the amount of the sum subscribed, as is to be done for the Association in Calcutta for building the Bonded Warehouses. If such an Act cannot be obtained, it is proposed to make it one of the fundamental rules of the Association, that should the debts ever exceed a certain portion of the Joint-Stock funds, the Association should be at once dissolved, and its affairs wound up. It would be made incumbent on the directors to publish quarterly a statement of the accounts. The amount of the shares is fixed at 600 Rupees each, and would be called for in three or four instalments, with intervals of two or three months between the payment of each instalment."

This was followed in March, 1838, by Messrs. Syme & Co., being appointed Agents of the New Bengal Steam Fund, and up to that time 2,475 shares had been subscribed for in England and India by 706 individuals and firms, and it was proposed to put on a small steamer between Bombay and Socotra to complete a regular mail every fortnight between England and India. The end of this was that, in 1841, the Committee of the New Bengal Steam Fund made an agreement with the East India and Peninsular and Oriental Steam Navigation Companies, and the Shareholders took a transfer of their shares to the P. & O. Company, and that important undertaking arrived at a definite point, and held its first half-yearly meeting in that year.

A buffalo started off in a furious state one Saturday evening, and after injuring a number of persons and tossing Mr. Catchick, the Armenian Priest, and goring him severely, it attacked a pony and gharry in St. Andrew's Church compound and killed the pony, and was shot by the police the next day in the jungle, a mile from the town. On St. Andrew's Day, Dr. Montgomerie was Chairman of the Scotch dinner, the Stewards being Messrs. Carnie, Fraser, Charles Spottiswoode (partner in John Purvis & Co.) and Davidson.

Up to this time, no Chinese woman had ever come to Singapore from China, and the newspapers said that, in fact, only two genuine Chinese women were, or at any time had been, in the place, and they were two small-footed ladies who had been, some years before, exhibited in England. The Bugis trade in the season for this year, which lasted from July to November, was 169 boats from Bali and the Celebes, in equal proportion; the total tonnage was nearly 5,000 tons, and the number of men 5,038.

Mr. Thomas Scott and Mr. Charles Spottiswoode joined Mr. John Purvis in December and the firm was then called John Purvis & Co.

In this year Mrs. Whittle had a Boarding and Day School in North Bridge Road, the charges for Boarders were $12 and for day Scholars $5 a month.

In this year Mr. Benjamin Peach Keasberry came to Singapore. He was the youngest of the three sons of Colonel Keasberry, who was appointed Resident of Tegal, in Java, during the British occupation. Mr. Keasberry was born at Hyderabad in India 1811. His father died when he was a few years old, and the widow married a merchant in

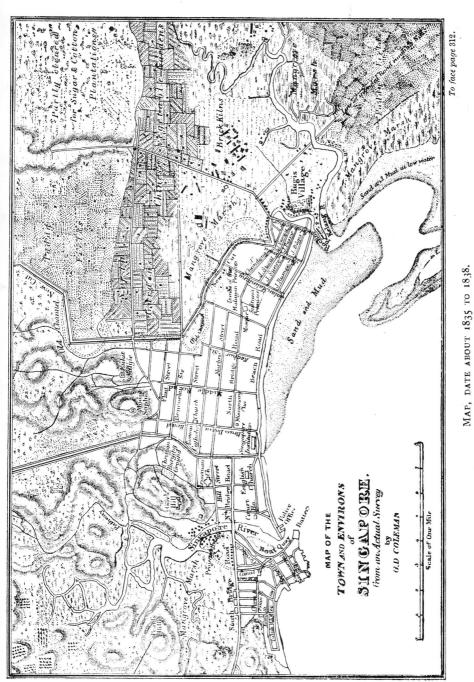

To face page 312.

MAP OF THE
TOWN AND ENVIRONS
of
SINGAPORE.
from an Actual Survey
by
G.D COLEMAN

Scale of Our Mile

MAP, DATE ABOUT 1835 TO 1838.

Soerabaya named Mr. Davidson. The three boys were sent to school at Mauritius and afterwards to Madras. When they grew up the elder brothers went to Soerabaya, and the youngest stayed in Singapore and opened a store. As it did not do much good, he went to Batavia, and was a clerk in a firm there, but making the acquaintance of Dr. Medhurst, of the London Missionary Society, he went to live with him, and joined him in his work, learning printing, bookbinding and lithography, which he found very useful afterwards in Singapore. About 1834 he received some money from his father's estate and he went to America, where he studied at College for three years, and in 1837 married Miss Charlotte Parker of Boston. He came to Singapore with his wife as Missionaries to Malays under the American Board of Commissioners for Foreign Missions. He remained in Singapore until his death.

The two brothers John and Alexander Stronach of the London Missionary Society were in Singapore then, and also Messrs. North, Dickenson, Tracy and Travelli of the American Board. In 1839 the American Board removed their men to China, and Mr. Keasberry joined the London Missionary Society, and learned Malay from Munshi Abdulla. He then started a small school at Rochore, where a few boys were taught printing, &c., under agreement to remain for a certain period. Preaching in Malay was carried on in an attap building in North Bridge Road nearly opposite where the Chinese Gospel House is now. Mr. Keasberry lived in the house still standing on the plot in Brass Bassa Road behind the present Raffles Hotel.

In 1843 by his exertions in collecting subscriptions in Singapore the Malay Chapel in Prinsep Street was built and opened. The opening sermon was preached by the Rev. Samuel Dyer of Penang, and the second by Dr. Legge, afterwards well-known at Oxford, both of the London Missionary Society, at that time on their way to China. The jubilee of the Chapel was held on the 7th February, 1893, when it was associated with the memory of Mr. Keasberry, as one of the earliest, most respected, and most well-known pioneers in mission work in the Peninsula. Although it was eighteen years after his death, the Chapel was crowded with those who had known him in Singapore.

In 1846 Mr. Keasberry, being a widower, married Miss Ellen Scott, a niece of Captain William Scott, and when, in 1847, the London Missionary Society ordered all their men to China, Mr. Keasberry would not leave Singapore, as he had some boys bound to him for several years, and was doing so much useful work in the place. So he severed his connection with the Society and remained from 1847 as a self-supporting missionary, occupying himself with his school, his preaching, and the printing establishment by which he supported the school. He held regular services in the Chapel and visited the neighbouring islands and the Carimons in his sailing boat.

There is a letter among the papers in the Raffles Institution which he wrote on 2nd July, 1847, to the School Committee of the Singapore Institution, in which he asked the patronage of the Committee for his boarding school for Malay boys which he had established eighteen months before, in connection, he said, with the Mission of the London Missionary Society. He had expected that Society to support his School, but they declined, owing to the state of the funds, and he was obliged to rely upon local resources. He said that he had not room for more than the thirteen boys he had, which caused an expense of $250 a year, some of the boys paying $2 a month, and the printing establishment partly supporting the School. This was the beginning of the house at Mount Zion at River Valley Road. It was a plank and tile-roofed house, which was pulled down and rebuilt in 1851 with some money left to Mr. Keasberry by his step-father Mr. Davidson. In the original bungalow were several Malay youths of good birth. Governor Butterworth sent the two eldest sons of Tumongong Ibrahim to school with Mr. Keasberry, and the elder, the late Sultan Abubakar of Johore, always spoke with the highest respect and gratitude of "Tuan Keasberry" and erected the monument over his grave. In 1858 there was a Malay girls' school taught by Mrs. Keasberry, at Mount Zion. About 1862 Mr. Keasberry opened a Mission station at Bukit Timah, and a chapel was erected there, which was supported by the members of the Malay Mission until his death when the Presbyterian Church was asked to take charge of it.

Mr. Keasberry wrote a number of books in Malay, and printed the Bible in Malay. His press was always resorted to by the European merchants to print their bills of lading, policies, &c., and Mr. Keasberry was always at work in the Square in the printing office, which was called the Mission Press. It eventually passed to to Mr. Neave and afterwards became Fraser and Neave, Limited. Mr. Keasberry's name had become a household word in Singapore. He died quite suddenly while preaching in the Malay Chapel on 6th September, 1875, after a residence in Singapore of 38 years, at the age of 64 years.

Mr. George Windsor Earl's book, "The Eastern Seas in 1832-34" was published in London in this year. He had been a sailor, in command of vessels, and in 1832 he came from Western Australia to Java. The greater part of his book contains descriptions of Batavia, Soerabaya, Borneo and Siam. The last three chapters relate to Singapore where he arrived for the first time from Batavia on 6th February, 1833, and after a short voyage elsewhere, remained in Singapore from June in that year to February, 1834, when he sailed for England. The reviews remarked that his statements were not always accurate, especially regarding the amount of trade. The height of Bukit Timah was stated at 1500 feet (it is really about 500) and the paper pointed out other mistakes of fact regarding the dates of building the Roman Catholic and Mr. Keasberry's Chapels. Mr. Earl said in the book that it was the custom on the morning of Christmas Day before the merchants came into town (they did not apparently keep a holiday) for the boatmen to deck the entrances of their town houses with plantain stems and green boughs, which was not done with a view to a Christmas Box, as the residents rarely knew by whom it was done, and the godowns of those who were in the habit of treating them with rudeness were sometimes neglected. Mr. Earl returned to Singapore in 1856 and practised in High Street as an Advocate and Law Agent. On 1st June, 1857, he was appointed Police Magistrate in Singapore. In 1859 he was Assistant Resident Councillor and exchanged offices with Mr. Willans at Province Wellesley; he then acted for Mr. Braddell in Penang and returned to Province Wellesley in 1860, and was Resident Councillor there and in Penang until 1865, when he died, two days after leaving Penang, on his way home.

Mr. Moor's Notices of the Indian Archipelago and adjacent countries, a book of about 300 pages with charts and maps, printed in Singapore, was published in December. It was a compilation from papers in the Singapore newspapers, and contains a great deal of information which (as the *Free Press* remarked in reviewing the book) would have been entirely lost but for the industry of Mr. Moor. It contains very little that relates to Singapore, but contains much information about the states in the Malay Peninsula and neighbouring countries.

The commercial activity of the Chinese was always greatly excited on the arrival of the junks from China. The first junk generally arrived a little before Christmas, and the vessels remained in the harbour from December until June. Boats were always going to and fro among the shipping, giving the roads, Mr. Earl says, the appearance of a floating fair. As a large junk came in, the boats used to go out when a long way off and as she neared the town she gained an accession of bulk at every fathom, until at last the unwieldly mass slowly trailed into the roads surrounded by a dense mass of boats. The Chinese master strutted about on the top of the thatched habitation on the quarter deck, with all the importance of a mandarin. For a day or two little business was done, as the time was spent in building roofs over the vessels to shelter the goods which were to be exposed for sale on the decks.

The arrival of the first junk was a time of great excitement. It was most anxiously looked for, and when a Malay sampan, which had been on the look out to the eastward, brought the news that a junk had been seen, there was a tremendous bustle among the Chinese community, running in all directions to tell their friends, so that they might hasten off to the vessel to learn the news from China. Some of these junks were very large vessels, up to seven hundred tons or more, manned and navigated entirely by Chinese.

Some of the small junks, varying from one hundred and fifty to three hundred tons, were fast sailing craft and came down expressly for opium, for which they paid in silver. They used to leave early in May; and smuggle the opium into Canton by bribing the Mandarins. All the large junks sailed on their return voyage by the end of June. In 1841 a few of them waited till the middle of July, hoping to get opium cheaper when the others had left, but they got into the monsoon, and one or two were lost with valuable cargoes, and the lesson was not lost on their successors. The Chinese in Singapore sent remittances by them to their families in China, usually of money, but sometimes rice and various useful articles. The servants used to want an advance for this purpose, and it was said that the masters of the junks, who received a percentage on the sum transmitted, were extremely honest in the transactions.

The Bugis Traders used to arrive in October and November, with coffee, tortoise shell, or gold dust, which they sold to the Chinese. About two hundred of these boats used to come annually, each manned by about thirty men. They used to walk all round about the place before making a bargain and buying the return cargo of opium, iron, piece goods, gold thread, &c.; they seldom, if ever, took money away with them.

Native vessels also used to come down from Siam and Cochin China. The rajahs there fitted out square-rigged vessels and loaded-them on their own account. They brought principally sugar and rice, and gamboge which was shipped to London, and cocoanut oil for Singapore use.

A large number of Arab vessels under the Dutch flag came from all parts of Java, fitted out and owned by Arabs residing in Java. They were credited with notorious smuggling, for which the numerous small rivers in Java gave many facilities. They were built of teak, ranging from 150 to 500 tons, and were fine vessels.

From May to October used to come boats from Sambas and Pontianak and Borneo, bringing pepper, camphor, rattans, &c., but they were greatly hampered by piracy until Sir James Brooke and Captain Keppel in the *Dido* gave them a check they could not get over, as Mr. G. F. Davidson remarks in his book, from which many of the above statements are taken.

There was an extensive trade also between Calcutta and Singapore throughout the year. Vessels brought raw-cotton and cotton goods, opium and wheat, and carried back tin, pepper, sago, gambier, and especially treasure; dollars were often very scarce after two or three of the clippers had left.

Mention has just been made of the junks in 1841 having tried to beat up to China against the monsoon. Mr. W. H. Read says in his book that it was in 1832 that the opium clipper *Red Rover* first accomplished this. The story is as follows:—"In January, 1832, a vessel called the *Red Rover*, commanded by Captain Clifton, started from Calcutta, and, touching at Singapore, plunged into the unknown terrors of a strong north-east monsoon, in the hope of reaching Whampoa in due time. Bets were heavy as to whether she would reach her destination or not. One morning, about a month after her departure from Singapore, the mercantile community was thrown into a state of considerable excitement by the appearance of a crippled vessel, flying a St. Andrew's white cross on a blue field— 'Jardine's private flag.' Her main-top-gallant mast was gone; the fore top-mast, evidently a jury one, had a royal set for the top-sail. The mizen mast looked all askew, and, in fact, the 'bonnie barkie' was a wreck. Of course, the 'I told you so' were triumphant. 'Impossible, we knew it.' Their opponents were as dejected as the others were jubilant. Meanwhile, Captain Clifton came on shore to breakfast with his agent. The worthy skipper's face was a picture of melancholy. He was limp with fatigue. He threw his hat on a table, tumbled into a chair, and seemed as if about to burst into tears. His host and others tried to cheer the mortified mariner, who refused to be comforted; but, like many others on similar occasions, he rather overdid his part. A suspicion was raised in the mind of one of those present, who, quietly rising from his seat, went into the verandah and examined the cast-away hat, withdrawing from it a Macao newspaper only a week old. The 'gaff was blown,' as the vulgar expression is; the secret was out, and the wily captain burst into a hearty laugh. He had beat up against the monsoon in eighteen days without losing a spar; all the ravaged look of his vessel was a comedy, and the 'I told you so' party, frightfully 'sold,' suddenly collapsed. The end of the *Red Rover* was sad. After many adventurous but successful voyages, she disappeared in the Bay of Bengal."

Mr. Thomas Church who had been appointed Resident Councillor in this year, had been, in 1819, a young assistant Magistrate at Bencoolen under Mr. E. Presgrave. On the abolition of the Bencoolen Government he was transferred to Penang, and in 1828 he was at Malacca as Deputy Resident, and went up to the Penghulu of Naning to try to settle the dispute which afterwards led to the so-called war in 1831.

He had been Police Magistrate and Assistant Resident in Penang and Malacca for five years, and was higher in rank than Mr. Bonham. He had retired from the service in 1835 and gone home, but he soon got tired of it, being a very active man, repented of his resignation, and petitioned the Company to be allowed to rejoin, which was done on condition of his being placed at the bottom of the list for promotion. He went to Calcutta, on his way to the Straits, and waited on Sir Charles Metcalfe, then acting Governor-General, who asked him for a record of his previous services. Mr. Church, unfortunately for himself, was, to say the least, reticent about his previous resignation, and Sir C. Metcalfe, supposing that he was older in the service than Mr. Bonham, sent him on to the Straits to relieve that gentleman of the acting Governorship. He did so and administered the Government in Singapore for a few months. But then matters were cleared up and positions reversed, which led, naturally, to a great deal of talk in the place. Mr. Bonham was confirmed as Governor in 1837 and Mr. Church received the appointment under him of Resident Councillor, and Singapore was, for the first time (Cameron, page 21) made the permanent residence of the Governor. Mr. Bonham was Governor until 1843, when Mr. Church according to practice, should have succeeded him, but the story went that it was known in Calcutta that he did not give good dinners (so it is written) and the difficulty was felt to be insurmountable. At any rate Governor Butterworth was appointed.

Mr. Church was in charge of Singapore while Colonel Butterworth was absent on leave from 1851 to 1853, when Mr. Blundell acted for the Governor, but remained at Penang. Mr. Church wrote to the Governor-General stating his claims to act for Governor Butterworth, but Lord Dalhousie on 9th January, 1852, replied that the Government of India fully appreciated his ability, energy, the success of his services in Singapore, and the value of his long experience and intimate acquaintance with the Settlement; and would have reposed the charge in his hands with perfect confidence. But as Mr. Blundell had once before been Governor of the Straits, and when he was removed, it became the subject of a despatch from the Court of Directors, the terms of that despatch were such that the Government could not have declined to appoint him to act again, without obvious disregard of the views of the Honorable Court and consequent injustice to Mr. Blundell. Lord Dalhousie added that though his letter might not remove Mr. Church's disappointment, yet it would satisfy him that Mr. Blundell's appointment arose from no other cause than his peculiar claims, which gave him the preference; while the Government highly and justly appreciated Mr. Church's long, able, and valuable services in the same sphere.

Mr. Church was distinguished by a most assiduous discharge of his public duties, giving up his whole time and attention to them for many years. In addition to his other labours, he disposed of the greater part of the civil business of the Court at Singapore, the visits of the professional judges being rare and hurried. Mr. Church was a very useful public servant, thoroughly familiar with the duties of his office, punctual and laborious in their discharge, and unaffectedly anxious for the welfare and advancement of Singapore, which owed a great deal to him. In August, 1856, he sent in his resignation, having been Resident Councillor for nineteen years, at the time when such an energetic, practical, and unassuming head of affairs was peculiarly valuable.

The following address was presented to him by the Chamber of Commerce, and was very much more than a mere formal compliment. "Sir,—The Singapore Chamber of Commerce, having learnt that your official connection with Singapore is about to terminate, desire respectfully to express the high sense they entertain of the zeal and assiduity with which you have discharged your public duties during the many years you have filled the office of Resident Councillor at this station.

"The Chamber have fully appreciated the ready attention you have at all times given to the representations of the mercantile community; and your conciliatory behaviour to all classes, and particularly to those native traders on whose presence so much of the prosperity of the trade of Singapore depends.

"The great facilities which you have afforded for the transaction of business by a liberal interpretation of official rules and requirements, and the disposition you have ever shewn to dispense with unnecessary formalities which might give rise to vexations, obstacles, and delays, deserve the fullest acknowledgment on the part of the mercantile community. But, in a more special manner, their grateful thanks are due to you for the important assistance rendered not only to them but to the whole community, by your voluntarily taking upon yourself the punctual and laborious discharge of judicial duties for so many years, when the absence of a resident professional judge would otherwise have been very detrimental to their interests.

"Although differences of opinion may at times have existed between you and the mercantile community on particular subjects, the Chamber fully believe that you have at all times been actuated by a conscientious sense of duty and have ever had the sincerest desire to promote the commercial interests of this place.

" The Chamber regret that failing health should have been the immediate cause of your leaving this Settlement, in the prosperity of which they doubt not you will still continue to take much interest, and, in conclusion, the Chamber beg to offer their best wishes for your future welfare and that your health may be benefited by a return to your native land.

Signed in name, and by authority,
of the Singapore Chamber of Commerce,

C. H. HARRISON,
Chairman.
A. LOGAN,
Secretary.

A Malay letter written to him by the Tumongong expressed his earnest thanks in eastern phrases for the help and advice Mr. Church had given to him, which had converted his country " into a populous country again." And the law agents of that time, Messrs. W. Napier, A. Logan, R. C. Woods and A. M. Aitken, addressed Mr. Church with warm acknowledgments of the great labour and responsibility he had undertaken on the Bench, outside his own proper duties, and the high opinion they had entertained of his impartiality and judgment. The letter was of more value as it was written in October, 1855, on the occasion of his having stated in Court that he found it would only be possible to take peculiarly urgent cases, as he found it caused too serious an interruption to the discharge of his other work. And yet (in spite of a very careful turn of mind that will be spoken of presently) nothing is heard of any suggestion of extra salary, or of any other desire than to do all the good he could in his station.

Mr. Church's reply, dated 12th October, 1855, is worth recording :—
" Gentlemen :—

" I have had the honor to receive your obliging communication of the 8th instant. The anomalous constitution of Her Majesty's Court of Judicature in the Straits combined with the peculiar position of this Station induced me to undertake duties involving weighty responsibility necessarily attendant on the administration of justice.

" In the infancy of the Settlement the judicial business was comparatively light and simple, and no material interruption in the performance of the executive duties was experienced for some years. Singapore has, however, annually assumed a greater degree of importance. Commerce and population have vastly increased, and consequently the judicial business also ; it is a source of satisfaction to find the Home Authorities have at length determined to nominate a professional Judge to this important Station, a measure calculated to prove advantageous to the public and a great relief to the Executive.

" The testimony borne by gentlemen who, from professional position, are the most competent to form an opinion of the benefit which has resulted to the Community by my holding Civil Sittings, is particularly welcome and gratifying, and more than a compensation for the additional labour and mental anxiety which I have occasionally undergone in my earnest desire to impart substantial justice, and come to a right judgment.

"To you, Gentlemen, individually and collectively, I request to tender my cordial thanks for the valuable assistance afforded during the protracted period I have presided in Court and for the kind expressions towards me recorded in your letter under acknowledgment."

The social side of Mr. and Mrs. Church's life was a source of never failing amusement to the community, in a very amiable spirit. It is related that Mr. Bonham, when Governor, was found in his office one day with a large bottle of fluid magnesia on his table. "Not sick, I hope" said a friend. "Oh, dear no," said the Governor, "but I am going to dine with Tom Church to-night." Mr. Church always lived at the house, now standing, at the corner of Coleman Street and the Esplanade, opposite the Cathedral. It was afterwards the Masonic Lodge until the present Lodge was built in Coleman Street; then it become part of the Hotel de l'Europe, and is now part of the land that was bought for offices for the Municipality in 1899. In 1844 Mr. Church gave a dance and the Hon. Captain Keppel sent his band from the *Dido*. He was always famed for the band on his vessels. The brandy supplied to the band was not to their taste, and the Captain's Diary (we know now from the Admiral's last book) remarked at the time "Band got drunk." A few days after Mr. Napier gave a dance, and after it was over the band (who got good drink and enough of it, or more) marched away to Tom Church's, a trifle out of their way, and played the Rogues' March in the Compound, and then walked down to their boat on the beach (there was no sea-wall then) and went off to the *Dido*, which sailed at daybreak homeward bound.

Another well-worn anecdote was this. One forenoon in the office, a Kling tamby came and offered Mr. Church a very nice looking fowl pie, which Mr. Church bought as a great bargain, as he thought, to please Mrs. Church, for a dollar. But on reaching home, it was not a success, for he found Mrs. Church had sold it to the tamby for fifty cents, as it had not been cut at a party at their house the previous evening. It was further related that on one occasion when a very high official functionary came from Calcutta, he was placed in a small room on the lower floor, and the wash-hand stand was a cracked basin on an empty case stood on end.

One day there was a fire in town, at which some sailors rendered valuable assistance, and one of the old residents, a Magistrate, highly respected, took upon himself to give them some refreshments which they had well-earned. The bill, which amounted to some $6 or $7, was sent in the next day to Government, but the Resident Councillor, who was more than economical, refused to pay a cent; "it was absurd to throw away such a heap of money for nothing." So the worthy J. P. sent round a circular, asking for subscriptions, of not more than five cents each. He, of course, obtained the money at once, and sent the receipted bill and subscription list to Mr. Church to be kept among the Government records. An old Singaporean writes "Poor Mr. Church was a good-hearted, and in some things generous man, but liberality was not his forte." His handsome gift of a clock to the Church has been described on page 290. Mr. Church's eldest son Major Robert Church, of the Madras Army, now a retired Lieutenant Colonel, was

Private Secretary and A.D.C. to Governor Butterworth. His second son, now Major General Thomas Ross Church, C.I.E., was married to Miss Florence Marryat, daughter of Captain Marryat, the famous sea-novelist, in whose steps she followed as a novel-writer, but of a very different type. The notice of the marriage appeared in the *Singapore Free Press* of 23rd June, 1854, as follows:—"At Penang, on the 13th June, by the Revd. E. R. Maddock, T. Ross Church, Esq., 12th Regt. M. N. I., to Florence, the Fourth Daughter of the late Captain Frederick Marryat, R.N., C.B." Captain Marryat had died in 1848; he had been promoted and made a C.B. for his services in the Burmese War, but when H. M. S. *Larne* was here in 1840, Captain Blake was in command of her, and not Captain Marryat. It has been said that Captain Marryat was known in Singapore, and some circumstances seem to point to it. He was certainly in command of H. M. S. *Larne*, when she was on the station in the Burmah War, as has been said on page 281; and it used to be said that some of the stories in his novels, particularly O'Brien's famous duel in "Peter Simple" were founded on occurrences in Singapore, as a very similar duel took place many years ago in North Bridge Road, where a billiard room and public house stood, long since pulled down to build shop houses. This is however, quite uncertain, as no confirmation has been obtained up to the time this chapter is written. It is also thought that the children of Mr. Church and Captain Marryat were brought up, or at school together, in England.

Mr. Church died in London at 2 Hamilton Place, St. John's Wood, on 10th August, 1860. Singapore may well wish to see his like again. Mrs. Elizabeth Church returned to Singapore, and though possessed of large means, lived in the most frugal manner possible, and kept all her money, a very large sum indeed, in deposit notes in the Oriental Bank, on the failure of which the amount was necessarily somewhat decreased. She died here on 31st October, 1884, in Killiney Road, at the age of eighty years. She was only known to people in general, because she used to drive out in the evening in a very old pony gharry: and turning over the newspaper of that time, it is found that no notice whatever was taken of the occurrence, though she was certainly a part of the history of the place, for her husband was one of the most hardworking, conscientious men that ever came to Singapore.

CHAPTER XXVI.

1838—1839

1838.

IN January a number of small lots of ground on the northern side of Brass Bassa Road were sold by the Government at auction under the New Land Regulations, the term of 999 years having been abandoned. The longest term for any of these leases was 99 years, with a proviso that substantial buildings should be erected; or for 60 years when the nature of the building was left to the option of the purchaser. The result of reducing the term was that only one-third was realized of the price for which such land had been sold six or seven years before under a system of permanent leases, as they were called, for 999 years. In consequence of the defective state of the communication between the locality of the lots that were sold and the mercantile part of the town, the newspaper urged that the money received from the sale should be applied to local improvement.

This change in the regulations had been made by Mr. W. R. Young, the Land Commissioner who was sent from India. There were many complaints about the great expense to the Settlement, Mr. Young's salary alone being Rs. 3,000 a month; and about the futile result of his proceedings. The Bengal Government had been asked to allow waste jungle land to be cleared and planted, and at a great expense sent the Commissioner to say that it would be allowed on payment of an annual quit-rent for 20 years, and the land would then be resumed by Government, which created much dissatisfaction. Mr. John Crawfurd wrote a very long letter on the subject to the East India and China Association which was reprinted in the *Free Press* on 11th October.

The old question of a gambling farm was raised again in this year and was advocated by the press, one of the principal grounds being the connivance of the police; for the paper said that if it was otherwise the whole force must have been blind, as a short walk in town would show twenty shops where gambling was carried on almost openly every night.

Small-pox was very bad in the middle of the year, over three hundred persons dying within three months, and it was proposed to establish a Vaccination Society, which the Recorder suggested in his charge to the Grand Jury, referring to the benefit vaccination had conferred on the population of Ceylon.

In June, the Chamber of Commerce petitioned the House of Parliament against the heavy duty on tin imported into Great Britain from the Straits. The quantity of tin exported to London and Liverpool in 1837, had been 10,688 cwt.

In July, the steamer *Diana* left for Malacca and Penang, and it is a curious sign of the times that complaints were made by some of the merchants that they had not heard of her intended departure and had missed the opportunity to write. So it was suggested that it would be a good plan to circulate a notice among the merchants when a steamer was intended to leave. The *Diana* was the first steamer employed in the Straits; and besides going after pirates, for which Captain Congalton became very famous, she took the Recorder on circuit; so the views of Singapore became quite changed about the utility of steam-vessels, the paper remarking that "the use of the *Diana* afforded signal example of the advantageous and useful purposes for which steam-vessels could be employed in the Straits and that it was desirous that it should be extended and its powers more variously employed in every direction round Singapore. By means of steam-vessels the influence round the Peninsula might be strengthened, so as to be used at all times with benefit and effect; while commerce would increase under the security which it would afford; and steam navigation appeared to the writer to open up prospects, both political and commercial, embracing the most happy results."

In August the Government authorised the building of a new bridge to supersede the old bridge which had been so troublesome; it was to be placed further up the river, near where the Powder Magazine was then standing, the road at the foot of Government Hill (now called Hill Street) being intended to lead across it. It was expected to be completed in eighteen months.

In September the Chamber of Commerce succeeded after some delay in getting the Government to allow letters for England to be received at the Post Office for transmission by the overland Mails *via* India. The postage through India was paid here and the steam postage was collected in England.

The following are some passages from a letter written by Mr. Waghorn to the merchants here and in China about his proposed scheme for the overland route and mails to China :—" The time then is come for you to establish a chain of steam communication between Canton and Galle, and thus identify and connect China with the Calcutta line at that place. There are many advantages attendant upon such an establishment, not only to your own commercial pursuits but also to every other relation connected between Europe and China, all so evident to the politician, merchant, and individual, that it would be loss of time my dilating or dwelling upon them. I therefore will at once go to the outline of a plan, in my opinion, best adapted for the outset of steam navigation between China and England. One vessel is sufficient to begin with, making quarterly trips between Galle and Canton, in dates suited to meet the Calcutta steamer at Galle. Such a vessel should be about 800 tons, with engines of 220 horse power, and space for 100 tons of valuable freight, touching both ways at Singapore for fuel, letters, passengers, &c., &c. Raise £50,000 in shares, to pay for this first vessel, and for a year's coal at Galle, Singapore and Canton. Let this vessel be built by first rate builders and fitted by a first rate engineer; let any future vessels that you may be disposed to put upon the line be exactly upon the same principal and size, &c., &c., so that what is serviceable for one of your steam-vessels may always be applied to the others.

"Of course, the Calcutta line cannot long remain with one solitary steam-vessel between there and Suez. Another and another will soon be put on, and after they are, it will be for yourselves to put on a second vessel, and have more frequent trips between you and Galle. Java, as a matter of course, will connect herself with your line at Singapore, so will New Holland, and by-and-bye Australia, and many other places in the East. Steam navigation has already added as much, perhaps more, to England's greatness, than any other science, except education, that God has given to man. Its advantages to our Chinese connections are yet to be practically developed; in my opinion the sociality it will bring about, will, ere some thirty years hence, induce a British Viceroy of India to pay a visit of friendship by steam to His Celestial Majesty in China.

"When the writer began his advocacy of steam navigation between England and India, he found the Directors of the East India Company opposed to anything of that nature with India. He found Her Majesty's Postal Department averse to steam-vessels as packets. He found the Admiralty of opinion that the Government thought of doing away with theirs, because they were not safe in bad weather. He found himself deemed a visionary, nay, a madman, by the Government Officials, for maintaining that steamers could go easily in 50 days between India and England, *via* the Red Sea. It must not be surprising if some little egotism has crept into his own opinions, now that he has lived to see the matter compassed with ease in 40 days, and speedily it will be reduced three days more in Egypt, when the Government and Company do the needful in that Country.

"The above statement is made to give you an earnest of his future labours, to assist and devote himself to such an object with China, as in like manner he devoted himself to get it to India. Having seen it done to India, he now looks onwards to China, and hopes to see you all "doing" towards its being done, between Canton and London in 55 days, *via* Galle. My wish is to be entrusted with placing a first steam-vessel between Galle and Canton (as I would call at Galle on the way out) to bring you the first mail by the Red Sea. All this would be gratifying to me, and I particularly wish to be instrumental in doing it."

The Singapore Community continued to bestir themselves on the subject of steam communication, and the following is a report of a public meeting that was held on the subject:—"At a public meeting of the inhabitants of Singapore held at the Reading Room on Monday, the 17th December, 1838, for the purpose of taking into consideration the suggestion of the Madras Committee for establishing a steamer between Ceylon, the Straits, and China, in connection with steamers to be established between India and Suez, in the event of the comprehensive scheme not being carried into effect, Mr. W. D. Shaw having been called to the Chair, the following Resolutions were unanimously carried:—

First.—That this meeting views with feelings of satisfaction the disposition on the part of the Bengal and Madras Committees to co-operate cordially on the subject of steam communication between India and England.

Second.—That in the event of the comprehensive scheme (namely, an unbroken communication by steam between Calcutta and London, *via* Suez) not being carried into effect, the Madras plan for forming a Company to 'perfect the communication on this side of the Isthmus, is the best that could, under the circumstances, be adopted.

Third.—That this meeting, from such a view of existing circumstances as they are enabled to take, are of opinion that the establishment of a branch steamer between Galle, the Straits, and China, would eventually succeed.

Fourth.—That a Committee be formed for the purpose of procuring every information relative to the establishment of steam communication between Point de Galle, the Straits, and China, with a view to ascertain how far the undertaking would be likely to succeed with reference to the outlay and probable returns, and for the purpose of corresponding generally with the Committees of Bengal and Madras.

Fifth.—That the said Committee consist of the following seven gentlemen, three to form a quorum :—

Dr. Montgomerie, Messrs. Balestier, Napier, Connolly, Boustead, Brennand and MacDonald.

In August a waterspout passed over the harbour and town, dismasting one ship and sinking another and carrying off the corner of the roof of a house in its passage landward. It is referred to in 3 Logan's Journal, page 628.

1839.

In this year, we find the first account of the complete New Year's Day Sports on shore and on the water, which did not differ much from those of the present day, except that it was then a day set apart by the mercantile community to amuse the natives only.

The following was the account of the Sports in the *Free Press.* "The European Gentlemen of the Settlement have for some time back observed the laudable practice of ushering in the New Year with sports and pastimes among the native population, in which suitable rewards are appropriated to those who compete. Boat-racing is the most favourite and most attractive of these diversions. Indeed it is remarked how very few games or exercises of an active and athletic nature the Malays have ; even boat-racing, as a sport, is an exotic : and the only games peculiar to them appear to be a sort of foot-ball and kite-flying, the latter being an exercise practised in various ways in many parts of the civilized world, in a manner of which the poor Malays have not the smallest idea. In their sampans, however, whether pulling or sailing, they beat in their own waters every competitor. The first race was a pulling match, the reward for the winner was $15. The next was a sailing match between Malay sampans, about ten of them mustering for the race. They made a beautiful start of it : their long light, sharp hulls, cutting through the water under a fresh breeze in the best style—

'So shoots through the morning sky the lark,
Or the swan through the summer sea.'

"The run was about four miles, which was accomplished in a very short space of time, the first boat being rewarded with a prize of twenty, and the second with one of ten dollars. A race of common Malay sampans, manned with Kling boatmen, was then well contested and excited a considerable degree of interest.

"After these were over, the Sports on shore commenced with a pony race mounting native riders. A very grotesque congregation of men and horses assembled at the starting post, very few of whom reached the winning post. Some wrestling then ensued, in which the only competitors were Klings, who made far better work of it than we ever saw done by the more lusty Chinamen, whom we have sometimes seen vying with each other in the same contest. A great deal of foot-racing, &c., &c., then became the order of the day, and continued until four o'clock, when the ground began to get clear of its various multitudes, all of whom seemed equally delighted with the Sports, not the least interesting or important of which were the scrambles for copper pice which some lively young gentlemen were ever and anon projecting into the air. The weather was delightful, cloudy and breezy."

In January a facetious individual put an advertisement in the paper offering $1,000 reward to any person who could succeed in making a safe and easy conveyance to travel over (or rather through) the road leading to the Sepoy Lines in particular, and the Singapore roads in general; iron and wood having been found too weak, and springs and wheels impracticable.

The beginning of Banks in Singapore was an adventure of John Gemmill's, who issued in January the following original advertisement:—

"The undersigned will cash good Bills, the drawers and acceptors being residents of Singapore, or will advance money on Goods deposited with him, at such rate and terms as may be agreed upon.

"Deposits in money in sums of not less than $100 will be received by the undersigned, bearing interest at six per cent. per annum, if allowed to remain at least one month, when, after three days' notice, the principal and interest will be paid if demanded, but if withdrawn in less time, no interest to be allowed but the principal only be repaid at three days' notice.

"John Gemmill trusts that the merchants and other gentlemen of the Settlement will facilitate his views in thus publicly circulating capital, although on a small scale, as they may tend to shew the necessity of a Singapore Bank, of the expediency of which he has had even a little experience himself.

"As he does not presume to cash all the Bills, &c., that may be required, a Journal will be kept to shew what extent of specie transactions might be done."

The twentieth anniversary of the foundation of the Settlement was commemorated by a public ball on the evening of the 5th February, and a dinner on the 6th February. The *Free Press* remarked:—"It was curious to find in Lady Raffles' Memoirs that the 29th February was given as the day on which the British flag was first hoisted at

Singapore, an error probably of the printer's devil, as there was no doubt as to the 6th being the day, having often been commemorated here by gentlemen who themselves witnessed the ceremony of hoisting the flag by Sir Stamford Raffles." Several United States ships were in harbour, with a Commodore, and there were several public entertainments given; ending with the flag-ship, the United States frigate *Columbia*, giving a large dinner and dance on board the frigate.

The planting of gambier and pepper was increasing very much, and the following article, which shows how it was then carried on, was published in March:—"The increase which has taken place in the cultivation of gambier and pepper by the Chinese settled in the interior, requires that we should give some account of the extent to which it has now advanced, as it is the only cultivation on the island which has yet assumed any degree of commercial importance; and the following particulars have been obtained as well from parties who are themselves owners of plantations, as from those whose course of business engages them in extensive transactions with the planters. It is well known to our local readers that the cultivation of pepper and gambier is always carried on in conjunction, the support which they mutually afford each other being, it seems, indispensable to the existence of either of these plantations, commonly termed *bangsalls*. There are now altogether about 350 in the island, which we may divide into plantations of the first, second, and third class.

"A plantation, or *bangsall*, of the first class, occupies an area equal to about 350 fathoms square for its gambier, and generally employs from ten to eleven men, the proprietor included. Its average monthly produce is equal to between 17 to 18 piculs a month, or about 210 piculs annually. To supply firewood for the boiling-house it is necessary to have a tract of jungle in the immediate vicinity; and it is a serious objection to any locality for gambier-growing if it has not, at the commencement, an available extent of jungle for fuel equal to the area which is occupied by the plant, and which it is computed will supply firewood for a term of 25 years. Thus, a plantation of this size will consume in that space all the fuel which can be supplied by an extent of jungle 350 fathoms square. The annual produce of pepper on a plantation of this description is about 125 to 150 piculs. It seems that there are at present rather under than above thirty bangsalls, which severally yield these quantities.

"Plantations of the second class average about 150 piculs of gambier annually, and about 80 piculs of pepper, employing eight or nine men; while those of the third class, about 100 to 120 piculs of gambier, and about 50 piculs of pepper, there being seldom more than seven men to the latter. The same remarks regarding fuel apply, of course, to these as to the larger bangsalls.

"The aggregate produce of the whole 350 bangsalls in gambier and pepper is stated at fully 4,000 piculs a month, or 48,000 piculs annually, of the former, and 15,000 piculs a year of the latter. This is more than double the quantity of gambier produced in 1836, during which year it began to experience the effect of favourable prices in England, and is fifty per cent. in advance of the quantity of pepper stated to have been produced during the same year.

" Nearly all these plantations were commmenced by individuals without capital of their own, who began on small advances from the Chinese shopkeepers in town, on the security of a mortgage of their ground : and out of every three of them it is probable there are two which are subject to encumbrances of this description, the advances sometimes running on at a very high rate of interest, and often made in clothes and provisions at higher than the market rates : and the consequence is that instances are of daily occurence in which plantations are changing hands, and the original settlers often absconding, leaving considerable debts behind them.　　Notwithstanding all this, however, the Chinese in town who support the planters, and the better class of planters themselves, affirm that a plantation is almost sure to clear off the original advances, and finally yield a fair profit, if the planter is steady and industrious, and abstains from gaming and opium-smoking, both of which are the besetting sins of that class of Chinese who settle in the interior of the island, every third man of whom, it is admitted by themselves, is an opium-smoker, while the infatuation of gaming often produces the most ruinous consequences.　　In the interior, too, the practice of gambling on credit is common, and the unfortunate sufferer in those blind games of chance, to which they are so strongly addicted, is often induced to grant his promissory note for what he has lost, which, in due course, will assume the form of a mortgage over his plantation, after which an action at law, and a sale by the Sheriff, very soon leaves him altogether minus.　　On such occasions, the planta-tions generally pass into better hands, and are bought by men who have some little capital of their own ; and it is astonishing how far a small sum of a man's own money will go towards making him become a comparatively extensive proprietor.　　It was only the other day that the bangsall of one of those improvident characters above referred to was sold by auction for $1,400, and was purchased by a party who had only $200 of his own money, obtaining the additional requisite advance by agreeing to mortgage his new acquisiton for the accommo-dation.

" Many of the old gambier plantations, and there are some, it seems, 18 years old in the island, have, it is stated, considerably diminished in value of late years, as well from the soil being partly exhausted, as from the want of firewood, all the jungle in the neighbourhood having been cleared away, and requiring them to proceed to a considerable distance to bring it.　　This is the great drawback, and in consequence of it alone, many plantations have declined one third from their original value : and from the same cause several bangsalls have been given up altogether, and the ground abandoned to that inveterate enemy of all cultivation, the lallang grass.　　On these occasions, the boiling of gambier is altogether discontinued, and the pepper vines are allowed to drag on, until, deprived of the aid the soil receives from the boiled leaves of the gambier, they die away entirely.　　According to the Chinese, the leaves of the gambier, which are merely strewn over the ground in which the pepper vines are planted, rather protect than enrich the soil, and the rain, they say, washes a substance off it into the earth which prevents the growth of any noxious weed to interfere with the vines.

" Whether or not pepper would succeed here with the aid of some other manure besides gambier, is an experiment which has not, we believe, been tried, but it is manifest that gambier would never pay, if grown by itself, at present prices. The gross value of the annual produce (210 piculs) of the most extensive plantation of gambier on the island at the market rate of $2 per picul is only $420 which would barely suffice to pay the mere wages of the ten men engaged on it, if taken even at $3.50 a month, although the proper average is perhaps $4 per month for each man. Even joined together, gambier and pepper are certainly not an enriching cultivation, and if it requires little outlay of capital, taken all in all, it brings little in. Thus, taking the price realised for 48,000 piculs gambier at

$2 per picul we have $96,000
for 15,000 piculs pepper at $5 per picul ...   75,000
                                                        _____
value of the total annual produce of both   ... $171,000
                                                        _____

which, if we allow altogether 3,000 Chinese, and it is probable there is fully that number, to find work on the plantations, gives exactly $57 a year to each individual engaged. Rating the wages of each at $4, this would amount to $144,000 a year, which deducted from the above sum of $171,000 leaves $27,000 to be divided among 350 proprietors, giving an average of profit for each plantation of only $77 and a fraction annually, without making any deduction for interest of capital laid out, materials used, carriage, and a variety of *et ceteras*. According to the statements of the Chinese themselves, the best of these plantations, when clear of all encumbrances, yield the proprietor an annual profit of about $400, while the lowest barely pay their way. There seems not the least doubt, however, that the cultivation of gambier and pepper will go on increasing from year to year, until the island is bare of fuel to boil the former, unless some decline in the price of the article should take place, which now seems unlikely, or unless Government should interpose with what some would account an injudicious, and some a judicious, measure to check its progress. There is, in the meantime, one beneficial result accruing from the activity with which the cultivation of gambier is now prosecuted in the interior, that it finds employment for numbers who, in a different state of affairs, were formerly found leaguing themselves together in bands for the purposes of midnight robbery and depredation, often causing the greatest alarm even in the immediate suburbs of the town."

In April, first originated the strange notion that has been heard of several times since in Singapore. The Chinese community imagined that the blood of thirty-six men was required for the sanctification of the new Church, and that the Government had actually set on foot a system of Thuggee for the secret apprehension and sacrifice of the required number of victims. Respectable and intelligent Chinese made enquiries about it, and believed that nine heads had been already secured. It was thought at the time that the report had arisen from the church-yard having been enclosed, but we know now that the same singular notion has occurred several times since, and also in

Calcutta, and in Hongkong in 1886 when 500 children were said to have been buried to secure the completion of the Taitam Water Works, so that reason was not the true one. The neighbourhood of the Church got an extremely bad character among the lower class of the natives, and all manners of stories were in circulation about people being carried off on the road by the side of the Brass Bassa Canal, so that none of the natives would venture out after dark. There is an account of this to be found in Mr. Thomson's translations from the Hakayit Abdulla. There is an amusing account of another scare, and of a circular issued by the head Chinese related in the record of the year 1853. In 1885 it occurred again, and natives in the town, especially children, were afraid to go out at night. The Malays said that heads were required for the New Market at Teluk Ayer, as the Government could not build it without one hundred heads. A very well known Arab gentleman said that it had sprung from two murders, lately committed, in one of which a woman's head had been cut off.

On the 28th May, in the Shipping Report appears the arrival at Singapore of the British Schooner *Royalist,* Captain Brooke, 142 tons, from the Cape and England. The paper took no notice of it, and no one anticipated what was to spring from the first visit of Mr. James Brooke to Singapore. On the 28th July, the *Royalist* sailed on a cruise to Borneo. She returned to Singapore in October, and the *Free Press* of the 24th of that month contained a long letter from Mr. Brooke describing his voyage to Borneo.

In July the Government proclaimed a reward of $50 for every tiger brought into the town, it had been previously $20. Four men had been carried off within two miles of the town in three months, in the neighbourhood of Serangong Road, which induced the Government to increase the reward. A few days after the reward was offered, several more lives were lost. One was that of a woman killed near Sandy Point; the other a Chinaman who was carried off at three o'clock in the afternoon while working in his gambier plantation. The other coolies immediately raised a great clamour, beating gongs, &c., to alarm the tiger, and on going a little way into the jungle the dead body was found, very much mangled.

The month of August was the most rainy month then on record in the place, there were 26 rainy days during which 28 inches of rain fell, although the average for a whole year was only about 84 inches. In the first fifteen days, twenty-one inches fell, and sometimes more than four inches in the day. In one heavy thunderstorm the raingauge, which held only two and a half inches, overflowed in the course of an hour.

An analysis was made in Calcutta of water brought to Singapore from the famous hot springs at Ayer Panas, in Malacca, with the following result :—It was found to contain a small portion of sulphuretted hydrogen, with traces of carbolic acid and azote: 500 grains of the water, evaporated to dryness, left only 1.09 grains of dry residuum, which contained the organic matter called Glairine, sulphate of lime, muriate of soda, with traces of silicate and iron. It was said to be only valuable for its thermal, and not for its medicinal qualities. At the springs, the temperature was about 130 degrees of Fahrenheit. When cold it is very palatable drinking water.

In the *Free Press* for this year, a large part of the first page of the paper was taken up at a various times by the publication, in native characters, of translations of proclamations, and of some of the newly enacted Indian Acts.

Much attention had been given during the preceding five years to coffee planting, and the following account, showing how history repeats itself, of the formation of a company sixty years ago, was of interest about 1884, when similar projects were frequently started, but did not succeed.

In October, the Singapore Joint Stock Coffee Company was started, the author of which was a M. Le Dieu, a French resident in Singapore, and the prospectus was published at full length in the paper, but is too long to reprint. After a long preamble about the prospects of agriculture in Singapore, it went on as follows:—" These reflexions proceed from the consideration of a proposal to establish a joint stock company in this place for the cultivation of coffee, which cannot fail to have the most auspicious influence on the prosperity of the Settlement. Agriculture is yet in its infancy in Singapore; but the results already obtained have been sufficiently advantageous to induce several families to invest considerable property in the soil. Coffee seems to be one of the productions most calculated to succeed, as it is estimated to make a return of the full capital expended in four years. To what a pitch of agricultural and commercial prosperity would not then Singapore attain if we saw the half of the island covered with plantations of Coffee ? In limiting the produce of each plant to only one pound in the year, and ten dollars per picul as the price of the coffee, this would yield an annual revenue of \$2,488,320.

" It is proposed to establish a Society for the cultivation of Coffee in Singapore, under the authority of Government, to be called the (National) Agricultural Society of Singapore. The Capital to consist of one hundred shares of dollars 100 each."

During the next year, several calls were made, and a good deal was written to the paper about it by the shareholders and also by the promoter. The end of it was that some of the Committee sent the following address to the paper, and in October, 1841, the plantation was sold at auction:—" An Advertisement in the last number of the *Free Press* calls on us to pay up the third instalment of shares pursuant to the resolution passed at a Meeting held on the 25th January, but it being generally known that had there been a fuller meeting (twelve persons only being then present, including M. Le Dieu with his three votes) and had proxies been allowed, there would have been a great majority against any further payment towards the coffee plantation, and even as it was, strong dissatisfaction regarding the excessive expense already incurred was manifested by those who have had ample experience in planting, and are well capable of judging what ought to have been effected with the sum already expended." At the same meeting a Committee of five persons was appointed to superintend further operations, which were to be conducted with the greatest economy. This Committee met by appointment four days after the general meeting at the house of the new Secretary, Bishop Courvezy,

and after various separate calculations submitted by two or three of
the members, a resolution was passed that the whole concern should be
disposed of to the best advantage.

The paper in noticing the sale said that the result did not speak
well for the agricultural capabilities of Singapore, but that it would
soon publish some remarks by an old Straits hand on the subject, and
the writer referred to, in alluding to coffee planting in the island,
wrote as follows :—" The Coffee plant thrives well here when judiciously
shaded from the sun. But this essential application, it is to be feared,
has been neglected by the planters. The cultivation hitherto has been a
failure. The coffee tree, if properly shaded, thrives in the Penang Settlement even on the poorest soils, and on soils of every description, but fails
on the hills where it is not sheltered from the sun. The chief objection taken to the cultivation here, at Singapore, lies, as in the case
of cotton, in the irregularity of the crops. In the same plantation the
trees will be found in every stage, from budding to fruiting. When I
say that the attempt has failed, it is with these reservations. By
selecting appropriate soil and by judicious shading, the trees may
perhaps be brought to a fair average condition. The soil here, which
seems best adapted to the tree, is that where the peat and sand are
mingled in due proportions : next to this description of soil, the most
preferable would seem to be the slightly undulating lands and the
slopes at the base of the hills, and the hollows, not the swampy
hollows, and especially the spots admitting of this description where
the soil is reddish. But after all it will depend on the quantity of
such soils, whether the speculation will not be a losing one. To cultivate coffee successfully a large expanse of land is required.

" The coffee plants on the tops and upper slopes of the hills do not
give much promise of success. Like those which were planted on the
Penang hills, which for two or three years throve better, owing to the
superior elevation and shelter, than they have done on the hills here,
they manifest a strong tendency to overgrow themselves in the centre
shoot, and to decay prematurely. Topping is, under such circumstances, the only chance they have of surviving, and where the tree is
luxuriant it is a measure both of convenience and necessity at all
times and in all situations. If Coffee is destined to thrive on the
higher lands, it will probably be shewn by the spirited example of
Dr. d'Almeida, who has selected a gently undulating and broad ridge
for his plantation, with a soil of a friable texture and which may
prove also available for cloves. The late Coffee Company had also a
plantation on the same description of soil. This soil contains from 65
to 70 per cent. of silex. The plants in both of these localities are not
old enough to permit a decided opinion to be given as to their chance
of success. There may be, perhaps, about five hundred acres under
coffee cultivation, but not exclusively so, as the plants are intermixed
in some estates with other cultivated trees. The Coffee produced is
all of fair average quality : I have not obtained any estimate of the
quantity of coffee now produced."

The Coffee Company's plantation was on the left hand side of
Serangoon Road, about five miles from town. It was never successful.

The first vessel built at Singapore was launched by Mr. Melany at his yard in May. It was a schooner of about 100 tons, called the *Sree Singapura*, built for a European firm called Shaw & Stephens.

Gaston Dutronquoy, a painter, arrived in March and advertised that he would paint miniatures, portraits, &c. In May he opened a hotel called the London Hotel which was first in High Street and afterwards where the Hotel de l'Europe is now at the corner of High Street and the Esplanade.

The *Free Press* said that on 12th October the Right Reverend Father in God, Paul, the Armenian Bishop, with Mr. Deacon Martirus, embarked under a salute from the shore of eleven guns, on board a Dutch brig, which also saluted him with eleven guns, on his way to Batavia. This is mentioned on account of the salute to an Armenian Bishop.

A native advertised that he had been curing horses in Singapore for upwards of thirteen years, and that he would undertake the cure of all diseases. This may have been the man who sent in a bill many years afterwards, " for curing your horse till he died."

On Monday the 25th November, Sir William Norris, the Recorder, opened the Assizes in the New Court House which was then used for the first time, on which he congratulated the Grand Jury, and also on the prospect of a proper house of correction being built soon.

This New Court was part of the present Court House. It had been built by John Argyll Maxwell, the merchant, in 1826 and 1827, under the superintendence of Mr. Coleman, the Architect, and was sold by him on 1st September, 1829, to John Cockerell and George Gerard Larpent. On 1st September, 1841, it was advertised for sale by auction by Guthrie & Co., and was bought on behalf of Government by Mr. Church. It was transfered to him on 26th October, 1841, for $15,600, and on 10th October, 1842, by him to Governor Bonham, on account of the East India Company. The boundaries on two sides were High Street and the Singapore River, the area was 82,080 square feet, and had a river frontage of 240 feet.

CHAPTER XXVII.

1840.

THE first China junk of the season arrived on the 9th January, and the junks in the first fortnight brought down ten thousand chests of tea. The junks took back produce to China in exchange.

In January, the assessment on houses in town was fixed at eight and a half per cent. and on property of a like nature situated outside the limits at five per cent. The tax on horses and carriages was then imposed for the first time, at which there was a good deal of remonstrance, but as the roads were very bad, and continual complaints were being made about them, it was hoped the money so raised might be all applied in repairing them.

On the 14th January, the British brig *Brigand* which had come in from Calcutta two days before, sailed for China. On the following night, while off Pedra Branca, Captain McGill, her master, who was well known and esteemed in Singapore, was murdered by two of the crew, John Williams, a European sailor, and Florentine de la Cruz, a Manilaman. They threw the body of the Captain overboard and asserted that the second mate, who was missing, had been lost overboard by accident in the disturbance. The body of the Captain was never found, and nothing could be proved of the fact beyond some remarks made by Williams when the Captain and second mate were found missing, and the poop, where the Captain was asleep, covered with blood. Williams confessed his guilt before he was hung. The trial was held on Wednesday, the 4th March, from 10 a.m. to 8.30 p.m. and both men were executed on Friday the 6th.

Each month an account appears in the paper of deaths by tigers, and in April the first hunt took place, of which the following account was published in the *Free Press*:—"A Singapore Tiger Hunt.—A friend of ours, when out snipe-shooting a day or two ago, in that jungly locality behind Buffalo Village [this would be about where the Race Course is now], rather unexpectedly came upon what was nothing more nor less than a tiger, very harmlessly employed in taking his morning siesta beneath the shade of some bushy underwood with which the ground is there completely overgrown. Finding himself unperceived, and feeling no disposition to intrude further upon the privacy of the dangerous slumberer, as his gun only contained a charge of snipe shot, our sportsman made as hasty and noiseless a retreat as he could. Returning into town, the rencontre was forthwith made known to several of his friends, who very soon became convinced that a crusade against the tiger was the best employment in which they could be engaged for the day, and the Mantons and Mortimers of four doughty sportsmen, who felt certain of demolishing their grim antagonist, were in immediate requisition. A detachment of some five and twenty convicts, variously armed, was also procured, and although a considerable time was expended in all this preparation, not a doubt was entertained but that the tiger would be found snug in the same berth in which he had been seen in the morning. As they approached the spot, the hopes of the party were considerably raised by meeting with a grass cutter, breathless with exhaustion, who said he had been, but a few minutes before, within an ace of scraping acquaintance with the gentleman they were in search of. But unfortunately, the tiger was not found, although most diligent search was made for him."

In May, the first vessels of the China expedition for the "Opium War" began to arrive, and the troops disembarked and encamped on the plain where the esplanade is now, until the whole expedition was ready to proceed up the China Sea. The plain was covered with tents, and various temporary structures were put up. The following is an article in the newspaper of the 21st May :—

"There have been various rumours within the last few days regarding the intended departure of the force assembled here; and there is no doubt of an early movement, although it may be judged necessary to wait for the arrival of the *Marion* with the Staff on board, before anything is definitely arranged on the subject. Eighteen troop and store transports are already in the roads: but detachments of H. M. 18th Regiment and of the Volunteer Corps have still to arrive, and may be expected in the course of a few days, which will then complete the whole of the land forces, with the exception of the small addition expected from home, to be employed in the expedition. The full extent of the naval armament is not exactly ascertained, but from all accounts, the more formidable portion of it is still on its way from home, and the Cape Station; although we have already in China, the *Druid*, 44, *Volage*, 28, *Alligator*, 28 (on the way up), and *Hyacinth*, 18; and here the *Wellesley*, 72, *Larne*, 28, *Cruizer*, 18, and *Algerine*, 10, besides the *Conway*, 28, and *Favorite*, 28, still to join. There still remains however, the *Melville*, 74, from the Cape carrying the flag of Admiral Elliot, and several corvettes from the same station: with the *Blenheim*, 72, the *Blonde*, 44, *Pique*, 42, *Andromache*, 28, *Nimrod*, 18, from home. In this estimate, we do not include the steam vessels, which it seems will be supplied entirely from the steam flotilla in India, to consist of the *Atalanta* and *Madagascar*, already in the roads, and the new steamers *Queen* and *Sesostris*, the former of which is daily expected from Calcutta."

On the 4th June, the *Free Press* wrote as follows :—" On Saturday forenoon the 30th instant, H. M. ships-of-war *Wellesley*, *Cruizer*, and *Algerine*, troop-ship *Rattlesnake*, and H. C. Steamer *Atalanta*, with sixteen sail of transport vessels, got under weigh for China presenting a fine and animating spectacle as they steered out of the roads in three divisions, with one of Her Majesty's ships at the head of each. They were followed next day by the steamers *Queen* and *Madagascar*, into the former of which the staff from the *Marion* had been trans-

ferred; and of the two ships-of-war remaining in the roads, the
Conway will, we understand, move forward in the course of to-day :
the *Larne* waiting to take on the April mail, which may now be
expected almost daily to arrive from Calcutta by the steamer *Enterprise*.
We are not aware whether any day has been specified for the departure of the other transports, now in the harbour, but the *Marion* must,
of course, remain until she repairs the damages sustained in her masts
and rigging during the voyage from Calcutta. It has been very
generally surmised that the preliminary operation of the expedition
will be to batter down the Bogue forts : and we believe there is no
doubt that such are the instructions of Sir Gordon Bremer. But we
understand the campaign is to be opened by also taking possession of
Macao at the same time, we presume under some arrangement effected
at home between the British and Portuguese Governments."

On Tuesday forenoon, the 16th June, H. M. Sloop-of-war *Pylades*,
anchored in the roads from the Cape on the 27th April, announcing
the approach of the *Melville*, 74, bearing the flag of Rear-Admiral the
Hon'ble G. Elliot, Captain the Hon'ble R. Dundas, which entered the
harbour in the course of the same day, followed by H. M. Frigate
Blonde, 42, Captain Thomas Bourchier, both having left the Cape on
the 30th April.

On the following day, the Admiral landed under the salute due to
his rank, as Commander-in-chief of Her Majesty's Naval Forces to the
eastward of the Cape. It was stated that Admiral Elliot received
notification of his appointment to succeed Sir Frederick Maitland, who
died, only three days before he left the Cape, during which interval the
Melville made up her full war complement of men, made every requisite
addition to her ammunition, &c., and took in the necessary supply of
stores and provisions.

The paper also referred to the seizure of some Chinese junks in
the following article :—" Almost immediately after the appearance in
harbour of the Squadron that has just arrived from the Cape, a China
junk that had got under weigh on her return homeward, was followed
and overtaken by H. M. Frigate *Blonde*, and taken possession of by a
party sent from on board that vessel, a proceeding which was shortly
after followed by the seizure of three other Chinese Junks (being all
that were then in the roads) much to the surprise of the European
community of the Settlement, and greatly to the consternation of the
Chinese, as well on board the junks as on shore, many of the latter
being interested to a large extent in their cargoes. Yesterday, however,
Admiral Elliot directed the release of the junks, and they are now at
liberty to proceed on their voyage, at least if their apprehensions as
to what may befall them on the coast of China, will permit them.
According to the information we have been able to obtain on the subject, there is no doubt that Admiral Elliot was acting merely in pursuance of his orders in taking possession of the junks. But, as the
Chinese here had sometime ago received something like an assurance
from the local Government that their junks would not be molested, we
may infer that on being made acquainted with the fact, Admiral Elliot
assumed the responsibility of setting them again at liberty, in preference
to detaining them under such circumstances."

To face page 344.

CATCHICK MOSES.

On the 2nd March, the firm of Sarkies & Moses was established by Aristarchus Sarkies. He had come to Singapore in 1820, and began business on his own account on 1st August, 1828. Mr. Catchick Moses, his nephew, came from Calcutta in that year and was in the office of Boustead, Schwabe & Co., as an apprentice, for five years. Then he made some trading voyages to Calcutta and back on his own account, and in 1840 he joined his uncle in the firm of Sarkies & Moses. Mr. Sarkies died when 65 years old on 8th March, 1841, at his house in Armenian Street, which is still standing and now called Zetland House, opposite St. Andrew's House. Mr. Catchick Moses died at his house the Pavillion on Oxley Hill, when 80 years old, on 2nd October, 1892; his widow died on the 17th September, 1895. The family now consists of three sons, two of whom carry on the firm of Sarkies & Moses, the name of which has never been changed, and two daughters one of whom is married to Mr. Jacob Carapiet. Mr. Catchick Moses was a man of a very kind disposition, and was much respected in Singapore. The natives in former days used often to go to his house in the early mornings for advice, and to settle their differences. He was a good billiard-player, using his left hand, and he had the curious habit of shaving himself with his left hand, while walking up and down the verandah of the house, without a glass. He made his will about seven years before his death, and gave it to his children to read, so that they could ask him about it if they did not understand it, so as to avoid any discussion after his death. During the later years of his life he did not conduct the business, but he used to come down to town and sit in the office, and go back home at four o'clock in a small palanquin which had been built for him by Mr. G. H. Brown some generations before. He was one of the three local residents who alone wore tall black beaver hats. The other two were Mr. Christian Baumgarten, the Registrar of the Court and afterwards a practising lawyer, and Mr. M. J. Carapiet, an opium merchant. The joke used to be that Mr. H. M. Simons used to present the last with his hats, and that they passed round among the three until they were altogether past wear. It was in Zetland House that Mr. R. C. Woods lived when he started the *Strait Times* newspaper. Mr. Moses was one of the last of the old residents of the place.

The following is the first account we have met with of a Chinese procession in the town : it was published in April :—" For some days past, the town has been resounding with the clangour of Chinese gongs, and the streets crowded with processions of this noisy race, in honour of a goddess, or the statue of one, that has been recently imported from the Celestial Kingdom, but the procession which took place on Monday was really something worth looking at. It extended nearly the third of a mile, to the usual accompaniment of gongs, and gaudy banners of every colour, form, and dimension. But what particularly engaged the attention of spectators, and was the chief feature of the procession, were the little girls from five to eight years age, carried aloft in groups on gaily ornamented platforms, and dressed in every variety of Tartar and Chinese costumes. The little creatures were supported in their places by iron rods, which were concealed under their clothes, and their infant charms were shewn off to the greatest advantage by the rich and peculiar dresses in which they were arrayed, every care being taken to shield them with umbrellas from the effects of the sun's rays, which shone out in full brightness during the whole time the procession lasted. The divinity herself was conveyed in a very elegant canopy chair, or palanquin, of yellow silk and crape, and was surrounded with a body guard of celestials, wearing tunics of the same colour. We have not been able to ascertain the various attributes of the goddess, but it seems she is highly venerated : and a very elegant temple, according to Chinese taste, has been built in the town for her reception. She is called by the Chinese Tien-Seang-Sing-Bok, which, we believe, may be translated Holy Mother of the Gods, being the deity who is commonly termed the Queen of Heaven. She is supposed to be the especial protectress of those who navigate the deep; at least, it is to her shrine that the Chinese sailors pay the most fervent adoration, there being an altar dedicated to her in every junk that goes to sea. The procession, we are informed, is regarded as a formal announcement to the Chinese of her advent in this Settlement, and the exhibition, with the feasting attendant thereon, is stated to cost more than six thousand dollars."

The Singapore Institution School was growing larger, and a Mr. Dickenson of the American Mission was engaged as second Master. There was an American Mission School for Chinese and Malay boys on what was known as Ryan's Hill, the expense of which was met by the Board of Foreign Missions in America. There were a few Malays and some Chinese, who had to be bound to the Manager to remain at school for a certain period. Ryan's Hill was on the way from the then Jail, now the site of the Central Police Station, towards Tanjong Pagar, it was afterwards called Dickenson's Hill, then Bukit Padre, and is now known as Bukit Passoh.

The *Free Press* of the 11th June contains a long letter from Mr. James Brooke about his voyage in the *Royalist* to the Bugis countries and the Celebes. At this time, C. Goymour, who came out with Mr. Brooke in the *Royalist* as steward, opened a public house in the Square which he called the Royalist Hotel. Afterwards he took the house in High Street, which the Guthries, and at that time Mr. and Mrs. James Guthrie, had occupied, and opened it as the Adelphi Hotel. Goymour used to ride in the races, ponies in those days, and so obtained a certain notoriety, but he was an illiterate man, not much appreciated.

The tigers were continually becoming more bold, and in July, five men were killed, all within two miles of the town, in the course of eight days, and in November, the first one was caught alive in a pit of which the following was an account :—" The news of the capture and death of a tiger, last Saturday night, on a Chinaman's plantation close to that of Mr. Balestier, the American Consul, gave general satisfaction, being the first of these destructive animals which they had succeeded in catching alive. A pit was dug, where his track had been observed, the mouth of which was lightly covered over, and two or three dogs tied as bait; the ruse luckily took, and when advancing to his imagined prey he was himself precipitated into the pitfall, where he was very soon despatched, being pounded to death with stones. He was a large animal, measuring 9 feet 2 inches from the nose to the tip of the tail, which was only 35 inches long: the circumference round the fore arm being 26 inches. The captors have claimed and obtained from the local authorities the promised reward of a hundred dollars, besides having sold the flesh of the animal itself to the Chinese, Klings, &c., (among whom its virtues are much celebrated) for six fanams a catty, by which they realised about seventy dollars more."

In June new regulations were issued as to the occupation of Agricultural land. Leases were offered for twenty years, renewable for thirty years at the option of the lessee, but free for two years, then three years at four annas an acre, five years at eight annas, and afterwards at one rupee an acre a year. It was said that such short leases did not give any encouragement to agricultural undertakings.

Mr. Balestier's godown on the river bank was robbed by a sailor, presumably an American, who secreted himself in the godown after he had been shipped before the Consul in the office on that day by the Master of an American Vessel in the Roads. He robbed a drawer of about $100, and was trying to open the iron chest (primitive safe) when he was heard. It was about nine o'clock and bright moonlight. He made his escape over the roof and dropped into the mangroves on the river side, when all trace of him was lost. Two days afterwards his corpse, fully dressed except his shoes, which he had left on the roof, was found among the piles of the new bridge which was being built. He proved to be a notorious fellow who had been discharged from jail some time before.

On the 30th October, the H. C. S. vessel *Nemesis* arrived, being the first steamer round the Cape. She was 168 feet long, 29 feet beam, 650 tons and 120 horse power. She carried two 32 pdr. guns, and a crew of fifty seamen. She was nearly flat bottomed, and could be lightened to four feet, but had two wooden false keels of six feet depth, one aft and one forward, which could be let down through the bottom of the vessel. The paddle floats could be unshipped for sailing. She had left Portsmouth on 8th March, and was a show vessel at the ports she had called at, the Governor of the Cape and a large party having visited her there. She was the first of her construction which had rounded the Cape, being of iron, and greatly astonished the natives of Singapore. She was a famous vessel against the pirates in Singapore afterwards.

In December in this year, cholera broke out in Malacca, and soon reached Singapore. At Malacca, the Revd. Josiah Hughes, the Residency Chaplain, and the Revd. John Evans, the Principal of the Anglo-Chinese College, died of it within three days of each other.

There was no jollification at all on St. Andrew's Day this year, which caused some remarks in the newspaper. There is an advertisement in the paper, in December, by Boustead, Schwabe & Co., that the letter bag of a sailing vessel for London was to be closed at their office at 4 p.m. on a Saturday afternoon, and another that the books of the Singapore Reading Room were to be sold by auction. But it was proposed to start it again subsequently. The paper for this year contains many references to the advances of Russia towards India, and to their proposed expedition to Khiva.

In December, 1840, the total population of the Island and its dependencies amounted to 39,681, including both the floating population and the military force of the Station, and the body of Convicts from India. The previous Census published had been for 1836, when the total inhabitants amounted to 29,984, exclusive of the floating population, military force and convicts: and as without these, the new Census numbered only 33,969, the increase in the fixed population during the four years that had elapsed since the former was taken, amounted to little above 4,000, of which fully three-fourths were Chinese, but it was believed the Census was rather under than above the mark. There were in the interior of the island 477 gambier and pepper plantations, while in 1836 there were only 250. There were in use on the island, during the year, 170 four-wheeled and 44 two-wheeled carriages: 266 ponies, and 77 carts. The total amount of taxation paid to Government, which consisted solely of the Farms and the Assessment, amounted to $106,125. and the total rental of the island, estimated according to the rate levied as assessment, amounted to $136,129, of which $7,600 was the proportion of what was termed the country.

Dr. Robert Little, M.D. (*Edin.*), arrived in Singapore on the 11th August in this year in the vessel *Gulnare*. He lived at first in the Dispensary in the Square, and Dr. M. J. Martin lived in the adjoining building which still forms part of John Little & Co.'s premises. From 1843 to 1846 Dr. Martin lived at Annanbank in River Valley Road, and Dr. Little, his partner, afterwards lived at Bonnygrass House, and did so for nearly forty years. It was originally built by Mr. Adam Sykes, of Robert Wise & Co., who lived close by with his wife. In 1846 Dr. Little was one of those who took steps to form a Presbyterian Congregation here. In 1848 he wrote a long paper in the second volume of Logan's Journal on the use of opium in Singapore: and in the same volume and in the fourth, his long papers on fever being caused by coral reefs, which led to much animated discussion; and in the third volume he wrote a treatise on the diseases of the nutmeg tree in Singapore. In October, 1848, the *Free Press* said:—" On Friday last a special Court was held by the lay Judges, for the purpose of swearing in Mr. R. Little, Surgeon, as Coroner. The appointment of Mr. Little to the office cannot be looked upon but as a very judicious one, and it is to be hoped that the Government will, in their appointments generally, seek to carry out the principle which seems to have guided them in this instance, namely, to nominate those possessing the best qualification for office, instead of allowing other considerations, not connected with fitness for the required duties, to have a paramount influence."

In June, 1855, Dr. Little issued a circular and advertisement asking the European community to meet at the News Rooms at 2.15 on the 30th June, to take the necessary steps to establish a sanitarium on Gunong Pulai, but nothing came of it, and it has been proposed several times since with the same result.

It is the highest land within thirty miles of Singapore, and Dr. Little coveted the top, and wanted the East India Company to make a road to it. In those days the Bengal Civilians thought Singapore to be the very place to come to for health, and the Doctor pictured to himself villas, hotels, billiard tables, and soda water manufactories on the very top of his elysium, with mail-coaches to arrive there. A party of six was got up, of which J. T. Thomson, the surveyor, was one, and he has left us an amusing account of it. They went up the river Skudai as far as possible in a boat and then walked all day through the jungle, sighting a tiger on the hill, and just at dusk reached a small hut made by the convicts who had gone on ahead. After a meal of hot rice and jam (and whisky) they sang to a violin which an Irishman had brought with him. They did not sleep much, and in the morning they toiled up to the summit, only to find that they had gone to the wrong place and the highest point was on another much higher hill, and there was a great gulf fixed between. On arriving at the summit they had a clear view of the coast of Sumatra and of Bukit Timah. The thermometer was only five degrees below that on the plain, and their provisions were run out, so they all came down again.

Near the foot of the hill a large animal was heard close to them, and ten minutes afterwards, in winding round the ravine, at the bottom of which was a clear flowing rivulet, Mr. Robert McEwen (of W. R. Paterson & Co., afterwards of McEwen & Co., and then of the Borneo Co.), espied a large animal and near it another of a similar kind. Immediately the gun was cocked, every breath hushed, bang went the piece, and a roar was heard. Another ball followed, and the animal tried to mount the hill, but another brace of balls from the same hand turned him, and he made for the other side; by this time one of the convicts came up, but his gun was not loaded, which, however, was soon done, and, with a Malay servant who had seized a Chinaman's *parang*, followed the animal. The convict hit him again, still he rushed, crushing all before him, but his fore leg being broken by the first shot, he made but little progress; at last, he stood near a tree, and the Malay boy with his *parang* only, rushing on him to have the first stroke, he turned round and charged him, the boy jumped behind the tree, and in an agony of pain the mighty beast, blind from his fury, struck his horn against the trunk, snapped the end off, and receiving a ball from the convict, who had again loaded, he fell.

Having cut off his ear, the Malay boy rushed through the wood, and having found the party, who were trying to find him, he proclaimed with a shout of exultation that it was a rhinoceros. It was the female, the male having escaped, and it may be worthy of note that the bullets were made of tin and lead, and fired from a smooth bore. As soon as the *parang* could do it, she was decapitated, then shorn of her feet and ears, and lastly of her tail. The interior was examined, and the contents of the stomach found to consist of partially digested grass and leaves; the examination, however, was but a brief one from fear that the male would return, and there being only two balls remaining; nor was this fear an ideal one, as he made his appearance next day to the Chinamen who went to skin the body, and routed them out. Loaded with the skull, which was carried by the convicts, they made the best of their way to the Punguloo's house, which they reached in three hours, so that they had come from the top of the hill in four and a half hours, excluding stoppages, having taken a whole day to find their way up. At 2 p.m., they got into their boat, twenty souls and luggage to boot, and rowed down the river,

much assisted by a rapid current which, however, owing to the tortuous
nature of the stream, and the sunken and projecting trees, endangered
their safety frequently, for had it not been for the strength of the
boat, the alertness of the steersman, and the dexterity of the gun-boat
men, six or seven times they would have been upset. Two of the
party, Mr. Thomson and Dr. Little, had arranged to ride across the
island from Kranji by the road then just newly finished (1855). Their
horses were expected to be at the first gambier *bangsal*, to which they
found their way in the dark through thick, high scrub. The Chinese
had lately been attacked by some Malays, and had just built a stockade
round their house, and thinking the two travellers were Malays,
they came out, in a fright, with spears and swords, and the Doctor
(who Mr. Thomson says was a brave man) got nearly stuck with a
spear. Then the Chinese saw his white dress and recognised him as an
orang puteh, and welcomed them with great joy. They got into town
by early morning and thus ended Doctor Little's inroad upon the
jungle of the Malay Peninsula, and the first ride across the island by
Bukit Timah Road. The excursion had taken four days; the head of
the rhinoceros was to be seen for many years at the Borneo Co.'s
offices at the corner of Malacca Street.

Dr. Little was one of the first unofficial members of the Legislative
Council in 1867, and did a great deal of public work in Singapore. Until
1847 he was a partner with Dr. M. J. Martin, as Martin and Little,
Surgeons, in the Square. In 1847 Dr. Martin left Singapore and Dr.
Little continued the practice alone. In 1859 he was joined by Dr.
Robertson, and it was called Little and Robertson. Dr. Little died at
Blackheath, London, on 11th June, 1888.

Dr. Little was the eldest of three brothers who all spent the
greater part of their lives in Singapore. Their grandfather was the
minister of the village of Applegarth in Scotland, as his fathers had
been for some generations before him. Their father was a lawyer in
Edinburgh.

The second son, John Martin Little, and his younger brother,
Matthew Little, eventually were the partners in John Little and Co.,
which arose out of the establishment of their cousin or uncle, Mr.
Francis S. Martin, as a store-keeper and auctioneer in 1842. On 30th
August, 1845, he made over his business to Mr. John Martin Little
and Mr. Cursetjee Frommurzee, who carried it on as Little, Cursetjee
& Co., on the same premises as those occupied by Mr. Martin, where
John Little & Co., Limited, still are. Cursetjee was the son of From-
murzjee Sorabjee, a Parsee merchant who established his firm in
Singapore in 1840, and died on the 17th February, 1849. Cursetjee
afterwards did business on his own account, and was very popular in
Singapore. He had an English wife. He died here in 1881. On 1st
July, 1853, the partnership of Little and Cursetjee was dissolved, and Mr.
J. M. Little was joined as a partner by Mr. Matthew Little, and the
business was continued under the name of John Little & Co. In July,
1900, it was converted into a limited company, solely for the convenience of the transmission of interests in the business, but retained
in the same hands. Mr. J. M. Little died at Blackheath in 1894.
Mr. M. Little left Singapore in 1877 to reside permanently at

This is a reproduction of a small print of 1854, showing a portion of Raffles Square, with John Little & Co.'s premises as they were then. The building on the right is the site of the present Dispensary, where Dr. M. J. Martin, and afterwards his partner Dr. Robert Little, at one time lived.

Hampstead. The three brothers had a large part in the social and general life of Singapore in its early days, and some of their children are now in the Straits and in Borneo.

In the *Free Press* of November is a notice stating that Mr. August Behn and Mr. V. Lorenz Meyer had commenced business on the 1st November, under the firm of Behn, Meyer & Co. They continued as the partners until 1850, when Mr. F. A. Schreiber, who had joined as a clerk in 1847, became a partner. In 1852, Messrs. Behn, Schreiber and Arnold Otto Meyer were the partners, the latter having been a clerk since 1850. In 1857 the partners were Schreiber, A. O. Meyer and Johannes Mooyer, who had been a clerk since 1852. In July, 1863, Mr. Ferdinand Von der Heyde became a partner.

In November, Mr. A. G. Paterson, the agent, came to open a Singapore branch of the Union Bank of Calcutta, the first Bank in Singapore. It was open for business on the 1st of December, and the hours were from 9.30 to 3. Advances were made on goods to three-fourths of the value, and ninety per cent. on bullion, &c., with interest at 9 per cent. on the former, and seven on the latter. Discount varied from 8 to 10 per cent. In 1842 the Bank appointed a Committee of three merchants to assist the Singapore Agent in managing its affairs, which was strenuously objected to on the ground that they might use the knowledge they gained to the prejudice of the business of their neighbours.

CHAPTER XXVIII.

1841

THE New Year's Sports took place as usual, a silver cup being given for a well contested pony race on the Esplanade.

The paper of the 14th January contained the first published accounts of the assessment, which look very small if compared with the present day. The total collection for the year was $14,196 and disbursements $12,258. The new carriage and horse tax had realised nearly $3,000. On Twelfth Night there was a Fancy Dress Ball.

In February the paper first mentions the island of Hongkong as likely to be ceded to the British. There were a few villages on it, and in the official notification Captain Charles Elliot, the British Plenipotentiary, in a circular dated in Macao on the 20th January, stated that the British Government sought for no privilege for the exclusive advantages of British ships and merchants, but offered the protection of the British flag to the subjects and ships of all foreign powers that might resort to the British Possession.

In March the paper contains the first reference to Mr. James Brooke's visit to Sarawak in the *Royalist*, and stated that he had been assisting the Rajah there in restoring order in the country, as it had been thrown into a state of rebellion, which had prevented the inhabitants from following their ordinary pursuits. Mr. Brooke had come over to Singapore, but intended to return to Sarawak.

The Opium Farm was let for the year 1840–41 for $6,250 a month, and the spirit farm for $3,750, being $1,375 over the preceding year. In 1836 when the population was 30,000 the revenue for the farms was Rs. 259,885, and in 1841, with a population of 40,000, it was Rs. 324,244. The total revenue for 1841 was estimated at about Rs. 366,000 which was thought fully adequate to meet all the charges of administration, including the expenses of the troops.

On the 30th March a tiger carried off a Chinaman from the public road within two miles from town, in the view of several persons, and dragged him into the jungle. There were a good many cases of a serious form of cholera in the town, particularly in Teluk Ayer, in April.

In November, Mr. J. T. Thomson, the Government Surveyor, came to Singapore, and the Government called upon all holders or occupiers of land to point out their boundaries preparatory to the issue of leases. The paper mentioned the matter in the following article:—"It is now, we believe, a considerable time since the Bengal Government authorised the appointment of Surveying Officer for this Settlement: and we are glad to find a competent individual has recently been placed at the head of the Survey Department for the island, and is about to enter upon the discharge of his arduous and important duties. The object, we presume, to which the labours of the surveying officer will be directed, with as little delay as possible, will be the measurement of the lands in the interior occupied by Chinese squatters, and laying down, as far as circumstances at present will permit, the boundaries of the various lots. Under the system which has hitherto prevailed, every Chinese, who had a mind to become a planter, selected the spot of ground which he thought would suit best his purpose, and forthwith began felling the jungle and clearing as he pleased, without being called on to contribute anything in the shape of rent to the Government. At first, this very simple and primitive mode of proceeding went on very smoothly; but, as the plantations multiplied and began to approximate each other's limits, disputes about boundaries commenced, and of later years have been the constantly recurring cause of strife and contention among the Chinese occupants; and, in particular, the right to reserve a certain extent of forest in the neighbourhood of each plantation, to supply their gambier-furnaces with fuel, has been the fertile source of disputes, and sometimes of bloodshed. When such quarrels occurred between parties of the same tribe, or belonging to the same brotherhood, they were generally settled by the intervention of friends on both sides, but, as the matter now stands, there is not a single week passes without applications being made by squatters for the assistance of the authorities to protect them from the alleged encroachments of some neighbours engaged in the same kind of cultivation as themselves.

"The lands here particularly referred to consist entirely of the pepper and gambier plantations of the Chinese, of which, it is computed there are now, large and small, throughout the island about five hundred, and of which the aggregate produce is estimated at piculs 60,000 of gambier, and piculs 15,000 of pepper, and, from what we learn, the majority of the planters are desirous to hold their grounds under a grant, and become regularly authorised tenants of Government under the rent they will be required to pay, in preference to going on under the existing arrangements, which must ultimately produce a degree of confusion that it will not be easy to remedy."

Mr. John Turnbull Thomson (the name has been often wrongly spelt, in books on the Straits, as Thompson) did a great deal of work in the place. In particular he was the architect and builder of the Horsburgh Light-house, of which an account is given in a special chapter in this book. He was appointed Government Surveyor and left Singapore in 1856, as is related in that year. He called upon occupiers of land to point out their boundaries, and went to Malacca and Penang in the course of his work. He designed, Major McMair tells us, the European hospital and Tan Tock Seng's hospital at Pearl's Hill which were afterwards taken for military purposes, and the European hospital was then first placed on the swampy spot at Bukit Timah Road, and Tan Tock Seng's hospital was built on a still worse swamp in Serangoon Road, a piece of mischief which has been the cause of continual complaint and is not remedied yet. Mr. Thomson will be remembered by the books he wrote about the Straits, with considerable pains and certainly no prospect of any pecuniary return for his time and trouble, like others who had done the same. In 1865 he wrote his "Glimpses of Life in the Far East" and in the same year the second volume of the same work, entitled a Sequel to it. The books consist of short chapters, written in an amusing way, about the ways and the inhabitants of Singapore. In 1874, while in New Zealand, he published in London a book of 350 pages being translations made by him (for he was a very good Malay Scholar) of parts of the Hakayit Abdulla, which are made more interesting by Mr. Thomson's remarks upon the Munshi's stories, at the end of the various chapters. He was a pupil of Abdulla's, who wanted him to translate his Hakayit, but Mr. Thomson said he had no leisure for such a work, which would have filled two large-sized volumes. He says Abdulla was known among the Natives as Abdulla Padre, because he was so much associated with the protestant missionaries in Malacca, and rendered them the principal assistance in translating the Scriptures for printing, but that he never changed his own views of the Koran which he was convinced were sufficient for him.

There are a number of papers by Mr. Thomson in Logan's Journal:—

The newspaper contained an account of the installation of the new Tumungong, Dain Kechil, on the 19th August at New Harbour in the presence of the Governor and the Bandahara of Pahang who had come to Singapore. There was a banquet afterwards at which the Governor, the Resident Councillor, and others were present.

The following statements of the revenues and disbursements of the three settlements in the years 1835, 1836 and 1837 were published in the *Free Press*. The figures which were in rupees have here been turned into dollars, as being more convenient, at exchange 218 rupees per 100 dollars, the exchange at that time:—

Revenue.		1835.		1836.		1837.
		$		$		$
Penang	...	80,312	...	83,944	...	86,237
Singapore	...	122,600	...	119,265	...	114,219
Malacca	...	29,000	...	29,816	...	24,530
Total	...	$ 231,912	...	$ 233,025	...	$ 224,986

VIEW OF THE TOWN FROM GOVERNMENT HILL, NOW FORT CANNING. BY J. T. THOMSON.

To face page 354.

Expenditure.	1835.		1836.		1837.
	$		$		$
Penang ...	122,936	...	101,834	...	136,238
Singapore ...	131,195	...	113,302	...	111,009
Malacca ...	38,073	...	51,375	...	51,834
Total ...	$ 292,204	...	$ 266,511	...	$ 299,081

The paper remarked that the charges for the troops were not included, and that the expenses were unequally distributed between the three places, but that the revenue was correct.

In November the Government issued a notification that fifty feet on the north side of the Canal from the Bridge near Buffalo Village to the base of Bukit Timah had been reserved and marked out for a public road. This is the reserve upon which the railway is now being built. The road was afterwards made on the other side of the Canal.

The following account of Singapore, with many interesting details, is taken from a Journal kept by Major Low during 1840 and 1841. The Journal is of great length, and we take the following extracts from it, as they are interesting when compared with the present time :—

"There are not many of what are commonly called sights at Singapore, but if there be no *lions*, there are unfortunately many tigers, as the facility with which these disturbers of the peace can cross the narrow channel which separates the island from the continent, will always prevent the nuisance from being entirely abated, although if the people continue on the alert they may be kept at a distance from the town.

"The absorbing sight here to a well-wisher to his native country, must be the forest of masts which graces the spacious and secure harbour, the flag-staff constantly decked with flags, and the ever busy crowds in the streets of the town and suburbs. At such a small island as this is, everything else in it becomes almost insignificant when compared with it as a prominent, although small part, in the system of Britain's widely extended maritime influence. Upwards of fifty square-rigged vessels may be seen lying in the harbour, forming the outer line of shipping. Inside these, in shallower water, may be counted, from seventy to a hundred vessels (under the denominations of Junks and Prahus), from China, Siam, Cochin-China, Borneo, and other places. The throng of boats plying in the river, to and from the shipping, scarcely ceases at night; and large passage boats are constantly passing to and from Rhio, and to and from Malacca. There are also brigs commanded by Chinese and others which keep up a constant intercourse and traffic between Penang and Singapore, touching generally at Malacca on the way. The voyage either way may average from eight to ten days. Direct, the passage is often made in five or six days.

"The merchants' warehouses are conveniently situated close to the bank of the river or creek, and a large space remains still to be similarly occupied on the branches of the creek, which are now being brought into the form of canals. The town is quite unfortified and a few guns only are drawn out on the beach. It would necessitate a very large expenditure to fortify the place in such a manner as to protect the town in any useful degree. No works could fully protect it against the fire of ships-of-war, and the strongest would only expose it, by encouraging resistance, to surer destruction from shot or shells. Like Penang and Malacca (for the Fort of Penang is indefensible against European tactics, and that of Malacca was long ago destroyed when it was restored to the Dutch), Singapore must depend for safety in time of war upon those wooden walls which are in truth the only Colonial bulwarks which can in the long run be depended on, where the vulnerable points are sea-ports. The harbour is so large and free from dangers, that vessels can at once without the aid of a pilot take up a convenient position.

"The only English buildings of note are the church and the building in which the Government Offices and Court-house are combined. The Armenian Church is a neat, classic edifice, but unavoidably small. There is a Hindu Temple and a Mosque or two, holding out no great attractions to travellers. The Chinese Temple, which has been lately erected, will quite satisfy those who have it not in their power to visit China. It is of elaborate workmanship and very curious in its way, although the taste displayed is quite in keeping with the other tastes of the Chinese. The granite pillars and much of the stone ornamental work have been brought from China, and the latter is exceedingly grotesque. The building will, when quite finished, have cost, I am informed, $30,000. The outlay already has been $23,600. A large portion of this sum has been defrayed by the owners of Chinese Junks from Amoy, and other Chinese ports, and from Siam and Java. The interior and the cornices are adorned with elaborate carving in wood. Outside are painted tiles and edging of flowers, fruits, &c., formed out of variegated pottery, which is broken to pieces, and then cut with scissors.

"Singapore cannot yet boast of either a Theatre or Assembly-Rooms. These, it may be presumed, will be preceded by, if not combined with, an exchange.

"The Garden houses are in a handsome style of architecture and are almost invariably of two stories. But old Indians are apt to prefer the bungalow style on the score of superior coolness. The climate, however, is here so mild and equable, that any little deviation to the Venetian mode is not attended with the inconveniences it is accompanied by in India. The Chinese build their houses with brick and mortar when they can afford it, the Malays seldom or never. The streets of the town are spacious and they are crowded with native shops. A stranger may well amuse himself for a couple of hours in threading the piazas in front of the shops, which he can do unmolested by the sun, at any hour of the day. Europe shops, as they are termed, are not numerous, nor, although respectable, are they in keeping with such a mart, but the frequent investments of all sorts of supplies which are sent out to, and exhibited in, the merchants' warehouses prevents this deficiency from being felt. There are three hotels here which are well conducted and conveniently situated. A Frenchman, Mr. Dutronquoy, has opened the most spacious one of the three. It has now become fashionable for travellers to resort to these, instead of being, as formerly, liable to be cast away, as it were, unless provided with a passport to hospitality. There are table d'hotes at these hotels and conveyances are provided.

"House-rent is not perhaps high, considering the style of building. A comfortable two-storied house with dining-room, drawing-room, and from four to six bed-rooms may be had at from 35 to 60 dollars a month, the rent varying with the site. Some have been rented at 100 dollars. But these are of the largest description and cost about $10,000 each in building, an ordinary one can be built at from 3,000 to 5,000 dollars. Singapore is rather an expensive place to reside at, everything, with the exception of English supplies, being much dearer than in India.

"Servants are a heavy item. Thus, for a moderate family, there is a butler at from 7 to 8 dollars a month, two under-servants at 5 dollars each, a maid (or Ayah) or nurse 5 to 6 dollars, tailor 7 to 8 dollars, cook 7 to 8, with an assistant, perhaps, at 5 dollars, washer-man 5 to 6 dollars, two grooms at 5 dollars each, grass-cutter 2 dollars, lamp-lighter and sweeper 4 dollars, scavenger 1 dollar, water-man 4 dollars. All of these wages can hardly be less than from 66 to 70 Spanish dollars a month. But it must not be imagined that comfort is ensured by the keeping of so many servants (for excepting the ladies' maid and nurses there are no women-servants); on the contrary, a family is worse served by these than it would be in England with one-third, perhaps one-fourth of the number. Warehouses have estimated rentals of 100 dollars down to 30 or less.

"After breakfast, most of the servants walk off to the bazaars for their own pleasure, and as there are no knockers to, or names engraved on, the outer doors or gates of the houses here, and as few people sit in the lower story during the forenoon, but use it chiefly for dinner, a stranger has some difficulty, while paying morning visits, in avoiding intrusions at wrong houses, for there is often no one to announce him, and unless he makes a disagreeable use of his lungs, he must be the porter of his own card upstairs, and perhaps have half an hour's leisure to admire the prints and articles of bijouterie with which most parlour tables are plentifully garnished, before the inmates of the house become aware of his presence.

"Residents generally dine at four or five o'clock. But the hour for a large party is seven. Perhaps the former hours are the most conducive to health. The punkah cannot, on such occasions, be dispensed with, more than in India, and American ice would be a very luxurious addition.

"The Native festivals here are, of course, numerous. If every class was to have its own way, the town would be in a continual clamour by noisy and riotous processions. When the Chinese run riot, it is generally in the streets during processions. They have a wholesome antipathy to coming to very close quarters, and therefore prefer long poles to shilelahs. With these they contrive to break a few bones, and poke out some eyes, but it is amusing to see how soon the most furious onset either of Chinese or Klings can be turned aside, and the parties put to flight, by the appearance of a constable and a few police peons. Whenever a Chinese is assaulted, those of his clan who are at hand haste to his assistance, and in five minutes a pitched battle will be got up, and bricks, stones and poles will be in full play.

"I believe the abomination of swinging on tenter hooks passed through the tendons of the back, as practised by Hindoos in India, is still practised once a year in this Settlement, as also the walking through fire. But it is to be hoped that these barbarities will be done away with ere long, as positive nuisances.

"The climate of Singapore is warm but undoubtedly salubrious. Fahrenheit's thermometer seldom rises above 82 during the hotest time of the day, in the months when rain falls copiously. February, March and April are perhaps the hottest and driest months, yet showers frequently fall during these. Indeed, a drought of six months duration would probably not only render the place very unhealthy, but destroy the whole cultivation of the island. A six weeks drought is of rare occurrence, and even during the severest drought the dews fall heavily, and the valleys at sunrise are shrouded in mist. About 90 inches of rain fall upon an average in a year, and the average number of wet days is about 170. In these two instances, the climate here agrees closely with that of the Penang station. But at the latter the rains are less dispersed throughout the year than they are generally at Singapore, and fall also more copiously within certain months, especially in April, May, August, September and October.

"The showers at Singapore are commonly very short, few enduring beyond a quarter of an hour. But they are generally heavy, which might not have been expected when the deficiency of high hills is considered. A completely rainy day seldom occurs. Thunder and lightning happen likewise much less frequently than they do at Penang, where they are often of daily occurrence for a month and longer, and happen during about one-third of the days in the year. This frequency of electric change in the atmosphere is owing, at Penang, to the mountainous nature of the island and of the adjacent coast. But although Singapore is perhaps on the whole a moister climate than that of Penang or Malacca, it is yet subject to periodical droughts: one happened this year (1841) during the months of February, March and April, which was only relieved by a few partial showers. The wells which supply the town with water to drink, and which range along the base of the hills close to it, became nearly dry, because they were wholly sustained by the filterings of these hills, or slopes. Yet the streams which drain the central parts of the island continued to yield a plentiful supply.

"The soil of Singapore may be thus classified:—First the clays: then the sandy soil: thirdly the soils composed of both these: and lastly the peaty soil covering either clay or sea mud. The hills and slopes are composed of the first and third classes, although the clay is in excess, while the valleys and plains embrace the second and fourth descriptions, and occasionally the clays, as an upper stratum. Were the peaty covering to be left out of consideration, the flat lands in the valleys would be brought within the class of clays. There is no soil in the island (sufficiently extensive to be really useful) which can be called favourable, or which exhibits a due admixture of earthy and decomposed vegetable matter. The earthy matter is either in excess, as in the clays and sands, or the vegetable superabundant, as in the peats, and as a whole the soil of the island is of a very inferior description.

"The nucleus of the island is granite, but this circumstance is of little importance to the agriculturist, because the granite is, except at Bukit Timah, overlaid by the clays of the sandy strata: and, as at this last locality, it is not sufficiently micaceous or porphyritic to yield a good soil by decomposition. It would appear, after such an examination as the cleared portions of the island have allowed me to make, that the soil deteriorates as we advance to the interior, where, although it is more uniform than along the sea shore near the town, yet derives little benefit from the circumstance. The ridges in the neighbourhood of the bay, which forms the spacious harbour, exhibit the highest patches of the red soil, although but a few of these only are moderately fertile. The ridge, which stretches some miles from the North extremity of the Singapore plain to the Sirangoon river, has generally a light soil, with from 66 to 70 per cent. of silica or sand.

"The soil of the island graduates from the deep and iron clay, to the gritty gravelly iron soil, containing rounded and broken masses of scoreous or lateritic iron stone, either embedded in it or loosely scattered on the surface: next comes a clayey soil tinged by the oxides of iron with shades of red and yellow: and lastly there is a white and hard clay: and all of these varieties are to be found within the compass of three or four acres: owing, as before noticed, to the high inclination of the sandstone strata. Although the hills and ridges have doubtless for ages been clothed in tall forest with a close underwood, yet there is hardly any vegetable soil beyond a few inches in depth to be found on any of them. Where such has been formed, the heavy rains have doubtless washed it down to the swamps.

"The quantity of rice produced on the island is extremely small, since there is but a very small extent of rice land available, which will always prevent any large number of Malayan agriculturists from settling here. The island is supplied with rice chiefly from Siam, Java, Manila, Rhio, &c. The Malayan population has been gathered from almost every shore and island to the eastward. The greatest number find employment in fishing, petty traffic, and day-labour, and the remainder cultivate, as squatters, scattered patches of land, on which they grow sweet potatoes, plantains, Indian corn, and tropical fruits. Sugar has of late years begun to attract the attention of Singapore capitalists; and whatever may be the result, still the spirited pioneering of the new path exhibited by two members of the settlement deserves applause and success. The former, Mr. Balestier, has erected a steam-engine (besides distilling apparatus), and the latter, Dr. Montgomerie, has water-power for the machinery.

"The rate of wages for agricultural labour is not exorbitant, but ranges from three and a half to four dollars a month. But it would require perhaps more labourers to combat the clay soil of Singapore than to work the friable volcanic soil of Java or the alluvial deposits of the other countries above alluded to. Notwithstanding the numerous attempts which have been made to decry the cultivation of the cocoanut trees on the island, it bids fair for success. No tree of this kind can be more flourishing than those in the plantations which stretch along the sea shore to the N. E. of the town, and which are growing on the island called Blakang Mati, or Dead Back by the Malays (with reference to some murders committed there as some people say, but most likely from the sterility of the southern slopes of the island, where there is no cultivation) and if they can be kept as free as they now are from that pest the elephant beetle, they will become perhaps the most valuable of any species of agriculture property on the island, because most lasting, and the least liable to suffer from the fluctuations of commerce.

"The locality first described is very sandy, and the soil is occasionally intermixed with a dark half-peaty, half sea-mud soil. The tree is also growing with vigour at the base of the hills, in clay and even in the peaty soil. The sea beach is, however, undoubtedly to be preferred. There are perhaps about 50,000 trees now planted out and occupying about 660 acres of land. Many expedients have been tried in the Straits to get rid of the beetles. Such as salt, lime, and fine sand, &c., all of which are poured in amongst the upper shoots and branches. But as these destructive insects fly at night and come from any distance and in any numbers, without being observed, nothing has succeeded perfectly except the manual process of picking them out of the trees with a long iron skewer having a barbed end. The baker here depends entirely on the cocoanut tree for toddy or yeast.

"Cotton has been tried, but although the plant thrives luxuriantly, and bears a sufficiency of pods, the climate is thought too wet for its profitable cultivation. As the pods thus ripen during every month in the year there is no regular season for plucking. So that it would be necessary to keep labourers employed all the year for this purpose. The frequent rains, too, it is said, greatly injure the cotton when the pods burst. It is not likely that it would be, even under more favourable aspects, a very profitable speculation here.

"There are now planted out in Singapore, as nearly as can be discovered and estimated, about twenty-five thousand nutmeg trees. In this number, there are about four or five hundred which have been bearing for considerable terms of years, including about two hundred or so from 18 to 21 years of age. The remainder consist of trees of all ages downwards, from about eight or ten years of age to one. The land occupied by these trees may be from about 550 to 600 acres. In the whole collective area there is only a very limited proportion of the best, but a large proportion of the worst soil.

"It has become fashionable in these Eastern Isles where the imagination, like the jungle, is so apt to luxuriate, to pitch upon some trees of uncommon growth, and situated in the most favoured spots, as standards of comparison, and as sure indices of prospective wealth, in a species of cultivation which, beyond all others, demands the soberest exercise of the judgment, and the most liberal sacrifice

of preconceived opinions and exaggerated expectations, before we can
venture on a computation of the probable (certainly always more or
less uncertain) results. Like most fruit trees, some nutmeg trees
will bear large and others scanty corps. The annual rent will always
vary considerably, for a full crop can hardly be expected beyond
once in three years.

"The betel-nut tree deserves consideration for although it would
not be worth the while for a capitalist to speculate upon it, still,
as the nut is exportable, it is of more value than produce which
must, from its perishable nature, be consumed on the spot. It is a
hardy tree, and only requires to be kept free from the lalang grass
and jungle for two or three years, after which it will afford sufficient shade to prevent that grass growing strongly.

"I have already noticed that Straits fruit trees promise well
generally. The base of the hills and gentle slopes and undulations
are well suited to them. The mangosteen seems to thrive on the flat
clayey land, while orange trees, the pummelo, jacks, durians and others,
will be best planted on other sites. Some of these trees, the jack for
instance, thrive well on the stony red iron soil. The Cinnamon tree
may yet come to the aid of the planter. It has been introduced on
the island, and thrives very well, but a very small number of trees
only have as yet been planted out.

"The Cocoa, or tree yielding the chocolate bean, may be advantageously cultivated here. It has been long acclimatised in Penang,
and chocolate of a fair quality is manufactured for the use of the
Roman Catholic Mission by its padres. It is a hardy tree, and
seems to grow wherever it has been planted there, both on the hills
and plains.

"The teak tree thrives at Singapore, and might be usefully
employed along with the cocoa tree to line the boundaries of estates.

"The pine-apples of Singapore and the islets in the vicinity,
are of a superior quality. They are large, sweet and well-flavoured,
and they are cultivated in such abundance up the steep sides of
these hilly islands, that they are sold in the market at three for
one of a cent of a dollar, and are thus eagerly consumed by the
lower classes. But it is not a wholesome fruit, and, doubtless, it
assisted the cholera in the ravages it made here last spring, when
it is believed from six to seven hundred natives died of that dire
disease, and several Europeans seamen died on board vessels in the
harbour. The pine-apple grows best on the arid rocky slopes, on the
worst red soil, and it partakes outwardly of this red colour. If the
pine-apple fibre comes into repute in England, which it is likely to
do, then there will be a wide field here for its manufacture.

"The Agricultural Society has not effected anything as yet in the
horticultural department, which, I believe, it was intended that it
should embrace. The Chinese and Malays raise in their own way all
the vegetables which are brought to market. These are sweet
potatoes, bad yams, kaladie, or the arum colocasia (of R) which is
cultivated in swampy places. The root is single, oblong and bulbous,
and it is eaten as a substitute for the potato. The stalks and leaves
are sold as fodder for pigs. The native vegetables are rather small,

yet they are of good quality, and for a garden of a moderate extent, a soil can readily be made to suit every species which the climate will permit to grow. From all that has been stated, it would appear that the cultivation of this island is still in its probationary period.

"The Chinese have been the chief cultivators of gambier and pepper but then they have no attachment to the soil. Their sole object is to scourge the land for a given time, and when worn out to leave it a desert. And what, we may enquire, is to become of the thus empoverished land covered with the jungle they leave in the rear on their onward progress over the island. A fifty years' fallow would barely return it to its pristine condition; and what agriculturist would be so rash as to embark on a large scale in the attempt to renovate it? In short, it seems clear that, if no general cultivation of a more permanent nature than pepper and gambier can be advantageously established, the forest must ultimately re-assume its dominion. The only remaining chance therefore would seem to be the planting of cocoa-nut, areca, and other indigenous fruit trees and incorporating them gradually with sugar cane and trees yielding an exportable produce. As the case stands, it is clear that if there should be any considerable prolonged fall in the prices of pepper and gambier, the cultivation of these articles, and consequently of the greatest cultivated portion of the island would cease. The area of the island has been stated at about 120,000 acres. But as far as the above two products are concerned, the quantity of land available for them might not be reckoned at above one-fourth of the whole, supposing that pepper and gambier must continue to be cultivated together and cannot prove profitable separately, because the proportion of pepper land is much smaller than that suited to gambier. Then a very large deduction would be required for the jungle land which must be attached to each plantation for the supply of fuel; and these plants or trees cannot, until a long period of years has elapsed, be successfully raised a second time on the same soil.

"Buffaloes and oxen are chiefly used for draft, but are very expensive, as they are subject to frequent murrains and are not reared on the island, but are brought from Malacca, Penang, and other countries. Some black cattle have been brought from the Island of Bali near Java. They are of brown colour. The horns are sharp and diverging. The head and muzzle are shaped like those of the elk. Ponies with small carts have lately been introduced; and the Chinese, in order to evade the tax on carts drawn by cattle or horses, have started a three-man cart or truck, which is propelled by them, one man guiding it by the pole, and one pushing at each hind corner of the cart.

"The conveyances used for pleasure or convenience on the island are Palankeen carriages drawn by one pony, and led, not often driven, by a groom, with an occasional out-rider behind. Four-wheeled open carriages drawn by horses or ponies are also common, as are gigs. Very good palankeen carriages are made on the island. The other carriages are brought from India. With the exception of a few Arabs, the residents content themselves with ponies. They are chiefly obtained from Java. But they are not so smart and powerful as those from Sumatra. A good pony may be got in Singapore at from 60 to 100 dollars.

"A draftsman at Singapore will always have employment for his pencil in the specimens of his kind, from almost every corner of the globe, which he will find grouped in the bazaars. He may portray the species in most of its phrases, from the highest state of civilization to which it has attained, down to that one where matter seems almost divested of mind.

"The two chief roads are those leading to Bukit Timah, the highest hill on the island, and Serangoon, which is the name of a creek and also of a district. Each of them is about seven miles long, and without any material deviations from the right line. There are three other good roads, besides cross ones, leading into the country, of from two or three miles in length. When proceeding at sunrise, along any one of the roads leading directly towards the interior, the difference of the temperature of the air there and on the beach is very perceptible. On the latter it is warmer by several degrees. A fog floats along the valleys during some months, and at the early period of the day is dense as any Calcutta one, but it rarely lasts beyond seven o'clock. These roads are either bordered by canals, in which flow free streams of fresh water, or by dry ditches, so that some foresight and nerve are required in driving the generally badly broken-in ponies. Although the early morning is the most delightful period of the day in this climate, still one meets but a sprinkling then of seekers of health of either sex. The fashionable time for exercise is betwixt five and half past six o'clock in the evening, or till it becomes nearly dark. The ride or drive is finished off by a few turns on the Course [now called the Esplanade]. This last is an oblong square of about five hundred by seventy yards, and is bounded by the sea or harbour on one side, on the opposite side by splendid garden houses, at the southern extremity by the Court House and Public Offices, and at the northern by the Institution, in which direction the garden houses stretch away for about half a mile in a single line open to the sea. The tars from the shipping frequent also this gay square, to display their equestrian tactics on the foresaid hard-mouthed ponies; while two select bodies of local politicians frequent a convenient old battery, the low walls of which serve for benches, although our researches cannot precisely enable us to tell which are the opposition ones. [This was in the centre of the sea front and was known as Scandal Point.] The old battery beyond this one, is now a green mound, which the Institution boys use as a play ground.

"As the streets would soon be encumbered and rendered impassable were the markets not confined to one spot, a very commodious one has been erected by Government, which is subject to due regulations. It is an octagonal building of 120 feet diameter, and is let out to the highest bidder [this was at Teluk Ayer]. It is probable, however, that a second will be required ere long to meet the increasing population, for the present one is already too crowded. As it is, it requires the constant vigilance of the police to prevent the streets being blocked up by vendors of pork, fruits, vegetables,

&c. Chinese cooks with portable kitchens perambulate the streets at all hours, and distribute viands, which, however tempting to their own class, could hardly be adventured on by others, since the materials of which they are composed may, for ought anybody knows to the contrary, be the flesh of dogs, lizards, and rats, all of which come within the scope of the Chinese cook's oracle. The fish market is indifferently supplied, and perhaps this is partly owing to the luxurious habits of the wealthier Chinese, who as the fishermen are chiefly composed of their own people, can easily obtain the best fish before they go to market.

"The shipping is supplied with water by boats kept by five private individuals, or rather companies, provided with force pumps. The charge is from 50 cents to one dollar a ton, according to the place from which water is to be brought. Each boat costs originally from 500 to 1,000 dollars. The water is obtained partly from a Government aqueduct and party from wells; which last are sunk to the depth of about ten or twelve feet. These are for the most part private property. The water is good, being filtered through the sand stone and clay of the rising grounds. But after heavy rain it is turbid for a day or two. It is of a quality betwixt hard and soft.

"Singapore, Malacca, Penang and Moulmein are the Sydney, convict settlements, of India. There are upon an average about 1,100 to 1,200 native convicts from India constantly at Singapore. These are employed in making roads and digging canals; and undoubtedly without them the town, as far as comfort in locomotion is concerned, would have been now but a sorry residence. The convict whose period is short contrives to save something out of his allowance, and on the expiration of his time, he generally sets up as a keeper of cattle, or a letter-out of bullock carts, carriages and horses: and, undoubtedly, some of these men are as well, if not better, behaved than many of their native neighbours of higher pretensions. There are regulations by which the convict is encouraged by certain rewards, or remissions short of emancipation, to orderly conduct.

"Game is scarce, if we except snipe. Some quail and grey plover are found in the cleared islands. There are no extensive lakes, or tanks, and therefore few water-fowl. Wild hog is abundant in the jungle, where are also found, as before noticed, tigers; also elk, small deer, the plandok, or deer about the size of a bear, monkeys, wild cats (beautifully striped), civet cats, lemurs, flying foxes, small squirrels, &c. Happily the jackals imported from Bengal have become extinct. Flocks of paroquets of a greenish colour are occasionally found in the interior, but they keep to the highest trees, and rarely come within shot. The dial bird, or *morei* is the nightingale of the Straits. It is about the size of a lark, has a black body with some white feathers in the wings, and the half of the lower part of the body is also white. It has a rather long and sharp beak and long tail. It is a very lively bird, and it may be tamed so as to require no cage, unless to protect it from the cats, and from the large rats which infest the Straits. The male bird appears to be the songster, and he serenades the hen while she is engaged in domestic cares. He may sometimes be heard an hour before dawn waking the grove with his pleasing notes, and he is so little afraid of man that he will sing for hours close to, or even on the top of a house; it is the most common bird to the eastward. There are one or two smaller birds whose rather plaintive notes may be occasionally heard. There are no crows on the island, nor are birds of prey numerous.

"When the Bugis vessels arrive, they hold a sort of fair on the beach, where they display for sale their sarongs, or pretty coloured plaids or peticoats, for they answer for both purposes—the chief manufacture of that country. These cloths are famed amongst the Malays for their strength of texture, but English trade has here too wrought a change; instead of using the thread wove in their own country they carry English thread back with them. The value of the plaid has thereby decreased, those made from English thread being thought less durable. These vessels also bring numbers of the parrot tribe, lories, &c., and for about a month the streets resound with the discordant screams of these beautiful birds; the usual price of an untaught bird is from six to eight dollars, but if accomplished in the *unknown* tongues, their price is unlimited.

"Singapore is not much afflicted with insects. Mosquitoes are rather numerous at times, but they can be kept off by gauze curtains at night, when they are most troublesome. The white ant is here, as everywhere in the East, the most destructive insect, although never personally annoying. Common ants of various kinds find their way into houses, but they may be got rid of by pouring boiling water into their nests on the ground floor. A very slim species of hornet constructs its clay nest on the walls and beams and behind pictures, and having deposited an egg, and laid up in it a supply for the future caterpillar, of a sort of greenish spider, which it contrives to reduce to a half torpid state, it closes the nest and leaves the spot. Scorpions and centipedes occasionally intrude themselves into the houses, but they are seldom large. The nuisance so prevalent in India of swarms of flying ants, beetles, and other insects covering the table cloth and falling into the dishes and glasses at an evening dinner is little known here.

"One of the greatest nuisances in the Settlement is the legion of dogs of most anomalous breeds which infests the streets both day and night. An annual edict goes forth against them, yet their numbers are never perceptibly thinned. Next in order come crackers and fireworks, which, in defiance of policemen, are let off without regard to place or time, to the great danger of bad riders and people in carriages with unruly horses.

"As no one thinks of shutting the door of his house during the day, and, perhaps, often not at night, he ought not to wonder if he is robbed now and then. Hawkers, coolies or porter-distributers of advertisements, and others, of various and equally erratic habits, scruple not to perambulate a house till they find some one to attend to them.

"The Chinese uphold here, as they do in other places where they have settled out of China, the *Kongsis* or Secret Societies of which the Emperor of China is so much afraid. The chief one here is the *Tean Tay Hueh*, which boasts, it is believed, about from five to six thousand members, who are bound by oath to support each other on all occasions, and to screen their brethren from public justice : but reserving to their secret tribunal the power to punish offences committed within the society, by its own members, but not by others against it— all such being given up to English law. I have not learned what the badge of this lodge is, for everything regarding it is about as mysterious as Freemasonry, of which it is a perverted type. The meetings of this Society are held at a Temple in the outskirts of the suburbs at Kampong Glam. The Society is governed by a Council of four officers, each of whom represents a tribe. The tribes are the Amoy the Kheh, the Teouchoo, and the Macao. Some of these societies are avowedly for good purposes, such as relieving distress within the limits of the Chinese population, and this is more required now than it was when pork was taxed for the same purpose, and it is a tax which was and would be more willingly paid by the Chinese than any other, so long as the proceeds, as before stated, should be, as formerly, appropriated for the benefit of their poor. The Klings, Chinese and Bengalees are the most quarrelsome sections of the population, but the largest proportion of charges of felony is found on the side of the Chinese : who, in the main, at this island, are little better than the refuse population of China.

"Gambling is carried by the Chinese to a great height. The Police force of the island consists of the Sitting Magistrate as Superintendent, three European Constables and an Assistant Native Constable, 14 Officers and 110 Policemen. It would be reckoning very wide indeed of the mark were any one to believe for a moment that any native police can resist temptation, even when that is of a much weaker kind than it is under any circumstances here exposed to There are now about a hundred gaming establishments in the town in full play, besides many more in the Country districts. The Chinese show in China by their secret opposition to the arbitrary rule under which they groan, how strong the arm of that law must be which can check their deeply rooted vices. As the English law rests, it would be a hopeless task to attempt putting down gambling or gaming amongst the Chinese, for in the Eastern Settlements the vice presents to the jurisconsult a problem which neither European codes, nor the experience of Europeans who have been on the spot, have as yet satisfactorily solved. It is the aim of the law to check an evil or a crime, or if it cannot be checked, to modify, abate, and neutralize it by legislative expedients. But the law, as it here exists is inadequate in this instance to accomplish either."

Major, afterwards Lieut.-Colonel James Low, of the Madras Army, was for many years employed in the Civil Service in the Straits, as Magistrate, head of the police, etc., and in political missions, principally in Penang, from where he finally quitted the Straits for Europe in March, 1850. He wrote numerous articles on the agriculture, geology, antiquities, and history of the Straits and the Malay Peninsula and Siam, which shewed his great perseverance and zeal in the pursuit of knowledge. The first five volumes of Logan's Journal contain no less than thirteen of his papers, and he published

several pamphlets which are now unobtainable. He left Singapore
in March, 1844, and it seems to have been thought for the last time,
as the *Free Press* of 4th July contained the following account
(shortened) of a farewell dinner that was given to him:—"It was
not the intention of the community to allow Major Low to leave
the Settlement, without carrying with him some suitable manifestation of their sentiments and feelings in his favour; and it was decided
to give him a public dinner on his retirement from his present duties,
in consideration of his long and useful career in the Straits and of
the good feelings entertained towards him by the country. The dinner
took place on Saturday last, at the house of the Recorder, and a
numerous assemblage, including nearly every one of the principal
gentlemen of the Settlement and many military officers of the station,
sat down to table, J. Balestier, Esq., being in the Chair, and Lieut.
Elliot, of the Madras Engineers, officiating as Croupier. The health of
Major Low was proposed from the Chair with appropriate remarks,
and was received with cheers which could not fail to have been highly
gratifying to the worthy Major, who returned thanks. The toasts and
speeches usual on such occasions followed, and the evening wore on
amidst the uninterrupted enjoyment of all present, until the company
broke up about three o'clock."

It was in this year that Mr. William Henry Macleod Read came
to Singapore. He left England in the sailing vessel *General Kyd*
on 18th March, and arrived in Singapore on the 12th September.
Mr. Johnston left Singapore in December, and never returned.
On the 1st January, 1842, the *Free Press* contained a notice that
his father Mr. C. R. Read ceased to be a partner in A. L.
Johnston & Co., and that Mr. W. H. Read was admitted in his
stead. He was then living in Battery Road, on the side nearest
the river. In 1848 the house which had been built by Mr. A.
L. Johnston was pulled down, as it was becoming rotten and
riddled by white ants. It stood between Fort Fullerton and a
little above the present site of Flint Street, and faced Battery
Road, standing in a compound. The back gave on to the river, and
it was called *Tanjong Tangkap*, because the jealous brother merchants
said it was a trap to catch shipmasters on their first arrival as
they came into the river. In 1848 A. L. Johnston & Co.'s godown
was built on the opposite side of Battery Road, where the Hongkong and Shanghai Bank is now, and Mr. Read, on his marriage
at that time, went to live at Beach Road, generally called Campong
Glam in those days, in Mr. Gilman's old house. Soon after his
arrival he began to interest himself in the social life of the place,
as he did all the years he was in Singapore, and at the first
races in February, 1843, he rode the winner of the first race, of
which the *Free Press* said "The excellent jockeyism of the young
amateur who rode the *Colonel* excited general admiration," and he
was one of the stewards of the Race Ball. In March on the same
year Mr. Read (W. H. as he was usually called) got up the first
Regatta in the harbour, of which Admiral Keppel speaks in his
book. In 1844 the paper mentioned that he was Treasurer of the
first public Library in Singapore. In 1845 the first Masonic Lodge

was opened, and Mr. Read was the second to be initiated, Mr. William Napier being first; and Mr. Read was the first Provincial Grand Master. In April, 1851, a public Meeting was held to establish the Sailors' Home, and Mr. Read was appointed Honorary Secretary. In 1859, at a Meeting in the News Rooms to consider the proposal to start a Volunteer corps, Mr. Read's name was the first to be signed on the roll. He had a thorough knowledge of French, speaking and writing it fluently (having been for some time at school in France) which was not usual in those days, and it was probably partly for this reason that he became Consul for Holland in Singapore in 1857, at a time when there were no Dutchmen in the place. It was necessarily a somewhat difficult post to fill, under the circumstances, as the strained relations between the Dutch and the English in these seas, and especially so close to Rhio and Java, have always left some trace behind them, and it speaks well for the Consul's diplomatic, as well as for his undoubted patriotic, character, that both sides were satisfied with his conduct of the public affairs of the country he represented. He was made a Knight of the Netherlands Lion, by the King of Holland and was received with great courtesy at the Hague; while he was in February, 1886, made a C. M. G. by Queen Victoria. He was the first unofficial member of the Legislative Council at the Transfer in 1867, which was largely due to his exertions, and to the influence he had in England. He had very great influence with the native rajahs in the surrounding states, who often came to him in their troubles; and especially with the old King of Siam. It was partly owing to him that the Native States in the Peninsula came under English protection. In the report in the *Singapore Free Press* in March, 1866, of the speeches at a public dinner in the Town Hall, the Recorder, Sir Richard McCausland, in proposing Mr. Read's health, spoke of him as follows:—it summed up, in Sir Richard's genial Irish manner, the many sides of Mr. Read's doings in Singapore:—" I shall not venture or attempt to enumerate all the public services which Mr. Read has rendered; for the omission of any one might be fatal to the task. But whether it be Free trade, or Freemasonry; Gas works, or a Gambling Farm; a Secret Society which has just started up or a Grand Jury presentment to put it down; a Screwpile Pier, or a Railway; Patent slips and Docks; the Suez Canal, or any other diggings of *The Delta!* and lastly, but by no means least, the total and absolute transfer of the entire of the Straits Settlements and its Government from the cold embraces of poor old John Co., (now alas no more) to the fostering care of a Colonial Secretary, and the tender mercies of a Chancellor of the Exchequer,—for each and all these services the inhabitants of Singapore, and I myself among the number, feel deeply indebted to our worthy Chairman, William Henry Read." For nearly fifty years, his signature Δ or *Delta* was constantly to be seen in the correspondence columns of the newspapers. When he resigned the post of Consul-General for the Netherlands, in 1885 the Singapore paper published a translation of a passage from the Batavia newspaper as follows:—

"It is with great regret that we have read the announcement that our Consul-General at Singapore, Mr. W. H. Read, intends to

To face page 368.

W. H. M. READ, C.M.G., K.N.L.
From a photograph taken in 1901.

resign that post on 1st March next. Never has the care of our interests abroad been confided to a more able, more honest, more disinterested and more vigilant agent, than, during nearly a quarter of a century, to Mr. Read in the Straits. We believe that we are the exponents of the wish of every one who means well with the Netherlands and this Colony, when we recommend the Government to take it into consideration to do their utmost to dissuade Mr. Read from his intention."

In 1901, Wells Gardner & Co. published a small book in London, entitled "Play and Politics, Recollections of Malaya by an Old Resident," which it was known was written by Mr. Read. It was dedicated to Sir. Andrew Clarke, formerly Governor of the Straits. It was a reprint of some papers written to amuse some young members of the families of his nephews and nieces, and contains amusing stories of old days here.

Certainly no one here ever worked more unselfishly or unsparingly for the good of the place, and how much it owed to him there are few now to remember. Public men work for various reasons, and often for somewhat selfish objects, but Mr. Read gave his time and his unsparing energy for the good of the place, even to the detriment of his own personal and pecuniary interests, solely from a wish to help the place with which he, his father and his family, had been so long connected. The history of Singapore for forty-six years was also the history of himself, and it was curious that the information of the Queen having been pleased to create him a C. M. G. reached him on the eve of the anniversary of the foundation of this Settlement and close to his own birthday; for he was born, on the 7th February, 1819, within a very few hours of the time when Sir Stamford Raffles hoisted the flag here. Mr. Read visited England eleven times between 1841 and the 28th February, 1887, when he finally left. The first time he remained seven years in Singapore, and was then away for two years and a half, and that was his longest absence at one time. Read Road and Read Bridge were named after him, and the Freemason's Lodge at Kuala Lumpur was called after him. His portrait, painted by his friend and connection, Mr. James Sant, R.A., hangs in the Town Hall, and the community, European as well as Native, who always looked to him, as their predecessors had done to Mr. Johnston, gave tokens in many ways of their appreciation of his character.

CHAPTER XXIX.

1842.

THE usual sports were held on New Year's Day; and a pony race, for a silver cup of $100, had the following entries :—

Mr. W. Napier's	*Runnymede*	Mr. T. Dunman's	*Bellows-to-mend.*
,, C. Carnie's	*Hardmouth*	,, Seth's	*Jockey.*
,, M. T. Apcar's	*Snipe*	,, Santos'	*Doctor.*

During the sports, a tiger was brought in from one of the gambier plantations, and made an excitement during the races.

Mr. James Brooke was then at Sarawak, and the *Free Press* of the 13th January spoke of his proceedings there as follows, in an article on the future of Borneo :—"It may be said that an opening has already been made for us in Borneo by our enlightened and enterprising countryman Mr. Brooke, of whose undertakings the pages of this journal have from time to time furnished some account. That gentleman has lately entered into an engagement with the Rajah Moodah Hassim of Sarawak, a Borneo prince of amiable character and most favourably disposed towards the English, which has placed him in authority over that territory, and he is now devoting his talents, energy, and fortune, to develop its resources, promote its trade, and extend some of the blessings of a civilized life to its population. This, however, is an enterprise which, to be carried out to the successful issue it promises, requires means that a private gentleman can scarcely be supposed to command for such a purpose, and calls for personal privations and personal sacrifices which few possess the resolution to make; least of all, those who enjoy the means of living in luxury and ease in their own country, and it is right that the attention of the British public at home, as well as in India, should be drawn to the exertions Mr. Brooke is making to extend the name and character of his countrymen, and open new markets for their manufactures, as well as new scenes for the exercise of more generous principles than are always comprised in the mere extension of commerce. That his efforts will be appreciated as they deserve, we will not permit ourselves to doubt; but they will also require to be seconded in order to produce results worthy of the generous and important views under the influence of which he has commenced his undertaking."

On the 13th January, occurred the heaviest fall of rain that had then been recorded on the island; it began at midnight and rained without stopping for twenty hours, 9·37 inches of rain falling. The Brass Bassa Canal overflowed its banks, owing to the obstruction caused at the convict Jail, and the whole of Kampong Bencoolen

was flooded, the space between the Jail and Rochore Canal being one
sheet of water about two feet deep, and all the roads got into a
most wretched state. An experience which continues at intervals to
the present time.

On the 25th December, 1841, the ship *Viscount Melbourne* had
left Singapore for Macao, and on the 17th January a boat was
seen coming into Singapore River to Mr. Johnston's landing steps
at Tanjong Tangkap. Dr. Little and Mr. Read saw the boat coming up
to the steps, and the former helped a lady on shore, with a little
boy of two years old and a baby of only a few weeks. They had
been thirteen days in the open boat at sea. The elder of these
children, Mr. George Dare, was not cured of a taste for the sea by the
experience, and the baby was Mr. Julius Dare, who for many years
was a very prominent player in amateur theatricals here, but was
afterwards resident in Yokohama, where he died suddenly of cholera
in 1879, and his mother died there five days after him. The vessel
had been wrecked on the Luconia Shoal in the China Sea, and the
passengers and crew left her in five boats. There were fourteen
Europeans and thirteen natives and servants in the boat in which
the children came. One of the European sailors died in the boat,
and water and biscuits, which were all the crew had, were very short.
On Sunday morning, four days after they left the ship, the boats
saw a *proa* bearing down on them, and the following account of the
adventure was written by a very young officer, an apprentice who
was in one of the boats, as he explains:—"About six A.M., as we
were all assembled in the launch, hearing the captain read prayers,
we saw a *proa* bearing down towards us. The captain ordered us
to take the serang (boatswain over the lascars), along with us and
speak to them, to learn if they were friendly; for we much feared
they were pirates. If there was danger, we were to hoist a signal,
and they would come to our assistance. We accordingly started
to meet them; we waved a white cloth in token of amity,
and they did the same. When we got alongside of them we spoke,
the serang acting as interpreter; they said that they came to
conduct us safely in-shore, and that one boat was there already.
So by this we suspected that they had taken them prisoners,
and wished to entice the rest of us to the same fate. They now
said that they wished to see the captain; so we pulled back, and
they soon came up with the launch, where all were ready, cutlass in
hand, to receive them, in case of treachery. They tried all they could
to persuade us to go with them, and finally began to make fast to the
launch with a rattan rope. When they found that we would not go
with them, they assumed a very threatening aspect; so, there being so
few of us who could fight, and our fire-arms being useless on account
of the preceding rain, the captain gave orders to cut and run. The
cook with one blow of his cutlass severed their rope, and we all made
sail. When they saw this, they made sail in chase of us. We gained
upon them at first, when, to our surprise, they opened fire upon us,
first from their rifles, and finally from a swivel, the last shot passing
through a blanket that was rigged as a screen from the sun at the
back of the captain and passengers. It passed betwixt the captain

and Mrs. Dare, and then scraping a piece off the skull of one of the lascars, who sat in the bow of the boat, it buried itself in the water. Another shot, cut away the leech of the second cutter's lug. They gained rapidly on our boat, we not being so well manned or skilful as the rest. When within a few fathoms they made signs for us to desist pulling, at the same time taking aim at us. Mr. Parkhouse, who was pulling the next oar to me, when he saw the rifle pointed towards us, dropped his oar, exclaiming, 'Good God! there is one of us gone.' It was of no use persisting further, so they ran alongside. The *proa* was about the size of a sloop, neatly built of teak, but cleverly covered with matting and bark, to make her appearance as lubberly and clumsy as possible. She had two long straight poles for masts, and a large lug made of matting to each. Besides this, they pulled fifteen sweeps a side. When they first ran alongside the launch, there appeared to be only five or six half-naked fellows, who were fishing; but now her decks were crowded with Malays, armed and dressed in fancy costumes. Krises, very dangerous, crooked, poisoned swords, clubs, spears and guns, altogether made them have a very ferocious appearance. They jumped into our boat; seized upon us; and would, I think, have despatched us at once, had it not been for the interference of one who seemed to be their chief, who, dashing away the swords of the most forward, ordered all but two to get into their own craft and to proceed in chase of our other boats, which by this time had got pretty far in advance. They accordingly set their sails, and stood for the other boats, whilst we were obliged to steer for the land. Our preserver, a gentlemanly thief, was still with us, and he now began to lay his hands upon all our things, tying them all up in a blanket. But when those in the *proa* saw this, they, thinking, I suppose, that they were sent after a shadow, whilst he was making sure of the substance, turned back, and running alongside, began to clear the boat of everything—clothes, provisions, and even our drop of water, about two gallons, for the sake of the keg. As they took our muskets, pistols, and other arms, they repeatedly, jumped for joy, exclaiming, 'bagus' (very good). When they came to our sextant, they seemed much puzzled to know what it was, and made signs to me to show them the use of it, which I did. We repeatedly made signs to the chief to let us go after the boats, which by this time were nearly out of sight; to which he nodded his head assentingly, and shook us by the hand. Mr. Parkhouse now very foolishly pulled a small bag from his pocket, containing a fifty rupee note and some silver, which he gave to the chief, at the same time pointing to our other boats. Directly he got this, the rest began to strip us for more. They took his watch, Mr. Dainty's watch and ring, but on me they only found a Dutch silver piece. There was a case of herring-paste, which they made me taste before they would take it. They also threw our bag of biscuit into the water. When having taken everything, they now, to our great delight, told us we might go. They gave us a small basket of sago, and about three pints of water. The chief politely shook hands with us all; then stepping on board the *proa* they made sail towards the shore. Luckily for us, one of our boats was just in sight, that

containing Mr. Penfold, who had offered the captain, if he would give
him six Englishmen, he would rescue us, or share our fate, for they
never thought we should return. Guess then our joy, when we saw
him lying-to, though a great way off. We made sail, and stood
towards him, pulling at the same time with all our might, uncertain
for some time whether we gained upon them or not. Had it been
night, we should have missed them, and must, unprovided as we were,
have died a miserable death; worse, indeed, than the one from which
we had escaped. We came up with him fast, and in two hours after
leaving the *proa*, ran alongside of them, and pleased enough they were
to see us. Just as we reached them, away went our mast, and the
cutter took us in tow. We soon came up with the launch, when the
captain welcomed us heartily. Our boat not being worth repairing
was condemned. Half of our crew went in the second cutter. Mr.
Dainty and myself into the launch. The sails and oars being taken
out of her, she was scuttled, and cast adrift. We arrived at Singapore
at about three p.m., after being twelve days in our boats. The second
cutter had got in early in the morning. The first cutter did not get
into Singapore until a fortnight after we left, having been to Sambas.
The lascars, who deserted us, had been taken as slaves, and did not
regain their liberty until twelve months after."

The Government chartered a vessel, the *Royalist*, and the
American Commodore, as there was no English man-of-war in the harbour,
offered to send two vessels under his command in search of the
missing boats. One boat arrived at Singapore from Sambas a few
days afterwards, and the remaining boat reached Sarawak, and the
crew were well treated by the Rajah; the *Free Press* remarking that
this might be taken in extenuation of his ill treatment of shipwrecked
people on former occasions. This was before the days of Rajah Brooke's
rule there, of course. Captain George Julius Dare was a well known
Singaporean. He had been a navigating officer, in those days called
the master, in the Navy, and married at the Cape when on that
Station. His grandfather, Mr. Julius, then helped him to build a
vessel of his own, and he afterwards built others, trading out to China
with three different vessels of his own. In this year he was passing
through Singapore, on his way from Bombay to China, and left his
wife on shore at a boarding house kept by Mrs. Clark at the south
west corner of North Bridge Road and Middle Road, where the baby
Julius, who has been mentioned, was born. About two months afterwards Mrs. Dare left in the unfortunate *Viscount Melbourne* for
Macao, with the two children, to join her husband there. Captain
Dare sold his vessel for a very handsome price, remitting home the
money at the exchange of about six shillings to a dollar! In 1845 he
went home, and returned and settled down in Singapore in February,
1848. These particulars are found in the evidence he gave in favour of
Sir James Brooke, on the famous enquiry related under the year 1854.
He commenced business in Singapore as a shipchandler and commission
agent in the Square. There were then four shipchandlers' firms,
namely, W. S. Duncan, John Steel & Co., Whampoa & Co., and
Mr. Dare. His first clerk, and until 1857, was Mr. Franz
N. H. Kustermann, afterwards of Rautenberg, Schmidt & Co., and

head partner of it in 1874. In 1855 Mr. Dare went to England, leaving a man in charge, whose name there is no necessity to mention. He was a very plausible man, with a particularly pleasant manner, but he turned out untrustworthy and ruined the business, as well as his employer. Mr. Dare died in London, 50 years of age, in 1856. He had a family of nine children, one of his daughters married Mr. William Ramsay Scott; another, Captain C. J. Bolton, very well known and a great favourite in Singapore, who commanded Jardine Matheson & Co.'s crack opium schooner, and when steam came, the *Glenartney*. He is living now in Essex. Another daughter was married to Mr. Whitworth Allen, who was in Singapore and Penang for many years, now retired from business. Another to Mr. Jackson, now Sir Thomas Jackson, K.C.M.G., of the Hongkong and Shanghai Bank; and another daughter to Dr. William Hartigan of Hongkong.

During the rule of the Dutch in Malacca and only a few weeks before the English flag was last hoisted, human beings were treated as mere goods and chattels and set up at public sale like horses and cattle. At a public meeting in 1829, it had been decided by the inhabitants to abolish all slavery in 1842, so the following notice was issued by Governor Bonham:—

GOVERNMENT NOTIFICATION.

The period having arrived for carrying into execution the humane, disinterested and noble pledge of the Slave-holders at Malacca, the Governor deems it right to republish for general information, and in order to remove from the minds of the few slaves who may yet be in existence, all apprehension or doubt of their right henceforth to be considered as free and no longer subject to be treated as slaves under any denomination, colour, or pretence whatever. An authentic copy is subjoined of the resolutions passed at the public meeting of the inhabitants of Malacca held on the 28th November, 1829, and at their request conveyed to the Governor through Mr. W. T. Lewis, who presided on the occasion.

The Governor takes the opportunity of congratulating the European and other inhabitants of Malacca on the completion of their generous purpose and the satisfaction which they cannot but feel in having thus of their own free will come forward and emancipated their fellowmen from the degraded condition of slavery. He is aware that the slaves in question were generally speaking born and bred up under their master's roof, and having for a series of years been supported with kind and considerate treatment and that they came into the possession of their owners at a period and under a Government when slavery was tolerated by Law. The spontaneous emancipation, therefore, of their slaves by the inhabitants of Malacca, under such circumstances, cannot fail to be highly gratifying to, and warmly appreciated by, the British Authorities, as well as the Supreme Government of British India, to which latter authority the Governor will have great satisfaction in reporting that the last remnant of slavery which existed in the British Settlements in the Straits of Malacca has been for ever abolished by the unanimous accord of the inhabitants themselves.

(Signed)   S. G. BONHAM,
Governor of P. W. Island,
Singapore and Malacca.

Gang robberies began to become frequent again in this year. In March, a gang of between thirty and forty Chinese, part of them armed, and with lighted torches, attacked and plundered the store of a money-changer, who had established his quarters in the verandah

of the extensive buildings belonging to Mr. Boustead [next to where
Elgin Bridge is now] on the river side, broke open his chests, and
carried off every farthing he possessed; amounting according to his own
account to 1,500 dollars, but believed to be more accurately stated at
about half that sum.   They were seen by one of the night-watchmen,
who said he was driven off by a shower of stones when he attempted
to check them, and that he gave the alarm; but the robbers
accomplished their purpose and effected their retreat without further
molestation or interruption, leaving the owner of the property with
several wounds on his head and other parts of his person in addition
to his loss.   And in May, in a house close to the Jail [the site of
the present Central Police Station] at about three o'clock in the morning,
a gang consisting of about fifty men, all well armed with broad
hatchets, &c., broke into a native dwelling house.   As soon as the
entrance was gained, the robbers prevailed upon the men by threats,
to keep quiet and offer no resistance at the peril of their lives, whilst
they commenced breaking open seven chests that were in the house, and
contrived to get possession of 700 dollars in money and goods, and
copper utensils to the value of about 500 dollars more.   Whilst the
thieves were in the act of walking away with their booty, the police
peons, whose station was not far off, got the alarm, and immediately
rushed to the spot to afford assistance.   The major part of the robbers
succeeded in getting off, leaving only five of their companions behind
in the hands of the peons who, with difficulty, succeeded in capturing
them.   These men were supposed to have come from the back of the
Government Hill, landing at the New Bridge in boats, and to have
gone up by one of the new roads to avoid the Police.

The following remarks in the *Free Press* of this year give some
details of the value of land at this time:—"A Government sale that
took place in March proves the high rates paid for ground.   The
ground we allude to consists of lots in Upper Circular Road, comprising an area of two acres which realised no less a sum than $12,746.
And in July, two and a half acres of land, divided into sixty-four lots,
realised Cs. Rs 22,172 besides a quit rent of nearly Rs 300, the leases
being for ninety-nine years like all the other town lots sold at that
time."

In April, the Governor advertised for tenders to convey 350 tons
of coal to the new Settlement of Hongkong at a rate not exceeding
six dollars a ton.

In May, the Government refused to allow the Klings to have a
procession and to carry their *taboot* about the town, and on the
following day all the Klings, men of every trade and profession at
Singapore, struck work, and even the petty shop-keepers amongst
them closed their shops, refusing to engage in buying or selling with
the European portion of the community; in short, there was a strong
feeling of dissatisfaction manifested by this class of the population,
which finding vent in the way above described, caused a temporary
inconvenience, especially among the merchants, from their being
deprived of the services of their boat-men and boats.   After a day or
two, the Chinese turned to and did some of the boat-work, which had the
effect of opening the eyes of the refractory Klings.   In June, a

Singapore merchant wrote to the paper complaining of the inefficiency of the Police, as there had been four gang robberies and eight murders in ten days.

The following appeared in the *Free Press* in May:—

PROSPECTUS FOR A THEATRE.

The dearth of all amusement in Singapore has induced several gentlemen to suggest the establishment of theatrical performances by subscription; it has therefore been deemed advisable to circulate this paper, with the view of ascertaining the sentiments of the Gentry and Community in general, as to the desirableness of a scheme of this description.

It is therefore respectfully requested, that those gentlemen who are desirous of patronizing the *Drama* will signify the same by subscribing their names to a List lying at the shop of Messrs. Rappa & Co., and the amount they may wish to subscribe.

It may be expedient to state, that so soon as a sufficiency of funds have been subscribed, an intimation will be given to the subscribers, and Messrs. Rappa & Co., have kindly offered to collect the subscriptions; whilst a Committee of Gentlemen will be nominated to superintend the disbursements and erection of a building.

The list of subscribers included Dr. Martin, Dr. Little, Mr. Carnie, Dr. d'Almeida, Messrs. Gilman, James Fraser, John Connolly, W. Napier, W. R. George, J. Guthrie, T. O. Crane and A. Sykes.

About this time, in 1841-42, the principal European inhabitants lived at Kampong Glam, now called Beach Road, where the old houses (the first built in the Settlement) began disappearing about 1880 to make way for Chinese shop-houses and one large Chinese temple. On the Esplanade, in the same house which is now the main building of the Hotel de l'Europe at the corner of the High Street, Mr. Boustead lived; Dr. W. Montgomerie, the Residency Surgeon, occupied the next, and Mr. Church, the Resident Councillor, lived in the third. Mr. Church's house was afterwards the Freemasons' Lodge, and the building where the ladies used to go, and tiffin was laid at the time of the New Year's Sports. These last two buildings are now the Municipal Offices. The Raffles Institution, a small school then, was inhabited by Mr. Moor and his family, Mr. Dickinson, the second master, and Padre Milton, the Chaplain. Then came Mr. and Mrs. W. R. George, where the Raffles Hotel has been built, and then came a bungalow built and inhabited by Dr. Alexander Martin, who died here. He was also Senior Sworn Clerk of the Supreme Court, in those days when there were more appointments than competent persons to fill them, and "one man in his time played many parts." This house was subsequently occupied by Captain Stephens, who commanded the *Elizabeth*, the first sea-going vessel that was built here. He afterwards became a merchant, and joined Mr. Clark, who had been in Guthrie and Clark, but they each started a separate business not long afterwards. Then came Mr. and Mrs. John Purvis, who lived in the next large house, which was afterwards occupied by Mr. and Mrs. D. S. Napier, and afterwards as a hotel by Mr. Chevalier. In after years it was occupied for some time as the quarters for the Telegraph Company's clerks, when the line from Europe was first opened. Miss Grant occupied a house as a missionary school, and Mr. and Mrs. J. H. Whitehead's house (of Shaw, Whitehead & Co.) was next Middle Road. After that were Mr. and Mrs. McMicking (of Syme & Co.), and Dr. d'Almeida and his family, which is the only house of the row that is still standing, in a dilapidated state. In the same row were Mr. and Mrs. E. J. Gilman, Mr. and Mrs. James Fraser, Mr. and Mrs. Bernard, and the last house belonged to Mr. Ker, and Mr. M. F. Davidson lived in it. The houses on Beach Road had nearly all a separate building for billiard tables. Mr. C. Carnie lived in Rochore Road, off where Carnie Street now is. Dr. d'Almeida had a large piece of building land between Middle Road and where Bugis Street is now, and between Victoria Street and North Bridge Road; he had a small orchard and fish-pond there.

In Battery Road, lived Mr. A. L. Johnston, Mr. J. C. Drysdale, Mr. Robert Bain, and Mr. Read (all of A. L. Johnston & Co.). Dr. Little lived at the Dispensary, and Dr. M. J. Martin lived in the building which now forms part of John Little & Co.'s premises. Mr. McEwen, G. Stewart and T. Dunman lived at the corner of Malacca Street, where the Borneo Co.'s office was for very many years in the Square. Mr. Moses lived in the premises which is still occupied by the firm of Sarkies & Moses, as an office. The building had first been Dr. d'Almeida's dispensary, and afterwards was occupied by Mr. and Mrs. Wingrove. Mr. Simons Stephens (of the firm of Apcar and Stephens) lived with his family at the corner of the Square, next Battery Road. Messrs. Spottiswoode and Connolly's office was where the building erected for the Oriental Bank now is, and had a small compound facing the Square. Mr. F. S. Martin had his store where Little's is. Where the Mercantile Bank is now, Mr. and Mrs. T. O. Crane lived. In High Street, Mr. J. Guthrie, Mr. and Mrs. Armstrong, and Mr. Napier, the lawyer, lived. In Coleman Street, Mr. Coleman, and Mr. Dutronquoy's Hotel. Major and Miss Low lived in the Pavilion in North Bridge Road, and Mr. G. F. Davidson and Padre Beurel in Brass Bassa Road.

In the country, Dr. Martin lived at Annanbank in River Valley Road, from 1843 to 1846, and Dr. Little, who was his partner, then lived in Bonnygrass House, Mr. and Mrs. Adam Sykes (of Robert Wise & Co.) were his neighbours. Dr. Oxley lived on his hill, where the Pavilion, No. 2, now is. Mr. Carnie lived on Cairn Hill, and had planted the two beautiful waringa trees which grew to such a great size, and were cut down in 1884 only, to make room for the large house which was built then, and has been occupied by the Chartered Bank Managers. Mr. Thomas Hewetson lived at Mount Elizabeth, the furthest house in Tanglin. Mr. Behn, V. L. Meyer, and Schreiber (of Behn, Meyer & Co.) at Mount Sophia. Lieutenant Charles Morgan Elliot, of the Madras Engineers, who was sent here to make the magnetic surveys of the surrounding waters, lived at Kallang, on the right bank of the river next to the long iron bridge on the south side. Mr. Ker lived at Bukit Chermin at New Harbour, in the house he built on the hill, which has since been re-built.

Horses were then very rare, ponies and carriages in fair proportion to the upper classes, but a lot of walking was done in those days. People dined at half past four, and sauntered afterwards to the Saluting Battery, better known as Scandal Point, where a sharp eye was kept on Tanjong Tangkop. where Mr. Johnston's hospitable house was situated. A fives court was the only athletic sport then existing, and cards, chiefly *loo* and *vingt-et-un*, were the usual evenings' refuge. The Governor, Mr. Bonham, kept open house at the present Fort Canning, and the Navy House was at the foot of the hill, next to the present Masonic Lodge, where the office of the Government Analyst is now, at the corner of Coleman Street; it has been discontinued for very many years. In those days it was a point of policy to show attention to Naval Officers, and provide for their convenience when on shore.

The following passage appeared in the *Free Press* of 1842, in an article describing the general appearance of the town :—

"A stranger visiting Singapore cannot fail to be struck by the signs everywhere exhibited of the Settlement being in a high state of prosperity and progressive improvement. He lands on the side next the town, he beholds the pathway in front of the merchants' godowns cumbered with packages, and if he glances into one of these godowns he will see it piled with packages and bales of goods from all parts of the world. If he goes amongst the native shops, he finds them filled with clamourous Klings and long-tailed Chinese, all busily engaged in driving bargains. Passing on, he comes to where, near the Jail [present Central Police Station], the swamp is being filled up and covered with shops, which are seen in every stage of erection, some with the foundations merely laid, and others nearly completed. If he wishes to leave the town, he crosses the Singapore river ·by a new bridge which was built two years ago, but the construction of which does not reflect much credit on the Architect, it being exceedingly high, and shaking a vehicle in crossing in a very unpleasant manner. The scene now undergoes a change: in place of the narrow and crowded streets of the town, the stranger finds himself amongst rows of neat villas each standing in its own enclosure. The Governor's residence is to the left, upon a small hill commanding a fine view of the town and harbour, the flag-staff is also placed there, and at all hours of the day may be seen covered with flags announcing the approach of ships from every quarter of the globe. Many villas are also in the course of being built, betokening, by the demand for comfortable houses, the rapid increase of population and wealth. If he should go into the country, the many thriving plantations of spices and other tropical products, among which are to be noted one or two sugar estates, present an equally pleasing sight, and give promise of a long continuance to the well being of the Settlement."

In this year appears the first advertisement that has been met with of Mr. Francis S. Martin, who was a store-keeper and auctioneer, and was afterwards joined by Mr. John M. Little, and resulted in John Little & Co.'s firm eventually. The P. & O. Company were creeping on towards Singapore, though they did not reach here until 1845, and the *Free Press* contained a copy of their half-yearly Report, in which a dividend was declared of three and half per cent. for the six months.

The criminal assizes in August lasted a whole fortnight, there being 77 prisoners. There had been no assizes held for six months. One case was a murder case against fifteen Chinese, for a row in a junk in the harbour, in which the police were attacked and six peons were killed; the identification failed and the prisoners were discharged. There was one other case of murder, and the man was transported to Bombay for fourteen years.

On the 13th September, Mr. Abraham Logan advertised that he had commenced practice in Singapore as a Law Agent and Notary Public. He afterwards was one of the leading lawyers of the place, and for a long time proprietor and editor of the *Free Press*. He was born at Hatton Hall, Berwickshire, on 31st August, 1816. He practised in Singapore for many years, first with his younger brother, James Richardson Logan, who was born at the same place on 10th April, 1819, and arrived in the Straits in February, 1839. In 1853, J. R. Logan went to Penang, and Abraham practised alone for some years, and in 1862 was joined by Mr. Thomas Braddell. Mr. Logan went to Penang in 1869, and died there on 20th December, 1873. In Singapore he lived for many years at Mount Pleasant, Thomson's Road. His brother was the founder and editor of the Journal of the Indian Archipelago. He died in Penang on 20th October, 1869, and a monument was erected to his memory, by the people of the Straits Settlements, in front of the Supreme Court in Penang, the lengthy inscription on which speaks of his death, in the prime of his manhood, as a public calamity, and of his having always been first, and sometimes standing alone, in promoting the welfare of the Settlements; and also of his having founded the Journal of the Indian Archipelago.

On the 19th September, appeared an extraordinary edition of the *Free Press*, announcing the conclusion of the China war, the cession of Hongkong in perpetuity, the opening of the ports of Canton, Amoy, Foochow, Ningpo and Shanghai, and payment of twenty-one millions of dollars indemnity. The news was carried from Nankin to Calcutta by the *Tenasserim* steamer, which called in at Singapore, carrying Sir Henry Pottinger's despatches; Mr. J. D. Vaughan was a midshipman on board her; she had been engaged in all the naval actions up to the end of this war.

The accounts of the Straits at this time, after deducting the expenses for troops and convicts, which were not then considered to form a proper charge against the revenue, showed a surplus of about Rs. 57,000. At Penang there was a deficiency of Rs. 56,000, at Malacca of Rs. 90,000, and at Singapore a surplus of Rs. 203,000. The expenses for troops however amounted in the Straits to Rs. 633,000 and for convicts to Rs. 89,000, so the total deficiency for the year 1841-42, in the official returns, was Rs. 665,000.

It was in this year that the first Consul for France, Mr. Eugene Chaigneau, was appointed in Singapore. The wall along the river side at Boat Quay was built at this time, replacing piles and little private piers in front of the godowns. In Vol. 4 of Logan's Journal, in a paper by Colonel Low, it says that about this period cholera prevailed for a short time in Singapore, proving very fatal in several confined localities, where the houses were mean and filthy, and the people living in them dirty in their habits. From two to three hundred persons died.

On the 16th April, a weekly newspaper was started, called the *Straits Messenger*, published on Saturdays. It was eight pages of small size, and consisted almost entirely of cuttings from English and foreign papers. It had only a brief existence, and for this reason was not mentioned on page 153. There were several such papers at various times. The *Singapore Local Reporter* ran a short time in 1852-53, but there are few, if any copies of the papers to be found. The *Messenger* was conducted by Mr. Edwards, who had formerly had a small newspaper in Malacca, and much amusement was caused in Court by his method of defending himself in a case for libel, heard before Mr. Bonham, Mr. Church, and a jury. The result was a fine of Rs. 200. The subject of the libel was a statement that had been made in the paper regarding Lieut. Maidman, of the Madras Native Infantry, in regard to his behaviour in the Roman Catholic Church. Mr. Edwards, who was a native of Africa, died at the age of 34 years, in March, 1843, which stopped the paper. He had been an entirely self-taught man, and was said at the time to have been a striking instance of natural ability overcoming difficulties.

In December appeared the notice of the first races, and the Stewards announced that the course and stand being almost finished, they had fixed the 19th February, being the anniversary of the foundation of the Settlement (!) for the first meeting. The Secretary signed as Templeton, which was the *nom-de-plume* of Mr. Charles Dyce.

Two Bugis men had a row in the town, one stabbed the other with his *kris*, and he died in the hospital. The other man ran into the jungle pursued by a mob of two or three hundred people, who attacked him with spears and anything they could lay their hands on, and killed him. Some police peons were on the spot, but the mob were in such an excited state that they could not restrain them. A coroner's inquest was held on his body and the verdict was justifiable homicide.

The total imports into Singapore in 1841-42 were $14,000,000, and the exports $11,500,000, being an increase of about one million in each case over the preceding year. The examination of the Institution School was held in December, by Mr. Church and the Chaplain, Mr. Panting. The average attendance at the school was about 125 boys. The Chinese boys were taught English for two hours a day, and their own language during the remainder.

The firm of W. R. Paterson & Co., which led on to McEwen & Co., and so to the Borneo Company, Limited, commenced in this year. In 1846 (the year when the first Directory of Singapore was published), the five partners were W. R. Paterson and William Morgan in Glasgow, Francis Richardson in Manila, Henry Vernede in Batavia, and Robert McEwen in Singapore. Mr. John Harvey was then a clerk. In 1849, Mr. Paterson left the firm; in 1850, John Black, William Martin, and V. L. Helms were among the clerks; and in 1852, John Martin and Robert Harvey.

In 1852 the firm of McEwen & Co., was established, the first partners were Wm. Morgan and Robert McEwen at Glasgow, Vernede and Richardson at Batavia, and Charles Bannatyne Findlay and John Harvey at Singapore. The clerks were William Martin and Robert

Harvey. In 1854 the firm was composed of Morgan, Richardson, Findlay and Harvey, and Mr. Samuel Gilfillan and George Armstrong were among the clerks. In 1857 Mr. William Adamson was one of the clerks.

On 31st July, 1857, the Borneo Company, Limited, was established in Singapore. Mr. John Harvey was Managing Director in the East, Mr. John Black was Manager at Batavia, and Mr. Samuel Gilfillan at Bangkok, the firm of McEwen & Co., having been dissolved on 20th April. Messrs. H. W. Wood and Auchincloss were clerks. In 1859, Messrs. S. Gilfillan and H. W. Wood were Managers, and Mr. C. E. Crane was a clerk. In 1860, Messrs. Gilfillan and Auchincloss were managing; in 1862, Mr. W. Adamson, and the clerks were Messrs. Tidman, Mulholland and Crum. In 1863, Messrs. Gilfillan and Adamson were in Singapore.

The firm of Paterson & Co., was dissolved on 30th April, 1842, and the new firm of Martin Dyce & Co., was established. The partners in Paterson & Co., had been William Richard Paterson, Charles Carnie, George Martin and Alexander Dyce, with houses at Singapore, Batavia, and Manila, and the house of Paterson, Martin & Co., at Glasgow. On 30th April, George Martin, Charles Carnie, and Alexander Dyce advertised in the *Free Press* that Mr. John Campbell had joined them as a partner, and the new firms were called Dyce Martin & Co., at Singapore, Batavia and Manila, and Martin Dyce & Co., at Glasgow, but the latter name was soon afterwards used for the eastern firms. Martin was in Glasgow, Carnie at Singapore, Dyce at Manila, and Campbell at Batavia. Charles Andrew Dyce and Andrew Farquhar were then clerks. In 1858, Mr. Carnie left the firm, and Thomas H. Campbell, who had been a clerk since 1847, became a partner. David Rodger, to whom there is a window in the Cathedral, was a clerk in 1858, and W. C. Hannay in 1859, and were both afterwards partners.

In this year Mr. William Willans Willans, who was a nephew of Mr. Thomas Church, was appointed clerk in the Land Office. He held at different times almost every official office. In September, 1849, the *Free Press* said: "Mr Little, the Surgeon, having resigned the coroner-ship, Mr. Willans, nephew to the Resident Councillor, chief clerk in the Treasury, Official Assignee, &c., &c., has been sworn in as coroner. He is a young gentleman of great activity, but how he will be able to do all the duties of his multifarious employments, we are quite at a loss to conceive." He was in the service for forty years, and there never was a more hard-working, punctual, accurate official in the place. He had the respect of all. He was an excellent magistrate, and a very competent and careful treasurer. He was a member from the first of the executive and legislative councils after the Transfer. He married one of the daughters of Governor Blundell; and Mr. Adolf Emil Schmidt of Rautenberg, Schmidt & Co.; Mr. K. B. S. Robertson of the Police under Mr Dunman; Captain George Tod Wright, Marine Magistrate and in the Master Attendant's Office; and Mr. J. M. Moniot, the Government Surveyor; all married daughters of Mr. Blundell. Mr. Willans retired in May, 1882, on a pension of $3,600 a year, and is now living in England.

In the year 1842 Mr. Samuel Bateman, who had been land agent in England to the Earl of Dudley, and was a land surveyor by profession, had left England for Australia, but did not stay there, and came up to Singapore in 1843 and remained until his death. In August, 1843, with the authority of the Board of Trade in England, he established a Shipping Office for seamen, which was largely availed of. In 1850 Governor Butterworth wrote to him that in the event of a Government Shipping Office being established, his claim to consideration to be appointed Registrar would not be lost sight of. In 1858, when Governor Blundell had succeeded Colonel Butterworth, the Legislative Council at Calcutta introduced a Bill similar to the English Merchant Shipping Act of 1854, and Mr. Bateman, having again applied to the Governor, Mr. Blundell replied that his application would be given every consideration: All the European firms had signed a letter recommending him to Government for the post of Registrar of Seamen. The appointment was not made until Colonel Cavenagh had succeeded Mr. Blundell, and, to the general dissatisfaction, he appointed Mr. W. Wilkinson who had been Master's Mate of H. M. S. *Royalist*. Mr. Bateman then became an Auctioneer and Land Agent. He had a printing office and stationery shop connected with his shipping office, when he first came to Singapore, and did a great deal of surveying in the town, for which reason he had refused the appointment of Postmaster in Hongkong which had been offered to him by Sir Henry Pottinger. He died in Singapore in 1866 at the age of sixty-six years, a well known Singaporean.

CHAPTER XXX.

1843.

A MERCHANT wrote to the paper on New Year's day that 200 barrels of gunpowder were stored in a godown in the Square, and wanted the Insurance offices to take up the matter. Another complained that when the guard was relieved at the Court House, a swarm of pariah dogs came with the soldiers, and attacked the natives passing by, and threw them down and tore their clothes, which seemed to amuse the sepoys, who did not try to stop them till the fun became too serious. So he proposed, as the only effectual way to reduce the super-abundance of dogs, that a tax of $2 per annum should be put upon each; which has often been suggested since.

The advertisements contained notices that Mr. John Purss Cumming and Mr. Gilbert Angus Bain were admitted partners in Maclaine, Fraser & Co., and Mr. John Myrtle in Geo. Armstrong & Co., in January. H. E. Sir Hugh Gough, who had been commanding the Force in China, embarked on board H. M. S. *Endymion* in January, for Calcutta, with his staff; the troops had been returning from China since September on the conclusion of the war. At the same time, Mr. Bonham, the Governor, left in the Company's steamer *Diana* for Penang, in order to go to Calcutta from there in the steamer *Queen*. He went to Europe on leave, and did not return. He carried with him the best wishes of the people. He had tried in every way to advance the interests of Singapore, and during twelve years as Resident Councillor and Governor, had seen Singapore increase in importance every year until it was among the first of the commercial ports of India. He was distinguished by liberal hospitality, and especially during the continual passage of troops and men-of-war on their way to China on the expeditions

Mr. Bonham, afterwards Sir George Bonham, was very popular among the Europeans and natives. He commenced life in the East in the Civil Service in Bencoolen, and had a considerable knowledge of mankind, and, like a sensible man, exerted himself to keep things in easy train and make them pleasant when he could. He had been a quarter of a century in the East, and had made many friends and supporters. He was described as honest, upright, just and generous. He had fine grey hair, a snub nose, and spoke with a stutter and a lisp, but his upright carriage, amiable jocularity, and high sense of honour, sunk them under his gentlemanly qualities. In March, 1848, he passed through Singapore on his way from England, to take up his appointment of Governor of Hongkong and Plenipotentiary and Superintendent of trade in China. He was greeted very warmly in

Singapore, the natives no less than the Europeans coming forward to express the respect and esteem they bore towards him, and their congratulations on his new appointment. He was created a baronet for his services in China, having been Governor of Hongkong from 1848 to 1854.

It was in this year that the Charter was given to Hongkong. The place was ceded to England in January, 1841, and the cession was confirmed by the Treaty of Nankin, in August, 1842. Unlike Singapore, the place was carried on at considerable cost until 1854, Parliament in 1843 voting £50,000 in addition to the military expenses. If Sir Stamford Raffles had commenced the establishment at Singapore in a similar way, it would have been stopped at once.

Mr. E. A. Blundell was appointed by the Governor-General to act until further orders, and Mr. Samuel Garling acted as Governor until Mr. Blundell came, who did not arrive in Singapore until the 23rd July, and on the following day the public were surprised by a report that he had received the intelligence that his appointment was cancelled, and another Governor was being sent in his place. He left on the 27th in the *Diana* for Penang, on his way to Calcutta. The Indian Government, on the 14th June, had appointed Colonel Butterworth, C.B., of the 2nd Madras European Regiment as Governor. The *Free Press* made the following remarks upon this :—" The new Governor of the Straits is Col. Butterworth of the Madras Army. This sudden turning of Mr. Blundell to the right about is, we suppose, the winding up of Lord Ellenborough's conduct to that gentleman, and is upon a par with the other extraordinary behaviour of his Lordship, who seems to place his special delight in depressing and mortifying the civil service, and bestowing all the lucrative and honourable posts on the military. The unceremonious and arbitrary manner in which he has presumed to treat Mr. Blundell, is only a continuation of that course of proceeding which he has pursued towards the Civil Servants. Mr. Blundell, we doubt not, will receive that justice at the hands of the Directors which such an old and valuable servant is justly entitled to, and there are many ways in which the injustice he has suffered can be repaired; but the Straits Settlements are also entitled to complain, and the injustice inflicted on them does not stand such a good chance of being remedied. These Settlements may justly protest against their being deprived of the services of Mr. Blundell, who of all men in the service out of the Straits, was the person best fitted to fill the office of Governor with advantage to all parties. From his previous residence in the Straits, Mr. Blundell is familiar with the language and customs of the people. Ever since he left the Straits he has been resident in the Tenasserim Provinces, and there the whole object of his long Government has been directed to the fostering and promoting their trade and agriculture, and his exertions have been eminently successful.

" That the same qualities which had proved so highly beneficial elsewhere would have been equally serviceable in the Straits is very manifest. In Penang the decaying trade requires to be watched over, and where opportunity occurs, to be reinvigorated by the judicious interference of the local Authorities with the Supreme Government or with the neighbouring states. The agriculture of Penang, which must

To face page 384.

Governor William John Butterworth, C.B.

constitute the main prop and stay of the prosperity of that place, is virtually dependent on the views which are adopted by the Governor, and the help he may be inclined to give.

"In Singapore, Mr. Blundell in like manner might have been highly useful in applying his practical knowledge in carrying the recent measure regarding the sale of land into effect, in opening up new districts, and in encouraging cultivation. At the present time such a person would have been of eminent service in watching the effect which the changed nature of our relations with China will no doubt produce upon the commerce of Singapore; and representations coming from one in his situation, who was evidently so well acquainted with his subject, would have been more favourably regarded than had they been merely by the merchants themselves, whose demands, however just and reasonable, are apt to be looked upon with suspicion and grudgingly acceded to For all these reasons, we esteem Mr. Blundell as the person best fitted for the Government of the Straits, that could have been picked out of the whole service. If the Supreme Government is determined to make room for military gentlemen wherever they can find or effect an opening, we think those whose local experience might be immediately subservient to the public good should have the preference. Instead of removing Lieut.-Colonel Hutchinson, after being three years in the Straits, to the command of the 2nd European Regiment (Lieut.-Colonel Butter-worth's) why was he not detained here in the capacity of Governor? Major Low, whose civil experience in the Straits has been most extensive, might well put in his claim when Military Governors are the order of the day."

The Municipal accounts were published in the paper in January. The assessment on houses in town was then eight per cent., and four per cent. on those in the country. The expense of Police for the year was $12,000, and $1,900 was spent upon the roads. The coolies employed on the work were convicts, and were paid Rs. 4 a month for able-bodied men and R. 1 for feeble men. A sum of $18.62 was spent to enclose the Esplanade!

They was a long series of robberies, and attacks by numbers of armed Chinese about this time, and a public meeting was called, of which the following are the minutes:—

"At a Public Meeting of the Inhabitants of Singapore, held at the office of Messrs. Hamilton, Gray & Co. on the 10th February, 1843, Thomas Oxley, Sheriff, in the Chair, the following Resolutions were read from the Chair, and unanimously adopted:—

1st. Resolved.—That house-breaking and robbery by gangs of Chinese have become so frequent and daring as to create general alarm for the security of property in the Town and Suburbs.

2nd. Resolved.—That the impunity with which these outrages are committed is the main cause of their frequency and audacity, and that it is chiefly attributable to the very inefficient state of the Police department that offenders of this description escape apprehension or detection.

3rd. Resolved.—That it is the opinion of this Meeting that the improved efficiency of the Police, and a more energetic management of that department are absolutely necessary towards effecting a remedy for the grievances under consideration.

4th. Resolved.—That it is the opinion of this Meeting that as one necessary step towards securing greater efficiency in the Police, an addition ought to be made to the number of European Constables and Peons, that the utmost vigilance and activity are necessary on the part of these officers in the discharge of their duty, and that their personal attendance at the Police during the day ought to be dispensed with, except on occasions of positive necessity.

5th. Resolved.—That it appears to this Meeting also highly necessary to establish a Harbour or Water Police to prevent escape seaward, in which direction it is known offenders often fly with their plunder, and that to render effectual this means of preventing escape, the Chinese junks should be required to anchor at a greater distance from the shore, moored in regular divisions, and marked each with a number so as to be readily identified, an arrangement which would be attended with salutary effects in other respects.

6th. Resolved.—That the existence of organized associations of Chinese in this settlement under the designation of *Huey* or Brotherhood is notorious; that the members of these societies often league together for unlawful purposes, the execution of which is facilitated by this system of combination, and that there is no doubt whatever the gang robberies in question are chiefly committed by individuals enrolled in fraternities of this description.

7th. Resolved.—That it is an understood fact that many of the Chinese Shop-keepers and Traders in the Town, particularly the native born subjects of China, pay regular sums to these Associations, as protection money for their own property, or as a contribution in the nature of *black-mail*, and that it rarely or never happens that the Chinese are themselves sufferers from the depredations complained of.

8th. Resolved.—That it is highly expedient a law should be passed having for its object the suppression of these Brotherhoods so far as the same may be effected or influenced by legal enactments, and in particular that it should be made penal for any person or persons to pay or receive any sum of money as protection money of the nature specified in the preceding Resolution.

9th. Resolved.—That the Resolutions now passed be transmitted to the Hon'ble Samuel Garling, Acting Governor, through the Committee of the Chamber of Commerce, accompanied with a letter from that Body in support of the firm conviction of this Meeting (inadequately conveyed in these Resolutions), that the grievances in question demand immediate and energetic measures on the part of the local Government.

The Chamber of Commerce recommended that the Police Force should consist of one Deputy Superintendent of Police, six European Constables, seven Jemadars or Sergeants, eleven Duffadars or Corporals, and one hundred and fifty Peons, which it was thought would necessitate the highest rate of assessment (ten per cent.) being put into operation.

Tiger stories were very numerous, there being five cases reported in the paper as having occurred in six days, in the jungle, chiefly among the Malay wood-cutters. A tiger and tigress were killed on a plantation on Bukit Timah Road one mile from town. The following grumble appeared in the paper in February:—" Why are the Verandahs in Kling Street, and in fact in almost all the streets, allowed to be choked up with the wares of Klings and Chinese, thereby preventing people from walking under them? I wish to ask if they have any right to do so? Proprietors of godowns in the Square are not allowed to use the Verandah to put goods under. Certainly it is rather surprising that this nuisance should be suffered. We believe that the meaning of the clause which is inserted in all the building leases, obliging parties to make a Verandah in front of their houses six feet wide, is or was intended to provide for the accommodation of the public by furnishing them with a walk where they might be in some degree free from the sun and dust, and be in no danger of sudden death from the numerous Palankeens that are always careering along the middle of the way. But this seems to have been forgotten, and the natives have very coolly appropriated the verandahs to their own special use by erecting their stalls in it and making it a place for stowing their goods."

The following advertisement appeared in the *Free Press* in February :—

A RACE BALL

Will be held on the evening of Monday, the 27th instant, at the residence of the Hon'ble the Recorder.

Dancing to commence at 8 o'clock.

STEWARDS.

Lieut. Hoseason.	William Napier, Esq.
Lewis Fraser, Esq.	James Guthrie, Esq.
Chas. Spottiswoode, Esq.	Charles Dyce, Esq.
W. H. Read, Esq.	Dr. Moorhead.

Full Dress.

and the *Free Press* gave a long account of the First Races in Singapore which were held on Thursday and Saturday the 23rd and 25th February. The first race was at 11 a.m., and called The Singapore Cup, of $150. Mr. W. H. Read rode the winner. There were four races the first day, and three the second; followed by some matches to fill up the time. The races were held on the same course as at present, but the stand was on the opposite side, near Serangoon Road.

The ship *Edward Boustead*, 484 tons, left Liverpool on 14th August, 1842, and arrived at Singapore on 14th December, consigned to Boustead, Schwabe & Co.; she sailed again for London on 11th March, 1843.

H.M.S. *Dido* had left England in January, and passed through Singapore in May, 1842, on her way to China in the war. She returned to Singapore on 30th December, and was in the Straits or Borneo until 30th June, 1843, when she went again to China. She returned to Singapore in February, 1844, and was again in the Straits and Borneo until October, when she sailed for England, and was paid off. It was during this commission of the *Dido*, and her expeditions to Borneo against the pirates, and assistance rendered to Rajah Brooke, whose doings Singapore looked upon as almost a part of its.

own history, that Captain Keppel made so many friends in the place. He had previously been in Singapore a few days only on two occasions, when he was a Lieutenant of the *Magicienne*, as said on page 218, in September, 1832, and April, 1833, but his book "A Sailor's Life under Four Sovereigns" gives from his diary many occurrences while he was here in the *Dido*, and mention is made of Mr. Church, Wm. Napier, Wm. Scott, Rajah Brooke, Captain C. M. Elliot, W. H. Read, Balestier, and many others whose names are mentioned in this book.

The *Dido* was a beautiful corvette of 734 tons, 18 guns. Admiral Keppel often used to remark, half a century later, that he could never leave her without rowing twice round her in his boat to have a look at her. The present Rajah of Sarawak, Sir Charles Johnson Brooke, mentions in his book about Sarawak, that he first went there "a small midshipman" in the *Dido* with Captain Keppel.

In one week in March, the paper contained an account of four Kling men having been murdered in a boat at Tanah Merah; they were found with their hands tied behind their backs and strangled. The Powder Magazine of Tock Seng on Kallang River was broken open by a large gang of Chinese robbers, and large quantities of powder carried off. And the same night a gang of armed Chinese landed from a boat at New Harbour and attacked several houses, but the Tumongong turned out with his followers and beat them off in gallant style and captured eighteen men. On the same night, a quantity of coal stored at Sandy Point was set on fire by an incendiary.

There was a regatta held in March, with ten entries of yachts, of which the *Victoria* and *Maggie Lauder* came in at the head. Captain Keppel, of the *Dido*, was umpire, and Mr. W. H. Read, Secretary. There is an account of it in Admiral Keppel's last book. The *Free Press* said that the community were much indebted to the Captain of the *Dido* for sending his band to play for two or three hours every evening on the Esplanade, which attracted all the Singaporeans. The paper contained a long account of the *Dido's* attacks on pirates; her boats used to be sent away round the island whenever a native boat brought in any suspicious intelligence, and on one occasion Captain Keppel put a number of the crew into Chinese topees as a blind. In May the *Dido* sailed for Borneo with Mr. James Brooke on board. Captain Keppel and the officers and crew of the *Dido* were the life of the place whenever she came into port. Regattas and picnics were held, and from the Captain downwards they seemed to vie with each other in making their stay as jolly as possible, and the arrival of the vessel in the harbour was an event in those days of no telegrams.

Major C. E. Davis, who had been the principal assistant to Colonel Farquhar, and married one of his daughters, died in Calcutta in his 53rd year on the 8th March in this year. The *Englishman* spoke of him as a sterling and very amiable man.

The following articles appeared in the paper of 20th April:—

"We have much pleasure in announcing to our local readers that it is the intention of the Agents of the Steam Ship *Victoria* to despatch her on Wednesday, the 26th instant, on a trip to Malacca and Penang and back. The following are the rates proposed to be charged:—

Cabin passengers to Penang and back	...	...	Drs.	100
If to Penang only	...	...	...	...	...	,,	50
If to Malacca only	...	...	...	...	...	,,	25
Steerage passengers with berths	...	...	...	,,	12
Deck	...	...	...	...	...	...	...	,,	8

Provisions for this class not included.

"We understand this trip is intended as an experiment, and if it is found that the expenditure so incurred is not so great as at present anticipated, a modification of the above rates will be made in future. It is proposed that the *Victoria* shall leave here on Wednesday, the 26th instant, at 2 o'clock p.m., start the next day from Malacca at 2 o'clock p.m. when she will be at Penang on the following morning, where she will remain until Tuesday morning, when she will return on the same plan. This is the first experiment ever tried here, and we trust that sufficient encouragement will be given to induce the owners of the *Victoria* to continue her in the Straits. Many of the community who have never visited the other Settlements in the Straits will, we are assured, gladly avail themselves of so desirable an opportunity"

"We have lately been much gratified by seeing the manly game of Cricket resumed in this Settlement. A very interesting match is now being played between the officers of H. M. S. *Dido* and Singaporeans. We observed among the players several excellent bowlers."

The following is taken from a paper that appeared at this time:—"To an old inhabitant of Singapore who knew it only a few years back in its primitive Malayan state of jungle and marsh, it is a source of gratification to observe the many improvements which are now in progress, not only in the extension of the town, but in the construction and repair of useful roads which run in various directions over the country. It is pleasing to observe with what rapidity little gardens and large plantations spring up on each side of these roads, to the extent of several miles, and we have no doubt that were the whole island judiciously intersected with roads, it would soon be cleared of jungle and become a highly productive settlement. Commercial prosperity has given an impetus to agricultural enterprise for some time past, and the Government ought to foster and encourage it by every means within its power. Can it be said to do so at present? We *know* that most of the planters would cry out against us were we to state that it does. They would exclaim that they commenced their plantations under very great discouragements and hold them, even now, only by a sort of tacit permission. Such a state of things ought not to be allowed to continue any longer, the Government ought speedily and openly to declare the terms on which planters are to have their possessions, and the more liberal these terms are the sooner will the whole island come within the reach of the present march of improvement.

"A large portion of the island is covered with plantations of gambier and pepper, owned by Chinese squatters, and as these two products have become important articles of commerce, every encouragement ought to be held out to continue and extend their cultivation, by

granting these industrious people permanent leases and by opening more
roads into the districts occupied by them.   The Chinese are not slow
in taking advantage of the facilities afforded by the new roads as far
as they go, as we observe them now conveying their produce into
town by carts, whereas formerly files of them might be seen trudging
over rough, steep and circuitous paths leading to the town, each man
loaded with a couple of baskets slung on a pole and carried over the
shoulder.   The extension of water communication inland will also, we
trust, be attended to in time, not only on account of the drainage of waste
lands, but as affording a cheap means of conveying produce to town."

The following is the statement of the Excise Farm, from 1826 to
1843-44.   It includes the Opium and Spirit Farms, and small amounts
for Serih (about \$100 a month) Pawn-brokers (about \$30 a month)
the two markets at Teluk Ayer and Kampong Glam (about \$80 a
month) and Toddy and Ganja (about \$20 a month).

1826-27	Excise Farms,	per month,	Drs.	3,540
1827-28	Do.	do.	„	3,668
1828-29	Do.	do.	„	4,613
1829-30	Do.	do.	„	3,718
1830-31	Do.	do.	„	7,042
1831-32	Do.	do.	„	6,672
1832-33	Do.	do.	„	7,113
1833-34	Do.	do.	„	7,470
1834-35	Do.	do.	„	8,970
1835-36	Do.	do.	„	9,031
1836-37	Do.	do.	„	8,556
1837-38	Do.	do.	„	8,298
1838-39	Do.	do.	„	8,429
1839-40	Do.	do.	„	7,908
1840-41	Do.	do.	„	10,356
1841-42	Do.	do.	„	12,034
1842-43	Do.	do.	„	12,100
1843-44	Do.	do.	„	15,050

In June, a fire of a serious nature occurred, which at one time it
was feared would have laid a considerable part of the town in ashes.
It broke out in Lorong Teluk in the early part of the day, and there
was fortunately little wind at the time.   A great deal was said about
the necessity for a fire brigade of some kind, or rules and regulations
for similar occasions, and the paper made the following remarks:—" It
is really wonderful that fires of a most destructive and extensive nature
do not more frequently happen in Singapore.   There are such a
number of old wooden houses in Singapore, and the habits of the
natives in their use of fire are so extremely careless, that it is very
surprising that we have not a weekly conflagration.   The streets
and houses are crowded and connected with each other in such a
manner that were a fire to reach any height, the whole town would
be almost sure to go.   The immense quantities of goods stored in the
godowns of both European and Native merchants would cause the loss
in such an event to be immense, and the consideration of these things,
and also of the loss of life which would very probably ensue amongst the
crowded population, seem to call for some measures being adopted for
preventing them as far as possible."

Another fire, which destroyed eighteen shops, occurred in Teluk
Ayer in September.

There were long advertisements in the paper this year of lotteries in Calcutta, for which the tickets were Rs. 50, and the highest prize was Rs. 20,000. Another was for Rs. 100,000 with tickets of Rs. 100.

The total number of square-rigged vessels coming into Singapore in 1842-43 was 870, being 286,351 tons, and 2,490 native vessels of the tonnage of 69,268 tons—a considerable increase in each case over the preceding year.

In July, a man was killed by a tiger about a mile behind the Sepoy lines. The body of his dog was first found, then one of his bangles which had dropped from his arm, and, lastly, the remains of the man, partly devoured. At the same place bones and other remains of human bodies were found, from which it was judged that no less than ten persons must have been destroyed at that spot by the tiger. A number of Convicts, under the direction of Captain Stevenson, went on the look out for the brute, and it was confidently expected that they would be able to destroy him, but they did not meet it.

The paper in August spoke of the loss of life by tigers, and its consequent effects, as follows:—

"The head and shoulders of a man who had been killed by a tiger were brought to the Police Office on Monday last. They were found in Bukit Timah road, about three miles from town. A tiger is at present prowling about in the cocoa-nut plantations in Siglap District to the no small apprehension of the owners. We are concerned to learn that the destruction of human life by tigers has been fearfully on the increase lately, so much so indeed that the gambier and pepper planters who have hitherto thought it for their interest to affect to discredit the accounts of the ravages, and did all they could to conceal the deaths from this source, have at last been forced to admit the existence of this evil in its fullest extent, and to take steps to bring the subject to the notice of Government. We are informed that a deputation of Chinese planters waited upon the Resident Councillor on Saturday. We have conversed with a Chinese who is largely concerned in the gambier and pepper trade, and he states that to so great a height has the dread caused by the increased destruction of the coolies by tigers risen, that a number of plantations have been abandoned solely on account of the numerous deaths therein from tigers. Formerly the Chinese in town who make advances to the cultivators used to visit the plantations occasionally for the purpose of looking after their interest, but now they shudder at the thought of venturing into the jungle, and are forced to trust altogether to the honesty of their debtors. The value of these plantations has naturally decreased, in one case from $300 to $25 ; the reason is to be found in the circumstance that a number of coolies had been taken off by tigers, and that in consequence the plantation had got a bad name, and it would have been extremely difficult for the purchaser to procure labourers to live upon it. The rapid increase of the tigers is ascribed to the reduction of the Government reward which formerly used to be paid for every tiger brought in, and without the prospect of which the men are unwilling to take the trouble and risk of entrapping them. The trouble is not so slight as might be supposed, as the construction of a pit, in the proper manner, fully occupies a man for a month.

There are usually so many persons engaged in the capture and destruction of a tiger that, when the present reward of fifty dollars is divided amongst them, the share of each is exceedingly small. The one hundred dollars, which used to be given, (although even it was inadequate) yet, of course, formed an object of more importa ce in their eyes and held out some incentive to exertion. The low price of gambier and pepper has, together with a dread caused by the tigers, produced a great despondency on the part of the planters, and should any but the most favourable and liberal measures in connection with the sale of the lands under the late regulations be pursued towards them, we may expect to see them throw up the cultivation altogether, and it is impossible to contemplate without most serious apprehension the results which this would produce. The many thousands of Chinese coolies who are at present employed in these plantations would be deprived of work, and most undoubtedly would endeavour to gain a dishonest livelihood by sallying forth at night from their coverts in the jungle, and robbing in the neighbourhood of the town Against an irruption of this kind, the police would be powerless, and even though the military were to be availed of, the disparity in numbers and other circumstances would render the issue extremely doubtful. The reward ought to be raised to its former rate or even higher, and the gambier planters ought to be encouraged to make traps in the vicinity of their plantations as numerously as possible. It has been suggested to us that amongst the convicts there are a number of expert tiger hunters, who would be induced to hunt them, if they were promised a ticket of leave on p o lucing a certain number of heads; and other rewards might be held out to them which would probably induce them to engage in the pursuit with alacrity."

And in October the paper again wrote:—"The Chinese who live in the jungle, it is known, never think of giving information of the ravages committed by tigers, so that it is only by enquiry that the facts become known. Their feelings of superstition in regard to tigers may perhaps be one cause of this, for we have been informed that they believe that when a person is killed by a tiger, his *hantu* or ghost becomes a slave to the beast, and attends upon it; that the spirit acts the part of a jackal as it were, and leads the tiger to his prey, and so thoroughly subservient does the poor ghost become to his tigerish master, that he often brings the tiger to the presence of his wife and children, and calmly sees them devoured before his ghostly face. The old *payongs* or umbrellas which may often be seen stuck on the tops of newly made graves are intended to mark the spot where a tiger-slain body is deposited, but from what motive they are placed there we have not been able to learn. That the general belief as to the extent of the deaths caused by tigers and their prevalence on the island is not based on false grounds, we can attest, having made considerable enquiry on the subject. We are informed on the best authority that in one district between Bukit Timah and the old Straits, six persons on an average are every month carried off from the gambier plantations, and that not one of these cases is ever made known to the authorities. Lately in the Kallang district a cow, which was grazing at no great distance from a house on one of the large plantations, was attacked by a tiger which carried it off. On Monday morning the body of a Chinaman was brought to the Police Office having been found at a short distance beyond the Sepoy lines near the road leading to New Harbour; the body was quite fresh and apparently newly killed, the companion of this man who had gone with him into the jungle has not since appeared, so that it may be concluded that the tiger had also killed him, and carried away the body to his lair."

In November what was called the first tiger hunt took place. There were three letters written to the *Free Press* about it, at different times, and the following account is a mixture of the three, consisting of sentences from the various letters, the names of the persons alluded to being now added in brackets, one of the three writers, who is still alive, having made a memorandum of their names. Information was received in town that a tiger had been caught in a trap in the jungle on the left of Bukit Timah Road near the third mile stone, not far from the present Botanical Gardens. In a few minutes vehicles of every description went conveying Europeans from town. The tiger was in a pit, ascertained afterwards to be 24 feet deep. The mouth was closed with heavy logs, through which the tiger was seen lying at the bottom in about two feet of water. He had evidently made several attempts to spring out of the pit. "There was considerable excitement, and our chief police Magistrate (Major Low) forgot to cap his gun; and our chief surveyor (Mr. J. T. Thomson) fired away his ramrod. The tiger received the first fire with sovereign contempt, the second produced a growl, and after allowing the smoke to clear, he was seen from the marks of blood to be evidently badly wounded. As he did not move, a dapper-little man (Mr. W. H. Read) thought it might be dead, and got a long bamboo, which was lying near, and gave him a prod. There was a terrible roar, and a great stampede of nearly all the sportsmen, helter-skelter through the brushwood in all directions. The tiger made a double spring at the side, and then at the mouth of the pit, and its fore-claws reached to within a foot and a half of the top, when Dr. Oxley, who with Mr. Read and one or two others had stood his ground, fired both barrels down its throat and it fell back dead, never moving again." Mr. Charles Dyce wrote that he had been accustomed to tiger hunting in India, but the same mode could not be adopted in Singapore, the jungle being of a different character; indeed the only plan likely to be successful was by traps. He said it was to be regretted that the local government had not taken some pains to prove this to the cultivators, as many lives might have been spared. As soon as all was over, Mr. W. R. George offered to act as guide by a near cut to the Bukit Timah Road, where the carriages had been left. After following him for several miles, up hill and down dale, they found themselves at Tanglin Road with two miles to walk home, under a very hot sun. They consoled themselves by saying that they had seen more of the interior of the island than any of them had ever seen before. Their only regret was the discovery that their guide had left before the termination of the walk, several of them being anxious to *thank* him for his exertions.

In the same week the paper said:—"On Tuesday evening, a Chinaman, while engaged in constructing a tiger pit at the back of Mr. Ballestier's sugar plantation, was pounced upon by a tiger, who, after killing him and sucking the blood, walked into the jungle leaving the body behind. We suppose the tiger knowing the object of the Chinaman's labours took this opportunity of giving a striking manifestation of his profound disapproval of all such latent and unfair methods of taking an enemy at disadvantage."

The same paper contains an account of the stranding of H. M. S. *Samarang* in Sarawak river, and her being raised, after she had fallen over and filled, by Captain Belcher. The manner in which this was done is to be found in English works on seamanship to this day.

It was proposed to start a public library by subscriptions, as the want of it was much felt, and a prospectus, printed at length in the paper of the 24th August, was circulated.

In September, Mr. Thomas Dunman first entered the Police Force, and the paper mentioned it in these terms:—"The Government have appointed Mr. T. Dunman to the Office of Deputy Magistrate and Superintendent of Police. From Mr. Dunman's activity and intimate acquaintance with the manners and habits of the natives, we anticipate that he will be able to introduce a more efficient system of Police, especially if he is allowed, as we hope he will be, to devote his time exclusively to this office. Although we cannot expect to see crime put an end to, yet we have no doubt that with an improved police, and an able and active Deputy Magistrate, much will be done."

Mr. Dunman, afterwards one of the most widely known residents of Singapore, was a clerk in Martin Dyce & Co., and was not one of the covenanted service. It turned out to be a most fortunate choice, and the police, which had been a very inefficient body, was, by his exertions, made efficient, and it has never been the same again since Mr. Dunman resigned in 1871. The office was a very responsible one, involving hard work and active attention by day and night. There had been no proper police, and gang robberies had been very prevalent, so the European Mercantile community had sent strong remonstrances to Calcutta, and the Government there was forced to pay attention to the matter, and consented to the appointment, but in a very grudging way. Mr. Dunman soon put the police into a state of discipline, gang robbery was put down, and the country roads became safe. He was a man of much delicacy of feeling and benevolent disposition. Mr. Thomson in his book "Sequel to Life in the Far East" in speaking of the uncovenanted officers of the East India Company's service, says "It was Congalton who swept the Malay waters of pirates; it was Dunman who first gave security to households in Singapore by raising and training an efficient police force; and it was Coleman who laid out the city of Singapore in the expansive and well arranged plan admired by strangers." And in other books Mr. Dunman's work is spoken of in a similar way.

In the early days of Singapore, and before then, no Englishman had a right to land in India, without an authority from the Court of Directors in the India House at Leadenhall Street. All those in the service of the Company for Civil or Military employment went out under a bond or covenant for a term of service, and were called covenanted servants. So that Europeans in India became divided into two classes—covenanted, and free. A free trader meant the ship of a private merchant, such as London, Liverpool, or Glasgow. A free merchant meant a private European settled in India; and a free settler meant a private planter. Thus all Europeans were bond or free, and the "bond" had all the good things for themselves. A good deal on this subject, and the disadvantages it caused to the general good are to be found in Mr. Thomson's books. The amusing letters referred to in page 197 of this book, have been found, after that page was printed, set out at length at pages 22 to 28 of the "Sequel to Glimpses at Life in the Far East," including that of Mr. William Scott, afterwards Scott of Raeburn and of Lessurden in Roxburghshire, and of James Scott, the uncle of the novelist.

The appointment of Mr. Dunman was therefore unusual, taken as he was from a mercantile office into the service. One secret of his success, no doubt, arose from this, as he was known and liked in the place among all classes of the community, European and native, who were willing to give him information and assistance. They looked upon him as a friend, and not as a military martinet. They never saw him in a uniform and spurs. His time was not spent in sitting in an office under a punkah, answering frivolous enquiries and minutes about petty police details, as in the present day, but in going about the town and country. A good deal of his time was however, taken up by sitting as a Police Magistrate, which he was made in 1844; but it was afterwards stopped, as it engaged too much of his time. One morning a gentleman went to him, and complained that he had met him driving up Orchard Road late at night without lights, and Tom Dunman admitted that it was not the right thing, but he took care to drive carefully, and his object was to see whether the police at the station were looking out, and that if he had lights it defeated his object. He did not spend all day in office and all night in bed, and it was no unusual thing, especially if there was any feeling of insecurity about, to meet him the same night in widely different directions. He was not unfrequently out at four in the morning, and home at midnight.

If anything occurred that required consideration or explanation, he would drive over to the public office where the Court is now, and walk into the room of the Resident Councillor, Mr. Church or Colonel Macpherson, and talk it over. No time wasted on argumentative minutes. He was thoroughly trusted by the heads of the Chinese, and of the secret societies, who knew they could trust him not to divulge the sources of his information. One of his successors did so on one occasion, and it was fatal ever afterwards to one source of doing good police work. All through the place there was the feeling that the police were the friends of orderly people, and therefore had their ready support and countenance. A police force, especially in the Straits, that tries to assert its own importance and hectors and worries the people, may be able to make a fine show on a parade, but misses one of its first duties, and is a hindrance and annoyance to the community. Mr. Dunman's police showed that it is possible to be on good terms with the bulk of the people, and to do the work in a way that enlists the sympathy of those whose interests they are employed to protect. There was an *esprit-de-corps* in the force that has not continued under military officers, and the men worked to please Mr Dunman, because they knew he took an interest in them and their belongings. He might be seen in the evenings in the stations, where he had a night class for learning to read and write, as a man could not be promoted to corporal until he could write. The Malay sergeant-majors in Mr. Dunman's time occupied a very good position among their own people, and were respected, and respected themselves in consequence. Men of good class joined the police under such system, it is not so now. The secret seems to be that to make a good working police in such a cosmopolitan place, it is desirable to appoint a man who has had the opportunity to learn the manners and habits of the natives, and who is known to them, not as a government official, but as one who has an interest in the place. A military officer from some distant place, or a police officer from some other country where circumstances are very different, does not readily appreciate the nature of the work; and does not gain the co-operation of those around him, in obtaining information which others desire to conceal.

For many years Mr. Dunman practically controlled the police, but the Resident Councillor was, ex-officio, Commissioner. In 1856 strong opinions were expressed that the duties of Commissioner of Police should not be hampered with Magistrate's work and duty in the Resident Councillor's office, as they were incompatible with each other. Governor Blundell held the same view and sanction was given by the Governor-General in Council from Calcutta to make the office of Commissioner of Police a separate and distinct appointment, and it was conferred on Mr. Dunman whose long experience in police matters peculiarly qualified him for the situation; and it was said by the paper at the time to be a rare example at that time of the right man in the right place.

On 1st June, 1857, the Resident Councillor ceased to hold the office, and Mr. Dunman was made Commissioner on a salary of Rs 1,000 a month, and Mr. George W. Earl, who was practising as a lawyer in High Street, was made Magistrate. Mr. Dunman then gave his whole time to the Police, and the *Free Press* remarked that this speedily made another marked improvement in the force. On 20th January, 1851, he received his final appointment as Superintendent of Police for Singapore, which the paper remarked was a very tardy act of justice which had been repeatedly demanded by the community.

Mr Dunman had a large cocoa-nut plantation, some 400 acres, at Tanjong Katong, where he built his own house, and three bungalows on the seashore, the first of the Tanjong Katong waterside houses for honeymoons and holidays, and they were not added to for many years. Now the whole beach is overrun with them, and the land divided and sub-divided to such an extent and built over that the enjoyment is gone. References to his planting coffee and cocoa-nuts are to be found in volume 4 of Logan's Journal at pages 104 and 141. He had a piece of land at the north east corner of Brass Bassa Road and Victoria Street, known as Dunman's Corner, and a road in Kampong Kapor was named after him, while the large open space behind the present Magistrates' Courts was called Dunman's Green, as he got it filled up when it was a disagreeable swamp opposite the Police Station and Magistrate's Court, then on the opposite side of the road, where the present Central Police Station now is. In Mr. Read's book at page 165 is an account of "A Practical Joke," which was only one of many of Mr. Dunman's little amusements in that way. He is well described in it as a very popular personage and a general favourite.

Mr. Dunman received the commendation of the Governor-General in Council for his services during the Chinese riots in May, 1854, and Governor Butterworth gave him a sword for the same reason. He resigned in 1871, and after remaining four years in Singapore, looking after his plantation at Tanjong Katong. retired to England, and died at Bournemouth on 6th October, 1887, 73 years of age. He had married, as has been said on page 189, one of the daughters of Mr. T. O. Crane, a grand-daughter of Dr. d'Almeida; and had a number of children who were some of the most popular young people of Singapore.

The following notice was advertised by Government in September. It was no doubt one of the first examples of Mr. Dunman's good sense, as there had been numerous gang robberies near the town, by bodies of fifty and sixty men.

The idea of frightening away robbers by firing blank cartridge after sunset is as futile as it is absurd, and calculated to annoy the community.

The police become indifferent to alarms thus given. or their attention is distracted thereby, from the general duties of their station.

The practice therefore of discharging fire arms, letting off crackers, and beating of gongs during the night. is hereby strictly prohibited.

All persons who shall hereafter be found transgressing this Order shall be prosecuted.

W. J. BUTTERWORTH,
Governor.

In October, it was proposed to abolish the Grand Jury, its abolition was condemned by the community then as it was afterwards in 1873, when it was abolished.

The first mention we have found of fortifying Singapore occurs in the *Free Press* of the 9th November in this year, and is as follows :—

" In an article which we extract from the Calcutta *Englishman*, we observe our contemporary deprecates the idea of fortifying Hongkong, as calculated to inspire alarm and dread into the minds of the Chinese, and he recommends that, instead. Singapore should be fortified, which, he observes, could give no just offence to any Power, and would make Singapore what it ought to be in time of war, the key of the Eastern Seas, and the rendezvous of fleets and convoys. He adds that at present it could not resist a single frigate. Without entering upon the point mooted by the *Englishman* as to the policy of fortifying Hongkong, we are sorry to inform him that the measure he proposes in lieu of it, is, unfortunately, impracticable.

"The town is so placed that no amount of expenditure would make it even tolerably secure, much less afford any shelter or protection to the shipping. A single ship of war could with ease and safety lay the town in ruins, and no fortifications can be constructed so as to completely prevent this. The only effectual method of preserving the town of Singapore in the event of its being threatened by a hostile force would be by stationing a sufficient number of men-of-war for its protection. We sincerely hope, however, that no occasion may ever arise to make it necessary to take any such precautions, but that Singapore may continue to be, as heretofore, a place devoted to commerce and the medium of diffusing the manufactures of civilised and peaceful Europe amongst the surrounding nations, and that, as she has hitherto been only the scene of peaceable and unwarlike commerce, so she may long remain unvisited by the horrors and miseries of wars."

The bridges and roads were in very bad condition at this time, and the paper was full of complaints, so the Sheriff called a public meeting of the inhabitants to express a general opinion upon the subject and to memorialize the Government.

The paper spoke of the state of affairs as follows:—"The roads are daily becoming more impassable, so that in the course of another fortnight, especially if the present rainy weather continues they will be quite useless. Bridges are giving way in all directions, and on several roads all passage is prevented. Meanwhile the Superintendent of Roads pursues his operations on the Government hill heedless alike of the complaints and sufferings of the public, and regardless of all suggestions that he should mend his ways. It would seem, too, as if the works on the hill were destined to be of some duration, as we observed on Sunday that the mound, on the construction of which the convicts have been employed for several weeks past, had given way in one place, and they have ever since been employed in filling up the gap. If the country roads are not repaired speedily we would advise the assessment payers to stop the supplies, as really we cannot suppose that Government would attempt to enforce the collection of funds for a purpose to which they are not applied."

In November, Messrs. Boustead, Schwabe & Co. issued a notice that they had opened a house in China in connection with Messrs. Butler, Sykes & Co., in Manila, and Messrs. Sykes, Schwabe & Co., in Liverpool. The partners in their several establishments continuing as before:—Mr. Edward Boustead, managing in China, Mr. Benjamin Butler at Manila, Mr. Gustav Christian Schwabe at Liverpool, and Mr. Adam Sykes at Singapore.

St. Andrew's Day was celebrated by a dinner, of which the following was an account:—"On Thursday, the 30th November, the sons of St. Andrew assembled in great force at Dutronquoy's to drink punch in honour of their patron Saint. We counted some 75 gentlemen at table, which is not so bad for Singapore, and we should decidedly say from the circumstance that old 'Andrew' was *looking up*.—Dr. Montgomerie was in the chair, and Mr. William Napier, Croupier. Dr. Montgomerie in his usual able manner proposed the following toasts:—The Queen, the Pious Memory of St. Andrew, the

Navy (acknowledged by the Hon'ble Captain Hastings), the Governor and the land we live in, our guests, the President of the United States (acknowledged by Mr. Balestier). Mr. William Napier, with an appropriate speech—the "Land o' Cakes," the Army (acknowledged by Captain Philpot), Memory of Burns and Scott, King of the French (acknowledged by Mr. Chaigneau). Memory of Raffles, &c. Mr. M. F. Davidson,—Memory of Wallace and Bruce. Mr. G. G. Nicol,—The Kirk of Scotland. Mr. Charles Dyce,—Mrs. Butterworth and the ladies. Many excellent songs were sung. We left the company busy brewing the mountain dew into punch, and listening to the enlivening strains of the beautiful band of the 4th Regiment which was kindly allowed to attend the party."

The following curious account of a discovery of old cannon balls in Johore appeared in the newspaper:—

"A number of iron and stone cannon balls to the amount of 240 were, a few days since, discovered at Johore buried about eight feet in the ground. We have seen two of these balls, and to judge from the appearance of the iron one, it must have been laid a long time in the ground, being much corroded; this ball is about 13½ inches or thereby in circumference, the stone one about 16½ inches. How these balls found their way to Johore is a matter of considerable uncertainty, but the most probable conjecture seems to be that they had been brought there by some foreign invader. We find that in 1608 the town of Johore was attacked and burnt by the Portuguese, who indeed had long before visited Johore in a hostile manner, as about the year 1538, Paul de Gama attacked it but was defeated and slain by the Lacsamana, and shortly afterwards Don Estevan de Gama took and plundered the town. Between the years 1588 and 1606, the Dutch visited Johore, and entered into a friendly treaty with the Rajah. It is very likely that the Dutch on this occasion presented the Malays with cannons and ammunition, which the latter no doubt would be eager to acquire, considering that they were in a constant state of warfare with the Portuguese, who had driven them from Malacca. An old iron cannon which, we believe, has long been an object of great reverence amongst the Malays, and which was lying on a hill near the former capital of Johore, has been within these few days sent by his Highness the Tomungong to the authorities here. It is of very ancient appearance and much broken at the mouth, so that it may have very likely burst at some period in its history. On it are the letters E. R. with a large rose between them. This would seem to prove that it was of English manufacture, probably of the time of Queen Elizabeth, but how it found its way to Johore, unless through the agency of the Portuguese or Dutch, we cannot conjecture. The iron ball above alluded to fits this gun, and they may have both been brought at the same time."

Bukit Timah was first made accessible at the end of this year, and the following was written about it at the time:—"The other day we paid a visit to Bukit Timah, which, thanks to the labours of the Superintendent of Roads, is now accessible by a good carriage-way reaching to the top of the hill, where Captain Stevenson has likewise constructed a small hut, provided with table and benches for the accommodation of visitors. We were quite delighted with the view which is obtained from this place. The hill would afford capital sites for two or three bungalows, and would, we think, be an excellent sanitarium, there being a decided change of temperature from the town. It is, of course, not so cold as the great hill in Penang, but that is almost too violent and sudden a change from the excessive heat of the plain, while the climate of Bukit Timah, though not sufficient to make the invalid shiver and seek refuge beneath a couple of blankets like the Penang Hill, is perceptibly cooler and fresher than the plain, producing an agreeable exhiliration of spirits. The prospect, too, regarding which nothing appears ever to have been said, is nearly if not quite equal to Penang, though differing considerably in its features. Instead of the large extent of cultivation which composes the foreground of the Penang view with its trim rows of nutmegs and other fruit trees, dark masses of primeval forest stretch away from Bukit Timah on every side. But the landscape is altogether very varied and presents a rare collection of grand and pleasing forms. To the south we have at our feet a considerable part of the island of Singapore composed of small hills mostly covered with dense jungle, though near the town cultivation usurps its place. In the middle distance, the town of Singapore stretches itself along the bay, which is crowded with shipping, while in the far distance, are seen the blue hills of Battam, and the cloud-crested peak of Bintang. On the west, numerous islands are scattered over the still waters of the Straits. the Carimons are visible at a greater distance, and further still we have a faint view of the coast of Sumatra. The view to the North is composed of one continuous mass of dark forest reaching to the distant hills of Johore. So narrow is the channel which separates the island from the mainland in this direction, that nowhere is it distinguishable save at one place where a small part of its water is seen glittering amid the surrounding woods, like some small inland lake. The entrance to the sea of China is visible to the East Such are some of the most noticeable views, and taken together they are well worthy of admiration, and could not fail of rendering Bukit Timah a most desirable and agreeable place of residence for the invalids of Singapore, were it not that the dwellers on the hill would be exposed to the visitations of tigers, which abound in the neighbourhood, and are occasionally seen or heard on the hill itself. One thing that strikes a person very forcibly in surveying the island from this height is the small amount of cleared and cultivated ground compared with that still in jungle. It is only in the immediate vicinity of the town that there appears any proper clearing, and this shows but a very insignificant part of the whole island. Judging from what has hitherto been done, we should say that many years must elapse before the island will be cleared, and we should much doubt whether the whole of it will ever be so."

At this time, photography first found its way to Singapore, as appears from the following advertisement; which reads quaintly now:—

Mr. G. Dutronquoy respectfully informs the ladies and gentlemen at Singapore, that he is complete master of the newly invented and late imported Daguerreotype. Ladies and Gentlemen who may honour Mr. Datronquoy with a sitting can have their likenesses taken in the astonishing short space of two minutes. The portraits are free from all blemish and are in every respect perfect likenesses. A Lady and gentleman can be placed together in one picture and both are taken at the same time entirely shaded from the effects of the sun. The price of one portrait is ten dollars, both taken in one picture is fifteen dollars. One day's notice will be required.

London Hotel, 4th December, 1843.

The Rev. Samuel Dyer of the London Missionary Society died at Macao on the 24th November. He left England and came to the Straits in 1827, where he was for sixteen years at Penang, Malacca, and Singapore. He compiled vocabularies of Chinese, and made punches and matrices for casting two founts of Chinese type. A great proportion of the Chinese characters usually met with in the generally used Chinese works in later years were cast from them.

The *Free Press* contained a notice of the death of Mr. F. G. Bernard "formerly of Singapore" at Batavia on the 19th December.

Two of the Company's small gun-boats were lost in August. The *Pearl* was wrecked near Malacca, and the *Diamond* went to try to save her stores, &c. On her return to Singapore off Pulo Midan, in a squall, the mainsail could not be lowered as the ropes jammed, and the boat went down. After being in the water for twelve hours, holding on to floating wreck, a Malacca boat picked up sixteen of the crew, and another boat seven more, but the gunner, serang, and nine sailors of the *Diamond* were drowned.

The first bridge across the river was of wood joining North and South Bridge Road where Elgin Bridge is now. This was built about 1822. The second was built in 1840 by Mr. Coleman, of brick work, joining Hill Street and New Bridge Road, and was called after him. The first bridge became dilapidated and was removed in 1843. The Government having land to sell near Coleman Bridge objected to rebuilding the lower bridge, and on a deputation going to see Governor Butterworth about it he said, in his usual inflated style, that they might make up their minds that the bridge would not be made, as he was a determined man. The community who went chiefly on foot in those days objected to having to walk round such an unnecessary distance to cross the river, and it led to public meetings and correspondence. Some time afterwards it was found that in grants of land in that part of the town it had been agreed by Government to maintain a bridge. So it was built and was called Elgin Bridge after the Governor-General of India. The story of the dispute is told in Mr. Read's book.

At this time, the firm of Middletons, Blundell and Co., commenced business. The four partners were Charles, James, and Alfred Middleton in Liverpool, and William Blundell in Singapore. Charles Hercules Harrison was then a clerk, and in 1850 became a partner. In 1851 the name was changed to Middletons and Co., the partners being the same as before. In 1852 the clerks were William Graham Kerr, and John Haffenden. In 1854 Charles Middleton left the firm. In 1860 the name was changed to Middleton, Harrison and Co., the partners then being Alfred Middleton and C. H. Harrison.

It was in this year that Dr. Montgomery left Singapore. It has been mentioned on page 60 that he belonged to the Bengal establishment, and came to Singapore as Assistant Surgeon with the Bengal Native Infantry in 1819, and, on page 56, that he was then spoken of by Colonel Farquhar as a very young man who would be left in charge of the Settlement if anything occurred to himself. He was one of the first Magistrates appointed by Raffles, and his name has been very frequently mentioned in this book. In a paper by Dr. T. Oxley, at page 22 of Volume 1 of Logan's Journal, he says that the first notice of gutta percha seems to have been by Dr. Montgomerie in a letter to the Bengal Medical Board in 1843, in which he recommended it as likely to prove useful for surgical purposes. Dr. d'Almeida took some in that year to London, and gave it to the Royal Society of Arts, but no notice was taken of it, beyond acknowledging the receipt. During his long residence in Singapore, from 1819 to 1843, Dr. Montgomerie entered extensively and zealously into agricultural pursuits, which did not prove remunerative. The river, 2¾ miles from town, divided his estate, now known as Woodsville, from Mr. Balestier, and he had a large water-wheel and mill a few hundred yards up the stream from the bridge in Serangoon Road, which was called Montgomerie's Bridge. He built the small house now called Woodsville Cottage, and lived there. Mr. R. C. Woods afterwards purchased the plantation and called it after himself. Dr. Montgomerie had 510 nutmeg trees in 1848, but the principal cultivation was sugar, which he pursued very energetically, and engaged in the manufacture on a considerable scale for a number of years, but had to relinquish it with great loss. He was a brother of Major-General Sir P. Montgomerie, K.C.B., of the Madras Artillery, who highly distinguished himself in the China Expedition. In a Scotch newspaper in 1845, there is an account of a meeting of the Provost, Magistrates and Town Council of Irvine, when an address was presented to the two brothers, in which it was said that Dr. Montgomerie, who had been long abroad, had acquired an equal celebrity in the medical profession, as his brother, the colonel, had in a military capacity. After being some years at home on furlough, Dr. Montgomerie went to Bengal, where he was appointed Garrison Surgeon at Fort William. In the war with Burmah he accompanied the troops as Superintendent Surgeon, and received the marked approval of Government. He died from an attack of cholera at Barrackpore, in India, on 21st March, 1856.

At the time of his death the *Free Press*, in answer to some remarks as to the discovery of gutta percha in the London *Morning Hearld* gave the correct version of it as follows:—

"The long and meritorious services of Dr. Montgomerie would alone have entitled his son to a place in the list of nominations to the military service of the Honourable Company, and the friend who thus asserts his title to a discovery which probably the doctor himself does not claim, can scarcely be considered as having acted wisely. The facts of the case, as they appear to us after close examination, are as follows:—The first discoverers of the properties of the gutta were, undoubtedly, the Jakuns, or inland tribes of the Malay Peninsula, who have been in the habit of moulding it into handles for their chopping-knives, swords, and krisses from time immemorial; and the first to introduce it to the notice of Europeans was a Malay of Singapore, who, in the year 1842, commenced manufacturing riding-whips of gutta, which had all the tough and elastic properties for which the *shamboks* or rhinoceros-hide whips of South Africa are so celebrated. These were made up in bundles of twenty each, and sold in considerable number, chiefly to commanders of ships going home, and it is stated that some of them were exhibited in a shop-window in Oxford Street, London, as early as 1843. Of course, under these circumstances, the material could scarcely fail of coming under the notice of European residents here, and in the early part of 1843, Dr. Montgomerie noticed it as likely to prove useful for surgical purposes in a letter to the Bengal Medical Board; and in July, 1843, the Calcutta *Englishman* contained an account of a remarkable variety of caoutchouc, sent from Singapore by Dr. W. Montgomerie, the Senior Surgeon, with a detail of its properties and probable uses, which was known as gutta percha or gutta tuban. It excited a great deal of attention. But the first to introduce it to the notice of scientific men at home was Dr. Almeida, also an old resident in this Settlement, who took with him some specimens, both raw and manufactured, when leaving for England in the latter part of 1842. A portion of this was presented to the Royal Asiatic Society of London in April of the following year, and it was submitted to the inspection of Dr. Royle, a high authority on raw produce, but with no other result than a letter of thanks from the Secretary of the Society to the donor. Subsequently, in 1845, Dr. Montgomerie sent some specimens to the London Society of Arts. These were taken in hand by Mr. Solly (also a leading member of the Asiatic Society), by whom its singular and valuable properties were ascertained and developed, and the natural result was that the gold medal of the Society was given to Dr. Montgomerie, who had presented it. It is singular that the properties for which the gutta was most admired by the aborigines of this Peninsula, namely its applicability for handles to cutting instruments, from the firm grip that its solid yet slightly elastic principal gives to the holder, seems never to have been developed in Europe, although cavalry sabres and other weapons of the kind, would be much improved by its use." The insulation of submarine cables was an unknown quantity when that was written. A few years afterwards Logan's Journal, published in 1847, continued an article on *Gutta Percha*, its botanical description and economic uses, by Dr. Oxley, who claimed to be the discoverer of one of its most important applications, which led to a controversy that has existed ever since. The *Free Press* remarked about it:—"Our opinion is that both Dr. Little and Dr. Oxley are discoverers, and the only advantage on Dr. Oxley's side consists in his having first promulgated the discovery to the world. It is probable, however, that if he has been the first to announce it, the merit of the application will generally be given to him. This ought to incite Dr. Little, and all other discoverers, not to lose any time in future in publishing their discoveries, else they may find themselves anticipated by others equally ingenious and more prompt in giving them publicity.

"It was very surprising that such a useful substance as gutta should have remained so long unnoticed, as it appeared that it had long been in some limited use by the natives in these parts. Doctor

Montgomerie, who first introduced it to the notice of Europeans, stated that so far back as 1822, he had obtained the name of it, at Singapore, while making inquiries relative to caoutchouc. He had some specimens brought to him, particularly one called *gutta girek*, and was told that there was another variety called *gutta percha* and sometimes *gutta tuban;* which was said to be harder than the *gutta girek*; but none was brought to him at that time, and he lost sight of the subject, having returned to the Bengal presidency. On his return to the Straits, he observed at Singapore, in 1842, the handle of a *parang* in the hands of a Malay wood-cutter made of a substance which appeared quite new to him. This he found was *gutta percha*, and it could be easily moulded into any form by simply dipping it in hot water, while on cooling it regained unchanged its original hardness and rigidity. Dr. Montgomerie made several experiments which sufficed to convince him of the exceeding value of the substance, but he was prevented by bad health from prosecuting the enquiry as he wished. He, however, sent some of it to the Bengal Medical Board strongly recommending its adoption for the formation of many surgical instruments, and it seemed to have met the approval of the Board, though whether they made any experiments on it did not appear. Dr. Montgomerie also sent some to the Society of Arts, London, for investigation and analysis, for which he was awarded the Society's gold medal. The Doctor likewise ascertained from Bugis traders that it grew at Coti on the South-eastern coast of the island of Borneo, and Mr. Brooke informed him that 'the tree is called *Naito* by the Sarawak people, but that they were not acquainted with the properties of the sap; it attains a considerable size, even as large as six feet diameter; and was plentiful in Sarawak and Borneo.' Dr. Montgomerie suggested that it might be applied in printing for the blind, and also in the formation of embossed maps for that unfortunate class, little thinking of the multitudinous uses to which it was to be applied in a few years."

It is very curious that the same number of the paper which mentioned it, said also in a small paragraph to fill up a column, that a proposal had been made to connect the Channel Islands and Southampton by a submarine telegraph, consisting of one wire by which a bell could be run by the electric current. In 1851, Professor Wheatstone made the first cable with gutta-percha.

The article just mentioned on gutta percha was republished in many periodicals both in India and Europe, and was acknowledged to be the best and most complete description that had then been given. It was then called *Gutta Taban* in Malay. The exportation began in a very small way, but increased very largely in a remarkably short time, as the Malays found there was a demand for it, and it began to come in from Sumatra and Borneo as well as from Johore, Malacca and Pahang. In 1844, one picul and 68 catties only were exported. In 1845, 169 piculs; in 1846, 5,364; in 1847, 9,296 piculs; and in the first seven months of 1848, 6,768 piculs. The whole export, with the exception of 1,000 piculs to the United States, was 21,600 piculs, valued at $274,190. The price began at $8 a picul, rose to $24, and in 1848 was $13. In September, 1853, the *Free Press* said that gutta percha had reached the " enormous price " of $60 a picul. The "enormous price" in 1901 was $700 a picul, but in 1853 sub-marine telegraph cables and bicycle tyres were not in use.

Dr. Montgomerie was succeeded as Senior Surgeon, Straits Settlements in 1846 by a very well known Singaporean, Dr. Thomas Oxley. He had been for about four years in Malacca where he performed the manifold duties of Police Magistrate, Superintendent of Police, Collector of Assessment and Commissioner of the Court of Requests, for which as the *Free Press* remarked, he received the salary of Rs. 200 a month in addition to his allowance as Assistant Surgeon, and in order to take up the duties had left a remunerative practice in Singapore, and a great deal of useful work, especially that of Honorary Secretary of the Raffles Institution. He wrote many scientific papers, some of what are in Logan's Journal; namely, On Gutta Percha (Vol. 1, page 22); On Nutmegs (Vol. 2, page 641 and N. S. Vol. 1, page 127); On Amoks (Vol. 3, page 532); On Zoology (Vol. 3, page 594); and on Botany (Vol. 4, page 436).

Dr. Oxley's name is still well known owing to the land which he bought from Government being known as Oxley's Estate. It was then of little value, and in the jungle; and is now one of the most densely built-on districts near the town. He purchased it on 18th March, from the East India Company for Rs. 2,342-0-3. The area was acres 173.3.18, for ever. It was bounded by River Valley Road, Tank Road, Orchard Road and Grange Road; but it extended along River Valley Road beyond Grange Road so as to include what is now called Moss Bank, which contained about 28 acres. The square now contained in the four roads, and usually called Oxley's Estate, bounded by Grange Road, contains therefore about 145 acres. On the top of the hill stood the house called the Pavilion, still standing, which was built by Mr. George Gorden Nicol, who lived there until he built Chatsworth. Dr. Oxley lived there for many years. Admiral Keppel tells the story of being there at breakfast one morning when they heard the children calling out in a side room in an excited way. On going in to see what it was, the children were seen dancing in great glee backwards and forwards towards a cobra, which was standing erect in the corner spitting at them, which they thought great fun, as they had no idea what it was. Snakes were very common in those days, now they are very rarely seen. Dr. and Mrs. Oxley left Singapore finally for England with five children in the P. and O. Mail on 23rd February, 1857, and he died in England in March, 1886.

Dr. Oxley had a large nutmeg plantation on all the high ground on Oxley Estate, and Mr. G. F. Davidson in his book said: "Dr. Oxley's is by far the finest nutmeg garden on the island. He has spared neither trouble nor expense in bringing his plants forward and has five thousand of the finest nutmeg trees I ever saw. Nothing can be finer than their beautiful position, tasteful outlay and luxuriant foliage."

The cultivation of nutmegs was thought at that time to be a sure road to a speedy fortune, and their failure caused very serious loss and great discomfiture in Singapore. The trees prospered well and paid very largely, when a sudden calamity fell upon them which was ascribed to several widely-differing reasons. As the matter was of very serious consequence to most of the European residents, an attempt has been made to collect some details of the cultivation, and where the plantations were, and of the reasons to which the total failure was attributed.

In August, 1819, Raffles sent from Bencoolen to Colonel Farquhar 125 nutmeg plants, 1,000 nutmeg seeds, and 450 clove plants and seeds which were planted on Fort Canning. The nutmegs prospered and became the means of extending the cultivation in the neighbourhood. The cloves never came to much, as in the three years from 1845 to 1847 only three piculs were produced. In 1848 there were about twenty nutmeg plantations belonging to Europeans, of which the following is an account. The Natives were said to have 7,000 trees in various places.

PROPRIETORS.	No. of TREES.	SITUATION.
A. Guthrie - . -	2,250	Everton, near Spottiswoode Park
Dr. Montgomerie - -	1,800	Duxton, do.
Joaq. d'Almeida - -	700	Raeburn, do.
Dr. Oxley - . -	4,050	Oxley Estate
C. R. Prinsep - . -	6,700	Prinsep's Estate where Government House and Mount Sophia are now.
T. Hewetson - . -	1,515	Mount Elizabeth
C. Carnie - . -	4,370	Cairn Hill, Orchard Road
José d'Almeida - -	1,023	Mount Victoria, Stephen's Road
Dr. M. J. Martin - -	1,530	Institution Hill, River Valley Road
W. W. Willans - -	1,600	Grange Road near Tanglin Barracks
Dr. Montgomerie - -	510	Serangoon Road, third mile Kallang Dale
Sir J. d'Almeida - -	4,000	Bandulia, five miles, Serangoon Road
T. Dunman - . -	1,000	Near Bandulia
G. G. Nicoll - . -	8,000	Sri Menanti, Grange Road, where he built Chatsworth
J. I. Woodford - .	600	Bukit Timah Road, six miles
W. Cuppage - . -	1,250	Orchard Road, right hand side, Emerald Hill, Railway Bridge now
W. Scott - . -	5,200	Scott's Road, Claymore Estate

As to the cause of the simultaneous death of the trees Mr. W. H. Read writes in 1902, referring to this subject; " Nutmegs flourished till George Windsor Earl (I think it was) went in a chartered vessel to the Moluccas to bring a select quantity of plants from there. They were carefully placed in the hold of the vessel, and were sold to the various planters on arrival of the ship in Singapore. After a short stay in the nurseries, they were planted out among the trees, which were already giving magnificent results, and a few months later a disease spread among the plantations. Prinsep, Nicol, d'Almeida and others were the sufferers and the nutmeg was killed out in the Straits. Prinsep's plantation used to yield 22,000 nuts a day, and in six months went down to 2,500, and others in proportion. It was supposed that the rot had been propagated in the gin cases and non-aired hold of the ship, and our own small plantation at Dalvey was wiped out at once. An attempt with sound seed might now succeed." Mr. George Rappa's opinion is that the trees died off because the soil did not extend deep enough, and the roots rotted away in the hard clay underneath it. Mr. H. A. Crane says that after a certain time, when the trees had reached a certain age, about 25 to 30 years, white ants attacked the roots and the stems of the trees, and destroyed them.

END OF VOLUME I.

To face page 310

ABRAHAM SOLOMON.

To face page 240.

VIEW OF THE COURT HOUSE.
[*From an old picture by Begbie, about 1834.*]

An Anecdotal History
Of Old Times . .
In Singapore . . .

(With Portraits and Illustrations)

FROM

The Foundation of the Settlement under the Honourable the
East India Company, on February 6th, 1819,

TO THE

Transfer to the Colonial Office as part of the Colonial
Possessions of the Crown on April 1st, 1867,

BY

CHARLES BURTON BUCKLEY.

IN TWO VOLUMES—VOLUME II.

SINGAPORE :
PRINTED BY FRASER & NEAVE, LIMITED.
1902.

CHAPTER XXXI.

1844.

ALMOST every issue of the weekly paper contained accounts of several deaths by tigers, and the "Tiger Club" was frequently mentioned. The Club killed a large one three miles from town on a gambier plantation about New Year's day. A week after, one of the Native Infantry was killed by a tiger, and the party went out and wounded it, but it escaped in the thick jungle. A day or two after, they disturbed another tiger and two cubs. The Tiger Club gave a reward of $100 to a Chinaman who caught a tiger in a pit where it was shot. Two men in the plantation had been killed by tigers.

Gang robberies were very frequent in the town, large gangs of Chinese attacking shops. The following is an account of such robberies in one paper, and it is only one of many:—"On the night of the 17th January, a most daring robbery was perpetrated in the town by a gang of Chinese. About 10 o'clock a band of between 50 and 60 Chinese armed with muskets, pistols, swords, spears and shields attacked the shop of a money-changer named Mohamed Abdulkader, on Boat Quay. He was sleeping in the verandah outside his shop which was locked, and was awakened by the Chinese beating some rattan shields; then they lighted three or four paper matches and broke open the shop, which they immediately plundered. The robbers wounded two Klings near the shop, and then carried away five bags of money and gold. One of the constables, who (a European, presumably) was going his round with a peon at the time, came on the Chinese while plundering the shop. They immediately knocked the peon down, and fired several blank cartridges at the constable, who, thereupon went to procure assistance, but by the time he succeeded in collecting the guardians of the night and returned to the spot, the robbers could not be overtaken.

"Another robbery took place about two o'clock on the morning of the 23rd January. About forty Chinese attacked the house of a Kling writer named Andry Narrain (adjoining the Hindoo Temple) which they broke open, and about ten of them armed with swords and axes entered the room where the owner was, and, whilst some by threatening signs kept him quiet, others broke open three boxes from which they took $130, and 3½ buncals of gold, which they carried off. One of the inmates of the house was severely wounded on the head and body. The robbers had their faces blackened so that they could not be identified, and they preserved a strict silence. They were two or three peons on the spot, but though they sprung their rattles, no efficient force came till after the robbers had gone away."

The first Chinese Hospital or Poor House had been built from the proceeds of the Government Pork Farm, which had been imposed for that express purpose. The building was finished in 1834, but the Government used it as a Convict Jail, because the Convict lines, that had been commenced before the Poor House, were not finished, and not sufficiently large to contain all the convicts; and the poor were put in an attap bungalow run up for the occasion, to which exception was made. Complaints were also made of the number of sick Chinese who came from the plantations in Rhio and other Dutch places, to take advantage of the hospital, which was not intended for them.

This year saw the commencement of the present Tan Tock Seng's Hospital. The *Free Press* of the year wrote of it thus, beginning on the 25th January:—" We are glad to learn that there is now every chance of a suitable hospital for the reception of diseased and aged Chinese paupers being erected, and what is still more gratifying, chiefly through the means of the Chinese themselves. Cham Chan Sang, a Chinese merchant, who died a few days ago, has by his will bequeathed $2,000 to the hospital, and we understand that a short time ago another wealthy Chinese merchant, Tan Tock Seng, presented $5,000 towards this object. We have no doubt that we shall hear of their example being generally followed by their fellow-countrymen in the Settlement, so that sufficient funds will speedily be obtained. A number of diseased Chinese, lepers and others, frequent almost every street in town, presenting a spectacle which is rarely to be met with, even in towns under a pagan Government, and which is truly disgraceful in a civilised and Christian country, especially one under the government of Englishmen.

" A public meeting of the inhabitants was held on Saturday last to take into consideration a letter which had been received by the Governor from the Bengal Government. This letter is an answer to one from the Governor, enclosing the draft of an Act for the suppression of mendicity and loathsome exposure at Singapore, and relative to the erection of the hospital, for which purpose Tan Tock Seng had offered $5,000. The Deputy-Governor seems to have got the idea that it is merely to please the fastidious " European, and quasi Europeans," that the hospital is to be erected, and he therefore thinks that the Chinese, who are almost the only parties who would be benefited by the hospital, ought not to be made to pay for its support, but that the whole community ought to be taxed for it. We believe that the Chinese would have had no objection that the funds required should be raised by a pork farm, and this tax would have pressed very lightly upon them.

"The monthly expenditure of the hospital might, we understand, be calculated at from $450 to $500 per month, say $6,000 per annum. This sum the Bengal Government seem to think must be raised by means of a new tax or rate, and it was one of the objects of the meeting to show that such a measure would be unnecessary. From official documents it was shewn that there existed a large surplus both on the general revenue and in the Assessment fund, and it appeared to the meeting that, before a new tax was imposed upon the inhabitants, the funds arising from those already existing ought to be exhausted.

"The recommendation of the meeting that the proposed Pauper Hospital and the European Seamen's Hospital should be under one roof would be advantageous in many ways. We sincerely trust that nothing may happen to mar or hinder establishment of the hospital. It has long been required; and, so far back as 1829, called from the Grand Jury a very strong representation."

RESOLUTIONS OF A PUBLIC MEETING HELD AT SINGAPORE, ON SATURDAY, THE 3RD FEBRUARY, 1844.

TAN TOCK SENG IN THE CHAIR.

A letter from the Under Secretary to the Government of Bengal to Colonel Butterworth, C.B., Governor to Prince of Wales' Island, Singapore and Malacca, No. 1244, dated at Fort William, 18th December, 1843, having been read by the Chairman—

1st. It was proposed by E. J. Gilman, seconded by Tan Kim Seng, and unanimously carried:—That it appears to this meeting that the Government of Bengal is under a misconception in supposing that the proposed erection of a Pauper Hospital for the reception of the Chinese is to " please the European and quasi European," portion of the inhabitants, and that the Chinese are indifferent on the subject : that on the contrary it is the opinion of this meeting that the Chinese are, as a body, most anxious that the same should be carried into effect.

2nd. It was proposed by C. Spottiswoode, seconded by T. O. Crane, and unanimously carried :—That it is the opinion of this meeting that the erection of a Pauper Hospital is absolutely necessary, and that the funds for the support of the same should be provided from the General Revenues of the island.

3rd. Proposed by W. Napier, seconded by Syed Omar and unanimously carried:—That it is the opinion of this meeting, that, with reference to the last published Official Statement of the Revenue and Expenditure of this island, any further tax for the purpose of supporting a Pauper Hospital is unnecessary.

4th. Proposed by the Chairman, seconded by M. F. Davidson, and unanimously carried :—That on its being decided that a Pauper Hospital be built, it is desirable that the Executive Government do take measure for the prevention of the importation of sick paupers into the island.

5th. Proposed by C. A. Dyce, seconded by J. Guthrie and unanimously carried :—That funds having been provided for the erection of a European Hospital, it is the opinion of this meeting that it would be expedient and desirable to unite the proposed Pauper and European Hospitals under one roof, as in that event the funds would be amply sufficient to erect a large, convenient, and sightly building, divided into distinct establishments, for Europeans, Chinese, and other Natives of Asia.

6th. Proposed by W. R. George, seconded by W. H. Read, and unanimously carried :— That the proceedings of this meeting be forwarded to the Hon'ble the Governor, with a request that the local Government will afford their countenance and support to the same.

7th. Proposed by the Chairman, seconded by T. Smith and carried unanimously :—That a petition to the Supreme Government embodying the foregoing resolutions be drawn up in English and Chinese, and signed by the inhabitants, and that it be thereafter sent to the Honourable the Governor for transmission to Bengal."

On Monday morning, the 25th July, 1844, the foundation stone of the new Pauper Hospital at Pearl's Hill was laid in the presence of the Hon'ble Thomas Church, Resident Councillor, Tan Tock Seng, by whose munificence the funds for the building had been supplied, and a number of other gentlemen. A brass plate was deposited beneath the foundation stone, on which was engraved the following inscription :—

The Foundation Stone

of

The Chinese Pauper Hospital

Singapore,

was laid on the XXVth May, MDCCCXLIV,

during the Government of

The Hon'ble Colonel W. J. Butterworth, c.b..

Governor of Prince of Wales' Island, Singapore

and Malacca.

The Hon'ble T. Church, Esquire,

being Resident Councillor at Singapore.

The funds for the erection of this building were

furnished by the humane liberality of

Tan Tock Seng, Esq.. J.P.,

Chinese Merchant in Singapore.

It was the wish of several brethren of the Mystic craft that the ceremony of laying the foundation of the building, which was to be appropriated to those purposes of charity and benevolence which are recognised by Masons as among the fundamental articles of their constitution, should be performed with Masonic honours, but it was unfortunately found to be too late to make the necessary arrangements.

The foundation stone of the European Seamen's Hospital was also laid at this time on the same hill. The two buildings, still standing, were designed by Mr J. T. Thomson, the Government Surveyor, and were said to be very handsome edifices, adding much to the appearance of the town. The Government had been slow to recognize the necessity for providing a hospital, and as the first introduction of anything like one was due to private enterprise, it was not thought to be astonishing that it was left to generous minded individuals to do what they could to alleviate the necessities of the sick poor.

As the Chinese who flocked into the Settlement were mostly of a poor class, it followed as a matter of necessity that some of them would at some time or other be thrown on the charity of the public. Men in failing health, exposed to all the vicissitudes of the climate, soon became helpless and unable to earn their living ; while others, from neglect of superficial scratches or slight wounds, soon suffered by their abrasions becoming sloughing ulcers, and they became street mendicants, to the annoyance of the general public. On this account

Tan Tock Seng, a generous-hearted and philanthropic Chinese gentleman, built the hospital at his own expense, and his son Tan Kim
Ching added to its accommodation. The Government provided only
medicines and medical attendance. The dieting was met by contributions and subscriptions from all classes of society. The management of
the financial department was in the hands of a Committee, Hoo Ah
Kay, Whampoa, being the Treasurer, and Seah Eu Chin looking after
the food supply.

The paper in November, 1852, contained the following paragraph
about the Pauper Hospital:—" For some time past the patients admitted
into Tan Tock Seng's Hospital have been far more numerous than
there are any means of accommodating, and the consequence has been
a great overcrowding, so that the diseases of the patients instead
of being alleviated have in fact been aggravated by their reception
into the Hospital. The Committee of management have for some time
past been fully alive to the inadequacy of the accommodation and
most anxious for its increase, and indeed had procured plans from
Mr. Thomson, the Architect of the original building, for its
enlargement, but the want of funds has hitherto prevented them from
making the additions required. Under these circumstances, some of the
principal Chinese residents met the Officiating Governor yesterday, for
the purpose of considering what steps should be taken; when the
difficulty was solved by Tan Kim Ching, the son of the founder
of the Hospital, offering to defray the entire cost of the additions,
estimated at two thousands dollars, provided Mr. Thomson's plan
was adopted. This act of liberality on the part of Tan Kim Ching
thus removes the main difficulty, and his generous example has been
followed by others of his countrymen increasing the monthly subscriptions, so as to allow of the benefits of the Hospital being materially
extended. The monthly income of the Hospital, however, will still
be inadequate to meet its requirements, and we therefore trust many
others will be induced to contribute towards its maintenance and
thus assist in conferring a great boon on their helpless fellow-creatures
who must otherwise be left to perish in their misery."

Here (wrote Dr. Rowell in 1885) one would wish to inscribe in
letters of gold not only the names of the Founder, his son, and of the
Treasurer and Purveyor as given above, but, chief of all, of that early
Committee of management, the names of Colonel Macpherson, Resident
Councillor, Thos. Dunman, Commissioner of Police, and Mr. R. C.
Woods; not that there were not others, but these were the most
prominent. But for them, the Poor Fund would have dwindled away
as a lump of ice in the sun at a very early stage of its existence, as
it did when they passed away from the scene of their labours. Mr.
Dunman knew how to put the "screw" on in the shape of "fees for
processions," "fees for permission to carry fowling pieces on sporting
expeditions," in fact, he was a sturdy beggar for helpless beggars, and
when he entered the doors of Chinese Towkays with a subscription
paper, it was not for nothing; he was not to be refused. In his
private diary are frequent entries such as " Received through Inspector
Cox from the pawnbrokers' shops a subscription of $60 to Tan Tock
Seng's Hospital."

The following inscription was engraved on stone and fixed at the hospital gate :—

THIS HOSPITAL
FOR THE
DISEASED OF ALL COUNTRIES
WAS BUILT A.D. 1844.
AT THE COST OF
SEVEN THOUSAND DOLLARS
WHOLLY DEFRAYED BY
TAN TOCK SENG.

———

THE WINGS WERE ADDED
AND LARGE IMPROVEMENTS EFFECTED
AT THE COST OF
THREE THOUSAND DOLLARS
WHOLLY DEFRAYED BY
TAN KIM CHING.
SON OF THE FOUNDER.

———

This tablet is erected by the Committee of Management, 1854.

The paper in September, 1857, contained the following passages in an article about the hospitals :—" The Indian Government (on account of the expenses of the Mutiny) have ordered all public works, not absolutely necessary, to be stopped. We hope this will prevent the hospitals being scattered as proposed at distances apart from each other, so that more medical officers would be necessary. The European Hospital, it is said, is to be erected on the Race Course, while Tan Tock Seng's Hospital is to be situated on the ground lately bought by Government on Balestier's plantation. In the case of Balestier's plantation is it very well ascertained that the locality is perfectly salubrious? [Quite prophetic words.] If the Government is quite determined that the Hospitals shall be removed from their present positions [Pearl's Hill], we would suggest that the Singapore Institution [Raffles] and the ground attached to it would be much better adapted for Hospitals than the places at present intended. It is easy of access from the harbour and the town, and sufficient room for both; the Trustees would probably be willing to listen to a proposal to transfer the schools to another site, and to concur in requesting the Legislature to give the requisite power to do so."

This arose from the buildings for the Hospital on Pearl's Hill being wanted after the Mutiny for military purposes and, together with the European Seamen's Hospital, being converted into the present Ordnance and Commissariat Offices. The present Chinese Hospital was then built on a swamp on Balestier plain, bordering on Serangoon road, which was given for the purpose by Government, in place of that erected by Tan Tock Seng, and the tablet was removed to the new hospital, were it remains.

The new Government building was much larger than the building at Pearl's Hill. As the Settlement grew larger and richer, the poor also increased. Three blocks of brick buildings forming three sides of a square were put up for the sick, while the fourth side facing the road was for the adminstrative requirements. Some have thought that the building on Serangoon road was at first intended for Indian troops, and never occupied by them. But it seems more likely, so far as can be gathered from old papers, that they were built specially for the hospital. But even these buildings soon proved insufficient; there were some 400 paupers crowed into them in a very short time after they were occupied.

Looking at the hospital, at the present time, it is impossible to realise what it was then. Dr. Rose, the then Head of the medical department, never took a stranger visiting Singapore near the place. He felt thoroughly ashamed of it. His representations to remove difficulties in the way, to improve the state of the wards, their floors, their drains, to relieve their overcrowded state, were all of little avail. The low ground prevented proper drainage. The food supply was limited, a fixed quantity without reference to the numbers in hospital was issued daily; the fund could not do otherwise, so that when the hospital population was large, the share failing to each was proportionately small. Many a time did good old Mr. Dunman send for them a hand-cart load of slaughtered fighting cocks picked up in a raid on cock-fighters. Tan Kim Seng sent them once a year (Chinese New Year) a ration of pork and a few cents each. The average death rate was about two a day.

Notwithstanding the frequent urgent representations by those who were in charge, the then Government took no steps to alter or improve its condition. In fact, the time were bad, for the "Transfer" was being agitated. The Government of India did not care to interest themselves in this question, but left it for the new Government to settle; and even when the transfer took place, the first Governor was unpopular, and the expenditure incurred for Imperial purposes was too large to allow the question of comfort and better accommodation for paupers to be considered. Dr. Randell was the first to take the bull by the horns. He was at that time Acting Assistant Colonial Surgeon, and finding no hopes of anything likely to be done to improve the hospital, he took it upon himself to calculate what number could be kept there with the likelihood of deriving benefit by treatment, allotting what he considered the least safe superficial space for each patient. Then, keeping those who were most in need of treatment, he turned all the others out, and further admissions were regulated, either by the urgency of the case, or by vacancies in the wards.

The large number of mendicants thus thrown on the public, forced the Government to take the first steps toward increasing the accommodation, and the erection of a ward outside the hospital enclosure was decided on. Commission after commission was nominated to consider what was to be done, and a poor rate was proposed, as the Poor Fund was gradually disappearing.

As times became better, and the revenues increased, ward after ward was put up, and Mr. Tan Beng Swee built a tile-roofed ward at his own expense; eventually the Government granted votes for the maintenance of the hospital on a more liberal basis. Afterwards under the careful management of Dr. Rowell, P.C.M.O., it became a well organised hospital and a pride to the Settlement. The whole place was a model of a poor-house and Infirmary combined.

The Lepers, who were located in a miserable, dirty shed, had a decent place in a detached ward, and from time to time were sent to the Leper Asylum at Palau Jerajak at Penang. On the whole, too much praise cannot be accorded to all those who helped to bring about the happy change, and it was said in 1884 that it had become as much a contrast to what it was in 1862, as a palace is to a pig-sty.

But statistics have again and again proved that the removal from the high airy site on Pearl's Hill to the water-logged ground on Serangoon Road has been the cause of serious and frequently fatal illness among the patients. From time to time some of the Committee have tried to find a scheme to move the hospital to some healthy site, and the matter came to a head about 1898 when the disease of beri-beri took a hold of the place and caused very fatal consequences. Again a determined effort was made to induce the Government to face the evil, and to sell the present site and rebuild the hospital elsewhere. The matter was referred to London, and an attempt is now being made, in 1902, to overcome the evil by the erection of a novel kind of experimental but very expensive ward, with an iron frame, and sides of very perishable material that can be quickly removed and burnt. The fact will remain to the end of time, or of the present hospital, that the Government took over the original building of Tan Tock Seng, for a purpose that might certainly have been accomplished equally well in another spot, and allowed the hospital to remain in a swamp, which should have been the last place to be chosen for the purpose. By some strange fatality, the opinion of the then Senior Medical Officer, Dr. Joseph Rose, was overruled in selecting the site, and the result has been most unfortunate. Statistics shewed clearly that the germs of disease were so rampant in the hospital, that those who came in for treatment for one complaint died in the hospital from another disease they contracted in it.

Now to take the case of the European Seamen's hospital. For a long while after the occupation of Singapore, there was no Government Hospital for the sick seamen of vessels lying in the harbour. The only hospital on shore for sick seamen then, was one established by Dr. Martin, situated where the Singapore Dispensary now stands in the Square. It was started a few years before 1840, in which year Dr. Robert Little arrived and joined Dr. Martin. The charge was $1 a day, but when the Government opened a hospital and charged one rupee (45 cents) the private hospital was driven out of the field; and as soon as it was quite discontinued, the Government charged one dollar.

The Government opened a place as the "European Seamen's Hospital." Accounts are very confusing as to the locality of the first hospital for this need, but it was afterwards built on Pearl's Hill at the same time as Tan Tock Seng's Hospital. There it remained till the Indian Mutiny occurred, and the construction of Fort Canning was decided on. Temporary accommodation was then found in Armenian Street for the European Seamen's Hospital, and finally, about 1861, the new buildings in Bukit Timah Road were occupied.

Referring to the time when the authorities were looking for European barracks, and it was proposed to place them in Balestier road, on the plateau near where the Quarantine Camp now stands, but which was rejected because of the vicinity of the swampy race-course on one side and the low land of Balestier's plantation on the other,

Dr. Rose once remarked that though the site was condemned for the soldiers, it seemed to be thought good enough for the sick, for they placed a hospital on each of the objectionable grounds, viz., the Seamen's Hospital on the Race Course, and the new Pauper Hospital on Balestier plain. And, as if to make matters worse, a Lunatic Asylum was placed on one side of the hospital, while on the other side were the cattle sheds (Kandang Kerbau) of the Public Works, and a crowded filthy native locality.

In building the new hospital, provision was made also for a Police Ward for members of the Police force and for injuries, accidental or homicidal, amongst natives. These two hospitals constituted two blocks running parallel to each other: and a small bungalow was run up between the Police Ward and the Lunatic Asylum for the reception of Officers.

However, everyone concerned tried to do his best to make the insufficient accommodation that was provided as comfortable as means and the surroundings permitted, and the name of the Institution was quietly changed to "The General Hospital," which was largely used both by H. M. Ships and mercantile marine: in fact, there was often a pressure for room, and Sir Harry Ord was considering the advisability of building a third block, when a long expected event brought about unlooked for relief. The opening of the Suez Canal revolutionized the trade of the port, and instead of having a large number of English vessels in harbour for weeks, waiting for cargo, Canal steamers sprang up. remaining only a few hours in port. The floating population thereby decreased, and consequently there were fewer patients seeking admission into the hospital. But in June, 1873, cholera, in an epidemic form, broke out it Kampong Kapor and the Lunatic Asylum. The patients of the General Hospital were hastily removed to the buildings at the Sepoy Lines left vacant by the removal of the Indian native regiment, but temporarily occupied by the Police. The hospital on Bukit Timah Road was reserved for a Cholera Hospital, which had to be supplemented by a temporary structure on the Race Course Plain. At the outbreak of this epidemic, Dr. Randell, the then Principal Civil Medical Officer, was on sick leave in England, and the removal was effected by Drs. Anderson and Hampshire, Dr. Randell returned about August, when cholera was declining. He at once made up his mind not to return to the old place, and strong representations were made to the then Governor, Sir H. Ord; but, though he quite agreed with the P. C. M. O., he felt (as he was about resigning office) that the initiation of the change should be left to his successor, Sir Andrew Clarke. One of the first public places visited by the new Governor, was the old hospital; and the following day, he went to the Sepoy Lines, and decided that the hospital was not to revert to its old quarters at Kandang Kerbau: and, to have good grounds on which to base a statement to the Secretary of State, a Commission was appointed to report on the advisability of the removal; and who can say how many quires of paper, and how much valuable time, was spent in arriving at a conclusion?

The revenues of the Settlement were progressing, the new Governor was a favourite after Sir H. Ord, and things worked smoothly; there was no dissenting voice in Council, so plans for a new hospital were made and submitted to the Secretary of State; but, as is well known, Government is never in a hurry, so it took months before the Secretary of State had leisure to look at the plans, and even then, only disapprove of them as being too large, too expensive, &c., &c., and suggesting alterations. Fresh plans were made and re-submitted, which were eventually approved of. All these steps took time, but at last the present hospital was put in hand and was completed and occupied in August, 1882. The European Hospital (which was on a very much better site than that of. the Tan Tock Seng's Hospital on Serangoon Road) was rebuilt at the Sepoy Lines on rising ground in a healthy place; but Tan Tock Seng's Hospital (which is only for the poor) remains in the swamps, and continues to claim its victims there to this day, in 1902.

The time of the receipt of letters by the overland route, at this period, was still very uncertain. In one week in February, for example, instalments for three mails came in, and in the very reverse order to that in which they ought to have been received. On a Tuesday, a portion of a mail posted in England in December, arrived by way of Calcutta; on the next day, a part of the November mail arrived by way of China; and four days later, the brig *Sea Horse* from Bombay brought the October mail. So that the mail, not unusually, took over four months to reach here, which was longer than an average passage by a sailing vessed round the Cape. It was proposed to get the P. & O. service established to Singapore, and that " Pulo Labuan, near Borneo," should be made a point of call for British men-of war to coal on the voyage between Singapore and Hongkong when conveying the mails from here. The *Sea Horse* brought forty convicts from Bombay under an armed guard, being part of a famous robber gang known as the Bunder Gang.

The Races were held in March, on Tuesday, Thursday and Saturday, the same days of the week as at the present time, but they took place in the morning. The evening before each . race day a dinner was held at the Race Stand open to all members.

The steamer *Royal Sovereign* made a few trips to Malacca and Penang, but it was an unprofitable venture, and the natives did not appreciate the superiority of steam over sailing vessels. The fares were $12 to Malacca and $30 to Penang; and $2 and $5 for deck passages. Mr. Whampoa provided the meals, for which an extra charge was made. The steamer had been sent here in 1843 in the hope of forming a Company to purchase her. Syme & Co. were the agents of the steamer.

The following is an account, in a private letter, of a voyage overland via Calcutta, at this time, which was very different from the experiences of the present day:—" I left Calcutta for Europe by the steamer *Hindostan*. She is a splendid vessel, and everything from Calcutta to Southampton went on smoothly, the table was good, we had good wines, and everything in first rate style, even the passage across the desert down the Nile and on the canal, was comfortable. We had English coachmen to drive us through the desert, the stations attended by English women, clean and well provided. I took my passage back at Malta, and paid for myself and native servant to Alexandria £24.10. I have nothing to complain of on board the *Great Liverpool,* I was comfortable, and the table and wines were good. I paid at Alexandria, for myself and servant, £25 to Suez besides £2 for extra baggage; you cannot imagine how bad was our scanty and miserable food. The transit was equally bad, we were driven by Arabs, of which they know nothing, and the consequence was, that some of the vans were capsized, some of the ladies had black eyes, and not a little burning, and I was once obliged to walk four miles, as the horses would not start. For economy's sake the stations are now managed by Arabs, and these people have such a tendency to dirtiness, that the rooms and everything else were swimming in their element. We had nothing but Irish stew all the way. At Suez, I found the *Hindostan,* and you will hardly believe that I was again obliged to submit to the greatest imposition; the purser made me pay down for my passage and for native servant, from Suez to Calcutta, the exhorbitant sum of £172, and this for a miserable dark cabin, rejected by every other passenger, without light and air, a single berth, and a sofa half under the berth, and only about eight inches lower, and only fit for a child or any one that had lost his legs. The fare was indifferent; the claret sour; the sherry muddy and bad, brandy and gin the worst that could be had. The passengers being more than there were seats for in the saloon, about ten or twelve of them were cast upon the deck, where their meals arrived generally cold; in any other part of the world, the captain or purser should in duty bound, apologize for it, and should have said 'Gentlemen, there is not room for the whole of you in the saloon, therefore, if you wish, some of the gentlemen below will take it by turns, and you will go down.' This would have smoothed our feelings. I am confident you would not like much the overland route."

In May, a Hindoo festival took place, which the *Free Press* described as follows:—"On Thursday last the Hindoo festival called Churruck Poojah was celebrated in the usual manner, to the disgust and serious annoyance, we doubt not, of all right-thinking persons. The horrible ceremony of swinging round a high pole suspended by a hook inserted in the back, was performed by two men, not only with the sanction of Government, but on a piece of ground at the race course allowed by the authorities for the purpose. We think that Government is blameable and altogether in the wrong in permitting this or any other cruel and disgusting native rite to be practised in these Settlements. There may be some appearance of reason in saying that in Hindostan the Hindoos ought to be allowed to practise their rites and ceremonies without molestation or hinderance, and that it might be dangerous and impolitic to forbid them. But even this argument, untenable as we deem it, and which in India, in the case of Suttee, a practice regarded by Hindoos as of the most sacred and paramount nature, has been successfully disregarded, does not apply with any great force here, since the Hindoos are mere foreigners in these Settlements, which may be looked upon as founded and settled by Europeans and therefore to be governed according to their laws and customs. Not only is the practice which we condemn, abhorrent to the feelings of Europeans, but we are afraid that it produces anything but a good effect on other classes of Asiatics who crowd to witness it. On Thursday evening, the number of Chinese much exceeded the Hindoos or any other class. The · practice is alike unchristian and inhuman, and we therefore trust that this is the last time that it will be permitted to pollute the island. In the evening, after dark, the Hindoos came along the Beach Road at Kampong Glam in procession with lighted torches making a great noise. It is surprising that serious accidents did not occur."

In June, the presentment of the Grand Jury contained the suggestion that the verandahs should be kept clear of obstructions. The paper said it was very desirable, but could only be done by an Act of the Legislative Council, except in those cases where proprietors of houses had exceeded their limits and constructed their verandahs on the public property, in which cases Government could impose such conditions as might be necessary.

H. M. S. *Samarang* arrived in Singapore in July, with her Captain wounded in an attack by pirates, the account of which shows how serious the piratical attacks were in those days. The *Free Press* described it as follows:—"H. M. Surveying Ship *Samarang*, Sir E. Belcher, K.C.B., arrived on the 2nd instant from Borneo. We understand that Sir Edward, while employed in the ship's boats making scientific observations off the coast of Gilolo, a considerable island lying East of the Northern limit of Celebes, was attacked by a large party of Illanoon pirates, consisting of ten prahus, with about sixty men in each. The boats of the ship had silenced several of the prahus which were afterwards taken possession of and destroyed, when a shot from one of them struck Sir Edward Belcher, passing through one thigh and lodging in the other, and knocking him overboard. Sir Edward was, we understand, in the act of directing a rocket against one of the prahus, when the shot reached him, and is the only one of the party who was seriously hurt, but it was not until considerable execution had been done among the piratical force, that the party returned to the ship, which immediately bore up for Singapore. The shot which struck Sir Edward, when cut out, was found to be an iron swivel ball, of more than an inch in diameter; but he is progressing favourably, and will, no doubt, be able to take part in the operations which the Admiral will, we trust, ere long, direct to be pursued against the pirates in that quarter of the Archipelago, whose repeated outrages against Europeans we have recorded of late."

An effort was made at this time to improve the town, and the following notice was issued by the Supreme Court. It referred to a very large number of houses in Teluk Ayer Street, Pekin Street, Market Street, Circular Road, Boat Quay, and neighbouring streets, and the notice, although very closely printed, filled nearly a column of the paper. In Chinchew Street, for example, it named thirty-seven houses:—

NOTICE.

Whereas, it having on the 15th of June last past, been presented to the Judges of Her Majesty's Court of Judicature of Prince of Wales' Island, Singapore and Malacca sitting as a Court of Oyer and Terminer and General Gaol Delivery at Singapore by the Grand Inquest then and there assembled, that the several houses or buildings, situated in several streets hereinafter mentioned in the town of Singapore, marked and numbered over the door or entrance of the said several houses or buildings, respectively, are public nuisances by reason of the very decayed and unsafe condition of the said several houses or buildings, and whereas, it being desirable that the public nuisances should be speedily removed and abated, notice is hereby given to the several and respective proprietors, tenants, sub-tenants, occupiers or holders of the aforesaid several houses or buildings, as above specified, must be pulled down within the space of three months, from the date hereof, or legal proceedings will be instituted with the view of abating the said public nuisances."

Then followed the particulars of the streets and houses.

In August, a public meeting was held to establish a Library, to be kept in the Singapore Institution. Mr. J. C. Smith was the first Secretary and Librarian, and Mr. W. H. Read, Treasurer. The following were the first shareholders, who each contributed $30. The monthly subscription was $2.50. The rules, &c., will be found printed in the *Free Press* of the 15th August:—

Almeida, Joaquim	Dyce, C. A.	McMicking, G.
Bain, G.	Fraser, L.	Martin, M. J.
Butterworth, Col.	George, W. R.	Middleton, A.
Blundell, Wm.	Gilman, E. J.	Myrtle, J.
Caldwell, H. C.	Guthrie, James	Napier, W.
Church, Thos.	Harrison, C. H.	Purvis, John
Crane, T. O. B.	Ker, Thos. B.	Read, W. H.
Cumming, J.	Little, Dr.	Saul, R. P.
Davidson, M. F.	Logan, A.	Sorabjee, Frommurze
Drysdale, J. C.	Logan, J. R.	Stevenson, Captain
Dunman, Thos.	McEwen, Robert	

The following is an account of the first sale of horses from Sydney:—" On Tuesday, the 20th August, the recent importation of horses and sheep from Sydney was sold by public auction. The sheep were first put up in lots of five, and went off briskly at $4.60 to $5 each, which was considered a good price. As the time approached for the sale of horses " Tattersall's " became rather crowded with Europeans, Jews, Parsees, Arabs, and the various tribes of settlers, which presented an animated scene. The result of the sale was very satisfactory, the highest bid was $350, and the lowest $100, making an average of $211 each for 11 horses. Some Sydney potatoes were also sold at $2.30 per picul. We believe that the importation of these horses, &c., was, in some degree, experimental, and from the satisfactory result of the sales we may expect to see it repeated. We have no doubt that a small annual importation of horses, and a larger one of sheep, potatoes, &c., would always take, and there are, no doubt, other products of New South Wales which might also find a market here. The present importation has been made by Messrs. Boyd & Co., of Sydney, and we believe that various articles of Straits and other Eastern produce will be taken as a return. Although, perhaps, it may not be possible to make the whole of the returns in produce, yet a part of them might, we daresay, be very profitably made in sugar, spices, &c. Some gambier has also been taken, for the purpose of tanning, but we understand that the high price of labour in New South Wales forms a bar to the establishment of any extensive manufacture there, it being found more profitable to send the articles home in an unmanufactured state ; and thus hides instead of being tanned and converted into leather on the spot, are sent to England as they come off the cattle, with the addition of salt to preserve them from decay. We have no doubt that a considerable outlet for Colonial produce may be found in China, the Straits, and Continental India, and an increased intercourse could not fail of being mutually advantageous."

There was a dearth of bricks in the Settlement at this time, as there was so much building going on. The paper wrote as follows :— "We may notice the high price of bricks in the Settlement. We believe they are at present $18 per laksa, whereas a few months ago they were only $10 or $12. We believe this arises from a monopoly of the article having been secured, it is said, in anticipation of the wholesale destruction of the wooden houses in town, which, it was thought, would follow on the presentment of the Grand Jury. This expectation turns out to be fallacious, as it is discovered that only those houses which are really dangerous to the public can be ranked as nuisances, and, as such, are indictable, and, of these, we believe, the number is not large. It is very much to be regretted that the advance should have happened at this juncture, as it will enhance the cost of the two hospitals very considerably, to the public loss in one case, and, in the other, to that of the humane individual at whose cost it is erecting, Tan Tock Seng." Bricks in 1902, are selling at $50 to $140 a laksa.

In September Captain Faber, of the Madras Engineers, the newly appointed Superintending Engineer, arrived from Madras. Mount Faber was called after him. He was the gallant officer who, on being told that he had built a bridge over the river so low that the tongkangs could not pass under it at high tide, had the bottom of the river dredged under the bridge to float them through. Some of his architectural and engineering failures are alluded to further on in the year 1846. One of his gallant successors spent many vain efforts and no little of Mr. Tan Beng Swee's money in endeavouring to make water run up hill, when the first fruitless attempt was made to bring water into the town.

From time to time, attempts continued to be made to make planting pay on the island, and about this time sugar was being cultivated on a large scale at Serangoon on Balestier Plain and elsewhere, as was said in the last chapter; the paper wrote on the subject in October, as follows:—" In Singapore, the cultivation of sugar has been prosecuted by two enterprising and persevering gentlemen, Messrs. Balestier and Montgomerie, who have successfully established the fitness of the soil and climate of Singapore for sugar culture. The cultivation is rapidly extending, and large tracts of ground are being brought under the operation of the husbandman. The system of contracts with the Chinese has, by experience, been found to be the best plan of proceeding. By it not only is a better cane produced, but the crop is more abundant. The plan is this; the ground is cleared, planted, and the whole management of it undertaken by the Chinese, who bring the crop to maturity and cut it down. It is carted from the ground by the manufacturer to the mill, and the Chinese are allowed at a certain rate upon the out-turn. The sum at present given is about $1.50 per picul. An acre of cane produces from thirty to forty piculs of sugar. The quality of the sugar, which is as material a point as the quantity, is first rate, consisting of a fine strong grain excellently adapted for the purposes of the sugar refiner.

"There is much land on the island well suited for the growth of the sugar-cane, and were parties encouraged, by a relaxation of the heavy duties, against which Singapore planters will now have to contend, to embark in the cultivation, Singapore could annually send home a very large supply of sugar to the home market. We may here take the opportunity of remarking that very erroneous and unfavourable ideas have been formed as to the adaptation of Singapore for agriculture. This, no doubt, may have in part arisen from some inferior soils having been at first selected for planting operations, and the result of the cultivation of which has been rather discouraging. It is admitted that the climate of Singapore is admirably suited for most kinds of tropical cultivation and the quality of the soil is, therefore, the essential point of enquiry. On this head, it might be sufficient for answer to instance the beautiful plantations of different kinds of fruit and spice trees which are to be found in the neighbourhood of the town. Whether the capabilities of the soil are to be availed of to any great extent will depend, in a great measure, on the amount of encouragement and protection which Straits agriculture may experience from Government." Subsequent experience taught a different lesson, as the plantations entirely failed. Mr. Balestier, the American Consul, had his plantation where Balestier Plain is now, and Dr. Montgomerie on the other side of the Kallang stream where Woodsville is now. It was called Kallang Dale, and Mr. R. C. Woods changed the name to Woodsville after he built the large house there.

On 18th September the following notification was issued by Government. It is inserted here because the matter has come to the front several times since :—

"Authentic intelligence having been received, that a naturalized British subject, but of Chinese origin, had incurred some risk of seizure, and persecution by the Chinese authorities, in consequence of his appearing at one of the Ports in China lately thrown open to British shipping as supercargo of a British vessel—and as the cases of the same kind are likely to occur from the growing trade in British ships between the Ports in China and the Straits Settlements, it is hereby notified, with a view to protect persons so situated, that the Resident Councillors at Penang, Singapore, and Malacca, will be prepared to furnish a certificate when required, intimating that they are naturalized British subjects. This document will be lodged with the Consul at the first Port the vessel may touch in China."

A letter from Mr. John Crawfurd at this time said that it was not improbable that a Royal establishment might be formed in the island of "Labuwan" off the Borneo river, for a steam station for coal. A notice was issued by the Police that shoals of sharks, of immense size, had been seen, and a great number caught in the roads in a few days in the middle of September, and warning sailors against bathing in the sea.

The following is the first reference we have met with to the possible annexation of the Native States :—"We consider the suggestion to acquire some of the neighbouring Native States for the purposes of agriculture as worthy of attention. There is no doubt that the change from the Native to the British rule would be very beneficial to the States themselves, as at present they are in a condition very little removed from downright barbarism. Their rajahs are in general grossly ignorant and of the most puerile and depraved habits; when not engaged in some petty warfare with a neighbour, their whole time is spent in cock-fighting and gambling. Their subjects, insecure in their possessions, and without a motive to exertion, give way unrestrainedly to the indolence so congenial to a Malay, and with the exception of the scanty fields of paddy, which is to supply their food, and a few cocoanuts, which surround their villages, the soil is uncultivated. The only sign of activity displayed is in the working of the tin mines in some of these states, and these are carried on by Chinese from the British Settlements. Were these states to be under English Government, we might expect to see them exhibiting in the course of a few years, a very different appearance from what they do at present. Their soil would be made to yield those rich and abundant crops for which nature intended it, and their mineral wealth would be fully developed. A large and comparatively wealthy population would cause a large demand for the manufactures of England, and she would, in return, receive those supplies of sugar which she so much requires, besides an abundance of other tropical productions." All which has since been exemplified in the Protected Native States.

CHAPTER XXXII.

1845.

———

O N Saturday, the 18th January, a public meeting was held, having been called, as usual in those days, on a requisition to the Sheriff, Captain Faber and all the community attended. Mr. Thomas McMicking was the Chairman. The first part of the proceedings related to the Land Question, about which the Government had proposed to make more stringent regulations, to which the planters took exception. The next subject was the expenditure of the assessment fund, which Mr. W. H. Read brought forward, showing that the money was not properly applied, the Government paying out of the assessment funds for public works that properly pertained to Government alone. The following is the report of the latter part of the meeting, the rest of the report being too long to reproduce:—

"Mr. Read concluded by moving:—That the Hon'ble the Governor be requested to allow the assessment funds to be controlled by a Committee of three persons—one appointed by the Government, and two by the assessed. Mr. Lewis Fraser seconded the motion.

Considerable discussion ensued on the terms of the motion, and two amendments were brought forward, one by Mr. Dyce, to the effect that the assessment fund should be controlled by a committee of conservancy to be chosen by the payers of assessment exceeding a certain amount—the executive being still vested in the Government;—and the other by Dr. Little to the effect that the Governor-General of India in Council be memorialized to allow the assessment to be managed by the rate-payers. The three propositions were put to the vote, when Mr. Read's motion was carried by a large majority.

Mr. M. F. Davidson then, after a few appropriate observations, in which he remarked that it was not for the purpose of supplying an additional sitting Magistrate or Assessing Officer that the inhabitants agreed to the assessment being raised to 10 per cent., but in order that an increased efficiency of the Police might be secured by an improved and thorough superintendence, moved:—That it is the opinion of this meeting that the Deputy Superintendent of Police cannot effectively perform the duties of his situation, and at the same time those of a sitting Magistrate, and that the Government be requested to make such arrangements as will relieve him of all duties foreign to his office as Deputy Superintendent of Police.

Mr. Alexander Guthrie seconded the motion, which was carried *nem con.*

Mr. R. Bain proposed, seconded by Mr. Davidson:—That the Local Authorities be requested to alter the present foot-bridge over the river near Syed Omar's godowns [where Elgin Bridge is now] into a Carriage Bridge with as little delay as practicable, which the meeting unanimously agreed to.

On the motion of Mr. Guthrie, seconded by Mr. Crane, the following gentlemen, viz., M. F. Davidson, W. H. Read and C. Spottiswoode, were appointed a Committee to address the Governor on the three last resolutions, and to procure, so far as practicable, their being carried into effect.

The meeting was held at noon, in Mr. Read's house. There was no public building that could be used for the purpose in those days.

In January, the Chamber of Commerce addressed a long letter to Government on the subject of the copper currency which was in a very deranged condition as the Government had no copper coinage for the Straits at that time, and the change for a dollar consisted of all kinds of tokens which the merchants imported from England.

Sugar planting in the jungle in those days was not unattended with danger. Gang robberies were not unfrequent, and the following is an account of an attack on one of the planters:—"On Saturday morning, the 15th March, about half-past two o'clock, the house of Monsieur Beauregard, a French gentleman, who is forming a sugar plantation in Pyah Lebar district, and who resides on the spot, was attacked by a gang of about thirty Chinamen, who were headed by two Malays. They were provided with fire-arms, and fired seven times, wounding M. Beauregard, and six of his labourers slightly, but they did not succeed in getting possession of the house, being driven back by M. Beauregard, who fortunately had a good supply of fire-arms which he used with such success that, after he had fired six shots, the robbers retreated, carrying with them their dead and wounded. From the great quantity of blood which was afterwards observed upon the ground, it is conjectured that four or five men, at least, must either have been killed or desperately wounded. Two Chinese servants had their swords taken from them by the assailants, but they were not hurt, which, with other suspicious circumstances, renders it extremely probable that they were in the counsels of the gang. As soon as information was conveyed to the Police Office, Mr. Dunman, Deputy Superintendent, and a large body of peons, proceeded to the spot, where they arrived during the forenoon. They searched the jungle in the neighbourhood without finding any traces of the gang, although 120 men were employed in the search the whole day. The houses at the piratical village at Siglap were likewise searched, as well as all boats leaving the neighbourhood, but without success. "The coolness and courage with which Monsieur Beauregard withstood such a large body of men is deserving of the highest praise, and shows that, with resolution and a good supply of arms, a single European need not despair of beating off a gang of Chinamen, though thirty times his number, if only on the alert in time. At the same time we must observe that if it is wished that Europeans should settle in the island as cultivators, means must be taken by an improved system of Police to give them some security of life and property. At present there is no sufficient Police in the country parts; there are a few

Thannahs here and there, but it can scarcely be expected that two or three Klings should boldly face a large gang of thirty or forty reckless Chinamen, and we do not therefore blame the men so much as the system. There ought to be European constables with an adequate force stationed at some central place in the cultivated districts, whose special duty it ought to be to act as a night patrol, going in different directions in their beat in parties of four and five, and provided with the means of summoning others to their aid in the event of their falling in with any gang of evildoers."

It was in this year that the Peninsular and Oriental Company made the first contract for the conveyance of the mails to China *viâ* Ceylon. The contract was for 140 hours from Ceylon to Penang, and 45 hours from there to Singapore, and 170 hours from there to Hongkong. The steamers were to remain 48 hours here. The service was once a month. The first mail steamer, the *Lady Mary Wood*, arrived on the 4th August, having been eight days from Galle. She brought the mails from London of 24th June, having taken 41 days. The paper spoke of this matter as follows:—" The arrival of the first direct Overland Mail for the Straits and China is an event of some importance, and deserving of special notice at our hands. It is a further addition to the great lines of steampackets by which Great Britain is brought into such close contact with her more distant Colonial possessions. The American and West Indian Colonies have long had regular lines of steamers between them and the Mother Country, and now in the East it only wants an extension of the chain to Australia to render it complete. This we believe will not be long withheld, the growing importance of the Australian Colonies, and the advantages resulting to Government itself from quick and regular communications with distant possessions, will speedily bring about the accomplishment of this line. It seems almost certain that Singapore will be the station where the junction of the Australian line with the Indian one will take place, so that with the Dutch monthly steamer and perhaps the Manila one in addition, Singapore bids fair to become a steam-packet station of considerable importance.

The number of letters carried by the succeeding steamer, the *Braganza*, from Europe was 652, and newspapers 673; total number of covers 1,325. The number taken by the *Lady Mary Wood* on her return voyage homewards on 1st September, was:—

Europe	...	...	... 3,989
Penang	...	...	... 165
Ceylon	...	...	... 74
Bombay	...	...	... 242
Madras	...	...	... 281
Aden	...	...	... 6
Total amount of covers	...		4,757

The passage money was £160, including transit through Egypt and steward's fees.

There was a good deal of excitement in the Square because the prepaid letters by the first homeward mail were all left behind! and the following appeared in the paper:—"We regret to notice that a great number of letters sent to the Post Office and intended for despatch to Europe by the steamer *Lady Mary Wood*, although sent to the Post Office a few minutes before two o'clock (the advertised latest hour), were not forwarded to their destination, but returned to the senders. The letters in question were sent by two commercial houses whose communications and correspondence were extensive, and who throughout the day were dispatching letters to the Post Office so soon as they were sealed, in order that the Post Office servants might experience as little inconvenience as possible. In the instance of these letters some excuse is raised which is not withal very reasonable. The whole of the "rejected addresses" were epistles to foreign countries, and as such, had to undergo various entries in sundry books of the Singapore Post Office to ensure the certainty of reaching their destination. Although in good time, that is, several minutes before the advertised hour of closing the mails, the letters were returned; because, as alleged, there was no time to perform all the manipulations necessary in the instance of foreign letters. But a still worse casualty occurred: *the whole of the prepaid letters were forgotten!* They had been placed in a very snug corner, but were overlooked.

The Chamber of Commerce addressed the Governor very warmly upon the subject, and Mr. William Scott and Mr. Cuppage, who were in charge of the Post Office, got a good deal of warm language. The merchants made legal protests against the Post Office authorities, holding them liable for any loss that might ensue, but they were only waste paper, as the Indian Postal Act exempted them from responsibility. The paper said shortly afterwards that the energy of the Chamber had worked wonders. The forgotten letters were sent on by the steamer *Fire Queen* to Calcutta some days after, to go from there by any opportunity. Spottiswoode & Connolly were the first Agents of the P. & O. Company.

The *Lady Mary Wood* was built in 1842, her gross tonnage was 556, and the horse power 250, she was, of course, a paddle wheel steamer.

The following statement in the *Free Press* for March shows what the native trade by junks was at that period:—"Below we give a statement of the number of junks which have arrived this season up to the 24th instant, greatly exceeding the arrivals last year at the same time. The arrival of immigrants has also been very large, being at the 19th instant, 6,883, of whom 1,168 have come by square-rigged vessels, a new feature in the history of Chinese immigration, and 5,715 by junks. The number of immigrants last year was about 1,600, and the year before 7,000, but judging from the number who have already arrived, we may anticipate that this season they will not fall much short of 9,000 or 10,000. They are chiefly dispersed through the Straits Settlements and the neighbouring Dutch one at Rhio. In the Straits there will be an increased demand for labour for the sugar estates, which

will absorb some of the surplus, and we understand that the cultivation of gambier is being carried on in Johore rather extensively
by the Singapore gambier planters. We do not know what number
go to Rhio, but we should think that it cannot be on the increase,
as we are informed most of the gambier and pepper plantations in
the vicinity of Rhio have already been, or will soon be, exhausted
and abandoned. The distance from the town at which operations
will consequently have to be carried on, by increasing the cost of
carriage, etc., will, no doubt, lessen the profits of the cultivation
and tend in some measure to check it."

*Arrivals of Chinese and Cochin-Chinese junks during the present
season from 2nd December to 24th March.*

Whence.		Number.			Tons.
	Canton	5	...	...	737
	Shanghai	4	...	...	1,150
	Amoy	5	...	...	1,300
	Kongmoon	1	...	...	150
	Hongkong	1	...	...	62
From China.	Honghoy	1	..	...	100
	Chonglim	5	...	...	1,700
	Chowan	3	...	...	325
	Macao	1	...	...	800
	Swathow	3	...	...	700
	Tywan	2	...	...	174
	Eagling	1	...	...	125
		32			7,323
From Cochin-China.	Long Loy	1	...	...	355
	C. China Proper ...	1	...	...	500
		34			8,178

In the same month, the paper spoke of the mouth of the river,
which is still attracting attention : "The entrance to the river undoubtedly requires to be deepened, but how is it to be done? If
we are not mistaken, the present Assistant Resident tried his hand
at it, but after having broken in pieces a large stone at the
entrance of the river, a famous historical relic, and one of the very
few of which Singapore could boast, he abandoned the task." This
is the famous stone that has been already spoken of at page 89.

The *Free Press* of 27th March contained the following remarks
upon the expedition to Borneo :—"H. M. steamer *Driver*, of which
we some weeks ago announced the departure for Borneo with a
political mission on board, returned into the roads last Saturday
morning, having effected the passage over from Sarawak in 48 hours.
The mission, which consists of Captain Bethune of the Royal Navy,
whose general and scientific attainments are well known, associated
with Mr. Brooke, visited Borneo Proper, and, as we have been
informed, met with the most favourable reception from the native
rulers of that place, who have long been desirous to secure the

friendship and alliance of the British Government. Everything proceeded to the satisfaction of the mission, while the island of Labuan and the adjacent waters were carefully surveyed with a view to the advantage of forming an establishment there under the British crown, but what the ultimate determination on this head may be, or whether another locality will be finally chosen, has not transpired. Of Labuan we ourselves know only the geographical position, and a few other particulars which are, we believe, pretty generally known, but there is no island on the coast of Borneo of which we have received any information which appears to equal Labuan in the advantages it offers for a Settlement, not the least of its recommendations being that it yields excellent coals, of which a specimen has been brought over in the *Driver*. In connection with the affairs of Borneo, we ought not to omit to mention that Mr. Brooke has been appointed by Her Majesty's Ministers the Confidential Agent of the British Government in Borneo. What powers this designation includes we are not yet aware, but it will be a source of gratification to all those who feel an interest in the progress of civilization and improvement in these countries, to find that gentleman occupying a situation which will enable him to advance the great objects which he has all along had in view in his enterprising career on the Coast of Borneo—namely, the welfare of the inhabitants, by extinguishing piracy; the consequent security of property; and the extension of our commerce on principles which would secure the friendship and gratitude of the natives. There is no person of whom we have heard who possesses in the same degree as Mr. Brooke that union of qualities which fit a man to be at the head of a movement in this part of the world which has these great and important objects in view."

The Races were held in March, on two days in the afternoon. A "four-in-hand club (ponies)" turned out with a drag, as a novelty. Rear Admiral Sir Thomas Cochrane was here, in his flagship the *Agincourt*, and there was a large party from his vessel at the races. The Chamber of Commerce tried to induce him to allow one of the men-of-war to carry mails between Singapore and Ceylon for a few months until the P. & O. was properly established. The following was an account of the result :—

"His Excellency Sir T. Cochrane, in replying to the Hon'ble the Governor's letter forwarding the request of the Chamber, says that it will at all times afford him the highest gratification to render himself or the squadron under his command useful in forwarding the views and wishes of so respectable a body of gentlemen, and to find that he and the squadron have been made in any manner instrumental in promoting their interests or prosperity, and he therefore greatly regrets that on the present occasion he is unable to comply with their request. There are, His Excellency observes, only three large steamships under his command, one of which is stationed in India, another in China, and the third in the Straits of Malacca and Java Sea for the express purpose of protecting the commerce of the Straits Settlements, and the numerous vessels that trade to the Indian Archipelago; and one of the chief objects of his Excellency's present visit to Singapore is to ascertain how Her Majesty's ships dedicated to the important duties of the Straits can best render their services to the commerce of their country; on which subject he looks forward to the Chamber affording him any suggestions which they may be able to offer.

"The Admiral is fully alive to the great inconvenience to which our Eastern and Northern correspondence is at present exposed, an inconvenience, he remarks, felt still more severely at Hongkong than in the Straits from its more remote position, and he would most willingly give his best endeavours to remove it, but he would not, under any circumstances, feel himself justified (without orders from home) in appropriating a steam-ship-of-war to Post Office duties, entailing a heavy expense, uncompensated by the profits on passengers and cargo available to a private steam-ship."

On the 7th April, the Rev. Edward White, M.A., the Residency Chaplain, died very suddenly at the age of 52 years. He was much respected in the place. The tombstone in the old church yard says that it was erected by the congregation of which he was in charge for eight years, and the tablet in the Cathedral has been noticed on page 298. It was a military funeral, and the service was read by Mr. Thomas Church. Mr. White died in Coleman Street. He was succeeded by Mr. Moule, who came from Calcutta, and commenced duty on Sunday, the 18th May.

The *Free Press* in June contained the following paragraph. The foolish action of the Government in condoning the mischievous and vexatious actions of Opium and Spirit Farmers (in order to keep them in good humour and maintain the revenue) continues to this day:—"On Friday the Spirit Farmer was charged before Captain Adam Cuppage, 27th Madras Native Infantry, Stipendiary Magistrate, and Messrs. John Purvis and James Guthrie, Magistrates, at the Police Office, by W. H. Miles, keeper of the Union Hotel, with having sold him spurious or adulterated Brandy. The Brandy was produced and was admitted by the Farmer to be the article that he had sold to Mr. Miles. Several respectable dealers were called who gave it as their opinion that the stuff was not Brandy at all, and Mr. John Steel stated that it appeared to him to be a compound of Arrack, burnt Sugar and Tobacco! The Farmer in defence said that he bought the Brandy from Mr. Purvis in bottle and emptied it into a cask. Mr. Purvis sent for a muster of Brandy of the same quality he had sold to the Farmer as second quality Brandy, which was found to be a wholesome spirit and quite different from the Farmer's compound. The Magistrates then fined the Farmer Rs. 1,000. We are informed this is the third conviction of the Spirit Farmer for selling adulterated liquor, but that on the two former occasions the fines, Rs. 1,000 in each case, were remitted by the Authority in whose discretion the exacting of it or otherwise, is placed. This has no doubt tended to make the Farmer confident in following his evil practises, but we trust that for the protection of the public, the fine will be exacted to the last pie."

In July in the next year the following appeared in the paper, on the same subject, and is quoted here on account of the remarks by Mr. Church, the Resident Councillor:—" On Monday an action was tried in the Court of Judicature before the Hon. the Resident Councillor at the instance of a respectable Chinese merchant named Ang Ah, against some peons of the Opium Farmer, who under pretence of searching his person for illicit Opium, had seized hold of him on the street, and were dragging him away by his tail to the Opium Farmer's Office, when he was with some difficulty rescued from their hands by Mr. Frommurzee Sorabjee who was passing at the time, and who compelled them to take Ang Ah to the Police. The peons alleged that they found in Ang Ah's purse a small box containing some Opium valued at 3 sucoos:—Ang Ah on the other hand asserted that while some of the peons seized him behind, he caught the hands of one of them in front who was endeavouring to convey the Opium into his purse. The case was heard at the instance of the Farmer by the Sitting Magistrate and the Superintendent of Police, who after hearing the evidence for the charge, dismissed the Complaint, and thereupon Ang Ah brought an action against the peons to recover damages for the assault which they had committed upon him. After evidence had been given of the assault and for the defence the Hon. the Resident Councillor gave judgment for the Plaintiff, awarding $65 as damages. His Honor remarked that though it certainly was necessary that the Revenue should be protected it was also necessary, perhaps more so, that the public should be protected. Large powers were given to the Revenue peons under the Acts regulating the Farms, which it was necessary they should exercise with caution, and it had been proved that they had not done so in the present case, but on the contrary, had been proved to have committed a very gross assault upon a most respectable individual. The assault we have reason to believe was prompted by a wish to annoy Ang Ah, because he has recently become renter of the Opium Farm lately established in Johore by the Tomoongong, whose Chinese settlers daily increase, to the serious detriment of the Singapore Revenue Farmers; who between immigration and the suppression of gambling, experience a daily diminution of their receipts. Indeed we hear that the decrease in the sale of Opium and Spirits amounts to so much as clearly 100 dollars per diem respectively."

During this year, the Bukit Timah road was roughly opened up beyond Bukit Timah as far as Kranji. In May, Ellenborough Market was being built. Tan Tock Seng was making preparations for commencing the erection of the Ellenborough Buildings. The Seamen's Hospital on Pearl's Hill was completed. The following is taken from the paper in May:—" The preparations for removing the signal station from Blakan Mati towards Tulloh Blangah Hill are advancing rapidly to completion, the latter having been cleared, a convenient road to the top constructed, and huts for the accommodation of the convicts erected. It is a very good station, commanding an extensive prospect seaward as well as landward, and would form a desirable site for a bungalow. One of the reasons, and, if we mistake not, the chief one, assigned by medical men for the unhealthiness of Blakan Mati, was its being covered with pine-apples, the miasma arising from the decaying leaves of which was thought to be of a very injurious nature, yet the same cause is likely to render the Tulloh Blangah station as unhealthy, since the range along which the road runs, and till within a short distance of the site of the intended flag-staff, is thickly planted with young pine-apples! We dare say the Tomoongong, who is the proprietor of the ground, would be easily induced to substitute some less obnoxious cultivation, were the reasons for objecting to the cultivation of pine-apples on that spot explained to him."

In July, the Government advertised that the hill would, in future, be named Mount Faber, which called forth the following remonstrance in a letter to the *Free Press*:—

"In the first place, who is the ''orrid cockney' who changed the pretty and appropriate Malay name of the Hill? and why, having done so, call it after one who, although he is the Superintending Engineer in the Straits, is not, and most probably never will be, much known to the good folks of this Settlement? Have we not sundry Governors and others high in office, from Sir T S. Raffles down to our most worthy Resident Councillor himself who are deserving of the 'honour and glory'? Or is it because the present nominee has constructed a stupidly narrow road to the top of the Bukit—two persons meeting can barely pass each other—that so much renown is bestowed upon him?"

An artist named Beverhans visited Singapore during this year, and painted several portraits which are still to be seen. Among others one of Mr. Whampoa

The rate of postage *via* Marseilles on overland letters at that time was 2*s.* 2*d.* for a letter not exceeding a quarter of an ounce. The newspaper rate was 5*d.*

The gambier plantations in Singapore were becoming so thick, that the Chinese began to open up gardens in Johore, which have since grown to such a large extent. In June, the following was written about them:—" For some time past, it has been known that a considerable immigration of Chinese gambier and pepper planters from Singapore to the opposite country of Johore has been going on. From a memorandum made by a gentleman who lately visited the different points in Johore where the planters have settled, it appears that, within the last six months, 52 plantations have been commenced:—20 on the Sakodie river, 12 on the Sungei Malayu, 15 on the Sungei Danga, and 5 at Sungei Tambroh. There are about 500 people in all engaged in these plantations, and it is thought, and with probability, that the immigration will increase as the gambier and pepper plantations on this island wear out, which, from their age, many of them are fast doing. At Rhio, also, it is understood that most of the gambier and pepper plantations are nearly exhausted, so that the planters will be obliged to seek for new localities, which they will probably find in Johore.

At the end of August a public meeting was held on a requisition made to the Sheriff to consider entering into arrangements to obtain regular supplies of ice, and a committee of James Stephen, Lewis Fraser, and W. H. Read was appointed to see the Governor on the subject. As the Ice committee at Hongkong had arranged to have two vessels of Ice yearly sent from America, it was suggested that Singapore could compass one ship load.

The following letter in the paper in September, is the first mention of a country bungalow at Changhi:—"As the Changhi hut is now becoming the fashionable resort for pic-nic parties, I wish the Superintendent of Roads would take a ride down some morning to see the *holy* state of the roads between Arthur's Cottage and the river at Changhi; in fact 'tis almost unsafe for a conveyance to go there until it is repaired."

The following is taken from the *Free Press* of November:—"We are glad to learn that some intentions are entertained of forming a Company for making a dry Dock at Singapore, but we have not yet heard any particulars, nor how far the affair has progressed to a bearing. We understand, however, that the proposed site is in New Harbour, on Pulo Brani or some other island in that locality. New Harbour presents many advantages for a place of this kind, being smooth as an inland lake, and having a rise and fall of tide of about 12 feet. The undertaking, we should think, cannot fail to be profitable to the projectors. With so many steamers which already, and ere long will, arrive at our port monthly, and which will all, at times, have to encounter rough weather and adverse monsoons, a dry dock into which they can go and refit is almost indispensable. We shall, in all likelihood, before the lapse of another year, have steamers arriving here monthly from the following places:—Ceylon, Calcutta, Hongkong, Australia, Batavia and Manila. Indeed, steamers at present arrive from all these places except the two last, and, being generally vessels of a large size, there would be great difficulty in repairing one of them with the present means for the purpose in the Straits. A steamer, owing to her paddle boxes, cannot be hauled down upon the beach, and even for large sailing-vessels it is a very objectionable operation, exposing them to the risk of receiving much injury. Her Majesty's vessels, likewise, have at present no other place than Trincomalee to which they can go to repair, and a dry dock at Singapore would be peculiarly advantageous to them. They could come down from China, go into dock, refit, and be back at their station in a very short space of time. All these things considered, the scheme wears a most promising appearance—both of advantage to the public, and of remuneration to the undertakers—and it will therefore give us much pleasure to have it in our power on an early occasion to record that it has been commenced, or that active measures are in progress for its being so."

In January, 1846, it was mentioned again, and we publish the whole account, as it is interesting as compared with what has since been accomplished by our Dock Companies:—"Some weeks ago, we noticed that a proposal had been originated for constructing a Dry Dock at Singapore, and we are now happy to announce that the project has assumed such a practicable bearing as to enable us to lay a sketch of the details before our readers. The place pitched upon for a site is *Pulo Brani*, in New Harbour, almost directly opposite to the Tomoongong's House, a spot selected some time ago by Mr. C. Prinsep as a suitable location for a Patent Slip, but which, we believe, he has most readily ceded to the superior claims of the

Dry Dock. The situation has been carefully surveyed by practical persons, and is the most suitable and convenient in every respect in the neighbourhood of Singapore.

"It is proposed to construct a Dock of the following dimensions, by which it will be capable of accommodating vessels of the largest class :—

Length	300	feet.
Width	68	„
„ at Gate	48	„
Depth	15	„

"It will be approached by a canal 70 feet in width, and extending 280 feet from the dock gate. As the ground is soft, vessels will be able to lie in the canal for a tide if necessary. At the proposed entrance of the canal, there is a perpendicular bank running in a semi-circular form across the small bay in the centre of which the dock will stand; close to this bank the depth of water is 3½ fathoms, and at a short distance there will be placed mooring buoys, attached to which 8 or 10 vessels may lie in security free from the current. It is proposed to construct the masonry of the most substantial description. The bottom of the dock will consist of large logs of timber of the hardest description which can be procured, 120 feet long by 40 inches in diameter. It is proposed to build the dock on the same principle as that pursued in erecting the new Liverpool Graving Docks, with the exception of the gates, which will not be hung, but be one solid mass—which is considered a better plan than the others, being more easily worked, more durable, and less costly. As the rise and fall of water is only 11 feet, a small steam-engine will be required to pump the additional 3 or 4 feet out of the dock when necessary, but this, at the utmost, will not cost above £100 sterling. It is calculated that the dock would be so far ready in eight months after commencement, as to be available for the reception of sailing vessels, and would be entirely completed in twelve months.

"With regard to the financial part of the scheme, the following is a rough estimate of the probable cost and of the returns likely to be derived; and the latter, we believe, will be allowed by all our readers conversant with the subject to be a very moderate calculation.

"COST OF CONSTRUCTION AND ANNUAL CHARGES.

"A dry dock complete, with steam-engine, buoys, gate, capstans, posts, chains, counting-house, &c., it is estimated will not cost more than ... ... $ 80,000

Interest on $80,000 @ 10 per cent. per annum ...	$ 8,000
Annual repairs	1,000
Clerks' salaries, $140 per month; Watchmen, $10 ...	1,800
	$ 10,800

RECEIPTS.

Entrance fee on 30 vessels a year @ $100 each ...	$ 3,000
Remain in dock 2 days each after the first 24 hours, 60 @ $40	2,400
Two Large Bombay Ships, entrance $200	400
Remain in dock 4 days each or 8 days @ $60 ...	480
Two P. & O. Co. steamers, China line, require docking every three months, 8 @ $500	4,000
Two P. & O. Co. steamers, Australian line, require docking every three months, 8 @ $500	4,000
Two Dutch steamers will bring in yearly entrance fee ...	1,000
Two H. C. steamers will bring in yearly entrance fee ...	1,000
Twenty-one steamers in dock, one day each @ $80 ...	1,680
H. M. steamers and men-of-war, yearly, say	1,500
	$19,460
Excess of income	$ 8,660

or above 10½ per cent. clear annual profit, no doubt increasing in after years."

In September, the following was written:—"The Committee of Government *employés* nominated by his Honour the Governor to report on the proposal for the formation of a Dry Dock, have submitted a report to the local Government, which has been transmitted by the Governor to the merchants at whose instance the Committee was organised. In this report, is is stated that the Committee have fixed on a spot at Pulo Brani, which they recommend to be made the site of the proposed work, and which site they state 'whether for ease of construction or facility of approach at all times, may probably vie with any in the world.' Four estimates for the construction of the Dock had been submitted to the Committee, viz.:—

No. 1 of Wood	14 feet water, to cost	...	$ 76.290.28
No. 2 „ Brick	14 „ „ „	...	89,735.22
No. 3 „ Wood	18 „ „ „	...	87,658.52
No. 4 „ Stone & Brick 18 „ „ „	...	105,953.86

The last is the estimate which the Committee recommend for adoption, and they state that the estimate seems to possess such a degree of correctness as would allow the arrangements to be proceeded with, without any great chance of the actual cost being found to differ very widely from it. They have recommended the large size, as its adoption would probably lead to the P. & O. Company taking a considerable interest in the undertaking on account of the number of steamers they will have ere long plying in these seas."

It was in this year that the Esplanade was enclosed, as appears from a passage in the paper; the sea-wall was not yet built:— "We understand that it is in contemplation to enclose, with posts and chains, the whole of the space fronting the sea called Esplanade. This will be a decided improvement. and will secure pedestrians

within the enclosure from the danger attendant on the present
not infrequent use of this open spot as a race ground."

The following account of the introduction of Freemasonry into
the Straits was published in a Madras Review in March of this year,
and is interesting to the large number of the craft in Singapore :—

"In 1809, a warrant of constitution was first received in Penang
from the M. W. G. M. the Duke of Athol, though Lodges of instruction had been held for three or four years previously, during which
period two applications for charters had miscarried, it was supposed
by capture by the French of the vessels the letters were sent in,
with whom we were at that time at war. By this warrant of constitution the worthy Brother T. W. Court, was appointed Master, and
Bros. A. B. Bone and S. Stewart, Wardens. The Lodge met with
only partial success, and never at any time numbered above fifteen
members. The high rate of fees (three hundred and fifty dollars for
the three degrees), and the exclusive spirit with which the Lodge was
conducted, will readily count for its want of success; and though
there were several worthy and very zealous Brethren connected with
it, it gradually sunk into decay, and became finally extinct in 1819.

"In 1821, Brigadier O'Halloran, commanding the troops in Penang,
assisted by Bros. R. B. Smith and P. Ogilvie, obtained a warrant
from the Provincial Grand Lodge of Bengal, and established a military
Lodge designated "Humanity with Courage," and in a short space of
time Masonry became so popular in Penang, that almost every civilian
of respectability was ranged beneath its banners; but in 1825, Bro.
W. Stewart, an eminent Mason, commanding the barque *Lallah Rookh*,
of Liverpool, visited the Lodge, and pointed out its irregular and
unconstitutional proceedings, in making civilians in a military Lodge.
The result was an application, through Bro. Stewart, to the United
Grand Lodge of England, which was graciously and favourably
received by the M. W. the G. Master, H. R. H. the Duke of Sussex,
who renewed the warrant of the Atholl Lodge (Neptune, No. 344),
and confirmed the proceedings of the military Lodge. directing all
its members to be admitted on the register of the Grand Lodge.
The craft after this continued to prosper, under the vigorous management of Colonel Sale, of the Madras Army (brother of the illustrious
hero of Jellalabad), but after his return to the Coromandel Coast,
in 1828, it fell into great disrepute, owing to the improper proceedings and intemperate conduct of the Brother who was elected his
successor. The zealous and unwearied exertions of several eminent
Brethren who afterwards presided in the Lodge, among whom may
be named the late Bros. T. M. Ward, J. P. Grant, J. Wallace, G.
Pinnock, of the Madras Army, Bro. A. B. Kerr, now of that service,
and J. C. Smith, of Singapore, failed to meet with that success their
abilities and distinguished conduct, as Masters of the Lodge, deserved.
The odium of the past misconduct of a few appears to have been
indelible, and at the time I am now writing, and owing to these causes,
and the diminished commercial importance of the Settlement, with
the consequent great reduction in the number of its European inhabitants,
Neptune Lodge is again extinct, and little hope can reasonably be
entertained of its ever being revived.

"In 1843, the Lodge voted a silver vase to Bro. J. C. Smith, as a mark of its high esteem of his character and services during the fifteen years he had been connected with it; and at the same meeting a special vote of thanks was tendered to the late Bro. F. Dunnett, then about to proceed to China: and those only who knew him and loved him as a man and a Mason can sufficiently understand the high claims of this most excellent Brother to this distinction. Honoured be his memory! for Masonry and friendship will very seldom meet with one so worthy of such laudation.

"In 1844, an absurd attempt was made to constitute the then decaying Lodge into a Provincial Grand Lodge, in order to preserve the fading honour of the notable P. G. Master of Sumatra, who by some species of ingenious sophistry, peculiar to himself, has managed to claim Penang as a portion of *his* province, "the Rising Sun" in Sumatra having set beneath the Masonic horizon for more than twenty years, and his only other Lodge, in the moon, being beyond the reach of human ken. This ridiculous attempt was very properly and effectually resisted by the worthy Bro. R. W. Stonehewer, then presiding as Master of No. 293, and the late Bro. W. Anderson, who ably supported him in protecting an unfortunate but honourable section of our ancient and honourable Fraternity from being decorated with the loathsome trappings of a corpse, and rendered the object of contumely and contempt to the Craft in general. The worthy P. G. Master, deputed a Master Mason, who had systematically withheld his support from this declining Lodge, to take upon himself the office of D. G. Master, or in the event of his being disposed to display a magnificient self-abnegation of the appointment, to nominate any other equally deserving Brother he might select for this exalted office. So much for the legality of the contemplated proceedings of this Provincial Grand Master. The attempt was met with the scorn and contempt it so richly merited; for verily the purple of Sumatra is at discount in the Malacca Straits, however much it may be esteemed at the Board of General Purposes, Grand Festivals and other high places in the metropolis of the Craft and of the world.

"The vase voted to Bro. J. C. Smith was sent to Bro. T. O. Crane, for the purpose of being presented to him at Singapore, with a request that he would assemble as many Brethren as he could to be present on the occasion; and Bro. Crane having then, in a very appropriate speech, expressed his regret that he had not an opportunity of doing it in a Lodge after the proceedings of the day were over, the practicability of establishing a Lodge in Singapore was discussed, and Bros. Smith and Crane were requested to draw up the necessary petition to the United Grand Lodge of England for a warrant of constitution. This was eventually obtained through the kind instrumentality of Bros. D. Davidson and H. B. Webb. Bros J. C. Smith, C. A. Dyce, and T. O. Crane were appointed the first Master and Wardens of Zetland Lodge, No. 748. Some unavoidable delay occurred in the receipt of the warrant, and the Lodge was not regularly constituted until the 8th December last, when that interesting ceremony was performed by Bros. R. Taylor, P. M. of Social Friendship, 326. He went down from Malacca for this purpose, and the new Master and Wardens were then installed in due and ancient form. Zetland Lodge has been fitted up in a manner which does the highest credit to its members, and few stations in India, as I said before, can boast of a Masonic temple so creditable to themselves and the Craft. In four months there have been upwards of twenty initiations, and from the well-known respectability and indefatigable zeal of the officers and members of the Lodge, a permanent and most satisfactory career of success and usefulness may very reasonably be calculated upon. Zetland Lodge has voted a handsome Past Master's jewel to Bro. R. Taylor, in acknowledgment of his zeal and services.

"*List of the Officers of Zetland Lodge*, No. 748, established in Singapore, December 8th, 1845:—W. Bro. J. C. Smith, K.R.C., K.I. and M. W. Master; Bros. C. A. Dyce, S.W.; T. O. Crane, J.W.; J. B. Cumming, Sec. and Actg. Treas.; T. Smith, R.A., S.D.; W. Gibb, J.D.; J. Craig, I.G.; W. Rainford, Tyler."

On the 8th December, the first Masonic Lodge called *Zetland* was opened. The following account was given in the paper:—

"Pursuant to the Warrant of Constitution lately received from the Grand Lodge of England [dated February, 1845], 'Zetland Lodge, No. 748,' was opened in due form on Monday evening last, the Worshipful Master and Officers being installed and invested with their respective badges. There appears to be every prospect of this Lodge meeting with great success from the number of members already belonging to it, as well as from the numerous list of respectable candidates for *legitimate* admission to the mysteries and privileges of the ancient and honourable fraternity."

The Lodge was held in a house in Armenian Street. Mr. Wm. Napier was the first brother initiated, Mr. W. H. Read was the second, at the first meeting of the Lodge; and Mr. J. D. Vaughan at a meeting in the January following.

The following list of the Officers and Members was in the Directory at the commencement of 1846:—

W. Bro. J. C. Smyth	... ...	Worshipful Master.
Bro. C. A. Dyce, M.M.	... ...	Senior Warden.
„ T. O. Crane, M.M. ...	...	Junior Warden.
„ J. B. Cumming, M.M.	...	Secretary and Treasurer.
„ T. Smith, R.A.	... ...	Senior Deacon.
„ W. Gibb, M.M.	... ...	Junior Deacon
„ J. D. Scott, M.M. ...	...	Inner Guard.
„ W. Rainford, M.M.	...	Tyler.

Members:—E. A. Q. Apel, J. D. Booth, J. Chimmo, J. Craig, S. F. Cumming, C. J. J. Curteis, G. S. Darby, D. Davidson, T. Dunman, B. B. Keane, L. Fraser, W. S. Lawson, J. Myrtle, W. Napier, W. H. Read, W. Rodyk, W. Scott, J. Simson, J. Thomson, E. J. White and R. W. Wiber.

The *Singapore Free Press* had then been established ten years, and the following was written about it. In Mr. Horace St. John's *Indian Archipelago*, he said:—"The year 1835 is distinguished in the history of Singapore as that in which the *Free Press* was established. It is among the ablest and most influential journals in the East, conducted with remarkable vigour, and animated always by the

spirit of genuine liberality. It has made, indeed, a European reputation—among all, I mean, who turn their attention to the politics,
commerce, or social progress of the British Settlements in that remote
quarter of the world." Another writer said in that year:—"The
Singapore Free Press is the most noted paper in the East. The
central position from which it is published enables it to command the
best intelligence from China, Australia and the Islands, for which
reason a collection of the late numbers is the most acceptable present
in an Indian port. Its liberal and rational views, just and moderate
arguments, and the total absence of any little party spirit or prejudice,
give it higher claims on our esteem, and render it decidedly one of
the first British Colonial Journals."

On the 15th July, appeared the first number of the *Straits Times*.
It had been advertised as a new Journal to be issued on the morning
of Tuesday, the 15th July, and to be continued weekly. The printing
material had been ordered from England by Mr. Marterius Thaddeus
Apcar, of Apcar and Stephens, of Singapore, with the intention of
starting a newspaper with Mr. Edwards as Editor; but he had died,
and then the firm of Apcar and Stephens suspended payment, and
Mr. Gilbert McMicking was the Assignee of their estate. Mr. Catchick
Moses, to oblige Mr. Apcar, took over the printing material, and Mr.
R. C. Woods came from Bombay looking for employment, having
been obliged to leave there, and started the paper as Editor. It was
not a financial success at first, and Mr. Moses, after a year or so
gave up his connection with it, letting the price he had paid to Mr.
Apcar go against the deficiency, and Mr. Woods carried it on. It
consisted of eight folio pages, the subscription was $1.75 a month, or
$16 a year. The following is the commencement and some passages
from the opening article :—

"Good morning to you, kind reader! So you expect from us
some declaration of our 'intentions,' and the course we intend pursuing in
the management of the *Straits Times?* Like a candidate for other
honours than those we now seek, we proceed to declare our sentiments, whilst we aver the honourableness of our intentions. We have
mounted our *Pegasus*, which is a quiet and well-disposed animal, such
indeed as a gentleman of a certain age (like ourselves) ought to ride.
We desire to travel smoothly along, and therefore pray the 'powers
that be,' to keep the road of public economy in an efficient state;
never allowing the ruts to get too deep, nor placing obstructions in
the middle of the way, because our *Pegasus* is apt to shy, it might
kick, or do even greater violence. We have said our quadruped
possesses a good disposition, may it not be *crabbed*. What Tristam
Shandy said of his *Neddy*, so say we of ours :—'It is, if you recollect,
a quiet beast, he has scarce a hair or lineament of the *ass* about him.'
We have gone astride on him frequently 'to canter it away from the
cares and solicitudes of life'—now jogging, trotting, galloping; now
'going it' with the fleetness of an Arab. The *beau ideal* of a good-
tempered animal, our *Pegasus* will be found to prick his ears and laugh or
neigh as modestly as Aunt Cleary—but no more. We promise that its
past training will not altogether be lost upon it, and, in the disinterested
sympathy of our hearts, wish ourselves a pleasant ride of it."

In the middle of November, it turned into an issue twice a week, on Wednesdays and Saturdays, of four folio pages; but in January, 1849, it returned to its former mode of publication and appeared once a week only, on Wednesdays.

There was some correspondence in the newspaper about the keeping of St. Andrew's Day, which led to a Ball and Supper at the New Public Rooms (no doubt, including the new theatre) at which Messrs. Charles Carnie, C. A. Dyce, Lewis Fraser, Alexander Guthrie, Dr. Robert Little, R. McEwen, William Napier, Archibald and Charles Spottiswoode, and J. Stephen were the Stewards. The paper remarked that the Raffles Club, which had existed in the early days from 1825 to 1835, ought to be revived, as they used to have very animated festivities on the anniversary of the Settlement and other annual celebrations.

On the 25th November the Theatre which had been built by Subscription at the Assembly Rooms at the foot of Fort Canning, was opened with a comedy and a farce. The prices were $2 and $1, and the performance began at 8 o'clock. There is no description of the building, but the paper said that the stage was larger than that at the old theatre, which was in Dutronquoy's Hotel, the Drop Scene, painted by one of the Amateurs, most likely Mr. Charles Dyce, was a view of Singapore from Sandy Point. There was an Amateur Orchestra, which was highly praised.

The following passages are part of an account of the progress of Singapore in the year 1845, which was written at the close of the year:—

"A new importance has been attached to Singapore during the past year from its having become the focus where steamers from different places periodically congregate with news from Europe and various quarters of the Far East. During the present year, these ramifications are likely to be increased by lines to Australasia and Manila. The Calcutta line, though for the present apparently suspended, will not, in all probability, be long unoccupied either by the Peninsular and Oriental Navigation Company or some other association, who will not fail to derive a handsome profit from it. The discovery of extensive beds of good coal in Borneo, adapted for the use of steamers, is of much importance, and will greatly facilitate the perfecting of the arrangements for steam navigation in this quarter of the world. Though nothing definite has transpired as to the results of Capt. Bethune's recent mission to Borneo, there is every reason to believe that during the present year a British Settlement will be formed in Borneo.

It is a subject of much congratulation to find, on casting a glance over our columns for the past year, that there exists almost no record of any cases of piracy in our harbour similar to those which, a year or two ago, were so frequent in occurrence and so detrimental to our native trade. This change has been brought about by the activity of Her Majesty's and the East India Company's vessels of war, which have always been on the alert, and is, no doubt, also greatly due to the terrible lessons read to the pirates of Borneo during the past and the preceding years by

His Excellency the Admiral, the Hon. Capt. Keppel, Sir E. Belcher, &c. The native traders may now resort to our port, even though unarmed like the Cochin-Chinese, with very little dread of violence by the way.

"The local Authorities having discovered that slave-dealing existed to a considerable extent in some of the neighbouring States, accompained by circumstances of much cruelty, have exerted themselves with much success in rescuing the unfortunate victims of it, and endeavouring to suppress the traffic.

"The recent visit of the H. C. steam-vessel *Phlegethon* to Cochin-China has manifested the favourable disposition of the English and Cochin-Chinese Governments towards each other, and may have the tendency to encourage the resort of Cochin-Chinese trading vessels to this port, an event which the suppressing of piracy, from which the unarmed Cochin-Chinese traders who ventured to come to Singapore used to suffer so severely, may help to promote.

"In regard to more purely local subjects, the Post Office has been improved to meet the enlarged demands upon it, consequent on the extension of the overland steam arrangements to this port. It is still susceptible of much improvement, which will, no doubt, be effected during the present year. Renewed efforts are being made by the local Authorities and the mercantile body to procure the erection of a light-house at the South entrance of Singapore Straits. The heavy loss of property, even during the past year, attributable in a great measure to the want of such a conspicuous guide by day as well as by night, is an unanswerable argument both for its necessity and speedy erection.

"A majority of the Chamber of Commerce have declared an opinion in favour of the introduction of an Insolvent law into the Settlement—an opinion which is acquiesced in by the great majority of traders, European and Native. Unless, however, the Indian Law Commissioners are prepared with their general scheme of an Insolvent law for India, there is no probability of an Insolvent law being introduced into the Straits during the present year, as the existing Insolvent law in operation at the Presidencies is acknowledged to be defective, and the Supreme Government would therefore, we presume, be unwilling to sanction its application to the Straits, since the amended scheme for the whole of India will probably be ready in the course of a year or two.

"A considerable number of local improvements have been effected during the past year, the chief of which may be indicated as the extension of the roads in the interior. The line known as the Kranjie road, extending from Bukit Timah to the Old Straits, about 8 miles in length, was completed during the past year, and is now very extensively used by the gambier and pepper cultivators on the line for conveying their wares to town, instead, as heretofore, of transporting them round by the Straits in large boats. A similar line of road has been commenced from within a short distance of Singapore to a different part of the Old Straits, which promises to be a most useful as well as an exceedingly picturesque road. This road is the first the construction of which has been commenced by private contractors in terms of the permission accorded by the Supreme Government some months ago. The contractors and labourers are all Chinese, and they are found to make the roads much more quickly, as well as cheaply, than has ever been effected by means of convict labour. The funds from which these roads are to be constructed are those derived from the sale of the Government lands, and we suppose that provisions have been, or will be, made from this source for keeping these and the other country roads in repair, otherwise they will soon become comparatively useless. It is hopeless to look to the assessments for this purpose, as they are found barely adequate to keep up the present avowedly inefficient Police force and effect the imperfect cleansing of the town. Besides, it does not seem at all fair to tax the inhabitants of the town for keeping up the roads in the country, and, therefore, until the increase and extension of cultivation allow of the levy of an assessment adequate for the purpose, which may perhaps be about 20 or 30 years hence, the roads ought to be kept up out of the proceeds of the land sales, which the making of roads is calculated greatly to promote.

"Improvements in town also proceed apace. Many—or we may say with truth, most—of the old wooden houses which in the beginning of the year gave such a ruinous and decaying look to the town, have now been replaced by handsome and substantial looking brick houses, and, ere many months more have passed, the principal streets bid fair to shew nothing but brick edifices, confining the wooden erections to the poorer parts of the town. The Seamen's Hospital has been finished and opened for the reception of patients; and Tock Seng's Hospital is approaching completion. A large space of ground, heretofore a swamp overflowed by the tide, and known to older residents by the name of Kampong Malacca, has been partially filled up and laid out into building lots, which will, no doubt, be exposed to sale during this year. A commodious public market [Ellenborough Market] is being constructed in this quarter, and Tan Tock Seng is far advanced with the erection of an extensive range of shops on a uniform plan and with more pretensions to architectural beauty than the general run of such *boutiques*. This quarter is to bear the name of "Ellenborough Buildings!" The improvements on Government Hill, comprehending the enlargement of the burying ground, are now nearly completed, and will add much to the beauty of this part of Singapore. A want of sufficient drainage is still apparent in many places in and near town, and there are one or two noisome swamps in town the filling up of which with wholesome earth would greatly conduce to the comfort and health of the inhabitants.

"The trade of the Settlement during the past year must, on the whole, be pronounced to have been prosperous; but it has been the quiet, monotonous prosperity of steady, moderate, or even low prices, with little of the excitement of speculation, or large losses balanced by large profits, which has so often prevailed in former years. The story told by the shop-keepers and small native dealers is that they have to encounter much rivalry for small profits, but at the same time their profits have been tolerably certain, affording, with judicious management, a fair price for their labour and a fair return for their capital, which is generally of a very limited nature.

"The importing merchants and extensive native dealers give nearly the same report as regards their trade; the more sanguine and speculative will pronounce 1845 to have been a bad year, while the plodding and steady will probably admit it to have been "not so bad." Its characteristic may be said to have been low prices and want of speculation.

"It would be at best a delicate task to enter upon the moral statistics of the Settlement, and in this place it would not be much use as the changes which one year can effect must be very slight indeed. We may notice, however, that the Library has been in operation for some time past, and that, scanty as are its stores, the increasing number of those wishing to avail themselves of its benefits, augurs well for the intellectual and moral habits of the European portion of the community. It may, indeed, be remarked that here, as in other parts of India, an evident change is taking place in the general tone of society—a change which the diminishing number of old stagers deplore and exclaim against, while the recent arrivals from Europe are somewhat surprised and pleased to find here so little difference from the tone of good society among the middle classes at home. The regular and rapid intercourse now maintained with the Mother Country, by tending to keep alive home feelings and affections, and the constant supply of new intellectual food which every mail brings, keeping the sojourner in India almost on a par with those at home as regards the literature and science of the passing day, must contribute materially to bring about this alteration."

CHAPTER XXXIII.

1846.

IN March, a fire broke out in Market Street, at ten o'clock at night, just behind the Square. The Police gongs were beaten and the bell of St. Andrew's Church was rung. There was no water to be got for some time, and a deal of thieving went on. A general store of Ching Wan & Co. was burned down, also a godown of Chin Sing & Co., full of rattans, but as there was no wind, the fire was then stopped. The necessity of some organization like a Fire Brigade was again prominently discussed, but it was not formed.

The following is an account of a Hoey riot in March, which caused a good deal of talk at the time:—"On Tuesday last, the town of Singapore was comparatively in a state of siege, in consequence of some apprehensions on the part of the authorities that disturbances would arise on that day: indulgence in such fears, if not in a great measure the working spirit of the commotion, contributed greatly to extend it, by causing alarm in the breasts of the quiet, loyal, and well disposed. The Head of the Hoeys, a secret and powerful society of Chinese, expired about eighteen days ago, and an application was made last week to the Magistrates to grant permission to bury the body with due form, procession, and the outward display usual on the occasion of the funeral of the chief of the order. The Magistrates consented to allow a procession to be formed, provided the number of followers did not exceed one hundred, and with the condition that the procession would pass through the direct line of road to the burial ground. The Heads of the Hoey acquiesced in the arrangement. Early on Tuesday morning, the whole Police force was mustered, and was chiefly located near the Chinese Temple at Rochor, outside the town. About 10 o'clock a.m., information was received at the Police Office that several thousands of Chinese were assembled in front of the temple at Rochor, where the body of the deceased was placed, and that the whole of them were resolved on passing through the town, staying in such streets of it as they thought proper, to perform ceremonies, and alleging that they had received permission from the Resident Councillor to proceed the way they listed; a sanction neither applied for, nor likely to be granted. Captain Adam Cuppage, 27th Madras Native Infantry, who was Assistant Resident, and Mr. Dunman, Deputy Superintendent of Police, proceeded to Rochor, expecting that by confronting the procession at the place where it was forbidden to go, they would effectually deter the rabble from entering the town. As soon as the men with banners in advance of the procession diverged into the road leading to Kampong Glam, the Police Magistrates told them to halt; they did so. In the meantime a parley was attempted. Captain Cuppage remained on the bridge at Rochor, where a party of Police peons was stationed, and Mr. Dunman, accompanied by a Chinese interpreter, proceeded to the front of the temple. Mr. Dunman addressed the chiefs of the Hoey and remonstrated with them on their want of faith in collecting together nearly six thousand persons instead of one hundred to follow the body to the grave: they, in reply, declared themselves unable to restrict the numbers or control them. Mr. Dunman was about to return to consult with Captain Cuppage when a Chinese cooly called out "*Pah-pah,*" meaning "beat." Mr. Dunman seized him by the throat, and dragged him away and gave him in charge to Captain Cuppage. The latter delivered him over to the constables to convey to the Thannah, but on the way a rescue was effected. As soon as the cooly was seized, the mob commenced beating the Chinese interpreter with the iron instruments they place on their hands, and also jumped upon him. Mr. Dunman returned to the assistance of the interpreter; with the butt end of a musket he drove off the people that were maltreating the interpreter, and brought the latter away in triumph; an act of humanity and gallantry that cannot be too loudly praised. The rescue of the cooly gave an impulse to the mass; the procession moved on, each member of the Hoey declaring that he would proceed along Kampong Glam. The order for the advance was hailed with a general shout, and on they went.

"Information was sent to the civil authorities' stating to what length the Chinese had gone, and that the civil force was incapable of controlling the mass of people which was now fast increasing, threatening the town with pillage and destruction. An express was despatched for the troops, who were soon in readiness, and arrived in time to prevent the procession passing near the Court House and up Hill Street. The avenues thus being closed, the Chinese turned down Coleman Street into South Bridge Road, thence over the bridge to the burial ground beyond the Cantonment. By the judicious placing of the troops at the avenues leading to South Bridge Road, the procession was prevented from passing into the town, and, by stopping the lines of communication, any addition to the number of followers was prevented."

Long letters were written to the paper about the necessity of putting down the secret societies, and the peace of the town was considerably disturbed for a fortnight, when the Hoeys finally made terms with each other. The following proclamation was issued in Chinese, and posted up through the town and on the temples:—

"To the Chinese living in Singapore this notice is given, and they are to conform strictly thereto. The practice of assembling in large numbers and proceeding along the public roads with flags, music, or arms of any description is forbidden, and, if attempted, will be at their peril. No processions will be allowed having any connection with illegal societies of any description, and should this order be infringed, all guilty persons will be considered as disturbers of public peace, and if, on being duly warned, they fail to disperse, will ba treated as such."

The following account of the attack on the house of Mr. Thomas Hewetson on Mount Elizabeth, appeared in the paper in April. Mr. Hewetson was a clerk to the Magistrates, and the event is still remembered in Singapore, although the particulars are forgotten :—

"On the night of the 30th March, a most daring and successful gang robbery was perpetrated in the house of Mr. T. Hewetson, about two miles from town. The house is situated on an eminence in his plantation, which is completely surrounded by a large hedge. It appears that a gang of 200 Chinese proceeded to Mr. Hewetson's a little after midnight, and after taking the most deliberate precautions by posting sentinels at the entrance into the plantation from the public road, the main body proceeded to the house, where they overpowered the watchman and other persons near the premises, beating and dispersing them. They then surrounded the house, which is a bungalow built of wood upon high posts. Mr. Hewetson, who had not long retired to rest, heard, between half-past 12 and 1 o'clock, a great noise under the house, stamping of feet and clashing of sticks, and his men calling out "China, China." This continued for about 8 or 10 minutes before the Chinese came up to the back verandah of the house, where they commenced battering at the door opening into the verandah, which was secured by a strong wooden bar. While they were trying to break in, Mr. Hewetson fired through the door, and continued doing so as fast as he could load, which kept them in check for about 20 minutes. They then succeeded in making an opening in the door of about one inch and a half by six inches, through which they thrust their spears, endeavouring to enlarge the opening, Mr. Hewetson at the same time firing through upon the robbers. In about ten minutes more the door was almost shattered to pieces, when Mr. Hewetson retired with his family to a loft in the top of the house to which access is had by a trap door. The Chinese, being undisturbed, soon broke the outer door, and at once proceeding to the door of a small room in which Mr. Hewetson kept his money and plate, &c., they quickly forced it and broke open a number of boxes, almeirahs, &c., from which they abstracted about 400 dollars, silver spoons, clothes, a box containing a number of papers, &c., &c. Having thus effected their purpose, they immediately left the house, being saluted by a parting shot of slugs from a blunderbuss, and would appear to have immediately separated, as Mr. Gilbert Angus, who lives about half a mile from the spot, and had been awakened by the shots and screams of the female members of Mr. Hewetson's family, on going up with some of his men, met about 15 armed with sticks coming from Mr. Hewetson's who, on his calling on them to stop, prepared to attack him, on which he fired a pistol, which appeared to drop one of them, and, drawing his sword rushed under their guard and endeavoured to cut some of them down. He was, however, immediately assailed by all the number, and receiving some severe blows on his head, shoulders, and hands, he was stunned, and dropped his sword, on which the men immediately made off. This was the only resistance, independent of that offered by Mr. Hewetson and his people, which they encountered, although it was near two o'clock before they left the house, as the Police did not arrive until some time afterwards.

"They would appear to have proceeded with their attack with the utmost coolness and confidence. The room in which Mr. Hewetson stood when firing through the door was lighted by a lamp, which enabled the robbers to watch his movements. There were traces of blood in the verandah and on the ground, so that some persons must have been wounded, but to what extent is of course unknown. We are informed that the Klings, Malays, Javanese and other Natives residing in a circuit to the North West and South of Mr. Hewetson's were aware at 11 o'clock p.m., that something was in the wind, as they state that they heard the concerted signals made by the Chinese for assembling."

Three Chinese were convicted of being concerned in the gang-robbery, and the Recorder sentenced them to transportation to Bombay for fourteen years, and, in passing sentence, dwelt at length on the dangerous and unlawful nature of the secret societies with which it had been proved the prisoners were connected.

The house was the first built on Mount Elizabeth, near the top of the hill at the right hand side of the road. There is an attap bungalow still on the site, which is quite closely surrounded by tile-roofed houses.

In consequence of the Chinese riots, a proposal was made to establish a Volunteer Force, but it was not realised for nearly ten years afterwards.

At the Assizes in April, the Grand Jury in their presentment complained of the state of the Police, and of the continuance of certain nuisances in the town, such as the swamp in front of the goal, and the broken down foot-bridge. It would have attracted no particular notice but for the extraordinary behaviour of the Governor, Colonel Butterworth, who, as was usual in those days, sat on the Bench, as one of the Judges, with the Recorder, Sir William Norris. The Governor complained of the Grand Jury having spoken of the Police as *disgraceful*, and of other matters as *unfair* on the part of Government, lost his temper, threw the blame of any delay or shortcomings on the Bengal Government, and went into a long tirade on the subject of his own devotion, zeal and energy for the welfare of the Settlements. It was an explosion which caused a great deal of talk, and was spoken of as an "extraordinary performance, which, for the sake of the dignity of the Bench, as well as of public functionaries, it was hoped we ne'er may look upon its like again."

The following extract from the *Free Press* is interesting as the recommencement of the gambling farm argument:—

"On the 29th April, Charles Cashin, formerly a police constable, was found guilty of having received bribes from the keepers of gambling shops, to connive at their existence, and on the 1st instant, was brought up to receive sentence. The Hon'ble the Recorder, in passing sentence, said that it had been fully proved that the prisoner had been guilty of a gross neglect of duty. It appeared that he was well acquainted with the extensive gambling which was carried on, he knew of it, and ought to have informed against it that it might have been put down, instead of which he received a bribe to sanction its continuance. The Court must therefore pass sentence upon him. It has been asserted by the public journals that it was impossible to put down gambling: his Lordship could not agree with them; he did not see the impossibility; he thought it could be put a stop to if the police did their duty. It was only through the corruption of the police that such sinks of iniquity were permitted to exist. If the constables were honest men, the evil would be put a stop to, but he must declare his opinion that not only the prisoner but all the constables had been guilty of receiving bribes for conniving at this system. (The prisoner here interrupted his Lordship and said that for three years past all the constables had received $20 each monthly, from the keepers of the gambling shops, that the evidence against him was all false, and that the constable who had brought the charge against him had himself received bribes. It was a conspiracy against him to deprive him of his situation, and get it for another person.) The Recorder then proceeded to say that he believed they were all implicated, and that if they did their duty, gambling might be put down. If the constables had any honesty they would come forward and confess their fault, and he was sure their doing so would be in their favour, if they resolved on pursuing a better course in future. The prisoner Charles Cashin was then sentenced to be imprisoned for eighteen months, and to pay a fine of 1,000 dollars, and to be further imprisoned until the fine was paid.

Some of the constables present then came forward and represented that they felt much hurt at his Lordship's observations regarding them. They denied their guilt, and said that they had endeavoured to put down the gambling shops, but that an order had been issued forbidding them to interfere with them! His Lordship said he thought there must be some mistake, he could not think how such an extraordinary order could have been given, but even if it had, it was their duty to disregard it, and to enforce the law. The constables explained that the order was verbal.

Mr. Dunman, Deputy Superintendent of Police, was then sent for, and admitted that such an order had been given. It was not given by him, but by Major Low, the former Superintendent of Police. Previously, orders had been given to the police to put down the gambling shops, and to stimulate them to do their duty and to counteract the effect of the bribery on the part of the keepers of the gambling shops, the police had been promised half of whatever money was found upon the table. They had accordingly gone to work, but it was found that the whole time of the police was engrossed by it to the total neglect of their other duties, and it was therefore found necessary to annul the order. In reply to an observation from the Recorder, Mr. Dunman said he considered it impossible to put down the gambling shops. They had communications with the neighbouring houses so that the persons engaged could always make their escape, but he thought the most insuperable obstacle was in the power which the keepers of the gambling shops possessed of corrupting the police. The Recorder observed that that was the very thing he thought ought to be remedied; the police ought to be honest. Mr. Dunman said with a native police it was impossible, where could you get an honest native of the grade of a policeman? The police were in the regular pay of the keepers of the gambling shops, and it could not be prevented with the large means of bribery which the gambling shops in Singapore, one hundred and ninety-one in number, afforded."

It appears from the following passage that gambling was permitted at the Chinese New Year:—

"The active measures taken against the gambling shops in consequence of the Recorder's remarks, have had a most serious effect upon the Revenue Farms, the Opium and Spirit Farms especially, the renters of which have experienced a very large decrease in their sales. Such an effect was to be anticipated, and perhaps a knowledge of this has been the cause of the leniency with which the gambling shops have heretofore been treated. It is well known that it is at the instance of the Opium and Spirit Farmers, that the fortnight's license for open gambling at the Chinese New Year is granted by those in authority. Would it not be better to have a gambling farm at once, than all these miserable shifts and inconsistencies, apparent disapprobation, and virtual countenance?"

In July, a suggestion was again made to establish a Savings Bank, which Sir Benjamin Mulkin had advocated in 1833. There was some correspondence on the subject, but nothing was done.

There is a tablet in St. Andrew's Cathedral to Captain Maitland, R.N., as is said on page 298. The following is an extract from a lengthy report in the *Free Press* of his services:—

"We regret having to announce the death of William Maitland, Esq., Commander, R.N., at the early age of 44. Captain Maitland, who has commanded H. M. steamer *Spiteful* on the Indian Station for the last three years, was a nephew of the late Earl of Lauderdale, and also of the late Admiral Sir Frederick Maitland, entered the Royal Navy at an early age, and during the earlier part of his career served for several years in the West Indies, where he was actively employed against the pirates. In 1841, when 1st Lieutenant of the *Benbow*, he distinguished himself in the operations on the coast of Syria, and for his services there received his promotion as Commander. In December, 1842, Captain Maitland commissioned the steamer *Spiteful*, and arrived on the Indian Station in August, 1843. Since his arrival in the East he has been actively employed in various parts of the Station—in China, in India, and in the Archipelago. During the late war, in the Punjaub, the *Spiteful* was employed in conveying troops to various points, and only a month or two ago, in Borneo, Captain Maitland's duties were laborious and incessant. The flag of Rear-Admiral Sir J. T. Cochrane, was hoisted on board the *Spiteful* during the ascent of the river Bruni and the attack on the capital, and it is supposed that the fatigue which Captain Maitland underwent on this occasion may have assisted in bringing on the attack which carried him off. The *Spiteful* came up here from Borneo with despatches, and on the news being received of the wreck of the *Frederick IV.*, a few days after the steamer's arrival, she immediately proceeded to the spot to render assistance. The exposure and fatigue which Captain Maitland here underwent brought on a return of bilious remittent fever, under which he had suffered severely about two years previously; the attack was of a most severe nature, and although at one time he rallied, and hopes were entertained of his recovery, these proved fallacious, and he sunk under the strength of the disease, having expired on board his vessel in the roads at midnight on Monday, 11th August."

The proceedings of the English Government and Mr. Brooke in Borneo, were attracting considerable attention in Europe at this time, the recent volumes of Captain Keppel—" The Narrative of the Expedition to Borneo of H. M. S. *Dido*"—having placed the whole subject in a clearer and more distinct light than formerly, and shown what were the precise objects which the English Government, or rather its agent, Mr. Brooke, had in view. The Dutch journals were filled with violent denunciations of the faithlessness of England, which was accused, in the negotiations regarding Labuan, &c., of having violated the treaty of 1824, and they called for an instant vindication of the rights of Holland; the English journals, on the other hand, generally upheld the necessity of our occupying Labuan, though some of them sided with the Dutch in their interpretation of the treaty of 1824, but contended that it did not apply to that part of Borneo to which our operations were confined; the French journals held the balance and arbitrated between the two parties. The subject was discussed in a lively and acute manner in the French periodical, the *Revue des Deux Mondes*, of 15th May.

It appears from a remark in the newspaper in June, that the neighbourhood of Mount Elizabeth was notorious for tigers at this time. The police peons making their rounds in Orchard Road one Sunday night, disturbed a tiger close to the road at Mr. Hewetson's gate, the present entrance to Mount Elizabeth.

It was in that year that the fire-wells were made near the Square, which were adopted as a precautionary measure in consequence of the frequency of fires, and the total absence of water at low tide. They were filled up twenty years ago. They were large wells in the centre of the roads, several in the Square and Malacca Street, covered by square plank flap-doors, which lay level with the road.

In Java, at this time, slavery was still openly recognised, and in the *Java Courant* advertisements of men, women and children for sale were mixed up with sales of horses, wine, &c. The *Free Press* printed some of these advertisements as an example; the following is one of them:—

To be sold by private contract; a family of very good slaves consisting of seven persons; other information will be given by

VOUTE & GUERIN.

Voute & Guerin will, at the auction, on Monday, 11th instant, at Rijswijk, sell on account of the estate of the late Mrs. Petel the following slaves, viz.:—

Dantong, aged 48 years, cowherd.
Pelo, otherwise *Constantie*, aged 37 years, washerman.
Malative, aged 17¼ years, lady's maid.
Mochamat, aged 14½ years, house-boy.
Antionetta, aged 13½ years, lady's maid: and
Selana, aged 2½ years:
together with an entirely new Brussells-waggon.

On Tuesday, the 31st August, the Sword of Honour, which the late Sultan of Johore carried with him on state occasions, and which was often seen at Government House on the Queen's birthday, was presented to the Tumoongong. The following inscription is on the sword:—Presented in the year 1846 to the Tumoongong of Johore Sree Maharajah, by Lt.-Col. Butterworth, c.b., Governor of Prince of Wales' Island, Singapore and Malacca, as a testimony of the high estimation in which the services of the Sree Maharajah in the suppression of piracy are held by the Government of India. The following account of the ceremony was written at the time. Government House was then where Fort Canning barracks are now:—" In consequence of the assistance rendered by the Tumoongong of Singapore in the suppression of piracy, the Indian Government determined upon presenting His Highness with a Sword His Honour the Governor, being desirous of fulfilling the wishes of the Supreme Government in the most public manner, invited nearly the whole of the community to be present at the interesting ceremony which took place on Tuesday last at the Government House. For the convenience of the public generally, several tents were pitched on Government Hill, and preparations made on the most liberal scale. The natives seemed to consider it a holiday, and at an early hour Chinese, Malays, Javanese, Chuliahs, Hindoos, &c., &c., were seen swarming into the town from all quarters, and long before the appointed hour Government Hill presented a very animated scene. Guns were taken from the Battery and placed near the House, two companies of the 27th M. N. I. accompanied by all the Officers and the band, were in attendance.

" At two o'clock, His Highness left the Court House, accompanied by the Resident Councillor, the Sultan of Johore, the Sultan of Lingin, Tuanku Jaffar, Major Carthew, &c., and on arriving at the foot of the hill proceeded in the Governor's carriage until he reached the guard of honour, when he alighted and walked to the Government House, a salute being fired. After a short interval, during which His Highness was introduced, with his friends, to some of the ladies, the Governor handed him to the verandah, the sword being placed on a table, and opposite the numerous followers of the Tumoongong were arranged. Another salute was fired on presenting the sword. The Tumoongong was evidently delighted with the attention of the Governor in inviting the ladies, and such a numerous company of gentlemen—including the officers of H. N. M. steamer *Merapi*, the Military, and Foreign Consuls, &c.—to meet him. Shortly after the ceremony, His Highness left with the same honours as on his arrival. About 3 o'clock the guests, amounting to 90, sat down to a splendid tiffin at the hospitable table of the Governor, who spoke as follows :—

" ' It is almost superfluous to mention the purpose for which we are assembled here this morning, and more so to enter into details of the rapine and murders formerly committed in these seas by formidable bodies of what are justly termed the enemies of all mankind—pirates—now for the most part subdued and dispersed by the gallantry of our Navy, ever first and foremost to meet danger and difficulty in every shape.

" ' Happily, for some time past, piracy has been rarely heard of in the vicinity of our own shores, and when isolated cases have occurred, the perpetrators have generally been apprehended, through the exertions of the local authorities, and the able and willing assistance afforded by the neighbouring chieftains of Pahang, Tringanu and Lingin, but more especially by the powerful aid of His Highness Sree Maharajah, the

Tumoongong of Johore, to whom I am directed to present this sword, in testimony of the estimation in which his services in the suppression of piracy are held by the Government of India.

"'I congratulate you, Sree Maharajah, on the high compliment that has been paid to you, and I can assure you that I experience the most deep and heartfelt satisfaction in being called upon to present you with this token of the esteem of our most just and ever generous Government.

"'Let me say a word or two, to one and all of the Malayan and Chinese people here assembled. The sole desire of the Government of India is, that you should live in peace and happiness, enjoying the benefit of the traffic which is carried on with all parts of the Eastern Archipelago; but this is impossible if piracy prevail, and I would therefore urge you to exert yourselves to discover and give information of the haunts of these enemies of all mankind, these pirates, if any still there be located at Singapore, assuring yourselves in so doing of the protection and reward of Government.'

"To which the Tumoongong replied 'Colonel Butterworth, in laying at your feet my sincere thanks for the high distinguished honour which you have conferred upon me, I am much pleased that my conduct should have met with the approbation of Government, and that my humble exertions should have been conducive to the welfare of this community. Highly do I value this splendid testimonial of your approbation, with pride shall I wear it, and as an heir-loom it will be handed down to my posterity. My gratitude for the good wishes which you have now uttered, it is difficult for me to express, and the kind consideration which you have always shown towards me is engraven on my heart; with pleasure have I witnessed the zeal with which you have carried out so many public improvements, and with admiration will future ages view these splendid monuments of your fostering care over all classes of this community. You govern wisely; may you govern long, and may He who rules the destinies of Mahometans and Christians watch over and aid you in all your wise and good works.'"

The total receipts of Singapore for the official year 1845-46, exclusive of military and convicts, which it was considered should be debited to India, amounted to Rs. 530,000, and the disbursements to Rs. 253,500. The latter included one-third of the Governor's and Recorder's salaries and of the expenses of the Colonial steamers, the other two-thirds being considered as debited to Penang and Malacca. The result of the year was an excess of revenue in Singapore alone of Rs. 276,492, or about $140,000. The excise farms produced Rs 425,000, being Rs. 2,500 increase over that of the previous year.

It was in this year that the Oriental Bank started. Mr. Cargill and Mr. Scrymgeour arrived in Singapore on the 8th February, to establish the Branch. The head-quarters of the Bank were then at Bombay, and branches had already been opened at Calcutta, Ceylon, and Hongkong. The following circular was issued in Singapore, and business began on the 1st May:—

ORIENTAL BANK.

Arrangements having been made towards establishing a Branch of the Oriental Bank in this place, the Office will be open for general business on the 1st proximo, in the meantime proposals to transact business will be entertained.

EXCHANGE.

The Bank draws as follows:—

On the Union Bank of London from one day sight fixed to six months sight fixed.

On the National Bank of Scotland and branches at one day sight.

On the Branches of the Provincial Bank of Ireland at one day sight fixed.

And on Bombay, Calcutta, Colombo, and China at any term.

The Bank undertakes to remit money to Great Britain by each Overland Mail, free of charge, for Constituents, at the current Exchange, payable in any town where there is a Bank or Banker.

The Bank has also on hand Bank of England Post Bills in convenient sums for parties proceeding to Europe.

INTEREST ALLOWED.

On Fixed Deposits for three months certain, repayable on thirty days' notice, three per cent. per annum.

Ditto, for six months with ninety days' notice, four per cent. per annum.

On Current Deposits or Floating Accounts, no interest is allowed, and no commission charged.

INTEREST CHARGED.

On Loans and Cash Credits

For 2 months on Deposit of Goods and other securities, 11 per cent. per annum.

For 3 months on Deposit of Goods and other securities, 12 per cent. per annum.

DISCOUNT.

On Local Bills and Promissory Notes.

for 1, 2, and 3 months—10, 11 and 12 per cent. per annum.

The rates of advances on Goods and other securities, and particular rules as to current and other accounts, can at all times be ascertained on application at the Office.

WM. ANDERSON,
Interim Manager,
Singapore Branch.

Commercial Square, 21st April, 1846.

In October, the roof of the covered landing place which was being erected in the river, where the landing steps are now near the front of the Government Offices, gave way and seriously injured several workmen. The pillars were too thin and the roof came down with a rush. The paper in speaking of it said of the engineer in charge:—

"Captain Faber has hitherto been rather unfortunate in his architectural and engineering undertakings in Singapore. First, Faber's Bridge could not be made to maintain its proper position until after several attempts; next, the walls of the new market, after it was finished, were found to be cracking most alarmingly in several places, owing to the ends of the building proving too heavy in comparison to the sides, and, from the treacherous nature of the soil, which had not been sufficiently guarded against, beginning to sink very fast. The pediments, which were of an ornamental character, were therefore obliged to be removed, and the building now presents, when viewed from either end, a bald and meagre appearance. The next undertaking of any moment was the landing place, which has proved equally, or more, unlucky. The new gaol, we hope, will afford Captain Faber an opportunity of redeeming his reputation.

The paper in November contained the following paragraph:—

"We have much pleasure in noticing that a place for bathing is likely to be fenced in from the harbour in front of the Esplanade, where the Singaporeans will be enabled to enjoy the delightful recreation of sea bathing. A meeting was held on Friday last to discuss the subject, and consult about the necessary arrangements, when a managing committee was appointed to carry out the views of the subscribers. We wish the project all success, and trust it will receive all the support that our community can give it." The proposal was never carried out, but sometimes on moonlight nights as late as 1870, a few young people used to go and swim off the centre of the Esplanade.

In November, a meeting was held of gentlemen favourable to the establishment of a Scotch Church at Singapore. The meeting took place in Little, Cursetjee & Co.'s godowns, and the following is an account of what took place:—

"A meeting of the Scotch Presbyterians was held on Friday, the 27th November, for the purpose of taking steps for forming a Presbyterian Congregation in Singapore and procuring a Clergyman of that denomination to settle amongst them; G. G. Nicol, Esq., being in the Chair. The meeting, which was pretty numerous, was of the most satisfactory nature. The following are the resolutions which were come to:—

"1st.—Proposed by Mr. Stephen and seconded by Mr. Fraser:—That for the sake of unanimity the minority accede to the wishes of the majority as to the proper plan for securing the services of a Presbyterian Clergyman.

"2nd.—Proposed by Mr. McEwen and seconded by Dr. Little:—That the London Missionary Society be requested to select a Clergyman for the European population of Singapore, on the understanding that one from *any* of the Evangelical denominations of Scotch Presbyterians will be cordially received without reference to his particular views in regard to Church Government.

"3rd.—Proposed by Mr. Thomson and seconded by Mr. Duff:—That the following be appointed a Committee to carry out the views embodied in the previous resolution, with powers to convene another meeting to report their proceedings: Messrs. Nicol, W. Scott, Robert McEwen and A. Logan.

"4th.—Proposed by Mr. Scott and seconded by Mr. Logan:—That the Chairman be requested to intimate to the Revd. Mr. Moule that the present movement has not by any means originated in any feeling of personal dissatisfaction with him, and that nothing but a preference for a Clergyman of their own denomination would induce the meeting to take the present step.

"Thanks were then voted to the Chairman, and the meeting dissolved.

"The Committee, we understand, have taken steps to accomplish the duties confided to them, and, after the departure of the Europe mails, will commence ascertaining the extent of funds which will be available for the furtherance of the scheme. There can be no doubt that those who are in ability to do so, will subscribe liberally; and we should think that it will be very gratifying to those old Singaporeans who are Presbyterians, who have retired from the Settlement with competencies, to have it in their power to assist in securing for their countrymen who have yet to pass a long period in the place, the aid and comfort which a clergyman of their own persuasion imparts, and the absence of which must have often been to them a source of regret. Should it be necessary to appeal to the community generally, the large contributions made by the Presbyterians towards the erection of St. Andrew's will, no doubt, be a motive with their brethren of the Church of England to the exercise of a similar liberality in purse and feeling."

In December, Captain Rodney Mundy, R.N., carried out a brief negotiation with the Sultan of Brunei, and the following treaty was made for the cession of Labuan; the island was formally taken possession of on the 24th December :—

"1. Peace, friendship, and good understanding shall subsist for ever between Her Majesty the Queen of Great Britain and Ireland, and his Highness the Sultan of Borneo, and their respective heirs and successors.

"2. His Highness the Sultan hereby cedes in full sovereignty and property to Her Majesty the Queen of Great Britain and Ireland, her heirs and successors, for ever, the island of Labuan and its dependencies, the islets adjacent.

"3. The Government of Her Majesty the Queen of Great Britain and Ireland hereby engage, in consideration of the cession above specified, to use its best endeavours to suppress piracy and to protect lawful commerce, and the Sultan of Borneo and his ministers promise to afford every assistance to the British authorities.

"Done and concluded at Bruné the 18th day of December, 1846.

"(Signed) THE SULTAN OMAR ALLI.
(„   ) G. RODNEY MUNDY."

There is a copy in the Library of Captain G. Rodney Mundy's book, published by Murray in 1848, called "A Narrative of Events in Borneo and the Celebes from the Journals of Sir James Brooke, and An Account of the Cruise of H. M. S. *Isis.*" He died as Admiral of the Fleet on the retired list about 1884. The book contains a picture of the signing of the treaty of 18th December. Captain Mundy was sixteen months in command of the squadron in the Straits and on the Coast of Borneo. His book contains a good deal about Captain Keppel and the *Dido*, which he says (page 100) made the quickest run on record from the Straits to England. He speaks of the kindness he met with from Mr. W. H. Read and Dr. Oxley, and of Captain Charles Morgan Elliot having remained two months with him at Sarawak, having taken over his observatory and all the apparatus of a man of science (page 335). There are a number of pictures in the two volumes.

The *Free Press* every year contained a long account of the annual examination of the Raffles Institution School, this year occupying nearly half of the matter in one issue. In 1846 it was conducted by the clergy and a gentleman from Sir Thomas Cochrane's flagship, the *Agincourt*, and some of the boys' papers are printed, of which the following is one, which will amuse some of our readers now, as the same "author" gave two lectures in 1878, which were printed, entitled "Singapore Thirty Years Ago" which contained very much more interesting and useful information than Mr. George Norris's first attempt thirty-five years before at describing the Settlements :—

"Singapore is a small island to the south of the Malayan Peninsula, and it is separated from it by a narrow strait. The principal productions of this island are nutmegs, gambier and sago. There are many Chinese here and one-fourth of them are said to be robbers. Large junks come from China once a year to Singapore for the purpose of trade. Many of the Chinese are employed as carpenters. This island was discovered by Sir T. S. Raffles, late Governor of Bencoolen, and bought for a sum of money from the Malays. It is now a flourishing seaport, but since the war with China, Singapore has declined a little in commerce."

It was in this year that a long-remembered practical joke took place The Editor of the newly established *Straits Times* boasted that he had the earliest information of every possible event, which was not the opinion of the community. One day he announced in his paper that he had received certain information from a Calcutta Opium clipper which passed through without anchoring, about the result of the recent opium sale; but as the Captain of the vessel had requested him to keep it secret he could not reveal it to the public until after the arrival of the next clipper. Now the opium market was worth watching in those days, and the movements of vessels carrying it either from Bombay or Calcutta were pretty well known, and the clipper that passed through could not possibly have had the news of the sale, as she had left Calcutta long before it took place. Two days afterwards, the *Antelope*, Captain Dumaresque, from Bombay, passed through, having left Bombay before the news of the sale could have reached there. So, as a number of merchants were looking at her, it was suggested to sell the Editor, and the joke being appreciated, a note was drawn up purporting to be written by the Captain of the *Antelope* with the result of the sale, &c., &c., and signed P. Dumaresk. The prices given were three hundred rupees over the probable sale prices, and the captain's name was spelt wrong, but the editor did not stop to consider this. A sampan boy was called for, and his part of the play explained to him; so he jumped into the water (there was no sea wall then) gave his clothes a squeeze, and ran to the Editor's godown. He opened the letter, gave five dollars to the boy (who bolted at once) rushed to the printing press, and announced to the astonished Square that he had been placed through the kindness of Captain Dumaresque in possession of the result, &c., &c. The sampan boy ran back to the jokers, who added a few more dollars to his store and sent him away to Pulo Damar, his home, for a fortnight. In the meantime the conspirators sent round the Square to tell all likely to be interested about the joke, so that no false speculation should take place, and when the famous slip came out all were prepared. The Editor, furious, inserted the following paragraph in the *Straits Times*, which made the joke all the better, and the writer went to see the "forged note," and to earn the fifty dollars if he could recognise the writing, but he didn't! The Editor soon learnt all about it, and did not raise another laugh against himself by trying to hang anybody, and became quieter afterwards.

"The late Opium Sale.—In a postscript to our last issue, we inserted what purported to be an account of the fourth Calcutta Opium Sale, addressed to us with the signature of Captain P. Dumaresque, late of the *Antelope*. In our anxiety to maintain the character of our journal for early intelligence, we gave insertion to the postcript which was received by us at an early hour: having experienced kind favours at the hands of the Commanders of American vessels, we were led to believe that the note in question was genuine. We subsequently shewed the letter of Captain Dumaresque to Mr. Balestier, the American Consul, who at once pronounced the document to be a forgery. From this circumstance the note appeared to be a hoax, apparently written by some one in Singapore for the purpose not only of deceiving us, but also misleading the public. The affair, although perpetrated as a hoax, is a much more serious matter than the writer in his ignorance and affrontery suspected, and, under the old law, if proved against him would have subjected him to what he deserved—the gallows. In the present state of the law, the author of a forgery is liable to transportation for life, an amount of punishment richly deserved.

"We have endeavoured to trace the note in question to the source whence it emanated, without, at present success; but we do not yet despair of discovering the scoundrel who villainously suggested the hoax. To facilitate the enquiry, we hereby offer a reward of *fifty dollars*, payable on conviction of the party; for the information of the public, as well as to aid in the detection of the offender, we also notify that the forged note is open for inspection at our office. We are led to adopt the above course, not only on account of the enormity of the offence committed, but also in justice not merely to Captain Dumaresque, but all Commanders of American Clippers from whom we have invariably received every kindness, and a promptitude in conveying information worthy of the gentleman-like conduct and spirit of the worthy commanders of American Opium Clippers."

The practical joker was Mr. W. H. Read; reference to it will be found at page 136 of his little book "Play and Politics."

In this year was published in London Captain the Hon. Henry Keppel's "Narrative of the Expedition to Borneo of H. M. S. *Dido* for the suppression of piracy; with extracts from the Journal of James Brooke, Esq., of Sarawak." The book is in the Library. The *Free Press* had long extracts from it, and spoke very highly of it.

In this year also a small book of 312 pages was published in Leadenhall Street, London, by Madden and Malcolm, called Trade and Travel in the Far East or Recollections of 21 years passed in Java, Singapore, Australia and China. It was written by Gordon Forbes Davidson. There is no copy in the Library. He was in business for a time in Singapore, but not much is known of him, he lived where the Bethesda now stands in Bras Bassah Road, and was lame, one leg being short. There is an advertisement in the *Free Press* on 18th February, 1840, that he had started business as Davidson & Co., as a merchant and general agent. He left England, the book tells us, in 1823 for Java, and came to Singapore for the first time in July, 1826; and speaks of it as being in a lovely situation, and of great prosperity, but he was of opinion that the trade had reached its maximum and that the town had attained its highest point of importance and prosperity, and as its being a beautiful and healthy town, but over-built. His misgivings as to the trade arose from the recent establishment of Hongkong, and the opening of the China ports, which he thought

would divert the trade that came to Singapore, in the same way as
the establishment of Singapore had very much injured Penang, giving
to the streets there a deserted appearance which he thought they would
never recover. His views, which events have proved to be unfounded,
have from time to time been expressed by others, and the volume of
trade and the value of property have been thought to have reached
their highest, but still its prosperity continues to grow. The book
speaks about Captain Keppel in the *Dido* and Sir James Brooke,
then Mr. James Brooke, putting down the pirates in Borneo, and
of the recent discovery of coal there. Also of heavy losses to the
European merchants in Singapore by the unlimited credit given to
the Chinese traders, and of an attempt, frequently suggested since,
but not practicable, of insisting on a cash system. He wrote highly
of the healthy climate of the place, saying that the European
residents of sixteen and twenty years standing spoke volumes for it,
and that during eighteen years in this part of the world he had
never known any endemic disease to prevail, and that the cemetery
was filled by the death of people from India, who came for health,
and would have died six months sooner, had they not come to
breathe the pure air of Singapore. The greater part of the book contains descriptions of Java, China and Australia.

In this year was published the first Directory. It was compiled
by Mr. R. C. Woods, who had come from Bombay in 1845, and
had started the *Straits Times*. There are only one or two copies
of it. The part relating to Singapore took a few pages, and the
greater part of it was a General Directory of the Habitable Globe,
and an Epitome of the Universe, as the title page expressed it,
and a reprint of a few of the Indian Acts in force in the Straits
and Government regulations. Directories of the place continued to
be published yearly from that time.

In this year the firm of A. L. Johnston & Co., consisted of
A. L. Johnston, James Cunison Drysdale and W. H. Read, Mr. Robert
Bain was a clerk and became a partner in 1848, as well as Mr.
Michie Forbes Davidson. Mr. Bain left the firm in 1857. On 1st
January, 1863, Mr. Robert Banlay Read became a partner, Mr. M. F.
Davidson leaving the firm, and some time afterwards joining Boustead
& Co.

CHAPTER XXXIV.

1847.

IN January, Sir Colin Campbell issued instructions for some officers of Artillery to proceed to Singapore to enrol Malays to go to Hongkong to be attached to the company of gun lascars of the Royal Artillery there.

Efforts were frequently made to promote agriculture, and in this year an attempt was made to establish sugar cultivation in Malacca, as appears from the following passage in the newspaper:—"Most satisfactory tidings, we are glad to say, have been received regarding the proposed establishment of an association for the cultivation and manufacture of sugar at Malacca. The plan has been taken up with much spirit in England. The names of the Earl of Harewood, Lord George Bentinck, Lord Howard de Walden, Sir Willoughby Cotton and others, who have interested themselves in the scheme, give a guarantee for the stability of the undertaking. We have seen the printed prospectus, from which it appears that the "Malacca Sugar Company" is to have a capital of £500,000, divided into 10,000 shares of £50 each. 1,000 shares are to be reserved for the Straits. It is proposed to commence the manufacture in the first instance by purchasing cane from the Chinese cultivators, and we believe that a gentleman may be expected to arrive in the course of two or three months hence from England, to have the necessary works erected. Four thousand acres of land on the Lingy river have been procured from Government, which will be cultivated by the company. The soil, we understand, is of the most fertile description and has been approved of by several experienced planters who have viewed it. A deposit of £1 per share will be made when the company is organized, which it is calculated will enable them to proceed so far as to manufacture 100 tons of sugar weekly. Not more than two calls of £2 each will be made afterwards, for carrying on the cultivation and manufacture of sugar, and this, it is estimated, will enable the company to produce 50,000 tons annually. From the cheapness and abundance of labour and other favourable circumstances, it is thought that the cost of production and manufacture will be so low that a profit on the outlay will secure splendid dividends at little more than half the present price of the article, thus holding out the hope of being able to afford to the consumers of this important necessary of life, the prospect of a large reduction in price. This is important news, and we trust that the company will prosper, not only for its own sake, but for the benefit its success will confer on the poor consumer at home, as well as on the Settlement of Malacca, and indirectly on the other Straits Settlements." It did not prove successful, however; any more than the large plantations in Singapore.

It was said in 1884, when a number of very serious cases of hydrophobia occurred, that it had been unknown in Singapore until that time, but an account of a death from hydrophobia appears in the *Free Press* of February, 1847; it was the case of a Chinaman who had been bitten four months before, and died in the hospital. Two months afterwards, a boy died in the Pauper Hospital, one month after being bitten. In consequence of these cases, the following notice was issued by the Magistrates on 15th April:—

In consequence of the great increase of pariah dogs and several cases of hydrophobia having occurred within a very short period:—Notice is hereby given, that all dogs found straying in the Streets and Roads on the first three days of each month (Sundays excepted) will be destroyed, without further notice.

The *Free Press* of 11th February contained the following paragraph:—"It having been ascertained that Whampoa, the younger, whose name is known far and wide in these eastern parts, and is familiar to not a few even in distant Europe, was about to leave this by the next steamer on a visit to his native country, a few of his friends, amongst the European mercantile community chiefly, resolved to show their respect and esteem for him by entertaining him at dinner. The dinner accordingly came off on Monday evening at the London Hotel, when about 20 sat down, C. Carnie, Esq., in the Chair, and W. S. Duncan, Esq., Croupier. The health of their guests having been given, Whampoa returned thanks in a most neat and feeling manner in English; and on the health of Kim Seng, one of our most respected Chinese merchants, who was also present, being drank, Kim Seng replied in a clever and humorous speech in Malay which delighted all present. A number of other toasts were also given, and the evening was spent in much harmony and merriment."

"On the morning of Saturday, the 6th February, 1847, the foundation stone of the new gaol (afterwards the Civil Jail, within the walls of the Criminal Prison) was laid by the architect, Captain Faber, Superintending Engineer, in presence of their Honours the Governor and the Resident Councillor. Below the stone was deposited the following inscription engraved on a brass plate:—

This Foundation Stone
of
H. M. Jail at Singapore,
Was laid by Captain FABER, Madras Engineers,
Superintending Engineer, Straits Settlements,
On the 6th February, 1847—
The 27th Anniversary of the Formation
Of a British Settlement
On this Island.
The Hon'ble Colonel W. J. BUTTERWORTH, C.B.,
Being Governor of Prince of Wales' Island,
Singapore and Malacca,
and
The Hon'ble T. CHURCH,
Resident Councillor at Singapore

VICTORIA,
Queen of Great Britain and Ireland.

The Right Hon'ble Lord HARDINGE, G.C.B.,
Governor-General of British India.

GOD SAVE THE QUEEN.

In a bottle, likewise placed below the stone, the following statistical information relative to the Settlements, written on parchment, was enclosed :—

The Trade for the year 1845-46 of Prince of Wales' Island, Singapore and Malacca, aggregated the sum of Company's Rs. 52,190,685 in Merchandize, and Company's Rs. 9,705,061 in Bullion and Treasure; making a grand total of Rs. 61,796,746 (exclusive of the trade between the three Settlements) as follows :—

		Imports.		Exports.		Total.
P. W. Island	Rs.	6,614,794	...	6,528,452	=	13,143,246
Singapore ...	,,	26,616,448	...	21,162,987	=	47,779,435
Malacca ...	,,	509,872	...	364,193	=	874,065

Grand Total Company's Rs. 61,796,746

The Revenue and charges for the year 1845-46 of Prince of Wales' Island Singapore and Malacca including Civil, Military, Marine, Judicial, Convicts, &c., &c., were as follows :—

Charges
P. W. Island Co.'s	...	...	Rs.	402,783.15.11
Singapore ,,	...	...	,,	497,186.14. 5
Malacca ,,	...	...	,,	231,158.12. 5

Rs. 1,131,129.10.9

Revenue.
P. W. Island Co.'s	...	...	Rs.	185,443. 2. 9
Singapore ,,	...	...	,,	530,040. 15. 7
Malacca ,,	...	...	,,	64,408. 9.11

Rs. 779,892.12.3

Total deficit at the three Settlements Rs. 351,236.14.6

N. B. ½ Company European Artillery, 1 Company Golundauze, 1 Regt. Native Infantry, 2,234 Convicts, 1 steamer and 4 gun-boats."

On the 12th February there was a large fire in Kampong Glam, of which the following is an account :—" About one o'clock in the afternoon it was discovered that a fire had broken out near the old Thannah at Kampong Glam. Exertions were used as soon as possible to suppress it, but the wind being very high at the time, and the attap and wooden houses amongst which it originated unfortunately offering every facility to its progress, it rapidly increased, and the flames soon extended across the road to the range of houses formerly belonging to the Sultan. In order to prevent the fire communicating to the houses of the Europeans on the Beach Road, it was resolved to pull down a number of attap houses immediately adjoining the bungalow occupied by Mr. Gilbert McMicking and this was immediately set about; but the wind shifting, the attap houses were soon in a blaze, and the kitchen in Mr. McMicking's compound caught the fire and then a bungalow situated in the adjoining compound belonging to Mr. William Wemyss Ker. The whole of this range of houses at this time seemed to be in very great danger, the heat and smoke rendering it almost impossible to work with effect. The excitement was general, and the occupants prepared for a move by packing up their plate and valuables. The heat of the houses was almost unsupportable and their destruction seemed certain, but the wind fortunately abated and the engines were got to work in the compound where the fire was already in progress. Mr. Dutronquoy of the London Hotel and a party of French sailors mounted the roof of Mr. McMicking's bungalow, and by great exertions in throwing water on the tiles saved the building, and the fire was prevented from spreading further along this range. Another party of Europeans, headed by a number of the Magistrates, by great activity, and at considerable risk, succeeded, by pulling down houses, in saving Kampang Jawa from entire destruction. The Police engine was in this quarter, but could not be worked owing to the scarcity of water, and the flames extended so far across the road as to render it difficult to prevent the engine being destroyed by them. About half-past five p m. the fire was confined to a range of buildings belonging to Syed Omar, which were not entirely gutted before midnight. The number of houses destroyed is estimated at about 273, consisting of brick, wooden, and attap tenements. The value of these buildings was very considerable, and the quantity of property in them destroyed by the fire was very large, the amount being roughly estimated at from 80 to 90,000 dollars. The Governor and Resident Councillor were early on the spot, and were active in their efforts to render every assistance, by directing the demolition of houses where it was considered necessary. The former indeed exposed himself to considerable risk, having been at one time nearly surrounded by the burning houses, from which position the smoke and flames made escape a matter of difficulty. One European at considerable hazard went into a house and brought out a cask of gunpowder which was safely deposited on the beach."

In February, a general order was issued by Governor Butterworth, by instructions from the Governor-General of India, throughout the three Settlements, to the following effect:—

"1.—The Governor-General is pleased to direct that all public works carried on by order of the Government, whether under the direction of its own officers or through the agency of contractors, shall be discontinued on the Sunday.

2.—Cases of urgent necessity, in which delay would be detrimental to the Public Service, are to be considered as cases of exception, and all such cases will be immediately reported to the Military Board for their special orders, and for the information of the Government. The officer in charge of the work will act on his own discretion, where delay in waiting for the sanction of the Board would be attended with injurious consequences.

3.—The cessation of work on the Sunday shall be an understood condition in all future contracts for Public Works, whether an express provision to that effect be inserted in the deed of contract or not. No claim therefore of addition to the amount of the contract on account of the suspension of labour on Sundays shall be admitted in reference to any engagements executed subsequently to the date of this notification.

4.—An order to this effect has been enforced, since January, 1843, by the Bombay Government, and the Governor-General has much satisfaction in extending the rule which it enjoins to the other Presidencies subordinate to the Government of India."

In May, Sir William Norris, the Recorder, left the Straits, and Sir Christopher Rawlinson was appointed in his place. In the same month, Mr. James Brooke received despatches from the English Government appointing him H. B. M.'s Commissioner and Consul-General to the Independent States of Borneo. He left Singapore, under a salute, by the E. I. Co.'s steamer *Nemesis* for Sarawak and Brunei. The *Free Press* spoke of the appointment as follows:—" This appointment, besides the advantages which our interests in these parts may expect to derive from the experience and ability of Mr. Brooke, is satisfactory as marking that the British Government are not disposed to give way to the extravagant and unjust pretensions of the Dutch; but that, on the contrary, it is intended to maintain our right to an equal footing in the Archipelago, and to all the commercial and political advantages which may arise from the exercise of a legitimate influence. We hope that Mr. Brooke's appointment is only the first of a series of measures for effecting such a desirable end."

On the 6th July, Mr. Brooke went on a visit to England in the P. & O. Mail from Singapore. Before he left, he presented over one hundred volumes to the Singapore Library.

A meeting was called on the 20th May, in Mr. Carnie's office, for the purpose of making preliminary arrangements for periodical assemblies; and the paper, in giving notice of it, said:—" The proposal for these assemblies has our warmest wishes for its ultimate success, promising as it does to supply a defect in our social system in Singapore— that of the want of any means of periodically bringing together the members of its small society on a friendly and social footing. The plan, we hope, will meet with the countenance of those who, from position, are entitled to take the lead in Society, and who, no doubt, feel gratified whenever they have an opportunity of lending their aid to the promotion of a social and harmonious feeling in the different members of community. It may be added that extravagance will be eschewed in all things, so that subscribers will have no reason to fear that, in lending themselves to the plan, they will be led into expenses not compatible with a prudent economy." It was decided at the meeting that a ball should be given every two months.

The following passage in the *Free Press* referred to matters which did not come to any successful result; but the future of Borneo and the Native States was then becoming recognised:—

"Nearly every mail from home brings intelligence of the increasing interest which the Far East is exciting, and of the measures which are being projected for making her resources, natural and commercial, available through the capital and enterprize of Europe. Some months ago we had the "Malacca Sugar Company" projected, with a large proprietary and capital, to carry on the manufacture of the cane. Then we had the appointment of a Consul-General and Commissioner to Borneo, followed up by a Commercial and Political Treaty with the Sultan of Borneo, while last mail brought us the intelligence of the Government having at length resolved to proceed in earnest with the settlement of Labuan, Mr. Brooke having been appointed Governor of that place, and other offices being spoken of. We have heard that there is yet a further Association being organised in England for carrying on operations in this part of the world on a large scale. The title of this body is, or is proposed to be, "The Company of the Eastern Archipelago," which proposes to go to work with a capital of £500,000. From what we can learn, Borneo is the contemplated field of operations, and it is probable that they will begin with purchasing the Antimony Monopoly. There can be little doubt that such a Company will find an ample scope for its enterprize, whether it is confined to Borneo, or embraces the wider range of countries which its title would seem to point out. Borneo, no doubt, alone offers the most varied objects to which the capitalist might direct his attention when in search of means for profitable investment. Her soil in some parts is admirably fitted for every species of tropical cultivation, whether we look to the rearing of spices, or wish to follow the less tedious cultivation of grain. In other parts, her soil teems with mineral wealth—diamonds, gold, &c.—not omitting what now-a-days holds no mean place amongst minerals—coal, which is found abundant and good in various parts of Borneo. The forests of Borneo also abound in many valuable natural productions, which an active commerce would, no doubt, bring to light in abundance. If the Company should desire to extend their views to other places, the Malay Peninsula offers an ample field in its capacity for cultivation, its extensive deposits of gold, tin and coal, and its numerous other resources, many of which, up to the present time, have been but imperfectly, or not at all, explored. In short, it only requires that capitalists should deviate a little from the beaten path of buying and selling, and make use of the influence and opportunities which their wealth would give them to find in the Malay Archipelago almost unbounded stores of the most valuable articles of commerce ready to be called forth by an intelligent and prudent search for them."

At this time, there were very serious riots and much loss of life in the Dutch residency of Rhio between the Chinese Societies Quan Tek Hoe and Tan Tae Hoe, and the latter getting the worst of it fitted out expeditions from Singapore. Enquiry was made, and Constable Simonides, accompanied by a small party of peons, left Singapore for the purpose of making a tour of observation in the jungle. He gradually shaped his course towards Selitar, but so totally was he left without guide or any means of ascertaining his way in the jungle of Singapore, as it was then, that five days elapsed before the spot aimed at was reached. On arriving at a large *bangsal* on the Neo Yang Kwan, a branch of the Selitar river, the party stopped there under pretence of being tired and wishing to rest themselves. Quietly looking about them, they found in the river on which this *bangsal* was situated, six large boats, each armed with two *lellas*, while a large collection of other kinds of arms was observed in one of the boats, and there were also noticed traces of warlike stores in the house. The owner of the plantation immediately made his appearence, and was at once taken into custody by the constable, who threatened to shoot him if he made the least resistance or gave the least alarm. The house was then searched in his presence, and there were found in it five brass *lellas* (cannons) one of them about five feet long and of proportionate bore, while the other two were each about four feet in length; five iron *lellas*, twelve matchlocks, several muskets, about four dozens of iron-pointed spears and triangles, battle axes, knives, long sharp-pointed poles, shields, &c.; a considerable quantity of gunpowder in barrels, and a number of priming cannisters. The owner of the house, Neo Liang Quan, in explanation of his having so many of these articles in his possession, stated that they had been brought shortly before by some of his friends from Rhio in his boats, in which they had taken refuge, the boats being then at Rhio for gambier. This explanation did not seem at all satisfactory to the constable, who brought the man away together with as many of the munitions of war as his party could carry. Subsequently three of the iron guns were recognised as being the property of the Yam Tuan of Rhio, by whom it appears they had been lent to Chinese of the Quan Toek Hoe, who were apprehensive of being attacked by the other party. It appeared that Neo Liang Quan was originally an inhabitant of Rhio, which he left many years ago on account of debt, and settled in Singapore, where he would appear to have prospered, being the owner of a number of valuable plantations, but was a person of very doubtful character who had been in prison for two years in Rhio.

It was then discovered that a Chinese expedition had left Singapore shortly before in two divisions, one party of boats leaving the Old Straits by the Changie entrance and making for that part of Battam Island at the entrance to the Straits of Rhio, while the other party emerged from the Old Straits by the Tanjong Goul entrance. Proceeding in this manner, they easily arrived at the scene of the intended operations, a small strait separating the island of Gallat or Gallang from the island of Gampang. This the two squadrons invested at opposite ends, and then swept rapidly inwards, destroying everything before them, until the two parties met each other. Their plans were laid with the greatest skill, and the effect was most complete. They took the inhabitants of the different *bangsals* or *kampongs* most completely by surprise, affording time neither for defence nor escape. The inhabitants were given to the sword, while everything in the different *kampongs* was destroyed, the houses and their furniture being burnt, and all the trees, pepper vines and gambier plants cut up and laid waste. Twenty-eight *bangsals* or plantations were thus treated in the course of one night, upwards of one hundred persons having been killed; their bodies having been found, in nearly every case, deprived of the heads, and shockingly mangled and disfigured.

In September, the Bengal Government authorised the construction of a wall along the front of the Esplanade to prevent the sea encroaching. There were very frequent complaints of the state of the roads, the Grand Jury at nearly every Assizes presenting them as very badly kept-up, and the following squib was put in the *Free Press* by a local wit :—

GRAND STEEPLE CHASE

For a purse of Fifty Dollars

Added to a Sweepstakes of $10 each

On Tuesday, the 16th Inst., 4 p.m.

The Course is from Coleman's Bridge along New Bridge Road over the unfinished Faber's Bridge and along South Canal Street into Upper Macao Street, passing over the Buffalo Carts and through or over the Palanquins in Macao or George Street, into South Canal Road, over the sand bank and brick heaps past Messrs. Purvis & Guthrie's godowns, into Market Street over the crockery and crates of earthenware, through Malacca Street into Commerical Square, over the logs of timber at Messrs. Syme & Co's., thence into Battery Road over the hills of the red earth and granite at Messrs. Fraser's and ditches and timber at Messrs. Middleton's into Boat Quay, past W. S. Duncan's and from that to the winning post at Bain's Bridge along Boat Quay.

The roads must have been suffcently bad even in the town, for Dr. Charles Curties, a private practitioner in High Street, in Singapore for many years, was driving one night along the road near Rochor Police Station, which the paper called "one of the principal roads of the town," and there was such a hole where the side of the road had fallen in, that the pony and buggy were thrown into the canal, the pony killed, and Dr. Curties injured.

During this year two Petitions were sent to the Houses of Parliament. One was regarding an Indian Act (No. III. of 1847) which took the appointment of the Police Officers out of the hands of the Court of Judicature and Quarter Sessions, and gave it to the Crown; and, secondly, asking that the Municipal funds should be placed under the management of a Committee chosen by the rate-payers, which had always been the case, but was rendered doubtful, in the opinion of the Recorder, Sir W. Norris, by another Act. The petition which was sent to Mr. John Crawfurd for presentation to Parliament, was as follows:—

"Unto the Honourable the Knights, Citizens, and Burgesses in Parliament assembled.

The Humble Petition of the undersigned, merchants and others, inhabitants of Singapore,

Respectfully Sheweth,

"That on the 19th day of February last an Act was passed by the Legislative Council of India being No III. of 1847, entitled "An Act to provide for the appointment of Constables and Peace Officers, at the Settlements in the Straits."

"That on the draft of this Act being published for general information in October, 1846, Your Petitioners considering that it was unnecessary and uncalled for, and that if passed into law it would tend to impair the respectability and usefulness of the Magistrates, by stripping them of powers and functions wherewith they had been invested by the Crown; and that the public safety and comfort would also be diminished by the efficiency of the Police force being impaired through the operation of the said Act, addressed a respectful Memorial to the Right Hon'ble the Governor-General of India in Council praying that the said draft Act might not become law; of which memorial and the documents appended thereto, copies are hereunto annexed.

"That, nevertheless, the said Act was in due time passed, and has now been in operation for some months, and your Petitioners from what they have observed of its effects upon the Police force, are still more impressed than before with a conviction of its tendency to impair the efficiency of the Police, as well as to diminish the authority of the Magistracy.

"That your Petitioners would most respectfully suggest, that not only ought the entire appointment and management of the Police force to be vested in Her Majesty's Court of Judicature of Prince of Wales' Island, Singapore and Malacca in its General and Quarter Sessions of the Peace, as it was previous to the passing of the said Act No. III. of 1847, but that the Assessment funds which are raised for the payment of the Police force and for other strictly municipal purposes ought to be managed by a Committee of the rate-payers or other popularly elected body; and your Petitioners consider that the powers of management given to the Governor of Bengal, or his nominee, by Act No. XII. of 1839, by virtue of which the said Assessment is levied, are very objectionable, as confiding to one person the exclusive management of funds raised for municipal purposes, and over which the payers have no control.

"Your Petitioners therefore humbly pray that it may please your Honourable House to adopt measures for repealing the said Act, No. III. of 1847: And also that the funds raised from the inhabitants of the Straits Settlements for the payment of the Police and other municipal purposes, may be placed under the management of a Committee chosen from the payers, or some other popularly elected body acting in conjunction with the executive officers of Government in the Straits. (Signed by 215 persons.)"

The other Petition, which was of great length, referred to the conduct of the Dutch Government in throwing all the hindrances and restrictions it could in the way of British trade with the Dutch possessions; an infringement of the provisions of the Treaty of 1824, which had perpetually been made a subject of complaint in Singapore since it was concluded. A memorial was sent at the same time to Lord Palmerston, and the following passages taken from it show the nature of the grievance:—

"That frequent complaints have been heretofore made regarding the conduct of the Authorities of the Netherlands Indian Government in respect to British Trade in the Eastern Archipelago, by which, in various ways, the provisions of the Treaty of the 17th March, 1824, which fixed the respective rights of the Governments of Great Britain and Holland, and of their subjects in the Eastern Seas, have been violated, and British subjects and trade deprived of those advantages guaranteed to them by the said Treaty.

"That, notwithstanding the many remonstrances and representations made by the British Government to that of Holland, on the subject of these violations of the Treaty of 1824, and by your Lordship in particular so lately as 1841, your memorialists regret that they have to complain of further acts on the part of the Netherlands Indian Government by which British Commerce is seriously impeded in the Indian Archipelago, and that freedom and equality of trade with the native powers, provided for by the Treaty, completely prevented, as regards British subjects.

"That your Memorialists, without entering into any lengthened specification of these acts of the Netherlands Indian Government, by which they appear to be aiming at establishing an exclusive dominion and monopoly of trade in the Indian Archipelago, would respectfully request your Lordship's attention to the copy of a Petition which has been addressed by the mercantile body in Singapore to the House of Commons, and to the other documents which are annexed to this Memorial, from which it appears that British trade has been completely excluded from all ports but one of the large and important Island of Celebes, the effect of which is to deprive British subjects of the liberty of trading with one of the richest parts, as regards valuable articles of commerce, of the Archipelago, and the natives of which have ever shewn the strongest desire to cultivate a commercial intercourse with the subjects of Her Majesty.

"That, through the proceedings of the Dutch Authorities in the Eastern Seas, the trade of British subjects has been and now is impeded and hampered, and prevented from attaining that extent, and being of that profitable nature, which the desire of the natives for English manufactures, and their increasing commercial enterprize and ability to furnish valuable articles of produce in exchange, would, without doubt, insure, were no obstacles to interpose to that freedom and liberty of trade which the I., II., III., and IV. articles of the Treaty of 1824 were intended to secure."

The first number of the *Journal of the Indian Archipelago and Eastern Asia* was published in June. It was the first attempt to promote a literary or scientific periodical in the British Settlements in the Far East; such works as the *Malacca Gleaner,* formerly published in Malacca, had missionary purposes for their chief end; and any notices·of neighbouring countries, or their inhabitants, languages, &c., were made subsidiary to their main design. The *Chinese Repository* partook in a large measure of the same character. The Dutch had scientific periodicals in Java, but very few English, even of the residents in Java, could read Dutch. The Straits newspapers had, in a large measure, supplied the want. The *Singapore Chronicle* had many valuable contributions on the history of the Archipelago, written by Crawfurd, Dalton, Medhurst, and others, a portion of which were (as has been said) collected by Moor; while the *Free Press* had many similar papers. Such articles, however, find a more appropriate and lasting place in the pages of a volume, which is in a handier form than the sheets of a newspaper. There is a note in the Journal which says that the publication did not nearly repay its cost, but this was to be expected in the small community of Singapore where it is easy to borrow a copy which some one else has paid for. But Mr. James Richardson Logan, like Mr. William Napier in regard to the *Free Press*, or Mr. Moor, or others after him, did not look for any pecuniary return, and was contented to bear the loss for the sake of the advantage to the Settlement. It may be useful here, as it is not easy to ascertain it elsewhere, to state how many volumes were published and the years: It was published in monthly or occasional numbers, as opportunity offered, and in bound volumes at the close of each year. Being edited by J. R. Logan who wrote very lengthy papers in it, it became known as Logan's Journal, which is the name used throughout this book for brevity's sake.

VOL.	YEAR.			
1	1847	429	pages	and Index.
2	1848	848	,,	and Appendix, 62 pages.
3	1849	766	,,	and two App. 16 and 48 pages.
4	1850	767	,,	
5	1851	740	,,	
6	1852	699	,,	
7	1853	378	,,	
8	1854	504	,,	
9	1855	528	,,	and Appendix, 48 pages.
New Series				
1	1856	317	,,	and Appendix, 151 pages.
2	1858	458	,,	

It has been proposed several times to publish an Index to the volumes, but it has not been carried out. In the *Journal of the Straits Branch of the Royal Asiatic Society* for December, 1886, No. 18, there is an Index by Dr. Dennys to the headings of the various articles only; it does not index the names of the authors or any of the contents of the articles. The last named Journal was commenced in 1877 and has continued in a spasmodic way until the present time, as the matter available for such a publication is necessarily of a limited character.

It must have been somewhere about this time that a French Scientific Expedition, so called, was sent out from France. There is nothing in the book to fix the date except that Louis Philippe lost his throne after it was written. Nothing would be known of this expedition in Singapore but for the publication of a book in 1855, by James Blackwood, London, called " Six months among the Malays and a year in China " by an author, described as the Physician to the Scientific Mission sent by France to China, and author of " Romance of Travel." It would not be noticed here, except that it contains 200 pages about Malacca, Singapore, and Penang, with such ridiculous traveller's stories, and exaggerations, that there is nothing to be learned from it. There is probably only the one copy in the place on which these remarks are founded. The true object of this " Scientific Expedition " creeps out on page 201, after the preliminary chapters about the Straits. It says " On repairing to China, Mr. de Legrene received a special order from H. M. King Louis Philippe to select from the Malay Archipelago some beautiful perfumed oasis, bathed by the waters of the Indian Ocean, upon which it would be possible to found an establishment; the old King having an extreme desire that France should not be destitute of a spice island, but possess a pearl in the magnificent treasures of Oceania, the most precious of which were under the respective dominion of England, Holland and Spain."

The way the expedition tried to carry out the King's wish was to let a young lieutenant and two cabin boys go away up a river at the island of Basilan. They get into a row, reason unknown but may be surmised, and two of the Frenchmen were killed. The man-of-war afterwards bombarded the island, and the author says that they destroyed everything, left not a single blade of grass on the spot, and burnt houses and boats. He winds up by saying that the return of the sailors on board was not the least interesting part of the affair, for they dressed and conducted themselves in a manner befitting a carnival, some carrying krisses, bucklers, and, on their bayonets, horns or other part of the buffaloes they had killed." This was the only result of King Louis Philippe's ambition in the neighbourhood of the Straits.

It is worthy of notice, however, that the French official, at the end of his three chapters on the three Settlements of the Straits, says:—"It must be confessed that the English people, who have ever been the guardians of freedom, and who have never employed any other than legal means for the establishment and maintenance of their rights and institutions, are, of all other nations, the most staunch protectors of human liberty in the present day." For which plain truth, as exemplified in the Straits, he may be forgiven his wonderful account of a great dinner at Mr. Balestier's modest house on Balestier Plain, which he describes as containing five immense rooms, lighted with wax candles contained in glass vessels (they were no doubt cocoanut oil lights in tumblers hanging inside inverted glass globes), and all the rarities and curiosities of India and China being contained in a long gallery (probably five glass-fronted almeirahs, which passed to Mr. Woods's house at Serangoon, close by) and a vast library, composed of valuable books in every European language, and of its being a fairy palace of the east, with Asiatic luxury all round, a soft perfumed atmosphere, and a young Chinese domestic in each corner employed in working very large fans! Then there is a ridiculous description of a visit to Whampoa's house close by, where the author passed the night; and these are fair samples of the contents of the book. Certainly some wonderful accounts of the place have appeared in books long since forgotten. Accidentally, while writing this very chapter, we came across a book, published in America, by a globe-trotter who spent three days in the place, and he says that Singapore was founded by Sir Stamford Raffles, "who married the daughter of the Sultan of Johore."

CHAPTER XXXV

1848.

———

AT this time, encouraged by their success in the expedition to Rhio, mentioned on page 464, another regular Chinese expedition of over a hundred men started from Singapore on a marauding foray. Their pretended errand was to collect gutta percha on some of the islands in the Straits. They cleared out at the proper office and received the usual pass, and bent their course to Muar in the Peninsula, where they made an attack upon a *kampong*, but were repulsed. They then crossed over to Siak in Sumatra and tried their luck, but were again unsuccessful, being driven away. Thence they came down to a small island, Pulo Buru, south of Pulo Supang, to the southward of the Carimons, where they again experienced discomfiture in their attempts to plunder some houses, some of their party being killed and others wounded. The Malays who were in the houses also suffered, but not so severely as the Chinese. While near this island, they attacked a Malay boat, the crew of which, five in number, they put to death, and taking out the rice, &c., they scuttled the boat. After their last repulse, they appear to have thought that the fates were against them, for, after burying their dead on a small island on their route, they returned to Singapore as empty-handed as when they left. They then resolved to try their fortune on land, in Singapore town; and, on the morning of the 22nd May, a large detachment of the gang, about forty or fifty in number, attacked a house in Kampong Glam inhabited by Malays; and, after forcing open the door by an extempore battering-ram, and wounding some of the inmates, who thereupon all fled, they plundered it, carrying off about thirty or forty dollars and other property. Their ill-luck still, however, attended them, as, the alarm having been raised, they were followed by the mounted patrol, which had been lately established, the police being provided with some ponies for the purpose, who chased them along the Changie Road, wounded some of them, and recovered all the stolen property and some of their weapons, which in their flight they threw away.

In the month of February, there was much excitement one day in the Square by a report that a large body of Chinese had landed from boats and attacked Mr. W. W. Ker's house at Bukit Chermin, in New Harbour, where he lived. But it turned out to be a false report. A number of Chinese who had been in Singapore delivering gambier, &c., were returning to their plantation at Sungei Jurong, in two large *tongkangs* with a goodly provision of pork, rice, &c., intended for the celebration of the Chinese New Year. When in the narrow strait at Batu Blayer, they met two other large boats with Chinese who were proceeding to Singapore. A number of Malay fishing boats were also in the strait, and in the confusion of the large boats meeting and passing in such a narrow passage, one of them got entangled in the fishing apparatus belonging to a Malay boat. One of the Malays in the boat struck a Chinaman, upon which a great clamour was raised by the latter, which induced some Malays, who apprehended an attack, to set off to Teluk Blangah with the intention of procuring assistance. The Chinamen, alarmed at this, resolved to appeal to Mr. Ker for protection. They accordingly brought their boats to anchor at the foot of the hill on which the house stood, and two of them ascended to the house, but were informed that Mr. Ker was in town. It would appear that they resolved on waiting his return, and that the servants left in charge of the house, alarmed by seeing so many persons collected near the house, beat a gong and gave the alarm. This speedily brought a number of the Tumongong's followers, by whom the Chinese were surrounded and taken into custody. Their story was, in some measure, corroborated by Eu Chin and other respectable residents in Singapore, and ultimately all were released.

A subscription was made in the Square to put wooden railings round the enclosure. Copper cents were very scarce, and were retailed at 82 to 85 for a dollar. The Chinese sent in petitions to Government on the subject, as it made things dear for the poorer classes.

At the beginning of this year, the closing of the P. & O. Mails was first signalled from the Government Hill [now Fort Canning] flag-staff—the red ensign being used for the Europe mail, and the yellow flag for China, and a gun was fired when the steamer arrived during the night. By the contract, the mail steamer had to wait in Singapore forty-eight hours. The first time the yellow flag was used, a report got about that a plague had broken out on board one of the Arab pilgrim ships, which caused alarm in the town among the natives for a few hours, from a belief that that signal was made to warn people of it.

It had been customary to allow gambling at the Chinese New Year, or at any rate not to interfere with it, and contributions were made by the Chinese for charitable purposes as a sort of considera-tion for allowing a violation of the law. Objections were made in the Square to its being permitted any longer and it was stopped. The firing of crackers was also objected to. The following is a trans-lation of a Chinese placard that was posted about the town in con-sequence:—

We think that it is now more than twenty years since Singapore was estab-lished; and annually the firing of crackers during the Chinese New Year was allowed. But this year the constables on no account will allow gambling, or even the firing of crackers. We wish to ascertain why during the Kling and Malay New Year firing of crackers is allowed. Is it because we Chinese are not equal to the Klings or Malays? If there are any intelligent Chinese amongst us, they would have gone to the police and remonstrated about last night's affair, and also we can join in a body and put a stop to all business in the market, which will be but proper. But if that cannot be done, do not bid at all at the sale of the Farms this year. If any one shall bid he shall be reckoned worse than a dog.

The above was only one of a number of objectionable placards of a similar nature, which were issued, some of great length, and all having for their object to show that the Chinese were oppressed by the police. The following was part of another placard:—

The island of Singapore contains a great number of Chinese; some are shop-keepers, others are working-men; some of them rich and some are poor people, all of one nation. All the other natives together are not so numerous. The police watch the Chinese only; no other nation is watched. Kling amusements are not interfered with; the Malays play, fire crackers, and shoot and are not interfered with. The Police do not interfere nor apprehend them. The Chinese have a feast once a year; they have amusements, fire crackers and gamble, and are taken up. Chinese selling articles in the street (which they bear on the shoulder) are seized by the peons by their bajus, beaten, and knocked down, and then confined in the *Thanahs*; they are seized as thieves. When they are taken to the police, sentence is pronounced without the case being inquired into. People carrying night soil, &c., are fined one or half a rupee. These are jungle people, how can they bear such a rule?

Formerly, at Malacca and Pulo Pinang, there were many Chinese and nobody interfered with them.

Singapore is a new place. When it was first opened the Chinese could work and do what they liked, then it was well, and at that time Mr. Bonham was here and had a great name which was known in Europe and till now he retains his name.

The state of the island was very disturbed at this time, and murders were frequent. In one week in January, there were four, near the town. The grand jury in their presentment attributed the grave nature of the crimes at that time to the combination which existed among the Chinese secret societies, and suggested that strong parties of not less than twenty well-armed men, the most active and intelligent of the police, should be detached for the special purpose of patrolling the island.

The following are extracts from a forcible statement drawn up by Mr. John Crawfurd and presented to the members of Parliament to enable them to judge of the question raised in the petition from Singapore regarding the police, which was sent home the year before:—

"The industry of the inhabitants of Singapore has created the whole fund from which the whole revenues are levied. This is made evident enough when the fact is adverted to, that eight-and-twenty years ago the island, which has now 50,000 inhabitants, was a jungle, with 150 Malay fishermen, imbued with a strong propensity to piracy, and no wealth at all, unless it were a little plunder. At the present time, the entire revenues may be safely estimated at not less than £50,000 per annum, being equal to a pound sterling a head, which is equal to about five-fold the ratio of taxation yielded by the population of Bengal.

"The revenues are divided into two branches, although the division be, in reality, little better than arbitrary—the General and the Police; or taxes, and rates. The first consists of excise on wine, spirits, and opium; of quit-rents; of the produce of the sale of wild lands; of fees and fines; of postages, &c., The second is a percentage on the rental of houses. The general revenue amounted in 1845-46, in round numbers, to £14,000, and the local one to £7,000; making a total of £21,000—a sum which, if expended with a just economy, ought to be adequate to every purpose of Government in a small sea-girt island, with a population for the most part concentrated in one spot.

"From this statement it is plain enough that, whether the police force is paid wholly out of the police revenue, or partly from the police and partly from the general revenue, it must, in any case, be paid out of the produce of the industry of the inhabitants—a fund wholly created within the short period of twenty-eight years. I cannot see, then, with what show of reason it can be said that the Executive Government pays the police, simply because it is the mere instrument of disbursement.

"Singapore is not, like Hindustan, a country conquered, or one received by inheritance from a despotic Government. On the contrary, it is strictly a Colony planted in a desert, the offspring of British enterprise and capital—just as much as were New England or New York. The constitution of society in it, moreover, differs wholly from anything found in Hindustan, the practices followed in which have been, notwithstanding, quoted as precedents.

"If, indeed, experience had shown that the administration of the police of Singapore was most advantageously lodged in the hands of the Executive, expediency might be pleaded in its favour. The very reverse, however, has proved to have been the case; for it has been the corruption and inefficacy of the police, so managed for many years, that has raised the whole question. I cannot but think that what holds good everywere else, must hold good also in Singapore—that the administration of mere local affairs must, from its very nature, be best conducted by those who are in a position to understand it best, and who have the most immediate interest in conducting it efficiently and economically. These are, assuredly, the inhabitants of each locality, and not the Executive Government, which has abundance of other and larger matters on its hands. But it is not theoretically alone that I came to this conclusion. It is with me the result of a personal experience, gained on the very spot itself.

"The practice with respect to the colonies under the management of the Crown has, of late years, certainly been rather to extend than to curtail the privileges of the inhabitants; and it is to be hoped that the East India Company will feel disposed to follow a course which, by conciliating the people, secures harmony, strengthens the hands of the local Government, and consequently contributes largely to facilitate the conduct of the administration. I trust, therefore, that the home authorities will refuse their approbation to this Act of the Indian Government, abrogating the very small instalment of rights conferred by Royal Charter on the inhabitants of Singapore; of rights, it must not be forgotten, exercised by parties selected and named by the Indian Government itself.

"In so far as concerns the framing of laws for Singapore and our other Malayan Settlements, the Supreme Government is in a very different position from that in which it stands on the continent in India, where there is ever at its disposition, men of first-rate talent, and long and varied experience in every department of administration. Respecting the Malayan Settlements, on the contrary, the Governor-General in Council can obtain no information from parties on the spot; for, in reality, less is known of them in Bengal than in England, because there is less intercourse.

In legislating, therefore, for the Malayan Settlements, the Supreme Government must depend wholly on the degree of knowledge and enlightenment which may happen to be possessed by the local Governor, with the assistance, at each of the three Settlements, of a kind of Assessor, under the name of a Resident Councillor, but without Deliberative Councils, or a legal adviser, which are so ably supplied in every other part of India. The local Governor, then, who may happen to be, and most probably is, a Military or Civil Officer of the Indian service, without any knowledge of the languages, manners, and character of the great majority of the inhabitants of the Settlements over which he presides, and with a natural bias in favour of his own authority, is the only party from whom the materials for legislation are procurable. He, accordingly, transmits the crude drafts of Regulations for the Settlements to the Supreme Government. On the sole confidential recommendation, then, of such a party, laws are passed, as in the instance now under consideration, repugnant to the feelings and interests of the community at large, and in despite of their earnest and respectful remonstrances."

This statement of Mr. John Crawfurd was, possibly, the commencement of the state of feelings which led, twenty years afterwards, to the Transfer of the Settlements from India to the Colonial Office as a Crown Colony. The *Free Press* in commenting upon it, thus remarked upon the grievance which eventually became the *casus belli* with the Bengal Government:—

" How correct these observations are, will, we believe, be admitted by all unprejudiced persons having any acquaintance with the actual condition of matters in the Straits Settlements, although probably they will be questioned by those who are the objects of them. Too many instances, unfortunately, exist of the ignorance of the Supreme Government of the real condition of the Straits Settlements, to make their denial of the truth of Mr. Crawfurd's statements of much value; and it is to be hoped that, instead of attempting to palliate or conceal their ignorance, they will take the more manly and honest course of admitting it, and earnestly casting about for the means of effecting a change for the time to come, and procuring the information which they are so lamentably deficient in, and the want of which has betrayed them into so many blunders and acts of injustice.

" That our accusations against the Indian Government of neglect and incompetence in the administration of the Straits Settlements are not mere vague assertions founded on prejudice and misconception, we shall prove by adducing evidence from their own acts. For this purpose, it is not necessary to take a very long retrospect. The legislation and administration of the past year or two are quite sufficient to compel the admission of every impartial mind that the Indian Government is either very ignorant of, or unpardonably inattentive to, the real interests and well-being of the Straits Settlements.

" The Act for the Regulation of the Copper Currency of the Straits Settlements affords an illustration of the ignorance of obstinacy of the Supreme Government. In this Act they were not content with making the necessary provisions for introducing the new coinage, but by an ill-judged prohibition they put an entire stop to the circulation

of a currency which had been rendered necessary by their own long
continued neglect, and which had for many years been the only one
available for local purposes. This was found well adapted for many
purposes, although an authorised coinage of a cent and its fractional
parts was desirable as a legal standard of value, and for the use
of those who did not require so minute a coin as the *doit*. All
that was desirable would have been attained by making the cent and
its fractional parts the legal tender, leaving it optional to receive or
reject the *doit* as suited the convenience of the people. But this
course was not pursued, the *doit* being totally prohibited, and the
consequence of this prohibition is that, at the present moment, the
poor experience a loss to the extent of at least 40 per cent. on their
means of livelihood, by being compelled, in purchasing their daily
food, to pay a quarter of a cent for what they used to obtain for
the sixth or seventh of a cent.

"The Act to allow of the reception of the transported convicts
of Hongkong into the Straits Settlements, is another instance of the
most complete ignorance on the part of the Supreme Government
of the Straits Settlements, or if that is disclaimed, of the most wanton
tampering with the safety and welfare of the inhabitants. We believe
the plea of ignorance will not avail the Indian Government in this
instance, as the Straits Executive officers, much to their credit, most
earnestly remonstrated against the measure, pointing out the grave
objections which existed to it in the nature of the population and
other circumstances. That their estimate of the characters likely to
be introduced was just, is but too well confirmed by the catastrophe
which it is our painful duty to record in another column as having
befallen the *General Wood*, which was conveying ninety-two of these
Hongkong convicts to undergo their sentences at Penang. We may
be sure that these persons, when in the Settlements, would not have
been found a whit less evilly disposed, or less anxious for their escape,
than what they were on board ship; and the peculiar facilities surrounding them would have led to attempts, renewed until successful.
In Singapore they are surrounded by their countrymen, all linked
together by the oaths and bonds of the secret societies to which, nearly
to a man, the Chinese here belong. These criminals also belong to
the same societies, and once beyond the walls of the convict gaol,
what more easy for them than to gain protection and assistance from
their countrymen? The many plantations in the jungles of Singapore,
as well as on the opposite coast of Johore, tenanted solely by Chinese,
afford admirable places of refuge, at all times open to them. Thus
the Chinese convict has every inducement to escape in the succour
and assistance he is sure to find when once he has broken away—
facilities which do not at all exist to the Indian convict. Can anything
be conceived more stupid than to make such places as these the
stations for Chinese convicts?

"The recent draft Act for the amendment of the existing Assessment Act betrays also the supreme contempt for the wishes of the
inhabitants of the Settlements, which characterises many other Acts
of the Indian Government. The communities of the Straits have
expressed their desire to be allowed to participate in the adminis-

tration of the funds raised for municipal purposes. So far, however, from the Indian Government complying with this most reasonable request, they propose the miserable expedient of a Committee of persons to be nominated by the Chief Authority, who, of course, will take care to select only those perfectly compliant in all things; and even against the proceedings of such a Committee, fettered and bound as they would be, the Chief Authority may appeal to Bengal, and have them disallowed.

"Other instances might be adduced to shew that the Straits Settlements do not receive from the Supreme Government that attention which is required for their proper management, and for the well-being and comfort of the inhabitants. We do not cherish any hope that changes for the better will be made during the few years which have to elapse before the expiry of the present Charter of the East India Company, but it may be of use to give the subject prominence now with the view of its attracting attention when the time shall arrive for making provisions for the future government of our Indian possessions."

A short paragraph in the *Free Press* of the 10th February gave the key note to the story of the tragedy of the *General Wood*. It said, "The *General Wood* left this on 3rd January for Penang, with ninety-two convicts on board; there was no military guard with them. She had not arrived at Penang up to the latest dates. It is hoped she may be kept out by baffling winds."

The community of Singapore had protested against convicts being sent from Hongkong to Singapore, and it is a remarkable thing that on the 27th January, there had been a long article in the newspaper arguing again the reasons against it. Such as that the Chinese on Singapore composed 40,000 of the whole population of 60,000; that a vast majority of these belonged to the lowest class; many lived in the interior of the island, hardly accessible to the police; and that convicts from Hongkong would be of very much the same class, active and dangerous, and sure to open communication with the Chinese outside the Jail. This article was afterwards referred to in the London *Daily News* of 26th April, which spoke of the tragedy of the *General Wood* as a tale of piracy and murder, which the Oriental Seas alone could furnish. On the 2nd January, shortly after midnight, the British ship *General Wood*, belonging to Jardine, Matheson & Co. of Hongkong, of 740 tons, left Singapore for Penang and Bombay. She had come from Hongkong taking Chinese convicts from there to Bombay. She remained in Singapore from 23rd November to 2nd January, for vessels took their time in those days, and, after taking in a few transported convicts from Singapore, went on her way. In Singapore the convicts were loosed from their handcuffs and leg irons, and were employed in hoisting in cargo and other work. At night they were secured. It was pointed out to the chief officer that they seemed to try to ascertain the position of the ship's arms, &c., but he made light of it. Early in the morning of the 20th February three of the passengers landed in a native *prahu*, and the story went all round Singapore that the convicts had risen on the crew the night after the vessel left Singapore, and, after sailing about for twenty days, had wrecked her off Pulo Laut, North Natunas.

There were three passengers on board—Lieutenant Seymour, of the Indian Cavalry, and his wife, a daughter of Mr. W. R. George, and Mr. Andrew Farquhar, a grandson of Colonel Farquhar, who had all three gone on board at Singapore as passengers to Bombay. The Captain and the three European mates were all murdered. Lieut. Seymour was cut over the knee and thrown overboard, but he got hold of a rope and held on for some hours and eventually clambered on board. Mr. Farquhar tried to get on deck, but was attacked and jumped overboard, and held on to the rudder until the morning. At daybreak he tried to get on deck, but was struck with a cutlass on the hands and fell back again to the rudder, and after some hours he was allowed to come on deck. Nineteen lascar sailors were murdered, and three native passengers and several servants. A European sailor on board working his passage from Hongkong to Bombay in the ship, was fearfully beaten over the head, and afterwards went down in the vessel. Mrs. Seymour's ayah jumped overboard and was drowned.

The following account of the tragedy appeared in the *Free Press*, as well as a long letter from Lieut. Seymour, one of the three passengers :—

"The vessel sailed on the morning of the 2nd January, and after 6 p.m., came to an anchor to the eastward of the Carimons. Four of the Chinese convicts, who were employed to cook for the rest, eight who were sick, and a Malay and Chinese sent on board at Singapore, also convicts, had not the chain passed through their leg-irons as the others had. The key by which the chain was secured was in posssesion of the sepoy who kept watch over them at the main hatch. Two lascars were placed in the main hatchway, one on the forecastle and another on the poop The havildar stated that two sepoys were keeping guard over the convicts on the main, and one on the after-hatchway. The lascars on watch had no arms. The syrang stated that it was drizzling and he went to sleep under the fore-castle on the port side. About 1 o'clock a m. he heard the Chinese calling out, and he got up and ran forward. He met the sepoy from the after-hatchway running forward, and asked him what was the matter, and was told the Chinese had got on deck. He met the second officer at the main-hatchway, who ran forward, and he saw no more of him. It was very dark and he could find no weapon in the hurry of the moment. The Chinese made a rush forward and secured all the ship's arms. There were about nine muskets in the third officer's cabin, six boarding pikes on a rack between the stanchions of the poop rail, and a box containing cut-lasses, bayonets, tomahawks and pistols, under the starboard poop ladder which were immediately seized by the convicts. A number of the crew got into the rigging, and many of them, including some native passengers, were murdered. The manner in which some of these were put to death is said to have been atrociously cruel, being tied to the mast, and literally cut to pieces by the convicts with savage exultation. The Captain, after displaying an utter want of presence of mind, tried to cut away one of the boats, but being unsuccessful hung on by a rope for some time and was then drowned.

The first and second Officers also, after receiving a number of wounds, jumped into the sea and were drowned. Others were thrown over, or themselves jumped over, some being drowned and others ultimately saved. After the convicts had got possession of the vessel they lighted up the deck with cups filled with oil and cotton. At day-light those of the crew who had taken refuge in the rigging were induced to come down on the promise, conveyed to them through two Chinese belonging to the crew, that the convicts would not harm them. They compelled the gunner's mate to bring up the ammunition and loaded all the muskets. A brig was lying at anchor at the distance of about a quarter of a mile, but she had no communication with the *General Wood*. At day-light about eighteen or nineteen lascars were missing, three Chuliah passengers, and two of the servants. The convicts ordered the lascars to loose the sails and get the ship under weigh. The syrang being told to heave up the anchor, intended to make a long job of it in hope of attracting the notice of the brig, but the convicts abused and threatened him, saying that a steamer would be sent after them, and he was delaying in order to get them secured again. They then slipped the chain and the ship got under weigh. One of the Chinese lascars said he knew the way back to China, and directed the ship's course, the gunner being made to trim sails and one of the seacunnies to steer. He took them through Durian Straits. About noon they passed a Dutch barque at about a mile's distance, which shewed its ensign, made a signal, but the convicts would not allow any flag to be hoisted in return. The ship anchored near a small island, and a number of the Chinese landed, taking four of the crew. While they were on shore a large junk hove in sight and the ship was got under weigh to speak her. The people who had gone ashore pulled out and boarded her. It seems the convicts tried to persuade the people in the junk to convey them to China, but they refused, as they were bound to Singapore. On the island they asked a Malay if he knew the way to Cochin-China. On the 19th, they hove to near another island and some of them landed and brought back some fowls and cocoanuts. They took a lascar as interpreter, but kept a vigilant watch over him to prevent his communicating unobserved with the people of the island. On the 21st, about 9 a.m., they struck upon a reef about a mile and a half from land. The sea at the time was quite smooth and a moderate breeze blowing. The long boat was hoisted out and the cutters lowered. The greater number of the convicts, passengers, and crew went to the island (Salaout) in the boats, about sixteen lascars and fifteen convicts being left on the ship to await the return of the boats. The water rose rapidly in the vessel, and at about 1 p.m. she slid off the rocks and went down in deep water. The gunner, syrangs, first tindal and lascars saved themselves in a small China boat and reached the shore about 3 p.m.; the rest left on the ship were supposed to have been drowned. The long boat and cutters also reached the shore in safety. The Chinese proposed killing the passengers, but were dissuaded from it by some of the lascars. The passengers got safely on shore, and found refuge in a Malay hut. The lascars made a rush into the jungle. The next morning they found the long boat gone and some of the Chinese left, who were secured by the Dutch and Malays on the island. They were then taken to Sedanow or Boongooran, where the passengers and crew received every attention from the Datoh Kaya, and were at last sent to Singapore where they arrived on Saturday the 19th February.

Messrs. Jnc. Purvis & Co., the agents in Singapore for Jardine Matheson & Co., asked the Government to send the E. I. Co.'s steamer *Auckland* to search for the convicts who had escaped in the ship's boats, and to endeavour to save her hull and cargo, and through the intervention of Mr. Church and Captain McQuhae of H. M. S. *Dædalus*, the *Phlegethon* was sent. In April, news came from Bangkok that Chinese, supposed to be some of the escaped convicts, cast-away there on an island named Pulo Ubi, had been seen by a vessel named the *Celerity*, and the *Phlegethon* went there to search. On the 26th April the trial of the nineteen men sent by the Orang Kaya took place. A temporary gallery was put up in the Court for the accommodation of ladies, many of whom, including Mrs. Butterworth and Mrs. Church were present. The Judges were Col. Butterworth, Sir Christopher Rawlinson (the Recorder), and Mr. Church. It lasted four days; the jury found all the prisoners guilty, but on the first count of the indictment only, which was for piracy simply, the other counts being for murder and piracy with violence. The following remarks then took place:—

The Recorder :—Then you find all the prisoners guilty of taking possession of the ship by violence?

Foreman :—No, my Lord; we find them guilty on the first count only.

The Recorder :—Then you mean to say by your verdict that the prisoners at the bar used no violence in taking possession of the ship?

Foreman :—Yes, my Lord.

His Lordship desired to know if the jury entertained especial grounds for recommending some of the prisoners to the merciful consideration of the Court; the foreman stated that he had not been instructed as to the reasons, but some of the jury desired especial recommendations. His Lordship said that if the jury were satisfied there was but little or conflicting evidence on which to convict, they ought to have acquitted such of the prisoners.

The jury, while finding all the prisoners guilty, recommended a number to mercy and three of the prisoners "particularly to mercy." On which the Recorder remarked that the jury had taken a most lenient view of their case. They, the jury, as judges of the evidence, had arrived at the conclusion (he knew not how, he knew not why), that notwithstanding a number of murders had been committed before possession was gained of the vessel, still they, the prisoners, in the minds of the jury, were not guilty of the violence which was proved, if they believed the witnesses, to have been enacted on board the vessel. His Lordship did "*not believe that any human being present, except that jury, would have arrived at the conclusion they did.*"

On which the *Free Press* remarked:—"This verdict has excited considerable comment, and we have heard that some of the explanations of the Hon'ble the Recorder were misunderstood by the Jury. It is, however, better that they should lean to mercy, than that through any panic or other feeling they should convict indiscriminately. When it is considered that the trial lasted three days, the Court on each day commencing its sitting at 9 o'clock a.m., and continuing it to a late hour, that there were nineteen prisoners, the case of each of whom was to be viewed separately and distinctly, that the witnesses were numerous, and in some cases rather suspicious, that the evidence, from the very nature of the case, the revolt having happened in the dead of the night, was vague and inconclusive; taking all these into account, we conceive that, without much fuller and more accurate notes than we imagine any of the Jury took, it was almost impossible to return a very discriminative verdict, unless indeed the Jury had considered it consistent with their oaths to follow implicitly the summing up from the Bench. The Court met on Saturday at noon, when sentence of death was directed to be recorded against the whole of the prisoners, and five of them— the carpenter, the two Chinese sailors, and two of the convicts— who appeared to have taken an active part in the affair, were sentenced to be transported to Bombay for life. The Court took further time to determine what should be done with the others. In passing sentence the Hon'ble the Recorder made some strong remarks on the verdict of the Jury, which he said (although he could not arrive at the grounds on which they had formed their opinion of the case) the Court was bound to endeavour to give effect to it; that, although sentence of death against them all would be recorded on the first count, yet he felt so hampered by the verdict of the Jury, they he could not allow that sentence to be carried out. His Lordship hoped that his thus acting on what he believed to be the constitutional view of the law, would not be attended by evil consequences."

On Monday, the 8th May, the H.C. steamer *Phlegethon*, Capt. Niblett, returned from her visit to Pulo Ubi, having on board twenty-eight Chinese said to be part of the convicts escaped from the *General Wood*. The men offered some resistance when it was wished to apprehend them, and one or two were killed or died from the wounds then received. It appeared that fourteen of the convicts left Pulo Ubi in the long boat with the intention of trying to find their way to China, five went to Siam, and three took their departure for Singapore on board a junk. Most of the officers and crew of the steamer contracted fever while lying at Pulo Ubi, and their fuel and water had got very low on their way back when they fortunately fell in with H.M. Steamer *Fury*, which supplied their wants and took them in tow.

The *Phlegethon's* boats had rowed round Pulo Ubi, and found the retreat of the convicts in a joss-house near the shore, and a number of articles belonging to the *General Wood*, including the chronometer and a card-case of Mrs. Seymour's, which left no doubt that they were on the right track, and, after a great deal of trouble, and stratagem, as the island was ten or twelve miles in circumference and abounding in caves and thick jungle, the captain pretended to give it up in despair, and the vessel went away, leaving some of the crew disguised as Cochin-Chinese; and thirty convicts were eventually captured. The account given by the prisoners was that they were about seven days at sea and arrived at Pulo Ubi early in February in two boats, sixty in number. After sailing about the island to reconnoitre, they landed well armed at the village and immediately took possession. The inhabitants, about thirty in number, fled to the jungle, and they helped themselves to everything. The largest boat, in which it is supposed most of the valuables and treasure were deposited, they never left without a strong guard, anchoring in deep water every night; this boat they decked over and otherwise disfigured. In the night, with about twelve of their number, they left, promising to send a junk for the remainder; the other boat was sunk on the appearance of the *Celerity*. Others had also left by various opportunities. The following seemed to be the end of the whole number :—

Drowned at Natunas	...	...	...	...	15
Captured by the natives	...	...	...	...	18
Gone to China in long boat		...	...	...	12
Do. Siam in Pukat	...	...	...	...	5
Do. Singapore do.	...	...	...	...	3
Do. Hainam do.	...	...	...	...	3
Do. Chinchew do.	...	...	...	...	2
Captured by the *Phlegethon*	...	...	...	30
Left on Pulo Ubi	...	...	...	...	5
				Total Chinese convicts	93

A special criminal sessions was held, on the 18th May, to try the convicts brought back by the *Phlegethon*, and they were all convicted. The paper in remarking upon the execution of those convicts who were hanged (three men only, in consequence of the verdict of the first jury), made the following final remarks on the subject :—

"From the confessions of some of the convicts, made since sentence was passed upon them, it would appear the Chinese carpenter of the *General Wood* was the sole concocter of the desperate resolve to rise and seize the vessel. This arch-villain, who had joined the ship but a month or two before, was no sooner at Singapore than he communicated his design to some of the convicts, when the plot was readily entered into. From the confession made, it would appear that one prisoner, a cook who was hanged, was loose on the night of the disturbance, and prepared billets of firewood by tapering the ends conveniently to handle; it was then arranged that sixteen on one chain were to be released by the one at the head of the chain forcing the lock, and the duty of these sixteen was to separate themselves into four parties, and that the parties were to single out the captain and three mates as their victims. The sepoy in charge of the key was first killed, and the key taken from him; the other convicts were then released and they went on deck to carry out their desperate resolution. The captain, it would appear, was killed and thrown over-board, as also the chief mate; the second mate was wounded but missed, and although search was made throughout the vessel no trace of him could be found. Lieut. Seymour at both trials stated that Chinese placed lights near his face apparently examining him for some one for whom they were in search, it forming no part of the original plot to kill the passengers, of whose presence on board they were scarcely aware. Prisoners Nos. 1 and 10 (the latter admitted as Queen's evidence) were of the party who killed the captain and mate. The unfortunate third mate, who, after manfully resisting the Chinese until nearly exhausted, managed to escape up the mizen mast into the mizen-top, was dragged down by Wong Ah Leang and despatched with a sword ; a blanket was then thrown over him ; at daylight, on observing a brig at anchor not very far distant, they were fearful of throwing the body overboard lest it should float and be discovered, so the corpse was rolled up in wax cloth and kept till the evening when it was cast into the sea. From all we learn it would appear that the prisoners pointed out as having taken an active part was substantially correct, and that amongst the worst actors in the dreadful tragedy were some of those convicted at the first trial, but by an unfortunate verdict permitted to escape the extreme penalty of the law."

The Government sent some handsome presents to the Orang Kaya and people of the Natunas for their assistance to the passengers and crew of the *General Wood,* and for the capture of the convicts ; among other things was a six-pounder brass gun with a suitable inscription.

The tragedy of the *General Wood* raised an outcry against convicts being sent from Hongkong to Singapore ; for a few years Chinese had been transported from there, and strong representations had been made on the subject. It was afterwards stopped. With reference to the previous cases of similar murders, the first case seems to have occurred on board the *Freak* in 1841 ; another on board the *Harriett Scott,* in September, 1843, which vessel was carrying convicts from Penang to Hongkong. The next case was the *Ariel,* in the following year, when the Captain was murdered. This was followed by the *Lowjee Family,* a large country-ship, in November, 1844. Another case of which the date has not been traced was the *Virginia.*

At a meeting of the Chamber of Commerce in March, a letter was addressed to the Resident Councillor soliciting the interference of the authorities for the protection of the freedom of the trade of the port against certain alleged encroachments on the part of the Tumonggong of Johore. The Chamber stated that, for some time past, complaints had reached them of the systematic proceedings adopted by the Tumonggong to monopolize the trade in gutta percha. That in declarations before them it was represented that native boats bringing supplies of gutta for sale in Singapore had been forcibly intercepted by the Tumonggong's followers. That, further, the Chamber was informed that the Tumonggong had boats stationed at different points to intercept all *prahus* with gutta destined for Singapore ; that the latter were boarded by armed Malays, and every means taken by outward display and show of authority to frighten the natives into compliance with the Tumonggong's terms. It was stated that the gutta trade had assumed considerable importance, amounting to between 10,000 and 12,000 piculs, valued at from $150,000 to $200,000 per annum, and that, of this, about nine-tenths of the import had been, in defiance of all opposition, secured by the Tumonggong, whence it was inferred that extreme influence of some kind was used, or some part of it would have found its way to parties who offered much higher prices for it than that which the native traders received from him. The Chamber then stated the serious and disadvantageous consequences likely to arise if such a state of things was permitted, and they remarked that they had been credibly informed that boats from Siak had actually gone to Malacca to dispose of their gutta percha to avoid being exposed to the interference they would experience were they to bring it to Singapore. The Chamber also represented that by the Treaty or Agreement under which the East India Company became possessed of Singapore, the Sultan and Tumonggong of Johore engaged to maintain a free and unshackled trade everywhere within their dominions, and to admit the trade and traffic of the British nation to all the ports and harbours of the Kingdom of Johore and its dependencies on the terms of the most favoured nation.

The *Free Press* remarked:—" It will be perceived that this is a serious question, into which it behoves the authorities to make a most thorough investigation. Should it turn out as represented, we trust the Government will make His Highness thoroughly aware that such conduct on his part, or that of his followers, cannot on any account be tolerated for a moment, and that should it be in future attempted, he will be visited with their serious displeasure."

In April, Mr. Balestier's estate was put in trust for his creditors. Mr. Balestier had been in Singapore since 1834, and in 1837 he had been recognised as American Consul. He had opened a large sugar plantation on the land still known as Balestier Plain, which swallowed up a great deal of money of Russell & Co. of China. The plantation was advertised for sale in April, by the Trustee, Mr. Joseph H. Weed, and the particulars show how different Balestier Plain must have been then from its desolate state now. The enterprise was a complete failure. Mr. Balestier's house has disappeared altogether. The following was the advertisement:—

"The sugar plantation known as the Balestier Plantation, situated two miles from the centre of the Settlement of Singapore, consisting of one thousand acres of ground, lying in one body, two hundred and twenty of which are planted with sugar canes. The soil is good and produces on an average from twenty to twenty-five piculs of raw sugar per acre, from cane juice standing at from $9\frac{1}{4}°$ to $11°$ of saccharometer. Two crops are obtained in two years, viz., one of planted canes and one of Ratoons. Every field is surrounded by a broad ditch serving the purpose of drainage by irrigation, and all communicating with a canal fourteen feet in width and upwards of two miles in length, running through the whole extent of the property, and on which the canes are carried in boats to the mills and the crops taken directly to the shipping in the roads, if required. One or two water wheels may be easily worked on this stream. The buildings consist of one two-story dwelling house for a large family and necessary out-houses in good repair. An out-house for the Superintendent, a boiling house with a set of flat bottom pans—two of thick copper and three of iron—all connected and communicating with one another by means of valves, copper skimmers, filterers, &c., making five to six thousand pounds of sugar per day. An engine house and a ten-horse steam engine from the Low Moor Factory and a horizontal iron mill for crushing the cane, all in excellent working order; a curing or draining-house with an ample stock of earthen pots and jars, and 250 wooden drain-ing boxes of the capacity of four piculs, or five hundred pounds of sugar each, in which the sugar is bleached. A store room is attached, with bins to receive the sugar after being dried on a drier close by. And of a distillery consisting of two copper perpetual Stills, Baglioni's patent, and fermentation vats, all in working order; adjoining is a godown and large receiving casks. The estate is stocked with two Sydney horses and a young elephant used in ploughing; bulls and bullocks used to the plough and carts; carts and ploughs of various sizes. English and American cultivators, extirpators, harrows and a great quantity of iron pipes and implements of husbandry useful on a plantation, in-cluding a rotary fire engine. In the garden, near the dwelling house, are many trees of China fruit, and rare plants and flowers. The property will be sold at a great bargain with the standing crop. Picked Chinese and Klings, male labourers, are to be had in any number at three Spanish dollars per month, they finding themselves in everything.

The London *Daily News* published at full length the petition sent by the Singapore Chamber of Commerce to the House of Commons on the subject of the encroachments of the Dutch on our trade, and wrote lengthy leading articles on the subject. Lord Palmerston deputed Mr. James Brooke, who was then in England, to enquire and report on the subject. The Dutch were much annoyed at the action taken by the Singapore merchants, Dutch papers calling it an unjustifiable proceeding, and using other strong adjectives rather than arguments.

Mr. T. W. Salmond, who had been Resident Councillor at Malacca, died in Penang on the 12th of March, in his forty-first year. He joined the Bencoolen service in 1824, and when it was broken up was transferred to the Penang Civil List, where he held various appointments until 1841, when he went to Malacca as Resident Councillor. He was much esteemed, and a large number of natives attended his funeral.

In April, Captain Russell succeeded Captain Ross as Master Attendant; he had been the Commander of H. C. steamer *Nemesis*. On the 25th May, H. M. S. *Dædalus*, which had been here and in China for some years, left for England. Captain McQuhae had con-stantly exerted himself for the protection of trade, and he was very popular in Singapore. On his way home, he met the sea-serpent, the first of its notoriety, which caused so much discussion in Singapore and England at the end of the year, and *Punch* laughed at so much. The story is told in Mr. Richard Proctor's book called *"Pleasant Ways in Science"* in the chapter headed *"Strange Sea Creatures,"* and if the whole chapter is read, there may be found reason to think that such a thing may have a real existence; and that those who gave credit to "old McQuhae," as Admiral Keppel calls him in his book, were in the right and the wiseacres in the wrong. But he was called "Sea-serpent McQuhae" to the end of his life.

On Saturday evening, the 20th May, H. M. S. *Meander*, a 44 gun frigate, Captain the Hon. Henry Keppel, arrived from England, having as passengers, Mr. James Brooke, Governor of Labuan, Mr. and

Mrs. William Napier and their daughter, Mr. Hugh Low (in after years Sir Hugh Low, Resident of Perak), Mr. Spencer St. John (afterwards Sir Spencer), Secretary to Sir James Brooke, and some others. Miss Catherine Napier was married in St. Andrew's Church, Singapore, on the 12th August, 1848, to Mr. Hugh Low, and Admiral Keppel in his book, published in 1899, speaks of it as "a cheery wedding."

Mr. Brooke and the other Officers of his Government landed on Monday evening and were received with every honour. The Governor, Resident Councillor, European residents, and a large concourse of natives were present.

The *Free Press* wrote of Mr. Brooke's return as follows:— "We sincerely congratulate Mr. Brooke on his return to the scene of his labours in the East. The honourable post which he has been selected by Her Majesty's Government to fill, will enable him to give great assistance in advancing the general interests of commerce, as well as the welfare and civilization of Borneo, and we have no doubt that each and all of these objects he will devote himself to. The formation of a Crown Colony in the Indian Archipelago may be looked upon as the commencement of a new and most prosperous era in the history of British Commerce in the Eastern Archipelago. Already we have a foreshadowing and manifestation of it in the active commerce which has sprung up between this place and Bruni, since our relations with that country were re-organized. On Tuesday evening, the 23rd, the eve of the anniversary of Her Majesty's birthday, the Government House presented a scene of great festivity in honour of the occasion. Invitations to a ball and supper had been issued to about one hundred and fifty, including the Officers of H. M. Ships now in the harbour. Dancing was kept up with great spirit till midnight, when the party sat down to an elegant supper, in the course of which his Honour the Governor proposed Her Majesty's health, which was drunk with the utmost enthusiasm. A novel and striking effect was produced by simultaneously lighting blue lights, at a given signal, on the different elevations round the town, causing the appearance of a sudden illumination. A number of the principal native residents, Chinese, Arabs, &c., were also invited, and numerous others gained admittance to the grounds, to witness a display of fire-works which had been provided for the evening's entertainment."

A Public Company, called the "Eastern Archipelago Company," instituted for the extension of commerce in the China seas, and for promoting the civilization of Borneo, with a capital of £200,000, was started in this year, and a notification was issued signed by James Brooke, as Governor of Labuan, that the island of Labuan had been formally taken possession of by Great Britain, and would be open to settlers from the 1st August, as a free port. An office of the Labuan Government was opened in Singapore. W. R. Paterson & Co. were the Agents.

The Eastern Archipelago Company was started with Mr. Brooke's sanction, but had at bottom a scheme to buy out his rights in Sarawak, and to make money out of the country for money's sake, of which Mr. Brooke was not aware. It was this that led to serious trouble for him afterwards, as will be told later on.   Admiral Keppel in his last book says that he had the opinion that Henry Wise, Rajah Brooke's agent in London, who was at the bottom of the matter, managed to get Brooke, Napier and other truthful witnesses away from England in order to further the scheme to float what was afterwards shown to be a fraudulent concern.

The following letter to the *Free Press*, in June, gives the particulars of a matter that is still remembered here, as an example of the extraordinary engineering feats that have been attempted by Government Military Engineers in Singapore:—"Allow me through the medium of your paper, to congratulate Singapore upon its possessing a genius in its Superintending Engineer worthy to rival the ingenious Paddy, who finding his blanket rather short for him cut a piece off the bottom to join to the top that it might cover his head.   I have always admired the said Paddy with extreme veneration for the brightness of his conception, but he must for the future be content with a secondary place and give way to Major Faber.   The Grand Jury presented that two Bridges across the Canal were, by their flatness, obstructive to the traffic during high water, and recommended their being raised in the centre.   Major Faber set his face decidedly against any such alteration, but proposed that the bed of the Canal should be excavated, and so, of course, to lower the level of the water!   A most admirable plan, if only the sea will reduce its level or change its nature, to please a Superintending Engineer of the Hon'ble Company; which perhaps Major Faber has already contracted with it to do.   I firmly believe this must be the case, as I can hardly fancy that a Major of Engineers, and no doubt a scientific man, would have put forth such a proposition without some agreement of the kind."

The newspaper on 1st June said: "Mr. E. A. Blundell, formerly Acting Governor of these Settlements, and who was one of the victims of Lord Ellenborough's military furor, arrived here last week from Calcutta by the schooner *Eliza Penelope*, having been appointed Resident Councillor at Malacca.   Mr. Blundell was sworn in on Tuesday, and took his departure for Malacca yesterday.   We hope, for the sake of justice as well as for the interests of these Settlements, that Mr. Blundell's appointment to Malacca is only preliminary to his restoration to the Government of the Straits Settlements, and that our present worthy Governor (Colonel Butterworth) will receive an appointment in his own profession, in which he will be able to display, to the advantage of his country, those military talents which are comparatively lost in a civil employment."

It was in the *Eliza Penelope* that Mr. James Meldrum, now Dato Meldrum of Johore, came from Calcutta to Singapore for the first time, arriving there on 27th May, 1848, the only other passenger, the Dato now says, being Mr. Blundell; and it is curious to find that the *Eliza Penelope* was the famous old paddle wheel steamer *Diana* of Captain Congalton, under a new name, which has been described on page 281.

Mr. Joseph Harvey Weed, the Acting American Consul, who was the trustee of the affairs of Mr. Balestier, died in June.

On the 1st August, Mr. G. J. Dare and Mr. Alfred Bernard opened the firm of G. J. Dare & Co., as Auctioneers, Shipchandlers and Commission Agents. In the same month Mr. Alexander Dyce, of the firm of Martin, Dyce & Co., died at sea on the passage from Manila to Singapore. Mr. Alexander Dyce had been in Manila, and his brother Mr. Charles Dyce in Singapore; their brother was the famous Royal Academician who painted some of the frescoes in the House of Lords.

The following is an account, from the *Free Press*, of the launch of the little gun-boat *Ranee*, for Sarawak, into the river from where Hallpike Street is now:—" On Monday, the 4th August, there was launched from the building-yard of Messrs. Wilkinson, Tivendale & Co., in the presence of Sir F. E. Collier, c.b., Naval Commander-in-chief of this Station, the Hon. T. Church, Esq., Resident Councillor, and Captain Young, of the H. C. steamer *Auckland*, a small steamer of elegant proportions, designed by Mr. Bulbeck, Carpenter of H. M. S. *Meander*. Miss Church, the daughter of the Hon. the Resident Councillor, christened the vessel by naming her the *Ranee*. She is intended for immediate active service for the suppression of piracy in the Borneo and Sulu seas. She will leave this on Saturday next, in charge of Mr. Baker of H. M. S. *Meander*, in company with the H. C. war-steamer *Auckland* for Sarawak, where she will join the *Meander*, and be under the orders of Hon. Captain Keppel and Sir James Brooke. This small steamer is 60 feet in length, breadth of beam 8 feet 6 inches, fitted with a 4-horse power engine by Messrs. Seaward, of Limehouse, and with her armament and men, it is stated will not exceed a draught of 26 inches. She has a very handsome appearance afloat, is built entirely of teak, coppered and copper-fastened, and reflects the highest credit on her constructors and the Chinese artisans in their employment. Her armament is to be two long brass guns and rocket tubes. We wish her every success, although the power is stated by those conversant with steam navigation to be totally insufficient for the intended purpose."

The price of gambier was then very low, about 80 cents a picul, and the prospects of the Chinese planters were very bad, and the cultivation was, in a great many instances abandoned; in Province Wellesley the sugar cultivation was also in a very depressed state.

The new Insolvent Act of Parliament, for India, and extended to the Straits, was put in force here in September, and the Chamber of Commerce passed some resolutions which were entered in the Records of the Chamber; among them was the following:—

" The punishments to be inflicted by clauses 25, 50, 51, 52 and 70 form an important and most salutary feature in this Act. On the strictness and just severity with which these powers are carried out will mainly depend the success of the measure and its advantage to the Straits Community, for it cannot be denied that peculiar and local causes, the unsettled and migratory habits of native traders here, their generally low origin, the difficulty of detecting, and impossibility of punishing frauds as public crimes, have induced much laxity, recklessness and demoralization among many classes of traders, it being estimated that from two-thirds to three-quarters of native failures in Singapore are fraudulent. This may, for some time, render necessary a vigorous and unsparing application of the powers of punishment now conferred. Henceforward imprisonment will become, not as now—incarceration of the debtors' body as security for debt—but a punishment inflicted upon him as a public criminal, and it will be most desirable that this broad distinction be clearly brought to the understanding of native traders coming within the jurisdiction of the Court."

A Masonic banquet was given in June, of which the following was an account, which we print as it contains reference to some well-known names:—

"On Saturday, the 24th June, being the anniversary of the festival of St. John the Baptist, the Brethren held a special meeting at high twelve for the purpose of receiving in due form James Brooke, Governor, and W. Napier, Lieut-Governor, of Labuan, who afterwards remained to witness the initiation of a new candidate for admission to the Masonic mysteries and privileges—Lieut. H. W. Comber of H. M. S. *Meander.*" He is now a retired Rear Admiral. The Lodge was then in North Bridge Road on the West side, near where Hock Lam Street is now.

"In the evening these distinguished visitors, with Captain the Hon'ble H. Keppel, were invited to meet the Past Master and Brethren at a Farewell Banquet given to the Worshipful Master Brother W. H. Read, on the occasion of his expected early departure to Europe. The Brethren with their distinguished guests sat down to a sumptuous dinner at 7 o'clock. The Worshipful Past Master was in the Chair; the Worshipful Master on his right, Brother Brooke on his left. The Senior Warden acted as Croupier; the Hon'ble Captain Keppel on his right, the Hon'ble Brother Napier, on his left. All the other officers of the Lodge were in their appropriate seats and the other brethren took their places under the direction of the Stewards for the occasion, Brothers J. B. Cumming and M. F. Davidson. In front of the Lodge a beautifully illuminated square and compasses was exhibited, and the interior of the Banquet Room throughout the evening presented an unvaried scene of harmony and animated enjoyment. Much of the success of the evening's entertainment is to be attributed, we believe, to the delightful complacency of Brother Brooke. In the hands of a gentleman of his polished demeanour, it may be easily conceived he had no difficulty in exhibiting to perfection the beautiful masonic lesson—that all masons are, as brethren, upon the same level—yet masonry takes no honour from any man that he had before, for masons are bound not to derogate from that respect which is due to any brother, were he not a mason: these great truths and principles were most happily illustrated on this delightful occasion. We believe we may venture to say that this festival will be a Red Letter Day in the annals of 'Zetland in the East,' and in the memory of every one who had the gratification of participating in its enjoyment."

In July it was proposed to start a local Marine Insurance Company. There were then 18 agencies in Singapore for different companies, and it was ascertained that the amount of premiums received during the preceding four years had been between $112,000 and $123,000, yearly. It was said that a local company would obtain a large share of the business. It was never carried out, and it was not until over thirty years later that the first local assurance company was established, and was afterwards wound up.

The paper in August contained the following paragraph : —

"It is our duty this week to chronicle the disappearance of the well-known mass of rock situated on the Singapore side of the Western entrance to New Harbour, called by natives *Batu Belayer*, and by Europeans *Lot's Wife*. This rock, which was composed of a mass of very hard conglomerate, partially crystallised, has been known to navigators in the Straits for many hundreds of years, and we believe figures upon old charts engraved upwards of 200 years ago." It was blown up.

The following letter to the *Free Press*, in August, shows that the question of the necessity for the defence of Singapore was then quite appreciated by the mercantile community. Admiral Sir Francis Collier had just arrived from England in the P. & O. Mail and had hoisted his flag on Captain Keppel's ship the *Meander* :—

"The present is a favourable moment for calling attention to a subject which is of paramount importance to Singapore. I mean the great advantages which would accrue to this Settlement were it made the Principal Naval Station in these Seas. The arrival of the gallant Admiral, now here, is the most favourable moment that for years has offered for attaining the end in view. Seeing that not only is the Admiral enabled to form his own judgment upon personal examination, but that Captain the Hon'ble H. Keppel is also here, it would be presumption to call his attention to the concentrical position we hold in the direct route between India and China, and within three days' sail of the Straits of Sunda, which may be looked upon as the prison-house of our China trade whenever a European War shall tempt an enemy's cruisers, whether legitimate or ruthless Privateers, to lie in wait there, should the seas in that neighbourhood not be protected by the English Ensign.

"It is therefore the more selfish note of self interest that I would sound. This will not only be believed as sincere, but will relieve me from the imputation of offering him that which, if feasible, will no doubt have already been suggested by that distinguished officer, Captain Keppel, who is as highly respected for his professional talents as he is esteemed for that urbanity which has made him ever so deservedly popular in Singapore.

"The eclat which Singapore would derive from becoming the nominal head-quarters of the Naval Commander-in-chief would be understood by all, while the benefit arising from the circulation of money expended in the construction of Public Works, would be more substantial, especially if the docks, which *must* sooner or later be built here, should be taken in hand by Government instead of being deferred till private enterprise carry out the undertaking. But the most important advantage we should obtain would be the safety and security which would thus be conferred upon our Settlement whenever a war breaks out, as break out I fear it must ere long. The idea of fortifying Singapore, about which so much noise was made, seems to be given up, so we must trust to the 'wooden walls.' Should this become the chief Naval Station, these natural guardians of a defenceless but valuable seaport like ours, and which will then probably become a rendezvous for our merchantmen when either waiting for convoy or in want of shelter from the enemy's cruisers; then these natural guardians will always be upon the spot in greater or less force."

On Tuesday, the 22nd August, Mr. Brooke was created a K.C.B., the Queen's warrant, addressed to Mr. William Napier, Lieutenant-Governor of Labuan, having been received in Singapore while he was still here, with instructions from Prince Albert to omit nothing in the ceremony that might evince the esteem entertained by the Queen for Mr. Brooke. The ceremony took place in the Public Assembly Rooms, at the foot of Fort Canning, and the *Free Press* contained a very long account of the most elaborate ceremonial that had ever taken place in Singapore; from which we take the following :—

"The investiture took place in the Public Assembly Rooms, which were fitted up in a suitable manner. At one end of the large room a dais or platform had been run across the whole breadth of the apartment, and, raised two steps above this, a chair was placed to represent a throne, under a canopy of crimson velvet edged with gold lace, the dais and steps of the throne being covered with red cloth. The whole apartment was very tastefully decorated with flags, while the main entrance of the building outside was ornamented with a variety of shrubs and flowers. The accommodation for visitors consisted of rows of chairs running down both sides of the throne-room on a graduated rise, leaving an open space in the centre which was also covered with red cloth, for the processions to advance towards the throne, comfortable seats for 240 spectators being thus provided. Facing the throne, the Royal Marines of H. M. S. *Meander* were ranged along the other end of the room, to act as a guard of honour, the Band of the same vessel being stationed in the gallery erected in the apartment. In the spacious portion which is on a level with this room, a flank Company of the 21st Regiment M. N. I. was stationed, to act as a guard of honour to Sir James Brooke, the Band of the same Regiment being also stationed in the portico. A little after 11 o'clock visitors began to arrive in considerable numbers, and at about half-past eleven Mr. W. Napier drove up to the rooms, and was shortly followed by Sir J. Brooke, who was received with the usual military honours by the guard of the 21st Regt. At 12 o'clock the Royal Standard was hoisted on a flag-staff on Government Hill under a salute of 21 guns from the battery on shore and the ships of war in the harbour, which was the signal for the ceremonial to commence. The procession now moved from the banqueting room, where they had assembled, entering the throne room by a side door at the end, and passing in front of the guard of Marines. The guard of honour of Royal Marines saluted the Lieutenant-Governor in the usual manner as he passed their front, and the Band of H. M. S. *Meander* struck up *God Save the Queen* as the procession entered, and kept playing as it moved up, until Mr. Napier had taken his seat on the throne—when the music ceased. [Here follows a list of the first procession, which included Mr. John Connolly, the Sheriff; Mr. Hugh Low; Major Faber; the Rev. H. Moule, the Chaplain; and twenty others.]

After a little time Mr. Brooke's procession began to move, entering the throne room by the door opposite that by which the other procession entered, and passed in front of the guard of Marines, and up the centre towards the throne. [Here follows a list of the second procession, which included Dr. Treacher, Colonial Surgeon of Labuan; Mr. Thomas Dunman, Superintendent of Police; Mr. St. John, one of Sir James Brooke's Secretaries; Dr. Oxley; Mr. Behn, Hamburg Consul; Mr. Nicol, Danish Consul; Sir Jose d'Almeida, Consul-General for Portugal; Mr. C. Johnston (now Rajah of Sarawak) Aide-de-Camp to Sir J. Brooke; Mr. Thos. Church, Resident Councillor; and over twenty others; and was followed by Captain Keppel and Mr. Brooke himself.]

Mr. Low, Secretary to the Government of Labuan, then read and published the following letter from His Royal Highness Prince Albert, Great Master of the Order, communicating the Royal Warrant for the investiture, viz:—

Buckingham Palace,
23rd May, 1848.

Sir,—The Queen having been graciously pleased as a mark of Her Royal approbation of the services of James Brooke, Esquire, Governor and Commander-in-Chief in and over the Island of Labuan, to appoint him an Ordinary Member of the Civil Division of the Second Class or Knights Commanders of the Most Honourable Order of the Bath; I am to signify to you Her Majesty's pleasure that you should invest him with the Insignia of that Class and Division of the Order (herewith transmitted) in conformity to the enclosed Royal Warrant; and it being Her Majesty's intention that the same be done in the most honourable and distinguished manner that circumstances will allow of, you will concert and adjust with him such time and manner for investing him with the Insignia of a Civil Knight Commander of the said Most Honorable Order, and at the same time mark in the most public manner Her Majesty's just sense of the zeal and ability displayed by Mr. Brooke in the service of his country.

I am with consideration,
Sir,
Yours, &c.,
ALBERT,
Great Master.

To WILLIAM NAPIER, ESQ.,
&c., &c., &c.,
Lieut.-Governor of Labuan.

The Mandate of the Sovereign having been read, the Revd. H. Moule, Residency Chaplain, read an appropriate prayer. Mr. Napier after a long speech, eulogistic of Sir James, invested him with the order, after which Sir James Brooke made the following reply:—"The honour you have now conferred upon me by command of Her Most Gracious Majesty has naturally excited in my breast feelings both of gratitude and of pride. I feel myself grateful to my Sovereign for this mark of distinction; and proud that the Queen should have deemed me worthy to receive it.

"With the approval of his Sovereign her grateful subject may be absolved from the task of speaking of his own service: he can only hope that the future may be as the past has been, and that he may be enabled faithfully to discharge his duty to his Queen and to his country.

"Were I to say, Sir, that this decoration could either stimulate or increase the loyalty I entertain towards Her Majesty, I should be doing less than justice to myself; for my feelings of loyalty, in common I trust with those of every British subject, are not susceptible of increase. I value this distinction, I value it most highly, as a token of her Majesty's most gracious approbation, and sanctioned by this approbation, I shall wear it with the proud consciousness of having won it in this far and distant part of the world.

"Sir, as the Representative of the Crown on this occasion, you will permit me to express my acknowledgments for the kind and flattering terms you have used in speaking of me; and to say that I trust our future career together may be distinguished by the confidence and good will which has ever existed between us. Sir, I beg to thank you for the manner you have discharged the duty which Her Majesty the Queen has done you the honour to entrust to your hands."

A numerous party assembled at the Ball in the evening given by the Lieut-Governor of Labuan to meet Sir James Brooke, and dancing was kept up with great animation until a late hour.

This was an occasion that was long remembered by the community of Singapore, and by Colonel Butterworth, the Governor, who lost his watch, and by Mrs. Butterworth, who had all her jewellery stolen the same night from Government House (on Fort Canning) after the Ball. The *Meander*, left on the following day for Labuan with Sir James Brooke.

The following letter from "An old Resident" (Mr. W. H. Read) appeared in the *Free Press* in 1884, the time some of these papers were first being published:—"The Ball-room in the Assembly Rooms was fitted up for the occasion, a dais was erected, and three chairs placed thereon, the middle one, as is usual on such occasions, representing the Royal Throne. Mr. Napier was an old resident in Singapore, and a general favourite; but his peculiar way of carrying his head, of brushing his hair, and swagger of body, had earned him the title of 'Royal Billy.' Fully impressed with the importance of the functions he had to perform (and, perhaps, a little bit more so than was necessary), the Lieut.-Governor endossed his uniform, begirt himself with his sword, and was marshalled into the room prepared for the ceremony, in 'due and ample form.' His head was higher than ever, his hair more wavy, and with the strut of a tragedy tyrant, he proceeded to mount the steps of the dais, and, to the horror of the assembled spectators, sat down on the Royal Throne! There was a general titter, and the Admiral, Sir Francis

Collyer, who was present, made an exclamation more vigorous than polite in its language. The ceremony proceeded, and Sir James Brooke made a suitable reply, which, as a local paper observed, 'alone saved the whole from becoming a burlesque' so utterly did 'Royal Billy' overact his part. Peace be to his ashes! A better fellow, and a truer friend, or a sterner enemy, did not exist, and one soon forgot his little failings in the society of a man of so amiable a character, and so well up in most subjects. He it was who started the *Free Press*, and was for years its Editor, handing over his pen to Mr. Abraham Logan, when he left for home in 1846 or 1847, coming out again in the *Meander* in 1848, on the Labuan Staff, with Mr. Low, now Sir Hugh, as his Secretary."

It was on May 30th in this year that Captain Keppel wrote in his diary, on board the *Meander*,

"In pulling about in my gig among the numerous prettily wooded islands on the westward entrance to the Singapore river, I was astonished to find deep water close to the shore, with a safe passage through for ships larger than the *Meander*. Now that steam is likely to come into use this ready made harbour as a depot for coals would be invaluable. I had the position surveyed, and sent it with my report to the Board of Admiralty; as it was, the forge was landed, and artificers employed under commodious sheds, all under the eyes of the officers on board."

These repairs of the *Meander* were, therefore, the first repairs done in New Harbour, on the spot where the Tanjong Pagar wharves now extend for some mile and a half, crowded with steamers. The diary on 24th August, 1849, while Captain Keppel was still in the *Meander*, contained this:—"Having reported to the Admiralty over twelve months ago the natural advantages of the inner Harbour of Singapore as a coaling station, and no notice having been taken of my letter, I now sent a similar statement, with survey to the Secretary of the P. & O. Company." So it was Keppel who first sailed through New Harbour, and Singaporeans often said that it should have not been called New Harbour, which meant nothing, but Keppel Harbour. This was eventually done on 19th April, 1900, when the old Admiral was on a visit to Singapore, and staying at Government House with the Acting Governor, Sir Alexander Swettenham, who made it an occasion of much pleasure to the old man in his ninety-second year, whose name had been at the very top of the Active List of the Navy for ten years. The road to New Harbour was called Keppel Road fifteen years before, which pleased the Admiral very much; and when the name of the Harbour was changed, the men of war, the Governor's yacht, a number of merchant steamers, and a great tail of steam launches, steamed through the narrow passage, through which the *Meander* first passed, and Sir Alexander Swettenham broke a bottle on a large iron buoy in the centre of the passage, and everyone near shouted when he called out the new name, and it was taken up all down the line. It may be mentioned that the *Meander* shoal in New Harbour was discovered by the keel of Captain Keppel's ship!

Captain Keppel had pointed out to the Admiralty and to the P. & O. Company the present site of the Tanjong Pagar Docks and

Wharves on the main island, but a wiseacre of a Naval Officer who came a few years after him managed to persuade the Admiralty to put their wharf on Pulo Brani, on the opposite island, where there are cross tides, and dangerous mooring. Perhaps it was as well for the trade of the place, and the great steam traffic that has grown up since, that Captain Keppel's advice was disregarded by the Admiralty, or a few men of war would have occupied the ground that is now invaluable for shipping. The Navy never use the site on Pulo Brani, but go to the Dock Company's Wharves on the site which Captain Keppel originally advised.

The *Meander* was in Singapore for several months in both 1848 and 1849, and the Admiral's book contains many references to what he did, and to former residents.

The following appeared in the *Free Press* on 4th September, it seems to have been somewhat prophetic of after times : " At various times we have had occasion to find fault with the Peninsular and Oriental Company and their behaviour towards the public, and, from all we can learn, the monopoly which they have acquired between England and her Eastern possessions has not in any way quickened their desire to meet the public convenience. On the contrary it has the usual effect of monopoly, an exclusive concern for their own interests, and a complete disregard for that of others. The passengers from China and the Straits especially suffer from the conduct of the Company, which having secured their money, gives itself no further trouble about them. There is no accommodation reserved for passengers from the East in the Red Sea steamers, so that if the steamer from Calcutta and Madras is full, the unlucky Far Easterns must wait in Ceylon for a month before they can have the chance of going on ; and for this heavy expense the Company, as far as we are aware, make no allowance. Further, a person taking a first class passage is only entitled to a cabin on the orlop deck lighted by a scuttle, which in general is only opened in the Red Sea, and if there is an empty cabin on the main deck, £50 in addition is charged, or the cabin is locked up and kept empty. These facts may serve as illustration of the way in which the Company do business, and of the care they bestow upon the comfort of those who pay them all they choose to ask for passage."

A few weeks afterwards a correspondent asked the Editor why the P. and O. charged $25 passage money from Penang to Singapore, and $50 from Singapore to Penang ; and the Editor gave it up.

The *Free Press* contained the following account of the celebration of St. Andrew's day, and of an exhibition of fireworks at New Harbour in the same week :—

"St. Andrew's day was celebrated on Thursday last by the patriotic sons of Scotia in Singapore with an enthusiasm and devotion which proved that they were scions of no degenerate race. A number met at dinner in the public rooms in the evening, where they gave a free vent to their feelings of nationality, and the song and pledge went round to a late hour. A number of eloquent and inspiring addresses were delivered by different gentlemen during the evening and the whole passed off with that cordiality and unanimity of sentiment and feeling, which give the chief charm to such festive meetings."

" The Tumonggong received the company in a rustic pavilion which had been erected at Pantei Chermin, on a rising ground overlooking the New

Harbour, and it was decorated with much taste. The building was soon filled by such an assemblage of the 'beauty and fashion' of the station, as we never remember to have witnessed before. The arrival of the Governor and Mrs. Butterworth, announced by the firing of a salute, was the signal for the commencement of the exhibition, and then firework succeeded firework in rapid succession, rockets, blue-lights, flower-pots, wheels, ducks, and last, though not least, the Chinese drums with their minute population, who spend their brief existence in public in the uncomfortable position of suspension by the pigtail surrounded by an atmosphere of squibs and crackers that would choke even a Salamander.

"The views interiorly and exteriorly were most striking, comprising as they did every degree of civilization from the wild *orang laut*, the excited Malay, the solemn Arab, and the grinning celestial, to the pale European beauty. A supper was provided for those who wished to partake of it, and was done due credit to, and about ten o'clock the whole party betook themselves to their carriages, and then came the tug of war. Many were the mishaps which ensued. The road, previously not in a very first-rate condition, had got dreadfully cut up by the passage of the numerous vehicles going to the village, and in returning many carriages fairly stuck fast, including, we have heard, those of high functionaries, who were thus, for once in their lives, practically convinced of the inconveniences which the public suffer when the roads get out of order. The only material injury we have heard of as resulting from this state of the roads, besides broken harness, strained vehicles and jaded horses, was that inflicted on the company by being deprived of the pleasure of listening to the music of the band of the twenty-first Regiment, it having been found impossible to get the instruments through. Notwithstanding these little drawbacks, however, those present were much delighted with the night's exhibition, and grateful to His Highness for the trouble he took in thus providing for their amusement."

The paper remarked on the improvements that had been made at New Harbour by the Tumonggong, as follows:—"The great changes, and in most instances improvements, which have taken place of late years in Singapore, both as regards the architecture of the town, and the cultivation of the country, are nowhere so strikingly manifested as at Teluk Blangah, the residence of His Highness the Tumonggong. There, within a few years past, but especially in more recent times, the whole aspect of things has been changed, and everywhere improved. A few years ago, Teluk Blangah only presented the appearance of a very dirty Malay village, the royal residence being merely distinguished from its neighbours by being of brick, and if possible dingier and dirtier than the rest. Now everything has put on a new face. The money, which has flowed so copiously into the Teluk Blangah coffers, through the successful dealings of His Highness and his followers in the gutta trade, has been more judicially applied than is generally the case when Malays become possessed of a little cash, and instead of being expended on evanescent shows and spectacles, or squandered at the gambling-table and cock-pit, it has been laid out in improving the outward appearance of Teluk Blangah. His Highness has built for himself several extremely neat houses and *baleis* in the European style, which are gay with green and white paint, and many of his followers have done the same, their smart, green venetianed, tile-roofed houses, being an extreme contrast to the rude huts in which they formerly were content to live. The old palace, now the residence of the mother of the Tumonggong, has also been cleaned up and white-washed, and altogether has a very nice appearance.

"In addition to these Malay residences, several large European houses have also been constructed in the close vicinity of Teluk Blangah, and we have heard of others about to be erected. No less remarkable is the spirit of agricultural improvement which seems to have seized upon the Tumonggong and his followers. The hills overhanging the village, and which heretofore were covered with a thick jungle giving shelter and cover to the tigers, are now being rapidly divested of their coverings, and planted with fruit and spice trees. Much of this improvement is no doubt owing to the advice and example of the European gentlemen, whose opinion His Highness has the sense to ask, and still greater sense to follow; but even making allowance for all this, enough still remains to show that there must be a real desire to adopt the comforts and conveniences, and the more settled and industrious habits of civilized life, instead of adhering to the rude habitations and the idle and equivocal habits which formerly were the marks and distinguishing characteristics of the Teluk Blangah Malays."

In December, the paper wrote as follows, and the proposal was carried out thirty-seven years afterwards:—"Now that the Esplanade is nearly closed in and the green sward protected from the incursions of pony-racing, drunken sailors, we trust the crowning improvement will not be forgotten. In the centre of the Esplanade there ought to be placed a suitable monument to mark the achievements of the founder of this Settlement—Sir Thomas Stamford Raffles. The example of that great and good man ought prominently to be set forth, and where so appropriately as the scene of his labours? What is so attractive to the imagination, as the memorial raised to a great man by his admiring fellow-citizens? Monuments are the appropriate rewards of virtue, the evidences of a country's gratitude. We throw out this hint in the hope that some of the influential members of society will take the initiative."

The following account of the Masonic Dinner on St. John's Day appeared in the *Free Press*. It is reprinted here as it will be interesting from the record it gives of some of the best known Singaporeans of the time. Mr. Robert Duff was then the resident partner in Shaw, Whitehead & Co., a firm established in 1834; Mr. Michie Forbes Davidson and Mr. Robert Bain were partners in A. L. Johnston & Co.; Mr. J. C. Smith was Head-master of the Institution Free School (the Raffles); Captain Charles Morgan Elliot, of the Engineers, was here on special duty for the magnetic survey department; Mr. Caldwell was Senior Sworn Clerk of the Court; Frommurzjee Sorabjee was a Parsee merchant; Dr. Charles Curties and Dr. Allen were Surgeons and Medical Practitioners; Mr. F. A. Cargill was the Manager of the Oriental Bank; Mr. G. H. Brown had come down from Penang in 1847 and was organist of the old St. Andrew's Church; Mr. Tivendale was a shipwright in High Street, under the name of Wilkinson, Tivendale & Co., and Mr. J. G. Barnes was third master in the Institution School:—

"The Annual Festival of the Sons of St. John was celebrated on the evening of the 27th December by the members of the Lodge 'Zetland in the East,' by a magnificent banquet, to which all the brethren on the island and a number of other guests, who did not belong to the craft of Freemasonry were invited. The company sat down to dinner at half-past seven o'clock— the Band of the 21st Regiment, by the kind permission of the Officers, being in attendance. The room was brilliantly lighted up, and the arrangement of the table, strikingly elegant and tasteful, did much credit to the Brethren who had so well discharged the office of Stewards. The new canopy in the East was very beautifully fitted up, and, with the illuminations, transparencies, Master's pedestal covered with Masonic implements, and other suitable decorations with which the room was ornamented, presented a spectacle seldom, if ever before, equalled in this Settlement on the occasion of a public dinner."

In the course of the evening, a number of toasts were given with the usual honours and appropriate airs, and the paper contained a long report of the speeches made by those already mentioned.

"We should have premised that the members of Lodge 'Zetland in the East,' pursuant to summons, assembled on Wednesday morning, at 6 o'clock, for the purpose of witnessing the installation of the Worshipful Master elect for the ensuing year, and the investiture of the several Officers, viz.:—

Bro. J. B. Cumming	...	Worshipful Master.
„ M. F. Davidson	...	Senior Warden.
„ F. A. Cargill	...	Junior Warden.
„ J. C. Smith	...	Treasurer.
„ C. J. Curties	...	Secretary.
„ G. J. Dare	...	Senior Deacon.
„ H. A. Allen	...	Junior Deacon.
„ G. H. Brown	...	Organist.
„ T. Tivendale	...	Inner Guard.
„ J. G. Barnes	...	Tyler.

"There was a very full attendance of the Brethren on this occasion, as well as several visitors from foreign and other Lodges, and the arrangements for the imposing ceremony had been so well made, the Lodge Room so much improved by its enlargement to more than double its former size, and the fitting up of the chair and other decorations so tasteful and appropriate, that it was acknowledged by all to have been one of the most gratifying gatherings the craft had ever held in Singapore."

The *Free Press* at the end of the year in its review of the events of the preceding twelve months, which had been a very exciting time all over Europe, alluded to the local commerce of the year as follows:—

"The state of trade during the past year has not been of a very cheering character, although, fortunately, Singapore was unmarked by the fall of any of its mercantile houses, as happened nearly everywhere else. The disastrous events in England (the Chartist Riots, &c.) and elsewhere, by which trade for a time was almost paralysed, no doubt contributed in a great measure to bring about the depression in our trade complained of, although other local causes no doubt also existed. The great fall which took place in what may be called two of the principal staple productions— gambier and gutta percha—had a very injurious effect, influencing as they did so many, more or less, directly concerned in their cultivation, manufacture or collection. Another cause of the dulness of trade was a considerable decrease in the China junk trade, and the non-arrival of anything like the usual number of Bugis boats, as well as the comparatively greatly less value of the cargoes of such as did arrive. These and other causes have produced a great exhaustion of means on the part of many of the smaller native traders—Kling and Chinese—amongst whom several failures took place. The very low price to which gambier fell, produced much distress among the planters, who found it almost impossible to obtain the means of existence. The price of rice fortunately kept at a moderate rate, otherwise it is probable that much severe suffering would have ensued amongst these unfortunate persons, and they might have been led to endeavour to procure the means of existence by having recourse to gang robberies and other dishonest courses. The cultivation of gambier has much diminished, while that of pepper is being increased as much as possible."

It was in May of this year that Mr. Robert Barclay Read first arrived in Singapore. He came out to A. L. Johnston & Co., when he was twenty years old. He became a partner when Mr. M. F. Davidson retired from the firm in 1862. He resided in Singapore for thirty-six years, and died at Yokohama, where he had gone in ill health, on 27th October, 1884, 56 years of age. He was very popular in the place, a leading spirit in all its affairs, like his cousin, Mr. W. H. Read, both commercial and social. He was Consul for Sweden and Norway, and during the absence of Mr. W. H. Read, he officiated as Acting Consul-General for the Netherlands. For his long services, the Swedish Government made him a Knight of the Order of Wasa, and the Dutch Government conferred on him the Knighthood of the Netherlands Lion for his valuable assistance in discovering and following up the threads of a conspiracy against their authority in Palembang in 1880. At one time he held a seat in the Legislative Council and he was a Director of the Tanjong Pagar Dock Co., Limited. Socially, Mr. Read was, for years, the life and soul of the place. He had a good appreciation of the enjoyments of life, and, especially in his younger days, the capacity for inspiring and diffusing them. He was an enthusiastic yachtsman and took great delight in his cruises. He had also very good dramatic taste. In the Amateur Theatricals of those days he was always considered an indispensable associate. In all Club matters he invariably took the liveliest interest, and was always ready to assume his share of the duties which such institutions entail. He was for a long time President of the Singapore Club, and a handsome centre piece was subscribed for by the members after his death to be kept in the Club in memory of him.

The Court for the relief of Insolvent Debtors was established on 1st November, 1848. Mr. W. W. Willans was the first Official Assignee. There were four lawyers in Singapore, and ten Justices of the Peace, merchants ; the police force consisted of a Superintendent, a Deputy, 5 European constables, and 187 natives.

CHAPTER XXXVI.

1849.

AT the beginning of this year the *Free Press* Office was moved from High Street to No. 1, Malacca Street, at the corner of Commercial Square, which the Oriental Bank had just quitted; and Mr. Abraham Logan had bought the newspaper, on 1st November, 1848, from Mr. W. R. George. The paper was published on a larger sheet.

Mr. John James Greenshields became a partner in Guthrie & Co.; and Mr. Charles Hercules Harrison in Middleton, Blundell & Co., at the beginning of the year. On the 2nd April, Mr. Henry Charles Rautenberg and Mr. Frederick George Schmidt, of Hamburg, established the firm of Rautenberg, Schmidt & Co. Mr. Rautenberg had been an assistant in a German firm here called F. E. Walte & Co., which was established in 1845. Mr. Walte, the sole partner, had died in Singapore on the 22nd September, 1847. In 1852 Mr. Schmidt was the sole partner and remained so until 1858. During those years G. Cramer, Otto Puttfarcken, and Otto Rheiner had been clerks. On 1st October, 1858, the partners were F. G. Schmidt Gustavus Cramer, and Adolph Emil Schmidt. In 1863 Mr. Franz Kustermann became a partner, and Mr. Conrad Sturzenegger in 1865.

On the 24th March, Mr. John Connolly, one of the oldest merchants in Singapore, died. He was a partner with William and Charles Spottiswoode in Spottiswoode & Connolly, whose offices were where the Oriental Bank was afterwards. Mr. John Connolly, Jnr., Mr. A. J. Spottiswoode, and Mr. William Mactaggart were assistants in the firm at the time of Mr. Connolly's death. Mr. Connolly was Sheriff of the Settlement in 1848.

On the 12th January, Mr. Simon Stephens (of Stephens & Joaquim) died, at the age of 45 years. He came to Singapore in 1829, and commenced business, which he carried on with much enterprise and varying success until 1845, when he failed and retired from business until 1848, when he commenced again under very favourable circumstances. He had great influence among the native community, who often went to him for advice and assistance. On the 17th February, Frommurzee Sorabjee died at Parsee Lodge, in his 43rd year. He was very popular in Singapore as the proceedings at the Masonic banquet in the preceding year show. He was the father of Cursetjee Frommurzee, a partner for many years with the Littles.

The sports took place as usual on New Year's Day, and to show how they were carried out at the time, we take the following account from the *Free Press* :—

" New Year's Day was celebrated with the usual rejoicings, the Esplanade being crowded with the natives who had assembled to enjoy the accustomed sports and pastimes. There was an abundance of amusement suited for every taste, from a well-greased climbing pole for those inclined to display their powers of perseverance, to dancing girls for those fond of the ballet. There were three hack-pony races with a number of entries, foot races, and a pig race, or rather a race after a pig. The most exciting sport, however, was a game at football in which all joined, and which was kept up capitally for about half an hour. The day was fine, a breeze for the most part prevailing, and the varied and gay costumes of the natives, and especially of the Malays, who were present in large numbers and dressed in their best, formed altogether a very animated and enlivening scene, enhanced by the good humour and spirit of enjoyment which seemed to animate all. The aquatic sports were no less well got up and successful. There were sailing races, yachts, sampans and tongkangs, as well as sampans, &c., rowing, which were all well contested, and proved highly interesting and exciting."

The Hon. Samuel Garling, the Resident Councillor at Penang, on leaving that Settlement had a number of cases on board a barque called the *Cape Packet* which was burnt in the harbour there. The paper remarked that Mr. Garling had a collection which could not well be replaced, and papers intended for publication, the loss of which resembled that of Sir Stamford Raffles at Bencoolen on board the *Fame*.

The same paper announced the death of Mr. Jackson, the Assistant Resident, Magistrate, and Superintendent of Police in Singapore, which was a mistake. A letter to the *Free Press* in speaking of it as being likely to inflict pain upon persons at a distance who might hear of it, spoke of the general indignation that was felt at the statement, and said that it was not the first of its kind, and, without some mark of reprobation, was not likely to be the last; and it was suggested to publish a "*Straits Times* Obituary" of personages who had been embalmed in its pages during the period of their natural lives.

The proprietors of the Singapore Library, which was kept in the Raffles Institution building, proposed to form a Museum, and a resolution was passed at their annual meeting on the 31st January "that a Museum with a view principally to the collection of objects illustrating the General History and Archæology of Singapore and the Eastern Archipelago be established in connection with the Singapore Library; that it be called the 'Singapore Library Museum' and that it be deposited in the rooms of the Library." The commencement of the collection was made by the presentation of two curious gold coins given by the Tumunggong.

Amoks were not infrequent in those days; the following account of one appeared in the *Free Press* in February :—" On Friday last a Bugis armed with five nebong spears (selegie) while in a state of frenzy, wounded one Chinaman in the knee and another in the abdomen, the latter case being one of some danger. He threw spears at several other persons, but without wounding them, and an alarm having been raised, Constable Taylor proceeded to the spot armed with a musket, and called upon the man to surrender. This he refused to do, and threatened the Constable with a spear, on which the latter fired and wounded the Bugis in the thigh, and being taken to the Hospital the man died the next day. A Coroner's inquest was held on the body, when a verdict of " Justifiable Homicide " was returned.

The number of persons killed in the jungles of Singapore by tigers at that time was very great. The paper said that the tigers seemed coming gradually nearer to town and increasing in numbers, so that unless something was done much more effectual than before, men and beasts might be carried off in the close vicinity of the town. The *Free Press* contained the following characteristic anecdote of a Malay :—" Two Tigers were noticed last week at Tulloh Buddoh. A person who saw them being asked, 'And what did you do on seeing them,' replied, ' Kalau saya tiada angkat saya punia kaki lakas, jangan kata saya punia nama Bujang'." Within a short time two persons were killed by tigers near Bukit Timah, two at Tanah Merah, and two at Tulloh Mata Ikan. The Government in April sanctioned an expenditure for the construction of tiger pits, and in August the *Free Press* said :—" The attention of his Honour the Governor having been directed to the continued deplorable ravages committed by tigers on this island, he has expressed himself ready to adopt any measures which may tend to remove the evil. It has been suggested that persons are to be found in the vicinity of Calcutta trained for the purpose of destroying tigers, and his Honour has writen to the Bengal Government requesting that half a dozen of these Shikarries should be sent to the Straits for a limited period, to be employed in the destruction of these animals. The Governor has also directed that in the meantime, should it be deemed expedient, a certain number of volunteers from the 3rd class convicts should be permitted to beat the jungle once every month, with tomtoms, horns, &c., which, if they do not lead to the destruction of the tigers, may frighten them away from the island, to which they come from the neighbouring state of Johore. The first of these measures may probably be productive of advantage, but we should be doubtful whether the last will be of much benefit. The tigers have too large a space to range in to be easily driven out, and the only effect will be to make them shift from one locality to another."

Singapore had then been established forty years, and some statistics may be useful :—

The public revenue of Singapore for the year 1848-49 amounted to Rs 393,232, consisting of :—

Excise Farms*	...	...	...	...	Rs. 327,257
*Opium	...	...	$7,030		
Spirit	...	...	3,050		
Siri	...	...	805		
Pawnbrokers	...	...	300		
Toddy and Bhang		...	115		
Markets	...	...	855		
Per Month		...	$12,155		
Fees, Courts of Judicature and					
Requests	...	...	...	...	Rs. 22,061
Quit-rents	...	...	...	...	„ 20,935
Sale of Lands	...	...	...	...	„ 5,056
Miscellaneous	...	...	...	...	„ 17,923
					Rs. 393,232

The expenditure amounted to Rs. 620,826 consisting of :—

Local charges ...	... Rs.	169,874
General charges	... ,,	43,557
Buildings ...	... ,,	55,373
Contingencies ...	... ,,	34,148
Military ...	... ,,	263,754
Convicts ...	... ,,	54,120
	Rs.	620,826

The total imports into Singapore in 1848–49 amounted in value, according to the official returns, to $12,379,801, shewing an increase over the previous period of 1847–48 of $81,477. The total amount of exports was in value $11,049,969, being less by $138,887 than in the previous year. The number of immigrants from China to Singapore during the season 1848–49, was reported at 9,817, but it was supposed that not many of these persons remained in Singapore, most of them going to other places in the Archipelago. The agriculture of Singapore was then beginning to assume a considerable importance. The plantations of nutmegs and cocoa-nuts were coming rapidly into full bearing, and the planting of the former, to some extent, was carried on during 1849, both by European and Chinese planters. It appears from a statement of the cultivation then prepared by the Government Surveyor, that there were 1,190 acres planted with 71,400 nutmeg trees, the produce of which in nutmegs and mace, amounted to 656 piculs, yielding an annual value of $39,360. As a great part of the plantations were very young, this afforded no criterion of what the produce would have been if the whole had come into full bearing. There were 28 acres planted with clove trees. Cocoa-nut cultivation occupied 2,658 acres, the number of trees being 342,608, and the produce yielding a value of $10,800. The quantity of land planted with betel-nuts was 445 acres, having 128,821 trees thereon, and giving $1,030 annually. The fruit trees occupied 1,037 acres, and their produce was valued at $9,568. The gambier cultivation covered an extent of 24,220 acres and the produce was valued at $80,000. The pepper cultivation was stated at 2,614 acres, yielding $108,230 annually. The vegetable gardens covered 379 acres, and the produce was stated at $34,675. The siri or pawn vines extended to 22 acres, and yielded $10,560, while sugar-cane, pineapples, rice or paddy engrossed 1,962 acres, and the estimated produce was valued at $32,386. The quantity of ground under pasture was 402 acres, valued at $2,000 annually. The total gross annual agricultural produce of the island was valued at $328,711.

The total receipts by the Municipal Committee in 1848 were Rs. 68,519; of which about Rs. 43,000 were assessment on houses in town at ten per cent. under Act 12 of 1839; Rs. 1,500 taxes on land and country houses at five per cent.; Rs. 11,000 taxes on private conveyances and horses; and Rs. 6,500 police fines, &c. The disbursements were about Rs. 55,000 on the Police, which was entirely paid by the Municipality; Rs. 6,300 on roads and bridges; Rs. 6,000 on town cleaning. The receipts exceeded the expenditure by Rs. 6,000.

The *Free Press* in March contained the following paragraph :—" The Police having found themselves unable to compose the differences existing between the different societies of Chinese in Singapore, which for some

time past have been producing scenes of riot and violence, Seah Eu Chin
has been called in to their assistance, and we are glad to hear has succeeded in effecting a treaty of peace, though probably not of friendship,
amongst the belligerents, whom he has bound over in heavy penalties to
keep the peace in time to come.   This is only one of many instances in
which Eu Chin's aid has been found of great use in controlling his countrymen, and it strikes us it might lead to good results were His Honour the
Governor to include the name of Eu Chin, one of the best informed and
most literate Chinese in the Settlement, in the next Commission of the
Peace which is issued."

In the same month the paper said:—"Sultan Allie of Johore, who is
at present at Malacca, has been lately treating with various parties for
the sale of a portion of his territories.   His first negotiations, we understand, were with Mr. Tock Seng, but they went off on some point or other.
Since then, we are informed, certain arrangements have been made or
proposed by the Resident Councillor at Malacca, for the cession by the
Sultan to the East India Company of the district of Muar lying on the
Southern boundary of our Malacca territory.   The country is described to
be generally a beautiful level plain, with a rich soil, admirably adapted in
many places for paddy and other cultivation.   It also abounds in tin, which
if properly worked, would yield a large revenue to Government.   The acquisition of this country would also give the command of the river Muar up
to Mount Ophir.   At present the navigation of the Muar is by no means
safe, the river being infested by gangs of robbers, and the exactions of the
petty Malay chiefs, who dwell upon its banks, are so intolerable that the
trade between Malacca and Ulu Muar is almost extinct, although with
proper protection it could not fail to be considerable."

In March the Insolvent Court was opened by Sir C. Rawlinson.
Mr. Simonides, of the Police Force, J. H. Benjamin, and Mark Moss,
traders, were the insolvents who opened the proceedings of the new Court.
The second having been five years and a half in the goal was discharged.
The others were granted orders of protection.

The newspapers used to publish a report of the Charge of the Recorder to
the Grand Jury, and in March the Recorder fell foul of both the newspapers
for not reporting correctly what he had said.   The *Free Press* spoke of this
as follows:—"We have given as good an outline as we could of the Charge
the Recorder delivered to the Grand Jury, but it is necessarily much less full
than the address itself.   His Lordship more than once in the course of his
speech complained (we beg pardon, his Lordship never complains, he only
stated) that on previous occasions he had been misrepresented and said he
must rely upon his growing character in the Settlement to vindicate him
from the imputation of having said what had been attributed to him.   It is
true that we do not pretend to give the *ipsissima verba* of what falls from
his Lordship's eloquent lips on the occasions when we deem it worth while
to report him, but we listen attentively to what he said and take notes, and
the statement which we give we generally find pronounced correct by
others who have been present.   Indeed, we think that our report of what
his Lordship says is more likely to be correct than his Lordship's recollection of it, seeing that he does not commit his speeches to writing, and it is
probable that he is led by a vivid imagination and an active fancy to say
more than he intended, and to diverge considerably from the course he

had previously laid down, as well in the manner as in the matter of his address. It is a pity therefore that he does not take the plan which was generally followed by his predecessor, and is adopted, we believe, by the present Judges at Bombay and Madras, viz. :—to write down what he has got to say, and after he has delivered his charge, to allow a copy of it to be handed to the newspapers. By adopting this course all chance of misrepresentation is avoided, and the charge itself is ensured that correctness and judicial gravity which is befitting such an occasion, but which is apt to be lost sight of when there is nothing to trust to but the inspiration of a vivid and somewhat discursive imagination."

The following are a few paragraphs from the presentment of the Grand Jury in April. Mr. Charles Carnie was foreman. " The Grand Jury present as nuisances the parapets of solid masonry round the public wells in Commercial Square and at the crossing behind the Portuguese Church and in other similar situations, one of them having in addition a surrounding railing. These wells being situated on the public streets, the Jury consider as very likely to occasion dangerous accidents. They therefore recommend that the parapets be removed and the mouths of the wells be again made level with the street and covered in as before, and that they be provided with pumps placed at the side of the road for the supply of water to the public. The Grand Jury would further suggest that two or more wells for the supply of water to the public be constructed in the enclosures in Commercial Square, and that the water be drawn off by means of pumps which would prevent their becoming public nuisances from persons bathing at them." At that time there were wells in the centre of the streets near the Square with wooden covers on hinges lying flat with the road over which the traffic went. They were of great use in fires, as the hand engines could not suck the water from such a distance as the sea, and one engine was put to pump the sea water into the well, and another engine to pump from the well on to the fire. The Borneo Company's Offices and godown in Malacca Street were saved in this way, by the use of the well in the middle of Malacca Street, when the adjoining buildings were on fire.

" The Jurors present that the river's mouth still remains in the same obstructed state so frequently presented by previous Grand Juries. This causes so much detriment to the trade of the port, that the Grand Jury would earnestly suggest that some means be speedily taken to apply a remedy, and they urge this the more as they widely differ in opinion from views expressed by the Superintending Engineer to the Grand Jury, touching the importance of the interests involved.

" The Grand Jury regret to find that although a very considerable period has elapsed since Tan Tock Seng, Esq., presented a Chinese Pauper Hospital to the public, no apparent steps have been taken to apply this building to the purpose for which it was intended, and that diseased and starving paupers still abound upon the public streets. Former Grand Juries have, at the suggestion and request of the Chinese inhabitants, the countrymen of these paupers, pointed out the means of raising funds for the support of this Hospital by the re-imposition of a Pork Farm, and the present Grand Jury would reiterate the recommendation, believing it to be the most unobjectionable and unburdensome means of raising an ample revenue for this purpose.

"The Grand Jury fully concur with the Hon'ble the Recorder in condemning as a most serious public nuisance the practice of allowing native processions in the public streets, attended as these generally are by such large crowds, and accompanied by unwieldy machines, torches, &c., blocking up the thoroughfares and rendering them dangerous for persons requiring to pass along them on their lawful business. The Grand Jury further present that the privilege of these processions being allowed to pass through the public streets being confined to certain classes only of the native community, the Klings and Convicts, a feeling of dissatisfaction is caused on the part of the numerous portion of the inhabitants, namely, the Chinese, in many of whose customs such processions form leading features, and who therefore feel aggrieved that that should be rigidly denied to them which is so fully allowed to other classes of the population, and even to the Convicts. The Grand Jury recommend that all processions, firing of crackers, and such other dangerous practices in the public streets, should be rigidly prevented, the natives being required to confine their celebrations to those places where they will not constitute a public nuisance."

A Cochin-Chinese *prahu* on arriving here was boarded by a number of Chinese, who insisted on turning over all the goods and seeing every part of the vessel, and who on being opposed in attempting to go into a cabin in which was a French missionary, tried to do so by force, and otherwise conducted themselves in an insolent manner, evidently with the purpose of extorting money. They were prevented from succeeding in their designs, whatever they were, by the Missionary, and left the vessel uttering threats against the Cochin-Chinese, and saying that when the boat left Singapore on its return, they would take care to punish them, which was reported to the Police. When the boat was ready to sail a French Missionary took passage in it, and the Revd. Mr. Beurel, recollecting the threats held out against the Cochin-Chinese some months before, and alarmed for the safety of his countryman (the Cochin-Chinese being completely unarmed and several cases of piracy having lately occurred) applied to the Master Attendant, Captain Russell, to permit a gunboat to escort the *prahu* beyond Pedra Branca. He was referred to the Resident Councillor, Mr. Church, who stated that one of the gunboats had already gone to that quarter with four boats belonging to the Tumonggong, that the other gunboat in the harbour could not be spared, and that therefore the request could not be complied with, adding that it was nonsense to be afraid of an attack, there was no danger at all, and with this assurance dismissed the application. The boat sailed, the only weapons on board being two muskets, and a pistol in possession of the Missionary, which he had provided himself with, intending to throw it away after he had fairly passed the dangerous latitudes of Romania and Bintang, and got into the China Sea. When the boat had reached the narrowest part of the strait between Point Romania and Bintang, they unfortunately had a contrary wind which rendered their progress very slow, and they were alarmed by seeing a boat, numerously manned, push out from the Romania shore and rapidly approach them. Part of the men in her were pulling and part had arms in their hands, the crew consisting of Malays with two Chinese. When the boat came near, the Cochin-Chinese hailed them to keep off, but the only reply to this was a discharge of fire arms. The Cochin-Chinese fired their two muskets in return, and the

French gentleman also fired his pistol, but from being heavily charged it burst and knocked him down, inflicting a very severe wound in the face. The Cochin-Chinese on this, lost all courage, and would probably have surrendered, but the breeze fortunately carried them beyond the reach of their assailants, and they regained Singapore very considerably frightened, and but little disposed to put any further trust in the Resident Councillor's opinions on the subject of pirates, or the degree of danger to be apprehended from their attacks.

Bank notes were first issued in Singapore in May by the Oriental Bank. They were of $5 and $100.

In May the *Free Press* wrote of gambling as follows—"Last week we stated that public gambling shops were very numerous, and we believe that ever since the Chinese New Year they have been augmenting. At that time ten were opened, which have now increased to upwards of thirty, five of which are in the immediate vicinity of the new market. Several cases were brought before last Quarter Sessions, but the offenders were very leniently dealt with, the fines inflicted being of the most moderate description, and utterly inadequate to put a stop to the evil. It is well known that the persons interested in the gaming houses combine to pay the fines of persons convicted at Quarter Sessions for gambling or keeping gambling houses, so that fines of one, five, and ten dollars, are of very little moment to them. It is a pity that such a state of things should exist, as there is no doubt that it tends much to the increase of crime, and the Municipal Committee ought to try and devise some means of putting an end to it."

The following is taken from the newspaper of the same month ; thefts of the kind described were continually being reported in the paper :—"The thieves are at present exceedingly industrious in providing their little consignments for the junks, previous to their annual departure, and there is the usual active demand for telescopes, clocks, watches, and other articles of elegance and utility, which prevails amongst the Chinese light-fingered gentry of Singapore at this season. It may not therefore be amiss to address a few precautionary words to our local readers on the subject. It is notorious that a person may walk through almost every European house on the beach in Kampong Glam, at certain periods of the day, without meeting a single inmate, or being exposed to challenge for the intrusion. This is well known to the thieves and taken advantage of accordingly. A number of Chinese boys neatly dressed (generally servants out of place) go with notes, written for them, to a gentleman's house and meeting no one below, proceed upstairs ; if they encounter any person, this note is presented, and, of course, the boy is told the person to whom it is addressed does not live there, and the bearer takes his departure, having made some useful observations for future operations, and perhaps even picking up some little " unconsidered trifle." If no one is found upstairs, then the Chinaman takes as many useful, portable articles, such as telescopes, &c., as he can put his hands upon, with which he quietly makes off, and they are speedily stowed away in the capacious hold of a junk. Another class of thieves consists of respectably dressed Chinamen who visit houses carrying a carpenter's rule in their hand, and ask for work, or request permission to take the pattern of a table, &c. These agents also help themselves to what they can find, if unobserved. Another source of the mischief is engaging servants without making any enquiries as to their characters of their previous employers. Written characters are plentiful amongst them, and are usually handed about from one to another, and afford therefore very little guarantee in engaging a servant that he is a trustworthy person, or that the character he produces was originally written for him. Means might easily be devised, through a system of registry, of keeping a check upon servants, and it would tend to improve their honesty were they to find that it was matter of much difficulty to procure employment with a black cross against them in the register."

A public meeting, which was very numerously attended, was held on the 20th July, Mr. W. W. Ker in the chair, to consider the proposed Indian Act on Excise law. In September, Mr. J. S. Sparkes, the P. & O. Agent, announced " a very considerable reduction in passage money from Singapore to Southampton." A first class passage for a gentleman in a general cabin was $590.40, and for a lady in one of the ladies' general cabins was $628.80.

It was in this year that the landing place was built, which was taken away about 1880, near the Dalhousie monument. The paper spoke of it as follows :—" It will be gratifying to our local readers to learn that the preliminary operations for constructing a ghaut or landing place on the beach have commenced. The place selected, the foot of High Street, is the most eligible that could have been hit upon." In July the new bridge over the canal at Boat Quay, adjacent to Messrs. Guthrie & Co.'s offices there, was opened with due ceremony.

In September, Mr. Blundell was made Resident Councillor of Penang, and Captain Ferrier, Resident Councillor of Malacca. There was a big fire at Kampong Malacca in September, which destroyed 210 native houses. A Police corporal was suffocated in it.

On the 22nd September, the mercantile community gave a dinner to the Hon'ble Captain Keppel of H. M. S. *Meander*, which had come down from China, and was bound to the Australian station. The following was the account of it in the *Free Press* :—" On Saturday, the mercantile and other friends of Captain the Hon. H. Keppel, of H. M. Ship *Meander*, gave a public entertainment to this highly esteemed officer on the occasion of his leaving the station. The dinner was given in the Masonic Hall, which the W. Master and Brethren of ' Lodge Zetland in the East' very kindly allowed the use of for the purpose, this mark of personal respect and public esteem being paid to a distinguished member of their Order. Between 40 and 50 gentlemen sat down to dinner at half-past six o'clock, J. Purvis, being in the Chair, W. W. Ker, Croupier. The arrangements were all of the most excellent description, and did great credit to the activity of the stewards, Messrs. J. Guthrie, M. F. Davidson, L. Fraser, J. B. Cumming, R. Duff and C. Spottiswoode, who had only a single day to complete them.

" As soon as the cloth was removed, the usual loyal toasts were given from the Chair, after which the Chairman rose to propose the health of the honoured guest of the evening. The Chairman prefaced the toast by a few well-merited complimentary remarks on the esteem in which Captain Keppel was held by the community of Singapore, and indeed by every community and every society in which he had mixed since he first came on the station. The Chairman then alluded to his own intercourse with Capt.

Keppel, and warmly eulogised his frank and affable manners both in private society and in matters of duty. He concluded by proposing—'Health, long life and prosperity to Captain Keppel, and may we at no distant period hail his return to these shores as Admi. il Keppel.' The toast was received with deafening applause and nine times nine. [He did come back as Commander-in-Chief on the China Station on March 31st, 1867.]

"Captain Keppel returned thanks in a feeling and eloquent speech, his manner evincing that he deeply appreciated the warm manner in which the Chairman's remarks had been received by the company. He said he felt deeply gratified by the present proof of the approbation and regard of the mercantile community of Singapore. Among those present were several old friends, others, though known more recently, were not less entitled to his kindly remembrances, while to all were due his thankful acknowledgments for the cordial manner in which they had received the toast. He had spent many happy days in Singapore, to which he looked back with much pleasure, and he could assure them all that nothing would give him greater pleasure than to have it in his power to forward the interests of Singapore, which he hoped ere long to see attain that importance which its central position and its great resources would ultimately command. Captain Keppel concluded by saying that the marked kindness and attention he had constantly received from his numerous friends in Singapore, during the long time he had been connected with them, were indelibly fixed in his heart, and no change of scene or place could ever efface them, and he added that it would give him the highest satisfaction to renew this pleasing intimacy either here or in England, should he ever be favoured with an opportunity of meeting any of them again.

"Then followed the health of Colonel Butterworth and Lady Butterworth, Mrs. Keppel, and other toasts. Mr. Church in proposing the toast of the Merchants of Singapore said that little more than a quarter of a century had elapsed since Singapore was but the rendezvous of a few *prahus*, and now through the energy of its merchants it had risen to be one of the great commercial depots of the East, and an outlet for an immense amount of the manufactures of Great Britain, which benefited very largely thereby. This much it owed to its merchants, and were it deserted by them, it must return to its primitive jungle.

"The Band of the *Meander* was in attendance, and played suitable airs to the various toasts, and a beautiful selection of Opera music during the evening. The company began to break up about half-past ten, and thus terminated one of the most pleasant meetings which had ever taken place in Singapore."

A select committee of the House of Commons was appointed during the year to enquire into the steamers in the Navy, and the *Free Press* reprinted part of the evidence given by Captain Chads (formerly of the *Andromache* in Singapore, as related in page 279) as follows :—" Capt. Chads thinks iron very inferior to wooden vessels for warlike purposes, and that iron vessels ought to be avoided as much as possible. No iron vessel can be built to resist shot unless it is of such a weight that it will not float. The shot goes right through the vessel, and the fractures are such that they cannot be repaired, while should it strike a rib upon going out, the ship must go down."

In this year the Supreme Court in Singapore awarded £20,700 to Captain Farquhar of H. M. S. *Albatross* and other persons for the destruction of the Sarebas pirates in July. The expedition under Captain Farquhar had fallen in with a fleet of upwards of a hundred war prahus, manned by at least 3,500 men, and, which was proved on the confession of the pirates themselves, to have been committing outrages both by sea and land. Admiral Sir Arthur Farquhar, K.C.B., is still alive. He was promoted for his services against the pirates in 1849.

The entire police force in this year was 218.

CHAPTER XXXVII.

THE HORSBURGH AND THE RAFFLES LIGHTHOUSES

ON 20th November, 1836, a public meeting had been held at Markwick's Hotel at Canton, at which Mr. Jardine presided, to consider the best means of making some lasting tribute of respect to the late Captain Horsburgh, and the great services he had performed for the cause of commerce and navigation. It was decided that a lighthouse on Pedra Branca in the Straits near to Singapore would be the most suitable. Subscriptions were made at Canton, Bombay and Penang. The list at Canton was headed by Mr. W. Jardine with $500. The rest of the subscribers were principally merchants and captains and officers of ships, the only considerable exception being the Chinese Security Merchants who contributed liberally. The Bombay Chamber of Commerce collected Rs. 4,299, and the Penang Chamber of Commerce Rs. 404. The Canton subscriptions amounted to $4,191, but Jardine, Matheson & Co. liberally gave compound interest until 1847, when the fund was paid over, and it had accumulated to $7,411.13.

James Horsburgh, F.R.S., was born at Elie, in Fife, Scotland, in 1762, and made many voyages to India and China, and, by the study of books and experiments, he familiarised himself with lunar observations and scientific subjects connected with navigation, and when in port occupied himself with constructing charts. In 1819 he was appointed Hydrographer to the East India Company. He died in 1836, in his 74th year. He was called " The Nautical Oracle of the World," and it was said by the East India Company that his charts and books had been invaluable safe-guards to life and property in these seas.

All vessels leaving Singapore for the East and China pass close to Pedra Branca. It was so called owing to its aspect of perfect whiteness, and Mr. J. T. Thomson said the name could not be more appropriate, because of its being covered with the dung of the numerous sea-birds that frequented it as a resting place. In the English translation made in the year 1598 of the work of the early Dutch voyager Van Linschoten, written in 1583, he speaks of " Pedra Bianque, or white rock, where the shippes that come and goe to and from China doe oftentymes passe in great danger and some are left upon it, whereby the Pilots when they come thither are in greate feare for other way than this they have not."

In November, 1844, Mr. J. T. Thomson prepared plans and estimate for a lighthouse on Peak Rock, which is part of the Roumania group; and afterwards the Lords Commissioners of the Admiralty and the India House thought it was too far within the Straits, which prevented it from being a good leading mark for vessels, while Pedra Branca from its advanced position was the first object that vessels ran for, and being clear of all dangers in its northern proximity could be approached by a direct course and closely passed. Peak Rock on the contrary had several out-lying reefs, and a vessel making for a light on it would have to alter her

HORSBURGH LIGHTHOUSE, OCTOBER, 1851.

To face page 510.

course as it was neared, and on a dark night run on the Roumania shoal on one side by keeping too distant, or on the out-lying rocks on the other side by keeping too near.

Nothing having been done for over eight years the Singapore Chamber of Commerce took up the matter again in 1845, and on 20th November a deputation from the Committee of the Chamber waited on His Honor the Governor. The Governor readily supplied the information sought. It appeared that a proposition by a former Governor involving a large establishment and the stationing of a detachment of troops on a small island, had caused the scheme to be temporarily laid aside. That funds subscribed in China to the Horsburgh testimonial, amounting to $5,513, were forthcoming and would be paid into the hands of Government whenever a pledge was given to construct a lighthouse in the vicinity of Pedra Branca. The Governor had in October, 1844, availed himself of the presence of H.M.S. *Samarang* to obtain a report from the distinguished scientific officer, Captain Sir Edward Belcher, C.B., who cheerfully gave his services to promote the erection of a testimonial to the hydrographer Mr. Horsburgh The Malayan authorities of Johor, in whose territory the Roumania island is situated, not only offered the island for a lighthouse, but expressed satisfaction at the prospect of its erection. The Governor mentioned to the deputation of the Chamber that he had visited the proposed site in the H. C. Steamer *Diana*, having with him the Superintending Engineer of Public Works in the Straits, whom he had instructed to make an estimate of the cost of the proposed erection. This officer considered that from one to one-and-a-half lacs of rupees would be necessary to complete the work of masonry. This being beyond the sum likely to be available, the Governor instructed Mr. Thomson, the Government Surveyor, to submit an estimate, which had been done by that gentleman with great care and detail, and which was accompanied by an offer from a Chinese contractor to erect a granite base of 16 feet for $2,667, and further, if required, a brick tower (exclusive of lantern and lamps) for $4,338 additional, or, in all, $7,000. The Governor seemed to think that an iron tower on the granite base would be preferable to brick, and had suggested the sending of one from England similar to one erected at Bermuda, at a cost of £1,500. Mr. Thomson described the rock as hard grey granite very suitable for building, and not liable to be washed away by the waves in bad weather. Mr. Thomson proposed the entrance to the lighthouse should be by a movable ladder, or basket and crane, from the top of the granite basement, thereby obviating the necessity of scarping the rock to guard against surprise by pirates. On the 1st November the Chamber of Commerce passed the following Resolution :—

" That the East India and China Association in London, the Calcutta and Bombay Chambers of Commerce, Captain Bedin of Madras, the subscribers in America (through J. Balestier, Esq., U. S. C.), and the subscribers in France (through the French Consul) be addressed with a copy of the report read this day, and be requested to make the funds subscribed available for the erection of a lighthouse as a Memorial to the late hydrographer, James Horsburgh."

T. O. CRANE,
Secretary.

On 21st June 1847, Mr. Thomson had instructions from Mr. Church to take steps for the erection of the lighthouse on Pedra Branca, and on 1st December before the north-east monsoon came on, he put up brick pillars on various parts of the rock to test the force of the waves. On 1st March, 1848, he found all the pillars on the north side, which were thirteen feet above sea level, entirely swept away. This was held to show that a brick building would be insufficient, and it was decided to construct it of granite set in the best hydraulic cement. This was the first lighthouse in this part of the world built in granite masonry, and it was certainly the crowning point of all good work done Mr. Thomson in Singapore during many years. There is a long account in 6 Logan's Journal of the building of the lighthouse, with the calculations as to the curves of the shaft, copies of the estimate, plans of the building and of the light apparatus, and elaborate details of the way in which the work was carried out under very considerable difficulties, from the absconding of the Chinese contractor with his advance; the difficulty of keeping up communication with the rock; and of obtaining water, to economise which they used to bathe in the fresh water (for Chinese coolies would not use salt water) before using it for making mortar. Three of the stone cutters were killed in a boat by pirates. Among other things there is a good account of the way in which the Chinese coolies lift very heavy weights by cross stretchers, by which means Mr. Thomson says stones were lifted weighing nearly seven tons. There is a little lithographed sketch pasted on to the page to illustrate this, in the manner we are familiar with when the Chinese carry their very heavy coffins through the streets. There is also a very full description of the tools used by the natives, and the way they work, and their wages, and the value of their labour as compared with European workmen, which would be of considerable interest and use to engineers in this part of the world. There are also some useful details about squalls and waterspouts, birds and fish, seen at the lighthouse while under construction.

On 4th December, 1849, Mr. Thomson was informed by Mr. Church that the Court of Directors of the East India Company had sanctioned the construction. On the 14th January materials were collected and by the end of March work was begun on the rock, Mr. John Bennett going with Mr. Thomson as foreman. The following is the account of the laying of the Foundation Stone on the 24th May, 1850, taken from the *Singapore Free Press* :—

"The Hon'ble the Governor of the Straits Settlements, Lieutenant-Colonel Butterworth, c.b., having requested the Brethren of the Lodge 'Zetland in the East,' to lay the Foundation Stone of the Horsburgh Testimonial, or Lighthouse For All Nations, with the honours of their craft, on the 24th May—the anniversary of Her Majesty's Birthday—the Worshipful Master and Brethren of the above Lodge, in number about thirty, accompanied by several visiting Brethren, started for Pedra Branca on the morning of the 24th in the H.C. Steamer *Hoogly,* and the barque *Ayrshire* in tow of Her Majesty's Steamer *Fury.* Several distinguished visitors, including His Excellency Rear-Admiral Sir F. Austin, c.b., Naval Commander-in-Chief and suite, the Hon'ble Thomas Church, the Resident Councillor, Lieut.-Colonel Messiter, Commanding the troops, several of the foreign Consuls, and merchants of Singapore, availed of His Honour the Governor's invitation to witness the ceremony, and accompanied him in the *Hoogly.* The party arrived at Pedra Branca about 11-30 a m., and having disembarked, the Masonic body marched in the following order of procession to the summit of the Rock :—

The Band.

Tyler with drawn Sword.

Brethren not members of the Lodge,
two and two.

Cornucopia with Corn
borne by the Wor. Past Master Bro. J. B. Cumming.

Two cups with Wine and Oil:
The Wine borne by Bro. T. O. Crane and the Oil
by
Bro. Greenshields.

The Organist, Bro. G. H. Brown.

The Inner Guard, Brother Thomas Hewetson
bearing the Inscription Plate.

The Secretary, Brother T. H. Campbell
bearing the Book of Constitutions on a silk cushion.

The Treasurer, Bro. J. C. Smith
bearing the purse containing Coins to be deposited in
the Stone.

The Corinthian Light
borne by Brother H. Minchin Simons.

Brother W. Paterson, bearing the Mallet.

The Junior Warden, Brother R. Bain
bearing the Plumb Rule.

The Banner of the Lodge.

The Senior Warden, Brother J. Jarvie
bearing the Level.

The Chaplain, Bro. the Rev. F. W. Linstedt
bearing the Sacred Law on a cushion.

Junior Deacon	The Worshipful	Senior Deacon
bearing his	Master Bro.	bearing his
Wand.	M. F. Davidson.	Wand.

Having halted and formed a passage for the Worshipful Master to pass through, the Chaplain, the Past Master with the Cornucopia, the Senior and Junior Wardens, the Brethren with the wine and oil, and the Deacons with their wands, followed the Worshipful Master to the Foundation Stone, where they were received by the Governor, who, in the following words, requested them to proceed at once with the ceremony :—

"Worshipful Master and Gentlemen of the Lodge Zetland in the East,—I have solicited the favour of your laying, on this the anniversary of our beloved Queen's Birthday, the foundation stone of the lighthouse to be erected on this spot for the safety of the mariner, and in commemoration of that celebrated hydrographer James Horsburgh, F.R.S., to whose labours the mercantile world is so much indebted for the easy navigation of these seas. The philanthrophic object of the building appears especially to call for the exercise of that craft which has charity and good-will to all mankind for its ground-work ; and it affords me deep and unfeigned gratification to see so large an assembly of Masons here this day from the newly formed Lodge 'Zetland in the East' at our little emporium, Singapore, for the purpose of taking part in this day's ceremony, to which, Gentlemen, I will thank you to proceed with the least practicable delay."

The Worshipful Master having taken up his position on the East side of the Stone, with the Lodge Chaplain, the Revd. Brother F. W. Linstedt, on his right, and on his left the Past Master, with the Senior and Junior Wardens, Treasurer, Secretary, and other office-bearers immediately around him, requested the Chaplain to open the ceremony with prayer, which he did in a suitable and appropriate form. The architect of the building, J. T. Thomson, Esq., now submitted his plans of the construction for the Worshipful Master's inspection, and having received his approval, they were returned to the Architect for his guidance. The Worshipful Master received from the Treasurer and Secretary a bottle containing the current English coinage, also an original edition of the Horsburgh Directory, a copy of the newspapers and the other publications at Singapore ; he deposited the bottle with the coins in the cavity prepared for its reception. The Inner Guard then presented the Worshipful Master with a copper plate bearing the following inscription :—

In the year of Our Lord 1850
and
in the 13th year of the reign of
Victoria
Queen of Great Britain and Ireland
The Most Noble
James Andrew, Marquess of Dalhousie, Kt.,
being Governor-General of British India :
The Foundation Stone
of the Lighthouse to be erected at Pedra Branca and
dedicated to the memory of the celebrated
Hydrographer
James Horsburgh, F.R.S.,
was laid on the 24th day of May,
the anniversary of the Birthday of
Her Most Gracious Majesty,
by the
Worshipful Master M. F. Davidson, Esq.,
and the
Brethren of the Lodge Zetland in the East,
No. 748,
In the presence of the Governor of the Straits Settlements,
and many of the British and Foreign Residents of Singapore.
J. T. Thomson,
Architect.

The inscription having also been placed in the cavity, the Worshipful Master received from the architect a silver trowel with some cement with which he proceeded to close the cavity; this having been done and the stone lowered into the bed, he directed the Architect to see that it was properly adjusted. The Square, Level, and Plumb and Rule were then handed to the Worshipful Master, who applied each instrument successively to the stone, and having struck it three times with his mallet, said :—" May the Great Architect of the Universe grant a blessing on this stone which we have now laid, and by His Providence enable us to finish this and every other virtuous undertaking." The Brethren replied, "So mote it be," and gave the usual Masonic salute. The Worshipful Master next called for the Cornucopia containing corn, and the cups with wine and oil, and having poured the contents of each successively over the stone, said:—"May the All Bounteous Author of Nature bless our Island, of which this Rock is a dependency, with Corn, Wine and Oil, and with all the necessary comforts and conveniences of life." The Brethren again responded, "So mote it be," and saluted as above. The Chaplain pronounced an appropriate prayer and the Worshipful Master then addressed the Governor and gentlemen present in the following speech:—

"It will be impossible to convey to you in adequate terms, the very high sense entertained by myself and brethren of the honour you have done us, in having thus publicly called upon us to assist with our Masonic art, in laying the foundation stone for the Lighthouse about to be constructed on this spot, in commemoration of the services of that distinguished Hydrographer, James Horsburgh, by whose enterprising genius and surpassing zeal, the navigation of these intricate seas has been so greatly facilitated. As a body, we feel justly proud of the distinction thus conferred upon us in having committed to our care the commencement of a work of such vast importance to every maritime nation in the world, and so perfectly accordant with those principles of philanthropy which form the basis of our ancient institution; and I shall ever esteem it one of the happiest circumstances of my life that the Brethren of Lodge Zetland in the East have been called upon to exercise their craft in so laudable and great an undertaking during the period that I enjoy, through their kind suffrages, the honour of occupying the Master's chair.

"All present must regard it as a most auspicious event that this noble work has been begun on a day held in the highest veneration by every British subject, as being the anniversary of Her Most Gracious Majesty's Birthday; and to you, Hon'ble Sir, is the credit due of having selected this most fitting mode of testifying our loyalty to our beloved Sovereign on the occasion; who I feel assured could desire no greater and more pleasing proof of our attachment to her royal person, than our being engaged, as we are this day, in laying the foundation of a structure which will tend to promote the welfare of so many of her subjects. It would perhaps, be a very difficult task to foresee the extent of usefulness to the commerce of our own country, and to that of equally civilized powers; but when we contemplate its effects in fostering our intercourse with the semi-barbarous nations of Eastern Asia which surround us, whose want of skill in the art of navigation render them so frequently a prey to the mysteries of the mighty deep, and tends so materially to restrict their advancement, we shall be lost in a maze of conjecture and surmise.

"The disastrous effects resulting from the absence of a Lighthouse in this locality, the loss of human life and the extensive destruction of property, have been too frequently and too severely felt within late years not to render it a matter of the deepest concern to all who feel an interest in the prosperity of commerce and the welfare of their fellow-creatures, that this work which, under your auspices, we have now so happily begun, should have been so long deferred. I should therefore be doing you a great injustice, were I to refrain from noticing how much the world is indebted to you, Hon'ble Sir, for having brought the necessary arrangements to a conclusion, which, but for your unceasing and strenuous advocacy of the cause, might still have been protracted to an indefinite period. Nor can I permit this opportunity to escape me of offering you my most heartfelt congratulations that your long and useful career as the chief authority in the Straits of Malacca, which has tended so much to the improvement and embellishment of the Settlements under your rule, should be crowned by a labour calculated to be an era in their history, and to reflect everlasting honour on yourself. Doubtless the recollection of this day's proceedings will form, in after years, when you may be removed from the scene of your present labours, not the least pleasing of your reminiscences ; and that you may long live to enjoy the contemplation of your past useful and honourable career, is my sincere wish. I feel that I should ill acquit myself of the task you have assigned me, were I to omit to pay a just tribute to the munificence of those merchants and mariners to whose liberality we are indebted for the nucleus of the fund raised for the erection of the edifice of which we have this day laid the foundation stone. Thanks are also due to the Hon'ble the Court of Directors of the East India Company for having advanced the remaining sum necessary to effect this desirable object.

"The merits of the distinguished man to whose memory the Lighthouse is to be dedicated, are too universally acknowledged to need any lengthened panegyric on my part. His comprehensive charts, and elaborate and invaluable sailing directions, the labour of years of untiring exertion and devotion, stamp him as a man of almost unexampled genius and industry. To the navigator of these seas, the name of Horsburgh is almost as familiar as his own, and among those who are engaged in commerce in this quarter of the globe, who is there that does not feel and acknowledge the deepest debt of gratitude to him ? To the memory of one so devoted to the cause in which almost his whole life was spent, what more appropriate testimonial could be offered than the edifice now to be erected ? And I supplicate the Supreme Architect of the Universe so to bless the work, that it may long withstand the ravages of time, and bid defiance to the billows of destruction that surround it, to be a tower by day and a light by night, to guide the mariner in his course, for ages to come, and that succeeding generations, whilst they admire the genius of him to whose memory it is raised, may have cause to regard with gratitude those to whom its erection is due."

The Governor replied as follows :—

" Worshipful Master and Gentlemen of the Lodge Zetland in the East;

" I thank you for the able manner in which you have been pleased to perform this day's most interesting ceremony. I have ever honoured the Craft of Masonry ; and the solemnity which has characterised this day's proceedings has made me feel the deepest respect for what I had **previously honoured.**

" The kind terms in which you, Gentlemen Masons, have been pleased to speak of myself cannot fail to be deeply gratifying; and what has passed this day will indeed have a most prominent place amongst the many pleasing recollections which I shall take with me to my native land, when leaving the Straits, where, I may truly say, I have honestly laboured to the utmost of my ability for the advancement of the three stations.

" I should be wanting in justice to the mercantile community and mariners in China if I omitted to notice what you mentioned of their liberality for their donations towards the Horsburgh testimonial, which, magnified by the munificence of Messrs. Jardine, Matheson and Co., in allowing compound interest on the sum raised in 1842, most certainly enabled me to call upon the Government of India for aid in this matter. The call was readily responded to and favourably received by the Hon'ble Court of Directors as our presence here this day bears evidence. But, Gentlemen, there is one other person whose zeal in this cause must not be lost sight of. I allude to one of the oldest and most respected residents of Singapore, John Purvis, Esq., who has narrowly watched and earnestly aided the authorities on this occasion, and whose suggestions for the more safe and speedy navigation of the Straits of Malacca, subsequently enlarged upon and recommended by that excellent body, the Singapore Chamber of Commerce, I hope eventually may be carried into effect. Gentlemen, I entrust the completion of the building, of which you have now laid the foundation stone, to that valuable and indefatigable public servant and able architect, Mr. Thomson, with the utmost confidence; and I again thank you most sincerely for the labours of this day, and for the impressive manner in which you have exercised your Masonic Craft on the occasion; accompanied by the warmest expressions of loyalty to our most Gracious Majesty Queen Victoria, who, whilst some of the greatest Potentates of the Earth have either fallen from or tottered on their thrones, has remained firmly seated, supported solely by the affections of her people; and how far-spread and deep-rooted are those affections the sentiments promulgated by the little band here collected on this isolated spot, will still further testify to the world at large. Let us now unite in three hearty cheers to the health, prosperity and long continued reign of Our Queen : God bless her.

" The Brethren then opened a passage to allow the Governor to return and the party embarked at 2 p.m. on board the *Hoogly*, where a dejeuner was prepared to which His Excellency the Naval Commander-in-Chief, the Governor, and his guests, did ample justice; displaying their loyal attachment to our beloved Sovereign and acknowledging the kindliness of their host by enthusiastic acclamations."

On the 15th October the monsoon prevented any further work and on the 21st all that could be made secure was left and the rest left to be washed away; at 5 p.m. all took their departure. On the 5th April, 1851, work began again, and Mr. Church went out occasionally to see how it went on. In August the lantern and machinery arrived; and the men-of-war lent a hand; and on 21st September the lighthouse was completed. A fortnight before, an English barque the *Metropolis* laden with tea had struck on a rock, twelve miles from the lighthouse, and was abandoned by the crew.

On Saturday, the 27th September, Governor Butterworth accompanied by Sir William Jeffcott, the Recorder, Colonel Messiter, and a large party of gentlemen, including many of the oldest residents, proceeded to Pedra Branca in the *Hoogly* for the purposes of witnessing the illumination for the first time. The steamer left the roads at 8 o'clock in the morning, and anchored a little to the westward of the rock at 1 p.m. The afternoon was spent in inspecting the tower and lantern, together with the numerous conveniences that had been constructed for the comfort of the light-keepers, including a store and a kitchen cut out in the solid granite, and a jetty of timber, secured by guys of massive chain-work, to facilitate landing during the north-east monsoon; and the visitors anticipated that this first Pharos of the Eastern Seas would prove the great Lion of the Straits for a long time to come. The *Free Press* spoke of it as an edifice of which Singapore might well be proud, and described it in the following way :—

" The granite blocks which form the walls were quarried and shaped at Pulo Ubin ; the timber used in the building is the growth of our island ; the brass rails of the stair-case were moulded and turned in this Settlement ; and last not least the Architect and Engineer, Mr. J. T. Thomson, acquired the skill and experience, which enabled him to erect so rapidly this chaste and stately building, during a long and useful career as Government Surveyor at Singapore. The cast-iron dome and lantern are the only outside productions. For these we are indebted to Messrs. Stevenson of Edinburgh, the Engineers of the Northern Lighthouses, and from the completeness of the details there can be little doubt that all the modern improvements have been introduced. The lamps are arranged on the frame in three groups, and consist of three lamps each, backed by a silver reflector to concentrate the rays of light. The frame revolves horizontally, by means of a clock-work-like apparatus, once in three minutes, so that the brilliant flash which lasts about 15 seconds is presented to the distant beholder once a minute. The guests, in number about fifty, sat down to dinner on board the *Hoogly* at half-past five, and soon after the removal of the cloth, a simultaneous rising announced that the process of illumination had commenced. Three hearty cheers welcomed the light, the meteor-like brilliancy of which will probably serve to guide the midnight path of the mariner for a thousand years to come. The light was lighted regularly from the 15th October.

The lowest floor of the building is 16 feet 9 inches above high water, the centre of the light is 96 feet 9 inches, and the top of the tower is 109 feet 6 inches. The light is visible fifteen nautical miles. The expense to completion was $23,665.87 ; the lantern apparatus and lightning conductor cost £1,324.9.6. This exceeded the original anticipated outlay by $843.17 but was less than the amount sanctioned by $960.63.

It was at first a revolving bright light, which gradually attained its brightest period every minute. The rooms are reached by ladders, with brick partitions and doors to shut in the rooms. Since its construction $24,752 more has been spent on alterations and a new light. The total cost to date being $48,377. It is now a revolving light of the new order, with a flash every ten seconds, visible for twenty miles. The shaft was originally painted white, but is now in black and white stripes. At the time it was erected it was the only lighthouse in India on a small solitary rock far out to sea. It is distant nine miles from Point Roumania, the nearest point of land; and thirty-seven miles from Singapore. There is a large reef of rocks, measuring about 450 feet in one direction by 200 feet in the other. At low water a number of detached rocks are seen in the locality; at high water Pedra Branca has the appearance of a heap of boulders loosely piled together. The proximity was long noted for its great danger to shipping. Between 1824 and 1851, sixteen large vessels were totally lost there, and two others were stranded, besides other minor accidents. A Portuguese Brig the *Dourado* went down with $500,000 on board, and a British Barque the *Sylph* went ashore with $557,200 worth of opium. It was also a favourite place of attack for pirates, the people in the vicinity as well as the crews of the Chinese Junks being notorious for committing depredations on all whom they thought they could safely attack, and having no compunction in murdering all their victims in order to destroy all traces of evidence against them.

The following inscriptions are in a panel in the wall of the Visitor's Room, which is on the sixth floor, just under the Light Room —

Pharos Ego
Cui nomen praebuit
Horsburgh Hydrographus
In maribus Indo Sinicis praeter omnes proeclarus
Angliae Mercatorum nisi imprimus indole
Ex imperii opibus Anglo Indici denique constructa
Saluti nautarum insignis viri memoriae
Consulo
A.D. MDCCCLI
W. J. Butterworth, c.b.,
Prov: Malacc. Proef.

A.D. 1851
The Horsburgh Lighthouse
is raised by the British enterprise of British Merchants,
and by the liberal aid of the East India Company,
to lessen the dangers of navigation,
and likewise to hand down,
so long as it shall last,
in the scene of his useful labours,
The Memory of the Great Hydrographer
whose name it bears.

Col. W. J. Butterworth, c.b.,
Governor in the Straits of Malacca.

J. T. Thomson,
Architect.

The Raffles Lighthouse.

In July, 1838, it was proposed to build a lighthouse on some one of the islands at the western entrance of Singapore Straits; and Barn Island, Alligator Island, and the Coney (where the light now stands) were each suggested as the most advantageous. Mr. Coleman thought the Coney island was too small, having only a superficial area of seventy feet by twenty-two, and only thirty feet above the sea-level, while Barn Island was seventy, and Alligator Island one hundred, but the position of the Coney was considered the best of the three. Captain Begbie in his book written in 1834, said, "The cluster of islands on the sea; Barn Island, Alligator Island, the Rabbit and Coney (two small islands which bear a strong similarity in figure to the animals whose name they bear) present a labyrinth through which the mariner has to thread his way." The island on which the lighthouse is built is fifteen miles south-west of Singapore, and marks the outer and south channel round St. John's Island to the Singapore roads.

It was not until 1854 that the project was carried into execution and the following account of the proceedings at the laying of the foundation stone is taken from the *Free Press* :—"Wednesday the 24th May, being the anniversary of the birthday of Her Majesty, had been fixed upon for laying with Masonic honours, the foundation stone of the Lighthouse on the Coney, at the entrance to the Straits of Malacca. The Hon'ble Colonel Butterworth, c.b., Governor of the Straits Settlements, proceeded to the place in the H. C. Steamer *Hoogly*. Amongst the gentlemen who accompanied the Governor were the Hon'ble the Resident Councillor, the Hon'ble Sir W. Jeffcott, Recorder; Colonel Cameron, Commanding the Troops in the Straits; the Hon'ble Captain Elliot, H. M. S. *Sybille*; Captain Blane, H. M. S. *Rapid*; Captain Saunderson, H. M. S. *Lily*; M. D'Egremont, Consul-General for Belgium; M. Gautier, Consul-General for France; and the other Consuls, a number of the merchants, and the Worshipful the Acting Master, Mr. W. H. Read, and a party of the Brethren of Lodge Zetland in the East. About twenty of the Masons embarked on board the Sultan of Linga's Schooner *Young Queen*, which was taken in tow by the *Hoogly*, and the whole got under weigh about half-past ten in the forenoon. The day was singularly favourable for the excursion, being cloudy with light breezes, while only a very slight shower fell. The Band of the 43rd Regiment M. N. I. was on board the *Hoogly* and beguiled the time with music. The vessels anchored off the Coney about 1 p.m. when the Masonic party disembarked and proceeded to make arrangements for the ceremony. When all was ready the Hon'ble the Governor landed and was received by the Worshipful the Acting Master and the Masons who then proceeded to the spot in the following order :—

Tyler with drawn Sword.
Members of the Lodge and other Brethren
two and two.
Banners
borne by Brothers Gordon and Passmore.

Cornucopia with Corn
borne by W. Brother M. F. Davidson.
Two Cups with Wine and Oil
borne by Bro. T. O. Crane and Bro. C. Baumgarten.
The Architect, Brother J. Bennett
with the Plan of the Building.
The Inner Guard, Brother J. Baxter
bearing the Inscription Plate.
The Secretary, Brother F. H. Gottlieb
bearing the Book of Constitutions.
The Treasurer, Brother J. C. Smith, with a bottle
containing Coins and the Papers to be deposited
in the Stone.
Banners
borne by Brothers Macey and Frommurzee Cursetjee.
The Corinthian Light borne by Brother G. Shambler.
The officiating Junior Warden, Brother J. Sparkes
bearing the Plumb Rule.
The Senior Warden, Brother W. C. Leisk
bearing the Level.
The Square borne by Brother A. Middleton.
The Banner of the Lodge borne by Brother C. Perreau.
The Past Master, Worshipful Brother J. Jarvie
bearing the Sacred Law.
The Officiating Worshipful Master, Brother
W. H. Read.
supported by two Brethren bearing wands.

The company having arranged themselves round the foundation stone, the Hon'ble the Governor addressed the Masonic party as follows :—

"Worshipful Master and Gentlemen, I had the gratification four years since of enlisting your services, on the anniversary of our beloved Queen's Birthday, in the performance of a most philanthrophic work; and for a similar object I have again solicited the exercise of that craft, which, as I then observed, has charity and good-will to all mankind for its ground-work, and I have selected a return of the auspicious day for the present ceremony of laying the foundation stone of a lighthouse on this spot as a future guide to the mariner in the navigation to the entrance to the Straits of Malacca, and to the haven of Singapore, which Settlement owes its great and growing importance to that most eminent statesman Sir Stamford Raffles, whose name the building will bear. I now beg the favour of your proceeding with the work, and your acceptance of the Trowel which I have had prepared, as a momento of the call that has been made this day upon the Lodge Zetland in the East.

"The Revd. C. J. Quartley, M.A., late Chaplain at Singapore, then offered up prayers including the following :—O Eternal Lord God, who spreadest the Heavens, and rulest the raging of the Sea, be pleased to receive under Thy Almighty protection and gracious favour, the work which is here this day begun. Do Thou, without whom nothing is strong, nothing is holy, preserve it during its construction from the fury of the elements, and from the ill-designs of our enemies; and when through Thy goodness it shall be completed, grant that it may afford the means of security to all who shall be in danger in these seas. Do Thou hold their souls in life, rescue them from the jaws of death, preserve their ships and goods, hear their prayers when they call upon Thee, and save them out of all their distress. And when thus delivered by Thy mercy may they, knowing how terrible Thou art, and how greatly to be feared, adore Thy Divine Majesty, acknowledge Thy power, and implore Thy goodness. Help, Lord, and save for Thy mercy's sake in Jesus Christ. Amen.

"The Acting Worshipful Master then gave three strokes with his gavel, and requested the Treasurer to deposit in the cavity a bottle containing an inscription on parchment and the current coins of the Settlement. The Secretary then read the inscription on the plate which was as follows:—

In the Year of our Lord
1854,
and in the Seventeenth Year of the reign of
VICTORIA,
QUEEN OF GREAT BRITAIN AND IRELAND,
The Most Noble
James Andrew Marquis of Dalhousie, Kt.
being Governor-General of British India,
The Foundation Stone
of the Lighthouse, to be erected on the
Coney, and dedicated to the Memory of
SIR STAMFORD RAFFLES, Kt.,
LL.D., F.R.S. and S.A.L.S.,
to whose Enlightened Policy, the Mercantile
World is indebted for the selection of
SINGAPORE AS AN EMPORIUM,
and for the Freedom of its Commerce from
all restraints,
was laid on the 24th of May, the anniversary
of the birthday of
HER MOST GRACIOUS MAJESTY,
by the
WORSHIPFUL MASTER
and the
BRETHREN OF THE LODGE ZETLAND IN THE EAST,
No. 748,
In the presence of
COLONEL BUTTERWORTH, C.B.
The Governor of the Straits Settlements, and
many of the British and Foreign Residents at Singapore.

"The plate was then placed over the cavity, the cement was spread by the Acting Worshipful Master, and the upper stone lowered, the Band playing 'Rule Britannia.'

"The stone was then tested with the Plumb, Level and Square by the proper officers, who reported that the craftsmen had done their duty. The acting Worshipful Master then took the plumb, level and square and having therewith tested the stone, declared it to be correct and laid according to the rules of the ancient craft. The corn being then handed to the acting Worshipful Master he sprinkled it on the stone, saying :—'I sprinkle this corn as an emblem of plenty : may the blessings of bounteous heaven be showered down upon us and may our hearts be filled with gratitude.' To which the Brethren responded : 'So mote it be.' The cup containing the wine was then presented to him. He poured some on the stone saying :—'I pour out this wine as an emblem of joy and gladness : may our hearts be made glad by influence of divine truth and may virtue flourish as the vine.' To which the Brethren responded : 'So mote it be.' He then took the ewer with oil, and pouring it on the stone, said :—'I pour out this oil as an emblem of peace : may peace and harmony, good-will and brotherly love abound among us for ever.' To which the Brethren responded as before : 'So mote it be.'

"The following supplication was then offered up : 'Brethren, having now with your assistance laid the first stone of this building according to the rules of our ancient craft, let us implore the blessing of the Great Architect of the Universe upon this our present undertaking, and may He be pleased to bless this building and grant that it may tend to His glory, to the advancement of science and to the promotion of the prosperity of this Settlement.' 'So mote it be.'

"The plans of the building having then been submitted to the acting Worshipful Master, he inspected them and said : 'Brother Architect, in the presence of this numerous and influential assembly and of these members of our ancient and honourable fraternity, I have much pleasure in expressing to you how well pleased I am with the plan which has been exhibited, and having ascertained that the foundation stone is fitly placed, I have to request that you will promptly bring this good work to a speedy termination, feeling sure that you will perform it so as to benefit your reputation.' The acting Worshipful Master, Mr. W. H. Read, then addressed the Hon'ble the Governor in the following terms :—

"Colonel Butterworth, as you observed, it is now four years since you called upon us to assist with our Masonic art, in laying the foundation stone of a Lighthouse about to be erected on Pedra Branca, in honour of that distinguished Hydrographer, James Horsburgh, and you have now, Honourable Sir, again requested our assistance at a similar ceremony, when about to raise a monument to the memory of that eminent statesman Sir Thomas Stamford Raffles. If it was peculiarly gratifying to the Brethren of the Craft to meet your views when about to honour him, who had, by his indefatigable geographical researches and untiring perseverance, so greatly facilitated the navigation of these seas, how much more must they feel honoured on the present occasion, when assembled to lay the foundation stone of a building, not only peculiarly useful in itself, but moreover destined to perpetuate to distant ages the name of him to whom England owes so deep a debt of gratitude for the political foresight and surpassing sagacity displayed in the selection of Singapore, as 'a great commercial emporium and a fulcrum whence we may extend our political influence,' and I cannot refrain from congratulating myself on the prominent part I am appointed to take in this imposing ceremony, when I call to mind the intimacy with the members of his family which I have so long enjoyed, and their friendship which I still continue to possess.

"Under the peculiar circumstances in which our native land is now placed on the threshold of a war of undoubted severity and uncertain duration, the selection of this day for the purpose to which we have devoted it, is not the least felicitous conception connected with its proceedings; it awakens with double force those feelings of patriotism and devotion to Her Most Gracious Majesty, which must ever animate the hearts of all true Britons; and sincerely do I trust that it will please the Great Disposer of Events to crown the arms of England with victory, and grant to our Sovereign many years of peace, happiness and prosperity, enshrined in the hearts of her devoted subjects, by unceasing watchfulness over their welfare. The continued exertions, which you, Hon'ble Sir, have so constantly devoted to the important object for which this building is designed, are now approaching a successful termination, and it cannot but be most gratifying to you to assist at this commencement of the second link of that chain of lights which will at no distant period illumine the Straits of Malacca, the safe and speedy navigation of which has now become of paramount importance, and it will ever be a proud reminiscence, when you have retired from these scenes of your active labours, that you have left your name prominently connected with one of the most beneficial public works in the East.

"It is beyond the imperfect powers of my abilities to give due praise and honour to the gifted statesman to whom this building is dedicated, and it would indeed be presumptuous to attempt to speak in adequate terms of his noble qualities, his varied talents, his ardent patriotism and his guileless philanthropy : his acts, his works, his letters, bear ample testimony of these. Here he established Free Trade in the midst of Monopoly, and with prophetic confidence looked forward to the day when the British flag should wave over these seas in protection of its freedom and in the promotion of its spirit. Here he fondly anticipated the time when commerce and civilization, joined hand in hand, should redeem the natives of these countries from their benighted state of barbaric ignorance. He looked upon this as the mission of his native country, as the glorious task of a people grateful for the blessings showered down from on High upon a favoured land." Mr. Read then quoted the words of Sir Stamford in his address on the founding of the Institution, which have already been printed at the end of the first chapter in this book, on page 16.

To which the Governor made the following reply:—" Worshipful Master and Gentlemen,

" The imposing and impressive manner in which you have exercised your craft, cannot fail to have left on the minds of all present a feeling of deep respect for the order of Masonry, and I thank you, Gentlemen, for having complied with my request. To you, Reverend Sir, I am most grateful for the solemn blessing you have invoked on the undertaking, through which and the acknowledged skill of the able architect, Captain Man, and his zealous assistant, Mr. Bennett, we may confidently hope it will realize the object contemplated. It has afforded me infinite satisfaction to mark the sense so universally entertained of the services rendered to the commercial world by the enlightened policy of the founder of Singapore, by dedicating the building to his memory, under the designation of the Raffles Lighthouse. To this circumstance and to the Masonic Ceremonies, I, in a great measure, attribute the large attendance here his day, but in a greater still to its being in honour of Her Majesty's birthday. I will therefore ask you, Gentlemen, to unite with me in three hearty cheers for Her Majesty Queen Victoria, and for the successful termination of the war, in which Great Britain is now engaged to support the weak against the mighty power of the oppressor."

" Three cheers were then given with right good will and thus terminated this very interesting ceremony. The company then re-embarked and returned to Singapore, the *Hoogly* again taking the Schooner in tow. Dinner was served on board at five, and after the excellent fare provided had been done ample justice to, the health of Her Majesty the Queen was drunk with all the honours, followed by that of His Majesty the Emperor of the French, and other appropriate toasts. M. Gautier, Consul for France, proposed the united Armies and Navies of the two powers, which was suitably responded to by the Hon'ble Captain Elliot, r.n., and Colonel Cameron. The party on board the Schooner appeared to be a very " jovial crew " keeping it up in famous style. The vessels came to anchor about half-past seven, and thus ended an excursion, at which every one present seemed thoroughly to enjoy himself."

The inscriptions placed on a Tablet in the visitor's room are as follows :—

Haec Pharos
ex Imperii Anglo-Indici opibus extructa,

STAMFORDI RAFFLES
oppidi in insula Singapura conditoris,
cujus per prudens consilium et munificum
isthæc regio fruitur
Porto immuni
et ad mercatoram maribus in Indicis agendam
opportunissime sito,
nomen et memoriam apud posteros servet.

A.D. MDCCCLIV.
Gul: Joh: Butterworth, c.b.,
Prov: Malaccæ Prœf:

The Raffles Lighthouse
erected in the year of Our Lord
1854
by the Honourable East India Company
and dedicated to the Memory of
SIR STAMFORD RAFFLES,
The Founder of Singapore,
to whose liberal and comprehensive Policy
This Settlement is indebted for its
Free Port
and the unrivalled position it now holds
as an Emporium
in the Indian Seas.
Colonel W. J. Butterworth, c.b.,
Governor of Prince of Wales' Island,
Singapore, and Malacca."

The light which was lit from the 1st December, 1855, is a fixed bright dioptric light of the third order. The centre of the light is 106 feet above high water mark, and is visible about twelve nautical miles.

As compared with the Horsburgh Lighthouse it was a very easy work, there being ample surface on the hill at some height above the sea. Whereas on Pedra Branca there was scarcely two feet to spare round the building on the surface of the rock, and the waves washed right over it.

CHAPTER XXXVIII.

1850.

O N Sunday night, the 17th February, shortly before midnight, the
E. I. Company's man-of-war *Feroze* anchored in the roads, having on board the Marquis of Dalhousie, Governor-General, and the
Marchioness of Dalhousie, attended by a numerous suite, which included
Sir Henry Elliot, K.C.B., the Foreign Secretary to the Government of
India, and a brother of Captain Charles Morgan Elliot, of the Engineers, who was so well-known in Singapore. Lord Dalhousie had been
in bad health, and came down here for a sea voyage. The following
account of the three days' stay of the Governor-General in Singapore
is taken from the *Free Press*. The Dalhousie Monument was erected
during the year in commemoration of his visit :—

"At an early hour on Monday morning the Governor, Colonel
Butterworth, C.B., repaired on board the *Feroze*, when it was arranged
that the landing should take place at half-past nine o'clock. Long
before that hour arrived, the roads leading to the landing place were
thronged with natives, all in their gala dresses, hastening towards the
scene of debarkation, where the 51st Regiment M. N. I. was drawn
up. Two lines of sampans, manned chiefly by the Tumonggong's
followers, in bright *bajus* and *sarongs,* formed a lane from the entrance
of the river to the shipping, through which the procession of boats
bearing his Lordship and suite passed to the landing place, where the great
body of the European residents, H. H. the Tumonggong and sword-
bearers, the Heads of the Chinese tribes, and other principal native
inhabitants, were drawn up to receive him. It was altogether a very
impressive scene, and calculated to produce a striking effect on those
who were not aware how large and motley a population the blessings
of free trade have collected together in this remote part of the world.
Here were representatives of every commercial nation under the sun,
assembled together to welcome one of the leading advocates of those
principles of free trade under which our Settlement has prospered,
and which now seem destined to effect a bloodless revolution throughout the world.

"During his short stay, the Governor-General was actively
employed in visiting the public buildings and institutions, and making
himself acquainted with the affairs of the Settlement. We understand
that the general result proved highly satisfactory to his Lordship, who
was lavish in his expressions of surprise at the evidently prosperous
condition of our community; which, by the bye, seems to have been
heretofore very little known and appreciated at head quarters. His
Lordship's visit occurring during the season of Lent, prevented the
display of those festivities which usually accompany the *progresses* of
great personages, but the principal members of the community had an

opportunity afforded them, by the hospitality of Colonel Butterworth, of meeting the Marchioness of Dalhousie, whose amiable character and unaffected goodness and kindness of manner has left among the smaller circle in which her position threw her, an impression not less pleasing than that produced by the Governor-General.

"Tuesday was the day fixed by his Lordship for holding a general levee at the Court House, and receiving the various addresses. The first address was that of the Masonic Lodge 'Zetland in the East,' his Lordship being the Grand Patron of the order in India. The deputation presenting the address consisted of about forty of the members of the Lodge, who were most kindly received, and left deeply impressed with the courtesy of their Grand Patron. The next was that of the Singapore Chamber of Commerce, which was presented by Mr. George Garden Nicol, the Chairman, and a numerous deputation. On the conclusion of the reply his Lordship addressed the Chairman, and after remarking on the wide circle of countries and nations represented by the members of the Chamber, took occasion to inform the deputation of the appointment by Her Majesty of Sir James Brooke to a special Mission to Siam and Cochin-China, with a view to place British trade there on a more satisfactory footing; and his Lordship expressed his hope that it would be successful. The Deputation then withdrew.

"The address of the Chinese merchants was then presented, and was answered in the same kind way, but, from some oversight, it was not interpreted to them in Chinese. From all we have heard, we may assure the Chinese merchants that his Lordship was greatly pleased with them, and much impressed with their peaceful and respectful manners, their great industry and enterprise, and the large share they have had in bringing about the prosperous condition of the Settlement. We understand he was greatly struck with the Chinese aspect which they have given to so large a portion of the town. After the levee was over, his Lordship, entering the Hall where the party was assembled, renewed the expression of the deep gratification his visit had afforded him, and his regret that, owing to the state of his health and the lateness of the season, he was reluctantly obliged to shorten his visit which he would otherwise have gladly prolonged.

"The forenoon of Wednesday, the day fixed for his Lordship's departure, was signalised by a display of feeling on the part of the Chinese community, which we believe to have been quite spontaneous. About 9 o'clock the road up Government Hill was occupied by a long train of toy carriages, splendidly painted and gilded, some drawn by ponies, others by men, which were filled with gaily dressed Chinese children, sent by their mothers to wait upon Lady Dalhousie. It was altogether a most pleasing spectacle, and as a display of feeling on the part of our large Chinese community, is not devoid of importance. Her Ladyship, as well as Lord Dalhousie, received their youthful visitors with the utmost kindness, and appeared to take great delight in the novel and interesting sight. The great kindness and personal notice bestowed by her Ladyship on the children during the visit, have, almost more than anything else, gained the hearts of the Chinese.

" Lord and Lady Dalhousie visited the Chinese temple at Teluk Ayer, and his Lordship also found time to visit some of the plantations in the vicinity of the town.

" Lord Dalhousie embarked at half past two o'clock p.m., under a salute of 19 guns, the attendance at the landing place being similar to that which had assembled to honour his arrival. His Lordship, after shaking hands with a few of the spectators, again expressed his great regret at the shortness of his stay, but hinted at the possibility of his return hereafter. Three hearty cheers followed his stepping into the *Feroze's* barge, and thus terminated what we truly hope is only Lord Dalhousie's *first* visit to Singapore. Perhaps no public man ever succeeded in producing so general a feeling of confidence and satisfaction among a large community as the Governor-General has done during this short visit. This may, in some degree, be attributed to his Lordship's kind and courteous manner; but the great cause is the matter-of-fact and business-like style in which his Lordship handled every subject that was brought under his notice, and the evident intention that he displayed of making his visit, not one of ease to himself, but of advantage to the community that he has been called upon to govern."

The *Free Press* spoke of the result of the visit as follows:—

"The three days' visit of the Governor-General to Singapore, has, we trust, produced as pleasant an effect on the noble lord as it has done on the community of Singapore. The liberal policy so freely avowed by his Lordship, his manly frankness of address, and the sound and matured judgments which characterised his conversation and remarks, have gained him golden opinions, which we hope nothing hereafter may arise to disturb or alter. His Lordship has gained some knowledge, from personal observation, of the circumstances of the Settlement, and the inhabitants have gained some knowledge of his Lordship; better aids to a mutual understanding than could be accomplished by petitions, memorials, and dispatches discharged at each other at some thousands miles' distance, although of the utmost voluminousness and frequency.

"Although the visit of the Governor-General has been so short as not to allow him to do more than cast a very hasty glance at matters of business, yet the better understanding he must have acquired of the Settlement and its people must have convinced him of the great advantages which would result to the Straits Settlements from more frequent visits to them by high functionaries of Government. His Lordship cannot be expected to renew his progress through his Far Eastern dominions, but he might urge the Deputy-Governor of Bengal, under whose control they are more immediately, or some other members of council, to make the tour from time to time. Such an inspection, we are convinced, would be attended with the happiest results, in establishing and maintaining a more cordial feeling between the governors and the governed. It may be a matter of little consequence to the former, but to the latter of what vital importance.

"For many years past, the reception given to the representations of the communities in the Straits Settlements in high quarters, and in some instances the legislation on Straits affairs, have given rise to a very general impression that there existed in the Supreme Government, or some member of it, an unfavourable feeling towards these Settlements; an impression which, whether well or ill-founded, it must be desirable to remove. That this feeling does not now exist with the Governor-General, or any of the Officers of Government who accompanied him, may be confidently hoped for, and that it should never again arise, would be secured by the personal experience in the members of the Supreme Government, of which a visit to the Straits, from time to time, would put them in possession. The Governor-General has learned from personal observation that Singapore is not a mere fishing village, and that it is something better than a convict station. May the favourable opinion that has been thus formed, be strengthened and perpetuated, and the result in time to come cannot fail to be beneficial to the Settlement."

The Governor-General presented one thousand Rupees to Tan Tock Seng's hospital during his stay. Tan Tock Seng died, at the age of 52 years, a fortnight after Lord Dalhousie left Singapore. He was a native of Malacca, but had lived almost all his life in Singapore, to which he came soon after its establishment, with no money, his only capital being industry and economy, like Eu Chin and so many of our best Chinese residents. Tock Seng started as a vegetable, fruit and fowl-seller, going into the country to buy and retailing in the town. Having saved a little money he opened a shop on the river-side. Afterwards he joined in some speculations with Mr. Whitehead, and it was chiefly by this means he made most of his money. He was made a Justice of the Peace by Colonel Butterworth, the only native who had been appointed up to that time, and was very often occupied in settling disputes between his countrymen. His charities were very extensive and constant, and he was accustomed to bear the expense of burying poor Chinese. He built the hospital of which there is an account in another Chapter, which was called after him, and it was said that if he had lived he would have left considerable sums for its maintenance, as well as for other charitable purposes. He left a widow, three sons and three daughters. His eldest son, Tan Kim Cheng, followed in the footsteps of his father. He carried on a large business, owning rice mills in Saigon and Siam, and steamers. He was Consul for Siam and had a title conferred on him by the King. He died in Singapore in 1892. His eldest son, or eldest male descendant, is a Statutory Member of the Committee of Management of Tan Tock Seng's Hospital, under the Ordinance by which the hospital was incorporated in 1880.

On Saturday, the 23rd February, a public meeting of the European and Chinese inhabitants was convened by the Sheriff to consider the best way of commemorating the visit of the Governor-General. Mr. William Wemmys Ker was in the Chair. Mr. G. G. Nicol and Mr. M. F. Davidson moved the first resolution as follows :—

"That it appears to this meeting the most proper mode of commemorating the Governor-General's visit to Singapore, would be by the erection of an Obelisk or triumphal Column on some part of the Esplanade (the centre being reserved for the intended monument to Sir Stamford Raffles) or such other conspicuous site as may be fixed on hereafter."

Mr. G. W. Earl and Mr. Joaquim d'Almeida proposed :—

"That the testimonials shall consist of two towers to be erected, one on or near the St. John's or eastern entrance, and the other near the Tree Island or western entrance of the narrow Straits of Singapore: the one to be called Raffles and the other the Dalhousie Light, and that the authorities be applied to apportion part of the funds raised by tonnage dues on shipping to the maintenance of their respective lights."

After a long discussion, Mr. Charles Spottiswoode and Mr. Lewis Fraser proposed :—

"That the recent visit of this Governor-General of India, and the addresses and discussion it has occasioned, are eminently calculated to call to mind the origin of Singapore, and all those great principles connected with the extension and freedom of commerce, which led to its establishment as a British Settlement and free port, and which principles are now for the first time fully recognised and acted upon by the Supreme Government; it is the opinion of this meeting that the most fitting mode of at once commemorating Lord Dalhousie's visit and the sound commercial views which mark his administration, is to erect a durable public monument, on a conspicuous site, to the memory of Sir Stamford Raffles, the founder of this Settlement, handing down to posterity, as such a monument must do, the high sense entertained by this community of the extraordinary sagacity and penetration of that great man in planning the formation of a British Settlement to the Eastward, and the indomitable energy and perseverance with which he overcame all obstacles and carried it into effect, while it will perpetuate the remembrance of the wise commercial policy which characterises the present Government of India under the administration of the distinguished nobleman who has so recently left these shores."

Whereupon Dr. Little and Mr. James Guthrie proposed that the meeting should be adjourned for a week, but Mr. Davidson and some others objected, and it was decided to continue, and after Mr. T. A. Behn had explained the proposal in Malay for the benefit of the Chinese, a committee was appointed to decide the matter ; and the following correspondence took place :—

To the Hon'ble Colonel BUTTERWORTH, C.B.,

Governor of Prince of Wales' Island,

Singapore and Malacca.

Sir,

We have the honour to inform you, that the mercantile and other non-official members of our community, Europeans and Asiatics, deeply impressed with a sense of the great benefits the Settlement cannot fail to derive from the recent visit of the Most Noble the Marquis of Dalhousie, Governor-General of India, the auspicious circumstances attending it, the unfeigned gratification all classes derived from personal intercourse with one so distinguished by public character and private worth—and more especially his earnest recognition of those great principles of freedom from all commercial restrictions to which the prosperity of the Settlement is due, and with which it must ever be identified—resolved to commemorate the event by the erection of a Testimonial in honour of his Lordship, and we were appointed as a Committee to carry out this resolution.

The necessary funds being raised (by subscriptions limited to $5) we have now the honour to state that the plan of an Obelisk, designed by Mr. Thomson, and submitted to you herewith, has been approved of, and it being our opinion that the most suitable spot for its erection would be at the new landing place, at the point of intersection of the Beach Road and that leading to High Street, we request that permission may be granted for its being erected on that site.

We are also directed to convey to you the unanimous wish of the subscribers, that in further commemoration of the visit, the new landing place should be called the *Dalhousie Ghaut* and we confidently anticipate your compliance with this wish.

We have the honour to be, &c.,

G. G. NICOL,	
M. F. DAVIDSON,	
J. GUTHRIE,	
TAN KIM SENG,	Committee of the Dalhousie
JOAQUIM D'ALMEIDA,	Testimonial.
H. C. CALDWELL,	
ANG CHOON SENG,	
SEAH EU CHIN,	

To which the following was the reply : --

GENTLEMEN,—I have the honour to acknowledge the receipt of your letter under date the 30th instant, intimating that the mercantile and non-official members of the Community at this Station, Europeans and Asiatics, have resolved to commemorate the advent of the Most Noble the Marquis of Dalhousie, Kt., Governor-General of British India, by the erection of an Obelisk, the funds for which have been raised by subscriptions limited to five dollars, and requesting that the new jetty may be termed the *Dalhousie Ghaut*.

I shall have great gratification in communicating to the Most Noble the Marquis of Dalhousie, Kt., Governor-General of British India, the high estimation in which his visit to this Station is held by all classes of the community, and the manner in which you have determined to commemorate that event.

The site selected for the Obelisk appears peculiarly well-adapted for the purpose, and it is a pleasing satisfaction to me to sanction its erection on the spot indicated by you, as also to authorize the new jetty being termed the *Dalhousie Ghaut*.

I have the honour to be, &c.,

W. J. BUTTERWORTH,

Governor.

Singapore, 31st May, 1850.

The list of subscribers was afterwards published in the *Free Press* it contained over 200 names, and amounted to $1.305.

It is curious to observe that in the first resolution of the meeting on 23rd February it was mentioned that the centre of the Esplanade was intended to be reserved for the intended monument to Sir Stamford Raffles, which was actually carried into effect in 1887. The Dalhousie monument was in the way when the Esplanade was widened thirty-five years afterwards, and it was proposed to do away with it, but Governor Sir Cecil Smith most wisely declined to accede to this, on the ground that the acts of former generations of this place should not be allowed to fall into oblivion, and it was replaced on the same line, as regards a harbour mark, but a little nearer the new sea wall.

The public revenue of Singapore for the year 1849-50 amounted to Rs. 386,119, and the proper local expenditure to Rs. 258,333. To the expenditure must be added Rs 200,892 for military, and Rs. 58,222 for convicts, making the total expenditure Rs. 517,447, and thus leaving a deficiency to be borne by India of Rs. 131,328. The total value of the imports into Singapore for the official year 1849-50 amounted to $13,313,041

Exports for the same period $10,455,521

Total value of trade 1849-50 ... ... $23,768,562

The total population, which was ascertained by a census in December, 1849, was 59,043, of which 198 were Europeans, 304 Eurasians, and 24,790 Chinese. This was a very trifling increase over the census of 1848, and was attributed to the decrease in the number of coolies working in the interior of the island, in consequence of the low price of produce and the exhaustion of much of the soil, for which reasons many had left and opened new plantations in Johore.

The number of Chinese immigrants who arrived from China for the year ending 30th April was 10,928, of whom 7,726 were brought by junks, and 3,202 arrived in square-rigged vessels.

Two of the earliest settlers in Singapore, and who were peculiarly distinguished by the aid they lent in advancing the prosperity of the Settlement, were removed by death during the year. One of them, Mr. A. L. Johnston, the contemporary of Sir S. Raffles, and who was much in the confidence of that eminent man, although he had resided in Europe for several years before his death, to the last took a most lively interest in Singapore, and by his will left a handsome donation to the Institution. The other, Sir Jose d'Almeida, resided in Singapore to the last, and pursued with untiring zeal those agricultural experiments to which he was always attached, and which assisted so much in inspiring others with a taste for similar undertakings. Accounts of both these old pioneers of Singapore have already been given in this book, on pages 62 and 184.

The *Free Press* contained the following account of a Masonic Ball given on the 25th January :—" The ball and supper given by the Brethren of the Lodge ' Zetland in the East' to the Singapore community, took place at the Masonic Hall on Friday last, and was very numerously attended, the company assembled having amounted to little short of three hundred. The front of the Hall was brilliantly lighted by variegated lamps arranged in Masonic devices, and the interior was decorated in a style which did great credit to the taste of the Committee of Management. Dancing commenced soon after eight o'clock. The full Masonic costume of the Brethren, and, above all, the presence of a Knight Templar and his page in the splendid full-dress of the order, added much to the brilliant appearance of the assemblage. The Governor arrived about nine o'clock, and seemed to be much gratified by the scene that presented itself. Soon after midnight the company adjourned to a spacious *salle à manger* which has recently been erected at the back of the Hall, (to which it is attached by a covered gallery) where the supper-tables were laid out, loaded with the delicacies that our Settlement affords. After supper the dancing was renewed and kept up with great spirit far into the small hours of the morning when the company dispersed evidently much gratified with their entertainment. We have been confidently informed by those whose experience of Singapore dates farther back than ours, that this has been one of the most brilliant and well-conducted assemblages that has ever taken place at Singapore. The Masonic brethren have great advantages in getting up affairs of this kind. They form an organised body, accustomed to act in concert, so that the making up of the committee, generally the most difficult part of the task, is to them, a work of comparative ease."

The list of members of the Masonic Lodge showed 91 members, including the Hon. Henry Keppel, and 5 honorary members, including Rajah Brooke.

In February, Sir Christopher Rawlinson, the Recorder, was promoted to the Madras Bench, and Sir William Jeffcott was appointed and took his place in April.

On the 1st March, Mr. T. A. Behn and V. L. Meyer dissolved partnership, and the firm of Behn, Meyer & Co. was continued under the same name by Mr. T. A. Behn & Mr. Frederick Albert Schreiber ; Mr. Arnold Otto Meyer signing by procuration. In May, the firm of Middletons Blundell & Co. was dissolved, Mr. William Blundell leaving the house, and it was continued as Middletons & Co. by Mr. James Middleton, Mr. A. Middleton and Mr. C. H. Harrison.

In March the newspaper gave the following account of the weather ; and of a duel in Singapore, an occurrence almost unknown here :—" During the greater part of last week the visitations of thunder and lightning were frequent, betokening that Dame Nature was breaking up the North-east monsoon. On Friday several loud claps of thunder took place immediately overhead, which caused much alarm amongst the natives. The electric fluid struck the flagstaff on Government Hill, and split the masts to shivers, peeling the copper off the heel. The electric fluid injured some of the venetians of Government House, as also the aviary, but without doing further mischief. Happily no lives were lost."

" On Thursday morning last an ' affair of honour ' came off, in the neighbourhood of the Race Course, between two European gentlemen, Messieurs S. and P. Mr. S. fired and the shot whizzed close past his antagonist's ear ; Mr. P. discharged the contents of his pistol into the air. The Police had received information, but were not on the spot until too late to save—powder and shot !"

In April the paper spoke of the hill now called Government Hill, as follows :—" Within the last few days that part of the high bamboo hedge encircling Mr. Prinsep's Estate, which bounds the low ground separating the public road from Bukit Selegie [this would be where Selegie Road is now], has been cut down, opening up a view to the lovers of the picturesque equally unexpected and enchanting. The dark masses of the fruit-trees growing in the low ground contrast agreeably with the lighter foliage of the nutmeg trees on the slopes, the large trees at the feet and on the sides of the hills, and the glimpses here and there caught of Mount Sophia and Bukit Selegie form altogether a picture as rare as it is pleasing, reminding the European resident of scenes in the old country, which he little expected to find so vividly brought to his recollection by anything in our tropical landscape. There are few properties in Singapore which can offer such varied scenery as that of Mr. Prinsep, most of them being still too new and wearing too formal and raw a look, yet there are none which would not form a more pleasing object to rest the eye upon than a close and high bamboo hedge, excluding at once the air and the light; and we, therefore, hope that the landed proprietors generally in the neighbourhood of the town will have sufficient philanthropy and consideration for the comfort of their fellow-citizens to follow the good example thus set them."

The following is a copy of the Minutes of the first meeting of the Committee to send exhibits to the Great Exhibition of 1851 :—

" *Proceedings of the Singapore Committee for the furtherance of the objects of the great Exhibition of 1851, under direction from the Bengal Government and Central Committee of Calcutta, held this 16th May, 1850.*

PRESIDENT :

Hon'ble Colonel Butterworth, C.B., Governor.

MEMBERS :

Hon'ble T. Church, H. C. Caldwell, G. W. Earl, Captain Man, G. G. Nicol, W. W. Ker, Tan Kim Seng, Syed Omar, and T. Oxley, Member and Secretary.

His Honour the Governor having opened the proceedings by calling attention to the importance of the subject, and thanking the members for the alacrity with which they had responded to his wishes, lists of various articles were submitted by several members of the Committee, each member being individually responsible for obtaining those articles he was best acquainted with, after which the following resolutions were passed :—

1st Resolution.—That the Secretary be requested to write to the Central Committee reporting the proceedings of to-day, and furnishing at the same time a list of the articles procurable, with the names of the gentlemen who have undertaken to procure them.

2nd Resolution.—That each party who has undertaken to procure the several articles be furnished with a a list thereof by the Secretary.

3rd Resolution.—That the prices of all the articles at the places where procurable be shewn on the final list to be submitted to the Central Committee, and transmitted with the article to be exhibited.

4th Resolution.—That each member furnish a short account of the several articles supplied by him.

5th Resolution.—That an outline map shewing the geographical position of each place from whence the articles are procured be forwarded for the information of the Central Committee.

6th Resolution.—That it is the opinion of this Committee, recorded for the information of the Central Committee, that the whole of the articles enumerated in the lists now before them cannot exceed a sum of three thousand dollars, inclusive of the arms and Malay musical instruments.

7th Resolution.—That the Secretary be requested to write to the Central Committee soliciting their opinion as to whether the products and manufactures of the Philippines are to be included in the operations of the Singapore Committee. These the Committee beg to observe will probably be costly and are not considered in their present estimate.

8th Resolution.—That the Committee take leave to point out that the Malay arms and musical instruments are by far the most expensive articles in the lists submitted, a set of the latter is likely not to cost less than 1,000 rupees, they therefore request the sanction of the Central Committee before purchasing these articles.

9th Resolution.—That His Excellency Sir James Brooke, K.C.B, be requested to favour the Committee by making his valuable services and influence available to them for obtaining specimens of Bornean products and manufactures, provided he has not received instructions from the Home Government to make collections for them."

In June, the Naval Commander-in-Chief, Admiral Austin, stopped the P. & O. Mail, as is related in the following extract from the *Free Press* :—" The inhabitants of Singapore on Monday forenoon were surprised at the report of heavy guns, immediately after the departure of the *Pekin*, which was soon ascertained from those cognizant of naval forms to be a " recall," or order for the detention of the *Pekin*, which vessel had made a few revolutions when the signal was made from the steam-sloop *Fury*, on board which ship the Naval Commander-in-Chief's flag is at present flying. These sounds, however, were imagined by those on board the *Pekin* to proceed from some junks saluting prior to their departure, and she held on her way without attending to them. It appears that important public despatches had been left behind, and it was therefore necessary that they should be sent after the *Pekin*. The *Fury* was at this time undergoing some requisite adjustment of her ponderous machinery, and one boiler was under repair, besides other causes of detention, the details of which we are not cognizant of, yet at noon she was ready for the chase, on which she started precisely 3 hours 7 minutes in arrear of the run-away mail. A stern chase is generally denominated a long chase, but in the present instance such proved not to be the fact. The *Pekin* was sighted shortly after 2 o'clock, and the distance between each rapidly decreased. When the *Pekin* was some five miles ahead "blank cartridge" from the bow gun, we hear, was fired, but no notice being taken, it was determined to send a shot in the same direction so as to fall on the starboard quarter, which had the desired effect, and the *Pekin* at last pulled up."

Such an occurrence was not unusual in former days. One Admiral, about 1862, we think it was Admiral Kuper, shot away part of the fore-rigging of a P. & O. steamer in Japan for not heaving to, when signalled to do so: The master of a P. & O. steamer in Singapore in 1867 having made some demur as to waiting a short time to take Admiral Keppel's despatches on board, was effectually prevented from going to sea, if he had intended to do so, by a manned-and-armed cutter being laid alongside the vessel at the New Harbour wharf ; the letters, however, were on board before the advertised hour for sailing. Another steamer during the Abyssinian war, in 1867, neglecting to heave to when passing through the old harbour, when H. M. S. *Satellite* signalled to her to do so, had two blank guns fired at her, and then a shot was sent across her bows. The shot was so well in front of her, that it nearly hit the powder magazine, anchored outside the harbour !

The newspaper in September contained the following paragraph :—" A plan has been set agoing for building three bungalows on Bukit Timah by subscription, which has met with the cordial approval and assistance of the authorities. This scheme promises, if carried out, to prove of much benefit to the residents here, by providing the means of a change of scene and, in a slight degree, of climate also, without the trouble and expense of a sea voyage. The subscription list is being rapidly filled up, and operations will be commenced as soon as practicable. Some six or seven years ago we pointed out the eligibility of Bukit Timah for the purpose to which it is now proposed to apply it, and as the favourable opinion which we then expressed of the spot has undergone no change, we have much pleasure in recommending those who may not have yet subscribed, and who are desirous of having the means of a seasonable change of scene, &c., at their command at a very moderate expense, to lose no time in putting down their names." The proposal was not carried out, and the Government bungalow was built on the top of the hill many years afterwards.

The following shews how the Secret Societies carried on their proceedings in those days:—

" A case which exposes to view the criminal and pernicious tendency of the system of the *hoés* was brought before the Criminal Session last Saturday, and Tan Ah Tow, one of the headmen and judges at the *Kongsi* house at Rochore, was put on his trial, charged with misprision of felony and an aggravated assault. It was fully proved by the evidence produced that five Chinamen, the owners of a boat which had been stolen, had succeeded after a search of fourteen days in finding it in the Serangoon river with a number of weapons in it, commonly used by our petty pirates, securing three of the thieves at the same time, whom they were conducting to the Police Office, when they met the prisoner at Gaylang, who ordered them to let go the thieves who were his men, and directed them to appear at the *Kongsi* house on the 9th of June, when he would decide upon the merits of the case. Fear compelled them to act as they were directed. On the appointed day they went all five to the *Kongsi* house, found there only one of the thieves, about thirty other Chinese, and the prisoner in the chair, who directed them to return all the articles found in the boat to the thieves, and to keep the boat, while they were told they would be punished. Not submitting to that decision, the prisoner directed them to be beaten, which was done with fists, stones, and the handles of umbrellas. Found guilty, the Hon'ble the Recorder sentenced him to imprisonment for six months and to a fine of 200 dollars."

" The Court House during that trial was crowded by a number of the leading men of the society, who, at the close of it, manifested great satisfaction at the penalty; some even were heard to say that the penalty being levied by a collection, the same would come to one cent a head, there being 20,000 members of the society in the Island. It ought to be noticed that each person on entering the society pays two dollars entrance fee, has not to pay any monthly contribution, but is bound to pay any sum when called upon by the *Kongsi*. It is of common occurrence to see the *hoé* raising sums of 500, 1,000, and 2,000 dollars in a few days, and it can easily be ascertained, the Police Authorities being acquainted with the fact, that 20,000 dollars were raised in 8 days on account of the disturbances at the burial of the late chief of the society, besides the burial expenses, which amounted to nearly 5,000 dollars."

The firm of Hinnekindt Fréres was established in this year by Eugene and Henri Hinnekindt. In 1854 Mr. L. Cateaux joined, and it was styled Hinnekindt Frères & L. Cateaux.

In the Singapore Directory for this year were the names of the officers of the 51st Regiment Madras Native Infantry, which had arrived in Singapore on the 28th April, 1849. The name of the youngest lieutenant, of whom there were ten, was William Dalrymple Maclagan, who had been stationed at Malacca, where he was still remembered by those alive there only a few years ago, but had just gone home on two years' leave to Europe. His father was a distinguished military officer. The Archbishop was born in Edinburgh in 1826. He left the army, and graduated at St. Peter's College, Cambridge, in 1856, and entered the Church, being first curate at St. Saviour's, Paddington, and in 1875 Vicar of St. Mary Abbots, Kensington, then he was Bishop of Lichfield, in 1878, and in 1891 Archbishop of York. He still speaks of his pleasant recollections of the Straits. It is remembered in Malacca that the Archbishop wrote some music which was played there, and it may interest the choir of St. Andrew's Cathedral to know that he is the composer of not less than five of the tunes in Hymns Ancient and Modern, Nos. 280, 318, 445, 454, and 269; and is also the author of the words of four others, Nos. 116, 122, 425, and 428, "The Saints of God! their conflict past" which Sir John Stainer's beautiful tune has helped to make so well known. The Archbishop crowned Queen Alexandra in Westminster Abbey on August 9th, 1902.

CHAPTER XXXIX.

1851.

ON the 1st January, it was advertised that Mr. W. W. Shaw and Mr. Joseph Wise were admitted partners in the firm of Boustead & Co. Mr. Boustead went to England and never returned to Singapore.

In January the Bishop of Calcutta with Archdeacon Pratt visited the Straits and went on to Sarawak to consecrate the Church that had been built there. The Sunday morning when the Bishop preached in the old St. Andrew's Church, there was a regular downpour, and the rain made such a noise on the roof that his voice could not be heard, and complaints were already made about the building, which leaked so short a time after it had been erected. It may be worthy of note as a custom that has long ceased, that the paper said that the Bishop landed " under the accustomed salute due to his rank. "

In a short manuscript note made by Mr. Braddell of a despatch by the Court of Directors on 15th January, it says that they had laid down, in concurrence with the Governor General, that the Indian Coasts could not be defended against a European enemy and even in salient points must depend as heretofore, and that hopefully, on the fleet. It was a sufficient object to defend against privateering and petty attacks in the absence of men-of-war; and approved of the suggestion that two Batteries of four heavy guns each (with one if necessary for Back Bay [?], would do for Singapore, and a few heavy guns be substituted for those now in position at Penang and Malacca.

The *Free Press* contained, in January, the following paragraph about the rainfall :—" The continued heavy rains, which fell last Sunday and Monday in torrents, caused the Brass Bassa Canal and the Rochore River to overflow their beds; the mass of water, being met by the rising tide, found no outlet, and reached a height unprecedented in men's memory at this Settlement. At the bridge at the Buffalo Village the water stood, for about three hours, 15 inches higher than at the inundation during last year. Considerable damage was done to public and private property, but the poor inhabitants are of course the greatest sufferers. The seawall along the Esplanade tumbled down into the sea for a length of about 80 feet, and at three other places the wall is in a most precarious state and threatens to tumble down; the whole will have to be rebuilt. A portion of the western wall surrounding the Pauper Hospital has also come to the ground, the foundation having been undermined, and giving way to the current of the water from the Brass Bassa Canal. In High Street the wall surrounding a gentleman's compound was washed away. The roads are horribly cut up, all the soft parts are washed away, and the bare rocks appearing on the surface make them at some places nearly impassable. Bencoolen Street and Middle Road are in a sad predicament from these causes, a great number of native houses are destroyed, rice and vegetables were found on the public roads, having been washed and deposited there by the water of the currents. Large pieces of timber, cocoa-nuts, dead pigs, &c., were floating in our streets, and a number of policemen and convicts had enough to do next morning to remove all the obstacles which obstructed the thoroughfares."

On Monday, the 20th January, Mr. Thomas Dunman received his final appointment as Superintendent of Police for Singapore, which the paper remarked was a very tardy act of justice, which had been repeatedly demanded by the majority of the community. There were four European Constables in the Police Force at that time, namely, McDonald, with a monthly salary of $55 ; Shea, $50 ; Hale, $45 ; and Berthier, $40 ; which were considered by the Municipal Committee to be liberal salaries. A Mr. Hammond, of the Bengal Civil Service, was appointed in January to be Assistant Resident and Superintendent of Police and Police Magistrate. He seems to have been a curious example of the administration of injustice, and there were frequent allusions to him and his doings in the newspapers. He was removed after he had carried on his eccentricities for about a year and eventually took orders in the Church in England! The paper, after a lengthy comment upon some of his acts, concluded on one occasion as follows :—

"Now all this is very improper, not to say dangerous. Freaks and eccentricities which, exercised on another stage, would only be simply amusing, assume a very different aspect when perpetrated on the magisterial bench, and when the consequence is the illegal restraint of persons. The administration of justice is brought into contempt, and the public is the sufferer from the incompetence or folly of the Magistrate. It is high time that the Government should take the matter into its most earnest consideration. The interests of the community are involved in a most serious manner. All charges of crime and misdemeanour must come before the Magistrate in the first instance, and with him rests the duty of preparing cases for trial in the higher Court. No excellence in this higher Court will insure an efficient administration of justice, if the person with whom rests the preliminary arrangement and preparation of the evidence is ignorant of his duty or neglects it. The sitting Magistrate is, besides, invested with extensive summary jurisdiction, and for the proper exercise of it requires a sound judgment, competent knowledge of the law of evidence, and an acquaintance with the character of the population.

"Few, if any, of the persons who have filled the Magisterial office for some years past, have been at all qualified for the situation. They have been utterly wanting in the requisite knowledge, training and experience. They have been appointed beeause the office, or its emoluments, was convenient to them, not because they were suited for the office. Military officers, innocent of any knowledge cf law, have been promoted to the bench, as if, from sitting in the seat of their predecessor, they could by some mesmeric process be imbued with the requisite skill for discharging their duties. Young Bengal civilians have been turned loose upon the community, to work their will and play such antics as they chose, and wild work some of them have made of it. It is time this haphazard mode of filling the Magisterial chair should cease. The interests of the community are too much jeopardised by it, and experience has shewn its utter unfitness and danger."

The following amusing example of one of his proceedings was sent to the *Free Press* by one of the parties aggrieved:—" On Wednesday, a Chinaman was observed by two of Mr. Bernard's servants running out of the front entrance of Mr. Bernard's house. They immediately pursued him and caught him at the compound gate. The thief was given in charge to a peon, and taken to the Thannah at Buffalo Village The following day, 1st instant, Mr. Bernard attended the Police Office with the two servants who had apprehended the man. Mr. Hammond, the Sitting Magistrate, was on the Bench alone. The case was entered into, and the following were the facts sworn to:—The two servants deposed that they saw the prisoner running out from the front staircase of Mr. Bernard's house; that they caught him at the gate, and that they never lost sight of him. The peon deposed that the prisoner was the man given into his charge, that he was taken to the Buffalo Village Thannah, and on searching him there, a silver watch was found secreted in his baju. The silver watch was produced, was sworn to as being the one found on the prisoner, and identified by Mr. Bernard as belonging to him. Of course, it might naturally be concluded, that after such evidence, the Magistrate could have done nothing else than commit the prisoner for trial at next sessions; more especially as Mr. Hammond had been made acquainted with the fact of the prisoner being a notorious thief, and that he still bore the marks of his last whipping all over his back. Still more than this, the prisoner had not a word to say for himself, not even a question to put to any of the witnesses. Mr. Hammond, however, in the excess of his Magisterial acuteness had discovered a mare's nest; was pleased to say that there were great discrepancies in the evidence and therefore would discharge the prisoner, who accordingly was discharged! You may well conceive the astonishment of the whole court at the above decision, worthy indeed of a Squire Western, but most certainly unexpected in a Magistrate of the H. E. I. Company. Surprised as all those in court were, certainly the most astonished person was the prisoner, who required to be told a second time, before he would believe that he was discharged; then, not waiting to receive the congratulations of his friends, he immediately disappeared, and made himself so scarce that when a peon was sent to observe which way he went, the innocent and injured man was nowhere to be seen. As a climax to the absurdity of the proceedings, Mr. Hammond returned the property to Mr. Bernard! How he could reconcile that with the discharge of the prisoner, I leave wiser heads than mine to determine. Mr. Bernard, I am told, on leaving the Police Office waited on Mr. Church, the Resident Councillor, related to him the circumstance, and received a promise that he would enquire into the case and do whatever was in his power to remedy it. Now, when a man holding such a responsible position, commits an injury to the community by acting in the manner described, it becomes a public duty to expose him, and to teach him that his being clad with a " little brief authority" does not license him to act in such a way. Since the foregoing was written, the Chinaman has again been apprehended by virtue of a warrant, and on Tuesday last was brought before the Sitting Magistrate when he was committed for trial at next sessions, on the very same evidence that at his first examination had been deemed insufficient."

On the 7th February, by the P. & O. Mail s.s. *Pekin*, Sir James Brooke, K.C.B., returned to Europe, and among the passengers was Mr. W. W. Ker who had been (the *Free Press* said) a resident in Singapore for twenty-two years, and finally retired with a handsome competency and the best wishes of his numerous friends.

There was an epidemic of cholera in Singapore and the neighbouring Dutch ports at this time, which lasted for three or four months; the deaths in Singapore from this cause were supposed to approximate two or three hundred, almost all confined to Malays and Chinese. No records were kept in those days of any burials, so it was almost purely conjectural.

The Grand Jury, in their presentment in February (C. Carnie, Foreman), made the following complaint:—" The Grand Jurors again present those injurious Chinese Secret Societies. They do not deem it necessary to dwell at length upon the pernicious influence of these bodies, the cases that have been brought before the Court this Session, the depositions taken before the Grand Jury which are now handed to your Lordship, the well-known dread Chinese of all classes entertain of the power of these Societies, the illegal acts that have been lately perpetrated all over the island by these people, numerous *bangsals* belonging to Chinese Christians having been destroyed, exhibiting a most dangerous combination against public security and peace; and the more recent outrageous attack upon the police in the vicinity of Bukit Timah, must place this important subject in so strong a light before you, that in recommending that the most stringent means should be adopted to put a stop to such a nefarious system for once and for ever, the Grand Jurors feel confident that they but re-echo the sentiments of your Lordship and propose that which you have already determined to carry out."

The interior of the island had been in a most disturbed state, owing to an active persecution having broken out against the Chinese converts to the Roman Catholic Church, who were scattered over the island as planters, and whose numbers were steadily increasing. A very slight pretence was laid hold of for putting in practice a general sacking and pillaging of the plantations belonging to the Christian Chinese and for carrying off individuals and holding them to ransom in large sums. These proceedings were generally ascribed to the influence, more or less openly exerted, of the Tan Tae Hoè, and probably of the other Secret Societies, from whose ranks the

Christian converts were withdrawn, and whose power and influence were of course diminished in proportion to the success of the Roman Catholic Missionaries. Besides withdrawing members from these Secret Societies, the conversion of the Chinese in the interior had the effect of placing everywhere throughout the island, men who were subject to influences adverse to the interests of the Societies, who were thus deprived of that complete immunity from surveillance which constituted one of the sources of their power. With these Chinese converts disseminated throughout the island, the Hoès could no longer hold their meetings, or execute sentence on refractory or defaulting members with the same security which they had enjoyed when there was no check upon their proceedings. This led to a general attack upon the Christian Chinese thoughout the island.

The paper contained the following accounts, among many others, of the proceedings of the Societies:—"Everywhere, at Serangoon, Bukit Timah, Bookoh Khan, Lauw Choo-khan, Nam Tokang, Chan Chwee-kang, even at Kranji, Propo, and Benoi, the *bangsals* and plantations of the Christians have been attacked by sets of 20 to 50 men, who rob all the property and destroy what they cannot carry away. The Christians came to town from all parts of the country as to a place of refuge, and people yesterday in flourishing circumstances are to-day reduced to the greatest misery. No less than twenty-seven plantations have been attacked within the last week; and the list of planters ruined last Sunday, proves there exists a conspiracy throughout the whole island, following the directions of one set of headmen.

"The authorities, although only at the eleventh hour, after the devastation of so many plantations and the ruin of hundreds of industrious and quiet people, have taken some measures, which, it is hoped, will keep the robbers in check; the police force at Bukit Timah has been reinforced with ten policemen, twelve men taken from the crew of the gunboat are directed to patrol the country in every direction under the guidance of the youngest constable. The gun-boat is stationed in the Old Straits to intercept all property which the criminals might try to transport to the coast of Johore, and a reward of $25 for the apprehension of every robber has been promised by the authorities. I must however notice, that the Revd. Mr. Issaly who had gone to Sungei Benoi to attend a sick Christian woman, the wife of a Christian planter, being informed that a band of heathen Chinese intended to attack him, took refuge in the jungle, where he remained for 24 hours, and finally escaped on reaching the coast, where he met a boatman who, for the exorbitant sum of $8, carried him to town. It has been ascertained that during Mr. Issaly's concealment the plantation was attacked and robbed of all that was on it.

"The force of police and crew of the gunboat *Charlotte* under Mr. Henry Kraal [afterwards in 1886, one of the Bailiffs of the Supreme Court] went to execute half a dozen warrants issued on the application of as many Christian planters, who had been robbed of all their property. After securing some prisoners and stolen goods in the village at Sungei Kranji, *alias* Bookoo Khan, they were returning to their station with the prisoners and goods, when at a short distance from the village, being on the high road, they suddenly heard the Chinese alarm signals sounded with horns, tom-toms, and the firing of crackers; and in less than 5 minutes a crowd of Chinese, armed with swords, lances, forks, knives, headed by 8 or 10 leaders furnished with the well-known rattan shields (if new and well made impenetrable to a musket ball) commenced a most decided attack for the rescue of the prisoners. A few moments afterwards another party of about 50 Chinese, armed in the same way, but also provided with a few matchlocks and muskets barred the highroad. The Constable in the van, and Mr. Kraal in the rear, cautioned the rioters against any violence in the manner prescribed by law; this producing no effect, Mr. Kraal caused a few shots to be fired over the heads of the men approaching from the rear, which, however, produced no other result than to encourage them to advance faster. The Constable in the van, having to contend with a smaller force, picked out four men, and made a rush against the people who fronted him, and dispersed them, and they ran right and left into the jungle. They joined however, the party attacking the rear and came with a rush against the police, firing a few shots.

" A volley was then fired amongst them, which caused them to advance with more caution, and allowed the officers to continue their route; but repeated attacks, which required continual repulses, caused the march to be very slow. The rioters were most determined, and the firing lasted during an advance of more than two miles. Finally the death of three of their leaders, who fell at a distance of about 20 feet from the police force, stopped them, and the officers were able to reach their station with their prisoners and the goods. All the ammunition except a few cartridges had been expended. It has since been ascertained that five of the attacking Chinese were killed and a great number wounded.

" The authorities on being informed of these facts sent the gun-ner of the steamer " *Hoogly* " with twelve men of its crew to re-inforce the police, and the crew of the gunboat and thirty convicts were directed to join this force, but by some misunderstanding only seven of the last reached the station in the early morning of Sun-day. The force consisting now of 38 men, of whom 28 were armed with muskets, it was resolved to make a round to the sea to look after the gunboat, which was left with only 7 or 8 men in the Old Straits, to exchange some of the men and to take provisions and ammunition. The detachment, leaving a small reserve at the station, traversed in silence the distance of 7 miles during the night, and arrived a little after sunrise at the Old Straits, without meeting any-thing; but returning home, and approaching the village, the road was again found barred by a numerous band of Chinese, while the signals of alarm were again heard. Necessity again compelled the police to fire into these dupes of the Hoé, after all peaceful means to disperse them had been unsuccessful. They rushed on and were rewarded by the death of two of their number, and the wounding of some others, which caused them to disperse after carrying away their dead and wounded.

"On Monday evening the full complement of the convicts having come up, a detachment of fifty Sepoys headed by a European Officer, Lieutenant Wilson, also arrived. On Tuesday the police force, reinforced by Constable Hale and some peons, and followed by the military, departed to execute twenty-two warrants issued at the instance of the Catholic owners of as many plantations which had been pillaged. The force arrived at 4 o'clock in the morning at Kranji Village, without having been observed. Halting there for a few minutes, the light of a dammar carried by one of three armed Chinese was seen to descend a hill. The greatest silence was preserved until they were at a few yards distance, but still on the steep declivity of the hill; there they discovered the force, threw their light away and disappeared. At the same moment a shot was fired by a concealed rioter, and the noise and cries of a multitude of people from every direction, saluted the discovery of the police party, which succeeded in surprising a great number of "bangsals," in some of which robbers were identified and some stolen property recovered. It being however now about ten o'clock a.m., and alarm being everywhere given, the force returned by two different paths; the Sepoys took a short one to reach the high road, while the police returned by a circuitous route, in order to surprise and disperse the Chinese concealed amongst the bushes and jungle opposite the village of Kranji on the east side of the road. The Sepoys arriving first on the spot, halted, and were saluted by the customary Chinese alarm signals. The police coming a little later from the east, a number of about two hundred Chinese were surprised and dispersed without a shot being fired, decamping like hares chased by hounds. Here the Sepoys departed, there being no more than two *bangsals*, situated at the other side of the river and village, to inspect. Leaving a guard for the prisoners, Constable Hale, Mr. Kraal, and the special constable passed the village, which was for the greatest part deserted, but passing the bridge a great number of Chinese appeared on the different hills in a threatening manner, and two shots were fired by them at the party, by whom a volley was fired in return, and a chase commenced, to secure some of them and the white flag carried by them. Four men were shot by the volley, amongst whom was an old man, the guardian of the Chinese brick temple, who certainly had no lawful business in the centre of a crowd of such vagabonds, whose number is differently given up by the European officers, according to the different sections of the hills on which they were acting; for Mr. Kraal calculated the number to whom he was opposed, to amount to about fifty, while Constable Hale could discern on his side about eighty or ninety, and the special from his position, about one hundred and twenty or one hundred and fifty.

"A Christian planter named Tan Ah Choon, who had been informed that his plantation was to be attacked and robbed, took all the money he could collect, amounting to more than $80, and two piculs white pepper, and departed for the town with two or three coolies, but was stopped near Amokiah by some Chinese, who seized and carried him into the jungle with the decided intention to murder him after having robbed him. The coolies escaped and reported the fact ; on which Mr. Dunman with a small number of peons went himself in search. On the road a man informed him that Tan Ah Choon had been carried to Loh Siah's plantation. The chase was continued, some *bangsals* were passed, where Chinese were gambling to their heart's content ; and Mr. Dunman finally succeeded in delivering Tan Ah Choon, who was in the custody of three of his captors in Loh Siah's premises, who himself was secured. The other criminals escaped, having been informed by the calls and cries of the nearest neighbours of the approach of the Police. Here is a most visible proof of the effects of the power of the Hoé. A man is kidnapped, carried through some crowds of Chinese, without any person interfering to prevent the crime, and these same men save the criminals by their calls and signals. Tan Ah Choon's plantation has since been robbed of nearly all its contents."

In April, a subscription was made for the purpose of making a steel engraving of the painted likeness of the late Mr. A. L. Johnston, of which there are now copies in the Library, and in several of the mercantile offices.

On the 22nd April, a meeting was held to establish a Sailors' Home, and a Committee appointed composed of Mr. James Guthrie, Captain J. S. Sparkes of the P. & O. Company, Mr. John Harvey, and Mr. W. H. Read as Honorary Secretary. It was proposed that a fancy dress ball should be given in aid of the funds, and it took place on the 15th May in the Assembly Rooms, single tickets were $5, and family tickets $7.50.

A new flag-staff was put up on Mount Faber in May, and within a month it was struck by lightning and destroyed ; it happened before daybreak, before the signal-men had come to work. The mast was split into pieces and fragments of it were thrown to a considerable distance.

On the 17th April, Mr. H. C. Rautenberg, the senior of the two partners in Rautenberg, Schmidt & Co., and Mr. Hurtlaub, the junior assistant employed in Behn, Meyer & Co.'s, left Singapore with two other gentlemen for Rhio in a boat belonging to the Tumongong. They met with a strong current and a high sea in the Straits, and a squall caused the boat to heel over and take in so much water that she sank about two miles from the shore. One of the gentlemen clung to the mast of the boat and another kept himself afloat by means of a cushion and a mat, and were picked up by a fishing boat after being several hours in the sea. Mr. Rautenberg and Mr. Hurtlaub were drowned. The whole of the Malay crew and a Chinese servant got safely to shore. Mr. Frederick George Schmidt remained the sole partner in the firm until 1858, when Gustav Cramer and Adolph Emil Schmidt became partners.

In one week at that time several tigers were shot by natives in the jungle, and Dr. d'Almeida gave a reward of $50 in addition to the same amount given by Government. It was stated on good authority that in the Serangoon district alone more than thirty persons had been killed by tigers within a few weeks. The following account of deaths by tigers in the same month is taken from the *Free Press* :—" While some Malays were collecting rattans and cutting wood in a piece of jungle near Mr. Dunman's plantation at Serangoon, they were alarmed by hearing a tiger making his approach through the underwood. They immediately commenced a retreat, but had not cleared the jungle when the tiger came up with them and singling out the fattest man in the party sprang upon him. It had dragged the body some distance ere the man's companions recovered from the fright into which they had been thrown, and pursued him with their *parangs,* on which the tiger dropped the body and retreated. The poor man was found in the agonies of death with his throat and face severely lacerated. The body was brought away, but the tiger, it would appear, was determined to have his meal, for the same night he carried off a Chinaman at a short distance from the scene of his morning's exploit. The Chinaman's friends on making a search found the body, with one of the legs wanting. The tiger is described as being of a large size and remarkable for having large white spots, from which it is conjectured that he is well advanced in years." The same animal killed another man in the next week.

The Rev. H. Moule, who was Chaplain longer than most of those who were sent from Calcutta to Singapore, died on 3rd June, 1886, at 81 years of age. He had left Singapore in 1851. He was Secretary to the Raffles Institution and was famous for good speeches at wedding breakfasts. He enjoyed his pension for many years and was Rector of Road cum Woolverton at the time of his death. He was a good judge of a horse, and it was said that as he would not go to the Races (as it was wrong) he stole a quiet look behind a bush when opportunity offered. He was afterwards the originator of the earth closet system which was known by his name, and which was extremely remunerative.

The Municipal Committee, as it was called, consisted in that year of Mr. Thos. Church, the Resident Councillor, Captain Henry Man, the Superintendent of Convicts and Commissioner of the Court of Requests, Mr. Mickie Forbes Davidson of A. L. Johnston & Co., and Mr. T. A. Behn of Behn, Meyer & Co. The following are parts of the Minutes in June :—

" It having been brought to the notice of the Committee that syces and others are in the habit of exercising horses on the reserved Plain [the Esplanade] to the serious inconvenience and danger of pedestrians, resolved, that a sum equal to a moiety of the cost of a chain sufficient to enclose the Plain be authorised, provided the Government will undertake to defray the other half, and that in the meantime measures be adopted to put an end to the dangerous practice alluded to."

" A letter dated the 19th June from Syed Ali Al Junied was read, stating that he had viewed with concern the great inconvenience to the public generally, and the suffering of the poorer classes in particular, from the want of an adequate supply of good and wholesome water during the dry months, and expressing a wish to be allowed to sink and construct at his exclusive expense, four capacious wells for the use of the community.

" The Committee deemed it right to record the high gratification they experienced at this mark of spontaneous liberality and benevolence on the part of Syed Ali Al Junied, which will be the means of conferring a boon on the inhabitants of the town and insure (with the other wells) an ample supply of good water thoroughout the year. It was therefore resolved that Syed Ali's offer be accepted and a letter of thanks embracing the foregoing remarks written to that gentleman. It was also resolved that a transcript of Syed Ali's letter to the Committee be sent to his Honour the Governor, and that the local authorities be requested to allow the services of the Government Surveyor, in communication with Syed Ali Al Junied, to be made available in the selection of the most eligible sites for the wells."

One of these wells was that in Selegie Road near the Dhobie Green, one at Campong Malacca, one at Campong Pungulu Kessang, and one at Teluk Ayer.

The Court at this time was held in the building now attached to the Government Printing Office. The paper alluded to the arrangements as follows :—" Some time ago it was found that the existing accommodation for the Court of Judicature at Singapore was too limited, and it was therefore resolved to add several rooms to the existing Court-room, for the use of the Recorder, the Registrar and his establishment, &c. The present Court House is a badly ventilated room, built on to one end of the Government Public Offices, and bounded close on the other side by a private house and a ship-builder's yard. This inconvenient site was originally chosen, it is presumed, for the accommodation of the executive Officers of Government, who also generally officiated as Judges, and who having turned the proper Court House into public offices, probably still wished to have the Court-room under the same roof, that they might pass from their own offices to the Bench without having to quit the building. The Registrar's establishment was in some of the rooms belonging to the public offices, and thus had the appearance of being a mere department of the local Government, a circumstance which has led to considerable confusion of ideas in the minds of both Europeans and natives, not unattended with objectionable results. Of late it has been found very inconvenient that there should be no separate accommodation for the Recorder, the Registrar and his Establishment, Juries, &c., and plans were therefore prepared for additional buildings estimated to cost some Rs7,000. These it was proposed to erect in rear of the present Court-room, and although the many disadvantages of the site were pointed out, and it was urged that for a very trifling addition to the estimate, a handsome suite of buildings might be erected for the use of the judicial establishment, altogether detached from the Government Office, the original design has been adhered to. The result bids fair to bear out the strong objections which were made, the new rooms being ill-ventilated and dungeon-like receptacles, which would be more suitable for condemned cells, than apartments for the Recorder and the Officers of the Court."

A public meeting was held on the 22nd September to consider a proposal of the Government at Bengal to introduce a stamp tax in lieu of the *Siri* Farm which the Government proposed to abolish. Mr. John Purvis was in the chair, and some lengthy resolutions were passed, to the effect that the Settlements paid their own expenses, if the cost of the convicts and the troops was borne, as it was said it should be, by the Indian revenue. The following were three of the resolutions carried at the meeting, which was very largely attended :—

"Proposed by Lewis Fraser, seconded by C. H. Harrison, and carried unanimously :—

3rd.—That Singapore was established, and is kept up, for the chief purpose of affording an outlet to the manufactures and productions of Great Britain and India, and is now yearly acquiring increased value to these countries as a naval and steam station.

Proposed by Gilbert McMicking, and seconded by Hoot Seng :—

5th.—That although a stamp tax may be a proper source of revenue in other places, this meeting considers that in Singapore it would prove burdensome and vexatious, especially to the commerce of the port, because the trade, unlike that in England or India, where goods are generally sold for cash, is here wholly carried on by a system of credit. That from the habits and customs of the native traders, who resort here in large numbers, the tax would prove especially obnoxious to this class, and would tend much to shake their confidence in that freedom from all imposts affecting trade, which they have hitherto been accustomed to meet with at Singapore, and this meeting therefore earnestly deprecates the imposition of a tax which would have such an injurious effect.

Proposed by William Paterson, seconded by Joaquim d'Almeida, and carried unanimously :—

6th.—That excluding the charges for Military and Convicts, there has been for many years past an annual surplus of revenue at Singapore (amounting according to the Government returns for 1850-51 to Rs195,000) and therefore any additional tax in lieu of the Rs25,000 at present derived from the *Siri* farm is quite uncalled for."

On the night of Monday the 21st July, the P. & O. Steamer *Erin* from Calcutta ran into the same Company's steamer *Pacha*, which had left Singapore the afternoon before, off Mount Formosa. The *Pacha* went down in a few minutes. The *Free Press* alluded to the circumstances as follows :—

"The *Pacha's* masts immediately fell over the side and she went down within less than seven minutes after the accident, in about 25 fathoms of water. The whole of the passengers, officers and crew were saved, except two cabin passengers (Dr. Briscoe and Mr. Hendowin) two Chinese deck passengers, the 3rd officer, the Clerk in Charge, and ten of the European crew, who were all drowned. The *Erin* sustained considerable damage, and the water rushed in at her bows, but being built with watertight compartments, it was found that only two filled, and as the pumps were got to work with the engines, it was found that the water could be kept sufficiently under to enable her to reach Singapore. A considerable part of the goods in the *Erin* is of course damaged by salt water and the whole are being landed. She has upwards of 1,000 chests of opium for China, much of which is damaged. The extent of the injury to the *Erin* has not yet been accurately ascertained, but it will require some days before she can be sufficiently repaired to enable her to prosecute her voyage. The *Pacha* had on board upwards of $400,000 of specie shipped in China, and $30,000 shipped in Singapore, and very little of the latter, which belonged chiefly to natives, was insured. Considering the immense amount of property in the *Pacha,* and the possibility of Malay divers and others endeavouring to remove it clandestinely, we are surprised that a vessel of war has not ere this been despatched to the spot. There were two steamers lying in the harbour yesterday, one of which surely might have been spared. The *Leitnitz* and the *Faize Allum* which arrived here to-day, picked up a quantity of China silk, piece goods, clothes, &c., near the scene of the wreck."

The damaged opium was sold in Singapore at auction at prices very far below its usual value, averaging about $315 a chest, and the purchasers here, of whom Thomas O. Crane & Co., were the largest, realised about a hundred per cent. on the speculation when it was sent on for sale in China, after having been opened and dried in Singapore. This led to much dispute and litigation, the Insurance offices refusing to pay. The *Erin* was repaired and sailed for China on the 9th August. The Calcutta and Bombay papers contained numerous proposals to form companies to raise the vessel, which was in 25 fathoms of water, for the large amount of treasure.

In 1853, Mr. Lovi, a practical engineer of much talent in cases of sunken vessels, and who had often been engaged by the British Government in cases of great difficulty, came out from England with the sanction of the underwriters, to try to recover the treasure, and entered into an engagement to raise it. He was unsuccessful for a long time. It is said that after searching for six months for the *Pacha*, he first ascertained her position from a peculiar quiver of his compasses as he passed over the ship. He fixed a buoy to it, and returned to Singapore for his diving gear and assistance. When he got back, the buoy had been stolen, and, as he had not taken the bearings, he dragged for four months more before he found the place again. The vessel was standing upright in the sand, which was nearly up to her bulwarks. A number of skeletons were on the stairs and the landing below, as if the passengers had been crowded together in trying to ascend. Mr. Lovi began to recover the treasure, but in April, 1856, while in an open boat going to his schooner the *Wizard* at anchor near the wreck, he had a stroke of the sun, and was forced to return to Singapore in an open boat, which took four days. He arrived on a Sunday, and died in Singapore on the following Saturday night, of congestion of the brain, while those whom he had left working on the spot were getting up the treasure. The dollars were sent to the Mint at Calcutta. The silver had become as black as ebony, and each roll was as firmly fixed as if it had been a bar, and not separate coins. Treasure and bullion to the extent of between sixty and seventy thousand pounds were recovered.

Mr. Thomas Scott, of Guthrie & Co., (who must not be confused with a former merchant of Singapore of the same name, mentioned in this book, who died at Calcutta at the age of 34 years on 7th July, 1848,) arrived in Singapore for the first time on 7th July, in the British Barque *Coaxer*, 316 tons, which had sailed from Liverpool on 16th February. He is the only passenger mentioned in the *Free Press* list of arrivals by that vessel. On the next day he went to Malacca with his uncle in a schooner, for a trip, and after being for a few months in another business, he joined Guthrie & Co., as a clerk, and became a partner in that firm in

1857. He died in Scotland on 28th June, 1902, having been a partner in the firm for forty-five years. In 1876 he founded the branch firm of Scott & Co., London. He was one of the promoters and afterwards largely concerned in the affairs of the Tanjong Pagar Dock Company. He was one of the first unofficial members of the Legislative Council, when it was established in April, 1867, and he was Chairman of the Committee of the Chamber of Commerce for many years. His portrait given by Chinese subscribers is in the Town Hall. Mr. Scott married the elder daughter of Major McNair, who survived him, and he left one son and one daughter.

In September, the barque *Fawn* of Calcutta arrived here from China, on her first voyage, being quite a new ship. She had been aground and was hove down at Sandy Point for repairs. A great part of her crew of Bengal lascars quitted the ship and refused to proceed in her to Calcutta, although they had four months' pay to receive on arrival there. When the vessel was ready to proceed on her voyage it was necessary to get other men, and twenty-nine Singapore Malays were shipped, who were said to be a very superior set of men. The shipping master who procured them cautioned Captain Rogers as to his treatment of this new crew, warning him that Malay and Javanese sailors would not allow themselves to be struck like Indian lascars. The ringleader in the tragedy which afterwards occurred had sailed as tindal with a Captain sailing out of Singapore, who described him as a fine spirited fellow and a good sailor. The *Fawn* sailed on the 28th September, having on board, besides Captain Rogers and his first and second mates, four European passengers, Mrs. Rogers the Captain's wife, Mrs. Bechem and child, and Elphick a horse-keeper.

On the sixth day of the voyage, about four o'clock in the afternoon, the chief mate saw the burra-tindal smoking down the forehatch, and found fault with him for so doing, asking him if he wanted to set the ship on fire. He then kicked him, got him on the deck and punished him with a rope's end in presence of the whole crew, the Captain and his wife being on deck and observing what was going on. About midnight or a little after, the Serang and two Bengal lascars, who were sleeping forward, were aroused by the tindal, who told them that the Captain was killed and thrown overboard. It appeared that the Captain was asleep on the poop, and was killed without resistance. The Serang on being thus roused by the tindal ran into the caboose, one of the lascars on to the flying jibboom, and the other to the foretop. One of these lascars said that at daylight he saw the tindal and about 16 or 18 of the crew round the second mate, wnom they were striking with hatchets. He made a most determined stand, but was eventually overpowered and killed. The chief mate and Elphick succeeded in shutting themselves up in one of the cabins where they defended themselves, and it is said that from twenty to twenty-four hours elapsed from the death of Captain Rogers before the chief mate was overpowered. Finding that he had taken refuge in the cabin, the crew made an opening in the deck, through which they poked at him with oars and other implements and wounded him; but at last, probably imagining that he would soon be overpowered, he jumped out of the port and was drowned. In what manner Elphick met his death the witnesses did not say. Mrs. Rogers, Mrs. Bechem and her child, and two or three native women, were then put into one quarter boat, the vessel going through the water at the time. Either through the falls breaking or from the boat being carelessly lowered, it was upset, and all in it, except the native women who laid hold of the falls, were drowned. When Mrs. Bechem was in the water she held up her child, and one of the men that was tried, asserted that he threw her an oar, for doing which he alleged he was beaten by the tindal. Mrs. Rogers sank immediately.

In the evening the tindal went round to each man asking what side he was going to be on, threatening that if he was on the Captain's side, the tindal and his people would kill him. In consequence of this, apparent unanimity was secured. The ship was scuttled on both sides and set on fire, and finally run on shore at Bruas, about forty-five miles south of Penang. She grounded in 1½ fathoms and about 200 fathoms from the beach. At this time a vessel was in sight going down the Straits, which was afterwards known to be the *Rajah*, of Liverpool, which vessel saw the *Fawn* run ashore and set on fire, but, strange to say, the Captain did not try to render any assistance, saying in Singapore that he did not think there was anything wrong with the vessel. If he had stopped, the unfortunate females, who were brutally treated by the crew before they were drowned, might have been saved. About nineteen of the crew, including the tindal, went on shore, and fourteen took to the long boat, in which they reached Singapore, on the 10th October. They anchored at Passir Panjang, and two of the Bengal lascars, finding the rest asleep, got out of the boat and came on shore. A Malay on board seeing them leaving, also joined them, and all three came into the town, where the Malay left the lascars, who then went to the Resident Councillor and reported what had occurred. The remaining men proceeded to Sandy Point where they landed, letting the boat go adrift. The Chinese carpenter gave himself up to the Police, and two Cochin Chinese, who had turned Mahomedans, and three Javanese, were captured. Rewards were offered for the apprehension of those still at liberty, and a most vigorous search was made for them.

Those of the crew who went to Bruas were captured and taken to Penang, and seven of the Bengal lascars and two women gave themselves up to the Police there. The H. C. steamer *Hooghly* with the gun-boat in tow, proceeded to Bruas, and succeeded in capturing the persons remaining there, amongst whom were the ringleaders. The vessel was found to have been completely destroyed and sunk, with only her stem and stern-post visible. Sixteen of the crew were tried in Penang before Sir Wm. Jeffcott, the trial lasting two days, and the Court sitting till 8-30 and 9 o'clock at night. Four of the prisoners, the worst of the men, were hanged, and the rest were sentenced to transportation for life. It is worthy of remark that the whole attack was confined to Malay and Javanese sailors; the Indian lascars took no part in it; and it was frequently remarked at the time, that while lascar seamen will not face a danger or difficulty, but rely more on prayers than any exertions during a storm, the Malays act well in any such circumstances, but will resent any blows which the lascars will quietly submit to. In the case of the *Fawn*, it unfortunately happened that the ill-fated officers had been accustomed to Bengal lascars, and probably had a very imperfect idea of the danger to which they subjected themselves by continuing towards their Malay crew a treatment which the Bengalees endured without retaliation.

This is the case which is the subject of a chapter headed " An English ship taken by Malays" at page 293 in Mr. J. T. Thomson's " Life in the Far East," but the name of the ship was not given.

The following Proclamation was issued in Singapore on 6th September. The three settlements were placed directly under the Supreme Government of India instead of under the Presidency of Bengal, constituting, practically, a separate presidency like Madras, Bombay and Bengal :—

Fort William, Home Department, the 1st August, 1851.

PROCLAMATION.

Whereas the Hon'ble the Court of Directors of the East India Company have by Virtue of the power vested in them by Sec. 21 of the Act 6 Geo IV. cap 85, been pleased to declare that the settlements of Prince of Wales' Island, Singapore, and Malacca shall cease to be subordinate to the Presidency of Fort William in Bengal, and have invested the Governor of the said Settlements with the powers heretofore exercised therein by the Government of the Presidency of Bengal, subject to the control of the Government of India, it is hereby notified for general information that from and after the first day of September next ensuing, the Governor of Prince of Wales' Island, Singapore, and Malacca will exercise those powers of local administration in regard to those settlements which have hitherto been exercised by the Government of Bengal.

The *Free Press* in November contained the following paragraph :— " During the past week the police have been informed of three men having been killed by tigers. It is estimated that at least one man is taken daily by tigers in this small island. The Government some years ago reduced the reward for killing these animals from $100 to $50, because they seemed to be then pretty well extirpated; but although they have again increased to an alarming and destructive extent the Government reward still remains at the minimum. Experience has shown that the reward of $50 for each tiger killed is not sufficient to tempt natives to devote themselves to tiger hunting in Singapore. Government ought therefore to try whether a higher reward will not lead to this. If it appeared that rewards of $150 or $200 had induced a number of natives to take up the trouble of rendering themselves expert in slaying tigers, the amount might then be reduced, and it would probably be found that 50 or 100 dollars was a sufficient inducement to the hunters to continue their search for tigers. At present the loss of life caused by these ferocious animals is really shocking, and we must say that it is a disgrace to a civilized Government that more urgent measures are not adopted to put a stop to it. We are aware that Government has caused traps to be constructed, but this is not sufficient, they must by the offer of a high reward induce more active means to be taken for ridding our jungles of tigers."

In November, Colonel Butterworth, after being eight years Governor of the Straits, went to Australia for the benefit of his health. A number of addresses were presented to him at the Government House where Fort Canning is now, from the Chamber of Commerce, the Consuls, Chinese merchants and others. In replying to that from the Chamber of Commerce, the Governor said that he owed his warmest acknowledgments to the Chamber for the terms in which his administration of the Government had been noticed by it, and that it had proved a great satisfaction to him to have such a body as the Chamber of Commerce to refer to in matters connected with the trade of the port, the entire freedom of which it had been his earnest endeavour most scrupulously to maintain. And among the passages in his reply to the Chinese was the following :—"I take the advantage of this opportunity to notice the obligation the Chinese community, and the public generally, are under to Seah Eu Chin for his management of the Pauper Hospital, which involved great responsibility, pecuniary and otherwise, prior to the establishment of the present very efficient Committee, one of whose members, my friend Tan Kim Seng, is at the head of this deputation. I commend to the special attention and liberal support of the Chinese community, the aforesaid institution, founded by Tan Tock Seng, whose premature death prevented his endowing it, as he had proposed, with funds sufficient for the maintenance of a given number of its inmates."

The Tumongong of Johore was absent at the time the Governor left, but his sons also presented an address, to which the Governor replied expressing his regret at the absence of the Tumongong, and his acknowledgment of the ready help he had always received from him in the suppression of piracy. Colonel Butterworth left in the British barque *Penelope*, 344 tons, for Adelaide, and returned by the P. & O. steamer viâ Ceylon in November, 1853, having been away for two years. Mr. Blundell, the Resident Councillor of Penang, officiated during Colonel Butterworth's absence, but remained in Penang, Mr. Church, the Resident Councillor, being in charge at Singapore.

The following is an account of the opening of Kim Seng & Co.'s new godowns in Battery Road, which are those that were occupied by Hamilton Gray & Co. for many years, later by Stiven & Co.

"Baba Tan Kim Seng, Justice of the Peace, one of the most wealthy and influential of our Chinese merchants, celebrated the completion of his new godowns in Battery Road, by entertaining the European community and his native friends with a ball and supper. The offices which occupy the upper floor of the godowns, were the scene of the entertainment, the front room overlooking the river being fitted up as a dancing saloon; and so admirably adapted did it prove, that we feel sure many of Kim Seng's fair guests regretted that so spacious and airy an apartment should ever be put to any other use. Dancing commenced soon after 8 o'clock, and was continued with great spirit until midnight, when the company sat down to an elegant supper at which the host presided, who welcomed his guests in a short but expressive speech which elicited thunders of applause from his audience. Kim Seng's health was proposed by

Mr. Thomas Church in appropriate terms and drunk with the greatest enthusiasm by his guests. Dancing was renewed after supper, and kept up until the small hours. So perfect were all the arrangements of this truly elegant entertainment, that it will not easily be forgotten by those who were present. The band, consisting of more than twenty performers, was brought from Malacca expressly for the occasion. Nor were the native friends of the host forgotten, some of the side rooms being laid out with tables of refreshments suited to their varied tastes, but they seemed to be chiefly occupied in gazing on the lively scene that was passing before them. The variety of costumes among the spectators added much to the striking appearance of this truly cosmopolitan assemblage."

In the 5th volume of Logan's Journal, published in this year, there is at page 254 a most curious and amusing description of the Durian fruit, there spelt Duryœn, translated from Linschottens's Voyages.

Mr. Jonas Daniel Vaughan settled down in Singapore and the Straits in this year. He had first passed through Singapore in January, 1842, when he was a midshipman in the East India Company's Steam Frigate *Tenasserim* on her way to China. He was engaged in all the naval actions to the end of the first China War, and the frigate then carried the despatches of Sir Henry Pottinger to the Governor General of India at Calcutta, announcing the peace concluded at Pekin at the end of that year. Mr. Vaughan then served on the Straits station as an officer of the Company's armed steamer the *Phlegethon* from September 1845 to the end of 1846. He was at the capture of the city of Brunei, and the destruction of the forts and strongholds of the Lanun pirates in several rivers on the north-west coast of Borneo, under Captain Rodney Mundy, afterwards Admiral, who mentions Mr. Vaughan in his book. He afterwards became Chief Officer of the Company's war steamer *Nemesis*, the "Fighting *Nemesis*" as she was called.

In 1851, when at Canton, he was offered by Colonial Butterworth, the Governor of Singapore, the appointment of 1st Officer of the *Hooghly*; afterwards he was Superintendent of Police at Penang, and he held it until June 1856. Then he was removed to Singapore as Master Attendant. From 1861 to 1869 he was Magistrate of Police and Assistant Resident Councillor, and in September of that year he retired from the service and practiced as an Advocate and Solicitor of the Supreme Court. During his absence on leave in England, he had, in June, 1869, become a barrister of the Middle Temple. For a short time he was acting as one of the Puisne Judges of the Supreme Court at Singapore.

The cause of Colonel Butterworth having sent to offer Mr. Vaughan the post in Penang was greatly to his credit. When passing through Singapore in 1842, he liked the place and set to work to learn Malay, which he afterwards knew very well and could read and write fluently. Colonel Butterworth came across him at Government house, and learned that the young man wished to come to the Straits; and seeing his knowledge of Malay, offered him the appointment, when he had the opportunity to help him.

Mr. Vaughan was a man of considerable ability. He wrote a good deal of useful matter in the newspapers in former days, and occasionally acted as editor for a time when others were absent, and with an unselfish object, for newspapers in those days did not allow of any pecuniary return. He wrote a very long and interesting paper on the Malays of Penang and Province Wellesley in Logan's Journal for 1857, at page 115. He also wrote a work on the manners and customs of the Chinese of the Straits Settlements. He was a good singer and musician, and a capital amateur actor, indeed he had remarkable ability in that direction. One anecdote may be told of this.

In December, 1866, when the community was much smaller than it is now, and the English and Germans mixed together a great deal in social life (though the Germans had their own Club and the English had the Tanglin Club as at present) the Germans had arranged to play a comic travesty of one of the old operas, and some English were to play a farce to fill up the programme in the Town Hall. It was for Tan Tock Seng's hospital. The morning before it was to take place, the Manager of the Chartered Bank, who then joined in Amateur Theatricals, went round to a clerk in the oldest mercantile house in the place, and told him that there had been a hitch about the farce, which the English had promised to play, so the Germans were dropped into a hole. This was to be avoided at any cost. After a hurried talk, the two went off to the Police Court and saw Mr. Vaughan, who said he knew of a farce for four people; two men, a lady, and a servant girl. In those days ladies never appeared on the stage, and it would doubtless surprise those of the present day to see how readily and successfully the female characters were played by young men. Costume and paint go a long way, if they can only remember to take short steps. Mr. Vaughan said he had to play an old London cabman, which it was clear would be very funny in any case. A fourth amateur was found in the Accountant of the Mercantile Bank. Mr. Vaughan sent to the house to ask his wife to send down the little book, and by eight o'clock all had roughly copied their parts. Farces in those days lasted about 25 minutes, just long enough to make people want to laugh more; and were not spun out, as they are now, for two hours or more, on no more material than then sufficed for the half-hour.

There was a rehearsal at Mr. Vaughan's house at 8 p.m., another the next morning early, and again at tiffin time in the Square in the tiffin room in the Bank, and lastly on the stage at 5 p.m.; and it was played with very great success that night. Mr. Vaughan had a very long, large, white beard which he tucked into a buttoned up great coat and put a great woollen comforter round his neck. The husband's dress was only ordinary clothes and false whiskers, and the two female costumes were easily fixed up with the help of two ladies, as amateur theatricals were common in those days. At the rehearsal it was found that there was a difficulty because the lady of the house (Chartered Bank) had to change her dress, and he declared it was impossible to do it in the time allowed in the dialogue. Mr. Vaughan said he need not hurry because there was some luncheon on the table in the piece, and there could be something real to eat, and he and the servant girl could easily fill up the time. Accordingly they sat down in the absence of the mistress, not far from the footlights, and their gravity was much upset by hearing a remark by Governor Cavenagh, who was sitting in front, that the servant girl would get very drunk on the sherry; for it was well known that the individual in girl's clothes never drank anything but water, and does not to this day. The bottle had been filled up with tea and water to the required colour.

The paper the next day said that the success of the little piece was not alone due to the skill displayed by each actor, but also to the way in which they acted together; that the costumes were particularly good on the female side; and the farce was a great success. It was a case of four rehearsals, and thirty hours notice, and it may be taken as a suggestion that rehearsing for weeks and months, as is done at the present day by amateurs in Singapore, till every one is sick and tired of the whole thing, may be no advantage.

Mr. Vaughan died at sea, when on his way back to Singapore in a small steamer from a trip to the Native States, on 17th October, 1891. He was missed in the morning, and it was supposed that he had been standing during the night at the side of the vessel and had slipped and fallen overboard. He had always taken a great deal of interest in the place and its affairs, and had spared himself no trouble in assisting in public matters, and his unfortunate and sudden death was very much regretted in the place.

There have been several sensational trials in Singapore, but that which caused a greater excitement than any, before or since, was a murder trial in February in this year. The prisoner's name was Hajee Saffer Ally; he was the Malay and Tamil Interpreter in the Police Court, and a man of great importance among his own class and beyond it. Inchi Abdullah wrote, and Mr. Keasberry printed, a book in Malay, containing all the story of the murder, with a very good portrait of Saffer Ally in the dock as a frontispiece, but it is not obtainable now. The facts, which were very curious, and the means of discovery, which were very romantic, were briefly as follows :—In September, 1850, a little Arab (slave) boy of twelve years of age, in Saffer Ally's employ, was found by a policeman in the road shockingly maimed, burned with hot irons, and wounded. He said he had been ill-treated by Saffer Ally and others, and had escaped. The boy was sent to the hospital, and by means (as was said afterwards) of a false uniform and a false letter, the boy was taken away from the hospital, after Saffer Ally and his eldest son, and four others, had been committed for trial. When the Assizes came round in October, the boy was not to be found, and Sir William Jeffcott, the Recorder, who seems to have had a suspicion of foul play, said that it was a most horrible case, and that the utmost endeavours must be made to find the boy; he refused to hear the case in his absence; and the prisoners were committed to goal, in default of finding heavy bail.

Saffer Ally, however, did get bail, and was at large on a certain evening, which fact was proved at the subsequent trial for murder, with some difficulty, as it was Saffer Ally's principal line of defence. However, it was at last proved beyond a doubt. Mr. Thomas Dunman, the head of the police, found that the boy had been taken in a sampan to Rhio, but brought back again, and then all trace of him was lost. A man who lived in a native house, only separated from the next one by a partition, heard a Kling man in the adjoining house, talking in his sleep, crying out that he had killed a boy. The listener went and gave information, and the Police learnt that the boy was likely to be found somewhere up the Singapore River. For two days the police rowed up and down, and at last observed a bad smell issuing from bubbles in the water which burst on reaching the surface. A peon dived down and eventually the whole body of the boy was found, with the head nearly cut off, the feet tied together, one rope round the neck, and another round the waist, made up into a kind of net-work, held down by a large stone. Then they found the boat, which Saffer Ally had borrowed (to carry some firewood, as he said) with all the boards blood-stained, close to his house on the river.

Dr. Oxley proved that the body was that of the boy who had been injured; Mr. A. J. Kerr the Registrar of the Court, Mr. R. C. Woods, Mr. Thomas Dunman, and many others, were witnesses at the trial, which was held before Colonel Butterworth, the Governor, Sir W. Jeffcott, the Recorder, and Mr. Church, Resident Councillor, in the building which is now behind the Government Printing Office. Mr. William Graham Kerr, book keeper to Martin Dyce & Co., was foreman of the Jury. The excitement was greater than had ever been known here, and although it rained heavily all day, an enormous crowd was congregated outside the doors all the time of the trial, which commenced at 9 a.m., and finished after nine o'clock at night; the prisoners charged being convicted. One of those concerned in the murder was made Queen's Evidence, and gave a circumstantial account of the murder, which was committed on the night of the great Hindoo festival. They were hung exactly a week after the trial, on the 21st February, 1851, at the (then new) gaol at the Sepoy Lines. Great preparations had been made to give much ceremony to the burial of Saffer Ally, but the Government, on Thomas Dunman's advice, refused to give up his body, and he was buried in the gaol, which grievously disappointed his friends, who deemed the absence of funeral rights as the heaviest punishment that could be inflicted. The body was buried secretly in quick-lime in the jail, as it was thought an attempt might be made to remove it, and the knowledge of the spot died with Mr. Ganno, the jailer, many years afterwards.

Thirty-four years afterwards, Saffer Ally's son, named Akbar Ally, followed in his father's steps, as a complete rogue, and was tried in September, 1885, for forgery; and the natives crowded the court inside and outside, as on his father's trial. The case was again a remarkable one, for the prisoner had been for years a clerk in a certain class of lawyers' offices, where such men can do a lot of villainy, as the natives appear to trust them more than their masters. It turned out, as the Chief Justice said, that it was only one of a whole series of frauds, carried on under the cover of his employment, in the most audacious manner. A Kling named Aaron Pillay, Tamil Inspector in the Supreme Court, had died about twelve years before, leaving a widow and three sons. His mother and his widow took out probate of his will. One son was a spendthrift and asked the prisoner to borrow money for him. The prisoner asked him

where the mother kept the title-deeds of his father's property, so the son
abstracted them, and a forged conveyance was made by the prisoner, who
forged the signatures of both the women. It was found out because the
mother had died two years before her signature was forged to the conveyance, but the prisoner had forgotten it! The case lasted till after dark,
and the prisoner was convicted and died in the Jail.

CHAPTER XL.

1852.

O N the 26th January a public meeting was held in the Singapore Reading Rooms to consider the necessity of the appointment of a resident local Judge in the Settlement. The reasons for this were explained in the *Free Press* as follows :—" From time to time for many years past, we have pointed out the serious defects existing in the provisions for the administration of justice at this Settlement, and advocated a remedy being applied, by the appointment of a professional Judge for Singapore. The community, we are glad to find, have now become fully alive to the evils of the present system, and on Monday last at a very numerously attended meeting of the inhabitants, called by the Sheriff, the subjoined resolutions on the subject were passed. The large fixed population of Singapore, and her valuable trade, would of themselves warrant the demand for an improved judicial system, but when we consider the very great number of persons who resort here temporarily for purposes of trade, and the large extent to which the interests of merchants at a distance are involved in the commerce of Singapore, the necessity for an efficient and expeditious administration of justice, civil and criminal, becomes the more apparent. We trust that the representations about to be made to the Court of Directors and Board of Control, will meet with early and favourable attention, and that such arrangements will be made as will allow of the appointment of two professional Judges in the Straits, thus putting an end to the present absurd and anomalous system, which in practice leads to such an irregular and imperfect administration of the law.

Proposed by Joaquim d'Almeida, seconded by John Harvey, and carried unanimously :—

That, considering the population of this island is estimated at 80,000 inhabitants, of which 60,000 are residents, and that the trade aggregates upwards of six millions sterling per annum, it is the opinion of this meeting that this Settlement is of sufficient importance to warrant an entire revision of the present arrangements for the administration of justice.

Proposed by Robert Duff, seconded by Charles Spottiswoode, and carried unanimously :—

That whilst they record with pleasure their appreciation of the zealous ability with which the Resident Councillor has hitherto discharged his arduous duties as Judge in Civil cases, this meeting feel that it cannot be expected that either he or his successors can, without detriment to their other important duties, conduct the increasing business of the Court with that satisfaction to the public which they might expect from a professional Judge.

Proposed by Gilbert McMicking, seconded by James H. Adams, and carried unanimously :—

That, though three criminal sessions in a /year, as now proposed, may be sufficient to meet the requirements of the resident inhabitants of this Settlement, yet, taking into consideration how often the ends of justice are defeated by the departure of prosecutors, which it is impossible to prevent, it is the opinion of this meeting that the services of a resident Judge are also in that department of Justice imperatively called for.

Proposed by W. H. Read, seconded by R. C. Woods, and carried unanimously :—

That, for the reasons already mentioned, it is the unanimous opinion of this meeting that the appointment of a resident professional Judge for this Settlement is of absolute necessity.

Proposed by Captain Sparkes, seconded by Wm. Paterson, and carried unanimously :—

That a Committee consisting of the Chairman, A. Logan, W. H. Read, and R. C. Woods, be appointed to embody these resolutions in a Memorial to the Hon'ble the Court of Directors and the Board of Control."

Nothing being done, another public meeting was held on 13th April, 1853, and it was decided to send a memorial to the Governor-General urging the immediate appointment of a Resident Professional Judge.

The paper contained the following notice of the death of Captain Elliot in August :—

"It is with much regret that we observe the death of Captain Charles Morgan Elliot, of the Madras Engineers, announced in the Madras papers. Captain Elliot resided for five years at Singapore in charge of the Magnetic Observatory, and subsequently made an extensive voyage through the Archipelago for the purpose of continuing his observations. The results of his labours were afterwards given to the world in the Philosophical Transactions of the Royal Society, which learned body testified their high sense of Captain Elliot's scientific character by electing him a Fellow. After residing some time in England, superintending the printing of his observations, Captain Elliot returned to the East for the purpose of continuing his magnetic pursuits and intended in the course of them to re-visit Singapore in 1853, for the purpose of revising his former observations. We are sure Captain Elliot's premature loss will be lamented by a very wide circle of friends, for wherever he went he secured to himself the attachment of those with whom he came in contact by his singularly frank and engaging disposition."

Captain Elliot was a younger brother of Sir Henry Myers Elliot, the Foreign Secretary to the Government of India; who came to Singapore with Lord Dalhousie as mentioned on page 527. Captain Keppel, Mr. W. H. Read, and Captain Elliot were great friends, and in his book "A Sailor's Life Under Four Sovereigns" Admiral Keppel mentions in volume 1, page 290, speaking of 1843, "visited Elliot at the Observatory." This was a building near Captain Elliot's house, which stood near the main road on the side of the Kallang

River, at the corner on the right hand side just before crossing the long iron bridge on the Gaylang Road. Part of the house is still standing, now occupied by the Chinese coolies of a saw mill. The observatory was a commodious shed, containing the usual meteorological instruments, with a tower, some 30 feet high, at a short distance, for observing the direction and velocity of the wind. A rain guage was also kept there, and the newspapers referred to the results of Elliot's observations for many years, as the only scientific records that had been taken. He was in Singapore from about 1841 to 1847, when he went to England and did not return. He was sent to Singapore for the purpose of laying down on the charts the position of Singapore and the surrounding countries by magnetic survey. All the neighbouring charts fifty years ago bore his name, and it is worth notice that he was very accurate, while the Dutch charts have been shown by the latest surveys to have been as much as four miles out at the southern extremity of the island of Lingga. Many years after Captain Elliot's death, an officer in the Royal Engineers, one of the sons of Charles Darwin, the famous naturalist, was sent to Singapore to lay down its position accurately and the telegraph lines were arranged to communicate at a certain moment direct through to Greenwich, which was the first chance of extreme accuracy for ascertaining Greenwich time. It was found that Singapore on the charts had been laid down a little over one mile out of its true position, which was considered remarkable under the difficulties of former days, dependent upon chronometers and observations. In the *Free Press* of 9th May, 1848, is an advertisement by Mr. J. T. Thomson that the house lately occupied by Captain Elliot on the banks of the Kallang River, surrounded by cocoanut trees, was to be let. It was described in the advertisement as most advantageously situated in the most thriving district in Singapore, and possessing excellent communication with the town both by land and water. In the appendix to vol. 3 of Logan's Journal there happens to be a description of the observatory, as Dr. Little and Captain Elliot were at cross purposes about the correctness of some of the thermometrical tables, and the controversy (from page xxxviii) is very amusing. Captain Keppel, when in the *Dido*, used to row up the river in his gig to see Captain Elliot. In volume 3 of Logan's Journal is an account of a voyage in one of the East India Company's steam cruisers in 1846, with Captain Elliot on board, to Borneo and Sarawak, when Captain Mundy took possession of Labuan. One of Sir Henry Elliot's grandsons, and a grand nephew of Captain Elliot, is now practising at the Bar in Singapore.

The Singapore newspaper reprinted this year from the *Madras Times* and other papers some observations on the P. & O. Company's treatment of passengers, including the following remarks of a military officer, who was many years in Singapore :—"I feel, for I know it is true, that the conduct of the P. & O. Company towards their passengers, is one of neglect and indifference. As long as they can obtain the present mail contract, they do not care one farthing about us or our comforts. For a rival company to start in England will be difficult, nay I consider impossible. It therefore must be a hopeless monopoly, the English Government helping, and we must bide our time. But I am of opinion that it is derogatory to the dignity of human nature to submit to be treated like a bale of cotton or a box of bullion. The passage in the Red Sea was made on the very ancient steamer *Oriental* having boilers completely worn out, at 8½ knots an hour."

In September, there was a large fire in Kampong Glam, of which the paper gave the following account :—" On the evening of Thursday, the 16th instant, a fire broke out in 23, Arab Street, Kampong Jawa, at about 7 o'clock, which speedily spread among the attap and wooden houses in that quarter, rendering all attempts to check it in the outset unavailing. The Sultan's Mosque and a number of houses behind it were in danger at one time. The number of houses burnt amounted to 135, of which 101 were inconsiderable habited by Javanese, 21 by Malays, 8 by Chinese and 5 by Klings. The number of persons burnt out are reckoned at 1,500. A good deal of pillaging took place and several attempts were made to break into houses at a distance from the fire."

During a thunderstorm in the harbour the ship *Wigrams* was struck by lightning, but owing to her being provided with a copper lightning conductor she escaped damage. At the time when this occurred, two large cargo boats, laden with gunpowder, were lying alongside the ship, but fortunately they were not touched by the lightning and were immediately cast off and anchored some distance astern. There were no regulations then as to the storage of gunpowder. The attention of Government was thus directed to the subject. The *tongkangs* with powder on board used to anchor in the river.

On the 6th November, Syed Omar bin Ali Al Junied died at the age of sixty years. He had been in Singapore for 31 years and was one of the most respected of the native merchants. He was a native of Arabia, and carried on a most extensive business and realised a large fortune. He was a nephew of Syed Mahomed bin Haroon al Junied, who came from Palembang in the very early days of Singapore, and built the house in High Street, near where the Eu Chin family house is now, at the side of the river. His old house has been pulled down. He was buried in Syed Omar's cemetery at Victoria Street.

Syed Omar also came from Palembang and when his uncle Syed Mahomed died, he carried on the business, as Syed Allie bin Mahomed Al Junied, the son, was then only nine years old. Syed Omar bought the land at the southwest corner of High Street and North Bridge Road, and the house which he built is still standing. It was this Syed Omar that gave the large Mahomedan burial ground at Victoria Street which is generally known by his name, and he was buried there. He left five sons, but none of them are now alive, three died at Mecca and two at Singapore. There are about ten grandchildren now in Singapore. He also built the mosque at Bencoolen Street. His son Syed Abdulla built the mosque at Kampong Malacca.

Syed Allie bin Mahomed Al Junied lived in the house which was afterwards bought by the Eu Chin family, in High Street and carried on a large business in Singapore. He gave a large piece of land in Victoria and

Arab Streets to Tan Tock Seng's Hospital, and also gave the burial ground called Bukit Wakoff at Grange Road. He made all the wells behind Fort Canning, and at Selegie Road, Pungulu Kisang, and Teluk Ayer. They were very large wells, with granite sides, which the Municipality not long ago filled up and carried the granite away. This was a mistake, as the water near Fort Canning was very good indeed, with no houses near the wells, and in very dry weather it would have been a great help, to say nothing of destroying for no purpose charitable works which cost a good deal of money. The road called Syed Allie Road at Kampong Kapor was called after him. He bought it as a garden for Rs. 400 from Inchi Sidik, a Malacca lady, and he also bought about 70 acres of the adjoining swampy land. He died 44 years old, in Singapore, on 9th December, 1858. His estate was wound up by his son, Syed Allowie, the only survivor of his four sons, and he filled the land up by degrees, and formed Weld Road and Jalan Besar, while the Municipality built the three bridges at Bencoolen Street, Arab Street and Jalan Sultan at his expense. The land is worth now sixty or seventy cents a foot, and shop-houses on it let at $25 to $35 a month. The members of this family of Al Junied subscribed largely to the fund for building the present Town Hall.

Another old Arab family in Singapore is that of the Alkoffs. Syed Mahomed bin Abdulrahman Alkoff traded in Singapore with Java, and bought land and houses in Singapore when they were cheap. He had no sons, and his younger brother Sheik Alkoff came to Singapore, having inherited his estate, and traded. His son Syed Ahamed bin Sheik Alkoff, a man with very large landed property in the place, is in Singapore.

In the very early days of the Settlement an Arab named Abdulrahman Al Sagoff came to Singapore. He had gone from Arabia to Malacca, where he had traded, going in his own vessels to Java. He continued to trade from Singapore, and died at Grisseh, in Java, not far from Soerabaya. His son Ahamed married in Singapore one Raja Sitti, who was the daughter of Hadjee Fatima, a very well known Malay lady in Singapore, who was of a very good family of Malacca, connected with many of the Rajas in the Malay States in the Peninsula. She had married a Bugis Prince from the Celebes, the son of the Raja of those countries. She carried on a large trade, owning many vessels and prows, and it was only after her death that the business came to be called after her son-in-law, Syed Ahamed, being known by all Singapore as the business of Hadjee Fatima, although Syed Ahamed looked after it. Hadjee Fatima built a house in what is now known as Java Road, but was then country, in Campong Glam. It was twice attacked by robbers and set on fire, in the days when gang robberies were so alarming, as has been stated elsewhere. So after it was burnt a second time, she erected the present mosque on the spot, and built another house for her family. The mosque and several houses for the poor were erected in Java Road, and they are kept up by the family to this day, all the expenses for imaum and charity being entirely defrayed by the Al Sagoff family. Twice every year large feasts are held there at which several thousands attend, of all ranks and classes of the Mahomedan creed. One of these is held on the anniversary of the death of Hadjee Fatima, and the other on that of the birth and death (which both

occur on the same day of the year) of the Prophet Mahomed. Hadjee
Fatima died at the age, as her descendants believe, of 98 years.
Her son-in-law, Syed Ahmed bin Abdulrahman Al Sagoff, died in
Singapore a very rich man, having carried on a very large trade, owning steamers and sailing vessels. He was buried in the private burial
ground behind Hadjee Fatima's mosque. His son, Syed Mohamed
bin Ahmed Al Sagoff, still carries on business in Singapore, but
makes frequent visits to Europe, Jeddah, and other places, for the
sake of his health.

Another Arab merchant who was for many years in Singapore
and at one time owned several large trading vessels, and towards
the end of his life some steamers, was Syed Massim bin Salleh Al
Jeoffrie. He came with the nakodah of an Arab vessel, and saved
a few dollars on some of the voyages, with which he opened a small
shop in Arab Street and gradually made a great deal of money.
But times changed, and towards the end of his life, he became nearly
blind, and his business fell off, and he died in May, 1894, about
eighty years of age. He was very well known and liked in Singapore by many of the European community.

The Government made at this time eight pits and nine traps
for tigers in various parts of the island. In a pit at Serangoon on
Dr. d'Almeida's plantation a tiger fell into a pit 20 feet deep, and
succeeded in scrambling out again, although there were several feet
of water at the bottom. The son of the headman at the village of
Passier Reis was in the jungle cutting wood in January when he
was seized by a tiger. Hearing his cries, his father ran out and
found the tiger dragging him into the jungle. He grasped his son
by the legs and tried to drag him away, but the tiger kept his
hold, growling furiously, and it was only on several persons coming
up and assisting him that he let go his hold and ran into the
jungle. The unfortunate young man was quite dead when the tiger
dropped him. The newspaper in February said that a Chinaman walking on the road near Kranji was sprung at by a tiger, but escaped
by opening his umbrella in its face, and the tiger ran one way and
the Chinaman the other. On 14th May the *Free Press* said that
it had been usual to say in former years that at least one man a
day was killed in Singapore, but it seemed to be much exceeded
then, as no less than ten persons had been killed by tigers in the
Kranji district in the course of only two days.

On 15th March a public meeting was held to protest against
a tonnage duty being imposed, with a view to meet the expense of
maintaining the Horsburgh Light House. It was a repetition of what
had taken place in 1838. The first resolution, proposed by Gilbert
McMicking and seconded by W. H. Read, was : " That as this Settlement was formed with the intention that it should be a free port,
and as the East India Company have hitherto strictly carried out
such intention, and as no grounds of sufficient importance exists to
necessitate a departure from the liberal policy hitherto pursued—
this meeting is of opinion that on no account, except in a case of
most urgent necessity should the freedom which is so requisite for
the existence and prosperity of this port be infringed."

The proposal was afterwards modified, and the light dues confined to square rigged vessels only, and not charged to native shipping.

Another public meeting was held on 14th August, which expressed satisfaction at the concession, but still objecting to the duty on any vessels at all. The Act was twice amended, and in January, 1853, the *Free Press* said: "If the Government committed a mistake at first in framing the Act, misled by bad advisers, every honour must be accorded to it for the readiness which has been shown to rectify its errors."

In August, two gentlemen went after a tiger at Bukit Timah and one of them fell into a tiger pit 24 feet deep, but escaped with severe bruises and dislocations. The police then ordered marks to be put up near the pits, so as to give warning of their position.

On 21st October the Tumongong gave a large ball in the Assembly Rooms, and on the 26th Captain Marshall, the P. & O. Agent, gave a ball in the recently completed offices at New Harbour, in honour of that and also of the opening of the line from Singapore to Australia; the *Chusan*, 700 tons, having arrived from Australia, the first vessel on that line. The vessel lay close by, and was illuminated, and there was a display of fireworks on board. The paper remarked that the *Chusan* brought only a small quantity of gold, but it realised such a high price that large exports were expected to be made from Australia to Singapore.

At a meeting of the Chamber of Commerce held on the 23rd November, the following resolution was passed:—

"The Chamber of Commerce, taking into consideration the present lax and irregular system prevailing, unanimously resolves that none of its members shall henceforth sell goods of any description at a longer credit than Three Months."

This resolution was rendered necessary by the facilities which the position of Singapore afforded to defaulting debtors to make their escape from their creditors, facilities aided very much by the imperfect working of the Insolvent Court, the sole Judge of which was resident for much more than half the year at such a distance from Singapore as to render it impossible to obtain his aid in those cases of emergency which every now and then occurred.

On 14th December a public meeting was held to take into consideration the measure contemplated by the Government to abolish the dollar currency and substitute rupees as the legal currency in the Straits. George Garden Nicol was chairman. It was decided that it would be inexpedient and would injure commercial interests very seriously.

It was towards the end of 1852 that a meeting was held to establish a Singapore Cricket Club.

The firm of Hamilton Gray & Co. had been established in 1832. In 1846 the partners were Walter Buchanan, William Hamilton, and William Macdonald in Glasgow, and Ellis James Gilman and George Garden Nicol in Singapore. In 1853 John Jarvie was a partner. In 1855 Reginald Padday and C. H. H. Wilsone were clerks and afterwards became partners.

Mr. G. G. Nicol left the firm in 1860, and was for many years the Chairman in London of the Chartered Mercantile Bank of India,

London, and China, and a Director of the Eastern Extension and
Australia Telegraph Company, and of the London and Joint Stock
Bank.   He is frequently mentioned in this book; he died in England
on 16th January, 1897, at the age of 83 years.

The firm of William Macdonald & Co. started in 1852, the first
partners of which were Robert Duff in Singapore and William Macdonald
(who then left Hamilton, Gray & Co.) in Glasgow. In 1855 Garlies
Allinson became a partner and Farleigh Armstrong was clerk. In
1858 William Ramsay Scott was a clerk. In 1859 John Earn
Macdonald was a partner, and W. R. Scott in 1864. Mr. Whitworth
Allen was a clerk from 1859 to 1864, after which he went to Penang.

CHAPTER XLI.

1853.

FROM the beginning of this year the monthly P. & O. Mail was changed into a mail twice a month. The first left London on the 8th of each month, which came direct from Galle to Penang, Singapore and China. The second left London on the 24th, and went from Galle to Calcutta and then to Penang and onwards. The first was due in Singapore about the 15th of each month, the contract time being 38 days. The second about the 10th of each month, the contract time being 47 days. The homeward mails left Singapore on the 17th and 28th the first *via* Bombay and the second *via* Calcutta ; the contract time for both to Marseilles being 44 days. The steamers went on to Southampton. The passage money from Singapore to Southampton was $528, and it was raised soon afterwards, in consequence, as the advertisement said, of the increased cost of coal, &c., to $600, equal at the exchange at that time to £142.10. The delay occasioned by the steamer going round *via* Calcutta caused so much delay that the two mails arrived very near each other, and this was avoided in 1857 by the mail being transhipped at Galle. The P. & O. Company opened their office in Singapore at this time. Mr. Henry Thomas Marshall was the first agent, with John Say Sparkes as a clerk.

In January, Mr. Lewis Fraser of Maclaine, Fraser & Co., who was then living at the large house on Campong Glam beach, returned to Europe. The following is an account of a ball given in his honour on the 21st : "During the week that has elapsed since our last issue, Singapore has been more than usually gay. On the 21st the Freemasons of Lodge 'Zetland in the East' gave a ball and supper in the Assembly Rooms as a farewell token of their regard for our townsman Mr. Lewis Fraser and his lady, who are about to leave the Settlement. The assembly was numerous, and the rooms were most tastefully decorated with various masonic emblems. The Military band was in attendance, and everything went off in excellent style. At supper, Mr. W. H. Read, the present Master of the Lodge, proposed the toast of the evening in a short but appropriate speech, and after it had been drunk with masonic honours as well as the hearty cheers of the uninitiated, Mr. Fraser made a suitable reply. After the company left the supper table, the dancing was resumed and kept up with great spirit to an advanced hour."

The following paragraph was in the paper in February. "It will be seen from the proceedings of the Municipal Committee, that a very great improvement is projected in Commercial Square, by the removal of the ugly wall which at present surrounds the centre of the Square, the widening of the road and introducing a good drainage. We should think all the proprietors and tenants of houses in the Square will at once give their assent to the measure, and we trust that ere many months elapse, the plan of the Committee will have been carried out."

In March the Governor-General sanctioned the erection of a screw pile lighthouse at the two and a half fathom bank in the Straits in place of the floating light, cost not to exceed Rs. 35,000; a lighthouse of masonry on the Coney Island, and also of fixed beacons on the Blenheim, Pyramid, and Bambeck Shoals.

In May, another of the cooly vessel piracy cases occurred, and was discovered by accident by a Kling boatman who was outside the harbour looking for in-coming vessels. He fell in with a vessel to the eastward of Pedra Branca which he was not allowed to board, but which he was informed by persons on board was an American vessel, with a crew of Manilamen, and that the Captain and the officers had been cut off by the crew. These facts were reported to the Police, but as no vessel was sent out by the authorities, who were under the impression that the ship had proceeded up the China Sea, the boatman again went out to the eastern entrance of the Straits of Singapore, and succeeded in falling in with the vessel near the place where he had first met her. This time he was allowed to get on board, and on being requested to conduct the vessel to Rhio promised to do so, but he brought her to anchor about ten miles on this side of Pedra Branca and on some pretence or other came to Singapore and reported that she was a cooly laden ship, and that all the officers and most of the crew were absent from the vessel. On this a merchant brig consigned to A. L. Johnston & Co., the *Rival*, Captain Franklyn, was induced to proceed in search of the vessel, and arrived in her neighbourhood about seven o'clock on the evening of Sunday, the 8th May. Captain Franklyn proceeded alongside in a boat and hailed the people on deck, requesting to be allowed to come on board, but this was refused. It was seen that preparations had been made for resistance, and Captain Franklyn was told if he did not keep off he would be fired upon, and he noticed that a man stood beside one of the guns with a lighted match in his hand. Captain Franklyn then returned to the *Rival* for assistance, and dividing his small party between two boats, again returned to the vessel, and boarded her at two points. The persons on board offered some resistance, but were driven back, and about twenty of the Chinese jumped overboard and were supposed to have been drowned. The rest were got below and a watch kept on board until day-light when the chain was slipped, and the two vessels being got under weigh they succeeded in reaching the harbour in the afternoon. During the night two attempts were made by the Chinese to rush on deck, but unsuccessfully On investigation it turned out that the vessel was Spanish, bound from China to Lima with 200 coolies. Her officers, who were English, had been murdered.

The following paragraphs are taken from the presentment of the Grand Jury in August, of which Mr. Thomas Owen Crane was the foreman. "The Jurors present the necessity of adopting stringent measures to detain witnesses in very grave cases until the trial of the prisoners, particularly where Hoeys are concerned, as the Jurors have reason to believe that the witnesses are frequently tampered with and disposed of, as the secret societies may think proper; consequently

defeating the ends of justice and encouraging crime. The Jurors beg
to recall your Lordships' attention to the oft-repeated complaint against
the dangerous and increasing evil of the secret societies, and urge the
necessity of ample authority being given to the Executive in the new
Police Act, to put down effectually the growing power of a body of
men, committing daily acts of daring violence and injustice, treating
with contempt the wholesome laws of a British Settlement, and likely,
if allowed to remain unchecked, to endanger seriously the peace and
safety of this community.

"The Jurors again present the impropriety and danger attending
the unrestricted sale of arsenic and other poisons in the bazaar.

"Having visited the Institution, the Jurors found the building
apparently in good repair, but the grounds are much in want of
efficient draining. They also examined the boys, and, as far as
time would allow, endeavoured to ascertain whether the system
pursued was adapted to the capabilities of the pupils. They see no
reason to find fault in this respect, but attribute the falling off in
the numbers attending, to the establishment of other schools and to
the distance the Institution is situated from the populous part
of the town. The Jurors therefore suggest that the present
building and the ground belonging to it, be let out on building leases and a school constructed in a more central position—and
they are of opinion that the Green in front of the Police Office is
an appropriate spot for that purpose. The Jurors beg here to record their regret that the state of education among the Natives is
not in a higher state of cultivation in this Settlement, and trust that
the Authorities will take such measures as will promote that blessing among those who are so much in need of it, and which is
the only effectual means of promoting civilisation and checking
crime."

In August, Mr. John Turnbull Thomson, the Government Surveyor,
left Singapore on sick leave, and did not return. The following
is taken from the *Free Press* of that month:—

"A meeting of the European community took place at the News
Room, for the purpose of considering the most appropriate manner
of marking their sense of the public services of Mr. Thomson, the
Government Surveyor, who is about to proceed to Europe on sick
leave. The meeting was the most numerously attended which we
have witnessed for some time past, and the strongest desire was
manifested to testify in the most unequivocal manner the public appreciation of Mr. Thomson's valuable services. The eloquent remarks
of Mr. Napier sufficiently showed what were Mr. Thomson's merits
in regard to the designing and erection of the Horsburgh Lighthouse, but he could have pointed to many more of Mr. Thomson's
undertakings, which show with what zeal and ability he has served
his employers, and how much Singapore has benefited by his labours.
Irrespective altogether of the duties of his office of Government
Surveyor, which we believe have always been discharged in a manner calling forth the approbation of his superiors both here and in
Bengal, Mr. Thomson designed and superintended the building of
the two Hospitals, which are certainly the most ornamental of our

public edifices; he also added a spire to St. Andrew's Church, designed and superintended the Ellenborough Buildings, threw the bridge across Kallang, renewed Presentment Bridge, and lowered and repaired Coleman's Bridge. Several of the longest lines of roads were executed by him, besides many minor public works. Not content with his labours on shore, in conjunction with the late Captain Congalton, Mr. Thomson made a very elaborate survey of the Straits of Singapore, which was laid down by him and afterwards engraved. He also surveyed the Seebu Channel on the East Coast of the Malay Peninsula and New Harbour in Singapore, both of which have been engraved by the Admiralty. Such are some of the works which Mr. Thomson has actually carried into execution, but in addition to these, numerous and important as they are, he has furnished plans and estimates for many others. The most important to the public of such plans are perhaps those for a screw pile lighthouse on the Two and a Half Fathom Bank, and for a light-house of masonry on the Coney. It will be matter of regret should anything occur to prevent the early return of Mr. Thomson to carry out these and other important public works, to which the experience he has now acquired would enable him to do such ample justice.

"It must be in the highest degree gratifying to Mr. Thomson, that he not only carries with him the best wishes and fullest recognition of his merits, on the part of the community amongst whom he has spent the last twelve years, but that the Government which he has so faithfully and effectively served, also acknowledge his varied services in the most ample manner. This will probably compensate somewhat for the absence of more substantial reward, from the hope of which, no doubt, the rigid rules of Government exclude their uncovenanted servants, however great their deservings."

In acknowledging the testimonial, a piece of plate, Mr. Thomson wrote from Edinburgh in November, 1853:—"It was with feelings of deep regret that I was forced away from so beautiful and pleasant a Settlement as Singapore, where I had passed the best part of my life, and to which I was bound by so many ties of frendship, but I trust that, if my health be restored, I may not be long absent."

Mr. Thomson went to New Zealand and was Surveyor-General at Dunedin. While at Otago in New Zealand in 1873, he wrote the Translations from the Hakayit Abdulla, which have been mentioned on page 28, with comments of his own. The book was published by Henry S. King & Co., London, in 1874, and in the preface he speaks of the ever recurring interest he had in Singapore. He made the translations from a copy he had been given by Abdulla himself, and the translation is remarkable as having been made eighteen years after Mr. Thomson left the Straits, and he had been away from any Malay-speaking people. Mr. Thomson, whose name should always be remembered in Singapore, died in New Zealand at the end of 1884. He had a large family of daughters, about ten, most of whom were married. His first cousin, Mr. Thomas Scott Thomson, has been a resident in Singapore since 1859.

Search has been made in the Survey Office to try to obtain information about the town in former days from copies of old maps.

There is one made in 1842 by Mr. J. T. Thomson, and it gives the names of the Streets in Campong Bencoolen as they were then. North Bridge Road, Victoria Street, Queen Street and Bencoolen Street are still called by the same names, but the present Waterloo Street was then called Church Street, and Prinsep Street was called Flint Street. The Mission Chapel is shown on it, as standing at the north east corner of North Bridge Road and Brass Bassa Road, and the Institution building consisted of three blocks with two narrower portions connecting them.

The next map is also by Mr. Thomson, dated 1842-3-4-5. The Post Office is shown near the river, where the Government offices now stand, and Tanjong Mallang is marked between Fort Palmer and Tanjong Pagar village, about where the sunken hulks are now at the eastern end of Tanjong Pagar Wharves.

The next is a map lithographed in Calcutta in 1857, also by Mr. Thomson. Waterloo and Prinsep Streets were still called Church Street and Flint Street. What was called the Mission Chapel in the former map, at Brass Bassa Road, is now put as the English Chapel. Commissariat Office buildings, showing a considerable size, are opposite the site of the present Ice House in River Valley Road. A large building called the new Court House is placed exactly where the present Library and Museum stand on Fort Canning Hill, but it can only have been a proposed building (like the suggestion to build a new Court House next to the Roman Catholic Church, as mentioned on page 265) for no building was commenced on that spot before the present Library. The Masonic Hall is marked at the house vacated by Mr. Church, at the corner of the Esplanade and Coleman Street.

There is also a map lithographed in London in 1854, in a very dilapidated state. It is interesting as showing exactly where the old Assembly Rooms were, and the size of the building, which had been sought for in vain for some time when writing this book. It stood at the corner at the foot of Fort Canning and River Valley Road; that is, at the north-west corner of Hill Street and River Valley Road, opposite the present Ice House, facing Hill Street, not far from the road. The plan shews that it was about 150 feet long by 80 feet wide, and had a portico in the centre of the front. It was built of lath and plaster and attap, open beneath, with a large room to the left as you entered, for a ball-room, dinners, &c., and a room for a theatre, with a well for the orchestra next the footlights, on the right hand side of the building. It was constructed under the superintendence of Mr. McSweeney. It had been proposed to have a Masonic Lodge, and a Public Library there also, but they came to nothing. The two large banyan trees which stood towards each end of the building are still there.

Another of Mr. Thomson's plans was lithographed in Calcutta in 1846, but it does not give any further information than those already spoken of.

Mr. Thomson took trigonometrically the heights of a number of the principal eminences of the ranges in the neighbourhood of Singapore town and vicinity, above the level of low water, at spring tides.

The following are some which can still be traced by the same names. They have been arranged here alphabetically. The first name was that used by Mr. Thomson, and the explanations added are a description from which the different places are likely to be identified at the present time, in 1902:—

Feet.

Broad Fields	75	(W. Paterson) Paterson Road.
Blaken Mati large hill or Bukit Serapong ...	301	
Bukit Chermin	106	(W. W. Ker) Keppel Harbour.
Bukit Timah	519	
Cairn Hill	113	Orchard Road.
Claymore	74	Burial Ground, Orchard Road.
Draycott	84	Behind Tanglin Club, Steven's Road.
Dunearn	75	Bukit Timah Road.
Government Hill	156	Fort Canning.
Green Hill	67	(Caldwell's) Chancery Lane, Thomson Road.
Guthrie's Hill	106	Tanjong Pagar Dock, entrance, Manager's House.
Institution Hill	121	River Valley Road.
Lady Hill	108	Between Orchard Road and Steven's Road.
Lessuden	72	Teluk Ayer, Chinese Club House.
Line Hill	124	Sepoy Lines, General Hospital.
Monastery	72	Keppel Harbour.
Monk's Hill	78	(C. Carnie), Bukit Timah Road, 1¾ miles.
Mount Elizabeth	82	Orchard Road, corner of Scott's Road.
„ Emily	135	Now Government House.
„ Faber	300	New Harbour.
„ Harriet	103	(W. W. Willans) part of Tanglin Barracks.
„ Palmer	119	Near Tanjong Pagar.
„ Sophia	108	Sophia Hill.
„ Victoria	100	(Almeida's) Steven's Road, corner of Almeida Road.
„ Wallich	144	Blasted to fill up Teluk Ayer Bay.
„ Zion	45	(Keasberry) River Valley Road.
Pavilion	108	(Oxley) Tank Road.
Peak Island	101	Near St. John's Island.
Pearl's Hill	170	Commissariat and Water Reservoir.
Rosemary Hill	115	Opposite Mount Echo.
St. John's Island	189	
Sri Menanti	81	(G. G. Nicol) Junction River Valley and Tanglin Roads.

The paper in April said that tigers were particularly destructive then in Johore, several persons being killed every day. And that the alligators in the Gaylang and Kallang rivers were doing much harm; even snapping at natives sitting in boats, and carrying off many ducks and fowls.

It was at this time that a number of Europeans abandoned the diggings at the foot of Mount Ophir where they had been led into the belief, possibly by the name, that gold would be found. Several of them died there, some were in the hospital in Malacca in April in a precarious state, and the rest were forced to leave through illness. The paper remarked that the gold obtained was trifling in quantity if any at all, and that no better result had been anticipated. The paper in the same month contained a long account of the prospectus for a large Dutch Company to work tin mines at the Carimons, which was expected by the Dutch to do great things, but resulted in much the same way.

The state of affairs in the Native States was thus alluded to in the paper in June :—

" There seems to be a spirit of anarchy and confusion reigning throughout many of the Malay States at present, which may probably lead to considerable changes ere long. Thus, in the north part of the Peninsula, we have the Rajah of Pera, apparently hard pressed by his rebellious subjects and obliged to send to his neighbours for assistance. In the south of Sumatra, we have the Sultan of Jambi reported to be at issue with his liege lords, the Dutch Government, the end of which will most assuredly be the annexation of Jambi to the N. I. territories in Sumatra. In the same quarter, the Sultan of Lingga is reported to be on terms of most bitter enmity with his hereditary Prime Minister, the Viceroy of Rhio, and as the latter lives under the protecting shadow of the Dutch, we suppose he has considerable confidence in defying his superior's anger. The Viceroy in a fit of piety lately shut himself up for six weeks, during which he meant to devote himself wholly to meditation and prayer, absolutely excluding all cognisance of sublunary matters. On the east side of the Malay Peninsula, we have the Bandahara of Pahang renouncing his allegiance to his lawful sovereign the Sultan of Johore, and asserting an independent position. His power, however, is said not to be of a very stable nature, as his subjects are discontented with his rule, and are only kept quiet through the influence of his father who, although he has renounced his power in favour of his son, still commands the respect of his former subjects. The Pahang potentate is on bad terms, too, with his neighbour the Rajah of Tringanu, and as the latter is supported by his relative, the Sultan of Lingga, a struggle between the two would probably be protracted and costly. The Tringanu chieftain, on the other hand, has his own peculiar anxieties. He has incurred suspicion of being piratically disposed, and although the Government of India has peremptorily refused to take notice of his delinquency, the question has not yet been finally disposed of and may still be again re-opened."

And in October the *Free Press* contained the following on the same subject :—" In another column we give the observations of the

Earl of Albemarle in moving for the correspondence relative to the seizure of a Chinese junk at Tringanu, and the murder of its crew by orders of the Rajah of that place. His Lordship has stated the case with great accuracy, although he has fallen into a few errors regarding the statistics of Singapore. Instead of a population of 200,000, our numbers only amount to 60,000, of whom two-thirds at least are Chinese. The export trade is not entirely in the hands of the Chinese, although they have a good share in it, but is largely participated in by the Europeans, the Bugis, &c. His Lordship has probably been led by mistake to attribute to Singapore the whole population of the three British Settlements in the Straits of Malacca, which is estimated at from 200,000 to 220,000. It would be pro- ductive of great benefit to British interests could attention be drawn to the present state of our relations with the different Malay states on the Peninsula of Malacca. These states might be made very valuable to commerce from the immense mineral riches they contain, as well as from the fertile soil which exists in abundance, admirably fitted for tropical cultures of all kinds. These resources at present are almost wholly neglected, the native population, under ignorant and generally debased rajahs, being little addicted to habits of in- dustry, the insecurity of life and property which prevails in these states destroying the motives to exertion. With proper management on the part of our government, and without directly interfering to any considerable extent with the internal government of these states, a great change for the better could be introduced. The proximity of the British Settlements would enable the government to exert such a moral influence on the rulers of these states that they would readily follow such a course as might be indicated to them. Some trouble might be found at first in teaching them the value of the advice tendered, but a judicious and patient representative of govern- ment would very speedily be able to bring them round to his views. No attempt of the kind has ever been made, our only mode of dealing with these states being, in general, utter neglect, and occa- sional threats and coercion when a powerful neighbour like Siam has required our interposition. The non-interference system, however, has been the favourite one of late years, and their determination to adhere to it, in all events, may be taken as the solution of the strange behaviour of government in regard to the outrage on the junk *Kim Eng Seng.* It is highly probable that other civilized powers may ere long acquire a knowledge of the value of the Peninsula of Malacca, and desire to possess a footing upon it, and our government will then find that it would have been wise to have obtained a wholesome influence over the neighbouring states, and to have been in a position to have practically in their own hands the power of de- termining whether it would be convenient to allow the establishment in their close vicinity of rival European or American settlements.

The following is an amusing account of a famous " head scare ;" in addition to what has been said on page 337 :—

" For about ten days past a most extraordinary delusion has prevailed amongst the native population, and especially the Chinese section. It is believed that the evil spirits which are said to have their abode in St. Andrew's Church, have lately proved so restless as to oblige the Europeans to desist from having public worship there and take refuge in the Court House. It is further believed that the only way of pacifying these evil spirits is to make them an offering of a large number of heads of human beings, and that the Government has therefore issued an order to the convicts to provide the required heads by way-laying and murdering unwary passengers at night! Absurd as such an idea must seem to any one possessed of common sense, such is the little knowledge which the great mass of the native population apparently possess of the European character and institutions, and the gross superstition with which they are leavened, that this notion has obtained very general credence and a great panic consequently prevails. People are afraid to go out at night, and the most extravagant reports are circulating as to the number of victims who have already been sacrificed, some go so far as to reckon them above thirty. The Government, with the view of allaying the excitement, some days ago issued a notice declaring these reports to be false, and offering a reward of five hundred dollars for the discovery of the persons propagating them. This measure would not appear to have been productive of the end desired, as placards were thereafter posted up in Chinese denouncing the Government notice as an attempt to throw dust in the eyes of the people, and hinting pretty plainly the propriety of adopting re-taliatory measures against the Europeans! Although it is not anti-cipated that any actual breach of the public peace will ensue, yet it has been deemed proper to take all reasonable means of allaying the uneasiness on the part of the native population, and amongst other steps we understand that orders have been given that the first class convicts, who are allowed to reside beyond the convict lines, must not quit their houses betwixt the hour of eight in the evening and five in the morning.

"Some of the more enlightened of our Chinese merchants have taken pains to disabuse their countrymen of the ridiculous impressions which have taken hold of them, and a Committee consisting of Messrs. Tan Beng Swee, Tan Kim Cheng, Tan Chin Seng. Seah Eu Chin and Hoo Ah Kay (Whampoa,) have prepared an address which has been signed by about thirty Chinese merchants, and which it is intended to have lithographed and distributed. The following is an abstract of this address, which, we believe, will prove interesting to our readers :—

"Reports have lately arisen about people being beaten to death at night, which are utterly false, yet they have obtained great prevalence, for it is the nature of such rumours that if one repeats them, a hundred persons believe them. These reports have, no doubt, arisen from thoughtlessness. A Chinese was lately beaten by some Malays when bathing at their well, this happened when these reports prevailed, and the occurrence was magnified and received as a confirmation of them, and they were therefore held as being quite true. At the moment when people heard this they did not reflect that Malays are not pleased that persons should drink or bathe at their wells; if it had happened at any other time it would have been thought nothing of. The Government issued a notice telling the people that such reports were false and unfounded. This notice ought to have been believed and respected, but instead of attending to it, how could you put up such improper placards? You do not think of the paternal and compassionate character of the Government, which even offers rewards for the destruction of the tiger which kills people. How then could the Government order people to be killed under the pretence that they were to be offered to evil spirits? The Europeans do not believe in evil spirits.

" The English law is that if a man commits murder he must be punished by death. If this is so, how is it possible that it could be so much violated as it would be by people being killed without their having been guilty of any crime? It you will only reflect on these things it will be apparent that these reports are all nonsense. To persist, therefore, in affirming such absurdities is very wrong. The Government of this country is very benevolent; much more so than that of other countries. The law for all classes and nations in this island is the same. It is not as in other countries, where there are different laws for the different sections of the population. In this port vessels can freely enter, and they are not obliged to pay any duties, but only to report themselves. Persons can also go and cultivate land in the country, and gain a livelihood without paying any taxes. The privileges which the Government allows to the people are they not very extensive and of long continuance? How can you then be so ungrateful as not to acknowledge this, but on the contrary to put up these improper placards? You are people without reflection! You do not consider how high are the Heavens, and how deep the earth! You say that the Europeans dare not go to their Church for fear of the evil spirits, but we know that this is not the reason, but because the Church is out of repair and therefore dangerous. It must therefore be repaired before people can go to it.

" Another report is that twenty or thirty persons have been murdered. You do not reflect that men are not small objects which can disappear without being noticed! Just let us know from what street or place in Singapore persons are missing and cannot be found? If none are missing it is quite clear none have been killed. Were it true we also would have heard of it. The result of all these foolish reports is that poor persons cannot earn their livelihood being afraid to venture out in the mornings and evenings. We also are Chinese and consequently cannot see these things without taking notice of them. We have therefore framed this address to remove the false impressions existing in the hearts of the people, and also to point out the impropriety of adopting such coarse and objectionable language as that contained in these placards. If any of your friends are really beaten or murdered, let us know and we will take you to the Authorities, who will investigate the matter, but if you bring us false stories you will incur disgrace and punishment."

It was in this year that the different flags were first used to distinguish the closing of the various mails :—Calcutta by a blue ensign; Australia, a white; Europe, a red; and China, a yellow flag; which have been used ever since except that to Australia.

There was a small outbreak in the gaol in July of which the following was an account in the *Free Press* :—

"On the evening of Sunday, the 3rd September, a number of the Seikh convicts confined in the Convict Gaol made an attempt to escape, which, as far as regarded some of them, was temporarily successful. About one hundred of these men, who are generally powerful, daring fellows, had contrived to arm themselves with sticks and billets of firewood, and suddenly made a rush upon the peons on guard, whom they knocked down. Thirty of these desperadoes, although in irons, contrived to get through the door of the gaol before it was closed by one of the peons who had been knocked down in the first rush. Those of the Seikhs who were still in the gaol were quickly overpowered by the other convicts, who did not exhibit the slightest sympathy with them, even the class of heavy defaulters, who are kept in irons, giving their aid with alacrity in securing them. The peons and others than gave chase to the run-aways, and soon overtook and secured twenty-seven, some of them receiving rather hard knocks when they would not surrender quietly. The whole have since been brought in. These Seikhs were forwarded from Allipore gaol and are described as insubordinate and dangerous characters. The ill-success which has attended their attempt to run away, and the severe punishment which it has brought down upon them, will, no doubt, prevent them from trying to make their escape for some time to come."

Piracy was still very frequent around Singapore, especially against the Chinese and other native trading vessels, and the Chamber of Commerce corresponded with the authorities and the Admiral of the station who promised to station a man-of-war at Singapore when he had one available.

The following is an extract from the Report of the Sailors Home :—

"So long as the number of Punch Houses continues so large, the Committee fear their efforts to preserve the improvident sailor from the pernicious effects of debauchery will not meet with such success as they would wish, but the gradual restriction in the issue of licenses to these haunts of vice by the Magistrates, leads them to hope that, by sure and certain steps, the object of their desires will be finally attained. Your Committee deem it right here to call the general attention to the low coffee houses and spirit shops in the out-skirts of the town, where there is but too much reason to fear the un-wary sailor is stupified by deleterious spirits, and unscrupulously rob-bed, and they hope that steps will be taken to mitigate this serious evil."

The Sailors Home had been commenced in High Street. An ac-count of it is on page 125 of Mr. W. H. Read's book. The Govern-ment paid Rs. 100 for the rent. The house became too small for the purpose, and the present premises, which had been occupied by Mr. Balestier, were bought in 1857, the Government advancing Rs. 12,000, or ten years' annual subscription, and the building was formally conveyed to Government as a security. When the ten years expired, it was formally returned to the Committee. The building was much enlarged by extending the two ends in 1877.

In September, the supply of rice for local consumption was thus referred to in the *Free Press*:—"Considerable alarm was felt some days ago on account of the small stock of rice in Singapore for local consumption, the great bulk of the article having been shipped for China, or at least bought for shipment to that quarter. The retail price also rose to a very high figure, being equal to $100 per koyan, while at ordinary times it never much exceeds $60 and is often considerably below that rate. This high price, we believe, still continues, although some further supplies have come in and more are expected. At one time it was calculated that there was not above ten days' consumption in the place. The population of Singapore, and at the Chinese settlement in Johore, which is wholly dependent on Singapore for their supplies, amounts to 100,000 at least, and calculating the daily consumption of rice by this number at one catty a head, a very moderate estimate, will give us 1,000 piculs a day. For our supplies of rice we are wholly dependent on other countries, not a single grain being grown on the island, and it will therefore be easily seen how important it is that nothing should occur to prevent the market being at all times abundantly supplied. Should the supply be interrupted through any cause, and become exhausted, there is no means of averting a famine, since the island, unfortunately, produces no other articles of food which could serve as a substitute for rice even for a few days."

The following passages are taken from an annual retrospect of the year in the pages of the *Free Press*:—

"Notwithstanding the existence of various circumstances which were calculated to exercise an unfavourable influence on the trade of Singapore during the year, such as the disturbances in China, the ravages committed on the native trade by pirates, &c., it is a subject for congratulation to find, from the returns, that our commercial prosperity continues unabated, and that the large increase which we had to notice in the trade of 1852 has been fully equalled by that in 1853. The trade of Singapore appears to be augmenting at the rate of one million sterling a year!

"During the year, a very large trade was carried on with Australia, and although subject to considerable fluctuations, as was to be expected from the extraordinary state of things in the Colonies, we have no doubt that the permanent trade between Singapore and Australia will in future form a very important item in our commercial returns. Prices of produce generally ruled high during 1853, and a very large demand existed for most of our staple products. Gutta Percha, in particular, which a few years ago was sold at $10 per picul, in consequence of the active competition, was at one time run up to the high rate of $75 per picul. Prices have since receded, but gutta still brings $30 to $35, and appears again advancing in price.

"The *prahus* from the eastward, comprising the Bugis traders, &c., arrived in considerable numbers this year. Those parts of their cargoes which consisted of articles chiefly adapted to the Chinese market, such as tripang, agar-agar, birds' nests, rattan and garro wood, &c., had to be sold at very losing rates, while the produce adapted for the Europe and Indian markets, such as gold dust coffee, oil, rice, wax, tortoise-shell, sago, gutta percha, &c., brought very remunerative prices.

"The revenue of Singapore during the official year 1852-3 amounted to Rs. 457,207, and the expenditure to Rs. 442,342, thus leaving a surplus of Rs. 14,865. In the expenditure, the charges for military and convicts are included. It would thus appear that the revenue of Singapore is advancing in proportion with its trade. The amount derived from the Revenue Farms (Opium, Spirits, Toddy, Market, Pawn-brokers, &c.) amounted to Rs. 340,089.

"The number of Chinese immigrants into Singapore during the official year 1852-3 amounted to 11,484. Towards the end of the year, large numbers of Chinese began to arrive in square-rigged vessels and junks. Many of these were from Amoy, and had taken part in the disturbances there. The rebels in that quarter are understood to have received very considerable supplies from Singapore, and more were on the point of being sent, when the news of their having evacuated Amoy reached this. Amongst the arrivals from Amoy were the wives and families of several of our most respectable Chinese merchants, and a number more are still expected. Should the practice of the wives and families of our traders following them from China hereafter continue, it may be expected to exercise a beneficial influence on the Chinese part of our population.

"In February, the draft of an Act was published to repeal that passed some time previously for levying tolls for defraying the cost and maintenance of the Horsburgh Light-house, &c. This draft made some desirable modifications in the manner of levying the tolls, and entirely exempted native craft, but it being considered that the rates proposed were unnecessarily high, and that they would unduly press upon the class of vessels called Straits Traders, memorials were addressed to the Governor-General in Council and by the Chamber of Commerce, praying for some modifications of the Act in these respects. To these representations a reply was received from the Supreme Government, promising to reduce the duty on Straits traders to one half of what will be exigible from other classes of vessels liable, and although refusing for the present to alter the duty as regards other vessels, yet distinctly pledging the Government to lower it, should experience show that the aggregate amount of duty levied is more than enough to meet what is legitimately chargeable to the lighting of the Straits. This promise and the resolution adopted by the Government to proceed without delay with the erection of other lights were considered satisfactory.

"A proposition was submitted to the Supreme Government to make the Company's rupee the sole legal tender throughout the Straits Settlements. This proposal was generally deprecated in Singapore, and the community were glad to learn that the Governor-General in Council had discountenanced the plan.

"During the course of 1853, the urgent necessity which existed for the permanent presence of a professional Judge at Singapore again engaged public attention, and the Grand Jury in April earnestly pressed the matter in their presentment. The Chamber of Commerce also addressed a Memorial to the Governor-General in Council on the subject."

The Governor and Mrs. Butterworth returned to Singapore from the Australian Colonies by the P. and O. Steamer on the 9th November, and were entertained at a Ball on 6th December, at what Mr. John Purvis was Chairman of the Committee, and Mr. T. O. Crane proposed the health of Mrs. and Miss Butterworth. The next week Colonel Cameron and the officers of the 43rd Madras Native Infantry gave a similar entertainment. In February the Sultan of Lingga had given a large fancy dress ball to the European community in the Assembly Rooms.

It was in this year that Miss Sophia Cooke came to Singapore. The Society for the Promotion of Female Education in the East had been extended to Singapore in 1843. It had been founded in 1834, the first Society for sending Woman Missionaries to the women of the East, and Singapore was one of its first Stations and was the last to be transferred, when the Society came to an end on the 9th January, 1900, to the Church of England Zenana Missionary Society. In Singapore the School has always been known as the Chinese Girls School, and perhaps better known as Miss Cooke's School, as she was so much respected in the work which she carried on for forty-two years. The work was begun by Miss Grant, who reached Singapore in 1843, and took over a School which Mrs. Dyer of the London Missionary Society had begun. In 1853, Miss Cooke came out. The house was built in 1861, and the School was supported by half-yearly sales of work sent out from England and of other gifts. For some years there was a mortgage on the building which was finally paid off about 1898. In September, 1895, Miss Cooke died in Singapore. Her name is still a household word with many in the place, as she did a great deal of work among the European Police force and Soldiers and Sailors. After her death Miss Ryan, who had been for very many years associated in the work with Miss Cooke, carried on the School for two years until November 1897, when Miss Gage-Brown came from England. In the beginning of 1901 there were sixty-two Chinese Girls in the School.

CHAPTER XLII.

1854.

THE following is part of a long account of a ball given in the Assembly Rooms on Monday, the 6th February, by Governor Butterworth and Mrs. Butterworth to commemorate the celebration of the thirty-fifth anniversary of the foundation of the Settlement :— "The ball-room was very tastefully fitted up, the principal decoration being a large transparency, representing, in one division, Singapore as it might be supposed to appear before it became a British possession, thick jungle clothing the whole landscape, and the only indication of the presence of man being one solitary fishing *prahu* in the bay, adding, if anything, to the feeling of loneliness and desolation. In contrast to this, the other division shewed us Singapore in 1854. The sombre jungle had disappeared and was replaced by the warehouses and residences of our merchants ; and Churches, Court-houses, and Schools told that order and civilisation had been firmly established, while the residence of the Governor, on the eminence overlooking the town, presided over the whole. Instead of the solitary *prahu* in the harbour, ships of every size and form, from the graceful clipper to the clumsy junk, and numerous native crafts, crowded the foreground, and completed the striking contrast. The whole was executed by Captain Dun, of the 43rd M. N. I., and does great credit to his taste and abilities as an artist. In front of the transparency a pedestal supported the bust of Sir Thomas Stamford Raffles, the founder of Singapore. Dancing was commenced at 9 o'clock, and at half-past eleven the company proceeded to supper, which was laid out in the lower room, where two long tables afforded ample accommodation to the whole of the guests. After supper the health of the Queen was drunk in the loyal manner which is characteristic of the Singapore community. Colonel Butterworth then rose and spoke nearly as follows :—

"'We are assembled here this evening to commemorate the formation of this Settlement ; and when we picture to ourselves what I daresay is remembered by the honourable gentleman opposite me, Mr. Purvis, as well as by my most highly esteemed and excellent colleague, Mr. Garling—whose signature I find attached to the first official document on the records of this Station, dated 6th February, 1819—I say when we picture to ourselves the appearance the island then bore, and contrast this with the aspect it has now assumed, we cannot but feel profound admiration of the consummate judgment and wonderful foresight displayed by that eminent statesman, whose name I mention with every degree of reverence and respect—Sir Stamford Raffles—a respect I propose to testify in a manner which I am sure will be as pleasing to this community, as gratifying to myself. I refer to my intention of designating the lighthouse, about to be erected on the Coney, at the entrance of the harbour—the "Raffles Light-house"—in memory of the Founder of Singapore. Here there have been no adventitious circumstances, such as the discovery of vast mineral deposits, or any very favourable agricultural results, to aid the advancement of this Settlement—nothing, in fact, but what that great man foresaw and foretold, when he selected this spot for its geographical position, and, stepping in advance of the age, pronounced it to be a Free Port—looking to its becoming the chief emporium in these seas for British merchandise, and the produce of the Indian Archipelago. How fully this has been realised, a glance of our 'Trade Statements' will satisfactorily shew. It will therein be seen that at the expiration of the first five years, the Imports and Exports were valued at two and a half millions sterling; that at the close of the next ten years they amounted to three and a quarter millions sterling, and on the termination of the subsequent ten years, to five millions; and by the last returns, to six and a half millions, exclusive of goods transhipped—an advance regular and unprecedented—whilst in place of the few *prahus* which might be seen in 1819, no less than 1,068 square-rigged vessels and 2,360 native boats visited this island during the past year. At the close of the last Chinese war and the opening of the five ports, the culminating point of the Singapore trade was stated to have been reached. Since then, however, it has increased by a million sterling. Again, on the establishment of the colony of Labuan, the like evil prognostications arose, but Singapore is now more prosperous than ever, the Imports and Exports being greater at the end of the last official year than at any time since the formation of the Settlement. Now, Ladies and Gentlemen, let me ask you to drain your glasses, in drinking to the continued prosperity of Singapore with Free Trade in its fullest integrity.'"

"Mr. Purvis then addressed the company as follows:—'I am very sure that nothing can be more gratifying to a large portion of this company than the very interesting speech of our worthy Governor, and I beg to assure Colonel Butterworth that the sentiments he has generously and warmly expressed on behalf of Singapore are duly appreciated. The hoisting of the flag, thirty-five years ago, is to all of us a matter of history, inasmuch as none of us were present on that interesting and auspicious occasion, but as a very few days more will complete the thirty-second year of my residence here, I may be said to have known the Settlement from its infancy, and when I look back to the day of my first landing here and contrast the then state of the Settlement with what it is at this moment, I do indeed see much to astonish me; for it must always be borne in mind that we have had no auriferous soils to fall back upon, or to aid us in our forward march, and yet Singapore had a hidden treasure which has happily developed itself in industry and intelligence! For it is to those sources, aided by a liberal system of Government, that Singapore is indebted for the proud position she now holds, and so long as that system shall be maintained, so long will Singapore continue to flourish and the Government be respected by every nation and people with whom we may hold intercourse. On a recent occasion I alluded to the 'true interests' of the Settlement, and I will now mention one of the most important. It is this:—To preserve Singapore in all integrity a Free Port! The principles adopted by Sir Stamford Raffles, he left as a legacy to Singapore for its rule and guidance, and as the Government are trustees to the bequest, I feel assured it will be faithfully carried out.'"

The following remarks in the *Free Press* in March, are worthy of notice in the light of the present day, and the progress that the Native States have made since Sir Andrew Clarke adopted the policy of assisting them :—"After Raffles and Crawfurd, we had a succession of officials who were either imbued with the prejudices and feelings of the higher authorities, or were of too little weight at head-quarters to induce any great degree of attention to their representations. They knew that the Supreme Government did not wish to have any trouble regarding the politics of a quarter so distant from the seat of Government, and they very dutifully shaped their line of conduct accordingly. Hence a course of utter neglect towards the Native States in our vicinity. These States have been steadily retrograding, and we have never made the slightest effort to arrest their decay, although it is very evident that a systematic and judicious interposition on our part might have told powerfully in promoting their welfare. The rich natural resources of these States have, therefore, remained utterly neglected, or only partially and most defectively availed of. And this has proved directly prejudicial to Singapore, for had these States improved in their resources, their produce would have been greater and their capability of consumption more extensive, and while their produce would have flowed into Singapore, to the same market they would have resorted for their supplies of those articles of luxury or utility which their own industry did not furnish, but which it enabled them to procure from elsewhere. In some cases the conduct of the Government has been even of a more reprehensible character. Witness the whole of the course pursued in regard to Keddah, which is so justly reprobated by Raffles in the extracts before us. In that case we not only refused that assistance to Keddah which we were bound by treaty to afford, but we actually joined with its ruthless oppressors in destroying it. The consequences have been that it has diminished in population and resources, that its government has been feeble, and that in place of benefiting us to any extent by its commerce and industry, it has only proved an asylum and hiding place for the bands of robbers who have for many years infested our territories in Province Wellesley. Everywhere else we find the Native States, which we have so completely neglected, feeble and despotic in their governments, their populations diminishing and their trade dwindling away. Yet in their fertile alluvial lands, forests abounding with valuable natural productions, and soils rich in minerals, might be found the sources of a solid prosperity were the energies of their inhabitants only stimulated by judicious encouragement from our Government, our relations with them so formed as to allow others to turn these advantages to account with a reasonable prospect of security to life and property."

This was the year of the biggest Chinese riots that have been known in Singapore, which upset the whole island for ten or twelve days. It arose between the Hokiens, from the province of Hokien in China, and the Teo Chews from the province of Quantung, because the Hokiens refused to join in a subscription to assist the rebels who had been driven from Amoy by the Imperial China Troops. We proceed to give an account of them at some length, with the proceedings that subsequently took place in connection with them. The riots arose, as they have done since, without any apparent cause, as the small dispute which commenced them was not, of course, the real *casus belli*, which originated in the proceedings of the Secret Societies, with a predetermination to fight out their quarrels in spite of the authorities. There were 400 or more persons killed, a great number wounded, and about 300 houses burned. The police force proved to be in good order and quite equal to what could be expected from their small number as compared with the thousands of Chinese. The military in the Settlement only numbered about 300 in all, and after providing for the necessary guards there were only 150 to 180 men available. The whole community turned out as special constables, and to them, as in after times, the return to law and order was principally due.

On Friday, the 5th May, about mid-day, a dispute arose between two Chinese, the one a Hokien man and the other a Macao man, about the weight of a catty of rice which the one was selling to the other. High words ensued, and the quarrel of each was quickly adopted by his countrymen among the bystanders. Blows followed, and the report being rapidly circulated through the neighbouring streets, the adherents of each faction came pouring in by hundreds to take part in the broil, which then assumed a very alarming character. The fighting spread into the adjoining streets, in all of which the shops were at once closed, and sticks, stones and knives were used freely on the streets, and bricks thrown from the upper windows whenever an opportunity offered of assailing their enemies on the street. Several shops and houses were broken into, rifled of their contents and the inmates maltreated, and the work of plunder once commenced would soon have become general throughout the town, had not the military made their appearance, after Mr. Dunman, the Superintendent of Police, had stated his inability to suppress the riot.

Governor Butterworth had, unfortunately, thought very little of Mr. Dunman's apprehensions, and, in spite of his remonstrance, mounted his white horse, and rode into the town. It was probably Hill Street near River Valley Road where he was pelted by the mob, who did not of course know who he was, and they had no quarrel with any Europeans; but he rode into the row, and had to retire, and a nephew of the Recorder, attempting to rescue a Chinaman who was being assaulted, was knocked down by a brickbat and badly hurt, and several others were roughly treated. The Governor then listened to Mr. Dunman's opinion, and the troops were sent for; when they came, quietness generally ensued, but, as they marched in a body, their effect was confined to one street at a time, and the fighting began as soon as they had passed. The Governor and Resident Councillor, with some of the Magistrates, also passed through several streets where the riot had been greatest, and, as might have been expected, their appearance was almost always followed by a cessation of the fighting and plundering, and, by degrees, the presence of the authorities and the soldiers produced an air of quietness which seems to have generated a great misconception of the true nature of the disturbances that had taken place. The troops were dismissed to their barracks, and as the Chinese do not like to fight in the dark, the evening passed over without any signs of a serious intention to renew the riot. Many flattered themselves that the affair was at an end, and that nothing more would be heard of it.

The following morning, however, was calculated to undeceive all those who thought that the Chinese had had enough of it the day before. They must have been busy organising themselves during the night, for in the morning with day-break the fighting and plundering began in different parts of the town, and, in spite of the Police, the shops and houses of many of the Chinese inhabitants were broken and pillaged. Wherever, in fact, a few of the one faction happened to have their houses or shops in a locality inhabited chiefly by the other, they were set upon at once, their goods either stolen or destroyed, and themselves severely bruised or wounded and in some instances murdered. A gentleman who was assisting in escorting the goods of a Chinaman to a place of safety was knocked down and severely cut about the face and head. The military were again called out, a corps of Marines landed from H. M. Ships *Sybille*, *Lily*, and *Rapid*, and although the troops were confined to marching in a body through the worst streets as on the day before, the presence of an armed force operated as a check upon the rioting, and during the day there was comparative quietness, the rioting being confined to desultory attacks upon passers-by in the streets. At ten o'clock a meeting of the European inhabitants was called for noon, and in the meantime a deputation of them waited upon Colonel Butterworth to represent the serious character which the tumult was assuming. His Honour thanked the European community for their co-operation, and said that every exertion would be used by the authorities to put an end to the disorders that had occurred, and that with the assistance of the Senior Naval Officer, he did not doubt they would quickly succeed in restoring quiet. He did not consider that the matter was so serious as was represented, and thought he could manage it himself; another error which, as the result proved, was a serious one.

At noon the Europeans met and determined to offer their services as special constables. They proceeded in a body to the Police Office, where they were met by the Governor and Resident Councillor. About seventy gentlemen, comprising the greater part of the European residents and a few of the commanders of merchant vessels lying in the harbour, were sworn in, Mr. W. H. Read being the first to be sworn; he has written an account of the matter in his book at page 95, in the chapter called " The Chinese Secret Societies." The Governor thanked them for the manner in which they had come forward to give their assistance and expressed his hopes that quiet would speedily be established. About fifty of the leading Chinese merchants and others were with some difficulty collected at the Reading Rooms, in Commercial Square, being escorted there by some of the special constables. They were addressed by the Resident Councillor, who exhorted them to use their influence in restoring order, and after some deliberation they signed a paper to that effect, but subsequent events proved that they either possessed very little command over their countrymen, or that they were afraid to exert themselves. None of the shops were open, and the Oriental Bank and all the godowns of the merchants were closed.

On Sunday, a strong body of the special constables was ordered to be on duty by 4 o'clock in the morning; and it was fortunate that this was done, as there were evident symptoms that an extensive system of depredation had been determined on for that day. Probably the Chinese calculated that the European community would observe their day of rest as usual, and not come into town at all, or only to go to church at 11 o'clock. As day-light began to dawn, it became clear to the gentlemen on duty that an extraordinary influx of people must have taken place during the previous day and night. The regular police were wholly knocked up with the work of the two previous nights and days, and the body of special constables on duty had almost the entire charge of the town. They were divided into parties, each numbering eighteen or twenty men, and headed by two Magistrates, and when day broke upon their patrols, appearances were anything but encouraging. Few Chinese ventured into the streets at first, but in Circular Road, the upper part of Market Street, Teluk Ayer, and other places in the vicinity, there seemed to be a complete ferment within doors. In some of these places the houses appeared to be crammed full of men, and all were convinced that but for the presence of the special constables, part of the town would have been pillaged, and not improbably burnt down by the hundreds of men whom the heads of the Secret Societies had called in from the jungles and the junks in the harbour. A little before six o'clock, an attempt was made to commence operations by plundering a house at the corner of Circular Road and South Bridge Road, but luckily one of the patrolling parties happened to be near, and were in time to prevent it, and to disperse the mob. Considerable rioting took place in Philip Street (where the rioters were armed with knives and swords), Market Street, and Amoy Street, where a party of seven special constables and four police peons took upwards of fifty of the rioters into custody.

Colonel Butterworth and the authorities now became thoroughly awake to the extent of the danger which threatened. All the *pukats* and other Chinese boats, which were swarming with men and afforded the most convenient receptacles for plunder, were ordered into the middle of the river to prevent communication with the shore, and seven boats belonging to the men-of-war were kept rowing about to prevent any attempt at landing, and other signs of more prompt action became apparent, should any further attempts at plunder be made. These measures and the attitude assumed by the authorities and European community appeared to frighten the rioters from any further serious attempt in town, and they then betook themselves to the suburbs and country in the vicinity. In the afternoon a party of Hokien men, who had been to procure rice, were attacked by some Teo-Chew men and robbed of their provisions; but the Hokiens having got a reinforcement from some of the plantations near, and accompanied by the Police, succeeded in beating their opponents, one of whom was killed. Ten or twelve of, the Teo-Chew men were taken into custody. The opium shop from which these men had rushed out was burnt down the same evening, probably by some of the Hokien men. About eight in the evening an armed party of Chinese with banners and gongs made their appearance at Rochore, defied the police to fight, and proceeded to break open and pillage the houses and shops of some of the inhabitants. The constables fired over their heads at first, but that having no effect the officer ordered his men to fire upon them before they would disperse. Two men were shot dead, and several were wounded. In the town all remained comparatively quiet during the night, both the Marines and Sepoys being posted in the town for fear of any outbreak.

The scene of operations appeared on Monday to have been fairly transferred to the country districts, and murder, burning and pillage prevailed in all directions. In the Tanglin district, a number of houses and *bangsals* were attacked and burnt, several persons were killed, and numbers wounded. In the Bukit Timah district the Police stationed at the village of Bukit Timah were threatened with an attack by a large body of men, and were at last so closely pressed that they were obliged, in self-defence, to fire upon the Chinese, several of whom were wounded.

Mr. Cluff, the Deputy Superintendent of Police, having proceeded along Thomson Road for some distance beyond the Police Station at Chan Chu Kang, to ascertain the state of matters in that part of the island, was met on the road by a woman who reported that her husband and child had been murdered and their house burnt down. She was put into Mr. Cluff's palankeen, and after proceeding a little further on the road three Chinese were met, whom the woman declared to be of the party which had murdered her husband. They were taken into custody by the Police. Several Chinese with arms were then met and apprehended, and Mr. Cluff returned towards the Station, but before he reached it a great many Chinese gathered round the small party and demanded the release of the prisoners, which Mr. Cluff refused, at the same time threatening to fire upon them if they continued to press so closely upon his party. The woman was then observed in the palankeen, and a rush made to get hold of her, the Chinese exclaiming that they must murder her also. The palankeen was much broken and battered in the attempt to get possession of the unfortunate woman, but Mr. Cluff at last succeeded in lodging her and his prisoners in the Police Station, which was an attap-covered building situated on the slope of the hill. Here the numbers of the Chinese rapidly increased, and they threatened to burn down the Station unless the prisoners and the woman were given up. Mr. Cluff at length thought it prudent so far to comply with their demand as to release the men who had been taken with arms in their hands, refusing at the same time to give up the others on any terms whatever. Having sent intimation of his situation to town, two Magistrates, with a party of troops and some special constables, were sent in palankeens to his assistance. Being joined by Mr. Cluff they proceeded to a village about a mile and a half beyond the Station, where the woman stated that the persons who had murdered her husband resided. On approaching the village a few of the special constables proceeded in advance for the purpose of drawing out the Chinese, and the latter were inclined to fall into the trap, but some Sepoys made their appearance at the moment, and the Chinese dispersed into the jungle, where they could not be pursued. Some houses belonging to the rioters were burnt down and the whole party returned to town.

In the Payah Lebar district, the persons belonging to the two tribes which chiefly inhabit that locality had entered into a compact that they would not molest each other, but the Teochew people violated the agreement by turning out considerable bodies and attacking the Hokien Chinese, who were taken quite unprepared as they relied on the engagement which had been made. A number of houses were plundered, several burnt to the ground, and the inmates killed and wounded. A large body went to the Station which had been recently established at the village of Gaylang, and told the Jemadar that they intended to burn the village, that if he did not interfere they would not harm him, but if the contrary, he and his party would all be put to death. The Jemadar refused to parley with them and on their attempting to attack the village, fired several times, after which the Chinese retreated. One man was killed and several wounded. All the Chinese *pukats* were that evening turned out of the river by a party of special constables.

On Tuesday, a number of houses were burnt in Tanglin, and persons killed or wounded. One of the magistrates on his way to town having learned that a party of some hundreds were advancing from Bukit Timah, immediately turned back, and assisted by four special constables and a few peons, Boyans, and Chinese, formed a barricade at the first Station on the Bukit Timah Road. They then advanced along the road towards Bukit Timah, and near Cluny encountered a large body of Chinese, armed, and having gongs and banners. This party was driven back for some distance, shots being exchanged with them. They, however, so greatly outnumbered the magistrate's force that the latter was obliged to give way for about one hundred yards, but Constable Berthier with a party of peons at this time came up, and thus reinforced they returned to the attack and succeeded in driving back the Chinese, who at last took shelter in a *bangsal* and some negotiations ensued. In the meantime, another party, consisting of a Magistrate, a number of special constables, and police peons, &c., went round by the hills and through the jungle. They met a very large body of Chinese, whom they repeatedly fired upon and at last forced to give way, some taking to the jungle, but the greater part retiring upon the other body of their countrymen, whom they joined in the *bangsal*.   Fifteen Chinese were killed in this affray, and many more must have been wounded.

A detachment of troops was sent out to help them, but being without a guide, missed its way and did not join the specials until the evening.   In the Payah Lebar and Siglap districts, the unfortunate Hokien people continued to suffer severely, their huts being everywhere burnt by their enemies, who murdered men, women and children.   The corpses in this and other localities were found in many instances frightfully mutilated.   A Magistrate with a party of fifty Malays, &c., went out to Thomson Road, from whence they followed a number of armed Chinese to near Serangoon, but owing to the obstruction offered by the jungle they did not succeed in bringing them to a stand.   Several prisoners were taken.   In the evening a party of forty Malays were sent to Siglap to reinforce the police. A party of some hundreds of Chinese, armed, and having flags, gongs and horns, attempted to pass the Police Station at the fifth mile-stone in Thomson Road, in the direction of town, but the Jemadar and police peons stationed there opposed their progress, and on their still persisting, fired several rounds upon them, when they retired.   They afterwards returned to within half a mile of the Station, but finding that the police were on the alert they did not attempt to advance.   One of the special constables, Mr. Rohde, an assistant in Apel & Co., who accompanied one of the parties, received a stroke of the sun, from the effects of which he died the same evening.

In the evening, at about seven o'clock, the Police were fired upon from a house in Church Street at a short distance from the Police Office, on which Mr. Dunman, Sitting Magistrate, proceeded to the spot with a party of Sepoys and having read the Riot Act, the house was fired into and then entered, a quantity of arms being found in it, and several prisoners taken.   One of the special constables, Charles Cashin, had the end of one of his fingers carried away by a shot from this house.   In the next house, which was also entered, a Chinese trader of some influence and standing was apprehended, there being a large quantity of arms in it.   At a later hour, some special constables detected a party of Chinese in the act of setting fire to a house in Teluk Ayer.   The greater number escaped, but about a dozen were apprehended.   In the course of the night two of the special constables, while on their way to Commercial Square, were fired at, one in Market Street, but they both escaped without injury.   During the night, a Chinese was found murdered in Circular Road.

The following proclamations were issued by the Government on the 6th and 8th :—

Several evil disposed persons having caused a disturbance between certain classes of the Chinese population, the Governor of the Straits Settlements calls upon all Chinese interested in the peace and quietness of the town, to aid him in putting an end to this feud.

With this object in view, all persons found fighting with sticks or throwing stones will be apprehended and punished according to law, and all householders giving shelter to such persons either directly or indirectly, shall be forthwith apprehended and prosecuted.

The Governor does not wish to resort to the aid of the military, but if these disturbances continue the parties concerned must abide by the consequences.

During the present disturbances in town, all junks now in the harbour must anchor in the position which will be pointed out by the Master Attendant, who has authority to cause the removal of all such vessels as thereby directed.

On Wednesday, the 10th, the disorder in the country districts still prevailed. It was resolved to despatch the steamer *Hooghly* with Sepoys and Malays to be landed at different points round the island so as to co-operate with the parties which had been sent out, and especially with a detachment of Sepoys under Colonel Cameron, which proceeded towards Buddoh, information having been brought in that the Chinese had collected in force near that place. Colonel Cameron and his party therefore started by land, and the *Hooghly* left in the afternoon. It had been reported that the Chinese were on the town side of Buddoh, and it was intended that the party from the steamer should land at Buddoh and take them in the rear, while Colonel Cameron attacked them in front. It turned out, however, that the information was defective, as Colonel Cameron reached the convict lines at Buddoh without seeing any sign of the rioters. Here he was joined by the party from the steamer, and the convicts having stated that the Chinese were to be found further on, the party proceeded. The road about two miles beyond Buddoh was over a hill, and on the crown of this a barricade was found, placed across the public road so as to effectually stop all passage. It was not quite finished, but it was apparently intended to be made of considerable strength and was protected by an attap roof. No one was on the watch, or considerable resistance might have been offered. Colonel Cameron, who was on horseback on the right flank of the detachment, caught sight of about one hundred and thirty Chinese apparently waiting for dinner. For a minute they appeared stupified at the appearance of the military, and then bolted into the jungle in all directions. The soldiers came up at a run and immediately opened fire, but the jungle came so close up to the spot where the Chinese were found, that they were out of sight in a moment. Only four men were made prisoners. The place where the Chinese were found had a very large attap roof over it, apparently intended for a house which would hold some hundreds of people. Close to it was a new Chinese house made of wood, fitted up in a very neat style, with all the usual accompaniments of a Chinese dwelling, such as an altar, joss, &c. This, it is supposed, was the residence of the leader of the party. In a corner of the large building was found a kind of cage, consisting of two stories, and very strongly constructed, probably intended as a receptable for the more valuable plunder. A larger boiler was found full of rice, which was being cooked, and there was an abundance of fowls, pork, &c., besides two large barrels of arrack. A little further on, on the opposite side of the road, a new house was met with, surrounded by a strong stockade about twelve feet high, and from this and another hut near it, a number of Chinese were observed to flee into the jungle. The whole of these buildings were burnt down, and the stockade across the road having been destroyed, the party returned towards Singapore.

The following proclamation was issued on the 11th :—

The Governor of the Straits Settlements calls upon the Chinese to remember that the British Authorities are placed in this Country to afford protection to all classes, to whatever sect belonging, whether engaged as merchants, traders. shopkeepers, gardeners, gambier-planters, or coolies, from whom nothing further is required than to obey the Laws. and not disturb the peace of the community with their private quarrels, as some of them have been doing of late.

These people must fully understand that this is not their country, and they must learn to attend to their own business, instead of molesting each other by going about the country to destroy the houses and property of their neighbours, and that if they continue in the perpetration of these outrages, they must expect to be treated like madmen.

The authorities have not, and will not take part with any sect or class of Chinese, but they are determined not to permit fresh disturbances to take place, and it is therefore hereby notified by the Governor of the Straits Settlements that all persons found committing acts of violence on their neighbours or their neighbours' property, or assembling with arms in their hands, will be hunted from place to place, until they are taken or destroyed.

W. J. BUTTERWORTH,

*Governor of Prince of Wales' Island,
Singapore, and Malacca.*

On Thursday quiet prevailed in town. Business was being fast resumed, many shops were opened, and the handicraftmen steadily at work. From the country, the different parties landed from the *Hooghly* at Changi, Serangoon, Thomson Road, and Kranji, returned to Singapore. The Changi division came upon the remains of the stockade destroyed on the previous day by Colonel Cameron, which was still burning. The party which landed at Kranji found the Chinese gathered in force with arms, and about twenty armed Chinese having fired at them, they were obliged to return the fire. Two men were seen to drop down dead and one man was wounded in the arm. The headman of the village and some others were captured and brought to town. The people at the village said they had armed themselves, as they were afraid, having heard that the Hokien men were going to attack them that evening. This statement was so far corroborated by the fact that letters had been received in town from parties in the village in which the anticipated attack had been mentioned.

The other divisions did not meet any opposition. The whole of the roads radiating from Singapore to different parts of the island were thus traversed from one end to the other, and with good effect, as the Chinese are described to have been quite surprised at seeing these large parties of armed men approaching them from the back of the island. The Malays are said to have behaved very well under the European gentlemen by whom they were accompanied.

It being reported that the Chinese were again assembling at the *bangsal* in Bukit Timah Road, where they had come to a stand on Tuesday, the detachment of military stationed in that quarter, accompanied by a Magistrate and some special constables and peons, went to the spot. The Chinese, however, had retired, but having found extensive preparations for feeding a large body of men, an ox stolen from a neighbouring plantation having been slaughtered and great quantities of rice boiling, as well as arms and ammunition, the place was burnt. Twenty-two prisoners were taken.

In the morning, Constable Berthier proceeded to Siglap with ten peons, and when near Doctor Little's bungalow, a Chinese reported that his friend had been killed at a hut near the bungalow. The constable proceeded to the spot, and found that the man had been killed by a sword cut across the face. Another Chinese gave information of another man having been murdered, and this corpse was also seen by the constable. The person who was said to be the leader of the gang by which these murders were committed was captured. It being stated that the band of Chinese who had plundered the district of Gaylang lived about two miles from Mr. Caldwell's residence, Constable Berthier, accompanied by Dr. Little and some other European gentlemen, proceeded in that direction. As they approached Mr. Caldwell's house they met eight or ten Chinese, most of them armed with muskets and spears. They said that they were running away because a gang of plunderers had threatened to burn their property. They were sent to Dr. Little's bungalow. As they approached the *bangsal* in which the guide said the band was concealed, they came upon about thirty Chinese armed with spears, two of whom carried flags. The party fired upon them, when one fell, and it is believed that several more were wounded. The man who fell was taken up to be conveyed to the house but expired on the road. Another man was taken who had been hit on the head slightly. Both of these men were identified by the guide as having been of the party which had burnt his house and murdered his brother. In the *bangsal* a quantity of arms were found, and from its whole appearance it was supposed to have been a refuge of the plunderers. and was accordingly burnt down. The party then returned to Siglap and from thence to town.

In the evening about half past five o'clock a Bugis ran *amok* on Boat Quay, and stabbed no less than six Chinese, some of whom received very severe wounds. He then threw himself into the canal opposite Mr. Purvis' godowns, where he took shelter beneath the bridge. He was repeatedly called upon to come out of the water and give himself up, but refused, saying he wished to die and they had better shoot him where he was. As he was armed with a kris which he refused to surrender, and the tide was running up very strongly, rendering it difficult to approach him in a boat, the police were at last ordered to fire upon him, but although thirty or forty shots were aimed at him, none of them appeared to take effect, and he was at last captured, after being severely wounded, while in the act of getting ashore, having swum a considerable distance up the canal. He was taken to the hospital, where it was found he had received twenty-three sword wounds, but not one bullet had touched him. He died shortly after 10 o'clock.

On Friday, a Chinese was found murdered near the foot of Government Hill. Two Malays were also murdered by Chinese in the Payah Lebar district. Several parties of armed Chinese were seen in this district and chased, but took refuge in the jungle, where. for want of guides, it was found impossible to follow them. A large force was reported to have assembled in the jungle, between the Serangoon and Gaylang Roads. Four detachments of Sepoys, each of twenty men, were stationed on Thomson Road near the fifth mile stone, in the Tanglin District, in Gaylang at Dr. Little's bungalow, and on the Bukit Timah Road at the house of Mr. M. F. Davidson, still called Dalvey.

On Saturday morning a Chinese was murdered in the Tanglin district. The police tried to beat the jungle between the Gaylang and Serangoon Roads, but all the paths were found to be obstructed by trees being felled across them, the logs, by which the swamps are crossed, removed, &c. In various districts, besides burning down the houses, the nutmeg, cocoa-nut, and other fruit trees were cut down by the rioters.

The riots subsided, after having lasted for ten or twelve days, and murder, fire-raising, robbery, and wanton destruction of houses, plantations, gardens, and fruit trees, having happened daily during that time.

There was great uneasiness at Malacca, all kinds of rumours being propagated there about what was occurring in Singapore. The Secret Societies in Singapore wrote to Malacca inviting their friends there to commence a riot, but without effect. A public meeting was held at the Residency. Mr. J. H. Velge in the Chair, and resolutions adopted calling on the Government to take immediate steps to prevent similar disturbances there.

In Johore, there was some trouble, as the coolies were short of rice, the supplies from Singapore being temporarily stopped, as all trade was suspended.

The lock-ups and gaol were crowded with prisoners, about five hundred men having been arrested, and a special sessions was held on Tuesday, the 6th June, before Colonel Butterworth, Sir Wm. Jeffcott, the Recorder, and Mr. Church. The following were the Grand Jury :—

Michie Forbes Davidson.—*Foreman.*

José d'Almeida.	William Stewart.
James Mottley.	Walter Scott Duncan.
Dunjeebhoy Hormusjee.	Henry M. Simons.
John S. Scrymgeour.	William Martin.
Clement Fabian Demée.	John Purss Cumming.
Cachick Moses.	William Mactaggart.
John Jarvie.	John Russell.
John Purvis.	F. Geo. Schmidt.
Thomas Owen Crane.	Leopold Catteaux.
Reinhard Rittershaus.	M. G. Mackertoom.
Charles H. Harrison.	A. James Spottiswoode.

The following are a few passages from the remarks to the Grand Jury made by Sir Wm. Jeffcott about the riots :—

" These people had hitherto lived peaceably together, transacting business with each other and living intermingled in the same streets. Without any apparent cause, however, a spirit of discord appears suddenly to have arisen amongst them, which on the 5th of May last broke out in acts of violence, riots occurring in different parts of the town, and at length resulting in houses being attacked and plundered. This state of things continued for seven or eight days, although after the first three days the rioting in town gradually diminished. The police were incessantly employed, the military were called out, and the marines landed from the ships-of-war: and with a most praiseworthy alacrity, the European inhabitants came forward and offered their services as Special Constables and had afforded most valuable assistance in preserving order, for which they were entitled to the gratitude of the community.

"After the first two days, the disturbances spread into the country, where, his Lordship regretted to say, they assumed a very different character. The riotous proceedings there were much more serious and aggravated, and quickly led to the plundering and burning of property, and eventually to the destruction of life and the committal of excesses of every kind of the most barbarous nature. The Grand Jury could easily understand how this difference should have taken place. While in town the people are comparatively civilised, the mass of the population in the jungle consists of men who have never for any length of time come in contact with Europeans or with the more orderly part of the town residents, and who live in a state of secluded semi-barbarism in the jungle, with little or no idea of what law or order is. When, therefore, the disturbances spread amongst them, they naturally plunged at once into far greater excesses than had characterised the town population, and the consequence was, that for a series of days the rural districts were the scene of the most lamentable outrages—huts and villages being burnt down in every direction, and murders committed, many of which had come to their knowledge, while it was to be feared many more had been perpetrated but remained unknown. Another cause, perhaps, of the different character which the disturbances in the country had assumed compared with those in the town, might be found in the fact that while in the town the two parties were nearly equal, in the country one of them had a great preponderance, and had the other party in a great measure in their power."

The Sessions lasted seventeen days. Six men were sentenced to death, but only two were executed; sixty-four were sentenced to various terms of hard labour, and eight were transported for fourteen years. There were about two hundred and fifty prisoners tried.

In this year the Indian Council introduced a Bill to make the anna and pie of the copper currency in India, legal tender in the Straits for fractions of a rupee. The intention was to force out the dollar, and make a rupee currency; and for this purpose the Treasury in Singapore were told to substitute the rupee for the dollar in their payments, which was partially carried out from May to the end of the year, at the exchange of Rs. 220 per $100. The *Free Press* remarked on this as follows:—"The present Bill is but a step further in the same direction, and it behoves the community of this place, as well as the two other Straits settlements, to lose no time in offering their determined opposition to the progress of these mischievous and most ill-judged measures. We dare not hope that much regard will be paid to any remonstrances that may proceed from this, but it is due to the community itself to record its decided opposition to these measures, both in principle and detail, and the doing so will also prevent an argument which would otherwise certainly be brought up, when the future and still more decisive steps are to be taken, that they had tacitly acquiesced in the change. A public meeting has been called for this day to consider the subject, and we sincerely hope it may result in unanimous and firm representation against such causeless and wanton tampering with the life-blood of our commerce—the circulating medium."

The rupee was first coined in 1835, and declared a legal tender throughout the territories of the East India Company, which included the Straits, but had no special reference to them. In 1844, the copper currency was extended to all the territories, but it never became actual currency in Singapore.

The dollar, which had been the coin of commerce in the Archipelago for centuries before we obtained any footing in it, became by necessity the circulating medium in English places when they were established, and it has continued ever since to be the *real* currency of the Straits Settlements. Subsequent to 1835, the dollar fully retained its place, and, so far as the Straits were concerned, the two Indian Acts of 1835 and 1844 were a mere dead letter. In 1847, the then Government of India (acting with rather more enlightenment than their successors in 1854), accepted the state of things which they saw was unavoidable, and as the want of an authorised copper currency to represent the fractions of a dollar, had long been productive of great inconvenience, and had led to the introduction of copper tokens or doits (manufactured by private individuals and of varying inferior value), coined in the Indian Mints the cents, half and quarter cents of a dollar for Singapore, and passed the Act of 1847 declaring them to be the *only* legal copper currency of the Straits. These coins quickly superseded the former tokens and doits, driving them entirely out of the market, and formed the only copper currency of the Settlement both legally and actually.

In this year therefore the Company's silver rupee was by law a legal coin in the Straits, but it never was used. The dollar was the only silver coin current in the Straits, and by the law of custom it was also a legal coin. The Company's cent, half and quarter cent, were actually and also by force of law, the only copper currency. No one was dissatisfied with this state of things. It worked well, and the commerce of the Settlement throve under it. The only thing desired was that the Hon'ble Company should coin a dollar of its own, with half and quarter dollars, and do away with some inconveniences which arose from the want of silver of a smaller denomination, but no one in the Straits desired to get rid of these insignificant inconveniences by the use of the Rupee.

In this state of matters, this Bill was brought forward to effect the following alterations :—

First.—The dollar and the rupee were to remain as before—both legal coins.

Second.—The cents of a dollar, and half and quarter cents, were no longer to be the *only* legal copper currency.

Third.—The Company's pice, double pice, half pice and pie, were to become a legal copper currency along with the cent and its parts.

Fourth.—Each of these two copper currencies was to become a legal tender, not only for fractions of its own representative in silver, but also for the other silver coin. That is, cents were to remain a legal tender for fractions of a dollar, and were to become a legal tender also for fractions of a rupee; and pice and pie, besides becoming legal tenders for fractions of a rupee (which at that time they were not in the Straits), were to become also a legal tender for fractions of a dollar."

A public meeting was held on the 13th October, at which the following resolutions were passed:—

Proposed by W. H. Read, and seconded by T. H. Campbell:—
"That this meeting regrets that the former representations which have been submitted to the Bengal Government on the subject of the currency have not met with the attention and consideration to which, it is submitted, they were entitled, and it deprecates the introduction of the Company's Rupee as an unlimited legal tender, at a fixed rate, as injurious to the trade of the Settlement, and as inexpedient and impolitic under any circumstances."

Proposed by J. Jarvie, and seconded by W. Mactaggart:—"That this meeting objects in the strongest manner to the introduction of the copper coins at present current in continental British India, as cumbersome and totally unsuited to the requirements of the Straits Settlements, and opposed to the system of decimal currency now in the course of being introduced into Great Britain, and at present existing in this Settlement."

Proposed by M. F. Davidson and seconded by Mr. Allinson:—
"That this meeting recommends that a petition embodying the previous resolutions be laid before Parliament, and that the following gentlemen be appointed as a committee to draw it up:—Messrs. Purvis, Jarvie, Read, Logan, and Guthrie.

A petition was drawn up to the Legislative Council of India, and the following is the substance of the letter sent with it to the Governor:—

"For many years past (and in regard to Penang and Singapore, it may almost be said, since their commencement) the currency of the Straits Settlements has been the dollars of 100 cents. Considerable inconvenience was occasionally experienced from there being no regular copper currency, the want of it, in Singapore at least, being supplied by tokens or doits, imported from England, and which had a very extensive circulation over the Indian Archipelago, having a varying value of from 360 to 600 to the dollar. In 1847, however, a convenient copper currency was furnished by the Indian Government in the form of a cent, half and quarter cent, and these have since been found perfectly adapted to the purpose required, the only matter of complaint being an occasional short supply. These coins are not only the exclusive copper circulating medium of the Straits Settlements, but have obtained a considerable currency in various Native States in the Archipelago.

"The Supreme Government has proposed at different times to introduce the Indian currency into the Straits Settlements, but has refrained from carrying this into effect in compliance with the strongly expressed opinion of the inhabitants against it. During the course of last year, the subject was again revived, but although all classes of the community were found decidedly opposed to the introduction of a rupee currency into the Straits, the Supreme Government has so far persevered in its intention as to make it imperative that all payments from, or sums received by, the local treasuries should be in rupees. This experiment has fully confirmed the unfavourable anticipations which were formed regarding the use of the rupee as a circulating medium, it having produced much general inconvenience and inflicted serious loss on those parties who, from their position in regard to Government, have been obliged to accept payments in rupees.

"The rupee and its fractional parts, whether of silver or copper, we are convinced, will never become acceptable in these Settlements as a circulating medium, and any attempt to force them upon the community by legislative enactment cannot be too strongly deprecated, as it will, without doubt, seriously injure trade and give rise to very general inconvenience. The decimal system of currency and accounts has long been established in the Straits, and has been found greatly to facilitate commercial transactions. To introduce the rupee as the legal currency, would involve a complete change in this respect (for a double currency, so totally dissimilar as the dollar and rupee, we are convinced, would not be found compatible) and would be an abandonment of a system, the superior advantages of which are now so fully recognised and which it is so anxiously sought to introduce into Great Britain and other countries where a different one now prevails.

"If the Supreme Government, instead of imposing upon these communities a currency which meets with general disapproval and which can only be productive of serious evils, were to issue a Company's dollar, and fifty, twenty-five and ten cent pieces (similar to those coined by the Bengal Government in 1787 for Prince of Wales' Island) a boon of the greatest value would be conferred on these Settlements and (with the present copper currency of cents, half and quarter cents) as perfect a monetary system as could be desired, would be established.

"Not only, moreover, would this currency be of the greatest value to the Straits Settlements, but we have no hesitation in asserting that it would be found highly profitable to Government, as the dollar, and half dollar at least, would become popular not only over the whole of the Archipelago and adjacent countries, but would, in the opinion of the most experienced merchants, in a very short time become the chief circulating medium of European commerce in China if not of the whole Chinese Empire."

The question of the currency and of a British dollar for the Straits, continued to be agitated for some time, and caused great discussions in the Council in India. In England the old veteran Governor John Crawfurd, with a number of old Singaporeans, including Messrs. Nicol, Guthrie, Gilman, Fraser and Paterson, waited upon the Board of Control, and went a long way to convince the mind of the President; and on the receipt of the advice of their proceedings, a public meeting was held here on the 11th August, 1855, with Mr. James Guthrie in the chair, at which a long list of resolutions were passed, copies of which were sent to all the Chambers of Commerce in any way connected with the Straits, and petitions were sent in January, 1856, to both Houses of Parliament. Mr. Crawfurd took the matter up *con amore*, and the petition to the House of Lords was taken charge of by Lord Albemarle, Admiral Keppel's brother, by whom on Monday, 21st April, 1856, the following notice was given :—

"The Earl of Albemarle to present a petition from the European, the Chinese, and other Asiatic merchants of Singapore, remonstrating against the introduction by the Government of India of a novel and highly inconvenient currency instead of a long established, convenient, and satisfactory one; thereby throwing confusion into the commerce of that and the associated British Settlements in the Straits of Malacca."

The petition to the House of Commons was placed in the hands of Mr. Gladstone, and the *Free Press* remarked that it was hoped the Court of Directors would be convinced, by the steps that had been taken, that Singapore would never submit to having the barbarous monetary system of India (—1=16=12—) substituted for that (1=100), which had so long prevailed!

The Earl of Albemarle gave a very admirable explanation of the views of the mercantile community here, and state· the case with much ability. On the 1st July, 1856, another public meeting was held, Mr. W. H. Read in the chair, and a number of resolutions were passed, among which were the following:—

Proposed by J. d'Almeida, and seconded by R. Padday:—"That the manifest advantages of the dollar over the rupee currency having been thus clearly demonstrated by experience, this meeting earnestly urge the Supreme Government forthwith to coin a Company's dollar, and the sub-divisions thereof, in silver, of the intrinsic value of the Mexican dollar, say, 416 grains troy of silver."

Proposed by A. J. Spottiswoode, and seconded by W. Howard:—"That the respectful and cordial thanks of this Community be tendered to the Right Honourable the Earl of Albemarle for the deep interest he has evinced in the Straits Settlements, and for the eloquent address to the House of Lords in which he so ably exposed the evils entailed by the attempted alteration in the currency."

The result was that the Bill did not pass, and the dollar continued to be the legal tender in the Straits, as it is to this day. The mercantile community gained their point, which was a vital one for the commercial interests of Singapore.

The Chamber of Commerce then attacked the Government on the question, and in January, 1858, the Grand Jury, with Mr. John Harvey as foreman, in their long presentment, spoke as follows of the matter:—"The Grand Jurors take occasion here to refer to a subject which has been frequently pressed on the attention of the Government by the inhabitants of this Settlement, viz., the propriety of establishing a Mint at Singapore, and the Grand Jurors are persuaded that such an establishment for the coinage of British dollars, half dollars and quarter dollars, in silver; and cents, half cents, and quarter cents in copper, would be found most profitable to the Government, at the same time that it would eminently conduce to the increase of its trade, and to the extension of commerce generally, throughout the neighbouring countries."

And the following was part of the letter of the Recorder, Sir Richard McCausland, sent into Government, as usual, expressing his own opinions on that passage of the presentment:—"The pressure upon the poorer classes arising from the scarcity of decimal copper coins, with which they are familiar, has long been felt, and loudly complained of; and so long ago as August, 1856, hopes were held out by the Hon'ble Mr. Allen that this should speedily be removed, yet the evil has ever since continued in an increased degree. With respect to the establishment of a Mint at Singapore, the coinage of British dollars with their subdivision in silver, would greatly increase the trade of Singapore with all the ports and islands of the Eastern Archipelago. The constant demand for a supply of silver in the East, as the circulating medium, would always keep it at a price that would amply repay the expenses of a Mint and the cost of coinage, whilst the very fact that British money could be procured for their produce would act as an incentive to the Native traders to resort in greater numbers than ever to the port of Singapore, and would add considerably to the moral force and prestige of the British name throughout all the neighbouring states and countries."

To which the Governor, Mr. Blundell, replied as follows :—" The Government Mints, both at Calcutta and Madras, have been directed to do all in their power to remedy the evil complained of in the want of copper cents and fractions of cents, and the subject of establishing a Mint either here or at Hongkong is considered to be under reference to High Authority in England."

And in May the Secretary to the Government of India wrote to the Governor here :—" I am directed to acknowledge the receipt of your letter No. 27, dated the 23rd ultimo, forwarding a memorial from the Chamber of Commerce at Singapore on the subject of the deficiency of copper coins in the Straits Settlements, and referring to your previous letters relative to the suggestion that a supply of cents and fraction of cents be obtained from private Mints in England, and that a Mint be established at Singapore for the coinage of dollars and fractions of a dollar.

" *2nd.* In reply, I am desired to inform you that the question of establishing a Mint in Singapore was referred in April to the Hon'ble Court, who informed this Government in reply that they had been in communication with the Lords of Her Majesty's Treasury on the subject ; that Sir John Bowring had recommended the establishment of a Mint at Hongkong, and that the subject was still under the consideration of Her Majesty's Government, promising to address this Government again when the decision of Her Majesty's Government was made known to them. A further communication will be made to you when the determination of Her Majesty's Government is made known to this Government by the Hon'ble Court."

In September, 1858, the *Free Press* contained the following article :—
" We learn from the China papers that the Lords of Her Majesty's Treasury have rejected the proposal of Sir John Bowring to establish a Mint at Hongkong for the coinage of British dollars. The reasons for this rejection are :—1st, that British sterling money has been adopted as a standard of value at Hongkong, and that to substitute a silver standard would render it necessary to re-adjust the rates at which the dollar should be received in payment of duties, &c.; 2nd, that Sir John Bowring has greatly under-rated the cost at which a dollar could be coined; 3rd, that the benefits of the measure would only or chiefly accrue to the merchants of Shanghai if successful, while, if it failed, the cost would fall upon the revenues of Great Britain ; 4th, that the evils complained of might be solved by any united effort to adopt the Mexican dollar as the recognised measure of value and medium of exchange, and that there is no fear of the supply of the Mexican dollars failing.

" The Treasury seems to be aware that British sterling money can never become current in this part of the world, but it nevertheless refuses to give a British standard coin, regarding the success of which there can be no reasonable doubt, and prefers to leave the vast commerce carried on by its subjects in China and the Eastern Seas dependent for the supply of a circulating medium upon a distant foreign state. On this point the *North China Herald* well remarks :—The

supply of Mexican dollars may be at present unlimited, but we have
no security that this will continue, and as little that the coin will be
maintained at its present purity. Both of these contingencies are
more than possible; we know that Brother Jonathan is, as he would
say, "Bound to have Mexico one of these days," and even if this
much coveted morsel should be long delayed, nothing will seem more
natural to a Spanish-American Republic than to debase a coin for
which there exists a great demand. Let either of these occur, and we
are landed in all the evils formerly occasioned by the scarcity of the
Carolus dollar, and that too at a time when our relations with China
will probably be vastly more extended than they are now. At present
the Mexican dollar comes to us by way of London, with very heavy
charges in the shape of commissions, insurances, and costly overland
freight. Most of this would be saved by having a Mint on the spot, and
the Sycee silver would afford a large supply of the material for coinage."

In September was commenced the enquiry connected with Rajah
Brooke and the pirates, which, though it had nothing directly to do
with the history of Singapore itself, was a matter of considerable consequence to the place, and drew a great deal of attention in other
places to the Settlement and the conduct of the residents.

In 1849 the London *Daily News*, the organ of Mr. Cobden and
his party, being misled, commenced an attack upon Sir James Brooke,
misrepresenting the operations by Captain the Hon. Henry Keppel and
the Rajah as a brutal war of conquest, waged against tribes who were
not at war among themselves; and asserting that the Sarebas and
Sekarran pirates were innocent traders, and that the Rajah was using
the English Navy for his own private ends. In September, 1849, the
Free Press remarked that there was such a coincidence, even in words,
between the statements in the *Daily News* and the Singapore *Straits
Times*, that there could be no doubt they were both derived from the
same source. In February, 1850, the *Free Press* spoke of the reckless
misstatements and fictions of the Singapore correspondent of the *Daily
News*, to which no credit was given by the Government officials, or by
the merchants of Singapore.

In July a Court of Enquiry was held in Singapore on board H.
M. S. *Hastings*, the flagship of Admiral Austin, C.B., on an officer of
H. C. S. *Nemesis*, a doctor, for having furnished information to the
Straits Times, relative to the proceedings on the coast of Borneo in
March and April, 1849. It terminated in the officer's favour; he himself, and the officers who gave evidence, saying the statements contained in the communications to the *Straits Times* were false and calumnious
and denying all knowledge of them. The inference was that the statements were concocted in the office of the newspaper; but the reason
for doing this did not transpire for some time.

In August, 1850, the London *Times* reported that Mr. Drummond
in the House of Commons had spoken of Henry Wise (who was a
dismissed and discredited agent of Rajah Brooke) as having been an
anonymous slanderer of Sir James Brooke for the preceding three years,
and as wanting to turn Labuan and Sarawak into a means for his
own aggrandisement, and to make Sir James a jobber with him
in the promotion of a Company.

In a long article in the London *Times* of 23rd July, 1852, on the subject of the debates in the House of Commons about the Borneo pirates, it spoke of its having been the fashion to impute the inevitable slaughter that had occurred, as having been attributed by those who attacked Rajah Brooke, to the deliberate malignity and unbounded appetite for blood of the Governor of Labuan (Sir James). It went on to say that the whisper of private enmity soon increased to a public cry, and the manœuvres of a dismissed and discontented agent. It said that Pamphlets had been concocted, and a Clergyman or two incited to rouse the sympathies of peace meetings in favor of the pirates. It had turned out upon enquiry that the flotilla that had been attacked was manned by a set of as pitiless ruffians as ever sailed upon the sea, and the fact had been clearly established. And after referring at length to the facts in vindication of the Rajah's character, and quoting statements made in the debate, and remarking that Mr. Hume had made himself the common cesspool into which every slander against Sir James Brooke might be poured, and that a wicked and infamous libel, written by Mr. Wise, had been put into the hands of every member of the House ; the article in the *Times* concluded as follows :—
" Mr. Hume, as will be seen by reference to his speech allowed himself, unconsciously no doubt, to be made the organ of conveying Mr. Wise's misstatements to the House. But this is not all. It was stated in the House last night that Mr. Wise had falsified Sir James Brooke's journal. Even twisted from its real meaning, what has been made out ? One single act of trading on the part of Sir James Brooke ? Not one. Twelve years have elapsed since he left this country. The real fact is that so far from having been a gainer, Sir James Brooke has diminished his private fortune [The *Times* might more correctly have said had spent his whole fortune, £30,000], in his endeavours to carry out the civilization of the Archipelago, and the paltry salary he draws as Governor of Labuan is devoted to the same object."

The agitation went on in the usual Exeter Hall fashion, fomented by well intentioned people, no doubt, made catspaws and fools of ; and on 4th August, 1854, a notification was issued in Singapore, signed in Calcutta on 7th July, by Lord Dalhousie, the Governor-General, Sir Barnes Peacock and three others, appointing Charles Robert Prinsep, Barrister-at-law and Advocate-General of Bengal, and the Hon'ble Humphry Bohun Devereux, of the Civil Service, to enquire into certain matters connected with, and arising out of the position of Sir James Brooke as H. M. Commissioner and Consul-General in Borneo. The notification was of some length. A few days afterwards a notice was issued, signed by K. B. S. Robertson as Clerk to the Commissioners, that the sitting would commence on Monday, 11th September.

As will be seen from a remark in an article in the *Friend of India* quoted further on, the attack had been founded on an old letter or memorial which had been taken round Singapore for signature by Robert Carr Woods in 1851. As has been said on page 438, he had come from Bombay six years before, and his anticipations of making his newspaper a pecuniary success had not reached his expectations.

The enquiry was held in what was then used as the Court House ; the very building is still standing, filled up with bales of paper and printing materials, being now used as the store room of the Government Printing Office, the new office having been built on to it in front, facing High Street.

How the signatures to the letter had been obtained, and the object of Mr. Woods in forwarding it, came to light in the enquiry, and afterwards. The paper which was struggling on its early way had been subsidised by the detractors of the Rajah.

The Commission was opened on Monday, 11th September, 1854, Sir James Brooke accompanied by Mr. W. H. Read entered and took his seat. Mr. Woods (Editor of the *Straits Times*) came forward and asked for heads of the charges. The Commission expressed disappointment at the attempted delay and adjourned to Thursday when the Court House would not be required for any other purpose. On Thursday they sat again, when Sir James Brooke was present. Mr. Woods did not come. There was a pause for some little time, after which no one appearing, Mr. Prinsep remarked "That it certainly appeared to the Commissioners somewhat extraordinary, that after the petition which had been sent from Singapore so numerously signed, and in consequence of which the present Enquiry had been instituted, no one should now come forward, either to bring a charge against Sir James Brooke or to offer any substantiation of the charges previously made. Her Majesty had paid a high compliment to those demanding this Enquiry against a servant upon whom she had conferred great distinction, and it not only seemed extraordinary to him, but must appear very unaccountable to people at home, that after they (the Commissioners), had been sent here at great expense to enquire into the validity of these charges, there should appear not a soul to bring them before the Commission. As for what Her Majesty's Ministers would think it was not for him to conjecture."

They adjourned to Tuesday when Mr. Woods came, and a great deal of evidence was taken. One gentleman well known here, was Captain George Todd Wright, of the Government steamer *Hooghly*. He said in reply to the Commissioners that he had signed the memorial. Mr. Woods had told him several of Sir James Brooke's friends had signed it, so he did so, saying " Anything for Sir James, I will willingly sign." He did not read it. Mr. Thomas Tivendale, also very well known here, was a witness. He had a shipbuilding yard on the river side, opposite where the Hotel de l'Europe is now, next to the present Government Printing Office. He said in reply to Sir James Brooke that he had signed the memorial; he would not have done so, but he was misinformed by Mr. Woods. He told Mr. Woods that he had no time to read it and asked him to call on Monday. but Mr. Woods said he need not be afraid to sign it, as it was merely for the suppression of piracy on the coast of Borneo, and had been signed by all the principal merchants in the place. He said if that was the case there could be no harm in signing it, and did so. He decidedly should not have signed it if he had known its contents. On Sunday he discovered its contents. On Monday he went to the Court House, to Mr. Woods, who was deputy sheriff at the time, and asked him to take his name out; he said it could not be done, it must go home with the others. Another witness, Mr.

George Julius Dare, said that he first sailed out of Calcutta to China in 1823, and between Singapore and China from 1840 to 1845, when he went home, and returned in 1846 and had been settled on shore in Singapore since 1848. He said that the description put opposite to his name on the memorial had not been made by him and he had never authorised it, and the statement in it was untrue, that he had traded exclusively with the Eastern Archipelago for ten years. Even witnesses called against the Rajah, whatever their private feelings against him, proved that he had been in the right. The proceedings as they went on, and they continued until nearly the end of October, became more and more decisive in favour of the Rajah, and the whole thing broke down after 56 witnesses had been called to support a case against him.

Years afterwards, in 1861, at the public entertainment given to the Rajah, which is spoken of further on, under that year, Mr. Woods, when everyone went up at the close of the evening to wish the Rajah good-bye, asked Mr. Read whether he thought the Rajah would shake hands with him. Mr. Read told the Rajah, who said "Let him come; let bygones be bygones." And as Woods walked back down the room with Mr. Read, he said "Well, it has not done him any harm after all, and it has educated my boys." Subsequent events shewed that the result was very unfortunate in each case.

Mr. Woods lived to do much good work in after years for the community in Singapore, and died much respected, but the result of his earlier days in Singapore is expressed thus by Admiral Keppel in his last book, in 1899, (volume 2, page 62) in a passage headed "Persecution of Sir James Brooke":—"I cannot close my diary for this year without mention of the sore trouble in which my friend Brooke was involved. The commencement, indeed, of the persecution from which he emerged stainless, but at the cost of mental anxiety which ultimately caused his death." The gallant sailor says also that Wise was improperly allowed access to the Rajah's journal which contained disparaging references to himself. Then came the formation of the Eastern Archipelago Company, without Brooke's sanction, which had only one object, to make money. A law suit brought by the Rajah against the Company in England ended in his favour, and a false certificate was shewn to have been put on the prospectus of the Company, out of which Wise had reaped a very large sum. He induced Mr. David Hume to take up the matter, being a man who liked to air a grievance, and tried to turn the tables on the Rajah. His object, it was thought, being to get the Rajah, Captain Keppel, William Napier and others, out of England in order to float the Company.

Rather than refer to anything that was written in Singapore on the result of the enquiry, it seems better to turn to what may be fairly considered an independent expression of opinion. The London *Times* has already been referred to; the following passages are part of an article in one of the leading Calcutta newspapers, *The Friend of India*, on 9th November, 1854:—"Sir James Brooke after clearing the Northern Archipelago of pirates, and after establishing the only orderly Government ever known in Borneo was suddenly assailed at home, by accusations of having butchered unoffending natives. The Aborigines Society took up the cause of the Dyaks. The unscrupulous malignity of a dismissed agent was aided by the mistaken philanthropy of hundreds, and by the incessant invective of a newspaper. The Rajah was supported only by the House of Commons, the Ministry of the day, and the Indian public. The House twice acquitted him. But the tide turned. The coalition Ministry were anxious to conciliate the Rajah's opponents. On the strength of an old letter signed in 1851 by many residents of Singapore, they requested the Governor-General to appoint a Commission to examine into rumours. They found, on their arrival at Singapore, that the Commission was an absurdity. Not only there was no ground for the charges, but there were no charges at all. One individual did not remember why he signed it, another had done so because he had read stories in English newspapers; while a Dutch Resident, who alike by instinct and policy was hostile to the Rajah, stepped forward in the name of humanity to defend him. At last Mr. Prinsep with just indignation reproved the conduct of those who on such grounds had asked for a Commission. A knot of individuals at Singapore have chosen to run down one of the most successful of British pioneers. They have accepted every calumny, rejected every reply, taken advantage of the clamour of a misguided section of the British public, and at last when the enquiry has been ordered, have shrunk from substantiating their charges. We leave them to the contempt they have so assiduously earned."

These last remarks, which make an effective tail-end to an article, were fair enough of the name of the editor of the *Straits Times* had been written instead of "a knot of individuals at Singapore;" and much stronger language might have been fairly used. It has been said that this calumny of Sir James Brooke, founded on falsehood and strutted up with newspaper lies, is the one big blot on the history of Singapore. The community, however, were, in part, to blame. As soon as it was seen that the paper was propagating falsehoods, as must have been apparent (see the case of the Court of Enquiry on board the *Hastings*) the community had the remedy in their own hands; but unfortunately experience shewed that, as in other places, a newspaper disseminating lies and slanderous remarks, even on those who are far above being affected by its knavery, finds a class of readers who support and pay for it, for the gratification, it must be supposed, of their own idle curiosity. The opinions expressed in a newspaper are only of the value which the knowledge or judgment of the writer can give to them, he is but an individual, whose opinion, unless there is the opportunity to judge of his competency, may be worth nothing at all. As the vast majority of the newspaper reading public have not the discrimination to realize this, and some are so foolish as to take statements of opinion as incontrovertible, because they read them in print, it is the duty of those with more intelligence to do what they can to prevent the mischief by withdrawing from the paper what they contribute to the sinews of war, without which it cannot continue to misrepresent the truth, or the opinions of the public ; unless, indeed, it is subsidised for evil purposes by those who are willing to expend money in such a manner, in the hopes of gaining much more, on the supposition that the world is largely composed of foolish or ignorant people.

Lastly the Calcutta *Gazette* of 28th October, 1855, reproduced in the *Free Press* of 29th November, in a notification as long as that appointing the Commissioners, conveyed the opinion of Her Majesty's Government on their report. It completely cleared Sir James from the charges so long and so virulently made. It is too long to quote, except one sentence :—" The enquiry which has ended in the complete exculpation of Sir James Brooke from the charges made against him, has, at the same time, brought to light abundant evidence of the beneficial results of his administration of the affairs of Sarawak, which are exhibited by the establishment of confidence and the increase of trade, and are such as to deserve the approbation of Her Majesty's Government."

The name of Charles Robert Prinsep was a household word in Singapore as early as 1842, though it is not known now whether he actually came here before he was sent with Mr. Devereux for the Brooke enquiry. It seems more than probable that he had been in Singapore many years before, because for years before this he had owned the Prinsep nutmeg estate, which Dr. Oxley estimated in July, 1848, at 6,700 trees. It extended from Stamford Road to Bukit Timah Road, as far inland as Cairn Hill, or thereabouts. Behn, Meyer & Co.'s people lived on it, in a bungalow on the hill where the Colonial Secretary's house is now ; and Charles Scott who looked after the Prinsep estate, lived in an attap house on the exact site of the present Government House, where, after his time, Mr. W. H. Read and his cousin Mr. R. B. Read were living when Governor Ord had the land bought to build the present Government House.

When Mr. Prinsep came to Singapore for the Brooke Commission, he was almost in his dotage and died soon afterwards. He was much in favour of the Rupee currency, and had great arguments with Singapore people about the Rupee and Dollar question ; Devereux, the other Commissioner chaffing him, and adding fuel to the fire.

At the time of the commencement of the Crimean War there were three men-of-war here, one corvette of 1,633 tons, the *Sybille*, and two sloops, the *Rapid* and *Lily*, of about 400 tons each. There was very little alarm felt here ; fortifications, or rather the want of them, were talked of, and the three men-of-war went out cruising occasionally. One result of the big riots and the Crimean war combined was the formation of the Volunteer Corps. A meeting was held in the News Rooms on Saturday, the 8th of July, to consider the proposal to establish a corps. Mr. John Purvis was in the chair, and he said that the large attendance present showed in a favourable manner how the proposal had been entertained for the establishment of a Volunteer Corps. Believing that the feeling in its favor was general, he had taken upon himself to convene the present meeting. Although he (Mr. Purvis) was not at liberty to mention names, he believed the establishment of a Volunteer Corps had been suggested by the highest authority in India; and he felt assured that a measure of this nature would receive the hearty concurrence and co-operation of Governor Butterworth; indeed, His Honour had intimated his readiness to head the corps. The object of the proposed Singapore Rifle Corps was, in cases of great emergency, to assist the Police in the preservation of order, and to resist the invasion of a foreign foe. The readiness which all had evinced, in the recent Chinese *émeutes,* to stand forward and prepare to act at once, had been of signal service to the Government. The manner in which the Governor had expressed his sense of the patriotism which inspired and prompted them cheerfully to aid in the suppression of the riots, was a sufficient guarantee that nothing would be wanting on the part of the head of the Executive in consulting the wishes of the meeting. They were all aware, and ready to admit, that however valuable their services in the late riots, the good effected would have been much greater had they been regularly drilled, and accustomed to act in concert. To meet any future emergency, and to act with effectiveness, he trusted those present were prepared to incorporate themselves and establish a Volunteer Rifle Corps.

After some desultory conversation, and the proposal and amendment of sundry propositions, the following resolution was finally passed:—

Proposed by H. C. Caldwell and seconded by M. F. Davidson— "That it is the opinion of this meeting that a Volunteer Rifle Corps will be of manifest advantage to the Settlement; that the following gentlemen do form a committee, viz., Messrs. Purvis, Guthrie, Napier and W. H. Read, to offer the services of the Corps to Government, and that His Honour the Governor be requested to propose a set of Rules and Regulations for the guidance of the Corps.

Before the meeting broke up thirty-two signatures were affixed to the Volunteer roll, to which twenty-nine were soon added, making the total number 61. The name of Mr. W. H. Read was the first on the roll.

The subscription in Singapore to the Patriotic Fund for the widows and orphans of soldiers and sailors employed in the Crimean war, was collected by Rev. C. Gladwin, the Chaplain of Singapore; and amounted to the handsome sum, in those days, of £900.

Sunday, the 16th July, was appointed by Royal Proclamation to be held throughout India and the Straits as a day of general humiliation and prayer for the success of our arms in the Crimea. A few days after, the ships went out to look for a Russian transport that was reported to be near. It was supposed that a squadron of six Russian vessels was cruising in the China Sea.

In the month of September, the P. & O. mail from London was delivered in thirty-four days, which was considered very remarkable; and the paper said : " When the lines of Railway through France and Egypt are completed we may expect to receive our mails from England in thirty or thirty-one days." They have since been delivered on one occasion in twenty days.

The Assembly Rooms at the foot of Fort Canning falling into disrepair led to the building of the present Town Hall which was not completed until 1861. The following extracts from the proceedings of the Municipal Committee explain how the change began :—

" The Chairman submits the following letter with enclosure from the Trustees of the Public Rooms. The Committee highly approved of the suggestion, to substitute for the present frail structure, a handsome building (to be designated the Town Hall) commensurate with the commercial importance of Singapore, and will gladly, as Trustees for the public, take charge of the edifice when finished, and also contribute towards its construction, the amount to be thus appropriated to be determined by the Committee when the views of Government are known, and the extent of support which may reasonably be expected from the State and the community.

To the Honourable T. Church, Esq.,
Resident Councillor, Singapore.

Sir,—I am directed by the Trustees of the public rooms to communicate to you that in consequence of the dilapidated state of the Public Rooms, a meeting of the shareholders took place on the 9th instant, at which a Report drawn up by the Trustees, was read and the following resolution passed :—" That instead of rebuilding the public rooms by shares, a subscription be raised for the purpose of erecting a handsome building as a Town Hall, to which it is to be hoped the Government and Municipal Committee will subscribe liberally, and on which condition the present shareholders abandon all claim to the ground, and to what remains of the present building. The new building to be placed under the management of the Municipal Committee." From the Report mentioned above you will learn that the estimated cost of reconstructing the upper portion of the building amounts to about $3,300, but should the proposal for a Town Hall be adopted, a much larger sum would be necessary, as the building would require to be entirely new and of a size and appearance suitable to the wants of this increasing Settlement, and for this purpose five or six thousand dollars it is considered would be required. So large a sum as this there is no probabilty of raising without the aid of Government and the Municipal Committee, but it is thought if they will come forward and together grant one half, that the other moiety could be raised by donation from the public.

It is quite unnecessary to point out to you the great need there now exists for a building of this description in this Settlement, which may be applied to all public purposes, as that the want of it is very frequently felt.

Trusting therefore that the proposal will meet with your approval and support.

I have the honour to be Sir,
Your obedient servant,
M. F. DAVIDSON,
Secretary, Public Rooms.

Singapore, 24th October, 1854.

On 15th November a meeting of the subscribers was held at the News Rooms, Mr. Crane was in the chair. The subscriptions had amounted to $5,089 and at least $500 more was expected. A Committee of Messrs. M. F. Davidson, T. O. Crane, A. T. Spottiswoode, James Guthrie and Dr. Little, were appointed as trustees, and to enter into communication with the Government and Municipality for the purpose of carrying out the object, and to use their utmost endeavours to obtain a site worthy of the importance of the proposed Town Hall.

The Government and the Municipal Committee agreed to give a sum of money for a Town Hall equal to that subscribed by the community, and the present site was suggested as the most suitable. The Post Office and powder magazine were then standing near it. and it was said that the former ought to be put on the Square side of the river, which was done many years after, and that the magazine ought to be removed from a place so dangerous to the dwelling houses in High Street.

The presentment of the Grand Jury in November contained the following paragraph regarding the Court House, which was part of the present Government Printing Office. Tivendale and Co., the ship-wrights, had a yard where Hallpike Street is now. On one occasion when a Judge had newly arrived he sent the Sheriff to stop the hammering but the shipwrights sent to say that they were building a boat for Captain Keppel and had to finish it, and a compromise was arrived at by mutual concession so that the work of the Court might go on.

"The Grand Jury present this Court House as being in every respect unsuited for the purposes to which it is applied. It is, as your Lordship designated it, a mere shed, squeezed in between the building containing the Government Offices and the back wall of the compound, by which wall alone, at the distance of a few feet, it is separated from an extensive ship-building yard, and it possesses almost none of the accommodation proper to a Court-room. There is almost no space for the public, and in the little that does exist, the usual convenience of seats is wanting—wooden trestles of the rudest description being introduced when any furniture of that kind is deemed necessary. The place is enclosed on one of its sides by Government offices, and on another side by the Chamber (so called) allotted to your Lordship ; and as the wall of the compound above-mentioned runs along the whole length of a third side, the consequence is that the Court-room is ill-ventilated, being in fact all but inaccessible to any current of air, and the atmosphere in the Court is frequently pervaded by an effluvium alike offensive and unhealthy. Another frequent and most unseemly result of the near proximity of this Court House to the ship-building establishment is that the voice of the Judge, the jury, the witness, or the advocate is occasionally so completely drowned by the piercing and discordant sounds, as to interrupt the business, and place this Court in the extraordinary position of being forced either to submit to this disturbance of its solemn procedure, or to interfere with the private and vested rights of the citizen ; for the Grand Jury are informed, and believe, that the ship-building yard with all its noises, etc., existed on the same spot before the erection of this Court House."

Another presentment made by the Grand Jury in December alluded to a number of other grievances ; the inconvenient position of the Post Office ; the state of the old Fish Market at Teluk Ayer ; the number of sago manufactories in the precincts of the town which then amounted to thirty, manufacturing nearly 8,000 tons a year ; the want of bridle-paths across the island ; the small proportion of native females, only one to eleven of the population ; and other matters. The three following paragraphs we reprint at length :—

"The Grand Jury again present the inefficient state of the drainage of the town. This, like many other subjects of public complaint, has frequently been presented by Grand Juries ; and, although the Executive has as often expressed its desire to effect a reform in this respect, there has as yet been nothing done towards an efficient drainage upon a general and uniform plan. The air is still polluted throughout the length and breadth of the town by the sickening malaria arising out of a double row of open drains in every street, which are never thoroughly clean, and generally more than half full of filth. The Grand Jury are exceedingly sorry to feel themselves compelled to say that in this particular, which is universally admitted to be one of the most essential towards the health of large towns, as in all other and less important matters where the expenditure of a little money is required, there is a degree of dilatoriness and disinclination to act which is far from creditable to the Executive authorities, and which is undoubtedly one of the greatest misfortunes under which this Settlement has long laboured.

"The last three heads of the Presentment may be said to fall within the sphere of the Municipal Committee, and along with these long-standing nuisances, the Grand Jurors beg to present the body called the Municipal Committee of Singapore. The members of this Committee are all nominated by the Government, two of these members are Government officials, and the Resident Councillor is Chairman *ex-officio*, with a casting vote in every equal division. As might have been expected from its constitution, and as its action has proved, it is a mere Government Bureau, whose object and effect is to render the raising of money from the public more easy, and its extraction from the Government for the public use more difficult. It answers these purposes so well as to stand seriously in the way of the public welfare ; and the Grand Jurors have therefore felt themselves called upon to present it, and to crave your Lordship's assistance in obtaining its reform ; or, if that may not be, then its entire abolition. At present it serves only the purposes of a shield to receive and break the shocks which would otherwise fall directly upon the Executive authorities.

"The Grand Jurors present that, though the population of the town and suburbs of Singapore amounts to close upon 70,000, and the trade aggregates nearly £10,000,000, there does not exist a Government Educational Institution of any kind, at least such as deserves the name. The Grand Jurors are aware that small donations are given to the Raffles Institution; but that is a school maintained by public subscription, and is utterly inadequate to the wants of the Settlement. There are also other schools, Protestant and Roman Catholic, but all of them are provided for by private subscriptions; and the Grand Jurors are of opinion that it is most discreditable that a British Settlement which has so increased in population and in wealth, should have reached that point without any provision having been made by Government for the education and improvement of the mass of children who must be growing up in ignorance or vice."

It was in this year that the ice-house was first established, and stocked with ice from America, by Messrs. Whampoa & Co. Small quantities had occasionally being brought from Batavia shipped in tin boxes!

Some 56-pounder guns were mounted at Fort Fullerton, where the Post Office is now, and the concussion brought down the ceilings of the godowns, which led to a protest from all the mercantile firms near the Square, who said they should claim against the East India Company for any loss or damage to their property. The *Free Press* said that it was hoped that the Fort would speedily return to its former condition of a saluting battery, as it was useless against an enemy.

It was in this year that Mr. Alfred Russel Wallace, the well known author of "The Malay Archipelago" came to Singapore, and was backwards and forwards on his expeditions as a naturalist until 1862, when he returned to England, and published his book six years afterwards. It has run through a great many editions. He says in describing Singapore that few places are more interesting to a traveller from Europe, as it furnishes examples of a variety of Eastern races, and of many different religions and modes of life. Mr. Wallace used to live for weeks at a time with the Roman Catholic Missionary at Bukit Timah, going after birds and botanical specimens, and hunting for insects among the fallen trunks and old sawpits, which he says was nervous work, as tigers were heard to roar once or twice in the evening, and one might be lurking close by. He expresses the usual opinion, referred to more than once in this book, that tigers killed a China-man a day on an average. As bearing upon what has been said on page 257 about the stipends and means of living of the Roman Catholic Priests, there is a passage in the book in which he speaks of the work done by the Missionary in whose house he stayed. He says : " He was truly a father to his flock ; he preached in Chinese on Sundays, had evenings in the week for discussion and conversation on religion, a school to teach their children, and his house was open to them day and night, and if they were in want he shared with them what he had. The result was his flock trusted and loved him, for they felt sure that he was their true friend, and had no ulterior designs in living among them." He says that the Missionary was allowed about £30 a year on which he lived, and the natives seeing him living with none of the luxuries of life, were convinced that he was sincere in what he taught, and had really given up home and friends, and ease and safety, for the good of others. The Rev. A. Manduit was the Vicar of St. Joseph's Church, at Bukit Timah, at the time Mr. Wallace speaks of having lived at the house attached to the Church. It was quite in jungle-land in those days.

The firm of Peres, Zapp and Ritterhaus began in this year. The three partners were Carl August Peres in Solingen, and Rudolph Zapp and Reinhard Ritterhaus in Singapore. In 1858 it was called Zapp, Ritter-haus & Co. Mr. Bauer and Mr. Staehelin were afterwards clerks, and in 1863 it became Zapp, Bauer & Co., and in 1867 Staehelin and Stahlknecht.

In this year Kerr, Whitehead & Co. commenced business ; Mr. William Graham Kerr being in Singapore and Mr. William Cullen Whitehead in England. The firm continued until 1858. Mr. Kerr died many years afterwards in Bangkok ; he had been a clerk in Martin Dyce & Co., before he started business with Mr. Whitehead.

CHAPTER XLIII.

1855.

IN January, Colonel Butterworth went on a visit to Calcutta, and Mr. Blundell, the Resident Councillor of Penang, took temporary charge there. The Governor was away about a month. In March, he resigned and left for Europe, and Mr. E. A. Blundell was appointed Governor ; Mr. Lewis, Resident Councillor at Malacca, to take Mr. Blundell's place in Penang ; Captain Henry Man, Superintendent of Convicts at Singapore, to be Resident Councillor at Malacca, and Colonel Ronald Macpherson, Superintendent of Convicts at Penang, to the same position in Singapore. A public meeting was held, Mr. Purvis in the chair, to prepare an address, and on Tuesday, the 20th March, addresses from the Chamber of Commerce, the Foreign Consuls, the European Community, the Chinese, Mahomedans, and others were presented to him. Shortly before he left, he laid the foundation stone of the present Town Hall, the account of which in the *Free Press* was as follows :—

" The foundation stone of the proposed Town Hall was laid on the afternoon of Saturday, the 17th March, by the Hon'ble the Governor, in presence of a large assemblage of the inhabitants.

" Before commencing the ceremony, Mr. M. F. Davidson, the Secretary to the Trustees for the building fund, addressed the Governor as follows :—' In the name of the Trustees and as Secretary to the Town Hall, I have the pleasing task of requesting you to lay the Foundation Stone of that building in which you have taken so great an interest, and the ultimate success of which will be so much indebted to you. When you first came to this Settlement, Singapore had no place of public resort, and for general purposes it was necessary to have recourse to the private dwellings of the inhabitants. Soon after your arrival, encouraged by your patronage, and the liberal support you afforded the measure, the Public Rooms were built. These being no longer adapted to the requirements of this Settlement, the project of a Town Hall was mooted, when you again came forward, and not only by the exercise of your influence procured a munificent donation from the Supreme Government, but it is to your exertions that we owe this highly eligible site for a building which, when finished, will, we trust, prove worthy of the situation. I now beg, Hon'ble Sir, that you will be pleased to proceed to lay the Foundation Stone of the Singapore Town Hall.'

" Colonel Butterworth then proceeded to lay the foundation stone, and afterwards made the following address :—' I feel extremely gratified at having been requested to perform the pleasing office now completed, of laying the Foundation Stone of your Town Hall ; and I desire most earnestly to impress upon you, Ladies and Gentlemen, the great satisfaction I must ever derive from the reminiscence of this day, in the knowledge that I am thus associated with a building which is to be devoted, not only to the grave deliberations of your Civic Senators, but also to the Graces, as well as to the Muses. I earnestly trust that all may lead, under Divine Providence, to the continued prosperity of this highly favoured Island, and tend still further to cement the unity of feeling at present existing in this happy community.' "

The following is a copy of the inscription on the plate which was deposited beneath the stone :—

In the year of our Lord
1855
And in the 18th year of the Reign of
QUEEN VICTORIA,
The Most Noble
The MARQUIS OF DALHOUSIE, Kt.,
Governor-General of India,
The Foundation Stone
of the
Town Hall,
Was laid on the 17th day of March,
By the
Honourable Colonel Butterworth, C.B.,
Governor of the Straits Settlements,
In presence of many of the
British and Foreign Residents
of this Settlement.

The site had been selected by a Committee composed of Messrs. M. F. Davidson, R. Little, C. Spottiswoode, T. O. Crane and J. Guthrie, and sanctioned by the Governor on 9th February. The Government of India gave a grant of $3,000, and the subscriptions were expected to reach $6,000.

In March, the Supreme Government sanctioned a loan to the Municipal Committee of the funds that might be required for the drainage of the town, at four per cent. interest, but nothing was done to any purpose. The very low level at which the town lies in regard to the sea being a serious difficulty, which, however, is ameliorated by the rise of the tide through such drains as there are, and their consequent frequent flushing.

A local Committee was appointed to send articles to the Paris Exhibition which took place in that year; and fifty lists of articles were forwarded, and expenses incurred to the extent of $324·57.

In the same month the celebrated singer, Catherine Hayes, came to Singapore and gave a Concert in the Public Rooms. The charge was $3, which was thought a high price, and the Concert commenced at 8 o'clock.

It was in this year that the treaty was made between the two Chiefs, Sultan Allie and the Tumonggong of Johore, which led to so much discussion afterwards. It provided for their rights; and the Tumonggong was declared to be sole and absolute sovereign of Johore except the Kassang territory now commonly called Muar, which is about 260 square miles, and withdrew all claim to that Kassang territory which was declared to be the Sultan's territory under a provision that he should not alienate it without offering it in the first place to the Hon'ble the East India Company and then to the Tumonggong of Johore.

Sultan Allie died in 1877, and on his death Muar passed to the territory of Johore, as the Straits Government declined to take it. Muar, during the rule of Sultan Allie, remained in a state of torpor, and under the hands of his successors it has become a flourishing and rising province.

As the signing of the treaty was carried out with much ceremony, some particulars are taken from the accounts in the newspaper :—

"On Saturday, the 10th March, in pursuance of instructions from the Supreme Government, the Sultan of Johore was formally recognised by the local authorities. This was Sultan Allie the son of Sultan Hoosain, not the ruler of Johore proper, who was then called the Tumonggong. The ceremony took place at noon, in the large room of the Government Offices. At the head of the room, on a scarlet covered platform, were placed three chairs for the Governor and the Sultan and the Tumonggong of Johore ; above the chairs were the English Union Jack and the East India Company's flag ; the Consular flags were drooping from the cornices round the room, other flags being arranged in festoons above them. Immediately behind the Governor's chair was the marble bust of Raffles, executed by Chantry, placed on a pedestal ; on each side of the platform was placed a table, on one of which was a State sword, on the other was placed a silver inkstand, the State seals, and three copies of the treaty about to be concluded between the two native Princes. We ought to mention that the different national flags were so arranged that their respective Consuls sat beneath them. On each side of the scarlet platform, chairs were placed for the sons of the Sultan and the Tumonggong. The chairs on each side of the entrance to the platform were occupied by ladies. The lower part of the room was occupied by officers of the 38th and 43rd M. N. I. and other gentlemen. In the portico fronting the audience chamber was stationed a guard of honour of the 38th M. N. I., and also as many chairs for the public as the limited space would permit.

"At noon Governor Butterworth took his seat ; the Sultan was led into the portico by Mr. Church and Major Campbell, and was received by a guard of honour. On Mr. Church handing the Sultan into the audience room, His Highness was received by the Governor ; on shaking hands with the Sultan, His Honour, addressing the guests assembled, in a firm voice, said he took advantage of the occasion publicly to recognise his friend Tuanku Allie as Sultan of Johore, in succession to his father. The Sultan was then placed on a seat on the Governor's right, under a salute of 11 guns. After a short pause, His Highness the Tumonggong arrived, and the guard of honour in the portico again presented arms. The Governor received His Highness with a cordial shake of the hand, and introduced him to the Sultan under a salute of nine guns, whereupon the Tumonggong

made obeisance to the Sultan, and was then handed by the Governor to a
seat on his left hand; the Tumonggong's sons Inche Aboobakar (afterwards
Sultan of Johore) and his brother Inche Abdul Rahman were placed near
His Highness. The Governor called upon Mr. Church to read the
treaty.

" The treaty having been read in English by Mr. Church, and in Malay
by Inche Bujal, it was signed and sealed in due form, another salute of
eleven guns was fired, and the guard again presented arms."

Many important changes had taken place during the twelve years
Colonel Butterworth had been Governor of the Straits. Direct steam
communication with Europe was completed soon after he came. The
Horsburgh and Raffles light-houses were both erected and a floating light
placed on the North Sands, and a lantern for the harbour light at Singapore. He did much to obviate the unwise measures which the Bengal
Government tried to force on Singapore regarding the silver currency in
rupees. He abolished the Sireh Farm, which was considered an oppressive tax by all the natives. During his time, a Seamen's Hospital, a
Pauper Hospital, and the new Gaol (now being pulled down) were erected,
and also the new House of Correction; the sea-wall along the Esplanade
was built; Johnston's Pier and Dalhousie Pier were erected; and many
of the bridges and roads made. The Volunteer Corps was established,
and a good deal done towards the foundation of a system of education both
by himself and Mrs. Butterworth.

The following was the address presented to him by·the Chamber of
Commerce, and the Governor's reply :—

" The Singapore Chamber of Commerce, in common with the rest of the community, viewing with much regret the approaching termination of your official connection
with these Settlements, are anxious before your departure to record their sense of the
great benefits you have conferred upon the commerce of Singapore during the many
years you have filled the office of Governor of the Straits Settlements.

Your earnest advocacy of every measure calculated to promote the interests of
the trade of Singapore,—your readiness to receive suggestions for its benefits,—your
prompt interposition in endeavouring to avert, by every means in your power, whatever may have seemed calculated to injure or interfere with that freedom from useless
restrictions, which has been the peculiar characteristic, as well as the mainspring of
the prosperity, of the commerce of Singapore,—the ready access to your presence
which you have afforded to all,—and the courtesy which has invariably marked your
intercourse with us—have all been fully appreciated by the mercantile community of
Singapore, and we now beg to express, although inadequately, our grateful
acknowledgment of them.

The very remarkable increase which has taken place in the commerce of Singapore
under your Government, has afforded triumphant testimony of the soundness and
wisdom of those principles of commercial policy which its illustrious founder Sir
Stamford Raffles initiated from the first day he took possession of Singapore, then an
almost uninhabited island; and it must be extremely gratifying to you, Honourable
Sir, who have so steadily maintained and upheld those principles, to find that during
the course of your Government the trade of Singapore has risen from 24,620,243
Dollars, its amount in 1843, when you first assumed the charge of these Settlements, to
the large sum of 36,655,557 Dollars, as shown in the official returns for the past year.
This advance has been owing to no adventitious circumstances. It has been steadily
progressive, resulting from the natural expansion of trade,—at first attracted by the
peculiarly favourable position of Singapore and its entire freedom from imposts or
restriction, and then fostered and encouraged by wise Government.

In now taking leave of you, Honourable Sir, the members of the Chamber of
Commerce beg respectfully to offer their warmest wishes for your health and prosperity, and they venture to express the hope that those high qualifications for Govern-

ment, which has been so beneficially exercised for the well being and advancement of these Settlements, may yet find a still wider field of employment in the service of your country.

Signed in name of the Singapore Chamber of Commerce:

J. GUTHRIE,

Singapore, 20th March, 1855.   Chairman.

To which the Governor replied :—

"Gentlemen,—Your very flattering and most gratifying recognition of the deep interest I have ever taken in the commercial prosperity of Singapore, is more highly appreciated by me, than I can find words to express.

That illustrious statesman, as you have justly termed Sir Stamford Raffles, the Founder of all the growing greatness of this wonderful Emporium, has been my guiding star. and I have viewed as a legacy to his successors, the scrupulous maintenance of Singapore as a Free Port. I am grateful for your pleasing acknowledgment that I have not been unmindful of this great trust.

Receive, Gentlemen, my warmest thanks for the ready assistance you have afforded me from time to time, in many of the important questions that have been before us, and with a profound sense of the kind feelings which have dictated your good wishes I will say—Farewell!"

A public subscription was made to present General Butterworth with a testimonial and to have the portrait painted which is now in the Town Hall. The following account of the plate and of the Governor's career appeared in the *Illustrated London News* of 26th July, 1856 :—

"A very gratifying testimonial of public esteem has recently been presented to General W. J. Butterworth, c.b., late Governor of Prince of Wales' Islands, Singapore, and Malacca. The gift originated in a public meeting held at Singapore on March 30th, 1855, when the inhabitants of the Settlement resolved to present General Butterworth with a piece of plate, of not less value than £500 sterling, as a mark of the high sense entertained by them of his valuable services as Governor of the above Settlements, for a period of nearly twelve years. It was also resolved by the ladies of Singapore, to present Mrs. Butterworth with a silver tea and coffee service.; and, furthermore, General Butterworth was requested to sit for his portrait, to be placed in the Town Hall of Singapore, in memory of the esteem and respect in which he is held by all classes of the community. The portrait has accordingly been painted, and will be transmitted to Singapore by an early opportunity ; and the plate, which has also been completed, has been presented to General and Mrs. Butterworth now in England.

"General Butterworth, who has received these distinguished honours, was trained at the Hon. East India Company's military establishment, Addiscombe, and passed for the Artillery. Previously, however, to his quitting England for India, actuated by the prospect of more speedy promotion, he sought and received permission to exchange into the Infantry of the Madras Presidency, whither he proceeded in 1818. On his arrival he obtained a Lieutenancy in the Second Battalion 19th (now 38th) Regiment and was appointed to the Rifle Corps.

"He subsequently joined the Light Field Division of the Mahratta Army, under the late Sir Theophilus Pritzeer, k.c.b., and was at the siege of Ghopart Droog. On the day of assault the company of the

Rifles to which Lieutenant Butterworth was attached not being detailed for duty, he earnestly volunteered, and was allowed to accompany the escalading party. For his services on this occasion he was in 1821 made Adjutant of the 38th Native Infantry.

"In 1822, he was compelled to proceed to England on medical certificate. On his return, having in the meantime attained the rank of Captain, he joined the army in Ava, under Sir Archibald Campbell, and in 1825-26 was in most of the skirmishes with the enemy, and at the taking of Moolawm. At the termination of hostilities he was nominated Deputy Assistant Quartermaster-General of the Army; and, in 1828, promoted to the Assistant Quartermaster-Generalship, in which capacity he was posted in 1834 to the western column of attack on Coorg, under the command of the late Brigadier Sir David Foulis, K.C B., and was three times wounded whilst heading the advance to the capture of the several stockades in the Higgular Ghauts. For his services at this period he received the special thanks of Government in general orders, and was recommended for the Order of the Bath.

"On the formation of the field force, under command of Brigadier-General Taylor, C.B., Captain Butterworth was again detached, as Assistant Quartermaster-General of that force, and distinguished himself on several occasions, particularly in the attack on the Khonds at Nowguan, on 1st June, 1836. During this campaign he attained his Majority. At the restoration of peace he returned to head-quarters, obtained the thanks of Government, and was shortly afterwards made a Companion of the Bath.

"Having from time to time acted as Deputy Quartermaster-General of the Army, Major Butterworth was in 1839 permanently appointed to that office. In 1841, he obtained the Lieutenant-Colonelcy of his regiment; and in the same year, being again obliged to seek the restoration of his shattered health, he went on medical certificate to the Cape of Good Hope. During his visit to the Colony he was presented to the Earl of Ellenborough, then on his way to assume the Government of India; by whom, in 1843, he was appointed Governor of Prince of Wales' Island, Singapore, and Malacca.

"Lieutenant-Colonel Butterworth was promoted to the Colonelcy of the 2nd Regiment during his tenure of that important office— a period of twelve years, two of which were passed in the Australian Colonies in consequence of the declining state of his health; which, eventually, in March, 1855, forced him to relinquish the Government of the Straits of Malacca, just as he had attained the rank of Major-General.

"The able manner in which Major-General Butterworth discharged the arduous duties intrusted to him is amply testified in a letter from the Government of India; and also by the addresses presented to him on his vacating the government for a time, and afterwards on his final resignation of it. The importance of this highly honourable post may be estimated by the fact of the annual trade of the three Settlements amounting to upwards of ten millions sterling.

"The plate consists of a centre ornament, thirty-nine inches high, and two side ornaments, twenty-two inches high; total value £700. The centre ornament has branches for nine lights and four glass dishes for flowers, &c. The base supports a very rich group of figures, representing commerce exhibiting to Britannia a portrait of the General : with the figures of a Chinese, a Malay, and an Indian Jew, over whom Britannia holds her shield in allusion to her protection. The standard of the East India Company is also introduced. The inscription is as follows :—

" ' Presented to Major-General W. J. Butterworth, c.b., by the inhabitants of Singapore, to mark their sense of the important services rendered to the Settlement during the period of his Government, to express their acknowledgment for the readiness with which he at all times identified himself with the true interests of the place, and to record their admiration of the ability and energy which characterised his administration as Governor of Prince of Wales' Island, Singapore, and Malacca, from 1843 to 1855.'

" The two accompanying ornaments support baskets for flowers, and are enriched respectively with a group of tigers under pitcherplants, and a buffalo with two deer under fern-trees.

" The ladies' testimonial consists of an elegant silver tea and coffee service, and was accompanied by an address stating it to be presented :—

" ' To Mrs. Butterworth, by the ladies of Singapore, whose names are hereon inscribed, to testify their regard, and in affectionate remembrance of her uniform courtesy and kindness to them during the period of eleven years in which her husband, Major-General Butterworth, c.b., was Governor of Prince of Wales' Island, Singapore, and Malacca. December, 1855.' (Then follow the names of the several lady-subscribers to the testimonial.)"

Governor Butterworth was a handsome patron of sports on land and water. He gave a cup annually for the horse races, and kept a boat, an improved sampan, for sailing after office hours in the harbour, and he sailed his boat on New Year's Day. He was not popular at first in Singapore, as he began with much pomposity ; and a joking remark in a private letter of Sir James Brooke, which unexpectedly became known, described him as "Butterpot the Great." Mrs. Butterworth was very good to the school children, and both she and her husband frequently passed an hour in the schools. The Colonel used to time his morning walk so well at 5.30, that he was said to be as good as a watch when the guard turned out to meet him. He had a great fancy for the two silver sticks, only to be seen now in Court, which used to follow him about on many occasions.

Like several other public officers who have left the Straits, the late Governor lived but a short time to enjoy his rest, for he died at Millmead House, Guildford, on the 4th November, 1856, eighteen months after he left Singapore.

He was spoken of in print by a well known Singapore an as " A perfect gentleman, though a good deal of a military ' bahadour.' He laboured hard to introduce black coats and continuations into our social habits, but, in those uncivilised times, white was the order of the day among ' men.' The ladies used to prefer clean white to dubious black. However, he laboured in vain, and except, of course, at Government House, white prevailed. One evening at some public dinner, at which he was present, and all were in respectful black, his health was proposed, and received a warm acknowledgment of cheers. Something had nettled His Excellency, and in reply he gave a lecture to all hands, winding up by informing the enthusiastic public that 'sincerity was not proved by loud applause!' This rather annoyed some of the audience, and two days after, at a theatrical representation, it was determined to pay him off. The after-piece was *Bombastes Furioso,* and when that eminent General dismissed his troops, he exclaimed, in response to their loud acclamations :—" Silence in the ranks, cease, cease your braying ; sincerity's not proved by hip, hip, hip, hurraying." The Governor looked serious at first, and a thunder-cloud overspread his brow, but, immediately recovering himself, he burst out laughing, and applauded heartily. He told the actor afterwards : 'A very good hit, a very good hit ! and well done too !!' Local allusions were often 'gagged' into the plays in those days, and Hongkong many years after did the same, to the intense annoyance of thin-skinned officials, especially H. E. Pope Hennessy, but to the intense enjoyment of the public. It is said that Mr. Balestier had one day a note from Col. Butterworth, whose caligraphy was shocking. He returned it with a remark " Can't read the Governor's handwriting."

The total trade of the three Settlements in 1853-54 amounted to Rs. 107,675,802, an increase over the previous year of Rs. 20,480,300, or above two million pounds sterling. These figures were dependent upon the returns of the mercantile community, and the real state of the trade was no doubt larger. The Opium Farm of Singapore was let in this year for Rs. 27,100 a month, and the Spirit Farm for Rs. 9,510.

On Thursday, the 8th March, there was a review of the newly enrolled Volunteer Corps, of which the *Free Press* wrote as follows :— " The Singapore Rifle Corps paraded on Government Hill on the afternoon of Thursday last, and went through a pretty stiff drill, after which they were reviewed by the Hon'ble the Governor, who then addressed them in complimentary terms on the efficiency they had attained, and assuring them how proud he should have been to have headed them in actual service. His Honour requested that his name might remain upon their roll, and concluded by reading some despatches from the Court of Directors and Supreme Government of India, noticing in terms of approbation the promptitude with which the Singapore Volunteers had come forward with the offer of their services, and expressing the hope that their example might be followed in other parts of India. The Corps, although they turned out on this occasion in somewhat diminished numbers, appeared, as far as an unprofessional eye could judge, to go through their manœuvres with steadiness and precision, and we have no doubt they will highly distinguish themselves whenever they may be called upon to take the field."

Mr. Edmand Augustus Blundell, the new Governor, joined the Penang Civil Service on 6th August, 1821, and was afterwards a Commissioner of the Tennaserim Provinces. He was Acting Governor of the Straits in June 1843, and then went to England. After he returned he was Resident Councillor at Malacca, and in 1848 he wrote a paper in volume 2, page 726, of Logan's Journal, on Malacca. In

1849 he was Resident Councillor at Penang, and Acting Governor in 1851. In 1855 he would probably have been appointed Governor, but for Lord Ellenborough's attachment to Colonel Butterworth.

In April, during a squall, a house in Kampong Malacca was struck by lightning, and four natives were killed; they were lads sleeping near each other. Sir Wm. Jeffcott, the Recorder, who went to the spot, helped the mother afterwards with money, as the lads had been her chief support. She was with them in the room when they were struck.

This year was remarkable for an increase in piracy, the native trade suffering very severely from it. The most formidable pirates were Chinese, who waylaid and fired on the junks and other native traders, attacking them, in their voyages to or from Singapore, in the China Sea and the Gulf of Siam. The pirates resorted to Singapore without fear, and in May a public meeting was held to memorialise the Secretary of State. Mr. Guthrie was in the Chair and the following resolutions were passed:—

" Proposed by Tan Beng Swee, and seconded by J. P. Cumming, That this meeting views with deep concern the ravages committed by pirates, Chinese particularly, in the immediate vicinity of this port, to the great destruction of human life, and detriment to trade.

Proposed by W. H. Read, and seconded by Tan Kim Ching :—That in order to remedy the present insecurity of life and property, petitions be prepared and forwarded to the Supreme Government, the Houses of Parliament, and the Admiral on this Station, urging them to take vigorous measures to suppress piracy in these parts.

Proposed by R. Duff, and seconded by J. d'Almeida :—The Singapore community are so thoroughly convinced of the necessity of protection to the junks now about to leave for China, and so indignant at the long continued supineness of the Authorities on the subject of Chinese piracy, that— if the men-of-war now in the roads will not interfere—the community itself agree to subscribe to hire an English vessel to see the junks safely beyond the Gulf of Siam, and that the local Government be requested to license said vessel.

Proposed by Dr. Little, and seconded by T. O. Crane :—This meeting highly approves of the conduct of the local Government in detaining the suspicious junks now in the harbour until the trading junks are safely beyond their reach.

Proposed by J. d'Almeida, and seconded by A. J. Spottiswoode :— That the following gentlemen be appointed a Committee to carry out the foregoing resolutions :—Messrs. Guthrie, Read, Logan and Duff."

The paper was full of accounts of piratical murders, and the Government steam-vessel *Hooghly* was too slow to be of any use, and there were very few men-of-war near Singapore. Eventually orders came from the Admiralty to the Admiral on the Station to send a vessel to the Gulf of Siam. The Government at last began to take away the rudder of doubtful piratical junks in the harbour, and prevent them leaving until they were searched for arms. In some cases, junks were fully manned, but without any cargo.

The number of covers that passed through the Post Office in April of this year was 31,683.

It was in May of this year that the Bengal Government sanctioned building the new Church (the present Cathedral) as said on page 493. The *Free Press* said "The Government of India, has approved the plan submitted to them of the proposed structure, which is described as being a very handsome one and a great improvement upon the former building. If it is practicable to change the site of the building, we should recommend, in place of the present one, the piece of level ground half way up the Government Hill, and which is marked by a withered tree. This site is airy and at the same time easily accessible from all quarters, and would advantageously display the architectural beauties of the new edifice. It would, moreover, leave the whole of the present Church compound available for other public buildings, such as the new Court House, for which at present there seems some difficulty in finding a suitable locality." The suggestion was, fortunately, not carried out, and the new Church was built on the former site, which was much more suitable.

In the month of May it became known to the inhabitants of Singapore, that a European of the name of Thom, who had been convicted in the Supreme Court at Calcutta of murdering his wife, and sentenced to transportation for life, was to be sent to Singapore to undergo his sentence. The natural inference from this was that, as the Australian Colonies were no longer available as penal Settlements, the Supreme Government intended to convert the Straits Settlements into a receptacle for the European felons of India, as they already were for native convicts. A meeting of the inhabitants of Singapore was immediately held, which was numerously attended by the Europeans and Chinese residents. Resolutions were adopted energetically protesting against the further degradation, which it was anticipated, the Government intended to inflict upon Singapore. A memorial was drawn up, addressed to the Governor-General, which the Hon'ble the Governor refused to forward, as, in his opinion, it was couched in rather more violent language than seemed consistent with official usage, and it was, therefore, sent direct to the Governor-General. The Governor, at the same time, is understood to have pointed out the strong objections which existed to making this a penal station for European convicts, and the result of the agitation on the subject was, that the Government of India speedily intimated that it had no intention of transporting European convicts to Singapore, and that Thom had only been sent here in consequence of the Supreme Court having named it as the place to which he was to be transported. Petitions were made to Parliament, and Mr. John Crawfurd wrote a long memorandum on the subject, which was laid before Parliament, dated from the Athenæum Club, London, August 30th, 1855. The result was that the Secretary to the Government of India wrote to say that the Government had no intention to transport European convicts to Singapore and that a Bill would be brought before the Legislature to change Thom's sentence, which was done, and he was removed.

In May, Mr. Moniot, who had been Government Surveyor at Penang, was appointed to Singapore for the purpose of reorganising the Survey Department here—a periodical attempt at settling an old grievance with the usual insufficient means to carry it out.

Deaths by tigers during this year became very numerous, and a great deal of attention was drawn to the subject. The Calcutta paper, the *Friend of India,* suggested that so many deaths were scarcely likely to be caused by tigers, and that it was possible the Chinese secret societies might imitate tigers' wounds on murdered persons! And the London *Punch* of October 27th had the following paragraphs :—

A SCHOOL FOR TIGERS IN THE EAST.

" Rapid Depopulation of Singapore by Tigers.—Two deaths by tigers every week (says the *Singapore Free Press*) are read of in the papers, just about as much a matter of course as the arrival or departure of the P. & O. Company's steamers. It is notorious that during the last fifteen or twenty years many thousands of men have lost their lives from this cause. Yet the only measures adopted by Government, so far as we know, to prevent this enormous sacrifice of life, have been to dig tiger-pits in various parts of the island (which we are now told did little or no good). and to give a reward of one hundred Company's rupees for every tiger killed on the island. The reward is, for all practical purposes, ineffective ; it ought to be increased to two hundred and fifty rupees ; for the price of procuring the destruction of one tiger in the jungle of Singapore is a hundred dollars, and the thing cannot be done for one hundred and ten Company's rupees. Such is the position in which we are now placed.'

" If the population of Singapore is really being converted into food for tigers, and the inhabitants are departing as regularly as the steamers, it is high time that something should be done to save the remnant of the populace. Considering that the tigers have evidently got the upper hand, we think they show a sort of moderation in taking only two inhabitants per week. and there is consequently no hope of any further diminution, for it is clear that the brutes are already on what may be considered low diet. We cannot be surprised at the anxiety of the Editor of the *Singapore Free Press,* who may any day be selected as a moiety of the weekly allowance of the somewhat abstemious tigers. who appear to be practising the negative virtue of moderation and regular living. Since the Government will not, or cannot. take the matter up, and put the tiger down, we would advise the population of Singapore to enter into an arrangement with the brute-slayer at the top of the Haymarket, and we have no doubt that Mr. Cumming would be hailed as the Coming Man, if he were to offer his services.

" The Singapore journalist expresses his fear that the ' evil will go on increasing,'—or in other words, that the population will go on diminishing—and we fully sympathise with his editorial fears ; for even should he be so lucky as to escape till after every other inhabitant is disposed of, it would be but a sorry consolation to feel oneself constituting the last mouthful at a feast of tigers.

" We suspect that our Eastern contemporary is either indulging in a little romance, or is agitated by fears that have grown up under the enervating influence of the climate, for we cannot suppose that the people and the Government are quietly submitting to the gradual consumption of the inhabitants in the manner described, and our friends at Singapore will excuse us. therefore, if we have treated somewhat lightly a subject that we should certainly regard as no joke, if we put faith in the statements on which we have commented."

On the 25th May, Mr. John Kinsey Salmon died, at the age of sixty years. He was a native of Flintshire, and one of the old Bencoolen Officers under the East India Company, and lived during the latter years of his life, with a pension, in Singapore.

In July, a subscription was made towards the Roman Catholic Church in Malacca, of which the paper spoke as follows :—

" We have now before us plans of a handsome and spacious Gothic Church in course of erection at Malacca, under the direction of the Rev.

Mr. Barbe, the R. C. Minister at that station. The cost of the building is estimated at $9,000 ; but such are the circumstances of the Roman Catholic Christians at Malacca, that only about 300 to 400 dollars have been raised there. The sum of about $1,100 was granted by the mission at Penang. Most persons would have despaired of ever accomplishing the completion of so great an undertaking ; not so the French priests, whose zeal in whatever they may embark knows no hindrance. By the personal exertions of the Rev. Mr. Favre, in the United States, the Mauritius, and elsewhere, more than $6,000 have been obtained which, with the sums above mentioned, have been expended on the Church. It appears, however, that the sum of $1,000 is required to complete the building, and to obtain this sum the Rev. Mr. Barbe is about to make an appeal to the Singapore community."

It was in this year that the nutmeg disease got to such a head. The *Free Press* of 12th July published long papers by Dr. Oxley and others, on the disease, and its possible remedies.

The following is an account of the total amount of Municipal Assessment and Taxes during the preceding six years, in round numbers :—

1849	.. $28,600
1850	... 28,800
1851	... 31,000
1852	... 32,000
1853	... 34,000
1854	... 40,000

The expenditure was always from $2,000 to $3,000 in excess. It was in this year that the cross road from Seletar to Bukit Mandai was made.

In August, the new clipper ship *Kate Carnie,* named after Mr. Carnie's sister, built under Captain Rodger's superintendence, came out from home. She made the best passage then known—88 days from England and 28 from the Cape. She was very well known here during the next ten years, being a famous opium clipper, and commanded by Captain Rodger, whose son was then in Martin Dyce & Co.'s firm and became afterwards a partner in that house, and to whose memory there is a window in the Cathedral.

On the 11th August, a public meeting was held in the News Rooms in Commercial Square at which nearly every European in the place was present. Mr. James Guthrie was in the Chair. It proved to be the beginning of the agitation for the Transfer from the East India Company. The primary cause of the meeting was the Act which had just been published introducing the copper currency of India in addition to the cents of the Spanish dollar. The second resolution proposed by Mr. W. H. Read and seconded by Mr. W. G. Kerr, was as follows :—

"2.—That by the passing of the Act 17 of 1855 this meeting is forced into the painful conviction that the Legislative Council of India, in treating with utter disregard the remonstrances of the inhabitants, have shewn that they are neither to be moved by any prospect of doing good, nor restrained by the certainty of doing evil, to the Straits Settlements, and that it is therefore the bounden duty of this community to use every exertion and to resort to every means within its reach to obtain relief from the mischievous measures already enacted, and to escape from the infliction of others of the same nature, more comprehensive, and still more hurtful."

In this year a table of precedence as regarded the East Indies was issued by the Queen, and proclaimed in India and the Straits. The Governor-General headed the list, of course, and it is only referred to here as showing where the Straits came—which was away at the foot, the Governor and the Recorder coming after the Puisne Judges of the Courts of Calcutta, Madras and Bombay.

Reviews of the troops were held several times during the year on the Esplanade. In December, a full dress parade of all troops was held, and the proclamation relating to the taking of Sebastopol was read and a royal salute fired.

In August, Mr. George Wahab, of the London Police, arrived and took up his position of Deputy Superintendent of Police. He was engaged in England by Mr. A. Guthrie, at the request of the Municipality. The following is an extract from the Minutes of the Municipal Committee in August :—

" The Committee notice with regret, the continued and increasing obstructions in the verandahs, some of them so completely closed in as to exclude the public. The early attention of the Police is requested to the evil, as it is apprehended that unless prompt measures are adopted, the rights, convenience and interests of the community will permanently and materially be impaired."

" At the suggestion of Mr. Harvey, the all important question of the drainage of the town is again brought under review. The increase of the town population, together with the densely crowded state of many of the houses, vividly and daily remind the members individually and collectively of the imperative necessity for an immediate amelioration of a state of things fraught with so direful consequences. The Committee have no hesitation in reiterating their deliberate opinion, that, considering the site of the town was selected by the Government Officials and a large sum has already been paid into the local Treasury for lands sold, and holders of property pay an annual quit-rent exceeding 20,000 Rupees to the State, it is for the Executive alone to undertake the efficient drainage of the town ; this measure the Committee conceive cannot be deferred without imminent risk, and possibly loss of life, to an extent fearful to contemplate. Should the Government of India still withhold their aid after this representation, the Committee will then, under the exigence of the case, be constrained to accept as a loan a sum not exceeding 100,000 Rupees, to be disbursed as required. The Committee, however, can offer no positive guarantee for the regular payment of the interest or the gradual liquidation of the principal, this must necessarily depend on the amount of the funds available by the Committee at the close of each year."

On September 12th, a branch of the Mercantile Bank of India, London and China (as it was then styled) was opened here by Mr. Walter Ormiston as Manager.

On the 22nd October, the Recorder, Sir William Jeffcott, died at Penang at the age of 55 years. He was the second Recorder in the Straits who had died in office, the first being Sir Francis S. Bayley, who died at Penang in 1824, about two months after his arrival. Sir

William was only ill for a few days, and was at the same time suffering under considerable anxiety of mind as to his future position in reference to the new arrangements of the Judicial system in the Straits, and was annoyed at indirectly learning that the Singapore division of the Court had been assigned to him, as he much preferred Penang as a place of residence. He was an Irishman. A Dublin paper in 1842 said:—"As a lawyer, he was among the most rising on the Munster Circuit. Nearly related to the late lamented Chief Baron Wolf, he possessed much of his ability, integrity and sterling independence of character. Indeed, Mr. Jeffcott has established a reputation at the Bar of being a sound and safe lawyer."

In that year he went to Australia as a Judge, but returned to Ireland and resumed practice at the Bar, and held an appointment under the Attorney-General there. In 1849, he succeeded Sir Christopher Rawlinson as Recorder in the Straits, when the latter went to Madras as Chief Justice. During his residence in the Straits, Sir William Jeffcott sustained the character which in his earlier years he seems to have gained at the Irish Bar, of being a sound and painstaking lawyer, and, without evincing any extraordinary legal attainments, he commanded respect by the earnest manner in which he discharged his judicial functions. Any slight irritability he occasionally allowed to be seen was sufficiently explained and excused by the fact that he laboured under a painful internal disorder. Soon after his arrival in the Straits Sir William Jeffcott shewed his anxiety to administer justice in the most efficient manner that the circumstances of these Settlements would permit, and for that purpose made an alteration in the periodical circuits of the Court, by which Singapore was visited three times in the year, instead of only twice, as formerly. Sir William Jeffcott was highly esteemed in private life. He was of a generous and benevolent disposition, and never failed to respond in the most liberal manner to all appeals for assistance, whether on behalf of individuals or institutions, which were made to him, and these were by no means infrequent. He took a deep interest in the cause of education in the Straits, and embraced every opportunity which presented itself of promoting its improvement. He was offered a Judgeship both at Calcutta and Bombay while he was in the Straits, but he declined both. Minute guns were fired from Fort Fullerton in Singapore, on the news of his death reaching here. He was succeeded, in the following year, by Sir Richard McCausland.

As an example of the way in which the Municipality worked with the public at that time, the following is taken from their minutes in October regarding the way in which the present road to Tanjong Pagar was widened. It was then only used as a road to Mount Palmer and a small village.

"The Hon'ble T. Church, Esq.,
    Chairman of the Municipal Committee,
            &c.,   &c.,   &c.

" Sir,—We beg to inform you that all the Proprietors of Land on the south side of the Tanjong Pagar Road, have agreed to give up a sufficient space of their ground, to form a ditch inside of the present hedge, so as to follow the widening of the road to that extent. This would be of great convenience to the public, the present road being so very narrow and dangerous.

" This road, you are aware, has long been, and still is, in a very bad state, and we would therefore hope that no time will be lost in carrying out the above desirable improvement and putting it in a thorough state of repair.

We have, &c.,

J. Guthrie,

Cursetjee Frommurze. "

" The Committee fully recognise the desirableness of making the improvement and reform adverted to, and relying on the assurance that all parties are willing to surrender the requisite space, the Committee are prepared to commence on the work at an early date, in the hope and expectation that the Executive will contribute a moiety of the outlay, as the road in question leads to ' Lake's Battery ' recently constructed on Mount Palmer."

There were three fires towards the end of the year, after the lapse of a considerable period without one. The first was a fire at Tanjong Ru, the second at Kampong Malacca, and the third, in November, at the corner of Kling and Philip Streets. At the latter eleven houses were burnt out, some of which were stored with very combustible materials—turpentine, oil, &c.; and twenty houses were pulled down or injured in stopping it. The whole of the burnt block belonged to Syed Ali bin Mahomed Al Junied ; and the *Free Press* said : ' Being a Mussulman he is, of course, uninsured, but it is understood that he is better able to bear his loss than many of his less fortunate tenants. The loss was about $33,000."

In the beginning of December, there was a very unusual amount of rain, the country was flooded and the roads in many places were almost impassable. Serangoon district was a vast lake, and communication had to be made by sampans. It rained without intermission from 7 a.m. on the 30th November to 4 a.m. on the 2nd December. And as the tide continued about high water mark for three consecutive days, the rain remained on the low lands and overflowed the roads, to the depth of two feet in places. There was heavy weather in the China Sea, and the P. & O. steamer had to lay to off Point Romania for twenty-four hours, as the atmosphere was so thick with heavy rain, that no one could see half the length of the vessel.

In December, a schooner, the *Alma*, with gunpowder on board, was struck by lightning in Malacca and blown up, one man out of the crew of twelve being recovered: This again drew attention to the want of control of the storage of gunpowder in the town and harbour of Singapore.

The following account of the practices of small Kling shop-keepers in Singapore was published at this time by a Malay resident :—

" Many of my nation, the *Orang Malayu*, who come from sequestered localities and the interiors of rivers, people who are very simple, and men of the different tribes of Bugis, who are not accustomed to resort to Singapore to trade, are cheated and deceived in the cloth shops of the Klings because their shops being shut in by screens of cloth next the public street are nearly quite dark, and the verandahs are also rendered impassable by benches and stools on which many persons sit. In the darkness and confusion thus produced, goods which are coarse become fine; good silver money is transmuted into copper; doits, which were sufficient in tale, lose part of their number; and measurement becomes deficient. The sellers are rude and overbearing to the simple buyers and insist on their purchasing. From these causes how often are people cheated and deceived and suffer loss. If they don't submit to the exactions of the Klings, then a row is kicked up and the buyers are hustled about by the Klings. Hence disturbances take place, but the police cannot readily find out the scene of disturbance on account of the screens of cloth which enclose the verandahs."

At this time the syces of private carriages and hacks always ran along with the pony and never sat on the carriage. Colonel Butterworth imported a large carriage and four horses, and when attending the evening service at St. Andrew's on dark nights, the syces ran at the sides of the horses with lanterns.

The North Western Bank of India, of which the head office was at Calcutta, opened a branch at 19, Malacca Street on 20th December. David Duff was the Agent.

CHAPTER XLIV.

1856.

O N New Year's Day a picnic party composed of a large number of the merchants went out on a trial trip, and the result is told in the following account in the *Free Press*. The steamer was afterwards sold to pay the damages:—" The screw steam-ship *Labuan*, Captain Browne, belonging to the Eastern Archipelago Company, previous to proceeding on her voyage to Labuan, made a trial trip in the direction of the Raffles Light-house; her machinery, &c., having undergone alterations and repairs since her arrival here. She left the anchorage about seven in the morning, and after having passed the barque *Zarah*, which sailed the same morning for Akyab, rounded the Light-house and steamed towards Singapore on her return. Soon after this, at about ten o'clock, the *Labuan* and the *Zarah*, which was coming towards her close hauled to the wind, came into collision, when the steamer took the barque directly amidship on the star-board side, carried away the barque's mainmast with her bowsprit, and, with her bowstay, which consisted of a strong iron chain, literally sawed the barque in two. The *Zarah* sank within three minutes of the contact. The officers and crew were all saved and taken on board the *Labuan*. The hull of the steamer was apparently uninjured and scarcely appeared to touch the other vessel, but her bowsprit was snapt by the collision, and becoming entangled with the rigging of the *Zarah*, was dragged out, together with the topmast and rigging, when the barque sank. The whole party were down below at a meal, and the Captain had been called down for a minute when they heard the crash, and only reached the deck in time to see the barque's masts disappearing beneath the waves."

In January the Rev. Mr. Sames who had kept a school in Malacca for some years and had a free school for native boys in Hill Street, at the old Assembly Rooms at the foot of Fort Canning, left Singapore in consequence of ill health and went to England.

At this time a question was raised by the Police about the horse sales in the Square, and the *Free Press* remarked that it was a practice as old as the Square itself and it would be a great injustice to stop them. The practice was continued until about 1890, when it ceased because of the large traffic through the Square. It had been a great convenience to all, as it was a good opportunity, after tiffin time, to see what was offered, and there was little difficulty in finding buyers.

On Tuesday evening, the 4th March, the Bishop of Calcutta laid the foundation stone of the present St. Andrew's Cathedral, as already stated on page 293.

The paper in April contained the following paragraph:—" The small cutter *Tear an' Ages* which left this about a month ago with the mails for

Java, returned on the 1st instant. She made the run down to Batavia in six days. The voyage altogether was a venturous one at this season of the year for a craft of her size, as she is not more than 40 tons burthen." In those days when the mail steamers broke down, mails were forwarded by any available opportunity, generally by men-of-war, but in default of anything better, the little Singapore yacht undertook the experiment.

The *Tear an' Ages* belonged to Mr. Cursetjee Frommurzee and Mr. W. H. Read. The name of the boat was to have been the *Ariel*, but at the launch, an officer of the Artillery, an Irishman, and a General Officer now, chaffing and laughing, did not notice the chocks being knocked away, and the cutter had already gone some distance, when he dashed after her, with a "Tear an' Ages," and broke the bottle over the bows. "By Dad," said he, "and what's her name?" It was too late to alter it then. She was afterwards sold to Bishop McDougall and named the *Southern Cross*, as a mission boat, and was subsequently bought as a gunboat by the Sarawak Government, and, as the *Badger*, fought a gallant action, under sail, with two Lanun *prahus*, crippling one, which was afterwards abandoned, and damaging the other considerably. The *Badger* was wrecked on the bar of the Bintulu river. Her run to Batavia would have been quicker, but the nights were dark and the skipper cautious, so he anchored. The residents at Batavia got up a handsome subscription to pay the expenses of the trip.

In April, the whole community gave a Ball to the Commodore and Officers of the French Squadron, which took place in the P. & O. Company's establishment at New Harbour. The English Admiral, Sir James Stirling, came from Hongkong the same afternoon, and, being about the time of the Crimean War, the proceedings were very enthusiastic.

In April the *Free Press* mentioned that Captain Keppel had been appointed to command the gunboat flotilla to proceed to the Baltic if the Crimean War should not be concluded; and printed parts of a speech by Sir Charles Wood, the First Lord of the Admiralty, in the House of Commons, in reference to the matter, in which he said "Captain Keppel has seen more active service than almost any other officer of his rank, and if my Hon. friend were to poll the entire navy, he would find its unanimous opinion to be that there is not a better, or more gallant, or more deserving officer in the service. Captain Keppel has distinguished himself on every occasion in which his services have been called into requisition, the most recent instance is during his command of the Naval Brigade before Sebastapol."

The Municipal Committee this year consisted of Mr. Church, the Resident Councillor, as Chairman, and four members; Captain R. Macpherson, Superintendent of Convicts, *ex-officio*; John Harvey of McEwen & Co.; H. M. Simons of Ker, Rawson & Co.; and H. T. Marshall, the Superintendent of the P. & O. Company. Mr. J. Moniot was in charge of the Government Survey Department.

The German Club, called the Teutonia Club, was started on the 28th June by about seven members, and the first committee was composed of Otto Puttfarcken, Arnold Otto Meyer, and Franz Kustermann. It was opened in a house in North Bridge Road, behind where Raffles Hotel now is, but a little way further towards Rochore than the end of that building. The Club was removed about six months afterwards to Blanche House, which is still standing on Mount Elizabeth, near the present Club building. The first club house was built about 1862, and many entertainments were given in it. On 25th June, 1886, a celebration on a very large scale was given in it to celebrate the thirtieth anniversary of the Club, and some excellent poetry in German, written by Mr. H. Ebhardt, was recited, a translation being given to the English guests. It was in this building that Prince Henry of Prussia was entertained by the Club in February, 1898. The building becoming too small for the increased German community, the present much larger and handsome building was built, and opened with a large ball on 21st September, 1900.

There were two Government bungalows at that time; one at Changie and the other at Bukit Timah, near the road; a Government Notification issued in September stated that they were expressly constructed for the use of officers on duty in the rural districts, but were open to the use of others at other times.

In July, it was decided to construct a wooden foot-bridge across the river a little above where Cavenagh Bridge now stands, the estimated cost was $9,835.49, which included a carriage way of sixteen feet wide. There were then only two bridges—Coleman's, built in 1840, and Thomson's, in 1844—and as the Post Office was across the river, communication from the Square had to be carried on in boats, which was very inconvenient. The projected plan was not followed out, and some time after a foot bridge only, with a toll of a quarter of a cent, was put up.

Mr. Carpenter, who painted the two well-known views of Singapore, was here in September. The *Free Press* spoke of him as follows :— Mr. Carpenter, an English Artist who has been resident here for some time, has just completed a view of Singapore, in oil colours, which is by far the best *likeness* of this place which we have ever yet seen. It is taken from Mount Wallich, and includes the whole of the town, while the back ground embraces an extensive panorama from Bukit Timah to Johore Hill. The foreground contains characteristic groups of Malays, &c. Mr. Carpenter proposes, if a sufficient number of subscribers can be obtained, to have this picture engraved in line, in the best style, and we are sure it will form a very desirable acquisition to all who are in any way connected with Singapore. The picture for the present is to be seen at the news-room in Commercial Square, but it will ere long be transmitted to London, so that those who have not yet had an opportunity of inspecting it should lose no time in paying it a visit." The lithographed copies, of which there were many for a long time hanging in the houses in Singapore, were made in 1858.

The curious way in which the convicts from India were kept under control, which led, however, to no evil results, and provided a body of men who did a great deal of good work in road making, building the Cathedral, Government House, and other public works, is shown by the following account of some of their proceedings in this year :—

"It appears that the authorities, having at last made up their minds to forbid the convicts from exercising privileges which are denied to some of the free inhabitants of Singapore, gave orders that on the occurrence of the last Mohurrum the convicts should not be allowed to carry their *taboot* in procession through the streets as in former years, but that their demonstrations should on this occasion take place within their own lines. This did not please these men, who had been accustomed to enjoy a degree of license strangely inconsistent with their condition, and accordingly on the evening of Wednesday last, the 10th September, some hundreds of them forced their way out of the lines, and carrying their *taboot*, and lighted by torches, they marched in procession to the house of the Resident Councillor, where they vented their displeasure by noisy cries and excited gestures and afterwards proceeded to the Government Offices, where they were at last prevailed upon by two of the officers, who had previously in vain attempted to restrain them, to return to their quarters.

" Such an outbreak will no doubt appear strange to persons who are unacquainted with the way in which the convicts are managed in the Straits and the degree of license accorded to them. In former years they were allowed to indulge in their Saturnalia without restraint, their *taboot* was the gayest, and their processions the noisiest to be seen on the public streets. With only one or two European officers over them, the whole of the staff of Jemedars, peons, &c., are convicts, who must of course to a great extent be identified in feelings and interest with those over whom they are placed. Large gangs are dispersed over the country in open lines, without any adequate guard or control over them, and these persons can have very little feeling of restraint. They look upon themselves as superior to the rural population and fully demonstrate this by their behaviour. Whatever may be the theoretical rules for their management, practically they are allowed a degree of liberty and freedom from discipline which is inconsistent with their *status* as convicts."

On 21st March, by the P. & O. Mail steamer *Madras* the new Recorder, Sir Richard Bolton McCausland, arrived from England with Mrs. McCausland. Sir Benson Maxwell, who was the new Recorder for Penang, came at the same time. Sir Benson had been on a Commission concerning the conduct of the Crimean war, and in the *Free Press* was a quotation which had been taken from *Punch*, though it did not say so. The lines attracted general notice in England.

"Whom shall we hang
Is off to Penang
With a place of £200 a year ;
The book was a sham,
and we think my Lord Pam
Buys his whitewash excessively dear."

Whether it was a misprint in the *Free Press* by printing £200 instead of £2,000, or whether the writer was mistaken, cannot now be traced, as there is no copy of *Punch* of 1856 to be found in Singapore ; but the salary of the Recorder of Singapore was Rs. 25,000, and that of Penang Rs. 20,000 a year.

The Court was opened on 22nd March by the Recorder, and the new Charter of the Court of Judicature of Prince of Wales Island,

Singapore, and Malacca was proclaimed; after which the Recorder took the oaths of office under the usual salute, Sir P. B. Maxwell being present on the Bench.

One result of the new Charter was that eight gentlemen, who were Justices of the Peace, wrote a long letter to the Governor dated 24th July resigning the office. They were Messrs. T. H. Campbell, T. O. Crane, J. J. Greenshields, C. H. Harrison, John Harvey, H. T. Marshall, W. Paterson, and W. W. Shaw.

A public meeting was held at the News Rooms in Commercial Square on 29th July, at 2 p.m., for the purpose of taking into consideration the Draft Municipal (Straits) Act and other matters of importance to the Settlement. Mr. W. H. Read was called to the Chair, and made some remarks on the objects for which the meeting was held. He then adverted to the proceedings which had recently taken place with reference to the appointment of peace officers, and which had led to the whole of the independent and unpaid Justices of the Peace resigning office. As this subject was not without bearing on the questions which they had met to discuss, and as he saw several of the ex-Justices present, he hoped they would allow the correspondence which had passed between them and the Governor, to be read for the information of the meeting, which was done, and the following resolutions were passed:—

Proposed by W. G. Kerr, and seconded by A. J. Spottiswoode:—

That the thanks of the Community be given to the ex-Magistrates, for their dignified and spirited conduct in resisting the despotic measures of the Government.

Proposed by J. B. Cumming, and seconded by D. Duff:—

That this meeting objects to Act XIII of 1856, as regards the Constitution and Management of the Police Force—being of opinion that the Rate-payers who furnish the funds for its maintenance, are entitled to a share in its control, and therefore earnestly protests against the arbitrary and unconstitutional measure which places the entire power in the hands of the Government.

Proposed by A. J. Spottiswoode, and seconded by R. C. Woods:—

That this meeting claims as a right that which has been already conceded by the Bengal Legislative Council in the preamble of Act III of 1847, to wit; that "it is expedient that all constables and subordinate peace officers and other persons appointed to perform duties of police should be appointed by the Authorities from whom they receive their pay and no others;"—this meeting therefore submits that if the appointment of police officers is vested in the local Authorities, the Government should defray the expenses thereof, and on no account should the assessment funds be applied to such purpose.

Proposed by J. Harvey, and seconded by T. O. Crane:—

That this meeting adheres to the opinion expressed at and adopted by the public meeting held on the 27th September, 1853, that the number of Municipal Commissioners should consist of seven elective and two Government members, it being of opinion that by a less number the interests of the Rate-payers would not be adequately represented.

Proposed by C. H. Harrison, and seconded by H. T. Marshall :—

That Section 16 of the Municipal Assessment Straits Bill, by which power is given to the Governor or Resident Councillor to fill up vacancies occurring in the Municipal Committee is decidedly objectionable, and this meeting is of opinion that such vacancies should be supplied by a new election.

Proposed by J. J. Greenshields, and seconded by T. H. Campbell :—

That this meeting indignantly protests against the insidious introduction of the Rupee Currency by the provisions of the Acts under review.

Proposed by T. O. Crane, Esq., and seconded by W. Howard, Esq. :—

That a Committee, to consist of the following Gentlemen, be appointed to petition Parliament against the objectionable Acts of the Bengal Legislative Council :—Messrs. Logan, Read, Woods, Harvey and Cumming.

A reference to events which occurred in former years may probably be useful in order to understand the reasons which induced the Justices to take such a strong measure.

By the Letters Patent from the Crown (popularly called the Charter) by which the former Court of Judicature of Prince of Wales Island, Singapore and Malacca had been constituted, power was given to the Court at their General and Quarter Sessions to nominate and appoint constables and subordinate peace officers. The Justices of the Peace were authorised to sit at such General or Quarter Sessions, and to have a deliberate voice in the proceedings. For a considerable time no attempt seems to have been made to exercise the powers given to the Court in its General or Quarter Sessions to regulate the Police, the executive making appointments and exercising a general management through the Sitting Magistrate, who was usually the Assistant Resident, and who also officiated as Collector of Municipal Assessment, which was disbursed by him under the control of his superiors. Matters went on in this manner for a number of years, but in 1843 the daring outrages committed by the Chinese drew the attention of the community to the inefficient state of the Police, and a public meeting was held at which certain representations were made to the Government for the improvement of the Police force. These were given partial effect to, and amongst other measures adopted by the Government was the appointment of a Deputy Superintendent of Police, subordinate to and under the control of the Sitting Magistrate, who continued to act as Superintendent. This was soon perceived to be a very objectionable arrangement, especially as the Sitting Magistrate, as then appointed, might generally be expected to be a person of much less experience in Police affairs than the Deputy, who was liable to have his plans thwarted by a prejudiced or ignorant superior. This actually occurred, and in addition it was found convenient to transfer the collection and disbursement of the assessment to the Deputy Superintendent, who thus had duties imposed upon him which interfered very materially with a proper superintendence over the Police force. The evil effects of such a state of matters were not long in manifesting themselves, and in 1846 the Police as to discipline and efficiency was in as defective a state as it had been in 1843.

In opening the Criminal Sessions in April, 1846, the Recorder, Sir W. Norris, in his charge to the Grand Jury, adverted in forcible terms to the very inefficient state of the Police and made several suggestions for its reform. The Grand Jury in their presentment dwelt at considerable length on the subject, pointing out what they conceived to be the causes of what they did not hesitate to designate "the present disgraceful inefficiency" of the Police. One of the reforms recommended by the Grand Jury was the separation of the offices of Sitting Magistrate and Superintendent of Police, which latter office they were of opinion should be conferred on the Deputy Superintendent, Mr. Dunman, who ought to devote his whole time and attention to the duties of his office, being relieved from the collection of the assessment and from acting as a Sitting Magistrate. The Justices of the Peace, finding that by the Charter they were clothed with certain powers of control over the Police, conceived that it was time for them to undertake a duty which they had perhaps too long neglected, and accordingly a sitting of the Court of Quarter Sessions was held to consider the matter, which was attended by the Recorder, the Resident Councillor, and nearly all the Justices of the Peace. It was proposed at this meeting that the sole superintendence of the Police should be given to Mr. Dunman, the Deputy Superintendent, who was to have the entire management of the Police, subject only to the control and direction of the Court of Quarter Sessions. This was opposed by the Resident Councillor who considered it would be productive of much inconvenience to remove the Police from under the control of the Executive. The Recorder and the great majority of the magistrates did not adopt this view, and the proposed changes were accordingly made, the Resident Councillor protesting against them. Under the new system of management thus introduced, the Police force rapidly improved.

The Magistrates in Quarter Sessions were not, however, long allowed to exercise the power, of which their first use had proved so beneficial to the community. Without waiting to see whether the alterations made by the Court of Quarter Sessions would succeed or not, the Government of India hastened to publish the draft of an Act which, by the terms in which it was conceived, betrayed no small degree of pique at the course taken by the Court of Quarter Sessions. By that Act the appointment of Constables and Peace Officers was to be vested in the Governor of Bengal and the Governor of the Straits Settlements. The Community of Singapore petitioned the Governor-General in Council against this Act and prayed that the appointment and control of the Police might be left with the Court of Quarter Sessions. No attention was given to this memorial, and in due time the Act was passed and came into operation as Act III of 1847. Three of the non-official Justices immediately upon the Act being passed resigned their offices, and some of the Justices at Penang took the same step. From this time the office of Justice of the Peace in Singapore was held in little esteem, very few non-official persons being found willing to accept it.

Governor Butterworth would seem at last to have become aware of the mistake which had been committed by the passing of Act III of 1847, and in the end of 1853 he induced a number of gentlemen to allow their names to be put in the Commission of the Peace on the understanding that the obnoxious Act was to be repealed, and there was also a prospect of the appointment and control of the Police being vested in a popularly elected Municipal body, a course which had before been recommended by the community, and which seemed equally satisfactory with restoring the power of the Magistrates, as in either case the Act would be repealed, and the management of the Police left with those in whom the community could place confidence for its right administration.

Things remained in this state when the Letters Patent reconstituting the Court of Judicature arrived from England, and as it was found that they contained the same powers as the former Charter in regard to the appointment of peace officers, it was conceived that the authority of the Court in its Quarter Sessions of the Peace was thereby revived, and the Justices were therefore prepared to exercise their functions in that respect. Mr. Blundell, the Governor, however, took a different view and thought that his powers under Act III of 1847 remained unaffected, and proceedings to try this question were taken in Court, with the result that the Recorder held that the opinion of the Governor was the correct one, and that the powers of the Justices in Quarter Sessions were not resuscitated by the recent Letters Patent. The Legislative Council of India in the meantime passed their Police Act, which extended to the Straits as well as to the Presidency Towns of India, and by it the complete nomination and control of the Police was committed to an officer to be appointed by Government with the title of Commissioner of Police, and which office in the Straits Settlements it was proposed to confer on the Resident Councillors.

Whatever, therefore, may have been the grounds on which Colonel Butterworth conceived himself warranted in holding out hopes that the power of the Court of Judicature in General or Quarter Sessions would be restored, the Government of India did not do it, and the Justices of the Peace, who had held office on the faith of Colonel Butterworth's representations, had but one course left when it was seen that these representations would not be given effect to.

On 2nd June Captain John Russell, the Postmaster and Master Attendant resigned, and Mr. Vaughan, who was then Superintendent of Police at Penang, was appointed in his place; which gave, the paper said, general satisfaction, as he had every qualification for the office. A letter very numerously signed by the merchants, was sent to the Government, suggesting that the Post Office was becoming of great importance and recommending Mr. Cuppage, if the work could be separated from the duties of Master Attendant and Marine Magistrate, which were enough for one official. It was not done for many years afterwards.

In June the *Free Press* said " The Singapore petition about the Rupee Currency has been presented to the House of Lords by the Earl of Albemarle, and his Lordship appears to have made himself fully conversant with the subject, and to have stated the case of the petitioners with much ability. The reply to the elaborate exposition of Lord Albemarle made by Lord Granville is anything but satisfactory. Lord Granville says that the matter is not so simple as Lord Albemarle seems to think. We are at a loss to conjecture where the difficulty lies. To any person possessed of common sense it must be very obvious that a purely decimal system, represented by a suitable silver and copper coinage, is infinitely superior to a barbarous currency like that of India. The difficult point is the strange infatuation of the Indian Government, including the Legislative Council, which induced them to persist in doing their utmost to overturn the decimal currency established in the Straits and to substitute the inconvenient Rupee system, in spite of the strongest remonstrances from those who were to be the victims of their meddling. Lord Granville states that the Spanish Dollar was never a legal tender and never had been authoritatively settled as such. There may never have been a distinct legislative enactment to that effect, but in every other way it was sanctioned and recognised as the legal currency of the Settlement. For many years all the transactions of government were in dollars, the Charters of Justice emanating from the Crown mentioned dollars, all suits in the Courts of a pecuniary nature referred solely to dollars, and merchants and all other sections of the inhabitants carried on their dealings and kept their accounts entirely in this coin. Moreover, government further recognised this currency by supplying a copper coinage adapted to it and to it only. These are facts which show that whether or not the dollar had ever been settled as a ' legal tender ' in the Straits, there can be no doubt that it was long the actual and only currency."

A public meeting was then called by the Sheriff in the Square on Tuesday, 1st July, to take the question into consideration, and the objections by the whole community to a Rupee currency were insisted on as warmly as ever. The attempt of the Government in India to force a double currency had proved a source of general inconvenience to everyone, including the officials.

A member of the Legislative Council of India, known as Rupee Allen, who was supposed to have taken the Straits affairs under his particular care, came to Singapore from Calcutta in October, and was actually seen in the Square. So a few merchants sought an interview with him, to expose again the mischief which it was endeavoured to force upon the trade of the place, but he said he was not "at home" and went back as ignorant as he came ; the newspaper remarking that he was one of these small minds who think it an affront to ask them to reconsider a matter after they have expressed their opinion upon it, and consider discussion a bore, and so gain the contempt of many and the respect of none.

Whampoa & Co. had been importing ice from America, but the consumption was only from 400 to 500 lbs. a day, and it required a sale of 1,000 lbs. to meet the cost and expenses, so they stopped it.

At a public meeting held in July a resolution was adopted by a majority but subsequently withdrawn, which proposed to appoint a committee for the purpose of drawing up petitions to Parliament with a view to an address to the Crown, praying Her Majesty to make Singapore a Crown Colony.

In September, Ker, Rawson & Co., advertised for sale by auction the late Dr. Montgomerie's nutmeg plantation at the junction of New Harbour and Tanjong Pagar Roads, with the dwelling houses called Craig Hill and Duxton, area about 32½ acres, with 1,700 nutmeg trees.

Mr. Thomas Church left Singapore, for the last time, on Monday, 22nd September, after having been Resident Councillor for over nineteen years, as already stated on page 326. Mr. Henry Somerset Mackenzie, a Bengal Civilian, from Penang, took Mr. Church's place, Mr. Braddell was Police Magistrate at Penang, and Mr. Willans at Malacca.

Two small gunboats, called the *Malacca* and *Singapore*, were launched in October. They were built by Tivendale & Co., and the paper said they promised to be very efficient craft, going fast either with oar or sail and being of very light draught in the water. They were manned by eleven men each, armed with pistols and cutlasses, and each boat carrying a brass 3-pounder gun. They were stationed so as to make a complete sweep round the island, and it was their duty to be constantly on the move, looking into the different creeks and rivers and other resorts of sea robbers.

In October the paper said:—"The Rajah of Siak has arrived here with thirty prahus and about 500 followers. His object, we understand, is to fit out an expedition for the purpose of bringing to submission a number of refractory chiefs who refuse to recognise his authority and who have kept Siak in a state of disorder for a year or two past. He has purchased a schooner and other vessels of smaller size, and is laying in a large supply of arms and ammunition of all kinds. As soon as he has repressed the civil commotions in his country, the Rajah intends to turn his attention to the development of the resources of his state, and for this purpose, we hear, he will avail himself of European agency. From the close proximity of Siak to Singapore the Rajah will have peculiar facilities for carrying his intention into effect, if he proceeds upon any well regulated plan. Coal, tin and gold are said to exist in considerable quantities, while the usual articles of produce which the Malayan forests yield, such as wax, rattans, gittah taban, canes, dammar, &c., &c., are found in abundance." All this came to nothing.

In December Mr. C. R. Rigg, who had been Coroner, was made the Secretary to the Municipal Commissioners, in anticipation of the passing of the new Municipal Act. He was Secretary until he left Singapore in 1866, and did a great deal of good work.

In December Mr. A. M. Aitken, who had in 1852 been admitted one of the Law Agents of the Court as they were then styled, and was afterwards called to the Bar in 1864, was appointed Registrar of the Court, in room of Mr. Caldwell. The cause of it created a great deal of excitement in the place at the time. The reasons for this can be seen from the following passages taken from an article in the *Free Press* of 11th December. Mr. Caldwell in after years paid off by far the greater part of his creditors in Singapore in full:—

"Some three weeks ago unpleasant rumours began to circulate regarding Mr. H. C. Caldwell, Registrar of the Court of Judicature here, to the effect that he had misappropriated a large sum of money entrusted to his care for investment, and that he had tried to conceal his defalcations by rendering false accounts to his principal, apparently showing that the money was out at loan on mortgage. Very little credit was at first given to these reports, as Mr. Caldwell had always borne the highest character for integrity and there had been nothing in his mode of living, &c., showing any expenditure beyond what was amply covered by his official emoluments. About a fortnight ago, however, these rumours began to acquire consistency and strength. and were at last proved to be but too true, by Mr. Caldwell being deprived of his office, the Judges of the Court having called upon him for explanations which he was unable to give. Thus lamentably was terminated an official connection with the Court of 28 years, during the course of which Mr. Caldwell had enjoyed the confidence and respect of his superiors and of the public, who looked upon him as a most zealous and upright public servant.

"The enquiries which now took place on the part of persons interested in property entrusted to Mr. Caldwell's care, in the various capacities of agent, trustee, executor and, through his office, as administrator in intestate and other estates, revealed that his misappropriations had been extensive and general, not even his most intimate friends being spared. The confidence placed in Mr. Caldwell's integrity by every class of the community was so unlimited, that the property confided to his management, in the various capacities above mentioned, was very large, and from all that we can learn the amount which he has fraudulently made away with cannot be less than one hundred thousand dollars, and will probably be found considerably in excess of that sum. Although repeatedly pressed for an explanation, Mr. Caldwell would not give any intelligible account of the manner in which he had disposed of this large sum. Ultimately a criminal charge was made against him by one of the severest sufferers from his frauds, but on the officers proceeding to his house to take him into custody, Mr. Caldwell had disappeared, although seen and conversed with only a few hours previously, and, notwithstanding the most perserving search since, no clue has been obtained to his hiding place. Some persons think that he has succeeded in leaving the island, while others believe that he still remains in Singapore, concealed by some of his native friends. The shock which this occurrence has inflicted on the community has been great, for very seldom has any one enjoyed such universal respect and esteem as were accorded to this unhappy man. We have delayed as long as we could from alluding to this matter, in the hope that something might transpire which would give it a less repulsive aspect, but any such expectation appears now to be vain, and it would therefore serve no good purpose to remain longer silent."

Mr. Aitken held the post for a short time, and in 1857 Mr. Christian Baumgarten was appointed and held it until 1874, when he practised at the Bar, and Mr. Charles Eugene Velge, one of the sons of Mr. John Velge, spoken of at page 185, was appointed Registrar.

On the 18th December, a public meeting, very numerously attended, with Mr. W. H. Read in the chair, was held, and the following resolutions were passed :—

Proposed by W. Napier, and seconded by W. Paterson

That the imposition of tonnage or port dues on shipping is an unwarrantable attack upon the freedom of this port, which this meeting views with apprehension and regret; as being in direct violation of the principles upon which this Settlement was established, and calculated to endanger the very existence of its trade.

Proposed by J. Harvey, and seconded by J. B. Cumming.

That the following gentlemen be requested to form a Committee to draw up a Memorial to the Legislative Council in India, embodying these views :—Messrs. W. H. Read, John Purvis, Wm. Napier, A. Logan, Joaquim d'Almeida and W. G. Kerr.

The paper remarked on this as follows :—

" The feeling of the meeting, which was very numerously attended by the European and Chinese merchants, as well as other parties interested in the welfare of Singapore, was unanimous, and strongly expressed against the proposition. This is not the first time, by any means, that it has been sought by the Government of India to introduce duties at Singapore, in one form or another. So far back as 1826, the subject was mooted by the East India Company, but the proposal met with such a warm opposition in England, that it was abandoned for the time being. About ten years later, the Indian Government again brought it forward, the pretence for doing so being the great expense incurred in putting down piracy in these seas. The merchants petitioned both Houses of Parliament, and the result was, that although in the meantime the authorities in India had modified their scheme and restricted it to the levy of port or tonnage dues, positive orders were sent from home that no measure of the kind was to be attempted, and that if already in operation it was to be forthwith annulled. Statesmen of all parties in England have ever recognised the importance of maintaining in all its integrity the system on which Singapore is conducted, and which has been productive of such beneficial results to the trade of England as well as to that of India. Our immediate rulers in India, however, have never been able to regard the Settlement of Singapore through any other medium that a revenual one; and whenever, therefore, there has been an excess of expenditure over receipts, whether arising from ordinary sources of disbursement or from measures required for the protection of trade, they have frowned upon the unfortunate place, and the one sole remedy propounded—the only suggestion they have had to make on the subject—is the imposition of duties on the trade."

The result of this protest, supported by the action of old Singaporeans in London, who went to the Board of Control on the subject, was that the Directors at Leadenhall Street sent out positive instructions to Bengal to do nothing at all in the matter, and again in the history of Singapore the merchants maintained the freedom of the port.

In 1854 the local Presbyterians considered the advisability of having a Minister of the Presbyterian order in Singapore. A committee was appointed, and Dr. Guthrie, the famous Edinburgh preacher, was requested to find a suitable Minister, and the Rev. Thomas McKenzie Frazer, M.A., arrived in October, 1856. In the same year a Chinese catechist named Tan See Boo came from Amoy, recommended by Dr. Carstairs Douglas and other missionaries there. He worked in a small building, used as a Mission Chapel, in the compound of Miss Sophia Cooke's Girls' School in Sophia Road. Miss Cooke took much interest in the matter and had induced Mr. Humphrey, the Church of England Chaplain, to begin mission work among the Chinese some months before the Presbyterians were actually at work. See Boo, who, was one of the earliest Presbyterian converts in China, had been working with the Episcopalians for a time, but was afterwards ordained an Elder in the Presbyterian Church. In September, 1860, Mr. Frazer went to Australia; and in June, 1861, the Rev. John Matheson arrived. He left for home in 1866, and died at Alexandria; having been very much respected in Singapore. The Rev. W. Jeffrey arrived from home in 1866, but not long afterwards he left the Presbyterian communion and joined the Plymouth Brethren in Singapore. Mr. Alexander Grant, M.A., a Presbyterian missionary from Amoy, and Tan See Boo, doing the same. In 1870, the Rev. M. J. Copland, the fourth minister, arrived, but he died suddenly in the following year, on 19th February, 1871.

The Rev. William Dale began his ministry in November, 1871 and in April, 1872, the Presbyterian Church took an important step and entered into the Synod of the English Presbyterian Church. Before that the local Church had had no direct ecclesiastical connection at home.

In May, 1872, as the Session had lost its Chinese Mission by the deflection of Messrs. Grant and See Boo, they decided to take over for a time Peter Tychicus and the Tamil congregation, and thus became more interested than before in Mr. Keasberry's Mission. On his death in 1875 the Bukit Timah Chinese Mission passed under the care of the Presbyterian Church, and ten years later the Presbyterians also took charge of the Chinese work at the Prinsep Street Chapel, which since 1885 had been under the charge of the Rev. J. A. B. Cook. Mr. Dale was succeeded by the Rev. W. Aitken, M.A., who left in 1883. The Rev. A. S. MacPhee, M.A., B.D., was then appointed and remained until 1889, when the Rev. G. M. Reith came, and was succeeded by the Rev. S. S. Walker in 1896.

The services were formerly held in the building known as the Mission Chapel, originally built by the London Missionary Society, at the corner of Brass Bassa Road and North Bridge Road opposite the present Raffles Girls School, and in 1876 that site, which had been purchased by the Presbyterian congregation from the London Missionary Society on 3rd August, 1866, was sold and the present Church in Stamford Road was built, the Government giving the land free for the use of the members of any denomination of Christians holding as their confession of faith the ecclesiastical documents received by the different branches of the Presbyterian Church and known as the Westminster Standard.

In December the screw steamer *Sir James Brooke* commenced to run between Singapore and Sarawak, and it was in this year that the steamers of Jardine Matheson & Co., and Apcar & Co., commenced to run between Calcutta and China. These steamers were the first regular vessels to trade with the Port in addition to those of the P. and O. Company.

A large number of new houses had been built during the year, but, notwithstanding this, rents rose very much and continued to advance, and the value of fixed property, whether in town or country, was double or treble what it had been three years before. The demand for residences in the country exceeded the supply. A new Court House was proposed, and the side of Government Hill below the cemetery was suggested, but it would have been inconvenient. The Victoria Brick Bridge over the Rochore river was built in this year. A new steam wharf and coal shed for the use of the Borneo Company and Jardine Matheson & Co's. steamers (since called the Borneo Wharf) was building, and at the west of New Harbour Mr. Badenock commenced a dry dock under the superintendence of Captain Cloughton, the spot selected being where a patent slip had been commenced but had not succeeded. The premises were known afterwards as the New Harbour Dock. The construction of a dry dock at Pulo Brani was also being attempted at this time.

It was in this year that Lieut. John Frederick Adolphus McNair, R.A., came to Singapore. He left England for Madras in 1846, a little over seventeen years of age. One of those young Englishmen, of whom there were so many in the history of India in former days, who had the resolution to leave home when almost school-boys (and whose parents were brave enough to let their boys go), at a time when life in India was far different from what it is now; when such a voyage was a matter of many months; and when a return home was looked upon as a very distant and, perhaps, unlikely event, so much less was known about the country in those days. In 1853 he went to Malacca in command of the detachment of Madras Native Artillery stationed there. He made friends with Mr. J. B. Westerhout, who was so well known among the up-country natives, and was the person in Malacca to whom the Government looked for advice and assistance in dealing with the neighbouring Malay States. He used to go long journeys with him into the interior, and as he had been a student of geology in England with an eminent geologist, he sent to Calcutta specimens of various metals, &c., which he found in his journeys. He made a collection also of the woods and resins of the country, which was sent to the Government of Madras. He had been scarcely a year in Malacca when he was sent to take command of the Artillery in Labuan, and in July, 1856, he was called to Singapore to act as Adjutant to the Artillery in the Straits, with his head-quarters at Singapore. While he was in Labuan he had travelled over part of Borneo Proper, and made a valuable collection of shells which were afterwards placed in the Cuming collection now in the British Museum. The Governor of the Island there was an eager coadjutor in that work; he was Mr. Low, now Sir Hugh Low, afterwards in Perak. He had not been long in Singapore before he was appointed Private Secretary and A.D.C. to the Governor—a post very different in the days of the East India Company to what it is at present. The most analogous now is that of the Colonial Secretary; for all the correspondence of the Government then passed through the hands of the Private Secretary. It was while he was so employed that the Indian Mutiny broke out, and Lord Elgin was here on his way to China in 1857, as is related in the next chapter.

In December, 1857, he was appointed Executive Engineer and Superintendent of Convicts in the Straits. This involved the charge of all the public works, and what was quite as important, of the

Criminal Jail, holding, in very insecure walls, some three thousand prisoners from India, Ceylon and Hongkong. He had passed in Hindustani in India and spoke it well, and he acquired a remarkable personal influence over the gangs of prisoners, which was frequently noticed. He had been fortunate in succeeding two such officers as Colonel Man and Colonel Macpherson, who like himself had been in the Madras Artillery. They had brought the jail into order, and organised gangs of convicts as artificers in various trades. Those convicts were of much use to Singapore, at a time when labour was scarce and required for other than public purposes; for the long roads across the island were made by them, the Cathedral was built by them, and later on Government House, while they were in charge of Major McNair. In 1861, while he was in England, he learnt photography, so that he might teach others to take the pictures of the convicts, and he introduced it in the Government service here, and afterwards at Penang. It was no uncommon thing for ladies and gentlemen to go and be photographed in the Jail by the Major. There was not the competition in photography then that there is now, when it is so much better known. It is noteworthy that in the charge of so large a number of convicts (many times the number there is in our jail now), he was at one time assisted by only one European Warder, the remainder of the petty officers being recruited from among the prisoners. An account of this is to be found in the book lately written by Major McNair and Mr. W. D. Bayliss, who was his assistant and Superintendent of Works and Surveys for many years in Singapore, entitled "Prisoners their own Warders" published in one volume in London in 1899.

No doubt the system had its defects, and that there was a wide difference between the jail as it is now, filled with offenders sentenced in Singapore, and a jail which contained criminals who came from distant places and did not know the local language, and had no friends outside the walls to help them to escape from the island if they succeeded in getting clear of the jail; but notwithstanding, it was often a wonder to many to find so large an establishment of the worst characters of India kept in check by what was, practically, almost personal influence alone.

The jail was one of the most remarkable sights in the place, and no one came on a visit from India in those days without going over it before he returned. For all sorts of things—from coir matting and rattan chairs down to waste paper baskets—every one went to the jail, and the rattan lounging chairs the Chinese now sell here so largely were invented there, beginning with a cumbrous, heavy chair, which was the first pattern, down to the shapes we see now.

In 1867 the Major returned from a visit to England. He came out with Governor Ord, and was appointed Colonial Engineer to the Straits Settlements—the new name of his office in the Colony, which was then taken over from India. The first works he had to take in hand were Government House and the Water Works, which latter had been commenced, ignominiously smashed up, and been commenced again, and failed again, under other hands, and were at last constructed in his time. He made three schemes for the works, and one was approved in England by Sir Robert Rawlinson and sanctioned by the Secretary of State. Though the Major had to bear the brunt of the credit (?) of the extra expense caused to the Colony, it should be said, in justice to him, that he was not in any way responsible for the former designs, and that the successful issue was due to his working while on leave in England with Sir Robert Rawlinson, who was afterwards made the responsible adviser of Government in the matter. By one of those who knew of the former fiascos, how one Engineer thought water would run up hill without a head on it, and another thought to lower the surface of a stream by digging away at the bed of it, it was said that the best epitaph for Major McNair's services in the Straits would be : "The Water-works were finished in his time, and the Water ran through the pipes." There is a road called after the Major behind Tan Tock Seng's hospital in Serangoon Road.

In 1868 he went with the expedition to view the eclipse at Whae Wan on the East Coast of the Peninsula, which caused the death of the old King of Siam, who went to the same place, and caught fever, of which he died, consequent, as some thought, on *curing* himself with too many Holloway's Pills. In 1875 the Major went as Chief Commissioner in Perak during the disturbances, an account of which is to be found in his book called "Perak and the Malays" published in London in 1878. He was afterwards Resident Councillor of Penang, and was obliged to give up the post in 1884, on medical advice, after thirty years of hard work, and has since lived at Brighton. His eldest daughter married the late Mr. Thomas Scott, of Guthrie & Co., and the youngest daughter Mr. Charles Stringer of Paterson, Simons & Co.

The Major went on several missions to the surrounding countries, besides the one to Siam, and was very well acquainted with all the neighbouring places and their inhabitants, and his name was well known among them. He was permitted to accept the order of the White Elephant of Siam, and made a C.M.G. in 1879. He belonged to several of the learned societies in England, and took a great deal of trouble to send curiosities and specimens of fruit and other products to Europe. He acted as Colonial Secretary in Singapore at one time, and there was scarcely any official in the service who knew as much as he did about the Straits. The always ready kindness and hospitality of himself and Mrs McNair were known to all, and, especially in the old days, to young men just out from England in a strange place, to whom such friends were a world of good. His very courteous manner to everyone, and his consideration, especially for all those employed under him, will long be remembered.

Among the list of passengers who arrived from Europe on the 16th December by the P. & O. Mail is found the Name of Mr. Charles Dunlop, who came out from Glasgow to Maclaine, Fraser & Co., at nineteen years of age. He was afterwards a partner in that firm, and subsequently for some years in Powell & Co., and has now been longer resident in Singapore than any other European here.

CHAPTER XLV.

1857

O N the 2nd January all the shops remained closed, the markets were deserted, and the boatmen and hack-gharry syces refused to work. The Municipal and Police Acts had been brought into force without their objects being properly made known to or under-stood by the natives, and considerable misconception prevailed about them, which led to a general combination among the native population.

An attempt to induce a shop-keeper to open his shop, led to a riot in which the police were roughly handled, and as the state of affairs in China had given rise to some feelings of ill-will towards Europeans on the part of some of the lowest classes of the Chinese, matters began to assume a somewhat serious appearance. In those days there were very few Singapore-born Chinese in the place.

A public meeting was called by the Sheriff at one o'clock in the afternoon. Mr. John Purvis was Chairman, and a committee of nine European gentlemen, with Whampoa and Tan Kim Cheng, was appointed to wait at once upon the Governor, asking him to issue a proclamation calling upon people to return to their business, and saying that any acts of intimidation would be severely punished; and that the Governor was at all times ready to listen to proper complaints, respectfully made, and that the translations of the Acts would be revised.

The following proclamation was issued in Chinese the same day : "Now on account of all classes of the people closing their shops, and not wishing to do business because they have heard that the words of the new Act are not clearly understood; people do not understand it, therefore it is difficult for them to obey, and in consequence the present misunderstanding has arisen, and the closing of the shops has taken place. Now be it known that within one month hence the definitions of the Act will be more clearly explained, in order that it may be fully understood. If in the body of the Act there is anything objectionable to the mass of the population, such as know thereof may come within one month to the Court, and to the Governor may make known their complaint. Now you ought all to open your shops and transact your business as usual and do not disobey this. This is given to understand."

An adjourned meeting was held the next day, Saturday, at 3 p.m., when the greater part of the shops had been opened, and a long discussion took place incidentally about the probable advantage that would result, if the Settlements were transferred to the direct rule of the Crown. Some amusement was caused by a counter-proclamation in Chinese being read. It had been found pasted over the Government proclamation; the purport being that no faith was to be put in the Governor's promise to have the law explained; that he only wished to gain time and secure provisions; while the Chinese were quite ready with guns to sweep away every barbarian from the island.

Mr. W. H. Read proposed, seconded by Mr. T. O. Crane, a resolution, which was carried unanimously, as to the danger of the Secret Societies, on whose headmen the people evidently relied in the disturbances; and the same committee as before was asked to wait upon the Governor, and satisfy themselves that the authorities were prepared to suppress any outbreak that might arise.

The Military and the Volunteer Rifles were in readiness, and some large guns were mounted on Government Hill (now Fort Canning) and Pearls Hill. An additional regiment was soon afterwards sent from Madras.

At the Assizes in the following week the Grand Jury in their Presentment at the close of the Session dwelt at considerable length on the dangers to the peace of the Settlement arising from the Secret Societies or Hoés amongst the Chinese being allowed to exist unchecked, and suggestions were offered as to the best means of dealing with these societies.

The enforcement of the Police and Conservancy Acts by the Police gave rise to another disturbance in February, confined however to one section of the Native population, the Klings, and was unfortunately attended with considerable bloodshed and loss of life. The Imaum of the Mahomedan Mosque in Telloh Ayer Street had obtained a license to celebrate a festival extending over several days, on the condition that the proceedings should terminate each evening at ten o'clock. On the evening of the 5th February, Arthur Pennefather, one of the Police Inspectors, going his rounds between ten and eleven, accompanied by a Police Sergeant and several peons, found a large assemblage of Klings at the Mosque, completely blocking up the road in Telloh Ayer and Japan Streets, there being also obstructions in the shape of stakes and plantain trees stuck in the ground. The Inspector ordered the obstructions to be removed by the peons, but this was resisted by the Klings. The Inspector then sent to the Police station for a reinforcement, he himself remaining on the spot with the Sergeant. Seven or eight policemen presently arrived, some of them armed with loaded muskets. The Inspector then again ordered the Imaum to remove the obstructions, and on his declining to do so, the police peons were ordered to take up the stakes. On their attempting this, the mob assailed them with sticks and stones, and the Sergeant and one of the peons were knocked down, the latter being rendered senseless. He was taken up by some of his comrades, and the party retired towards the Police Station in Telloh Ayer Street, followed by the mob, who continued to throw missiles. When near the Station the Police fired over the mob, who retreated, and the party then gained the Station. The mob then assailed the Station with brickbats, stones, &c., and the Police replied by firing from both the ground and upper floors. One person was shot dead, one died next day from his wounds, and eleven others were so severely wounded that they were sent to the Hospital. Inquests were held on the bodies of the persons killed, and, in both, verdicts were returned of justifiable homicide. The Commissioner of Police (Mr. Mackenzie, the Resident Councillor) after the first inquest, with the consent of the Governor, dismissed the Inspector, Sergeant, and one of the peons, and reduced some of the native police, who had been concerned in the affair, in rank. This decision was come to because the Commissioner was of opinion that the conduct of the Inspector was most rash and precipitate, that fire arms had been used without sufficient cause and that this had provoked the riotous and illegal attack of the mob. Considerable excitement was induced amongst the European residents by this decision of the Commissioner; they thought it was not justified in face of the verdict of the Coroner's Jury, who had completely exculpated the police from blame, and they also conceived it was calculated to prejudice the interests of Inspector Pennefather, against whom proceedings had been taken before the Police Magistrate, which resulted in his being committed to take his trial for manslaughter at the next Criminal Sessions.

A public meeting was held on 26th February, at which over 80 Europeans were present, with Mr. C. H. Harrison in the chair, and remonstrances were addressed to the Governor, who however declined to restore the dismissed persons to the positions they had previously held in the Police force. The difference of opinion between the Governor and the European residents generally was so wide, that at one of the meetings a Committee was actually appointed " for the purpose of drawing up a resumé of the general policy of His Honor the Governor, pointing out the repeated instances in which it has been at variance with the true interests of the Settlement, and begging that the present serious difference of opinion between the Executive and the public of Singapore be taken into the earnest consideration of the Supreme Government."

This threatened indictment of the Governor was not however carried out; the Inspector was brought to trial at the Criminal Session held in April, and after a trial lasting eight days was acquitted of the charge against him.

The *Free Press* remarked that upon a review of the case it appeared that the police acted with a want of that forbearance and good temper which was requisite, and had recourse to unnecessary violence, calculated to provoke the mob, though it could not excuse it in the extremities to which it went. The conduct of the authorities in afterwards dealing with the case was undignified, and wanting in that spirit of fairplay and impartiality which ought to characterise those in high office towards their subordinates.

In February the petition against levying tonnage dues in the Straits ports was sent to Calcutta by the Committee appointed on 18th December. As soon as the information reached England in March, a number of gentlemen connected with the Straits had taken up the matter there with great vigour. A memorial to the President of the India Board was prepared and presented, and the deputation met with a most attentive hearing. No positive assurances were given, but it was obvious that if it were pressed from Calcutta it would receive no countenance at the India office. A copy of the memorial was in the *Free Press* of 30th April. The names make a rough sort of directory of the old Singaporeans in England, and of the large firms in London connected with the trade of Singapore, at that time ; so they are inserted here, in alphabetical order ; first of individuals, and then of London firms, which comprised some very eminent houses :—

W. S. Binny	Arbuthnot, Latham & Co.
Edward Boustead	Ashton & Co.
Thomas Church	Borneo Co., Limited
J. A. Crawford	Chalmers, Guthrie & Co.
John Crawfurd	Crawford, Colvin & Co.
J. P. Cumming	D. Dunbar & Sons
Robert Diggles	Forbes, Forbes & Co.
James Fraser	Gregson & Co.
Lewis Fraser	Harvey, Brand & Co.
Samuel Garling	R. & J. Henderson
Ellis J. Gilman	Fred. Huth & Co.
Alex. Guthrie	Jardine Skinner & Co.
James Guthrie	W. S. Lindsay & Co.
W. W. Ker	Matheson & Co.
Geo. G. Nicol	Oriental Bank Corporation
J. Padday	Palmers, Mackillop, Dent & Co.
W. W. Shaw	P. & O. Company
J. N. Smith	Wm. Jas. & H. Thompson
Chas. Spottiswoode	Rawson Sons & Co.
William Spottiswoode	Small & Co.

On the 6th February a regatta took place in the morning, and in the evening the members of Lodge Zetland in the East, No. 748, gave what they modestly called an evening party, but was a most successful ball and elaborate supper.

On the evening of Saturday 14th February, the Singapore Volunteer Rifle Corps was presented with a set of colours which had been prepared for it by Mrs. Butterworth, the widow of the late Governor, under whom the Corps was embodied, and who continued its Colonel up to his death. Brigadier McLeod permitted all the troops in Singapore to be paraded on the Esplanade. The Corps wore a band of crape on the arm as a sign of mourning for their late Colonel. Governor Blundell presented the colours to Mr. W. H. Read, the Senior Lieutenant, and addressed the Corps.

Mr. Read replied ; and the following is the final passage of his reported speech :—" We seek not the glory of the battle-field, nor to embroider the names of victories on these colours. Ours are less martial, more peaceful aims. Our object is to assist in protecting the lives and property of the public, and to shew the evil-disposed how readily Europeans will come forward in the maintenance of order and tranquillity. Should we ever be called upon to act, we shall be found prepared to do our duty, contented with the approbation of the Government and the applause of our fellow citizens."

In March the Dutch barque *Henrietta Maria* was brought into Singapore by part of the crew of an American merchant vessel, having been found in a disabled state in the China Sea. The vessel had left Macao for Havana, with upwards of 300 Chinese coolies on board, but the coolies had risen during the passage down the China Sea, and seized the vessel. A great many of the Chinese had left the ship, and the Captain and the greater part of the crew were stated to have gone away in a boat. When the vessel was taken possession of by the American salvors, there were only four men of the original crew, together with about one hundred of the Chinese, on board. On the arrival of the vessel at Singapore, Governor Blundell communicated the circumstances to the Dutch Resident at Riow, and a Dutch vessel of war having been sent to Singapore, the Governor delivered the *Henrietta Maria* to her, in spite of the protests of the United States Consul; the American flag, which the Consul had authorised the salvors to hoist on the vessel, being hauled down by the Master Attendant. An American man of war arrived some time afterwards at Singapore to enquire into the circumstances, and some correspondence ensued between the commander and the authorities. The affair having been reported to the Supreme Government by the Governor, his conduct in giving up the vessel to the Dutch authorities was pronounced illegal, and he was desired to make proper compensation to the salvors.

A number of petty cases of piracy occurred in the waters near Singapore, and Chinese pirates as usual were busy in the Gulf of Siam and China Sea at the season when the junks and other native craft passed through on their way to or from Singapore. The state of affairs in China in this year prevented the promised measures being taken by Commodore Henry Keppel for an organised system of operations against the pirates in the neighbouring seas.

As the remarkable establishment of Sir James Brooke's Government in Sarawak had almost seemed part of the history of Singapore, great excitement was caused on the arrival of the schooner *Good Luck*, on 10th March, with the news of the very serious outbreak of Chinese there in February, attended with considerable loss of life and destruction of property, which did not, however, more than very temporarily interfere with the prosperity of the place. The Chinese acted with great secrecy and determination, and dropping down the river to Kuching in large numbers, on the night of the 17th February they attacked the houses of the Europeans connected with the Government and the stockaded posts in which were lodged the treasure, opium, ammunition, &c. The houses occupied by Sir James Brooke, Mr. Arthur C. Crookshank the magistrate, and Mr. Middleton were burned down. Sir James Brooke narrowly escaped with his life, Mr. and Mrs. Crookshank were severely wounded, two of Mr. Middleton's children perished in the flames, and Mr. Nicoletts, a relation of Sir James Brooke, and Mr. Willington, a metallurgist in the service of the Borneo Company, were slain.

The Chinese went up the river, but again returned to Kuching in large force on the 22nd, took possession of the town and burnt down a part of the Malay kampong. They did not long however enjoy their triumph, for the Borneo Company's Steamer *Sir James Brooke* having arrived from Singapore, she proceeded up to Kuching

on the 23rd and by the fire of her guns soon cleared the town
of the Chinese. They retreated in much disorder, and the Malays
and Dyaks having rallied and collected in great numbers, an un-
relenting pursuit of the Chinese was kept up and they were finally
driven into the Dutch territories.

In March Boustead & Co. advertised for sale the house of Mr.
William Napier in the "Tang Leng" district, 3½ miles from town.
It was afterwards, and is now, known as Tyersall. The house had
been built in 1854, and the grounds had an area of 67 acres.
The house was pulled down when the late Sultan Aboobakar of
Johore built the present Istana on the site.

On 19th March, H.M.S. *Raleigh*, Captain Turner, bearing the
broad pennant of Commodore Keppel, c.b., sailed into New Harbour. On the 24th she came into the roads and saluted the shore.
As the old Admiral was in Singapore when this chapter was being
written, he was asked (while he was sitting on an easy chair,
looking across the Straits, from the verandah of Dato Meldrum's
house in Johore) if he remembered how it came about that he sailed
the *Raleigh* into New Harbour instead of into the Roads. He said
that he did it because he had surveyed New Harbour while he
was in the *Meander*, and had the same master, (navigating officer)
with him in the *Raleigh* who had surveyed it with him, so he felt quite
confident about it, although others had been afraid to go in! It seemed
very curious to be talking in this part of the world, to the old
Admiral of the Fleet, close on his 93rd year, hearing details of those
old days. He said he thought that he came in late in the evening.

Admiral Montagu tells in his book, mentioned later on, how
Keppel carried on to be at Hongkong in time for the fray, after
leaving Penang, and the frigate was running with the main-deck
guns dragging through the water, as the Commodore would not
allow a scrap of sail to be taken in during the squalls.

An address signed by the whole of the mercantile community
was presented to him on the 20th, and contained the following
passage :—"We hail with pleasure your appointment as a guarantee
on the part of Her Majesty's Government for the future efficient
protection of trade and commerce, by confiding a high command to
so distinguished and energetic an officer as yourself, whose experience in the East has been so extensive, while your appreciation
of Singapore is peculiarly gratifying to us."

And the reply contained the following :—"It is with no small
feelings of pride and gratification that I have to acknowledge the
kind and flattering "welcome back" I have this day received in an
address signed by the Merchants and other Gentlemen residents at
Singapore. I plead guilty to a long standing and deep interest
in all that concerns this rapidly rising Settlement. By zealously
performing those duties for which I may be selected by an energetic
and distinguished chief, I shall hope to retain the good opinion of
my kind friends at Singapore."

The *Raleigh* was a magnificent frigate of 50 guns, the last of
the old sailers ! She was said to be the fastest sailing frigate
afloat, and had a crew of 600 men, besides super-numeraries.

The vessel was nicknamed in Singapore the "House of Lords," as there were in her so many officers of illustrious family, who became distinguished men in after years. The first lieutenant was Mr. Goodenough, who was killed in Australia while Commodore, universally lamented. The second is now the Earl of Clanwilliam, who came here afterwards as the Admiral of the Squadron with which the two sons of the Prince of Wales came to Singapore. The third was Prince Victor of Hohenlohe. Among the midshipmen was Captain Keppel's nephew, his sister's son, now Sir Henry F. Stephenson, K.C.B., Equerry to the King, who was the Senior Officer in command of the Channel Squadron at Spithead at the great Jubilee Review in June, 1897. In the Admiral's last book he says that at the time of the bombardment of Bomarsund in the Crimean War : "On one occasion when my officers had taken my nephew Harry Stephenson on shore, a round shot buried itself within a few yards of them. They dispersed in haste, all but young Harry, who picked up a pointed stick and commenced digging at his first trophy." He came again to Singapore when he commanded the *Carysfort* in Admiral Clanwilliam's squadron with the Princes, the two sons of the Prince of Wales, and Admiral Keppel's only son was then a midshipman in his ship. Lord Charles Scott, the senior midshipman of the *Raleigh*, has been many times in Singapore since then. He was Captain of the *Icarus* and afterwards of the *Bacchante*, in which the two Princes were midshipmen. In 1902 he is Commander-in-Chief at Plymouth. There were others on board whose names are now well-known.

The *Raleigh* only stayed a few days, and on her way to Hongkong was passing near Macao, when she struck on a sunken and uncharted rock. The *Free Press* contained a long account of the accident. The Admiral tells us about her loss, and the well-known story of his saluting, as she was sinking, a French man-of-war that was near, and the French Admiral's exclamation, "*C'est magnifique !* A British frigate saluting the French flag while sinking !" But the Admiral does not say, what the old story told, that he was the last man up the ladder from the main deck when the last shot of the salute had been fired. The ship was never raised.

After the loss of the *Raleigh*, Commodore Keppel was in the Fatshan Creek action on the 1st June, 1857, what has been spoken of as "the greatest cutting-out action of modern times." In the Junior Army and Navy Club in London is a picture of Commodore Keppel in his boat, with his dog "Mike" barking in the bows. The boat was sunk, the bowman killed, a sailor cut in two, a third's arm shot off, and while Prince Victor was leaning forward to tie it up with his neck-cloth, a shot passed through both sides of the boat wounding more of the men. A long account of the action was in the *Free Press* on 29th October, 1867, and a copy of the picture was in one of the London illustrated papers on Jubilee Day in 1897. There is also a full account of it in Mr. W. H. Read's book called "Play and Politics."

In April Dr. Little advertised the land at Institution Hill for sale in lots of one or more acres each for house-building, but it was not sold.

In May, as in India during the two months before, rumours began to arise, in a vague uneasy way, about threatenings of coming trouble in India. There were only suspicions, apparently founded on nothing but talk in the bazaar. It now seems possible that the convicts in Singapore may have had, as many natives in India had, some news of what was in the wind. This seems to be likely, as on Friday, 7th August, a state prisoner, named Kurruck Sing, who had been released some time before from confinement in the Jail, and allowed to reside outside, was seized and taken on board H. M. S. *Racehorse*, a gunboat in the harbour. He had been detected in tampering with the Sikh convicts in the Jail, and was sent away to Penang.

On Sunday, 31st May, the opium steamer *Fiery Cross*, Captain Grant, arrived from Calcutta, and the first news reached Singapore of the Mutiny. The *Free Press* said that it was hoped the Mutiny might not spread, and added that if the European troops in India should not be thought sufficient to maintain order in the crisis, it was probable the whole or the greater part of the force, then on its way from England to China, might have its destination temporarily changed to India. And that however much the postponement of operations in China might be regretted, everything would have to yield to the paramount necessity of maintaining our power in India, and teaching the misguided sepoys that the only ultimate result of revolt on their part would be to ensure a certain and terrible retribution.

Mr. Abraham Logan was writing the *Free Press* at that time, and his words are noteworthy, as matters turned out. Lord Elgin had arrived the day before the paper appeared, and it is possible Mr. Logan may have heard that day what the Plenipotentiary had decided during the night to do. If he had not, the passage was a remarkable one.

The Right Hon'ble Lord Elgin, the 8th Earl, was afterwards a distinguished Viceroy of India. He had been appointed British High Commissioner and Plenipotentiary in China, and had left England with his staff, in the P. & O. Mail on 26th April, and arrived at Point de Galle, Ceylon, on 26th May. There he heard of the outbreak of the 3rd Bengal Cavalry and other native troops at Meerut in the Punjab, but it was thought that it might be a slight matter. He arrived at Singapore on Wednesday, 3rd June, to wait the arrival of H. M. S. *Shannon*, a steam frigate, Captain W. Peel, c.b., which had come round the Cape, as his Embassy Ship, to convey him to China.

On page 95 it has been said that there had been a tradition that he, Lord Elgin, walked up and down all night on the long front verandah of the old Government House, now Fort Canning, and decided in the morning to divert the troops going to China. As the sheets of this book have been printed, a copy has been sent to England in order that a few old Singaporeans there might read them and make any remarks. One of these was Major McNair, often spoken of elsewhere in this book, and just as this Chapter has to be written, letters have been received from him which put the matter beyond a doubt.

Whether Lord Elgin did or did not actually walk up and down the verandah (as tradition has said, and the writer, who heard it here only seven years afterwards, believes) is not of any consequence ; but the main fact, which has been doubted, as will be shewn presently, is now beyond question, for we have the story from one who was present. It may be remarked that Mr. John Cameron, who wrote his book in 1864, also seven years afterwards, said, at page 24, that Lord Elgin " all that night paced up and down his room in the Government bungalow where Fort Canning stands now, holding interviews with the naval and military officers of the expedition, and next morning at daylight a steamer was despatched to the Straits of Sunda with the order which, it is believed by many, saved the British Empire in India." This is confirmatory of the tradition spoken of, but it was not in the mind of the writer when page 95 was written, but has been noticed in hunting into the matter for this chapter.

The way in which a doubt arose as to this very important decision having been made in old Government House, was a passage in a book entitled " Life and Times of Sir George Grey " which stated that Lord Elgin had no knowledge of the diversion of the troops for China to India in 1857, until informed of the fact by Sir George Grey, at that time Governor of the Cape ; and that the credit for the first " timely and invaluable aid," also mentioned by Lord Malmesbury as due to Lord Elgin, was really due to the action taken by Sir George Grey. This led to a letter of some length clearly disproving this, written by Sir Henry Loch, then Governor of the Cape, which appeared in the London *Times* in October, 1892 in which he said that it was the information in Singapore that decided Lord Elgin to take the course he did.

Mr. Loch was an Attaché to Lord Elgin's Embassy in 1857. He was afterwards Sir Henry Loch, Governor of the Cape, and later was created Lord Loch, the first Baron. He died in 1900.

Now follows a copy of what Major McNair wrote in December, 1901, to Mr. W. H. Read on the subject :—" Did you notice by the way, that in the description of the old Government House, on page 95, Buckley says that there was a tradition that Lord Elgin had walked up and down the verandah one whole night, thinking what was best to be done about sending troops to Calcutta to help to quell the Mutiny ?—There was some truth in the remark, for I was present at the interview between Lord Elgin and Governor Blundell when the serious news came from Calcutta. Lord Elgin asked the Governor, who knew about India and its people, whether he thought the revolt was likely to spread ; and when he replied in the affirmative, His Lordship decided to divert the troops to India then on their way to China. This was accordingly done, and orders were sent to turn the troop-ships on to Singapore en route to Calcutta.

" The late Lord Loch was Private Secretary to Lord Elgin and I was Private Secretary to Governor Blundell at the time, and we were present at this remarkable interview; which, it was afterwards said, had resulted in the saving of Calcutta by the timely arrival of re-inforcements from the Straits, the Mauritius and the Cape ; and those from the Straits were the first to arrive on the scene. There is no doubt the anxiety might have caused Lord Elgin a sleepless night, but I cannot vouch for his nocturnal peripatetic walking about the verandah of old Government House."

With this testimony of Lord Loch and Major McNair in strict accord, there is no room for doubt; and it is very satisfactory that the mention of the tradition, in a casual way, while writing on another subject, has brought Major McNair's most interesting letter in time to insert it here.

Lord Roberts of Kandahar in the sixteenth chapter of his book "Forty-one Years in India" says:—"It was cheering to learn that Lord Elgin, taking a statesmanlike view of the situation, had diverted to India the force intended for the China Expedition." But he added this foot-note:—"Since writing the above, it has been brought to my notice that the promptitude with which the troops were diverted to India was due in a great measure to the foresight of Sir George Grey, the Governor of the Cape, who, on hearing of the serious state of affairs in India, immediately ordered all transports which touched at the Cape on their way to take part in the China Expeditionary force, to proceed directly to Calcutta, instead of to Singapore."

The letters of Lord Loch and Major McNair show that Lord Roberts was not correctly informed in the qualification he put upon what he had first correctly written. The matter seems clear, also, for other reasons. There was quick steam communication, for those days, between Calcutta and Singapore, by the opium steamers which had only commenced to run in 1856, and the news only reached here three days before Lord Elgin arrived, when the transports were probably past the Cape on their way towards Singapore and China. Whether there was steam-communication between Calcutta and the Cape at that time, cannot be ascertained in Singapore when this is written, but, it is extremely unlikely, and in the absence of direct proof to the contrary, it seems impossible that any definite news could have reached Sir George Grey in time to divert the transports. It also seems to the writer to be most unlikely that Sir George Grey would have taken upon himself the grave responsibility of taking them from under the orders of Lord Elgin, when the latter could divert the ships himself (as he did) if he saw sufficient reason to do so.

It has been said speaking of the responsibility which Lord Elgin took in this matter, that if the state of affairs in India had been exaggerated, as was quite possible, or if the Mutiny had been suppressed before the troops arrived, which was also possible, so far as could be known in Singapore that night, his reputation would have been ruined.

The *Shannon* arrived on the 10th, and left for China on 23rd June, and before her arrival the Earl of Elgin and Kincardine held a Levée at Government House, on Saturday the 6th, and was presented by Mr. W. Paterson with an address from the Chamber of Commerce, referring to the critical state of our relations with China. In his reply Lord Elgin said that it was gratifying to witness the progress of the community of Singapore, which, under the influence of wise and just laws, was daily advancing in prosperity and wealth; and comparing it with the sad condition of Canton where bad faith and misgovernment had paralysed trade, and spread hunger, desolation and ruin. The Chinese merchants also presented an address speaking of their great advantage of being under English Government.

On the morning of the 10th Lord Elgin went with a party of gentlemen to pay a visit to the Perseverance Sugar Estate of J. d'Almeida & Sons, and went over the works. On Friday evening, the 12th, the mercantile community entertained the Earl at a Ball and Supper at the Masonic Lodge.

On 28th July the *Shannon* with Lord Elgin, and the *Pearl*, both steam vessels, arrived together from Hongkong, and left for Calcutta on the 30th. They were the vessels from which the famous naval brigade was formed at Calcutta to go up-country in the Mutiny. The *Shannon* was commanded by the gallant Captain Peel, afterwards Sir William Peel, who was seriously wounded in command of a battery at Lucknow. An account of his death is at the end of Chapter XXIX of Lord Robert's book, " Forty-one Years in India." In the *Shannon* also was a young lieutenant, twenty-two years of age, now Admiral of the Fleet Sir Nowell Salmon, v.c., g.c.b., an account of whose exploit at Lucknow is in Chapter XXIV of the same book ; he was afterwards in Singapore when he was Commander-in-Chief on the China Station in 1888.

The *Pearl* was commanded by Captain Sotheby, who died Sir Edward Sotheby, k.c.b., in January, 1902, a retired Admiral. After the *Raleigh* was wrecked, three of her midshipmen, Lord Charles Scott, the Hon. Victor Alexander Montagu and H. F. Stephenson were told that they were appointed to the *Pearl* in Hongkong, while they were having break-fast with Mr. John Dent, and left for Singapore and Calcutta the next day. Admiral Montagu, now retired, one of the sons of the Seventh Earl of Sandwich, has written a book called " A Middy's Recollections, 1853 to 1860," published by Adam and Charles Black, London, in 1900. It con-tains a great deal about Admiral Keppel, the Crimean War, the Fatshan Creek action, and the Indian Mutiny, and has a picture of the *Princess Royal*, of 91 guns, in the Crimean War, which was flagship in China in 1866, and pictures of the *Raleigh* and the battle of Fatshan, showing the sinking of Commodore Keppel's galley ; and a picture of the *Pearl*. The Admiral says in his book that the three midshipmen thought then that following Keppel in China would have been more to the point, as they could not anticipate the Naval Brigade in India, which got them their promotion and the thanks of both Houses of Parliament, and a great re-ception in Calcutta when they got back to the *Pearl* in February, 1859, having left her to go with the Naval Brigade in October, 1857, a period of eighteen months away from their ship, which is probably unexampled in the service.

The *Pearl* was a steam corvette of 21 guns, 1,469 tons, 400 horse power, and was often in Singapore. It was of her that an amusing story was told of Captain John Borlase, afterwards a retired Admiral, who took her out to China under sail, and on entering Hongkong harbour, with all plain sail set, being one of the old school of course, he forgot the ship had got steam up. He took in sail as he neared the shipping in the most seamanlike way, but to his horror the vessel went on in spite of taking in sail after sail, and cannoned from the bows of one vessel at anchor against another vessel, and fought her way through the shipping, until it struck him there must be something more than the wind driving the ship, and he called out " Good ——, I forgot I was a steamer. Stop the —— thing down below." Little harm was done, and soon afterwards Captain Borlase engaged the batteries at Kagosima in Japan, in 1863. This was the same ship which Commodore James G. Goodenough, in Australia, commanded at the time of his unfortunate death. The *Pearl* was also in Singapore, when she came again from England, from October, 1866 to April, 1867, when Admiral Keppel hoisted his flag in her on the day of the transfer on 1st April, and the *Pearl* accompanied his yacht, the *Salamis*, to Sarawak. She afterwards went north, and eventually went home by the Pacific, to be paid off, and was broken up long ago. As Sir Walter Besant made the old sailor say in "By Celia's Arbour," "it seems a shame to break such brave ships up, and they ought to be painted every year and kept for the boys and girls to see."

Lord Elgin was three times in Singapore in 1857; once on his way to China, then on his return to Calcutta, and again on his return to China from India. He died in November, 1863, on his way to Lahore, while Governor-General of India, in which he had succeeded Lord Canning. In Sir Algernon West's Recollections published in 1899, he says :—"Lord Elgin, Lord Dalhousie, and Lord Canning, fell victims to the climate and responsibilities of our Indian Empire : they were swept away, as Mr. Gladstone said, 'in the full maturity of their faculties, and in the early stages of middle life.' Someone has said that 'forty is the age of youth, and fifty the youth of old age,' and they, before they reached that age, had all sought their rest."

There were several accidents to the troopships. The famous *Himalaya*, that had been bought into the Navy from the P. & O. at the time of the Crimean War, and did such good work for some forty years, (she was broken up in 1896) brought out the 90th Regiment (the Perthshire Volunteers) and got aground on a shoal in Banka Straits, but got off again. When she arrived in Singapore "this magnificent steamer was an object of much curiosity at the P. & O. Company's Depôt, and the numerous visitors to her were very courteously received by her officers, notwithstanding the very hurried nature of her brief stay in port." The regiment's band, over 50 strong, played on the Saturday evening on shore at New Harbour.

A long remembered incident was the total loss of H. M. Steam Troopship *Transit*, 3,000 tons, 450 horse-power. The wreck was sold by auction at the Master Attendant's Office in Singapore on 10th September. She was lost on a sunken rock off Cape Oelar, Island of Banca. The troops were brought to Singapore in the Straits Steamer *Hooghly*, and a chartered American vessel the *Beaver*.

The troops on board were 193 Medical Staff Corps, 30 Royal Engineers, 286 of the 90th and 119 of the 59th Regiments. The ship went down so quickly that only part of the arms were got out, and the officers and men did not save any of their clothes, many of them leaving her without shoes or stockings as the decks were being washed when she struck. The officers and crew came to Singapore in the Borneo Company's steamer *Sir James Brooke*.

The *Transit* had a most unfortunate voyage all the way. She left Portsmouth on 8th April for China, and the next day returned in a sinking state, having during the night grounded on her anchor.

All hands disembarked, the vessel was repaired, and all on board ready to start again on 15th April. But in going out of the dock she ran into the gate, injured the propeller, and, as it was afterwards known, seriously shook and loosened her stern, which was not apparent at the time. Then she got into rough weather in the Bay of Biscay, and a lot of water got in at the stern post. She put into Corunna to repair, and set off again.

She made good weather as far as the Cape, as long as the wind was on the beam, but before the wind she rolled very much, and took in lots of water. The injury at the stern showed itself again, the seams opened, and at each roll of the ship, water rushed in. In the course of one day no less than 600 tons of water were pumped out, and it was feared she would go to the bottom, but fortunately the weather improved, and they made Java Head.

They were steaming at their best, number one, speed of 8 knots, when the vessel ran hard on to a sunken rock not on the chart, bumped violently three times, and settled down about six miles from shore. Perfect discipline was maintained, the boats were got out, but they only held 200 men, and the ship seemed likely to go down before half could be landed. Captain Chambers ordered them to be landed on a reef two miles away, which was uncovered as it was low water. So all went first to the reef, and then to the shore; and the last trip was accomplished just in time, as the tide on the reef was rising, and was up to the knees of those who remained to the last. The discipline was compared at the time to that at the memorable accident of the *Birkenhead.* The soldiers all went on to Calcutta in the *Shannon* and the *Pearl.*

Neil, Outram and Havelock Roads in Singapore town were, about this time, named by the Municipality after some of the heroes in the Mutiny.

One of the measures adopted by the Government of India for meeting the emergency in which the Mutiny had placed it, was the passing of a legislative measure by which the Press was subjected to the most rigid fetters. Although this Act was at first chiefly justified on the ground of the seditious character of the native publications, no exemption was made in favour of the English press. This Act was applied everywhere throughout British India without exception, and the newspapers in the Straits, although they could not possibly exercise the slightest effect on the mutiny in India, found themselves subject to all the provisions of this most foolish Act. A public meeting was held on 28th July, Mr. M. F. Davidson in the Chair, to publicly protest against the application of this law to the Straits. The Act excited so much disapprobation both in India and England that it ceased in June, 1858.

In May Mr. T. A. Behn, who had retired from Behn, Meyer & Co., gave $500 each to the Sailors Home, Mr. Keasberry's Malay Schools, Tan Tock Seng's Hospital, and the Seamen's Hospital, which the *Free Press* said was an example that might be followed more extensively by retiring millionaires of Singapore.

It was in this year that the Governors of the different Presidencies, and other heads of Departments in India were ordered to make Annual Reports, and the first Report on the Administration of the Straits, during the year 1855-56, was made by the Governor.

It having been reported in August that the local government intended to allow the convicts the liberty of parading the streets during the Mohurram festival, the withdrawal of which in the previous year had led to very riotous acts on their part, a number of gentlemen addressed the Governor pointing out the inexpediency of allowing the convicts any such license. The Governor in reply stated that permission had been given to the convicts to parade certain streets outside their lines—and that this permission had been granted under the conviction that to refuse it would have the effect of needlessly exasperating the convict body, and of driving them to acts of desperation more dangerous to the peace and good order of the town than those which occurred the previous year. The convicts, after all, declined to avail of the permission given them! The large number of convicts in Singapore, and the reported intention of Government to send here a number of the most dangerous prisoners confined in Alipore Gaol, as well as sepoys and others convicted of participation in the mutiny in India, led to the inhabitants memorializing the Governor General in Council on the subject, protesting against such additions being made to the convict body in the Straits and praying that transportation to this quarter should be wholly discontinued. The Memorial was transmitted through the Governor, who was understood to be favorable to its general purport, having apparently considerably modified his opinions regarding a class whom in 1856 he had designed as "harmless settlers."

On 9th September it was stated in the *Free Press* that the Government would probably construct a Naval Dock at Pulo Brani, as it was under contemplation; which had been brought about by Commodore Keppel; and that considering the value of the services he had always sought means of rendering to Singapore, and in order to connect his name permanently with the benefit he had contributed to confer on the place, it was suggested that " the name of New Harbour be changed to Keppel Harbour." This was done in 1900, as has been said on page 493.

On 3rd October, a dinner was given to Commodore Keppel in the Hotel de l'Esperance, on the Esplanade, called afterwards the Hotel de l'Europe. Mr. John Harvey was in the Chair. The paper said that excellent speeches were made by Sir Richard McCausland the Recorder, who was a very witty, genial Irish speaker, and others. The *Free Press* remarked that the loss of his beautiful frigate the *Raleigh* has caused much disappointment in Singapore; that his gallant conduct in the Fatshan Creek action had added to the brilliant reputation he had already earned; and that the public dinner was characterised by a degree of enthusiasm not often witnessed on such occasions. The Commodore heard of his promotion to Rear Admiral and that he was made a K.C.B., just at the time. In his diary he said: "Waited on by a deputation of the merchants to invite me to an Entertainment. Grand dinner given me by residents. Their kindness prevented me responding as I wished." On the next day it said :— " Afternoon passed agreeably at Angus' small bungalow, where Whampoa and Harrison dined,

Mr. Gilbert Angus and Mr. Whampoa, just spoken of, were at one time partners. Gilbert Angus came from Lerwick, the capital of the Shetland Islands, and had been in Java before he came to Singapore. He was afterwards book-keeper to Shaw, Whitehead & Co., in which Captain James Stephens and Michie Forbes Davidson (afterwards of A. L. Johnston & Co., and Boustead & Co.) were partners. While Mr. Davidson was away in Europe, Stephens took Mr. Robert Duff, then *per procuration* holder of Boustead, Schwabe & Co., as a partner; and, in consequence, Angus left the firm and joined Mr. Whampoa, in Whampoa & Co. Mr. Davidson returned, did not like the arrangement, and joined A. L. Johnston & Co. Mr. Angus had nutmeg plantations, and owned a number of the hills round Tanglin at different times, as well as land in other parts of the island. His name frequently turns up in title deeds relating to land in a most unexpected fashion. He also tried brick making after Mr. Hentig gave it up, but he did not succeed; indeed it may be said that he was not fortunate generally in his business pursuits. He was a Municipal Commissioner for some time, and knew a great deal about the place. He never returned to Europe, and died at his residence in Armenian Street on 24th March, 1887, at 72 years of age, having been born on the day of the battle of Waterloo. He had been an auctioneer latterly, and was in failing health for some time. He was one of the oldest residents and left a large family.

It was curious how many of the well-known residents in Singapore in its early days came from Lerwick. Besides Mr. Angus, Mr. William Paterson of Paterson, Simons & Co., came from there. Also W. C. Leisk, Lloyd's Surveyor and chronometer maker, and Andrew Hay, who was in A. L. Johnston & Co., and then a shipchandler with Duncan in Hay and Duncan, who also came from Lerwick where his father was Sheriff Substitute as mentioned on page 155. The two brothers Gilbert and Robert Bain, well known in the place, and partners at various times in A. L. Johnston & Co., Boustead & Co., and Maclaine, Fraser & Co., also came from Lerwick. It seems too late now to find out how it came about; probably one of the first was a sailor, or on board a vessel in the East as A. L. Johnston was, and he may have seen the prospective advantages of the place and sent the news to Lerwick.

Mr. Whampoa, whose name was Hoo Ah Kay, was certainly the best known and most liked Chinaman in the Straits. His father came to Singapore in its earliest days, and kept a shop to supply the shipping and town with beef, bread and vegetables, which grew into a large business. Mr. J. T. Thomson, in one of his books, says he first knew Whampoa when he was a young boy in his father's shop, which was at the corner of Bonham Street and Boat Quay in the direction towards Elgin Bridge. After his father's death, Whampoa carried on the business, and for many years, and after his death, the firm were contractors for the navy. He first had a plantation where the Tanglin Barracks are now; and long before they were thought of, he had bought a neglected garden two-and-a-half miles out of town on the Serangoon Road. He built a bungalow there and made a fine garden, and had curious dwarf bamboos, and plants cut into resemblances of animals. There was an aviary, and peacocks, bears, and other animals.

A night or two at Whampoa's bungalow was a frequent treat to naval
officers, with whom he was much brought in contact, and who had
much admiration for him.   There is a good picture of him in Admiral
Keppel's last book, who often mentions him.   For example in his
diary in 1848, Captain Keppel wrote :—" Our worthy old Purser, Sim-
mons, died while staying at Whampoa's country house.   He was a
fine specimen of his countrymen ; his generosity and honesty had long
made him a favorite.   Whampoa gave sumptuous entertainments to
naval officers.   At midnight, by the light of a full moon, we would,
visit the beautiful *Victoria Regia*, a magnificent lotus in a circular
pond, a present from the Regent of Siam who sent it through W. H.
Read."   And nine years afterwards, the Admiral wrote :—" Put up at
Whampoa's and how comfortable the old fellow made me."

All visitors to Singapore had heard of him before they landed,
and it was the first place enquired for when a drive was to taken
out of the town.   It was one of the most hospitable houses in Singapore.   It was the custom in the early sixties for gentlemen going out
to dinner to dress in white, with the exception of Government House ;
or a first visit soon after arrival in Singapore at a party where there
were ladies ; or Mr. Whampoa's ; where a black dress suit was always
worn.   It may have been noticed that at the first Race Ball, see page
387, the words *Full Dress* were at the foot of the advertisement.   It
meant evening dress, and not the white suit with jacket, as was usual
on all occasions then, and for many years, until about 1870 probably,
when evening dress superseded it.   At the dances in the old Assembly
Rooms white dress was worn.

Mr. Whampoa was almost, the only Chinaman in Singapore in those
days who spoke English ; which he did with ease, but with some
curious mispronounciations ; for example he asked Mr. Thomson to
scratch his father's portrait, and he used to point to it, and tell how
Mr. Thomson had scratched it for him.   If he could be induced to
sing a Chinese song, the only one he knew, it was very laughable,
and he was as much amused, and laughed as heartily as any one
else.   He was a very upright, kind-hearted, modest, and simple man, a
friend to everyone in the place.   Towards the later years of his life,
he launched out into general business and speculations, in company
with some European merchants in the place, which got him into
troublous times, without his own fault, but he weathered the storm,
with his fortune very much reduced, in which he had the sympathy of all.

Mr. Whampoa was born in Whampoa rear Canton in China
about 1816, and died in Singapore on 29th March, 1880, 64 years
old.   His father was in Singapore when he was born, but his
mother never came to the place.   He was for many years Consul for
Russia, and possessed a consular uniform and sword, which he used
to say he had only put on once, and that he looked so " ugly "
and was laughed at so much, from his curious appearance in it, that
he never wore it again.   He was one of the first Unofficial Members
in 1867 of the Legislative Council when it was formed, and was
made a C.M.G. in 1878.   He was certainly the most widely-known
and respected Chinaman there has ever been in Singapore.   His remains
were taken to China and he was buried on Danes Island, opposite Canton.

The large brick house in the old garden was built in later years, and the large dining room at the back was finished just in time to give a big dinner to Admiral Keppel when he came out again as Commander-in-Chief in 1867. After Whampoa's death Mr. Seah Leang Seah bought the property, and then called it Bendemeer. Before that it had always been known as Whampoa's.

On 17th November a public meeting was held about the convicts and their treatment, Mr. M. F. Davidson in the Chair, and a number of resolutions were passed protesting against mutineers being sent as convicts to Singapore, the number of convicts being already too many for safety, and a committee was appointed to draw up a petition which was afterwards sent to Calcutta. There were then over 2,000 convicts in Singapore, besides others in the place whose terms had expired, and only a small number of military and of the European community. It was curious that the Singapore convicts sent to Bombay were returned to Singapore on the expiry of their sentences, whereas those sent from Bombay to Singapore were so well off here that they remained in the place.

The Straits Settlements at this time were in the diocese of Calcutta, as has been said on page 299. Singapore was too distant from India, for the Bishop there to take much interest in the place, with so many important duties close to his hand, and when it was necessary in 1851 to consecrate the first Church of St. Thomas at Sarawak, which Mr. McDougall, afterwards the Bishop, had built, Bishop Daniel Wilson of Calcutta came down to Singapore, and went to Sarawak for the purpose, with the authority, and in the name, of the Bishop of London, under whose jurisdiction the Church in Sarawak was assumed to be.

In the same way Bishop McDougall performed certain acts in Singapore in the character of Bishop, as, for example, the consecration of the new Cemetery in the year 1865, afterwards spoken of, which was done under the special power of a commission from the Bishop of Calcutta, Singapore being out of Bishop McDougall's diocese.

In connection with the matter of the bishopric, the following passage was written in September, 1857, in a letter in Sarawak by Bishop McDougall. It is to be found at page 167 of the Memoirs written by his brother-in-law, published in London in 1889. " Much as I prefer Sarawak as a place of residence, I feel more and more that Singapore ought to be the centre of the Church's Mission for these parts, and the site of a Missionary College and Cathedral Church. If, as it is anticipated out here, the Straits stations are turned over to the Queen's Government, my station ought to be Singapore, and the noble Church there now in erection, with the design of which I have had a great deal to do, ought to be my Cathedral. The present free schools at Singapore, Penang and Malacca, would be excellent feeders for a Missionary College, as they contain lads from all parts of the Archipelago, as well as from Siam and Burmah. Why should not our Church take up as large a field as the Roman Catholics, who are making the Straits their *point d'appui* for their Missions, not only to the different parts of the Archipelago, but also for Siam and Cochin-China. ?... The more I think of these views, the more desirable I feel them to be for the Church's sake."

It is clear from this that the Bishop appreciated the result to be expected in the future of Singapore from the work of the Roman Catholic Church in the place. He could not anticipate the work that would be done by the American Methodist Episcopal Church to be started in the centre of the work of the Church of England thirty years later.

As has been said on page 299, Bishop McDougall resigned in 1868, and went to England, never returning to the East. He was a canon residentiary of Ely, then Archdeacon of Huntingdon, then of Winchester, and Archdeacon of the Isle of Wight, besides holding two livings at various times in different parts of England.

In May, 1861, Bishop McDougall wrote to England in connection with the proposed transfer of the Straits to the Colonial Office, urging that the opportunity should be taken to separate them from the diocese of Calcutta. Among other reasons he pointed out that the average term of service of the Bengal Chaplains in the Straits had only been about two years, and that the missionary work had been left to the Roman Catholics, who had a Bishop, and a considerable body of French clergy, and Sisters of Mercy, while little or nothing had been done for the Church of England.

The seat of the diocese was transferred, as he had proposed, to Singapore in 1870, but the good that he anticipated did not result. What his earnest, sturdy character, (he was spoken of in England after the Lanun pirates' episode, as a good specimen of the "Church Militant!") would have done in Singapore, who can say? The Cathedral was built ten years before the change, and the work of thirty years has only to show a small Church with occasional services in an unfrequented part of the town; and the Mission Chapel, house, and school mentioned on page 300, largely due to the Society for the Propagation of the Gospel.

If these are compared with all the churches, buildings and schools of the Roman Catholic Church; or with those of the American Methodist Episcopal Mission, a list of which, over a column long, appears each month in their *Malaysia Message*; it may well be asked what good has resulted from the change which Bishop McDougall expected to produce a great expansion of the Church of England in Singapore. St. Andrew's Cathedral is kept in repair, and the portion of the stipend received by the Bishop from the Straits Settlements, as well as the stipend of the Colonial Chaplain, are all paid by the Government, advantages which no other church possesses.

It has to be remembered, however, that the arrangement that was made in 1870, with the object of making Singapore the headquarters of the Bishop, could not have been anticipated by Bishop McDougall in one respect. The Bishop was consecrated in Calcutta as Bishop of Labuan, because a bishopric could not then be established in a foreign country, so Labuan was chosen as being a Crown Colony available for the purpose. The stipend was provided by the Society for the Propagation of the Gospel and the Rajah of Sarawak, and it was styled the Bishopric of Labuan and Sarawak. When the title was changed to that of Singapore, Labuan and Sarawak it was intended to give prominence to the position of Singapore as the head-quarters of the work. But the stipend given by the Government of the Straits Settlements, one hundred pounds a year, is very small compared with that contributed by the S.P.G. and Sarawak, so that the Straits cannot reasonably complain that only a small portion of the year is spent by the Bishop in Singapore. A house was built by subscription among the congregation as a residence for the Bishop, in the expectation that he would be able to give more time to the Church here, but the house is let for some eight months of the year. The result of the work of the Church of England in Singapore and the Straits during the last thirty-two years, can be fairly judged by comparison with what others, with far less opportunities, have been able to do.

In 1882 the question of the disestablishment of the Church of England, which was carried out in Ceylon and other Colonies, came under consideration in the Legislative Council, but as the three Roman Catholic members of the Council joined with the rest in urging the Colonial Office not to make the same change in the Straits, matters have hitherto remained as they were under the East India Company.

In 1871 Mr. Thomas Scott, of his own motion, had brought the question of the disendowment of the Church before the Legislative Council, but it was not much discussed and was negatived (to use Mr. Shelford's words in 1882) as a premature step. In February, 1882, the question had again been raised by the Secretary of State for the Colonies, and the debate was noteworthy for the speech made by Mr. James Graham, which will be found at page 5 of the Council Proceedings for that year. The speech was spoken of as one of the most interesting and eloquent of those recorded in the Council. Mr. Graham, as he said on this occasion, was not given to speak at length or warmly in the Council, and this made it the more remarkable. No doubt he felt on other occasions that both time and patience are thrown away in discussing questions which have been definitely decided in advance, to be carried by an official majority. One passage in Mr. Graham's speech showing one reason, in his opinion, for upholding the establishment, was as follows:—" It is, therefore, wise and politic of us to insure that a man of education and high moral character, a man in whom the poorest—whether belonging to the church or not—can find a faithful friend, shall be placed in every one of our provinces, interested in the moral and intellectual welfare of our people, and with the sole object of doing good to them."

On 26th November it was said in the *Free Press* that the occupation of the Cocos Islands had been objected to by Holland as a violation of their rights, and gave an account of the way in which Mr. J. Ross, a sailor, a native of the Shetland Islands, had acquired his authority there. For some years before 1827, Ross had traded in the Archipelago, principally on the Coast of Sumatra, in a vessel called the *Borneo*, which he built with native labour at the Cocos, where a man named A. Hare had settled about 1823, upon the southernmost island. When the price of pepper was fluctuating very much, in consequence of the resort of Americans to Sumatra, Ross bought, in conjunction with his principals in London, all he could get, whenever prices were low, and stored it at the quiet and un-inhabited Cocos Islands, in order to take the accumulated stock to London when prices rose. He landed with his wife and children on the Cocos in 1827, and built a house. The chief mate went in the *Borneo*, and Ross remained on shore. The firm in London with which he was connected failed, and he was left with his family cut off from the world. Then Hare became very disagreeable, and seems to have gone a bit off his head, and at last left the Cocos. Ross remained on Direction Island, chief and master of the whole establish-ment, which gradually increased in extent and importance. Hare had taken a number of slaves there, whom Ross declared to be free. A Dutch ship went in there for repairs in 1842, and the Captain des-cribed Mr. Ross as a man of about 60 years old, of healthy and venerable aspect, intelligent, acute and deep thinking. In 1846 Sir Edward Belcher, r.n., paid a visit in his ship to the island, and found Captain Ross, as he called him, still in the house he had put together in a hurry with the remains of shipwrecked vessels, very dark, wholly overshadowed by cocoanut trees, and infested by mosquitoes. Captain Ross died soon after that. On 8th January, 1889, Christmas Island, on which the Ross family from the Cocos Islands had effected a settlement, was annexed to the Straits Settle-ments; the Cocos or Keeling Islands were placed under the Govern-ment of the Straits Settlements on 1st February, 1886.

A matter for congratulation during the course of 1857 was the receipt of orders from the Court of Directors ordering the complete resumption of the use of the dollar currency in all Government transactions.

There were a number of casualties to vessels this year. The Singa-pore barque *Penang*, with passengers from Singapore to Malacca and Penang, was lost near the Raffles Light house, having been thrown on her beam ends in a squall, and while in this disabled state was sunk by a waterspout. Thirty-eight lives were lost. A French Steamer was burnt, and sank while at anchor in the roads, and four Singapore vessels were wrecked in the Java Sea.

The increase in the value of real property noticed in 1856, was fully maintained during the year, and building was also carried on to a large extent both in town and country, notwithstanding a very large rise in the price of materials and labour. The building of the Church and Town Hall went on slowly, and all other public works were stopped in the course of the year, by order of the Supreme Government, the disordered state of the Indian finances having necessitated the most stringent economy in every department.

During this year the *Corps Dramatique* of Amateurs gave several performances to raise funds for a new theatre, and the *Free Press* said that it would be well to combine the Town Hall and the Theatrical funds, because in such a small place a theatre in the Town Hall would be sufficient for the purpose. This was afterwards done, and is so to the present day.

At this time Mr. Adam Wilson, who had been the chief clerk in Martin Dyce & Co., obtained from the Sultan of Siak a grant of the island

of Bengcalis.   There had been a row going on between the Sultan and a
Rival Chief, and Mr. Wilson and N. M. Carnie went over there in a
schooner to help the Sultan.   The Dutch, asserting a claim under the
treaty of 1824, interfered, and some cannonading took place, Wilson's
party opposing the rival chief, from the Sultan's house, and taking 33
guns and 38 *lelahs*, while the Dutch gunboat was firing.   On their
way back to Singapore Wilson and his companions, in three boats, were
attached by two pirate prahus which fired into them, but finding they
had not unarmed traders to deal with, but Europeans and determined
Bugis men, they made off as fast as they could.   A sampan sent from
Bengcalis to Malacca by Mr. Wilson had been attacked and four men
killed shortly before.

The grant to Mr. Wilson, though it had been given with the
knowledge of the Governor of Singapore when the Sultan of Siak had
come for the purpose, came to nothing; and Mr. Wilson became
Secretary to the Singapore Exchange and was also a broker and
Auctioneer until 1866.

CHAPTER XLVI.

1858.

AT seven o'clock on the morning of 19th November, the Queen's Proclamation of 1st September, by which Her Majesty took upon herself the direct government of her Indian dominions, was read by the Governor. A platform under an attap covering, was erected for the purpose in the centre of the Esplanade, on which he took his place, surrounded by the Recorder, the Resident Councillor, and other officials, the Consuls of different nations, and several navy and military officers, and the Sultan of Johore being also present. The troops in garrison, the 43rd M. N. I., and Madras Artillery, and the Singapore Volunteer Rifle Corps were paraded, together with the Marines and a party of Sailors from H. M. S. *Amethyst* with the band of that ship.

The Proclamation was first read in English by the Governor, and a Malay version was then given for the benefit of the natives. A royal salute was fired by the Artillery, and a *feu de joie* by the troops. The Governor next proposed three cheers for the Queen. The day was observed as a holiday, but unfortunately it began to rain heavily early in the forenoon, and continued a perfect downpour until night, which interfered considerably with the enjoyment of the occasion. In the morning a number of yachts and ships boats were arranged off the Esplanade, under the management of Captain Marshall, the Agent of the P. & O. Company, tastefully decorated with flags, which added very much to the picturesque effect of the spectacle. The state of the weather had an unfavourable effect upon the arrangements for illumination in the evening, as Government House remained wrapt in darkness, and it was only at the Masonic Lodge and a few other houses in town, that any displays in the shape of illuminated emblems of loyalty were visible.

Captain Collyer of the Madras Engineers (after whom Collyer Quay is named) arrived in Singapore in January, 1858, for the purpose of reporting on the proposed plans for the fortification of Singapore. He was appointed Chief Engineer, and assumed charge of the office on the 1st August, 1858. The whole labour of the convict body, both skilled and ordinary, was placed at his disposal. Some of the military works comprised in the proposed fortifications were at once commenced, and the convicts were placed on Government Hill to form a battery; and on Fort Fullerton, with the view of rendering that Battery more serviceable by extending and widening it. The work executed by convicts in those two Batteries was considered to be of excellent quality, as good, if not probably better, than could have been obtained from free Chinese labour; and the convict body proved most useful in the new scheme of covering the hills and shores of Singapore with

Batteries, Redoubts, Barracks, Magazines, which, however, did not ultimately prove of any practical use, and they were, fortunately probably, never called on to justify their existence. Colonel Collyer left Singapore in 1862, as is stated under that year.

The Government started the *Straits Government Gazette* in January. The total amount subscribed in Singapore for the Calcutta Relief Fund was Rs. 14,000. In September, 1856, the German Club had given a Concert in the Masonic Hall for the fund. The Grand Jury, in January, suggested that the Post Office and Marine Magistrates Offices which were on the other side of the river, should be moved to Fort Fullerton, which was done, many years afterwards; and that a Court House should be built where the Post Office then was, behind the present Printing Office.

In February it was reported that the Governor, Mr. Blundell, had resigned. There were very conflicting reports as to the reason. In Penang, the moving cause was said to be the impossibility of his getting on with the Singapore people; while in Singapore it was said to be in consequence of the Governor General's despatches about the Chinese disturbances in Penang, in which Mr. Blundell's action was so strongly condemned that he said he could not remain unless the tone of the despatches was modified. There had been a collision, as it was called, in Penang between the Chinese and the Police about a temporary *wayang* (native theatre) that stood on the ground of a temple, and was roughly pulled down by an injudicious police inspector, which led to the use of firearms and several casualties, and then to a row in March, 1856. The *Pinang Gazette* said of Mr. Blundell's action that he had done many unwise things during his government of the Straits, but none which attained that which marked his treatment of the Chinese, or more undignified and childish than his reception of them. Mr. Blundell however remained until Col. Cavenagh was appointed in July, 1859.

In February Mr. Thomas Braddell, then Assistant Resident and Magistrate, went on leave to Europe, but before doing so he published a pamphlet entitled " Singapore and the Straits Settlements Described." It was written because of the agitation that was going on about the Transfer, and was highly useful and very opportune. He discussed the best way of governing and administering the Settlement, and several of his suggestions came into practice. He wanted the government of the Straits to be quite distinct from that of India, and that the sources from which the Officials were derived should also be distinct. On the latter point he said :—" It will be no easy matter to secure favour for a close Civil Service in the Straits, yet it seems difficult to provide for the necessary duties otherwise. If suitable persons were at all times procurable when vacancies occur, it would suffice. But it is well known that qualified persons are not so procurable ; and without some previous training as assistants, it cannot be recommended that inexperienced persons should be at once placed as heads of important offices. The end is to secure for the public service the best men, the difficulty is how to arrive at this. Probably a mixed plan might be adopted, a plan which would at all times secure gentlemen qualified by previous education and training for the ordinary duties, without at the same time preventing the employment of others not already in the service, who might show a peculiar aptitude for public business. The competition would doubtless act beneficially as a spur to greater exertion. Except in those cases, appointments could be made from young gentlemen sent out from home or engaged on the spot."

The Municipal Minutes of 8th March contained the following about the renaming of the streets, which is often a subject of enquiry on looking at old Maps of the town :—" The Canals not having names, and much confusion existing from the definitions of several streets and roads, the same name, in many instances, having been given to two and even three streets, it is Resolved : that the Canal from Ellenborough market to the Sepoy Lines be called ' Dalhousie Canal ' ; the road from the stone bridge over Dalhousie Canal to the police station on the River Valley Road to be the ' Havelock Road '; the road at present called Salat Road, from the corner where the Tanjong Pagar Road branches off, up to the junction of the old and new roads to New Harbour, to be called ' Neil Road ' ; the road from Neil Road at present called Cantonment Road, and that part of River Valley Road passing the present Sheriff's Jail to the Havelock Road police station, to be the ' Outram Road'; the quadrangle in front of the police office to be ' Trafalgar Square ' ; and Tavern Street and Commercial Square to be renamed ' Bonham Street ' and ' Raffles Place ' respectively. On the north side of the Singapore river the following streets (of which there are others bearing the same names on the south side) are renamed ; Church Street to be 'Waterloo Street'; Flint Street to be ' Prinsep Street ;' Market Street to be ' Crawfurd Street ' ; the street and road from Rochore Bridge to the Serangoon Road to be ' Lavender Street ; ' and the road between Seligie Street and Waterloo Street, which formerly was a side road into Rochore road, to be ' Albert Street.'

On 5th April the death was announced of Mr. Charles Scott, in Singapore, aged 56 years. The paper said he was one of the earliest settlers at Singapore and established himself as a merchant soon after the opening of the Settlement, and was for a number of years a member of the firm of Napier & Scott. He was one of the first Magistrates in 1823, and one of the earliest planters ; the nutmeg plantation, called Raeburn, was commenced by him, and the Hill was called Scott's Hill, on the way towards New Harbour. Mr. *William* Scott's plantation was at Tanglin in Scott's Road ; the two have often been mistaken for each other. Mr. Charles Scott afterwards went to Penang and was in business there for a long time, but finally passed the last days of his life at Singapore. He was a son of Mr. Robert Scott of Penang.

The Rev. W. T. Humphrey, who had been Residency Chaplain for three years, left for Calcutta in April. By his kindly and unassuming manners and earnest promotion of every good work among his parishioners, Mr. Humphrey (the paper said), had acquired the esteem of all who knew him, and his removal was very much regretted. In those days the Chaplains were frequently moved from one station to another, and only remained in Singapore for three or four years, an advantage when an undesirable Chaplain was appointed.

The paper a few days afterwards contained a notice of the death, at Bath, of the Rev. Charles James Quarterly, M.A., at the age of 48 years, who had been Chaplain in Singapore from 1852 to 1854.

Some Government correspondence on 13th April said that the European Artillery about to arrive in Singapore were to be put in the late Tan Tock Seng's Hospital pending the erection of the Barracks intended for them on the top of Pearl's Hill. They were eventually stationed on Fort Canning.

One hundred and ninety convicts, described as too dangerous to be kept in the Alipore Jail, arrived in May; and on Wednesday the 19th, a public meeting was held to consider the recent importations of convicts by the *Julia, John Bull* and *Carthage.* A Committee of Messrs. A. Logan, W. Howard, M. F. Davidson, R. C. Woods, J. J. Greenshields and John Purvis, was appointed to draw up a petition to Her Majesty's Government that no more convicts should be sent; and to wait upon the Governor to urge that the mutineer convicts in question should be deported from the place. The convicts were soon sent to the Andamans. The London merchants sent a memorial to the Board of Control in September protesting against turning the settlement into a convict station.

In May the Municipal Commissioners decided to appoint a Town Engineer, Surveyor, and Architect, and Mr. J. W. Reeve was the first Municipal Engineer. The Municipal Minutes of 27th May contained the following letter addressed to the Commissioners by Messrs. Marshall, Charles Spottiswoode, and T. O. Crane about the Assembly Rooms and the Town Hall, which contains an account of the growth of the scheme for the present Town Hall, and elucidates some points that have been raised from time to time about it:—

" Gentlemen:—A meeting of the subscribers to the Town Hall was held on the 8th current, when the Secretary and the Trustees furnished a statement of the progress of the building, and the accounts, estimates, and plans were laid before the meeting.

" The resolutions were submitted to the meeting and carried, to this effect:—

1.—That a deputation be appointed to wait on the Municipal Commissioners, at Singapore, for the purpose of ascertaining whether, in the event of the subscribers now making over the building in course of erection for a Town Hall to the Municipal Commissioners, the Commissioners will be prepared to raise money and complete the building according to the approved plan, and fully to carry out the original wishes of the subscribers.

2.—That the following gentlemen be requested to form a deputation to wait on the Municipal Commissioners for the purpose of carrying out the foregoing resolution, viz:—Messrs. H. T. Marshall, T. O. Crane and C. Spottiswoode.

3.—That at a Special Meeting to be convened by the Secretary, the deputation report the result of the interview with the Municipal Commissioners.

" In pursuance of these resolutions we now beg to lay before you a short account of the intentions of the Trustees and the extent to which they have been able to carry them out.

" About ten years ago the Assembly Rooms were erected by subscription at a cost of about $ 6,000, and two of the present Trustees of the Town Hall were appointed Trustees. This building was contracted for by Mr. McSwiney and passed by the Government Superintendent of Works, yet it was so imperfectly finished, so loosely put together, and constructed of such miserable materials, that first of all the tiled roof had to be taken off and an attap one put on, and before ten years had elapsed it was condemned by a professional builder as unsafe and not fit to be repaired. The Trustees in consequence came to the resolution that instead of repairing the building, it would be better to build another in a better situation, for the site of the Assembly Rooms was most objectional for many reasons.

" An arrangement was made with Government to give up the old Assembly Rooms, or their ruins, with the site, for one more suitable, and, when the river is bridged over at Whampoa's, more accessible to the commercial public; on the consideration that the building when finished would be given over to the Municipal Commissioners for the benefit of the Community.

" In 1855 a subscription paper to build a suitable Town Hall was put in circulation, and $ 5,923.75 was subscribed by the community, $3,000 were added by the Government in addition to $ 3,000 by the Municipal Commissioners out of their funds, these latter sums being in accordance with an understanding with His Honor the Governor that the public subscription would be doubled by the authorities. The sum of $11,999.75 was lodged in the Oriental Bank at 5 per cent. interest, which brought the whole amount to the credit of the Town Hall to $13,207.62. The Trustees bearing in mind the insufficiency of the Assembly Rooms, and how imperfectly that building represented the thriving Settlement of Singapore, advertised for plans for a Town Hall, not only in Singapore, but in Calcutta, and further instructed Mr. M. F. Davidson, who was going home, to put himself in communication with an Architect in England, in conjunction with Mr. W. Spottiswoode, whose long residence here would enable him to give much local information and whose architectural abilities were well known to the Trustees.

" No plans were sent from Calcutta; three were given in from Singapore, one of which was selected by the Trustees and the subscribers at a public meeting convened for the purpose. Some time elapsed before Mr. Davidson sent his plan from London. It was by Mr. Fergusson, who had been in Calcutta for many years and had visited Singapore, he is now the Manager of the Crystal Palace, and is the author of the popular book 'Handbook of Architecture.' His plan was so similar to Mr. Bennett's that had been selected, that the Trustees had no hesitation in adhering to Mr. Bennett's plan as the most appropriate one, and they were not a little proud that Singapore could furnish a design of such high Architectural pretensions. The Trustees had resolved that they would not be accessory to erecting a building which would only last a few years instead of many generations, or that from its unsightliness would be a disgrace to this rising town."

"On the 13th November, 1855, a public meeting of the subscribers was held and after an inspection of the plans, Mr. Bennett's was adopted; the amount subscribed was stated, and a rough estimate was given in by Captain Macpherson, the Government Superintendent of Works, of the probable expense of constructing a new Town Hall according to accompanying plan, No. 3, that is Mr. Bennett's; this amounted to $12,565.50, but if iron girders and a slate roof were adopted, it would amount to $15,315.50. Captain Macpherson further stated the estimate allowed a wide margin and he thought the cost would be somewhat less.

"On the faith of this, the Trustees commenced the erection of the Town Hall, considering that, even if the building should cost more than the amount raised, the Public would not be reluctant to supply the deficiency, either by individual subscriptions, or from the Municipal Funds.

"Mr. Clunis, Junr., was chosen to superintend the construction of the edifice and the selection of the materials, on account of his experience in the P. & O. Co.'s employment at the New Harbour, for which he was to receive the sum of $800 by instalments. Contracts were now attempted to be made with the Carpenters and Brick-layers, when Captain Macpherson's estimate was found too low, and Mr. Bennett gave in his, to the amount of $16,926.96.

"The Trustees could not find any one in Singapore who would contract for the whole building, so they necessarily had to divide the contracts, into those for materials and labour. The first contractor for timber received a small advance, disappeared, and has not been seen since. The present Carpenter, who contracted for the work at $3,000, and to supply timber at certain rates, has acted up to his contract, and will probably finish his work to the satisfaction of the Trustees.

"For the Bricklayers' work they could not get a workman to engage who could get guarantees, except one, who asked what we at that time considered to be ridiculous. After much consideration on the part of the Trustees it was decided to contract with a China-man called Goh Khoy, who, though he could give no security, was well known to the Trustees as a most skilful workman, and under Mr. Clunis's superintendence the work, it was thought, would be of a superior quality to what could be got by ordinary contract.

"Goh Khoy agreed to furnish labour to finish the buildings for $4,000, and it is likely that amount will not be exceeded, as he has only received about 'one half and the building is half finished, yet the amount subscribed is all expended save $78, and the Trustees have every reason to believe that every dollar has been faithfully laid out. From Mr. Clunis's statement now produced, it appears that the sum of $13,129.62 has been expended, and that at the present prices of materials and labour it will require $12,371.93 more to finish the building.

"The Trustees think that Mr. Clunis's estimate is rather over than under the mark, from a prudent fear of again under-estimating. Yet, at the least, $12,000 will be required to finish and paint the building according to the plan. To take into consideration the ways and means, a public meeting of the subscribers was called on the 8th ultimo, and in consequence of the resolutions already quoted, we now appear before you to request, that as the Town Hall is intended for the use of the public, and a portion of it especially for that of the Municipal Commissioners to whom, at its completion, it is to be handed over, that you, the Municipal Commissioners, will take over the building as it now stands, fulfil the contracts made by the Trustees, and finish it according to the plan now laid before you, from the funds of the Municipality, either raised by a loan expressly for the purpose, to be paid off by the next generation who have not subscribed but who will derive all the benefit from the building, or in any other way the Commissioners may think fit.

"Trusting this request may meet with your approval, we beg to lay before you our plans, estimate and papers.

H. T. Marshall, C. Spottiswoode, T. O. Crane."

The Commissioners assured the deputation that the application should have their most favourable attention, and resolved that the Chairman should solicit an interview with His Honor the Governor to consult on the subject of raising the necessary funds for completing the Town Hall, under the provisions of Section xxxv of Act xxv of 1856. Should this preliminary be satisfactorily arranged, the Commissioners would submit the plans and estimates to their Architect and require him to report on the work already executed and on what remained to be done; the Commissioners would then decide on their answer and lose no time in communicating it to the deputation.

On 17th June Mr. Charles Spottiswoode died at the age of 46 years. The *Free Press* spoke of him as one of the oldest and most respected merchants in the Settlement. He was living at Spottiswoode Park at the time of his death.

At this time the Municipal Commissioners gave notice that their meetings were open to the public, they were held at 2 p.m. on the 7th and 27th of each month, unless it fell on a Sunday, in which case the meeting was held on the Monday following.

At this time occurred the death of a Roman Catholic Priest at Penang, which is mentioned as it has often been spoken of in connection with the stories of deaths by tigers in the Straits. Father Louis Marie Couellan, who had been fourteen years in the Straits, had celebrated early mass at day-light on the first Sunday in Advent and was walking to take the service at Bukit Mertajam when he was faced by a tiger in the jungle path. He opened his umbrella to frighten it, and had time to climb up a tree. The tiger remained at the foot. The congregation at Bukit Mertajam, finding he did not come, set out to meet him. When they got near he called out to them that there was a tiger there, and it was then frightened away. Father Couellan died in Penang shortly afterwards of tetanus, from the effect of the encounter.

Mr. John Harvey, who was a prominent resident in Singapore left there in this year, having first arrived in 1843. He died, at the age of 50 years, in 1879. There is a tablet to his memory in the south aisle of St. Andrew's Cathedral.

In this year the firm of Busing, Schroder & Co. commenced business; also Lorrain Sandilands & Co. in which the partners were G. M. Sandilands in Penang, and John Buttery in Singapore. Mr. Walter Scott Lorrain was in Glasgow.

On 1st January Puttfarcken Rheiner & Co. commenced, the two partners being Otto Puttfarcken and Otto Rheiner, who had both been in Rautenberg, Schmidt & Co. since 1854.

The firm of Reme & Co. was also commenced in this year, by G. A. Reme. In 1861 Edward John Leveson, a very well known resident, joined as partner, and it was styled Reme, Leveson & Co. in 1862. They had both been clerks in the German firm of Apel & Co. which began in 1845. The firm was afterwards Reme Brothers.

In 1858 Mr. Philip Robinson, first established the business of Robinson & Co., which has grown into such a large shop. He came to Singapore in 1857 from Melbourne, where he had been in the firm of Passmore, Watson & Co. He was at first an assistant in Cursetjee & Co.'s shop for a few months, and in 1858 he joined James Gaborian Spicer, under the name of Spicer & Robinson. Spicer was keeper of the Jail for some years from about 1845, and then was in a shipwright's business called Spicer & Morrison. He did not remain long in the business with Mr. Robinson, and in 1858 he left it, and Mr. Geo. Rappa, Jnr., who is still in Singapore, joined Mr. Robinson as a partner. The business continues under the name of Robinson & Co., until the present time, his son Stamford Raffles Robinson taking his father's place, after he died in London in 1886.

Mr. Philip Robinson was one of the founders of the " Gospel House " in Bencoolen Street, which led on to the Bethesda in Bras Bassa Road. There was a library attached to the Gospel House for some years. The " tea meetings " which came into vogue afterwards in Singapore were first introduced by him. His family was well known in the west of England, and one of his brothers was Mayor of Bristol.

CHAPTER XLVII.

1859.

I N January attention was called to the action of the States General of Holland protesting against the proceedings of Rajah Brooke at Sarawak, which they said was contrary to the Treaty of 1824, and that it was of paramount importance that the Netherlands Government should oppose with all its might, if necessary, every British Government Settlement on Borneo.

So far from the Treaty supporting the interpretation put forward, it seemed to furnish very clear evidence, ·in the 3rd and 6th articles, that Great Britain could form new settlements in Borneo or elsewhere, whenever the British Government should deem it expedient to do so. The 8th article ceded to England all the establishments on the Continent of India, but the next article, in place of ceding all English establishments in the Eastern Seas or renouncing the right to form them thereafter, merely ceded the possessions in Sumatra and engaged that no British settlement should be formed on that island, and in the next article engaged that no British establishment should be formed upon any of the other islands of the Rhio-Lingga Archipelago, of which Singapore forms part, but to which the Dutch withdrew any objections they had made to its occupation by the English.

So far from England contemplating any such abandonment of the Indian Archipelago to the Netherlands, as was now contended by the Dutch, the British Plenipotentiaries, in the note subjoined to the treaty, stated that they "record, with sincere pleasure, the disavowal, on the part of the Dutch, of any design to aim either at political supremacy or at commercial monopoly in the Eastern Archipelago." Great Britain had the best right to complain of the numerous infractions of the treaty by the Dutch, which had often been allowed to pass without notice.

The Chartered Bank of India, Australia and China was established in Singapore on 19th February, and filled the blank caused by the withdrawal of the North Western Bank. Mr. James Fraser, of Maclaine Fraser & Co., was on the Board of Directors in London, and several of the most influential of the retired Singapore merchants were connected with it. Mr. David Duff was the first Manager, then called Agent, in Singapore.

On 28th March, Captain H. T. Marshall, for many years the agent of the P. & O. Company in Singapore, then called Superintendent, being about to leave for England, was entertained very handsomely at a large dinner of upwards of sixty persons, by the Freemasons at their Hall on the Esplanade, at the corner of Coleman Street. The chaplain the Rev. T. C. Smyth, M.A. (Cantab.), a high Mason, who was Chaplain for two years at that time, was in the chair, The P. & O. wharf and establishment at New Harbour, which were said to be superior to any other of the company on the line, was due to him, and he had done, the *Free Press* said, a great deal in the place in very many ways, Municipal, Educational, &c., and would be a great loss.

In April the Government steamer *Hooghly*, George Tod Wright, commander, attacked two Chinese pirate junks which had taken a junk the day before off the coast of Tringanu, and rifled her of opium and all she contained. The pirates were too heavily armed, and the *Hooghly* was drawing off, when the Siamese steamer *Chow Phya* came in sight at 6 p.m. on her usual run from Bangkok to Singapore. She had no guns, but she lent boats to attack the pirates in shore the next morning; when it was found the boats manned by native seamen could not advantageously attack the pirates, who were too strongly posted, so they withdrew. The fact was, the *Hooghly* was so old that she could only steam five to seven knots, and the Chinese junks could do more with a fair wind.

H. M. S. *Esk*, Captain Sir R. McClure, 1,175 tons, at once went out from Singapore, taking Mr. Warwick, the chief officer of the *Hooghly*, and not being able to find the two junks, lay in wait, by his advice, in Condore Bay, and on the second day the two pirates came sailing in. Between them they had 28 large guns. A Special Criminal Sessions was held on 4th June to try the pirates, 52 of them were tried, were all convicted, and sentenced to various terms of transportation to Bombay.

Sir Robert Le Mesurier McClure, K.C.B., of the *Esk*, had been knighted for services on an Arctic voyage. His book "Discovery of the North-West Passage by H. M. S. *Investigator* 1850-54" was published in 1857, and is in the Library.

The steamer *Chow Phya*, just mentioned, is worthy of notice, as she seems to have made a wonderful record of steamer life in Singapore. She was built at West Hartlepool in 1858, and was running for years between Bangkok and Singapore, owned by the King of Siam or his Prime Minister, after whom she was named. She was sold in what was thought to be her old age, many years since, but is still running regularly in the Straits, to Malacca and Klang, but is close to the end of her life now. She was built of very good half-inch iron plates, and there has been no vessel in the Straits like her.

Her captain in the Bangkok trade was very well known in Singapore; he died here in 1885, 62 years of age. He was the brother of the famous claimant in the Tichborne case. A very hard working, persevering man, quite a character in Singapore. The Engineer of the *Chow Phya* at the beginning was Mr. Hargreaves, one of the founders afterwards of Riley, Hargreaves & Co.

The beginning of submarine telegraph lines from Singapore was very unfortunate. In May the Dutch Government determined to lay a cable to Batavia, and obtained leave to lay it from Singapore. The line was completed on 24th November, and the merchants in Singapore sent a congratulatory message to which the Batavia merchants replied. The second message was from the Governor-General of Netherlands India to Governor Cavenagh, to which the latter replied. Then it snapped! A ship's anchor was thought to have broken the cable. It was repaired, but only remained a short time in operation, and after having been once or twice more repaired, it remained obstinately mute, and on examination was found so much injured, and in so many places, that the attempt to repair it was abandoned. An office, a two-storied building, had been erected on the left bank of the river, about where the back of the Government Offices are now, and was used afterwards as the Master Attendant's Office.

In May, Government Hill was undergoing a rapid metamorphosis from the peaceful and historical seat of the Governor's residence from the first days of Raffles, into what the newspaper described as a strong and extensive fortification, intended to be called Fort Canning after the Governor-General. The top of the hill was raised several feet to afford sufficient level surface, and when finished was to enclose an area of about seven acres. By the middle of May seven 68-pounders were in position facing the sea The work was carried out with 400 Chinese coolies. After it was completed, it was noticed that Pearl's Hill was higher, so the Government Military Engineer proceded to cut down the top of that Hill !

Fort Fullerton was also being enlarged to nearly three times its former extent, and was being armed with 56 and 68 pounders. It extended from the river to Johnston's Pier, with a house for the officer in the centre, and barracks· for the soldiers along the roadside, and was planted with trees. The estimated cost of the works was said to be $840,000. Smaller works were contemplated on Pearl's Hill and Mount Sophia, but were not carried out.

The Governor on leaving Fort Canning Hill went to live at the Pavilion on Oxley Estate. Mr. Schreiber · of Behn, Meyer & Co., had been living there, and was away in Europe. He came back, and Government House was moved to Leonie Hill, Grange Road ; the same house is still standing. It was rented from Mr. Thomas Hinton Campbell, of Martin Dyce & Co., who had gone home, and was vacated when the present Government House was ready for occupation in October, 1869.

Governor Blundell, just as he was about to leave, provoked a good deal of odium by proposing to sell part of the land in Campong Glam, lying between the road and the sea in front of the houses of the Europeans, on the Beach. There was a long correspondence in February, and meetings about it, and it was said that it was not only a question between the Governor and the owners of those houses, but one for the public at large, who were as much entitled as the house-owners to the use of the beach, which they had enjoyed since the formation of the Settlement. The plan was dropped, Mr. Blundell having first made the suggestion that the land should not be sold as long as the properties on the inland side of the road were used as European dwelling houses.

A serious misunderstanding arose in Penang between Mr. Blundell and the Recorder of Penang, Sir Benson Maxwell, about the illegal detention of a woman by the police in Province Wellesley. Both sides appealed to Lord Canning, the Governor-General. The eventual result was, that an enquiry was ordered to be held by Governor Cavenagh, and the woman was compensated.

In July it was announced that Mr. Blundell had sent in his resignation. He had been Governor since 1855. Sir John Inglis, the defender of Lucknow in the Mutiny, was mentioned as likely to be his successor, but Colonel Cavenagh was appointed, and arrived on Saturday, 6th August, from Calcutta, and Mr. Blundell made over to him on the Monday, and left for Calcutta, retiring on pension, but having been granted leave of absence for one month to visit Calcutta preparatory to resigning his office, Colonel Cavenagh to officiate as Governor during his absence on leave.

Colonel Orfeur Cavenagh received from Lord Canning the appointment of Governor of the Straits. He had twice distinguished himself in India ; he had been actively engaged in the Punjab war, where he lost a leg, and when the Mutiny broke out, he was Town Major in Calcutta. When he accepted the appointment he thought it would only be a short one, as the transfer was likely to take place, and he remarked in his book, written in 1886, and referred to hereafter, that he then little anticipated that his official career would be brought to an early close in 1867, when he naturally entertained expectations of succeeding to one of the prizes of the Indian Service. His term of office, however, extended quite as long as that of most of the Governors of Singapore, being only exceeded by those of Mr. Bonham and Colonel Butterworth.

In the *Free Press* of 7th July is a copy of a long "Memorandum on Pulo Penang," without date, signed by Arthur Wellesley, afterwards Duke of Wellington, relating to its position, need of defences, means of revenue, &c. It is a pity that such a thing should be lost. It contains a good deal of interesting matter, and, at a guess, was probably written about the beginning of last century, before Singapore was founded.

The construction of St. Andrew's Church went on so slowly that several jocose letters appeared in the *Free Press* upon the bankruptcy of the Government finances. Among others was this poetry :—

"If then would'st view the Church aright,
Go visit it on a moonless night,
For the gay beams of lightsome day
Gild, but to show, the sad decay,
Then roofless porches, choir, aisle, nave,
Are silent as the ocean wave.
Then the warm night's uncertain shower
Pours through the ruined steeple tower ;
Then from the roof, in puddles, flop
The rainy streamlets, drop by drop ;
And make one sigh in these hard days
At the dire waste the view displays.
Then go at once, nor wait the while,
Would'st view St. Andrew's ruined pile,
And, home returning, softly swear
Never was scene so sad as there."

In September José d'Almeida & Sons advertised Mount Victoria for sale, "with an area of over 100 acres of beautifully situated hillocks well adapted for country residences, consisting of three or more sites,

GOVERNOR ORFEUR CAVENAGH.

besides the house occupied by José d'Almeida, Esq., with a beautiful
view of the country round and part of the harbour; only a few minutes
drive from town; and the land planted with fruit and nutmeg trees
in bearing." And in December, Hamilton, Gray & Co. advertised for
sale "the valuable and extensive nutmeg plantation in Claymore and
Tanglin, called the Sri Menanti Estate, belonging to G. G. Nicol, Esq.,
consisting of six hills, about 150 acres in all, with one of the most
commodious and substantially built residences in Singapore, on a hill
about two miles from town, and a small bungalow on one of the
other hills."

On 18th November, 1857, Tan Kim Seng had offered $13,000 for
the purpose of bringing a sufficient supply of good water into the town,
which was much required, and to show the interest he felt in the place.
He said in his letter that he was told good water in sufficient quantity
could be got from and near Bukit Timah and there would be an ample
supply to be laid on to the principal thoroughfares in the town. The
Secretary of State for India, among others, expressed his warm acknowledgments for the public spirited liberality of Tan Kim Seng.

He was a native of Malacca and began life in humble circumstances.
By his perseverance, intelligence and integrity, he rose steadily in the
world and left a large fortune to his children. He was for many years a
Justice of the Peace, and was constantly referred to by his countrymen in
the settlement of their disputes. He took a warm interest in the welfare of the place in which he had thriven so successfully, and in addition
to this gift for supplying water to the town in Singapore, he gave the
large iron bridge over the river close to the Stadt House at Malacca, a
few feet only above the spot where Albuquerque's bridge was, as shown
in the old maps of Malacca.

Tan Kim Seng died at Malacca, at 59 years of age, on 14th March,
1864. His eldest son, Tan Beng Swee, took his place in many ways,
and used to go to Malacca once a year, and was said there to be a
generous man, but he did not follow his father's example as regards
Singapore. He died in Singapore at his house in River Valley Road on
4th November, 1884, and was buried in Malacca.

Nothing was done with Kim Seng's money until just before his
death. Plans had been made, and schemes suggested, and a great
deal of talk went on at the Municipal Meetings, and there was much
correspondence with Government about the delay, and several places
were proposed for the reservoir, such as New Harbour, Bukit Timah,
and Thomson's Road. A serious drought seems to have brought matters to a head, and the plans were sanctioned by Calcutta about
December, 1862, and it was said in 1864 that the work would be finished
in a year, but it never was.

Kim Seng's money was spent on a lot of earthenware drain
pipes which turned out no use, and for some time a number of
them lay at Kandang Kerbau, and could be had for the taking
away. And there was an advertisement in the paper that unless a
large quantity of water pipes on board a ship in the harbour were
taken delivery of, the master would get rid of them in some other
way. The only result of Kim Seng's gift was that the money was
all wasted by the Government Engineer, who hoped to make water

run up hill through the pipes, and in 1882 the Municipality erected the large fountain close to Johnston's Pier with the inscription : "This fountain is erected by the Municipal Commissioners in commemoration of Mr. Tan Kim Seng's donation towards the cost of the Singapore Water-Works."

Rules were published towards the end of the year requiring persons seeking employment in the Government service to pass in the Malay language within twelve months after appointment.

The enhanced value of land, noticed in 1858, was fully maintained for a considerable part of the year, but towards the end there was a re-action. The demand for land in town and country seemed to have been fully satisfied, and it was difficult to sell at all.

In this year the business of G. Kaltenbach & Co. was established. In 1862 F. Engler joined and it became Kaltenbach, Engler & Co. They had a large store at the south west corner of the Square, where Katz Brothers, Limited are now, but a much smaller building than the present one.

The Netherlands Trading Society opened their branch in 1859, and Mr. H. J. van Hoorn was the first Manager in Singapore, where he died in November, 1865, at 46 years of age. Mr. Richard Owen Norris was the first clerk, and has continued in the office to the present day, his long local knowledge of, and warm interest in, the history of Singapore are well known, and he has been of very great and most ungrudging service in the compilation of this book.

The firm of Smith, Bell & Co., also began business in Singapore this year, John Knox Smith being the resident partner.

CHAPTER XLVIII.

1860.

ON 10th March official notification was received by the Government that the port and river of Saigon were opened for trade. There was an anchorage duty of two dollars a ton, and an import duty of 20 per cent. on the value of opium, but no other duties at that time. It would have been well for the place if it had remained so.

Orders were received from Calcutta in March to push on the completion of the barracks on Fort Canning Hill, and steps were taken to acquire the present land at Tanglin for European barracks.

Mr. Carrol shot a very large tiger at Sungei Lunchu in Johore, which had killed a number of people.

In this year John Baxter and John Lawrence Kirby started as Marine Surveyors for Lloyds and other Insurance Companies. Mr. Baxter had been in Siam, building vessels for Tan Kim Ching, and was afterwards a partner in Tivendale & Co., shipwrights at Singapore river next the Court House. He was a native of Port Glasgow in Scotland, and was a well-known character in Singapore for many years and died here in October, 1892, leaving money to the Presbyterian Church to provide a manse, from which the house in Cavenagh Road was purchased and re-built subsequently. He was the honest, bluff old Scotsman, of whom an anecdote is told on the last page of Mr. W. H. Read's book "Play and Politics."

Mr. Kirby had been in Duncan Dunbar's famous Indian merchant service between England and India. He was very popular in Singapore, and famous for his good natured jokes. The following is an example.

At that time there was, of course, no direct telegraphic communication with Europe, and as everyone was eager to hear the news on the arrival of the mail, and as it took some time to sort the letters and newspapers at the Post Office it was arranged that the large parcel of copies of the *London and China Express*, with a sort of *precis* of the latest news, should be sent by post to Colombo. There the purser of the P. & O. took them from the Post Office, and on reaching Singapore, when the mail got near the wharf, they were thrown from the steamer, and taken up to town in a hack gharry to John Little & Co.'s, where people used to wait to get them as soon as they were likely to reach there. There was a somewhat irascible manager in the shop on the occasion in question, which Captain Kirby took advantage of. Just as the mail had come in one morning, he took an old copy of that paper off the file, and asked another person to go with him with another old copy. They stood at Little's door and pretended to read. Very soon some one came running up, "What, got the papers already?" and, not waiting for an answer, rushed inside where the manager was sitting near the back. More came up, and ran in. Then a loud dispute was heard inside, the people asking for the *China Express*, and the manager very angrily saying that they were not come, to what the equally excited reply was that they were, as Kirby was reading his at the door. Kirby, when the dispute got warm, pocketed his paper, and walked quickly away round the corner to his office.

On 6th June, Dr. Charles Julius Curtis died in Singapore. He had been a medical practitioner for many years and coroner. He was succeeded by Dr. John Scott, who came from Penang, and accompanied Tumongong Abubakar to England in 1866.

On 20th July a public meeting was held at the News Room about the proposed extension of the Indian Income Tax bill to the Straits. Mr. W. H. Read was in the chair. It was shewn that the revenue was more than equal to all the expenditure which could with justice be charged against the local government, and that there was no necessity for any additional revenue, and that the surplus in Singapore, which was about £35,000 (Rs. 356,030) was more than sufficient to cover any deficiency that might exist at Penang or Malacca.

The following resolutions were agreed to by the Meeting :—

Proposed by Joaquim Almeida, and seconded by R. C. Woods :—
That the inhabitants of these settlements have a constitutional right to be consulted before a tax, arbitrary, impolitic, and inexpedient, is forced upon them.

Proposed by J. Davidson, and seconded by Joze d'Almeida :—
That an income tax is of a nature especially unsuited to the natives of these settlements, who are peculiarly averse to all inquisitorial measures, and view with deep distrust all new taxes of an unknown nature.

Proposed by C. H. H. Wilsone, and seconded by N. B. Watson :—
That the provisions of the proposed Act are framed in total ignorance of the financial position and resources of these Settlements, and the character of their inhabitants.

Proposed by J. J. Greenshields, and seconded by W. Paterson :—
That the imposition of the Income Tax on the Straits Settlements, under present circumstance,—besides being unconstitutional—is unreasonable and unnecessary : 1st., because the revenue is already sufficient to meet all legitimate charges, and 2ndly., because the transfer of these Settlements to the Colonial Office has been already determined upon, and will be carried into effect so soon as the necessary arrangements can be made : these Settlements are now virtually one of Her Majesty's Colonies.

Proposed by Dr. Scott, and seconded by W. Paterson :—That Petitions to the Houses of Parliament and the Legislative Council of India, embodying the resolutions of this meeting be drawn up, and transmitted with as little delay as possible."

A Committee, consisting of the following gentlemen, was formed for the purpose of drawing up the Petitions to Parliament and the Legislative Council of India, namely, the Chairman, A Logan, R. C. Woods, J. J. Greenshields, Wm. Paterson, James Davidson, A. M. Aitken and C. H. Harrison.

A copy of the Petition was printed in the *Free Press* of 2nd August. The Calcutta Government soon afterwards dropped the question.

In the accounts referred to in connection with that matter it is noticed that at that time an annual sum of Rs. 24,245 was spent for house rent and batta (extra pay) for the Senior Naval Officer, and Rs. 8,539 for batta to H. M. Ships.

In October the newspaper said:—"Orders are said to have been recently received from the Government of India for the erection of a battery at Sandy Point. It will probably be an expensive work, owing to the difficulty of making a secure foundation at that place. This will be another item in the bill which the Indian Government is running up for the fortifications at Singapore, and which has already been found such a serious obstacle to the transfer of the Straits Settlements to the Colonial Office. The extensive scale on which these fortifications are being constructed is wholly uncalled for and will prove a source of embarrassment to the colony in the future." The battery was never constructed.

In October Mr. Charles Emmerson came to Singapore, and advertised that he had commenced to practise as a member of the College of Veterinary Surgeons. He was the first to practise in Singapore. He afterwards commenced a very small tiffin room in Battery Road, in addition to his other occupation, and it grew into a hotel on Beach Road, occupying two large houses, and to the tiffin rooms at Cavenagh Bridge which are still known by his name. He was a very popular amateur actor for many years in low comedy characters. He died in Singapore in 1883.

The first performance in the theatre in the Town Hall was given on 24th October in aid of the funds required for completing the building. The plays were a comedy called *The Folies of a Night* and the farce *A Storm in a Teapot*. It was repeated with *Bombastes Furioso*, which was often performed in Singapore, in place of the farce.

In October the Rajah of Pahang and the Rajah of Kedah, with a number of followers, paid visits to Singapore.

In November the Calcutta Government sanctioned the erection of a lighthouse on Cape Rachado.

The Indian Penal Code having been passed, Mr. Willans, the Magistrate of Police wrote the following letter to the Resident Councillor on 3rd November. The recommendation was forwarded to Calcutta with the Governor's entire concurrence. "Having perused the Indian Penal Code recently passed by the Legislative Council of India, I much regret to find that the Straits Settlements have been excepted from its provisions. The Code in question is a most important enactment and contains within itself a full and lucid exposition of its provisions. Its application to this Settlement would I feel assured be of infinite advantage and I would respectfully submit for the consideration of His Honor the Governor the desirability of procuring, if possible, its extension to the Straits; such extension would I believe be acceptable to the inhabitants. I am aware that these Settlements were at the last moment excluded from the provisions of the Act in consequence of their probable transfer to the Colonial Office, but as such transfer, if at all, may not take place for a considerable time, I would most respectfully urge that it is undesirable this Community should be debarred from so important an improvement in the Law for an indefinite period. Should such transfer be carried into effect earlier than expected and a Legislative Council granted for the Colony, some length of time would possibly elapse before such Council could prepare and pass so complete a measure of Criminal Law, while if the Code was in force at the time of transfer, any alteration that might be considered expedient could be easily made by Council."

Mr. Willans proved quite correct, for the Code was not introduced into Singapore until 1871.

The following was in the newspaper in November, 1860 :—" On the evening of Monday, 26th November, 1860, the Singapore Volunteers were reviewed by the Hon. the Governor, Colonel Cavenagh, on the Esplanade. The volunteers mustered in full force under their commandant, Captain Read, and on the arrival of His Honor, accompanied by Brigadier Burn and Staff, presented arms. They then marched past in slow and quick time, and went through a number of Light Infantry manœuvres, advancing, firing, halting, changing front in one direction and in the other, forming square, retiring, and finally, having fired two volleys with remarkable precision, they formed up in their original position and again presented arms.

"The Governor then addressed the corps in animated language. He alluded to the formation of the corps, which had the honor to be the first enrolled in India and was therefore entitled to bear upon its colours the inscription *Primus in Indis*. He dwelt upon the great utility of volunteers in general, and adverted to his own experience as having commanded the Calcutta volunteers during the Indian rebellion, when they were found so eminently useful in preserving confidence and order in the Capital, and in allowing the regular troops to be employed in active operations against the mutineers. His Honor adverted to the great and wonderful progress such institutions had made in the mother country of late, and as in these days no dependence could be placed in the duration of peace, the gallant speaker said he thought it behoved all good and true subjects to stand forward in the general defence. Colonel Cavenagh then eulogised those of our fellow citizens who, though not British subjects, yet showed their appreciation of the protection bestowed by our laws and of the benefits they thereby derived, by swelling the numbers of the volunteers, and he concluded by expressing a hope that those young men who had not yet joined the corps would no longer hesitate to enrol themselves as members of the Singapore Volunteer Rifles.

"The Governor complimented the volunteers on their soldierly appearance and the steadiness and precision with which the various manœuvres had been gone through. Much of which was owing to the indefatigable exertions of the gallant Captain and other officers of the Corps, who were no doubt highly gratified at the result of their assiduity having elicited the commendations of so competent an authority in these matters as Colonel Cavenagh. The spirited address of the Governor was followed by three hearty cheers for His Honor. The spectators then gave three cheers for the gallant corps, which marched off to the Masonic Lodge. The excellent Band of Her Majesty's 40th Regiment M. N. I. attended, by the kind permission of the officers of the Regiment, and added much to the gaiety of the scene."

The screw steamer *Sir James Brooke* owned by the Borneo Company, Limited, was totally lost on the 17th September, on the rocks off Point Romania. She was on her way to Singapore from Bangkok with a cargo of rice.

In the latter part of the year a number of failures occurred among the Chinese traders. In most cases private arrangements were made, and a composition accepted with security, but it was thought that in some cases insolvency had been declared while the parties were quite able to pay in full, and that it was done to save a considerable percentage on their liabilities, and was not weighed against the effect which such a course might have upon their future credit as traders. Credit was obtained so very easily, that even repeated insolvency only operated against a trader for a time.

A census was taken by the Police during the year, the total population being reckoned as 80,792, of whom Europeans and Eurasians were 2,445, and Chinese 50,043.

The new General Hospital and the Lunatic Asylum at Kandang Kerbau were completed and occupied. The whole expense of the former had been Rs. 51,086; and of the latter Rs. 46,259. The foundations of Cape Rachado Lighthouse were cut and materials collected, the expense being Rs. 20,200.

The Agri-Horticultural Society was established in this year, the Government giving the large extent of ground at Tanglin, where the gardens still are, for the purpose. They were supported for some years by private subscription, but were afterwards taken over by the Government.

The rendezvous at Singapore of the vessels carrying troops and stores for the operations in China, both from Europe and India, caused much activity in the harbour, and the war was prosecuted so quickly that before the close of the year a number of transports with troops who had been engaged in the hostilities, passed westward again through the harbour. Besides visits from the Earl of Elgin and Baron Gros the French Plenipotentiary, on their way to China, Singapore was visited by the Russian Envoy and Plenipotentiary to China, Japan, and Siam with a numerous suite, who remained in Singapore for some days waiting for the Russian man-of-war which met them in the harbour.

The firm of Stelling, Hooglandt & Co., was begun on 1st February, 1860, by G. H. P. Stelling, and Willem Hooglandt the partner resident in Singapore.

CHAPTER XLIX.

1861

A T 7-30 p.m. on 16th January an earthquake was felt at Singapore, lasting about a minute; the direction appearing to be from S. W. to N. E. There were two shocks, the undulations being very distinct, and producing in many persons a feeling of nausea, and the idea that the house was going to tumble down; doors rattling and hanging lamps swinging about, for some minutes. Those who were upstairs ran down. It was felt also in Malacca and Penang.

As far as is ascertained, there had been three previous instances of earthquakes felt in the Settlement. The first at 9 p.m. on Sunday, 24th November, 1833, when a shock lasting upwards of a minute was felt, and followed by two more; one at 3, and the other at 4-30 a.m. That was also felt at Malacca and Penang.

The next was in 1837, when a large wave broke on the sea-shore at Teluk Ayer. The third was half an hour after midnight on 6th January, 1843, which was also felt in Penang.

Earthquakes are of so frequent occurrence in Sumatra, Java, &c., that it is well to give these instances to show how little effect they have had at Singapore, where the oscillation is always attributed to a volcano in some of those directions, that of 1833 having been attributed to Gunong Berapi in Sumatra.

The most noticeable occurrence of this kind heard in Singapore was, of course, that of Krakatoa, in the Straits of Anjer, about 500 miles from Singapore, on 26th to 28th August, 1883. On Sunday afternoon, the 27th, about 5.45 o'clock, during the chanting of the Psalms in St. Andrew's Cathedral, a loud explosion was heard, which was the first to be noticed. It was thought that, contrary to rules, the blasting of the rocks in a hill at Tanjong Pagar, which had been going on for some time in order to reclaim Teluk Ayer Bay, was being continued on Sunday; and faint rumblings and explosions, heard at intervals that evening and during the night, were thought to be caused in the same way. Those in the country thought it was saluting, or signals from the Fort, and some natives thought it was a battle between the French and Chinese. But about 11 a.m. on the Monday morning a very much louder report was heard, which was the last, and when some one in the Supreme Court suggested that the noises must be occasioned by an eruption, the speaker was laughed at. Shortly after noon a telegram came from Java that the natives were all flying, the sky in darkness, and general consternation. Then the telegraph cable broke, and nothing more was heard until a day or two afterwards, when a Dutch gunboat, which had been near the mountain at the time, came into Singapore, and the Captain said it had been an awful experience, describing it by saying that they thought they were in hell: with the fire, the smoke, the thick darkness, except for the flashes of the fire, and the great weights of pumice stone and ashes that had to be constantly cleared off the ship's deck, or they would have sunk her.

Not long afterwards pieces of pumice stone, as big as a hat, were floating about outside the harbour, and Mr. George Dare brought pieces to the Club in his canoe. There was a scientific account of the disaster by Dr. Treub in the "Annals of the Botanical Gardens of Buitenzorg in Java," vol. 7. The tidal wave caused by the fight between fire and water, in which the water was the conqueror, was twenty-five metres high. It was thought that at least thirty thousand natives perished, but the loss of life could not possibly be ascertained.

Singapore lies in the centre of a circle, in peace and safety so far as human experience has hitherto shown; but on the circumference of that circle, there are volcanic eruptions in Java, causing widespread death and destruction; earthquakes in Manila, tumbling down buildings like houses of cards; typhoons in Hongkong, tossing large vessels on to the shore, destroying heavily built sea-walls in the Praya, and blowing away massive stone verandahs on the most solidly constructed buildings on the sea-front; cyclones in Calcutta, sinking ships and causing great damage and loss of life—while, in Singapore, convulsions of nature are unknown, and a Sumatra squall blowing away the attap roof of a house on a hill overlooking the present Ladies Lawn Tennis Ground on to the old Dhoby green, some thirty-five years ago, on the morning of the day when there was to be a dinner party in the evening as a house-warming, is, possibly, the worst that can be alleged against the forces of nature.

On 1st February the P. & O. advertised a rise in passage fares. To Southampton first class was $552, with $33.60 for the transit through Egypt. The Singapore paper remarked that in addition to the permanent complaints of bad fare· and overcrowded vessels, there had been an extraordinary number of breaks down in their steamers. The Calcutta *Friend of India* said at the same time that much grumbling, many threats, and frequent denunciations had been met by one virtue "the public can depend upon us for punctuality"; but even this consolation had been taken away.

During the race week in May, Tan Kim Seng gave a ball in the Masonic Lodge on the Esplanade to all the Europeans. In the same month it was reported that Sir James Brooke might be the Governor, if the transfer took place and Colonel Cavenagh returned to India. The paper said that the Rajah would govern the Straits with the vigour and sagacity that had distinguished his career in Borneo.

On 24th May, the Queen's birthday, the Volunteers paraded with all the troops on the Esplanade in the morning, and a salute was fired at the same time from the new Fort Canning.

In August there were very heavy wind and rain squalls on two days and a large three-storied godown which was being built on the left-hand side of Almeida Street, about half way down after leaving the Square, for José d'Almeida & Sons, which had just been roofed in, fell down; one man sleeping inside was killed. Busing, Schroder & Co., were the tenants.

An ice-making machine was set up in August, but it did not work satisfactorily. After the ice-house was built, a private company imported ice *pro bono publico,* and charged five cents a pound, which resulted in a heavy loss. The house then remained empty for a considerable time, when Mr. Tudor, an American, tried to keep up a supply; but it was constantly failing, and often at the hottest times. It was said in the newspaper that he lost $20,000 over it. When the ice failed, liquids used to be cooled by turning the bottles in pails with saltpetre. It was not for many years after this, that the supply of ice could be depended on. The local consumption was then so small, and there was no demand for steamers, except for the mails.

In May, Drs. Little and Robertson advertised that their Singapore Dispensary in the Square was put under the entire management of Mr. Robert Jaimie, who had come out from Edinburgh for the purpose. He lived for many years over the Dispensary in the Square, in the same building as at present, but latterly he lived at Serangoon on the large cocoanut plantation he bought there, as has been said on page 185. He is now living at Edinburgh.

On Monday, 7th October, Sir James Brooke was entertained by the whole community at a ball in the Assembly Rooms. It had been proposed to have a dinner but the ladies wished to take part in it. Sir James was on his way home on account of ill-health. He returned to Sarawak afterwards for a short time, and left there for the last time in October, 1863, and died at Burrator in Devonshire, on 15th June, 1868, where he is buried.

In this year the fortification and barracks on Fort Canning were completed, and the European Artillerymen were removed from the buildings on Pearls Hill, which were from that time occupied by the Commissariat Department. The attap barracks at Tanglin were so far advanced as to be capable of affording ample accommodation for a European regiment, but the newspaper said that they would probably remain empty and deteriorate rapidly in consequence ; which proved to be the case. The sea-wall, now called Collyer Quay, from Fort Fullerton to the old Teluk Ayer market, was nearly completed at the end of 1861, and the space behind it was being gradually filled in to allow of godowns being built, which it was said would greatly improve the appearance of the town; as they did five years afterwards.

The annual report for 1860-61 stated that Rs. 21,784 had then been spent on St. Andrew's Church, and that the building of the tower was in abeyance owing to the settlement of its foundation, and that the design would probably have to be changed for the sake of a lighter superstructure.

The German Club gave a performance in the Town Hall in September, in aid of the building fund. There was a heavy rainfall this year, as in other parts of the Indian Archipelago, greatly damaging the roads. The new Agri-Horticultural Society held two shows of fruit, vegetables and flowers, in June and December.

The Sultan of Tringanu and the Bandahara of Pahang visited Singapore; and the Prime Minister of Siam, Chow Phya Sri Surywongsie and two sons of the First King of Siam, with a large retinue, came in July on their way to Quedah, from where they went overland to Siam. There were then two Kings of Siam called the First and Second Kings.

In December the *Free Press* said that the Town Hall was assuming an appearance very creditable to the Settlement, but the work had been brought to a stand for want of funds, as the Treasurers were under an advance of $5,000, and the Committee would have to apply to the public for further money. The great advance in the cost of building materials which took place during its erection, caused the original estimates to be much exceeded.

In 1886, Mr. James Guthrie wrote from London, because he had heard that some question had arisen about the purposes for which the Town Hall had been built. He said, "As I had a good deal to do with it, perhaps my information may be useful. The ground was *given* by the Government—a free gift. The whole of the money was subscribed by the European and other residents, all of whom gave liberally, but, as often happens, the building cost a good deal more than estimated, so the movers in the good work had rather a troublesome time of it, but, I am happy to say, were again and again most kindly received, when appearing with an empty bag—never in my remembrance being refused a further subscription to the good work, in which all were interested. The building was at last completed, and an arrangement was made with the Municipal Commissioners, to take over the responsibility and management of the Town Hall, in consideration of which they were to occupy *one* or *two* of the rooms behind the dining-room for offices—the dining-room being available for theatrical perfomances, &c., the large room upstairs being intended for balls, &c., &c., and the small rooms for libraries, which it was thought might be more convenient there than at the Institution. In those days the Municipal Commissioners had a room for their Secretary in the Police Office, and held their meetings in the old Court-house."

On 26th December the *Free Press* remarked that the London papers said there was some prospect of the Prince of Wales passing through Singapore on his projected visit to India and Australia; but the Prince did not, of course, go further than India.

CHAPTER L.

1862.

I N January the Chamber of Commerce presented Captain Stanton of H. M. S. *Saracen*, surveying vessel, with a gold pocket chronometer which Mr. James Guthrie had selected in London, as an acknowledgment of the services rendered by him to commerce, by his surveys in Banca Straits in 1860.

The Tumongong of Johore, Daing Ibrahim Sri Maharajah, died at his residence at New Harbour on the 31st January, in his 52nd year. He was the second son of the Tumongong with whom Sir Stamford Raffles in 1819 entered into the negotiations which led to the Settlement. The *Free Press* said :—"This native chief, during the course of his long rule, conducted himself with great prudence and secured the friendship and support of the British Government, by whom he was presented with a sword of state for his exertions in putting down the piracy which at one period was so prevalent in the vicinity of Singapore. For many years he devoted himself to the improvement of his territory of Johore, in which he was very successful, the revenues at his death amounting to a very considerable sum, derived principally from the Chinese population that under his encouragement had settled in Johore and engaged in agricultural pursuits. He was succeeded by his eldest son, between whom and the Bandahara of Pahang a treaty was entered into at Singapore in June, with the sanction of the British Government, to regulate the countries of Pahang and Johore, their boundaries, jurisdiction and government, to prevent disputes hereafter and to perpetuate the amity existing between them."

Tumongong Ibrahim was succeeded by his eldest son, Ungku Wan Abubakar, who had been administering the Government for some years, as his father's health had been declining. Mr. Cameron in his book speaks of him as an amiable and high-minded gentleman, more desirous of peace and quiet than of great power, which was very true of the late Sultan Abubakar, as he was afterwards styled. Both he and his father have been referred to on page 45.

There were a number of cases of cholera amongst the native population in the beginning of the year. With the view of driving away this scourge the Chinese expended large sums in getting up processions, which for some days completely obstructed the principal thoroughfares in the town, and were accompanied by the burning of joss paper, the explosion of crackers and the beating of gongs, making it dangerous to attempt passing along the streets in carriages. The police were much blamed for the complete immunity they seemed to allow the Chinese in the perpetration of these nuisances, no attempt apparently being made to preserve any semblance of order.

In February, Colonel George Chancellor Collyer, who was styled Chief Engineer, Straits Settlements, retired from the service and left for Europe. The principal works he had carried out were Fort Canning, the reconstruction of the works at Fort Fullerton, the erection of the attap barracks for European troops (who did not come until the buildings had to be re-attaped) at Tanglin ; and the sea wall from Johnston's Pier to the old Fish-market at the east end of Teluk Ayer, which was called Collyer Quay after him. It had been designed by him in 1858, but was not completed when he left. Colonel Collyer, as regards the forts, could only carry out the orders from India, and they were not considered of any use. The Colonel, although he was a very busy man, always found time to give the benefit of his advice and suggestions to the Municipal Commissioners when they asked him, as they were often anxious to do, in which respect he was a favourable contrast to Colonel Faber, who acted for a time during Colonel Collyer's absence on sick leave, and declined to give such assistance. It was probably as well for the rate-payers, judging from the result of the public works Colonel Faber spent public money on.

Some people wanted to know why the good old Malay name of the hill at the New Harbour was changed to Mount Faber, who, a newspaper correspondent said, deserved no record in the place.

Colonel Collyer bestowed much pains on preparing a plan and estimate for a pier which he proposed should run out from the new sea-wall at Collyer Quay into 17 feet of water. His scheme was received with favor by the mercantile community, and it was proposed to carry it out by means of a Company, but it was afterwards said that that depth of water was too shallow for the class of vessels for which such a pier would be of the greatest utility, and the project was postponed for further information regarding the additional expense that would have to be incurred to extend it into the depth of water considered necessary.

As will be seen later, the Tanjong Pagar Dock Company, which probably sprung out of Colonel Collyer's scheme, began in the next year. At the time he proposed the pier, the godowns along Collyer Quay were just being planned, and goods landed from ships on to such a pier could have been readily stored near the shore end ; but the value of the property now, and the large traffic in the streets leading from the Quay to Boat Quay and the Chinese business portion of the town, would render such a scheme very inconvenient at the present day.

The Annual Report of the P. W. D. in June, 1862, said that the cost of Collyer Quay was defrayed by the merchants, the Government giving a certain amount of convict labour. The foundations could only be proceeded with once a fortnight, as it was built in one foot of water in ordinary tides. About two-thirds was completed at the beginning of 1861, and the work was not completely finished, and the roadway filled in for carriages to pass, for some three years afterwards. All the carriage and goods traffic was in the Square.

On 28th March a public meeting was held, which came to be called the Battle of the Bridges. It was held because it was given out that the Municipal Commissioners intended to place across the Singapore River at Flint Street an iron bridge that was coming out from England to replace the dangerous wooden bridge at Kallang.

Mr. John Purvis was in the chair, and he said a bridge at Flint Street should never have been thought of. Mr. N. B. Watson said a bridge near the mouth of the river would not help traffic to any extent, would prevent boats coming up the river, and injure the property on the river side, with which Mr. Reginald Padday agreed. Then Mr. Greenshields said the proper place for an additional bridge was at Market Street, as it was a wide street [it would not be thought so now, but it was wider than Flint Street] and Mr. M. F. Davidson agreed with him. Dr. Little said it would be a shame to use the new iron bridge at any other place than Kallang for which it was ordered, and much wanted [he had a plantation in that direction]. In his opinion the best site would be half way between Bonham Street and Market Street, with which Mr. José d'Almeida agreed. Then Mr. John Cameron said Bonham Street was the best place, as it was higher up than Flint Street, and boats would have more time to lower their masts.

Votes were then taken; 15 for Market Street, 13 for half way, and 12 for Bonham Street. Mr. Adamson then proposed that a bridge across the river near Ellenborough Market would be a great convenience, and tend to relieve the traffic over the other bridges, and that the iron bridge might be erected from Tocksing Street to East Road, which was carried by a majority.

The result was that the iron bridge ordered for Kallang River was erected there as first intended, and another iron bridge was placed where the first bridge had been, called Thomson's or Presentment Bridge, but was afterwards called Elgin Bridge after Lord Elgin. Both these bridges are still standing, but have been widened, the former when the steam tramways were made, which were afterwards abandoned. Both bridges were erected and opened during the year.

In May, Governor Cavenagh returned from Penang and occupied Leonie Hill House in Grange Road. Complaints were made about the inconvenience of the Governor's office being removed to the house, in place of being in town with the other public departments, as had before that been the case. The Governor's office was for a time at Leonie Cottage, a wooden house with an attap roof, which was said to be unsafe in case of fire; it was not likely, however, as fires in the country districts were almost unknown. The change led to much of the business which had before been transacted directly with the Governor in town, being passed through the hands of the Resident Councillor; but Colonel Cavenagh could always be seen at any moment in his office at Leonie Hill where he was always to be found without any ceremony, during office hours, working in a room downstairs.

The *Free Press* of 5th June contained a long account of the famous fight between the Sarawak steamer *Rainbow* and the six Lanun pirate boats on 22nd May. About 160 of the captives from Celebes, Pontianak, and other places, and two from Singapore were rescued, and testified their joy by kissing the hands and feet of those on board the *Rainbow*. Very many more were drowned, some of them having had their feet tied together by the pirates, who had treated their prisoners very brutally. The pirates fought to the last, and even after they were in the water would not allow themselves to be taken, and the destruction was most complete.

A great deal of notice was unfortunately attracted to the matter by the "extremely imprudent" (to use what was then spoken of as the mildest phrase) letter of Bishop McDougall of Sarawak. He sent a highly coloured narrative of his exploits, which filled three columns of the London *Times*; and praised his new double-barrelled gun, which never missed fire once in *eighty rounds*, without wanting to be cleaned; and more in the same way. No doubt the sinking of the *prahus* was perfectly just, and captives were released from inhuman captivity, and the pirates were as the Bishop styled them "pests of the earth."

The Singapore newspaper said that although there were some strange rumours in Singapore, at the time, about the exploits of the Bishop, the letter in the *Times*, and his desire to boast about his own warlike exploits, from behind the shelter of a bulwark, and in such language, came as a surprise to his acquaintances in Singapore, who had hoped that the knowledge would be confined to a few, and would never come to be the subject of very undesirable comment in the newspapers, such as the *Spectator*, *Examiner*, and other papers contained.

The Dutch Government sent a handsome gold chronometer to Captain Hewatt of the *Rainbow*, with an inscription that it was given in acknowledgment of his gallant and able conduct on 22nd May, 1862, by which a great number of Netherlands India subjects were delivered from the hands of pirates. It was publicly presented to him by Mr. W. H. Read at the Club House.

On 12th June a public meeting, called by the Sheriff at the written request of thirty-three of the principal European residents of the place, was held at the Town Hall to take into consideration the most efficient measures to adopt in order to control, if not repress, the vice of gambling then so prevalent. There was a large attendance, and it was admitted generally that gambling was carried on to a large extent, that it was very prejudicial to the place, and that bribery of the police, to obtain their connivance in allowing it, also prevailed.

Some said that it was not possible to prevent it, and to secure the integrity of the Police, without a farm. Others said it would be useless to propose it because of Exeter Hall and the House of Commons, and that Singapore would be disgraced in the eyes of the civilised world if it were allowed. Others said it was a social vice, not a crime against the public, and could not be stopped. A Chinese gentleman suggested that licensing should be tried for a limited time.

There was so much difference of opinion, that it was agreed a committee should be appointed to collect information, and report to an adjourned meeting. The matter seems to have ended there, as no report is to be traced. Notice had been drawn to the subject, because during the fortnight after the Chinese New Year, the police had allowed gambling to go on unchecked, and no satisfactory explanation of this circumstance had been given.

In the middle of this year a half holiday was first observed on Saturdays. The movement was started by Mr. Gilfillan of the Borneo Company and Mr. A. T. Carmichael of the Chartered Bank.

In September the Singapore Library was removed from the Raffles Institution to the Town Hall. It was in two rooms on the south side, downstairs.

Mr. Thomas Tivendale, who was for many years a very well known shipwright in Singapore, died on board the P. & O. Mail on his way home on 10th September.

On 1st July, 1863, Mr. Wm. Cloughton, the Director of the Patent Slip and Dock Company advertised that that Company had purchased the property and goodwill of the business of the late firm of Tivendale & Co., for repairing ships at Sandy Point alongside the Heaving down Hulk; and that the Dry Dock at New Harbour which had been opened in March, 1859, was 400 feet long, with 15 feet 6 inches depth of water.

In September the sum of £1,160, subscribed in Singapore for the relief of the Lancashire and Cheshire operatives, was sent to the Lord Mayor of London in aid of the Distress Fund, consequent on the effect of the American Civil War on the cotton trade.

In November the bombardment of Tringanu occurred, which led to a discussion in the House of Commons on 16th July, 1863, and was for some time a subject of comment.

In 1851 a Singapore trading junk had been seized and destroyed at Tringanu and thirty-five of the crew and passengers were put to death. Mr. Thomas Church, Resident Councillor at that time, went there to enquire into it, and made a demand for compensation which the Rajah of Tringanu refused to pay, and, unfortunately, no further proceedings were taken. This had nothing to do with the subsequent trouble, but it was thought that the misplaced leniency led the Rajah, who was still the chief of the country in 1862, to think that his disregard of the representations of the Straits Government would not involve him in any troublesome consequences.

An ex-Sultan of Lingga had gone to Tringanu, and repeatedly instigated attacks upon the neighbouring state of Pahang, which was invaded by one Wan Ahmad, acting under his orders, with a force from Tringanu, asserting that he was the only legitimate successor of his grandfather, Sultan Mahomed, as the ruler of Johore, Pahang, &c. The Siamese Government were informed of the inconveniences to trade arising from the man living at Tringanu, which was alleged to be a tributary of Siam, and of a Siamese gunboat having taken him from Bangkok to Tringanu on his way to join Wan Ahmad.

The King of Siam disclaimed all intention of supporting the ex-Sultan in attempting to disturb the peace of the Peninsula, and said he had given orders to the Rajah of Tringanu to send the ex-Sultan back to Bangkok, where he would be sent to reside in one of the interior Siamese provinces, so that he would be out of the way of stirring up mischief in the Malay Peninsula. As this was not done and the Siamese evidently intended to talk and do nothing more, and the approach of the north-east monsoon required that a stop should be put to the matter without delay, Colonel Macpherson, Resident Councillor, left for Tringanu on the 6th November in H. M. S. *Scout*, a 21 gun corvette of 1462 tons, for the purpose of removing the man and taking him to Siam.

Colonel Macpherson sent a letter on shore to the Rajah, saying what was wanted, and that he would land the next day. A long interview took place then, the Rajah alleging that the man was too ill to be moved, but a doctor of the *Scout* saw him and said there was nothing much the matter with him. Colonel Macpherson said it was desired to convey him in the manner most consistent with his own convenience, and he could go in his own state barge with his flag and that of the Rajah of Tringanu, in tow of a steamer, if he liked, but the Rajah positively refused to give him up.

Colonel Macpherson then said that if he were not given up by a certain time on the following day, he would resort to force. The time expired, and three guns were fired, and then a pause of some hours was allowed in the hope the Rajah would come to terms, but as he did not make any sign, the *Scout* and *Coquette*, a sloop of 677 tons which had also gone, opened fire upon the Rajah's *Kotta* or fort. The fire was kept up at intervals until dark, care being taken as much as possible to avoid injury to private property. A letter afterwards came from the Rajah professing great penitence for his conduct, and saying that the ex-Sultan had disappeared from Tringanu, and it was not known where he had gone to. It was understood that he was afterwards taken to Bangkok by the Siamese.

Mr. W. H. Read wrote to the *Free Press* at the time, saying that about twenty men had been killed at Tringanu, of whom eight at any rate had nothing to do with the matter, and suggesting that the object could have been realised by seizing the ex-Sultan, by which many innocent lives might have been saved; and that sufficient opportunity was not given to the King of Siam to take action himself It was on these grounds that Lord John Hay brought the matter before the House of Commons.

Mr. John Cameron, at page 137 of his book, makes a passing reference to this occurrence, and says:—"Our moral influence, added to a few days' vigorous bombardment [he is wrong here it was only a few hours] was used in favour of one claimant to the Bandaharaship of Pahang, whose family has after all been set aside, and the man whom we opposed now reigns peaceably and quietly, by the people's choice."

How this occurred may be found in the following paragraph taken from the *Free Press* of 2nd July, 1862 :—"By last accounts from Pahang we learn that Wan Ahmad has been left in indisputed possession of the country. After the death of the Bandahara at Pahang on the 2nd ultimo, the followers of his younger brother Tan Abdulrahman (or Ahman) installed the latter as Bandahara, but the greater part of the chiefs and people refused to recognise him, as he had long made himself very unpopular by his lawless conduct and his addiction to opium smoking. The support of the Johore Government was withdrawn, and under these circumstances he found himself unable to make head against his uncle Wan Ahmad, and he therefore withdrew to Kalantan, leaving the latter the only person then in Pahang in a position to assume the government. It will, we presume, depend very much upon Wan Ahmad's own conduct whether he will be left in undisturbed possession of Pahang or not. It is fortunate for him, as increasing his chances of ultimate success, that the ex-Sultan of Lingga is at present at a distance from Pahang, and not in a position to interfere in its affairs. If Wan Ahmad is wise enough to rid himself of his connection with the ex-Sultan and to endeavour to govern Pahang with moderation, maintaining at the same time peaceful relations with his neighbours, he will probably remain unmolested; but if he lends himself to intrigues of the ex-Sultan or any one else against Johore he will certainly involve himself in much trouble and probably endanger his position as ruler of Pahang."

The Lords Commissioners of the Treasury in England had raised questions about the sufficiency of the revenue of the Straits to meet the expenditure, and the transfer to the Colonial Office was hanging off in consequence. With the object of overcoming the objection, the Calcutta Government sent imperative orders in very curt terms to enforce the Stamp Act in the Straits. On some previous occasions the Government of India had expressed its desire to raise additional revenue by means of stamp duties, but on the remonstrances of the inhabitants it had as often abandoned the design.

In May, a notification appeared in the *Government Gazette,* stating that under instructions from the Supreme Government the provisions of the Stamp Act would be brought into force in the Straits Settlement on or about the 1st of November following. The Singapore Chamber of Commerce immediately memorialised the Governor-General in Council on the subject, setting forth that the imposition of stamp duties would be a heavy and peculiar burden on the trade, from the fact that in the Straits goods were always sold on credit, for which promissory notes were taken, whereas in India and elsewhere such sales were generally for cash, and that the taxation already levied in the Straits Settlements was not only much higher than what prevailed in India, but that it was more than sufficient to cover all the expenditure that with any justice could be charged against the local revenue. In answer to this, the Governor-General in Council caused it to be intimated that in his opinion there was no sufficient reason for exempting the Straits Settlements from the operation of the Stamp Act, and that he was therefore unable to comply with the prayer of the Chamber.

On Thursday, 10th July, a public meeting was held at the Town Hall on the subject, and was very largely attended. The meeting expressed regret that the memorial of the Chamber of Commerce had not met with more consideration from the Viceroy of India; and as the revenue of the Straits was sufficient to pay all the legitimate expenses, the imposition of additional taxation was vexatious and uncalled for. It protested against the Settlements being saddled with the whole of the military expenditure, and a committee of Messrs. W. H. Read, W. Paterson, J. J. Greenshields, Abraham Logan, James Davidson (Mercantile Bank), W. Mactaggart and Joaquim d'Almeida, was appointed to draw up a Memorial to the English Ministry on the subject, and to the Viceroy.

The assistance of gentlemen in England interested in the Straits was sought, and efforts were made by Mr. Crawfurd and others to induce the Secretary of State for India to reconsider the matter, but without result. The Governor-General in Council declined to accede to any delay pending these appeals to the Home Authorities, and adhered to his resolution that the Act should be brought into force at the time originally named. Officers were therefore appointed for carrying out the Act, but it was found that their arrangements could not be completed by the time fixed, and the Governor of the Straits Settlements, on his own responsibility postponed the period for bringing the Stamp Act into operation until the 1st of January, 1863, when it was accordingly initiated.

The determination thus shown by the Supreme Government to carry out the behests of the Secretary of State for India, in spite of all remonstrance, let to a renewed effort being made to have the Settlements placed under the Colonial Office, and thereby obtain such a degree of self-government as would be secured by having a Legislative Council on the spot.

The hurried way in which the Calcutta Government attempted to introduce the measure was amusing. It had to be postponed more than once for causes which showed how little was understood there about the Straits. The stamps sent were all in rupees, and there were no rupees in the place, and no rate of exchange was provided for. Then the number of stamps sent was altogether inadequate, and the natives could not understand about them. It all worked well enough after a time, but it always remained a question whether the community were not right in their objection, on the broad ground that it was an infringement of that free trade policy of Sir Stamford Raffles, which had made the place what it is, and which it is so essential to maintain, and for which the community has fought so many battles. It was looked upon as the thin edge of a wedge to be resisted to the utmost. It undoubtedly led more quickly to the transfer.

The French mail line of the Messageries Imperiales, as it was then termed, began to run towards the close of the year. Messrs. Hinnekindt Freres and L. Cateaux, a Belgian firm of very good standing, which began as Hinnekindt Freres in Singapore in 1849, were the Agents in the preliminary arrangements.

The first steamer of the company to arrive from Suez, bringing the mails from London of 18th October, was the *Imperatrice,* which arrived at Singapore on the 21st November. The steamer *Alphée* going homewards about the same time. It was then and for some years afterwards a monthly service, and was due to the opening of Cochin-China and the Port of Saigon by the French. Emperor Louis Napoleon took a great interest in the line, and it was said that the arrangement for the building of the steamers was due to him. The first steamers were built at La Ciotat near Marseilles by Scotch shipbuilders engaged from the Clyde to work there, and after a few vessels had been built, the French workmen went on alone, and built very fine steamers. The *Imperatrice* was afterwards called the *Provence,* on the downfall of the Emperor.

By that steamer on the 21st November, Mr. Paul Brasier arrived at Singapore to arrange to take over the Agency from Messrs. Hinnekindt. Mr. Brasier lived in Singapore for many years, and died here on 24th September, 1887, having been Agent for the Company all the twenty-five years, and it is not too much to say that the success of the line, and especially as regards the number of English passengers from Singapore who travelled by the French mail, was largely due to his being very much liked.

He lived with his family for a great many years at St. James, Keppel Harbour, where he died. He and Mrs. Brasier and their three children, who were all brought up in the place, attracted the friendship of all Singapore, with their amiable, courteous, and gentle characters. It was often said that Mr. Brasier, who was always cheerful and obliging, passed through a life of much trouble here. Mrs. Brasier died, and then his elder daughter who had married a French gentleman who was afterwards the Agent of the Company· at Madras, then the younger daughter, who was very much liked in the place, died here ; and when he died his son Réne, his only remaining child, was away at Hongkong. Mr. Réne continued in the Company's Agency here, and latterly was Agent, but he left Singapore in 1900 for Sydney, where he was appointed Agent, as the most important Branch in the East.

On 15th May, James B. Cumming, Simon F. Cumming and Hugh R. Beaver advertised that they had started the firm of Cumming Beaver & Co.

It was in this year that Mr. Thomas Braddell came to reside in Singapore. He had been Assistant Resident Councillor in Penang, and returned from leave after having passed for the Bar, and commenced practising in Singapore. He had been heard of in Singapore, as he had been in Penang and Malacca for eighteen years. He was one of the most useful and hardworking men that ever came to Singapore. It was said of him, after he died, that if he had had a longer education, he would have been a very eminent man. He left Ireland, where he was born, in 1823 at sixteen years of age, and went to a plantation in the West Indies. About 1844 he came to the Straits from Demerara, to manage the sugar estate called Otaheite in the Ayer Etam Valley at Penang, which belonged to Messrs. Brown & Co. About that time an alteration had taken place in the sugar duties in England, putting the British Indian produce on the same footing as the Colonies. This gave a great increase to the development of Province Wellesley ; therefore in 1846 Brown & Co. and Mr. Nairne formed a Company and opened the Batu Kawan Estate in Province Wellesley, of which Mr. Braddell became manager and owner of four-sixteenths of the property, Brown & Co. furnishing the funds. The venture was unfortunate, as the estate got inundated in a very high tide and the crop was lost.

Mr. Braddell left the estate, and was on 1st January, 1849, appointed Deputy Superintendent of Police at Penang, and a few months afterwards was transferred to the Municipality as Secretary. From that he took charge of the Police of Province Wellesley, and in 1851 was sent to Malacca, where he was for three years. Until this time he had been heard little of in Singapore, and he used to tell how he went between Malacca and Singapore in schooners and sampans. In 1856 he returned to Penang as Magistrate, and in 1859 he was called to the Bar in England by the Society of Gray's Inn.

He resigned his appointment in Penang in 1862, and came down to Singapore to practise in the Supreme Court. He joined Mr. Abraham Logan in 1862, and they had offices behind Battery Road at the rear of John Little & Co.'s premises. They worked together until Mr. Logan went to Penang.

In January, 1864, he was appointed Crown Counsel of the Straits Settlements, and prosecuted for the Crown at the Assizes. He held the appointment, continuing his large private practice, until April, 1867, when he was appointed Attorney General of the Straits Settlements, on the Transfer, and held the position until he retired on 31st December, 1882, on a pension of $4,090 a year, and died in London on 19th September, 1891, at 68 years of age.

A very great deal of work was thrown upon Mr. Braddell as the first law-officer after the transfer. Many new Ordinances had to be drawn, and the law officers of the Crown in London gave him great credit for his ability in dealing with many difficult subjects. This was especially the case with the Crown Suits Ordinance. He was a man of great quickness of perception, great energy of purpose, and unwearied industry. He was, in his comparatively younger days, when he first came to Singapore, one of the most popular men of the place. He was a capital billiard player, and was to be seen in the theatre when any travelling company gave performances there, which were poor enough; but he used to say that it passed an evening occasionally, however bad the players were, and made a little diversion from work.

It was always pleasant to the jury to hear him conducting the cases at the Assizes, for he was most essentially a kind-hearted, straight-forward man, with a very pleasant, perfectly audible voice, and a fluent, but very simple, speaker. He had a very pleasant face and manner, and it was said of him after the Transfer, that he was the only official who could carry off the civil service uniform which came into use then among some, but not all, the officials, for he had a fine figure, and was over six feet in height.

Mr. Braddell was a most indefatigable worker, and used to sit up very late at night at his work. At one time he intended to write a history of Singapore similar to the present work, and he filled a great number of foolscap sheets of common Chinese writing paper with rough copies of old documents and *précis* of the contents of many others. Some few of these were printed in Logan's Journal, but there are several hundred sheets of other matter, which have been very largely made use of in compiling this book, as they were given into the author's possession. There are some who wonder why Mr. Braddell, who was a very busy man, should have spent so much time and taken so much trouble, about the stories of this place; but he was one of those, like Mr. Crawfurd, J. T. Thomson, G. W. Earl, John Cameron, and others, who were very willing to use their spare time in endeavouring to record the history of the place, the growing importance of which they foresaw and appreciated. Mr. Braddell wrote a number of papers in Logan's Journal, which did not all give his name, but among the sheets above spoken of, (which with similar papers, although not so voluminous regarding Penang and Malacca would make a small volume of themselves) is

a list in his own writing of his contributions to the journal, which
were as follows :—

It was Mr. Braddell's manuscripts, which were in many cases only
decipherable by the compiler of this book, who was well accustomed
to his writing and method of contracting the words, that led,
more than anything else, to undertaking this book. It seemed impossible to let all his useful, voluntary, and persevering labour go
to the white ants for want of some one to turn it to the best
account he could. It is much to be regretted that he did not live
to read the proofs of this book, for he would have made it very much
better.

As will be understood from the long translations of Malay
works which he published in Logan's Journal, he was a very good
Malay scholar, at a time when there were few residents who read
and wrote it. The Malays had great respect for him, and the
chiefs in the Peninsula looked to him, as they did to Mr. W. H.
Read, as a friend to go to for advice. He was largely concerned
with Mr. Andrew Clarke, in the Settlement of the Native States
about 1874, and the appointment of the first residents.

He received the thanks of Government for his services on many
occasions, and had the Perak war medal. He was made a C.M.G.
in 1882. Three of his children are in the Straits now, one
daughter and two of his sons, the latter following his profession,
one of whom was for a time acting as Attorney General, while the
holder of the office was on leave. Thomas Braddell is a name that
should always be remembered with gratitude in Singapore, for it
owes him much in many ways.

THOMAS BRADDELL, C.M.G.

CHAPTER LI.

1863

IN January the Supreme Government directed the Governor to submit to the Chamber of Commerce, for their opinion, a Bill to authorise the levy of port dues in the Ports of the Straits Settlements. The opinion of the Chamber of Commerce was that the measure was totally uncalled for, and that if persevered in it would be highly damaging to the welfare of the ports in the Straits, which would thenceforth lose all claim to be called "free ports." The proposal was a favourite one with the Indian Government and had been frequently mooted by it, but as often had been discountenanced by higher authorities at home. The last occasion had been in 1857, when the Court of Directors objected to the levy of port dues in the Straits, and since that time nothing more had been heard of the subject until 1863. It was thought that the Secretary of State might have withdrawn the prohibition given by the Court of Directors, in which case the Indian Government would doubtless try to carry the measure through.

Colonel Cavenagh wrote to Calcutta supporting the view of the Chamber of Commerce, his despatch containing the following passage :— " Unlike the Ports of India, which are the natural portals of the commerce of the country, and to which therefore its carriers are compelled to resort, Singapore is a mere depôt, where goods, the produce of other countries, are stored, until a favourable opportunity for their reshipment to their final destination ; hence it is requisite to offer some inducement to vessels to enter and discharge their cargoes. This inducement has hitherto been its freedom from all port charges. Doubtless Singapore is much favored by its natural position, standing as it does between the China Sea and the Straits of Malacca, and surrounded by Native States, still its position alone would not have led to its prosperity, had vessels been deterred from visiting its harbour by the fear of being called upon for heavy payments in the shape of anchorage dues. "

In March several of the Singapore merchants then in London saw Sir Charles Wood, the Secretary of State for India, on the subject, and he was reported to have said that it was in consequence of the recommendation of the Chamber of Commerce that the prohibition sent by the Court of Directors at Leadenhall Street to Calcutta in 1857, against the levy of Port Dues in the Straits, had been withdrawn by him. The Chamber had always protested in the strongest manner against any Port Dues in the Straits, and strongly objected to Sir Charles Wood's statement.

In August the *Free Press* contained the following :—" Sir Charles Wood remains obstinate in his refusal to withdraw his sanction to the levy of tonnage dues in the Straits. This is probably not of much importance, practically, as the Government of India is pledged not to take advantage of the permission given to it by the Hon. Baronet to injure the trade of the Settlement, but it must make us all the more anxious to be removed from under the control of a person who has shown himself so wrong-headed and who has it so much in his power to damage our interests. The following is the latest appeal to Sir Charles Wood on the subject, and his answer:

To the Right Hon. Sir Charles Wood, Bart., Her Majesty's Principal Secretary of State for India.

Right Hon. Sir. By late advices from Singapore it appears the Supreme Government of India has suspended the act for levying Tonnage duties at Singapore and intimated its intention of abandoning it altogether; under these circumstances I trust you will see the inutility of persisting in cancelling (to the injury of many holders of property) the long standing prohibition to levying duties on the commerce of the Settlement, and that you will reimpose it, and thus replace Sir Stamford Raffles's proclamation in full force and integrity, as until that is done, the proprietors cannot feel secure in their property.

I have, &c., &c.,

C. R. READ.

8th June, 1863.

INDIA OFFICE, S. W.,

19th June, 1863.

Sir, I am directed to acknowledge the receipt of your letter of the 8th inst., and to inform you in reply that Sir Charles Wood does not see in the circumstances therein represented any reason for reimposing the prohibition against the levy of Tonnage duties in the Settlement of Singapore.

I am, &c.,

C. R. READ, Esq.

HERMAN MERIVALE.

In February a petition signed by eighty-six of the European inhabitants was sent to the Duke of Newcastle, Secretary of State for the Colonies, asking that Singapore should be transferred from the diocese of Calcutta, and made the centre of an Ecclesiastical policy as it was of a commercial system, and that with the Straits Settlements should be incorporated the bishopric of Labuan, with Singapore as the Bishop's residence.

In the *Free Press* of 16th July is a copy of a long report made by Captains Fraser and Forlong upon the proposed route across the Isthmus of Kraw to connect the Bay of Bengal and the Gulf of Siam; and on the 6th August some lengthy notes by Mr. J. D. Vaughan on the report, which had been read at the Royal Geographical Society on 26th January. It was said that there had been a tradition that there had formerly been a canal across the Isthmus. Mr. John Crawfurd, who was present at the meeting in London, made some lengthy remarks in objection to the scheme, from which the following extracts are taken :—

"Mr. Crawfurd said he had never visited the locality of the projected railway, but he knew pretty well what the nature of it was. Though this peninsula was called by the authors of the Paper a strip of land, it was in extent about twice the size of Ireland, containing an area of 60,000 square miles. The greater part of it was thick forest, and the land was not by any means fertile except in minerals, a little tin, iron and gold.

"He could not, however, agree with the authors of the Paper in believing that the projected plan was in the least degree feasible; on the contrary, he was sure it was impracticable. The distance from shore to shore was 65 miles, of which 15 miles were described to be navigable by the so-called Pakchan River. This in reality was not a river, but an estuary of the sea, with only four or five fathoms of water for half the distance, and but a fathom and a half on the bar at low water. Then came the projected railway of 50 miles, at the terminus of which, on the eastern side of the bay, there happened to be no harbour at all. Such a terminus would never do to carry on the great trade of Europe and India with China and Japan. Then, with respect to the monsoons, the rough monsoon in the Bay of Bengal is the south-west monsoon, just the very opposite of that which prevails in the China Sea and along the whole of the eastern coast of the Malay peninsula, where the north-east was the boisterous one; its strength is frequently that of an eight or nine knot breeze. A ship could not with safety lie at the terminus, and even a small vessel of about 120 tons had not been able to come inside the bar.

"As to the alleged dangerous navigation of the Straits of Malacca, the Straits of Malacca are about 500 miles long and about 300 miles wide at the broadest part. There are no storms: there are variable winds and squalls, called "Sumatras," because they always blow from the coast of Sumatra, which last about a couple of hours. The Peninsular and Oriental Company have been carrying the mails by this route for the last eighteen years. During that period their ships have made between 600 and 700 voyages through the Straits, and have met with only one accident, which was caused by two of their ships running against each other in the dark, when one of them went to the bottom. The merchants of Calcutta and Bombay send their opium to China by this route, and out of 300 voyages made by their steamers not a single loss has occurred. Steamers belonging to the Royal Navy are constantly passing and repassing through the Straits of Malacca, and he had never heard of one of them being lost. For the last ten years also the Dutch Government have been sending a vessel once a fortnight, and during the whole of that time have never lost a vessel. He, therefore, took it for granted that the navigation of the straits was not so dangerous as had been alleged."

In this year an iron steamer, the *Pluto*, was sent from Calcutta to take the place of the old worn-out *Hooghly*; she had more accommodation, but her speed was hardly any better, and she required as much tinkering as the *Hooghly* did. The Calcutta Government saddled the Straits with an inefficient craft that caused "more expense than a new vessel." There were at this time two old Thames penny-steamboats, called the *Tonze* and *Mohr*, of about 80 to 100 tons each, which used to lie in the harbour, and were supposed to be useful against pirates.

The shipwrights, Buyers and Riach, built a vessel called the *Singapore* for the Netherlands India mail line of Mr. Cores de Vries, she was 600 tons, the largest vessel constructed in Singapore at that time, 186 feet long, 24 feet beam, and 16 feet deep; of teak and copper fastened. The engines and rigging were to be supplied in Java.

In May the Chamber of Commerce sent Petitions to the Government and the Governor-General of India, pressing upon the Government the advantages that would result from coining a British dollar. It suggested that instead of the coins having the effigy of the reigning Sovereign on the obverse, it should only have the Royal Arms, and that on the reverse there should be an inscription indicating the nature of the coin, such as "One Dollar," surrounded by scroll work. By adopting this plan the general appearance of the coin would remain the same during successive reigns, the only change at different periods would be in the date of issue. The suspicion and distrust which any considerable change in the appearance of a coin would be apt to raise in the minds of the Chinese and other natives would thus be avoided, and the Chamber trusted that this would be held a sufficient justification for their venturing to suggest such an innovation in the usual practice of making the effigy of the reigning Sovereign a part of the design impressed on coins issuing from the Royal Mints."

A Memorial was also sent to the Chancellor of the Exchequer asking for the abolition of the heavy duty on pepper.

At this time the Oriental Bank was always known among the natives as the " Bank Besar," and the paper in June published statements made at the meeting in London in April, from which it appeared that the Bank was still very successful notwithstanding the great competition it had met with of late years. A dividend of 5 per cent. and a bonus of 3 per cent. were declared, making, with a previous payment in the course of the year, a total distribution of 15 per cent. for 1862. The Chairman stated that during the 12 years they had been in existence they had paid 160 per cent. to the shareholders; and had thus paid back the whole of the Capital and 60 per cent. besides. It is a pity it did not go on in the old way, and there was a very considerable stir in Singapore in 1884, when it stopped payment.

An excursion party was made up in June to Gunong Pulai, and they were away four days. The result of their observations was unfavorable to the idea of establishing a sanatorium there. The reduction in temperature was not found to be great; and the distance from Singapore would present serious obstacles in the way of procuring supplies and, in the case of invalids, medical assistance. For a mere change of scene it was thought that Bukit Timah presented nearly as great advantages as Gunong Pulai, and its accessibility from Singapore was a great recommendation in its favor. The height was taken by the mean of two-aneroids as 1906 feet, and by boiling water as 1833 feet. The difference by thermometer was taken as 8 degrees.

The only way at this time to cross the river from the Square to the Post Office and Stamp Office without going round over Elgin Bridge was in little *tambangs* or sampans, and the Municipal Commissioners (who must have been desperately anxious for funds, to descend to such small game to raise a revenue), farmed out the right of the ferry, and the farmer caused a strike among the sampan boys by asking too much from them for permission to ply. A wooden bridge on trestles, with a charge of a quarter of a cent (doit) was soon put up, and Europeans crossing over to the Esplanade after office, used to give a cent or two every now and then. All carriages drove down Kling Street and Circular Road from the Square.

A very bad case of *Amok* occurred on 1st July in Shaik Madarsah Lane, Campong Glam. A Javanese Sailor ran amok, cutting a woman nearly to pieces, mortally wounding a man and a child, and inflicting wounds more or less severe on three other persons. He then set fire to the house in which this took place, and brandishing a kris in one hand and a large knife in the other, defied all attempts to capture him. Inspector Cox having arrived on the spot repeatedly called upon him to surrender, but he refused and attempted to break through the partition into the neighbouring house. Inspector Cox then fired at him through the venetians, intending to disable him, but the ball went through the heart.

The following paragraph on the paper in July looks like the first symptom of the interminable Acheen war of a few years later :— "There is a report that the Rajah of Acheen,—not approving of chiefs on the East Coast of Sumatra, whom he considered as his vassals, hoisting the Dutch flag—intended to try to bring them back to their allegiance by force, should softer means fail, and the Dutch government is of course prepared to assist those who have shown themselves so willing to come under its sway. If there is really any truth in this, we are afraid the Achinese monarch is only precipitating his own destruction, and giving the opportunity so eagerly longed for by our astute neighbours, of bringing the whole island of Sumatra under their exclusive dominion."

A very large fire broke out on the afternoon of Wednesday, 19th August, in the neighbourhood of Upper Circular Road, which cleared away a great number of old houses, and led to the wide, open street that now stands there. The fire cleared away nearly the whole block of buildings as far as Carpenter Street, and did a great deal of good to the town.

On 1st September was issued a little prospectus, the beginning in a very small way of the Tanjong Pagar Dock Company, Limited, which has grown to such large dimensions. It stated that the Company with a capital of $125,000 in 1250 shares of $100 each with power to increase, was started, and that applications for shares could be made to Mr. M. F. Davidson, before the 10th instant, when a meeting would be called, allotment made, and directors appointed. On 14th September an advertisement signed by Mr. Thomas Scott (then a partner in Guthrie & Co.) as Acting Secretary, appeared, giving the names of the Committee as Messrs. G. Cramer (Rautenberg, Schmidt & Co.), M. F. Davidson (A. L. Johnston & Co.), S. Gilfillan (Borneo Co. Ltd.), C. H. Harrison (Middleton, Harrison & Co.), Tan Kim Ching, C. P. Lalla, Thos. Scott (Guthrie & Co.), and C. H. H. Wilsone (Hamilton, Gray & Co.)

Mr. Cameron in his book written in 1864 says:—"One plan was to build a series of wharves at the nearest point of New Harbour, where ships can lie alongside, and connect these with town by a tramway or railway. Another was to construct a pile-pier running right out from the busiest part of the town into deep water, to enable ships of all sizes to come alongside and load and discharge into trucks, which could afterwards be conveyed on tramways to the various godowns. The latter plan is one upon which Colonel Collyer, for some years Chief Engineer, spent a good deal of time and reduced into shape. Either plan appears to me feasible, and likely to prove profitable to the capitalists who would undertake it, and valuable to the town. The first has not many engineering obstacles, and the works connected with it could be made permanent, but the cost would be very great. The second plan, on the other hand, requires very limited outlay and though a considerable sum would have to be spent on renewing piles, yet similar undertakings in other parts of the world have, I believe, generally proved more successful than costly permanent erections. The water of Singapore harbour is never so seriously disturbed as to interfere with even the largest vessels lying safely alongside such a pier, and from the soundings obtained upon the site proposed, the bottom was found to consist of soft mud, so that ships might without danger ground at low water, should a pressure of business compel them to do so."

It was in 1865 that the works for the Naval Coal Depot at Pulo Brani were completed on behalf of the Admiralty. They consisted of two coal sheds, to hold 8,000 tons of coal, a small house for the Superintendent, and a quay wall and short wooden pier having 27 feet of water alongside at low tide. The site was ill-chosen, as the tides were dangerous, and in 1868 the famous transport *Himalaya* was in great danger owing to one of the mooring hawsers giving way and swinging round on the shore in the little bay ; it was said that her having steam up at the time was all that saved her.

The beginning of the present extensive works at Tanjong Pagar on the opposite side of Keppel Harbour was very unfortunate, but it led on to very great results. An earth and rock embankment, was being run out from the shore, and one afternoon about 3 p.m. a message came round the Square that there was a sight to be seen at Tanjong Pagar. All went down in gharries. The monsoon was just set in, and waves came rolling into the entrance from the old harbour. As each successive wave came, several yards of the embankment were swept away, and piece after piece went, until all the work that had been done disappeared, and nothing whatever remained to show for all the money that had been spent.

In September, 1865, some excitement was caused by the report that in blasting a hill at Tanjong Pagar for the Company gold had been discovered, but it proved not to be gold at all.

On 28th July, 1865, the following letter was sent to Governor Cavenagh :—" 1st.—We have the honor to apply for the right to construct and erect an Iron Screw Pile Pier from the vicinity of Princes Street extending into the Harbour in a southerly direction for a distance of about 2,200 yards, with a view to afford wharfage to vessels loading and discharging their cargoes at the port of Singapore.

2nd.—We have the honor further to apply for the right to build a seawall from the vicinity of Princes Street to that of Tanjong Mallang and to fill up the seashore so reclaimed, with the view of constructing warehouses and other buildings necessary to the aforesaid pier, and to render the same otherwise available for general building purposes.

3rd.—We purpose to provide the funds for the above undertakings by means of a Joint Stock Company, with a capital of £200,000 now being formed for this purpose, and to which the rights granted under this application are intended to be conveyed.

W. H. READ,

WHAMPOA,

E. J. LEVESON,

H. M. SIMONS."

This did not come to anything, but it will be noticed that the reclamation of Teluk Ayer Bay was then part of the scheme.

On 14th September the Bank of Hindustan, China and Japan, of London, established an Agency in Singapore, in charge of Messrs. Paterson, Simons & Co., which continued for many years.

The verandah question, which has reached such an acute stage at various times, commenced in October, when the *Free Press* said "The Municipal Commissioners have postponed carrying into effect their order that all the verandahs in town should be completely cleared from all obstructions, until the 1st January next. In coming to this resolution they have shown their wisdom; and we trust that during the interval they will consider whether it will not be prudent to modify somewhat the terms of their order, and confine themselves to enforcing what we believe the Court of Judicature has declared to be the right of the public in the verandahs, namely, a right of way or free passage along them. The Court has not said that the public has an exclusive right to the verandahs—or that the occupants of the houses, of which the verandahs form a portion, may not make such use of them as they find convenient, as long as they do not thereby prevent pedestrians from passing along them. That such use has been made of them for more than twenty years past, we can testify from personal experience, and we do not therefore very well see how the Commissioners can *legally* insist on their being entirely cleared.

"If it is considered desirable that the verandahs should be wholly set apart for the use of the public the aid of the legislature must be invoked. But the legislature in depriving the owners of town houses of part of their property will take care that they receive proper compensation for it. To do otherwise would be to commit an act of downright spoliation, to which we do not think any British legislature, however absolute its constitution, would lend itself."

In February, 1864, the Commissioners contented themselves with establishing the right of the public to a free passage along the verandahs; the rough and ready rule being that sufficient room should be left for two persons to walk abreast. This was in general readily complied with in places where people wanted to walk in the verandahs, and the owners of small shops had still the use of part of the space to show their goods, which was undoubtedly an advantage to the trade of the place, when the natives, and especially the Bugis traders, went walking in single file about the town, on the look out for bargains.

In the month of October a collision took place in the early morning in the Straits of Malacca between the steamer *John Bright*, on her way from Singapore to Bombay, and the French barque *Salazes,* bound from Singapore to Penang. The barque sank in a few minutes but no lives were lost. It led to a lot of litigation.

The Chinese, in October, gave a great deal of trouble to the police by their clan and faction fights and several murders occurred in the course of the disturbances. One of the most effectual means of repressing these broils was found to consist in calling on the more respectable Chinese traders to act as special constables. A large number of females arrived from China during the latter part of the year, several of them, it was stated, being imported by some of the Secret Societies as a means of increasing their influence. The attention of the Government and the Police was called to the abuses likely to arise from permitting this, and they were urged to take some steps to ameliorate the condition of these immigrants, which was represented as being a species of slavery of the worst description.

On 18th November the startling news was received that the Confederate cruiser *Alabama* had come out to this end of the world, and had burned two American ships near Sunda Straits. The paper said it was to be hoped that she might fall in with some of the Northern men-of-war, so that her career of semi-pirate, by attacking and burning defenceless merchant ships, might be put an end to. The vessel arrived at Singapore on the night of Monday, 21st December, and the next day she went into New Harbour to coal, and great numbers of natives went down to see her. She left on the morning of Thursday the 24th, and proceeded up the Straits of Malacca. About 2 p. m. of the same day she fell in with the British barque *Martaban,* Captain Pike, from Moulmein to Singapore, laden with rice. The *Martaban* was formerly an American vessel called the *Texan Star,* belonging to the port of Boston, but she was sold at Moulmein to a British merchant and obtained a Certificate of British Registry. When she met the *Alabama* she was about ten miles away from Mount Formosa. The *Alabama* fired a gun across her bows and sent a boat on board, the officer in charge of which demanded the ship's papers. The master of the *Martaban* produced his Register, Port Clearance and other papers, and was then requested to go with them to the *Alabama.* He refused to do this, on which the Confederate officer said he would take charge of the vessel until he could communicate with Captain Semmes. Two armed men were then called on board and the boat was sent back to the *Alabama.* It soon returned bringing Captain Semmes, who at once proceeded to the cabin where he sat down and called for the ship's papers. The Master handed the Certificate of British Registry to him which he perused, reading out aloud the name of the owner and the date of the Certificate, 10th December. Captain Semmes said that he was not to be humbugged by any sham papers and that Captain Pike ought to have had a Certificate that the transfer was legal, and mentioned some other documents that ought to have been produced. He then turned to Captain Pike and said " I shall burn your ship." Captain Pike protested against this, and said that his papers were legal, but Captain Semmes called his officer and said " You will burn this ship, Sir" and immediately returned to the *Alabama.* The first Lieutenant of the *Alabama* then came on board and took charge of the *Martaban.* In the meantime the officer who first boarded the barque ordered the lascar crew to hoist out one of the ship's boats and proceed in her to the *Alabama,* which they did. Captain Pike and his officers were told that they might take some clothes with them. Captain Pike was allowed to take two small trunks and the others one bag each, and they were assured that the property they took with them would be respected. Captain Pike placed in his trunks a bag containing Rs. 400 and some papers. The first lieutenant of the *Alabama* ordered the *Martaban's* anchor to be let go and the sails clewed up, and he directed some of his men to haul down the British flag which had been flying at the peak. The skylights were broken and tow steeped in tar was placed in the cabin and in the fore part of the 'tween decks. The officers of the *Martaban* were then ordered to proceed to the *Alabama* in their own boat, which had returned. Shortly after they reached the *Alabama* they saw the *Alabama's* boat returning and flames burst out from the *Martaban* at both ends. The *Alabama's* boat brought from the *Martaban* four bolts of cotton canvas and some twine, two chronometers, all the nautical instruments of the Master and Officers, a deep sea line and lead, two hams and all the poultry, an unfortunate cat being the only living thing left on board the *Martaban.* At 5 p.m. the *Alabama* proceeded up the Straits uuder steam and about midnight came to anchor about five or six miles off Malacca. At daybreak of the 25th Capt. Pike was called on deck and ordered to produce the keys of his trunks which were opened and the contents turned out. The rupees, a small toy pistol, a marine binocular and some papers were taken possession of. The bags of the officers were searched. Captain Pike and his officers were required to sign a paper stating that they would not serve against the Confederate States until regularly exchanged. The officers and crew of the *Martaban* were then embarked in one of the *Alabama's* boats under charge of two officers and proceeded towards the shore. One of the Confederate Officers landed to communicate with the authorities, and in about an hour he returned, when the persons belonging to the *Martaban* were put on shore. It was understood that Captain Semmes sent a letter to the authorities at Malacca stating that he was sorry to burn a vessel under the English flag, but he had his reasons for it! Captain Pike and his crew received every attention at Malacca and arrived in Singapore on the morning of the 29th. The paper said that Captain Semmes had committed a bold act in capturing and destroying a vessel sailing under a British register, and that his conduct savoured very much of downright piracy.

On the morning of the 26th December the *Alabama* captured two more American vessels in the Straits. These were the *Senora,* Captain Brown, and the *Highlander,* Captain Snow, both in ballast and bound from Singapore to Akyab. Both ships were destroyed within a mile and a half of each other off Pulo Loumat. The people who had been taken from the two ships were offered the choice of taking a cruise in the *Alabama* and being landed at the first port touched, or going adrift in their boats. They chose the latter alternative, and the *Alabama* was quickly steaming ahead leaving all the boats to get to land as they best could. During a squall which blew shortly after, one of the boats with eleven Africans, a portion of the *Senora's* crew, parted company from the rest and was not heard of again. The remainder got on board a small native craft, but afterwards were taken on board the French ship *Pujet* going from Singapore to Madras, which put them on board a vessel for Penang. The *Alabama* then cleared right away to avoid two American ships, the *Wyoming* and *Vanderbilt*, who were after her, and, five months afterwards, she was sunk by the *Kearseage* off Cherbourg harbour in France, on a fine Sunday morning in May, while the good folks were going .to Church.

At this time there was a little shed, about twelve feet square, in the centre of the south side of the middle road crossing the Square, in which was a telegraph line to the New Harbour Dock Company and the P. & O. wharf. It was the first telegraph line in Singapore, and was on a very small scale.

In November Mr. George Mansfield died in London. He had carried on business in Flint Street as a shipchandler as George Mansfield & Co., since 1861, and the business was continued under the same name by his manager, Mr. R. J. Wright, as a partner with Mr. William Mansfield.

CHAPTER LII.

1864

A S a great many reports were made of persons in the jungle in one locality having been killed by tigers, some pits were dug, and a party of police went out in January to a place where a cub had fallen into one of the pits. While they were standing in a circle round the pit, the tigress suddenly sprung out upon them, and one peon was shot, and died the same day, and the Deputy Commissioner had a bullet through his coat. The police then went away, and the cub being still in the pit, Neil Martin Cranie, who has been spoken of on page 221, went out. He sat down alone near one side of the pit, with his rifle handy over his knees, and threw some earth or stones into the pit. The growl of the tigress was heard, and she appeared in the jungle, on the opposite side of the pit, and sprung towards him over it. He fired while she was in the air, and she fell almost close to him. It was said at the time that it was no part of the duty of the police to kill tigers, which they did not understand, and that it would be better if they attended to their own business more, and if they were not sent out and allowed to shoot each other. A few days afterwards two men were killed three miles from town, and a tiger was seen at the second mile on the bridge at Bukit Timah Road.

The Siamese Government at this time was renewing its attempts to acquire rule over Perak, and it was said that the Rajah of Tongka, a Siamese feudatory, proposed to the Resident Councillor at Penang that the British Government should allow Siam to take possession of Perak, on the understanding that one-third of the revenue should be applied to pensioning the Perak Chiefs; one-third paid to the British Government; and the remaining third be retained by the Siamese. This was, of course, rejected, and the person who made it was warned that any attempt to disturb Perak would be resented by the English Government. It was looked upon as another attempt to assume rights over the whole of the Peninsula; and this was borne out by the way the ex-Sultan of Lingga had been twice allowed to leave Bangkok to stir up trouble in Pahang, notwithstanding the disclaimer of Siam that they were unable to prevent it.

A native was sentenced to six months imprisonment in Penang for having deceived by borrowing $200 on a piece of land, for which he had paid $23, and inserting $220 in the conveyance, in order to borrow a larger sum of money. It is mentioned because the practice is not unknown, and is a warning to those who lend money to natives on mortgage. Sir Benson Maxwell, in passing sentence, spoke strongly upon the conduct of the borrower.

Captain Nelson of the Madras Presidency, induced by the unceasing accounts appearing in the newspapers of the dreadful destruction of human beings in Singapore occasioned by tigers, wrote to the Government to suggest that an attempt might be made to poison the brutes by means of strychnine. He mentioned a case in which he succeeded in destroying a tiger, together with a great many vultures, jackals, dogs, &c., by putting strychnine on the carcase of a buffalo which the tiger had killed and only partly consumed, and to which he returned to complete his meal. The method recommended by Captain Nelson was to be tried here by Mr. Dunman, although he had doubts on the point, as repeated attempts had been made in Singapore to poison tigers, without any good result. Dogs had been tied up in the jungle in places resorted to by tigers, their necks having been previously shaved and rubbed with strychnine, means being taken to prevent their licking off the poison. Calves had also been tethered in the jungle with their necks prepared in the same manner, but none of the experiments succeeded, although from the marks of tigers' feet all round the bait in several instances, it was apparent that their notice had been attracted to it. In one or two cases strychnine had also been placed on the bodies of persons killed by tigers, but the tigers did not again touch them; and it had been generally observed in Singapore that the tigers did not return to eat bodies, whether of men or beasts, which they had only partly consumed.

On the Queen's birthday, 24th May, the gas was lighted in the town for the first time. The Gas Company had made a push to have the mains laid in the principal streets to allow of this being done. When the lamps were lighted, natives were seen going up to the lamp-posts, and touching them very gingerly at first with the tips of their fingers; they could not understand how a fire could come out at the top, without the post getting hot, which was by no means unreasonable, as they could not know what gas was.

The Singapore Gas Company, Limited, a London Company, did very good work for the town for thirty-eight years, and sold the business to the Municipality in 1901. Soon after the gas was introduced, petroleum oil came to the place, about 1868, and the first lamp came up from Batavia to Mr. W. H. Read. It was a chandelier in his drawing room, with six lamps, and astonished the natives not a little. Mr Read had to get the oil specially from Batavia, but its use became general before long, and no doubt seriously affected the Gas Company.

Mr. Whampoa had gas laid on all the way to his house at the 2½ miles on Serangoon Road, in June 1866; and it was proposed to light Tan Tock Seng's Hospital opposite with gas, as it was said by some of the Committee that paraffin oil lamps would set fire to the attap and plank wards, which others doubted. It was not done, and oil has been used to the present time, some thirty years, without any accident, and at a very considerable saving of expense. The native shops and dwelling houses in town used gas pretty freely at first, but it was replaced by oil in most instances in course of time.

In June the Parsee firm of Byramjee Hormusjee Cama & Co. opened a school in Tanjong Pagar Road in the bungalow that had been formerly occupied by Mr. Cama. He established the school which was carried on for many years, and was kept up at his expense, as a free school for Chinese and others. At the end of the month there were 103 pupils, mostly Chinese.

Mr. James Guthrie some years before had established at his own expense a school for Malay boys at Tanjong Pagar, the average attendance in 1864 being about forty pupils, the instruction being in Malay only. At the Cama School the boys were taught English.

There were some very large mercantile failures this year, two among the European firms, one of the oldest in the place having suspended payment with liabilities of over a million of dollars. Trade in Singapore had never had such a shock and there was almost a stagnation in the market as far as selling manufactured goods was concerned. Very heavy failures among the Chinese firms occurred in June, and in that month there was a foolish panic among the natives about the security of the bank notes, and there was a run upon the banks for silver in place of them. At the Chartered Bank they had a lot of dollars, so they insisted on paying cheques in silver only, and those who cashed the cheques found they had to take away a heavy load of dollars, instead of the convenient, and easily locked up bank notes, and the rush to cash the notes gradually ceased.

There were four Banks in the Square at this time. The Oriental Bank in what were called Spottiswoode's Buildings in the centre of the East side, where Wm. Spottiswoode & Co.'s offices formerly were, of which Mr. John S. Scrymgeour was Manager.

The second was the Chartered Mercantile Bank of India, London, and China in what was called Almeida's Buildings, at the centre of the south end of the Square, where Dr. Jose d'Almeida's offices at one time stood, and where the Mercantile Bank of India now stands; it was always spoken of as the Mercantile Bank, and Mr. James Davidson was Manager at this time; he left the Bank in consequence of its being heavily involved in the failure of the European firms just spoken of, and became a broker, the beginning of them in Singapore. The brokerage for a short time, till competition speedily set up, was one quarter per cent. each way! The mercantile community gave a large ball in the Town Hall to Mr. and Mrs. Davidson, who had been very generous hosts in the days when the guests used to sit down at a large dinner party at their house at 7 o'clock, the hour in those days, and did not rise until nearly midnight. It was the first ball, it is thought, in the Town Hall.

The third Bank was the Chartered Bank of India, Australia, and China at the north corner of the Square and Prince Street, of which Robert Duff was the first Manager, and Charles Smith Sherwood was Manager in this year, and Mr. James Greig was Accountant. This was always known as the Chartered Bank, to distinguish it from the Mercantile. These three Banks all carried on business for many years.

The fourth Bank did not remain long. It was the Asiatic Banking Corporation, with its office at the opposite end of the Square to the Mercantile Bank. Mr. John Steel of the Mercantile Bank was the first Manager, and John Jamieson Winton was Accountant, and afterwards Manager.

In consequence of the great loss by the failures of the Chinese firms, it was decided at a General Meeting of the Chamber of Commerce on 13th June, that from the 1st July the term of credit allowed to buyers of Imports should be reduced from three months to two, and those firms which were not members of the Chamber should be invited to carry out the resolution. It was generally agreed to, and it was hoped it would have a wholesome effect, but as happened before and since, some of those whom it suited to secure business by breaking their promise, unknown to their neighbours, soon broke up the rule which was really made for the advantage of all, if all had honestly abided by it. It was suggested that cash sales only should be made, but the proposal was not actually brought forward in the Chamber.

In the early days the Europeans had capital to use to find outlets for goods, and the Chinese dealer, who not seldom had a short time before been a cooly or salesman in a shop, or perhaps a "boy" or servant to his master in a European firm, had acquired special knowledge of the wants of some neighbouring markets, and perhaps had special opportunities of access to them. If this was carried on honestly, credit could be given with comparative safety. But times had changed, the few dealers had grown into many, and a composition of thirty per cent. was found by some of them to be a profitable way of winding up a business ; to begin again when the trouble had blown over. At times there was an epidemic of failures in the bazaar, which spread like typhus fever. The competition for business in the European, and especially in the German firms, led to more and more extended credit, and holding over of promissory notes after they were due, and then came the collapse, and the acceptance of a percentage of as much as could be squeezed out of the defaulter, rather than pottering over wretched insolvent estates for several, or many years, with an even worse result.

On the 24th November, in the evening, the French Mail Steamer *Hydaspe* left Singapore for Batavia. She was the commencement of the line of the Messageries Imperiales between Singapore and Batavia in connection with the mail steamer from Europe. She was in charge of a Dutch Pilot, and next morning there was some excitement in the Square at the news that the steamer had run hard and fast on the well-known Pan Shoal at the entrance of the Straits of Rhio, only 22 miles from Singapore. A large rock went right through her bottom, and several steamers tried to tow her off, but it was an impossibility, and she remained there afterwards as a warning to fools. She was sold by auction on 30th November, six days afterwards. A Samarang paper said that the pilot on board the *Hydaspe* was an Englishman, and that he had been bribed by a Singapore firm to put the steamer on shore. The Batavia newspaper however said that the pilot was a Dutchman, and that the latter statement was ridiculous.

On the 28th December, to provide funds for laying out the Gardens, a horticultural fete and fancy fair was held in the Mess House of the Tanglin Barracks, which was still unoccupied. It was held in the forenoon, and was made a good deal of.

This year ended up badly, with the first fire that was known to have occurred in the European quarter of the town, but by no means the last, and at a place close to which serious fires occurred several times afterwards. At midnight or shortly after, on Saturday morning, the 31st December, McAlister & Co.'s shipchandlery store at the corner of Battery Road and Flint Street, where the Chartered Bank stands now, was burned out, nothing but the walls of the two large buildings being left standing. How the fire was occasioned there was nothing to show. The adjoining building was occupied by Charles Wilson & Co. as a sail loft, who had lately begun the business. The fire communicated with the loft by the beams in the roofs. Their shipchandlery store on the other side of Battery Road was not on fire, but the sail loft was burned out. The next godown was that of Mr. Richard Brennand, who had been a clerk in Smith Bell & Co., and commenced business in his own name in 1863, while the next building was the shipchandlery store of George Mansfield & Co. There was one continuous roof over the whole of these premises, and the fire quickly spread along them, before there was time to check or control it. People came hurrying in from Tanglin, for there was no fire brigade at this time, and every energetic person gave all the help he could under the direction of Mr. Thomas Dunman of the Police and Major MacNair the Engineer. The doors were forced open, some boat crews landed from the ships in the harbour, and a number of Artillerymen came down from Fort Canning, but the merchant sailors and the soldiers could not resist the sight of so much liquor within reach, and were committing so much wanton destruction, that they did more harm than good, and the officers were asked to remove them. The Police had two hand fire engines; Guthrie & Co. had another; the convicts brought theirs from the Old Jail, and the marines and sailors from H. M. S. *Perseus* brought a small engine; but with rope, tar, oil, and all the combustible materials in shipchandlers stores, they did not do much. McAlister & Co.'s loss was about $45,000, the loss of the others was not so serious. A good deal of their goods were removed, but they were so much damaged by water that they had to be sold, and it was more than doubtful whether it was an advantage to carry them out, as they blocked up Battery Road, and sold for very little after all.

The annual Government Report for this year said that the convicts were employed in filling up the swamp at North Campong Malacca. That the old Court House [now the store room behind the Printing Office] had been fitted up and converted into the Post Office. That a Government Bungalow had been built at Changhi, and that the Dutch Telegraph Office [on the river-side near where the back of the Public Offices are now] had been purchased from the Netherlands Indian Government, and was used for the offices of the Master Attendant and Shipping Office. The spire of Andrew's Church had been completed, and four handsome iron gates had been purchased for the entrances to the compound.

On 4th July, the foundation stone of the new Court House was laid. Owing to the site selected having been part of the old river bed, the foundations gave a great deal of trouble. It was used for a few years as a Court, while the old portion of the present Court House was used for the Public Offices. An exchange was then made, and the large Court room was turned into the present Council Chamber, and afterwards the building was largely extended both back and front, at various times, to its present dimensions. Alexandra Road, connecting Passir Panjang and River Valley Roads was made in this year. In addition to being a useful line of communication, the side ditches improved the drainage of the neighbouring country. One half of the cost was contributed by Mr. Lozé, who had been book-keeper in Hamilton Gray & Co., and other land-owners; and Tampenis Road, formerly a mere bridle path was made into a cart track; and the A. B. C. or Ordnance Bridge, to connect North and South Campong Malacca, as well as Fort Canning with the Arsenal at Pearl's Hill, was completed.

In May there died an old inhabitant of Singapore, Syed Abdul-rahman bin Mahomed bil Fagi, better known as Tunku Tingga, about 90 years of age. He was a younger son of Syed Hussain, a wealthy Arab merchant of Penang, whose eldest son Syful Alum Shah, through his father's influence, became king of Acheen in 1815, the reigning sovereign being deposed by his subjects. Syful Alum Shah did not, however, long enjoy the kingly state, as the legitimate sovereign was restored to authority in 1819 by Sir Stamford Raffles, under the auspices of the British Government, Syful Alum Shah being allowed to retire to Penang, on a pension. Syed Hussain left considerable property, part of which, by his will, he devoted to charitable purposes. According to Mahomedan usages this ought to have been expended in alms, prayers, &c., but the then Recorder of the Straits, Sir W. Norris, directed that the money should be invested and the interest applied in annual grants to the Penang Free School and the Singapore Institution. This and other family matters so mortified Tunku Tingga, who was one of the executors of his father's will, that he left Penang and settled in Singapore about 1840, never afterwards revisiting Penang. To the last he always expressed a keen sense of the injustice which he conceived had been perpetrated by the decision of the Court. Tunku Tingga was a person of mild and pleasing address and was much respected by his countrymen and co-religionists. The Raffles Institution draws a share of the income to this day.

In this year Mr. John Cameron published his book "Our Tropical Possessions in Malayan India," being a descriptive account of Singapore, Penang, Province Wellesley, and Malacca; their peoples, products, commerce, and Government." The book is very readable, and the descriptions are very good and not highly coloured, as is too often the case with works of the kind. It was very useful in connection with the agitation for the Transfer, as it drew attention to the prosperity and value of the Straits Settlements, which were then little known or appreciated in England. The book was of most interest to those who wished to know something of Singapore, or intended to come here, and Mr. Cameron had the thanks of the community for his trouble. It had seven coloured lithographic illustrations.

It does not contain many details of the History of Singapore, but is full of matter which will always be interesting to those who reside in the place. There is one mistake about the History of Singapore which it may be well to notice here, as it was pointed out at the time, and would no doubt have been corrected if a subsequent edition had been issued. On page 206, it says that, after being a dependency of Bencoolen for four years, it was placed under the Bengal Government, and in 1825 Singapore and Malacca were united to Penang, and the incorporated settlements continued the fourth Presidency of India until 1829 when it was again placed under the Bengal Government *in which condition of dependency* it remained to the time the book was written in 1864. The fact was that the Straits were not a dependency of Bengal, but were exactly in the same position as the Governments of Bombay, Madras, and Bengal, though it was not styled the fourth Presidency of India. There was no connection after 1851, when the Governor-General of India in Council relieved Bengal of her "dependency" and made the Straits quite as much a Presidency as they had been from 1825 to 1829. They had no connection with the Bengal Government, the Governor corresponded direct with the Supreme Government of India just as the Governors of the other Presidencies did, and it continued so until the Transfer in 1867.

At the end of the book is a useful table of the fruits of Singapore, with their use, characteristics, and botanical names. Attention was called to the title of the book, as Malayan India, which some considered a misnomer, as the Malay Peninsula is not India; it arose it was suggested, from the Straits being associated in its Government with India.

John Cameron was a well-known and popular resident in Singapore for thirty years. He was a master mariner, commanding ships trading in Australia. He was so unfortunate as to lose two vessels, and after the second, some friends in Singapore in 1861 helped him to become editor of the *Straits Times*, which they bought ; and soon afterwards Captain Edward Maher Smith and he became joint proprietors of it. They also carried on business together as John Cameron Co., in the Australian trade. He continued to edit the newspaper until 1867, when Alexander Duff joined him. Mr. Cameron died at Monk's Hill on Bukit Timah Road on 29th December, 1881, at the age of 46 years. Captain E. M. Smith also commanded sailing vessels, trading out of Singapore, from 1850, and he was for a year, in 1856, in the ship-chandlers' store of Campbell & Co. For several years up to 1861 he commanded the *Louisa*, and in that year he settled on shore and was official assignee, and a ship surveyor, until 1866, when he became the first manager of the Tanjong Pagar Dock Company, and the great success of the undertaking was largely due to him in its young days. As a partner in John Cameron & Co., he had become responsible for a serious loss occasioned by the sinking in the harbour of a gunpowder-hulk which was owned by them, for which they were held liable in an action brought by the owners of the powder. This had caused the loss of all his savings, and he joined the Dock Company. He left the dock in 1881, and was succeeded by John Blair. Captain Smith retired to England, but came out again to Singapore after a few years to look after some investments that had been made by his agent, and he died in St. Thomas Walk on 29th July, 1886, at the age of 64 years.

The first Malacca steamers began to run in this year. They were two small steamers, 54 and 56 tons respectively, built in Singapore, called the *Enterprize* and *Fair Malacca*, and were very remunerative. They were always filled with passengers, and soon superseded the schooner trade between the two ports.

CHAPTER LIII.

1865.

A T this time the hotel at the corner of the Esplanade and High Street, opposite the Court House, was called the Hotel de l'Esperance, and was kept by a Frenchwoman. At the beginning of the year Mr. Casteleyns, a Frenchman who had kept a hotel on Beach Road called the Hotel de l'Europe, removed from there to the site of the former, and took the old name with him, and it has been known to this day as the Hotel de l'Europe. The hotel then had the two houses, to which the "barracks" were afterwards added, and the Freemasons' Hall occupied the third house at the corner of Coleman Street.

The bridge across the river at Hill Street, called Coleman's Bridge, was finished in February. It was of wood, not well constructed. It cost about $10,000, and was built by Government, who had a difficulty in getting the Municipality to take it over—they said it would not last, and they turned out right. An iron bridge, it was said, would have cost $25,000, and lasted many times as long.

On 24th February a proclamation was made by beat of gong that the Sarawak cents, which had been coming into circulation in Singapore to the great financial advantage of the Sarawak Treasury, and to the corresponding disadvantage of the Straits finances, would not be received in payment by the Treasury or the Municipality. The coolies called them *man* doits in contradiction to *woman* doits, as the former had the head of Sir James Brooke, and the latter the head of Queen Victoria. Some Chinese traders in Sarawak made a regular practice of shipping cents from there to make payments in Singapore, obtaining them at a large discount in Sarawak, where dollars were in request. It was a long time before the mischief was put an end to, but it was largely due to the apathy of the Singapore Government in not obtaining a sufficient supply of subsidiary coin, a mistake which continues to the present day. The profit on it might be made a constant source of revenue if the Government made it as easily to be obtained as postage stamps, in various parts of the town.

On the 15th March a meeting was held in the Exchange Room to consult as to the establishment of a local Marine Insurance Company in Singapore—Mr. James Davidson in the chair. It was proposed and carried " that a Marine Insurance Company should be formed in the place, and that it should be called the Singapore Insurance Company, Limited." It was proposed also that the capital should be $1,000,000 in a thousand shares of $1,000 each. An amendment was made, that the arrangement should be 2,000 shares of $500 each, but the former proposal was carried. A provisional

committee was composed of the following gentlemen :—Messrs. G. Cramer,
J. Davidson, C. H. Harrison, S. Gilfillan, C. H. H. Wilsone and Seah Teck
See. The proposal was dropped as it was found that the Indian
Act relating to Limited Companies expressly excluded Banks and
Insurance Companies from its provisions.

It was in April this year that the first burials took place in
the new cemetery in Bukit Timah Road. The cemetery on old
Government Hill, mentioned on page 96, ceased to be used, and the
Commissioners, in 1863 and 1864, had acquired the new site.

The tombstones in the old cemetery on the hill-side seem now
like a memorial of the fading-out of memory in Singapore of many
of the oldest inhabitants, rather than a monument of those who were
laid there. The tombs which are still standing are fast falling into
pieces and the inscriptions becoming illegible. From time to time,
by private persons and the help of the Public Works Department,
the inscriptions have been cleaned or repainted, and the fallen brick
work or granite stones replaced in position. When Sir Frederick
Dickson was Colonial Secretary he had this done, about 1886. It
seems a pity these old inscriptions should be lost, and the Government might, perhaps, employ a clerk for a month or two, to copy
such as are still legible, and then have them written alphabetically
in a book to be kept in the Library, the more so as the registers
of burials in that cemetery are not to be found. There may be
copies in Calcutta, but it seems very doubtful. The great dearth in
general of all the documents before the Transfer in 1867, is very
remarkable.

On the right-hand side close to the entrance through the big
archway is a very large, decaying tomb, which should always be
kept in order. It has inscriptions on four sides. On the front it
says that it is erected by Captain the Hon. Arthur A. Cochrane,
C.B., and some of the officers and crew of H. M. Ship *Niger*, in
memory of their fallen comrades. The other three sides explain it.
On one side the inscription is headed " Drowned," with four names,
ages, and ratings. Another side has " Died of Disease " with fourteen names, eight having died in Singapore. The remaining side is
" Killed in Action," and four names ; two names of those killed in
Commodore Keppel's famous action at Fatshan Creek, on " The Glorious
First of June," 1857 ; and two at Canton on January 5th, 1858. The
inscriptions can only be read with much difficulty, but a little paint
and a little care will easily renew them, as they are cut into granite
slabs.

On one occasion the compiler of this book, going to try to
ascertain the date of the death of an old Singaporean, found the
native care-taker using an old tombstone with an inscription on it,
as a curry grinding stone. The wall up the centre divides the Protestant from the Roman Catholic portion, about which there was
much correspondence between Padre Beurel and Governor Butterworth.
For some years no difference had been made, as was said to have
been the practice in India. When the new cemetery in Bukit Timah
Road was laid out, the two divisions were again separated by the
broad centre path leading from the present turnstile, which, within

the last few years, has taken the place of the large central arch-way, through which the coffins always used to be carried.

The area purchased for the new cemetery was acres 23-1-0, and on 17th February, 1875, the Municipality bought from the Administrator of Mr. Lozé's estate, as he had then died, a further area of acres 22-2-11.

According to the printed records of the Municipal documents, the cemetery had been purchased from the East India Company on 22nd January, 1864, by Indenture No. 72, of the District of Clay-more, for one Rupee, for ever. But this does not represent the truth, and Government and Municipal Records should not contain sug-gestions of what is incorrect.

The following passage in the *Free Press* of 8th June, 1865, remarking upon the Municipal Expenditure for the preceding year, first drew attention to the matter; it is speaking of the Municipal accounts, just published, of the year before :—

" The second item we have to censure is the outlay of $10,000 for the purchase of the piece of land now laid out as the New Christian Cemetery. The price to us appears exorbitant; we do not believe it would have fetched one fourth the sum at auction. We suppose the Commissioners had set their hearts on the land, and the proprietor knew it. Surely as much land could easily have been obtained in more suitable sites for a mere fraction of the sum. "

On making enquiry it is found that on 30th June, 1859, the East Indian Company granted the land in question for ever to C. R. Prinsep, spoken of in several places in this book, in consideration of a payment of Rs. 255.12.0. On 30th December, in the same year, his Singapore Agents leased it for 9,999 years to Syed Abdulla, and on 14th January, 1864, Syed Abdulla and C. R. Prinsep sur-rendered it to the East India Company. No consideration is stated for that surrender, in the note that is made of it on the back of the original lease in the Land Office Records, and the original deeds are not to be found, but eight days afterwards on 22nd January, the grant already mentioned was given by the Government to the Municipal Commissioners, who had before that paid $10,000 for the land.

The amount mentioned in the *Free Press* is correct. This is clear from the Municipal accounts for the year 1864, on page 307 of the *Government Gazette* for 1865, which shows that a loan of $28,000 was raised upon the Rates and Taxes, from which $10,000 was paid for " Purchase of Land for the Cemetery," and $1,005.94 for " Account of Drainage, &c., of the Cemetery." The other side of the account shows that $1,900 was received as " Government contribution towards the Cemetery," the reason for which is not traced, and $500 for " Price of a small piece of the Cemetery sold to Mr. Lozé." The Municipal Minutes also show that in October, 1863, there had been an arbitration awarding $10,000 as the value of the land. There is no doubt that there was some reason for the suggestion in the *Free Press* as to an excessive value having been paid, and the persons chosen as arbitrators seem not to have been selected on account of their impartiality. The matter was the subject of unfavourable remark for many years, as it was certainly a bad site, and a very dear bargain indeed at that time.

When this Cemetery was first used, it was a very dismal place, with no sufficient drainage and water-logged within a few inches of the surface. Mr. R. C. Woods, one of the Commissioners, took the matter in hand, and gave much of his spare time for several years to planting trees and laying out the ground, for horticulture was his favourite hobby. The community have been much indebted to him for making the place as ornamental as it could be made on such a site. This Cemetery is now, in its turn, about to be closed, as the parts still without graves are so low as to be quite un-suitable. It was only by heavy expense for drainage that the place could be used at all. When it was consecrated by Bishop McDougal, of Sarawak, the choir walked round the Protestant portion of the ground, and in places were stepping through water several inches deep.

In connection with this matter there is a minute to the Commissioners by Mr. MacRitchie, the Municipal Engineer, who, unfortunately for Singapore, died here in 1896, which in the light of the present day is remarkable and prophetic. It was dated 4th May, 1893, and little or no· attention seems to have been paid to it then. At that time the Chasseriau Estate on Bukit Timah Road was being sold, and it was disposed of by a Bank who held a mortgage on it for $30,000. Mr. McRitchie sent large plans with his minute, and said that 750 acres of the land would be a good site for another cemetery, and advised its purchase, on account of the bad and low state of the ground on Bukit Timah Road, which he condemned as unfit for use as a cemetery. He also recommended, and it was the principal object of the minute, that a large part or the whole of the Estate should also be purchased for the water-works reservoir. He said that the daily supply was 3,500,000 gallons a day, and that he expected it would in time reach $5\frac{1}{2}$ to 6 millions, which would far exceed the storage in the then existing reservoir and adjacent extensions. As a matter of fact, on one occasion in the present year, 1902, the supply on one day reached over 6,000,000 gallons. The result of not following the suggestions in the minute which were, no doubt, equally due to the late Mr. Howard Newton, the Assistant Engineer, is that the Com-missioners have lately made two purchases of a portion only of the same Estate for about $58,000, and will have to spend a very large sum to purchase another piece of land elsewhere for the cemetery.

The first funerals in the new cemetery were the result of a terrible accident now to be related. On Saturday afternoon, 15th April, there occurred the worst accident that had been known in Singapore.

The Tumongong of Johore had ordered a steamer from England. It was the first he had, and it had been suggested to him by Mr. James Meldrum of Johore that he should buy a steamer with a twin screw that was for sale by Lairds of Birkenhead. If he had done so, Johore would have possessed the first twin screw vessel. The agents in England, however, bought an iron screw steamer of about 75 tons, built at West Hartlepool, and she was named the *Johore*.

She arrived at Singapore in March, and was at the New Harbour Dock, always called in those days Cloughton's Dock, to be overhauled. She had been a very long time on the passage out, and it was thought afterwards that this was the fault of the engineer, and of the crew having been engaged by the month instead of for the voyage. She had actually been over as far as the Coast of South America on the way.

Easter Sunday was the 16th April, and in the preceding week the Tumongong had asked the Governor, and a number of the officials and leading people in the place, to go on a picnic round the island in the steamer on Easter Monday, to start from Dalhousie Pier at 8 a.m. Johnston's Pier was then a small place, little used; the men-of-war boats used to land at Dalhousie Pier, which was in front of the Dalhousie monument.

On Saturday all the silverware, &c., was taken on board the *Johore*, and arrangements made for the picnic. On the Saturday the engines were to be tried, and the steamer taken out into the Roads to lie off Dalhousie Pier, ready to start on Monday morning. A steamer was a new toy to the Malays, and a number of them were looking forward to the run out to the harbour, as a Saturday afternoon's amusement.

Steam was got-up at noon and it was intended that the vessel should leave at 2 p.m. At that time Inche Wan Abdulrahman, a younger brother of the Tumongong, went on board, and found there Mr. Wishart, the Superintendent of the New Harbour Dock Company, and Mr. Hugh Bain, the Engineer of the Company, who were seeing after some carpenters who were fixing seats for use on the Monday. They went on shore, and Inche Abdulrahman asked the Captain of the *Johore*, a Malay named Abdul Talip, why she did not start, and he replied that there was something wrong with the engines. Abdulrahman looked into the engine-room and saw them pulling at the starting lever, but the vessel did not move. At this time Hussein bin Abdullah, the eldest son of Abdullah Moonshi, the writer of the Hikayit Abdullah, who had come on board for amusement, came upon the bridge to Abdulrahman and said there was something wrong with the engines, and that the engineer, Mr. Miller, wanted to call Mr. Bain. There was a boat passing in which was Captain Cleghorn, the master of the Dock Company's tug steamer *Henrietta*. He was called on board and the boat was sent to fetch Mr. Bain, who came at once. Soon afterwards an explosion occurred, the effects of which were very remarkable. The boiler blew up, and the deck was covered with dead and dying men, the only persons who altogether escaped were those standing right in the bows. The bridge was entirely blown away; the funnel was blown on to the top of the port paddle-box, the mainmast was blown into pieces over the stern of the ship, the after-cabin was entirely destroyed and everything in it smashed to pieces, a gun which lay abaft the boiler was blown overboard with its carriage, &c., and all the platedware and tableware, which the Tumongong's table boys had been putting ready on the table, was blown overboard though the stern ports. The engines were broken and twisted, the engine-rooms, the engineer's cabin, and the house over the fore-cabin staircase were entirely blown to pieces, the port paddle box being smashed by the funnel and casing which had been blown on the top of it. The boiler was an extraordinary sight, the outside shell was blown open right against the foremast, the after part of the deck was blown entirely away, and the remainder of the deck raised 9 or 10 inches above its usual position, and the vessel's topsides opposite the boiler were blown out from 6 to 10 inches.

The number of persons killed was about thirty, of whom five were Europeans, two Chinese and the rest Malays. The vessel had been anchored about one hundred yards from the shore, and as soon as the report was heard, boats and sampans hurried off to the vessel. Captain Wishart was the first there, he picked up Inche Wan Abdulrahman and a Malay in the water. Abdulrahman was one of the few who escaped. He was standing on deck, when he heard to use his own words, " a hissing sound for a few seconds, and then a crash which threw him down, and he received a blow on his head from something, he could not tell what, because (a curious expression) everything became extremely dark." No doubt he was stunned and thrown overboard, though he thought he jumped into the sea. Inchi Jaffer bin Hadjee Mohamed, the present Dato Muntri, or Prime Minister, of Johore, was also thrown into the sea. He received severe wounds on his face and neck which covered him with blood; the large scar on his face was caused by this accident. He was picked up by another boat. Hussein bin Abdullah, the eldest son of Abdullah Moonshi, was killed.

His younger brother Ibrahim, the present Dato Bintara Dalam of Johore, escaped by an accident. He was schoolmaster then at the Telok Blanga Malay School, and had shut up the school, and was going to his house to change his coat before going on board. On his way to the wharf he stopped to look at some boys playing marbles, and spoke to Abdul Rahman bin Andak, a young boy, now the Dato Sri Amar d'Raja, c.m.g., who was crying, and this delayed Inchi Ibrahim, who heard the explosion while he was standing talking to the boys. Inchi Mahomed Yahya bin Abdulla, the Tumongong's cashier, was killed, his body was never found, nor was that of Mat, the Malay servant of Captain Abdul Talip. Captain Cleghorn's body was not found till Sunday morning. Inchi Abdulrahman went with a party of Malays, and recovered it in 5 fathoms of water close to where the vessel blew up. Inchi Abdul Talip, the Captain, was very much hurt but recovered; he died many years ago. Inchi Abdul Samat, now Dato Barat, was on board and unhurt.

Five Europeans were killed. Captain Cleghorn was the master of the *Henrietta*, John Young was the gunner of the *Johore*, the only European seaman on board, Henry Sandhurst was a boiler maker of the Dock Company who went on board with Mr. Bain. These three were buried on Easter Sunday afternoon, the 16th April, at 3 o'clock, the Rev. C. J. Waterhouse, m.a., taking the service. With the exception of a Dutch seaman, who had been buried the previous afternoon, these were the first burials in the new Cemetery. The graves have no headstones, but are situated at the corner of the first plot of ground on the right of the centre path after passing the path that turns to the right leading to the Chapel. That is to say, as you walk into the Cemetery, you first pass at once on your right the path along the boundary hedge, and then the plot on which the Chapel stands, then on the right is the path leading towards the Chapel door, and at the corner on the other side of that path, on the left hand if you turn down the path to the Chapel, is the site of these first graves. On the following day, Monday 17th, John Miller and Hugh Bain were buried close by in the same plot.

The explosion was no doubt caused by cold water being turned into an empty and red-hot boiler, the fault of the engineer, who was said to be unsteady on the voyage out and to have been the cause of the great delay. The steamer was made over to the Dock Company, for the Tumongong would have nothing more to do with her, and became a tug, in which way she was used for many years.

In May there were three flagships in the harbour, which probably never occurred before or since. Admiral Kuper was on his way home after the actions in Japan, in the *Euryalus*; Admiral King in the *Princess Royal* had arrived here from England to relieve him; and Commodore Montresor had come from India in the *Severn*, as Singapore was then on the Indian Station. There was a large dance given on board the *Severn* at Tanjong Pagar. She was a steam frigate, 35 guns, 2,767 tons, 500 horse-power. The *Princess Royal*, famous in the Crimean War, was a two-decker, 73 guns, 3,129 tons, 400 horse-power. The *Euryalus* was a steam frigate, the second of her name in the century. The first was at *Trafalgar*, the second at the Bombardment of *Svenborg* in the Crimean War, and at the Bombardments of *Kagosima* and *Simono-Saki* in Japan in 1863 and 1864; she was broken up a few years afterwards.

The barque *Ruby*, Capt. Harrison, sailed from Hongkong for Singapore on the 4th May. About 3 o'clock one afternoon three junks were seen approaching towards the ship, and they were immediately recognised as Pirates. In order to know exactly what these junks were, the *Ruby* deviated from her course by 3 points; but the junks followed her; she again altered her course, and they still followed. All the sails that could be employed at the time were set, but their endeavours to escape from the pirates were in vain. The wind falling light, the junks availed themselves of the use of their oars to reach the ship. The *Ruby* had two guns which were placed in the after part of the ship, and all the firearms were loaded and every preparation was made for defence. The junks commenced to fire, and the *Ruby* kept up a smart fire upon them in return, until about 7 p.m. when they found their ammunition was exhausted. They then held a consultation, when they agreed to abandon the vessel. They lowered their boats and shortly afterwards left the vessel to her fate, having done everything in their power to keep her from falling into the hands of the pirates. After being five days at sea, in the boats, they were picked up by the French Gunboat, *Merillas*, and they received from the officers the greatest kindness. They arrived at Saigon on the morning of the 20th and to their great surprise saw the barque *Ruby* lying in the harbour, having been recovered by the Hamburg barque *Canton*.

In 1864, Chinese pirates had attacked the brig *Louisa*, belonging to Singapore, and murdered the master and all on board except three persons who contrived to escape to a passing vessel. The same pirates also attacked a French gunboat which was obliged to retreat.

In June the newspaper contained the following paragraph:—"We trust the complication of affairs in Perak will lead to the Rajah appealing to our government for assistance; we could scarcely interfere without. There is not the slightest doubt that the natives would hail our arrival with pleasure. For several years a civil war devastated the kingdom, and since the rule of the present sovereign has been established, his efforts to restore order have been fruitless. Would not this be a favorable opportunity for us to offer to purchase the country? It would be a valuable acquisition to this Settlement, and we fancy the royal family of Perak would be delighted to get rid of it at any price." The country continued in such an unsettled state that ten years afterwards the matter settled itself in another way, and it undoubtedly became the valuable acquisition that was suggested.

One of the old liberated Bengal convicts died in July leaving fifty thousand dollars to be divided between his sons.

It was in this year that the Honorable Henry Stanley wrote a book containing various inaccurate statements about Singapore. One of them was an attack upon the judgment of Sir William Jeffcott in the case in which he had decided many years before to apportion some of the funds under a Mohamedan's will to the Free School in Penang and the Raffles Institution in Singapore. The author had paid a visit to Singapore not long before, and lived with an Arab, refusing the society of Europeans. The natives in Singapore believed him to be a Mohamedan, and he dressed as an Arab.

On the 15th August the first vessel passed through the Suez Canal from the Mediterranean to the Red Sea, but the Canal was not completed and opened for traffic until 17th December, 1869.

For some years there had been trouble at times arising from Secret Societies among the Klings, both Hindus and Mohamedans, called the Red and White Flag Societies, which led to street fights and bloodshed, for the two societies were always at variance, although the Mohamedan members of both had the same religious tenets. In 1864 serious disturbances had taken place during the Mohurrum Festival, and in May this year Governor Cavenagh and Mr. Dunman forbade the procession. In October what was called the Great Conspiracy Case against six of the head members was heard, two of whom were men of standing, Mr. Dunman and Mr. Weir giving them remarkably good characters in matters of business. They were all convicted, and sentenced to two years' imprisonment. This broke up the societies practically, which had been established after the Chinese Ghi Hin and Ghi Kok Societies, with which it was supposed they were connected.

The appearance of the harbour at this time was very different from what it is at the present time. The subsequent steamer traffic through the Suez Canal quite changed the shipping. The sailing vessels used to remain for several weeks, or even two months, discharging and loading in the Roads. There are now only about four of the long five-oared Malay or Kling sampans at Johnston's Pier, while at this time there were nearly a hundred. The masters of the ships, in order to avoid the European crew rowing in the sun, engaged a sampan to wait on the ship. There were so many vessels lying in the harbour that the horizon could not be seen for their hulls. Now, in 1902, there are only a few sailing vessels, and a small number of the local steamers. The wharves in Keppel Harbour, which were commenced about this time, have changed the appearance of the harbour, the steamers only remaining one or two days, and then speeding on their way. No doubt the harbour in the old days had a more imposing appearance. To form some idea of what it was, the shipping list for one day in this year has been counted. There were three small sailing ships discharging at the Borneo Company's wharf, no doubt with coal; and one small Swedish brig in Cloughton's Dock. At Jardine's wharf, which was alongside the Borneo Company's, was a barque of 484 tons, no doubt having brought coal, and loading for Bombay In the harbour were 154 square rigged vessels, of which 3 were British men-of-war, one of which was the *Princess Royal*, already spoken of. There were two British merchant steamers, the *Reiver* of Apcar & Co., running between Calcutta and Hongkong, and the Siamese steamer *Chow Phya*. There were two American steamers of about 160 tons each, apparently going to Shanghai, probably river boats; and two small Dutch steamers. The remainder were:—

80	British merchantmen.
19	Hamburg.
9	Bremen.
8	French.
5	Danish.
5	Prussian.
4	American.
4	Dutch.
3	Oldenburg.
2	Hanoverian.
2	Swedish.
1	Norwegian
1	Belgium.

143	

From time to time in Singapore small parties for practising music had been formed, but had never attained any length of life. In this year the Amateur Musical Society was formed among the English community, and mustered about thirty to forty members. The German Teutonia Club had had its Liedertafel for some years before. The high tenor voices of Mr. Otto Puttfarcken and another member were of invaluable service, and the singing of the club was unusually good. After they left, the Liedertafel was fortunate in having Mr. Bremer among their number; he had a powerful high tenor voice, and used to sing the leading melody clearly, over the voices of the other twelve or fifteen members. There has rarely been a singer like Mr. Bremer in Singapore, and he was always ready to help. On one occasion in the Town Hall he sang Balfe's "Come into the Garden, Maud" in a way those who heard it often spoke of afterwards.

The Amateur Musical Society was conducted at first by the organist of St. Andrew's Cathedral, but the mainspring of it was Mr. Neil Macvicar, who came out in 1860, at the same time as Mr. Arthur Knight, and was book-keeper in Martin, Dyce & Co. He was three years in their house in Batavia, and then came to Singapore. He used to play the piano accompaniments, and keep things going. The Singapore newspaper in December, 1865, said that the Trustees of St. Andrew's Cathedral had presented him with a watch and chain as a slight memento of their gratitude for his kind service to the congregation in playing the organ during ten months in the Cathedral. There was a small amateur orchestra also at this time, which played at the Amateur Musical Society's Concerts. It arose in this way :—

In the early days of the settlement, as has been said on page 185, the D'Almeida family was the musical nucleus of the place, and when an Amateur Dramatic Society was formed in 1860 or thereabouts, the amateurs, which included two of the D'Almeida family, got together a small orchestra for the purpose of playing at the performances.

The Dramatic Society was called The Savage Club, and was due to Mr. Steel, the Manager of the Mercantile Bank. They rented Barganny House, close to Tank Road, which had a large centre room, and used to give performances at more or less regular intervals for several years, and performed good standard plays, including some of Shakespeare, and modern comedies like "Still waters run deep" in a very capable way. Dr. Allen, a medical practitioner in the place, and Mr. Barclay Read and several others, were famous at this time. As the room would not hold at one time all those who were invited, for it was a private entertainment for the subscribers only, the performance was given twice, and the first part of the alphabetical names were asked the first time, and the remaining part to the second performance. Mr. José d'Almeida played the viola, Dr. Robertson, Mr. Edward d'Almeida, and Mr. G. H. Brown, the violins, and Mr. Knight the violoncello. There were one or two more; but their names are not remembered. This first amateur orchestra did not consist of more than about six players.

This little enthusiastic band played at the first concert of the Amateur Musical Society on Thursday, 28th December, and played the afterwards well-worn overture to the "Caliph of Bagdad" and Haydn's first quintett. Then the Society, which consisted of male voices only, sang four glees or part songs. In these days they seem as rather curious musical efforts, for they were sung from the usual setting for unequal voices, so that the tenors were often, if not usually, singing above the music written for the trebles, and the basses above the altos. However, it was thought satisfactory for "the good old days," as Mr. R. O. Norris always expresses it. The German Club singers on the other hand sang from music arranged for male voices, and having Mr. Bremer's powerful voice to lead, it was musically correct. There was a quartett; and a duet *The Larboard Watch*, well sung by the two brothers Thomas and Charles Crane, who are both now living in England; and the newspaper paid a compliment to the singing of the one solo, *The Village Blacksmith*, in which the compiler of this book made his first appearance and sang the first solo, it is believed, in the Town Hall; but he was soon afterwards eclipsed at the future concerts of the Society, by Mr. William Hole, at the present day in Johore, who had a much better voice. A negro melody, and Locke's old music to *Macbeth*, sung in the remarkable manner that has been described, ended this, the first concert in the Town Hall, and it is seen that the amateurs were informed in print, by the musical critic of the newspaper, that it was a splendid treat!

A few months afterwards, in September, 1866, the German Liedertafel and the Amateur Musical Society joined together in the Town Hall in a concert of sacred and secular music for the benefit of the Singapore Institution School, and on turning over the files of the old newspaper, it is remembered that the singer already spoken of as singing at the previous concert, sang the bass recitative and air "The people that walked in darkness," from Handel's *Messiah*, which obtained, the paper said, the first encore. It is remembered on account of a remark that was made by Mr. David Rodger, mentioned elsewhere in this book, who was not a musical man and probably attended the concert to please Mr. Macvicar, who was book-keeper in his firm. He said that he did not think anything of that song, for it sounded like a man groping about in the dark, and there was no tune in it. A curious appreciation, quite unintended, of the genius of Handel. Such were the musical efforts of Singapore thirty-seven years ago.

CHAPTER LIV.

1866.

I N March, very early on a Sunday morning, a large fire broke out in Battery Road, just as the fire at McAlister & Co.'s godowns close by had commenced on a Sunday about a year before. The godowns and offices of William Macdonald & Co., and the shipchandler's store of Barsoe & Ottzen were burned.

There was an American firm in Flint Street called Hutchison & Co., which was commenced in 1862. Mr. G. H. Dana, who was only a few years in Singapore, was a partner in it at this time. He was some relation of the author of the then well-known book "Two years before the Mast." His name has been remembered here by some occasional jokes he wrote in the newspaper under the name of "Extinguisher," which were published more than once afterwards in book form. They were not, perhaps, always in good taste, in consequence of the style of the composition, as will be understood from the following specimen, which was the first of them; but were certainly witty, which goes far as an excuse. Mr. Dana was popular in the place, of a merry and humourous turn of mind, with quaint Americanisms in his conversation.

The occasion which caused the commencement of the "Letters of Extinguisher" arose from Lieut. Henry Burn, the Master Attendant, having fined a number of Captains of vessels in the harbour fifty rupees each for not having a light burning at night on their vessels. There was a very angry correspondence in the papers, at his putting in force some old, useless and long-forgotten regulations which had never been made known, and were not applicable to the particular case, as the Captains said their ships were not in a fairway, properly understood, as required by the rule. The fines were all returned to the Captains by instructions from Governor Cavenagh.

The Master Attendant has been an officer in the then defunct Indian Navy, and was a younger brother of Mr. James Burn, who was the Resident Councillor and a very useful official. Mr. Henry Burn died a few years afterwards from the effects of a carriage accident, at the foot of the hill leading down to the town from River Valley Road. The carriage was thrown down into a swamp that existed there at the time, but has long been filled in, and substantial houses and engineering yards built over it. To show how the appearance of the place has changed, Dr. Little about 1866 had a large pond made and closed in at the foot of the hill, on the right hand side coming towards town, to supply water-boats with water for the shipping. The boats came up the river.

The following letter of " Extinguisher " caused a great deal of amusement at the time:—

" In the Island of Singapore, that lieth over against Malacca, which is in the far Indies, in the days of the reign of Col. Cavena', there dwelt many great and good men who were called Government Officials, because that they *fished* all they could out of the Government.

" But among these was one possessed of a little soul, who thought himself larger than other men, and wished others to think even as he did.

" And he said unto himself: ' What shall I do that I may cause my name to be heard, and make myself to be great, even above my brother officials ?'

" And he went about seeking how he might encompass his designs.

" And it is so happened that this man, whose name was Mustir-attindint, of the tribe of the Scots, had among his other duties with the vessels which traded in merchandise with far countries (and which lay in the harbour near Singapore), to see that the lamps of these vessels were trimmed and lighted when darkness covered the face of the Earth.

" Now this was done on the land by Celestials, which resembled men, save that they have tails, but on the water was it this man's work.

" And as he wandered along the shores of the Sea he espeid many of these carriers of merchandise with no light.

" And he said unto himself. ' I have not told unto those men who command these vessels that they must show a *burning* light, so to-morrow they will do even as to-day, and I will come down upon them in the dead of night with a lead pencil, and I will take the names of these vessels, and of their wicked masters (who, peradventure, are like unto the foolish virgins), and I will bind them that they pay unto me fifty shekels of silver, even fifty pieces of silver from each vessel, so that my name may shine like a *burning* light throughout the land.'

" Now it all came to pass even as he had said unto himself, and the men of the sea did pay each man fifty shekels of silver, but a cry went up from among these men, because of this unjust deed.

" Now it came to pass that this wail reached even to the ears of the Governor, who was a just man in all his walks, and who was called Cavena' (after the manner of the Scots) because that he would *never* " *cave in* " to the wrong.

" And he sent for Mustirattindint and said unto him. ' Why hast thou done this wrong thing ?'

" And Mustirattindint answered and said. ' Lo, I thought to do that which was pleasant and good in thy sight, and now thou upbraidest me.' And the Governor answered him, saying, ' Give back unto these men of the sea every shekel that thou hast taken so unjustly from them.'

" Then Mustirattindint subsided: And he went out from the Governor's presence, and wept bitterly.

EXTINGUISHER. "

On 8th March an extraordinary general meeting was held of the Tanjong Pagar Dock Company. Mr. C. H. Harrison was in the chair. Mr. John James Greenshields, of Guthrie & Co., said that it was found necessary to double the capital if the undertaking was to be proceeded with, as the original cost of the undertaking had been greatly underestimated. The capital which had originally been fixed at $300,000 was to be increased to $600,000. Mr. Samuel Gilfillan and Dr. Little then proposed it, and it was carried unanimously. No one then anticipated what the Company would grow into in the next thirty years.

There was an old Kling Mohamedan in the place who died at this time, who was a character. His funeral was a curiosity; a great feast was prepared in the Square at the house of one of the Mohamedans, and he was buried at Tanjong Pagar, with a great crowd following. He was thought to be a prophet for about fifty years, and used to go into shops and take what he wished, even from the money changers, which he invariably distributed among his poorer countrymen. All the hack-gharries were free to him, the syces being prevented from asking for their fare by the awe with which he inspired them.

On St. Patrick's Day, 17th March, a farewell dinner was given in the Town Hall to Sir Richard McCausland, the Recorder, the like of which, it was said, had not been seen in the place before. Tables were laid round three sides of the room, and were all occupied. Mr. W. H. Read was in the chair. A number of farewell addresses were presented to him by all classes of the community, and he left for Europe on the 22nd March, in the same mail as Tumongong Abu Bakar, of Johore, who went to England for the first time, accompanied by one of his cousins and the present Dato Muntri Besar, and Dr. Scott. They returned to Singapore in November.

Sir Richard McCausland was ten years on the Bench. In the first volume of Mr. Kyshe's useful and carefully compiled "Reports of Cases heard in the Supreme Court of the Straits," it is said that Sir Richard last sat on the 25th August, 1866, but this is a mistake. He retired on a pension, and lived for many years afterwards in Ireland. He was a very kind-hearted genial Irishman, a sound and experienced lawyer, and a thoroughly courteous gentleman on the Bench, in which he was an example to some of those who have succeeded him in the Courts of the Straits. It is a very necessary qualification, if justice is to be done to suitors in the Court, for the possibility of witnesses being insulted from the Bench is very detrimental to justice, as it renders it difficult to obtain their evidence.

The judges sent out from England to the Straits during the time of the administration of the East India Company undoubtedly did great credit to those who selected them. It is noteworthy that most of the judges before the Transfer, became in after years distinguished men. Of the six who sat in Singapore before Sir Richard McCausland, three became Chief Justices in Calcutta or Madras, and Sir Benson Maxwell, who has now to be spoken of, succeeded Sir Richard.

Sir Peter Benson Maxwell came to the Straits in 1856, as Recorder of Penang, as has been said on page 631, at the same time as Sir Richard McCausland came to Singapore. In 1866 he was appointed to Singapore. In that year he published his book called, " The Duties of Straits Magistrates," and the *Government Gazette* in May notified that all civil servants would in future be subjected to an examination as to their general knowledge of the rules laid down for their guidance in this book instead of " Saunder's Practice of Magistrates Courts," as had been prescribed in 1859.

The book was printed at the Government Printing Office, Singapore, and in Penang, and was written because one of his sons was appointed a Magistrate. It was a remarkable book, and of the greatest use to the legal profession. The fifth chapter on The Construction of Statutes, consisting of 39 pages, led in after years to Sir Benson's text book of the same name, first published in London in 1875. It has run through several editions, and has been referred to with approval in the House of Lords. Chapter vi. the last 132 pages in "The Duties of Magistrates," was on the law of evidence, and it was said that those who mastered it, had a grasp of the whole subject, so accurately and concisely was it written. A larger second edition was published in Calcutta, adapted to the Criminal Procedure Code in force there. This is still largely used ; the old Singapore edition is rarely to be seen.

Sir Benson was a most industrious man. His copy of " Chitty on Contracts," for example, was a mass of marginal notes and interpolated pages, which he wrote week by week from the reports in the London *Times*, as well as other Reports. His celebrated judgment in Regina v. Willans, in May, 1858, about a decision of Mr. W. W. Willans, when he was Police Magistrate in Penang, on a subject of the liability of a native labourer for a repeated act of breach of contract, went far beyond the point necessary to be decided in the case, but it proved of great use afterwards ; for Sir Benson having time on his hands, as work was slack at the time in the Court, took occasion to go into a wealth of study upon what law had been introduced and was applicable to, and in force in the Straits. He had so much reliance on his knowledge of the law, and his readiness to alter his view of it, if it were shown to be in doubt, that nothing that arose was left undecided, and the temptation of a weaker mind to avoid any doubtful or troublesome question, by deciding a case upon some point which had never been raised, as Sir Benson's successor did, never occurred to him.

Sir Benson used to be somewhat worried by some of the practitioners at that time who had been admitted to practice without examination as to their qualifications. He used often to say that " he wished they would read their Roscoe before coming to Court." One day a case was called on, and Mr. James Guthrie Davidson was for the plaintiff and Mr. John Simons Atchison for the defendant. Mr. Atchison had not arrived. Sir Benson said the case must go on, so Mr. Davidson began opening his case very slowly and at quite unnecessary length, repeating what he had to say, and when Sir Benson remarked that he understood it when Mr. Davidson had mentioned it before, Mr. Davidson commenced explaining it again still more lengthily until he saw Atchison coming hastily into the Court, when he suddenly pulled up, and said he would call his witnesses. Sir Benson said to him afterwards that he could not think what he was driving at, until Atchison came in, and Davidson replied that he thought it would have been better to wait until Mr. Atchison came, and they both had a good laugh.

These two lawyers were both men of whom Sir Benson had a very high opinion, and they did the bulk of the work at the bar. Atchison came out in 1859, being a relation of Mr. H. M. Simons, and had his office in Paterson, Simons & Co.'s godowns. He was a man, like Mr. Davidson, of exceptional ability. He was remarkably stout, and drank enormous quantities of soda water, taking two or three bottles at a time. Mrs. Atchison died on her way home, and was buried in Egypt; and Mr. Atchison died not long afterwards in Bangkok, where he had been retained in a heavy law suit. It was thought that he had had a stroke of the sun under the awning of the *Chow Phya* steamer, as he would not, or could not on account of his size, get easily below the deck.

Mr. J. G. Davidson was a nephew of Mr. James Guthrie, his mother being Mr. Guthrie's sister, and came to Singapore in 1861, joining Mr. R. C. Woods. He was a Solicitor of the Supreme Court of Scotland. He practised at the bar for many years, and in 1874 was appointed Resident of Perak after the death of Mr. E. W. W. Birch. In 1876 he resigned the appointment, preferring to practice at the bar, and joined Mr. Bernard Rodyk in Singapore. He was killed suddenly in a carriage accident in Orchard Road as he was driving from Ardmore to Church early on Sunday morning, 8th February, 1891, at 53 years of age. He was one of the foremost men in Singapore, taking a leading part in all that went on, especially in public matters, though he always declined to accept a seat on the Legislative Council. His sudden death was very much felt, and his loss was a serious one to Singapore. The newspaper spoke of him at the time as one of the oldest and most respected residents of the place. The remembrance of these two, the leading names in the bar in the Straits, arose naturally from reminiscences of Sir Benson Maxwell, in whose Court they figured so largely.

Sir Benson retired on 26th July, 1871; and in 1882 was appointed Judicial Commissioner, or under some similar title, to organise the Courts in Egypt after the British occupation ; a post of great importance at that time.

Four of his sons were well-known in the Straits. The eldest, called after his father, was a Magistrate in Penang, and went to the West Indies in the Colonial service, where he died not long afterwards. The second son, Sir William Edward Maxwell, K.C.M.G., died at sea on 14th December, 1897, on his way home to England in ill health from the Gold Coast, where he was Governor. He was for many years in the Straits and the Native States, and at one time Acting Governor in Singapore, shortly before he was appointed to the Gold Coast.

The third son, Robert William Maxwell, was for many years in the Straits Police Force, and when he retired from ill health in August, 1894, he was Inspector General of Police. He died in England in 1895. The fourth son was Francis R. O. Maxwell, who became a cadet in the Sarawak service in 1872, and was Resident at Sarawak in 1881. These three brothers, who were very much liked in the Straits, all died, strange to say, within a year or so of each other. There are several sons of Sir William in the Straits and the Indian Army. One of Sir Benson's daughters married Mr. E. E. Isemonger of the Straits Civil Service, now retired.

There was at this time a fresh-water swimming bath which Mr. W. R. Scott allowed the use of to certain subscribers, at Abbotsford; it was the only one in the place, but it was very little used. A meeting was held, a subscription made, and a bath was made of stakes on a sand bank off the beach, some way from the shore, at Tanjong Katong, with a dressing room at one end, on posts in the sea. It was only used for a year or two, as it necessitated a row of over a mile in a sampan from Johnston's Pier. Mr. Charles Crane was the working hand in it. A swimming bath in the sea was proposed many times in the older days of the Settlement, but this was the only attempt to carry it out.

Aitken, De Souza & Co., who were shipchandlers, had a short pier called De Souza's Pier on Collyer Quay, near the foot of Prince Street, which was useful for some years.

A large Fancy Fair was held in May at the unused Mess Room in the Tanglin Barracks, for the benefit of the Botanical Gardens, which were then supported entirely by private subscriptions under a Committee of the Agri-Horticultural Society. Mr. Lawrence Niven was the Superintendent of the Gardens, which were on the present spot. The Government in after years took it all over, but in Mr. Niven's days there used to be many more large beds of pretty flowers which made the Gardens look very attractive.

Mr. Jacob Clunis died suddenly in Singapore on 12th June. He came, it is thought, from Shetland, and was the P. & O. pilot. He is to be remembered here, like Captain Cloughton, as a very useful pioneer of docks in Singapore, as was written by an old Singaporean in 1885, " He, with the perseverance worthy of a better cause, started the project of a Dock, and, what is more, excavated one on Pulo Brani, but was finally ejected therefrom by the then Resident, Thomas Church, on the plea that the ground was required by the Naval Authorities for coal sheds. In vain did Jacob plead for compensation. He was told to whistle " jigs to the mile-stones," while his letters were sent from pillar to post, between the Hon'ble the E. I. C. and the Admiralty. He died, the grand old enthusiast, but never got a red cent."

His son, John Clunis, was a Civil Engineer, living in Oxley Road. He built the unusual looking house at the corner of Lloyd Road, which he intended to be the first of a row of a terrace of houses, adjoining each other. So that at first there was no window on one side. He built the present Town Hall, which has in it the one room in the place which is in proper proportions. The upper room is seventy-three feet long by forty wide, and is an accurately proportioned room. It has been usual to speak of the Town Hall upper room as being too small, some people being under the impression, apparently, that it is possible to build a room in a town, large enough to hold all those who may wish to come into it. It is needless to say that the largest buildings in London, or the world, would only hold a very small proportion of the population. It is of course practicable to build a larger room, as is to be shortly done by its side, but to speak of the present hall as a small one is a mistake. It is easy to compare it with well-known rooms in London; and those who think it small may probably be surprised to hear that it is a few inches longer and only five feet narrower than the House of Commons, and only two feet shorter and two feet wider than the famous large dining hall of the Fishmongers Company, on the north west corner of London Bridge. A place as large as the Colosseum at Rome, intended solely for spectacular purposes, can be reasonably enlarged to the length along which the furthest spectators can see sufficiently what takes place in the arena; but a room to be used for meetings, concerts, and public speaking, must be bounded, if it is to be used by people with ordinary voices, by the necessary size in which they can be heard. Even in the House of Commons complaint is often made of the voices not being heard in the Reporter's Gallery. The room is just of the right size for the principal uses for which it was intended, and it has been the scene of many historical events in the history of the place, and the large hall that is intended to be built on to it is intended to be 120 feet by 60, or 7,200 superficial feet, against 2,920 of the present hall. The larger room will, no doubt, be better suited for a Ball Room now the place has grown so much bigger, but that again will not hold all who wish to be present on such an occasion as the late visit of the Duke and Duchess of York, and there must be an end somewhere to the size of a ceiling without interior supports. The Town Hall in Bombay looks a much larger room on paper, but it is partly supported by large masonry pillars in the room, and the available space inside those looks little if any larger than the present Town Hall upper room. Mr. John Clunis went to Bangkok about thirty years ago, and did a great deal of work for the King or the Government there, where he died.

Another old resident in Singapore like Jacob Clunis, who died in July, 1885, was spoken of by an old resident in that year as follows:—

"During this week there has passed away in Singapore an old resident who certainly deserves a tribute of remembrance from Singapore. Mr. George Lyons came here many years ago, and at one time had a ship-building yard at Tanjong Rhoo with his brother. He had formerly worked in the Government dockyards in England, and had very high certificates for his ability there. He built the big iron bridge at Kallang river, beyond the gas-works, and also Elgin Bridge, which has stood so well. There is a story about that which is almost forgotten now. He put the whole bridge together bodily on North Bridge Road, and said he would run it across the river. Everyone laughed at him except one or two persons, old residents, who said that "Lyons was slow but sure." He got everything ready, and one morning there was no bridge to be seen; in four hours he had walked it across, and at midday the two sides were bridged over. He is said to have been one of the first who caught at the idea of Tanjong Pagar, and he began the first work of the present Dock Company there, about 1864. He also did a great deal of the work at the Borneo Company's wharves. He was a very hard-working, capable man, but times went hard with him;

he went to Deli, and did a good deal of road and bridge making there very successfully. He returned to Singapore, and undertook work at the light-house that is now being built on Pulo Pisang. He came to Singapore a short time ago saying that the place would be the death of him, and died on Tuesday last."

CHAPTER LV.

RAINFALL. CLIMATE. OLD AMATEUR THEATRICALS.

A FTER the last chapter of this book had been written it was suggested that something would be useful about the rainfall, &c. ; and from another source it was said that little or no notice had been taken of the amateur theatricals, which were one of the most popular amusements in former days, when golf, lawn-tennis, football and other athletic occupations (rather than recreations ?) were unknown. So this chapter has been added.

RAINFALL, &c.

The first particulars of the rainfall are to be found in a passage written by John Crawfurd, about 1828, as follows :—" In a place little more than eighty miles from the Equator there is of course little variety in the seasons. The greatest quantity of rain falls in December and January, but refreshing showers are experienced throughout the year. In 1820 rain fell on 229 days; in 1821, on 203 ; in 1824, on 136 ; and in 1825, on 171 ; giving an average, in four years, of about 185 rainy, and 108 dry days. The rainy months are the coldest, namely December and January; and the dryest months, April and May, the hottest. The lowest range of the thermometer within the year 1825 was 71 and the highest 89 degrees."

In George Windsor Earl's book published in 1837, he gave the rainfall for the year 1835; and Dr. Little in a paper in the second volume of Logan's Journal, gave the rainfall taken by Captain Charles Morgan Elliot in the years 1841 to September, 1845, which are as follows ; they have been placed in the same columns as Mr. Earl's for 1835 :—

MONTH.	1835	1841	1842	1843	1844	1845
January ...	18·5	3·7	22·6	18·0	10·2	5·7
February ...	1·5	6·7	10·9	3·0	6·9	4·2
March ...	10 8	5·0	7·2	8·0	4·1	3·0
April ...	3·2	3·1	10·0	5·6	12·3	7·2
May ...	5·0	6·1	9·0	9·0	7·8	5·0
June ...	6·5	7·5	6·3	2·3	6·0	5·3
July ...	4·6	7·4	5·0	8·5	5 8	3·4
August ...	6·9	7·0	6·0	5·5	5·7	6·7
September	3·6	4·2	4 2	4·0	5·0	10·2
October ...	10·8	4·0	21·0	12·1	10·2	...
November...	7·4	12·2	9·4	9·6	6·0	...
December ...	20·7	6·2	4·4	6·4	8·7	...
Total ...	99·5	73·1	116·0	92·0	88·7	

On which Dr. Little made the following remarks :—" Taking the average of the completed four years we have 92·5 as the annual fall of rain in Singapore from 1841 to 1844. The greatest fall of rain was in the month of January to the amount of 22·585, and the smallest in the month of April to the amount of 3·19. The year 1842, Dr. Little said, was considered a very wet year, 116·247 inches having fallen, against 73·126 in the preceding year. The months in which most rain fell were January and October, then April and November, and the least in March. Most rain falls in the north-east monsoon, and the dry weather may be said to exist in the south-west monsoon. No particular quarter of the wind seems to have much influence on the fall of rain. The tables show there is the greatest fall when the north-east is the general direction, nearly the same quantity when the south-west is the quarter, and not less during the continuance of the wind from the north-west. The only inference that can be drawn is, that when the wind is from the S. E. less rain falls. Many tropical countries have an equal quantity of rain, and even more, annually falling; but owing to the fall being confined to one part of the year, an equal benefit with Singapore is not received, nay even it is the occasion of much disease when the rain is followed by great heats. The rain in Singapore falling in showers throughout the year, and not confined to one season, gives a perpetual verdure to vegetation, cools the surface of the earth, and precipitates, as well as tends to diminish, the generation of any atmospherical malaria."

There is an interesting paper, written in 1887 by Mr. Vaughan (spoken of on page 555) on this subject; from which the following is taken :—

"We have now had observations upon the rainfall and temperature of Singapore regularly taken for a quarter of a century without a gap; by myself from 1862 to 1866, tables published in the *Government Gazette*; by Mr. Arthur Knight of the Audit Department from 1864 to 1886; and by the Medical Department from 1869 to 1886. We have also records of the rainfalls and temperature kept by Lieut. Charles Morgan Elliot, of the Madras Engineers (a brother of Sir H. M. Elliot, Secretary to the Government of India), from 1841 to 1845 at the Singapore Magnetic Observatory, which stood near the Kallang Bridge, not far from the Gas Works; I believe the ruins may still be seen. Elliot was one of the most promising men in the service of the East India Company, and would have made his mark in India had his life been spared; but he died young, shortly after leaving Singapore, at the close of 1845.

"The annual rainfall for the twenty-five years was as follows :—

1862	-	99·51 inches.	1871	-	109·45 inches.	1880	-	111·08 inches
1863	-	86·62 „	1872	-	75·30 „	1881	-	94·00 „
1864	-	86·92 „	1873	-	85·60 „	1882	-	88·16 „
1865	-	78·06 „	1874	-	87·05 „	1883	-	75·30 „
1866	-	90·52 „	1875	-	93·96 „	1884	-	80·13 „
1867	-	90·01 „	1876	-	89·91 „	1885	-	67·32 „
1868	-	75·55 „	1877	-	58·37 „	1886	-	95·19 „
1869	-	90·65 „	1878	-	103 16 „			
1870	-	123·24 „	1879	-	116·14 „			

"Captain Elliot's record gives an average of a little more than 92 inches per annum; which has been quoted by John Turnbull Thomson and Dr. Little and other writers on the subject, and may fairly be considered the average annual rainfall to this day. The above table shows with what regularity the annual rainfall ebbs and flows in decades.

"The greatest number of rainy days in one year was recorded by Mr. Knight at Mount Pleasant, *viz.*, 244 days. The greatest monthly fall was recorded in December, 1869, inches 20·66, and the lowest in February, 1864, 17/100 of an inch, was recorded by Mr. Knight, whilst no rain fell in town during that month. The lowest annual rainfalls occurred in 1877 and 1885, when 58 and 67 inches fell respectively. The greatest rainfall in twenty-four hours was 7·10 inches in 1884. The normal range of annual rainfall lies between 85 and 95 inches. In eleven years out of twenty-five, it kept within this range, rising in other seven years by thirty-eight inches, and falling below it for seven years more by twenty-seven inches. The average of annual rainfall at the Criminal Prison, Brass Bassa Road register, kept by Mr. Wheatley from 1870 to 1881, was ninety-two inches. If you will take the trouble and add together the falls of the three years 1869 to 1871, and again the falls of the three years 1878 to 1880, you will find only a difference of a few inches. If you will add the rainfalls from 1866 to 1874, four years on each side of the maximum in 1870, and the falls from 1875 to 1883, four years on each side of the maximum in the next decade, you find only a difference of three inches, and the average of the falls in each period to be about 92 inches. The maximum of wet days in one year was 244 in 1879 and minimum 119 in 1877.

" Droughts occur periodically, and are worth noting. The first during the twenty-five years lasted for thirty-five days, from the 27th of January to the 2nd of March, 1864, with the exception of the fall mentioned above of 0·17 of an inch at Mount Pleasant. The price of water in the Town rose to five cents a bucket, and much distress prevailed in consequence amongst the poor natives. These droughts, I have no doubt, led Mr. Tan Kim Seng to present the Government with his munificent gift of $13,000 towards the construction of water-works. There was a drought in 1877 that lasted from the 22nd September to the 23rd October, thirty-one days, and the natives suffered much. The water-works were finished in 1877 and opened in 1878. A drought of forty-nine days with slight sprinklings of rain, of no 'consequence, lasted from the 28th of January to 17th March, 1883, but happily the water-works were in full play and no evil consequences resulted. The water supply had, however, to be cut off for a few hours daily for several days."

For the sake of comparison with former years, the following figures are given as the rainfall for the three years 1890, 1895 and 1900 taken at the Kandang Kerbau Hospital :—

	1890.	1895.	1900.		1890.	1895.	1900.
January	8·77	5·47	7·98	July	20·76	8·91	5·58
February	12·47	2·88	4·14	August	8·09	7·72	9·59
March	9·91	6·05	6·73	September	8·29	4·15	2·42
April	7·97	12·78	17·91	October	9·07	9·69	5·54
May	3·37	7·34	6·13	November	13·43	11·68	12·72
June	6·61	7·78	8·53	December	11·67	13·96	4·11

Total for the years 1890, 120·41 ; 1895, 98·41 ; 1900, 91·38.

It has been mentioned on page 338, that in 1839 there was a very rainy month, over 4 inches having fallen in one day, which was then considered a remarkable record; but on Sunday, 29th May, 1892, 9·25 inches fell between 7 a.m. and 11 a.m. The heavy downpour flooded the town, and particularly Orchard Road, where the water was 2 ft. 6 in. deep at Government House Gates. In fact Orchard Road as far as the police station, except in one or two of the higher parts, was quite under water. The depths of the different parts of the road were taken and printed in the *Free Press* of May 30th; a gentleman had swum down Orchard Road with a three foot rule to gauge the depths; and the same day a gentleman canoed from Tanglin to the sea. Singapore lies so low that heavy rains bring up the water level temporarily to that of the sea. The storm waters can only get out of the big channels at low water, and the multiplication of these would have no effect in that respect, although they would assist materially in clearing away the storm waters at low tide. In 1892, when the tide went out, the water in Orchard Road. fell no less than four inches in an hour.

In John Cameron's book he says:—"In 1863 rain fell on 184 days, and the quantity was considerably in excess of that of temperate countries generally. It seldom rains a whole day through; the greater part is discharged in short but heavy showers, and in big drops like those from thunder-clouds at home. The effect of these is very refreshing; they generally come when the air is unusually close and warm, and though not lasting perhaps more than half an hour or an hour, they leave it both cool and purified. Another good point in the climate is the rare absence of a good stiff breeze from one quarter or another during the day, and of the soft land airs breathing out from the jungle at night, when all more boisterous winds are hushed to rest. To these land winds is due in a great measure the coolness of the nights, which will generally admit of good sound slumber, a *sine quâ non* to health here as elsewhere.

"By resorting to the neighbourhood of the jungle a degree at least of reduction in the temperature may be secured. In such places as Selitar, lying well in the interior, and with the primeval forest all round them, the additional coolness is palpable, and cannot be less than two or three degrees. Sea bathing is also a relief within easy reach, and is often availed of; but the neighbourhood of coral banks which are exposed at low water is avoided, as the exhalations produced by the heat of the sun have been found to be very unwholesome. The climate is also one in which more out-door amusement can be enjoyed than in that of most other tropical countries. From sunrise till eight o'clock in the morning, and from half-past four in the afternoon till sunset, the sun is comparatively harmless, and even in midday Europeans walk about the Square in town with apparent impunity. To be safe, however, the head should always be kept well covered, and with this precaution, the more out-door exercise indulged in the better."

As regards the climate, Mr. Crawfurd wrote in 1828 that it was hot but equable; but, from the absence of distinct seasons, necessarily monotonous. He added that the town was remarkable for its salubrity, the fevers and dysenteries of ordinary tropical countries being of very rare occurrence, and that he had no recollection of any European having fallen a victim to the climate in the long period of nine years since the formation of the settlement.

George Windsor Earl says in his book, published in 1837, that from his first arrival in Singapore, during twenty-two months, only two deaths occurred among the European residents, and neither of these arose from the effects of the climate.

G. F. Davidson in his book published in 1846, but probably speaking of about 1840, when he was carrying on business as Davidson & Co., said:—"Of the state of public health in Singapore I am able to report most favorably. Let any one go and see the European residents of sixteen and twenty years standing, and he will be able to judge for himself. During my acquaintance of sixteen years with this part of the world, I have never known any endemic disease to prevail; never heard of more than one European dying of cholera, or of more than three Europeans being attacked with that disease; never knew but one or two cases of liver-complaint in which the sufferers had not their own imprudence to thank for the attack; and, as far as my memory serves me, cannot reckon up two deaths among the European inhabitants in that long period. Some one may here whisper, "Look at the state of your Singapore burial ground." My reply is, that it is filled by the death of numbers who have, from time to time, arrived from Calcutta and other parts of India in a dying state, and who would have died six months sooner, had they not come to breathe the pure air of Singapore."

The following paper on the temperature of the place was written by Mr. Vaughan in 1887:—"Captain Elliot's tables are most useful in enabling us to come to a definite conclusion as to the changes in temperature that have taken place in Singapore during the last forty-five years. They may be put down as *nil*.

"Elliot's register gives the following means of all the observations of each hour for every day of the month from 1841 to 1845 :—

January	... ...	79·55
February	... ...	80·25
March	... ...	81·22
April	... ...	81·47
May	... ...	82·31
June	... ...	82·29
July	... ...	82·24
August	... ...	81·80
September	... ...	81·76
October	... ...	81·21
November	... ...	80·63
December	... ...	80·24

The mean temperature for ten years, 81·25.

"The means for the years 1885 and 1886 were as follows:—

January	...	...	80·3
February	...	...	80·0
March	...	...	81·9
April	...	...	82·4
May	...	...	82·5
June	...	...	82·0
July	...	...	82·0
August	...	...	82·0
September	...	...	82·0
October	..	...	82·0
November	...	...	80·9
December	...	...	79·2

The mean temperature for the two years, 81·50.

"The mean of the means of temperature for the last 17 years (1870 to 1886) given by Dr. Rowell is 81·20.

The mean temperature by Elliot for each year was as follows:—

1841	1842	1843	1844	1845
81·28	81·66	81·09	80·82	81·66

Mean of five years, 81·3.

" Let us take five consecutive years, 1881 to 1885, and the figures will be nearly identical—

1881	1882	1883	1884	1885
81·6	81·7	81·3	81·1	81·7

Mean of five years, 81·4.

"Or let us take another five years—

1871	1872	1873	1874	1875
80·8	81·5	81·3	80·7	81·0

Mean of the five years, 81·00

" As in Elliot's time the heat increased gradually from January to June, and decreased from July to December, so it does now. In 1886 the range was as follows:—

January	...	... 80·7	July	...	...	82·6
February	...	... 80·9	August	...	...	81·2
March	...	... 82·4	September	...	...	81·8
April	...	... 82 5	October	...	...	81 9
May	...	... 82·3	November	...	...	80·4
June	...	... 82·9	December	...	...	78·6

"The coldest years were 1869, 1870, and 1879, when the greatest rainfalls were recorded; the warmest were 1872, 1877, and 1885, when the lowest falls were recorded. It is a noteworthy fact connected with the climate of Singapore, that the warmer the day the cooler the night.

"The mean maximum of heat is about 87 degrees, and the mean minimum about 73°, the maximum in Elliot's time was 87·5° and minimum 74·7°; the maximum in the twenty-five years was 94° in April, 1878; and 93° in February, 1885, a warm year.

" The range of barometer is so trifling that it is scarcely worth noting. It was lowest in the wettest years, and highest in the driest. We have literally no season. There is very little difference in the rainfall in the two monsoons, a mere difference of about six inches in the year in favour of the N. E. monsoon; nor is there any perceptible difference in the temperature during the two monsoons. The N. E. monsoon prevails from November to April, and the S. W. monsoon from May to October. Singapore lies right athwart the track of both ; the one blowing across a vast expanse of water like the China Sea ; and the other across the Indian Ocean, both wafting clouds laden with moisture across the island, shedding their contents in the form of rain as they pass over. So long as the monsoons endure, so long will Singapore enjoy the refreshing showers, although every tree in the jungle should be levelled to the dust."

With this very interesting paper of Mr. Vaughan, who, from his experience of sea-faring life and his scientific accomplishments, was always listened to with respect on these subjects, we now turn to the remaining subject of

OLD AMATEUR THEATRICALS.

The earliest record of amateur theatricals in Singapore appears in the issue of the *Singapore Chronicle* of the 21st March, 1833. The theatre was in Cross Street, Teluk Ayer. Tickets were sold at $2 and $1 ; doors opened at 6, and the performance commenced at 7 o'clock. The amateurs soared high in those days. The play was Dr. Young's celebrated and much admired tragedy of *The Revenge.* It was followed by the laughable farce of *The Mock Doctor*, also by comic and sentimental songs, and a recitation from Campbell's *Pleasures of Hope*. No money was received at the door, but tickets were sold at Merryweather & Co.'s and other places.

The tragedy was an utter failure, and the amateurs, for their ambition, received severe castigation at the hand of the Editor. This is a portion of the article :—" On Monday evening last a company of amateurs performed, or rather attempted to perform, Dr. Young's celebrated and much admired tragedy of *The Revenge.* Considering the *quality and attainments* of the several actors, we must own we did not experience much disappointment in witnessing this performance, as it required no skill in vaticination to predict a failure. We must certainly allow them credit for their presumption in having fixed on so difficult a piece, but for no more. Instead of lachrymose effect, as is proper, the acting produced a very contrary one on the risible nerves of the audience, and, excepting the tedium produced in listening to a continued series of unintelligible dialogues the piece altogether afforded some amusement from the burlesque character of the performance. Tragedy is altogether beyond the reach of the present company of performers ; and if they wish to attract future audiences, they must confine themselves to the *low* comedy which seems to be their proper forte."

This proved a perfect damper, and the amateurs collapsed. On the 30th of July, 1834, sixteen months after, they essayed a comedy, and were more successful. The play was Goldsmith's admired comedy *She Stoops to Conquer.* Tickets were to be had at Messrs. Merryweather's at $3 each, and the performance commenced at half-past seven o'clock. The following significant paragraph appeared in the advertisement :—" N.B —The Manager pledges himself to the Ladies of Singapore that no improper characters will be admitted." The performance was thus reviewed in the *Chronicle* of July 31st, 1834 :— " The performance of *She Stoops to Conquer* took place on Wednesday evening, and, judging from the loud and continued plaudits of a respectable and well-filled house, it afforded universal satisfaction. To say that the amateur performers acted their parts well is only doing them bare justice ; indeed there were several who entered fully into the spirit of their parts, and acted much better than could have been anticipated." A few lines in this critique, which we quote, show that fifty years ago the amateurs could furnish a respectable orchestra, and that their services were as much appreciated then as those of Mr. Salzmann and our present musical amateurs are now. The Editor wrote :—" To the amateurs, who, though few in number, delighted the audience with several Italian overtures and some of Rossini's best airs, the community must feel much indebted. Their kindness is the more to be felt, as, had they not volunteered their services, the manager must have had recourse to those indefatigable scrapers of cat-gut, commonly known as the Malacca Fiddlers, whose exertions, we know well, would have destroyed all the harmony felt on so agreeable an occasion."

The theatre in Cross Street was abandoned for what was known as Chong Long's House in Kampong Glam, (see page 216) where the next performance took place. On the 27th of September, 1834, the much admired plays of *The Apprentice* and *The Mock Doctor* were brought out. Doors opened at 6, the performance commenced at 7, the price of tickets was reduced to $2 for boxes, $1 for gallery, and $0.50 for the pit. The performance, in consequence of the indisposition of some of the amateurs, had to be postponed to the 30th of the same month. It proved an utter failure, and was thus criticised by the *Chronicle* on the 2nd October :—" Estimating the performance by the quantity, we have some reason to talk— but as to the quality ' the least said the sooner mended.' We refer more particularly to last Tuesday's performance, which afforded abundance of amusement to some, both off and on the stage. The two farces are very humorous in themselves, and some of the characters on the part of three or four of the performers were well sustained ; but the whole would have gone off much better had several of them kept *sober*, and others remembered their parts better. The arrangements of the house were so good and made with so much attention to the modesty of the ladies, that not a single one was to be seen. The gentlemen, therefore, had the house to themselves, and many amused themselves in a variety of ways, of which we need take no notice. Such another exhibition, and farewell to Singapore theatricals say we." It was the death knell of amateur theatricals in Singapore for a time.

On the 14th of March, 1844, there was a revival performance under the management of Vincent Crummles, who was Captain Calbeck of the Madras Army. The plays were *Charles the Second* or *The*

Merry Monarch and *The Spectre Bridegroom*. In the second piece appeared for the first time Miss Petowker as Lavinia, and Mr. Johnson as Dickory. The theatre was in Dutronquoy's Hotel, then called the London, where the Adelphi now stands in Coleman Street. Miss Petowker for several years played ladies' parts. She had the smallest waist, and smallest foot, of any lady in Singapore, and was the envy of all the sex, for it was acknowledged she was the prettiest little chambermaid on the stage and a clever little actress, and played everything she attempted most successfully. One night, after a performance, she was taken to the house of a lady friend, where there was a lady visitor, who talked to the actress for some time and seemed much impressed with her ladylike bearing, &c., when the pert little woman came out with a rather strong expression which aroused the old lady's suspicions; so she walked up to Petowker and said in tragic tones, opening her eyes as wide as she could, "Why you naughty creature, you are a man," and so it was— Mr. W. H. Read! Since that he has played important parts in his own character on another stage quite as successfully, but he probably often looks back with pleasure to the days when he tripped the boards in petticoats. But when speaking of the "Soubrette" the *Prima Donna* should not be forgotten. Pretty, graceful, always well-dressed and careful in her acting, Miss Ledbrook for several years took the leading female parts, and was a decided public favourite. Some still alive remember the then well-known voice of Archie Spottiswoode. Lieut. Dunlop also took to the petticoat, but it took so much chalk and care to tone down his "black muzzle" to "maiden's blush" that he had to return to male attire. Mr. William Napier, the lawyer, afterwards the Governor of Labuan, Mr. C. A. Dyce in Martin Dyce & Co., Captain Scott, and others, enjoyed themselves in amateur theatricals that have not since been surpassed. The other amateur, Mr. Johnson, was Mr. Tom Dunman, the greatest low comedian Singapore has ever seen. In his amateur days, he was an assistant in Martin Dyce & Co.'s. His theatrical career was cut off after he assumed charge of the Police Force, when, on his appearance in the character of Captain Copp, he got a hint from the powers that he had better drop the stage. Colonel Butterworth and Mr. Thos. Church could not believe that private theatricals and the midnight watch after the Chinese thieves could go together. Mr. Dunman was also equally successful in his official career, which has been spoken of on page 394, and left Singapore one of the most popular men of the day, when he retired upon a well-earned pension.

The following are the remarks of the *Free Press* of the 14th March, 1844, on the above performance:—"On Tuesday evening, a few gentlemen amateurs performed the play of *Charles the Second* and the farce of *The Spectre Bridegroom* to a crowded audience. It is now some years since anything of the kind has been attempted in this Settlement, and although occasional efforts have been made to excite public attention to the subject, some obstacle has always been presented to the establishment of a theatre; the spirited proprietor of the London Hotel, Mr. Dutronquoy, has, however, at length converted a portion of his house into a small theatre, and we certainly think he deserves every encouragement from a liberal public."

In these two pieces, appeared Mr. Napier, Mr. Dyce, Mr. W. H. Read, Mr. Spottiswoode, and Mr. Dunman of Singapore; and Captain Calbeck and Lieutenant Dunlop of the 4th Madras Native Infantry, and Captain J. D. Scott of the Madras Artillery. Here is a short criticism written at the time by one who was in Singapore in 1887.

"Calbeck as Copp and Aldwinkle was splendid; also Dunman as Dickory. Napier as Charles the Second brought the house down by answering Lady Clara when she asks him at the commencement of the second act how His Majesty passed the night? 'Vara restless, vara restless,' in broad Scotch. Scott as Nicodemus kept his countenance wonderfully, and his 'I never eat cold pudding' elicited rounds of applause. Such a galaxy of amateurs has never been equalled in Singapore."

On the 18th of April, 1844, was performed *Miss in her Teens* or *The Medley of Lovers*, and *Fortune's Frolic*. Mr. Johnson (Tom Dunman) playing Robin Roughead, the principal part in the last; and Miss Petowker, Tag, the maid in the first. Here is the review of the *Free Press* on these two:—" Miss Petowker as Tag, the Maid, also displayed great cleverness. Mr. Johnson in the part of Robin Roughead was the star of the evening, and his acting was truly excellent. The hearty bursts of applause which the audience repeatedly granted him testified how successfully he had identified himself with the honest rustic whose sudden elevation to rank and fortune affords so many opportunities for the ludicrous and whimsical display of his untutored goodness of heart. The manner in which Mr. Johnson sustained this character would not have disgraced a practised actor. The pleasures of the evening were much enhanced by the performance of the Amateur Orchestra, which played some beautiful overtures with great skill and effect. It is seldom indeed that a small place like Singapore can boast of such a large number of really scientific and accomplished musicians as the gentlemen who so kindly lent their aid on Thursday."

In May, 1844, was played *The Haunted House* and *Bombastes Furioso* by the same company, Captain J. D. Scott being Manager. In June, Mrs. Deacle of the Theatre Royal, Dover, who had been starring in Calcutta with James Vining, the well-known London Tragedian, came down on a visit, with Captain Andrews and Lieut. Crossman of the Bengal Army— Calcutta amateurs—and gave several performances assisted by the amateurs. She built a theatre for herself, and called it, after the Calcutta Theatre, " Sans Souci." Singaporeans enjoyed a treat for some months, *Macbeth*, *Venice Preserved*, *Merchant of Venice* and other tragedies were played, and many farces and comedies. Before she concluded, she managed to secure the Theatre Royal, which was more suited for her performances than the temporary stage erected by her. Alluding to *The Merchant of Venice*, the Editor of the *Free Press* said:—" We will only say that it was an enjoyment of the very highest and most intellectual description. The character of Shylock was played by one of our Singapore amateurs, and was a most unexpected pleasure. Dress, look and delivery were all perfect, and from beginning to the end it was the Jew and nothing but the Jew." This was J. D. Horrocks, then employed in Shaw, Whitehead & Co.'s office. During this performance, Mr. W. Rodyk, afterwards for many years the Registrar of the Supreme Court in Malacca, sang *Billy Barlow* with great effect. An incident occurred to show that the opposition then shown by some clergy to the stage was in full force. One of the cloth, a clergyman of the Church of England, preached a powerful tirade against the stage and actors in general, and said that no modest woman should appear in such a character as Portia. This Revd. gentleman was severely handled in the papers by several writers, and the result of the sermon is thus recorded in the *Free Press* of 25th July, 1844:—' One good resulted from the sermon on Sunday, although not the one exactly intended by the Revd. gentleman, viz., persons who never visited a theatre before, went on Monday, and the house was crowded !"

Mrs. Deacle returned to Calcutta shortly after, and completed her engagement there. Admiral Keppel in his Diary on 23rd July, 1844, printed in his last book, vol. 1, page 339, said " Amateur Theatricals, ' The Merchant of Venice.' Read performed. Supped with Portia." And Mr. R. O. Norris on reading the above wrote this :—" How time flies ! I remember the days of 1844 very well, and read the recollection of old theatricals with great interest. The Theatre Royal was then in Coleman Street, and Padre White lived in the next house. Mrs. Deacle took for a time, the house, which was Mr. Kim Cheng's (south corner of Coleman Street and North Bridge Road), for her theatre. We, that is the boy-boarders at the Institution School, and the girls from Mrs. Whittle's School, used to go every month to Mr. White's, who, with his good lady and three big girls, used to be kind to us all ; magic lanterns, and lectures on botany, chemistry, and such things to amuse us and teach us what we could not learn in school. The boys were sent home with bread and jam, but the girls remained longer with tea and sweets as their share. One evening we were there, and a clergyman, Mr. Taylor, from Madras, when unfortunately Mrs. Deacle & Co. were rehearsing next door, and the Padre told us the house was a house of devils ! Rather strong that, but what a change now when Padres patronise theatres and horse races. I remember that we heard that evening the voice of Mr. Napier rehearsing. There were two good actors in the 21st Madras Native Infantry, named Bolton and Rideout, and the Square was represented by Messrs. Greenshields and Robert Duff, I do not doubt that some of the young ladies at Mrs. Whittle's school, now aged matrons, still among us, will recollect those days."

The year 1845 proved a dull one for amateur theatricals. After Mrs. Deacle's departure, Dutronquoy left Coleman Street for the Esplanade, taking his sign-board with him. He was the proprietor of the London Hotel—now the Hotel de l'Europe—for a few years. He disappeared, mysteriously, murdered it was whispered, whilst gold digging up in the Muar, and the hotel was carried on by his wife and son for several years. The Theatre Royal, Coleman Street, disappeared, and the Assembly Rooms were erected in the vacant spot at the foot of Fort Canning in Hill Street, not far from High Street. This building was distinguished by its ugliness. It possessed, however, a spacious ball-room, and a very passable theatre—the scenery for which was painted by C. A. Dyce. Mr. Dyce was a brother of the R. A. and an excellent artist. His drop-scene—a view of Singapore—was used for many years.

At the new Theatre Royal in the Assembly Rooms the first performance took place on the 25th of November. The play was *The Conquering Game* and the *Mummy*. Tickets at $2 and $1. Performance commenced at 8. We quote portions of the critiques from the *Free Press* of the 27th November, 1845 :—" The stage is more spacious than at the old theatre, and the accommodation for the performers combines more convenience and comfort. There are complaints, however, regarding the imperfect transmission of sound, the performers being quite inaudible in the back part of the theatre. The drop scene—a view of Singapore—does great credit to the amateur artist by whom it was painted. We also noticed a street which was exceedingly well painted. Our old friend Mr. Folair (Capt. J. D. Scott) as Charles XII, King of Sweden, sustained the character admirably. Miss Petowker (W. H. Read) as Baroness Ormsdoff was tastefully dressed and wore her honours with becoming self-possession and dignity. Miss Ledbrook (Spottiswoode) is always perfect, and as Catherine Ormsdoff was excellent. In the *Mummy*, Mr. Johnson (Dunman) as Toby Tramp, kept the house in roars of laughter. He met with a most flattering reception, which he well deserved, from the recollection of the many hours of laughter he created at the old theatre. The amateur gentlemen who attended the orchestra deserve the highest praise, the music was exquisite, and perhaps no part of India, of the same limited extent as Singapore, can boast of an equal number of efficient performers. The proprietors of the theatre ought to be, and we have no doubt are, very grateful for the assistance of these gentlemen. It gave us great pleasure to see the house so well filled (not a vacant chair to be had) and graced with the presence of all the beauty and fashion of the Settlement." The performance was repeated a week after.

The year 1846 proved a dull one, except that in it certain admirable actors made their first appearance in Singapore, to be mentioned hereafter. On the 25th May were played *The Little Back Parlour, Bombastes Furioso,* and *Nothing Superfluous.* On the 27th September, were played the farces of *Damp Beds* and *My Young Wife and Old Umbrella.* We take, from the *Free Press,* portions of the critique on the performance, which alluded to amateurs who are still well remembered in Singapore. The *Free Press* at this time was edited by Mr. William Napier, an accomplished actor :—

" After a considerable blank, the performances at our little Drury were revived on Friday evening last, and although we only recognised two of the *old stagers* on the boards, the whole went off with much spirit ; in fact, we confess ourselves to have been agreeably disappointed. The pieces chosen were humorous in the extreme, and the first, viz., *Damp Beds*, abounds with jokes, many of which, however, were omitted or rather forgotten, but what we heard were so palpable as to send us into roars. The acting of Mr. Jingle (J. D. Vaughan) as Whisk, was excellent throughout, and the complete self-possession and modulation of his voice convinces us that although new on the boards here, he is an old hand elsewhere. Jingle would prove a most valuable auxiliary to the little band ; such, however, we fear cannot be, as the duties of his profession call him hence in a very few days. Our old favourite Miss Quilp (W. Rodyk, of Malacca) was, as he always is, very effective in his part of the pert Abigail. Mr. Titmouse's first appearance (Lieutenant Sweet of the 21st Madras Infantry) was an admirable hit, his acting throughout of the vulgar upstart cockney who 'ain't to be done at no price,' was really good, and we hail this, his first appearance, as the promise of many future merry laughs; his appearance and manners are particularly droll, and we hope the manager will select a piece for next performance where the veteran Johnson and Titmouse can play together. We are sorry to see Mr. Fitzsnook (W. H. Read) playing in a new character, and sincerely trust he will again resume the old name, and captivate us as he did as the *Countess Ormsdoff* or as *Mrs. Pontifer*; the more especially, as Miss Ledbrook appears to have deserted the cause.

"In the second piece, Messrs. Fitzsnook, Snodgrass, and Jingle, and Miss Quilp, had almost nothing to do, the whole burden falling on Blueskin (Farleigh Armstrong's first appearance). *Gregory* was an admirable piece of acting, and kept the audience in a roar throughout; in fact, as we said before, all were mightily pleased. The excellent music of the 21st Regiment's Band added not a little to the evening's entertainment. With all due deference to Messrs. Crummles & Co., we decidedly object to their bamboozling Her Majesty's lieges by changing the actors' names so often—such mystification serves no other end than to puzzle people."

On November 24th, 1846, was performed *Charles the Second*, with Dunman as *Captain Copp*, his last appearance; and the farce of *State Secrets*, in which Tidman played the *Tailor of Tamworth*, the principal character. With the exception of the acting of these two, the performance was a failure. Dunman, as has been said, never played again. Miss Petowker's last performance was as *Fantine*, a low lodging housekeeper, and she looked the part to perfection. Archie Spottiswoode was Miss Ledbrooke and made up and played ladies' parts excellently well. The late Mr. William Rodyk, Registar of the Malacca Court, was the third female, and also played very well. One night when the *Dido*, Sir Harry Keppel's ship was here, after a performance, her Captain, Officers and amateurs, and Miss Petowker, played at leap-frog on the stage, and after their game adjourned for supper to the Navy House, which stood on the site occupied now by the Masonic Hall. The house belonged to Mr. Read's father.

In 1847, but one performance was advertised—On the 21st December, the laughable farces of *Animal Magnetism* and *But However*. No programme or critique appears in the *Free Press*, which was at this time edited by Mr. Logan, who was not a theatrical man, and the files of the *Straits Times* for this and other years were burnt.

In 1848, there were two performances—on the 29th August and 29th September. The programme of the first is given, but we cannot trace the amateurs. The plays were *His Last Legs* and *Twice Killed*. On the second night, the *Irish Lion* and *Meet Me by Moonlight* were played. There was no critique published on the performance.

During the next decade, the amateur performances were few and far between. There were none in 1851 and 1852. In 1853,

The Three Cuckoos, Little Back-Parlour and *Friend Naggles* were played. The performance was unfavourably reviewed by the press. No performance in 1854. In 1855, the amateurs revived, and performed in February, April, August and October. *Victorina, Mrs. Bunbury's Spoons, The Critic* and *Did You Ever Send Your Wife to Camberwell?* were the plays. Nothing in 1856. In 1857 the amateurs were very busy playing in aid of a fund for fitting up a new theatre at the Town Hall. They played *The Prisoner of War, A Thumping Legacy, Helping Hands, John Dobbs, Paul Pry* and *Slasher and Crasher*. In June of that year, the performance was under the patronage of Lord Elgin, who was on his way to India to help Lord Canning. There were no performances in 1858 and 1859; and one or two in 1860. *Folair*, Captain J. D. Scott, left with his battery for India, and for several years Mr. W. H. Read was the President and Stage Manager of the *Corps Dramatique*. Mr. Bono (Farleigh Armstrong, then in William Macdonald & Co.'s) improved on every appearance, and eventually became a worthy successor to T. Dunman; and for many years was the best low comedian on the stage. As the deaf ostler in *Deaf as a Post*, and many other characters, he was inimitable. During these ten years, the amateurs who played women's parts were Mr. McCleland of Spottiswoode & Co. as *Miss Glendiggings*; Mr. George Dare, *La Brani*, now in Singapore, and Mr. Julius Dare, his brother. Mr. McCleland was exceptionally good. The tragedian was Mr. E. J. Leveson of Reme Brothers, who, as *Mr. Gower*, played, as often as he could, parts suited to his talents. Unfortunately this was not often, as the amateurs wisely eschewed tragedies. He made a decided hit in the *Prisoner of War*. He was an accomplished actor and reciter. Of light comedians, none excelled Mr. Barclay Read of A. L. Johnston & Co., and Mr. William Adamson, then of the Borneo Company, now in England, and a C.M.G., the head of the London firm of Adamson, Gilfillan & Co., and taking much trouble in looking after the interests of Singapore, like others of the old Singaporeans. Mr. Weir, of Spottiswoode & Co., was also very good in this line; F. M. Goss of Ker, Rawson & Co., John Steel of Martin Dyce & Co., and afterwards of the Mercantile Bank; and last, though not least, *Perkyns* (John Armstrong) known as the kindest hearted amateur ever seen, and a dear good fellow off the stage. He was always ready to oblige the Manager, and played any part that wanted filling up. He dressed carefully and played everything he took in hand well. There were also Franklin Richardson Kendal, of the P. & O. Office, and others, all good actors.

In 1861, on the 4th April, there was *A Phenomenon in a Smock Frock* and *Mrs. Bunbury's Spoons*. On July the 26th, *Our Wife or The Rose of Amiens* was performed. In this appeared for the first time *Jupon* (Mr. F. D. Barnes of the P. & O. Company, who died lately the Managing Director of the Company in London), an actor possessing great powers in the famous Robson's line, and was much admired. In all these pieces, the two Armstrongs, McCleland, and Dare played. On the 18th October, was performed *The Chimney Corner* and *Boots at the Swan*. In the former piece *Jupon*, Barnes, played Robson's part very well indeed, but the critics did not flatter him. It was an exceedingly difficult part, abounding in passages of humour and pathos that are well known to those who have seen this piece and the *Porter's Knot*, both written for Robson, who was not less than a genius, and night after night brought tears into everyone's eyes in these homely characters, in the old, ill-appointed Adelphi theatre in London. No wonder if an amateur did not come up to so high a standard.

Mr. Vaughan as *Whisk* made his second appearance on the Singapore stage in the *Chimney Corner*; his performance was thus criticised by the *Straits Times* of the 19th October, 1861 :—" The only difference, in fact, which the *Chimney Corner* presents (alluding to the *Porter's Knot*) is in the introduction of the *Deus machina* in the person of the honest son's grandfather, an old man of ninety, most beautifully played last night by *Mr. Whisk*. We have not had the pleasure of seeing this gentleman perform before, but we heartily welcome him as a very great addition to our little *corps dramatique*. His assumption of the feeble, bed-ridden, half-blind, old man; his rendering of the broken, interjected sentences, which, having no reference to each other, but simply showing the fancies flitting through the old man's brain, yet so powerfully point the wit of the general dialogue, his make and gait, were admirably worked out, and we must assign to *Mr. Whisk* the place of honour in last night's performance." Farleigh Armstrong was the hero of the second piece; and played *Boots* exceedingly well. This was written by the late John Cameron who had assumed the editorial charge of the *Straits Times* on the 20th August, 1861.

A decided "sell" perpetrated by the *corps dramatique*, in 1861, deserves recording, as it caused a great deal of merriment at the time, and no little annoyance in some quarters. The *corps* advertised early in the year a performance of the *Merchant of Venice*, and a crowded house was the result. Instead of Shakespear, the audience had *The Merchant of Venice Preserved"*—a burlesque—which in the hands of *Bono* and others proved a success, but many were indignant, and the press levelled its thunders at the heads of the unfortunate amateurs. The critique called forth a number of letters abusing and defending the amateurs, and after a few indignant letters had been published on both sides, the storm subsided.

During 1856, the old Assembly Rooms at the foot of Fort Canning had been demolished, and a temporary theatre erected on their site, in which the amateurs performed to the end of 1861, chiefly in aid of funds required for the scenery, dresses and properties for the new Theatre in the lower room of the Town Hall. Mr. Barclay Read assumed the duties of Stage Manager and President of the *Corps Dramatique*. At the end of 1861, the Savage Club was started by Wm. Steel of the Mercantile Bank, and its birth was thus noticed by the *Straits Times* on the 7th December, 1861, in a leader headed "The Drama." We extract the following part referring exclusively to the new club :—" We are heartily glad to see the establishment in Singapore of a club, whose ostensible purpose is the furthering of theatrical performances in our Settlement. The Savage Club is by no means meant as an antagonistic body of performers to our old and justly esteemed corps at the Town Hall. It is simply designed in a graceful and generous spirit of rivalry, to incite the former corps to still further efforts, and to give to our European community an evening's entertainment which will afford them pleasure, and to the furtherance of dramatic performances in the East. The comparative dullness of the life we lead here, even as regards the Indian Presidencies, cannot be denied, and we joyfully hail another accession to our public fund of amusement."

During 1862, amateur theatricals flourished. The *Corps Dramatique* played two or three times at the Town Hall, and the Savage Club performed frequently. Mr. Steel of the Mercantile Bank, gave up his residence, the late Barganny House, for the performances. A pretty little theatre was fitted up in the drawing room and the admission to the performances was secured by a subscription of one dollar a month. With very few exceptions, all the European residents subscribed. Mr. Vaughan was President and Stage Manager, and Mr. Steel Secretary and Treasurer, a committee of three or four members assisted in the management. Barganny House being too small to accommodate all the subscribers at the same time, each performance had to be repeated. The Club played once in every month except during a few months in the middle of the year.

We give the following copies of the only two advertisements of the Club that we have been able to lay our hands on, which will give a fair insight into the Club's arrrangements :—

NOTICE.
" SAVAGE CLUB."
SEASON 1862.

The fourth performance of the season will take place at Barganny House on the 21st and 22nd proximo, at eight o'clock each night.
The following pieces will be presented :—
" ON AND OFF"
" NUMBER ONE ROUND THE CORNER, "
" COOL AS A CUCUMBER. "

The Singapore Amateur Instrumental Association will kindly assist on this occasion.

N.B.—Subscribers whose names commence with the letters I to Z are expected on the first and from A to H on the second evening.
Singapore, 3rd March, 1862.

———

" SAVAGE CLUB."
SEASON 1862.

The concluding performance of the season will take place at Barganny House, on Thursday and Friday evenings, the 11th and 12th December, 1862, when will be presented the much admired Drama in three Acts.
" PLOT AND PASSION "
and the Burlesque of
" FRA DIAVOLO OR THE BEAUTY AND THE BRIGANDS. "
With original music and new scenery, dresses and appointments.

The Singapore Amateur Instrumental Association will lend their valuable assistance.

Order of attendance: Subscribers I to Z on first and A to H on second evening of performance.

Singapore, 20th November, 1862.

The small subscription above mentioned sufficed to pay all the expenses of the Club, including scenery, dresses, properties and refreshments for the audiences. Besides the plays mentioned in the above advertisements, the following pieces were played during the year, also others that cannot now be ascertained: *Still Waters Run Deep, A Fearful Tragedy in the 7 Dials, Othello Travestied, The Turkish Bath*, the drama of *Robbers in the Wood*, and the burlesque of the same title; *Don Cæsar de Bazan, Burlesque of Medea, The Merchant of Venice* (Shakespeare's), *Fish Out of Water.*

The Club was the means of introducing a number of first rate actors to the public. The tragedian was the late Dr. H. A. Allen, a private practitioner, as *Mr. Courtney*. In melodrama De La Feuillade of the Borneo Company, as *Mr. Delaf*, excelled. In *Don Cæsar de Bazan* and *Desmarets* no one in Singapore could have touched him. He was for many years in John Little & Co., and afterwards in the Borneo Company. His father was French and his mother English. He was a very clever actor where a Frenchman had to speak broken English, such as "*The First Night*. In his way he was, probably, the best actor in the place. As a delineator of female characters, Mr. William Mulholland, of the Borneo Company as *Miss Booth* was never surpassed. He was afterwards for several years the Manager of the Company in London. He is now dead. As *Maritana* in *Don Cæsar* he was exquisite, and no stranger visiting the performance would have supposed that the character was represented by a man. His *Portia* was excellent. The late Mr. Winton, of the Hongkong Bank, as *Miss Wilton*, made his *debut*. The low comedian *par excellence* was Mr. Charles Emmerson as *Mr. Emery;* he was quite equal to any of his predecessors, and afterwards, at the Town Hall, proved an able successor to Farleigh Armstrong. Mr. Emmerson was a veterinary surgeon and hotel and tiffin-rooms proprietor.

Mr. Steel in *Still Waters Run Deep* and *Cool as a Cucumber* was very good. He changed his theatrical name from *Mr. Wills* to *Mildmay*, the chief character in the first piece. Mr. Vaughan played the leading character in *Fish Out of Water, On and Off, No. 1 Round the Corner*, and other farces. He changed his name from *Whisk* to *Sam Savory,* the hero of the first piece.

We here quote from the *Straits Times* of the 13th December, 1862, a portion of the critique on the last regular performance of the season, in order to show what an outsider thought of some of the actors:—
" The last performance has certainly proved the best of the season at Barganny House. At a time when their claims to support and consideration are about to come before the public, the Savage Club do well to strain themselves to the utmost, and their efforts of the last two nights will prove, we think, not to have been altogether in vain. Labouring under considerable disadvantages in stage accommodation

and scenic machinery, they are able to place on their boards a three-act drama in a style that certainly has not been surpassed by anything we have yet seen in the Town Hall Theatre. If there were fewer appliances, there was a greater exercise of taste and judgment, and the scenes 1 and 3 in Fouché's Closet could scarcly have been improved. *Plot & Passion* is placed in the period of the first Empire, when the schemes and intrigues of Fouché first taught the world the great value and enormous power of a well organised police. The plot of the piece is simple ; Marie de Fondanges is one of Fouché's agents, and is sent to decoy to Paris M. de Neuville, who has offended Fouché and fled to Prague; during her residence there she falls in love with Neuville, and in the end is enabled to save him from the toils of the wily Minister of Police. The principal character in the piece is Fouche, and the part was sustained by *Mr. Courtney* (Dr. H. A. Allen), who has only once before appeared on the Barganny boards. To great coolness, admirable ease and complacency, a good voice, and a very perfect French pronunciation, *Mr. Courtney* added sufficient passion and excitability to make his rendering nearer perfection than we are ever likely to see in Singapore again. *Mr. Delaf* (De la Feuillade of the Borneo Company) as *Desmarets* showed out to great advantage ; his acting was good, and his delivery was slower, and more distinct than on previous occasions ; we are inclined to divide between him and *Mr. Courtney* the first merit in last night's performance ; though the acting of the latter was decidedly the most masterly. *Mr. Mildmay's* (W. Steel) acting was good ; better than we remember it before, and the scene between him and Marie in Fouche's Closet, after his arrest, was really well done, and deserved the applause that followed it. The other male characters were subordinate ones, but were well enough rendered not to detract from the general effect of the piece. *Miss Booth* (Mr. Mulholland), *Prima Donna* of Barganny House, if not of the Singapore stage, sustained the only important female character in the piece—*Marie de Fontanges.* The part was a very heavy one, and required a more than usually retentive memory, together with a great deal of very fine acting. In all these essentials, however, *Miss Booth* was not wanting, and by her acting last night she adds another to the many laurels she has already gained upon the Amateur stage. Taking last night's performance of *Plot & Passion*, and considering it is a whole, we are ready to confess that we believe it by far the best piece that has been given on the Barganny boards— if not the best in Singapore. The burlesque that followed should have been left out. It was past eleven before it commenced, and the manner in which it was played did not justify the detention of the audience. The parts were very imperfectly committed, and the piece consequently broke down in several places. It would be unjust, however, not to record the praise which is due to *Mr. Emery* (Charles Emmerson) for his peroration of *Beppo*, which was really inimitable. ' Tis hard to put the hand where the tart can never be' was splendid, and richly deserved the encore which was given. *Miss Wilton* (Mr. Winton of the Hongkong Bank) also promises to be a valuable acquisition to the female strength of the Savage Club."

The Savage Club had a brief, but glorious career. Mr. Steel left Singapore for Bombay in 1863, and the performances collapsed,

Attempts were made at intervals to resuscitate the Club without success; and some of the members joined the rival corps. Others declined to do this on account of a little ill-feeling that arose between the two *corps* in consequence of the older one declining to let the Savage Club play at the Town Hall, because they had a claim to the theatre there, they having played to pay the expenses thereof; which was quite true. The Savage Club had to yield, but the ill-feeling engendered by the correspondence that appeared in the *Straits Times*, never wore off, and lost to the amateur stage several prominent actors who never played in public again.

In 1862, the *Corps Dramatique* played the *Critic, Catching a Mermaid,* and *Robert Macaire.* The first was got up regardless of expense, and gave great satisfaction. Mr. Barclay Read played *Puff* with eclat; but as the handsome, bold and rollicking highwayman *Macaire,* he surpassed himself. Mr. Tidman of the Borneo Company played the cowardly *Strop* splendidly. Mr. Vaughan was *Pierre,* The farce was very amusing, Farleigh Armstrong playing the chief part. Mr. Paul Frederic Tidman was the leading light comedian for some time after his debut and by far the cleverest actor of his time. He was in the Borneo Company, and afterwards in partnership with Mr. Wm. Mactaggart in London, as Mactaggart, Tidman & Co. He was the first Honorary Secretary of the Straits Association in London and was created a C.M.G., and died in 1891.

More than sufficient, perhaps, has now been collected from old papers to show the nature of the amateur theatricals in former days, and the subject may end here, as the names have been mentioned of all the leaders in an amusement which certainly did credit to the community.

CHAPTER LVI.

THE TRANSFER.

THIS chapter contains an account of the transfer of the Straits Settlements from the East India Company to the Colonial Office. It was always spoken of as "The Transfer," and was considered the most important event in the history of Singapore since the day when Sir Stamford Raffles founded the Settlement; and the prominent date of division in the history of the place. The causes which led up to the change will appear in the various petitions, letters, and papers that are reprinted here.

It has not been unusual of late years to hear it said in Singapore that there is little public spirit in the place, and that it would not exist if occasion arose when it might prove of much advantage. Whatever may be the case at the present time, it could not have been said with truth of the early days of the Settlement, as this book has clearly shown; and the patience and perseverance of the mercantile community during ten years in urging the importance of the Transfer, and in persistently following it up in spite of frequent discouragement, is proof that there was no lack of public-spirited members in the community at that time.

The principal cause of the movement was the feeling in Singapore, which had been growing for many years, that the Supreme Government in Bengal was able to give very little attention to the affairs of a place so far from Calcutta and so different from India in many respects. One small matter of grievance, for example, was that for more than twenty years the community had been complaining of the inconvenience of there being no regulations for the control of public conveyances, and no redress could be got, even in such a small matter, from Calcutta. A second point was the little attention that could be obtained with regard to the commercial relations of Singapore with the Native States in the Peninsula and Archipelago, the promotion of which had been one of the principal objects of Sir Stamford Raffles.

The Governor-General of India, with the engrossing duties entailed upon him by the Government of India, could ill spare the time to consider not only the internal government of the Straits Settlements, but also the matters of foreign policy connected with them. The French were commencing to take a peculiar interest in Cochin-China, which ultimately led to the occupation of Saigon. The Netherlands and Spain both had colonies close by, with which the interests of Singapore were connected, and all the correspondence on such matters had to reach the Foreign Office in London through the Governor-General, who might be at Simla, which caused delay for many weeks or months.

After the Indian Mutiny the Europeans in Calcutta had agitated the question of the Government of India being placed directly under the Crown, and the Straits Settlements being then part of the administration of India, this fact led to the opportunity of raising the question as regarded the government of the Straits.

A public meeting of the European inhabitants was held at the News Rooms on 15th September, 1857, called by the Sheriff on a requisition very numerously signed, for the purpose of considering the advisability of joining in the movement which had originated in Calcutta.

Mr. Joaquim d'Almeida, the Sheriff, was called to the chair, and after some discussion on minor points, the Meeting, being unanimous that it would be highly advantageous to transfer the management of India from the East India Company to the Crown, passed the following resolutions :—

Proposed by R. C. Woods, seconded by C. Spottiswoode :—" That this Meeting records its hearty concurrence in the prayer of the Calcutta Petition, dated 3rd August, and resolves to petition Parliament to present an address to the Crown, beseeching Her Majesty to place the whole of British India under the sole Government of the Imperial Parliament."

Proposed by J. J. Greenshields, seconded by J. Harvey :—" That the petition to Parliament set forth the grievance under which the Straits Settlements have laboured during the Government of the East India Company, and pray to be placed *directly under the Crown, with a separate Government*, and not as at present under a delegated authority in India."

Proposed by W. Paterson, seconded by J. B. Cumming, " That the following gentlemen be named a Committee to carry out the resolutions of the Meeting, Messrs. A. Logan, R. C. Woods, R. Bain, A. M. Aitken, and Joaquim d'Almeida."

The words above, here printed in italics, seem to be the first mention *in print* of what ended in the Transfer on 1st April, 1867.

The following was the Petition which was addressed to the two Houses of Parliament by the European inhabitants of Singapore, and was very numerously signed :—

" That your Petitioners have long felt aggrieved by the manner in which Singapore is governed by the East India Company. For a considerable time it was subordinate to the Bengal Presidency, and although of late years the Straits Settlements have been nominally a separate Government, placed directly under the Supreme Government of India, there has been little alteration in the system of management. Ignorant, apparently, of the many circumstances in which the Straits Settlements differ so widely from Continental India, the Supreme Government has almost invariably treated them from an exclusively Indian point of view, and shown a systematic disregard to the wants and wishes of their inhabitants, however earnestly and perseveringly made known. And only by appeals to the Imperial Government and Parliament, have needful improvements desired by the inhabitants of the Straits Settlements been brought about, or redress obtained for injustice inflicted on them by the Government of the East India Company.

" When, a few years ago, Parliament established a Legislative Council for India, your Petitioners hoped that a beneficial change would take place in the manner of dealing with questions affecting the welfare of the Straits Settlements, but they found that such expectations were fallacious. Unlike the several Presidencies and Governments of Continental India, the Straits Settlements are not represented in the Legislative Council, by any person having a competent knowledge of their requirements. On various occasions when proceeding to deal with matters connected with these Settlements, the members of the Legislative Council have confessed their complete ignorance of Straits affairs, but this has not induced them to hesitate in their action—or to take effectual means for acquiring the information acknowledged to be wanting. They have, on the contrary, passed Acts most detrimental to the interests of the Settlement, in spite of the earnest remonstrances and prayers of the inhabitants.

"The Straits Settlements are placed under the charge of a Governor, appointed by the Governor-General of India in Council. Without any Council to advise or assist him, this Officer has paramount authority within the Settlement, and by his reports and suggestions the Supreme Government and Legislative Council are in great measure guided in dealing with the affairs of these Settlements. It may, and indeed does in reality frequently happen, that this functionary, from caprice, temper or defective judgment, is opposed to the wishes of the whole community, yet in any conflict of opinion so arising his views are almost invariably adopted by the Supreme Government, upon statements and representations which the public have no knowledge of and no opportunity of impugning.

"In order to show that these assertions are not vague generalities, or made without sufficient facts to justify them, your Petitioners humbly submit the following statements:—

"The Settlement of Singapore was established as an outlet for British Commerce, and the preservation of its integrity as a Free Port has always been recognised by statesmen as essential to its prosperity and the full development of the objects contemplated in its formation. Thirty-nine years ago it was a haunt of savage Malay pirates and now it has a Trade of the annual value of ten millions of pounds sterling, steadily increasing from year to year. The Honorable the Court of Directors and the Government of India have never cordially recognised or appreciated the advantage which the free port of Singapore has afforded to the Commerce of Great Britain and India. Influenced solely by the desire to protect their revenue and ignoring all other considerations, they have at various times proposed to adopt measures that if carried out would have had the effect of ruining or seriously injuring the trade of Singapore. At one period they wished to impose Import and Export duties, at another Tonnage dues, and, passing over other projects never realised, they adopted measures in 1854 for introducing the Company's Rupee into more general circulation in the Straits Settlements, where hitherto a Dollar currency had almost exclusively prevailed. The Copper currency, consisting of Cents of a Dollar, previously supplied under the provisions of an Act of the Indian Government passed in 1847, was withheld, and the Indian copper money, which it is impossible to adapt to a Dollar currency was substituted in its place. The inhabitants of the Straits Settlements repeatedly and in the most earnest terms memorialized the Legislative Council and Supreme Government of India against these changes, setting forth the inconvenience and injury their adoption would occasion, but their representations were not listened to. In all these instances, the evil was only averted or redress procured by appealing to the Imperial Government or Parliament, from which that attention and justice were obtained which had been in vain prayed for at the hands of our more immediate rulers.

"From the very first establishment of Singapore the trading vessels, and more especially the native craft, resorting to it, have been much exposed to the attacks of pirates. No systematic measures of protection have ever been adopted or carried out by the East India Company, who have been content to leave the service to be performed by the Royal Navy. Her Majesty's Naval forces being liable to be called away to other duties, can only act at intervals; and hence for long periods the neighbouring seas have been left wholly or very slightly guarded and have at such times swarmed with pirates, to the great injury of the trade of this port.

"The Supreme Government of India has uniformly discouraged the local Government at Singapore from interfering with matters beyond the limits of the Island. The cultivation of friendly relations with Native States and Chiefs has been neglected, and the Government does not possess that influence in the Indian Archipelago which the interests of British commerce require, and which might have been acquired and maintained by a very slight exertion on the part of the Indian Government.

"Upon Singapore and Malacca being annexed to Prince of Wales' Island, the Recorder's Court established at the latter place was extended to the three stations, which were designated "The Settlements of Prince of Wales' Island, Singapore and Malacca." The Recorder resided at Prince of Wales' Island and made circuits to Singapore and Malacca twice in the year and at times even at longer intervals, principally with the view of discharging the Gaols, the civil suits at Singapore being nearly all tried and disposed of by the Governor or Resident Councillor, Civil Servants of the East India Company. In course of time the judicial business at Singapore increased largely, in consequence of its great commercial prosperity, and the officers of Government found that the discharge of their judicial functions interfered inconveniently with the performance of their other duties, while the community was dissatisfied at having the Law administered by unprofessional persons, at best very imperfectly acquainted with it. The Indian Government was besought to make those changes in the judicial system of the Settlement which had now become imperatively necessary. Much delay ensued, and some impracticable schemes were propounded, having for their principal object to dispense with professionally trained judges and to vest the administration of justice almost entirely in the local Officers of Government, Civil or Military servants of the East India Company, and at last the subject was postponed indefinitely. The inhabitants of Singapore, after much delay, petitioned both Houses of Parliament for redress, when two Recorders were assigned to the Straits, one of them being stationed at Singapore, with Malacca under his jurisdiction. Owing, however, to the long delay which had taken place, and the rapid increase in the wealth and population of Singapore, the judicial establishment that had been considered suitable ten years previously, and which was adopted in framing the new Charter, has been found very inadequate for the altered circumstances of the place, and the amount of judicial business has so much increased as to make it impossible for one Judge to dispose of it although sitting almost uninterruptedly in Court, from day to day, throughout the whole year.

" The native population of Singapore comprehends persons from all parts o the Continent of India, Arabia, the Indian Archipelago and China. In most instances, coming here solely for the prosecution of trade, or to acquire a competency, and without any intention or wish to become settlers for life, they do not feel that desire to conform to our institutions and laws which would no doubt arise were they bound to the place by family or other permanent ties. This is more peculiarly the case with the Chinese, who constitute the great bulk of the population. The Chinese residents are in most cases male adults, the females being in the proportion of one woman to eighteen men. Belonging chiefly to the lowest class, the Chinese immigrants are ignorant and turbulent, bringing with them from their own country those prejudices and feelings which animate their nation generally against foreigners. Here they find their secret societies and confederacies in full operation, and they fall into that system of self-government which, in this as in other Europeans Colonies to which the Chinese emigrate, is found to interfere so seriously with public order and the proper administration of justice. The principles on which these Societies are constituted and worked have a most baneful influence. They assume to themselves a jurisdiction extending even to life and death, and they exercise the great powers which their organization gives them, in hindering the constitutional administration of justice by shielding criminals and by suppressing and concealing evidence. The rivalries of hostile societies and clans give rise to disturbances and outrages, often of a very grave nature. To control such a population requires a firm and consistent though conciliatory course of action on the part of the Government. This has in a great measure been wanting in the Straits Settlements. At one time the attitude assumed by the officials is harsh and irritating; at another, finding or imagining themselves unable to control the Chinese, they have recourse to undignified compromises most damaging to their authority. For many years past the European inhabitants have urged upon the attention of Government the imperative necessity of measures being adopted for remedying this undesirable state of matters; they have suggested means by which the relations of Government with the Chinese population might be improved, and the effect of their peculiar habits and institutions in a great measure counteracted, without any violent interference with them; but such remonstrances and suggestions have been generally received with indifference, and sometimes without the slightest acknowledgment of their having been made.

" Although Singapore was established exclusively as a commercial emporium, yet from a very early period of its existence it has been used by the Indian Government as a station for the Convicts of Continental India; the felons sent here being those whose crimes are of the deepest dye and their period of transportation of a lengthened nature, frequently for life. Of late years, the number of such transported felons stationed at Singapore has been much increased, and your Petitioners are seriously apprehensive that it is the intention of the Government to make this Settlement a penal station on a large scale, and to send to it the worst and most dangerous of the criminals confined in the Indian Gaols. With such a large body of convicts there is no adequate provision for the protection of the life and property of the inhabitants. The convicts are only guarded by a few Sepoy troops who in courage are far inferior to the desperadoes they are set to watch over. The system of convict management and discipline has from the very first been of the most defective and loose nature. Large gangs of convicts are stationed in different parts of the island, in open lines, and with only native officers or peons (themselves convicts) to control them. They style themselves "servants of government" and their behaviour to the rural population is insolent and oppressive. Whatever may be the condition, morally or otherwise, of the native population, there can be little doubt that the presence of a large body of convicts, especially with such an imperfect state of discipline as that prevailing, must exert a decidedly injurious influence. Irrespective, however, of such considerations, your Petitioners entertain a strong feeling that a Settlement established and kept up as an Emporium of Trade should not be converted into a Penal Station for the felons of India. They earnestly desire to be freed from what they must ever consider the contamination arising from such a body of felons being placed amongst them.

"Your Petitioners therefore humbly pray, that your Honorable House will be pleased to adopt such measures as may be necessary for removing the Government of British India from the East India Company and substituting in its place the direct Government of Her Most Gracious Majesty the Queen; and further, that the Straits Settlements may be constituted a separate Government, directly under the Crown, and not, as at present, under a delegated authority in India.

In March, 1858, it was said that the Home Government had decided on the change, and to make the Settlement a Crown Colony, and the principal naval depot in the East. It was also reported that Sir James Brooke had been named as the first Governor of the Colony. This was, however, very premature, for it took nine years before the Transfer was carried out. The English Government had, at that time, a number of important matters in hand, while on the other hand Singapore was very little known or appreciated, and it was no doubt considered a very subordinate question which might very well stand over.

In the same month the Petition from Singapore was presented to the Houses of Parliament. Lord Albemarle, the elder brother of Admiral Sir Henry Keppel, was to have presented it in the House of Lords, but he was absent in Italy, and it was presented by Earl Granville. What he said on the occasion was not reported in the newspapers, owing no doubt to the crowd of what were thought much more important matters by the London daily papers. In the House of Commons the Petition was presented by Lord Bury, the eldest son of the Earl of Albemarle. The *Times* of 14th April contained a report from which the following is condensed.

"Lord Bury rose and said that the Straits Settlements were situated on the great highway of commerce between the east and the west, and the matter was one of national importance. He spoke of Sir Stamford Raffles having appreciated the valuable resources of Singapore and, after great trouble, having obtained leave to establish the Settlement, which in the course of a year had transferred to itself the trade before carried on at Penang. Singapore progressed most favourably under the East India Company, but when the trade of the Company with China ceased to be a monopoly it was consequently no longer a matter of importance to India whether Singapore continued to flourish or not. In proportion, however, as the interests of the East India Company in the place declined, it became a matter of national importance to England that its position should be maintained. The Straits Settlements were, in the strict sense of the word, Colonies; their population was not composed of conquered races but of bodies of men who had been attracted there by the security afforded by British rule. The trade had increased enormously, from £4,000,000 in 1840, to £15,000,000 in 1857. The Straits Settlements had properly no connection with India, they had ceased to be of any importance to that Empire since India had ceased to trade exclusively with China. In fact they appeared to be only regarded by the Indian Government as useful for a convict station, the whole of the convicts of Bombay, Madras and Bengal being sent there. The Company had wished to establish one uniform currency, and introduced the rupee and smaller Indian coins into the Straits, but great confusion had resulted. They had also attempted to impose tonnage dues upon shipping, and had only been stopped from inflicting this injustice by the remonstrances of the Home Government. All these things proved that the interests of the Settlements were much more Imperial than Indian, and would be better governed if they were brought immediately under the control of the Secretary of State for the Colonies. The population had no means of forwarding their views to head-quarters, and questions were decided entirely at variance with their feel- ings. Another point was that Singapore required protection against the aggressive policy of the Dutch, who prevented the native places from trading with the place and diverted their trade into Dutch ports.

" He said that since the Singapore petition had been sent home, all public works in the Straits Settlements had been stopped, because of the events which had happened in India, which was very hard as the Straits had nothing to do with India. These were the principal grounds for removing the Straits from the control of the East India Com- pany, and placing them directly under the authority of the Crown. Looking at the enormous progress they had made in a few years, the large European community there, and the peculiar position and advantages for trade, he hoped to hear from the Government a satis- factory answer, and moved for copies of the correspondence between Her Majesty's Government and the East India Company, in order that the House might have the advantage of listening to any discussion that might arise."

Mr. Baillie (the Secretary of the Board of Control of the East India Company) was free to confess, as the noble lord had stated, that the subject which he had brought under the notice of the House had not sufficiently occupied the attention of the Government. The fact was that they did not consider it necessary, at a time when the whole government of India was about to be discussed in the House, to deal with questions of detail respecting what must at present, at all events, be considered a portion of the Indian empire. Then, again, it would have been necessary, in taking this subject into consideration, to communicate with the home Government of India and the Governor-General; for, as the noble lord had stated, this Colony was one of the great penal stations for Indian convicts. With regard to the complaints made in the petition, he (Mr. Baillie) could not altogether admit their justice. It was alleged, first of all, that the Indian Government had made repeated attempts to impose duties on the trade of Singapore, which attempts had only been frustrated by appeals to the home authorities. Now, the petitioners could hardly complain that their interests were unattended to, when their grievances had thus been redressed. Again, with regard to the complaints about their currency, it was very natural that the Governor-General should desire to establish a uniform currency throughout the whole of the territories subject to his authority. But, after the complaints made at Singapore, this grievance also was redressed, and the currency which had been imposed on the Colony was changed back to the dollar currency. He thought that this, therefore, did not give the petitioners a right to complain. The only just ground of complaint which, in his opinion, those colonists could urge, was that Singapore had been made a penal settlement, and that no doubt was a complaint which was well entitled to consideration. (Hear, hear). It should, however, be borne in mind that Singapore had been made a penal settlement before it had risen to its present importance, and that the prosperity which it now enjoyed was to no small extent the result of convict labour. But, although he was prepared to admit that the complaint to which he had just adverted was one which was deserving of notice, he could by no means concur in the justice of the statement which had been made by the noble lord, to the effect that the expenses connected with the maintenance of the military establishment at Singapore were entirely defrayed by the colonists. Such was by no means the case, and he might add that the military defences of the colony involved a question of the utmost importance for the consideration of the Government; because, if Singapore were to become a Crown Colony this country would have to take upon itself the onus of defraying the charge for its military defence, a charge which could not be estimated at a less sum than £300,000 per annum. The House would recollect that at the commencement of the Chinese War great excitement prevailed in Singapore, inasmuch as there were 40,000 or 50,000 Chinese at the time in the Colony. It had, therefore, been deemed expedient to increase to a considerable extent its military defences, and he believed that there were at the present moment no less than three regiments stationed in the Settlement. At no period, indeed, could its garrison, in his opinion, be estimated at less than two regiments and a battery of artillery, the maintenance of which would cost this country nearly £300,000 per annum at the very lowest calculation; for that was an amount of expenditure which could not be thrown upon the resources of the colony itself, inasmuch as its revenue was barely sufficient to defray its ordinary civil expenditure and to admit of its furnishing £15,000 a year towards the outlay for military purposes. The subject, therefore, was one which was well worthy of serious consideration, and before Parliament proceeded to take any active steps with respect to it, it would do well, he thought, to bear in mind that the commerce of Singapore had within the last six years increased at least 75 per cent., a fact which afforded the best evidence of the prosperity of the Colony. (Hear). Under these circumstances he trusted that the noble lord would be satisfied with the explanation which he had given in reference to a subject which had not as yet been brought under the special consideration of the Government, and which, when the future Government of India was settled, might at any time press itself upon their attention. (Hear, hear).

Mr. Horsman (who at one time had large sugar plantations at Province Wellesley) said that, from all the information which he had obtained upon the subject, the case of Singapore appeared to him to be one of those instances in which a want of sympathy with the position of the inhabitants of our foreign settlements was exhibited, which was by no means creditable to the Legislature. (Hear, hear). He believed that history furnished no record of the advance in prosperity of a colony more rapid than was that of Singapore. Forty years ago it had been the haunt of pirates, and one of the most lawless districts which could well be conceived. It had within that period, however, risen to the possession of a trade of £10,000,000 *per annum*, a trade which had, as had been stated by the Honorable gentleman who had just spoken, increased 75 per cent. during the last six years. Now, the obstacles which had opposed themselves in the way of that remarkable progress had been overcome despite of the action of the Government of this country, and although the Honorable gentleman opposite seemed to think that nothing was more natural than that the Governor-General of India should deem the circulating medium of that country suitable to Singapore, the consequence had been that that step had led to the complete disturbance of the commerce of the colony. But a measure much more objectionable was that which had converted a small, but active and thriving, colony into a penal settlement for the very worst class of criminals in India, and imperilled its security by intrusting the guardianship of those criminals to a regiment of Sepoys. The real question for the consideration of the House was, what had Singapore to do with India? Why should that colony be governed in India? (Hear, hear). It carried on a larger trade with China than with India, and was inhabited by thousands of Chinese. As well, therefore, might Ceylon or Hongkong be placed under the Government of India (hear, hear), instead of under the control of the Colonial Office. The question was one which he thought was well worthy of the consideration of the Government, and he trust it would receive at their hands that degree of attention to which it was entitled.

Sir J. Elphinstone (the Member for Portsmouth) said, as one possessing some knowledge of Singapore, he wished to say a few words upon the occasion. He certainly had never until now heard any suggestion that Singapore should be placed under the control of the Colonial Office, and he was not at present prepared to give an opinion on the point. He had been at Singapore in 1820, when the Settlement was just formed. At that time it was an island inhabited only by a few Malay fishermen, but, being singularly well adapted by its position to intercept the whole trade of the Eastern Archipelago, Sir Stamford Raffles, one of the ablest men who ever visited the East, recommended its settlement. In consequence of its advantageous position the progress of the Settlement had been extraordinarily rapid, and it was now a vast entrepot for the commerce of that part of the world. At first it was necessary to send thither convicts to perform public works, and a very small military force was required to guard them; but as the Settlement increased in importance the elements of disorder increased likewise, for the population which resorted to Singapore was drawn from the most lawless and savage of eastern races; the Bugis, the Sarawak Dyaks, the Syaks, inhabitants of Sumatra, and other wild races, furnished their quota to the population of Singapore. In addition, however, there was a large Chinese population who resorted to the Settlement in order to make money, with which to return to China. Those men came unaccompanied by women, and they associated with the native women of the country, from which connection had sprung a race called Kling, a most disorderly people. It had become necessary to increase the military force to preserve order among those people, and not on account of the convict population in the Settlement, of whom he had never heard any complaints made, but from whom, on the contrary, the residents usually selected their domestic servants. (A laugh.) He once knew a lady, the wife of an Officer in high position, who told him she always selected her servants from that class, and upon his asking whether she preferred thieves or murderers for service in her nursery, replied that she always chose murderers (great laughter), their crimes having been generally committed from motives of jealousy, and, those motives ceasing, they were very desirable servants. He had never heard that the convicts were at all disagreeable to the residents in the Settlement, but he knew they were useful in constructing roads, bridges, and other public works, which otherwise would not be performed. He was inclined to agree with the Secretary to the Board of Control that it would be a great burden for this country to take upon itself the charge of maintaining peace among that mixed and lawless population. He had no doubt there might be defects in the management of the Straits Settlements, but there was one insuperable obstacle to the colonization of the island of Singapore, and that was the immense number of tigers which swam over from the opposite shore, from which Singapore was separated only by a small stream. The opposite coast was an impenetrable jungle tenanted by vast numbers of tigers, more bold and ferocious than any to be found in other parts of India; and scarcely a day passed without some native being carried off bodily by those animals. That circumstance operated to prevent the cultivation of spice and sugar, for which otherwise the country was excellently adapted.

Mr. Mangles (the Member for Guildford, a Director of the East India Company) did not wish on the part of the East India Company to put forth a decided claim to the control over the Straits Settlements, but he wished to correct some statements which were contained in a pamphlet written by an esteemed friend, Mr. John Crawfurd, the author of " Our Eastern Archipelago." In that pamphlet it was stated that the revenue of the three Straits Settlements, Malacca, Penang and Singapore, were burdened with charges which were never imposed upon the local revenues of any colony, and that out of it were defrayed the expenses of the military and naval services, and also for the maintenance of transported felons from Madras, Bombay and Bengal. The fact, however, was that the charge for the convicts was borne by the presidencies whence they were sent, all the military and naval expenses were also defrayed by India. (Hear, hear.) The gross revenues of the Straits

Settlements in 1855-6 was £97,904, the local charges, independent of the cost for military and naval purposes was £74,753, leaving only a balance of £23,151 to meet those expenses. The right Honorable member for Stroud had stated that the settlement of Singapore was exposed to danger from the convicts, but the last speaker had shown how unfounded was the apprehension. The real danger, and a most serious one it was, arose from the large Chinese population in the Straits Settlements, and he would warn the Honorable gentleman opposite and the House, that unless strong measures were taken, such as the Government of India were now considering, with respect to the Chinese population and their secret societies, the safety of those settlements would be greatly jeopardized. (Hear, hear). He did not know that the control of these settlements was of great importance to the Indian Government, especially as having lately taken possession of the Andaman Islands, they were no longer needed as a depot for their convicts, but he would advise the Government not to deal with this matter without consulting the Governor-General. If that officer should see no objection to the change, he did not know that the East India Company would be at all unwilling to part with its control over those settlements.

The motion for the production of correspondence was then agreed to.

The London *Times* thus remarked on the discussion :—" The leading idea of the speakers who took part in the discussion seemed to be that the authority over Singapore should be entirely taken away from the Government of India, and that it should be brought directly under the authority of the Colonial Office. What has Singapore to do with India? It carries on a larger trade with China than with India. The true idea of the settlement, colony, or by whatever name it may be called, is as the centre and citadel of British power in the Eastern Seas, and the great house of call between Great Britain and China. It is from this point chiefly that the ceaseless intrigues of the Dutch to exclude us altogether from the Indian Archipelago can be defeated. With the Straits of Malacca and the North-Western coast of Borneo in our possession, as long as we retain our naval supremacy, we could be secure of our communication with China."

There was a long article on the subject in the London *Examiner* of 24th April, which spoke of Lord Bury's speech as abundant in matter and lucid in manner, and ably supported by Mr. Horsman, but had been answered by orations which had neither of these qualities. Mr. Baillie had mistated the force of Sepoys in the Straits at more than seven times the actual garrison. The paper spoke of Sir J. Elphinstone as having outdone the Secretary of Control by still more extravagant statements. That honourable member, it said, had visited Singapore on a trading voyage the year after the place was founded, and laughed at all his statements about the population of Singapore consisting of the most lawless and savage of the Eastern races, the convicts, the *Syaks* of Sumatra, the race called Klings, and the tigers. It said that Mr. Mangles was more rational, as he was a man of ability and knowledge, but he was Chairman of the East India Directors, who were sure to find excuses.

The *Singapore Free Press* said :—"Straits matters begin to attract considerable attention and it is hoped that the subject will not be allowed to rest during the discussion of the change in the Indian Government, with which it is bound up, like a pamphlet on free trade or colonization, at the end of a huge volume on the annexation of Oude. The Singapore petition was presented to the House, and the views of the petitioners were warmly seconded by many speakers, but the majority know nothing, and care less, if possible, about the " Straits,". thinking perhaps for the first hour or so that the island of Perim and those " Straits" are in question, while some members exhibited all the characteristics of military heroes two or three centuries ago, and were not ashamed to argue that—as Singapore was originally a penal Settlement, and could in no way be looked upon as a colony, that as the large majority of the residents were aliens and the place was a mere resort for money-making traders, the claim to be considered separate from India was untenable. Such stuff as this is however being well answered out of doors. Sir James Brooke and Admiral Keppel dined the other day at Manchester, at a magnificent entertainment in their honor, when Sir James put the case in a very forcible manner. The *Times* too has taken up the matter very warmly and there is now a chance that our legislators, and the public, will learn something about the Indian Archipelago, and English, Dutch, Chinese and other interests. The Chinese war and the Indian rebellion have heated the iron, and it remains for those interested in the Straits Settlements, and in British commerce in the East, to hammer away incessantly until they obtain by clamour, if necessary, what is refused to reasoning."

The *Free Press* of 10th June, 1858, contained a copy of parts of a long memorandum drawn up by Mr. Crawfurd and circulated amongst Members of Parliament and others taking an interest in the Straits. It is too long to print here, and gave a number of statistics, which are mostly to be found elsewhere in this book, regarding the Settlements, their inhabitants, trade, and revenue. He showed that the revenue of the Straits, if taken per head of population, exceeded that of Continental India as 43 to 30, and that if the revenue were not burdened with military charges which were not made against the local revenue in any of the British Colonies, there would be a surplus at Singapore of £23,529, at Malacca of £3,840, and at Penang of £4,448.

Lord Canning, in a remarkably able minute on the proposed Transfer, written in November, 1859, said :—"It must not be overlooked that the revenues of the Settlement have been steadily increasing, and that while the receipts have risen from 873,692 rupees in 1854-55, to 1,323,368 rupees in 1858-59, (being an increase of 51 per cent. in four years) the disbursements for civil charges, not including the cost of the foreign convicts, have in the same interval risen from 722,107 rupees to 821,913, being an increase of 14 per cent. only. As there is no reason why the civil charges of the Settlement should be further increased, it may be anticipated that if peace should happily be maintained between England and the great European powers, the revenues of the Straits Settlements will in no very long time equal their full charges, military as well as civil. But even if it prove otherwise, and if it should be necessary for England to make some sacrifice in this respect, I hold a clear opinion that it ought to be made in justice alike to the Settlements and to India.

In another passage Lord Canning wrote :—" It is not easy to see any sound objection to the proposed transfer to the Colonial Office. Mr. Blundell, the late Governor, who was consulted, has urged none to which I can attach weight. He thinks that the native community, more particularly the Chinese, might, when informed of the change, be seized with suspicion and alarm. It is not apparent, however, why this should be the consequence of a change which would be attended, in the first place at all events, with no actual alteration of things in the Settlement itself. But even if Mr. Blundell's opinion be well founded, nothing beyond a little temporary inconvenience need be apprehended, for the Chinese are a very practical people, bent upon making money, and very indifferent to matters in which this is not concerned. As such, they are not likely to contend seriously or for long with a fancied grievance in which no substance or reality will be perceptible to themselves.

" But whether the main system of Government be altered or not, that under which officers are provided for service in the Straits is, so far as civil administration is concerned, a positive evil, which ought in any case to be remedied. Indian officers have no opportunities of acquiring experience of the habits or the language of either Malays or Chinese, and accordingly, when officers are sent to the Straits, they have every thing to learn. The Government of India is unable to keep a close watch upon their efficiency ; the field is so narrow as to afford little or no room to the Governor of the Settlements, for exercising a power of selection in recommending to a vacant office ; and there is consequently so complete an absence of stimulus to exertion, that it may well be doubted whether Indian civil officers sent to the Straits ever become thoroughly well qualified for, or heartily interested in the duties they have to discharge.

" The character of the Chinese, the most important and at times a very unmanageable part of the population of the Straits Settlements, is quite different from that of any people with which Indian officers have to deal. Democratic in spite of the outward form of their own government, enterprising and persevering, the Chinese are imbued with a strong tendency to self government, and are, therefore, the very opposite of our Indian fellow subjects. I am satisfied that if the Straits Settlements are to remain under the control of the Indian Government, it will be absolutely necessary to devise a plan, by which the persons employed in administering the civil government shall receive a special training ; and that without this the Indian Government cannot do justice to these Settlements."

And further on :—" Another very important point to be considered is the defence of the Straits Settlements, for which, in the event of danger from any formidable enemy, the Government of India could not with justice be made answerable. The past security which these settlements have enjoyed affords no guarantee of our capacity to defend them, for we have not been at war with any great power in these seas since the Government of India held the Settlement. It is necessary, of course, that Singapore should always be garrisoned, and this can be done by India in ordinary time without difficulty; but it is certain that the Settlements, if threatened with external danger, must be protected by the naval strength of Great Britain. It may be said that this is in a great degree true of India itself. So it is, but with this material difference, that whereas our Indian empire cannot, so long as we are strong in the interior of it, suffer from the enemy's ships anything worse than temporary insult and the ravage of its ports (very few, considering the extent of its seaboard), our settlement in the Straits might be wrested from us altogether if, even for a short time, a hostile fleet were stronger than our own in those waters."

The *Singapore Free Press* in May, 1864, in referring to Lord Canning's minute, said:—"We hope the Home Authorities may be able to understand thoroughly the state of the case, and that the exigencies of Singapore and the other Straits Settlements do not require any very costly military force. In the event of the Transfer, a man-of-war would probably be stationed in the Straits, and in the event of any disturbance with the Native States or a serious riot in the Settlements, the sailors would form the best force."

In January, 1859, that newspaper said that it was understood that no objection existed on the part of the Governor-General of India to the Transfer, and that the question was so far decided that only the details of the arrangements required to be settled and to receive the sanction of Parliament.

In the meantime a feeling had been gaining ground amongst some of the European residents in Singapore, that it might be more advantageous for the Settlements to be placed under the management of the Secretary of State for India, rather than under the Secretary for the Colonies. The chief reason formerly for desiring a change had been the interminable delay which arose from the multiplicity of channels through which representations from the Straits had to pass, before they found their way to the President of the Board of Control. This objection, it was suggested, would still to a great degree exist were the Straits Settlements to remain subordinate to the Government of India, but that it would be done away with, were they placed in direct relation with the Secretary of State for India, and furnished with a constitution which should embrace legislative powers. The petitions sent from Singapore to Parliament in October, 1857, had not contained a specific request to be placed under the Colonial Office, but only prayed "that the Straits Settlements may be constituted a separate Government, directly under the Crown, and not, as at present, under a delegated authority in India." The complete change in the whole form of the Indian Government which had since taken place, was not at that time anticipated, and as matters stood in January, 1859, it was said that it would not be inconsistent with the prayer of the petitions of 1857, to request that the Straits Government should be subordinated to the Secretary of State for India.

Whether such a course would be advisable was said by others to be very doubtful. The Secretary of State for India, for years to come, would find in the reorganization of the Indian Government, finances and army, sufficient matters to engross all his time and attention, and it was questionable whether he would be disposed to give much care to the concerns of the Straits Settlements. The Colonial Office, on the other hand, although at first sight it might appear to have an immense deal of business to attend to, had now comparatively little to do in the case of Canada, Australia, the Cape of Good Hope, &c., where the whole of their internal management was left to the Colonies themsèlves.

At one time a petition was drawn up to petition Parliament that the Straits should be disjoined from India and placed under the direct management of the Secretary of State for India, and that the Government of the Colony should have power to make laws and regulations for the government of the inhabitants. After a few signatures had been affixed to it, it was abandoned, and the general opinion was again in favour of a connection with the Colonial Office.

In February, 1859, the mail brought a report that Her Majesty's Government had finally decided on the transfer of the Straits Settlements to the Colonial Office, and that a Bill for the severance of their connection with India, and the creation of a separate colony would be immediately passed through both Houses of Parliament with as little delay as possible. It was also rumoured that the higher offices of Government, at present filled by officers of the Indian Army, would be occupied by gentlemen sent from England, the present incumbents returning to their respective presidencies.

It was said at this time that the East India Company had, uniformly discouraged, from a want of proper appreciation of the subject, the local Government of Singapore from dealing with any matters beyond the limits of the island. The cultivation of friendly relations with the neighbouring native countries had been neglected, and the Government did not possess the influence in the Archipelago which the interests of British Commerce required, and which might have been easily gained by a very slight exertion on the part of the Indian Government, and it was hoped that the transfer to the Colonial Office might lead to more attention being given to the subject.

The intention of Raffles in founding Singapore was to establish such an influence in the Archipelago, as would compensate for the return of Java and the other Dutch possessions. But since their restoration the Dutch had perseveringly and energetically applied themselves to the accomplishment of their long cherished design of extending their rule over the whole of the Indian Archipelago. They had acquired the Moluccas, the Key and the Arru Islands, and (on maps at least) claimed the greater part of New Guinea; and reduced Bali, Lombok, and Sumbawa to the rank of feudatories; claimed jurisdiction over the greater part of Borneo, and been very active at Jambi, Siak and other places in Sumatra. The Spaniards in a much smaller way, had followed this example, seized Sulo and adjacent islands, and formed a station on Palawan and elsewhere close to the coast of Borneo. The French were casting longing eyes at this part of the world, and having failed at Basilan in the Sulo Archipelago, to which place they had sent an expedition, referred to on page 468, they were laying the foundation of an extensive and important colony, having since 1857 carried on a troublesome contest with Cochin-China, and at last taken possession of Saigon.

It was added, to look much nearer home, that no systematic attempt had been made by the East India Company to carry out the views regarding the States in the Malay Peninsula alluded to in the address of Sir Stamford Raffles on the 1st April, 1823, when he contemplated founding the Institution. No systematic attempt had been made to keep up a friendly intercourse with the chiefs of the States on the Peninsula, and their power instead of becoming stronger, as the result of the education Raffles has wished to provide for their sons and the higher order of natives, had gradually become weaker, and confusion and misgovernment were the result.

During the course of 1860 it was known from England that Mr. Blundell, the late Governor of the Straits had written against the scheme, but Lord Canning had strongly recommended it, and his views had been adopted. Various reports reached Singapore regarding the matter. At one time it was assserted that Sir George Clerk, the Permanent Under-Secretary of the India Department would initiate the changes, with the appointment of Governor-General of Her Majesty's Insular Possessions in the Eastern Seas. Sir George Clerk, however, accepted the offer of Governor of Bombay.

The Colonial Office was making enquiries on various points. Among other things the Duke of Newcastle, the Secretary of State for the Colonies, enquired about the propriety of licensing gambling shops. Several of the old Straits residents in London expressed an opinion favourable to a Farm, chiefly because they thought that controlled and open gaming was better than clandestine, and to abolish gambling in such a population was an impossibility.

On 16th June, 1860, two Members of Parliament, Mr. Gregson, the member for Lancaster and Chairman of the East India and China Association, and Mr. Buchanan, with Messrs John Crawfurd, Alexander Guthrie, and James Guthrie, waited upon the Duke of Newcastle, and he received their suggestions very favourably.

Afterwards it was stated that the large sums required for the fortifications in progress at Singapore, repayment of which was claimed by the Secretary of State for India, prevented the Ministers proceeding with the Transfer, as in the state of the Finances they were averse to go to the House of Commons and ask a vote for the necessary expenditure. At a later date it was reported that the matter was proceeding, that a department of the Colonial Office had been assigned to Straits affairs, and that the Transfer would certainly be accomplished in 1861.

A public meeting was held in the Exchange-rooms on Wednesday, 22nd May, 1861, to consider important matters connected with the proposed Transfer. Mr. W. H. Read was called to the chair, and explained at considerable length the topics which would be brought forward. The following resolutions were then passed :—

Proposed by J. J. Greenshields, seconded by R. MacNeil :—
1. That it is the opinion of this meeting that the revenues of the Straits Settlements are sufficient to meet all legitimate expenses.

Proposed by W. Paterson, seconded by R. C. Woods—2. That the greatly increased expenditure for military purposes, entailed by the extensive system of fortifications now in progress, should not be borne by these Settlements, as it is undertaken for Imperial and not local interests.

Proposed by José d'Almeida, seconded by C. H. Harrison :—
3. That the surplus revenue, exclusive of military outlay, estimated at £ 50,600, is more than sufficient to defray the cost of a local corps of 1,200 men, which is considered ample to meet all the requirements of these settlements.

Proposed by R. C. Woods, seconded by A. E. Schmidt:—4. That it would prove injurious to British interests in these seas that the Governor of the Straits Settlements should also hold the appointments of H. M. Commissioner and Superintendent of Trade in the Eastern Archipelago.

Proposed by J. d'Almeida, seconded by R. MacNeil:—5. That a Committee composed of Messrs. W. H. Read, J. J. Greenshields, W. Paterson, R. C. Woods, and C. H. Harrison, be appointed to carry out these resolutions.

Notwithstanding the most persevering efforts of the friends of Singapore in London, the Transfer could not be accomplished before the adjournment of Parliament in August, 1861. The Officials more immediately concerned in the matter were anxious to facilitate it. The India Office was willing to part with the Settlements, and the Colonial Office to receive them, but the expense of the fortifications, on which India insisted, stood in the way. Mr. Gladstone, who delayed bringing the matter forward, perhaps saved himself a defeat in the House, for after a decisive report which had been made by a Committee on general colonial military expenditure, there did not seem much chance of a vote being carried for military works at Singapore. That Committee had fully supported, as applicable to many of the Colonies, the views expressed for many years in Singapore, that the principal mode of defence should be naval, and that it was inexpedient, if not impracticable to rely upon land works, as Fort Canning and Fort Fullerton would not protect the town from an attack by sea, and the probable result of their attempting to annoy a hostile fleet would be the destruction of the town.

The fortifications that were then referred to must not be confused with the forts of the present day. Fort Canning had seven 68-pr. guns, eight 8-inch shell guns, and two 13-inch mortars, with a few 14-pr. carronades, at a height of about 200 feet, on the hill over a quarter of a mile from the beach. Fort Fullerton was on the beach, with nine 68-pr. guns and one mortar. It began to be dismantled in 1865, as it was then admitted that it would draw the fire upon the most richly stored warehouses in the place. Fort Palmer was a small earthwork overlooking the eastern entrance to Keppel Harbour, and had five 56-pr. guns. Fort Faber was also an earthwork, halfway up Mount Faber, overlooking Keppel Harbour, with two 56-pr. guns, and two mortars on the top of the hill.

The total number of guns in the forts was thirty-six. The distance of the guns at Fort Canning from the beach put them at a great disadvantage against an enemy's ships at sea, and both that and Fort Fullerton would have drawn the fire right upon the centre of the town, while the two small works at Mount Palmer and Mount

Faber were of very little use. The military expenditure was, in consequence, regarded by the mercantile community as very unsatisfactory, and it swallowed up in 1863 nearly one half of the revenue.

The present defences (commenced about 1885) of New Harbour, and to a considerable extent of the Roads, were not then in contemplation. It was thought in those days, with much reason, that the money expended on what turned out to be obsolete and practically useless forts should have been spent on the formation of a dock and other works requisite to make it a first class naval station.

A memorandum, dated 21st April, 1862, was sent by Mr. John Crawfurd to the Colonial and India Offices, and the Chancellor of the Exchequer, &c., in order to shew that the revenue was amply sufficient to cover the expenditure, and that a large military force was not required for the internal safety of the Settlement, while it would be comparatively useless against an external enemy.

He said the public revenue, not including that of the Municipality, according to the official returns of 1860-61 were

Singapore...	...	...	£ 96,568
Penang ...	...	...	36,776
Malacca ...	...	...	16,454
			£ 149,798

and it steadily increased year by year, having been nearly £20,000 more than in the year preceding. The total revenue, on a computed population of 225,000 gave a rate of taxation of over 16s. a head, which was double the rate of any part of India, and higher than any of the Queen's fifty colonies, the more flourishing Australian ones excepted. After deducting the expenditure there was a balance for military purposes of £33,070; but among the civil charges of Singapore had been included £30,000, contributed towards the building of expensive barracks [Tanglin] for European troops, which had not been sent; so that the actual balance available for military purposes was £63,070, a sum quite adequate in his opinion for the payment of any garrison necessary for the safety of the Colony, which was only capable of effectual defence by a naval force.

It is remarkable that Mr. Crawfurd here named the very sum (£63,000) that was, after much controversy, not always of a very peaceable nature, settled as a fair proportion of military contribution by the Colony nearly thirty years later.

The memorandum went on to say that the interests of the Straits would be better understood in England than in India, while England had a much greater interest in them than India had.

A public meeting was held in the Town Hall on the 17th July, 1862, and W. H. Read proposed, seconded by C. H. Harrison :—"That the interests of Great Britain, both political and commercial are so intimately connected with the security of these settlements, that their transfer from the Indian to the Colonial Office is an imperative necessity."

Proposed by J. J. Greenshields, seconded by W. Mactaggart:—"That the present attempt to impose an objectionable tax upon these Settlements, notwithstanding repeated and urgent remonstrances on the part of the inhabitants forms a just ground for a renewal of their appeal to have the Straits Settlements transferred from Bengal and placed under the Colonial Department."

Proposed by Joaquim d'Almeida, seconded by W. Paterson:— "That Petitions be forwarded to Parliament, praying for the immediate transfer of the management of the Straits Settlements from the Government of India to the Colonial Office."

It was then proposed by J. J. Greenshields and seconded by Dr. Scott:—"That the following gentlemen form a Committee to carry out the foregoing resolution:— Messrs. W. H. Read, Abraham Logan, Joaquim d'Almeida, William Paterson, and William Mactaggart"; to which the name of Mr. Greenshields was added.

In April, 1863, a deputation of gentlemen interested in Singapore had an interview with Sir Charles Wood, the Secretary of State for India, which was not very satisfactory, as he raised questions about a harbour-master and establishment, pointed out the kind of tax that seemed to him most suitable for paying it, and insisted that the proposal had come, in the first instance, from the Chamber of Commerce in Singapore. This was not correct, as was shown in the next year, when the question cropped up again in the House of Commons.

On the 8th May, 1863, a number of gentlemen connected with the Straits waited upon the Duke of Newcastle, on the subject of the transfer of the management of the Settlement from the Government of India to the Colonial Office. The deputation consisted of Messrs. S. Gregson, M. P., W. Buchanan, M. P., J. Crawfurd, A. Guthrie, J. Guthrie, E. Boustead, L. Fraser, G. G. Nicol and F. Richardson. His Grace expressed his readiness to take charge of the Settlement, but said that it would be necessary to have the consent of the Treasury. The improved financial prospects of the Settlement were pointed out, and the Duke put a number of questions regarding different items of the expenditure which were answered by the members of the deputation, and the explanations appeared to be satisfactory. The courtesy of the Duke and his manner of discussing matters with the deputation was said to have offered a strong contrast to the demeanour of his colleague the Secretary of State for India.

On 15th October, 1863, the *Singapore Free Press* said :— " From all accounts, the arrangements regarding the transfer of the Settlement to the Colonial Office are proceeding satisfactorily and there appears every prospect of the measure being carried through early next year. The statements which have been submitted, official and otherwise, have given sufficient evidence that the revenue of the Settlements will be fully adequate to meet all ordinary expenditure, and the only hitch which is likely to occur is in regard to the Tanglin Barracks, on which, it would appear, it is reported some £20,000 will still require to be spent."

On 4th December, 1863, Sir Hercules Robinson, the Governor of Hongkong, on his way from home in the P. & O. mail to China, was directed to remain in Singapore, and in conjunction with the Governor and other officials to report upon certain points on which more information was thought desirable. The points in question were supposed to be financial. The most important one being whether the revenue was, or could be made, equal to the expenditure, so as to prevent the necessity of the Home Government applying to Parliament for a vote in aid of the Straits Revenue. Colonel Freeth of the Royal Engineers, stationed in Ceylon, had also received orders from England to proceed to Singapore. The military element in the Commission was predominant, Sir Hercules Robinson being the only civilian upon it.

The *Free Press* said "We trust this will not lead to the military force for the Settlement being fixed on such a scale as to swamp the transfer. The present force is sufficiently large and its expense might be materially diminished without impairing its efficiency. There is no necessity for a Brigadier, or a Colonel of Artillery, to command three companies. The Chief Engineer is an appointment which might also be dispensed with, as there is no part of his duties which could not be equally well discharged by the Executive Officers in the Straits, and if it is necessary that there should be a responsible chief of the Public Works Department the Executive Officer at Singapore could easily combine that duty with his own."

On 11th December, 1863, a meeting was held in the Town Hall, and a pamphlet says that, among others, there were present :—

Joaquim d'Almeida	...	J. d'Almeida & Sons.
Gilbert Angus	...	Auctioneer
John Armstrong	...	George Armstrong & Co.
John Simons Atchison	...	Advocate and Solicitor
P. W. Auchincloss	...	Borneo Co., Limited
John Bennett	...	Executive Engineer
Alfred George Farquhar Bernard		Auctioneer
James Berwick	...	Accountant, Oriental Bank
Richard Brennand	...	Merchant
Byramjee Pestonjee	...	Parsee Merchant
John Cameron	...	Proprietor *Straits Times*
Francis D. Cobb	...	Hutchinson & Co.
Thomas Owen Crane	...	Land Proprietor
James Guthrie Davidson	...	Woods & Davidson
Thomas Dunman	...	Commissioner of Police
William Renshaw George	...	in Jozé d'Almeida & Sons.
Henry Hewetson	...	Head Clerk, Land Office
Parsick Joaquim	...	Stephens & Joaquim
A. Letham	...	in Dahlmann & Co.
Matthew Little	...	John Little & Co.
W. Manford	...	in Wm. Spottiswoode & Co.
Arnold Otto Meyer	...	Behn, Meyer & Co.
Catchick Moses	...	Sarkies & Moses
James Murray	..	Syme & Co.
John Purvis	...	John Purvis & Son
Otto Rheiner	...	Puttfarcken, Rheiner & Co.
David Rodger	...	Martin Dyce & Co.
Dr. J. Scott	...	Medical Practitioner
Thomas Scott	..	Guthrie & Co.
John S. Scrymgeour	...	Manager, Oriental Bank.

Charles Smith Sherwood	...	Manager, Chartered Bank
Seah Eu Chin	...	Chinese Merchant
A. Velge	...	in Jozé d'Almeida & Sons.
Ernest Theodore Wagner	...	Busing Schroder & Co.
James Watson	...	Guthrie & Co.
J. J. Winton	...	Assistant, Mercantile Bank.
Robert Carr Woods	...	Woods & Davidson

Mr. Joaquim d'Almeida was in the Chair, and a Committee consisting of himself, Dr. Little, Messrs. Abraham Logan, H. M. Simons, A. O. Meyer, Thomas Scott, John Cameron and R. C. Woods, was appointed for the purpose of collecting information regarding the finances, resources, and commerce of the Straits Settlements, and, if expedient, to put themselves in communication with the Commissioners appointed by Her Majesty's Government to report upon the proposed transfer.

A long report, dated 9th January, 1864, was drawn up, and was published in pamphlet form, reiterating matters of complaint that have already been referred to in this book, and setting out a number of tables of statistics to shew that there was an excess of receipts over the expenses of the Settlement, and ending by saying, "While the freedom of its trade remains intact, uninterfered with by injudicious legislation or the introduction of unwholesome restrictions, its prosperity must be progressive, and its inhabitants be as happy as they are loyal and enterprising."

In June, 1864, a new obstacle arose in a demand by Sir Charles Wood that the Straits should take upon itself the whole of the local debt, on the ground that the Indian Government had consented to forego any claim for the money laid out in late years for public works. The local debt was mainly composed of money ordered by the Court to be invested by the Accountant General, and consisted of the property of minors and suitors. Instead of being invested in Indian public loans, it had been paid into the local treasuries on loan certificates, bearing interest at four per cent. and withdrawable on three months' notice. The local revenues were unable to meet the very heavy charges for military and convicts, and, for the convenience of Government in order to avoid drawing on India, this money of the Court was applied to the expenditure. It was, therefore, the debt of the Indian Government, and so Sir Hercules Robinson considered it.

The Chancellor of the Exchequer very reasonably objected to the Straits being saddled with a loan that would absorb for its interest the whole of the surplus revenue shown in the estimates of the Straits.

This trouble was got over, and soon afterwards the Treasury, the War Office, the India Office, and the Colonial Office were at last agreed on all details. A deputation of merchants of the Straits accompanied by Mr. Gregson, the member for Lancaster and Chairman of the East India and China Association, and by Mr. John Crawfurd, had an interview with Mr. Cardwell, the Secretary of State for the Colonies. They were as courteously received by Mr. Cardwell as by the Duke of Newcastle, and that was saying a great deal. It appeared that the Colonial Office was ready to take

charge of the Settlements at once: nor, indeed, did there seem to
be any difficulties in any other department, those that existed at the
Treasury and War Office having been overcome. An Act of Parliament of a few clauses was, however, necessary: and as, considering
the lateness of the season, there would be some difficulty in getting
it through the House of Commons during that sessions, the transfer
had to be delayed until the commencement of the next.

Further difficulties, however, occurred, and in the debate in the
House of Commons on the India Budget on the 21st July, 1864, Sir
J. Elphinstone said, "He understood an important alteration was to
take place with regard to the Straits Settlements, and he wished to
know what it was to consist of. When Sir Stamford Raffles established
the colony of Singapore in 1819, it was guaranteed as a free port. He
(Sir J. Elphinstone) was there in the year 1820, and he had been there
occasionally during the next 17 years. A more extraordinary increase
in any port had never occurred, except in some of the mushroom places
in America, than what had taken place at Singapore. The whole of
the trade of the Eastern Archipelago had been centred in that port,
and the progress of the colony had arisen from its immunity from all
port charges. He understood it was the design of the Indian Government to introduce port regulations for Singapore. Was that so? If
so, it would be most prejudicial." Sir Charles Wood replied, "That
no alteration in the position of Singapore was intended: but questions
had been raised by the Singapore Chamber of Commerce as to harbour
masters and also as to moorings, and it was stated that no objection
would be made to the levying of some small duty by the Indian Government if those alterations were made."

Mr. W. H. Read, who was Chairman of the Chamber of Commerce
at the time the correspondence took place between Government and the
Chamber on the subject, exposed in the letter we quote below, the
inaccuracy of Sir Charles Wood's statement. It is almost unnecessary
to state that the Chamber uniformly opposed the proposal to levy port
dues in the Straits Settlements, and in 1863 in consequence of Sir
Charles Wood having made a similar statement to that which he
had repeated in the House of Commons, the Chamber had addressed a
letter to the local Government, explaining the circumstances out of
which it was conceived Sir Charles Wood's misconception had arisen
and protesting strongly against the levy of port dues. It was requested
that this letter should be brought to Sir Charles Wood's notice, and it
no doubt was so, but the Secretary of State for India seemed to be
one of those unreasonable persons, who when they once make an assertion stick to it, in spite of all explanations, and however clearly it may
be shown to have been founded on mistaken grounds. Fortunately for
Singapore the Supreme Government of India was more amenable to
reason, and abandoned all intention of making use of the permission
given to it by Sir Charles Wood to interfere with the freedom of the port :—

To the Editor of *The Times*.

"Sir,—I have to request that you will allow me to correct a statement made by Sir Charles Wood when replying to Sir James Elphinstone
in the House of Commons yesterday evening.

"According to the report in *The Times* of to-day, Sir Charles Wood said 'that no alteration in the position of Singapore was intended: but questions had been raised by the Singapore Chamber of Commerce as to harbour-masters and also as to moorings, and it was stated that no objection would be made to the levying of some small duty by the Indian Government if those alterations were made.'

"This is not strictly correct. The facts are these, viz:—It was the local authorities who proposed levying a tonnage due to meet the expense of a harbour-master's establishment. The opinion of the Chamber of Commerce having been sought by the Governor of the Straits Settlements, the members unanimously rejected the proposal as an infringement of the liberty of the port, and have ever since energetically protested against the measure.

"The Indian Board will best meet the wishes of the Chamber of Commerce by leaving the port in the full enjoyment of that freedom which was guaranteed by Sir Stamford Raffles and confirmed by the Imperial Government.—I am, Sir, your obedient Servant,

W. H. READ,
Chairman of the Chamber of Commerce
at the time the proposal was submitted
by the Governor of the Straits."

Oriental Club, Hanover Square, July 22nd, 1864.

In October, 1864, it was reported that the Treasury had interposed its veto to the transfer on the ground that the estimated surplus of revenue over expenditure, shewn by the report of the Commissioners (£2,040) was not large enough to provide for contingencies, and that there was therefore the possibility of a demand being made upon the Imperial finances. It seemed strange that matters should have been allowed to advance so far before this objection was discovered. So late as the beginning of July it had been stated by the Treasury that there was no impediment in that department to the transfer, and the same statement was made by the War Office. Why this sudden distrust of the financial stability of the Straits Settlements should have been aroused it is difficult to conjecture. All the statements that had from time to time been submitted on the subject of the revenue of the Straits showed that for many years past it had been steadily augmenting, and there seemed to be no ground for supposing that it had reached its highest point, or that it would thereafter remain stationary or decline.

The following letter was then written, on 1st February, 1865, to Sir Frederick Rogers, Under-Secretary of State :—

Sir,—We, the undersigned Merchants and Owners of land in the British Settlements in the Straits of Malacca, now in England, on behalf of ourselves and of our fellow Colonists, European and Native, have once more the honour of bringing their case under the notice of the Right Honorable the Secretary of State, and to entreat the attention of Her Majesty's Government to the embarrassment and inconvenience to which their commercial and other interests have been subjected, through the long delay which has taken place in the transfer of the Straits Settlements from the Indian to the Colonial Branch of Her Majesty's Administration, earnestly trusting that the measure which they have so earnestly desired may be accomplished in the course of the ensuing Session of Parliament.

" Having recently received a copy of the Annual Official Report on the Straits Settlements, we beg to submit some important facts contained in it, which fully corroborate the statements and views which on a former occasion we had the pleasure of laying before the Right Hon'ble the Secretary of State. As usual, the Revenue has continued its progressive course. For the year 1862-63 it had been £186,572, while in 1863-64 it was £211,870, a rise of £25,298, equal to from 14 to 15 per cent.

" This improvement is the more remarkable, since the year in which it took place was one of considerable commercial embarrassment.

'' The increased Revenue now quoted is exclusive of a Municipal one raised entirely for local objects. In 1862-63 this fund amounted to £40,817, and last year it had increased to £41,449. The two branches of Revenue united give for 1863-64 a total of £253,219, equal to a taxation of a pound a head on the highest estimate of the population of the three Settlements. This may be compared with the rate in the Colony of Ceylon, which, notwithstanding the great improvement which has of late years taken place in the financial condition of that Colony through the administration of a skilfull and prudent Governor, has a revenue of no more than £ 800,000, a sum which on its computed population gives but eight shillings a head.

" The evidence now given in addition to the testimony formerly adduced will, we earnestly hope, satisfy Her Majesty's Government that the Revenues of the Straits Settlements are possessed in a very eminent degree of the quality of elasticity.

" It is easy, however, to show that if fiscal justice were done to the Settlements, the small surplus exhibited in the Public Returns, namely £ 2,129, might be raised to a very considerable one. Although several others are obvious, we confine ourselves to two subjects for retrenchment, namely the Convicts and the Military.

" The Convicts not only of Continental India but of Ceylon and Hongkong are a charge on the Straits Revenue. In the last year of the Public Account their number was 3,511, and their cost £ 26,450, exclusive of Superintendent, medical attendance and rent of expensive barracks. Some of the local officers seem to be of opinion that the convicts by their labour make a full return for this large expenditure incurred by them, but this notion will not bear examination, and is readily dissipated by a comparison of their work with that of free labourers. In England, it is well ascertained that it takes five convicts to perform the work of three free labourers. This proportion would reduce the numbers of the Straits convicts to about 2,100. But even from this reduced number there would of course have to be deducted 200 women, who are not called upon to work, the old, the infirm and the sick, so that the actual labourers would be reduced to a very inconsiderable number. The wages of a day labourer of Continental India or of Java, reckoned by the year, is about £ 9, and of a Chinese labourer £ 11. The money bestowed on the Indian Convicts, therefore would defray the cost of 2,716 Indian or Javanese free labourers or of 2,406 Chinese labourers, doing the same amount of work as the Indian or Javanese.

" According to this view nothing is gained but, on the contrary, much loss incurred, through the employment of convict labour, and the whole sum disbursed under this head, ought in fairness to be debited to the Governments transporting Convicts to the Straits, and consequently added to the surplus Revenue, raising the latter to £ 28,579.

" With respect to the Military expenditure, we very respectfully submit that it is inordinate and uncalled for. According to the Public Report the garrison of the three Settlements consists of two Batteries of European Artillery, a company of Native Artillery and two regiments of Sepoys of the Madras Presidency. The entire force numbers 1,811 persons, embracing the unusual number of 46 Commissioned Officers, among whom there are no fewer than seven Field Officers. The cost of this force, as far as it is borne by the Settlements, is no less than £63,400 a year, but this is exclusive of provisions and transport.

" For illustration we take the liberty of comparing the force thus described with the garrison of the Island of Ceylon, and we think it will be apparent to the Secretary of State, that it is far beyond what necessity and a just economy calls for. Ceylon is a country nearly as large as the Kingdom of Scotland, with a population of two millions or eight-fold that of the highest estimate of that of the three Settlements. The garrison of Ceylon according to the Public Returns amounts to no more than 2,400, being but 600 beyond that serving in the Straits Settlements. In Ceylon the Force is disposed over ten different and remote stations, the active portion is, it is understood, frequently employed in mere police duties. In the Straits, on the contrary, the Military duties are confined to three stations, the towns of the respective Settlements, all within range of the fire of shipping and they are not employed on any police services.

"Even if the present class of Native troops should be continued, there seems no reason why one Regiment of sepoys might not be dispensed with. One Regiment, with an exceedingly limited number of Commissioned Officers with it, was thought sufficient before the Sepoy rebellion, and now that it has been long quelled, two Regiments, with above forty Commissioned Officers, cannot be indispensable.

"We have the honor to submit to the Right Honorable the Secretary of State, our view of such a Military establishment for the Straits Settlements as, we venture to believe, would be adequate to the discharge of all the duties which could be reasonably looked for, having regard to their geographical and strategic position. Throughout the whole Indian Archipelago and in its neighbourhood there is not the remotest risk of invasion or attack from a native power, but this fact is so transparent that it need not be insisted on. Conspiracy against the Government in a heterogeneous population, consisting of many nationalities and differing in race, language and manners. and consequently incapable of combination, may be said to be next to impossible. If the inhabitants of the Straits Settlements cannot in a strict sense of the word be called loyal, the intelligent portion of them are unquestionably attached to the ruling Power by a thorough conviction of the advantages which they derive from its protection. The only danger incident to the Settlements would be from an European enemy in time of war. An enemy's cruisers might bombard and destroy any one of the Towns of the three Settlements, and most easily Singapore and Penang, the most valuable. From such a disaster our Fleet must always be our chief protection, for no amount of land force would be a security against such a catastrophe.

"The garrison required for the Straits Settlements is not one therefore which should aim at protection against foreign aggression, but one that will give confidence to its peaceful inhabitants, preserve internal order, and give security against lawlessness to property in goods, houses and warehouses, the value of which may be estimated by the fact stated in the Public Reports that the joint exports and imports of the United Settlements for the last year recorded amounted to the sum of £15,845,000.

"A certain portion of the garrison of the Settlements it is indispensably necessary should consist of European Troops of one kind or another, for it is their presence, and not that of a native force, whatever it may number or its quality, that gives both European and Native inhabitants a firm reliance on the stability of the Government.

"We respectfully repeat our former suggestion, that for this purpose a detachment of the Royal Marines, trained to the use of Artillery, and probably not exceeding two hundred in number, would be most eligible, efficient, and easily relieved description of troops. This Corps would receive valuable assistance from the drilled Volunteers, composed of Europeans and their descendants, which now exist at the three Settlements. It appears to us that all the duties at present performed by two regiments of Sepoys, numbering 1,475 men, might be as safely and effectually performed by a well organised native police corps, with an ample allowance of European commissioned and non-commissioned officers, after the organisation of the Metropolitan Police. Such a corps would consist of natives of Continental India and of Malays, in proper proportion, and of both descriptions there are ample materials to choose from on the spot; or a force similar to that recommended in the suggestions laid before His Grace the late Duke of Newcastle, dated 20th April, 1861, might be adopted: the cost of rations for which, including 200 Europeans, would, as therein stated, amount for the three Settlements to £44,250. Supposing, however, the Police force to be preferred, the cost could not exceed that amount, and deducting the above ample sum from the present Military expenditure of £63,400, a saving would be effected of very little short of £20,000. There is, however, we observe by the Public Report, a sum of £4,221 spent by the Government on Police objects exclusive of the large expenditure on Police paid by the municipal fund, and if this also is deducted, a saving would be effected of no less than £24,000. Should the retrenchments now suggested be considered practicable and carried out, the Straits Settlements would exhibit a surplus Revenue of £52,579, consisting of the following items namely:—

Present Surplus	...	...	...	£ 2,129
Abolition of convict Charge	...	...	...	26,450
Military saving	...	...	...	24,000

"Even, however, without adopting the scheme now exhibited, the reduction of the present garrison even by a single Regiment of Sepoys would reduce the Military expenditure by full one-third part of its present amount: that is, by the sum of £21,133, so that even in this case we should have a surplus of £49,712.

"Without adverting for the present to any other subjects for retrenchment, we feel ourselves obliged to remark that, however great has been the increase of the Revenue, within the last 12 years, it has increased by full 70 per cent; the increase of expenditure has, without any obvious good reason, always taken care to keep pace with it, and indeed often to encroach beyond its limits.

(Sd) J. Crawfurd	(Sd) W. W. Shaw
„ A. Guthrie	„ J. Harvey
„ J. Guthrie	„ F. E. Pereira
„ W. Mactaggart	„ W. H. Read
„ H. R. Beaver	„ G. Lipscompe
„ J. K. Smith	„ J. M. Little.
„ E. Boustead	

The *Singapore Free Press* contained the following remarks upon this letter :—" The letter contains a very clear statement of the financial position of the Straits Settlements, and it ought to dispel any doubts that may have still existed as to the sufficiency and elasticity of the revenue to meet all legitimate charges upon it, present and prospective. Before this letter reached its destination, however, it appears that the question of the transfer had again been taken up by the different Government departments having to do with it, and it was expected that the transfer would be carried through in the course of the present session of Parliament; one report says early in the session. There was still some little haggling about the so-called local debt, but the real nature of that debt having been at last ascertained, the Indian Office is disposed to give in, and take upon itself the burthen of what was in reality a loan from the suitors and depositors in the Court of Judicature to the Government of India, and which has since been paid off by that Government, so that it no longer exists. The only other matter of discussion, we understand, was on the subject of the military charges, the War Office stipulating for a larger European force than was considered necessary for the wants of the Colony. If this force is not to be for strictly local purposes, but is to be available for service in China or India in case of need, it seems scarcely fair to make the Colony bear the whole of its cost, as it might be withdrawn at the very moment when its services were most required; in the event, for instance, of some great movement amongst the people of China, the agitation of which would naturally be communicated to the Chinese in the Straits. If the Colony had no other military force than that so withdrawn, the public safety might be imperilled, and it is therefore obvious that it would be imprudent to expend the whole sum that can be applied for military purposes upon such a force. The garrison of marines suggested in the letter to Sir Frederick Rogers, would be liable to the same objections, and we believe, moreover, that the Admiralty would not give its consent to marines being employed in permanent shore duty in this part of the world. The sum proposed by the Commissioners in their report for military expenditure (£63,000) if judiciously applied, will be sufficient to provide for a proper permanent garrison and to allow of part of it being appropriated as a contribution towards the expense of any troops the Government may station here for general service. A further sum of £8,200 is allowed for the suppression of piracy, but as this duty could be much more efficiently performed by the Royal Navy than by the present local squadron, the latter might be safely abolished and the money appropriated for it could be added to the military contribution. With reference to the charge for convicts which it is properly proposed to disallow, we observe that the reduction will not amount to the whole sum disbursed; as while the places from which the convicts come will be charged with their maintenance, the same rule will have to be applied to the Straits Convicts sent to Bombay. Their numbers are however very much smaller than those of the Continental and Ceylon convicts in the Straits, and after a proper adjustment of the account the saving will still be very large."

In March, 1865, it was stated in the *London and China Express* that the obstacles to the transfer of the Straits Settlements had been satisfactorily cleared up, and a bill would be introduced in that Session of Parliament to effect the transfer from the Indian Government to the Colonial Office. And it was mentioned that the India Office had afforded every facility and that the Treasury made no further objection; and it was confidently expected that the Transfer would be an accomplished fact before the lapse of many months.

But in the House of Commons on the 6th May, 1865, Lord Stanley (the present Earl of Derby who had been giving his assistance to the Straits Merchants in the matter, being personally known to Mr. W. H. Read), asked the Secretary of State for India whether it was his intention to bring in a bill during the present session for the transfer of Singapore, Malacca, and Penang from the Indian to the Colonial Administration, and Sir Charles Wood was understood to say that he could not give a positive answer to the question of the noble lord. He assured him that, as far as the Indian Government were concerned, they had been quite ready to meet the wishes of the people of Singapore, but the Colonial Office had thought it requisite to institute certain inquiries to satisfy themselves that no burden would be imposed upon the estimates, and the final determination of the Department had not as yet been conveyed to him.

In April, 1866, Lord Stanley in the House of Commons asked Mr. Cardwell, the Secretary of State for the Colonies, to give some explanation as to the tedious delay which has been experienced in the transfer of the Straits Settlements from the Government of India to that of the Colonies. He said that for the past two years there had only been just one little difficulty to get over, but unfortunately when surmounted, the one little trouble was found to be hydra-headed. Mr. Cardwell admitted that the question of the military defences was still the stumbling block.

At last, on 13th June, 1866, the Bill was read a first time in the House. The following is an extract from a Treasury letter, dated 2nd June, " In order to avoid further delay, my lords consider it best that the fixed contribution of £59,300 a year should be adopted for the first five years, and, on this understanding, they assent to the introduction of the Bill into Parliament for the transfer of these Settlements. As regards that portion of your letter which refers to barrack accommodation for any troops stationed in the Settlements for Imperial purposes, my lords agree that no charge on this account ought to fall upon the Settlements. The only condition they have to make upon the subject is, that after sufficient barrack and hospital accommodation has been provided at the expense of the Settlements for the troops stationed there for local purposes, any existing barracks or hospitals which may be in excess of such accommodation, and which may be required by the War Department, shall be handed over to that department free of any charge, to be maintained at the Imperial expense during their occupation thereof. As regards the public debt of the Settlements, my lords conclude that the arrangement with the Indian Government, as explained in the Colonial Office letter of the 24th March, 1865, is to be carried out; that, as regards the convict expenditure, the whole of it from the date of transfer will be repaid by the Indian Government and that the notice for the removal of the penal establishment within three years of the date of such notice will be given not later than the date of transfer, which should take place, as recommended in the 65th paragraph of Sir Hercules Robinson's Report upon the Settlements, at the close of the colonial financial year, viz., December, 1866 or 1867, according as the necessary arrangements can be completed. As regards the civil establishment to be sanctioned for the Settlements, my lords will be prepared to approve of an establishment on the basis of that suggested by Sir H. Robinson, in Enclosure No. 6 of his report, subject to such modifications as experience may have since dictated, or which any change as regards the municipalities of the Settlements may hereafter render necessary."

The Act of Parliament of the 10th August, 1866, intituled " An Act to provide for the Government of the Straits Settlements " was Chapter 115 of 29 and 30 Victoria. It recited that it was expedient that the Islands and Territories known as the Straits Settlements, namely Prince of Wales' Island, the Island of Singapore, and the town and port of Malacca and their Dependencies should cease to form a part of India, and should be placed under the Government of the Queen as part of the Colonial Possessions of the Crown ; and enacted that the Settlements should at a time to be specified cease to be part of India, within the meaning of the Act of 21 and 22 Victoria, Chapter 126, which was an Act for the better Government of India.

By an Order in Council dated 28th December, 1866, the 1st April, 1867, was ordered for the Act to come into operation. By Letters Patent, dated Westminster, 4th February, 1867, the necessary authority was given constituting the new Government of the Straits.

The next and last Chapter of this book gives an account of the ceremony in the Town Hall, on Monday, 1st April, 1867, when the Indian Government formally transferred the Straits Settlements to the Crown.

CHAPTER LVI.

1867.

ON New Year's Eve, between 8 and 9 o'clock there was a fine display of fireworks on the Esplanade, and the usual sports took place the next day. The *Straits Times* remarked that, probably from the management having devolved upon younger men, the amusement of the natives was made subordinate to competitions for Europeans, artillerymen and others, which should be avoided, as the object of the sports had, from the first, been the amusement of the natives, and not the entertainment of the Europeans.

The Government holidays this year had been from 24th December to 1st January, but the merchants only observed half that time, and the Government arrangement tended to disorganise business, as the offices were all closed.

In January it was known that Colonel Ord was likely to be appointed the Governor under the new régime, and the paper said that one of the Ministers, in a conversation regarding the Straits, had said that he hoped Colonel Ord would keep quiet, and be guided in his administration of the government by the local authorities. It was a pity Colonel Ord did not do this. It had been intended to send out new officials from home to take charge of all the superior offices, but fortunately for the place it was not done, and Colonel Macpherson, the Resident Councillor, remained as Colonial Secretary, Mr. W. W. Willans the Accountant General was Government Treasurer, Major McNair was Colonial Engineer, and Mr. Thomas Braddell was appointed Attorney General, from 1st April.

In April for the formal ceremony for the assumption of the government of the Straits by the Colonial Office, Colonel Henry Man came down from Penang to represent the East India Company, as he was the senior official in the Straits after Governor Cavenagh had left. He had been Resident Councillor at Penang from 1860. He had entered the Madras Native Infantry as an Ensign in 1834, was Lieutenant in 1838, Captain in 1848, and died a General in England, after he had retired. He was in two campaigns in India in 1836, and there is a note by Mr. Braddell that he was in the second Burmese War in 1853, so that he must have rejoined the army again for a time in that year. In 1845 he was Superintendent of Convicts and Executive Engineer Officer in Singapore, and Major McNair speaks in his book "Prisoners Their Own Warders," in several places, of the good work Captain Man did in consolidating the work of the convicts. When he went to Malacca, as Resident Councillor, Captain Ronald Macpherson, of the Madras Artillery succeeded him as Superintendent of Convicts in 1855. He had joined the Artillery in 1836 and attained the army rank of Colonel in 1851. He was for several years Resident Councillor at Malacca from 1858 and in Singapore in 1860. He is also spoken of in Major McNair's book. Both Colonel Man and Colonel Macpherson did much good work in the Straits, and were very much liked. Colonel Macpherson was the first Colonial Secretary, but he and Governor Ord were not able to work harmoniously together, and the feelings of the community were with the Colonel. He died, much regretted in the place, on the day the Duke of Edinburgh was paying a visit to Johore, on 7th December, 1869, at 52 years of age, and there was a very large attendance of the military and of the community, at his funeral, which was also attended by the officers, sailors and band of H. M. S. *Galatea,* of which the Duke was Captain. He was buried in the cemetery in Bukit Timah Road, and a monument was erected in the compound of St. Andrew's Cathedral, of which he was the architect; a window was also put up in his memory over the west doorway of the Church, as has been mentioned on pages 294 and 298. The Colonel said in a speech which he made at the farewell dinner to Governor Cavenagh in this year, when his health was drunk :—" When I first visited Singapore, on my way to China, in 1841, I was so charmed with the place that I resolved to make, if possible, the Straits my Eastern home. In this I have very nearly succeeded. Here, the best and happiest portion of my life has been spent, here I have made many sincere and life-long friendships, and with the Straits are associated all the dearest and most cherished memories of the past."

On 22nd January the newspaper said that the appointment of Sir Henry Keppel to the command of the China station as communicated by telegram (part of the way) had given very general satisfaction in Singapore; and that it had been at one time expected that he might have succeeded Major-General Cavenagh as Governor, and his nomination as Admiral was less welcome. If the Admiral had come, matters would have gone much more smoothly, a great deal of irritation would have been avoided, and the Native States in the Malay Peninsula would have made a start, to the great benefit of the trade of the Settlements, several years before they did.

The following letter was addressed by the Municipal Commissioners (Colonel Macpherson, Thomas Dunman, J. D. Vaughan, W. H. Read, and R. C. Woods,—Henry Hewetson was Secretary) to Government about Cavenagh Bridge :—

"Sir :—I am deputed by my colleagues to request you will be good enough to ask His Honor the Governor to do us the favour of permitting the new Bridge which is proposed to be constructed across the river opening into Collyer Quay, to be called ' Cavenagh Bridge.

"The reclaiming of the submerged land from what was in former years the rear of an unsightly mass of buildings, and the constructing of a line of massive structures with an imposing sea frontage and a wide carriage way, is a work for the conception and

execution of which the public are indebted to the enlightened taste
and liberal support of His Honor ; and the Commissioners feel
assured that they express the wish of the public generally in
desiring that the connection link between the land so reclaimed and
the opposite side of the river, may be handed down to the future
residents of Singapore as the Cavenagh Bridge. If his Honour will
therefore do them the honour of acceding to their request, it will
be the endeavour of the Commissioners to have a Bridge constructed
in every respect worthy of the name."

The submerged land referred to was the sea-beach from
Johnston's Pier to Prince Street. Until the land was reclaimed, the
buildings had faced the Square, and only out-houses and sheds were
on the sea-shore. In 1866 almost all the present line of buildings
on Collyer Quay had been erected. A. L. Johnston & Co. occupied
the site where the new building of the Hongkong and Shanghai
Bank now stands. Where Guthrie & Co. are now was Martin
Dyce & Co.'s ; Guthrie's godowns having been for some 35 years on
Boat Quay, at the corner of Guthrie's Canal. Paterson, Simons &
Co. were already in their present offices.

Cavenagh Bridge was opened in 1869, and it was then suggested
by Governor Ord that it should be called "Edinburgh Bridge"
because it was first used about the time the Duke visited Singapore, but, quite properly, it was called, and still bears the name, of
the last of the Indian Governors. It was opened without any
ceremony whatever, carriages driving over it into town on the
morning that it was said to be ready for traffic.

On the afternoon of February 27th, the steamer *Agamemnon*,
the first of Holt's steam line to China, left Singapore for Hongkong.
At 8 p.m., twelve miles from Singapore, there was a collision between
her and the Labuan Company's steamer *Mona*, on her way from
Labuan to Singapore. The *Mona* was afterwards held to blame.
There had been a circus troupe in Singapore, called the Lenton
Troupe, and they were on board the *Agamemnon*. The stem of the
Mona crushed into a cabin of the *Agamemnon* in which two young
children, who used to perform on a trapeze, were asleep, without
injuring them ; while the Boneless Boy, who was a prominent feature
of the circus, and was asleep in the next cabin, had his leg
broken !

On the 28th February, a public meeting was held in the
Exchange, with Sir Benson Maxwell in the chair, and it was decided
to offer a public dinner to the Governor, and afterwards subscriptions
were made for a portrait of him to be placed in the Town Hall,
which was carried out subsequently. The dinner took place in the
Town Hall on the 12th March, Mr. W. H. Read being in the chair ;
and Colonel Macpherson, Sir Benson Maxwell, the Maharajah of
Johore, and others proposing various toasts.

On Friday the 15th, Governor Cavenagh left Singapore for the
last time in the Straits steamer *Pluto* for Penang. An Address by
the Chamber of Commerce was read to him at the Pier by Mr.
W. H. Read, and there was a guard of honour of the Volunteer
Corps ; and a number of other addresses were presented to him.

Colonel Cavonagh had assumed the Government of the Straits on 6th August, 1859, and was therefore seven years and eight months in the Straits. He took a great personal interest in his work, and was indefatigable in his efforts for the promotion of education, and identified himself with all the interests and the progress of the place. He stubbornly stood out against any attempt from Bengal to impose prejudicial taxation, such as an income tax and tonnage dues. He was especially known for the readiness with which he invariably made himself accessible to all classes of the community, who wished to lay their views upon any public matter before him, and he was a very liberal supporter of amusements and private enterprise. One evening when there was an amateur entertainment in the Town Hall for a charity, it was a regular Singapore wet night, and Governor Cavenagh sat alone in the front row, and there were only about six other people in the hall besides him. The amateurs, who had intended to give it all up, had a good laugh, and seeing him there, went through the concert with all the spirit possible.

In 1884 a book entitled *Reminiscences of an Indian Official*, by General Sir Orfeur Cavenagh, K.C.S.I., was published by W. H. Allen & Co., London, but it did not prove of much interest in the Straits. It is true that the last chapter, of 122 pages, related entirely to the former Governor's career in the Straits, but it was largely made up of reported speeches which he was accustomed to write out. Singapore expected to have found mention of those who worked here under him—a theme on which a good deal of local interest might have been gracefully said—but there was scarcely a mention of any one except Whampoa, of whom it was written " I paid him a visit to see his curiosities."

There was not much of general information concerning the Straits. The opening of the first telegraph cable to Batavia was duly chronicled, but it did not state that it broke down altogether almost immediately afterwards, and the congratulatory message which was despatched from Singapore, which was printed at full length, was therefore rather premature. The General took credit, fairly enough, for having established the Government Scholarships for the Boys' Schools, and those who had undertaken the task of conducting the examinations laughed in their sleeves at the story of how he had the examination papers printed at the Government Press "in the presence of my secretary, and then brought back to my private office," and yet (in the next page) how the Brothers' School spread a report that copies had been furnished to boys in the other schools. The most interesting passage was at page 352, in which he compared the Indian system of government with that of the Colonial Office, and the deductions he drew were certainly not in favour of the latter. The passage is as follows :—

" Under the Indian Government there were comparatively few officers, but they were well paid, and expected to do good work. The Governor was supreme, the whole of the patronage being in his hands. Officers felt, therefore, that their promotion must depend mainly on their own exertions, by showing that they were fit for advancement, for, as he was vested with great authority, so equally the Governor incurred great responsibility; as he selected his own instruments, he was in a great measure responsible for any failure on their part, hence he did his best to secure efficient men. Under the Colonial Office the officials were more numerous, but, upon the whole, not so well paid. The patronage rested with the Colonial Office, and consequently an officer did not look to his local chief to reward him acccording to his deserts, but to political friends at home who might have influence with the Secretary of State, and it was, therefore, within the bounds of possibility that an official might be promoted from whom the Governor had never experienced that cordial support which, to ensure due efficiency, every head of an establishment has a right to expect from his subordinates."

The other part of the book contained an account of his services in India, and of his assuming political charge of the Nepaulese Embassy to England, and was interspersed with a number of anecdotes, some of which are much more amusing than the concluding chapter on the Straits, where the General's career finished; he remarked that when he accepted the office of Governor here, he little anticipated that his official career would be brought to an early close at a time when he naturally entertained expectations of succeeding to one of the prizes of the Indian Service.

Governor Harry St. George Ord, C.B., for he was not then knighted, arrived in Singapore in the P. & O. Mail on Saturday, 16th March, the day after Governor Cavenagh had left for Penang. Major McNair accompanied Colonel Ord from England.

It was unfortunate that Governor Ord and Sir Benson Maxwell fell at once upon disputable ground which caused a good deal of talk, as the Recorder was generally known to be correct in the position he took up towards the Government, and because of his perfect independence, which was, as Mr. Cameron remarks in his book, a distinguishing mark of the Judges under the East India Company. The new Governor considered that he had the right to be styled His Excellency, even before he was sworn in, and a further cause of contention was the position of the Governor on the assumption that he represented the Crown or the Sovereign. Many years after this, in 1889 when a Singaporean met Sir Benson Maxwell in Rome, he referred to the subject, and it was amusing to hear how he remembered the cases, for he was a great case lawyer, as has been said on page 730, and prided himself on his memory. As to the first question, Sir Benson was technically correct; but by common consent and by courtesy, for so many years that it is beyond reasonable discussion, Governors of Crown Colonies have been addressed while in the Colonies by the style of Excellency. It is said that it is only certain Viceroys, Ambassadors to the Great Courts, and Plenipotentiaries, that can claim it as of right; and the Colonial Office does not address a Governor as His Excellency, but by his name.

The second contention was peculiarly within Sir Benson's knowledge. The point arises from time to time in many of the Colonies, where the newspapers speak of the "Sovereign's representative" or of the "Vice-regal party." The matter has been raised and swept aside in the Privy Council several times, as in the cases Sir Benson referred to. In the case of Cameron *v.* Kyte, an appeal from the Colony of Berbice, heard in 1835 before Lord Brougham, Baron Parke and others, it was laid down that the Governor was an officer, merely with a limited authority from the Crown, and his assumption of an act of sovereign power outside the limits of the authority given to him, would be purely void, and the Courts of the Colony could not give it any legal effect. And in the case of Sir George Hill, who was Governor of Trinidad, against Bigge, heard in the Privy Council before Lord Brougham, Lord Campbell, and two other Judges; Lord Brougham who delivered the judgment of the Court, said "If it be said that the Governor of a Colony is *quasi* Sovereign, the answer is that he does not even represent the Sovereign generally, having only the functions delegated to him by the terms of his commission, and being only the officer to execute the specific powers with which that commission clothes him." In that case the Governor pleaded in reply to a claim for a debt to some London jewellers, that he could not be sued. The Privy Council upheld the judgment of the Colonial Court which had been given against him for the amount of the debt, with interest, and all costs. But the Privy Council seemed to consider (though the point was not judicially decided, as it was not then in question), that though judgment was given against him, his person could not be taken in execution while he was actually on service as Governor.

On Sunday afternoon, March 31st, Admiral Keppel, who had been appointed Commander-in-Chief on the China Station, arrived in the P. & O. Mail from England. His flagship, the *Rodney*, which had flown his Commodore's flag in the Black Sea in the Crimean War, and when he was in command of the Naval Brigade, some 5,000 men, on shore, was on her way out by the Cape. He was accompanied by his flag-lieutenant, Harry F. Stephenson, spoken of on page 650, and Mr. William Bond Risk, his secretary. He went to stay with Mr. W. H. Read in the house where he was then living, which was pulled down when the present Government House was built on the same spot a year or two afterwards. In the Admiral's Diary on the following day was the following, which appears in his last book "A Sailor's Life under Four Sovereigns," (the old Admiral can now say Five) :—

"On looking out in the early morning from the verandah, an extensive view in front of the town and anchorage, and from behind of the country inland. How many associations of bygone days—some sad, but many more pleasant—were brought to mind. At noon repaired to Town Hall to assist in the inauguration of the new Governor and the transfer of the Straits Settlements from the Indian to the Colonial Government; an event in the history of Singapore."

The formal inauguration of the new government took place in the Town Hall at noon on Monday, the 1st April, and no public ceremony in Singapore had ever, probably, attracted so much interest. There was a great crowd of natives round the building and along the roads. Inside the hall there was a striking example of the much smaller number of the European population as compared with the present day, for there was room and chairs for all that wished to attend. The abolition of the time-honoured East India Company with its long and great history appealed to all, both Europeans and natives, and to this day the Government is still spoken of among the latter as the "Company." At the upper end of the room a sort of dais had been erected, just in front of the line of the gallery. The Volunteers formed a guard-of-honour in the front verandah. Among the naval and military officers in the room were Captain Ross of H. M. S. *Pearl*, Captain Edye of H. M. S. *Satellite* which was in the next year in the Red Sea in the Abyssinian War, and Captain Edye (who had been much liked in Singapore) heard while he lay dying in Hongkong, where he was buried, on the return of the ship to the China station from Abyssinia, that he was made a Companion of the Bath; Captain Suttie of H. M. S. *Salamis*, Admiral Keppel's despatch vessel; and Commander Menzies of the gun-boat *Osprey*; and Major-General Studholme Hodgson, Brigadier Ireland, Colonel Grant, R A., Colonel Lovell, C.B., R.E., Colonel Cooke of the 8th Madras Infantry, and many other naval and military officers.

The first to enter, a few minutes before noon, was the Acting Governor, the Hon'ble Colonel Henry Man, a fine soldierly looking man. He was received with a salute of 17 guns from Fort Canning, and by the guard of honour of the regiment downstairs and the Volunteers upstairs. Colonel Man went round the room shaking hands with the ladies, and waiting for the new Governor.

Then, under another salute, stalked in Governor Ord, without removing his hat, and sat down on a chair on the dais without taking any notice of any one. The impression thus created was never removed and was justified in the years that he remained in the Straits. Then another salute was heard, and a very short man, in an Admiral's uniform, his breast covered with medals (there was not room to put them all on) and the Order of the Bath over all, came up the verandah on the side facing the Esplanade, and, as he walked into the room through the last side door, taking off his hat with a bow to the company, with his smiling face, bright eyes and long eye-lashes, everyone stood up delighted to see him. He had only arrived the afternoon before. He went round a table that was placed in front of the dais, shaking hands with the ladies, Mrs. Jozé d'Almeida and others that he knew. As he was coming back Governor Ord motioned to him to come on to the dais, and sit on one of the three seats that were placed upon it. But the Admiral laughingly shook his head, and taking up a Town Hall chair, put it down on the floor near the dais, and sat down on it, and remained there.

The Order in Council constituting the Straits a Colony of the Crown was then read. It was dated at Westminster, 4th February, 1867. Then the Commission appointing Harry Saint George Ord, Esquire, Colonel in the Army, Lieutenant-Colonel of the Royal Engineers, and Companion of the Order of the Bath, was read. Sir Benson Maxwell administered the oaths of office to H. E. the Governor, and then to the newly appointed members of the Legislative Council, viz., the Hon'bles W. H. Read, F. S. Brown (of Penang), Thomas Scott (of Guthrie & Co.), and Dr. Robert Little. Mr. Whampoa was appointed subsequently. The Company then left the Town Hall, the members of the Council remaining to pass certain formal acts before separating.

CONCLUSION.

Singapore having been founded in the year 1819, the same year as the birth of Her late Majesty Queen Victoria, has been spoken of as " Her Birthday Isle;" and it has also been written that its success has been due to the " Magic of Free Trade," which is no doubt largely true. But there has been another kind of magic, which Sir Stamford Raffles, in a passage to be quoted presently, spoke of as " The energies of her sons."

In 1864, a Children's Evening Party at Christmas time, such as is common in England, was begun for the school children in Singapore, and has been continued year by year to the present time. It began with a small party of about twenty children, and has grown with the place to a large party of seven or eight hundred, until the Town Hall is not large enough to hold all. In 1887, there was a Fairy Play called "The Talisman of the Enchanted Island," written for the occasion, and acted by about seventy of the children for the amusement of all the rest. At the end of the play, in the great Fairy Palace of the Enchanted Island, with three little Fairies high up in the scene with electric lights on their dresses to represent the constellations of the Southern Cross, Mars, and Orion, which had been alluded to as part of the story, the Midshipman, the hero of the play, spoke the "tag," and these were the last lines :—

> And this our tale of Sailor and Princess,
> In depths of time, shall bring it sweet success ;
> Until our Isle, Enchanted then no more,
> Will to the world be known as Singapore ;
> A Magic Island still, its Magic then,
> The energy and work of Englishmen.

This book began by speaking of Sir Stamford Raffles, and it is fitting that it should close in the same way. He was in the service of the East India Company, and on the 1st April, 1867, India ceased to control the destinies of Singapore, which was the period fixed to close the records in this book. To what Singapore has grown since his day, it only remains to write.

Sir Stamford Raffles when, to use his own words, " it seemed possible that the English Ministry might sacrifice him, honour, and Singapore,'to the pretentions of the Dutch," was cheered by a vision of what Singapore might become. It is difficult to suppose that he can possibly have imagined then, what we see now.

But suppose that some Seer had led him up to the Forbidden Hill (Bukit Larangan) now called Fort Canning, and had shown him the jungle and the mangrove swamps transformed into a large and busy town ; the river flowing near the hill hidden by long ranges of buildings, large engineering shops, and godowns filled with produce ; and the harbour and all the wharves occupied by shipping, stretching far away before him. And if he had been told that the few Malays in the little attap campong, on which he was looking down, were the nucleus of a population of over a quarter of a million inhabitants; that the yearly shipping was over six million tons, taking the arrivals only; and that the trade of the settlements would become actually the third among the printed returns of Trade for the years 1900-1901 of all the British Colonies and Dependencies: *—Surely, the sight would have surpassed even his far-seeing conception of what the place was to be.

But some of the passages in his letters already quoted in this book must lead those who understand the importance of Singapore at the present day to wonder at his remarkable foresight, his tireless energy, and his great sagacity. They read like a prophecy. Some of these passages (on pages 6, 67 and 78) will bear repetition here :—

"This is by far the most important station in the East, and as far as naval superiority and commercial interests are concerned, of much higher value than whole continents of territory :—If no untimely fate awaits it, it promises to become the emporium and pride of the East.—It would be difficult to name a place on the face of the globe with brighter prospects. This may be considered as the simple, almost magical, result of that perfect freedom of trade, which it has been my very good fortune to establish."

There is a passage in the very long and eloquent Minute of Raffles (referred to on page 122) at the founding of the Raffles Institution, which has not been quoted in this book, and which it now seems a pity to omit:

"The acquisitions of Great Britain in the East have not been made in the spirit of conquest. A concurrence of circumstances not to be controlled, *and the energies of her sons*, have carried her forward on the tide whose impulse has been irresistible. Other nations may have pursued the same course of conquest and success, but they have not, like her, paused in their career and by moderation and justice consolidated what they had gained. This is the rock on which her Indian Empire is placed . . . . Our influence must continue to extend; the tide has received its impetus, and it would be in vain to attempt to stem its current; but let the same principles be kept in view, let our minds and policies extend with our Empire, and it will not only be the greatest, but the firmest and most enduring, that has yet been held forth to the view and admiration of the world. While we raise those in a scale of civilisation, over whom our influence is extended, we shall lay the foundations of our dominion on the firm basis of justice and mutual advantage, instead of on the uncertain and unsubstantial tenure of force and intrigue . . . . . Commerce is the principle on which our connections with the Eastern States is formed. . . . Education must keep pace with commerce in

---

* At the beginning of The Statesman's Year Book for 1902 is a Table which gives the total imports and exports of the Colonies and Dependencies of the British Empire for 1900-01. Total India, including the Feudatory States, is given as 151 millions ; then follows Canada with 78 millions ; and the third is the Straits Settlements with 57 millions sterling, the exchange being taken as 2/-. The next are New South Wales, 55 ; Victoria, 35 ; Cape Colony, 27 ; New Zealand, 23 millions ; with all the other Colonies tailing behind. Hongkong has no complete trade returns. Singapore is not given separately from Penang and Malacca.

order that its benefits may be ensured and its evils avoided; and in our connection with these countries it should be our care that, while with one hand we carry to their shores the capital of our merchants, the other shall be stretched forth to offer them the means of intellectual improvement."

Sir Stamford Raffles died, as has been said on page 12, at the early age of 45 years, and he had himself written, four years before, that he was "A little old man, all yellow and shrivelled, with hair pretty well blanched." To borrow some of the pathetic words in the concluding sentence of his Life by Mr. Hugh Egerton, mentioned on page 14, we cannot wonder that the end came so soon; but if men live not by the length of their days, but by the good they have done around them and by the work which they have accomplished, the memory of Raffles will survive as long as the Empire lasts.

And on the 6th of February (which may be called the 'Founder's Day' of Singapore) as year by year rolls by, and his memory is kept by the holiday that has become part of the history of the place, some of those in Singapore may well be reminded of some passages in the First Lesson for the day which had been read for centuries in the old chapel of Winchester College, at the service held in memory of its Founder over five hundred years ago, (*Ecclesiasticus* xliv, to verse 16) :—

"Let us now praise famous men......

Such as did bear rule in their kingdoms, men renowned for their power, giving counsel by their understanding......

Leaders of the people by their counsels, and by their knowledge of learning meet for the people, wise and eloquent in their instructions......

All these were honoured in their generations, and were the glory of their times......

The people will tell of their wisdom, and the congregation will shew forth their praise."

THE END.

INDEX.

Where a name is mentioned in many places, the principal reference is printed in blacker figures.

Q

R